NINTH EDITION

Shi & Singh's
Delivering Health Care in the United States

A SYSTEMS APPROACH

Leiyu Shi, DrPH, MBA, MPA
PROFESSOR, BLOOMBERG SCHOOL OF PUBLIC HEALTH
DIRECTOR, JOHNS HOPKINS PRIMARY CARE POLICY CENTER
DIRECTOR, JOHNS HOPKINS ASIA-PACIFIC CENTER FOR
　HOSPITAL MANAGEMENT AND LEADERSHIP RESEARCH
JOHNS HOPKINS UNIVERSITY
BALTIMORE, MARYLAND

World Headquarters
Jones & Bartlett Learning
25 Mall Road
Burlington, MA 01803
978-443-5000
info@jblearning.com
www.jblearning.com

Jones & Bartlett Learning books and products are available through most bookstores and online booksellers. To contact Jones & Bartlett Learning directly, call 800-832-0034, fax 978-443-8000, or visit our website, www.jblearning.com.

> Substantial discounts on bulk quantities of Jones & Bartlett Learning publications are available to corporations, professional associations, and other qualified organizations. For details and specific discount information, contact the special sales department at Jones & Bartlett Learning via the above contact information or send an email to specialsales@jblearning.com.

Copyright © 2026 by Jones & Bartlett Learning, LLC, an Ascend Learning Company

All rights reserved. No part of the material protected by this copyright may be reproduced or utilized in any form, electronic or mechanical, including photocopying, recording, or by any information storage and retrieval system, without written permission from the copyright owner.

The content, statements, views, and opinions herein are the sole expression of the respective authors and not that of Jones & Bartlett Learning, LLC. Reference herein to any specific commercial product, process, or service by trade name, trademark, manufacturer, or otherwise does not constitute or imply its endorsement or recommendation by Jones & Bartlett Learning, LLC and such reference shall not be used for advertising or product endorsement purposes. All trademarks displayed are the trademarks of the parties noted herein. *Shi & Singh's Delivering Health Care in the United States: A Systems Approach, Ninth Edition* is an independent publication and has not been authorized, sponsored, or otherwise approved by the owners of the trademarks or service marks referenced in this product.

There may be images in this book that feature models; these models do not necessarily endorse, represent, or participate in the activities represented in the images. Any screenshots in this product are for educational and instructive purposes only. Any individuals and scenarios featured in the case studies throughout this product may be real or fictitious, but are used for instructional purposes only.

30014-7

Production Credits
Vice President, Innovative Learning and Assessment Solutions: Ada Woo
Senior Director, Content Production and Delivery: Christine Emerton
Director, Product: Melissa Kleeman Moy
Acquisitions Editor: Sophie Fleck Teague
Senior Outsourcing Specialist: Carol Brewer Guerrero
Content Coordinator: Samantha Gillespie
Manager, Intellectual Properties and Content Production: Kristen Rogers
Content Production Manager: Belinda Thresher
Content Production Manager, Navigate: Michael Lepera
Intellectual Property Specialist: Carolyn Downer
Director, Product Fulfillment: Aaron McKinzie
Purchasing Manager: Wendy Kilborn
Senior Product Marketing Manager: Susanne Walker
Composition: Exela Technologies
Project Management: Exela Technologies
Media Development Editor: Faith Brosnan
Rights Specialist: James Fortney
Content Management: MPS Limited
Cover and Text Design: MPS Limited
Cover Image (Title Page, Part Opener, Chapter Opener):
   © Richard Sharrocks/Moment/Getty Images
Printing and Binding: Lakeside Book Company

Library of Congress Cataloging-in-Publication Data
Names: Shi, Leiyu, author. | Shi, Leiyu. Delivering health care in America.
Title: Shi & Singh's delivering health care in the United States : a systems approach / Leiyu Shi.
Other titles: Delivering health care in America | Shi and Singh's delivering health care in the United States
Description: 9th Edition | Burlington, MA : Jones & Bartlett Learning, [2026] | Preceded by: Delivering health care in America / Leiyu Shi, Douglas A. Singh. Eighth edition. [2022]. | Includes bibliographical references and index.
Identifiers: LCCN 2024045559 | ISBN 9781284297904 (paperback)
Subjects: MESH: Delivery of Health Care | Health Policy | Health Services | United States | BISAC: BUSINESS & ECONOMICS / Accounting / Financial
Classification: LCC RA395.A3 | NLM W 84 AA1 | DDC 362.10973–dc23/eng/20250211
LC record available at https://lccn.loc.gov/2024045559

6048

Printed in the United States of America
29 28 27 26 25   10 9 8 7 6 5 4 3 2 1

Brief Contents

Preface xi
About the Author xv
List of Exhibits xvii
List of Figures xix
List of Tables xxiii
List of Acronyms xxvii

CHAPTER 1 An Overview of U.S. Healthcare Delivery 1

PART 1 System Foundations — 47

CHAPTER 2 Beliefs, Values, and Health 49

CHAPTER 3 The Evolution of Health Services in the United States 105

PART 2 System Resources — 143

CHAPTER 4 Health Services Professionals 145

CHAPTER 5 Medical Technology 189

CHAPTER 6 Health Services Financing 237

PART 3 System Processes — 291

CHAPTER 7 Outpatient and Primary Care Services 293

CHAPTER 8 Inpatient Facilities and Services 347

CHAPTER 9	**Managed Care and Integrated Organizations**	387
CHAPTER 10	**Long-Term Care**	429
CHAPTER 11	**Health Services for Special Populations**	461

PART 4 System Outcomes — 517

CHAPTER 12	**Cost, Access, and Quality**	519
CHAPTER 13	**Health Policy**	573

PART 5 System Outlook — 611

CHAPTER 14	**The Future of Health Services Delivery**	613

Glossary — 653

Index — 675

Contents

Preface xi
About the Author xv
List of Exhibits. xvii
List of Figures xix
List of Tables xxiii
List of Acronyms xxvii

CHAPTER 1 An Overview of U.S. Healthcare Delivery 1

Introduction 2
Major Characteristics of the U.S. Healthcare System 9
Trends and Directions 17
Significance for Healthcare Practitioners 21
Significance for Healthcare Managers . . . 21
Healthcare Systems of Selected Other Countries 23
The Systems Framework 35
Summary 37
Terminology 38
Review Questions. 38
References 39

PART 1 System Foundations 47

CHAPTER 2 Beliefs, Values, and Health .49

Introduction 50
Significance for Managers and Policymakers 50
Basic Concepts of Health 50
Health Promotion and Disease Prevention 56
Public Health 61
Health Security in Action: COVID-19 69
Determinants of Health 71
Measures Related to Health 75
Anthro-Cultural Beliefs and Values 81
Healthy People Initiatives 87
Summary 93
Terminology 94
Review Questions 94
References 95

CHAPTER 3 The Evolution of Health Services in the United States 105

Introduction 106
Medical Services in the Preindustrial Era 107
Medical Services in the Postindustrial Era 112
Medical Care in the Corporate Era 128
Globalization of Health Care 129
The Era of Healthcare Reform 131
Summary 136
Terminology 137
Review Questions 137
References 138

v

PART 2 System Resources — 143

CHAPTER 4 Health Services Professionals ... 145

Introduction ... 146
Physicians ... 146
Dentists ... 159
Pharmacists ... 161
Other Doctoral-Level Health Professionals ... 161
Nurses ... 162
Nonphysician Providers ... 164
Allied Health Professionals ... 166
Health Services Administrators ... 169
Evolving Trends in the Healthcare Workforce ... 170
Summary ... 179
Terminology ... 179
Review Questions ... 180
References ... 180

CHAPTER 5 Medical Technology ... 189

Introduction ... 190
What Is Medical Technology? ... 191
Information Technology and Informatics ... 191
E-Health, M-Health, E-Therapy, and E-Visits ... 199
Telemedicine, Telehealth, and Remote Monitoring ... 201
Innovation, Diffusion, and Utilization of Medical Technology ... 203
The Government's Role in Technology Diffusion ... 208
The Impact of Medical Technology ... 217
The Assessment of Medical Technology ... 222
Summary ... 225
Terminology ... 226
Review Questions ... 227
References ... 227

CHAPTER 6 Health Services Financing ... 237

Introduction ... 238
The Role and Scope of Health Services Financing ... 238
Financing and Cost Control ... 239
The Insurance Function ... 240
Private Health Insurance ... 242
Trends in Employment-Based Health Insurance ... 251
Public Health Insurance ... 253
The Payment Function ... 268
National Health Expenditures ... 277
COVID-19 and Healthcare Financing ... 279
Summary ... 282
Terminology ... 283
Review Questions ... 283
References ... 284

PART 3 System Processes — 291

CHAPTER 7 Outpatient and Primary Care Services ... 293

Introduction ... 294
What Is Outpatient Care? ... 294
The Scope of Outpatient Services ... 295
Primary Care ... 296
Growth in Outpatient Services ... 310
Complementary and Alternative Medicine ... 328
Utilization of Outpatient Services ... 330
Primary Care in Other Countries ... 331
Summary ... 335

Terminology 336
Review Questions................. 336
References 337

CHAPTER 8 Inpatient Facilities and Services.................347

Introduction 348
Hospital Transformation in the United States 348
The Expansion Phase: Late 1800s to Mid-1980s................. 351
The Downsizing Phase: Mid-1980s Onward 353
Some Key Utilization Measures and Operational Concepts........ 355
Hospital Demand, Employment, Expenditures, and Profitability 359
Types of Hospitals 363
Expectations for Nonprofit Hospitals..................... 372
Some Management Concepts....... 373
Licensure, Certification, and Accreditation.................. 376
Magnet Recognition Program....... 377
Ethical and Legal Issues in Patient Care 377
Summary 379
Terminology 380
Review Questions................. 381
References 382

CHAPTER 9 Managed Care and Integrated Organizations 387

Introduction 388
What Is Managed Care?........... 389
Evolution of Managed Care 390
Historical Growth of Managed Care........................... 392
Efficiencies and Inefficiencies in Managed Care................ 395
Cost Control Methods in Managed Care........................... 396
Types of Managed Care Organizations 401
Trends in Managed Care 406
Impact on Cost, Access, and Quality...................... 408
Historical Managed Care Backlash and the Aftermath 411
Organizational Integration......... 412
Basic Forms of Integration 415
Highly Integrated Healthcare Systems...................... 416
Summary 420
Terminology 420
Review Questions................. 421
References 421

CHAPTER 10 Long-Term Care... 429

Introduction 430
Age, Functional Deficits, and Long-Term Care 430
The Nature of Long-Term Care...... 431
Long-Term Care Services 436
Users of Long-Term Care 441
Level of Care Continuum........... 442
Home- and Community-Based Services..................... 443
Institutional Long-Term Care Continuum 448
Specialized Care Facilities 452
Continuing Care Retirement Communities 452
Institutional Trends, Utilization, and Expenditures 453
Insurance for Long-Term Care...... 454
Summary 455
Terminology 456
Review Questions................. 456
References 457

CHAPTER 11 Health Services for Special Populations 461

Introduction 462
Framework to Study Vulnerable Populations.................... 462
Racial/Ethnic Minorities 463
The Uninsured 477
Children 478
Women 481
Rural Health.................... 484
Migrant Workers 486
People Who Experience Homelessness 487
Mental Health................... 490
The Chronically Ill Population....... 493
HIV/AIDS....................... 494
Addressing Disparities Across Subpopulations................ 500
Racism in Health Care............ 502
The Effects of COVID-19 504
Summary 505
Terminology 505
Review Questions................ 505
References 506

PART 4 System Outcomes 517

CHAPTER 12 Cost, Access, and Quality.................. 519

Introduction 520
Cost of Health Care 520
Reasons for Cost Escalation........ 527
Cost Containment: Regulatory Approaches................... 532
Cost Containment: Competitive Approaches................... 537
Cost Containment Under Health Reform...................... 539

Access to Care 539
The Affordable Care Act and Access to Care 544
Quality of Care 551
Quality Assessment and Assurance.................... 553
Public Reporting of Quality...................... 556
The Affordable Care Act and Quality of Care 559
Summary 562
Terminology 563
Review Questions................ 563
References 564

CHAPTER 13 Health Policy 573

Introduction 574
What Is Health Policy?............. 574
Principal Features of U.S. Health Policy........................ 576
The Development of Legislative Health Policy 584
Critical Policy Issues 587
Role of Research in Policy Development................... 593
Future Considerations in Domestic Health Policy................... 593
International Health Policy 600
Summary 605
Terminology 606
Review Questions................ 606
References 606

PART 5 System Outlook 611

CHAPTER 14 The Future of Health Services Delivery...... 613

Introduction 614
Forces of Future Change........... 614

Healthcare Reform in Transition 622
Innovations in the Healthcare Delivery Infrastructure.......... 626
Future Workforce Challenges 631
The Future of Long-Term Care 635
Global Threats and International Cooperation................... 636
New Frontiers in Clinical Technology 641

The Future of Evidence-Based Health Care..................... 643
Summary 644
Terminology 645
Review Questions................. 645
References 646

Glossary....................653
Index 675

Preface

With this ninth edition of *Delivering Health Care in the United States: A Systems Approach*, we celebrate 27 years of serving instructors, students, policymakers, and others, both at home and overseas, with up-to-date information on the dynamic U.S. healthcare delivery system. Every effort has been made to update the tables and figures in this edition and to keep the readers abreast of ongoing changes in the financing and delivery of health care.

The major event in 2020–2024 that gripped the entire world—with the United States being no exception—was the pandemic brought about by the novel coronavirus that caused the disease named COVID-19. This pandemic and its effects on health care are thoroughly discussed in several chapters of this text. Of course, the long-term effects of this disease, of the variants and mutations of the virus, and of the massive vaccinations against the disease on people's health and longevity are as yet unknown. Also unspecified at this time are what actions the global community can take to prevent such catastrophes in the future. Hence, this topic will remain of interest to public health experts for years to come.

Currently, both the political and cultural environments in the United States are in a state of flux; some observers even describe it as a pivotal moment. There can be no doubt that generational shifts will have consequences for the health and well-being of the U.S. population.

At the time of this writing, Donald Trump has been elected president and the Republican party gained control of both the Senate and Congress. However, given the disagreements within the Republican party, major stakeholders and interest groups, and the relative low emphasis by Trump on healthcare reform during the campaign, changes in U.S. healthcare landscape are likely to be incremental as in the past.

In the United States, it appears that we have entered an era of massive government spending of tax dollars with relatively little objective examination of the returns that such spending might bring. Hence, in future years, we can expect a significant examination and perhaps some overhaul of the U.S. healthcare delivery system in terms of its lack of efficiency. Amendments to the ACA will likely prevail with incremental expansion or reduction of coverage depending on compromise between the White House and the Congress. Regardless of which direction the U.S. healthcare system ultimately takes, the critical issues related to it—people's ability to access healthcare services when needed, the overall cost of health care and its affordability for individuals, and improvement of quality—are likely to remain. The vital test for the success of any future system-wide initiatives in health care will be the value produced for the money spent.

New to This Edition

This edition continues to reference some of the main features of the Affordable Care Act (ACA) wherever it is important to provide contextual discussions from historical and policy perspectives. As in the past, this text has been updated throughout with the latest pertinent data, trends, and research findings available at the time the manuscript was prepared. Copious illustrations in the form of examples, facts, figures, tables, and exhibits continue to make the text come alive. Following is a list of the main additions and revisions:

Chapter 1
- New information on the states' role in healthcare reform and innovation
- New information on integrated care to enhance quality and value
- Updated information related to nation-states
- Updated information on global health challenges and reform
- Added Global Health under the COVID-19 section

Chapter 2
- Updated information on health protection during global pandemics in light of the COVID-19 pandemic
- Updated information on health security in light of the COVID-19 pandemic
- Updated *Healthy People 2030*

Chapter 3
- Updated information on the legacy of the ACA
- New discussion about lessons from the past drawing from historical events

Chapter 4
- Updated discussion of issues in medical practice, training, and supply
- Updated information on the evolving trends in the healthcare workforce
- New discussion on the role of healthcare professionals and the social determinants of health

Chapter 5
- New information on the impact of medical technology with examples of applications in quality, cost, access, and equity
- New discussion about medical technology assessment around the world

Chapter 6
- Updated information on the effects of the ACA
- Updated information on private insurance and the COVID-19 pandemic
- Updated information on Medicaid under the ACA
- New section on payment innovations
- New information on the impact of COVID-19 on healthcare financing
- New section on payment methods and incentives

Chapter 7
- Updated information on the evaluation of PCAT
- Updated information on primary care and pandemics
- Updated information on PCHCs under COVID-19
- Updated information on primary care in other countries
- Updated information on best practices around the world

Chapter 8
- Updated information on the impact of managed care
- Updated information on hospital closures
- New section on the role of hospitals in an integrated care environment

Chapter 9
- Updated information on trends in managed care
- Updated information on the impact on cost, access, and quality

- New section on the Future of Managed Care

Chapter 10

- Updated information on institutional trends, utilization, and expenditures
- Updated information on impact on cost, access, and quality
- New discussion about long-term care and primary care

Chapter 11

- Updated figures regarding vulnerable subpopulations throughout the chapter
- New discussion about vulnerable populations under COVID-19
- Updated information on addressing disparities across subpopulations

Chapter 12

- Updated information on AHRQ quality indicators
- New discussion about the impact of COVID-19 on cost, access, and quality

Chapter 13

- Updated information on current domestic health policy initiatives
- Updated information on international health policy
- Additional case studies related to health policy applications

Chapter 14

- Updated information on the future forces
- Updated information on the direction of healthcare reform under the second Trump Administration
- New discussion on mega trends

As in the previous editions, my aim is to continue to meet the needs of both graduate and undergraduate students. I have attempted to make each chapter complete without making it overwhelming for beginners. Instructors, of course, can choose the sections they decide are most appropriate for their courses.

As in the past, I invite comments from our readers. Communications can be directed to the author:

Leiyu Shi
Department of Health Policy and Management
Bloomberg School of Public Health
Johns Hopkins University
624 North Broadway, Room 409
Baltimore, MD 21205-1996
lshi2@jhu.edu

I appreciate the work of Guoshu Kong and Yuling Li in providing assistance with the preparation of selected chapters of this text.

Instructor Resources

The following resources are available for qualified instructors only.

- Test Bank (Chapter Quizzes, Midterm, Final Exam)
- Slides in PowerPoint format
- Instructor's Manual

Student Resources

- eBook enhanced with:
  - Terminology and Acronym Flashcards
  - Chapter Review Slides
  - Interactive Glossary
  - Chapter Quizzes

About the Author

Dr. Leiyu Shi is the Professor of Health Policy and Health Services Research at the Johns Hopkins University Bloomberg School of Public Health. He is also Director of Johns Hopkins Primary Care Policy Center and the Director of Johns Hopkins Asia-Pacific Center for Hospital Management and Leadership Research.

Dr. Shi serves as Co-Editor-in-Chief of the International Journal for Equity in Health. He is author or editor of four Jones & Bartlett Learning textbooks and over 300 scientific journal articles. Thomson Reuters named him among the top-cited and most influential scientists in the world in a decade in the area of Social Science general. As a well-known expert on innovative practices and systems change, Dr. Shi consults extensively for hospitals, healthcare systems, and international agencies.

List of Exhibits

Exhibit 3-1	Evolution of the U.S. Healthcare Delivery System **107**	Exhibit 6-1	Essential Health Benefits Under ACA **244**
Exhibit 3-2	Groundbreaking Medical Discoveries **113**	Exhibit 6-2	Key Differences Between a Health Reimbursement Arrangement and a Health Savings Account **246**
Exhibit 3-3	ACA-Related Regulations **135**		
Exhibit 4-1	Definitions of Medical Specialties and Subspecialties **149**	Exhibit 6-3	Medicare Part A Financing, Benefits, Deductible, and Copayments for 2020 **255**
Exhibit 4-2	Examples of Allied Health Professionals **166**	Exhibit 6-4	Medicare Part B Financing, Benefits, Deductible, and Coinsurance for 2023 **256**
Exhibit 4-3	Strategies to Address Healthcare Professional Shortages **173**	Exhibit 6-5	Pros and Cons Regarding Medicare Advantage **259**
Exhibit 4-4	Summary of the Potential Benefits for the Team-Based Approach to Health Care **175**	Exhibit 6-6	Medicare Part D Benefits and Individual Out-of-Pocket Costs for 2023 **260**
Exhibit 5-1	The Role of Artificial Intelligence in Medicine **194**	Exhibit 6-7	How Payment for Outpatient Rehabilitation Works Under HCPCS **273**
Exhibit 5-2	The Effects of Electronic Health Records (EHRs) on Healthcare Delivery **197**	Exhibit 6-8	The Growth in Healthcare Expenditures by Major Categories **278**
Exhibit 5-3	The Benefits of Hospitals Participating in HIO **198**	Exhibit 8-1	Quality Benefits Noted in Physician-owned Specialty Hospitals **368**
Exhibit 5-4	Stages of Meaningful Use of Information Technology **199**	Exhibit 8-2	Key Hospital Metrics **376**
Exhibit 5-5	Reasons Behind the Revisions of Stark Law Regulation **206**	Exhibit 9-1	The Evolution of Managed Care: Capitation **391**
Exhibit 5-6	Pros and Cons of Right to Try Act 2018 **212**	Exhibit 9-2	Characteristics of Provider-sponsored Health Plans **405**
Exhibit 5-7	Dos and Don'ts When Bringing Drugs from Overseas **214**	Exhibit 9-3	Access to Mental Health Services Under Managed Care **410**
Exhibit 5-8	Process of Conducting Value Analysis **224**	Exhibit 9-4	How Providers Coordinate Patient Care **418**

© Richard Sharrocks/Moment/Getty Images

Exhibit 11-1 The Vulnerability Framework **462**
Exhibit 11-2 Predisposing, Enabling, and Need Characteristics of Vulnerability **463**
Exhibit 12-1 Regulation-Based and Competition-Based Cost-Containment Strategies **534**
Exhibit 13-1 Key Healthcare Concerns of Selected Interest Groups **579**
Exhibit 13-2 Arguments for Enhancing States' Role in Health Policy Making **581**
Exhibit 14-1 Potential Downsides of the Single-Payer System, or "Medicare for All" Proposal **624**
Exhibit 14-2 Paradigm Shift of Healthcare Delivery **626**
Exhibit 14-3 Critical Components of Value Based System **626**
Exhibit 14-4 Examples of Innovations in Health Care **629**

List of Figures

Figure 1-1	Basic healthcare delivery functions. **6**		**Figure 4-2**	Supply of U.S. physicians, including international medical graduates (IMGs), per 100,000 population, 1985–2019. **155**
Figure 1-2	External forces affecting healthcare delivery. **10**			
Figure 1-3	Relationship between price, supply, and demand under free market conditions. **12**		**Figure 4-3**	Trend in U.S. primary care generalists of medicine. **157**
Figure 1-4	Trends and directions in healthcare delivery. **17**		**Figure 4-4**	International medical graduates (IMGs) as a proportion of total active doctors of medicine. **159**
Figure 1-5	The systems model and related chapters. **36**			
Figure 2-1	The four dimensions of holistic health. **51**		**Figure 6-1**	Influence of financing on the delivery of health services. **240**
Figure 2-2	The Epidemiology Triangle. **53**			
Figure 2-3	Examples of preventive measures. **58**		**Figure 6-2**	Percentage of people by type of health insurance coverage 2022 (Population as of March of the following year). **241**
Figure 2-4	Core functions and essential services of public health. **62**			
Figure 2-5	Strengths and limitations of the GHS Index. **70**		**Figure 6-3**	Sources of Medicare financing, 2021. **261**
Figure 2-6	WHO Commission on Social Determinants of Health conceptual framework. **74**		**Figure 6-4**	Medicare spending for services. **262**
			Figure 6-5	Medicaid spending for services, 2021. **265**
Figure 2-7	Integrated Model for Holistic Health. **88**		**Figure 6-6**	Contributors to the growth in healthcare spending. **278**
Figure 2-8	Action model to achieve U.S. *Healthy People 2020* overarching goals. **89**		**Figure 6-7**	The U.S. healthcare dollar, 2021. **280**
			Figure 7-1	The coordination role of primary care in healthcare delivery. **298**
Figure 4-1	Ambulatory care visits to physicians according to physician specialty, 2016. **152**			

List of Figures

Figure 7-2	Percentage of total surgeries performed in outpatient departments of U.S. community hospitals, 1980–2015. **311**	Figure 8-8	International comparative hospital prices, 2017. **362**
Figure 7-3	Growth in the number of medical group practices in the United States. **313**	Figure 8-9	Proportion of total U.S. hospitals by type of hospitals, 2023. **363**
Figure 7-4	Ambulatory care visits in the United States. **314**	Figure 8-10	Breakdown of U.S. community hospitals by type of ownership, 2023. **365**
Figure 7-5	Medical procedures by location. **315**	Figure 8-11	Hospital governance and operational structures. **374**
Figure 7-6	Demographic characteristics of U.S. home health patients, 2018. **320**	Figure 9-1	Integration of healthcare delivery functions through managed care. **389**
Figure 7-7	Estimated payments for home care by payment source, 2017. **321**	Figure 9-2	Growth in the cost of U.S. health insurance (private employers), 1980–1995. **394**
Figure 7-8	Types of hospice agencies, 2014. **323**	Figure 9-3	Percentage of worker enrollment in health plans, selected years. **395**
Figure 7-9	Coverage of patients for hospice care at the time of admission, 2014. **324**	Figure 9-4	Care coordination and utilization control through gatekeeping. **397**
Figure 8-1	Trends in the number of U.S. community hospital beds per 1,000 resident population. **353**	Figure 9-5	Case management function in care coordination. **398**
Figure 8-2	The decline in the number of U.S. community hospitals and beds. **353**	Figure 9-6	Percentage of covered employees enrolled in HMO plans, selected years. **402**
Figure 8-3	Trends in average length of stay in nonfederal short-stay hospitals, selected years. **356**	Figure 9-7	The IPA-HMO model. **403**
		Figure 9-8	Percentage of covered employees enrolled in PPO plans, selected years. **406**
Figure 8-4	Average lengths of stay by U.S. hospital ownership, selected years. **357**	Figure 9-9	Percentage of covered employees enrolled in POS plans, selected years. **406**
Figure 8-5	Breakdown of U.S. community hospitals by size, 2019. **358**	Figure 9-10	Share of managed care enrollments in employer-based health plans. **407**
Figure 8-6	Change in occupancy rates in U.S. community hospitals, 1960–2019 (selected years). **359**	Figure 9-11	Beneficiaries (in millions) in Medicare Advantage Plans, Selected Years. **408**
Figure 8-7	Aggregate hospital costs and hospital stays by payer type, 2017. **361**	Figure 9-12	Organizational integration strategies. **413**

List of Figures

Figure 10-1 Percentage distribution of Medicare beneficiaries age 65 and over with limitations performing activities of daily living (ADLs) and instrumental activities of daily living (IADLs), by residential setting, 2017. **432**

Figure 10-2 Key characteristics of a well-designed long-term care system. **434**

Figure 10-3 Range of services for individuals in need of long-term care. **440**

Figure 10-4 Most frequently provided services to home health patients. **444**

Figure 10-5 Sources of payment for home health care, 2017. **445**

Figure 10-6 Distinctly certified units in a nursing home. **451**

Figure 10-7 Sources of Payment for nursing home care, 2018. **454**

Figure 11-1 Percentage of U.S. live births weighing less than 2,500 grams by mother's detailed race. **464**

Figure 11-2 Percentage of U.S. mothers who smoked cigarettes during pregnancy according to mother's race. **465**

Figure 11-3 Alcohol consumption by persons 18 years of age and older (age/sex adjusted). **466**

Figure 11-4 Use of mammography by women 40 years of age and older. **466**

Figure 11-5 U.S. life expectancy at birth. **467**

Figure 11-6 Age-adjusted death rates for persons aged 25 and over. **469**

Figure 11-7 Respondent-assessed health status. **471**

Figure 11-8 Current cigarette smoking by persons 18 years of age and older, age-adjusted, 2018. **471**

Figure 11-9 Percentage of female students of total enrollment in schools for selected health occupations, 2013–2014. **481**

Figure 11-10 Contraceptive use in the past month among women 15–49 years old, 2017–19. **484**

Figure 11-11 AIDS cases reported in the United States. **495**

Figure 11-12 Federal spending for HIV/AIDS by category, FY 2019. **499**

Figure 12-1 Average annual percentage growth in U.S. national healthcare spending. **521**

Figure 12-2 Annual percentage change in CPI and medical inflation, 1975–2019. **523**

Figure 12-3 Annual percentage change in U.S. national healthcare expenditures and GDP, 1980–2021. **523**

Figure 12-4 U.S. healthcare spending as a percentage of GDP for selected OECD countries, 1985, 2018, and 2021. **525**

Figure 12-5 Life expectancy of Americans at birth, age 65, and age 75, 1900–2021 (selected years). **528**

Figure 12-6 Change in U.S. population mix between 1970 and 2010, and projections for 2020 and 2030. **529**

Figure 12-7 Increase in U.S. per capita Medicare spending, 1970–2016 (selected years). **535**

Figure 12-8 Framework for access in the managed care context. **541**

Figure 12-9 Visit rates, by selected demographics, United States, 2018. **546**

Figure 12-10 Percentage of adults aged 18-64 with a dental visit in the past 12 months, by survey year and sex: United States, 2019 and 2020. **547**

Figure 12-11 Percentage of adults aged 18-64 with a dental visit in the past 12 months, by survey year and race and ethnicity: United States, 2019 and 2020. **548**

Figure 12-12 The Donabedian model. **554**

List of Tables

Table 1-1	The Complexity of U.S. Healthcare Delivery 3
Table 1-2	The Continuum of Healthcare Services 16
Table 2-1	Percentage of U.S. Population with Behavioral Risks 54
Table 2-2	Annual Percentage Decline in U.S. Mortalities from Breast, Cervical, Ovarian, and Prostate Cancers, 1991–2016 59
Table 2-3	Annual Percentage Decline in U.S. Specific Cancer Mortalities, 2016–2020 59
Table 2-4	Leading Causes of Death, 2017 63
Table 2-5	U.S. Life Expectancy at Birth—2002, 2007, 2015, and 2021 76
Table 2-6	Comparison of Market Justice and Social Justice 84
Table 2-7	*Healthy People 2020* Topic Areas 90
Table 4-1	Persons Employed in Health Service Sites 147
Table 4-2	Active U.S. Physicians According to Type of Physician and Number per 10,000 Population 148
Table 4-3	Number of People per Active Physician by Specialty, 2021 151
Table 4-4	Mean Annual Compensation for U.S. Physicians by Selected Specialties, 2023 157
Table 4-5	Percentage of Total Enrollment of Students in Programs for Selected Health Occupations by Race, 2008–2009 158
Table 4-6	U.S. Medical School Enrollment by Race, 2022–2023 158
Table 5-1	Examples of Medical Technologies 192
Table 5-2	MRI Units Available per 1,000,000 Population in Selected Countries, 2019 203
Table 5-3	U.S. Biomedical R&D Investment in 2020 207
Table 5-4	Summary of FDA Legislation 209
Table 6-1	Trends in Employment-Based Health Insurance, Selected Years 252
Table 6-2	Trends in Premium Costs, Selected Years 253
Table 6-3	Medicare: Enrolled Population and Expenditures in Selected Years 261
Table 6-4	Status of Hospital Insurance (HI) and Supplementary Medical Insurance (SMI) Trust Funds, 2015–2022 (Billions of Dollars) 262
Table 6-5	U.S. National Health Expenditures and Growth (Selected Years) 277
Table 6-6	Percentage Distribution of U.S. National Health Expenditures, 2010 and 2021 279

List of Tables

Table	Title	Page
Table 7-1	Owners, Providers, and Settings for Ambulatory Care Services	295
Table 7-2	Examples of Questions in the Primary Care Assessment Tools (PCATs)	305
Table 7-3	Selected Organizational Characteristics of U.S. Home Health and Hospice Care Agencies in the United States, 2018	321
Table 7-4	Patients in Home Health and Hospice Care Served at the Time of the Interview, by Agency Type and Number of Patients in the United States, 2007	322
Table 7-5	U.S. Physician Characteristics, 2019	330
Table 7-6	Principal Reason for Visiting a Physician, 2019	331
Table 7-7	Primary Diagnosis Group, 2019	332
Table 8-1	Discharges, Average Length of Stay, and Average Cost per Stay in U.S. Community Hospitals, 2016	355
Table 8-2	Inpatient Hospital Utilization: Comparative Data for Selected OECD Countries, 2021	358
Table 8-3	Share of Personal Health Expenditures Used for Hospital Care	360
Table 8-4	Changes in Number of U.S. Hospitals, Beds, Average Size, and Occupancy Rates	365
Table 8-5	The Largest U.S. Multihospital Chains, 2019	366
Table 9-1	Mean Annual Worker and Employer Health Insurance Premium Contributions for Family Coverage in Selected Years	395
Table 10-1	Association Between Age, Gender, Multimorbidity, and ADL/IADL Limitations	431
Table 10-2	Trends in Nursing Home Capacity, Utilization, and Expenditures, Selected Years	453
Table 10-3	Use of Nursing Home and ALF/Residential/Personal Care Facilities by Age Groups, 2016	454
Table 11-1	Characteristics of U.S. Mothers by Race/Ethnicity	464
Table 11-2	Age-Adjusted Death Rates for Selected Causes of Death, 1970–2018	467
Table 11-3	Infant, Neonatal, and Postneonatal Mortality Rates by Mother's Race (per 1,000 Live Births)	470
Table 11-4	Selected Health Risks Among Persons 20 Years and Older, 2013–2016	472
Table 11-5	Vaccinations of Children 19–35 Months of Age for Selected Diseases According to Race, Poverty Status, and Residence in a Metropolitan Statistical Area (MSA), 2017 (%)	480
Table 11-6	Mental Health Organizations, 2020	491
Table 11-7	Mental Health Providers by Discipline, Selected Years	493
Table 11-8	Diagnoses of HIV infection, by Year of Diagnosis and Selected Characteristics, 2016-2020—United States	496

Table 12-1	Average Annual Percentage Increase in U.S. National Healthcare Spending, 1975–2018 **521**		**Table 12-4**	Number of Healthcare Visits According to Selected Patient Characteristics, 2017 **545**
Table 12-2	Healthcare Expenditures as a Proportion of GDP and per Capita Healthcare Expenditures (Selected Years, Selected OECD Countries, 2019–2021 **524**		**Table 12-5**	Dental Visits in the Past Year Among Persons 18–64 Years of Age, 2017 **546**
Table 12-3	Visits to Office-Based Physicians, 2015 **544**			

List of Acronyms

A

AALL—American Association of Labor Legislation
AAMC—Association of American Medical Colleges
AA/PIs—Asian Americans and Pacific Islanders
AAs—Asian Americans
ACA—Affordable Care Act
ACNM—American College of Nurse-Midwives
ACO—accountable care organization
ACS—American College of Surgeons
ADA—American Dental Association
ADC—adult day care
ADLs—activities of daily living
AND—associate's degree nurse
AFC—adult foster care
AHA—American Hospital Association
AHRQ—Agency for Healthcare Research and Quality
AIANs—American Indians and Alaska Natives
AIDS—acquired immunodeficiency syndrome
ALF—assisted living facility
ALOS—average length of stay
AMA—American Medical Association
AMDA—American Medical Directors Association
ANA—American Nurses Association
APCs—ambulatory payment classifications
APN—advanced practice nurse
ARRA—American Recovery and Reinvestment Act
ASPR—Assistant Secretary for Preparedness and Response

B

BBA—Balanced Budget Act
BPCI—bundled payments for care improvement
BSN—baccalaureate degree in nursing
BWC—Biological and Toxin Weapons

C

CAH—critical access hospital
CAM—complementary and alternative medicine
CBO—Congressional Budget Office
CCAH—continuing care at home
CCRC—continuing care retirement center/community
CDC—Centers for Disease Control and Prevention
CDSS—clinical decision support system
CEO—chief executive officer
CEPH—Council on Education for Public Health
CER—comparative effectiveness research
CF—conversion factor
CHAMPVA—Civilian Health and Medical Program of the Department of Veterans Affairs
CHC—community health center
CHIP—Children's Health Insurance Program
CMGs—case-mix groups
C/MHCs—community and migrant health centers
CMS—Centers for Medicare and Medicaid Services
CNA—certified nursing assistant
CNM—certified nurse-midwife
CNS—clinical nurse specialist

xxvii

List of Acronyms

COBRA—Consolidated Omnibus Budget Reconciliation Act
CON—certificate of need
COPC—community-oriented primary care
COTA—certified occupational therapy assistant
COTH—Council of Teaching Hospitals and Health Systems
CPI—consumer price index
CPOE—computerized provider order entry
CPT—Current Procedural Terminology
CQI—continuous quality improvement
CRNA—certified registered nurse anesthetist
CT—computed tomography

D

DC—Doctor of Chiropractic
DD—developmental disability
DDS—Doctor of Dental Surgery
DGME—Direct Graduate Medical Education
DHHS—U.S. Department of Health and Human Services
DHS—U.S. Department of Homeland Security
DMD—Doctor of Dental Medicine
DME—durable medical equipment
DO—Doctor of Osteopathic Medicine
DoD—U.S. Department of Defense
DPM—Doctor of Podiatric Medicine
DRA—Deficit Reduction Act
DRGs—diagnosis-related groups
DSM-5—*Diagnostic and Statistical Manual of Mental Disorders, Fifth Edition*
DTP—diphtheria/tetanus/pertussis (vaccine)

E

EBM—evidence-based medicine
EBRI—Employee Benefit Research Institute
ECG—electrocardiogram
ECU—extended care unit
ED—emergency department
EHRs—electronic health records
EMT—emergency medical technician

EMTALA—Emergency Medical Treatment and Active Labor Act
ENP—Elderly Nutrition Program
ERISA—Employee Retirement Income Security Act
ESRD—end-stage renal disease

F

FD&C Act—Federal Food, Drug, and Cosmetic Act
FDA—Food and Drug Administration
FMAP—Federal Medical Assistance Percentage
FPL—federal poverty level
FTE—full-time equivalent
FY—fiscal year

G

GAO—Government Accountability Office
GDP—gross domestic product
GP—general practitioner

H

HAART—highly active antiretroviral therapy
HCBS—home- and community-based services
HCBW—home- and community-based waiver
HCH—Health Care for the Homeless
HCPCS—Healthcare Common Procedures Coding System
HDHP—high-deductible health plan
HDHP/SO—high-deductible health plan with a savings option
HEDIS—Healthcare Effectiveness Data and Information Set
HHRG—home health resource group
HI—hospital insurance
HIAA—Health Insurance Association of America
Hib—*Haemophilus influenzae* serotype b
HIO—health information organization

List of Acronyms

HIPAA—Health Insurance Portability and Accountability Act
HIT—health information technology
HITECH—Health Information Technology for Economic and Clinical Health Act
HIV—human immunodeficiency virus
HMO—health maintenance organization
HMO Act—Health Maintenance Organization Act
HPSAs—health professional shortage areas
HPV—human papillomavirus
HRA—health reimbursement arrangement
HRQL—health-related quality of life
HRSA—Health Resources and Services Administration
HAS—health savings account
HTA—health technology assessment
HUD—U.S. Department of Housing and Urban Development

I

IADLs—instrumental activities of daily living
ICF—intermediate care facility
ICF/IID—intermediate care facilities for individuals with intellectual disabilities
ICF/MR—intermediate care facilities for the mentally retarded
ID—intellectual disability
IDD—intellectual/developmental disability
IDEA—Individuals with Disabilities Education Act
IDS—integrated delivery systems
IDU—injection drug use
IHR—International Health Regulations
IHS—Indian Health Service
IME—Indirect Medical Education
IMGs—international medical graduates
IOM—Institute of Medicine
IPA—independent practice association
IRB—institutional review board
IRF—inpatient rehabilitation facility
IRMAA—Income-Related Monthly Adjustment Amount
IRS—Internal Revenue Service
IS—information systems
IT—information technology
IV—intravenous

L

LPN—licensed practical nurse
LTC—long-term care
LTCH—long-term care hospital
LVN—licensed vocational nurse

M

MA—Medicare Advantage
MACPAC—Medicaid and CHIP Payment and Access Commission
MACRA—Medicare Access and CHIP Reauthorization Act
MA-PD—Medicare Advantage Prescription Drug Plan
MA-SNP—Medicare Advantage Special Needs Plan
MBA—Master of Business Administration
MCOs—managed care organizations
MD—Doctor of Medicine
MDS—Minimum Data Set
MedPAC—Medicare Payment Advisory Commission
MEPS—Medical Expenditure Panel Survey
MERS—Middle East respiratory syndrome
MFP—Money Follows the Person
MHA—Master of Health Administration
MHS—multihospital system
MHSA—Master of Health Services Administration
MIPS—Merit-based Incentive Payment System
MLP—midlevel provider
MLR—medical loss ratio
MMA—Medicare Prescription Drug, Improvement, and Modernization Act
MMR—measles/mumps/rubella vaccine
MPA—Master of Public Administration/Affairs
MPFS—Medicare Physician Fee Schedule
MPH—Master of Public Health

MRHFP—Medicare Rural Hospital Flexibility Program
MRI—magnetic resonance imaging
MSA—metropolitan statistical area
MS-DRGs—Medicare severity diagnosis-related groups
MSO—management services organization
MSSP—Medicare Shared Savings Program
MUAs—medically underserved areas

N

NAB—National Association of Boards of Examiners of Long-Term Care Administrators
NAPBC—National Action Plan on Breast Cancer
NCCAM—National Center for Complementary and Alternative Medicine
NCCIH—National Center for Complementary and Integrative Health
NCHS—National Center for Health Statistics
NCQA—National Committee for Quality Assurance
NF—nursing facility
NGC—National Guideline Clearinghouse
NHC—neighborhood health center
NHE—national health expenditures
NHI—national health insurance
NHS—national health system
NHS—U.K. National Health Service
NHSC—National Health Service Corps
NICE—National Institute for Health and Clinical Excellence
NIH—National Institutes of Health
NIMH—National Institute of Mental Health
NP—nurse practitioner
NPP—nonphysician practitioner
NRP—National Response Plan

O

OAM—Office of Alternative Medicine
OBRA—Omnibus Budget Reconciliation Act
OD—Doctor of Optometry
OI—opportunistic infection
OPPS—Outpatient Prospective Payment System
OT—occupational therapist
OWH—Office on Women's Health

P

P4P—pay-for-performance
PA—physician assistant
PACE—Program of All-Inclusive Care for the Elderly
PAHPA—Pandemic and All-Hazards Preparedness Act
PASRR—Preadmission Screening and Resident Review
PBMs—pharmacy benefits managers
PCCM—primary-care case management
PCMH—patient-centered medical home
PCP—primary-care physician
PDP—stand-alone prescription drug plan
PERS—personal emergency response system
PET—positron emission tomography
PFFS—private fee-for-service
PharmD—Doctor of Pharmacy
PhD—Doctor of Philosophy
PHI—personal health information
PHO—physician–hospital organization
PhRMA—Pharmaceutical Research and Manufacturers of America
PMPM—per member per month
POH—physician-owned hospital
POS—point-of-service (plan)
PPD—per-patient day (rate)
PPM—physician practice management
PPO—preferred provider organization
PPS—prospective payment system
PRO—peer review organization
PSHP—provider-sponsored health plan
PSO—provider-sponsored organization
PSRO—professional standards review organization
PsyD—Doctor of Psychology
PTA—physical therapy assistant
PTCA—percutaneous transluminal coronary angioplasty
PT—physical therapist

Q

QALY—quality-adjusted life year
QI—quality indicator
QIO—quality improvement organization

R

R&D—research and development
RBRVS—resource-based relative value scales
RN—registered nurse
RUGs—resource utilization groups
RVUs—relative value units
RWJF—Robert Wood Johnson Foundation

S

SAMHSA—Substance Abuse and Mental Health Services Administration
SARS—severe acute respiratory syndrome
SAV—small area variations
SES—socioeconomic status
SGR—sustainable growth rate
SHI—socialized health insurance
SMI—supplementary medical insurance
SNF—skilled nursing facility
SPECT—single-photon emission computed tomography
SSI—Supplemental Security Income
STD—sexually transmitted disease

T

TAH—total artificial heart
TANF—Temporary Assistance for Needy Families
TCU—transitional care unit
TEFRA—Tax Equity and Fiscal Responsibility Act
TPA—third-party administrator
TQM—total quality management

U

UCR—usual, customary, and reasonable
UR—utilization review

V

VA—U.S. Department of Veterans Affairs
VBP—Value-Based Purchasing/Payment
VHA—Veterans Health Administration
VISN—Veterans Integrated Service Network

W

WHO—World Health Organization
WIC—Women, Infants, and Children (special supplemental nutrition program)

CHAPTER 1

An Overview of U.S. Healthcare Delivery

LEARNING OBJECTIVES

- Understand the basic nature of the U.S. healthcare system.
- Outline the key functional components of a healthcare delivery system.
- Provide a basic overview of the Affordable Care Act.
- Discuss the primary characteristics of the U.S. healthcare system.
- Emphasize why it is important for healthcare practitioners and managers to understand the intricacies of the U.S. healthcare system.
- Get an overview of healthcare systems in selected countries.
- Point out global health challenges and reform efforts.
- Introduce the systems model as a framework for organizing the book and studying the healthcare system in the United States.

The U.S. healthcare delivery system is a behemoth that is almost impossible for any single entity to manage and control.

Introduction

The United States has a unique system of healthcare delivery that is unlike any other healthcare system in the world. Almost all other developed countries have national health insurance programs run by the government and financed through general taxes. Nearly all citizens in such countries are entitled to receive healthcare services. Such is not yet the case in the United States, where not everyone is automatically covered by health insurance.

Although U.S. health care is often called a "system," this term may be misleading because a true, cohesive healthcare system does not exist in the United States (Wolinsky, 1988). The Agency for Healthcare Research and Quality or AHRQ's Compendium of US Health Systems defines a health system as "an organization that includes at least one hospital and at least one group of physicians that provides comprehensive care (including primary and specialty care)" (AHRQ, 2023). The World Health Organization (WHO) defines a health system as consisting of all organizations, people, and actions whose primary intent is to promote, restore, or maintain health, including efforts to influence determinants of health as well as more direct health-improving activities (WHO, 2007). The contrast between these definitions highlights the difference between a true health system and a mere healthcare system: the U.S. health system addresses health care rather than health. Indeed, a major feature of the U.S. healthcare system is its fragmented nature, as different people obtain health care through different means. The system has continued to undergo periodic changes, mainly in response to concerns regarding costs, access, and quality.

Describing healthcare delivery in the United States can be a daunting task. To facilitate an understanding of the structural and conceptual basis for the delivery of healthcare services, this textbook is organized according to the systems framework presented at the end of this chapter. Also, for the sake of simplicity, the mechanisms of healthcare delivery in the United States are collectively referred to as a system throughout this text.

The main objective of this chapter is to provide a broad understanding of how health care is delivered in the United States. Examples of how health care is delivered in other selected countries are also presented for the sake of comparison. The overview presented here introduces the reader to several concepts discussed more extensively in later chapters.

An Overview of the Scope and Size of the System

Table 1-1 demonstrates the complexity of healthcare delivery in the United States. Many organizations and individuals are involved in health care. To name just a few: educational and research institutions, medical suppliers, insurers, payers, and claims processors to healthcare providers. A multitude of providers are involved in the delivery of preventive, primary, subacute, acute, auxiliary, rehabilitative, and continuing care. A large number of managed care organizations (MCOs) and integrated networks now provide a continuum of care, covering many of the service components.

The U.S. healthcare delivery system is massive, with total employment exceeding 17.2 million people in 2018 in various health delivery settings (Kaiser Family Foundation, 2023). This number includes more than 9 million health practitioners and individuals in technical occupations, along with more than 6.7 million individuals in healthcare support occupations (U.S. Bureau of Labor Statistics, 2022a, 2022b; Kaiser Family Foundation, 2022). Approximately 5.6 million workers are employed in general medical and surgical hospital settings, while another 2.8 million are employed in physicians' offices (U.S. Bureau of Labor Statistics, 2022a, 2022b). The vast array of healthcare institutions in the United

Table 1-1 The Complexity of U.S. Healthcare Delivery

Education/ Research	Suppliers	Insurers	Providers	Payers	Government
Medical schools Dental schools Nursing programs Physician assistant programs Nurse practitioner programs Physical therapy, Occupational therapy, Speech therapy programs Research organizations Private foundations U.S. Public Health Service (Agency for Healthcare Research and Quality, Agency for Toxic Substances and Disease Registry, Centers for Disease Control and Prevention, Food and Drug Administration, Health Resources and Services Administration, Indian Health Service, National Institutes of Health, Substance Abuse and Mental Health Services Administration) Professional associations Trade associations	Pharmaceutical companies Multipurpose suppliers Biotechnology companies	Managed care plans Blue Cross/ Blue Shield plans Commercial insurers Self-insured employers Medicare Medicaid Veterans Affairs Tricare	**Preventive Care** Health Departments **Primary Care** Physician offices Community health centers Dentists Nonphysician Providers **Subacute Care** Subacute care facilities Ambulatory surgery centers **Acute Care** Hospitals **Auxiliary Services** Pharmacists Diagnostic clinics X-ray units Suppliers of medical equipment **Rehabilitative Services** Home health agencies Rehabilitation centers Skilled nursing Facilities **Continuing Care** Nursing homes **End-of-Life Care** Hospices **Integrated** Managed care organizations Integrated networks	Blue Cross/Blue Shield Plans Commercial insurers Employers Third-party Administrators State agencies	Public insurance financing Health regulations Health policy Research funding Public health

States includes approximately 6,129 hospitals (American Hospital Association, 2023), 15,600 nursing homes (Centers for Disease Control and Prevention [CDC], 2018), and 16,066 substance abuse treatment facilities (Statista, 2023). In 2022, 1,370 federally qualified health center grantees provided preventive and primary care services to approximately 30.5 million people living in medically underserved rural and urban areas (Health Resources and Services Administration [HRSA], 2022). Various types of healthcare professionals are trained in 180 medical and osteopathic schools (Association of American Medical Colleges, 2017), 67 dental schools (American Dental Association, 2022), 142 schools of pharmacy (American Association of Colleges of Pharmacy, 2022), and more than 2,600 nursing programs located throughout the country (Nursingschool411.com, 2023). Multitudes of government agencies are involved with the financing of health care, medical research, and regulatory oversight of the various aspects of the healthcare delivery system.

A Broad Description of the System

U.S. healthcare delivery does not function as a rational and integrated network of components designed to work together coherently. To the contrary, it is a kaleidoscope of financing, insurance, delivery, and payment mechanisms that remain loosely coordinated. Each of these basic functional components represents an amalgam of public (government) and private sources. Government-run programs finance and insure health care for select groups of people who meet each program's prescribed criteria for eligibility. To a lesser degree, government programs also deliver certain healthcare services directly to certain recipients, such as veterans, military personnel, Native American people/Alaska Native people, and some uninsured people. Nevertheless, financing, insurance, payment, and delivery functions largely remain in private hands.

The market-oriented economy in the United States attracts a variety of private entrepreneurs that pursue profits by facilitating the key functions of healthcare delivery. Employers purchase health insurance for their employees through private sources, and employees receive healthcare services delivered by the private sector. The government finances public insurance through Medicare, Medicaid, the Children's Health Insurance Program (CHIP), and a variety of state-initiated insurance programs for a significant portion of the country's low-income, older, disabled, and pediatric populations. However, insurance arrangements for many publicly insured people are made through private entities, such as health maintenance organizations (HMOs), and healthcare services are rendered by private physicians and hospitals. This blend of public and private involvement in the delivery of health care has resulted in the following characteristics of the U.S. healthcare system:

- A multiplicity of financial arrangements for healthcare services
- Numerous insurance agencies or MCOs that employ various mechanisms for insuring against risk
- Multiple payers that make their own determinations regarding how much to pay for each type of service
- A diverse array of settings where medical services are delivered
- Numerous consulting firms offering expertise in planning, cost containment, electronic systems, quality, and restructuring of resources

There is little standardization in this system because it is functionally fragmented and the various system components fit only loosely together. Because a central agency such as the government does not oversee the overall coordination of such a system, problems of duplication, overlap, inadequacy, inconsistency, and waste occur. Lack of system-wide planning, direction, and coordination leads to a complex and inefficient system. Moreover, the system does not lend itself to standard budgetary methods of cost control because individual and corporate entities within a predominantly private entrepreneurial system seek to manipulate financial incentives to their own advantage with no regard to their impact on the system as a whole. Hence, cost containment remains an elusive goal.

In short, the U.S. healthcare delivery system is like a behemoth that is almost impossible for any single entity to manage or control. The United States consumes more healthcare services as a proportion of its total economic output than any other country in the world. The U.S. economy is the largest in the world, and compared with other nations, consumption of healthcare services in the United States represents a greater proportion of the country's total economic output. Although the U.S. healthcare system can be credited with delivering some of the best clinical care in the world, it falls short of delivering equitable services to every person in the United States. It certainly fails in terms of providing cost-efficient services.

An acceptable healthcare delivery system should have two primary objectives: (1) enable all citizens to obtain needed healthcare services and (2) ensure that services are cost-effective and meet certain established standards of quality. While the U.S. healthcare delivery system falls short of both these basic ideals, the United States leads the world in providing the latest and the best in medical technology, training, and research. It also offers some of the most sophisticated institutions, products, and processes of healthcare delivery.

Basic Components of a Healthcare Delivery System

Figure 1-1 illustrates that a healthcare delivery system incorporates four functional components: financing, insurance, delivery, and payment. Hence, it is termed a **quad-function model**. Healthcare delivery systems differ depending on the arrangement of these components. The four functions generally overlap, but the degree of overlap varies between private and government-run systems, and between traditional health insurance and managed care-based systems. In a government-run system, the functions are more closely integrated and may be indistinguishable. Managed care arrangements also integrate the four functions to varying degrees.

Financing

Financing is necessary to obtain health insurance or to pay for healthcare services. For most privately insured people in the United States, health insurance is employment-based, that is, employers finance health care as a fringe benefit for their employees. A dependent spouse or the child(ren) may also be covered by the employed spouse's or employed parent's employer. Most employers purchase health insurance for their employees through an MCO or an insurance company selected by the employer. Small employers may or may not be in a position to afford health insurance coverage for their employees. In public programs, the government functions as the financier; the insurance function may be carved out to an HMO.

Insurance

Insurance protects the insured against financial catastrophe by providing expensive healthcare services when needed. The insurance function determines the package of health services that the insured individual is entitled to receive. In addition, it specifies how and where healthcare services may be received. The MCO or insurance company also functions as a claims processor and manages the disbursement of funds to the healthcare providers.

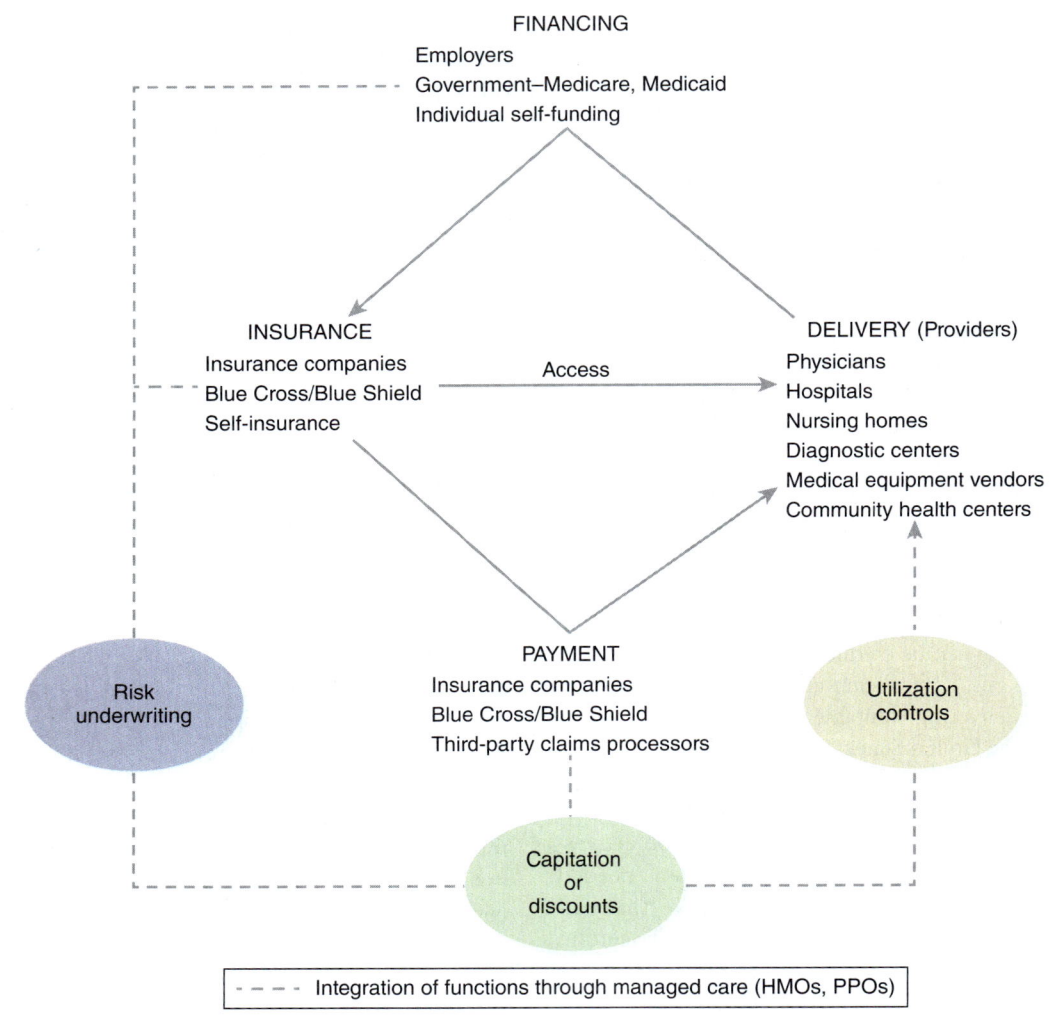

Figure 1-1 Basic healthcare delivery functions.

```
                          FINANCING
                          Employers
                          Government–Medicare, Medicaid
                          Individual self-funding

        INSURANCE                              DELIVERY (Providers)
        Insurance companies     Access         Physicians
        Blue Cross/Blue Shield                 Hospitals
        Self-insurance                         Nursing homes
                                               Diagnostic centers
                                               Medical equipment vendors
                                               Community health centers

    Risk                      PAYMENT                    Utilization
    underwriting              Insurance companies        controls
                              Blue Cross/Blue Shield
                              Third-party claims processors

                              Capitation
                              or
                              discounts

        Integration of functions through managed care (HMOs, PPOs)
```

Delivery

The term "delivery" refers to the provision of healthcare services by various providers. The term **provider** refers to any entity that delivers healthcare services and either independently bills for those services or is supported through tax revenues. Common examples of providers include physicians, dentists, optometrists, therapists in private practices, hospitals, diagnostic and imaging clinics, and suppliers of medical equipment (e.g., wheelchairs, walkers, ostomy supplies, oxygen). With few exceptions, most providers render services to people who have health insurance, and even those covered under public insurance programs receive healthcare services from private providers.

Payment

The payment function deals with **reimbursement** to providers for services delivered. The insurer determines how much is paid for a certain service. Funds for actual disbursement come from the premiums paid to the MCO or insurance company. At the time of service, the patient is usually required to pay an out-of-pocket amount, such as $25 or $50, to consult a physician. The remainder is covered by the MCO or insurance company. In government insurance plans, such as Medicare and Medicaid, tax revenues are used to pay providers.

Insurance and Healthcare Reform

The U.S. government finances health benefits for certain special populations, including government employees, older persons (people aged 65 years and older), people with disabilities, some people with very low incomes, and children from low-income families. The program for older persons and individuals with certain disabilities, which is administered by the federal government, is called **Medicare**. The program for the underserved, which is jointly administered by the federal government and state governments, is called **Medicaid**. The program for children from low-income families, another federal-state partnership, is called the Children's Health Insurance Program or CHIP.

However, the predominant employment-based financing system in the United States has left some employed individuals uninsured for two main reasons. The first is that some small businesses simply cannot get group insurance at affordable rates and, therefore, are not able to offer health insurance as a benefit to their employees. The second is because in some work settings, participation in health insurance programs is voluntary, so employees are not required to join. Some employees choose not to sign up, mainly because they cannot afford the cost of health insurance premiums. Employers rarely pay 100% of the insurance premium; instead, most require their employees to pay a portion of the cost. This is called **premium cost sharing**. Self-employed people and other individuals who are not covered by employer-based plans have to obtain health insurance on their own. Individual rates are typically higher than group rates available to employers. In the United States, employed people earning low wages have been the most likely to be uninsured because most cannot afford premium cost sharing and are not eligible for public benefits.

A further vulnerability under employment-based insurance becomes evident when a crisis slows down or even stops businesses, such as what occurred during the COVID-19 pandemic. As a result of economic pressures, companies had to lay off large numbers of employees to remain solvent. Those unemployed soon lost insurance coverage since it was tied to their employer. The disruption in insurance coverage was especially damaging because the newly uninsured faced challenges in accessing needed care, including care related to the crisis itself, such as testing and treatment for the coronavirus.

In the U.S. context, **healthcare reform** primarily refers to the expansion of health insurance to cover the **uninsured**—those without private or public health insurance coverage. The Patient Protection and Affordable Care Act of 2010, more commonly known as the Affordable Care Act (ACA), was the most sweeping healthcare reform in recent U.S. history. One of the main objectives of the ACA was to reduce the number of the uninsured. The ACA was rolled out gradually starting in 2010, when insurance companies were mandated to start covering children and adults younger than age 26 under their parents' health insurance plans. Most other insurance provisions went into effect on January 1, 2014, except for a mandate for employers to provide health insurance, which was postponed until 2015. The ACA required that all U.S. citizens and legal residents must be covered by either public or private insurance. The law also relaxed standards to qualify additional numbers of people for Medicaid, although many states chose not to implement the Medicaid expansion based on a 2012 ruling by the U.S. Supreme Court.

Under the ACA, individuals without private or public insurance had to obtain health insurance from participating insurance companies through Web-based, government-run exchanges; if they failed to do so, they had to pay a tax penalty. The exchanges—also referred to as health insurance marketplaces—would determine whether an applicant qualified for Medicaid or CHIP programs. If an applicant did not qualify for a public program, the exchange would enable the individual to purchase a government-approved health plan offered by private insurers through the exchange. Federal subsidies enabled people with income below a certain threshold to partially offset the cost of health insurance.

A predictive model developed by Parente and Feldman (2013) estimated that, at best, full implementation of the ACA would reduce the number of uninsured by more than 20 million. Nevertheless, by its own design, the ACA failed to achieve **universal coverage** that would enable all citizens and legal residents to have health insurance. Possible future scenarios for healthcare reform are discussed elsewhere in this textbook.

By March 2015, approximately 16.5 million uninsured people in the United States had gained health insurance coverage due to the Affordable Care Act ("Impact of Obamacare on Coverage," 2016). By 2016, an estimated 20 million had gained coverage (Uberoi et al., 2016), and by 2023, 41 states and the District of Columbia had expanded Medicaid through the ACA's provisions (Kaiser Family Foundation, 2023). The uninsured rate declined among all race/ethnicity categories, with the greatest decreases seen among Black and Hispanic people compared to White people (Uberoi et al., 2016). The uninsured rate declined from 22.4% to 10.6% among Black people, from 41.8% to 30.5% among Hispanic people, and from 14.3% to 7.0% among White people (Uberoi et al., 2016). Additionally, women experienced a greater decline in their uninsured rate (49.7% decline) compared to men (37.6% decline). Despite these gains, however, the ACA left more than 27.3 million people in the United States uninsured in 2016 (Cohen et al., 2016). A full critique of the ACA is provided in the *Health Policy* chapter.

During his first week in office in January 2017, President Donald Trump signed an Executive Order to repeal and replace the ACA (commonly referred to as Obamacare) in an effort to minimize the ACA's economic and regulatory burdens and to waive any requirement imposing a fiscal burden on states or families, individuals, healthcare providers, insurers, or other parties. By 2019, the Trump administration was able to alter significant portions of the ACA through administrative means (Simmons-Duffin, 2019). As a result, the number of uninsured increased significantly. From 2017 to 2018, the number of uninsured grew by almost 500,000 people for the second year in a row (Tolbert et al., 2019). However, under the Biden administration, the number of uninsured decreased by 1.9%, from 10.3% or 33.2 million in 2019 to 8.4% or 27.6 million in 2022 (National Center for Health Statistics, 2023).

Role of Managed Care

Under traditional insurance, the four basic health delivery functions have been fragmented in the United States; with few exceptions, the financiers, insurers, providers, and payers have been different entities. However, during the 1990s, healthcare delivery in the country underwent a fundamental change involving a tighter integration of the basic functions through managed care.

Previously, fragmentation of the four functions meant a lack of control over utilization and payments. The quantity of health care consumed refers to **utilization** of health services. Traditionally, the determination of the use of health services and the price charged for each service had been left up to the insured individuals and the providers of health care. However, due to rising healthcare costs, current delivery mechanisms have instituted some controls over both use and price.

Managed care is a system of healthcare delivery that (1) seeks to achieve efficiency by integrating the four functions of healthcare delivery discussed earlier, (2) employs mechanisms to control (manage) utilization of medical services, and (3) determines the price of services and consequently how much the providers are paid. The primary financier is still the employer or the government. Instead of purchasing health insurance through a traditional insurance company, the employer contracts with an MCO, such as an HMO or a preferred provider organization (PPO), to offer a selected health plan to its employees. In this case, the MCO functions like an insurance company and promises to provide healthcare services contracted under the health plan to the enrollees of the plan. The term **enrollee** (member) refers to the individual covered under the plan. The contractual arrangement between the MCO and the enrollee—including the collective array of covered health services that the enrollee is entitled to—is referred to as the **health plan** (or "plan," for short). The health plan uses selected providers from whom the enrollees can choose to receive services.

Compared with health services delivery under fee-for-service plans, managed care was successful in accomplishing cost control and greater integration of healthcare delivery. By ensuring access to needed health services, emphasizing preventive care, and maintaining a broad provider network, managed care can implement effective cost-saving measures without compromising access and quality, thereby achieving a healthcare budget predictability unattainable by other kinds of healthcare delivery.

Major Characteristics of the U.S. Healthcare System

In any country, certain external influences shape the basic character of the health services delivery system. These forces consist of the national political climate, economic development, technological progress, social and cultural values, physical environment, population characteristics (i.e., demographic and health trends), and global influences (**Figure 1-2**). The combined interactions of these environmental forces influence the course of healthcare delivery.

The following are ten basic characteristics that differentiate the U.S. healthcare delivery system from those practiced in most other countries:

1. No central agency governs the system.
2. Access to healthcare services is selectively based on insurance coverage.
3. Health care is delivered under imperfect market conditions.
4. Insurers from a **third party** act as intermediaries between the financing and delivery functions.
5. The existence of multiple payers makes the system cumbersome.
6. The balance of power among various players prevents any single entity from dominating the system.
7. Legal risks influence the practice behavior of physicians.
8. Development of new technology creates an automatic demand for its use.

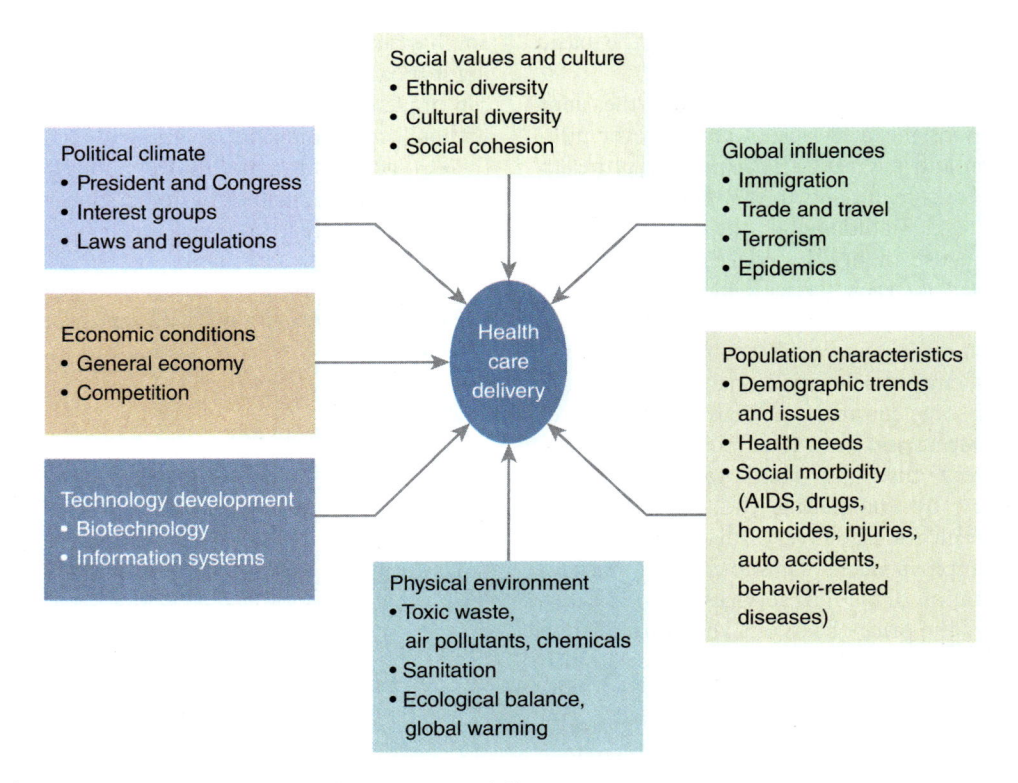

Figure 1-2 External forces affecting healthcare delivery.

9. New service settings have evolved along a continuum.
10. Quality and value are fast becoming the hallmarks of care delivery.

No Central Agency

Unlike healthcare systems in most developed nations, the U.S. healthcare system is not administratively controlled by a department or agency. Other developed nations have a national healthcare program, which entitles citizens to receive a defined set of healthcare services. To control costs, these systems use **global budgets** that determine total healthcare expenditures on a national scale and allocate resources within budgetary limits. As a consequence, both availability of services and payments to providers are subject to budgetary constraints. The governments of these nations also control the proliferation of healthcare services, especially costly medical technology. System-wide controls over the allocation of resources determine the extent to which government-sponsored healthcare services are made available to citizens. For instance, the availability of specialized services is restricted.

By contrast, the United States has a highly private system of financing and delivery. Private health insurance, predominantly through employers, accounts for approximately 34% of total healthcare expenditures; the government finances another 37% (Centers for Medicare and Medicaid, 2020). Private delivery of health care means that the majority of hospitals and physician clinics are private businesses, which operate independently of the government. No central agency monitors total expenditures through global budgets or controls the availability and utilization of services. Nevertheless, federal and state governments play important roles in healthcare delivery. They determine public sector expenditures and reimbursement rates for services provided to Medicare, Medicaid, and CHIP beneficiaries. The federal government also formulates **standards of participation** through health policy and regulation, meaning providers must comply with the standards established by the government to be certified to provide services to Medicare, Medicaid, and CHIP beneficiaries. Certification standards are regarded as minimum standards of quality in most sectors of the healthcare industry.

Partial Access

Access means the ability of an individual to obtain healthcare services when needed, which is not the same as having health insurance. People in the United States can access healthcare services if they (1) have health insurance through their employers, (2) are covered under a government healthcare program, (3) can afford to buy insurance with their own private funds, (4) are able to pay for services privately, or (5) can obtain charity or subsidized care. Health insurance is the primary means for ensuring access. Although the uninsured can access certain types of services, they often encounter barriers to obtaining needed health care. For example, while federally supported health centers provide physician services to anyone regardless of their ability to pay, such centers and free clinics are located only in certain geographic areas and provide limited specialized services. However, under U.S. law, hospital emergency departments (EDs) are required to evaluate a patient's condition and render medically needed services even if the patient is unable to pay. Therefore, even uninsured individuals are able to obtain medical care for acute illnesses, although with access barriers such as long waiting lines and medical debts. While one can say that the United States does have a form of universal catastrophic health insurance, it does not guarantee the uninsured access to continual basic and routine care, commonly referred to as **primary care** (Altman and Reinhardt, 1996).

Countries with national healthcare programs provide universal coverage. However, even in these countries, access to services may be restricted because no healthcare system has the capacity to deliver every type of service on demand. Hence, **universal access**—the ability of all citizens to obtain health care when needed—remains mostly an aspirational concept.

As previously mentioned, having coverage does not necessarily equate to having access. The cost of insurance and care and availability of services have continued to present barriers to receiving healthcare services in a timely manner.

Imperfect Market

Though the U.S. healthcare delivery system is largely in private hands, this system is only partially governed by free market forces. The delivery and consumption of health care in the United States do not quite pass the basic test of a **free market**, so the system is best described as a quasi-market or an imperfect market.

In a free market, patients (buyers) and providers (sellers) act independently, with patients being allowed to choose services from any provider. Providers do not collude to fix prices, and prices are not fixed by an external agency. Rather, prices are governed by the free and unencumbered interaction of the forces of supply and demand (**Figure 1-3**). **Demand**—the quantity of health care purchased—is driven by the prices prevailing in the free market. Under free-market conditions, the quantity demanded will increase as the price for

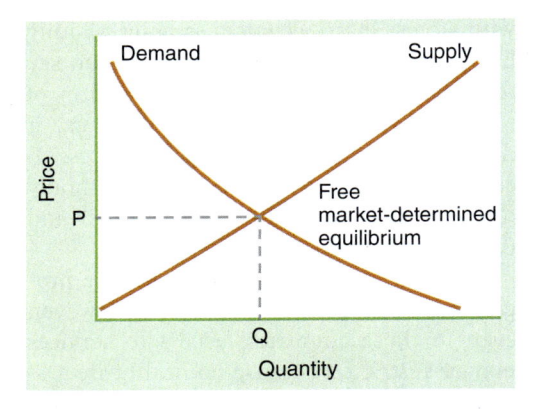

Figure 1-3 Relationship between price, supply, and demand under free market conditions.

a given product or service declines. Conversely, the quantity demanded will decrease as the price increases.

At first glance, it might appear that multiple patients and providers do exist. Most patients in the United States, however, are now enrolled in either a private health plan or one or more government-sponsored programs. These plans act as intermediaries for the patients, and the enrollment of patients into health plans has the effect of shifting power from the patients to the administrators of the plans. The result is that the health plans—not the patients—are the real buyers in the healthcare services market. Private health plans, in many instances, offer their enrollees a limited choice of providers rather than an open choice.

Theoretically, prices are negotiated between the payers and providers. In practice, however, prices are determined by payers, such as MCOs, Medicare, and Medicaid. Because prices are set by agencies external to the market, they are not governed by the unencumbered forces of supply and demand.

For the healthcare market to be free, unrestrained competition must occur among providers based on price and quality. However, the consolidation of buying power in the hands of private health plans has forced many providers to form alliances and integrated delivery systems on the supply side. In certain geographic sectors of the country, a single giant medical system has taken over as the sole provider of major healthcare services, restricting competition. As the overall United States healthcare system continues to move in this direction, it appears that only in large metropolitan areas will there be more than one large integrated system competing to get the business of the health plans.

A free market requires that patients have information about the appropriateness of various services to fit their needs. Such information is difficult to obtain because technology-driven medical care has become highly sophisticated. Knowledge about new diagnostic methods, intervention techniques, and more effective drugs is part of the domain of the professional physician, not the patient. Moreover, because medical interventions are commonly required in a state of urgency, patients have neither the skills nor the time and resources to obtain accurate information when needed. Channeling all healthcare needs through a primary care provider can reduce this information gap when the primary care provider acts as the patient's advocate or agent. In recent years, consumers have been seizing some measure of control over the flow of information: the Internet is becoming a prominent source of medical information for patients, and medical advertising is influencing consumer expectations.

In a free market, patients must directly bear the cost of services received. The purpose of insurance is to protect against the risk of unforeseen catastrophic events. Since the fundamental purpose of insurance is to reimburse major expenses when unlikely events occur, having insurance for basic and routine health care undermines the principle of insurance. When you buy home insurance to protect your property against the unlikely event of a fire, you do not anticipate the occurrence of a loss. The probability that you will suffer a loss by fire is very small. If a fire does occur and causes major damage, insurance will cover the loss, but insurance does not cover routine wear and tear on the house, such as chipped paint or a leaky faucet. However, unlike other types of insurance, health insurance generally covers basic and routine services that are predictable. Coverage for minor services, such as colds and coughs, earaches, and so forth, amounts to prepayment for such services. In this sense, health insurance has the effect of insulating patients from the full cost of health care. This situation may also create a **moral hazard**, in that once enrollees have purchased health insurance, they may use more healthcare services than if they were to pay for these services on an out-of-pocket basis.

At least two additional factors limit patients' ability to make decisions in the healthcare system. First, decisions about the use of health care are often determined by need rather than by price-based demand. **Need** has been defined as the amount of medical care that medical experts believe a person should have to remain or become healthy (Feldstein, 1993). Second, the delivery of health care can itself create demand. This follows from self-assessed need, which, coupled with moral hazard, leads to greater use, producing an artificial demand because prices are not taken into consideration. Practitioners who have a financial interest in additional treatments may also create artificial demand (Hemenway and Fallon, 1985), a scenario referred to as **provider-induced demand** or supplier-induced demand. Functioning as patients' agents, physicians exert enormous influence on the demand for healthcare services (Altman and Wallack, 1996). Demand creation occurs when physicians prescribe medical care beyond what is clinically necessary—for example, by making more frequent follow-up appointments than necessary, prescribing excessive medical tests, or performing unnecessary surgery (Santerre and Neun, 1996).

In a free market, patients have information on the price and quality of each provider. The current system, however, has drawbacks that obstruct information-seeking efforts. Item-based pricing is one such hurdle. Surgery is a good example that illustrates item-based (also known as fee-for-service) pricing. Patients can generally find information on the fees the surgeon would charge for a particular operation. But the final bill, after the surgery has been performed, is likely to include charges for supplies, use of the hospital's facilities, and services performed by other providers, such as anesthesiologists, nurse anesthetists, and pathologists. These providers, sometimes referred to as **phantom providers**, function in an adjunct capacity and bill for their services separately. Item billing for such additional services, which sometimes cannot be anticipated, makes it extremely difficult to ascertain the total price before services have actually been received.

Package pricing can help overcome these drawbacks, but it has made relatively little headway as a means of pricing medical procedures. **Package pricing** refers to a bundled fee charged for a package of related services. In the surgery example, this would mean one all-inclusive price for the surgeon's fees, hospital facilities, supplies, diagnostics, pathology, anesthesia, and postsurgical follow-up.

Third-Party Insurers and Payers

Insurance often functions as the intermediary among those who finance, deliver, and receive health care. The insurance intermediary does not have an incentive to be the patient's advocate on either price or quality. At best, employees can air their dissatisfaction with the plan to their employer, which has the power to discontinue the current plan and choose another company. In reality, however, employers may be reluctant to change plans if the current plan offers lower premiums than a different plan.

Multiple Payers

A national healthcare system is sometimes referred to as a **single-payer system** because it features one primary payer, the government. When delivering services, providers send the bill to a government agency, which subsequently sends payments to each provider. By contrast, the United States has a multiplicity of health plans. Multiple payers often represent a billing and collection nightmare for the providers of services, and they make the system more cumbersome in several ways:

- It is extremely difficult for providers to keep tabs on numerous health plans. It is challenging for providers to keep up with which services are covered under each plan and how much each plan will pay for those services.
- Providers must hire claims processors to bill for services and monitor receipt of payments. Billing practices are not standardized, and each payer establishes its own format.
- Payments can be denied for not precisely following the requirements set by each payer.
- Denied claims necessitate rebilling.
- When only partial payment is received, some health plans may allow the provider to **balance bill** the patient for the amount the health plan did not pay, that is, the difference between provider charges and insurance payment. Other plans prohibit balance billing. Even when the balance billing option is available to the provider, it triggers a new cycle of billings and collection efforts.
- Providers must sometimes engage in lengthy collection efforts, including writing collection letters, turning delinquent accounts over to collection agencies, and finally writing off as bad debt amounts that cannot be collected.
- Government programs have complex regulations for determining whether payment is made for services actually delivered. Medicare, for example, requires that each provider maintain lengthy documentation on the services provided. Medicaid is known for lengthy delays in paying providers.

It is generally believed that the United States spends far more on **administrative costs**—costs associated with billing, collections, bad debts, and maintaining medical records—than do the national healthcare systems in other countries (Himmelstein, 2014; Himmelstein et al., 2020).

Power Balancing

The U.S. healthcare system involves multiple players, not just multiple payers. The key players in the system have traditionally been physicians, administrators of health service institutions, insurance companies, large employers, and the government. Big business, labor, insurance companies, physicians, and hospitals make up the powerful and politically active special interest groups represented before lawmakers by high-priced lobbyists. Each set of players has its own economic interests to protect. Physicians, for instance, want to maintain their incomes and have minimum interference with the way they practice medicine; institutional administrators seek to maximize reimbursement from private and public insurers; insurance companies and MCOs are interested in maintaining their share of the health insurance market; large employers want to contain the costs they incur providing health insurance to their employees; and the government tries to maintain or enhance existing benefits for those covered under public insurance programs and simultaneously contain the cost of providing these benefits. The problem is that the self-interests of different players are often at odds. For example, providers seek to increase government reimbursement for services delivered to Medicare, Medicaid, and CHIP beneficiaries, but the government wants to contain cost increases. Employers dislike rising health insurance premiums. Health plans, under pressure from the employers, may limit fees for the providers, who then resent these cuts.

The fragmented self-interests of the various players produce competing forces within the system. In an environment that is rife with motivations to protect conflicting self-interests, achieving comprehensive system-wide reform has proved next to impossible, and cost containment has remained a major challenge. Consequently, the approach to healthcare reform in the United States has been characterized as incremental or piecemeal, and the focus of reform initiatives has been confined to health insurance coverage and payment cuts to providers rather than focusing on better provision of health care.

Litigation Risks

The United States is a litigious society. Motivated by the prospects of enormous jury awards, many people in the United States are quick to drag an alleged offender into a courtroom on the perception of incurred harm. Private healthcare providers, too, have become increasingly susceptible to litigation, and the risk of malpractice lawsuits is a real consideration in the practice of medicine. To protect themselves against the possibility of litigation, practitioners may engage in **defensive medicine**, the practice of prescribing additional diagnostic tests, scheduling return checkup visits, and maintaining copious documentation. Many of these additional efforts may be unnecessary, costly, and inefficient.

High Technology

The United States has long been a hotbed of research and innovation in new medical technology. The resulting growth in science and technology often creates demand for new services despite shrinking resources to finance sophisticated care. People generally equate high-tech care with high-quality care. They want "the latest and the best," especially when health insurance will pay for new treatments. Physicians and technicians want to try the latest gadgets. Hospitals compete on the basis of having the most modern equipment and facilities. Once capital investments in these new services are made, those costs must be recouped through utilization. Legal risks for providers and health plans may also play a role in discouraging denial of new technology. Thus, several factors promote the use of costly new technology once it is developed.

Continuum of Services

Medical care services are classified into three broad categories: curative (i.e., drugs, treatments, and surgeries), restorative (i.e., physical, occupational, and speech therapies), and preventive (i.e., prenatal care, mammograms, and immunizations). Healthcare settings are no longer confined to the hospital and the physician's office. Additional settings, such as home health, subacute care units, and outpatient surgery centers, have emerged in response to the changing configuration of economic incentives. **Table 1-2** describes the continuum of healthcare services. The healthcare continuum in the United States remains lopsided, with a heavier emphasis on specialized services than on preventive services, primary care, and management of chronic conditions.

Quest for Quality and Value

Even though the definition and measurement of quality in health care are not as clear-cut as they are in other industries, the delivery sector of health care has come under increased pressure to develop quality standards and demonstrate

Chapter 1 An Overview of U.S. Healthcare Delivery

Table 1-2 The Continuum of Healthcare Services

Types of Health Services	Delivery Settings
Preventive care	Public health programs Community programs Personal lifestyles Primary care settings
Primary care	Physician's office or clinic Community health centers Self-care Alternative medicine
Specialized care	Specialist provider clinics
Chronic care	Primary care settings Specialist provider clinics Home health Long-term care facilities Self-care Alternative medicine
Long-term care	Long-term care facilities Home health
Subacute care	Special subacute units (hospitals, long-term care facilities) Home health Outpatient surgical centers
Acute care	Hospitals
Rehabilitative care	Rehabilitation departments (hospitals, long-term care facilities) Home health Outpatient rehabilitation centers
End-of-life care	Hospice services provided in a variety of settings

compliance with those standards. There are higher expectations for improved health outcomes at the individual and community levels. The concept of continual quality improvement has also received much emphasis in managing healthcare institutions.

The healthcare landscape has witnessed significant changes in recent years, prompting the exploration and implementation of new delivery models. As an example, the accountable care organization (ACO) model advocated by the Center for Medicare and Medicaid Services (CMS) and the Center for Medicare and Medicaid Innovation (CMMI) aims at improving the quality of patient care while maintaining or reducing expenditures for Medicare services. This model rewards ACOs that can lower their healthcare spending growth while fulfilling quality of care performance standards with additional Medicare payments; conversely, it penalizes those that overspend their expected limit.

According to van Staalduinen et al. (2022), accountable care is when a physician, a team of healthcare professionals, or a medical facility takes the responsibility for enhancing the quality of care, coordinating patient care, and promoting positive health outcomes. In doing so, they aim to minimize care fragmentation and avoidable expenses for both patients and the healthcare system (van Staalduinen et al., 2022). ACOs have gained prominence as a mechanism for delivering coordinated care while controlling costs (van Staalduinen et al., 2022).

Another example of the quest for quality and value is value-based health care (VBHC), which provides financial incentives for achieving specified health outcomes. Bundled-payment models and pay-for-performance (P4P) models are two applications of VBHC. Bundled-payment models, such as the Bundled Payment for Care Improvement Initiative under Medicare, target specific treatments or conditions. P4P models provide incentives for measurable value, as is the case with the Hospital Value-Based Purchasing Program. To achieve high-value care, VBHC not only needs to incentivize high-quality care in conditions or treatments that can be measured, but also stimulate cost-conscious behavior, well-coordinated care, and preventive aspects (Cattel and Eijkenaar, 2019).

Value-based payment models gained momentum in recent years as payers and providers increasingly shifted away from fee-for-service reimbursement (van Staalduinen et al., 2022; Lewis, 2022). Shared savings arrangements and bundled payments were implemented to shift financial incentives toward achieving value and quality outcomes (Lewis, 2022). These approaches aimed to align provider reimbursement with patient outcomes and overall cost savings (Lewis, 2022). Recent evidence suggests that value-based payment models can drive improvements in care delivery, including reduced hospital readmissions, improved preventive services, and better chronic disease management. However, challenges remain, such as defining meaningful quality measures, establishing accurate risk adjustment methodologies, and addressing financial sustainability concerns (Werner et al., 2021).

Trends and Directions

Since the 1980s, the U.S. healthcare delivery system has continued to undergo fundamental shifts in emphasis, summarized in **Figure 1-4**. Other chapters discuss these transformations in greater detail and focus on the factors driving them.

Integrated Delivery Systems

One major shift in emphasis has been toward the implementation of integrated delivery systems (IDS). IDS has emerged as an effective approach to improve care coordination and continuity across the healthcare continuum (Burns et al., 2022). Integration involves the collaboration of various providers and settings, including hospitals, primary care practices, and post-acute care facilities (Al-Saddique, 2018). In a healthcare system plagued by fragmentation and lack of coordination, patients and providers alike seek to coordinate care more efficiently, create smoother transitions, reduce overlap, and control costs. Integrated delivery has emerged as an important component of healthcare delivery, particularly for patients with comorbidities. Recent literature highlights the positive impact of integrated delivery on patient outcomes, access to care, and cost efficiency.

Illness ⟶ Wellness
Acute care ⟶ Primary care
Inpatient ⟶ Outpatient
Individual health ⟶ Community well-being
Fragmented care ⟶ Managed care
Independent institutions ⟶ Integrated systems
Service duplication ⟶ Continuum of services

Figure 1-4 Trends and directions in healthcare delivery.

Examples of integration include single-specialty group practices, where physicians with a common specialty (e.g., cardiology) come together to form an alliance; multispecialty group practices, where primary and specialty care physicians share common administrative oversight and resources as they make referrals to patients to receive other services within the organization; virtual physician networks, where the Internet is used to facilitate access to physicians remotely, particularly for rural and underserved communities; physician-hospital organizations, where hospitals and their affiliated physicians form a partnership to contract health plans; management services organizations, where administrative and infrastructure support services are provided to contracted physicians; and clinically integrated networks, where physicians, hospitals, and providers form a joint venture and provide integrated services (Heeringa et al., 2020). The core functions of IDS are to provide comprehensive healthcare services, be accountable for the cost of the services and outcomes for patients, and improve healthcare coordination and integration. Well-known integrated delivery systems include Kaiser Permanente, Mayo Clinic, and Cleveland Clinic.

Pay-for-Value

Another shift in trends has been toward the concept of **pay-for-value**. Pay-for-value, as the name implies, is a method of payment in which providers are reimbursed based on the quality of health care they deliver. A few studies indicate that pay-for-value systems have, on average, reduced hospital readmissions and improved emergency department use. However, other strategies that have been used to implement such a system have generated mixed results (Cross et al., 2017; Cross et al., 2019; Rosenthal et al., 2016). Many of these mixed results can be attributed to the fact that pay-for-value systems are as various and diverse in their approaches as the settings in which they have been implemented, and this heterogeneity, in turn, leads to heterogeneous results.

Value-driven programs developed by CMS have demonstrated these mixed impacts in recent years (Figueroa et al., 2016; Gupta et al., 2018; Ody and Cutler, 2019; Ody et al., 2019; Papanicolas et al., 2017). Nevertheless, in 2019, CMS rolled out a plan for a new value-based program targeting primary care, called CMS Primary Cares. The hope is that by targeting a provider group that often acts as a first point of contact and strongly influences the trajectory of how patients' illnesses progress thereafter, CMS can significantly reduce costs by incentivizing primary care physicians to provide higher-quality care from the outset (CMS, 2019). Time and research are necessary to determine the long-term implications of this strategy.

Accountable Care Organizations

ACOs incorporate aspects of both integrated delivery and pay-for-value (Gold, 2015). They exist in both the public and private sectors of the healthcare industry, although the most well known and heavily scrutinized are those in the Medicare ACO program created under the ACA. The value of ACOs has been contested through the years, with some studies claiming decent impact and cost reductions, and others showing inconsistent results (Lam et al., 2018; Markowitz et al., 2019; Trombley et al., 2019; Zhang et al., 2019). Organizations of higher quality prior to entry tend to have more success when instituting such a program (Diana et al., 2019; Parasrampuria et al., 2018).

In 2018, CMS announced an overhaul of its primary ACO program, the Medicare Shared Savings Program (MSSP), in response to initial results from the previous six years. Titled "Pathways to Success," the overhaul advances five goals: accountability, competition, engagement, integrity, and quality. Previous research done by CMS indicates that ACOs that took on higher risk showed better outcomes. Therefore, the new rule reduces the amount of time that ACOs can remain in the program without assuming higher levels of risk, but also increases flexibility by expanding access to telehealth services (CMS, 2018; Verma, 2018, 2019).

Commercial ACOs also emerged, partnering with private payers to extend the accountable care model beyond Medicare beneficiaries. Research and evaluation studies were conducted to assess the performance of ACOs. Wilson et al. (2020) identified one recent systematic review and 59 primary studies and pointed out that ACOs help reduce costs, including outpatient expenses and the delivery of low-value services. A growing emphasis was also placed on population health management within ACOs, including preventive care, disease management, and addressing social determinants of health.

Promoting Health

The shift toward IDS, pay-for-value, and ACOs has been primarily driven by the desire to promote health while reducing costs. Another driving factor is a fundamental shift in the concept of health itself. Health is now increasingly seen as the presence of wellness rather than solely as the absence of illness. Such a change requires new methods for wellness promotion, although the treatment of illness remains the primary goal of the healthcare delivery system. The ACA has partially shifted the focus from disease treatment to disease prevention, better health outcomes for individuals and communities, and lower healthcare costs.

Managing Chronic Diseases

At present, the greatest challenge to the U.S. healthcare system is the quest to control costs while still meeting the increasing healthcare demands of an aging population—a population with more chronic diseases and comorbidities. Patients with multiple chronic conditions use health services the most (Sporinova et al., 2019). Managing chronic diseases has been a major focus of efforts to control healthcare costs. In particular, the patient-centered care approach founded on the chronic care model and continuous care is being implemented as a means to improve healthcare delivery performance, quality, and patient health outcomes. It represents a paradigm shift from the traditional hospital- and professional-centric approach to health care to an increasingly community- and consumer-centric approach (Donaldson, 2018; Miller and Baumgartner, 2016).

Patient-Centered Care

Traditionally, the complexity and various access points from which patients come into contact with the system have made it difficult to transition between providers, specialties, and locations of care. Chronically ill individuals with comorbidities who require treatment from various providers may therefore experience fragmentation and uncoordinated care. As a result, treatments may overlap, duplications may occur, and health outcomes may worsen (Frandsen et al., 2015; Juo et al., 2019; World Health Organization [WHO], 2018a).

The patient-centered care approach however strives to overhaul this pattern. As an example, patient-centered medical homes (PCMHs) and ambulatory intensive care units (A-ICUs) are being incorporated into ACOs. The main objective in establishing these programs is to better manage chronic conditions exclusively within a "clinically integrated, financially accountable primary care practice" (DeVore, 2014). Ultimately, providers hope these measures can address behavioral health needs, lower hospital utilization rates, decrease inpatient bed-days, shorten lengths of stay, limit admissions and readmissions, and minimize ED visits.

Mid-Level Healthcare Professionals

Mid-level healthcare professionals and health coaches are also important for managing chronic conditions and reducing costs. Health coaches, for example, complement medical professionals by getting to know patients through one-on-one contact and can keep the clinical staff apprised of financial struggles, issues with housing, family concerns, or other obstacles that may stand in the way of the patient following a prescribed care plan (DeVore, 2014). Health coaches do not need a medical degree, can be recruited from various professional backgrounds, and help improve the effectiveness and efficiency of care.

Telehealth and Health Information Technology

The COVID-19 pandemic quickly demonstrates that healthcare delivery could be made more effectively outside the traditional office visit with the help of technology and the Internet (National Academies of Sciences, Engineering, and Medicine, 2021, p. 115). According to National Academies of Sciences, Engineering, and Medicine (2021), telehealth use in primary care rose by approximately 50%, with both rural and urban healthcare providers experiencing an increase. Policy changes implemented in response to the pandemic further facilitated access to telehealth, removing barriers and encouraging its use in primary and specialty care (National Academies of Sciences, Engineering, and Medicine, 2021, p. 115).

The advancement of health information technology (HIT) has also helped improve access (Deloitte, 2017). During the COVID-19 pandemic, telemedicine received an even greater boost in growth. After Medicare expanded coverage of telehealth during the pandemic, utilization rates surged over 2000% from January to June (Patel et al., 2020). This growth, while partially borne out of necessity during the pandemic, is also in part driven by the increased demands for care owing to expansion of insurance coverage through the ACA; the health system may not have the capacity to treat each individual in person. For example, the Johns Hopkins Hospital at Home program delivers acute care services at the homes of patients with chronic illnesses who might otherwise need inpatient care. In this way, HIT increases access to care, particularly for patients living in rural areas where distance to the closest hospital is a major barrier.

Electronic health records (EHRs) have helped provide clinical measures and decision support tools, enabled providers to automate processes to reduce redundancy, and captured more clinical data (DeVore, 2014). Trends toward greater interoperability of health information systems, along with open-source interfaces, will allow for greater transparency, increased availability of data, and more creative use of data.

With the advancement in HIT and widespread Internet access, patients are becoming increasingly independent in making healthcare decisions and are more capable of communicating and interacting with health providers (Deloitte, 2020). HIT also helps streamline clinical processes and manage patients' health and payment information (Kelly, 2015). This technology can be used to monitor clinical quality and use measures to identify where improvements can be made (Kraschnewski and Gabbay, 2013). It has also demonstrated success in improving health outcomes and patient safety (Furukawa et al., 2017). On a community level, HIT provides a way for health professionals to keep track of population-level data and observe broader community trends. In all of these ways, it is further promoting the shift toward consumer- and community-centered care.

Emergency Preparedness

The COVID-19 pandemic quickly exposed the deficiencies in the U.S. public health and healthcare system from lack of emergency preparation at all levels, to shortage of health professionals and suppliers, lack of coordination across government agencies, between public and private sectors, and between public health and healthcare system (Todd, 2020; Xu and Basu, 2020; Schneider, 2020; COVID-19 National Preparedness Collaborators, 2021; Pollard and Davis, 2022). Despite the formation of various task forces, the fundamental problems, such as the limited status of public health and the disease-oriented nature of the healthcare system, remain intact.

Significance for Healthcare Practitioners

An understanding of the intricacies within the health services system would be beneficial to all those who come in contact with the system. In their respective training programs, health professionals, such as physicians, nurses, technicians, therapists, dietitians, and pharmacists, may understand their own individual clinical roles but remain ignorant of the forces outside their profession that could significantly impact both current and future clinical practices. An understanding of the healthcare delivery system can attune health professionals to their relationship with the rest of the healthcare environment. It can help them understand changes and the impact of those changes on their own practice. Adaptation and relearning are strategies that can prepare health professionals to cope with an environment that will see ongoing change long into the future, particularly as the U.S. healthcare system is expected to further evolve under subsequent efforts to reform the system.

Significance for Healthcare Managers

An understanding of the healthcare system has specific implications for both private and public health services managers, who must understand the macroenvironment in which they make critical planning and management decisions. Such decisions will ultimately affect the efficiency and quality of services delivered. The interactions between the system's key components and the implications of these interactions must be well understood because the operations of healthcare institutions are strongly influenced, either directly or indirectly, by the financing of health services, reimbursement rates, insurance mechanisms, delivery modes, new statutes and legal opinions, and government regulations.

For the foreseeable future, the environment of healthcare delivery will remain fluid and dynamic. The viability of delivery and the success of healthcare managers often depend on how the managers react to the system dynamics. Timeliness of action is often a critical factor that can make the difference between failure and success. Following are some more specific reasons why understanding the healthcare delivery system is indispensable for healthcare managers.

Positioning the Organization

Managers need to understand their own organizational position within the macro environment of the healthcare system. Senior managers, such as chief executive officers, must constantly gauge the nature and impact of the fundamental shifts illustrated in Figure 1-4. Managers need to consider which changes in the current configuration of financing, insurance, payment, and delivery might affect their organization's long-term stability. Middle and first-line managers also need to understand their roles in the current configuration and how these roles might change in the future.

How should resources be realigned to effectively respond to those changes? As an example, managers need to evaluate whether certain functions in their departments must be eliminated, modified, or added. Would the changes involve further training? Which processes are likely to change, and how? Which steps do the managers need to take to maintain the integrity of their institution's mission, the goodwill of their patients, and the quality of care? Well-thought-out and appropriately planned changes are likely to cause less turbulence for both the providers and the recipients of care.

Handling Threats and Opportunities

Changes in any of the functions of financing, insurance, payment, and delivery can present new threats or opportunities in the healthcare market. Healthcare managers will be more effective if they proactively deal with any threats to their institution's profitability and viability. Managers need to find ways to transform certain threats into new opportunities.

Evaluating Implications

Managers are better able to evaluate the implications of health policy and new reform proposals when they understand the relevant issues and appreciate how such issues link to the delivery of health services in the establishments they manage. Healthcare reform has brought more individuals into the U.S. healthcare system, creating greater demand for health services. Planning and staffing to ensure that the right mix of healthcare workers are available to meet this anticipated surge in demand are critical.

Planning

Senior managers are often responsible for strategic planning regarding which services should be added or discontinued and which resources should be committed to facility expansion. Any long-range planning must take into consideration the current makeup of health services delivery, the evolving trends, and the potential impact of these trends.

Capturing New Markets

Healthcare managers will be in a better position to capture new health services markets if they understand the emerging trends in the financing, insurance, payment, and delivery functions. New opportunities must be explored before any newly evolving segments in the market become crowded with competition. An understanding of the dynamics within the system is essential to forging new marketing strategies that will allow the institution to stay ahead of the competition and in some cases, to find a new service niche.

Complying with Regulations

Delivery of healthcare services is heavily regulated. Healthcare managers must comply with numerous government regulations, such as standards of participation in government programs, licensing rules, and security and privacy laws regarding patient information, and they must operate within the constraints of reimbursement rates. On a periodic basis, the Medicare and Medicaid programs have made drastic changes to their reimbursement methodologies that have triggered the need for operational changes in the way services are organized and delivered. Private agencies, such as the Joint Commission, also play an indirect regulatory role, mainly in monitoring the quality of services. Healthcare managers have no choice but to play by the rules set by the various public and private agencies that regulate the healthcare marketplace. Hence, it is paramount that healthcare managers acquaint themselves with the rules and regulations governing their areas of operation.

Following the Organizational Mission

Knowledge of the healthcare system and its development are essential for effective management of healthcare organizations. By keeping up-to-date on community needs, technological progress, consumer demand, and economic prospects, managers will be in a better position to fulfill their organizational missions to enhance access, improve service quality, and achieve efficiency in the delivery of services.

Healthcare Systems of Selected Other Countries

Except for the United States, the 25 wealthiest nations in the world all have some form of universal healthcare coverage (Rodin and de Ferranti, 2012; Shi and Greenhill, 2024). Canada and Western European nations have used three basic models for structuring their national healthcare systems:

- In a system based on **national health insurance (NHI)**, such as that found in Canada, the government finances health care through general taxes, but the actual care is delivered by private providers. In the context of the quad-function model, NHI requires a tighter consolidation of the financing, insurance, and payment functions coordinated by the government. Delivery is characterized by detached private arrangements.
- In a **national health system (NHS)**, such as in the United Kingdom, in addition to financing a tax-supported NHI program, the government manages the infrastructure for the delivery of medical care. Thus, the government operates most of the country's medical institutions. Most healthcare providers, such as physicians, either are government employees or are tightly organized in a publicly managed infrastructure. In the context of the quad-function model, NHS requires a tighter consolidation of all four functions.
- In a **socialized health insurance (SHI)** system, such as in Germany, government-mandated contributions from employers and employees finance health care. Private providers deliver healthcare services. Private, not-for-profit insurance companies, called sickness funds, are responsible for collecting the contributions and paying physicians and hospitals (Santerre and Neun, 1996; Shi and Greenhill, 2024). The insurance and payment functions are closely integrated in a SHI system, and the financing function is better coordinated with the insurance and payment functions than in the United States. Delivery is characterized by independent private arrangements, but the government exercises overall control of the system.

In this textbook, the terms "national healthcare program" and "national health insurance" are used generically and interchangeably to refer to any type of government-supported universal health insurance program. The following is a brief discussion of healthcare delivery in selected countries from various parts of the world to illustrate the application of the three models discussed and to provide examples of the variety of healthcare systems in the world.

Australia

In the past, Australia had switched from a universal national healthcare program to a privately financed system. In 1984, it returned to a national program—called Medicare—financed by income taxes and an income-based Medicare levy. This system is built on the philosophy that everyone should contribute to the cost of health care according to their capacity to pay. In addition to being insured by Medicare, approximately 55% of Australians carry private health insurance (Australian Government, Department of Health, 2019; Private Healthcare Australia, 2023) to cover gaps in public coverage, such as dental services and care received in private hospitals (Willcox, 2001). Although private health insurance is voluntary, it is strongly encouraged by the Australian government through tax subsidies for purchasers and tax penalties for nonpurchasers (Healy, 2002). Public hospital spending is funded by the government, but private hospitals offer better choices. Costs incurred by patients receiving private medical services, whether in or out of the hospital, are reimbursed in whole or in part by Medicare. Private patients are free to choose and change their doctors. The medical profession in Australia is composed mainly of private practitioners, who provide care predominantly on a fee-for-service basis (Hall, 1999; Podger, 1999).

In 2011, the Council of Australian Governments (COAG) signed the National Health Reform Agreement, which established the architecture for national health insurance reform. In particular, the Agreement provides for more sustainable funding arrangements for Australia's health system. In the same year, the National Health Reform Act 2011 established a new Independent Hospital Pricing Authority and a National Health Performance Authority. The Pricing Authority determines and publishes the national price for services provided by public hospitals. The Commonwealth Government determines its contribution to funding public hospitals on the basis of these prices. The Performance Authority is charged with monitoring and reporting on the performance of local hospital networks, public and private hospitals, primary healthcare organizations, and other bodies or organizations that provide healthcare services. The 2011 act also provides a new statutory framework for the Australian Commission on Safety and Quality in Health Care (Australian Government, 2011).

Australia focuses on developing various healthcare service delivery models to contain costs and provide quality and accessible care (Brownie et al., 2014). Notably, this country has encouraged interprofessional practice as a means to enhance socioeconomic development and improve health outcomes (Brownie et al., 2014). COAG defined new Australian Health Care Agreements (AHCAs), under which each state and territory funds a portion of the public hospital operation costs, commits to providing equitable access to free public hospital services based on clinical need, and agrees to match the rate of growth in the Australian government's hospital funding (Australian Institute of Health and Welfare, 2017). Australia has also developed a national primary healthcare strategy to better incentivize prevention, promote evidence-based management of chronic disease, support the role of general practitioners (GPs) in healthcare teams, encourage a focus on interprofessional team-based care, and address the increased need for access to various health professionals, such as practice nurses and allied health professionals. Other health reforms seek to achieve continuity of care, provide high-quality education and training for existing and incoming healthcare workers, and embed a culture of interprofessional practice (Brownie et al., 2014).

Current challenges faced by the Australian healthcare system include the following: the challenges of an aging population, the inequality of Aboriginal and Torres Strait Islander health, the twin health challenges of increasing levels of obesity and diabetes, and the organizational and structural challenges that the government faces with a publicly funded healthcare system (Day and Kerr, 2024).

Canada

Canada implemented its national health insurance system—referred to as Medicare—under the Medical Care Act of 1966. Medicare consists of 13 provincial and territorial health insurance plans, sharing basic standards of coverage, as defined by the Canada Health Act (Health Canada, 2013). The bulk of financing for Medicare comes from general provincial tax revenues; the federal government provides a fixed amount that is independent of actual expenditures. Public sector health expenditures account for 72% of the total Canadian healthcare expenditures. The remaining 28% consists of private sector expenditures, which include household out-of-pocket expenditures, commercial and not-for-profit insurance expenditures, and nonconsumption expenditures (Canadian Institute for Health Information, 2022). Many employers also offer private insurance that gives their employees supplemental coverage.

Provincial and territorial departments of health have the responsibility to administer medical insurance plans, determine reimbursement for providers, and deliver certain public health services. Provinces are required by law to provide reasonable access to all medically necessary services and to provide portability of benefits from province to province. Patients are free to select their providers (Akaho et al., 1998). According to Canada's Fraser Institute, specialist physicians surveyed across 12 specialties and 10 Canadian provinces reported a total waiting time of 20.0 weeks between referral from a GP and delivery of treatment in 2016—an increase from 18.3 weeks in 2015. Patients had to wait the longest to undergo neurosurgery, which had a wait time of 46.9 weeks (Barua et al., 2016).

Nearly all Canadian provinces—Ontario is one of the exceptions—have resorted to regionalization of healthcare services through the creation of administrative districts within each province. The objective of regionalization is to decentralize authority and responsibility so as to more efficiently address local needs and promote citizen participation in healthcare decision-making (Church and Barker, 1998). The majority of Canadian hospitals operate as private nonprofit entities run by community boards of trustees, voluntary organizations, or municipalities, and most physicians are in private practice. Most provinces use global budgets and allocate set reimbursement amounts for each hospital. Physicians are paid at fee-for-service rates, which are negotiated between each provincial government and medical association (MacPhee, 1996; Naylor, 1999).

In 2004, Canada created the 10-year plan to strengthen health care, which focuses on problems with wait times, healthcare human resources, pharmaceutical management, EHRs, healthcare innovation, accountability and reporting, public health, and Aboriginal health. Overall, progress has been made in these areas, but the goals have not yet been fully achieved (Health Council of Canada, 2013).

Although most Canadians are quite satisfied with their healthcare system, sustaining the current healthcare delivery and financing remains a challenge. Spending on health care has increased dramatically in recent decades, from approximately 7% of program spending at the provincial level in the 1970s to almost 41% in 2015 (Barua et al., 2016). It is expected to continue growing at a rate of about 5.3% annually through 2031 (Barua et al., 2017).

In line with global pressure for health reforms, Canada is also transitioning to patient-centered care (Dickson, 2016), but has not implemented major countrywide health reform since 2005 (Health Systems and Policy Monitor [HSPM], 2012). In addition to leadership challenges, two reasons that Canada has been reluctant to reform its health system are (1) resistance from long-standing professional associations and (2) a lack of follow-through from provincial governments (Dickson, 2016).

The 2014 version of the Canada Health Act expanded services such as nursing home intermediate care, adult residential care, home care services, and ambulatory care services (Canada Minister and Attorney General, 2016). Other initiatives include a collaboration between provincial and territorial governments to purchase drugs in bulk and cut costs in an effort to make drugs more affordable to patients as well as a program to improve access to high-quality mental health services, particularly for veterans and first responders (Granovsky, 2016).

Current challenges faced by the Canadian healthcare system include the following: the financial sustainability of the system as currently structured, questions about access to care (generally focused on system capacity), concerns about outpatient pharmaceuticals, debates about the appropriate role of the private sector, and continuing conversations about the importance of equity in assessing system performance (Duncan et al., 2024).

China

Since the economic reforms initiated in the late 1970s, health care in the People's Republic of China has undergone significant changes. In urban China, health insurance has evolved from a predominantly public insurance (either government or public enterprise) system to a multipayer system. Government employees are covered under government insurance as a part of their benefits. Employees of public enterprises are largely covered through public enterprise insurance, but their actual benefits and payments vary according to the financial well-being of those enterprises. Employees of foreign businesses or joint ventures are typically well insured through private insurance arrangements. Almost all of these plans attempt to contain costs through a variety of means, such as experience-based premiums, deductibles, copayments, and health benefit dollars (i.e., pre-allocated benefit dollars for health care that can be converted into income if not fully used). The unemployed, self-employed, and employees working for small enterprises (public or private) are largely uninsured. They can purchase individual or family plans in the private market or pay for services out of pocket. In rural China, the New Cooperative Medical Scheme (NCMS), discussed later, has become widespread; it relies on funds pooled from national and local governments as well as private citizens. Although the insurance coverage rate is high (more than 90%) in China, the actual benefits provided to the insured are still very limited.

Similar to the United States, China has been facing growing problems owing to its large uninsured population and healthcare cost inflation. Although healthcare funding has increased by 87% in 2006 and 2007, the country has yet to reform its healthcare system into an efficient and effective scheme. Employment-based insurance in China does not cover dependents, nor does it cover migrant workers, leading to high out-of-pocket cost-sharing as part of total healthcare spending. Rural areas in China are most vulnerable to poor access to health care because of a lack of insurance plans and accompanying comprehensive coverage. Medical costs are also increasing at an average annual rate of 10%, which is more than four times the rate of local consumer price inflation (Anderson, 2018).

In recent years, healthcare delivery in China has undergone significant changes. The former three-tier referral system (primary, secondary, tertiary) has been largely abolished. Patients can now go to any hospital of their choice as long as they are insured or can pay out of pocket. As a result, large (tertiary) hospitals are typically overused, whereas smaller (primary and secondary) hospitals are underused. Use of large hospitals contributes to both the escalation of medical costs and greater medical specialization.

Major changes in health insurance and delivery have made access to medical care more difficult for the poor, uninsured, and underinsured. Consequently, wide and growing disparities in access, quality, and outcomes are becoming apparent between rural and urban areas, and between the rich and the poor. After the severe acute respiratory syndrome (SARS) epidemic in 2003, the Chinese government created an electronic disease-reporting system at the district level. Each district in China now has a hospital dedicated to infectious diseases. However, there are still flaws in this system, particularly in monitoring infectious diseases in remote localities (Blumenthal and Hsiao, 2005), and public reporting is also subject to political and administrative supervision.

To fix some of its problems, the Chinese government has pushed through health reform initiatives in five major areas: health insurance, pharmaceuticals, primary care, public health, and public/community hospitals. In terms of health insurance expansion, it created the New Cooperative Medical Scheme to provide rural areas with a government-run voluntary insurance program. This program is intended to prevent individuals living in these areas from becoming impoverished due to illness or exorbitant healthcare expenses (Yip and Hsiao, 2008). In 2008, a similar program was established in urban areas, called the Urban Resident Basic Medical Insurance scheme. It targets uninsured children, older persons, and other nonworking urban residents, enrolling them into the program at the household level rather than at the individual level (Wagstaff et al., 2009).

The Chinese government has also increased its healthcare funding. In the past decade, government subsidies to public hospitals have more than tripled (Lyu et al., 2019). From 2008 to 2017, the government quadrupled its health expenditures from RMB 359 billion to RMB 1.52 trillion. In 2022, RMB 208 trillion was spent on health care (National Bureau of Statistics, 2022). Thanks to the increased healthcare funding, the rate of health insurance coverage hit a record high of 95% in 2013 and has remained stable ever since. However, due to the country's enormous population and significant disparities in regional economic development, insurance benefits still vary widely across China, with the majority of rural residents being unable to afford medical care should they become catastrophically ill.

To improve access to primary care, China has reestablished community health centers (CHCs) that provide preventive and primary care services so patients no longer need to seek expensive outpatient services at hospitals. The goal is to reduce hospital use and increase the number of CHCs that can provide prevention, home care, and rehabilitative services (Yip and Hsiao, 2008; Yip and Mahal, 2008). To date, the CHCs have not proved very popular among the public because of their perceived lack of quality and consequently their poor reputation (Wu et al., 2017). Although different models have been set up to showcase "success" stories from the tiered referral system, so far no sustainable approach has been identified due to systematic limitations in payment arrangement, personnel makeup, and administrative structure (Tam et al., 2018; Xu and Zhang, 2018; Yip et al., 2019).

Another major component of Chinese health reform has been the establishment of an essential drug system that aims to enhance access to and reduce out-of-pocket spending for essential medicines, since most of hospital revenue comes from drug markups. The reform policies specified a comprehensive system, including selection, procurement, pricing, prescription, and quality and safety standards (Barber et al., 2013). To reduce overprescribing, the government mandated the Zero-Markup Drug policy, starting from county-level hospitals in 2012 and then expanding to city-level hospitals in 2015. A fee schedule adjustment was implemented to compensate for revenue losses from the Zero-Markup policy. Under the fee schedule change, fees for labor-intensive health services were increased, though they remain lower than the market price. However, though the Zero-Markup policy reduced drug expenditures, the country's total health expenditures did not change. Notably, hospitals have sought to recoup revenue losses from drug markups by increasing the use of their basic health services and diagnostic tests.

In terms of public hospital reform, China's National Health and Family Planning Commission (previously the Ministry of Health) and State Council have detailed several health reform objectives, including cost containment (e.g., constraining drug prices), quality (e.g., improving staff performance), efficiency, and development of a hospital governance structure (Hsu, 2015). In an effort to control increasing healthcare expenditures, the central government has encouraged local governments to experiment with alternative payment methods, including global budgeting, diagnostic-related groups (DRGs), case-based payments, and capitation, to replace the fee-for-service payment system. Numerous pilot reforms have been launched in various cities in China, but no national implementation plan has been formulated (Yip et al., 2012). The public hospital reform is widely considered to be the least successful effort since the role hospitals will play in the postindustrial era is not yet fully conceptualized.

In 2012, China lifted restrictions on foreign investments in private hospitals in an effort to increase the number of hospitals and improve access to care (Hsu, 2015). By 2015, the State Council aimed to increase use of private health services by 20%. Health insurance reform is also being developed. The Chinese government plans to give tax breaks to private health insurance policyholders in an attempt to increase insurance coverage. Some of these tax breaks include allowing privately insured individuals to deduct RMB 2,400 per year from their assessable income for health insurance premiums (Hsu, 2015).

In 2015, China announced a 5-year plan for the health system, which outlined key areas for development by 2020 (Zhu, 2015). Despite broad reforms, the Chinese healthcare system continues to be plagued by resource shortages and underdevelopment in rural areas. Thus, the latest reform targets three main areas: infrastructure development, reduction of costs and expansion of insurance coverage, and investment in novel technologies. Importantly, these reforms will open up new opportunities for foreign investments.

Discussions on a transition from a fee-for-service to DRGs payment model started in 2018 when the National Healthcare Security Administration (NHSA) was newly built and then a pilot phase involving 30 cities across the country was announced that would run from 2019 to 2021 by using the CHS-DRG version, which comprises a total of 376 adjacent groups and 618 DRG subgroups (Yu et al., 2020). In November 2021, NHSA launched its 3-year payment reform plan (2022–2024) with the aim of fully implementing DRGs and DIP (Qian et al., 2021) model nationwide and covering 70% inpatient care costs by the end of 2024. An increasing number of studies show that the DRGs payment reform has a positive impact on lowering inpatient costs as well as improving medical quality (Lai et al., 2020; Li et al., 2023; Jian et al., 2015; Suwei et al., 2019; Yu et al., 2020), while it could also impair the equity of health care, especially for patients exempted from this payment scheme (Zou et al., 2020; Li et al., 2023), and provide inconsistent evidence on reducing total health expenditure and out-of-pocket payment.

Current challenges faced by the Chinese healthcare system include aging populations and an epidemiological transition from infectious diseases to noncommunicable chronic diseases, inequity in health and health care, air pollution and its health impact, inefficient healthcare delivery, and responses to the COVID-19 pandemic (Lu et al., 2024).

Germany

Health insurance has been mandatory for all citizens and permanent residents in Germany since 2009 (Blumel and Busse, 2016). As mentioned earlier, the German healthcare system is based on the SHI model, and voluntary substitutive private health insurance is available. "About 86 percent of the population receive their primary coverage through SHI and 11 percent through substitutive PHI" (Blumel and Busse, 2016), while special programs cover the rest of the population. Sickness funds act as purchasing entities by negotiating contracts with hospitals. However, paying for the increasing costs of medical care has proved challenging in Germany because of the country's aging population, fewer people in the workforce, and stagnant wage growth during recessions.

During the 1990s, Germany adopted legislation to promote competition among sickness funds (Brown and Amelung, 1999). To further control costs, its national system employs global budgets for the hospital sector and places annual limits on spending for physician services. Inpatient care is paid per admission based on DRGs—a system that was made obligatory in 2004 (Blumel and Busse, 2016).

Health reforms in Germany have focused on improving the efficiency and appropriateness of care. In 2011, the Pharmaceutical Market Reform Act introduced an assessment scheme for all new pharmaceuticals, under which only those drugs that offer additional benefits relative to existing alternatives can be reimbursed at a higher rate (WHO, 2014). The Hospital Financing Reform Act of 2009 requires performance-based flat rate grants for investments in hospitals rather than nonperformance-based flat rate grants on a case-by-case basis, as of 2012 (WHO, 2014).

One of Germany's biggest challenges is the division between SHI and private health insurance. The differences in risk pools, financing structures, access, and provisions in these alternative insurance plans contribute to inequalities in care (WHO, 2014). Additionally, more work is needed to improve the quality of medical services, patient satisfaction, and accessibility of healthcare services in rural communities (WHO, 2014).

More recent reforms in Germany have focused on improving services for SHI-covered patients and enhancing hospital quality. In June 2015, the Act to Strengthen SHI Health Care Provision gave municipalities the right to establish medical treatment centers, gave patients the right to see a specialist within 4 weeks, and promoted innovative forms of care in an effort to strengthen services for SHI-covered patients (HSPM, 2016). This act improves prevention services and health promotion through investments in schools, the workplace, and long-term care facilities. In addition, the 2016 Hospital Care Structure Reform Act introduced quality aspects in the regulation of hospital volume and payments (Blumel and Busse, 2016). Substantial funds will be invested to improve the hospital care structure in Germany.

Current challenges faced by the German healthcare system include cost containment pressure, especially with heavy national debts and inadequate funding for municipalities, integration of care, the aging population, the refugee crisis, and continued handling of COVID-19 (Ledlow and Kennedy, 2024).

United Kingdom

The United Kingdom follows the national health system model. Its health delivery system, called the National Health Service (NHS), is founded on the principles of primary care as espoused by the WHO (see Chapter 7) and has a strong focus on community health services. The government owns the hospitals and employs hospital-based specialists and other staff on a salaried basis. The primary care physicians, referred to as general practitioners (GPs), are mostly private practitioners. All NHS-insured patients are required to register with a local GP. In 2014, there were, on average, 7,171 patients per practice and 1,530 patients per GP (Thorlby and Arora, 2016).

The NHS emphasizes free points of access and equal access to all (HSPM, 2015). In England, the Health and Social Care Act abolished the Primary Care Trust and Strategic Health Authority in 2012, replacing them with the Clinical Commissioning Group. In 2013, the Better Care Fund was enacted to improve integration of health and social care. In 2014, the Care Act was introduced to cap out-of-pocket expenditures (HSPM, 2015).

Delivery of primary care occurs through primary care trusts (PCTs) in England, local health groups in Wales, health boards in Scotland, and primary care partnerships in Northern Ireland. PCTs have geographically assigned responsibility for community health services; each person living in a given geographic area is assigned to a particular PCT. A typical PCT is responsible for approximately 50,000–250,000 patients (Dixon and Robinson, 2002). PCTs function independently of the local health authorities and are governed by a consumer-dominated board. A fully developed PCT has its own budget allocations used for both primary care and hospital-based services. In this respect, PCTs function like MCOs in the United States.

Approximately 83% of U.K. health expenditures in 2013 went to the public sector (Office of National Statistics, 2015). Private expenditures involve mainly drugs and other medical products as well as private hospital care. Despite having a national healthcare system, 10.9% of the British population maintains private health insurance (Arora et al., 2013). Approximately 83% of total healthcare spending was government-financed in 2021 (Office of National Statistics, 2023).

England, Scotland, Wales, and Northern Ireland are taking their own approaches to health care. England is moving toward decentralization, reinforcement of an internal market, and more localized decision-making (HSPM, 2015). Scotland and Wales are dissolving the internal market and centralizing authority. While Scotland has embraced a publicly funded universal health system, England emphasizes private partnerships and internal competition. Costs are increasing in the United Kingdom owing to infrastructure improvements, technology innovations, an aging and growing population, more patients with chronic diseases, heightened focus on the quality of care, informed and empowered consumers, and innovative treatments (Deloitte, 2017).

In 2014, NHS England introduced the Five Year Forward View plan, which lays out strategies for addressing the most pressing challenges in the healthcare system (National Health Services England, 2015). This plan places a greater emphasis on prevention, integration of services, and patient-centered care. It lays out strategies and new care models with goals of integrating primary and acute care systems, creating multispecialty community providers, and fostering collaborations in acute care. These models will redesign services and change the way health services are administered, financed, and regulated in the coming years.

The latest health reform is the Health and Care Act enacted in April 2022 (The King's Fund, 2023). The main purpose of the Act is to establish a legislative framework that supports collaboration and partnership by working to integrate services for people, specifically the formalization of integrated care systems (ICSs). ICSs are partnerships that bring providers and commissioners of NHS services across a geographical area together with local authorities and other local partners to collectively plan healthcare services to meet the needs of their local population.

Current challenges faced by the British healthcare system include tackling deep and widening healthcare inequalities, addressing an unstable provider market, a workforce crisis, and high levels of unmet need, putting greater focus on and investment in prevention and public health as a result of the COVID-19 pandemic, achieving better coordination among health and care services, and encouraging greater use of digital technologies to improve people's health and experiences of services (Weeden et al., 2024).

Israel

Until 1995, Israel had a system of universal coverage based on the German SHI model, financed through an employer tax and income-based contributions from individuals (Stein, 2024). When the National Health Insurance (NHI) Law went into effect in 1995, it made insurance coverage mandatory for all Israeli citizens. Under the Israeli system, adults are required to pay a health tax. General tax revenues supplement the health tax revenues, which the government distributes to the various health plans based on a capitation formula. Each year, the government determines how much from the general tax revenue should be contributed toward the NHI. In 2013, public funds accounted for 60% of NHI revenues. The remaining share came from individuals' copayments, supplemental health insurance, and sales of health products (Rosen, 2016).

Health plans (or sickness funds) offer a predefined basic package of healthcare services and are prohibited from discriminating against individuals who have preexisting medical conditions. Later reforms have added mental health and dental care for children to the benefits package (WHO, 2015). The capitation formula has built-in incentives for the funds to accept a larger number of older people and chronically ill members. Rather than relying on a single-payer system, the healthcare reform supported the development of multiple health plans (today there are four competing nonprofit sickness funds) to foster competition among funds, under the assumption that competition would lead to better quality of care and an increased responsiveness to patient needs. The plans also sell private health insurance to supplement the basic package. The system is believed to provide a high standard of care (Rosen et al., 2016).

Israel has a highly efficient healthcare system due to the regulated competition between health plans, the country's strict regulatory controls on the supply of hospital beds, its accessible and high-quality primary care, and its reliance on EHRs (WHO, 2015). In 2014, the Ministry of Health created a national health information exchange for sharing clinical patient data across all general hospitals, health plans, and other providers in the country. Emerging challenges include a shortage of resources, both financial and staffing, and an increasing reliance on private financing, which affects equity and efficiency; the need to expand public financing and improve the efficiency of the public system; reduction of health inequalities, particularly for remote areas; shortage of advanced medical technology; and goals related to measuring and improving the quality of hospital care, reducing surgical waiting times, and enhancing the dissemination of comparative data on performance (Stein, 2024; WHO, 2015).

Japan

Since 1961, Japan has been providing universal coverage to its citizens through two main health insurance schemes: (1) an employer-based system, modeled after Germany's SHI program, and (2) a national health insurance program. Generally, large employers (with more than 300 employees) have their own health insurance programs. Nearly 2,000 private, nonprofit health insurance societies manage insurance for large firms. Smaller companies either band together to provide private health insurance or belong to a government-run plan. Day laborers, seafarers, agricultural workers, the self-employed, and retirees are all covered under the national healthcare program. Individual employees pay roughly 8% of their salaries as premiums and receive coverage for approximately 90% of the cost of medical services, with some limitations. Dependents receive slightly less than 90% coverage. Employers and the national government subsidize the cost of private premiums. Coverage is comprehensive, including most dental care and approved prescription drugs, and patients are free to select their providers (Matsuda, 2016). Providers are paid on a national fee-for-service basis set by the government and have little control over reimbursement (Ikegami and Anderson, 2012).

Several healthcare policy issues have emerged in Japan in the past few years. First, since 2002, some business leaders and economists have urged the Japanese government to lift its ban on mixed public/private payments for medical services, arguing that private payments should be allowed for services not covered by medical insurance (i.e., services involving new technologies or drugs). The

Japan Medical Association and the Ministry of Health, Labor, and Welfare have argued against these recommendations, stating such a policy would favor the wealthy and create disparities in access to care. Although the ban on mixed payments has not been lifted, Prime Minister Koizumi expanded the existing "exceptional approvals system" for new medical technologies in 2004 to allow private payments for selected technologies not covered by medical insurance (Nomura and Nakayama, 2005).

Another policy development in Japan is hospitals' increased use of a system of reimbursement for inpatient care services, called diagnosis-procedure combinations (DPCs). With the DPCs, hospitals receive daily fees for each condition and treatment, proportionate to patients' length of stays but regardless of the actual provision of tests and interventions. In theory, the DPC system will incentivize hospitals to become more efficient (Nomura and Nakayama, 2005).

Japan's stagnant economy in the past several years has led to increased pressure to contain the country's healthcare costs (Ikegami and Campbell, 2004). From 2000 to 2016, annual healthcare expenditure grew 40 times faster than the economy (Du and Reynolds, 2018). In 2005, Japan implemented reform initiatives in long-term care (LTC) delivery in an effort to contain the rapidly rising costs in this growing healthcare sector. The new policy required residents in LTC facilities to pay for room and board and established new preventive benefits for seniors with low needs. Charging nursing home residents a fee for room and board was a departure from past policies, which had promoted institutionalization of older people (Tsutsui and Muramatsu, 2007).

Despite their overall success, Japan's health and LTC systems face sustainability issues similar to those found in the United States, including rising costs and increasing demands for services. The Japanese government is considering and pursuing several options: preventive services, promotion of community-based services, and increases in taxes, premiums, and fees. In 2011, reform centered on the implementation of the comprehensive community care model. This model ensures access to LTC, medical or hospital care, preventive services, residential care facilities, and "life support" (or legal services) within a community where an older person lives. The focus on prevention and service consolidation is expected to result in healthier populations and therefore the decreased use of more expensive services.

More recently, health reforms in Japan have introduced the GP and family physician (FP) system. Starting in 2017, the Japan Primary Care Society initiated a training program to qualify doctors as GP/FP specialists (Takamura, 2015). By permitting the Japan Primary Care Society to run this program, the Japanese government aims not only to increase the number of systematically trained GPs/FPs but also to maintain good community care, improve health outcomes through prevention and primary care, and lower medical expenses. Challenges arising from the GP/FP reform include questions about where to place GPs and FPs (clinics or hospitals), how organ specialists currently providing primary care will be affected, and whether the GP/FP culture will be accepted by Japanese patients and citizens at large. During the COVID-19 pandemic, primary care capabilities played pivotal roles. In Japan, the primary care sector has performed the initial assessment, including testing for COVID-19, and triaged patients to determine those in need of hospitalization (Aoki and Shi, 2024).

Current challenges faced by the Japanese healthcare system include primary care system reform to enhance capabilities and measurement, care of older people and long-term care, dementia care, anti-smoking, diabetes prevention, and suicide prevention (Aoki and Shi, 2024).

Singapore

Prior to 1984, Singapore had a British-style NHS program, in which medical services were provided mainly by the public sector and financed through general taxes. Since then, the nation has designed a system based on market competition and self-reliance. Singapore has achieved universal coverage through a policy that requires mandatory private contributions but little government financing. The program, known as Medisave, mandates every working person, including the self-employed, to deposit a portion of their earnings into an individual Medisave account. Employers are required to match employee contributions. These savings can be withdrawn only for two purposes: (1) to pay for hospital services and some selected, expensive physician services or (2) to purchase a government-sponsored insurance plan, called MediShield, for catastrophic (expensive and major) illness. In 2015, MediShield became universal, compulsory, and lasting for a lifetime. Medisave has also been gradually expanded over the years to include more chronic conditions and health screenings (Liu and Haseltine, n.d.).

For basic and routine services, Singaporeans are expected to pay out of pocket. Out-of-pocket expenditures can be quite high, as only 25%–38% of health spending is publicly funded (Salkeld, 2014; Pacificprime.cg, 2023). Those who cannot afford to pay for healthcare services receive government assistance (Hsiao, 1995). In 2002, the government introduced ElderShield, which defrays out-of-pocket medical expenses for older people and individuals with severe disabilities who require long-term care (Singapore Ministry of Health, 2007). The fee-for-service system of payment is widely used throughout Singapore (McClellan and Kessler, 1999).

In 2006, the Ministry of Health launched the Chronic Disease Management Program. By now, this program covers 23 chronic diseases, including mental illnesses (Singapore Ministry of Health, 2022). More than 700 GP clinics and GP groups are supported by the Ministry to provide comprehensive chronic disease management to patients. Patients can use their own Medisave accounts or family members' accounts to pay for outpatient services under the program (Singapore Ministry of Health, 2012).

In 2017, the Ministry of Health issued HealthierSG 2022 (HS2022), the current healthcare master plan for Singapore (Choo and Shi, 2024). This plan aims to further enhance Singapore's healthcare system by focusing on three key areas:

- Keeping Singaporeans healthy: HS2022 aims to promote healthy living and disease prevention through initiatives such as healthy eating, physical activity, and early detection of illnesses.
- Improving the healthcare system: The plan focuses on improving the quality of care and patient outcomes through integrating care, enhanced health IT infrastructure, and strengthened partnerships with the private sector.
- Making health care affordable: HS2022 aims to ensure that health care remains affordable and accessible for all Singaporeans by implementing cost-effective measures and leveraging technology to reduce costs.

Future challenges in Singapore include adjusting copayments to avoid discouraging patients from seeking necessary primary care and preventive services that might lower their risk of developing chronic diseases. Overall, Singapore faces the challenge of ensuring positive health outcomes and containing costs, given an aging population that is facing an increased prevalence of chronic disease (Tan et al., 2014; Choo and Shi, 2024).

Developing Countries

Developing countries, which are home to almost 85% of the world's population, are responsible for only 11% of the world's total health spending—even though they account for 93% of the worldwide burden of disease. The six developing regions of the world are

East Asia and the Pacific, Europe (mainly Eastern Europe) and Central Asia, Latin America and the Caribbean, the Arab States, South Asia, and sub-Saharan Africa (United Nations Development Programme, 2019). Of these regions, the latter two have the least resources and the greatest health burden. On a per capita basis, the industrialized countries have six times as many hospital beds and three times as many physicians as the developing countries. People with private financial means can find reasonably good health care in many parts of the developing world. Unfortunately, the majority of these countries' populations have to depend on limited government services that are often of questionable quality when evaluated by Western standards. As a general observation, government financing for healthcare services increases in countries with higher per capita incomes (Schieber and Maeda, 1999; Shi and Greenfield, 2024).

Developing countries are moving toward adopting universal healthcare coverage in an effort to decrease the financial impoverishment of their populations due to healthcare spending, improve health, and increase access to care (Shi and Greenfield, 2024; Shi, 2023; Lagomarsino et al., 2012). Trends in health reforms in developing countries include increasing enrollment in government-sponsored health insurance, expanded benefits packages, decreasing out-of-pocket expenditures, and increasing the government's share of health spending. Countries that have successfully met the Millennium Development Goals—the world's time-bound and quantified targets for addressing extreme poverty in its many dimensions (income poverty, hunger, disease, lack of adequate shelter, and exclusion) while promoting gender equality, education, and environmental sustainability—have used a comprehensive set of strategies to reduce maternal and child mortality, improve healthcare financing, address workforce challenges, and improve quality of care (Ahmed et al., 2016; Shi, 2023).

Global Health Challenges and Reform

This brief review underscores the reality that *NO* countries in the world so far have found the perfect solution to addressing their multiple health challenges while containing escalating healthcare costs. As a result, healthcare reform is a common theme around the world and is achieving increasing prominence. Strengthening primary care programs is seen as a core strategy in delivering better health outcomes and achieving universal coverage while containing costs (Shi, 2023; Bitton et al., 2019), but it remains to be seen how this can be achieved within the current healthcare systems, given their multiple stakeholders and varied interests.

A huge gap in health care and health status persists between developing and developed countries. For example, in 2019, the global life expectancy at birth was 73.3 years of age, but life expectancy in the African region was only 64.5 years (WHO, 2022). In 2021, infant mortality rates varied between 1 death per 1,000 live births and 78 deaths per 1,000 live births. In 2014, infant mortality rates varied between 2 deaths per 1,000 live births and 110 deaths per 1,000 live births (World Bank, 2022). There were also wide variations in health care for pregnant women, availability of skilled health personnel for childbirth, and access to medicine.

The poor quality and low efficiency of healthcare services in many countries—especially services provided by the public sector, which is often the main source of care for people with limited financial resources—have become a serious issue for decision-makers in these countries (Sachs, 2012). This issue, combined with the rising out-of-pocket costs and high numbers of uninsured, has forced many governments to launch healthcare reform efforts. Many low- and middle-income countries are moving toward universal health coverage (Shi, 2023; Lagomarsino et al., 2012). International healthcare assistance continues to play a significant role in many developing countries. The United States' global aid for health care increased from $5.4 billion in fiscal year 2006 to $11 billion in fiscal year 2019, though the Trump administration proposed significant cuts in fiscal year 2020 (Kaiser Family Foundation, 2019). These cuts were not implemented, as the 2020 global health aid totaled over $11 billion (Kaiser Family Foundation, 2020).

Since 1999, the Bill and Melinda Gates Foundation (2017) has invested $7 billion in international healthcare delivery programs. This foundation's focus is on the coordination of delivery efforts, the strengthening of country health systems, and the building of integrated delivery systems. Funded initiatives include community healthcare worker programs, information and communications technology, and investment into data systems. From 2010 to 2015, United States Agency for International Development (USAID) dedicated $50 billion to strengthening international healthcare systems. From 2015 to 2019, USAID set forth a plan for continuing its progress by strengthening six interrelated healthcare system functions: (1) human resources for health; (2) health finance; (3) health governance; (4) health information; (5) medical products, vaccines, and technologies; and (6) service delivery (USAID, 2015). The ultimate goal is to strengthen these systems so they will contribute to positive health outcomes and create an environment for universal healthcare coverage.

The Systems Framework

A **system** consists of a set of interrelated and interdependent logically coordinated components designed to achieve common goals. Even though the various functional components of the health services delivery structure in the United States are, at best, only loosely coordinated, the main components can be identified using a systems model. The systems framework used here helps us understand that the structure of healthcare services in the United States is based on some foundations, provides a logical arrangement of the various components, and demonstrates a progression from inputs to outputs. The main elements of this arrangement are system inputs (resources), system structure, system processes, and system outputs (outcomes). In addition, system outlook (future directions) is a necessary feature of a dynamic system. This systems framework is used as the conceptual base for organizing later chapters in this text (**Figure 1-5**).

System Foundations

The current healthcare system is not an accident: historical, cultural, social, and economic factors all contribute to and explain its current structure. These factors also affect forces that shape new trends and developments as well as those that impede change. The chapters titled *Beliefs, Values, and Health* and *The Evolution of Health Services in the United States* provide a discussion of the system foundations.

System Resources

No mechanism for healthcare services delivery can fulfill its primary objective without deploying the necessary human and nonhuman resources. Human resources consist of the various types and categories of workers directly engaged in the delivery of health services to patients. Such personnel—physicians, nurses, dentists, pharmacists, other doctoral-trained professionals, and numerous categories of allied health professionals—usually have direct contact with patients. Numerous ancillary workers—billing and collection agents, marketing and public relations personnel, and building maintenance employees—often play important but indirect supportive roles in the delivery of health care. Healthcare

Environment

I. System foundations

Cultural beliefs and values and historical developments

Beliefs, Values, and Health
 (Chapter 2)

The Evolution of Health Services in the United States
 (Chapter 3)

System features

II. System Resources

Human Resources

Health Services Professionals
 (Chapter 4)

Nonhuman Resources

Medical Technology
 (Chapter 5)

Health Services Financing
 (Chapter 6)

III. System processes

The continuum of care

Outpatient and Primary Care Services
 (Chapter 7)

Inpatient Facilities and Services
 (Chapter 8)

Managed Care and Integrated Organizations
 (Chapter 9)

Special populations

Long-Term Care
 (Chapter 10)

Health Services for Special Populations
 (Chapter 11)

IV. System outcomes

Issues and concerns

Cost, Access, and Quality
 (Chapter 12)

Change and reform

Health Policy
 (Chapter 13)

Future Trends

V. System outlook

The Future of Health Services Delivery
 (Chapter 14)

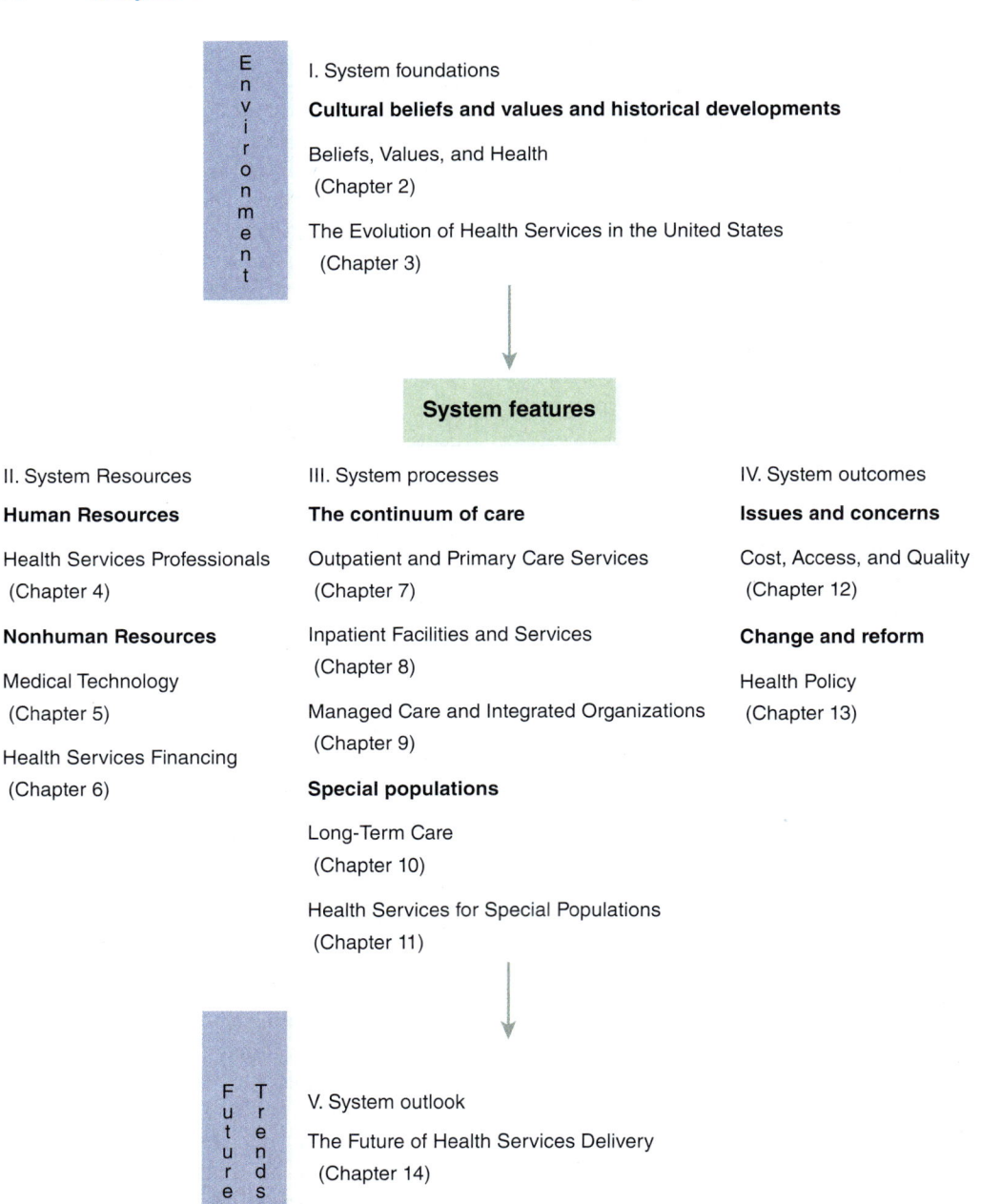

Figure 1-5 The systems model and related chapters.

managers are needed to manage various types of healthcare services. This text primarily discusses the personnel engaged in the direct delivery of healthcare services (in the *Health Services Professionals* chapter). The nonhuman resources include medical technology and healthcare services financing (discussed in the chapters with those titles, respectively).

Resources are closely intertwined with access to health care. For instance, in certain rural areas of the United States, access is restricted due to a shortage of healthcare professionals within certain categories. Development and diffusion of technology also determine the caliber of health care to which people may have access. Financing for health insurance and reimbursement to providers both affect access indirectly.

System Processes

System resources influence the development and change in the physical infrastructure—such as hospitals, clinics, and nursing homes—essential for the different processes of healthcare delivery. Most healthcare services are delivered in noninstitutional settings, mainly associated with processes referred to as outpatient care (discussed in the *Outpatient and Primary Care Services* chapter). Institutional healthcare services provided in hospitals, nursing homes, and rehabilitation institutions, for example, are predominantly inpatient services (discussed in the *Inpatient Facilities and Services* chapter). Managed care and integrated organizations (discussed in the chapter with that title) represent a fundamental change in the financing (including payment and insurance) and delivery of health care. Special institutional and community-based settings have been developed for long-term care (discussed in the chapter with that title). Delivery of services should be tailored to meet the special needs of certain vulnerable population groups (as described in the *Health Services for Special Populations* chapter).

System Outcomes

System outcomes refer to the critical issues and concerns surrounding what the healthcare services system has been able to accomplish, or not accomplish, in relation to its primary care objective—that is, to provide to an entire nation cost-effective health services that meet certain established standards of quality. The previous three elements of the systems model play a critical role in fulfilling this objective. Access, cost, and quality are the main outcome criteria to evaluate the success of a healthcare delivery system (as discussed in the *Cost, Access, and Quality* chapter). Issues and concerns regarding these criteria trigger broad initiatives for reforming the system through health policy (the topic of the *Health Policy* chapter).

System Outlook

A dynamic healthcare system must be forward-thinking In essence, it must project into the future the accomplishment of desired system outcomes in view of the anticipated social, economic, political, technological, informational, ecological, anthro-cultural, and global forces of change (described in the *Future of Health Services Delivery* chapter).

Summary

The United States has a unique system of healthcare delivery. Its basic features characterize it as a patchwork of subsystems. Health care is delivered through an amalgam of private and public financing, through private and public insurance programs; the latter reserved for special groups. Contrary to popular opinion, healthcare delivery in the United States is not governed by free market principles; at best, it is an imperfect market. Yet, the system is not dominated or controlled by a single entity, as would be the case in national healthcare systems.

No country in the world has a perfect healthcare insurance system, and most nations with a national healthcare program also have a private care sector, though these sectors vary in size. Because of limitations in resources, universal access remains a theoretical concept even in countries that offer universal health insurance coverage. The developing countries of the world also face serious challenges due to the scarcity of resources and strong underlying needs for services in those nations.

Healthcare managers must understand how the healthcare delivery system works and how it is evolving. Such an understanding can help them maintain a strategic position within the macroenvironment of the healthcare system. The systems framework provides an organized approach to an understanding of the various components of the U.S. healthcare delivery system.

TEST YOUR UNDERSTANDING

Terminology

- access
- administrative costs
- balance bill
- defensive medicine
- demand
- enrollee
- free market
- global budgets
- healthcare reform
- health plan
- managed care
- Medicaid
- Medicare
- moral hazard
- national health insurance (NHI)
- national health system (NHS)
- need
- package pricing
- phantom providers
- premium cost sharing
- primary care
- provider
- provider-induced demand
- quad-function model
- reimbursement
- single-payer system
- socialized health insurance (SHI)
- standards of participation
- system
- third party
- uninsured
- universal access
- universal coverage
- utilization

Review Questions

1. Why does cost containment remain an elusive goal in the U.S. health services delivery?
2. What are the two main objectives of a healthcare delivery system?
3. Name the four basic functional components of the U.S. healthcare delivery system. What role does each play in the delivery of health care?
4. What is the primary reason for employers to purchase insurance plans to provide health benefits to their employees?
5. Why is it that despite public and private health insurance programs, some citizens of the United States lack healthcare coverage?
6. What is managed care?
7. Why is the U.S. healthcare market referred to as "imperfect?"
8. Discuss the intermediary role of insurance in the delivery of health care.
9. Who are the major players in the U.S. health services system? What are the positive and negative effects

of the often conflicting self-interests of these players?
10. Which main roles does the government play in the U.S. health services system?
11. What are the trends affecting healthcare delivery in the United States?
12. Why is it important for healthcare managers and policymakers to understand the intricacies of the healthcare delivery system?
13. What is the difference between national health insurance (NHI) and a national health system (NHS)?
14. What is socialized health insurance (SHI)?
15. Provide a general overview of the Affordable Care Act. What is its main goal?
16. What is meant by value-based care?
17. What are the major and common challenges in healthcare reform around the world?

References

Ahmed, S. M., L. B. Rawal, S. A. Chowdhury, et al. 2016. Cross-country analysis of strategies for achieving progress towards global goals for women's and children's health. *Bulletin of the World Health Organization* 94: 351–361.

Agency for Healthcare Research and Quality (AHRQ). 2023. Compendium of US Health Systems. Available at: https://www.ahrq.gov/chsp/data-resources/compendium.html

Akaho, E., G. D. Coffin, T. Kusano, L. Locke, T. Okamoto. 1998. A proposed optimal healthcare system based on a comparative study conducted between Canada and Japan. *Canadian Journal of Public Health* 89: 301–307.

Al-Saddique, A. 2018. Integrated delivery systems (IDSs) as a means of reducing costs and improving healthcare delivery. *Journal of Healthcare Communications* 3: 19.

Altman, S. H., and U. E. Reinhardt. 1996. Introduction: Where does health care reform go from here? An uncharted odyssey. In: *Strategic choices for a changing health care system*. S. H. Altman and U. E. Reinhardt, eds. Chicago, IL: Health Administration Press. xxi–xxxii.

Altman, S. H., and S. S. Wallack. 1996. Health care spending: Can the United States control it? In: *Strategic choices for a changing health care system*. S. H. Altman and U. E. Reinhardt, eds. Chicago, IL: Health Administration Press. 1–32.

American Association of Colleges of Pharmacy. 2022. *Academic pharmacy's vital statistics*. Accessed September 2023. Available at: https://www.aacp.org/article/academic-pharmacys-vital-statistics

American Dental Association. 2022. *Dental Education*. Accessed September 2023. Available at: http://www.ada.org/en/science-research/health-policy-institute/dental-statistics/education

American Hospital Association. 2023. *Fast Facts on U.S. Hospitals, 2023*. Available at: https://www.aha.org/statistics/fast-facts-us-hospitals

Anderson, D. 2018. How employee insurance can help China manage its rising medical costs. Accessed January 2020. Available at: https://health.oliverwyman.com/2018/04/how_employee_insuran1.html

Arora, S., A. Charlesworth, E. Kelly, and G. Stoye. 2013. *Public payment and private provision: The changing landscape of health care in the 2000s*. Nuffield Trust. Accessed February 2021. Available at: https://www.nuffieldtrust.org.uk/research/public-payment-and-private-provision-the-changing-landscape-of-health-care-in-the-2000s

Association of American Medical Colleges. 2017. *2016 data book*. Accessed April 2017. Available at: https://www.aamc.org/data/databook/tables/

Australian Government. 2013. National Primary Health Care Strategic Framework. Accessed February 2021. Available at: https://www.health.qld.gov.au/__data/assets/pdf_file/0027/434853/nphc_strategic_framework_final.pdf

Australian Government, Department of Health. 2019. *Department of Health annual report 2018–19*. Canberra, Australia: Commonwealth of Australia. Accessed January 2020. Available at: https://www.health.gov.au/sites/default/files/documents/2019/10/department-of-health-annual-report-2018-19_0.pdf

Australian Institute of Health and Welfare. 2017. *Australia's health 2016*. Accessed April 2017. Available at: http://www.aihw.gov.au/australias-health/2016/health-system/

Barber, S. L., B. Huang, B. Santoso, et al. 2013. The reform of the essential medicines system in China: A comprehensive approach to universal coverage. *Journal of Global Health* 3: 10303.

Barua, B., M. Palacios, and J. Emes. 2016. *The sustainability of health care spending in Canada*. Vancouver, Canada: Fraser Institute.

Barua, B., M. Palacios, and J. Emes. 2017. The sustainability of health care spending in Canada 2017. Accessed January 2020. Available at: https://www.fraserinstitute.org/studies/sustainability-of-health-care-spending-in-canada-2017

Bill and Melinda Gates Foundation. 2020. *Global delivery programs*. Accessed February 2021. Available at: https://www.gatesfoundation.org/What-We-Do/Global-Development/Global-Delivery-Programs

Bitton, A., J. Fifield, H. Ratcliffe, et al. 2019. Primary healthcare system performance in low-income and middle-income countries: A scoping review of the evidence from 2010 to 2017. *BMJ Global Health* 4: e001551.

Blumel M., and R. Busse. 2016. *International health care system profiles: Germany*. The Commonwealth Fund. Accessed February 2017. Available at: http://international.commonwealthfund.org/countries/germany/

Blumenthal, D., and W. Hsiao. 2005. Privatization and its discontents: The evolving Chinese health care system. *New England Journal of Medicine* 353: 1165–1170.

Brown, L. D., and V. E. Amelung. 1999. "Manacled competition": Market reforms in German health care. *Health Affairs* 18: 76–91.

Brownie, S., J. Thomas, L. McAllister, and M. Groves. 2014. Australian health reforms: Enhancing interprofessional practice and competency within the health workforce. *Journal of Interprofessional Care* 28: 252–253.

Burns, L. R., I. M. Nembhard, and S. M. Shortell. 2022. Integrating network theory into the study of integrated healthcare. *Social Science & Medicine* 296: 114664.

Canada Minister and Attorney General. 2016. *Canada Health Act*. Accessed April 2017. Available at: http://laws-lois.justice.gc.ca/eng/acts/c-6/

Canadian Institute for Health Information. 2022. Accessed September 2023. Available at: https://www.cihi.ca/sites/default/files/document/health-expenditure-data-in-brief-2022-en.pdf

Cattel, D., and F. Eijkenaar. 2019. Value-based provider payment initiatives combining global payments with explicit quality incentives: A systematic review. *Medical Care Research and Review* Available at: https://doi.org/10.1177/1077558719856775

Centers for Disease Control and Prevention (CDC). 2018. *Nursing home care*. Accessed September 2023. Available at: https://www.cdc.gov/nchs/fastats/nursing-home-care.htm

Centers for Medicare and Medicaid Services (CMS). 2018. *CMS finalizes "Pathways to Success," an overhaul of Medicare's national ACO program*. Accessed November 2019. Available at: https://www.cms.gov/newsroom/press-releases/cms-finalizes-pathways-success-overhaul-medicares-national-aco-program

Centers for Medicare and Medicaid Services (CMS). 2019. *HHS news: HHS to deliver value-based transformation in primary care*. Accessed November 2019. Available at: https://www.cms.gov/newsroom/press-releases/hhs-news-hhs-deliver-value-based-transformation-primary-care

Centers for Medicare and Medicaid Services (CMS). 2020. *NHE fact sheet*. Accessed February 2020. Available at: https://www.cms.gov/Research-Statistics-Data-and-Systems/Statistics-Trends-and-Reports/NationalHealthExpendData/NHE-Fact-Sheet

Choo, R., and L. Shi, 2024. Chapter 35. Singapore. In Shi, Leiyu, and Greenhill, Richard (Eds.). Comparative Health Systems. (3rd ed.). Burlington, MA: Jones & Bartlett.

Church J., and P. Barker. 1998. Regionalization of health services in Canada: A critical perspective. *International Journal of Health Services* 28: 467–486.

Cohen, R. A., et al. 2016. *Health insurance coverage: Early release of estimates from the National Health Interview Survey, January–March 2016*. National Center for Health Statistics. Accessed February 2017. Available at: http://www.cdc.gov/nchs/nhis/releases.htm

COVID-19 National Preparedness Collaborators. 2021. Pandemic preparedness and COVID-19: An exploratory analysis of infection and fatality rates, and contextual factors associated with preparedness in 177 countries, from Jan 1, 2020, to Sept 30, 2021. *Lancet* 399(10334). Available at: https://www.thelancet.com/journals/lancet/article/PIIS0140-6736(22)00172-6/fulltext

Cross, D. A., P. Nong, C. Harris-Lemak, and G. R. Cohen. 2017. Sustained participation in a pay-for-value program: Impact on high-need patients. *American Journal of Managed Care* 23: e33–e40.

Cross, D. A., P. Nong, C. Harris-Lemak, and G. R. Cohen. 2019. Practice strategies to improve primary care for chronic disease patients under a pay-for-value program. *Healthcare* 7: 30–37. Available at: https://doi.org/10.1016/j.hjdsi.2018.08.004

Day, G. E., and B. Kerr. 2024. Chapter 36. Australia. In Shi, Leiyu and Greenhill, Richard (Eds.). Comparative Health Systems. (3rd ed.). Burlington, MA: Jones & Bartlett.

Deloitte. 2017. *2017 global health care sector outlook: Making progress against persistent challenges*. Accessed February 2021. Available at: https://www2.deloitte.com/tr/en/pages/life-sciences-and-healthcare/articles/2017-global-health-care-sector-outlook.html

Deloitte. 2020. *2020 US and global health care sector outlook: Laying a foundation for the future*. Accessed January 2020. Available at: https://www2.deloitte.com/us/en/pages/life-sciences-and-health-care/articles/global-health-care-sector-outlook.html

Diana M. L., Y. Zhang, V. A. Yeager, C. Stoecker, and C. R. Counts. 2019. The impact of accountable care organization participation on hospital patient experience.

Health Care Management Review 44: 148–158. Available at: https://doi.org/10.1097/HMR.0000000000000219

Dickson, G. 2016. Health reform in Canada: Enabling perspectives for health leadership. *Healthcare Manage Forum* 29: 53–58.

Dixon, A., and R. Robinson. 2002. The United Kingdom. In: *Health care systems in eight countries: Trends and challenges*. A. Dixon and E. Mossialos, eds. London, UK: European Observatory on Health Care Systems, London School of Economics & Political Science. 103–114.

Donaldson, S. 2018. Community-centered health home: Life on the other side of the wall. *Preventing Chronic Disease* 15: E66. doi:10.5888/pcd15.170510.

Du, L., and I. Reynolds. 2018. *Health-care paradox threatens to add to Japan's debt problems.* Accessed January 2020. Available at: https://www.bloomberg.com/news/articles/2018-12-13/health-care-paradox-threatens-to-add-to-japan-s-debt-problems

Duncan, P., M. E. Morris, G. L. Zori, and L. A. McCarey. 2024. Chapter 8. Canada. In Shi, Leiyu and Greenhill, Richard (Eds.). *Comparative Health Systems*. (3rd ed.). Burlington, MA: Jones & Bartlett.

Feldstein, P. J. 1993. *Health care economics*. 4th ed. New York, NY: Delmar.

Figueroa, J. F., Y. Tsugawa, J. Z. Zheng, E. J. Orav, and A. K. Jha. 2016. Association between the Value-Based Purchasing pay for performance program and patient mortality in US hospitals: Observational study. *BMJ (Clinical Research ed.)* 353: i2214. doi:10.1136/bmj.i2214

Frandsen, B. R., K. E. Joynt, J. B. Rebitzer, and A. K. Jha. 2015. Care fragmentation, quality, and costs among chronically ill patients. *American Journal of Managed Care* 21: 355–362.

Furukawa, M. F., W. D. Spector, M. Rhona Limcangco, and W. E. Encinosa. 2017. Meaningful use of health information technology and declines in in-hospital adverse drug events. *Journal of the American Medical Informatics Association* 24: 729–736. Available at: https://doi.org/10.1093/jamia/ocw183

Gold, J. 2015. *Accountable care organizations, explained.* Accessed February 2021. Available at: https://khn.org/news/aco-accountable-care-organization-faq/

Granovsky, D. 2016. A new government: A new open and collaborative era? *Canadian Nurse* 112: 15–18.

Gupta, A., L. A. Allen, D. L. Bhatt, et al. 2018. Association of the Hospital Readmissions Reduction Program implementation with readmission and mortality outcomes in heart failure. *JAMA Cardiology* 3: 44–53. doi:10.1001/jamacardio.2017.4265

Hall, J. 1999. Incremental change in the Australian health care system. *Health Affairs* 18: 95–110.

Health Canada. 2013. *Canada Health Act.* Accessed July 2013. Available at: http://laws-lois.justice.gc.ca/eng/acts/C-6/index.html

Health Council of Canada. 2013. *Progress report 2013.* Accessed July 2013. Available at: http://www.healthcouncilcanada.ca/rpt_det.php?id=481

Health Resources and Services Administration (HRSA). 2022. *National health center data.* Accessed September 2023. Available at: https://bphc.hrsa.gov/uds/datacenter.aspx

Health Systems and Policy Monitor (HSPM). 2012. *Health systems in transition (HiT) profile of Canada.* Available at: http://www.hspm.org/countries/canada22042013/livinghit.aspx?Section=6.1%20Analysis%20of%20recent%20reforms&Type=Section

Health Systems and Policy Monitor (HSPM). 2015. *United Kingdom.* Accessed May 2016. Available at: http://www.hspm.org/countries/england11032013/countrypage.aspx

Health Systems and Policy Monitor (HSPM). 2016. *Country page: Germany.* Accessed February 2017. Available at: http://www.hspm.org/countries/germany28082014/countrypage.aspx

Healy, J. 2002. Australia. In: *Health care systems in eight countries: Trends and challenges*. A. Dixon and E. Mossialos, eds. London, UK: European Observatory on Health Care Systems, London School of Economics & Political Science. 3–16.

Heeringa, J., A. Mutti, M. F. Furukawa, A. Lechner, K. A. Maurer, and E. Rich. 2020. Horizontal and vertical integration of health care providers: A framework for understanding various provider organizational structures. *International Journal of Integrated Care* 20: 2.

Hemenway, D., and D. Fallon. 1985. Testing for physician-induced demand with hypothetical cases. *Medical Care* 23: 344–349.

Himmelstein, D. U. 2014. *A comparison of hospital administrative costs in eight nations: U.S. costs exceed all others by far.* Accessed February 2020. Available at: https://www.commonwealthfund.org/publications/journal-article/2014/sep/comparison-hospital-administrative-costs-eight-nations-us

Himmelstein, D. U., T. Campbell, and S. Woolhandler. 2020. Health care administrative costs in the United States and Canada, 2017. *Annals of Internal Medicine* 172: 134–142. doi:10.7326/M19-2818

Hsiao, W. C. 1995. Medical savings accounts: Lessons from Singapore. *Health Affairs* 14: 260–266.

Hsu, S. 2015. *China's health care reforms.* Accessed May 2016. Available at: http://thediplomat.com/2015/05/chinas-health-care-reforms/

Ikegami, N., and G. F. Anderson. 2012. In Japan, all-payer rate setting under tight government control has proved to be an effective approach to containing costs. *Health Affairs* 31: 1049–1056.

Ikegami, N., and J. C. Campbell. 2004. Japan's health care system: Containing costs and attempting reform. *Health Affairs* 23: 26–36.

Impact of Obamacare on coverage. 2016. *Congressional Digest* 95: 7–32.

Jian, W., M. Lu, K. Y. Chan, et al. 2015. The impact of a pilot reform on the diagnosis-related-groups payment system in China: a difference-in-difference study. *Lancet* 386: S26.

Joshi, S., T. Nuckols, J. Escarce, et al. 2019. Regression to the mean in the Medicare Hospital Readmissions Reduction Program. *JAMA Internal Medicine* 179: 1167–1173. doi:https://doi.org/10.1001/jamainternmed.2019.1004

Juo, Y. Y., Y. Sanaiha, U. Khrucharoen, et al. 2019. Complete impact of care fragmentation on readmissions following urgent abdominal operations. *Journal of Gastrointestinal Surgery* 23: 1643–1651. doi:10.1007/s11605-018-4033-1

Kaiser Family Foundation. 2022. *Total health care employment*. Accessed September 2023. Available at: https://www.kff.org/other/state-indicator/total-health-care-employment/?currentTimeframe=0&selectedRows=%7B%22wrapups%22:%7B%22united-states%22:%7B%7D%7D%7D&sortModel=%7B%22colId%22:%22Location%22,%22sort%22:%22asc%22%7D

Kaiser Family Foundation. 2019. *The U.S. government and global health*. Accessed January 2020. Available at: https://www.kff.org/global-health-policy/fact-sheet/the-u-s-government-and-global-health/

Kaiser Family Foundation. 2020. *Breaking down the U.S. global health budget by program area*. Accessed February 2021. Available at: https://www.kff.org/global-health-policy/fact-sheet/breaking-down-the-u-s-global-health-budget-by-program-area/

Kaiser Family Foundation. 2023. *Status of state Medicaid expansion decisions: Interactive map*. Accessed September 2023. Available at: https://www.kff.org/medicaid/issue-brief/status-of-state-medicaid-expansion-decisions-interactive-map/

Kelly, M., C. James, S. Alessi Kraft, et al. 2015. Patient perspectives on the learning health system: The importance of trust and shared decision making. *The American Journal of Bioethics* 15: 4–17. doi:10.1080/15265161.2015.1062163.

Kraschnewski J. L., and R. A. Gabbay. 2013. Role of health information technologies in the patient-centered medical home. *Journal of Diabetes Science and Technology* 7: 1376–1385. doi:10.1177/193229681300700530.

Lai, Y., H. Fu, L. Li, W. Yip. 2022. Hospital response to a case-based payment scheme under regional global budget: the case of Guangzhou in China. *Social Science & Medicine* 292: 114601

Lagomarsino, G., A. Garabrant, A. Adyas, R. Muga, N. Otoo. 2012. Moving towards universal health coverage: Health insurance reforms in nine developing countries in Africa and Asia. *Lancet* 380: 933–943.

Lam, M. B., J. F. Figueroa, J. Zheng, E. J. Orav, A. K. Jha. 2018. Spending among patients with cancer in the first 2 years of accountable care organization participation. *Journal of Clinical Oncology* 36: 2955–2960. doi:10.1200/JCO.18.00270

Ledlow, G., and M. H. Kennedy. 2024. Chapter 15. Germany. In Shi, Leiyu and Greenhill, Richard (Eds.). *Comparative Health Systems*. (3rd ed.). Burlington, MA: Jones & Bartlett.

Lewis, S. 2022. Value-based healthcare: is it the way forward?. Future Healthcare Journal 9: 211–215.

Li, Q., X. Fan, and W. Jian. 2023. Impact of Diagnosis-Related-Group (DRG) payment on variation in hospitalization expenditure: evidence from China. *BMC Health Services Research* 23: 1–9.

Liu, C., and W. Haseltine. n.d. *International health care system profiles: Singapore*. Accessed January 2020. Available at: https://international.commonwealthfund.org/countries/singapore/

Lu, N., K.-C. Huang, and R. Guo. 2024. Chapter 31. China. In Shi, Leiyu, and Greenhill, Richard (Eds.). *Comparative Health Systems*. (3rd ed.). Burlington, MA: Jones & Bartlett.

Lyu, D., et al. 2019. *China is striving for the world's best, cheapest healthcare*. Accessed January 2020. Available at: https://www.bloomberg.com/graphics/2019-china-healthcare/

MacPhee S. 1996. Reform the watchword as OECD countries struggle to contain health care costs. *Canadian Medical Association Journal* 154: 699–701.

Markowitz, A. A., J. M. Hollingsworth, J. Z. Ayanian, et al. 2019. Risk adjustment in Medicare ACO program deters coding increases but may lead ACOs to drop high-risk beneficiaries. *Health Affairs* 38. Available at: https://doi.org/10.1377/hlthaff.2018.05407

Matsuda, R. 2016. The Japanese health care system, 2015. In: *International profiles of health care systems, 2015*. E. Mossialos et al., eds. New York, NY: The Commonwealth Fund. 107–114.

McClellan, M., and D. Kessler. 1999. A global analysis of technological change in health care: The case of heart attacks. *Health Affairs* 18: 250–257. Available at: https://www.commonwealthfund.org/publications/fund-reports/2016/jan/international-profiles-health-care-systems-2015

Miller, D., and E. T. Baumgartner. 2016. Lessons from the community-centered health home demonstration project: Patient-centered medical homes can improve health conditions in their surrounding communities. *Preventing Chronic Disease* 13: E102.

National Academies of Sciences, Engineering, and Medicine. 2021. Implementing high-quality primary care: rebuilding the foundation of health care. Available at: https://books.google.com/books?hl=en&lr=&id=O9zQDwAAQBAJ&oi=fnd&pg=PP1&dq=C.+Zhu+2015.+Healthy+China+2020.+Singapore:+People%E2%80%99s+Medical+Publishing+House.&ots=g0YteJ9a6c&sig=2ZTT4EfluvGywS2MNyr9shSwQkQ#v=onepage&q&f=false

National Bureau of Statistics, 2022. Accessed September 2023. Available at: https://data.stats.gov.cn/easyquery.htm?cn=C01&zb=A0S0U&sj=2022.%20

National Center for Health Statistics, 2023. U.S. Uninsured Rate Dropped 18% During Pandemic. Available at: https://www.cdc.gov/nchs/pressroom/nchs_press_releases/2023/202305.htm#:~:text=8.4%25%20or%2027.6%20million%20Americans,or%2033.2%20million%20in%202019

National Health Services England. 2015. *Five Year Forward View: Time to deliver.* Accessed February 2017. Available at: https://www.england.nhs.uk/wp-content/uploads/2015/06/5yfv-time-to-deliver-25-06.pdf

Naylor, C. D. 1999. Health care in Canada: Incrementalism under fiscal duress. *Health Affairs* 18: 9–26.

Nomura, H., and T. Nakayama. 2005. The Japanese healthcare system. *BMJ* 331: 648–649.

Nursingschool411.com. 2023. Nursing School and Program Guide of 2023. Available at: https://www.nursingschool411.com/#online

Ody, C., and D. Cutler. 2019. The Medical Hospital Readmission Reduction Program: Does it do any good? *JAMA Internal Medicine* 179: 1174–1175. doi: https://doi.org/10.1001/jamainternmed.2019.1003

Ody, C., L. Msall, L. S. Dafny, D. C. Grabowski, D. M. Cutler. 2019. Decreases in readmissions credited to Medicare's program to reduce hospital readmissions have been overstated. *Health Affairs* 38: 36–43. doi:10.1377/hlthaff.2018.05178

Office of National Statistics. 2015. *Healthcare expenditure, UK Health Accounts: 2017.* Accessed July 2024. Available at: https://www.nationalacademies.org/our-work/implementing-high-quality-primary-care

Office of National Statistics. 2023. *Healthcare expenditure, UK Health Accounts: 2021.* Accessed September 2023. Available at: https://www.ons.gov.uk/peoplepopulationandcommunity/healthandsocialcare/healthcaresystem/bulletins/ukhealthaccounts/2021#government-healthcare-expenditure

Pacificprime.cg. 2023. How does Singapore's healthcare system work? Available at: https://www.pacificprime.sg/blog/singapores-healthcare-system/#:~:text=Singapore%27s%20public%20healthcare%20is%20funded,Central%20Provident%20Fund%20(CPF)

Papanicolas, I., J. F. Figueroa, E. J. Orav, and A. K. Jha. 2017. Patient hospital experience improved modestly, but no evidence Medicare incentives promoted meaningful gains. *Health Affairs* 36. Available at: https://doi.org/10.1377/hlthaff.2016.0808

Parasrampuria, S., A. H. Oakes, S. S. Wu, M. A. Parikh, and W. V. Padula. 2018. Value and performance of accountable care organizations: A cost-minimization analysis. *International Journal of Technology Assessment in Health Care* 34: 388–392. Available at: https://doi.org/10.1017/S0266462318000399

Parente, S. T., and R. Feldman. 2013. Microsimulation of private health insurance and Medicaid take-up following the U.S. Supreme Court decision upholding the Affordable Care Act. *Health Services Research* 48: 826–849.

Patel, S.Y., A. Mehrotra, H. A. Huskamp, et al. 2020. Trends in outpatient care delivery and telemedicine during the COVID-19 pandemic in the US. *JAMA Internal Medicine* 181: 388–391 doi:10.1001/jamainternmed.2020.5928

Podger, A. 1999. Reforming the Australian health care system: A government perspective. *Health Affairs* 18: 111–113.

Pollard, M. S., and L. M. Davis. 2022. Decline in trust in the Centers for Disease Control and Prevention during the COVID-19 pandemic. *Rand Health Quarterly* 9(3): 23.

Private Healthcare Australia, 2023. Australians sign up to private health insurance in record numbers. Available at: https://www.privatehealthcareaustralia.org.au/australians-sign-up-to-private-health-insurance-in-record-numbers/

Qian, M., X. Zhang, Y. Chen, S. Xu, and X. Ying. 2021. The pilot of a new patient classification-based payment system in China: The impact on costs, length of stay and quality." *Social Science & Medicine* 289: 114415.

Rodin, J., and D. de Ferranti. 2012. Universal health coverage: The third global health transition? *Lancet* 380: 861–862.

Rosen, B. 2016. The Israeli health care system, 2015. In: *International profiles of health care systems, 2015*. E.Mossialos et al., eds. New York, NY: The Commonwealth Fund. 87–95. Accessed February 2017. Available at: http://www.commonwealthfund.org/~/media/files/publications/fund-report/2016/jan/1857_mossialos_intl_profiles_2015_v7.pdf

Rosen, B., R. Waltzberg, and S. Merkur. 2016. Israel: Health system review. *Health Systems in Transition* 17: 1–243. Available at: https://www.researchgate.net/profile/Sherry-Merkur/publication/303684696_Israel_Health_System_Review/links/58245b8b08aeebc4f898b52d/Israel-Health-System-Review.pdf

Rosenthal, M. B., M. B. Landrum, J. A. Robbins, and E. C. Schneider. 2016. Pay for performance in Medicaid: Evidence from three natural experiments. *Health Services Research* 51: 1444–1466. doi:10.1111/1475-6773.12426

Sachs, J. D. 2012. Achieving universal health coverage in low-income settings. *Lancet* 380: 944–947.

Salkeld, G. 2014. *Creating a better health system: Lessons from Singapore.* The Conversation. Accessed May 2016. Available at: http://theconversation.com/creating-a-better-health-system-lessons-from-singapore-30607

Santerre, R. E., and S. P. Neun. 1996. *Health economics: Theories, insights, and industry studies.* Chicago, IL: Irwin.

Schneider, E. C. 2020. Failing the test —the tragic data gap undermining the U.S. pandemic. *N Engl J Med* 2020; 383:299-302 doi: 10.1056/NEJMp2014836;

https://www.nejm.org/doi/full/10.1056/NEJMp2014836

Schieber, G., and A. Maeda. 1999. Health care financing and delivery in developing countries. *Health Affairs* 18: 193–205.

Shi, L. 2023. *Introduction to Health Policy* (3rd ed.). Health Administration Press, AUPHA.

Shi, L., and R. Greenhill (Eds.). 2024. *Comparative Health Systems*. (3rd ed.). Jones & Bartlett.

Simmons-Duffin, S. 2019. *Trump is trying hard to thwart Obamacare. How's that going?* Accessed February 2020. Available at: https://www.npr.org/sections/health-shots/2019/10/14/768731628/trump-is-trying-hard-to-thwart-obamacare-hows-that-going

Singapore Ministry of Health. 2007. *ElderShield experience 2002–2007*. Accessed February 2021. Available at: https://www.moh.gov.sg/docs/librariesprovider5/resources-statistics/information-papers/esh_experience_2002-2007.pdf

Singapore Ministry of Health. 2012. *Medisave for Chronic Disease Management Programme (CDMP) and vaccinations*. Accessed February 2021. Available at: https://www.moh.gov.sg/hpp/doctors/guidelines/GuidelineDetails/medisave-for-chronic-disease-management-program-and-vaccinations

Singapore Ministry of Health, 2022, *Medisave for Chronic Disease Management Programme (CDMP)*. Available at https://www.moh.gov.sg/hpp/doctors/guidelines/GuidelineDetails/medisave-for-chronic-disease-management-program-and-vaccinations

Sporinova, B., B. Manns, and M. Tonelli, et al. 2019. Association of mental health disorders with health care utilization and costs among adults with chronic diseases. *JAMA Open Network* 2: e199910. doi:10.1001/jamanetworkopen.2019.9910.

Statista. 2023. Total number of substance abuse treatment facilities in the U.S. from 2003 to 2020. Available at: https://www.statista.com/statistics/450281/total-number-of-substance-abuse-treatment-facilities-in-the-us/

Stein, C. 2024. Chapter 24. Israel. In Shi, Leiyu and Greenhill, Richard (Eds.). *Comparative Health Systems*. (3rd ed.). Burlington, MA: Jones & Bartlett.

Suwei, Y. U., L. I. Wenwei, W. E. Fengqing, et al. 2019. Impacts of hospital payment based on Diagnosis Related Groups (DRGs) with global budget on resource use and quality of care: a case study in China. *Iranian Journal of Public Health* 48: 238.

Takamura, A. 2015. The present circumstance of primary care in Japan. *Quality in Primary Care* 23: 262.

Takuya, A., and L. Shi. 2024. Chapter 32. Japan. In Shi, Leiyu, and Greenhill, Richard (Eds.). *Comparative Health Systems*. (3rd ed.). Burlington, MA: Jones & Bartlett.

Tam, Y., J. Y. Leung, M. Y. Ni, D. K. Ip, and G. M. Leung. 2018. Training sufficient and adequate general practitioners for universal health coverage in China. *BMJ* 362: k3128. doi:10.1136/bmj.k3128

Tan, K. B., W. S. Tan, M. Bilger, and C. W. Ho. 2014. Monitoring and evaluating progress towards universal health coverage in Singapore. *PLoS Medicine* 11: e1001695.

The King's Fund. 2023. The Health and Care Act: 6 key questions Accessed April, 2023. Available at: https://www.kingsfund.org.uk/publications/health-and-care-act-key-questions#:~:text=The%20main%20purpose%20of%20the,oversight%20of%20quality%20and%20safety

Thorlby, R., and S. Arora. 2016. The English health care system, 2015. In: *International profiles of health care systems, 2015*. E. Mossialos et al., eds. New York, NY: The Commonwealth Fund. pp. 49–58. Accessed February 2017. Available at: http://www.commonwealthfund.org/~/media/files/publications/fund-report/2016/jan/1857_mossialos_intl_profiles_2015_v7.pdf

Todd, B. 2020. The U.S. COVID-19 Testing Failure. AJN, *American Journal of Nursing* 120(10): 19–20 doi: 10.1097/01.NAJ.0000718596.51921.f2

Tolbert, J., P. Drake, and A. Damico. 2019. *Key facts about the uninsured population*. Accessed January 2020. Available at: https://www.kff.org/uninsured/issue-brief/key-facts-about-the-uninsured-population/

Trombley, M. J., B. Fout, S. Brodsky, J. M. McWilliams, D. J. Nyweide, and B. Morefield. 2019. Early effects of an accountable care organization model for underserved areas. *New England Journal of Medicine* 381: 543–551. doi:10.1056/NEJMsa1816660

Tsutsui, T., and N. Muramatsu. 2007. Japan's universal long-term care system reform of 2005: Containing costs and realizing a vision. *Journal of the American Geriatrics Society* 55: 1458–1463.

Uberoi, N., K. Finegold, and E. Gee. 2016. *Health insurance coverage and the Affordable Care Act, 2010–2016. ASPE Issue Brief*. Washington, DC: Office of the Assistant Secretary for Planning and Evaluation.

United Nations Development Programme (UNDP). 2019. *Human development reports: Developing regions*. Accessed February 2020. Available at: http://hdr.undp.org/en/content/developing-regions

USAID. 2015. *USAID's vision for health systems strengthening: 2015–2019*. Accessed February, 2021. Available at: https://www.usaid.gov/sites/default/files/documents/1864/HSS-Vision.pdf

U.S. Bureau of Labor Statistics. 2022a. *Occupational employment and wages, May 2022: 29-0000 healthcare practitioners and technical occupations (major group)*. Accessed September 2023. Available at: https://www.bls.gov/oes/current/oes_nat.htm#29-0000

U.S. Bureau of Labor Statistics. 2022b. *Occupational employment and wages, May 2022: 31-0000 healthcare support occupations (major group)*. Accessed September

2023. Available at: https://www.bls.gov/oes/current/oes_nat.htm#31-0000

van Staalduinen, D. J., P. van den Bekerom, S. Groeneveld, M. Kidanemariam, A. M., Stiggelbout, and M. E. van den Akker-van Marle. 2022. The implementation of value-based healthcare: a scoping review. *BMC Health Services Research* 22: 270.

Verma, S. 2018. *Pathways to Success: A new start for Medicare's accountable care organizations.* Accessed November 2019. Available at: https://www.healthaffairs.org/do/10.1377/hblog20180809.12285/full/

Verma, S. 2019. *Interest in "Pathways to Success" grows: 2018 ACO results show trends supporting program redesign continue.* Accessed November 2019. Available at: https://www.healthaffairs.org/do/10.1377/hblog20190930.702342/full/

Wagstaff, A., W. Yip, M. Lindelow, and W. C. Hsiao. 2009. China's health system and its reform: A review of recent studies. *Health Economics* 18: S7–S23.

Weeden, V., T. Garthwaite, S. Randall, and S. Tetlow. 2024. Chapter 13. United Kingdom. In Shi, Leiyu and Greenhill, Richard (Eds.). *Comparative Health Systems.* (3rd ed.). Burlington, MA: Jones & Bartlett.

Werner, R. M., E. J. Emanuel, H. H., Pham, and A. Navathe. 2021. *The future of value-based payment: A road map to 2030.* Available at: https://ldi.upenn.edu/our-work/research-updates/the-future-of-value-based-payment-a-road-map-to-2030/

Willcox, S. 2001. Promoting private health insurance in Australia. *Health Affairs* 20: 152–161.

Wilson, M., A. Guta, K. Waddell, J. Lavis, R. Reid, and C. Evans. 2020. The impacts of accountable care organizations on patient experience, health outcomes and costs: A rapid review. *Journal of Health Services Research & Policy* 25: 130–138.

Wolinsky, F. D. 1988. *The sociology of health: Principles, practitioners, and issues.* 2nd ed. Belmont, CA: Wadsworth.

World Bank Open Data 2022. Accessed September 2023. Available at: https://data.worldbank.org/indicator/SP.DYN.IMRT.IN?most_recent_value_desc=true

World Health Organization (WHO). 2007. Everybody's Business: Strengthening Health Systems to Improve Health Outcomes: WHO's Framework for Action. Available at: https://www.who.int/publications/i/item/everybody-s-business----strengthening-health-systems-to-improve-health-outcomes

World Health Organization (WHO). 2014. Germany: Health system review. *Health Systems in Transition* 16, no. 2. Accessed May 2016. Available at: http://www.euro.who.int/__data/assets/pdf_file/0008/255932/HiT-Germany.pdf?ua=1

World Health Organization (WHO). 2015. Israel: Health system review. *Health Systems in Transition* 17, no. 6. Accessed May 2016. Available at: http://www.euro.who.int/__data/assets/pdf_file/0009/302967/Israel-HiT.pdf

World Health Organization (WHO). 2018a. *Continuity and coordination of care.* Accessed April 2020. Available at: https://apps.who.int/iris/bitstream/handle/10665/274628/9789241514033-eng.pdf?ua=1

World Health Organization (WHO). 2022. The Global Health Observatory, 2022. Accessed September 2023. Available at: https://www.who.int/data/gho/data/indicators/indicator-details/GHO/life-expectancy-at-birth-(years)

Wu, D., T. P. Lam, K. F. Lam, X. D. Zhou, and K. S. Sun. 2017. Public views towards community health and hospital-based outpatient services and their utilisation in Zhejiang, China: A mixed methods study. *BMJ Open* 7: e017611. doi:10.1136/bmjopen-2017-017611

Xu L., and M. Zhang, 2018. Regulated multi-sited practice for physicians in China: Incentives and barriers. *Global Health Journal* 2: 14–31. doi:10.1016/S2414-6447(19)30117-4

Xu, H. D., and R. Basu. 2020. How the United States Flunked the COVID-19 Test: Some Observations and Several Lessons. *The American Review of Public Administration* 50: 568–576. Available at: https://doi.org/10.1177/0275074020941701

Yip W., and W. C. Hsiao. 2008. The Chinese health system at a crossroads. *Health Affairs* 27: 460–468.

Yip W., and A. Mahal. 2008. The health care systems of China and India: Performance and future challenges. *Health Affairs* 27: 921–932.

Yip, W. C., W. C. Hsiao, W. Chen, S. Hu, J. Ma, and A. Maynard. 2012. Early appraisal of China's huge and complex health-care reforms. *Lancet* 379: 833–842.

Yip, W., H. Fu, A. T. Chen, et al. 2019. 10 years of health-care reform in China: Progress and gaps in universal health coverage. *Lancet* 394: 1192–1204. doi:10.1016/S0140-6736(19)32136-1

Yu, L., and J. Lang. 2020. Diagnosis-related Groups (DRG) pricing and payment policy in China: Where are we? *Hepatobiliary Surgery and Nutrition* 9: 771.

Zhang, H., D. W. Cowling, J. M. Graham, and E. Taylor. 2019. Five-year impact of a commercial accountable care organization on health care spending, utilization, and quality of care. *Medical Care* 57: 845–854. doi:10.1097/MLR.0000000000001179.

Zhu, C. 2015. *Healthy China 2020.* Singapore: People's Medical Publishing House.

Zou, K., H. Y. Li, D. Zhou, and Z. J. Liao. 2020. The effects of diagnosis-related groups payment on hospital healthcare in China: A systematic review. *BMC Health Services Research* 20: 1–11.

PART 1

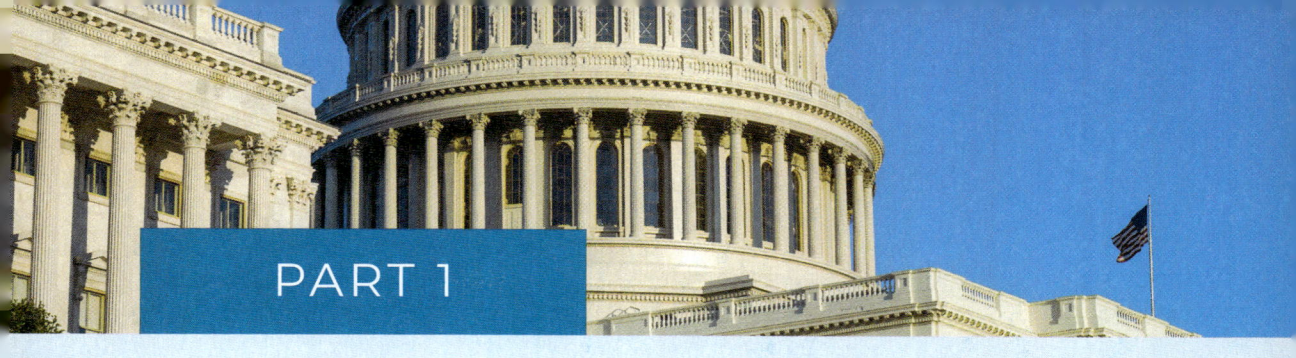

System Foundations

CHAPTER 2	Beliefs, Values, and Health 49
CHAPTER 3	The Evolution of Health Services in the United States 105

CHAPTER 2

Beliefs, Values, and Health

LEARNING OBJECTIVES

- Explore the integration of individual and population health.
- Study the concepts of health and disease, risk factors, and the role of health promotion and disease prevention.
- Summarize the disease prevention requisites under the Affordable Care Act.
- Get an overview of public health and appreciate its expanding role in health protection, both in the United States and globally, including preparedness against pandemics such as COVID-19.
- Explore the determinants of health and measures related to health.
- Understand American anthrocultural values and their implications for healthcare delivery.
- Evaluate justice and equity in health care according to contrasting theories.

This is the market justice system. Social justice is over there.

Introduction

From an economic perspective, curative medicine appears to produce decreasing returns in health improvement while increasing healthcare expenditures (Saward and Sorensen, 1980). There has also been a growing recognition of the benefits afforded to society by the promotion of health and the prevention of disease (including pandemics such as COVID-19), disability, and premature death. Even so, progress in this direction has been slow because of the prevailing social values, beliefs, and practices, which continue to focus on curing diseases rather than promoting health. The common definitions of health as well as measures for evaluating health status reflect similar inclinations. This chapter proposes a balanced approach to health, although achieving such an ideal is daunting. The 10-year *Healthy People* initiatives, undertaken by the U.S. Department of Health and Human Services (DHHS) since 1980, illustrate steps taken in this direction, even though these initiatives have been typically strong in rhetoric but weak in effective strategies and sustainable funding.

Anthrocultural factors reflected in the beliefs and values ingrained in American culture have been influential in laying the foundations of a U.S. healthcare system that has remained predominantly private as opposed to a tax-financed national healthcare program. Discussion of this theme begins in this chapter and continues in *The Evolution of Health Services in the United States* chapter, where failures of past proposals to create a nationalized healthcare system are discussed in the context of cultural beliefs and values.

This chapter further explores the issue of equity in the distribution of health services, using contrasting theories of market justice and social justice. U.S. healthcare delivery incorporates both principles, which are complementary in some ways and create conflicts in other areas.

Significance for Managers and Policymakers

The topics covered in this chapter have several implications for health services managers and policymakers alike:

- The health status of a population has significant bearing on the utilization of health services, assuming those services are readily available. Planning of health services must be governed by demographic and health trends and initiatives toward reducing disease and disability.
- The basic meanings of health, determinants of health, and health risk appraisal should be used to design appropriate educational, preventive, and therapeutic initiatives.
- There is a growing emphasis on evaluating the effectiveness of healthcare organizations based on the contributions they make to community and population health. The concepts discussed in this chapter can guide administrators in implementing programs that have the greatest value to their communities.
- Quantified measures of health status and utilization can be used by managers and policymakers to evaluate the adequacy and effectiveness of existing programs, plan new strategies, measure progress, and discontinue ineffective services.

Basic Concepts of Health

Health

In the United States, the concepts of health and health care have largely been governed by the medical model, more specifically referred to as the biomedical model. The **medical model** defines health as the absence of illness or disease. This definition implies that optimal health exists when a person is free of symptoms and does not require medical treatment. However, it is not a definition of health in the true sense. This prevailing view of health emphasizes clinical diagnoses and medical interventions to treat disease or symptoms of disease but fails to account for prevention of disease and health promotion. Therefore, when the term "healthcare delivery" is used, in reality, it refers to *medical* care delivery.

Medical sociologists have gone a step further in defining health as the state of optimal capacity of an individual to perform their expected social roles and tasks, such as work, school, and household chores (Parsons, 1972). A person who is unable (as opposed to unwilling) to perform their social roles in society is considered sick. However, this concept also seems inadequate because many people continue to engage in their social obligations despite suffering from pain, cough, colds, and other types of temporary disabilities, including mental distress. Their efforts are counterbalanced by individuals who shirk their social responsibilities even when they may be in good health. In other words, optimal health is not necessarily reflected in a person's engagement in social roles and responsibilities.

An emphasis on both the physical and mental dimensions of health is found in the definition of health proposed by the Society for Academic Emergency Medicine. According to this organization, health is "a state of physical and mental well-being that facilitates the achievement of individual and societal goals" (Ethics Committee, Society for Academic Emergency Medicine, 1992). This view of health recognizes the importance of achieving harmony between the physiological and emotional dimensions.

The definition of health developed by the World Health Organization (WHO) is most often cited as the ideal for healthcare delivery systems; it recognizes that optimal health is more than the absence of disease or infirmity. The WHO (1948) defines health as "a state of complete physical, mental and social well-being and not merely the absence of disease or infirmity." As a biopsychosocial model, the WHO's definition specifically identifies social well-being as a third dimension of health. For example, having a social support network is positively associated with resilience to life stresses, self-esteem, and social relations. Conversely, research shows that social isolation is associated with a higher risk of poor health and mortality (Pantell et al., 2013). As this chapter points out, health care should include much more than medical care and may be defined as a variety of services believed to improve a person's health and well-being.

In recent decades, increased interest has been directed toward **holistic health**, which emphasizes the well-being of every aspect of what makes a person whole and complete. Thus, **holistic medicine** seeks to treat the individual as a whole person (Ward, 1995). Within this approach, diagnosis and treatment would take into account the mental, emotional, spiritual, nutritional, environmental, and other factors related to the origin of disease (Cohen, 2003).

In addition to the physical, mental, and social aspects necessary for optimal health, the spiritual dimension is incorporated as a fourth element in holistic health (**Figure 2-1**). A growing volume of medical literature, both in the United States and abroad, points to the healing effects of a person's religion and spirituality on morbidity and mortality. The importance of spirituality as an aspect of health care is also reflected in policy documents produced by the WHO (2003) and other bodies.

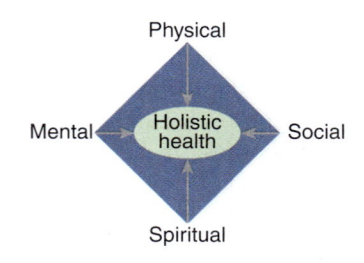

Figure 2-1 The four dimensions of holistic health.

Based on their extensive review of the literature, Chida et al. (2009) concluded that religious practice/spirituality is associated with reductions in deaths from all causes as well as from cardiovascular diseases. Patients with heart disease who attend regular religious services have been found to have a significant survival advantage (Oman et al., 2002). Spirituality has been shown to have a positive impact on a person's quality of life, well-being, and mental health (Peres et al., 2018). In addition, many studies have identified a positive relationship between religious practice and protective health behaviors (Chida et al., 2009). Some religious communities specifically promote healthy lifestyles in terms of abstinence from tobacco use and alcohol consumption and improvement in diet. An examination of the literature found a reduced risk for cancer in these communities (Hoff et al., 2008). Spiritual well-being has also been recognized as an important internal resource for helping people cope with illness. For instance, in a study conducted at the University of Michigan, 93% of the women undergoing cancer treatment indicated that their religious lives helped them sustain their hope (Roberts et al., 1997). Studies have also found that a large percentage of patients want their physicians to consider their spiritual needs, and almost half express a desire for the physicians to pray with them if they can (Post et al., 2000).

The spiritual dimension is frequently tied to one's religious beliefs, values, morals, and practices. Broadly, this dimension is described as meaning, purpose, and fulfillment in life; hope and will to live; faith; and a person's relationship with God (Marwick, 1995; Ross, 1995; Swanson, 1995). One clinically tested scale to measure spiritual well-being includes categories such as belief in a power greater than oneself, purpose in life, faith, trust in providence, prayer, meditation, group worship, ability to forgive, and gratitude for life (Hatch et al., 1998). In addition, several formal assessments have been developed to help physicians address the spiritual needs of their patients. One such tool is the HOPE Questions, which enable physicians to speak about spirituality with their patients so as to obtain important information about patients' views of health care and faith (Anandarajoh and Hight, 2001).

Respect for patient values and beliefs is increasingly recognized as an important aspect of culturally appropriate care by the medical community. Many medical schools and continuing education courses now offer formal courses in spirituality in medicine (Fortin and Barnett, 2004). Furthermore, the Joint Commission (2003) recommends that healthcare institutions accommodate and assess patients' spiritual beliefs and practices as a routine part of care.

The Committee on Religion and Psychiatry of the American Psychiatric Association has issued a position statement emphasizing the importance of maintaining respect for a patient's religious/spiritual beliefs. In fact, in 2013, "religious or spiritual problem" was included as a diagnostic category for the first time in the edition of the *Diagnostic and Statistical Manual of Mental Disorders,* Fifth Edition (DSM-5). The holistic approach to health also alludes to the need to incorporate alternative therapies into the predominant medical model.

Quality of Life

The term **quality of life** is used to capture the essence of overall satisfaction with life during and following a person's encounter with the healthcare delivery system. This term is employed in two ways. First, it is an indicator of how satisfied a person is with their experiences while receiving health care. Specific life domains—such as comfort factors, respect, privacy, security, degree of independence, decision-making autonomy, and attention to personal preferences—are significant to most people. These factors, in turn, are now regarded as rights that patients can demand during any type of healthcare encounter.

Second, quality of life can refer to a person's overall satisfaction with life and with self-perceptions of health, particularly after some medical intervention. The implication is that desirable processes during medical treatment and successful outcomes should subsequently have a positive effect on an individual's ability to function, carry out social roles and obligations, and realize a sense of fulfillment and self-worth.

Risk Factors and Disease

The occurrence of disease involves more than just a single factor. For example, the mere presence of the tubercle bacillus does not automatically mean the infected person will develop tuberculosis. Other factors, such as poverty, overcrowding, and malnutrition, may be essential for development of the disease (Friedman, 1980). Hence, tracing **risk factors**—attributes that increase the likelihood of developing a particular disease or negative health condition in the future—requires a broad approach.

One useful explanation of disease occurrence (for communicable diseases, in particular) is provided by the tripartite model, sometimes referred to as the Epidemiology Triangle (**Figure 2-2**). In this model, the **host** is the organism—generally, a human—that becomes sick. Factors associated with the host include genetic makeup, level of immunity, fitness, and personal habits and behaviors. For the host to become sick, an **agent** must be present, although the presence of an agent does not ensure that disease will occur. In the previous example, the tubercle bacillus is the agent for tuberculosis. Other examples of agents include chemicals, radiation, tobacco smoke, dietary indiscretions, and nutritional deficiencies. The third entity, **environment**, is external to the host and includes the physical, social, cultural, and economic aspects of the environment. Examples include sanitation, air pollution, anthrocultural beliefs, social equity, social norms, and economic status. These kinds of environmental factors play a moderating role that can either enhance or reduce susceptibility to disease. Because the three entities of host, agent, and environment often interact to produce disease, disease prevention efforts should focus on a broad approach to mitigate or eliminate risk factors associated with all three entities.

Behavioral Risk Factors

Certain individual behaviors and personal lifestyle choices represent important risk factors for illness and disease. For example, smoking has been identified as the leading cause of preventable disease and death in the United States because it significantly increases the risk of heart disease, stroke, lung cancer, and chronic lung disease (DHHS, 2004). Substance abuse, inadequate physical exercise, a high-fat diet, irresponsible use of motor vehicles, and unsafe sex are other examples of behavioral risk factors. **Table 2-1** indicates the percentages of the U.S. population with selected behavioral risks.

Acute, Subacute, and Chronic Conditions

Disease can be classified as acute, subacute, or chronic. An **acute condition** is relatively severe, episodic (of short duration), and often treatable and subject to recovery. Treatments are generally provided in a hospital. Examples of acute conditions include a sudden

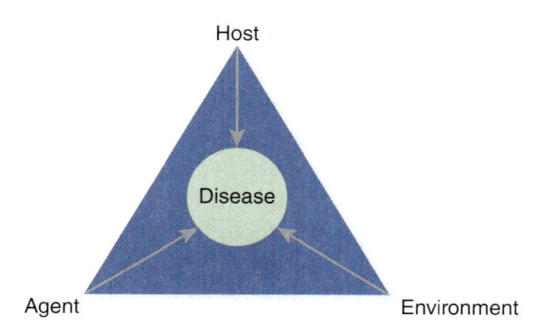

Figure 2-2 The Epidemiology Triangle.

Table 2-1 Percentage of U.S. Population with Behavioral Risks

Behavioral Risks	Percentage of Population	Year
Alcohol (12 years and older)	47.1	2019
Marijuana (12 years and older)	17.5	2019
Illicit drug use (12th graders)	14.8	2017
Illicit drug use (10th graders)	6.3	2017
Illicit drug use (8th graders)	2.0	2017
Cigarette smoking (18 years and older)	11.5	2021
Hypertension (20 years and older)	47, age-adjusted	2021
Overweight and obese (20 years and older)	73.6, age-adjusted	2017–2018
Serum cholesterol (20 years and older)	11.3, age-adjusted	2013–2018

Data from National Center for Health Statistics (NCHS). 2019. Health, United States, 2018. Hyattsville, MD: Department of Health and Human Services. Tables 20, 22, 23, 26; Substance Abuse and Mental Health Services Administration. (2020). Key substance use and mental health indicators in the United States: Results from the 2019 National Survey on Drug Use and Health (HHS Publication No. PEP20-07-01-001, NSDUH Series H-55). Rockville, MD: Center for Behavioral Health Statistics and Quality, Substance Abuse and Mental Health Services Administration. Retrieved from https://www.samhsa.gov/data/; CDC. 2023. Current Cigarette Smoking Among Adults in the United States. https://www.cdc.gov/tobacco/data_statistics/fact_sheets/adult_data/cig_smoking/index.htm#:~:text=In%202021%2C%20nearly%2012%20of,with%20a%20smoking%2Drelated%20disease

interruption of kidney function and a myocardial infarction (heart attack).

A **subacute condition** is a less severe phase of an acute illness. It can be a postacute condition, requiring continuity of treatment after discharge from a hospital. Examples include ventilator and head trauma care.

A **chronic condition** is one that persists over time and is not severe, but is generally irreversible. A chronic condition may be kept under control through appropriate medical treatment, but if left untreated, it may lead to severe and life-threatening health problems. Examples of chronic conditions are hypertension, asthma, arthritis, heart disease, and diabetes. Contributors to chronic disease include ethnic, cultural, and behavioral factors and the social and physical environment, as discussed later in this chapter.

In the United States, chronic diseases have become the leading cause of death and disability. Six in ten Americans have at least one chronic illness (Centers for Disease Control and Prevention [CDC], 2019b), and 8.7 out of every 10 deaths are attributable to chronic disease, with heart disease and cancer accounting for nearly 50% of all deaths (WHO, 2011). Cardiovascular diseases are responsible for one-fourth of all deaths annually. While heart disease is largely preventable, the burden associated with this disease continues to grow. Approximately half (47%) of Americans have at least one of the major clinical risk factors for cardiovascular disease: high low-density lipoprotein (LDL) cholesterol, high blood pressure, or smoking (CDC, 2019c). Other major risk factors include physical inactivity, diabetes, and obesity (Kannel and Abbott, 1984).

Cancer is the second leading cause of death in the United States, with more than 1.7 million people being diagnosed with cancer annually (CDC, 2022a). The most commonly diagnosed types of cancers are female breast cancer, prostate cancer, lung and bronchus cancer, and colon and rectum cancer (CDC, 2016a). Although the specific risk factors vary by type of cancer, general risk factors include family history, age, exposure to cancerous substances, diet, obesity, and tobacco use.

Over 90% of the nation's $4.1 trillion in annual healthcare expenditures are for people with chronic and metal health conditions (CDC, 2021). Totaling both direct and indirect costs, chronic conditions cost the U.S. economy $3.7 trillion in 2016, or 19.6% of the country's gross domestic product (GDP) (Waters and Graf, 2018). As of 2022, an estimated 37.3 million Americans were living with diabetes and another 96 million were living with prediabetes, a health condition that increases the risk of type 2 diabetes (CDC, 2022b). The major risk factor for diabetes is obesity. The estimated cost of diagnosed diabetes alone in 2017 was $327 billion, which included $90 billion in reduced productivity. The high costs of prescription medications, hospital inpatient care, and diabetes supplies contribute to the $237 billion in medical costs associated with this disease (American Diabetes Association, 2018). The economic burden of heart disease and stroke is also high, with these conditions costing the U.S. economy approximately $207 billion each year for healthcare services, medications, and lost productivity (Mozaffarian et al., 2016).

According to data from MEPS (Medical Expenditure Panel Survey), the annual direct and indirect cost of cardiovascular disease (CVD) in the United States is an estimated $378 billion, which includes $226.2 billion in expenditures and $151.8 billion in lost future productivity from 2017 to 2018 (Tsao, 2022). The direct medical costs for cancer are approximately $88 billion per year in the United States, and the economic burden of this disease is expected to increase significantly in the future due to the growth and aging of the population, improvements in survival, and increased costs of care (Yabroff et al., 2011).

Three main reasons underlie the increased prevalence of chronic conditions in the U.S. population:

- New diagnostic methods, medical procedures, and pharmaceuticals have significantly improved the treatment of acute illnesses, survival rates, and longevity, but these achievements have had the consequence of creating a larger population living with chronic conditions. The prevalence of chronic disease is expected to continue to rise with an aging population and longer life expectancy.
- Screening and diagnosis have expanded in scope, frequency, and accuracy (Robert Wood Johnson Foundation, 2010).
- Lifestyle choices, such as consumption of high-salt and high-fat diets and sedentary lifestyles, are risk factors that contribute to the development of chronic conditions.

Some risk factors that contribute to the most common chronic diseases can be modified through prevention. For example, smoking, obesity, physical inactivity, and poor nutrition are risk factors for most chronic diseases. Proven prevention methods include lifestyle change programs, though such programs are notoriously difficult to sustain. Increasing prevention efforts and awareness of the need to reduce cholesterol levels and hypertension so as to prevent heart disease and stroke remains a challenge (Franco et al., 2011). In the United States, obesity and diabetes rates have increased over the past several decades, at least in part due to changes in food consumption and technological advances, which have reduced energy expenditure in labor-intensive occupations (Caballero, 2007; Finkelstein et al., 2005; Franco et al., 2009). State and local health departments face their own challenges, such as budget restrictions, in enacting health promotion programs,. Moreover, many state and local programs directed at people with chronic diseases have been reduced or eliminated (Johnson et al., 2011). Chronic disease programs are not standardized or comprehensive in most healthcare settings (Bauer et al., 2014; Maylahn et al., 2013).

The CDC supports strengthened collaboration between public health agencies and private healthcare providers to prevent chronic diseases and improve population health. One comprehensive initiative geared toward meeting this aim was launched by the DHHS with the funding of $650 million allocated to the American Recovery and Reinvestment Act of 2009. The goal of this initiative, called Communities Putting Prevention to Work (CPPW), is to "reduce risk factors, prevent/delay chronic disease, promote wellness in children and adults, and provide positive, sustainable health change in communities" (DHHS, 2010a). By June 2013, CPPW had met 73% of its objectives (CDC, 2013a). It was successful in increasing access to environments with healthy food and beverage options in communities nationwide. It also created bike lanes in cities, supported the development of walking trails, and provided guidelines for daily physical activity in schools to increase access to physical activities. The program decreased exposure to second-hand smoke through expansion of smoke-free areas and expanded smoking cessation services. In addition, CPPW increased local capacity to improve public health interventions, developed products to support public health departments, and guided the development of programs to better support long-term community health. It is estimated that if these health improvements are sustained in CPPW communities beyond the intervention period, there will be 14,000 fewer deaths and $2.4 billion in healthcare costs will be averted through 2020 (Khavjou et al., 2014).

Health Promotion and Disease Prevention

According to WHO, health promotion is a process to enable individuals to have control over and improve their overall health status (2023). A program of health promotion and disease prevention is built on three main principles:

- Risk factors associated with host, agent, environment, and their health consequences are evaluated through a process called **health risk appraisal**. Only when the risk factors and their health consequences are known can interventions be developed to help individuals adopt healthier lifestyles.
- Interventions for counteracting the key risk factors include two main approaches: (1) behavior modification geared toward the goal of adopting healthier lifestyles and (2) therapeutic interventions.
- Adequate public health and social services, as discussed later in this chapter, include all health-related services designed to minimize risk factors and their negative effects so as to prevent disease, control disease outbreaks, and contain the spread of infectious agents.

Behavior changes are positive changes in health habits by using theory-based strategies from a combination of communication, psychology, sociology, and behavioral economics (Centers for Disease Control and Prevention, 2023). Behavior modification plays a significant role in health promotion. Many diseases, particularly preventable chronic ones, can be attributed, at least partially, to unhealthy lifestyle choices and behaviors. The widespread recognition of the roles that negative behaviors and lifestyles play in the onset of disease has led the National Institutes of Health (NIH) to call for "a unified, mechanisms-focused, science of behavior change that will transform how scientists tackle the substantial behavioral contributions to a wide range of health and disease outcomes" (Nielsen et al., 2018). The NIH cites the beneficial effects of previous behavioral change interventions as evidence to emphasize the importance of focusing on this area.

Since the public health interventions and mass media campaigns had been successful in the past, targeted issues have included tobacco, alcohol, and drug use as well as road safety, preventive behavior, nutrition, and healthy sexual behavior (Wakefield et al., 2010). The Diabetes Prevention Program (DPP), which was funded by the National Institute of Diabetes and Digestive and Kidney Diseases (NIDDK), also found that an intensive lifestyle intervention was more effective than an oral drug at preventing the onset of type 2 diabetes in high-risk participants. This reduced incidence was sustained after a mean follow-up period of 15 years, demonstrating the potential that behavioral interventions have for making long-term positive changes (Diabetes Prevention Program Research Group, 2015).

Not all behavioral interventions are successfully developed or carried out, however. Many previous campaigns have been launched with great fanfare, only to produce little or only short-term effects (Wood and Neal, 2016). Kelly and Barker (2016) discuss the tendency to fall back on behavioral change strategies that are based on what is assumed to be "common sense" instead of implementing those that are evidence-based and grounded in theory. They highlight six common perception errors that often hinder attempts to change behavior: (1) behavior change is just common sense; (2) success is just about getting the message across; (3) providing knowledge and information is enough to drive behavior change; (4) people act rationally; (5) people are irrational; and (6) there is no need to account for individual variance when predicting how people will respond (Kelly and Barker, 2016). When implementing behavioral change interventions, it is important to be mindful of these common misconceptions, which collectively oversimplify the process of behavior change. Although seemingly straightforward, human nature is complex and motivated by factors that are not necessarily easily identifiable.

Any successful behavioral change intervention will consider individual-level factors in conjunction with broader social and environmental contexts. Behaviors are not only influenced by single factors but are also a consequence of the social norms and environment around the individual. For example, someone who struggles with alcohol abuse may find it difficult to quit if they work in an industry with a heavy drinking culture, has a social network that primarily meets through drinking occasions, and has low self-efficacy about their ability to give up alcohol. Another individual may want to quit smoking but finds it hard to do so because of the immense stress they face as a single parent working a low-income job while raising their child in a high-crime neighborhood. For this individual, smoking is one of the only ways they are able to take any time to relieve their stress. Any behavior change program targeting these two individuals must recognize the barriers in their lives that make changing their respective behaviors less straightforward than it seems. These hypothetical examples illustrate how behavioral change strategies that are more comprehensive and make considerations for the multiple layers at play are more likely to be effective (Laverack, 2017; Young, 2014).

Various avenues can be used in motivating individuals to alter behaviors that may contribute to disease, disability, or death. Behavior can be modified through educational programs and incentives directed at specific high-risk populations. For example, in the case of cigarette smoking, health promotion efforts aim to build people's knowledge, attitudes, and skills to avoid or quit smoking. These efforts also seek to reduce the number of advertisements and environmental enticements that promote nicotine addiction. Likewise, financial incentives and disincentives, such as higher cigarette taxes, have been used to discourage purchase of cigarettes.

Therapeutic interventions fall into three areas of preventive effort: primary prevention, secondary prevention, and tertiary prevention. **Primary prevention** refers to activities undertaken to reduce the probability that a disease will develop in the future (Kane, 1988). The objective of primary prevention is to restrain the development of a disease or negative health condition before it occurs. For example, therapeutic interventions can include community health efforts to assist patients in smoking cessation and exercise programs to prevent conditions such as lung cancer and heart disease. Safety training and practices in the workplace can reduce serious work-related injuries. Prenatal care is known to lower infant mortality rates. Immunization has had a greater impact on the prevention of childhood diseases and mortality reduction than has any other public health intervention besides providing clean water (Plotkin and Plotkin, 2012). Hand washing, food refrigeration, garbage collection, sewage treatment, and protection of the water supply are other examples of primary prevention (Timmreck, 1994). Notably, food safety and proper meal preparation training could have prevented numerous outbreaks of potentially deadly infections, such as those caused by *Escherichia coli*.

Secondary prevention refers to early detection and treatment of disease. Health screenings and periodic health examinations are just two examples. Screening for hypertension, cancers, and diabetes, for example, has been instrumental in prescribing early treatment for these conditions. The main objective of secondary prevention is to block the progression of a disease or an injury—that is, to keep it from developing into an impairment or disability (Timmreck, 1994).

Tertiary prevention refers to interventions that could prevent complications from chronic conditions as well as further illness, injury, or disability. For example, regular turning of patients who are bed-bound prevents pressure sores, rehabilitation therapies can prevent permanent disability, and infection control practices in hospitals and nursing homes are designed to prevent **iatrogenic illnesses** (i.e., illnesses or injuries caused by the process of health care). **Figure 2-3** provides additional examples of preventive measures.

As shown in **Table 2-2**, prevention, early detection, and treatment efforts helped reduce mortalities due to breast cancer, cervical

Primary Prevention

(Health promotion and disease prevention)
Health education
Adequate housing
Exercise
Stress reduction
Favorable working conditions
Immunization
Environmental sanitation
Protection against occupational hazards
Highway safety

Secondary Prevention

(Early diagnosis and treatment)
Periodic health examinations
Health screenings
Case finding targeting high risks
Wellness visit
Preventive care

Tertiary Prevention

(Limiting disability and rehabilitation)
Subacute care
Convalescent care
Home care
Reduce complications
Prolong functional status
Maintain quality of life
Manage chronic diseases
Physical rehabilitation
Psychological rehabilitation

Figure 2-3 Examples of preventive measures.

cancer, ovarian cancer, and prostate cancer quite significantly between 1991 and 2016. This decrease was the first sustained decline since recordkeeping was instituted in the 1930s. **Table 2-3** shows reductions in other specific cancer mortalities from 2016 to 2020 for male and female Americans, respectively.

In addition to behavior modification, health promotion can include social and environmental interventions that target the root causes of ill health for the benefit and protection of people's health and quality of life. These interventions emphasize that many factors outside of the health system—such as socioeconomic status, food consumption, and learning environments—determine health and social well-being. Health promotion efforts aim

Table 2-2 Annual Percentage Decline in U.S. Mortalities from Breast, Cervical, Ovarian, and Prostate Cancers, 1991–2016

Type of Cancer	1991–1995	1994–2003	1998–2007	2001–2010	2009–2013	2012–2016
All cancers	3.0	1.1	1.4	1.5	1.5	1.5
Breast cancer	6.3	2.5	2.2	2.2	1.9	1.5
Cervical cancer	9.7	3.6	2.6	1.5	0.8	0.7
Ovarian cancer	4.8	0.5	0.8	2.0	2.1	2.3
Prostate cancer	6.3	3.5	3.1	2.7	3.6	0.8

Data from National Center for Health Statistics, Centers for Disease Control and Prevention, National Cancer Institute, SEER Cancer Statistics Review, 1975–2010; National Cancer Institute. 2020. State cancer profiles. Available at: https://statecancerprofiles.cancer.gov/recenttrend/index.php.

Table 2-3 Annual Percentage Decline in U.S. Specific Cancer Mortalities, 2016–2020

Male	Average Annual Percent Change (AAPC)	Female	Average Annual Percent Change (AAPC)
Thyroid	0.7	Uterus	0.8
Oral cavity and pharynx	0.4	Liver & Intrahepatic Bile Duct	0.5
Brain & ONS	0.4	Oral cavity and pharynx	0.5
Testis	0.3	Brain & ONS	0.3
Pancreas	0.2	Thyroid	0.0
Prostate	−0.6	Pancreas	0.0
Liver & Intrahepatic Bile Duct	−0.8	Cervix	−0.7
Esophagus	−1.3	Breast	−1.3
Kidney and renal pelvis	−1.8	Esophagus	−1.5
Myeloma	−1.9	Kidney and renal pelvis	−1.7
Non-Hodgkin Lymphoma	−2.0	Stomach	−1.8
Colon and rectum	−2.0	Myeloma	−2.0
All Sites	−2.2	All Sites	−2.0
Leukemia	−2.2	Colon and rectum	−2.1
Bladder	−2.3	Leukemia	−2.2
Stomach	−2.5	Larynx	−2.3

(continues)

Table 2-3 Annual Percentage Decline in U.S. Specific Cancer Mortalities, 2016–2020 *(continued)*

Male	Average Annual percent change (AAPC)	Female	Average Annual percent change (AAPC)
Larynx	−2.5	Bladder	−2.4
Melanoma of the skin	−2.9	Non-Hodgkin Lymphoma	−2.7
Hodgkin Lymphoma	−3.0	Ovary	−3.3
Lung and bronchus	−5.3	Melanoma of the skin	−3.8
		Lung and bronchus	−4.3
		Hodgkin Lymphoma	−4.8

SEER Cancer Statistics Factsheets: Common Cancer Sites. National Cancer Institute Bethesda, MD, https://seer.cancer.gov/statfacts/html/common.html

to improve health in different settings, such as schools, hospitals, workplaces, and residential areas. Consequently, a holistic approach should be implemented to address health issues by empowering communities and individuals to take control of their own health, developing public health leadership, establishing healthy public policies in all sectors, and building sustainable health systems.

Health Promotion and the Use of Social Media

Social media serves as an effective tool for promoting health communication strategies and disseminating health-related knowledge (Schimmelpfennig et al., 2021; Stellefson et al., 2020; Stock 2022). Studies show that the use of social media is effective to increase physical activities and improve well-being. Petkovic et al. (2021) point out social media interventions on health promotion reduce the risk of developing chronic diseases such as diabetes, heart disease, and cancer by advocating health behaviors to the public.

Health promotion-themed social media also plays an important role in addressing health disparities and promoting health equity (Vereen, Kurtzman and Noar, 2023). Vereen, Kurtzman and Noar (2023) have conducted a meta-analysis by synthesizing 17 studies with 3,561 participants from disparate populations and noting that distinct determinants impact populations experiencing health disparities, and tailored interventions can be designed to address these factors, enabling the development of culturally appropriate intervention materials that contribute to attaining the desired results. For instance, the studies demonstrating the most significant effect sizes highlight the development of content culturally suitable for various groups such as inner-city Black communities, blue-collar workers, and African American women (Vereen, Kurtzman and Noar, 2023).

Disease Prevention Under the Affordable Care Act

Prevention and wellness received significant emphasis within the Patient Protection and Affordable Care Act (ACA), which was passed in 2010. At least partially, as a result of the ACA's implementation, an estimated 137 million Americans, including 28.5 million children, received no-cost coverage for preventive services (Office of the Assistant Secretary for Planning and Evaluation, 2015). Significant progress has also been made in increasing access to clinical preventive services, improving financial capacity for local public health activities, and encouraging private employers to incorporate prevention and wellness incentives and programs into the workplace (Chait and Glied, 2018).

Specific ACA initiatives include the Prevention and Public Health Fund (PPHF) for national preventive efforts and programs geared toward improving health outcomes and enhancing quality of health care (American Public Health Association, 2013). The Office of the Surgeon General has developed a National Prevention Strategy to encourage partnerships among federal, state, tribal, local, and territorial governments; business, industry, and other private sector entities; philanthropic organizations; community and faith-based organizations; and everyday Americans to improve health through prevention (National Prevention Council, 2011).

As one example of a federally driven effort directed toward reducing chronic disease, the CDC has established the National Diabetes Prevention Program (NDPP). In 2012, six organizations received $6.75 million to develop partnerships with the aim of reaching people with prediabetes (CDC, 2013b, 2013c). Through the NDPP, organizations nationwide offer diabetes prevention lifestyle programs in healthcare clinics, pharmacies, wellness centers, worksites, and other community centers. These organizations also work to increase awareness of lifestyle changes, and they encourage healthcare professionals to refer patients with prediabetes to a lifestyle change program. The NDPP has also increased awareness across employers, some of whom now provide coverage for lifestyle change programs as health benefits for their employees. In addition, this program ensures quality and standardized reporting and monitors and evaluates program effectiveness (CDC, 2016b).

In 2011, $10 million in federal funding was made available to establish and evaluate comprehensive workplace wellness programs (DHHS, 2011b). Beginning in 2014, $200 million in wellness grants was made available to small businesses to encourage the establishment of wellness programs and employee health-promotion incentives (Anderko et al., 2012). In 2015, 46.8 million employees worked in firms that offered wellness programs. Although workplace wellness programs are diverse and vary in the services and activities offered, they are all required to promote health and/or prevent disease to qualify for federal funding support. Of the companies that provided health benefits, 50% offer wellness programs for tobacco cessation, weight control, nutrition, and other lifestyle or behavioral coaching (Mattke et al., 2013). Health-promotion activities, such as on-site vaccination services, biometric screenings, fitness benefits, and healthy food options at the workplace, are also common. The majority of workplaces that provide wellness programs offer a combination of screening and intervention services. These programs have been shown to generate savings in medical costs of approximately $3 for every $1 spent on the program and to reduce absenteeism (Baicker et al., 2010). As of 2017, almost half of all U.S. worksites offered some type of health promotion or wellness program (CDC, 2019a).

Public Health

Public health remains poorly understood by its prime beneficiaries, the public. For some people, public health evokes images of a massive social enterprise or welfare system. To others, the term means healthcare services for everyone. Still another image of public health is of a body of knowledge and techniques that can be applied to health-related problems (Turnock, 1997). However, none of these ideas adequately reflects what public health is.

The Centers for Disease Control (CDC) defines public health system as "all public, private, and voluntary entities that contribute to the delivery of essential public health services within a jurisdiction" (CDC 2019: Core functions and capabilities of state public health laboratories). These entities include but are not limited to public health departments at state and local levels, public safety agencies, environmental agencies, healthcare providers, human service and charity organizations, and economic and philanthropic organizations. The state and local public health departments are primarily responsible for vital statistics, communicable disease control, sanitation, laboratory services, maternal and child health, school-aged children's health, and health education of the general public.

The Institute of Medicine (1988) has proposed that the mission of public health should be understood as fulfilling "society's interest in assuring conditions in which people can be healthy." **Public health** deals with broad societal concerns about ensuring conditions that promote optimal health for society as a whole. It involves the application of scientific knowledge to counteract any threats that may jeopardize the health and safety of the general population. Because of its extensive scope, the vast majority of public health efforts are carried out by government agencies, such as the CDC in the United States.

Three main distinctions can be seen between the practices of medicine and public health:

- Medicine focuses on the individual patient—diagnosing symptoms, treating and preventing disease, relieving pain and suffering, and maintaining or restoring normal function. Public health, in contrast, focuses on populations (Shi and Johnson, 2014).
- The emphases in modern medicine are the biological causes of disease and the development of treatments and therapies. In contrast, public health focuses on (1) identifying environmental, social, and behavioral risk factors as well as emerging or potential risks that may threaten people's health and safety; and (2) implementing population-wide interventions to minimize these risk factors (Peters et al., 2001).
- Medicine focuses on the treatment of disease and recovery of health, whereas public health deals with various efforts to prevent disease and counteract threats that may negatively affect people's health.

Public health activities range from providing education on nutrition to passing laws that enhance automobile safety. For example, public health includes dissemination, both to the public and to health professionals, of timely information about important health issues, particularly when communicable diseases pose potential threats to large segments of a population.

Compared to medicine, public health involves a broader range of professionals. The medical sector encompasses physicians, nurses, dentists, therapists, social workers, psychologists, nutritionists, health educators, pharmacists, laboratory technicians, health services administrators, and so forth. In addition to these professionals, the public health forum includes professionals such as sanitarians, epidemiologists, statisticians, industrial hygienists, environmental health specialists, food and drug inspectors, toxicologists, and economists (Lasker, 1997). Refer to **Figure 2-4** for the core functions and essential services of public health.

Core Functions
Assessment
Policy Development
Assurance

Essential Services
Monitor health
Diagnose and investigate
Inform, educate, empower
Mobilize community partnership
Develop policies
Enforce laws
Link to/provide care
Assure competent workforce
Evaluate
System management

Figure 2-4 Core functions and essential services of public health.
Data from CDC. 2024. 10 Essential Public Health Services. https://www.cdc.gov/public-health-gateway/php/about/index.html

Table 2-4 Leading Causes of Death, 2017

Cause of Death	Deaths	Percentage of All Deaths
All causes	3,404,231	100.0
Diseases of the heart	695,547	20.1
Malignant neoplasms	605,213	17.5
COVID-19	416,893	12.0
Unintentional injuries	224,935	6.5
Cerebrovascular diseases	162,890	4.7
Chronic lower respiratory diseases	142,342	4.1
Alzheimer's disease	119,399	3.4
Diabetes mellitus	103,294	3.0
Chronic liver disease and cirrhosis	56,585	1.6
Nephritis, nephrotic syndrome, and nephrosis	54,358	1.6

Data from National Center for Health Statistics (NCHS). 2022. *Health, United States, 2021*. Hyattsville, MD: Department of Health and Human Services. Table 4.

Health Protection and Environmental Health

Health protection is one of the main public health functions. In the 1850s, John Snow successfully traced cholera outbreaks in London to contamination of the Broad Street water pump (Rosen, 1993). Since then, **environmental health** has specifically dealt with preventing the spread of disease through water, air, and food (Schneider, 2000). Environmental health science, along with other public health measures, was instrumental in reducing the risk of infectious diseases during the 1900s. For example, in 1900, pneumonia, tuberculosis, and diarrhea, along with enteritis, were the top three killers in the United States (CDC, 1999); that is no longer the case today (**Table 2-4**). With the rapid industrialization that occurred during the 20th century, environmental health faced new challenges due to serious health hazards from chemicals, industrial waste, infectious waste, radiation, asbestos, and other toxic substances. In the 21st century, the possession of chemical, biological, and nuclear agents by terrorists and rogue nations has emerged as a new environmental threat.

Health Protection and One Health

Along with environmental health, human health is also closely linked with that of animals. The study of how these three interact constitutes the One Health approach to public health. One Health brings together experts in public health, animal health, plant health, the environment, and more to achieve the best public health outcomes for all (WHO, 2017). Such an approach has become more widely recognized as multiple events in which diseases have been transferred from animals to humans (zoonotic disease) have occurred within the past few years.

One Health responds to the urgent need to reexamine how humans interact with their surroundings as the world continues to develop and industrialize. Close proximity between humans and animals, increasing international movement and travel, and changes in climate and land use (e.g., deforestation) all combined make the transfer of disease between humans and animals a distinct and real possibility. From 2013 to 2015, a deadly outbreak of Ebola virus in West Africa took more than 9,000 lives and infected more than 23,000 people (Meseko et al., 2015). Although the source of the virus has not been determined, scientists have indicated bats or nonhuman primates as potential animal reservoirs (CDC, 2019d). Environmental changes, including deforestation, road building, and the expansion of settlements in conjunction with a growing bushmeat trade, likely helped create an ideal setting for the transmission of disease (Wolfe et al., 2005). As the interface between humans and wildlife in this region became more intertwined, humans were at higher risk of exposure via infected animals (Mwangi et al., 2016). The environmental and wildlife context of the Ebola outbreak in West Africa highlights the relevance of the One Health approach.

The Zika virus outbreak in 2015–2016 serves as another example of the significance of One Health. Zika, a virus carried primarily by *Aedes* mosquitoes, causes fever, rash, headache, conjunctivitis, and muscle and joint pain on a usually mild scale (CDC, 2019e). However, because infection during pregnancy can cause congenital malformations such as microcephaly, Zika caused a global public health scare (WHO, 2018c). International movement and travel no doubt contributed to the virus ability to spread across countries and continents. The One Health approach tackles this issue by bringing together experts from various fields to address the ways in which Zika can be contained and prevented. Relevant measures include implementing stronger mosquito control, conducting better surveillance of new Zika cases, increasing awareness among the general public, particularly among high-risk groups, and continuing research on understanding Zika's mode of action within the human body (Sirec and Benedyk, 2018). As zoonotic diseases such as the Ebola and Zika viruses as well as the most recent 2019 novel coronavirus, start appearing with higher frequency and causing greater concern, the One Health approach will be crucial to anticipating and keeping future outbreaks under control.

Other examples of zoonotic diseases include rabies, salmonellosis, West Nile virus, and Lyme disease. In addition, antimicrobial resistance, food safety and security, and environmental contamination fall under the category of issues addressed by One Health (CDC, 2018). These problems present their own risks to human, animal, and environmental health and are important to anticipate and remediate.

Health Protection During Global Pandemics

Over time, public health has become a complex global undertaking. Its main goal of protecting the health and safety of populations from a variety of old and new threats cannot be achieved without global cooperation. On a global scale, influenza is the most common infectious disease, affecting nearly 3–5 million people annually and resulting in 250,000–500,000 deaths (Thompson et al., 2009). It spreads around the world in a yearly outbreak.

The global threat of avian influenza has also elicited a public health response. The CDC has launched a website dedicated to educating the public about avian influenza, the means by which it is spread, and past and current outbreaks. This website contains specific information for health professionals, travelers, the poultry industry, state departments of health, and people with possible exposures to avian influenza (CDC, 2007).

Although several strains of influenza exist, the subtypes currently circulating among humans are H1N1 and H3N2 (WHO, 2018b). After a novel H1N1 influenza virus emerged from Mexico in April 2009, U.S. health officials anticipated and prepared for an influenza pandemic, and these efforts stretched the response capabilities of the public health system. The virus affected every U.S. state, and Americans were left unprotected because of the unavailability of antiviral medications. Since then, a global effort has been undertaken to establish collaborative networks to exchange information and contain global pandemics (WHO, 2013).

Coronaviruses are believed to cause a large percentage of all common colds in adults (Committee on Infectious Diseases et al., 2015). However, some strains of coronavirus have particularly serious health effects, including the 2019 novel virus (discussed later). Severe acute respiratory syndrome (SARS) and Middle East respiratory syndrome (MERS) outbreaks occurred in 2003 and 2012, respectively. In 2003, SARS—a contagious disease that is accompanied by fever and symptoms of pneumonia or other respiratory illness—spread from China to Canada. Worldwide, more than 8,000 people were affected by this infection (CDC, 2012). MERS still occurs in parts of the Middle East. As of August 2023, a total of 2,605 laboratory-confirmed cases of MERS and 937 deaths were reported globally (WHO, 2023a). The WHO's *World Malaria Report* provides estimates of the global prevalence and mortality of malaria. In 2021, there were an estimated 247 million malaria cases and 619,000 malaria deaths worldwide (WHO, 2023b). The majority of cases occurred in Africa (95%), followed by Southeast Asia (2%) (WHO, 2022). The global incidence of malaria decreased from 82.3 to 57.2 cases per 1,000 population at risk between 2010 and 2019 (WHO, 2022).

The WHO (2023) has estimated that the worldwide tuberculosis (TB) epidemic led to approximately 10.6 million incidents of TB cases in 2021 (WHO, 2023c). Two-thirds of these cases were concentrated in eight countries: Bangladesh, China, Congo, India, Indonesia, Nigeria, Pakistan, and the Philippines (WHO, 2023c). Multidrug-resistant TB cases are especially problematic, with 484,000 new cases of rifampicin-resistant TB documented in 2018. An estimated 1.6 million deaths due to TB occurred in 2021 (WHO, 2023c). Nevertheless, the number of TB deaths is declining at a rate of approximately 2% annually, and an estimated 74 million lives were saved through TB diagnosis and treatment between 2000 and 2021 (WHO, 2023c). Even so, TB remains among the top 10 causes of death worldwide.

According to WHO estimates on the global human immunodeficiency virus (HIV)/acquired immunodeficiency syndrome (AIDS) epidemic, 39 million people were living with HIV/AIDS worldwide at the end of 2022; in that same year, 630,000 people died of AIDS-related illnesses (WHO, 2023d). The burden of the pandemic is greatest in the WHO African region, where nearly 1 in every 25 adults (3.9%) lives with HIV. In 2015, 800,000 people in this region died from HIV/AIDS. Approximately 66% of all new HIV infections occur in this region as well. At the end of 2022, 34.7 million people (89%) living with HIV globally were receiving life-prolonging antiretroviral therapy (ART) (WHO, 2023d) compared to 7.5 million people in 2010 and fewer than 1 million people in 2000. Additionally, access to ART to prevent transmission of HIV from mother to baby is increasing, with new HIV infections among newborns declining by 50% since 2010 (WHO, 2016b).

While some types of hepatitis are more problematic (i.e., hepatitis B and C) than others, all variants of this infection are viral in nature and present in the global population. An estimated 325 million people around the world live with viral hepatitis (Soucheray, 2017). In total, approximately 1.4 million people die from hepatitis each year globally (Jefferies et al., 2018). Hepatitis B accounted for approximately 820,000 deaths in 2019 (WHO, 2023e). In the WHO Western Pacific region and African region, 6.2% and 6.7% of the population are chronically infected with hepatitis B, respectively; in the WHO Eastern Mediterranean region, an estimated 3.3% of the general population is infected (WHO, 2019a). Approximately 58 million people have chronic hepatitis C, and approximately 290,000 individuals died in 2019 from related liver diseases (WHO, 2023e). The WHO Eastern Mediterranean and European regions are the most affected by the hepatitis C pandemic.

The most recent outbreak of the Ebola virus, which started in December 2013 and ended in April 2016, led to more than 28,000 cases and 11,000 deaths in Africa (WHO, 2016a). The countries most severely affected by this outbreak—Guinea, Sierra Leone, and Liberia—are all in West Africa. Now that the outbreak has ended, the current focus is on preparedness and prevention of future epidemics (WHO Ebola Response Team et al., 2016). In December 2016, scientists reported highly promising results for an experimental Ebola vaccine (Henao-Restrepo et al., 2017). In December 2019, the U.S. Food and Drug Administration approved Ervebo, the first vaccine cleared to prevent Ebola (US FDA, 2019).

The COVID-19 Pandemic

In late 2019, an unusual respiratory illness was reported in China. This disease was caused by a novel and highly infectious coronavirus, severe acute respiratory syndrome coronavirus 2 (SARS-CoV2). The WHO gave it the name of coronavirus disease 2019 (COVID-19). As of September 2023, more than 770 million cases were reported and more than 6.9 million deaths had occurred from this disease worldwide. Of these, more than 103 million cases and 1.1 million deaths were reported in the United States (WHO, 2023f).

On January 23, 2020, China imposed a quarantine on travel in and out of Wuhan, China, to prevent the spread of COVID-19. However, an estimated 5 million residents had already left the city before a lockdown was imposed (Luo et al., 2020). The early detected cases in other parts of the world were all related to travel in China. In response, several countries, including the United States, imposed travel restrictions on people coming from China in early February 2020. Imposing early travel bans was an effective measure in delaying the spread of the virus (Adekunle et al., 2020). Australian researchers concluded that the full **travel ban** implemented in Australia reduced the number of cases and deaths from COVID-19 in that country by approximately 87% (Costantino et al., 2020).

A worldwide response to the outbreak, including reliable information from and effective coordination by the WHO, did not come fast enough, and ultimately resulted in an inability to provide the necessary equipment, supplies, and hospital readiness in dealing with the cases very early during the pandemic. In the United States, to bridge the gap between public health and healthcare delivery, the federal government set up the COVID-19 Task Force headed by then Vice President Mike Pence. Along with the Federal Emergency Management Agency (FEMA), the Task Force was in charge of leading the nation's public health response and securing resources to distribute to the states (Kanno-Youngs and Lipton, 2020). FEMA also helped lead the Army Corps of Engineers in setting up emergency medical infrastructure with the Department of Transportation supporting supply chains (Miroff, 2020).

To increase the production of personal protective equipment (PPE), the Trump administration invoked the Defense Production Act (DPA), which allows the federal government to order the domestic production of necessary equipment in times of crises. The DPA has been used to command domestic companies to produce crucial equipment for dealing with pandemics, including ventilators, masks, and testing swabs. The Department of Defense started handing out federal funding contracts to boost such production (Ward, 2020). To address local shortages in health system capacity, the federal government enlisted the U.S. military to assist state and local governments. The military's two hospital ships were dispatched to New York and California, respectively, to provide extra beds and facilities; all states also activated their National Guard forces. Members of the Army Corps of Engineers were dispatched to multiple states to construct temporary COVID-19 hospitals. Army field hospitals were also deployed across the nation to provide additional care (Kanno-Youngs and Lipton, 2020).

In terms of testing and treatment costs, major insurance companies waived copayments for their insured (Simmons-Duffin, 2020). For uninsured patients with COVID-19, the federal government agreed to pay doctors and hospitals at Medicare reimbursement rates for their treatment, provided they accept the payment as full; in other words, they cannot ask patients to pay the difference (Armour, 2020).

For businesses, and in particular small businesses and those unemployed due to COVID-19, the U.S. Congress passed four pieces of legislation in 2020. The Coronavirus Preparedness and Response Supplemental Appropriations Act (2020) provided $8.3 billion in emergency funding to federal agencies. The Families First Coronavirus Response Act (2020) provided paid sick leave, tax credits, free COVID-19 testing, and expansions of food assistance, unemployment benefits, and Medicaid funding. The third bill, the Coronavirus Aid, Relief, and Economic Security Act (CARES), was a $2.2 trillion stimulus package that included loan programs for businesses, increased unemployment insurance, healthcare funding, direct payments to adults under a certain income threshold, and state/local aid (Zhou and Nilsen, 2020). An additional $484 billion relief package for small businesses and hospitals was passed at the end of April 2020 (Taylor et al., 2020).

Health Protection and Preparedness in the United States

After the horrific events of what is commonly referred to as 9/11 (the terrorist attacks on September 11, 2001), the United States began a new chapter in health protection. These efforts to protect the health and safety of Americans began in June 2002 when the then President George W. Bush signed into law the Public Health Security and Bioterrorism Preparedness Response Act of 2002. Subsequently, the Homeland Security Act of 2002 created the Department of Homeland Security (DHS) and called for a major restructuring of the nation's resources with the primary mission of helping prevent, protect against, and respond to any acts of terrorism in the United States. It also provided better tools to contain attacks on food and water supplies, protect the nation's vital infrastructures (i.e., nuclear facilities), and track biological materials anywhere in the United States. The term **bioterrorism** encompasses the use of chemical, biological, and nuclear agents to cause harm to relatively large civilian populations.

Today, health protection and preparedness comprises a massive operation to deal with any natural or human-made threats. Dealing with such threats requires large-scale preparations, including securing appropriate tools and training for workers in medical care, public health, emergency care, and civil defense agencies at the federal, state, and local levels. It requires national initiatives to develop countermeasures, such as new vaccines, a robust public health infrastructure, and coordination among numerous agencies. It also requires development of an infrastructure that can handle large numbers of casualties and isolation facilities for contagious patients. Hospitals, public health agencies, and civil defense must be linked together through information systems. Containment of infectious agents, such as smallpox, necessitates quick detection, treatment, isolation, and organized efforts to protect the unaffected population. Rapid cleanup, evacuation of the affected population, and transfer of victims to medical care facilities require detailed plans and logistics.

The United States has confronted several major natural disasters in the 21st century. Examples include Hurricane Katrina in 2005, Hurricane Sandy in 2012, and tornadoes in Oklahoma in 2013 as well as human-made mass casualties such as the Boston Marathon bombing on April 15, 2013. Health protection and preparedness have become ongoing efforts through revitalized initiatives such as the Pandemic and All-Hazards Preparedness Act (PAHPA) of 2006, which also authorized a new Assistant Secretary for Preparedness and Response (ASPR) within the DHHS and called for the establishment of a quadrennial National

Health Security Strategy (NHSS). The CDC has developed the National Biosurveillance Strategy for Human Health, which covers six priority areas: electronic health information exchange, electronic laboratory information exchange, unstructured data, integrated biosurveillance information, global disease detection and collaboration, and biosurveillance workforce. Based on the National Health Security Strategy developed by the DHHS in 2009, *Healthy People 2020* focused on four areas for reinforcement under an overarching goal to "improve the Nation's ability to prevent, prepare for, respond to, and recover from a major health incident": time to release official information about a public health emergency, time for designated personnel to respond to an emergency, Laboratory Response Network (LRN) laboratories, and time to develop after-action reports and improvement plans in states (DHHS, 2011a). A progress report shows that most states and localities have strong biological laboratory capabilities and capacities, with nearly 90% of laboratories in the LRN reachable around the clock (CDC, 2010b).

In 2011, the Health Alert Network (HAN) was established. This nationwide program is designed to facilitate communication, information, and distance learning related to health threats, including bioterrorism (DHHS, 2011a). When fully established, the network will link together local health departments and other components of bioterrorism preparedness and response, such as laboratories and state health departments.

One of the key concepts of preparedness is **surge capacity**, defined as "the ability of a healthcare facility or system to expand its operations to safely treat an abnormally large influx of patients" (Bonnett and Peery, 2007). The initial response is conducted at a local healthcare facility, such as a hospital. Strategies for expanding the surge capacity of a hospital include early discharge of stable patients, cancellation of elective procedures and admissions, conversion of private rooms to double rooms, reopening of closed areas, revision of staff work hours to a 12-hour disaster shift, callback of off-duty personnel, and establishment of temporary external shelters for patient holding (Hick et al., 2004).

If the local-level response becomes overloaded or incapacitated, a second tier of disaster response can be activated: community-level surge capacity. Cooperative regional planning necessitates sharing of staff and supplies across a network of regional healthcare facilities (Hick et al., 2004). An important aspect of disaster planning at the community level entails the transportation logistics for the region. The number of area ambulances and the means of accessing these resources during an event is crucial to delivering proper care to critical patients (Kearns et al., 2013).

The final tier of disaster response involves federal aid under the National Disaster Medical System (NDMS), which dates back to the 1980s and was designed to accommodate large numbers of military casualties. Disaster Medical Assistance Teams (DMATs) are a vital component of the NDMS that directly respond to the needs of an overwhelmed community. DMATs deploy with trained personnel (in both medical and ancillary services), equipped with tents, water filtration, generators, and medical supplies (Stopford, 2005).

Developments in technology have made major contributions to advances in disaster preparedness. For example, the United States is using new information and communication technologies to streamline emergency responses among various organizations. Social media is increasingly being used as a tool by governments, communities, and organizations for a range of purposes in disaster preparedness (i.e., detecting an event; connecting individuals following a disaster; and preparing and receiving disaster preparedness information, warnings, and signals) (Houston et al., 2015).

Despite the progress that has been made, disaster preparedness efforts in the United States remain fragmented and underfunded. For example, review, rotation, replacement, and upgrading equipment and supplies in the system on a regular basis remain challenging (Cohen and Mulvaney, 2005). Given the differences in institutional and local structures, it is difficult to develop clear and objective standards and methods while still respecting local authorities (Nelson et al., 2007). Other challenges include retention of high-quality staff in emergency departments and having insufficient funding and resources to provide education and training opportunities (Walsh et al., 2015).

The Global Health Security Index

In 2019, the Nuclear Threat Initiative (NTI) and the Johns Hopkins Bloomberg School of Public Health Center for Health Security launched the Global Health Security (GHS) Index, a comprehensive framework for assessing the health security capabilities of countries around the world. Drawing from publicly available data, including those of individual countries, academic literature, and the WHO, the GHS Index assesses the capabilities of 195 countries using 140 questions across six categories, representing 34 indicators and 85 subindicators.

The six main categories of the GHS Index are as follows (NTI and Johns Hopkins Center for Health Security, 2019):

1. Prevention: Prevention of the emergence or release of pathogens.
2. Detection and reporting: Early detection and reporting of epidemics of potential international concern.
3. Rapid response: Rapid response to and mitigation of the spread of an epidemic.
4. Health system: Sufficient and robust health system to treat the sick and protect health workers.
5. Compliance with international norms: Commitments to improving national capacity, financing plans to address gaps, and adhering to global norms.
6. Risk environment: Overall risk environment and country vulnerability to biological attacks.

Each of these six categories is scored out of a total of 100 points, with the overall score for each country being determined by the average of all scores in each category.

The GHS Index assessment concluded that national health security "is fundamentally weak around the world. No country is fully prepared for epidemics or pandemics, and every country has important gaps to address" (NTI and Johns Hopkins Center for Health Security, 2019). For the 195 countries assessed, the average total score on the index was 40.2. At least 75% of countries scored low on globally catastrophic biological risk-related indicators. Few countries were found to allocate portions of their national budgets to health security gap assessments and action plans. In none of the categories was any country able to score the maximum. The United States had the highest scores for categories 1, 2, 4, and 5 (83.1, 98.2, 73.8, and 85.3, respectively), while the United Kingdom scored the highest in category 3 (91.9) and Liechtenstein scored the highest in category 6 (87.9). The overall poor performance of countries on the GHS Index raises grave concerns about the worldwide capacity to handle and respond to a global pandemic. Since COVID-19, certain limitations were noted about the GHS Index. **Figure 2-5** summarizes the strengths and limitations of the GHS Index (Ravi et al., 2020; Abbey et al., 2020; Global Policy Journal, Beware of Mashup Indexes, 2021; Khalifa et al., 2021; Rose et al., 2021; An-qi et al., 2022; Ji et al., 2021; Haider et al., 2020).

Health Security in Action: COVID-19

The Global Perspective

COVID-19 has served as a real-world test of health security frameworks and strategies (WHO, 2021). Health security encompasses policies, protocols, and resources aimed at preventing, detecting, and responding to public health threats. The pandemic has underscored the need for robust preparatory plans, effective surveillance systems, and coordinated

Strengths
- Shape country risk landscapes to prevent, detect, and respond to outbreaks
- Measure and motivate sustainable financing at national, regional, and global levels
- Catalyze political will to fill gaps in health security capacity
- Complement ongoing efforts to build accountability for national preparedness
- Aggregate otherwise scattered qualitative and quantitative data into a consolidated, publicly available format that facilitates comparison and monitoring

Weaknesses
- **Dynamic Nature of Preparedness**: GHS Index's periodic assessments might not capture real-time changes and improvements.
- **Subjectivity and Weighting**: The methodology used to calculate scores might not fully capture the complex realities of health systems and preparedness in different countries.
- **Data Accuracy and Variability**: The impact of different preparedness components, like the robustness of the epidemiological workforce, vary throughout ongoing public health emergencies.
- **Limited Value in Assessing Certain Aspects**: The GHS Index has limited value in assessing a country's capacity to respond to the COVID-19 pandemic.

Figure 2-5 Strengths and limitations of the GHS Index.

responses to address emerging infectious diseases. The global spread of COVID-19 has demonstrated how a novel pathogen can quickly challenge health systems and necessitate rapid, well-coordinated actions across borders.

Kandel et al. (2020) did a study to review the existing health security capacities against COVID-19 and found that many countries have made substantial progress in developing effective levels of disease detection, which involves strengthening surveillance and laboratory capacities. For instance, the early detection of COVID-19 in China and the development of laboratory reagents for testing and genetically sequencing the novel virus are key steps that have supported the early response.

Lal et al. (2022) highlighted the critical importance of COVID-19 for preparedness and response mechanisms in managing health emergencies. Nations with well-developed health security strategies were better equipped to detect and respond to the virus early, implement testing and contact tracing, allocate resources efficiently, and engage in international collaboration. Adequate preparation and the ability to adapt response plans are central to minimizing the impact of future health crises. For instance, enhancing the governance and coordination of local and regional Health Information Systems (HIS) offers crucial information that enables governments to swiftly formulate policy choices, distribute resources, and shape readiness strategies based on up-to-date data.

Lal et al. (2021) compared three types of health systems (i.e., with stronger investments in global health security, and universal health coverage, and integrated investments in global health security and universal health coverage) in their response to the ongoing COVID-19 pandemic and synthesized four recommendations regarding integration, financing, resilience, and equity to reimagine governance, policies, and investments for better health toward a more sustainable future.

Malik et al. (2021) pointed out that since the idea of health security has primarily been conceptualized and put into practice based on a limited understanding of security rooted in the Westphalian tradition, they proposed the concept of human security as a more inclusive, integrated, and holistic guide. The key benefits of the human security approach includes (a) a universal outlook that transcends the "us" versus "them" division by recognizing human insecurity challenges in both developing and developed regions; (b) interconnectedness that avoids isolating security concerns by highlighting interlinked perceptions of security; (c) the indivisibility of threats that ties together humanity and the shared challenges it confronts; (d) an emphasis on collective efforts and international collaboration to tackle global human security issues; and (e) a focus on preemptive measures highlighting prevention over remedy.

The U.S. Perspective

The devastating impact of COVID-19 on the United States can be attributed to two primary failures in public health preparedness: a long-standing lack of emphasis on public health infrastructure, coupled with persistent underinvestment in population health and well-being, undermined the U.S. response from the beginning. As Maani and Galea (2020a) recount, public health funding has consistently been shunted to the side in favor of biomedical innovation and the quest to control rising healthcare costs. Funding for public health also tends to follow a reactionary trend, where emphasis is given only after a possible threat to population arises. Additionally, as a country that has continuously fallen behind its peers in terms of life expectancy and other crucial health indicators, the United States has failed to close the gap in improving health outcomes and increasing access to care. These problems disproportionately impact the most vulnerable groups and exacerbate social, health, and economic inequities (Maani and Galea, 2020b).

As a result of such inequities, vulnerable populations shouldered the worst of the COVID-19 pandemic, whose final damage remains to be seen. Not only did these groups experience higher case rates, but they were also put most socioeconomically at risk (Capatides, 2020; Yancy, 2020). Individuals with low income who relied on having a stable job to provide for themselves and their families faced the possibility of going hungry due to massive layoffs resulting from the virus economic repercussions. Those residing in rural regions also faced serious risks considering the demographic makeup of most populations in these areas (older, with a higher prevalence of chronic disease) and the higher barriers to accessing the needed care (Thompson, 2020).

Almost half a million American homes have inadequate plumbing, making the most basic action of handwashing to prevent infection much more difficult. Families living in homes lacking complete kitchens or facing overcrowding issues (approximately 5 million homes in total, combined) were confronted with further difficulties and increased risk in accessing food and isolating the sick (Ungar and Lucas, 2020).

The persistent socioeconomic and health inequities present in the United States likely exacerbated the domestic impact of COVID-19. This highlights the importance of investing in equitable population health programs and building a sounder public health infrastructure. Preventive services should receive more sustained funding and support, while higher cooperation and alignment levels among various healthcare services and providers should be maintained (Kwiatkowski, 2020; Maani and Galea, 2020a).

Many lessons can also be learned from the way other countries that successfully kept the number of COVID-19 outbreaks low. Of note, several Asian countries that were at severely high risk of bearing the brunt of global COVID-19 cases were able to turn the tide by imposing strict travel and quarantine measures early on, enforcing aggressive contact tracing, and conducting widespread testing (Lu et al., 2020). If the United States, with its strong existing capabilities, noted these lessons, the country could be better prepared to curtail the risk of future outbreaks.

Determinants of Health

Health determinants are major factors that affect the health and well-being of individuals and populations. An understanding of health determinants is necessary to plan and implement any positive interventions for health and longevity.

Blum's Model of Health Determinants

In 1974, Blum (1981) proposed an "Environment of Health" model, later called the "Force Field and Well-Being Paradigms of Health." Blum proposed that four major factors contribute to health and well-being ("force fields"): environment, lifestyle, heredity, and medical care. All of these factors must be considered simultaneously when addressing the health status of an individual or a population. In other words, there is no single pathway to better health because health determinants interact in complex ways. Consequently, improvement in health requires a multipronged approach.

The four wedges in Blum's model represent the four major force fields. The size of each wedge signifies its relative importance. Thus, the most important force field is environment, followed by lifestyle and heredity. Medical care has the least impact on health and well-being.

Blum's model also explains that the four main forces operate within a much broader context and are affected by broad national and international factors, such as a nation's population characteristics, natural resources, ecological balance, human satisfactions, and cultural systems. One of these factors is the type of healthcare delivery system. In the United States, the majority of healthcare expenditures are devoted to the treatment of medical conditions rather than to the prevention of factors that produce those medical conditions in the first place.

Environment

Environmental factors encompass the physical, socioeconomic, sociopolitical, and sociocultural dimensions. Among physical environmental factors are air pollution, food and water contaminants, radiation, toxic chemicals, wastes, disease vectors, safety hazards, and habitat alterations.

The positive relationship between socioeconomic status (SES) and health may be explained by the general likelihood that people who have better education also have higher incomes. The greater the economic gap between people with ample and limited financial resources in a given geographic area, the worse the health status of the overall population in that area is likely to be. It has been suggested that wide income gaps produce less social cohesion, greater psychosocial stress, and consequently, poorer health (Wilkinson, 1997). For example, social cohesion—characterized by a hospitable social environment in which people trust each other and participate in communal activities—is linked to lower overall mortality and better self-rated health (Kawachi et al., 1997, 1999). Even countries with national health insurance programs, such as the United Kingdom, Australia, Denmark, and Sweden, have experienced persistent and widening disparities in health according to SES (Pincus et al., 1998). The joint relationship of income inequality and availability of primary care has also been found to be significantly associated with individuals' self-rated health status (Shi et al., 2002).

Lifestyle

Lifestyle factors, also known as behavioral risk factors, were discussed earlier in this chapter. This section provides some illustrations of how lifestyle factors are related to health. Studies have shown that diet plays a major role in most of today's significant health problems. Notably, heart disease, diabetes, stroke, and cancer are some of the diseases with direct links to dietary choices. Throughout the world, incidence and mortality rates for many forms of cancer are rising, though research has clearly indicated that a significant portion of cancer cases are preventable. Researchers estimate that 30% to 50% of all cancers and as many as 30% to 35% of cancer deaths are linked to diet (World Cancer Research Fund and American Institute for Cancer Research, 2007). Research also shows that a diet rich in fruits, vegetables, and low-fat dairy foods, and a diet low in saturated and total fat can substantially lower blood pressure (for example, the DASH Eating Plan recommended by DHHS [2006]).

Increasing exercise and physical activity is a potentially useful, effective, and acceptable method for reducing the risk of colon cancer (Macfarlane and Lowenfels, 1994) and many other health problems. Smoking and alcohol consumption are also important lifestyle factors that impact health. In addition to increasing the risk of lung cancer, smoking increases the risk of coronary heart disease and stroke by 2 to 4 times (DHHS, 2014). Half of all cancer deaths and nearly half of all cancer diagnoses could potentially be prevented through a healthy lifestyle that includes not smoking, drinking in moderation, maintaining a healthy weight, and exercising regularly (Song and Giovannucci, 2016).

Heredity

Genetic factors may predispose individuals to certain diseases. While cancer is not entirely genetic, this disease can emerge when the body's healthy genes lose their ability to suppress malignant growth or when other genetic processes stop working properly (Davis and Webster, 2002). While people can do little about the genetic makeup they have inherited, their lifestyle and behavior can significantly impact their progeny. Finally, advances in gene therapy hold the promise of treating a variety of inherited or acquired diseases.

Medical Care

Although the factors of lifestyle, environment, and heredity are more important in the determination of health, medical care is nevertheless a key factor affecting health. Though Blum asserted that medical care is the least important factor in determining health and well-being, the United States focuses more on medical research and development of new medical technologies than it does on the other three factors. One salient point: significant declines in mortality rates were achieved well before the modernization of Western medicine and the escalation in medical care expenditures.

The availability of primary care may be one way in which income inequality influences population-level health outcomes. Research by Shi and colleagues (Shi and Starfield, 2001; Shi et al., 1999) suggests that access to primary care significantly correlates with reduced mortality, increased life expectancy, and improved birth outcomes. Access to primary care includes access to and use of preventive services, which can prevent illness or detect disease at an earlier, often more treatable stage. In the United States, individuals living in states with a higher primary care physician-to-population ratio are more likely to report good health than those living in states with a lower ratio (Shi et al., 2002).

Contemporary Models of Health Determinants

More recent models have built upon and extended Blum's framework of health determinants. For example, the model proposed by Dahlgren and Whitehead (2006) identifies age, sex, and genetic makeup as fixed factors, but that other factors can be modified to positively influence population health. While individual lifestyle factors can benefit or damage health, broader social, economic, cultural, and environmental conditions often have greater influence on both individual and population health.

Ansari and colleagues (2003) have proposed a public health model of the social determinants of health in which the determinants are categorized into four major groups: social determinants, healthcare system attributes, disease-inducing behaviors, and health outcomes. The WHO Commission on Social Determinants of Health (2008) concluded that "the social conditions in which people are born, live, and work are the single most important determinant of one's health status" (Satcher, 2010). The WHO model provides a conceptual framework for understanding the socioeconomic and political contexts, structural determinants, intermediary determinants

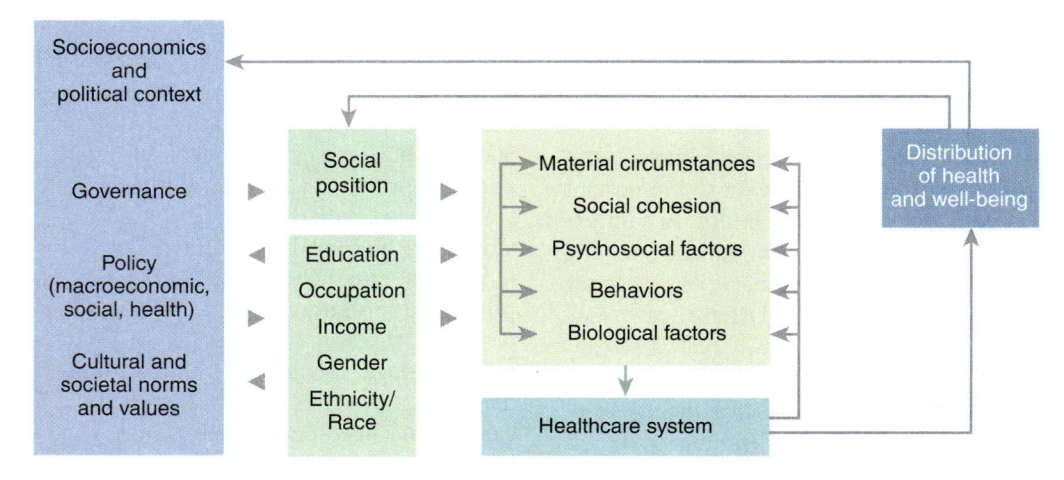

Figure 2-6 WHO Commission on Social Determinants of Health conceptual framework.

Reproduced from Centers for Disease Control and Prevention. 2010a. *Establishing a holistic framework to reduce inequities in HIV, viral hepatitis, STDs, and tuberculosis in the United States.* Available at: https://www.cdc.gov/socialdeterminants/docs/SDH-White-Paper-2010.pdf. Accessed April 2017. Modified from Solar, O., and A. Irwin. 2010. A conceptual framework for action on the social determinants of health. Social Determinants of Health Discussion Paper 2 (Policy and Practice). Geneva, Switzerland: World Health Organization.

(including material circumstances, social-environmental circumstances, behavioral and biological factors, social cohesion, and the healthcare system), and the impact on health equity and well-being measured as health outcomes (**Figure 2-6**).

U.S. government agencies, such as the CDC and DHHS, have recognized the need to address health inequities. The CDC's National Center for HIV/AIDS, Viral Hepatitis, STD, and TB Prevention adopted the WHO framework on social determinants of health as a guide for its activities.

Justification for Social Determinants

A substantial body of Social Science studies has consistently demonstrated a strong association between Socioeconomic Status (SES), which is measured as a combination of income, education, occupation, and health outcomes. The phenomenon known as "the socioeconomic gradient of health" is observed across countries with varying levels of economic development as well as within different social groups within a country. Specifically, it has been found that higher SES is generally associated with better overall health outcomes and vice versa (Adler and Ostrove, 2006; Goldman, 2001; Kaplan and Keil, 1993; Krieger et al., 2003; Marmot et al., 1984; Winkleby et al., 2006; Winkleby et al., 1992). Moreover, this positive relationship between the two is independent of factors such as the time period studied, geographical region examined, level of economic or healthcare development considered, methods used for assessing SES, and indicators employed to evaluate disease prevalence. Consequently, Link and Phelan (1995) proposed "The Fundamental Cause Theory of Health," which argues that social conditions play a prominent role in determining health.

The One Health Movement

One Health is a "collaborative, multisectoral, and transdisciplinary approach—working at the local, regional, national, and global levels — with the goal of achieving optimal health outcomes recognizing the interconnection between people, animals, plants, and their shared environment" (Centers for Disease Control and Prevention, National Center for Emerging and Zoonotic, 2022).

One Health has implications for healthcare delivery, including zoonotic disease prevention, antimicrobial resistance management, environmental health and food security, and health policy and education. First, zoonotic outbreaks, such as COVID-19, Ebola, and rabies, emphasize the need for early detection and collaboration with healthcare professionals and veterinarians to prevent further disease spreading between animals and people (Centers for Disease Control and Prevention, National Center for Emerging and Zoonotic, 2022). By employing the One Health framework, healthcare systems can take a proactive approach to overseeing animal populations, establishing strong surveillance systems, and promptly addressing potential risks to human health (Overgaauw et al., 2020). Second, antibiotic resistance (ABR) can also be addressed by using the One Health approach such as raising awareness and education about prudent antibiotic usage, fostering policies, advocacy, and antimicrobial stewardship (Aslam et al., 2021). Third, in terms of environmental health and food security, the One Health approach serves as guidance on food safety level for the healthcare professionals by integrating veterinary surveillance, food safety protocols, and monitoring of zoonotic pathogens (Rizzo et al., 2021; Naddeo, 2021). Finally, by bringing together expertise from public health, veterinary medicine, environmental sciences, and other fields, One Health enables a more comprehensive understanding of intricate health issues and therefore enhance preparedness, response capabilities, and overall healthcare delivery (Zhang et al., 2022).

Measures Related to Health

Certain quantitative measures are commonly applied to health, health status, and the use of health care. The conceptual approaches for defining health and its distribution form a vision for the future, and objective measures play a critical role in evaluating the success of programs and directing future planning activities. Practical approaches for measuring health are however quite limited, and mental health is more difficult to quantify and measure than physical health. An objective means of evaluating social and spiritual health is even more obscure.

The concept of population, as it applies to population health, has been borrowed from the disciplines of statistics and epidemiology. The term "population" is not restricted to describing the total population. Although commonly used in this way, "population" may also apply to a defined subpopulation—for example, age groups, marital categories, income levels, occupation categories, racial/ethnic groups, people having a common disease, people in a certain risk category, or people in a certain community or geographic region of a country. The main advantage of studying subpopulations is that it helps researchers trace the existence of health problems to a defined group. Doing so will avoid the likelihood of serious problems in a minority group being hidden within the favorable statistics of the majority. By pinpointing health problems in certain well-defined groups, targeted interventions and new policy initiatives can be deployed in the most effective manner.

Measures of Physical Health

Physical health status is often interpreted through **morbidity** (disease and disability) and **mortality** (death) rates. In addition, self-perceived health status is a commonly used indicator of health and well-being because it is highly correlated with many objective measures of health status. With this measure, respondents are asked to rate their health as excellent, very good, good, fair, or poor. Self-perceived health status is also a good predictor of patient-initiated physician visits, including general medical and mental health visits.

Longevity

Life expectancy—a prediction of how long a person will live—is widely used as a basic measure of health status. The two

Table 2-5 U.S. Life Expectancy at Birth—2002, 2007, 2015, and 2021

Year	Total	Male	Female
2002	77.0	74.4	79.6
White	77.5	74.9	80.1
Black	72.2	68.7	75.4
2007	78.1	75.5	80.6
White	78.5	76.0	80.9
Black	73.8	70.3	77.0
2015	78.7	76.3	81.1
White	78.9	76.6	81.3
Black	75.5	72.2	78.5
2021	76.1	73.2	79.1
White	76.4	73.7	79.2
Black	70.8	66.7	74.8

Data from National Center for Health Statistics (NCHS). 2022. Health, United States, 2021. Hyattsville, MD: Department of Health and Human Services. p.2.

common measures are life expectancy at birth (**Table 2-5**)—or how long a newborn can be expected to live—and life expectancy at age 65—expected remaining years of life for someone at age 65. These measures are actuarially determined and published by government agencies such as the National Center for Health Statistics (NCHS). The U.S. Census Bureau (2016) has projected that life expectancy in the United States will increase from 78.8 years in 2014 to 84.1 years in 2050.

Morbidity

The measurement of morbidity or disease, such as cancer or heart disease, is expressed as a ratio or proportion of those who have the problem and the **population at risk**. The population at risk includes all the people in the same community or population group who could acquire a disease or condition (Smith, 1979).

Incidence and prevalence are two widely used indicators for the number of **cases**, incidences of people who end up acquiring a negative health condition. Both incidence and prevalence rates can apply to disease, disability, or death.

Incidence counts the number of new cases occurring in the population at risk within a certain period of time, such as a month or a year (Smith, 1979; **Formula 2-1**). It describes the extent people in a given population acquire a given disease during a specified time period. Incidence is particularly useful in estimating the significance or magnitude of conditions of relatively short duration. Declining levels of incidence indicate successful health promotion and disease prevention efforts because they prevent new cases (Ibrahim, 1985). High levels of incidence may suggest an impending **epidemic**, a large number of people who get a specific disease from a common source.

Formula 2-1

Incidence = Number of new cases during a specified period/Population at risk

Prevalence determines the total number of cases at a specific point in time, in a defined population (**Formula 2-2**). Prevalence is useful in quantifying the magnitude of illnesses of a relatively long duration. Decreased prevalence indicates success of treatment programs by shortening the duration of illness (Ibrahim, 1985).

Formula 2-2

Prevalence = Total number of cases at a specific point in time/Specified population

The calculation of rates often requires dividing a small number by a large number to represent a defined population. The result is a fraction. To make the fractions meaningful and interpretable, they are multiplied by 100 (to get a percentage), by 1,000 (to get a rate per 1,000 people), by 10,000 (to get a rate per 10,000 people), or by a higher multiple of 10.

Disability

Disease and injury can lead to temporary or permanent disability as well as partial or total disability. Although the idea of morbidity includes disabilities as well as disease, specific measures of disability have been developed. Some commonly used measures are the number of days of bed confinement, days missed from work or school, and days of restricted activity. All measures are in reference to a specific time period, such as a year.

One of the most widely used measures of physical ability among older people in particular is the **activities of daily living (ADLs)** scale. The ADLs identify personal care functions a person with a disability may need assistance. Depending on the extent of disability, personal care needs can be met through adaptive devices; care rendered by another individual, such as a family member; or care in a nursing facility. Consequently, the ADLs scale is appropriate for evaluating disability in both community-dwelling and institutionalized adults. The classic ADLs scale, developed by Katz and Akpom (1979), includes six basic activities: eating, bathing, dressing, using the toilet, maintaining continence, and transferring from bed to chair. To evaluate disability in community-dwelling adults, a modified Katz scale, which consists of seven items, is used (Ostir et al., 1999). Five of these items—feeding, bathing, dressing, using the toilet, and transferring from bed to chair—have been retained from the original Katz scale. The additional two items are grooming and walking a distance of 8 feet. Thus, the modified scale includes items measuring self-care and mobility.

Another commonly used measure of physical function is the **instrumental activities of daily living (IADLs)** scale. This scale measures activities that are necessary for living independently in the community, such as using the telephone, driving a car or traveling alone on a bus or taxi, shopping, preparing meals, doing light housework, taking medicines, handling money, doing heavy housework, walking up and down stairs, and walking a half-mile without help. IADLs typically require higher cognitive functioning than ADLs. and as such are not purely physical tests of functional disability. The IADLs scale measures the level of functioning in activities that are important for self-sufficiency, such as the ability to live independently.

Mortality

Death rates are computed in different forms as indicators of population health. **Crude rates** refer to the total population because they are not specific to any age group or disease category (**Formula 2-3**).

Formula 2-3

Crude death rate = Total deaths (usually in 1 year)/Total population

Specific rates are useful because death rates vary greatly by race, sex, age, and type of disease or condition. Such rates allow healthcare professionals to target programs for the appropriate population subgroups (Dever, 1984). Examples of specific rates are the age-specific mortality rate (**Formula 2-4**) and the cause-specific mortality rate (**Formula 2-5**). The age-specific mortality rate provides a measure of the risk (or probability) of dying when a person is in a certain age group. The cause-specific mortality rate provides a measure of the risk (or probability) of dying from a specific cause.

Formula 2-4

Age-specific mortality rate = Number of deaths within a certain age group/Total number of persons in that age group

Formula 2-5

Cause-specific mortality rate = Number of deaths from a specific disease/Total population

The infant mortality rate (actually a ratio; **Formula 2-6**) is an indicator that reflects the health status of the mother and child throughout pregnancy and the birth process. It also reflects the level of prenatal and postnatal care (Timmreck, 1994).

Formula 2-6

Infant mortality rate = Number of deaths from birth to 1 year of age (in 1 year)/Number of live births during the same year

Demographic Change

In addition to measures of disease and mortality, changes in the composition of a population over time are important in planning health services. Population change involves three components: births, deaths, and migration (Dever, 1984). Migration refers to older individuals moving to the southern and southwestern United States, which requires planning of adequate retirement and long-term care services in those states. Longevity is also an important factor that determines demographic change. For example, lower death rates, lower birth rates, and greater longevity, taken collectively, indicate an aging population. This section presents measures of both births and migration.

Births

Natality and fertility are two measures associated with births. **Natality**, or the birth rate, is useful in assessing the influence of births on demographic change and is measured by the crude birth rate (**Formula 2-7**).

Formula 2-7

Crude birth rate = Number of live births (usually in 1 year)/Total population

Fertility refers to the capacity of a population to reproduce (**Formula 2-8**). Fertility is a more precise measure than natality because fertility relates actual births to the sector of the population capable of giving birth.

Formula 2-8

Fertility rate = Number of live births (usually in 1 year)/Number of females aged 15–44

Migration

Migration refers to the geographic movement of populations between defined geographic units and involves a permanent change of residence. The net migration rate (**Formula 2-9**) defines the change in the population as a result of **immigration** (in-migration) and **emigration** (out-migration) (Dever, 1984). This rate is calculated for a specified period, such as 1 year, 2 years, 5 years, and so on.

Formula 2-9

Net migration rate = Number of immigrants – Number of emigrants/Total population during a specific period of time

Measures of Mental Health

Measurement of mental health is less objective than measurements of mortality and morbidity because mental health often encompasses feelings that cannot be observed. In contrast, physical functioning, as reflected in behaviors and performances, can be more readily observed. Hence, measurement of mental health more appropriately refers to assessment rather than measurement. Mental health can be assessed by the presence of certain symptoms, including both psychophysiological and psychological symptoms. Examples of psychophysiological symptoms are low energy, headache, and upset stomach. Examples of psychological symptoms are nervousness, depression, and anxiety.

Self-assessment of one's psychological state may also be used for mental health assessment. Self-assessment can be obtained through self-reports of frequency and intensity of psychological distress, anxiety, depression, and psychological well-being.

Measures of Social Health

Measures of social health extend beyond the individual to encompass the extent of social contacts across various facets of life, such as family life, work life, and community life. Breslow (1972) attempted to measure social health along four dimensions: (1) employability based on educational achievement, occupational status, and job experience; (2) marital satisfaction; (3) sociability, determined by the number of close friends and relatives; and (4) community involvement, encompassing attendance at religious services, political activity, and organizational membership.

Social health status is sometimes evaluated in terms of social contacts and social resources. **Social contacts** are the number of social contacts or social activities a person engages in within a specified period. Examples are visits with friends and relatives as well as attendance at social events, such as conferences, picnics, or other outings. **Social resources** refer to social contacts that can be relied on for support, such as relatives, friends, neighbors, and members of a religious congregation. Social contacts can be observed, and they are the more objective of the two categories; however, one criticism of social contact measures is their focus on events and activities, with little consideration of how those events are personally experienced. Unlike social contacts, social resources cannot be directly observed and are best measured by asking the individuals direct questions. Evaluative questions include whether these individuals can rely on their social contacts to provide tangible support and needed companionship and whether they feel cared for, loved, and wanted.

Measures of Spiritual Health

Depending on the person's individual, social, and cultural context, spiritual well-being can have a large variety of connotations. Such variations make it extremely difficult to propose standardized approaches for measuring the spiritual dimension. Attempts to measure this dimension are illustrated by the General Social Survey, which includes people's self-perceptions about happiness, religious experiences, and their degree of involvement in activities such as prayer and attending religious services.

A wide range of tools for spiritual assessment are now available. Generic methods of spiritual assessment are not associated with any particular religion or practice, so they do not require a detailed understanding of any specific religious tradition (Draper, 2012). An example of a generic scale is the tool developed by Vella-Brodrick and Allen (1995), which evaluates items such as reaching out for spiritual intervention; engaging in meditation, yoga, or prayer; duration of meditation or prayer for inner peace; frequency of meditation or prayer; reading about one's religious beliefs; and discussions or readings about ethical and moral issues. Quantitative measurement scales are also available to assess dimensions such as general spirituality, spiritual well-being, spiritual needs, and spiritual coping (Monod et al., 2011), but their use has been confined mainly to clinical research.

Measures of Health Services Utilization

Utilization refers to the consumption of healthcare services and the extent these healthcare services are used. Measures of utilization can determine which individuals in a population group do or do not receive certain types of medical services. With this type of measure, a healthcare provider, such as a hospital, can find out the extent to which its services are used. Managers can use these measures to decide whether certain services should be added or eliminated, and health planners can determine whether programs have been effective in reaching their targeted populations. For example, managers can use these measures to ascertain how many hospital beds are required to meet the acute care needs of a given population (Pasley et al., 1995). Therefore, measures of utilization play a critical role in the planning of healthcare delivery capacity. Measures of utilization are too numerous to cover all of them here, but some common measures are provided (**Formulas 2-10–2-16**).

Crude Measures of Utilization

Formula 2-10

Access to primary care services = Number of persons in a given population who visited a primary care provider in a given year/Size of the population

(This measure is generally expressed as a percentage; that is, the fraction is multiplied by 100.)

Formula 2-11

Utilization of primary care services = Number of primary care visits by people in a given population in a given year/Size of the population

Specific Measures of Utilization

Formula 2-12

Utilization of targeted services = Number of people in a specific targeted population using special services (or visits)/Size of the targeted population group
   (The fraction obtained is multiplied by 100, 1,000, or a higher multiple of 10 to facilitate interpretation of the result.)

Formula 2-13

Utilization of specific inpatient services = Number of inpatient days/Size of the population
   (The fraction obtained is multiplied by 100, 1,000, or a higher multiple of 10 to facilitate interpretation of the result.)

Measures of Institution-Specific Utilization

Formula 2-14

Average daily census = Total number of inpatient days in a given time period/Number of days in the same time period

Formula 2-15

Occupancy rate = Total number of inpatient days in a given time period/Total number of available beds during the same time period
   or
Average daily census/Total number of beds in the facility

(This measure is expressed as a percentage; that is, the fraction is multiplied by 100.)

Formula 2-16

Average length of stay = Total number of inpatient days during a given time period/Total number of patients served during the same time period

Measures of Global Health

Global monitoring of changes in the health of various populations requires the use of "tried and true" global health indicators. Global health indicators can be divided into those that directly measure health phenomena (e.g., diseases, deaths, use of services) and indirect measures (e.g., social development, education, and poverty indicators); these are also referred to as proximal and distal indicators, respectively. As an example, when using population statistics to describe levels of educational attainment and access to safe water and sanitation, it is possible to accurately categorize a country as having a population with high, medium, or low burden of disease (Larson and Mercer, 2004).

The WHO (2015) compiles more than 100 indicators of a broad range of key public health issues. Commonly used indicators of life expectancy and mortality include life expectancy at age 60, healthy life expectancy at birth, infant and under-5 mortality rates, and the adult mortality rate. Cause-specific mortality rates are collected for selected communicable and noncommunicable diseases. Health services indicators reflect the extent people receive important health interventions. These services include unmet needs for family planning, prenatal care coverage, births attended by skilled health personnel, vaccination coverage, and other prevention and treatment coverage for common diseases among children. It is also important to report indicators of risk factors that are associated with increased mortality and morbidity. To assess the risk of transmission of diarrheal disease, for example, it is important to know what percentage of the population does not have safe water supplies and sanitation. Similarly, use of solid fuels in households is a proxy indicator for household pollution. Indicators of the prevalence of diabetes, hypertension, and obesity all signal the risk of cardiovascular disease and several types of cancer.

Indirect indicators of global health include health system indicators related to the workforce, infrastructure, medical technologies and devices, and government expenditures on health. Demographic and socioeconomic factors that are major determinants of health include primary school enrollment, population living in poverty, population size, crude birth and death rates, total fertility rates, and per capita gross national income.

Anthro-Cultural Beliefs and Values

A value system orients the members of a society toward defining what is desirable for that society. It has been observed that even a society as complex and highly diverse as that found in the United States can be said to have a relatively well-integrated system of institutionalized common values at the societal level (Parsons, 1972). Although such a notion still prevails, American society now includes distinct subcultures whose membership has increased significantly due to a steady influx of immigrants from different parts of the world.

The current system of health services delivery has its roots in the traditional beliefs and values espoused by the majority of American people. This belief and value system governs the training and general orientation of healthcare providers, the type of health delivery settings, the financing and allocation of resources, and access to health care in the United States. Among the main beliefs and values prevalent in the American culture are those outlined here.

1. The United States has a strong belief in the advancement of science and the application of scientific methods to medicine. This belief was instrumental in the creation of the medical model that primarily governs U.S. healthcare delivery. As a result, the United States has long led the world in medical breakthroughs. These developments have had numerous implications for health services delivery:
   a. They increase the demand for the latest treatments and raise patients' expectations for finding cures.
   b. Because medical professionals focus on clinical interventions, they do not provide adequate emphasis on the holistic aspects of health and use of alternative therapies.
   c. Healthcare professionals have been trained to focus on physical symptoms rather than the underlying causes of disease.
   d. Integrating diagnosis and treatment with disease prevention has lagged behind other concerns.

e. Most research efforts have focused on the development of medical technology. Fewer resources have been committed to the preservation and enhancement of health and well-being.
f. Medical specialists, using the latest technologies, are held in higher esteem and earn higher incomes than general practitioners.
g. The desirability of healthcare delivery institutions such as hospitals is often evaluated based on their acquisition of advanced technology.
h. Whereas biomedicine has taken central stage in the biomedical model, mental health diagnosis and treatment have been relegated to a lesser status.
i. The biomedical model has neglected the social and spiritual elements of health.

2. The United States has been a champion of capitalism. Due to the general public's strong belief in capitalism, health care has largely been viewed as an economic good (or service), not as a public resource.

3. A culture of capitalism promotes entrepreneurial spirit and self-determination. Hence, individual capabilities to obtain health services have largely determined the production and consumption of health care (i.e., which services will be produced, where and in which quantities, and who will have access to those services). Some key implications are as follows:
   a. Upper-tier access to healthcare services is available mainly through private health insurance. Those with public insurance fall in a second tier. The uninsured make up a third tier.
   b. A clear distinction exists between services for low-income and affluent communities, and between services available in rural and inner-city locations.
   c. The culture of individualism emphasizes individual health rather than population health. Consequently, medical practice has been directed at keeping the individual healthy rather than the entire community.
   d. A concern for the most underprivileged classes in society—the low income, older people, people with disabilities, and children—led to the creation of the public programs Medicaid, Medicare, and the Children's Health Insurance Program (CHIP).

4. U.S. healthcare delivery is guided by principles of free enterprise and a general distrust of big government. Hence, healthcare delivery is largely in private hands, and a separation exists between public health functions and the private practice of medicine.

Equitable Distribution of Health Care

Scarcity of economic resources is a central economic concept. From this perspective, health care can be viewed as an economic good. Two fundamental questions arise with regard to how scarce healthcare resources ought to be used:

- How much health care should be produced?
- How should health care be distributed?

The first question concerns the appropriate combination of health services that should be produced in relation to all other goods and services in the overall economy. If more health care is produced, a society may concomitantly devote fewer resources to producing other goods, such as food, clothing, and transportation. The second question affects individuals at a more personal level—namely it deals with who can receive which type of medical services and how access to services will be restricted.

The production, distribution, and subsequent consumption of health care must be perceived as equitable by a society. No society has found a perfectly equitable method to distribute limited economic resources. In fact, any method of resource distribution inevitably leaves some inequalities in its wake. Therefore, societies try to allocate resources according to some guiding principles that are deemed acceptable by the particular society. Such principles are ingrained in a society's value and belief system. It is recognized that, for example, not everyone can receive everything medical science has to offer.

A just and fair allocation of health care poses conceptual and practical difficulties. Hence, a theory of justice is necessary to resolve the problem of healthcare allocation (Jonsen et al., 2015). Even though various ethical principles can be used to guide decisions pertaining to just and fair allocation of health care in individual circumstances, the concern about providing equitable access to health services on a population level is addressed by two contrasting perspectives, referred to as market justice and social justice.

Market Justice

The principle of **market justice** leaves the fair distribution of health care up to the market forces in a free economy. In consequence, medical care and its benefits are distributed based on people's willingness and ability to pay (Santerre and Neun, 2010). In other words, people are entitled to purchase a share of the available goods and services that they value; they purchase these valued goods and services by means of wealth acquired through their own efforts. This is how most goods and services are distributed in a free market. The free market implies that giving people something they have not earned would be morally and economically wrong.

The *An Overview of U.S. Healthcare Delivery* chapter discussed several characteristics of a free market; these market characteristics are a precondition to the distribution of healthcare services according to market justice principles. As previously mentioned, health care in the United States is not delivered in a free market, but rather in a quasi-market. Hence, market justice principles are only partially applicable to the U.S. healthcare delivery system. Distribution of health care according to market justice is based on the following key assumptions:

- Health care is like any other economic good or service, and its distribution and consumption are determined by the free market forces of supply and demand.
- Individuals are responsible for their own achievements. With the rewards of their achievements, people are free to obtain various economic goods and services, including health care. When individuals pursue their own best interests, the interests of society as a whole are best served (Ferguson and Maurice, 1970).
- People make rational choices in their decisions to purchase healthcare products and services. Grossman (1972) proposed that health is also an investment commodity—in other words, people consider the purchase of health services to be an investment. For example, the investment has a monetary payoff when it reduces the number of sick days, making extra time available for productive activities, such as earning a living. Alternatively, it can have a utility payoff—a payoff in terms of satisfaction—when it makes life more enjoyable and fulfilling.
- People, in consultation with their physicians, know what is best for them. This assumption implies that people place a certain degree of trust in their physicians and that the physician-patient relationship is ongoing.
- The marketplace works best with minimum interference from the government. In other words, the market, rather than the government, allocates healthcare resources in the most efficient and equitable manner.

Under market justice conditions, the production of health care is determined by how much consumers are willing and able to purchase health care at the prevailing market prices. Thus, prices and ability to pay ration the quantity and type of healthcare services that people consume. The uninsured and individuals who lack sufficient income to pay for private healthcare services face barriers to obtaining health care. Such limitations are referred to as **demand-side rationing**, or "rationing by ability to pay" (Feldstein, 1994). To some extent, the uninsured may be able to overcome some of these barriers through charitable services.

Table 2-6 summarizes key characteristics of the market justice system and their implications. Market justice emphasizes individual—rather than collective—responsibility for health. It proposes private—rather than government—solutions to social problems of health.

Social Justice

The idea of social justice is at odds with the principles of capitalism and market justice. The term "social justice" was invented in the 19th century by the critics of capitalism to describe the "good society" (Kristol, 1978). According to the principle of **social justice**, the equitable distribution of health care is a

Table 2-6 Comparison of Market Justice and Social Justice

Market Justice	Social Justice
Characteristics	
■ Views health care as an economic good	■ Views health care as a social resource
■ Assumes free-market conditions for health services delivery	■ Requires active government involvement in health services delivery
■ Assumes that markets are more efficient in allocating health resources equitably	■ Assumes that the government is more efficient in allocating health resources equitably
■ Production and distribution of health care determined by market-based demand	■ Medical resource allocation determined by central planning
■ Medical care distribution based on people's ability to pay	■ Ability to pay is inconsequential for receiving medical care
■ Access to medical care viewed as an economic reward of personal effort and achievement	■ Equal access to medical services viewed as a basic right
Implications	
■ Individual responsibility for health	■ Collective responsibility for health
■ Benefits based on individual purchasing power	■ Everyone is entitled to a basic package of benefits
■ Limited obligation to the collective good	■ Strong obligation to the collective good
■ Emphasis on individual well-being	■ Community well-being supersedes that of the individual
■ Private solutions to social problems	■ Public solutions to social problems
■ Rationing based on ability to pay	■ Planned rationing of health care

societal responsibility, which is best achieved by letting the government take over the production and distribution of health care. Social justice regards health care as a social good rather than as an economic good, and suggests that it should be collectively financed and available to all citizens regardless of the individual recipient's ability to pay. The main characteristics and implications of social justice are summarized in Table 2-5.

Canadians and Europeans long ago reached a broad consensus that health care is a social good (Reinhardt, 1994). Public health also has a social justice orientation (Turnock, 1997). Under the social justice system, inability to obtain medical services because of a lack of financial resources is considered inequitable. Accordingly, a just distribution of health care must be based on need, not simply on the individual's ability to purchase such care in the marketplace (demand). The need for health care is determined either by the patient or by a health professional. The principle of social justice is also based on certain assumptions:

- Health care is different from most other goods and services. Health-seeking behavior is governed primarily by need rather than by the ability to pay.
- Responsibility for health is shared. Individuals are not held completely responsible for their condition because factors outside of their control may have brought on the condition. Society is held responsible because individuals cannot control certain environmental factors, such as economic inequalities, unemployment, or unsanitary conditions.
- Society has an obligation to the collective good. The well-being of the community is superior to that of the individual. An individual who is unhealthy is a burden on society. A person carrying a deadly infection, for example, poses a threat to society. Society, therefore, is obligated to cure the problem by providing health care to the individual. By doing so, the whole society will benefit.
- The government, not the market, can better decide through central planning how much health care to produce and how to distribute it to all citizens.

Just as true market justice does not exist in health care, social justice also does not exist. In the real world, no society can afford to provide unlimited amounts of health care to all of its citizens (Feldstein, 1994). The government may offer insurance coverage to all but must also find ways to limit the availability of certain healthcare services. For example, under the social justice principle, the government decides how technology will be dispersed and who will be allowed access to certain types of costly high-tech services, even though basic services may be available to all. The government engages in **supply-side rationing**, which is also referred to as **planned rationing** or nonprice rationing. In social justice systems, the government uses "health planning" to limit the supply of healthcare services, although the limited resources are often more equally dispersed throughout the country than is generally the case under a market justice system. The necessity of rationing health care explains why citizens of a country can be given universal coverage but not universal access. Even when a covered individual has a medical need, depending on the nature of health services required, they may have to wait until services become available.

Justice in the U.S. Health Delivery System

In a quasi perfect or imperfect market, such as the market for healthcare delivery in the United States, elements of both market and social justice principles exist. In some areas, the principles of market and social justice complement each other. In other areas, the two present conflicts. The two contrasting principles complement each other in the employer-based health insurance available to most middle-class working Americans (market justice) and the publicly financed Medicare, Medicaid, and CHIP coverage for certain disadvantaged groups (social justice). Insured populations access healthcare services delivered mainly by private practitioners and private institutions (market justice). Tax-supported county and city hospitals, public health clinics, and community health centers can be accessed by the uninsured in areas where such services are available (social justice).

Market and social justice principles create conflicts when healthcare resources are not uniformly distributed throughout the United States and when there is a general shortage of primary care physicians. Consequently, in spite of having public insurance, many Medicaid-covered patients have difficulty obtaining timely access, particularly in rural and inner-city areas. This conflict is partly created by artificially low reimbursement from public programs; in comparison, reimbursement from private payers is more generous.

Limitations of Market Justice

The principles of market justice work well for allocating economic goods when their unequal distribution does not affect the larger society. For example, based on individual success, people live in different sizes and styles of homes, drive different types of automobiles, and spend their money on a variety of things. In other cases, the allocation of resources has wider repercussions for society. In these areas, market justice has severe limitations:

- Market justice principles fail to rectify critical human concerns. Pervasive social problems, such as crime, illiteracy, and homelessness, can significantly weaken the cohesion of a society. Indeed, the United States has recognized such issues and instituted programs based on the social justice principle to combat such problems. These programs have added police protection, publicly supported education, and subsidized housing for many with limited financial resources and older populations. Health care is an important social issue because it not only affects human productivity and achievement but also provides basic human dignity.
- Market justice does not always protect a society. Individual health issues can have negative consequences for society because ill health is not always confined to the individual. The AIDS epidemic is an example of how a society can be put at serious risk by illness originally affecting just a few subpopulations. The initial spread of the SARS epidemic in Beijing, China, was largely due to patients with SARS symptoms being turned away by hospitals because they were not able to pay in advance for the cost of the treatment. Similar to clean air and water, health care is a social concern that in the long run protects against the burden of preventable disease and disability—a burden that is ultimately borne by society at large.
- Market justice does not work well in healthcare delivery. On the one hand, growing national economy and prosperity in the past did not materially reduce the number of uninsured Americans. On the other hand, the number of people who are uninsured increases during economic downturns. For example, during the 2007–2009 recession, 5 million Americans lost employment-based health insurance (Holahan, 2011).

Integration of Individual and Population Health

It has been recognized that the typical emphasis on the treatment of acute illness in hospitals, biomedical research, and high technology has not significantly improved the

U.S. population's health. Instead, the medical model should be integrated with a disease prevention, health promotion, primary care-based model to produce significant gains in health. Society will always need the benefits of modern science and technology for the treatment of disease, but health promotion and primary care can prevent and delay the onset of many diseases, disability, and premature death. An integrated approach will improve the overall health of the population, enhance people's quality of life, and conserve healthcare resources.

The real challenge for the healthcare delivery system is incorporating medical and wellness models within the holistic context of health. For instance, the Ottawa Charter for Health Promotion mentions caring, holism, and ecology as essential issues in developing strategies for health promotion (de Leeuw, 1989). "Holism" and "ecology" refer to the complex relationships that exist among (1) the individual, (2) the healthcare delivery system, and (3) the various physical, social, cultural, and economic environmental factors. In addition, as noted by an increasing body of research, the spiritual dimension must be incorporated into the integrated model.

Another equally important challenge for the healthcare delivery system is focusing on both individual and population health outcomes. The nature of health is complex, and the interrelationships among the physical, mental, social, and spiritual dimensions are not well understood. Translating this multidimensional framework of health into specific actions that are efficiently configured to achieve better individual and community health is one of the greatest challenges that today's healthcare systems face.

For an integrated approach to become reality, the best American ingenuity must be applied in addressing health-spending reductions and coordination of services among public health agencies, hospitals, and other healthcare providers. Community hospitals, in particular, are increasingly held accountable for the health status of the communities in which they serve. To fulfill this mission, hospitals must first conduct a health assessment of their communities. Such assessments provide broad perspectives of the local population's health and point to specific needs that healthcare providers can address. These assessments can help pinpoint interventions that should be given priority to improve the population's health status or address critical issues pertaining to certain subgroups within the population.

Healthy People Initiatives

Since 1980, the United States has developed a series of 10-year plans outlining certain key national health objectives to be accomplished during each of the 10-year periods. These objectives are developed by a consortium of national and state organizations under the leadership of the U.S. Surgeon General. The first of these programs introduced objectives for 1990 that provided national goals for reducing premature deaths among all age groups and reducing the average number of days of illness among persons older than age 65. A final review of this program concluded that positive changes in premature deaths had been achieved for all age categories except adolescents, but that illness among older people had not been reduced. However, this review set the stage to develop and modify the goals and objectives for the subsequent 10-year program (Chrvala and Bulger, 1999).

Healthy People 2000: National Health Promotion and Disease Prevention Objectives identified three main goals to be reached by the year 2000: (1) increase the span of healthy life for Americans, (2) reduce health disparities and wasteful care, and (3) promote individual responsibility and accountability for one's health as well as improved access to basic services. In a broad sense, these services include medical care, preventive

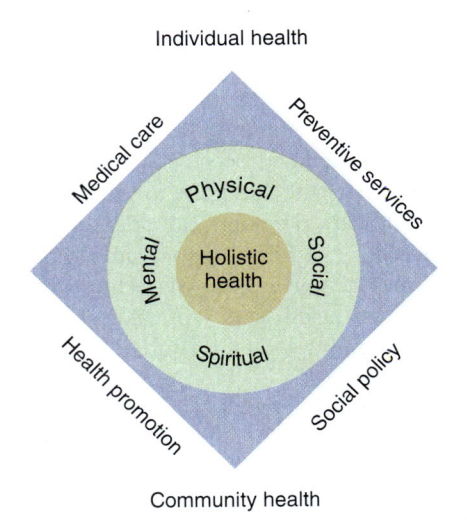

Figure 2-7 Integrated Model for Holistic Health.

services, health promotion, and social policy to improve education, lifestyle, employment, and housing (**Figure 2-7**). According to the final review, the major accomplishments of *Healthy People 2000* included surpassing the targets for reducing deaths from coronary heart disease and cancer; meeting the targets for mammography exams, violent deaths, tobacco-related deaths, and incidence rates of AIDS and syphilis; nearly meeting the targets for infant mortality and number of children with elevated levels of lead in their blood; and making some progress toward reducing health disparities among special populations.

Healthy People 2010: Healthy People in Healthy Communities continued the earlier tradition as an instrument to improve the health of the American people in the first decade of the 21st century. This initiative focused on two broad goals: (1) to increase quality and years of healthy life and (2) to eliminate health disparities. It went a step beyond the previous initiatives, however, by emphasizing the role of community partners (businesses, local governments, and civic, professional, and religious organizations) as effective agents for improving health in their local communities (DHHS, 1998). The final report revealed that 23% of the targets were met or exceeded and that the nation had made progress toward 48% of the targets. Specifically, life expectancy at birth, expected years in good or better health, and expected years free of activity limitations all improved, though expected years free of selected chronic diseases decreased. While many of the targets were met or in progress, the goal of reducing health disparities was not achieved. Health disparities identified in approximately 80% of the objectives did not change and even increased in another 13% of the objectives (NCHS, 2012). Hence, challenges remain in the reduction of chronic conditions and health disparities among population groups.

Healthy People 2020

Launched in 2010, *Healthy People 2020* (DHHS, 2010b) had a fivefold mission: (1) identify nationwide health improvement priorities; (2) increase public awareness and understanding of the determinants of health, disease, and disability and the opportunities for progress; (3) provide measurable objectives and goals that can be used at the national, state, and local levels; (4) engage multiple sectors to take actions that are driven by the best available evidence and knowledge; and (5) identify critical research and data collection needs. This initiative also had four overarching goals:

- Attain high-quality and longer lives free of preventable disease, disability, injury, and premature death.
- Achieve health equity, eliminate disparities, and improve the health of all groups.
- Create social and physical environments that promote good health for all.
- Promote quality of life, healthy development, and healthy behaviors across all life stages.

These overarching goals are in line with the tradition of earlier *Healthy People* initiatives but place particular emphasis on the

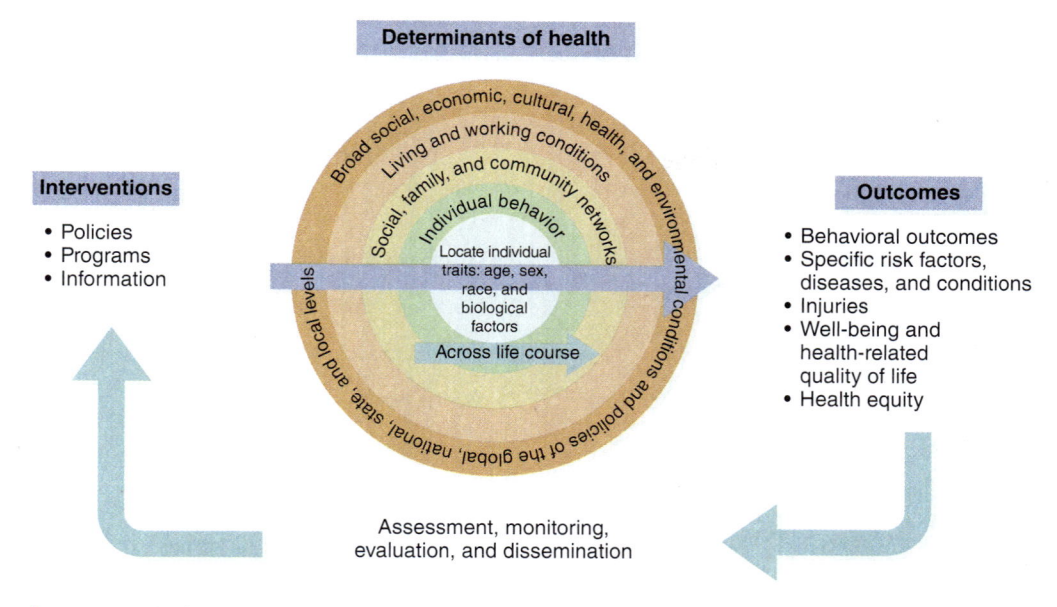

Figure 2-8 Action model to achieve U.S. *Healthy People 2020* overarching goals.

Courtesy of Department of Health and Human Services. 2008. The Secretary's Advisory Committee on National Health Promotion and Disease Prevention Objectives for 2020. 2008. Phase I report: Recommendations for the framework and format of *Healthy People 2020*. Section IV. Advisory Committee findings and recommendations. Available at: https://odphp.health.gov/our-work/national-health-initiatives/healthy-people/healthy-people-2020/secretarys-advisory-committee-2020. Accessed January 2025.

determinants of health. **Figure 2-8** illustrates the action model implemented to achieve the *Healthy People 2020* overarching goals. This model illustrates that those interventions (i.e., policies, programs, information) influence the determinants of health at four levels and lead to improvements in outcomes: (1) individual; (2) social, family, and community; (3) living and working conditions; and (4) broad social, economic, cultural, health, and environmental conditions. Results are to be demonstrated through assessment, monitoring, and evaluation, and the dissemination of findings will provide feedback for future interventions.

Healthy People 2020 differed from the previous *Healthy People* initiatives by including multiple new topic areas to its objectives list, such as adolescent health, genomics, global health, health communication and health information technology, and social determinants of health. *Healthy People 2020* had 42 topic areas, including 13 new areas (**Table 2-7**).

Measurement of Healthy People 2020

Healthy People 2020 established four foundational health measures to monitor progress toward achieving its goals: general health status, health-related quality of life and well-being, determinants of health, and disparities. Measures of general health status include life expectancy, healthy life expectancy, years of potential life lost, physically and mentally unhealthy days, self-assessed health status, limitations of activity, and chronic disease prevalence. Measures of health-related quality of life and well-being include physical, mental, and social health-related quality of life, well-being/satisfaction, and participation in common activities. Determinants of health are defined as "a range of personal, social, economic, and environmental factors that influence health status. Determinants of health include such things as biology, genetics, individual behavior, access to health services,

Table 2-7 Healthy People 2020 Topic Areas

1. Access to health services	22. HIV
2. Adolescent health[1]	23. Immunization and infectious diseases
3. Arthritis, osteoporosis, and chronic back conditions	24. Injury and violence prevention
4. Blood disorders and blood safety[1]	25. Lesbian, gay, bisexual, and transgender health[1]
5. Cancer	26. Maternal, infant, and child health
6. Chronic kidney disease	27. Medical product safety
7. Dementias, including Alzheimer's disease[1]	28. Mental health and mental disorders
8. Diabetes	29. Nutrition and weight status
9. Disability and health	30. Occupational safety and health
10. Early and middle childhood[1]	31. Older adults[1]
11. Educational and community-based programs	32. Oral health
12. Environmental health	33. Physical activity
13. Family planning	34. Preparedness[1]
14. Food safety	35. Public health infrastructure
15. Genomics[1]	36. Respiratory diseases
16. Global health[1]	37. Sexually transmitted diseases
17. Health communication and health information technology[1]	38. Sleep health[1]
18. Health care-associated infections[1]	39. Social determinants of health[1]
19. Health-related quality of life and well-being[1]	40. Substance abuse
20. Hearing and other sensory or communication disorders	41. Tobacco use
21. Heart disease and stroke	42. Vision

[1]New topic area.

and the environment where people are born, live, learn, play, work, and age." Measures of disparities and inequity include differences in health status based on race/ethnicity, gender, physical and mental ability, and geography (DHHS, 2010b).

Global health was also an important topic area in *Healthy People 2020*. The measurement of global health focused on two aspects: (1) measuring the reduction of global diseases in the United States, including malaria and TB; and (2) measuring "global capacity in support of the International Health Regulations to detect and contain emerging health threats" (DHHS, 2010b). The indicators include the number of global disease detection (GDD) regional centers worldwide, the number of public health professionals trained by GDD programs worldwide, and the number of diagnostic tests established or improved by GDD programs (DHHS, 2008, 2010b).

Achievement of Healthy People 2020

Ongoing review has focused on how well the healthcare system is working toward achieving the goals delineated in *Healthy People 2020* (2014). The findings of these ongoing studies are compared with baseline data from the beginning of the 10-year period to determine whether adequate progress has occurred.

In total, *Healthy People 2020* contained 42 topic areas with more than 1,200 objectives. A subset of 26 of these objectives, known as the leading health indicators (LHIs), was used to track the progress of the initiative and communicate high-priority health issues. Of the 26 LHIs, 4 indicators met or exceeded their *Healthy People 2020* targets, 10 showed improvement, 8 showed little or undetectable change, and 3 are getting worse. One indicator has only baseline data available.

Indicators for access to health services show little change in this area. Although the proportion of people with medical insurance has increased under the ACA, the target of 100% has not been reached. Similarly, access to a usual-care provider has increased but has not met *Healthy People 2020*'s target.

Many of the LHIs for clinical preventive services show improvement. The percentage of adults receiving colorectal cancer screenings, adults with hypertension whose blood pressure is controlled, and children receiving recommended vaccines all increased significantly, moving toward the *Healthy People 2020* target (Egan et al., 2014). In contrast, the rate of adults with diabetes who also have poor glycemic control has not shown any significant improvement.

Some environmental quality indicators not only met their *Healthy People 2020* goals, but actually exceeded them. The Air Quality Index, which assesses air quality changes by number and severity of unhealthy days, met its goal. Likewise, the goal for reducing the percentage of children exposed to secondhand smoke was achieved.

The LHIs for injury and violence have shown positive progress. Injury deaths decreased by 43% and the homicide rate declined by 13%—both of which meet the *Healthy People 2020* targets.

Maternal and child health LHIs were also significantly improving, with infant deaths and total preterm live births almost achieving their *Healthy People 2020* targets. Conversely, the LHIs for mental health appeared to be significantly worse than those measures at baseline. The suicide rate increased by 7%, and the percentage of adolescents with major depressive episodes increased by almost 10%.

Rates of obesity among adults, children, and adolescents all increased between 4% and 5%, although these changes are not statistically significant. Intake of vegetables remained stagnant. In a promising development, the percentage of adults meeting the federal physical activity guidelines increased by 13%, exceeding the *Healthy People 2020* target. In 2020, 25.3% of adults aged ≥18 years met the 2018 federal physical activity guidelines for both muscle-strengthening and aerobic physical activity. The percentage meeting both guidelines was highest in adults living in large central metropolitan (28.0%) and large fringe metropolitan areas (27.6%), followed by those living in medium and small metropolitan areas (23.4%) and lowest for those living in nonmetropolitan areas (18.1%) (CDC, 2022c).

In regards to oral health, the LHI was moving away from the target, showing a 6% decrease in the percentage of children, adolescents, and adults who had a dental visit in the past year. In contrast, the LHIs for reproductive and sexual health and social determinants showed some progress toward the *Healthy People 2020* goals.

Substance abuse indicators have been mixed. While the number of adolescents using alcohol or illicit drugs has decreased, the prevalence of binge drinking among adults has remained unchanged. The prevalence of adolescent cigarette smoking slightly decreased, with the overall cigarette smoking rate showing an even larger decrease of approximately 12%.

Healthy People 2030

In August 2020, the DHHS unveiled *Healthy People 2030*. The initiative contains 355 core objectives, including new objectives targeting opioid use disorder and youth e-cigarette use (DHHS, 2020). With new direction from the DHHS on areas of concern and target goals for health improvement, local communities across the nation can begin adopting strategies to meet the goals most relevant to their population groups.

Healthy People 2030's vision is to envisage "a society in which all people can achieve their full potential for health and well-being across the lifespan." Its mission, as a consequence, is "to promote, strengthen and evaluate the Nation's efforts to improve the health and well-being of all people." *Healthy People 2030* is guided by seven foundational principles:

- The health and well-being of all people and communities are essential to a thriving, equitable society.
- Promoting health and well-being and preventing disease are linked efforts that encompass physical, mental, and social health dimensions.
- Investing to achieve the full potential for health and well-being for all provides valuable benefits to society.
- Achieving health and well-being requires eliminating health disparities, achieving health equity, and attaining health literacy.
- Healthy physical, social, and economic environments strengthen the potential to achieve health and well-being.
- Promoting and achieving the nation's health and well-being is a shared responsibility that is distributed across the national, state, tribal, and community levels, including the public, private, and not-for-profit sectors.
- Working to attain the population's health and well-being is a major component of decision-making and policy formulation across all sectors (*Healthy People 2030*, 2020).

Its five overarching goals are as follows:

- Attain healthy, thriving lives and well-being, free of preventable disease, disability, injury, and premature death.
- Eliminate health disparities, achieve health equity, and attain health literacy to improve the health and well-being of all.
- Create social, physical, and economic environments to promote the full potential for health and well-being for all.
- Promote healthy development, healthy behaviors, and well-being across all life stages.
- Engage leadership, key constituents, and the public across multiple sectors to take action and design policies that improve the health and well-being of all (*Healthy People 2030*, 2020).

To achieve its goals, *Healthy People 2030* has outlined the following plan of action:

- Set national goals and measurable objectives to guide evidence-based policies, programs, and other actions to improve health and well-being.
- Provide accurate, timely, and accessible data that can drive targeted actions to address regions and populations with poor health or at high risk for poor health in the future.
- Foster impact through public and private efforts to improve health and well-being for people of all ages and the communities in which they live.
- Provide tools for the public, program planners, policymakers, and others to evaluate progress toward improving health and well-being.

- Share and support the implementation of evidence-based programs and policies that are replicable, scalable, and sustainable.
- Report biennially on progress throughout the decade from 2020 to 2030.
- Stimulate research and innovation toward meeting the *Healthy People 2030* goals and highlight critical research, data, and evaluation needs.
- Facilitate development and availability of affordable means of health promotion, disease prevention, and treatment (*Healthy People 2030*, 2020).

The framework for *Healthy People 2030* was approved in June 2018 (*Healthy People 2030*, 2020). It outlines a systematic approach to empower individuals to reach their full health potential throughout their entire lives (Hasbrouck, 2021; Benjamin, 2021; Gómez et al., 2021; Hoyer and Dee, 2022; Levine, 2021). It establishes a connection between a range of interconnected priorities and practical guidelines for implementing multisectoral policies aimed at achieving health equity and improving the social determinants of health. The framework acknowledges that better health and well-being can be attained more fairly and enhanced for everyone. The *Healthy People* objectives serve as a powerful call to action, presenting an ambitious blueprint for the nation's health over the next decade. These objectives encourage collaborative efforts among individuals, institutions, and organizations to elevate the overall health standards for all Americans. The significance of tracking progress toward these goals is emphasized, and it is crucial to find innovative ways to adjust and align objectives with the changing priorities of each subsequent decade.

Summary

The delivery of health care is primarily driven by the medical model, which emphasizes illness rather than wellness. Holistic concepts of health, along with the integration of medical care with preventive and health promotional efforts, need to be adopted to significantly improve the health of Americans. Such an approach would require individuals to take responsibility for their own health-oriented behaviors as well as the establishment of community partnerships to improve both personal and community health. Understanding the determinants of health, providing health education, using community health assessment, and promoting national initiatives such as Healthy People are essential to accomplish these goals. *Healthy People 2030*, launched in 2020, continues the goals of improving health and eliminating health disparities in the United States. Recently, public health has drawn increased attention due to the growing recognition of its role in health protection, environmental health, and preparedness for natural disasters and bioterrorism. Moreover, public health has now become global in its scope, especially in the wake of the COVID-19 pandemic. Programs to address the various facets of health and its determinants and ongoing initiatives in the areas of prevention, health promotion, health protection, and equality are complex undertakings that require substantial financial resources. Objective measures play a critical role both in evaluating the success of various programs and in directing future planning activities. The broad concern of achieving equitable access to health services can be addressed by considering the contrasting theories of market justice and social justice. Countries offering universal coverage have adopted the principles of social justice, under which the government finances healthcare services and decides on the distribution of those services. However, because no country can afford to provide unlimited amounts of health care to all citizens, supply-side rationing becomes inevitable in such a system. Many of the characteristics of the U.S. healthcare system trace back to the beliefs and values underlying the American culture. Under market justice, since not all citizens have health insurance coverage, a phenomenon called demand-side rationing is the result.

TEST YOUR UNDERSTANDING

Terminology

- activities of daily living (ADLs)
- acute condition
- agent
- bioterrorism
- cases
- chronic condition
- crude rates
- demand-side rationing
- emigration
- environment
- environmental health
- epidemic
- fertility
- health determinants
- health risk appraisal
- holistic health
- holistic medicine
- host
- iatrogenic illnesses
- immigration
- incidence
- instrumental activities of daily living (IADLs)
- life expectancy
- market justice
- medical model
- migration
- morbidity
- mortality
- natality
- planned rationing
- population at risk
- prevalence
- primary prevention
- public health
- quality of life
- risk factors
- secondary prevention
- social contacts
- social justice
- social resources
- subacute condition
- supply-side rationing
- surge capacity
- tertiary prevention
- travel ban
- utilization

Review Questions

1. What is the role of health risk appraisal in health promotion and disease prevention?
2. Health promotion and disease prevention may require both behavioral modification and therapeutic intervention. Discuss.
3. Discuss the definitions of health presented in this chapter in terms of their implications for the healthcare delivery system.
4. What are the main objectives of public health?
5. Discuss the significance of an individual's quality of life from the healthcare delivery perspective.
6. Which "preparedness"-related measures have been taken to cope with potential natural and human-made disasters since the tragic events of 9/11? Assess their effectiveness during the COVID-19 pandemic for the United States.
7. The Blum model points to four key determinants of health. Discuss their implications for healthcare delivery.
8. Why is the concept of "One Health" even more relevant in the wake of COVID-19 pandemic?
9. What has been the main cause of the dichotomy between the way physical and mental health issues have traditionally been addressed by the healthcare delivery system?
10. Discuss the main cultural beliefs and values in American society that have influenced healthcare delivery, including how they have shaped the healthcare delivery system.

11. Briefly describe the concepts of market justice and social justice. In what ways do the two principles complement each other, and in which ways are they in conflict in the U.S. system of healthcare delivery?
12. Describe how health care is rationed in the market justice and social justice systems.
13. To what extent do you think the objectives set forth in *Healthy People* initiatives can achieve the vision of an integrated approach to healthcare delivery in the United States?
14. What are the major differences between *Healthy People 2020* and the previous *Healthy People* initiatives? How does *Healthy People 2030* further advance the national objectives?
15. How can healthcare administrators and policymakers use the various measures of health status and service utilization? Please use examples to illustrate your answer.
16. Using the data given in the table below:
    a. Compute crude birth rates for 2005 and 2010.
    b. Compute crude death rates for 2005 and 2010.
    c. Compute cancer mortality rates for 2005 and 2010.
    d. Answer the following questions:
        i. Did the infant death rates improve between 2005 and 2010?
        ii. Which conclusions can you draw about the demographic change in this population?
        iii. Have efforts to prevent death from heart disease been successful in this population?

Population	2005	2010
Total	248,710	262,755
Male	121,239	128,314
Female	127,471	134,441
Whites	208,704	218,086
Blacks	30,483	33,141
Number of live births	4,250	3,840
Number of infant deaths (birth to 1 year)	39	35
Number of total deaths	1,294	1,324
Deaths from heart disease	378	363
Deaths from cancer	336	342

References

Abbey, E. J., B. A., Khalifa, M. O., Oduwole, et al. 2020. The Global Health Security Index is not predictive of coronavirus pandemic responses among Organization for Economic Cooperation and Development countries. *PloS One* 15: e0239398.

Adekunle, A., M. Meehan, D. Rojas-Alvarez, J. Trauer, and E. McBryde. 2020. Delaying the COVID-19 epidemic in Australia: Evaluating the effectiveness of international travel bans. *Australian and New Zealand Journal of Public Health* 44: 257–259. Accessed July

2020. Available at: https://doi.org/10.1111/1753-6405.13016

Adler, N. E., and J. M. Ostrove. 2006. Socioeconomic status and health: what we know and what we don't. *Annals of the New York Academy of Sciences* 896:3–15.

American Diabetes Association. 2018. Economic costs of diabetes in the U.S. in 2017. *Diabetes Care* 43. Available at: https://doi.org/10.2337/dci18-0007

American Public Health Association. 2013. *Prevention and Public Health Fund Allocations*. Accessed April 2017. Available at: https://www.hhs.gov/open/prevention/fy2013-allocation-pphf-funds.html

Anandarajah G., and E. Hight. 2001. Spirituality and medical practice: Using the HOPE questions as a practical tool for spiritual assessment. *American Family Physician* 63: 81–89.

Anderko, L., and K. Sebelius. 2012. Promoting prevention through the Affordable Care Act: Workplace wellness. *Preventing Chronic Disease* 9: E175.

Ansari, Z., N. Carson, M. Ackland, L. Vaughan, and A. Serraglio. 2003. A public health model of the social determinants of health. *Sozial und Präventivmedizin (Social and Preventive Medicine)* 48: 242–251.

An-qi, H. U., W. A. Ding, S. H. Jie, et al. 2022. Effectiveness analysis of global health security index (GHSI) assessment. 中华疾病控制杂志, (Journal of China Disease Control) 26: 1217–1223.

Armour, S. 2020. Trump administration to pay hospitals to treat uninsured coronavirus patients. *The Wall Street Journal*. Accessed May 2020. Available at: https://www.wsj.com/articles/trump-administration-plans-to-pay-hospitals-to-treat-uninsured-coronavirus-patients-11585927877

Aslam, B., M. Khurshid, M. I. Arshad, et al. (2021). Antibiotic resistance: One Health One world outlook. *Frontiers in Cellular and Infection Microbiology* 11: 771510. https://doi.org/10.3389/fcimb.2021.771510

Baicker, K., D. Cutler, and Z. Song. 2010. Workplace wellness programs can generate savings. *Health Affairs (Millwood)* 29: 304–311.

U. E. Bauer, P. A. Briss, R. A. Goodman, and B. A. Bowman. 2014. Prevention of chronic disease in the 21st century: Elimination of the leading preventable causes of premature death and disability in the USA. *Lancet* 384: 45–52.

Benjamin, G. C. 2021. Becoming the healthiest nation: The role of *Healthy People 2030. Journal of Public Health Management and Practice: JPHMP* 27: S218–S219.

Blum, H. L. 1981. *Planning for Health* 2nd ed. New York, NY: Human Sciences Press.

Bonnett, C., and B. C. Peery. 2007. Surge capacity: A proposed conceptual framework. *American Journal of Emergency Medicine* 25: 297–306.

Breslow, L. 1972. A quantitative approach to the World Health Organization definition of health: Physical, mental, and social well-being. *International Journal of Epidemiology* 4: 347–355.

Caballero, B. 2007. The global epidemic of obesity: An overview. *Epidemiology Review* 29: 1–5.

Capatides, C. 2020. Doctors Without Borders dispatches team to the Navajo nation. *CBS News*. Accessed May 2020. Available at: https://www.cbsnews.com/news/doctors-without-borders-navajo-nation-coronavirus/

Centers for Disease Control and Prevention (CDC). 1999. Achievements in public health, 1900–1999: Control of infectious diseases. *Morbidity and Mortality Weekly Report* 48: 621–629.

Centers for Disease Control and Prevention (CDC). 2007. *Information on Avian Influenza*. Accessed January 10, 2007. Available at: https://www.cdc.gov/flu/avianflu/

Centers for Disease Control and Prevention (CDC). 2010a. *Establishing a Holistic Framework to Reduce Inequities in HIV, Viral Hepatitis, STDs, and Tuberculosis in the United States*. Accessed April 2017. Available at: https://www.cdc.gov/socialdeterminants/docs/SDH-White-Paper-2010.pdf

Centers for Disease Control and Prevention (CDC). 2010b. Office of public health preparedness and response. *Public Health Preparedness: Strengthening the Nation's Emergency Response State by State*. Accessed April 2017. Available at: https://www.cdc.gov/phpr/publications/2010/phprep_report_2010.pdf

Centers for Disease Control and Prevention (CDC). 2012. *SARS Basics Fact Sheet*. Accessed October 2013. Available at: https://www.cdc.gov/sars/about/fs-SARS.html

Centers for Disease Control and Prevention (CDC). 2013a. *Community Based Interventions: Brief Executive Summary*. Accessed April 2017. Available at: https://www.cdc.gov/nccdphp/dch/programs/communitiesputtingpreventiontowork/pdf/community-based-interventions-executive-brief-update.pdf

Centers for Disease Control and Prevention (CDC). 2013b. *National Diabetes Prevention Program*. Accessed April 2017. Available at: https://www.cdc.gov/diabetes/prevention/index.html

Centers for Disease Control and Prevention (CDC). 2013c. *Recognized Lifestyle Change Program*. Accessed April 2017. Available at: https://nccd.cdc.gov/DDT_DPRP/Programs.aspx

Centers for Disease Control and Prevention (CDC). 2016a. U.S. cancer statistics working group. *United States Cancer Statistics: 1999–2013 Incidence and Mortality Web-based Report*. Accessed February 2021. Available at: https://www.cdc.gov/cancer/uscs/

Centers for Disease Control and Prevention (CDC). 2016b. *Facts about the National DPP*. Accessed February 2021. Available at: https://www.cdc.gov/diabetes/prevention/index.html

Centers for Disease Control and Prevention (CDC). 2018. *One Health Basics*. Accessed March 2020. Available at: https://www.cdc.gov/onehealth/basics/index.html

Centers for Disease Control and Prevention (CDC). 2019a. *CDC: Half of workplaces offer health/wellness *programs.* Accessed February 2020. Available at: https://www.cdc.gov/media/releases/2019/p0422-workplaces-offer-wellness.html

Centers for Disease Control and Prevention (CDC). 2019b. *Chronic Diseases in America.* Accessed January 2020. Available at https://www.cdc.gov/chronicdisease/resources/infographic/chronic-diseases.html

Centers for Disease Control and Prevention (CDC). 2019c. *Heart Disease Facts.* Accessed February 2020. Available at: https://www.cdc.gov/heartdisease/facts.htm.

Centers for Disease Control and Prevention (CDC). 2019d. *What is Ebola virus disease?* Accessed April 2020. Available at: https://www.cdc.gov/vhf/ebola/about.html

Centers for Disease Control and Prevention (CDC). 2019e. *Zika virus: Symptoms.* Accessed April 2020. Available at: https://www.cdc.gov/zika/symptoms/symptoms.html

Centers for Disease Control and Prevention (CDC). 2021. *National Center for Chronic Disease Prevention and Health Promotion.* Accessed September 2023. Available at: https://www.cdc.gov/chronicdisease/about/costs/index.html

Centers for Disease Control and Prevention (CDC). 2022. *National Center for Chronic Disease Prevention and Health Promotion.* Accessed September 2023. Available at: https://www.cdc.gov/chronicdisease/resources/publications/factsheets/cancer.html

Centers for Disease Control and Prevention, National Center for Emerging and Zoonotic Infectious Diseases (NCEZID). 2022. *One Health Basics.* Available at: https://www.cdc.gov/onehealth/basics/index.html#:~:text=What%20is%20One%20Health%3F,more%20important%20in%20recent%20years

Centers for Disease Control and Prevention (CDC). 2022c. *QuickStats: Age-Adjusted Percentage of Adults Aged ≥18 Years Who Met the 2018 Federal Physical Activity Guidelines for Both Muscle-Strengthening and Aerobic Physical Activity.* Accessed September 2023. Available at: https://blogs.cdc.gov/nchs/2022/07/08/6508/

Centers for Disease Control and Prevention (CDC). 2023. *Social and Behavior ChangeActivities.* Available at: https://www.cdc.gov/healthywater/global/sbc.html

Chait, N., and S. Glied. 2018. Promoting prevention under the Affordable Care Act. *Annual Review of Public Health* 39: 507–524. Available at: https://doi.org/10.1146/annurev-publhealth-040617-013534

Chida, Y., A. Steptoe, and L. H. Powell. 2009. Religiosity/spirituality and mortality. *Psychotherapy and Psychosomatics* 78: 81–90.

Chrvala, C. A., and R. J. Bulger, eds. 1999. *Leading health indicators for Healthy People 2010: Final report.* Washington, DC: National Academy of Sciences.

Cohen M. H. 2003. *Future medicine.* Ann Arbor, MI: University of Michigan Press.

Cohen, S., and K. Mulvaney. 2005. Field observations: Disaster medical assistance team response for Hurricane Charley. Punta Gorda, Florida, 2004. *Disaster Management and Response* 22–27.

Committee on Infectious Diseases, American Academy of Pediatrics; Kimberlin, D., et al. 2015. *Red book: 2015 report of the Committee of Infectious Diseases.* 30th ed. Elk Grove Village, IL: American Academy of Pediatrics.

V. Costantino, D. J. Heslop, and C. R. MacIntyre. 2020. The effectiveness of full and partial travel bans against COVID-19 spread in Australia for travellers from China during and after the epidemic peak in China. *Journal of Travel Medicine* 27. Accessed February 2021. Available at: https://pubmed.ncbi.nlm.nih.gov/32453411/

Coronavirus Preparedness and Response Supplemental Appropriations Act, 2020, H.R. 6074, 116th Congress. 2020. Accessed May 2020. Available at https://www.congress.gov/bill/116th-congress/house-bill/6074

Dahlgren, G., and M. Whitehead. 2006. *European strategies for tackling social inequities in health: Levelling up (part 2). Studies on Social and Economic Determinants of Population Health, No. 3.* Copenhagen, Denmark: World Health Organization. Accessed December 2010. Available at: http://www.euro.who.int/__data/assets/pdf_file/0018/103824/E89384.pdf

Davis, D. L., and P. S. Webster. 2002. The social context of science: Cancer and the environment. *Annals of the American Academy of Political and Social Science* 584: 13–34.

De Leeuw, E. 1989. Concepts in health promotion: The notion of relativism. *Social Science and Medicine* 29: 1281–1288.

Department of Health and Human Services (DHHS). 1992. *Healthy People 2000: National Health Promotion and Disease Prevention Objectives.* Boston, MA: Jones & Bartlett.

Department of Health and Human Services (DHHS). 1998. *Healthy People 2010 Objectives: Draft for Public Comment.* Washington, DC: U.S. Government Printing Office.

Department of Health and Human Services (DHHS). 2004. *The Health Consequences of Smoking: A Report of the Surgeon General.* Accessed February 2021. Available at: https://pubmed.ncbi.nlm.nih.gov/20669512/

Department of Health and Human Services (DHHS). 2006. *Your Guide to Lowering Blood Pressure.* Accessed December 7, 2013. Available at: http://www.nhlbi.nih.gov/health/public/heart/hbp/dash/new_dash.pdf

Department of Health and Human Services (DHHS). 2008. *The Secretary's Advisory Committee on National Health Promotion and Disease Prevention Objectives for 2020. 2008. Phase I report: Recommendations for the Framework and Format of Healthy People 2020. Section IV. Advisory Committee Findings and Recommendations.* Accessed February 2021. Available at: https://www.healthypeople.gov/sites/default/files/PhaseI_0.pdf

Department of Health and Human Services (DHHS). 2010a. *Summary of the Prevention and Wellness Initiative.* Accessed November 2010. Available at:

http://www.cdc.gov/chronicdisease/recovery/docs/PW_Community_fact_sheet_final.pdf

Department of Health and Human Services (DHHS). 2010b. *Healthy People 2020*. Accessed December 2010. Available at: http://healthypeople.gov/2020

Department of Health and Human Services (DHHS). 2011a. *National Health Security Strategy 2009*. Accessed August 2013. Available at: http://www.phe.gov/Preparedness/planning/authority/nhss/Pages/default.aspx

Department of Health and Human Services (DHHS). 2011b. *$10 Million in Affordable Care Act Funds to Help Create Workplace Health Programs* [News release]. Accessed April 2017. Available at: http://www.businesswire.com/news/home/20110623005954/en/10-Million-Affordable-Care-Act-funds-create

Department of Health and Human Services (DHHS). 2014. *The Health Consequences of Smoking—50 Years of Progress: A Report of the Surgeon General*. Atlanta, GA: DHHS, Centers for Disease Control and Prevention, National Center for Chronic Disease Prevention and Health Promotion, Office on Smoking and Health.

Department of Health and Human Services (DHHS). 2017. *2020 Topics and Objectives: Objectives A–Z*. Accessed April 2017. Available at: https://www.healthypeople.gov/2020/topics-objectives

Department of Health and Human Services (DHHS). 2020. *HHS Releases Healthy People 2030 with National Disease Prevention and Health Promotion Objectives for the Next Decade*. Accessed February 2021. Available at: https://www.hhs.gov/about/news/2020/08/18/hhs-releases-healthy-people-2030-with-national-disease-prevention-and-health-promotion-objectives-for-the-next-decade.html

Dever, G. E. 1984. *Epidemiology in Health Service Management*. Gaithersburg, MD: Aspen.

Diabetes Prevention Program Research Group. 2015. Long-term effects of lifestyle intervention or metformin on diabetes development and microvascular complications over 15-year follow-up: The Diabetes Prevention Program Outcomes Study. *Lancet: Diabetes & Endocrinology* 3: 866–875. Available at: https://doi.org/10.1016/S2213-8587(15)00291-0

Draper, P. 2012. An integrative review of spiritual assessment: Implications for nursing management. *Journal of Nursing Management* 20: 970–980.

Egan, B. M., J. Li, F. N. Hutchison, and K. C. Ferdinand 2014. Hypertension in the United States, 1999 to 2012: Progress toward *Healthy People 2020* goals. *Circulation* 130: 1692–1699.

Ethics Committee, Society for Academic Emergency Medicine. 1992. An ethical foundation for health care: An emergency medicine perspective. *Annals of Emergency Medicine* 21: 1381–1387.

Families First Coronavirus Response Act, H.R.6201, 116th Congress. 2020. Accessed May 2020. Available at: https://www.congress.gov/bill/116th-congress/house-bill/6201

Feldstein, P. J. 1994. *Health Policy Issues: An Economic Perspective on Health Reform*. Ann Arbor, MI: AUPHA/HAP.

Ferguson C. E., and S. C. Maurice. 1970. *Economic Analysis*. Homewood, IL: Richard D. Irwin.

Finkelstein E. A., C. J. Ruhm, and K. M. Kosa 2005. Economic causes and consequences of obesity. *Annual Review of Public Health* 26: 239–257.

Fortin A. H., and K. G. Barnett. 2004. Medical school curricula in spirituality and medicine. *Journal of the American Medical Association* 291: 2883.

Franco M., A. V. Diez-Roux, J. A. Nettleton, et al. 2009. Availability of healthy foods and dietary patterns: The multi-ethnic study of atherosclerosis. *American Journal of Clinical Nutrition* 89: 897–904.

Franco M., R. S. Cooper, U. Bilal, and V. Fuster. 2011. Challenges and opportunities for cardiovascular disease prevention. *American Journal of Medicine* 124: 95–102.

Friedman G. D. 1980. *Primer of Epidemiology*. New York: McGraw-Hill.

Grossman, M. 1972. On the concept of health capital and the demand for health. *Journal of Political Economy* 80: 223–255.

Goldman, N. 2001. Social inequalities in health. *Annals of the New York Academy of Sciences* 954: 118–139.

Gómez, C. A., D. V., Kleinman, N. Pronk, et al. 2021. Addressing health equity and social determinants of health through Healthy People 2030. *Journal of Public Health Management and Practice: JPHMP* 27(Suppl 6): S249–S257.

Haider, N., A. Yavlinsky, Y. M. Chang, et al. 2020. The Global Health Security index and Joint External Evaluation score for health preparedness are not correlated with countries' COVID-19 detection response time and mortality outcome. *Epidemiology & Infection* 148: e210.

Hasbrouck, L. 2021. Healthy People 2030: An improved framework. *Health Education & Behavior: The Official Publication of the Society for Public Health Education* 48: 113–114.

Hatch R. L., M. A. Burg, D. S. Naberhaus, and L. K. Hellmich. 1998. The spiritual involvement and beliefs scale: Development and testing of a new instrument. *Journal of Family Practice* 46: 476–486.

Healthy People 2020. 2014. *Leading Health Indicators: Progress Update*. Accessed April 2017. Available at: https://www.healthypeople.gov/2020/leading-health-indicators/Healthy-People-2020-Leading-Health-Indicators%3A-Progress-Update

Healthy People 2030. 2020. *Healthy People 2030 Framework*. Accessed January 4, 2020. Available at: https://www.healthypeople.gov/2020/About-Healthy-People/Development-Healthy-People-2030/Framework

References

Henao-Restrepo, A. M., A. Camacho, I. M. Longini, et al. 2017. Efficacy and effectiveness of an rVSV-vectored vaccine in preventing Ebola virus disease: Final results from the Guinea ring vaccination, open-label, cluster-randomised trial (Ebola Ça Suffit!). *Lancet* 389: 505–518.

Henry, R. C. 1993. Community partnership model for health professions education. *Journal of the American Podiatric Medical Association* 83: 328–331.

Hick J., D. Hanfling, J. L. Burstein, et al. 2004. Health care facility and community strategies for patient care surge capacity. *Annals of Emergency Medicine* 44: 253–261.

Hoff A., C. T. Johannessen-Henry, L. Ross, N. C. Hvidt, and C. Johansen. 2008. Religion and reduced cancer risk—what is the explanation? A review. *European Journal of Cancer* 44: 2573–2579.

Holahan, J. 2011. The 2007–09 recession and health insurance coverage. *Health Affairs* 30: 145–152.

Houston J. B., J. Hawthorne, M. F. Perreault, et al. 2015. Social media and disasters: A functional framework for social media use in disaster planning, response, and research. *Disasters* 39: 1–22.

Hoyer, D., and E. Dee, 2022. Using Healthy People as a tool to identify health disparities and advance health equity. *Journal of Public Health Management and Practice* 28: 562–569.

Ibrahim, M. A. 1985. *Epidemiology and Health policy*. Gaithersburg, MD: Aspen.

Institute of Medicine, National Academy of Sciences. 1988. *The Future of Public Health*. Washington, DC: National Academies Press.

Jefferies, M., B. Rauff, H. Rashid, T. Lam, and S. Rafiq. 2018. Update on global epidemiology of viral hepatitis and preventive strategies. *World Journal of Clinical Cases* 6: 589–599. doi:10.12998/wjcc.v6.i13.589

Ji, Y., J. Shao, B. Tao, , H. Song, Z. Li, and J. Wang. 2021. Are we ready to deal with a global COVID-19 pandemic? Rethinking countries' capacity based on the Global Health Security Index. *International Journal of Infectious Diseases* 106: 289–294.

Johnson N., P. Oliff, and E. Williams. 2011. *An Update on State Budget Cuts: At Least 46 States Have Imposed Cuts that Hurt Vulnerable Residents and the Economy*. Washington DC: Center on Budget and Policy Priorities.

Joint Commission on the Accreditation of Healthcare Organizations. 2003. *2003 Comprehensive Accreditation Manual for Healthcare Organizations: The Official Handbook*. Chicago, IL: Joint Commission.

Jonsen, A., M. Siegler, and W. J. Winslade. 2015. *Clinical Ethics: A Practical Approach to Ethical Decisions in Clinical Medicine*. 8th ed. New York: McGraw-Hill Professional Publishing.

Kandel, N., S. Chungong, A. Omaar, and J. Xing. 2020. Health security capacities in the context of COVID-19 outbreak: an analysis of International Health Regulations annual report data from 182 countries. *Lancet* 395: 10477–1053.

Kane, R. L. 1988. Empiric approaches to prevention in the elderly: Are we promoting too much? In: *Health Promotion and Disease Prevention in the Elderly*. R. Chernoff and D. A. Lipschitz, eds. New York, NY: Raven Press. 127–141.

Kannel, W. B., and R. D. Abbott. 1984. Incidence and prognosis of unrecognized myocardial infarction: An update on the Framingham Study. *New England Journal of Medicine* 311: 1144–1147.

Kanno-Youngs Z., and E. Lipton. 2020. As federal government mobilizes, local officials say response remains too slow. *The New York Times*. Accessed May 2020. Available at: https://www.nytimes.com/2020/03/23/us/politics/coronavirus-supplies-federal-response.html

Kaplan, G. A., and J. E Keil. 1993. Socioeconomic factors and cardiovascular disease: a review of the literature. *Circulation* 88: 1973–1998.

Katz S., and C. A. Akpom. 1979. A measure of primary sociobiological functions. In: *Sociomedical Health Indicators*. J. Elinson and A. E. Siegman, eds. Farmingdale, NY: Baywood. 127–141.

Kawachi, I., B. P. Kennedy, K. Lochner, and D. Prothrow-Stith. 1997. Social capital, income inequality, and mortality. *American Journal of Public Health* 87: 1491–1498.

Kawachi, I., B. P. Kennedy, and R. Glass. 1999. Social capital and self-rated health: A contextual analysis. *American Journal of Public Health* 89: 1187–1193.

Kearns R., M. W. Hubble, J. H. Holmes I. V., and B. A. Cairns. 2013. Disaster planning: Transportation resources and considerations for managing a burn disaster. *Journal of Burn Care and Research* 35: e21–e32.

Kelly, M. P., and M. Barker. 2016. Why is changing health-related behaviour so difficult? *Public Health* 136: 109–116. Available at: https://doi.org/10.1016/j.puhe.2016.03.030

Khalifa, B. A., E. J. Abbey, S. K. Ayeh, et al. 2021. The Global Health Security Index is not predictive of vaccine rollout responses among OECD countries. *International Journal of Infectious Diseases*: 113: 7–11.

Khavjou O. A., A. A. Honeycutt, T. J. Hoerger, J. G. Trogdon, and A. J. Cash . 2014. Collecting costs of community prevention programs: Communities Putting Prevention to Work Initiative. *American Journal of Preventive Medicine* 47: 160–165.

Krieger, N., J. T. Chen, P. D. Waterman, D. H. Rehkopf, and S. V. Subramanian. 2003. Race/ethnicity, gender, and monitoring socioeconomic gradients in health: a comparison of area-based socioeconomic measures—the public health disparities geocoding project. *American Journal of Public Health* 93: 1655–1671.

Kristol I. 1978. A capitalist conception of justice. In: *Ethics, Free Enterprise, and Public Policy: Original Essays on Moral Issues in Business*. R. T. DeGeorge and

J. A. Pichler, eds. New York, NY: Oxford University Press. 57–69.

Kwiatkowski, J. 2020. *COVID-19-Inspired Health Provider Innovation and Collaboration Should Continue.* Milbank Memorial Fund. Accessed May 2020. Available at: https://www.milbank.org/2020/05/health-provider-innovation-and-collaboration-should-continue/

Lal, A., H. C. Ashworth, S. Dada, L. Hoemeke, and E. Tambo, 2022. Optimizing pandemic preparedness and response through health information systems: Lessons learned from Ebola to COVID-19. *Disaster Medicine and Public Health Preparedness* 16: 333–340.

Lal, A., N. A. Erondu, D. L. Heymann, G. Gitahi, and R. Yates. 2021. Fragmented health systems in COVID-19: Rectifying the misalignment between global health security and universal health coverage. *Lancet* 397: 61–67.

Larson, C., and A. Mercer. 2004. Global health indicators: An overview. *Canadian Medical Association Journal* 171: 1199–1200.

Lasker, R. D. 1997. *Medicine and Public Health: The Power of Collaboration.* New York: New York Academy of Medicine.

Laverack, G. 2017. The challenge of behavior change and health promotion. *Challenges* 8: 25. Available at: https://doi.org/10.3390/challe8020025

Levine, R. L. 2021. Healthy People 2030: A beacon for addressing health disparities and health equity. *Journal of Public Health Management and Practice* 27: S220–S221.

Link, B. G., and J. Phelan, 1995. Social conditions as fundamental causes of disease. *Journal of Health & Social Behavior Spec* 80.

Lu, N., K. W. Cheng, N. Qamar, K. C. Huang, and J. A. Johnson. 2020. Weathering COVID-19 storm: Successful control measures of five Asian countries. *American Journal of Infection Control* S0196-6553: 30268–30266. Advance online publication. Available at: https://doi.org/10.1016/j.ajic.2020.04.021

Luo, G., M. L. McHenry, and J. J. Letterio. 2020. Estimating the prevalence and risk of COVID-19 among international travelers and evacuees of Wuhan through modeling and case reports. *PloS One* 15. Accessed February 2021. Available at: https://doi.org/10.1371/journal.pone.0234955

Maani, N., and S. Galea. 2020a. COVID-19 and underinvestment in the public health infrastructure of the United States. *Milbank Quarterly* 98: 250–259. doi:10.1111/1468-0009.12463

Maani, N., and S. Galea. 2020b. COVID-19 and underinvestment in the health of the US population. *Milbank Quarterly* 98: 239–249. doi:10.1111/1468-0009.12462

Macfarlane, G. J., and A. B. Lowenfels. 1994. Physical activity and colon cancer. *European Journal of Cancer Prevention* 3: 393–398.

Malik, S. M., A. Barlow, and B. Johnson, 2021. Reconceptualising health security in post-COVID-19 world. *BMJ Global Health* 6: e006520.

Marmot, M.l G., M. J. Shipley, and G. Rose. 1984. Inequalities in death—specific explanations of a general pattern? *Lancet* 323: 1003–1006.

Marwick, C. 1995. Should physicians prescribe prayer for health? Spiritual aspects of well-being considered. *Journal of the American Medical Association* 273: 1561–1562.

Mattke, S., H. Liu, J. Caloyeras, et al. 2013. *Workplace Wellness Study: Final Report.* Santa Monica, CA: RAND Health. Accessed April 2017. Available at: https://www.dol.gov/sites/default/files/ebsa/researchers/analysis/health-and-welfare/workplacewellnessstudyfinal.pdf

Maylahn C., D. Fleming, and G. Birkhead. 2013. Health departments in a brave New World. *Preventing Chronic Disease* 10: E41.

McKee, M. 2001. Measuring the efficiency of health systems. *British Medical Journal* 323: 295–296.

Meseko, C. A., A. O. Egbetade, and S. Fagbo. 2015. Ebola virus disease control in West Africa: An ecological, one health approach. *Pan African Medical Journal* 21: 6. doi:10.11604/pamj.2015.21.6.6587

Miroff, N. 2020. Coronavirus could be FEMA's biggest disaster ever, and it threatens to swamp the agency. *The Washington Post.* Accessed April 2020. Available at: https://www.washingtonpost.com/national/coronavirus-fema-biggest-disaster/2020/03/24/2e8602fe-6d50-11ea-96a0-df4c5d9284af_story.html

Monod, S. M. Brennan, E. Rochat, E. Martin, S. Rochat, and C. J. Büla. 2011. Instruments measuring spirituality in clinical research: A systematic review. *Journal of General Internal Medicine* 26: 1345–1357.

Mozaffarian D., E. J. Benjamin A. S. Go, et al. 2016. Executive summary: Heart disease and stroke statistics—2016 update: A report from the American Heart Association. *Circulation* 133: 447–454.

Mwangi, W., P. de Figueiredo, and M. F. Criscitiello. 2016. One Health: Addressing global challenges at the nexus of human, animal, and environmental health. *PLoS Pathogens* 12: e1005731. Available at: https://doi.org/10.1371/journal.ppat.1005731

Naddeo V. 2021. One planet, one health, one future: The environmental perspective. *Water Environment Research: a Research Publication of the Water Environment Federation* 93: 1472–1475. Available at: https://doi.org/10.1002/wer.1624

National Center for Health Statistics (NCHS). 2012. *Healthy People 2010 Final Review.* Hyattsville, MD: NCHS. Accessed August 2013. Available at: https://www.cdc.gov/nchs/healthy_people/hp2010/hp2010_final_review.htm

National Prevention Council. 2011. *Nation Prevention Strategy: America's Plan for Better Health and Wellness.*

Washington, DC: U.S. Department of Health and Human Services.

Nelson, C., N. Lurie, and J. Wasserman. 2007. Assessing public health emergency preparedness: Concepts, tools, and challenges. *Annual Review of Public Health* 28: 1–18.

Nielsen, L., M. Riddle, J. W. King, et al. 2018. The NIH Science of Behavior Change Program: Transforming the science through a focus on mechanisms of change. *Behaviour Research and Therapy* 101: 3–11. Available at: https://doi.org/10.1016/j.brat.2017.07.002

Nuclear Threat Initiative (NTI) and Johns Hopkins Center for Health Security. 2019. Global Health Security Index: Building collective action and accountability. Accessed May 2020. Available at: https://www.ghsindex.org/wp-content/uploads/2020/04/2019-Global-Health-Security-Index.pdf

Office of the Assistant Secretary for Planning and Evaluation. 2015. *The Affordable Care Act is improving access to preventive services for millions of Americans*. Accessed April 2017. Available at: https://aspe.hhs.gov/pdf-report/affordable-care-act-improving-access-preventive-services-millions-americans

Oman D., J. H. Kurata, W. J. Strawbridge, and R. D. Cohen. 2002. Religious attendance and cause of death over 31 years. *International Journal of Psychiatry and Medicine* 32: 69–89.

Ostir, G. V., J. E. Carlson, S. A. Black, L. Rudkin, J. S. Goodwin, and K. S. Markides. 1999. Disability in older adults 1: Prevalence, causes, and consequences. *Behavioral Medicine* 24: 147–156.

Overgaauw, P. A., C. M. Vinke, M. A. Hagen, and L. J. Lipman. 2020. A One Health perspective on the human-companion animal relationship with emphasis on zoonotic aspects. *International Journal of Environmental Research and Public Health* 17: 3789. Available at: https://doi.org/10.3390/ijerph17113789

Pantell, M., D. Rehkopf, D. Jutte, S. L. Syme, J. Balmes, and N. Adler. 2013. Social isolation: A predictor of mortality comparable to traditional clinical risk factors. *American Journal of Public Health* 103: 2056–2062.

Parsons, T. 1972. Definitions of health and illness in the light of American values and social structure. In: *Patients, Physicians and Illness: A Sourcebook in Behavioral Science and Health*. 2nd ed. E. G. Jaco, ed. New York: Free Press. 97–117.

Pasley, B. H., R. J. Lagoe, and N. O. Marshall. 1995. Excess acute care bed capacity and its causes: The experience of New York State. *Health Services Research* 30: 115–131.

Peres, M. F., H. H. Kamei, P. R. Tobo, and G. Lucchetti. 2018. Mechanisms behind religiosity and spirituality's effect on mental health, quality of life and well-being. *Journal of Religion and Health* 57: 1842–1855.

Peters, K. E., E. Drabant, A. Elster, M. Tierney, and B. Hatcher. 2001. Cooperative actions for health programs: *Lessons learned in medicine and public health collaboration*. Chicago, IL: American Medical Association.

Petkovic, J., S. Duench, J. Trawin, et al. (2021). Behavioural interventions delivered through interactive social media for health behaviour change, health outcomes, and health equity in the adult population. *The Cochrane Database of Systematic Reviews* 5: CD012932. Available at: https://doi.org/10.1002/14651858.CD012932.pub2

Pincus, T., R. Esther, D. A. DeWalt, and L. F. Callahan. 1998. Social conditions and self-management are more powerful determinants of health than access to care. *Annals of Internal Medicine* 129: 406–411.

Plotkin S. L., and S. A. Plotkin. 2012. A short history of vaccination. In: *Vaccines*. 6th ed. S. A. Plotkin et al., eds. Philadelphia, PA: W. B. Saunders. 1–13.

Post, S. G., C. M. Puchalski, and D. B. Larson. 2000. Physicians and patient spirituality: Professional boundaries, competency, and ethics. *Annals of Internal Medicine* 132: 578–583.

Ravi, S. J., K. L. Warmbrod, L. Mullen, et al. 2020. The value proposition of the global health security index. *BMJ Global Health* 5: e003648.

Reinhardt, U. E. 1994. Providing access to health care and controlling costs: The universal dilemma. In: *The Nation's Health*. 4th ed. P. R. Lee, and C. L. Estes, eds. Boston, MA: Jones & Bartlett. 263–278.

Rizzo, D. M., M. Lichtveld, J. A. Mazet, E. Togami, and S. A. Miller. 2021. Plant health and its effects on food safety and security in a One Health framework: Four case studies. *One Health Outlook* 3: 6. Available at: https://doi.org/10.1186/s42522-021-00038-7

Rose, S. M., M. Paterra, C. Isaac, et al. 2021. Analysing COVID-19 outcomes in the context of the 2019 Global Health Security (GHS) Index. *BMJ Global Health* 6: e007581.

Robert Wood Johnson Foundation. 2010. *Chronic care: Making the case for ongoing care*. Accessed April 2017. Available at: https://www.rwjf.org/en/library/research/2010/01/chronic-care.html

Roberts, J. A., D. Brown, T. Elkins, and D. B. Larson. 1997. Factors influencing the views of patients with gynecologic cancer about end-of-life decisions. *American Journal of Obstetrics and Gynecology* 176: 166–172.

Rosen G. 1993. *A History of Public Health*. Baltimore, MD: Johns Hopkins University Press.

Ross, L. 1995. The spiritual dimension: Its importance to patients' health, well-being and quality of life and its implications for nursing practice. *International Journal of Nursing Studies* 32: 457–468.

Santerre, R. E., and S. P. Neun. 2010. *Health Economics: Theory, Insights, and Industry Studies*. Mason, OH: South-Western Cengage Learning.

Satcher, D. 2010. Include a social determinants of health approach to reduce health inequities. *Public Health Reports* 4: 6–7.

Saward, E., and A. Sorensen. 1980. The current emphasis on preventive medicine. In: *Issues in Health Services*. S. J. Williams, ed. New York, NY: John Wiley & Sons. 17–29.

Schimmelpfennig, R., S. Vogt, S. Ehret, and C. Efferson. 2021. Promotion of behavioural change for health in a heterogeneous population. *Bulletin of the World Health Organization* 99: 819–827. Available at: https://doi.org/10.2471/BLT.20.285227

Schneider M. J. 2000. *Introduction to Public Health*. Gaithersburg, MD: Aspen.

Shi, L., and J. Johnson, eds. 2014. *Public Health Administration: Principles for Population-based Management*. 3rd ed. Burlington, MA: Jones & Bartlett Learning.

Shi, L., and B. Starfield. 2001. Primary care physician supply, income inequality, and racial mortality in U.S. metropolitan areas. *American Journal of Public Health* 91: 1246–1250.

Shi, L., B. Starfield, B. Kennedy, and I. Kawachi. 1999. Income inequality, primary care, and health indicators. *Journal of Family Practice* 48: 275–284.

Shi, L., B. Starfield, R. Politzer, and J. Regan. 2002. Primary care, self-rated health, and reduction in social disparities in health. *Health Services Research* 37: 529–550.

Simmons-Duffin, S. 2020. *Some insurers waive patients' share of costs for COVID-19 treatment*. NPR. Accessed May 2020. Available at: https://www.npr.org/sections/health-shots/2020/03/30/824075753/good-news-with-caveats-some-insurers-waive-costs-to-patients-for-covid-19-treatm

Sirec, T., and T. Benedyk. 2018. *Tackling emerging problems with One Health approaches: Zika virus*. Accessed April 2020. Available at: https://fems-microbiology.org/tackling-emerging-problems-one-health-approaches-zika-virus/

Smith B. C. 1979. *Community Health: An Epidemiological Approach*. New York: Macmillan.

Solar, O., and A. Irwin; World Health Organization (WHO). 2010. *A Conceptual Framework for Action on the Social Determinants of Health. Social Determinants of Health Discussion Paper 2 (Policy and Practice)*. Geneva, Switzerland: WHO.

Song, M., and E. Giovannucci. 2016. Preventable incidence and mortality of carcinoma associated with lifestyle factors among white adults in the United States. *JAMA Oncology* 9: 1154–1161.

Soucheray, S. 2017. *WHO: Viral Hepatitis Deaths Increasing*. Accessed January 2020. Available at: http://www.cidrap.umn.edu/news-perspective/2017/04/who-viral-hepatitis-deaths-increasing

Stellefson, M., S. R. Paige, B. H. Chaney, and J. D. Chaney. 2020. Evolving role of social media in health promotion: Updated responsibilities for health education specialists. *International Journal of Environmental Research and Public Health* 17: 1153. Available at: https://doi.org/10.3390/ijerph17041153

Stock, C. (2022). Grand challenges for public health education and promotion. *Frontiers in Public Health* 10: 917685.

Stopford, B. 2005. The National Disaster Medical System: America's medical readiness force. *Disaster Management and Response* 53–56.

Swanson, C. S. 1995. A spirit-focused conceptual model of nursing for the advanced practice nurse. *Issues in Comprehensive Pediatric Nursing* 18: 267–275.

Taylor, A., A. Fram, and K. Freking. 2020. *Trump signs $484 billion measure to aid employers, hospitals*. AP News. Accessed May 2020. Available at: https://apnews.com/article/77bcfddcdcc80a249e7def8410d630a8

Thompson, W. 2020. *COVID-19 now reaching into rural America*. U.S. News & World Report. Accessed May 2020. Available at: https://www.usnews.com/news/health-news/articles/2020-05-12/covid-19-now-reaching-into-rural-america

Thompson, W. W., E. Weintraub, P. Dhankhar, et al. 2009. Estimates of US influenza-associated deaths made using four different methods. *Influenza and Other Respiratory Viruses* 3: 37–49.

Timmreck, T. C. 1994. *An Introduction to Epidemiology*. Boston, MA: Jones & Bartlett Learning.

Tsao, C. W. 2022. Heart disease and stroke statistics—2022 update: A report from the American Heart Association. *Circulation* 145: e153–e639.

Turnock, B. J. 1997. *Public Health: What It Is and How It Works*. Gaithersburg, MD: Aspen.

U.S. Census Bureau. 2016. *An Aging World: 2015 International Population Reports*. Accessed February 2017. Available at: https://www.census.gov/content/dam/Census/library/publications/2016/demo/p95-16-1.pdf

U.S. Food and Drug Administration (FDA). 2019. *First FDA-Approved Vaccine for the Prevention of Ebola Virus Disease, Marking a Critical Milestone in Public Health Preparedness and Response*. Accessed January 2020. Available at: https://www.fda.gov/news-events/press-announcements/first-fda-approved-vaccine-prevention-ebola-virus-disease-marking-critical-milestone-public-health

Ungar, L., and E. Lucas. 2020. *Millions stuck at home with no plumbing, kitchen, or space to stay safe*. Kaiser Health News. Accessed May 2020. Available at: https://khn.org/news/millions-stuck-at-home-with-no-plumbing-kitchen-or-space-to-stay-safe/

Vella-Brodrick, D. A., and F. C. Allen. 1995. Development and psychometric validation of the mental, physical, and spiritual well-being scale. *Psychological Reports* 77: 659–674.

Vereen, R. N., R. Kurtzman, and S. M. Noar, (2023). Are social media interventions for health behavior change efficacious among populations with health disparities? A meta-analytic review. *Health Communication* 38: 133–140. Available at: https://doi.org/10.1080/10410236.2021.1937830

Wakefield, M. A., B. Loken, and R.C. Hornik. 2010. Use of mass media campaigns to change health behavior. *Lancet* 376: 1261–1271. doi:10.1016/S0140-6736(10)60809-4

Walsh, L., H. Craddock, K. Gulley, K. Strauss-Riggs, and K. W. Schor. 2015. Building health care system capacity to respond to disasters: Successes and challenges of disaster preparedness health care coalitions. *Prehospital Disaster Medicine* 30: 112–122.

Ward, A. 2020. *Exclusive: Senators urge Trump to use Defense Production Act to make more COVID-19 tests*. Vox. Accessed May 2020. Available at: https://www.vox.com/2020/5/6/21249233/coronavirus-defense-production-act-ppe-tests-trump

Ward, B. 1995. Holistic medicine. *Australian Family Physician* 24: 761–762, 765.

Waters, H., and M. Graf. 2018. *The cost of chronic diseases in the U.S.: Executive summary*. Milken Institute. Accessed January 9, 2020. Available at: https://assets1b.milkeninstitute.org/assets/Publication/Viewpoint/PDF/Chronic-Disease-Executive-Summary-r2.pdf

Winkleby, M. A., C. Cubbin, D. K. Ahn, and H. C. Kraemer. 2006. Pathways by which SES and ethnicity influence cardiovascular disease risk factors. *Annals of the New York Academy of Sciences* 896: 191–209.

Winkleby, M. A., D. E. Jatulis, E. Frank, and S. P. Fortmann. 1992. Socioeconomic status and health: how education, income, and occupation contribute to risk factors for cardiovascular disease. *American Journal of Public Health* 82: 816–820.

WHO Commission on Social Determinants of Health. 2008. *Closing the gap in a generation: Health equity through action on the social determinants of health*. World Health Organization. Accessed February 2021. Available at: https://apps.who.int/iris/bitstream/handle/10665/43943/9789241563703_eng.pdf?sequence=1

WHO Ebola Response Team. 2016. After Ebola in West Africa: Unpredictable risks, preventable epidemics. *New England Journal of Medicine* 375: 587–596. Available at: https://www.nejm.org/doi/full/10.1056/NEJMsr1513109

Wilkinson, R. G. 1997. Income, inequality, and social cohesion. *American Journal of Public Health* 87: 1504–1506.

Wolfe, N. D., P. Daszak, A. M. Kilpatrick, D. S. Burke. 2005. Bushmeat hunting, deforestation, and prediction of zoonotic disease. *Emerging Infection Diseases* 11: 1822–1827. Available at: https://dx.doi.org/10.3201/eid1112.040789

World Health Organization (WHO). 2021. Health systems for health security: a framework fordeveloping capacities for international health regulations, and components in health systems and other sectors that work in synergy to meet the demands imposed by health emergencies. Available at: https://www.who.int/publications/i/item/9789240029682

World Health Organization (WHO). 2023. *Health Security*. Available at: https://www.who.int/health-topics/health-security#tab=tab_1

World Health Organization (WHO). 2023. *Hepatitis C*. Accessed September 2023. Available at: https://www.who.int/news-room/fact-sheets/detail/hepatitis-c

World Health Organization (WHO). 2023a. *MERS Situation Update 2023*. Accessed September 2023. Available at: http://www.emro.who.int/health-topics/mers-cov/mers-outbreaks.html

World Health Organization (WHO). 2023b. *Malaria*. Accessed September 2023. Available at: https://www.who.int/news-room/fact-sheets/detail/malaria

World Health Organization (WHO). 2023c. *Tuberculosis*. Accessed September 2023. Available at: https://www.who.int/news-room/fact-sheets/detail/tuberculosis

World Health Organization (WHO). 2023d. *HIV and AIDS*. Accessed September 2023. Available at: https://www.who.int/news-room/fact-sheets/detail/hiv-aids

World Health Organization (WHO). 2023e. *Hepatitis B*. Accessed September 2023. Available at: https://www.who.int/news-room/fact-sheets/detail/hepatitis-b

World Health Organization (WHO). 2023f. WHO coronavirus disease (COVID-19) dashboard. Accessed September 2023. Available at: https://covid19.who.int

World Health Organization. 2023. *Health Promotion*. Available at: https://www.who.int/health-topics/health-promotion#tab=tab_1

World Health Organization. 2022. *World Malaria Report 2022*. World Health Organization. Accessed September 2023. Available at: https://www.who.int/news-room/fact-sheets/detail/malaria

Wood, W., and D. T. Neal, 2016. Healthy through habit: Interventions for initiating and maintaining health behavior change. *Behavioral Science & Policy* 2: 71–83. doi:10.1353/bsp.2016.0008

World Cancer Research Fund and American Institute for Cancer Research (AICR). 2007. *Food, Nutrition, Physical Activity, and the Prevention of Cancer: A Global Perspective*. Washington DC: AICR. Accessed February 2021. Available at: https://www.rwjf.org/en/library/research/2010/01/chronic-care.html

World Health Organization (WHO). 1948. *Preamble to the Constitution*. Geneva, Switzerland: WHO. Accessed April 2017. Available at: http://www.who.int/governance/eb/who_constitution_en.pdf

World Health Organization (WHO). 2003. *WHO Definition of Palliative Care*. Geneva, Switzerland: WHO.

World Health Organization (WHO). 2011. *Noncommunicable diseases country profiles: United States of America*. Accessed August 2013. Available at: http://www.who.int/nmh/countries/usa_en.pdf

World Health Organization (WHO). 2013. *Pandemic influenza preparedness framework*. Accessed August 2013. Available at: http://www.who.int/influenza/resources/pip_framework/en/

World Health Organization (WHO). 2015. *World health statistics. Part II: Global health indicators*. Accessed April 2017. Available at: http://www.who.int/gho/publications/world_health_statistics/EN_WHS2015_Part2.pdf

World Health Organization (WHO). 2016a. *Fact sheet: Ebola Virus Disease*. Accessed January 2017. Available at: http://www.who.int/mediacentre/factsheets/fs103/en/

World Health Organization (WHO). 2016b. Prevent HIV, test and treat all: WHO support for country impact: Progress report 2016. Geneva, Switzerland: WHO.

World Health Organization (WHO). 2017. *One health*. Accessed March 2020. Available at: https://www.who.int/features/qa/one-health/en/

World Health Organization (WHO). 2018a. *Global Health Observatory data: HIV/AIDS*. Accessed January 2020. Available at: https://www.who.int/gho/hiv/en/

World Health Organization (WHO). 2018b. *Influenza (Seasonal)*. Accessed January 19, 2020. Available at: https://www.who.int/news-room/fact-sheets/detail/influenza-(seasonal)

World Health Organization (WHO). 2018c. *Zika Virus*. Accessed April 13, 2020. Available at: https://www.who.int/news-room/fact-sheets/detail/zika-virus

World Health Organization (WHO). 2019a. *Hepatitis B*. Accessed January 11, 2020. Available at: https://www.who.int/news-room/fact-sheets/detail/hepatitis-b

Yabroff K. R., J. Lund, D. Kepka, and A. Mariotto. 2011. Economic burden of cancer in the United States: Estimates, projections, and future research. *Cancer Epidemiology, Biomarkers, & Prevention* 20: 2006–2014.

Yancy C. W. 2020. COVID-19 and African Americans. *Journal of the American Medical Association*. 323: 1891–1892 doi:10.1001/jama.2020.6548

Young S. 2014. Healthy behavior change in practical settings. *Permanente Journal* 18: 89–92. doi:10.7812/TPP/14-018

Zhang, X. X., J. S. Liu, L. F. Han, et al.2022. Towards a global One Health index: a potential assessment tool for One Health performance. *Infectious Diseases of Poverty* 11: 57. Available at: https://doi.org/10.1186/s40249-022-00979-9

Zhou, L., and E. Nilsen. 2020. The House just passed a $2 trillion coronavirus stimulus package. It now heads to Trump's desk. *Vox*. Accessed May 2020. Available at: https://www.vox.com/2020/3/27/21196202/house-passes-2-trillion-coronavirus-stimulus-package

CHAPTER 3

The Evolution of Health Services in the United States

LEARNING OBJECTIVES

- Discover historical developments that have shaped the U.S. healthcare delivery system.
- Understand the history of mental health care in the United States.
- Evaluate why the system has been resistant to national health insurance reforms.
- Explore the corporatization of health care.
- Identify the globalization of health care.
- Obtain a historical perspective on the Affordable Care Act, its legacy, and current status.

Where's the market?

Introduction

Delivery of health care in the United States evolved quite differently from the systems in Europe. The U.S. healthcare system has been shaped by the country's anthro-cultural values and a series of social, political, and economic antecedents. Because social, political, and economic contexts are not static, their shifting influences lend a certain dynamism to the healthcare delivery system. Conversely, cultural beliefs and values remain relatively stable over time. As a consequence of the persistent resistance of American anthro-cultural values to a government-run national healthcare program, initiatives toward establishing such a system had long failed to make any significant progress. Instead, the interaction of forces just mentioned led to certain compromises that resulted in incremental changes over time. Incremental changes, both small and large, since 1935 have gradually shifted U.S. health care from a mainly private enterprise to one in which both the private and public sectors have a substantial role in financing healthcare insurance for different population groups in the United States.

American medicine did not emerge as a professional entity until the beginning of the 20th century, with the progress in biomedical science. Since then, the U.S. healthcare delivery system has been a growth enterprise. The evolution of medical science and technology has played a key role in shaping the U.S. healthcare delivery system and has been a primary factor in fueling the growth of national healthcare expenditures. Advancement of technology has influenced other factors as well, such as medical education, growth of alternative settings for health services delivery, and corporatization of medicine. In many respects, healthcare delivery has also become a global enterprise.

This chapter traces the evolution of healthcare delivery through historical phases, each demarcating a major change in the structure of the delivery system. The first evolutionary phase is the preindustrial era from the middle of the 18th century to the latter part of the 19th century. The second phase is the postindustrial era beginning in the late 19th century. The third phase—called the corporate era—became recognized in the latter part of the 20th century. Corporatization of medicine has played a major role in the globalization of health care.

During the Obama presidency, healthcare reform took center stage in American politics. The Patient Protection and Affordable Care Act (ACA) was passed in 2010 to bring about sweeping changes in U.S. healthcare delivery. President Donald Trump's 2016 promise to "repeal and replace" the ACA has only partially materialized, mainly because in 2017, Republicans in the U.S. Congress failed to pass their own healthcare program to replace the ACA. Even President Trump's 2017 limited Executive Order 13765 (in anticipation of a repeal of the Patient Protection and Affordable Care Act) and Executive Order 13813 (allowing insurance companies to sell low-cost, short-term plans with lesser coverage) were later revoked by President Biden in 2021 after he took office (Whitehouse.gov, 2023). President Joe Biden reopened enrollment on ACA in January 2021, taking a step to help uninsured Americans that former President Donald Trump rejected.

The practice of medicine is central to the delivery of health care; therefore, a portion of this chapter is devoted to tracing the transformations in medical practice from a weak and insecure trade to an independent, highly respected, and lucrative profession. Developments since the corporatization stage, however, have made a significant impact on practice styles and have compromised the autonomy that physicians had historically enjoyed. **Exhibit 3-1** provides an overview snapshot of the historical developments in U.S. healthcare delivery.

Exhibit 3.1 Evolution of the U.S. Healthcare Delivery System

Development of Science and Technology

Mid-18th to Late 19th Century	Late 19th to Late 20th Century	Late 20th to 21st Century

■ Open entry into medical practice
■ Intense competition
■ Weak and unorganized profession
■ Apprenticeship training
■ Undeveloped hospitals
■ Almshouses and pesthouses
■ Dispensaries
■ Mental asylums
■ Private payment for services
■ Low demand for services
■ Private medical schools providing only general education
	■ Scientific basis of medicine
	■ Urbanization
	■ Emergence of the modern hospital
	■ Emergence of organized medicine
	■ Reform of medical training
	■ Licensing
	■ Specialization in medicine
	■ Development of public health
	■ Community mental health
	■ Birth of worker's compensation
	■ Emergence of private insurance
	■ Failure of national health insurance
	■ Medicaid and Medicare
		■ Corporatization
		  • Managed care
		  • Organizational integration
		  • Diluted physician autonomy
		■ Globalization
		  • Global telemedicine
		  • Medical tourism
		  • U.S. healthcare investment abroad
		  • Migration of professionals
		  • Global health
		■ Era of healthcare reform
		  • Affordable Care Act
		  • Prospects for new reforms

Consumer sovereignty	Professional dominance	Government and corporate dominance

Beliefs and values/Social, economic, and political constraints

Medical Services in the Preindustrial Era

From colonial times to the beginning of the 20th century, American medicine lagged behind the advances in medical science, experimental research, and medical education that were taking place in Great Britain, France, and Germany. While London, Paris, and Berlin flourished as major research centers, Americans had a tendency to neglect research in basic sciences and to place more emphasis on applied science (Shryock, 1966).

Native Americans' medical traditions are known to have used various herbs found in their natural environments. Various herbs were chewed, juiced, or used in concoctions. They were prescribed to treat various ailments not only among the Native populations but also among early North American settlers (Rana et al., 2014). Some of these remedies are still in use today outside mainstream medicine.

The practice of medicine in the United States had a strong domestic rather than professional character. Medical services, when deemed appropriate by the consumer, were purchased out of one's private funds because there was no health insurance. The healthcare market was characterized by competition among providers, and the consumer decided who the provider would be. Thus, the consumer was sovereign in the healthcare market and health care was delivered under free market conditions. Five main factors explain why the medical profession remained largely an insignificant trade in preindustrial America:

- Medical practice was in disarray.
- Medical procedures were primitive.
- An institutional core was missing.
- Demand was unstable.
- Medical education was substandard.

Medical Practice in Disarray

The early practice of medicine could be regarded more as a trade than a profession. It did not require the rigorous course of study, clinical practice, residency training, board exams, or licensing, without which it is impossible to practice today. At the close of the Civil War (1861–1865), "anyone who had the inclination to set himself up as a physician could do so, the exigencies of the market alone determining who would prove successful in the field and who would not" (Hamowy, 1979). The clergy, for example, often combined medical services and religious duties. The generally well-educated clergyman or government official was more learned in medicine than physicians were at the time (Shryock, 1966). Tradesmen, such as tailors, barbers, commodity merchants, and persons engaged in numerous other trades, also practiced the healing arts by selling herbal prescriptions, nostrums, elixirs, and cathartics. Likewise, midwives, homeopaths, and naturalists could practice medicine without being subject to any restrictions. The red-and-white striped poles (symbolizing blood and bandages) outside barbershops are reminders that barbers also functioned as surgeons at one time, using the same blade to cut hair, shave beards, and bleed the sick.

This era of medical pluralism has been referred to as a "war zone" by Kaptchuk and Eisenberg (2001), because it was marked by bitter antagonism among the various practicing sects. Eventually, in 1847, the American Medical Association (AMA) was founded with the main purpose of erecting a barrier between orthodox practitioners and the "irregulars" (Rothstein, 1972).

In the absence of minimum standards of medical training, entry into private practice was relatively easy for both trained and untrained practitioners, creating intense competition. Medicine as a profession was weak and unorganized. Hence, physicians did not enjoy the prestige, influence, and incomes that they later earned. Many physicians found it necessary to engage in a second occupation because income from medical practice alone was inadequate to support a family. It is estimated that most physicians' incomes in the mid-19th century placed them at the lower end of the middle class (Starr, 1982). In 1830, there were approximately 6,800 physicians in the United States, serving primarily the upper classes (Gabe et al., 1994). It was not until 1870 that medical education was reformed and licensing laws were passed in the United States.

Primitive Medical Procedures

Up until the mid-1800s, medical care was based more on primitive medical traditions than on science. In the absence of diagnostic tools, a theory of "intake and outgo" served as an explanation for all diseases (Rosenberg, 1979). It was believed that diseases needed to be expelled from the body. Hence, bleeding, use of emetics (to induce vomiting) and diuretics (to increase urination), and purging with enemas and purgatives (to clean the bowels) were popular forms of clinical therapy.

When George Washington became ill with an inflamed throat in 1799, he too was bled by physicians. One of the attending physicians argued, unsuccessfully, in favor of making an incision to open the trachea, which today would be considered a more enlightened procedure. The bleeding most likely weakened Washington's resistance, and historians have debated whether it played a role in his death (Clark, 1998).

Surgeries were limited because anesthesia had not yet been developed and antiseptic techniques were not known. Stethoscopes and X-rays had not been invented, clinical thermometers were not in use, and microscopes were not available to obtain a better understanding of pathology. Physicians relied mainly on their five senses and experience to diagnose and treat medical problems. Hence, in most cases, physicians did not possess any technical expertise greater than that of the mothers and grandparents at home or experienced neighbors in the community.

Missing Institutional Core

In the United States, widespread development of hospitals did not occur before the 1880s. A few isolated hospitals were either built or developed in rented private houses in large cities, such as Philadelphia, New York, Boston, Cincinnati, New Orleans, and St. Louis. By contrast, general hospital expansion began long before the 1800s in France and Great Britain (Stevens, 1971).

In Europe, medical professionals were closely associated with hospitals. New advances in medical science were being pioneered, which European hospitals readily adopted. The medical profession came to be highly regarded because of its close association with an establishment that was scientifically advanced. In contrast, American hospitals played only a small part in medical practice because most hospitals served a social welfare function by taking care of people with socioeconomic status, those without families, or those who were away from home on travel.

The Almshouse and the Pesthouse

In the United States, the **almshouse**, also called a poorhouse, was the common ancestor of both hospitals and nursing homes. The poorhouse program was adopted from the Elizabethan system of public charity based on English Poor Laws. The first poorhouse in the United States is recorded to have opened in 1660 in Boston (Wagner, 2005). Almshouses served primarily general welfare functions by providing food and shelter to the destitute of society. Therefore, the main function of the almshouse was custodial. Caring for the sick was incidental because some of the residents would inevitably become ill and would be cared for in an adjoining infirmary. Almshouses were unspecialized institutions that admitted impoverished and needy persons of all kinds: older adults, the orphaned, people who were mentally or physically ill, and people with disabilities. Hence, the early hospital-type institutions emerged mainly to take care of indigent people whose families could not care for them.

Another type of institution, the **pesthouse**, was operated by local governments (primarily in seaports) to quarantine people who had contracted a contagious disease, such as cholera, smallpox, typhoid, or yellow fever. The main function of a pesthouse was to isolate people with contagious diseases to prevent the spread of disease among the population. These institutions were the predecessors of contagious disease and tuberculosis hospitals.

The Dispensary

Dispensaries were established as outpatient clinics, independent of hospitals, to provide free care to those who could not afford to pay. Urban workers and their families often depended on such charity (Rosen, 1983).

Starting with Philadelphia in 1786, dispensaries gradually spread to other cities.

These private institutions were financed by bequests and voluntary subscriptions. Their main function was to provide basic medical care and to dispense drugs to ambulatory patients (Raffel, 1980). Generally, young physicians and medical students desiring clinical experience staffed the dispensaries as well as hospital wards on a part-time basis for little or no income (Martensen, 1996). This model served a dual purpose: it provided needed services to the poor and it enabled both physicians and medical students to gain experience in diagnosing and treating a variety of cases. Later, as the practice of specialized medicine as well as teaching and research was transferred to hospital settings, many dispensaries were gradually absorbed into hospitals as outpatient departments. Indeed, outpatient or ambulatory care departments became an important locale for specialty consultation services within large hospitals (Raffel, 1980).

The Mental Asylum

Mental health care was perceived as largely the responsibility of state and local governments. At this time, little was known about what caused mental illness or how to treat it. Although some mental health patients were confined to almshouses, asylums were built by states for patients with untreatable, chronic mental illness. The first such asylum was built around 1770 in Williamsburg, Virginia. When the Pennsylvania Hospital opened in Philadelphia in 1752, its basement was used as a mental asylum. Attendants in these asylums employed physical and psychological techniques, with the aim of returning patients to some level of rational thinking. Techniques such as bleeding, forced vomiting, and hot and ice-cold baths were also used.

Between 1894 and World War I, the State Care Acts were passed, centralizing financial responsibility for patients with mental disorders in every state government. Local governments took advantage of this opportunity to send all those persons with a mental disorder, including dependent older citizens, to the state asylums. The quality of care in public asylums deteriorated rapidly, as overcrowding and underfunding ran rampant (U.S. Surgeon General, 1999). Subsequent reforms are discussed in the section "Reform of Mental Health Care."

The Dreaded Hospital

Not until the 1850s were hospitals similar to those in Europe developed in the United States. These early hospitals had deplorable conditions due to a lack of resources. Poor sanitation and inadequate ventilation were hallmarks of these facilities. Unhygienic practices prevailed because nurses were unskilled and untrained. The early hospitals also had an undesirable image of being houses of death. The mortality rate among hospital patients, both in Europe and America, stood around 74% in the 1870s (Falk, 1999). People went into hospitals because of dire consequences, not by personal choice. It is not hard to imagine why members of the middle and upper classes in particular shunned such establishments.

Unstable Demand

Professional services suffered from low demand in the mainly rural, preindustrial society, and much of the medical care was provided by people who were not physicians. The most competent physicians were located in more populated communities (Bordley and Harvey, 1976). In the small communities of rural America, a strong spirit of self-reliance prevailed. Families and communities were accustomed to treating the sick, often using folk remedies passed from one generation to the next. It was also common to consult published books and pamphlets that gave advice on home remedies (Rosen, 1983).

The market for physicians' services was also limited by economic conditions in rural America. Many families could not afford to pay for medical services. Two factors contributed to the high costs associated with obtaining professional medical care:

- The indirect costs of transportation and the "opportunity cost" of travel (i.e., the forgone value of time that could have been used for something more productive) could easily outweigh the direct costs of physicians' fees.
- The costs of travel often doubled because two people, the patient and the caretaker, had to make the trip back and forth. For a farmer, as an example, a trip into town could mean an entire day's work lost. Hence, most families obtained only occasional intervention from physicians, generally for nonroutine and severe conditions.

Personal health services had to be purchased without the help of government or private insurance. Private practice and **fee for service**—the practice of billing separately for each individual type of service performed—became firmly embedded in American medical care.

Similar to physicians, dentists were private entrepreneurs who made their living by private fee-for-service dental practice. Their services were not in great demand, however, because there was little public concern about dental health during this era (Anderson, 1990).

Substandard Medical Education

From about 1800 to 1850, medical training was largely received through individual apprenticeship with a practicing physician, referred to as a preceptor, rather than through university education. Many of the preceptors were themselves poorly trained, especially in basic medical sciences (Rothstein, 1972). By 1800, only four small medical schools were operating in the United States: College of Philadelphia (whose medical school was established in 1756, which later became the University of Pennsylvania), King's College (whose medical school was established in 1768, which later became Columbia University), Harvard Medical School (opened in 1782), and the Geisel School of Medicine at Dartmouth College (started in 1797).

American physicians later established medical schools in large numbers, partly to enhance their professional status and prestige and partly to enhance their income. Medical schools were inexpensive to operate and often quite profitable. All that was required was a faculty of four or more physicians, a classroom, a back room in which to conduct dissections, and legal authority to confer degrees. Operating expenses were met totally out of student fees that were paid directly to the physicians (Rothstein, 1972). Physicians would affiliate with a local college for the conferral of degrees and use of classroom facilities. Large numbers of men entered medical practice, as education in medicine became readily available and unrestricted entry into the profession was still possible (Hamowy, 1979). Since few women went to medical schools in the earlier years, there were very few practicing female physicians. Gradually, as physicians from medical schools began to outnumber those from the apprenticeship system, the Doctor of Medicine (MD) degree became the standard of competence. The number of medical schools tripled between 1800 and 1820, then tripled again between 1820 and 1850, with 42 being in operation by 1850 (Rothstein, 1972). Academic preparation gradually replaced apprenticeship training.

At this point, medical education in the United States was seriously deficient in science-based training, unlike in European medical schools. Medical schools in the United States did not have laboratories, and clinical observation and practice were not part of the curriculum. In contrast, European medical schools, particularly those in Germany, emphasized laboratory-based medical research. At the University of Berlin, for example, professors were expected to conduct research as well as teach and were paid by the state. In contrast, in American medical schools, students were taught by local practitioners, who were ill-equipped in education and training. Unlike in Europe, where medical education was financed and regulated by the government, proprietary medical schools in the United States set their own standards (Numbers and Warner, 1985). A "year" of medical school in the United States generally lasted only 4 months, and only 2 years of attendance was required for graduation. In addition, American medical students customarily repeated the same courses they had taken during their first year during their second year (Numbers and Warner, 1985; Rosner, 2001). The physicians' desire to keep their schools profitable also contributed to low standards and a lack of rigor. They feared that higher standards in medical education would drive enrollments down, which could force the schools into bankruptcy (Starr, 1982).

Medical Services in the Postindustrial Era

In the postindustrial period, American physicians were highly successful in retaining the private practice of medicine and resisting government involvement in health care. Physicians delivered scientifically and technically advanced services to patients who were insured; became an organized medical profession; and gained power, prestige, and financial success. Notably, much of this transformation occurred in the aftermath of the Civil War. Social and scientific changes in the period following the war were accompanied by a transition from a rural, agricultural economy to a system of industrial capitalism in the United States. Mass production techniques used in the war were applied to peacetime industries. Railroads linked the east and west coasts of the country, and small towns became cities (Stevens, 1971).

The American system for delivering health care took its current shape during this period. The well-defined role of employers in providing worker's compensation for work-related injuries and illnesses, together with other economic considerations, was instrumental in the growth of private health insurance. Even though attempts to pass national healthcare legislation failed, the rising costs of health care prompted Congress to create publicly financed programs, such as Medicare and Medicaid, to cover the most vulnerable members of society.

Growth of Professional Sovereignty

The 1920s represented a milestone in the consolidation of physicians' professional power. During and after World War I, physicians' incomes grew dramatically and their prominence as members of a true profession finally emerged. Of course, this prestige and power did not materialize overnight. Through the years, several factors interacted to gradually transform medicine from a weak, insecure, and isolated trade into a profession of power and authority. Seven key factors contributed to this transformation:

- Urbanization
- Science and technology
- Institutionalization
- Dependency
- Autonomy and organization
- Licensing
- Educational reform

Urbanization

In 1840, only 11% of the U.S. population lived in urban areas; by 1900, the proportion of the U.S. population living in urban areas had grown to 40% (Stevens, 1971). As more and more Americans moved to the burgeoning towns and cities to find jobs, they were distanced from their families and the neighborhoods where family based care was traditionally given. Women began working outside the home and could no longer care for sick members of the family. Also, physicians became less expensive to consult as telephones, automobiles, and paved roads reduced the cost of time and travel and medical care became more affordable. Thus, urbanization created increased reliance on the specialized skills of paid professionals.

The trend away from home visits and toward office practice also began to develop around this time (Rosen, 1983). Physicians moved to cities and towns in large numbers to be closer to their growing markets. Better geographic proximity to their patients enabled physicians to book more patients in a given amount of time. Whereas physicians in 1850 saw, on average, only 5–7 patients per day, by the early 1940s, the average patient load of general practitioners had risen to 18–22 patients per day (Starr, 1982).

Science and Technology

Exhibit 3-2 summarizes some of the groundbreaking scientific discoveries in medicine during the postindustrial era. Advances in bacteriology, antiseptic surgery, anesthesia, immunology, and diagnostic techniques, along with an expanding repertoire of new drugs, gave medicine an aura of legitimacy and complexity. Now, medical practice could no longer remain within the domain of lay competence; instead, advanced technical knowledge became essential. Specialized training became necessary for using new technology in the diagnosis and treatment of disease. The therapeutic effectiveness of scientific medicine became widely recognized. Thus, physicians gained **cultural authority**—the general acceptance of and reliance on the judgment of the members of a profession (Starr, 1982) because of their superior knowledge and expertise.

Exhibit 3.2 Groundbreaking Medical Discoveries

- The discovery of anesthesia was instrumental in advancing the practice of surgery. Nitrous oxide (laughing gas) was first employed as an anesthetic around 1846 for tooth extraction by Horace Wells, a dentist. Ether anesthesia for surgery was first successfully used in 1846 at Massachusetts General Hospital. Before anesthesia was discovered, strong doses of alcohol were used to dull the sensations. A surgeon who could do procedures, such as limb amputations, in the shortest length of time was held in high regard.
- Around 1847, Ignaz Semmelweis, a Hungarian physician practicing in a hospital in Vienna, implemented the policy of handwashing. Thus, aseptic technique was born. Semmelweis was concerned about the high death rate from puerperal fever among women after childbirth. Even though the germ theory of disease was unknown at this time, Semmelweis surmised that there might be a connection between puerperal fever and the common practice by medical students of not washing their hands before delivering babies and right after doing dissections. Semmelweis's hunch was right.
- Louis Pasteur, a French scientist, is generally credited with pioneering the germ theory of disease and microbiology around 1860. Pasteur demonstrated sterilization techniques, such as boiling to kill microorganisms and withholding exposure to air to prevent contamination.
- Joseph Lister, a British surgeon, is often referred to as the father of antiseptic surgery. Around 1865, Lister used carbolic acid to wash wounds and popularized the chemical inhibition of infection (antisepsis) during surgery.
- Advances in diagnostics and imaging can be traced to the invention of x-rays in 1895 by Wilhelm Roentgen, a German professor of physics. Radiology became the first machine-based medical specialty. Some of the first training schools in X-ray therapy and radiography in the United States attracted photographers and electricians to become doctors in roentgenology (from the inventor's name).
- Alexander Fleming, a Scottish scientist, discovered the antibacterial properties of penicillin in 1929.

Physicians' cultural authority was further bolstered when medical decisions became necessary in various aspects of healthcare delivery. For example, physicians decide whether a person should be admitted to a hospital or a nursing home and for how long, whether surgical or nonsurgical treatments should be used, and which medications should be prescribed. Laws were later passed that prohibited individuals from obtaining certain classes of drugs without a physician's prescription. Physicians' decisions have a profound influence on other providers and nonproviders alike. The judgment and opinions of physicians even affect aspects of a person's life outside the delivery of health care. For example, physicians often evaluate the fitness of persons for jobs during the pre-employment physical examinations that many employers require. Physicians assess the disability of the ill and the injured in worker's compensation cases. Likewise, granting of medical leave for sickness and release back to work require authorizations from physicians. Health insurance pays for treatments only when they are rendered or prescribed by physicians. Other healthcare professionals, such as nurses, therapists, and dietitians, are expected to follow physicians' orders for treatment. Thus, during disease and disability, and sometimes even in good health, people's lives have become increasingly governed by decisions made by physicians.

Institutionalization

The evolution of medical technology and the professionalization of medical and nursing staffs enabled advanced treatments that necessitated the pooling of resources in a common arena of care (Burns, 2004). As had already occurred in Europe, in the United States, hospitals became the core around which the delivery of medical services was organized. Thus, development of hospitals as the center for the practice of scientific medicine and the professionalization of medical practice became closely intertwined.

Indeed, physicians and hospitals developed a symbiotic relationship. For economic reasons, as hospitals expanded, their survival became increasingly dependent on physicians to keep the beds filled because the physicians decided where to hospitalize their patients. Therefore, hospitals had to make every effort to keep the physicians satisfied, which enhanced physicians' professional dominance, even though they were not employees of the hospitals. Thus, physicians exerted enormous influence over hospital policy.

The expansion of surgery had profound implications for hospitals, physicians, and the public. As hospitals added specialized facilities and staff, their regular use became indispensable to physicians and surgeons, who in earlier times had been able to manage their practices with little reference to hospitals (Martensen, 1996).

Hospitals in the United States did not expand and become more directly related to medical care until the late 1890s. However, as late as the 1930s, hospitals continued to experience frequent deaths among their patients due to infections that could not be prevented or cured. Despite these problems, hospital use increased due to the great influx of immigrants into large American cities (Falk, 1999). From only a few dozen facilities in 1875, the number of general hospitals in the United States exploded to 4,000 facilities by 1900 (Anderson, 1990) and to 5,000 facilities by 1913 (Wright, 1997).

Dependency

Patients depend on the medical profession's judgment and assistance. This dependency is created because society expects a sick person to seek medical help and try to get well. The patient is then expected to comply with medical instructions. In addition, dependency is created by the profession's cultural authority because its medical judgments must be relied on to (1) legitimize a person's sickness; (2) exempt the individual from social role obligations, such as work or school; and (3) provide competent medical care so the person can get well and resume their social role obligations. Moreover, the need for hospital services for critical illness and surgery creates dependency when patients are transferred from their homes to a hospital or surgery center. The referral role (gatekeeping) of primary care physicians in some managed care plans has also increased patients' dependency on primary care physicians for referral to specialized services.

Autonomy and Organization

For a long time, physicians' ability to remain free of control from hospitals and insurance companies remained a prominent feature of American medicine. Hospitals and insurance companies could have hired physicians on salary to provide medical services, but individual physicians who took up practice in a corporate setting were castigated by the medical profession and pressured to abandon such practices. In some states, courts ruled that corporations could not employ licensed physicians without engaging in the unlicensed practice of medicine, a legal doctrine that became known as the "corporate practice doctrine" (Farmer and Douglas, 2001). Independence from corporate control promoted private entrepreneurship and put American physicians in an enviable strategic position in relation to hospitals and insurance companies. Later, a formally organized medical profession was in a much better position to resist control from outside entities.

The American Medical Association (AMA) was formed in 1847, but had little clout during its first half-century of existence. Its membership was small, with no permanent organization and scant resources. The AMA did not attain real strength until it was organized into county and state medical societies and until state societies were incorporated, delegating greater control at the local level.

Although the AMA often stressed the importance of raising the quality of care for patients and protecting the uninformed consumer from "quacks" and "charlatans," its principal goal—like that of other professional associations—was to advance the professionalization, prestige, and financial well-being of its members. The AMA vigorously pursued its objectives by promoting the establishment of state medical licensing laws and the legal requirement that, to be licensed to practice, a physician must be a graduate of an AMA-approved medical school. The concerted activities of physicians through the AMA are collectively referred to as **organized medicine**, to distinguish them from the uncoordinated actions of individual physicians competing in the marketplace (Goodman and Musgrave, 1992).

Licensing

Under the Medical Practice Acts established in the 1870s, medical licensure in the United States became a function of the states (Stevens, 1971). By 1896, 26 states had enacted medical licensure laws (Anderson, 1990). The licensing of physicians and upgrading of medical school standards developed hand in hand. At first, licensing required only a medical school diploma. Later, candidates could be rejected if the school they had attended was judged inadequate (Starr, 1982).

Through both licensure and upgrading of medical school standards, physicians obtained a clear monopoly on the practice of medicine (Anderson, 1990). The early licensing laws served to protect physicians from the competitive pressures posed by potential new entrants into the medical profession. As biomedicine gained political and economic ground, the biomedical community expelled providers such as homeopaths, naturopaths, and chiropractors from medical societies; prohibited professional association with them; and encouraged prosecution of such providers for unlicensed medical practice (Rothstein, 1972). In 1888, in a landmark Supreme Court decision, *Dent v. West Virginia*, Justice Stephen J. Field wrote that no one had the right to practice "without having the necessary qualifications of learning and skill" (Haber, 1974). In the late 1880s and 1890s, many states revised laws to require all candidates for licensure, including those holding medical degrees, to pass an examination (Kaufman, 1980).

Educational Reform

Reform of medical education started around 1870, as medical schools became affiliated with universities. In 1871, Harvard Medical School, under the leadership of a new university president, Charles Eliot, completely revolutionized the system of medical education. The academic year was extended from 4 to 9 months, and the length of medical education was increased from 2 to 3 years. Following the European model, laboratory instruction and clinical subjects, such as chemistry, physiology, anatomy, and pathology, were added to the curriculum.

Johns Hopkins University took the lead in further reforming medical education when it opened its medical school in 1893 under the leadership of William H. Welch, who was trained in Germany. For the first time, medical education became a graduate training course, requiring a college degree—not a high school diploma—as an entrance requirement. Johns Hopkins had well-equipped laboratories, a full-time faculty for teaching the basic science courses, and its own teaching hospital (Rothstein, 1972). Standards at Johns Hopkins became the model of medical education in other leading institutions around the country. The heightened standards made it difficult for proprietary schools to survive, and in time, those schools were closed.

The Association of American Medical Colleges (AAMC) was founded in 1876 by 22 medical schools (Coggeshall, 1965). Later, the AAMC set minimum standards for medical education, including a 4-year curriculum, though it was unable to enforce its recommendations.

In 1904, the AMA began to concentrate on medical education. It created the Council on Medical Education, which inspected the existing medical schools, and found that fewer than half provided acceptable levels of training. The AMA did not publish its findings but obtained the help of the Carnegie Foundation for the Advancement of Teaching to provide a rating of medical schools (Goodman and Musgrave, 1992). The Carnegie Foundation appointed Abraham Flexner to investigate medical schools located in both the United States and Canada. The Flexner Report, published in 1910, had a profound effect on medical education reform, and its recommendations were widely accepted by both the profession and the public. Schools that did not meet the proposed standards were forced to close. State laws were established, requiring graduation from a medical school accredited by the AMA as the basis for obtaining a license to practice medicine (Haglund and Dowling, 1993).

Once advanced graduate education became an integral part of medical training, it further legitimized the profession's authority and galvanized its sovereignty. Stevens (1971) noted that American medicine moved toward professional maturity between 1890 and 1914, mainly as a direct result of educational reform.

Specialization in Medicine

Specialization has been a hallmark of American medicine, albeit one that has resulted in an oversupply of specialists in relation to generalists. This distinctive aspect of medical practice in the United States explains why the structure of medicine did not develop around a nucleus of primary care.

Lack of a rational coordination of medical care in the United States has been one consequence of the preoccupation with specialization. In Great Britain, for example, the medical profession has divided itself into general practitioners (GPs), who practice in the community, and consultants, who hold specialist positions in hospitals. This kind of stratification did not develop in American medicine. In Great Britain, patients can consult a specialist only by referral from a GP. In several other European nations, primary care physicians (PCPs) are assigned the role of either complete or partial gatekeepers for specialty services (Willems, 2001). The Canadian healthcare system allows direct access to specialists, but a family physician's referral to specialist care is the norm (Hutchison et al., 2011). In the United States, only certain managed care plans use the **gatekeeping** model, which requires initial contact with a generalist and the generalist's referral to a specialist.

Reform of Mental Health Care

At the turn of the 20th century, the scientific study and treatment of mental illnesses, called neuropathology, had just begun. Later, in 1946, federal funding was made available under the National Mental Health Act for psychiatric education and research. Signed by President Harry Truman, this law was enacted in response to the large number of World War II veterans who suffered from "battle fatigue" (National Association of State Mental Health Program Directors [NASMHPD], 2014). At about the same time, several reports and studies exposed poor and abusive conditions in the state mental asylums.

In 1949, the National Institute of Mental Health (NIMH) was established with the goal of creating a better understanding of mental health issues through research. Six years later, the Mental Health Study Act of 1955 called for a thorough nationwide analysis of mental health and related problems. The task was assigned to a Joint Commission on Mental Illness and Health, which produced a comprehensive report, *Action for Mental Health*, in 1960. In 1963, President John F. Kennedy called for a shift from institutional care to community-based services and for integration of people with mental disorders into the mainstream of American life (Kennedy, 1963). There was also an emerging belief that early treatment of mental disorders and early intervention in the community would be effective in preventing subsequent hospitalization (Grob, 2005). In addition, reformers of the mental health system argued that long-term institutional care was neglectful, ineffective, and even harmful (U.S. Surgeon General, 1999).

By the 1960s, the concept of community mental health was born, and deinstitutionalization became a major thrust of mental health reform. By this time, new drugs for treating psychosis and depression had become available. The NIMH played a leading role in championing the substitution of confinement to asylums with community-oriented care (Grob, 2005). Passage of the Community Mental Health Centers Act of 1963, signed by President Kennedy, lent support to the joint policies of "community care" and "deinstitutionalization." Under this act, federal funding became available to build community mental health centers. For the first time, federal money was granted to the states for mental health treatment (Ramsey, 2011). This policy change ushered in the era of community mental health services and the end of the state psychiatric hospital as the core of the mental healthcare system in the United States (NASMHPD, 2014).

From 1970 to 2002, the number of state-run psychiatric hospital beds dropped from 207 to 20 beds per 100,000 population (Foley et al., 2006). The deinstitutionalization movement further intensified after the U.S. Supreme Court's 1999 decision in *Olmstead v. L.C.*, which directed U.S. states to provide community-based services whenever appropriate to people with mental illness. Today, state mental institutions still provide long-term treatment to people with severe and persistent mental illness (Patrick et al., 2006).

Around 1994, state-controlled money spent on community-based mental health services started to exceed the spending for institutionalized care. By 2012, fewer than 6% of people receiving mental health treatment used inpatient care (Substance Abuse and Mental Health Services Administration, 2013), and approximately 23% of all state funds for mental health were used for care in psychiatric hospitals (NASMHPD, 2014). By comparison, in the mid-1950s, inpatient services accounted for roughly 84% of the state and local funds devoted to mental health care (Fein, 1958). Income support programs for underserved people and people with disabilities—mainly Social Security Disability Insurance, Supplemental Security Income, and housing subsidies—played a critical role in achieving these remarkable results, along with the establishment of Medicare and Medicaid and the expansion of private insurance to cover mental health services on par with health care (Glied and Frank, 2016). As a result of these changes, mental health care in the United States is now an example of conjoint social and health policies.

Mental health parity acts were passed in 1996 and 2008 to address equality in insurance coverage for mental and physical health. The 1996 law did not mandate coverage for mental health but mainly focused on setting up annual or lifetime dollar limits in coverage and allowed waivers for certain cost increases. The 2008 law—the Mental Health Parity and Addiction Equity Act—added to the previous law by prohibiting differences in cost sharing between treatments for mental and physical health; it also applied to substance abuse, which the previous law did not (Mulvaney-Day et al., 2019). Both the laws, however, left loopholes in coverage for mental health treatments.

The 21st Century Cures Act of 2016 built on previous laws. It provided funds to strengthen parity laws, improve health care for people with serious mental disorders, fight the opioid epidemic, and advance research into treating Alzheimer's disease ("Major provisions of the 21st Century Cures Act," 2017).

Development of Public Health

Historically, public health has operated in the interest of health promotion and disease prevention through sanitary regulations, the study of epidemics, and vital statistics. Due to the growth of urban centers for the purpose of commerce and industry, unsanitary living conditions in densely populated areas, inadequate methods of sewage and garbage disposal, limited access to clean water, and long work hours in unsafe and exploitative industries led to periodic epidemics of cholera, smallpox, typhoid, tuberculosis, yellow fever, and other diseases. Such outbreaks required arduous efforts to protect the public interest. For example, in 1793, the national capital had to be moved out of Philadelphia due to a devastating outbreak of yellow fever. This epidemic prompted the city to develop its first board of health that same year. Subsequently, in 1850, Lemuel Shattuck outlined the blueprint for the development of a public health system in Massachusetts. Shattuck also called for the establishment of state and local health departments.

A threatening outbreak of cholera in 1873 mobilized the New York City Health Department to alleviate the worst sanitary conditions within the city. Previously, cholera epidemics in 1832 and 1848–1849 had swept through American cities and towns, killing thousands within a few weeks (Duffy, 1971). Until about 1900, infectious diseases posed the greatest health threat to society. The development of public health services played a major role in curtailing the spread of infection among populations. Simultaneously, widespread public health measures and better medical care were instrumental in reducing mortality and increasing life expectancy.

By 1900, most states had health departments that were responsible for a variety of public health efforts, such as sanitary inspections, communicable disease control, operation of state laboratories, vital statistics, health education, and regulation of food and water

(Turnock, 1997; Williams, 1995). Public health functions were later extended to fill certain gaps in the medical care system, though they were limited mainly to child immunizations, care of parents and infants, health screening in public schools, and family planning. Federal grants were also made available to state and local governments to support programs in substance abuse, mental health, and disease prevention services (Turnock, 1997).

Public health has remained separate from the private practice of medicine because of the skepticism of private physicians, who feared that the government could use the boards of health to regulate the private practice of medicine (Rothstein, 1972). Fear of government intervention, loss of autonomy, and erosion of personal incomes created a wall of separation between public health and private medical practice. Under this dichotomous relationship, the practice of medicine has concentrated on the physical health of the individual, whereas public health has focused on the health of whole populations and communities. The extent of collaboration between the two has been largely confined to the requirement by public health departments that private practitioners report cases of contagious diseases, such as sexually transmitted diseases, human immunodeficiency virus (HIV) infection, and acquired immunodeficiency syndrome (AIDS), and any outbreaks of cases such as the West Nile virus, coronavirus, and other types of infections.

However, in unprecedented times when the world has just experienced the once-in-a-generation shock of the COVID-19 pandemic, public health did not make a difference as expected and claimed as in times before. It is recognized that the lack of a timely, internationally coordinated evidence-based approach, the inadequate preparedness of health systems and the absence of effective global leadership has driven us to the current health, economic, and social disruptions (Cheema et al., 2020). It was reported by *The New York Times* that both the state and local public health departments across the United States have endured not only the public's fury but also widespread staff defections, burnout, firings, unpredictable funding, and a significant erosion in their authority to impose the health orders that were critical to early response to the pandemic.

Health Services for Veterans

Shortly after World War I, the U.S. government started to provide hospital services to veterans with service-related disabilities and for non-service-related disabilities if the veteran declared an inability to pay for private care. At first, the federal government contracted for services with private hospitals. Over time, however, the Department of Veterans Affairs (formerly called the Veterans Administration) built its own hospitals, outpatient clinics, and nursing homes.

Birth of Worker's Compensation

The first broad-coverage health insurance in the United States emerged in the form of worker's compensation programs, which were introduced in 1914 (Whitted, 1993). Worker's compensation was built on the theory that the employer was financially liable for the full cost of injuries and illnesses that were directly attributable to the workplace, regardless of who was at fault.

Worker's compensation was originally concerned with cash payments to workers for wages lost due to job-related injuries and disease; compensation for medical expenses and death benefits to the survivors were added later. Considering the trend, some reformers believed that since Americans had been persuaded to adopt compulsory insurance against industrial accidents, they could also be persuaded to adopt compulsory insurance against sickness. In essence, worker's compensation served as a trial balloon for the idea of government-sponsored universal health insurance in the United States. However, the growth of private health insurance, along with other key factors discussed later, has prevented any proposals for a national healthcare program from taking hold.

Rise of Private Health Insurance

Historically, private health insurance was commonly referred to as **voluntary health insurance** in contrast to proposals for a government-sponsored compulsory health insurance system. At least some private insurance coverage—albeit limited to bodily injuries—has been available since approximately 1850. By 1900, health insurance policies became available, but their initial role was to protect against loss of income during sickness and temporary disability (Whitted, 1993). Later, coverage was added for surgical fees, but the emphasis remained on replacing lost income. Thus, the coverage was, in reality, disability insurance rather than health insurance (Mayer and Mayer, 1984).

As detailed in subsequent sections, technological, social, and economic factors created a general need for health insurance. However, the economic conditions that prompted private initiatives, the self-interests of the well-organized medical profession, and the momentum of a successful health insurance enterprise gave private health insurance a firm footing in the United States. Later, the economic conditions during the World War II period laid the foundations for health insurance to become an employment-based benefit.

Technological, Social, and Economic Factors

The health insurance movement of the early 20th century was the product of three converging developments—technological, social, and economic. From a technological perspective, medicine offered new and better treatments. Socially, health care had become more desirable, and demand for medical services was growing. From an economic perspective, people could predict neither their future needs for medical care nor the costs, both of which had been gradually rising, and health care was becoming less affordable. These developments pointed to the need for some kind of insurance that could spread the financial risks over a large number of people.

Early Blanket Insurance Policies

In 1911, insurance companies began to offer blanket policies for large industrial populations, usually covering life insurance, accidents, sickness, and nursing services. A few industrial and railroad companies set up their own medical plans, covering specified medical benefits, as did several unions and fraternal orders. Nevertheless, the total amount of voluntary health insurance remained small (Stevens, 1971).

Economic Necessity and the Baylor Plan

The Great Depression, which started at the end of 1929, led to broad economic collapse and high unemployment rates. Hospitals faced economic instability and were forced to turn from philanthropic donations to patient fees for support. Patients, in turn, needed protection from the economic consequences of sickness and hospitalization because of the high unemployment risk and loss of incomes. During the Depression, occupancy rates in hospitals fell, income from endowments and contributions dropped sharply, and the charity patient load almost quadrupled (Richardson, 1945).

In 1929, the blueprint for modern health insurance was established when Justin F. Kimball began a hospital insurance plan for public school teachers at the Baylor University Hospital in Dallas, Texas.

Kimball was able to enroll more than 1,200 teachers, who paid 50 cents per month for a maximum of 21 days of hospital care. Within a few years, the Baylor plan became the model for Blue Cross plans around the country (Raffel, 1980). At first, other independent hospitals copied Baylor and started offering single-hospital plans. It was not long before community-wide plans, offered jointly by more than one hospital, became popular because they provided consumers a choice of hospitals. The hospitals agreed to provide services in exchange for a fixed monthly payment by the plans. In essence, these were prepaid plans for hospital services. A **prepaid plan** is a contractual arrangement under which a provider must deliver all needed services to a group of members (or enrollees) in exchange for a fixed monthly fee paid in advance. This concept was later adopted by managed care.

Successful Private Enterprise: The Blue Cross Plans

A hospital plan in Minnesota was the first to use the name Blue Cross in 1933 (Davis, 1996). The American Hospital Association (AHA) lent support to the hospital plans and became the coordinating agency to unite these plans into the Blue Cross network (Koch, 1993; Raffel, 1980). The Blue Cross plans were nonprofit—that is, they had no shareholders who would receive profit distributions—and covered only hospital charges, so as not to infringe on the domain of private physicians (Starr, 1982).

Later, control of the plans was transferred to a completely independent body, the Blue Cross Commission, which subsequently became the Blue Cross Association (Raffel, 1980). In 1946, Blue Cross plans in 43 states served 20 million members. Between 1940 and 1950, driven by the widespread adoption of these plans, the proportion of the U.S. population covered by hospital insurance increased from 9% to 57% (Anderson, 1990).

Self-Interests of Physicians: Birth of Blue Shield

Voluntary health insurance had received the AMA's endorsement, but the AMA had also made it clear that private health insurance plans should include only hospital care. Given the AMA's position, it is not surprising that the first Blue Shield plan designed to pay for physicians' bills was started by the California Medical Association, which established the California Physicians' Service in 1939 (Raffel, 1980). By endorsing hospital insurance and by actively developing medical service plans, the medical profession committed itself to private health insurance as the means to spread the financial risk of sickness and to ensure that its own interests would not be threatened.

Throughout the Blue Shield movement, physicians dominated the boards of directors not only because they underwrote the plans, but also because the plans were, in a very real sense, their response to the challenge of national health insurance. In addition, the plans met the AMA's stipulation of keeping medical matters in the hands of physicians (Raffel and Raffel, 1994).

Combined Hospital and Physician Coverage

Even though Blue Cross and Blue Shield developed independently (i.e., from the hospital and physician sectors, respectively) and were financially and organizationally distinct, they often worked together to provide hospital and physician coverage (Law, 1974). In 1974, the New York Superintendent of Insurance approved a merger of the Blue Cross and Blue Shield plans of Greater New York (Somers and Somers, 1977). Similar mergers occurred in other states. Today, the Blue Cross Blue Shield Association, which is a national association of 36 independent Blue Cross Blue Shield companies, provides health insurance throughout the United States and in more than 170 countries (Blue Cross Blue Shield, 2020).

Commercial Insurance

At first, the for-profit insurance companies were skeptical of the Blue Cross plans and adopted a cautious attitude toward entering the health insurance market. Their apprehension was justified because no actuarial information was available to predict losses. Nevertheless, within a few years, lured by the success of the Blue Cross plans, commercial insurance companies also started offering health insurance. By 1935, insurance companies covered 38,000 people under group hospital expense contracts through employers. The number of insured increased to 1.8 million by the end of 1940 (Reed, 1965).

Employment-Based Health Insurance

Between 1916 and 1918, 16 state legislatures, including New York and California, attempted to enact legislation mandating employers to provide health insurance, but these efforts were unsuccessful (Davis, 1996). Subsequent circumstances may have prompted it, but health insurance became employer-based through voluntary actions. Three main developments pushed private health insurance to become employment-based in the United States:

- To control high inflation in the U.S. economy during the World War II period, Congress imposed wage freezes. In response, many employers started offering health insurance to their workers in lieu of wage increases.
- In 1948, the U.S. Supreme Court ruled that employee benefits, including health insurance, were a legitimate part of union-management negotiations. Health insurance then became a permanent part of employee benefits in the postwar era (Health Insurance Association of America [HIAA], 1991).
- In 1954, Congress amended the Internal Revenue Code to make employer-paid health coverage nontaxable. In terms of its economic value, employer-paid health insurance was equivalent to getting additional salary without having to pay taxes on it, which provided an incentive to obtain health insurance as an employer-furnished benefit.

Employment-based health insurance expanded rapidly. The economy was strong during the postwar years of the 1950s, and employers started offering more extensive benefits. This expansion led to the birth of "major medical" expense coverage to protect against prolonged or catastrophic illness or injury (Mayer and Mayer, 1984). Thus, private health insurance became the primary vehicle for the financing of healthcare services in the United States.

The number of Americans with private health insurance began to fall in the late 1990s and early 2000s but has been rising slowly again since 2013, making around 60% of Americans covered under private health insurance by 2021(Statista, 2023). The U.S. individual health insurance market size was valued at $1.60 trillion in 2022 and is expected to expand at a compound annual growth rate of 6.08% from 2023 to 2030 (Grand View Research, 2022).

Failure of National Healthcare Initiatives During the 1990s

Starting in Germany in 1883, compulsory sickness insurance had spread throughout Europe by 1912. In the United States, the American Association of Labor Legislation (AALL) had been primarily responsible for leading the successful drive for worker's compensation. Some social academics and labor leaders were the prominent members of AALL, whose stated agenda was to initiate social reform through government action. Emboldened by its success in bringing about worker's compensation, AALL spearheaded the drive to establish a government-run health insurance system for the general population (Anderson, 1990). It also supported the Progressive (i.e., ideologically liberal) movement headed by former President Theodore Roosevelt, who was again running for the presidency in 1912 on a platform of social reform. Roosevelt, who might have been a political sponsor for compulsory health insurance, was defeated by Woodrow Wilson, but the Progressive movement for national health insurance did not die.

AALL continued its efforts to win support for national health insurance by appealing to both social and economic concerns. The reformers argued that national health insurance would relieve poverty because sickness usually brought wage loss and high medical costs to individual families. Reformers also argued that national health insurance would contribute to economic efficiency by reducing illness, lengthening life, and diminishing the causes of industrial discontent (Starr, 1982). At the time, the leadership of the AMA outwardly supported a national plan, and AALL and the AMA formed a united front to secure legislation meeting this goal. A standard health insurance bill was introduced in 15 states in 1917 (Stevens, 1971).

As long as compulsory health insurance was only under study and discussion, potential opponents paid no heed to it. Once bills were introduced into state legislatures, however, opponents expressed vehement disapproval of them. Eventually, the AMA's support proved only superficial.

Historically, the repeated attempts to pass national health insurance legislation in the United States have failed for several reasons, which can be classified into four broad categories: political inexpediency, institutional and public opposition, ideological differences, and tax aversion.

Political Inexpediency

At the time when they embarked on their national health programs, countries in Western Europe—notably Germany and England—were experiencing labor unrest that threatened their political stability. Social insurance was considered a means to obtain workers' loyalty and ward off political threats. Conditions in the United States by comparison were quite different. There was no real threat to the country's political stability. Unlike the governments in Europe, the U.S. government was highly decentralized and engaged in little direct regulation of the economy or social welfare. Although Congress had set up a system of compulsory hospital insurance for merchant seafarers as early as 1798, it was an exceptional measure.[1] Matters related to health and welfare were typically left to state and local governments, and as a general rule, these levels of government left as much as possible to private and voluntary action.

The entry of the United States into World War I in 1917 dealt a final political blow to the national health insurance movement, as anti-German feelings were aroused among the U.S. populace. The U.S. government denounced German social insurance, and opponents of health insurance called it a Prussian menace, inconsistent with American values (Starr, 1982).

After attempts to pass compulsory health insurance laws failed at the state levels in California and New York, AALL itself lost interest in an obviously lost cause. In 1920, the AMA's House of Delegates approved a resolution condemning compulsory health insurance (Numbers, 1985). The main aim of this resolution was to solidify the medical profession against government interference with the practice of medicine.

---

[1] Important seaports, such as Boston, were often confronted with the challenge of dealing with sickness or injuries of seamen. Congress enacted a law requiring that 20 cents per month be withheld from the wages of each seaman on American ships to support merchant marine hospitals (Raffel and Raffel, 1994).

Institutional and Public Opposition

Compared to Europe, American institutions were privately run. For example, American hospitals were mainly private, whereas in Europe they were largely government-operated facilities (Starr, 1982).

Anderson (1990) pointed to five main players in the private arena that viewed compulsory health insurance as encroaching on their interests. (1) Members of the medical profession saw erosion of their earnings because the primary source of their income would shift from individual patients to the government. (2) The insurance industry feared losing the income it derived from disability insurance, some insurance against medical services, and funeral benefits.[2] (3) The pharmaceutical industry feared the government would curtail its profits by acting as a monopoly buyer, and retail pharmacists feared that hospitals would establish their own pharmacies under a government-run national healthcare program. (4) Employers also saw the proposals as contrary to their interests. Spokespersons for U.S. business rejected the argument that national health insurance would add to productivity and efficiency. (5) It may seem ironic, but the labor unions—the American Federation of Labor, in particular—also denounced compulsory health insurance at the time. Union leaders were afraid the government would usurp their own legitimate role of providing social benefits, thereby weakening the unions' influence in the workplace. Organized labor was the largest and the most powerful interest group at that time, and its lack of support is considered instrumental in the defeat of national health insurance. John Murray (2007), an economic historian, proposed that while most historians have focused on the private entities just discussed, it is notable that the typical voter was not clamoring for some sort of government health insurance. To the contrary, whenever government-provided insurance programs were put on referendum ballots, they were resoundingly defeated.

Ideological Differences

In the American experience, individualism and self-determination, distrust of government, and reliance on the private sector to address social concerns—collectively considered to be typical American values—have stood as a bulwark against anything perceived as an attack on individual liberties. These beliefs and values have typically represented the sentiments of the American middle class, whose support was necessary for any broad-based healthcare reform. Conversely, during times of national distress, such as the Great Depression, pure necessity may have legitimized the advancement of social programs, such as the New Deal programs of the Franklin Roosevelt era (e.g., Social Security legislation providing old-age pensions and unemployment compensation).

In the early 1940s, during Roosevelt's presidency, several bills on national health insurance were introduced in Congress, but they all failed to pass. Perhaps the most notable bill was the Wagner-Murray-Dingell bill, drafted in 1943 and named after the bill's congressional sponsors. World War II diverted the nation's attention to other issues, however, and without the president's active support the bill died quietly (Numbers, 1985).

In 1946, Harry Truman became the first president to make an appeal for a national healthcare program (Anderson, 1990). Unlike the progressives, who had proposed a plan for the working class, Truman proposed a single health insurance plan that would

---

[2] Patients admitted to a hospital were required to pay a burial deposit so the hospital would not have to incur a funeral expense if they died (Raffel and Raffel, 1994). Therefore, many people bought funeral policies from insurance companies.

include all classes of society. At the president's behest, the Wagner-Murray-Dingell bill was redrafted and reintroduced. The AMA was vehement in opposing the plan. Other interest groups, such as the AHA, also opposed it. By this time, private health insurance had expanded. Initial public reaction to the Wagner-Murray-Dingell bill was positive; however, when a government-controlled medical plan was compared to private insurance, polls showed that only 12% of the public favored extending Social Security to include health insurance (Numbers, 1985).

During this era of the Cold War,[3] any attempts to introduce national health insurance were met with the stigmatizing label of **socialized medicine**—a label that has since become synonymous with any large-scale government-sponsored expansion of health insurance or intrusion in the private practice of medicine. The Republicans took control of Congress in 1946, and any interest in enacting national health insurance was put to rest. However, to the surprise of many, Truman was reelected in 1948, and he promised to establish a national health insurance system if the Democrats were returned to power (Starr, 1982). Fearing the inevitable, the AMA, in its preparation to battle Truman's plan, levied a $25 fee on each of its members to build a war chest of $3.5 million (Anderson, 1990), which was a substantial sum of money at the time. The AMA hired the public relations firm of Whitaker and Baxter and spent $1.5 million in 1949 alone, as it launched one of the most expensive lobbying efforts in American history. This campaign directly linked national health insurance with communism, so that the idea of "socialized medicine" was firmly implanted in the public's minds. In 1952, the election of a Republican president, Dwight Eisenhower, effectively ended any further debate over national health insurance.

Tax Aversion

Americans have generally supported the idea that the government ought to help people who are in financial need to pay for their medical care. However, most Americans have not favored an increase in their own taxes to pay for such care. This reluctance is perhaps why healthcare reform failed in 1993.

While seeking the presidency in 1991, then Governor Bill Clinton made healthcare reform a major campaign issue. Not since Harry Truman's initiatives in the 1940s had such a bold attempt to overhaul the U.S. healthcare system been made by a presidential candidate. In the Pennsylvania U.S. Senate election in November 1991, Democrat Harris Wofford had won while his call for national health insurance was widely supported by middle-class Pennsylvanians. Various public polls also seemed to suggest that the rising cost of health care was a concern for many people. These developments signaled that the time for national health insurance might be ripe.

After taking office in 1992, President Clinton made healthcare reform a top priority. His wife, Hillary Clinton, was given the leadership role for the Task Force on National Health Reform. A complex piece of legislation, the Health Security Act, was introduced in November 1993, but within the first year it died in Congress.

Some of the fundamental causes of the failure of the Clinton plan were no doubt historical in nature, as discussed previously in this chapter. According to one seasoned political observer, James J. Mongan (1995), the reform debate in Congress was not about the expansion of health insurance but rather about the financing of the proposed services. Avoiding tax increases, it appeared, took priority over expanding health insurance coverage and caused the demise of Clinton's healthcare reform initiatives.

---

3 Rivalry and hostility after World War II between the United States and the former Soviet Union.

Creation of Medicare and Medicaid

The year 1965 marked a major turning point in U.S. health policy. Up to this point, employer-sponsored private health insurance was the only widely available source of payment for health care, and it was available primarily to middle-class working Americans and their families. Many older adults, the unemployed, and the impoverished had to rely on their own resources, on limited public programs, or on charity from hospitals and individual physicians. Often, when charity care was provided, private payers were charged more to make up the difference, a practice referred to as **cost shifting** or **cross-subsidization**. In 1965, however, Congress passed the amendments to the Social Security Act and created the Medicare and Medicaid programs. Thus, for the first time in U.S. history, the government assumed direct responsibility for paying for health care on behalf of two vulnerable population groups—older adults and the low income (Potter and Longest, 1994).

During earlier debates over national health insurance, one thing had become clear: Government intervention was not desired by most Americans, but the public would not oppose reform initiatives to help the underprivileged and vulnerable classes, such as the poor or older adults. On their own, most of the people with limited financial resource or older adults could not afford the increasing costs of health care. Also, because the health status of these groups was significantly worse than that of the general population, they required a higher level of healthcare services. Older people, in particular, had higher incidence and prevalence of disease compared to younger groups. It was also estimated that less than half of the older adult population was covered by private health insurance. By this time, the growing older-adult middle class was also becoming a politically active force.

In 1957, a bill introduced in Congress by Aime Forand provided momentum for including necessary hospital and nursing home care as an extension of Social Security benefits for older adults (Stevens, 1971). By this time, "Social Security's old-age insurance program had been successfully institutionalized, providing a foundation for development of a health insurance program for seniors" (Starr, 2018). The AMA, however, undertook a massive public relations campaign that portrayed the proposed government insurance plan as a threat to the physician-patient relationship. The bill stalled, but public hearings around the country, which were packed with attendees who were older adults, produced intense grassroots support that pushed the issue onto the national agenda (Starr, 1982). A compromise bill, the Medical Assistance Act (Public Law 86–778), also known as the Kerr-Mills Act, was passed and went into effect in 1960. Under this act, federal grants were given to the states to extend health services provided by the state welfare programs to those low-income older people who previously did not qualify for such services (Anderson, 1990). Since the program was based on a **means test** that limited eligibility to people below a predetermined income level, it was opposed by liberal congressional representatives, who labeled it as a source of humiliation to older adults (Starr, 1982). Within 3 years, the program was declared ineffective because many states did not even implement it (Stevens, 1971). In 1964, however, health insurance for the aged and the low income became top priorities of President Lyndon Johnson's Great Society programs.

During the debate over Medicare, the AMA developed its own "Eldercare" proposal, which called for a federal-state program to subsidize private insurance policies for hospital and physician services. Representative John W. Byrnes introduced yet another proposal, dubbed "Bettercare." It proposed a federal program based on partial premium contributions by older adults, with the remainder subsidized by the government. Other proposals included tax credits and tax deductions for health insurance premiums.

In the end, a three-layered program emerged from the debates. The first two layers constituted Part A and Part B of **Medicare**, or **Title XVIII** of the Social Security Amendment of 1965, which sought to provide health insurance to older adults. Based on Forand's initial bill, the administration's proposal to finance hospital insurance and partial nursing home coverage for older people through Social Security became **Part A** of Medicare. The Byrnes proposal to cover physicians' bills through government-subsidized insurance became **Part B** of Medicare. An extension of the Kerr-Mills program of federal matching funds to the states, based on each state's financial needs, became **Medicaid**, or **Title XIX** of the Social Security Amendment of 1965. The Medicaid program was intended for indigent persons, based on means tests established by each state but was expanded to include all age groups, not just older adults with low income (Stevens, 1971).

Although adopted together, Medicare and Medicaid reflected sharply different traditions. Medicare enjoyed broad grassroots support and, because it was attached to the Social Security program, it made no class distinctions. Medicaid, however, was burdened by the stigma of public welfare. Medicare had uniform national standards for eligibility and benefits, whereas Medicaid varied from state to state in terms of eligibility and benefits. Medicare allowed physicians to **balance bill**—that is, charge the patient the amount above the program's set fees and recoup the difference. In contrast, Medicaid prohibited balance billing and, consequently, had limited participation from physicians (Starr, 1982). Medicaid, in essence, created a two-tier system of medical care delivery because, even today, many physicians refuse to accept Medicaid-covered patients due to the low fees paid by the government for their care.

Not surprisingly, shortly after Medicare and Medicaid became operational, national spending for health services began to rise, as did public outlays of funds in relation to private spending for health services (Anderson, 1990). For example, national health expenditures (NHE), which had increased by 50% from 1960 to 1965, jumped by 78% from 1965 to 1970, and by 71% from 1970 to 1975. Similarly, public expenditures for health care, which were stable at 25% of NHE for 1955, 1960, and 1965, increased to 36.5% of NHE in 1970, and to 42.1% of NHE in 1975 (based on data from Bureau of the Census, 1976).

Expansion of Medicare and Medicaid

Even though Medicare and Medicaid vastly expanded healthcare delivery in the United States, the Democrats' appetite for national health insurance did not die out. During the late 1960s and 1970s, Senator Edward Kennedy became the torchbearer, calling for building a national health insurance program based on Medicare. These efforts failed because President Richard Nixon countered that there would be too much government interference in health care if the program was fully financed by federal taxes (Starr, 2018). As a compromise, in 1972, Medicare was expanded to cover persons with disabilities receiving Social Security benefits and individuals with end-stage renal disease. After Nixon's resignation, Gerald Ford's successor, Jimmy Carter, did not push for national health insurance for fear of its fiscal consequences (Starr, 2018).

Beginning in 1984, Medicaid was first expanded to cover low-income pregnant women and children. After the presidencies of Ronald Reagan and George H. W. Bush, Clinton's initial proposal for expanding health insurance failed during the first term of his presidency, as discussed previously. During his second term, however, he was able to build on previous Medicaid expansions to create the Children's Health Insurance Program (CHIP) by providing federal funds to the states. Starr (2018) observed that "like Medicare, CHIP represented a retreat from covering everyone to expanding protection for an age group that evoked public sympathy." Unlike Medicare and Medicaid, however, the CHIP program was financed as a block grant that allowed the states to structure the program as the states saw fit. Medicaid was again expanded with the passage of the ACA to 41 states (including DC), covering nearly all adults with incomes up to 138% of the Federal Poverty Level and providing states with an enhanced federal matching rate (FMAP) for their expanded populations (KFF, 2023).

Medical Care in the Corporate Era

Early Developments

As pointed out previously, the corporate practice of medicine—that is, delivery of medical care by for-profit corporations—was historically prohibited by law, being labeled as "commercialism" in medicine. The AMA, however, recognized the need for certain industries located in remote areas—such as railroads, mining, and lumber companies—to employ or contract with practicing physicians. As early as 1882, companies such as Northern Pacific Railroad started to provide direct medical care to their employees.

In the early to mid-1900s, the healthcare delivery landscape began to change. Physicians in specialty practices were brought together into group practices. The Mayo Clinic, started in Rochester, Minnesota, in 1887, became the model for consolidating specialists into group practice—an arrangement that presented certain economic advantages, such as sharing of expenses and incomes. Family practitioners joined in, and many group practices started to offer multispecialty services. These innovations led to the formation of prepaid group plans.

In large urban markets, prepaid group plans began enrolling employee groups under capitated fee arrangements, through which these groups received comprehensive services for a fixed monthly fee paid in advance. The AMA opposed the first such plan, the Group Health Association of Washington (started in 1937 in Washington, DC) but was found guilty of restraint of trade, in violation of the Sherman Antitrust Act. This verdict may have been crucial in paving the way for the growth of other prepaid group practice plans. For example, the HIP Health Plan of New York, started in 1947, stood as one of the most successful programs, providing comprehensive medical services through organized medical groups of family physicians and specialists (Raffel, 1980). Similarly, Kaiser-Permanente, started in 1942, has grown on the West Coast.

The corporate era began in earnest in the latter part of the 20th century as employment of physicians by certain industries, group practices, and capitation plans sowed the seeds of managed care, which first appeared in the form of HMOs.

The HMO Act of 1973

The Health Maintenance Organization Act (HMO Act) of 1973 was passed during the Nixon administration, with the objective of stimulating growth of HMOs by providing federal funds for the establishment and expansion of new HMOs (Wilson and Neuhauser, 1985). The underlying reason for supporting the growth of HMOs was the belief that prepaid medical care, as an alternative to traditional fee-for-service practice, would stimulate competition among health plans, enhance efficiency, and control the rising healthcare expenditures. The HMO Act required employers with 25 or more employees to offer an HMO alternative if one was available in their geographic area. The objective was to create 1,700 HMOs to enroll 40 million members by 1976 (Iglehart, 1994). Ultimately, the HMO Act failed to achieve this objective. By 1976, only 174

HMOs had been formed, with an enrollment of 6 million (Public Health Service, 1995). Employers did not take the HMO option seriously and continued to offer traditional fee-for-service insurance until their own health insurance expenses started to grow rapidly during the 1980s.

Corporatization of Healthcare Delivery

By the dawn of the 21st century, the business environment in the United States—and indeed around the world—had become the domain of large corporations. At the same time, tremendous advances were occurring in global communications, transportation, medical and information technology, and international trade. Healthcare delivery has not remained immune to these transformations.

Managed care organizations (MCOs) are, in many regards, indistinguishable from large insurance corporations. The rising tide of managed care consolidated immense purchasing power on the demand side. To counteract this imbalance, providers began to consolidate their practices, and larger, integrated health care organizations began forming. As a result, many large hospitals and group practices have become part of larger health systems that deliver hospital services in addition to outpatient care, long-term care, and specialized rehabilitation.

In a healthcare landscape that is increasingly dominated by corporations, individual physicians have struggled to preserve their autonomy. As a matter of survival, many physicians have consolidated their services within large clinics, formed strategic partnerships with hospitals, or started their own specialty hospitals. There is also a growing trend of physicians choosing to become employees of hospitals and other medical corporations. Corporatization has shifted marketplace power from individuals to corporations. The days of consumer dominance in health care are long gone.

Globalization of Health Care

Globalization, from social and economic perspectives, has been another hallmark of the 21st century (World Economic Forum, 2023). **Globalization** refers to various forms of cross-border economic activities, characterized by transnational movement and exchange of goods, services, people, and capital. Corporatization, transportation, and telecommunications have been key enabling factors in globalization. From the standpoint of cross-border trade in health services, Mutchnick et al. (2005) identified four different modes of economic interrelationships:

- Telemedicine enables cross-border information exchange and delivery of certain services. For example, teleradiology (the electronic transmission of radiologic images over a distance) enables physicians in the United States to transmit radiologic images to Australia, where they are interpreted and the results reported back the next day (McDonnell, 2006). Telemedicine consulting services in pathology and radiology are being delivered to other parts of the world by cutting-edge U.S. medical institutions, such as Johns Hopkins Hospital.
- Consumers can travel abroad to receive elective, nonemergency medical care, referred to as **medical tourism**. Globalization has contributed to the standardization of medical knowledge, practice protocols, and technologies (Virani et al., 2020). It has also allowed some developing countries to tap into the growing market for medical tourism. Specialty hospitals, such as the Apollo chain in India and Bumrungrad International Hospital in Thailand, offer state-of-the-art medical facilities and surgical services to foreigners at a fraction of the cost for the same procedures done in the United States or Europe. Physicians and hospitals outside the United

States have clear competitive advantages: reasonable malpractice costs, minimum regulation, and lower costs of labor. Conversely, dignitaries and other wealthy foreigners come to multispecialty centers in the United States, such as the Mayo Clinic, to receive highly specialized services.
- Foreign direct investment in health services enterprises benefits foreign citizens. For example, Chindex International, a U.S. corporation, provides medical equipment, supplies, and medical services in China. Chindex's United Family Healthcare serves Beijing, Shanghai, and Guangzhou.
- Health professionals can move to other countries that have high demand for their services and offer better economic opportunities than their native countries. For example, nurses from other countries are moving to the United States and the United Kingdom to relieve personnel shortages in those nations. Healthcare workers from Indonesia are migrating to Japan for similar reasons (Shinohara, 2016).

To this list, we can add a few more aspects of the globalization of health care:

- Corporations based in the United States have increasingly expanded their operations overseas. As a result, an increasing number of Americans are now working overseas as expatriates. Health insurance companies based in the United States are, in turn, having to develop benefit plans for these expatriates. According to a survey of 87 insurance companies, health care is becoming one of the most sought-after employee benefits worldwide, even in countries that have national health insurance programs. Moreover, the cost of medical care overseas is rising at a faster rate than the rate of inflation in the general economy (Cavanaugh, 2008). Hence, the cost-effective delivery of health care is becoming a major challenge worldwide.
- Medical-care delivery by U.S. providers is in high demand overseas. American provider organizations—such as Johns Hopkins Hospital, Cleveland Clinic, Mayo Clinic, Duke University Medical Center, and several others—are now delivering medical services in various developing countries.
- The realities of globalization have resulted in a discipline called **global health**—that is, efforts to protect the entire global community against threats to people's health and to deliver cost-effective public health and clinical services to the world's population. It is now widely recognized that no country can ensure the health of its own population in isolation from the rest of the world (DeCock et al., 2013).
- In the last few years, the world experienced the major pandemic COVID-19, multiple geopolitical conflicts, and effects of climate and energy crises, all having detrimental impact on health and health care globally, with the most vulnerable populations being the most impacted. While triggering growth and innovation in the form of a surge in healthcare spending and investments, scientific advancements, improved digital innovation and connectivity and alternative care models, the pandemic also exposed global health disparities, had a detrimental impact on mental health and well-being, and exacerbated macro-economic issues and the climate crisis. Therefore, we cannot afford to ignore important contextual factors or the determinants of diverse socioeconomic and political contexts in which threats to health emerge and are sustained (Traore et al., 2023).
- The apparent failure of global health security to prevent or prepare for the COVID-19 pandemic has highlighted the need for closer international cooperation among health sectors to meet challenges,

including professional and institutional tensions, international legal system barriers, asymmetry in power and its impact on priority setting between countries, and chronic underinvestment for epidemic and emergency prevention (Elnaiem et al., 2023).

Cross-border collaborations in health care are on the rise, mainly triggered by the worldwide healthcare budgetary constraints. For example, the United States and Japan are collaboratively developing and testing medical devices (Uchida et al., 2013). India's Apollo Group is exporting telemedicine services from its Apollo Gleneagles Hospital in Kolkata (India) to patients in Bangladesh, Nepal, Bhutan, and Myanmar. This organization provides telediagnostic and teleconsultation from its center in Karaganda Oblast in Kazakhstan to that geographic region, and partners with Health Services America and Medstaff International in the United States for billing, documentation of clinical and administrative records, coding of medical processes, and insurance claims processing (Smith et al., 2009).

Globalization has also produced some negative effects. The developing world pays a steep price when emigration leaves these countries with shortages of trained professionals (referred to as "brain drain"). The burden of disease in these countries is often greater than it is in the developed world, and emigration merely exacerbates these countries' inability to provide adequate health care to their own populations (Norcini and Mazmanian, 2005). Globalization has also brought some new threats to health. For instance, the threat of infectious diseases has increased, as diseases appearing in one country can spread rapidly to other countries. For example, severe acute respiratory syndrome (SARS), H1N1 swine flu, and COVID-19 virus all originated in China and quickly spread around the world.

The Era of Healthcare Reform

Efforts to reform the healthcare system in a comprehensive way have had a checkered past in the United States, as discussed previously. Passage of the ACA in 2010 was a bold undertaking that sought to bring about major reforms. Under Donald Trump's presidency, the Republican Congress failed to "repeal and replace" the ACA, though some incremental steps were taken to dismantle the unpopular individual mandate.

The Affordable Care Act

On March 21, 2010, the U.S. House of Representatives passed, by a narrow vote of 219-212, the Patient Protection and Affordable Care Act, which was signed into law two days later by President Barack Obama. A week later, on March 30, the president signed the HealthCare and Education Reconciliation Act of 2010, which amended certain provisions of the first law, mainly to raise additional revenues through taxation to pay for expanded healthcare services. Together, the two laws constitute the principal features of what came to be known as the ACA, commonly known as Obamacare. Not a single Republican in Congress voted in favor of these bills.

At least six factors can be cited that led to the ACA's successful passage. First, the Democratic Party held not only the presidency, but also majorities in the two houses of Congress. That made it easier for Obama to push forward his agenda. In fact, in the early days of his presidency, Obama confidently stated that this was "the best chance of reform we have ever had" (White House, 2009).

Second, a public option[4] was initially included in the bill but was later dropped because of opposition from both Republican

---

4 A government-sponsored insurance plan as an alternative to private insurance.

and Democratic lawmakers. The public option was thought to be too radical of a change.

Third, deliberations in Congress over the reform bill took place behind closed doors, so that the American public had little to no participation and scant understanding of the resulting bill. Without any knowledge of the content in these proceedings, opponents were unable to mount a challenge to specific aspects of the ACA.

Fourth, the benefits of the proposed healthcare reform were overstated, making them more attractive to the public. For example, in a televised address to the nation on August 8, 2009, Obama claimed that his reform would "protect people against unfair insurance practices; provide quality, affordable insurance to every American; and bring down rising costs that are swamping families, businesses, and our budgets" (White House, 2009). In that same address, the president said, "Under the reforms we seek, if you like your doctor, you can keep your doctor. If you like your healthcare plan, you can keep your healthcare plan." This refrain was repeated numerous times to "sell" the plan to the American public. Once the ACA became law, however, it proved not to be what was promised.

Fifth, the ACA won the backing of major healthcare industry representatives. Even the AMA reluctantly pledged its support for the legislation, in a complete reversal of its traditional stance toward major healthcare reform proposals.

Sixth, subsequent to the Clinton presidency, the White House was held by a Republican, George W. Bush. For half of his eight-year tenure, both houses of Congress were under Republican control. Yet, Bush's focus remained on incremental reform, even though a large segment of the U.S. population did not have health insurance. While the United States was still mired in a deep economic recession, Obama made healthcare reform a top priority and tied his reform proposals to future economic growth and prosperity (White House, 2009).

The Patchy Legacy of the ACA

The Affordable Care Act (ACA), enacted in 2010, marked the most significant extension of healthcare coverage within the U.S. healthcare system since the establishment of Medicare and Medicaid in 1965 (The Assistant Secretary for Planning and Evaluation, 2023; U.S. Department of Health and Human Services. 2023). This comprehensive reform law substantially broadened access to health insurance for millions of Americans by following two primary avenues:

1. It granted premium tax credits to individuals whose incomes ranged from 100% to 400% of the federal poverty level (FPL). These credits were intended to reduce the expenses associated with obtaining individual market health insurance plans through newly established state marketplaces.
2. It enlarged the eligibility criteria for Medicaid to encompass adults with incomes reaching up to 138% of the FPL in states that chose to participate.

The ACA was partly successful in reducing the number of Americans without health insurance, although most of the increases in coverage were gained through increased enrollment in Medicaid. The ACA had mandated all states to expand Medicaid. This portion of the law, however, was struck down by the U.S. Supreme Court in 2012, so that expanding or not expanding Medicaid became a state-level decision. As of April 2019, overall Medicaid enrollment had increased by nearly 15 million from the pre-ACA baseline (Medicaid and CHIP Payment and Access Commission, 2020). However, many of these new beneficiaries would have qualified for Medicaid regardless of the ACA. Another 10 million (2018 figure) gained coverage by purchasing health insurance through government-established health insurance exchanges.[5] Nevertheless, despite the well-publicized promises of the ACA, 27.4 million Americans were uninsured in 2017, an increase from the 26.7 million uninsured in 2016 (Garfield et al., 2019). The primary gains under Obamacare were made by the newly qualified Medicaid beneficiaries and those who received adequate federal subsidies[6] to purchase insurance through the exchanges. Thus, Obamacare did help low-income people obtain health insurance. The largest decreases in insurance instability and uninsured spells (i.e., continuity of insurance) occurred among the ACA's intended population groups: adults aged 19–25, low-income families, and minority populations (Gai and Jones, 2020). The ACA also enabled people with preexisting medical conditions to obtain health insurance, as such people had encountered significant barriers prior to the passage of the ACA.

The ACA's regulatory mandates contributed to cost spiraling that had become out of control. All private and public health plans were required to include a list of "essential health benefits," regardless of whether an enrollee would benefit from any of them. Consequently, the average individual market premium more than doubled from $2,784 per year in 2013 to $5,712 in 2017, an increase of 105%, along with a substantial rise in deductibles that the patients are responsible for before health insurance starts paying. Thus, the label "affordable" in the law's title turned out to be a misnomer for many Americans. In addition, insurers offering ACA-mandated health insurance plans began dropping out. By 2018, more than half of U.S. counties on the federal platform had only one issuer, leaving millions of consumers with little to no choice for insurance (Centers for Medicare and Medicaid Services, 2018). Erosion of competition between insurers kept premium costs high.

The ACA also had a negative effect on employer-sponsored health insurance. Between 2012 and 2016, enrollment in fully insured group plans decreased 16% as employers switched to self-insured arrangements, and the number of small employers offering health benefits dropped 24% (Singhal et al., 2018).

While insurance coverage is often the focus of attention in most published reports, the ability to obtain healthcare services—that is, access—is much more valuable for assessing a program's success. Some evidence indicates that the ACA has led to an increase in preventive health care, along with improvements in affordability of care, regular care for chronic conditions, medication adherence, and self-reported health (Sommers et al., 2017). Yet, expanded access to services has come mainly from obtaining care from hospital emergency departments (EDs) and community health centers (CHCs) (Feinglass et al., 2017; Goozner, 2015). Medicaid expansion also buoyed CHCs' financial viability by increasing payments to these facilities (Tilhou et al., 2020). However, the ACA does not appear to have alleviated the problem of overcrowded EDs.

Court Challenges

From the ACA's inception, conservatives had challenged the constitutionality of Obamacare. Early on, the matter came before the U.S. Supreme Court. In a decision rendered on June 28, 2012 (in *National Federation of Independent Business v. Sebelius*), the Court upheld the constitutionality of the ACA on the grounds that Congress had the power to

---

5 The exchanges (also called marketplaces) were established by either the state or the federal government. Health insurance is sold on these exchanges by private insurance companies.

6 Subsidies in the form of tax credits are available to people with incomes between 100% and 400% of the federal poverty level.

tax, referring to the penalties that individuals had to pay if they chose not to have health insurance (known as the individual mandate). The ACA was again scrutinized by the U.S. Supreme Court in 2015. This time, in *King v. Burwell*, the Court was asked to decide whether people purchasing insurance through federal exchanges were entitled to subsidies because the natural reading of the law was that subsidies could be offered only to those who purchased insurance through state-established exchanges.[7] The Court ruled that subsidies could be legally given to purchasers on both types of exchanges.

Hours after taking the presidential oath of office on January 20, 2017, Donald Trump signed his first executive order to "waive, defer, grant exemptions from, or delay the implementation of any provision or requirement of the Act that would impose a fiscal burden on any State or a cost, fee, tax, penalty, or regulatory burden on individuals, families, healthcare providers, health insurers, patients, recipients of healthcare services, purchasers of health insurance, or makers of medical devices, products, or medications" (*Federal Register*, 2017). In effect, this executive order suspended the collection of individual penalties under the ACA. Subsequently, effective January 1, 2019, the individual mandate penalty was fully repealed under the Tax Cuts and Jobs Act of 2017.

In recent years, the ACA has again become a "political football." The U.S. District Court in Texas ruled in December 2018 (in *Texas v. United States*) that the entire ACA was unconstitutional because the individual penalty, viewed as a tax by the U.S. Supreme Court in its 2012 decision, had been nullified. On appeal, the Fifth Circuit Court upheld the unconstitutionality assertion but questioned as to how much of the ACA could be invalidated because one provision of the law was nullified. The U.S. Supreme Court once again heard the case in November 2020 and upheld the ACA in June 2021. Indeed, the ACA is highly complex and many of its features are firmly entrenched in the U.S. healthcare system. Hence, full replacement of the ACA will be a daunting task.

As for the American people, for a long time there was lack of consensus on the ACA's advantages. More recently, the ACA has drawn approval from a majority of Americans. A 2017 Pew Research Center poll found that, for the first time, a majority of American adults (54%) approved of the ACA, although 43% still wanted changes to the law (Fingerhut, 2017). As of March 2023, the result of *Kaiser Health Tracking Poll: The Public's Views* showed that 62% of the respondents had a favorable opinion of ACA, the highest share ever (KFF, 2023). Public views have been largely driven by partisanship: nearly nine in ten Democrats (87%) along with six in ten independents (58%) view the law favorably, while eight in ten Republicans (79%) hold unfavorable views (KFF, 2022).

Evaluation of ACA

Since the enactment of ACA (refer to **Exhibit 3-3** for a list of ACA-related regulations), a number of studies have been published summarizing the achievements of ACA, as illustrated below.

- Expanded Medicaid coverage: The ACA Medicaid expansion expanded Medicaid coverage to nearly all adults with incomes up to 138% of the FPL ($20,120 for an individual in 2023) and provided states with an enhanced federal matching rate (FMAP) for their expansion populations (KFF, 2023). To date, 41 states (including DC) have adopted the Medicaid expansion

---

[7] The ACA required each state to establish exchanges through which people could purchase health insurance. If a state failed to do so, the federal government would establish an exchange in that state.

Exhibit 3.3 ACA-Related Regulations

Year	Law	Development
2010	Patient Protection and Affordable Care Act (ACA)	■ Expanded Medicaid to cover uninsured working-age adults (18-65) earning under 138% of the Federal Poverty Line (and therefore not eligible for subsidies on the health insurance marketplace) along with some whose existing insurance plans were too expensive based on their income ■ Created health insurance marketplaces with three standard insurance coverage levels to enable like-for-like comparisons by consumers, and a web-based health insurance exchange where consumers can compare prices and purchase plans
2015	Medicare Access and CHIP Reauthorization Act (MACRA)	■ Many Medicare Part B services were reimbursed
2022	Inflation Reduction Act	■ Allowed Medicare to negotiate certain drug prices, caps Part D costs for seniors at $2,000 per month ■ Provided $64 billion for ACA subsidies through 2025, originally expanded under the American Rescue Plan Act of 2021

Data from Centers for Medicare & Medicaid Services (2022). The state of the ACA report. https://www.cms.gov/files/document/state-anniversary.pdf

and 10 states have not adopted the expansion (KFF, 2023).

- Increased cancer survival rate and reduced health disparities: The expansion of Medicaid was linked to a more significant rise in overall survival rates over a 2-year period (Ji et al, 2023). This increase was particularly noticeable among non-Hispanic Black individuals and in rural regions, underscoring the impact of Medicaid expansion in reducing healthcare disparities (Han et al., 2022). Medicaid expansion—particularly early expansion—was associated with increased rates of colorectal cancer screening among Black patients (Dee et al., 2022).
- More comprehensive and accessible health plans: According to the Biden Administration, starting in 2023, ACA insurance plans are required to have clinical considerations not influenced by age, anticipated lifespan, existing or anticipated disabilities, level of medical reliance, well-being, or other non medical factors (Policy Center for Maternal Mental Health, 2022).
- Increased access through expanded insurance coverage: Based on enrollment data from 2022 to early 2023, over 40 million people are currently enrolled in Marketplace or Medicaid expansion coverage related to provisions of the ACA, the highest total on record (The

Assistant Secretary for Planning and Evaluation, 2023).

- Decreased healthcare costs on the healthcare marketplaces: The affordability of health insurance coverage in the marketplace has reached unprecedented levels. As a result, 80% of individuals were able to find a monthly plan for $10 or even less. Moreover, during the 2022 Open Enrollment Period, 28% of all enrollees opted for coverage priced at $10 or less after benefiting from ACA subsidies (Centers for Medicare & Medicaid Services, 2022).

U.S. health policy has been increasingly characterized by extreme partisanship and political ideology. During the Trump administration, Congress accomplished very little even when the Republicans were in the majority. Subsequently, when Democrats became the majority in the House of Representatives, they were obsessed with investigations and impeachment of Trump and ignored healthcare reform. In this hostile political environment, Trump made some health policy moves through executive orders, while members of Congress could only complain and criticize. Notable among these changes were the expansion of short-term health plans that were cheaper than the plans available through the ACA-established exchanges, expansion of association health plans for small businesses and the self-employed, expansion of tax-advantaged health savings accounts, approval of more generic drugs and other measures to control the rising costs of prescription medications, price transparency measures, and expansion of Medicare Advantage plans to lower Medicare costs for seniors.

The Biden Administration reopened enrollment on the federal ACA in January 2021, with 4.4 million more people enrolled ever since and more than 40 million people up to March 2023 enrolled in Marketplace or Medicaid expansion coverage related to provisions of the ACA— the highest total on record.

Summary

The evolution of healthcare services in the United States, which has spanned approximately 150 years, has come a long way—from the delivery of primitive care to technologically advanced services delivered by small and large medical corporations that have increasingly crossed national boundaries. The need for health insurance was first recognized and addressed during the Great Depression. Unlike in Europe, where government-sponsored health insurance took root, health insurance in the United States began mainly as a private endeavor because of circumstances that did not parallel those in Europe. Even so, social, political, and economic exigencies and opportunities led to the creation of two major government health insurance programs, Medicare and Medicaid, in 1965. Since then, small-scale incremental reforms have been undertaken because they were politically and socially more acceptable than large-scale changes in how most middle-class Americans obtained healthcare services.

Historically, traditional American beliefs and values have acted as strong forces against attempts to initiate fundamental changes in the financing and delivery of health care. The ACA was passed without seeking consensus among Americans on how it fit with the basic values and ethics of the populace. Its provisions helped mainly low-income Americans obtain health insurance but placed greater financial burdens on the middle class. Repealing and replacing the ACA was one of President Trump's campaign promises. The task of actually undoing the ACA, however, is challenging and faces many hurdles. The Biden Administration has reinstated most of the earlier ACA provisions.

TEST YOUR UNDERSTANDING

Terminology

almshouse
balance bill
cost shifting
cross-subsidization
cultural authority
Dispensaries
fee for service
gatekeeping
global health
globalization
means test
Medicaid
medical tourism
Medicare
Medicare Part A
Medicare Part B
organized medicine
pesthouse
prepaid plan
socialized medicine
Title XVIII
Title XIX
voluntary health insurance

Review Questions

1. Why did the professionalization of medicine start later in the United States than in some Western European nations?
2. Why did medicine have a domestic—rather than professional—character in the preindustrial era? How did urbanization change that?
3. Which factors explain why the demand for the services of a professional physician was inadequate in the preindustrial era? How did scientific medicine and technology change that?
4. How did the emergence of general hospitals strengthen the professional sovereignty of physicians?
5. Discuss the relationship of dependency within the context of the medical profession's cultural and legitimized authority. What role did medical education reform play in galvanizing professional authority?
6. How did the organized medical profession manage to remain free of control by business firms, insurance companies, and hospitals until the latter part of the 20th century?
7. Discuss how technological, social, and economic factors, in general, created the need for health insurance.
8. Which conditions during the World War II period lent support to employer-based health insurance in the United States?
9. Discuss, with particular reference to the roles of (a) organized medicine, (b) the middle class, and (c) American beliefs and values, why reform efforts to bring in national health insurance have historically been unsuccessful in the United States.
10. Which particular factors that earlier may have been somewhat weak in bringing about national health insurance later led to the passage of Medicare and Medicaid?
11. On what basis were older adults and people with limited financial resource regarded as vulnerable groups for whom special government-sponsored programs needed to be created?
12. Which areas of healthcare delivery can be attributed to public health services?
13. Explain how contract practice and prepaid group practice were the prototypes of today's managed care plans.
14. Discuss the main ways in which current delivery of health care has become corporatized.

15. In the context of globalization in health services, what are the main economic activities as discussed in this chapter?

16. From the standpoint of health insurance, what were the main accomplishments of the Affordable Care Act?

References

Anderson, O. W. 1990. *Health Services as a Growth Enterprise in the United States since 1875*. Ann Arbor, MI: Health Administration Press.

Blue Cross Blue Shield. 2020. *The Blue Cross Blue Shield System*. Accessed May 2020. Available at: https://www.bcbs.com/about-us/the-blue-cross-blue-shield-system

Bordley, J., and A. M. Harvey. 1976. *Two Centuries of American Medicine 1776–1976*. Philadelphia, PA: W. B. Saunders.

Bureau of the Census. 1976. *Statistical Abstract of the United States, 1976*. Washington, DC: U.S. Department of Commerce.

Burns, J. 2004. Are nonprofit hospitals really charitable? Taking the question to the state and local level. *Journal of Corporate Law* 29: 665–683.

Cavanaugh, B. B. 2008. Building the worldwide health network. *Best's Review* 108: 32–37.

Centers for Medicare and Medicaid Services. 2018. *Premiums on the Federally-Facilitated Exchanges Drop in 2019*. Accessed May 2020. Available at: https://www.cms.gov/newsroom/press-releases/premiums-federally-facilitated-exchanges-drop-2019

Centers for Medicare & Medicaid Services. (2022). The state of the ACA report. Available at: https://www.cms.gov/files/document/state-anniversary.pdf

Cheema, S., M. Ameduri, A. Abraham, S. Doraiswamy, and R. Mamtani. 2020. The COVID-19 pandemic: The public health reality. *Epidemiology & Infection* 148: e223.

Clark, C. 1998. A bloody evolution: Human error in medicine is as old as the practice itself. *The Washington Post* Z10.

Coggeshall, L. T. 1965. Planning for medical progress through education. Evanston, IL: Association of American Medical Colleges.

Davis, P. 1996. The fate of Blue Shield and the new blues. *South Dakota Journal of Medicine* 49: 323–330.

DeCock, K. M., P. M. Simone, V. Davidson, and L. Slutsker, 2013. The new global health. *Emerging Infectious Diseases* 19: 1192–1197.

Dee, E. C., L. J. Pierce, K. M. Winkfield, and M. B. Lam, 2022. In pursuit of equity in cancer care: Moving beyond the Affordable Care Act. *Cancer* 128: 3278–3283. Available at: https://doi.org/10.1002/cncr.34346

Duffy, J. 1971. Social impact of disease in the late 19th century. *Bulletin of the New York Academy of Medicine* 47: 797–811.

Elnaiem, A., O. Mohamed-Ahmed, A. Zumla, et al. 2023. "Global and regional governance of One Health and implications for global health security." *Lancet* 401: 688–704.

Falk, G. 1999. *Hippocrates Assailed: The American Health Delivery System*. Lanham, MD: University Press of America.

Farmer, G. O., and J. H. Douglas. 2001. Physician "unionization": A primer and prescription. *Florida Bar Journal* 75: 37–42.

Federal Register. 2017. Minimizing the economic burden of the Patient Protection and Affordable Care Act pending repeal. Accessed November 2020. Available at: https://www.federalregister.gov/documents/2017/01/24/2017-01799/minimizing-the-economic-burden-of-the-patient-protection-and-affordable-care-act-pending-repeal

Fein, R. 1958. *Economics of Mental Illness*. New York: Basic Books.

Feinglass, J., A. J. Cooper, K., Rydland, et al. 2017. Emergency department use across 88 small areas after Affordable Care Act implementation in Illinois. *Western Journal of Emergency Medicine* 18: 811–820.

Fingerhut, H. 2017. Support for 2010 health care law reaches new high. FactTank. Accessed May 2020. Available at: https://www.pewresearch.org/fact-tank/2017/02/23/support-for-2010-health-care-law-reaches-new-high

Foley, D. J., R. W. Manderscheid, J. Atay, J. Maedke, J. Sussman, and S. Cribbs. 2004. Highlights of organized mental health services in 2002 and major national and state trends. In: *Mental health, United States, 2004*. R. W. Manderscheid and J. T.Berry, eds. Washington, DC: U.S. Government Printing Office. 200–236.

Gai, Y., and K. Jones. 2020. Insurance patterns and instability from 2006 to 2016. *BMC Health Services Research* 20: 1–12.

Garfield, R., K. Orgera, and A. Damico, 2019. The uninsured and the ACA: A primer: Key facts about health insurance and the uninsured amidst changes to the Affordable Care Act. Kaiser Family Foundation. Accessed May 2020. Available at: https://www.kff.org/report-section/the-uninsured-and-the-aca-a-primer-key-facts-about-health-insurance-and-the-uninsured-amidst-changes-to-the-affordable-care-act-how-have-health-insurance-coverage-options-and-availability-changed

Glied, S., and R. G. Frank. 2016. Economics and the transformation of the mental health system. *Journal of Health Politics, Policy and Law* 41: 541–558.

Goodman, J. C., and G. L. Musgrave. 1992. *Patient Power: Solving America's HealthCare Crisis*. Washington, DC: Cato Institute.

Goozner, M. 2015. Medicaid's enduring pay problem. *Modern Healthcare* 45: 24.

Grand View Research. 2022. U.S. Individual health insurance market size, share & trends analysis report. by type (public, private), by demographics (minors, adults, seniors), and segment forecasts, 2023-2030. Accessed October 2023. Available at: https://www.grandviewresearch.com/industry-analysis/us-individual-health-insurance-market-report

Grob, G. N. 2005. Public policy and mental illnesses: Jimmy Carter's Presidential Commission on Mental Health. *Milbank Quarterly* 83: 425–456.

Haber, S. 1974. The professions and higher education in America: A historical view. In: *Higher Education and Labor Markets*. M. S. Gordon, ed. New York,: McGraw-Hill.

Haglund, C. L,. and W. L. Dowling. 1993. The hospital. In: *Introduction to Health Services*. 4th ed. S. J. Williams and P. R. Torrens, eds. New York: Delmar. 135–176.

Hamowy, R. 1979. The early development of medical licensing laws in the United States, 1875–1900. *Journal of Libertarian Studies* 3: 73–119.

Han, X., J. Zhao, K. R. Yabroff, C. J. Johnson, and A. Jemal. 2022. Association between Medicaid expansion under the Affordable Care Act and survival among newly diagnosed cancer patients. *Journal of the National Cancer Institute* 114: 1176–1185.

Health Insurance Association of America (HIAA). 1991. *Source Book of Health Insurance Data*. Washington, DC: Health Insurance Association of America.

Hutchison, B., J. F. Levesque, E. Strumpf, and N. Coyle. 2011. Primary health care in Canada: Systems in motion. *Milbank Quarterly* 89: 256–288.

Iglehart, J. K. 1994. The American health care system: Managed care. In: *The Nation's Health*. 4th ed. P. R. Lee and C. L. Estes, eds. Boston, MA: Jones & Bartlett Learning. 231–237.

Ji, X., K. S. Shi, A. C. Mertens, et al. 2023. Survival in young adults with cancer is associated with Medicaid expansion through the Affordable Care Act. *Journal of Clinical Oncology* 41: 1909–1920.

Kaiser Family Foundation (KFF). 2022. 5 charts about public opinion on the Affordable Care Act. Accessed October 2023. Available at: https://www.kff.org/health-reform/poll-finding/5-charts-about-public-opinion-on-the-affordable-care-act-and-the-supreme-court/.

Kaiser Family Foundation (KFF). 2023. Kaiser health tracking poll: The public's views. Accessed October 2023. Available at: https://www.kff.org/interactive/kff-health-tracking-poll-the-publics-views-on-the-aca/#?response=Favorable–Unfavorable&aRange=twoYear

Kaiser Family Foundation (KFF). 2023. Status of state Medicaid expansion decisions: Interactive map. Accessed October 2023. Available at: https://www.kff.org/medicaid/issue-brief/status-of-state-medicaid-expansion-decisions-interactive-map/

Kaptchuk, T. J., and D. M. Eisenberg. 2001. Varieties of healing 1: Medical pluralism in the United States. *Annals of Internal Medicine* 135: 189–195.

Kaufman, M. 1980. American medical education. In: *The Education of American Physicians: Historical Essays*. R. L. Numbers, ed. Los Angeles, CA: University of California Press. 7–28.

Kelleher G. D., and G. Williams. 1994. The new sociology of the health service. *Challenging Medicine*. New York, NY: Routledge.

Kennedy, J. F. 1963. Message from the President of the United States relative to mental illness and mental retardation. *American Journal of Psychiatry* 120: 729–737.

KFF. 2023. Status of state Medicaid expansion decisions: interactive map. Available at: https://www.kff.org/medicaid/issue-brief/status-of-state-medicaid-expansion-decisions-interactivemap/#:~:text=The%20Affordable%20Care%20Act's%20(ACA,FMAP)%20for%20their%20expansion%20populations

Koch, A. L. 1993. Financing health services. In: *Introduction to Health Services*. 4th ed. S. J. Williams and P. R. Torrens, eds. New York: Delmar. 299–331.

Law, S. A. 1974. *Blue Cross: What Went Wrong?* New Haven, CT: Yale University Press.

Major provisions of the 21st Century Cures Act. 2017. *Congressional Digest* 96: 32.

Martensen, R. L. 1996. Hospital hotels and the care of the "worthy rich." *Journal of the American Medical Association* 275: 325.

Mayer, T. R., and G. G. Mayer. 1984. *The Health Insurance Alternative: A Complete Guide to Health Maintenance Organizations*. New York: Putnam.

McDonnell, J. 2006. Is the medical world flattening? *Ophthalmology Times* 31: 4.

Medicaid and CHIP Payment and Access Commission. 2020. Medicaid enrollment changes following the ACA. Accessed May 2020. Available at: https://www.macpac.gov/subtopic/medicaid-enrollment-changes-following-the-aca

Mongan, J. J. 1995. Anatomy and physiology of health reform's failure. *Health Affairs* 14: 99–101.

Mulvaney-Day, N., B. J., Gibbons, S. Alikhan, and M. Karakus. 2019. Mental Health Parity and Addiction Equity Act and the use of outpatient behavioral health services in the United States, 2005-2016. *American Journal of Public Health* 109: S190–S196.

Murray, J. 2007. *Origins of American Health Insurance: A History of Industrial Sickness Funds*. New Haven, CT: Yale University Press.

Mutchnick, I. S., D. T. Stern, and C. A. Moyer. 2005. Trading health services across borders: GATS, markets, and caveats. *Health Affairs* 24: W5-42–W5-51.

National Association of State Mental Health Program Directors (NASMHPD). 2014. *The Vital Role of State Psychiatric Hospitals*. J. Parks and A. Q. Radke, eds. Alexandria, VA: NASMHPD.

Norcini, J. J., and P. E. Mazmanian. 2005. Physician migration, education, and health care. *Journal of Continuing Education in the Health Professions* 25: 4–7.

Numbers, R. L. 1985. The third party: Health insurance in America. In: *Sickness and Health in America: Readings in the History of Medicine and Public Health*. J. W. Leavitt and R. L. Numbers, eds. Madison, WI: University of Wisconsin Press.

Numbers, R. L., and J. H. Warner. 1985. The maturation of American medical science. In: *Sickness and Health in America: Readings in the History of Medicine and Public Health*. J. W. Leavitt and R. L. Numbers, eds. Madison, WI: University of Wisconsin Press.

Patrick, V., R. C. Smith, S. J. Schleifer, M. E. Morris, and K. McLennon. 2006. Facilitating discharge in state psychiatric institutions: A group intervention strategy. *Psychiatric Rehabilitation Journal* 29: 183–188.

Policy Center for Maternal Mental Health 2022. Updates to ACA insurance plans for 2023 and the upcoming expiration of subsidies. Available at: https://www.2020mom.org/blog/2022/7/8/updates-to-aca-insurance-plans-for-2023-and-the-upcoming-expiration-of-subsidies#:~:text=Starting%20in%202023%2C%20ACA%20insurance,life%2C%20or%20other%20health%20conditions

Potter, M. A., and B. B. Longest. 1994. The divergence of federal and state policies on the charitable tax exemption of nonprofit hospitals. *Journal of Health Politics, Policy and Law* 19: 393–419.

Public Health Service. 1995. *Health United States, 1994*. Washington, DC: Government Printing Office.

Raffel, M. W. 1980. *The U.S. Health System: Origins and Functions*. New York: John Wiley & Sons.

Raffel, M. W., and N. K. Raffel. 1994. *The U.S. Health System: Origins and Functions*. 4th ed. Albany, NY: Delmar.

Ramsey, D. D. 2011. Evolution of mental health organizations in the United States. *Journal of Global Health Care Systems* 1: 1–11.

Rana, S., L. Verdin, J. Beasley, et al. 2014. Use of *Pseudognaphalium obtusifolium* in Native American traditional medicine and its possible health benefits. *NAAAS & Affiliates Conference Monographs* 2014: 437–453.

Reed, L. S. 1965. *Private Health Insurance in the United States: An Overview*. Bulletin, Social Security Administration. Accessed May 2020. Available at: https://www.ssa.gov/policy/docs/ssb/v28n12/v28n12p3.pdf

Richardson, J. T. 1945. The origin and development of group hospitalization in the United States, 1890–1940. *University of Missouri Studies* XX, no. 3.

Rosen, G. 1983. *The Structure of American Medical Practice 1875–1941*. Philadelphia, PA: University of Pennsylvania Press.

Rosenberg, C. E. 1979. The therapeutic revolution: Medicine, meaning, and social change in nineteenth-century America. In: *The Therapeutic Revolution*. M. J. Vogel, ed. Philadelphia, PA: University of Pennsylvania Press. 3–25.

Rosner, L. 2001. The Philadelphia medical marketplace. In: *Major Problems in the History of American Medicine and Public Health*. J. H. Warner and J. A. Tighe, eds. Boston, MA: Houghton Mifflin. 80–89.

Rothstein, W. G. 1972. *American Physicians in the Nineteenth Century: From Sect to Science*. Baltimore, MD: Johns Hopkins University Press.

Shinohara, C. 2016. Health-care work in globalization: News reports on care worker migration to Japan. *International Journal of Japanese Sociology* 25: 7–26.

Shryock, R. H. 1966. *Medicine in America: Historical Essays*. Baltimore, MD: Johns Hopkins Press.

Singhal, S., B. Latko, and C. Martin. 2018. The future of healthcare: Finding the opportunities that lie beneath the uncertainty. McKinsey & Company. Accessed May 2020. Available at: https://www.mckinsey.com/industries/healthcare-systems-and-services/our-insights/the-future-of-healthcare-finding-the-opportunities-that-lie-beneath-the-uncertainty

Smith, R. D., R. Chanda, and V. Tangcharoensathien. 2009. Trade in health-related services. *Lancet* 373: 593–601.

Somers, A. R., and H. M. Somers. 1977. *Health and Health Care: Policies in Perspective*. Germantown, MD: Aspen Systems.

Sommers, B. D., B. Maylone, R. J. Blendon, E. J. Orav, and A. M. Epstein. 2017. Three-year impacts of the Affordable Care Act: Improved medical care and health among low-income adults. *Health Affairs* 36: 1119–1128.

Starr, P. 1982. *The Social Transformation of American Medicine*. Cambridge, MA: Basic Books.

Starr, P. 2018. Rebounding with Medicare: Reform and counterreform in American health policy. *Journal of Health Politics, Policy & Law* 43: 707–730.

Statista. 2023. U.S. private health insurance - statistics & facts. Accessed October 2023. Available at: https://www.statista.com/topics/1530/health-insurance-in-the-us/#topicOverview

Stevens, R. 1971. *American Medicine and the Public Interest*. New Haven, CT: Yale University Press.

Substance Abuse and Mental Health Services Administration. 2013. *Behavioral Health, United States, 2012*. Rockville, MD: Department of Health and Human Services.

The Assistant Secretary for Planning and Evaluation 2023). Health coverage under the Affordable Care Act: Current enrollment trends and state estimates. Available at: https://aspe.hhs.gov/reports/current-health-coverage-under-affordable-care-act

The New York Times. 2021. Why public health faces a crisis across the U.S. Accessed October 2023. Available at: https://www.nytimes.com/2021/10/18/us/coronavirus-public-health.html

Tilhou, A. S., N. Huguet, J. DeVoe, and H. Angier. 2020. The Affordable Care Act Medicaid expansion positively impacted community health centers and their patients. *Journal of General Internal Medicine* 35: 1292–1295.

Traore, T., S. Shanks, N. Haider, et al. 2023. How prepared is the world? Identifying weaknesses in existing assessment frameworks for global health security through a One Health approach. *Lancet* 401: 673–687.

Turnock, B. J. 1997. *Public health: What it is and how it works*. Gaithersburg, MD: Aspen.

Uchida, T., I. Fumiaki, I. Koji, et al. 2013. Global cardiovascular device innovation: Japan–U.S.A. synergies. *Circulation Journal* 77: 1714–1718.

U.S. Department of Health and Human Services. 2023. Biden-Harris Administration celebrates the Affordable Care Act's 13th anniversary and highlights record-breaking coverage. Accessed October 2023. Available at: https://www.hhs.gov/about/news/2023/03/23/biden-harris-administration-celebrates-affordable-care-acts-13th-anniversary-highlights-record-breaking-coverage.html

U.S. Surgeon General. 1999. *Mental health: A report of the Surgeon General*. Rockville, MD: U.S. Department of Health and Human Services, Center for Mental Health Services, National Institute of Mental Health. Accessed November 2020. Available at: https://collections.nlm.nih.gov/ext/document/101584932X120/PDF/101584932X120.pdf.

Virani, A., A. M. Wellstead, and M. Howlett. 2020. The north-south policy divide in transnational healthcare: A comparative review of policy research on medical tourism in source and destination countries. *Globalization and Health* 16: 1–15.

Wagner, D. 2005. *The Poorhouse: America's Forgotten Institution*. Lanham, MD: Rowman & Littlefield.

Whitehouse.gov. 2023. Executive order on strengthening Medicaid and the Affordable Care Act. Accessed September 2023. Available at: https://www.whitehouse.gov/briefing-room/presidential-actions/2021/01/28/executive-order-on-strengthening-medicaid-and-the-affordable-care-act/

White House, Office of the Press Secretary. 2009. Weekly address: President Obama calls health insurance reform key to stronger economy and improvement on status quo. Accessed November 2020. Available at: https://obamawhitehouse.archives.gov/realitycheck/the-press-office/weekly-address-president-obama-calls-health-insurance-reform-key-stronger-economy-a

Whitted, G. 1993. Private health insurance and employee benefits. In: *Introduction to Health Services*. 4th ed. S. J. Williams and P. R. Torrens, eds. New York: Delmar. 332–360.

Willems, D. L. 2001. Balancing rationalities: Gatekeeping in health care. *Journal of Medical Ethics* 27: 25–29.

Williams, S. J. 1995. *Essentials of Health Services*. Albany, NY: Delmar.

Wilson, F. A., and D. Neuhauser. 1985. *Health Services in the United States*. 2nd ed. Cambridge, MA: Ballinger.

World Economic Forum. 2023. U.S. Global Health and Healthcare Strategic Outlook: Shaping the future of Health and Healthcare. Accessed October 2023. Available at: https://www3.weforum.org/docs/WEF_Global_Health_and_Healthcare_Strategic_Outlook_2023.pdf

Wright, J. W. 1997. *The New York Times Almanac*. New York, NY: Penguin Putnam.

PART 2

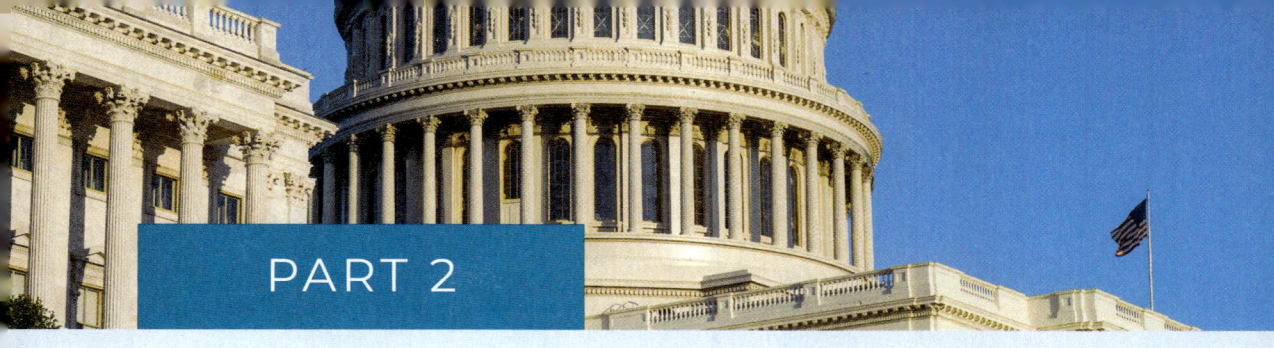

System Resources

CHAPTER 4	Health Services Professionals	145
CHAPTER 5	Medical Technology	189
CHAPTER 6	Health Services Financing	237

CHAPTER 4

Health Services Professionals

LEARNING OBJECTIVES

- Become familiar with the various types of health services professionals and their training, practice requirements, and practice settings.
- Differentiate between primary care and specialty care, and identify the causes of the imbalance between primary care and specialty care in the United States.
- Learn about the extent of maldistribution in the physician labor force, and comprehend the reasons for that maldistribution.
- Outline initiatives under the Affordable Care Act to relieve shortages of primary care providers and to ensure coordinated care delivery in team settings.
- Appreciate the role of nonphysician providers in healthcare delivery.
- Understand the role of allied health professionals in healthcare delivery.
- Discuss the functions and qualifications of health services administrators.
- Prepare for new trends in healthcare workforce development.
- Assess global health workforce challenges.

"Hmm, they're all beginning to look like me."

Introduction

The U.S. healthcare industry is the largest and most powerful employer in the nation, accounting for 12% of the total labor force in the United States (Kaiser Family Foundation, 2018). In 2020, the healthcare sector contributed 18.82% of the U.S. gross domestic product (World Bank, 2020). Although the number of jobs in many areas of the U.S. economy decreased with the economic recession beginning in December 2007, the healthcare sector continued its growth trend (Salsberg and Martiniano, 2018). Overall demand for all types of healthcare services is expected to continue increasing as the population ages, so that substantial growth is anticipated in health care and related occupations. It is projected that jobs in the healthcare sector will grow by 18.1% between 2016 and 2026, whereas the entire U.S. workforce will grow by only 6.1% during the same period (Center for Health Workforce Studies, 2018).

Health professionals are among the most well-educated and diverse of all labor groups. Almost all of these practitioner groups are now represented by their own professional associations, many of which are listed in **Appendix 4-A**. Health services professionals work in a variety of healthcare settings, including hospitals, managed care organizations (MCOs), nursing care facilities, mental health institutions, insurance companies, pharmaceutical companies, outpatient facilities, community health centers, migrant health centers, mental health centers, school clinics, physicians' offices, laboratories, voluntary health agencies, professional health associations, colleges of medicine and allied health professions, and research institutions. Most health professionals are employed by hospitals (31.7%), followed by physician offices (8.96%) and outpatient care centers (8.8%) (**Table 4-1**).

The expansion of the number and types of health services professionals is closely related to population trends, advances in research and technology, disease and illness trends, and changes in healthcare financing and delivery of services. New and complex medical techniques, equipment, and advanced computer-based information systems (ISs) are constantly being introduced, and health services professionals must continually update their skills and learn how to use these innovations. Specialization in medicine has also contributed to the proliferation of different types of medical technicians. The shift from acute to chronic disease as the dominant medical concern and a growing emphasis on prevention have created a greater need for professionals who are formally trained to address behavioral risk factors and the delivery of primary care. Finally, increased insurance coverage under the Affordable Care Act (ACA) has increased the demand for health services professionals.

This chapter provides an overview of the large array of health services professionals employed in diverse health delivery settings. It briefly discusses the training and practice requirements of various health professionals, their major roles, the practice settings in which they are employed, and some critical issues concerning their professions. Emphasis is placed on physicians because they play a leading role in the delivery of health care. At the same time, there has been increased recognition of the roles that nonphysician providers play, particularly in boosting the nation's primary care infrastructure.

Physicians

Physicians play a central role in the delivery of health services by evaluating patients' health conditions, diagnosing abnormalities, and prescribing treatments. Some physicians are engaged in medical education and research to find new and better ways to control and cure health problems. Many are involved in the prevention of illness.

Table 4-1 Persons Employed in Health Service Sites

Site	2000 Number of Persons (in thousands)	2000 Percentage Distribution	2019 Number of Persons (in thousands)	2019 Percentage Distribution
All employed civilians	136,891	100.0	158,600	100.0
All health service sites	12,211	100.0	22,262	100.0
Hospitals	5,202	42.6	7,055	31.7
Outpatient care centers	772	6.3	1,959	8.80
Nursing care facilities	1,593	13.0	1,765	7.92
Offices and clinics of physicians	1,387	11.4	1,994	8.96
Other healthcare services	1,027	8.4	1,297	5.83
Home healthcare services	548	4.5	1,483	6.66
Residential care facilities, without nursing	652	5.3	1,163	5.22
Offices and clinics of dentists	672	5.5	1,013	4.55
Offices and clinics of other health practitioners	143	1.2	367	1.65
Offices and clinics of optometrists	95	0.8	160	0.7
Offices and clinics of chiropractors	120	1.0	143	0.6

Data from Division of Labor Force Statistics, U.S. Bureau of Labor Statistics. 2019, 2020. *Labor force statistics from the current population survey*. Available at: https://www.bls.gov/cps/cpsaat18.htm. Accessed January 2020. https://www.bls.gov/opub/mlr/2020/article/job-market remains-tight-in-2019-as-the-unemployment-rate-falls-to-its-lowest-level since-1969.htm#:~:text=The%20number%20of%20employed 20people,partly%20reflecting%20slower%20population%20growth. Accessed September 2023; US Census Bureau, 2019 American Community Survey, 1-year estimates.

All states require physicians to be licensed to practice. These licensure requirements include graduation from an accredited medical school that awards a Doctor of Medicine (MD) or Doctor of Osteopathic Medicine (DO) degree; successful completion of a licensing examination, governed by either the National Board of Medical Examiners or the National Board of Osteopathic Medical Examiners; and completion of a supervised internship/residency program (Stanfield et al., 2012). The term **residency** refers to graduate medical education in a specialty that takes the form of paid on-the-job training, usually in a hospital. Before entering a residency, which may last 2–6 years, most DOs serve a 12-month rotating internship after graduation.

The number of active physicians, both MDs and DOs, has steadily increased from 14.1 physicians per 10,000 population in 1950 to 34.4 per 10,000 population in 2021 (**Table 4-2**). Of the 172 medical schools in the

Table 4-2 Active U.S. Physicians According to Type of Physician and Number per 10,000 Population

Year	All Active Physicians	Doctors of Medicine	Doctors of Osteopathy	Active Physicians per 10,000 Population
1950	219,900	209,000	10,900	14.1
1960	259,500	247,300	12,200	14.0
1970	326,500	314,200	12,300	15.6
1980	427,122	409,992	17,130	19.0
1990	567,610	539,616	27,994	22.4
1995	672,859	625,443	35,667	25.0
2000	772,296	692,368	44,723	27.0
2010	799,472	555,027	55,269	27.2
2013	829,914	559,713	60,172	29.4
2015	870,900	577,313	65,070	29.2
2021	949,658	624,987	78,904	34.4

Data from National Center for Health Statistics. 1996. *Health, United States, 1995*. Hyattsville, MD: U.S. Department of Health and Human Services. p. 220; National Center for Health Statistics. 2002. *Health, United States, 2002*. Hyattsville, MD: U.S. Department of Health and Human Services. p. 274; National Center for Health Statistics. 2016. *Health, United States, 2015*. Hyattsville, MD: U.S. Department of Health and Human Services. p. 282; National Center for Health Statistics. 2018. *Health, United States, 2017*. Hyattsville, MD: U.S. Department of Health and Human Services. Table 84; AAMC Center for Workforce Studies. 2014. *2014 physician specialty data book*. Available at: https://www.aamc.org/system/files/reports/1/2014physicianspecialtydatabook.pdf . Accessed January 2020; AAMC Center for Workforce Studies. 2012. *2012 physician specialty data book*. Available at: https://www.aamc.org/system/files/2019-08/2012physicianspecialtydatabook.pdf. Accessed January 2020; Association of American Medical Colleges. 2015. *Physician specialty data report: Active physicians with a Doctor of Osteopathic Medicine (DO) degree by specialty, 2015*. Available at: https://www.aamc.org/data-reports/workforce/interactive-data/active-physicians-doctor-osteopathic-medicine-do-degree-specialty-2015. Accessed January 2020.

America Medical Association. AMA Physician Masterfile (Dec.31, 2021). Population data are from the U.S. Census Bureau, Population Division, Release date: April 2020.

United States, 141 teach allopathic medicine and award an MD degree; 31 teach osteopathic medicine and award the DO degree (National Center for Health Statistics [NCHS], 2016).

Similarities and Differences Between MDs and DOs

Both MDs and DOs use accepted methods of treatment, including drugs and surgery. The two differ mainly in their philosophies and approaches to medical treatment.

Osteopathic medicine, practiced by DOs, emphasizes the musculoskeletal system of the body, such as correction of joints or tissues. In their treatment plans, DOs stress preventive medicine and take into account how factors such as diet and environment might influence natural resistance. They take a holistic approach to patient care. In comparison, MDs are trained in **allopathic medicine**, which views medical treatment as an active intervention to counteract and neutralize the effects of disease. MDs, particularly generalists, may also use preventive medicine, along with allopathic treatments. The osteopathic medical profession is one of the fastest-growing segments of health care, representing more than 11% of all physicians in the United States (AOA, 2022). More than half of DOs work in primary-care settings (NCHS, 2016).

Generalists and Specialists

Most DOs are generalists and most MDs are specialists. In the United States, physicians trained in family medicine/general practice, general internal medicine, and general pediatrics are considered primary care physicians (PCPs) or **generalists** (Rich et al., 1994). Most PCPs provide preventive services (e.g., health examinations, immunizations, mammograms, Papanicolaou smears) and treat frequently occurring and less severe problems. Problems that occur less frequently or that require complex diagnostic or therapeutic approaches are referred to specialists after an initial evaluation.

Physicians in non-primary care specialties are referred to as **specialists**. Specialists must seek certification in an area of medical specialization, which commonly requires additional years of advanced residency training, followed by several years of practice in the specialty. A specialty board examination is often required as the final step in becoming a board-certified specialist. Some common medical specialties are described in **Exhibit 4-1**. Medical specialties may be divided into six major functional groups: (1) the subspecialties of internal medicine; (2) a broad group of medical specialties; (3) obstetrics and gynecology; (4) surgery of all

Exhibit 4-1 Definitions of Medical Specialties and Subspecialties

Allergists	Treat conditions and illnesses caused by allergies or related to the immune system
Anesthesiologists	Use drugs and gases to render patients unconscious during surgery
Cardiologists	Treat heart diseases
Dermatologists	Treat infections, growths, and injuries related to the skin
Emergency medicine	Work specifically in emergency departments, treating acute illnesses and emergency situations—for example, trauma
Family physicians	Are prepared to handle most types of illnesses and care for the patient as a whole
General practitioners	Similar to family physicians—examine patients or order tests and have X-rays done to diagnose illness and treat the patient
Geriatricians	Specialize in problems and diseases that accompany aging
Gynecologists	Specialize in the care of the reproductive system of women
Internists	Treat diseases related to the internal organs of the body—for example, conditions of the lungs, blood, kidneys, and heart
Neurologists	Treat disorders of the central nervous system and order tests necessary to detect diseases

(continues)

Exhibit 4-1 Definitions of Medical Specialties and Subspecialties   (continued)

Obstetricians	Work with women throughout their pregnancy, deliver infants, and care for the mother after the delivery
Oncologists	Specialize in the diagnosis and treatment of cancers and tumors
Ophthalmologists	Treat diseases and injuries of the eye
Otolaryngologists	Specialize in the treatment of conditions or diseases of the ear, nose, and throat
Pathologists	Study the characteristics, causes, and progression of diseases
Pediatricians	Provide care for children from birth to adolescence
Preventive medicine	Includes occupational medicine, public health, and general preventive treatments
Psychiatrists	Help patients recover from mental illness and regain their mental health
Radiologists	Perform diagnosis and treatment by the use of X-rays and radioactive materials
Surgeons	Operate on patients to treat disease, repair injury, correct deformities, and improve health
General surgeons	Perform many different types of surgery, usually of relatively low difficulty
Neurologic surgeons	Specialize in surgery of the brain, spinal cord, and nervous system
Orthopedic surgeons	Specialize in the repair of bones and joints
Plastic surgeons	Repair malformed or injured parts of the body
Thoracic surgeons	Perform surgery in the chest cavity—for example, lung and heart surgery
Urologists	Specialize in conditions of the urinary tract in both sexes and of the sexual/reproductive system in males

Data from Stanfield, P. S., et al. 2012. *Introduction to the health professions.* 6th ed. Burlington, MA: Jones & Bartlett Learning.

types; (5) hospital-based radiology, anesthesiology, and pathology; and (6) psychiatry. The distribution of physicians by specialty appears in **Table 4-3**.

Work Settings and Practice Patterns

Physicians practice in a variety of settings and arrangements. Some work in hospitals as medical residents or staff physicians. Others work in the public sector, such as federal government agencies, public health departments, community and migrant health centers, schools, and prisons. Most physicians, however, are office-based practitioners, and most physician contacts occur in physician offices. An increasing number of physicians are partners or salaried employees, working in both hospitals and various outpatient settings, such as group practices, freestanding ambulatory care clinics, and diagnostic imaging centers.

Table 4-3 Number of People per Active Physician by Specialty, 2021

Physician Specialty	Physicians	People per Physician
All specialties	949,658	344
Internal medicine	120,342	2,714
Pediatrics	60,305	1,720
Obstetrics and gynecology	42,496	7,685
Anesthesiology	42,264	7,727
Psychiatry	38,424	8,499
General surgery	24,881	13,125
Emergency medicine	46,857	6,969
Orthopedic surgery	18,469	17,682
Radiology and diagnostic radiology	27,197	12,008
Ophthalmology	18,948	17,235
Neurology	13,853	23,574
Gastroenterology	15,678	20,830
Dermatology	12,767	25,579
Pathology, anatomic/clinical	12,180	26,812
Pulmonary diseases	4,867	67,099
Urology	10,081	32,395
Otolaryngology	9,616	33,961
Family Medicine/General Practice	118,641	2,753
Cardiovascular disease	22,262	14,669
Hematology and Oncology	16,673	19,587
Critical care medicine	14,159	23,064
Nephrology	11,554	28,265
Child and adolescent psychiatry	9,966	10,409
Infectious Disease	9,913	32,944
Physical Medicine and Rehabilitation	9,724	2,753
Endocrinology, Diabetes, and Metabolism	8,246	39,603
Plastic surgery	7,228	45,181
Preventive Medicine	6,555	49,820

(continues)

Table 4-3 Number of People per Active Physician by Specialty, 2021 *(continued)*

Physician Specialty	Physicians	People per Physician
Rheumatology	6,420	50,867
Pain Medicine and Pain Management	6,240	2,753
Geriatric Medicine	6,149	11,820
Neurological Surgery	5,748	56,814
Internal medicine pediatrics	5,701	57,283
Radiation Oncology	5,376	60,746
Allergy and Immunology	5,009	65,197
Interventional Cardiology	4,736	68,955
Thoracic Surgery	4,449	73,403
Neuroradiology	4,311	75,753
Vascular Surgery	4,039	80,854
Vascular and Interventional Radiology	4,011	81,418
Sports Medicine	3,208	101,798
Clinical cardiac electrophysiology	2,632	124,076

Data from American Medical Association. AMA Physician Masterfile (Dec.31, 2021). Population data are from the U.S. Census Bureau, Population Division. Release date: April, 2020.

In 2016, physicians in general/family practice accounted for the greatest proportion of ambulatory care visits, followed by those in pediatrics and internal medicine (**Figure 4-1**). Physicians in obstetrics and gynecology tend to spend the most hours

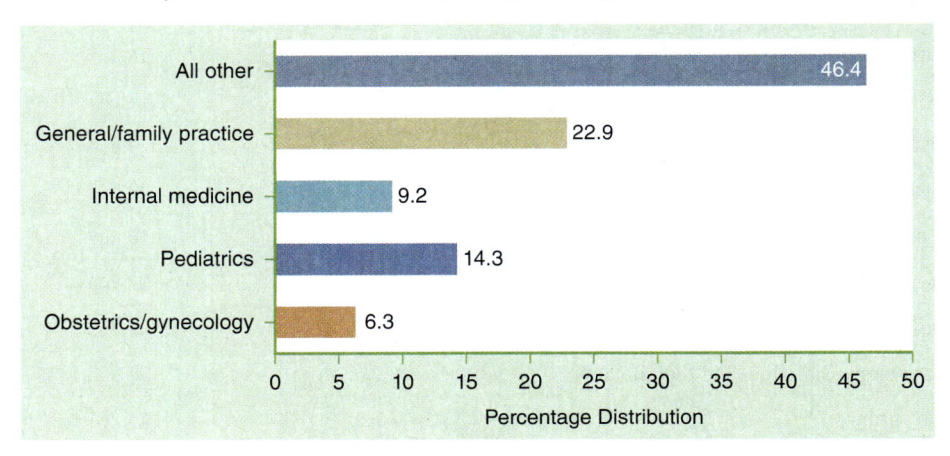

Figure 4-1 Ambulatory care visits to physicians according to physician specialty, 2016.

- All other: 46.4
- General/family practice: 22.9
- Internal medicine: 9.2
- Pediatrics: 14.3
- Obstetrics/gynecology: 6.3

Data from Willis, J. (2020). Primary Care in the United States: A Chartbook of Facts and Statistics. Robert Graham Center.

in patient care per week, even exceeding hours spent by surgeons (Health Resources and Services Administration [HRSA], 2008). Anesthesiologists have the highest average annual income (U.S. Bureau of Labor Statistics, 2019). Malpractice insurance premiums and operating expenses are the highest in obstetrics/gynecology.

Differences Between Primary and Specialty Care

Primary care can be distinguished from **specialty care** based on the time, focus, and scope of services provided to patients. The five main areas of distinction are as follows:

- In linear time sequence, primary care is first-contact care and is regarded as the entry point to the healthcare system. Specialty care, when needed, generally follows primary care.
- In a managed care environment where health services functions are integrated, PCPs serve as gatekeepers—an important role in controlling costs, utilization rates, and the rational allocation of resources. In the gatekeeping model, specialty care requires referral from PCPs.
- Primary care is longitudinal. In other words, primary-care providers follow through the course of treatment and coordinate various activities, including initial diagnosis, treatment, referral, consultation, monitoring, and follow-up. PCPs serve as patient advisors and advocates. Their coordinating role is especially important in ensuring continuity of care for chronic conditions. Because specialty care is episodic, it is more focused and intense than primary care.
- Primary care focuses on the person as a whole, whereas specialty care centers on particular diseases or organ systems of the body. Patients often have multiple problems simultaneously, a condition referred to as **comorbidity**. Treating comorbidities requires balancing multiple requirements, addressing changes in health conditions over time, and monitoring drug and disease interactions. Specialty care tends to be limited to illness episodes, the organ system, or the disease process involved. Comorbidities may necessitate referrals to multiple specialists, which present challenges in care coordination for PCPs.
- The difference in scope is reflected in how primary and specialty care providers are trained. Primary care students spend a significant amount of time in ambulatory care settings, familiarizing themselves with a variety of patient conditions and problems. Students in medical subspecialties spend significant time in inpatient hospitals, where they are exposed to state-of-the-art medical technology.

The Expanding Role of Hospitalists

Since the mid-1990s, an increasing amount of inpatient medical care in the United States has been delivered by **hospitalists**, physicians who specialize in the care of patients who are hospitalized (Schneller, 2006). Hospitalists do not usually have a relationship with the patient prior to or after hospitalization—only during the actual inpatient stay. Essentially, the patient's primary-care provider entrusts the oversight of the patient's care to a hospitalist upon admission, and the patient returns to the regular physician after discharge (Freed, 2004). In 2019, 44,037 adult hospitalists were recorded (Lapps et al., 2022).

The growth in the number of hospitalists is influenced by the desire of hospital executives, health maintenance organizations (HMOs), and medical groups to reduce inpatient costs and increase efficiency without compromising quality or patient satisfaction. Published research shows that using hospitalists does, in fact, achieve these goals (Wachter, 2004). Research findings have also put to rest initial concerns from PCPs, who were accustomed to the traditional method of rounding on their hospitalized patients. The debate over hospitalists has largely shifted from quality and efficiency of performance to optimizing hospitalists' skills and expanding their roles (Sehgal and Wachter, 2006). The American Board of Hospital Medicine (ABHM), founded in 2009 as a member board of the American Board of Physician Specialists (ABPS), is the only board of certification for hospital medicine.

Compared with the traditional inpatient-physician model, the hospitalist model has a number of advantages. The on-site availability of a hospitalist ensures that a dedicated provider is readily available to respond to acute medical crises, manage tests, and answer questions, thereby reducing the time needed for treatments and improving the efficiency of discharge planning. This allows the hospitalist more time to communicate with patients, their families, and patients' PCPs (White and Glazier, 2011). Studies have demonstrated that hospitalist care is associated with shorter lengths of stay, better quality of care, increased patient satisfaction, and lower inpatient costs (Chen et al., 2013; Coffman and Rundall, 2005; Goodwin et al., 2013; White and Glazier, 2011). Recent studies have also shown hospitalists are able to achieve better provider-patient communication (Abid et al., 2022) and reduction in administrative work (Yan, 2022).

Issues in Medical Practice, Training, and Supply

Research has shown that the way physicians practice medicine and prescribe treatments for similar conditions varies significantly. Physicians have at their disposal an increasing number of therapeutic options because of the exponential growth in medical science and technology. Conversely, increasing healthcare costs continue to threaten the viability of the healthcare delivery system. The difficult balancing act that physicians must perform—simultaneously taking into account the availability of the most advanced treatments, uncertainties about their potential benefits, and whether the higher costs of treatment are justified—contributes to a confusing environment. Hence, support has been growing for the development and refinement of standardized clinical guidelines that would streamline clinical decision-making and improve the quality of care. At the same time, some criticisms have arisen about the applicability, flexibility, and objectivity of such guidelines. Although the number of conditions for which guidelines are available is steadily increasing, guidelines for combinations of conditions (i.e., comorbidity) are not. Furthermore, many of the recommendations incorporated in the most well-accepted clinical guidelines allow for significant flexibility, making it difficult to determine whether care provided by physicians complies with recommendations made in the guidelines (Garber, 2005). In addition, the changing nature of chronic diseases and comorbidities is creating new challenges for disease-centered reactive practice patterns (Starfield, 2011). A better care model, such as the chronic care model, requires patient-centered, longitudinal, coordinated, evidence-based, and IS-supported care, which facilitates physician-patient interaction and patient self-management (Coleman et al., 2009).

Medical Training

The principal source of funding for graduate medical education is the Medicare program, which provides explicit payments to teaching hospitals for each resident in training. The government, however, does not mandate how these physicians should be trained. Medical and surgical services furnished by an intern or resident within the scope of his or her training program are covered as provider services, with Medicare paying for these services through Direct Graduate Medical Education (DGME) and Indirect Medical Education (IME) payments. DGME payments offset a portion of the direct costs associated with training physicians (e.g., resident stipends and benefits, supervising physician stipends and benefits). Teaching hospitals depend on IME payments to maintain state-of-the-art facilities and equipment (such as Level 1 trauma centers) and specialized services (e.g., advanced cancer care) that are critical both for training health professionals and maintaining community health (Association of American Medical Colleges [AAMC], 2014).

Emphasis on hospital-based training in the United States has produced more specialists than PCPs. Meanwhile, the healthcare delivery system is evolving toward a primary-care orientation (Centers for Medicare and Medicaid Services [CMS], 2019). The increasing prevalence of chronic diseases further highlights the deficiencies of the U.S. medical training model, which focuses mainly on acute interventions. Medical training in primary-care needs to be refocused on patient-centered care, general internal medicine, and longitudinal clinical experiences.

Supply of Medical Professionals

Aided by tax-financed subsidies, the United States has experienced a steady increase in its physician labor force (Table 4-2, **Figure 4-2**). In 2021, for example, there were 344 physicians per 100,000 population (NCHS, 2022). This growth, however, has mainly occurred among specialists.

In the near future, a large influx of individuals who are newly insured and seeking care is expected to strain the existing primary-care infrastructure and result in personnel shortages in primary care. Projected shortages are expected to reach between 46,900 and 121,900 physicians by 2032 (AAMC, 2019a). In primary care alone, projected shortages are expected to reach 21,100–55,200 (AAMC, 2019b). Physician retirement decisions are projected to have the greatest impact on supply, as more than 40% of all currently active physicians will be 65 or older within the next decade (AAMC, 2019b).

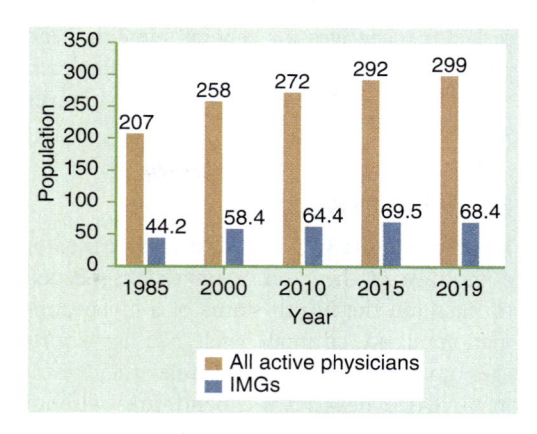

Figure 4-2 Supply of U.S. physicians, including international medical graduates (IMGs), per 100,000 population, 1985–2019.

Data from National Center for Health Statistics. 2018. *Health, United States, 2017*. Hyattsville, MD: U.S. Department of Health and Human Services. Table 83–84; U.S. Census Bureau. 2000. *Historical national population estimates: July 1, 1900 to July 1, 1999*. Available at: https://www2.census.gov/programs-surveys/popest/tables/1900-1980/national/totals/popclockest.txt. Accessed January 2020; U.S. Census Bureau. n.d. *Census 2000 data for the United States*. Available at: https://www2.census.gov/census_2000/census2000/states/us.html. Accessed January 2020; U.S. Census Bureau. 2019. *National population totals and components of change: 2010–2019: Annual estimates of the resident population for the United States, regions, states, and Puerto Rico: April 1, 2010 to July 1, 2019* (NST-EST2019-01). Available at: https://www.census.gov/data/tables/time-series/demo/popest/2010s-national-total.html. Accessed January 2020.

2019 data from: American Medical Association 2021. Physician Masterfile and Health, United States, 2020–2021 Table DocSt.

In 2013, $12 million in ACA funding was awarded to train more than 300 new primary-care residents during the 2013–2014 academic year; 32 teaching health centers in 21 states received funding (U.S. Department of Health and Human Services [DHHS], 2013). The ACA also provides for loan repayment for physicians going into pediatric, mental health, and surgical subspecialties—specialties known to have shortages—in exchange for professionals in these subspecialties providing care in medically underserved areas (MUAs). Additionally, the law authorizes grants to increase training in geriatrics and behavioral health and provides incentives for general surgeons who practice in MUAs (Congressional Research Service, 2017). The effects of these initiatives will not be known for several years.

Maldistribution

Maldistribution refers to either a surplus or a shortage of the type of physicians needed to maintain the health status of a given population at an optimal level. Neither shortages nor surpluses are desirable; they result in increased healthcare expenditures without yielding a positive return in health outcomes. The United States faces maldistributions in terms of both geography and specialty.

Geographic Maldistribution

One of the ironies of excess physician supply is that localities outside the U.S. metropolitan areas (i.e., counties with fewer than 50,000 residents) continue to have physician shortages. Nonmetropolitan areas have 50.2 PCPs per 100,000 population compared to 79.7 PCPs per 100,000 population in metropolitan areas (RHIhub, 2021). Rural areas, in particular, lack an adequate supply of both PCPs and specialists, even though residents in rural areas tend to be sicker, older, and financially poorer than those in nonrural areas. Whereas 19.3% of the U.S. population lives in rural areas, only 11.4% of physicians practice there (NCHS, 2014).

The DHHS designates as health professional shortage areas (HPSAs) those urban or rural areas, population groups, or medical or other public facilities that have a shortage of providers in primary care, dental care, and mental health care. In March 2023, there were 8,377 designated primary-care HPSAs, 7,414 dental HPSAs, and 6,643 mental health HPSAs in the United States (DHHS, 2023).

Several federal programs have demonstrated success in increasing the supply of primary-care services in rural areas. Some of these programs include the National Health Service Corps, which makes scholarship support conditional on a commitment to future service in an underserved area; the Migrant and Community Health Center Programs, which provide primary-care services to the low income and underserved using federal grants; and support of primary-care training programs and Area Health Education Centers.

Specialty Maldistribution

Besides geographic maldistribution of physicians, a considerable imbalance exists between primary and specialty care in the United States. Approximately 47.8% of physicians work in primary care; the remaining 52.2% are specialists (Kaiser Family Foundation, 2023). In other industrialized countries, only 25%–50% of physicians are specialists (Organization for Economic Cooperation and Development [OECD], 2016).

Figure 4-3 illustrates trends in the supply of PCPs. The proportion of active PCPs has been continually declining since 1949 and has reached its lowest point in recent years. Also, the number of physicians entering primary care has been decreasing. According to one study, only 21.5% of third-year internal medicine graduating residents reported general internal medicine as their ultimate career plan. Most of the residents reported subspecialty career plans (West and Dupras, 2012). Moreover, one in six general internists leaves his or her practice by midcareer either due to dissatisfaction or by moving into a subspecialty of internal medicine (Bylsma et al., 2010). The increasing number of international medical graduates (IMGs) practicing in the United States has helped alleviate these PCP shortages to some extent.

Growth of new medical technology is the one major driving force behind the increasing number of specialists. Health care is often delivered according to a model that concentrates on diseases and specialist care. Doctors, particularly specialists, increasingly rely on medical technology to diagnose and treat

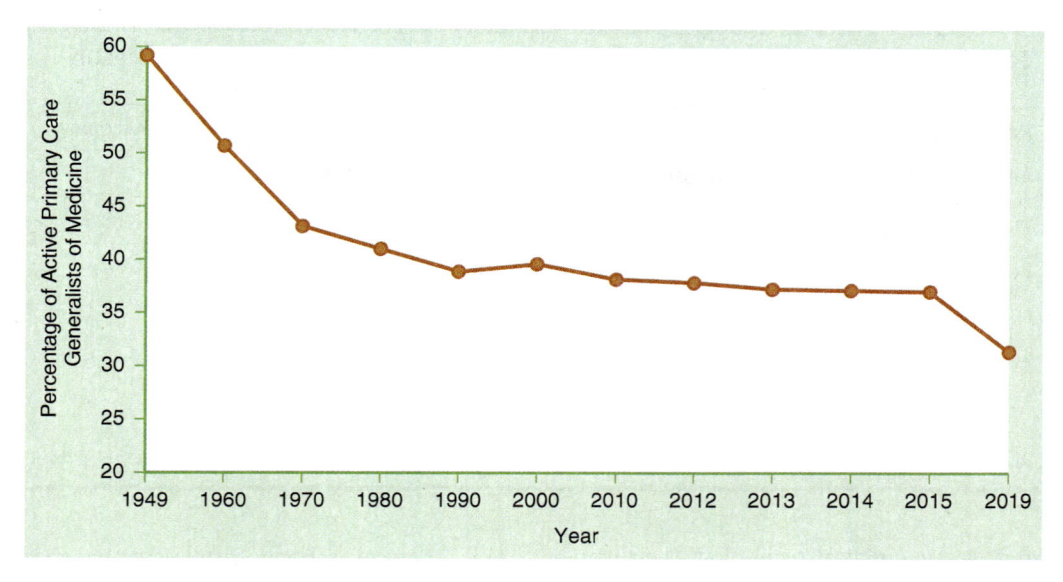

Figure 4-3 Trend in U.S. primary care generalists of medicine.

Data from National Center for Health Statistics. 2016. Health, United States, 2015. Hyattsville, MD: U.S. Department of Health and Human Services. p. 284; National Center for Health Statistics. 2018. Health, *United States, 2017.* Hyattsville, MD: U.S. Department of Health and Human Services. Table 85.

2019 data from Willis, J. (2020). Primary Care in the United States: A Chartbook of Facts and Statistics. Robert Graham Center.

diseases. Most hospitals with the latest medical technologies try to become clinical centers that offer all major specialty fields and employ these specialists as well. Additionally, medical students may be further attracted to go into subspecialties because their training is organized around medical technologies. Collectively, these factors may contribute to the expanding gap between the primary- and specialty-care workforces.

The higher incomes of specialists relative to PCPs have also contributed to the oversupply of specialists in the United States (Knight, 2019). In recent years, reimbursement systems designed to increase payments to PCPs have been implemented, but wide disparities between the incomes of generalists and specialists persist (**Table 4-4**). Specialists also tend to have more predictable work hours and enjoy higher prestige among their colleagues and the public at large (Rosenblatt and Lishner, 1991; Samuels and Shi, 1993). Likewise, higher status and prestige are accorded to specialists employing the latest

Table 4-4 Mean Annual Compensation for U.S. Physicians by Selected Specialties, 2023

Neurosurgery	$788,313
Cardiology	$544,201
Radiology	$503,564
Anesthesiologists	$462,506
General Surgery	$451,489
Internal medicine	$293,894
Occupational medicine	$292,814
Infectious Disease	$288,607
Geriatrics	$275,704
Family medicine	$273,040
Pediatrics	$242,832

Data from Doximity. (2023). 2023 Physician Compensation Report. https://press.doximity.com/reports/doximity-physician-compensation-report-2023.pdf

Table 4-5 Percentage of Total Enrollment of Students in Programs for Selected Health Occupations by Race, 2008–2009

Race	Allopathic	Osteopathic	Dentistry	Pharmacy
All races	100.0	100.0	100.0	100.0
White, non-Hispanic	61.7	70.0	59.9	58.9
Black, non-Hispanic	7.1	3.5	5.8	6.4
Hispanic	8.1	3.7	6.2	4.1
American Indian	0.8	0.7	0.7	0.5
Asian	21.7	17.1	23.4	22.1

Data from National Center for Health Statistics. 2012. *Health, United States, 2011.* Hyattsville, MD: U.S. Department of Health and Human Services. p. 355.

advances in medical technology. Unsurprisingly, such considerations influence medical students' career decisions.

In terms of racial and ethnic diversity in the health workforce, **Table 4-5** shows the percentage of total enrollment of students in programs for selected health occupations by race and **Table 4-6** shows the latest (2022–2023) U.S. medical school enrollment by race. Trends in racial and ethnic diversity vary considerably by occupation, although minorities tend to be more heavily represented among the lower-skilled occupations.

The medical education environment in the United States is largely organized according to specialties and controlled by those who have achieved leadership positions by demonstrating their abilities in narrow scientific or clinical areas. Medical education in the United States emphasizes technology, intensive procedures, and tertiary care settings, which are generally more appealing to medical students than the more rudimentary field of primary care.

The imbalance between generalists and specialists has several undesirable consequences. Having too many specialists has contributed to the high volume of intensive, expensive, and invasive medical services, and consequently, to the ongoing rise in healthcare costs in the United States (Greenfield et al., 1992; Rosenblatt, 1992; Schroeder and Sandy, 1993; Wennberg et al., 1993; Basu et al., 2019; Levine et al., 2019). Seeking care directly from specialists is often less effective than getting primary care because the latter attempts to provide early intervention before complications develop (Starfield, 1992; Starfield and Simpson, 1993). Higher levels

Table 4-6 U.S. Medical School Enrollment by Race, 2022–2023

Race	Number	Percentage
All races	96,520	100.0
White, non-Hispanic	43,818	45.4
Black, non-Hispanic	8,017	8.3
Hispanic	6,542	6.8
American Indian or Alaska Native	184	0.2
Asian	23,294	24.1
Multiple race/ethnicity	8,231	8.5
Non-US citizen	1,326	1.4

Data from AAMC. 2022 FACTS: Enrollment, Graduates, and MD-Ph.D Data. (May 30, 2023). https://www.aamc.org/media/6116/download?attachment.

of primary-care services are associated with lower overall death and lower mortality rates (Basu et al., 2019; Shi, 1992, 1994). PCPs have also been the major providers of care to minorities, people with low income, and people living in underserved areas (Ginzberg, 1994; Starr, 1982). They can play a major role in overcoming health disparities (Lee et al., 2016; Shi et al., 2013)—yet underserved populations suffer the most from PCP shortages.

International Medical Graduates

The ratio of International medical graduates (IMGs) to the overall U.S. population has steadily grown over time (Figure 4-2), although the ratio of IMGs to total active doctors of medicine practicing in the United States has declined slightly in recent years (**Figure 4-4**). Approximately 25.6% of professionally active doctors of medicine in the United States are IMGs, also known as foreign medical graduates (NCHS, 2018). This percentage translates into more than 222,000 active IMGs in the U.S. physician workforce (NCHS, 2018). In 2019, 58.8% of all IMGs matched to a U.S. residency program, up from 56.5% in 2018 and in keeping with the continuous upward trend (Educational Commission for Foreign Medical Graduates, 2019). Moreover, an increasing number of IMGs are filling family practice residency slots (Kozakowski et al., 2016). In 1995, only 6.3% of IMGs entered family practice residencies; by 2015, this percentage had increased to 11.3% (Boulet et al., 2006; Kozakowski et al., 2016). IMGs account for 39.8% of all physicians in internal medicine, 24.3% in pediatrics, and 30.2% in psychiatry (Educational Commission for Foreign Medical Graduates and Association of American Medical Colleges, 2021).

Dentists

Dentists diagnose and treat dental problems related to the teeth, gums, and tissues of the mouth. All dentists must be licensed to practice. The licensure requirements include graduation from an accredited dental school that awards a Doctor of Dental Surgery (DDS) or Doctor of Dental Medicine (DMD) degree and successful completion of both written and practical examinations. Some states

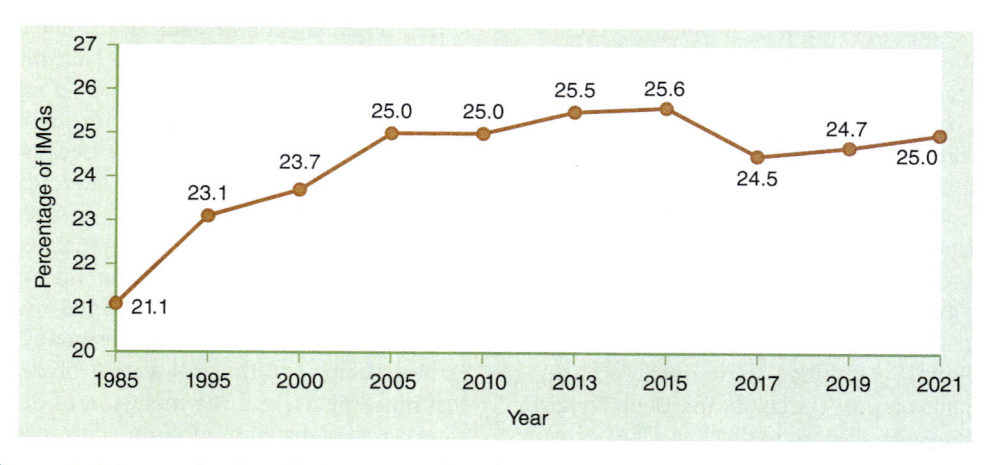

Figure 4-4 International medical graduates (IMGs) as a proportion of total active doctors of medicine.

Data from National Center for Health Statistics. 2016. *Health, United States, 2015.* Hyattsville, MD: U.S. Department of Health and Human Services. p. 283; Data from National Center for Health Statistics. 2018. *Health, United States, 2017.* Hyattsville, MD: U.S. Department of Health and Human Services. Table 84.

2017-19 data from American Medical Association (December 31, 2021). Active Physicians Who Are International Graduates (IMGs) by Specialty, 2021.

require dentists to obtain a specialty license before practicing as a specialist in that state (Stanfield et al., 2012). Nine specialty areas are recognized by the American Dental Association (ADA):

- Orthodontics: straightening teeth
- Oral and maxillofacial surgery: operating on the mouth and jaws
- Oral and maxillofacial radiology: producing and interpreting images of the mouth and jaws
- Pediatric dentistry: dental care for children
- Periodontics: treating gums
- Prosthodontics: making artificial teeth or dentures
- Endodontics: root canal therapy
- Public health dentistry: community dental health
- Oral pathology: diseases of the mouth

The growth of dental specialties is influenced by technological advances, including implant dentistry, laser-guided surgery, orthognathic surgery (surgery performed on the bones of the jaw) for the restoration of facial form and function, new metal combinations for use in prosthetic devices, new bone graft materials in "tissue-guided regeneration" techniques, and new materials and instruments.

Many dentists are involved in the prevention of dental decay and gum disease. Dental prevention includes regular cleaning of patients' teeth and educating patients on proper dental hygiene. Dentists also spot symptoms that require treatment by a physician. Dentists employ dental hygienists and assistants to perform many of the preventive and routine care services.

Dental hygienists work in dental offices and provide preventive dental care, including cleaning teeth and educating patients on proper dental care. Dental hygienists must be licensed to practice. The licensure requirements include graduation from an accredited school of dental hygiene and successful completion of both a national board written examination and a state or regional clinical examination. Many states require further examination on the legal aspects of dental hygiene practice.

Dental assistants work for dentists in the preparation, examination, and treatment of patients. Dental assistants do not have to be licensed to work; however, formal training programs that offer a certificate or diploma are available. Dental assistants typically work alongside dentists as they provide services to their patients.

Most dentists practice in private offices as solo or group practitioners. As such, dental offices operate as private businesses, and dentists often perform business tasks, such as staffing, financing, purchasing, leasing, and work scheduling. Some dentists are employed in clinics operated by private companies, retail stores, or franchised dental outlets. Group dental practices, which offer lower overhead and increased productivity, have grown slowly. The federal government also employs dentists, mainly in the hospitals and clinics operated by the Department of Veterans Affairs and the U.S. Public Health Service. Mean annual earnings of salaried dentists were $180,990 in 2022 (U.S. Bureau of Labor Statistics, 2023).

The emergence of employer-sponsored dental insurance caused an increased demand for dental care because it enabled a greater segment of the population to afford dental services. The demand for dentists is expected to continue to grow because of growth in populations, such as older adults, who have high dental needs, and an increase in public awareness of the importance of dental care to maintain good general health status. Demand will also be affected by the fairly widespread appeal of cosmetic and esthetic dentistry, the prevalence of dental insurance plans, and the inclusion of dental care as part of many public-funded programs, such as Head Start, Medicaid, community and migrant health centers, and maternal and infant care. In 2019, the Department of Health and Human Services awarded more than $85 million to 298 health centers across the United States to expand access to oral health services (DHHS, 2019).

Pharmacists

The traditional role of **pharmacists** has been to dispense medicines prescribed by physicians, dentists, and podiatrists, and to provide consultation on the proper selection and use of medicines. All states require a license to practice pharmacy. The licensure requirements traditionally included graduation from an accredited pharmacy program that awards a Bachelor of Pharmacy or Doctor of Pharmacy (PharmD) degree, successful completion of a state board examination, and practical experience or completion of a supervised internship (Stanfield et al., 2012). Since 2005, the bachelor's degree has been phased out, and a PharmD, requiring 6 years of postsecondary education, has become the standard. The mean annual earnings of pharmacists in 2022 were $129,410 (U.S. Bureau of Labor Statistics, 2023).

Although most pharmacists are generalists who dispense drugs and advise providers and patients, some become specialists. Pharmacotherapists, for example, specialize in drug therapy and work closely with physicians. Nutrition support pharmacists determine and prepare drugs needed for nutritional therapy. Radiopharmacists, or nuclear pharmacists, produce radioactive drugs used for patient diagnosis and therapy.

Most pharmacists hold salaried positions and work in community pharmacies that are independently owned or are part of a national drugstore, discount store, or department store chain. Pharmacists are also employed by hospitals, MCOs, home health agencies, clinics, government health services organizations, and pharmaceutical manufacturers.

In recent decades, the role of pharmacists has expanded from primarily preparing and dispensing prescriptions to include educating patients on drug products and serving as experts on specific drugs, drug interactions, and generic drug substitution. For example, under the Omnibus Budget Reconciliation Act of 1990, pharmacists are required to give consumers information about drugs and their potential misuse. This educating and counseling role of pharmacists is broadly referred to as **pharmaceutical care**. The American Council on Pharmaceutical Education (now the Accreditation Council for Pharmacy Education; 1992) defines pharmaceutical care as "a mode of pharmacy practice in which the pharmacist takes an active role on behalf of patients, by assisting prescribers in appropriate drug choices, by effecting distribution of medications to patients, and by assuming direct responsibilities to collaborate with other healthcare professionals and with patients to achieve the desired therapeutic outcome." This concept entails a high level of drug knowledge, clinical skill, and independent judgment. It also requires that pharmacists share with other health professionals the responsibility for optimizing the outcome of patients' drug therapies, such as health status, quality of life, and satisfaction (Helper and Strand, 1990; Schwartz, 1994; Strand et al., 1991). Physicians often consult pharmacists to identify and prevent potential drug-related problems and resolve actual drug-related problems (Morley and Strand, 1989). Recent studies also indicate that pharmacist-provided medication management can be beneficial for patients, especially those with multiple chronic conditions or complex medication regimens (Carter et al., 2012; Rafferty et al., 2016 Mack et al., 2023; Makhinova et al., 2023. Lokhande, et al., 2023).

Other Doctoral-Level Health Professionals

In addition to physicians, dentists, and some pharmacists, other health professionals have doctoral education, including optometrists, psychologists, podiatrists, and chiropractors.

Optometrists provide vision care, which includes examination, diagnosis, and correction of vision problems. They must be licensed to practice. The licensure requirements include obtaining a Doctor of Optometry (OD) degree and passing a written and clinical state board examination. Most optometrists work in solo or group practices, but some work for the government, optical stores, or vision care centers as salaried employees.

Psychologists provide patients with mental health care. They must be licensed or certified to practice. The ultimate recognition is the diplomate in psychology, which requires a Doctor of Philosophy (PhD) or Doctor of Psychology (PsyD) degree, a minimum of 5 years' postdoctoral experience, and the successful completion of an examination by the American Board of Examiners in Professional Psychology. Psychologists may specialize in several areas, such as the clinical, counseling, developmental, educational, engineering, personnel, experimental, industrial, psychometric, rehabilitation, school, and social domains (Stanfield et al., 2012).

Podiatrists treat patients with diseases or deformities of the feet, including performing surgical operations, prescribing medications and corrective devices, and administering physiotherapy. They must be licensed to practice. Requirements for licensure include completion of an accredited program that awards a Doctor of Podiatric Medicine (DPM) degree and passing a national examination by the National Board of Podiatric Medical Examiners. Most podiatrists work in private practice, but some are salaried employees of health service organizations.

Chiropractors provide treatment to patients through chiropractic (done by hand) manipulation, physiotherapy, and dietary counseling. They typically help patients with neurologic, muscular, and vascular disturbances. Chiropractic care is based on the belief that the body is a self-healing organism; thus, chiropractors do not prescribe drugs or perform surgery. Chiropractors must be licensed to practice. Requirements for licensure include completion of an accredited program that awards a 4-year Doctor of Chiropractic (DC) degree and passing an examination by the state chiropractic board. Most chiropractors work in private solo or group practice.

Doctoral nursing degrees include the Doctor of Nursing Practice (DNP), Doctor of Nursing Science (DNS), and Doctor of Philosophy in Nursing (PhD) (Ericksen, 2016). The DNS and PhD degrees are research focused, whereas the DNP emphasizes patient care and nursing practice (Ericksen, 2016). A doctoral degree is usually required to become a professor of nursing education or nurse researcher (Ericksen, 2016). Doctoral degrees are also preferred for nurse practitioners, clinical nurse specialists, nurse anesthetists, and nurse-midwives (American Association of Colleges of Nursing [AACN], 2014).

Nurses

Nurses constitute the largest group of healthcare professionals. The nursing profession developed around hospitals after World War I, primarily attracting women. Before that time, more than 70% of nurses worked in private duty, either in patients' homes or in hospitals for private-pay patients. Hospital-based nursing flourished after the war as the effectiveness of nursing care became apparent. Federal support of nursing education increased after World War II, with the passage of the Nursing Training Act of 1964, the Health Manpower Act of 1968, and the Nursing Training Act of 1971. However, despite federal support, state funding remains the primary source of financial support for nursing schools.

Nurses are the major caregivers for patients who are sick and injured, addressing their physical, mental, and emotional needs. All states require nurses to be licensed to practice. Nurses can be licensed in more than one state through examination or endorsement of a license issued by another state. The licensure requirements include graduation from an approved nursing program and successful completion of a national examination.

Educational preparation distinguishes the two non doctoral-degree levels of nurses. **Registered nurses (RNs)** must complete an Associate's Degree in Nursing (ADN), a diploma program, or a Baccalaureate Degree in Nursing (BSN). ADN programs take about 2–3 years to complete and are offered by community and junior colleges. Diploma programs take 2–3 years and are still offered by a few hospitals. BSN programs take 4–5 years and are offered by colleges and universities (Stanfield et al., 2012). **Licensed practical nurses (LPNs)**—called licensed vocational nurses (LVNs) in some states—must complete a state-approved program in practical nursing and a national written examination. Most practical nursing programs last about 1 year and include classroom study as well as supervised clinical practice. Nurse managers act as supervisors of other nurses; RNs supervise LPNs.

Nurses work in the same variety of settings as other healthcare professionals. In addition, they work in home health care, hospice care, and long-term care settings. A few work as private duty nurses in patients' homes. Nurses are often classified according to the settings in which they work—for example, hospital nurses, long-term care nurses, public health nurses, private duty nurses, office nurses, and occupational health or industrial nurses.

With the remarkable growth in the various types of outpatient settings (refer to the *Outpatient and Primary Care Services* chapter), hospitals and nursing homes now treat patients who are much sicker than before. As a consequence, more patients require a greater amount of care when in residence at these settings. Reflecting this new reality, the ratio of nurses to patients has increased, and nurses' work has become more intensive. The growing number of opportunities for RNs in supportive roles, such as case management, utilization review, quality assurance, and prevention counseling, has also expanded the demand for their services.

In 2022, registered nurses made up one of the largest occupations in the United States, with more than 3.07 million RNs earning an average salary of $89,010 per year (U.S. Bureau of Labor Statistics, 2023). Projections of the future need for nurses indicate there will be a deficit of 918,232 RNs in 2030 (Juraschek et al., 2012). To make the nursing profession more attractive, health services organizations need to initiate measures such as creating incentive packages to attract new nurses, increasing pay and benefits to current nurses, introducing more flexible work schedules, awarding tuition reimbursement for continuing education, and providing on-site daycare assistance.

A nationwide shortage of primary care providers inspired the Advanced Nursing Education Expansion Program, an ACA component that allocated $30 million to support academic training programs for nurse practitioners and certified nurse-midwives. The funds are expected to help pay for instructors and for students' housing and living expenses.

Advanced Practice Nurses

The term **advanced practice nurse (APN)** is a general classification of nurses who have education and clinical experience beyond that required of an RN. APNs include four areas of specialization (Cooper et al., 1998): clinical nurse specialists (CNSs), certified registered nurse anesthetists (CRNAs), nurse practitioners (NPs), and certified nurse-midwives (CNMs). NPs and CNMs are also categorized as nonphysician providers (discussed in the next section). Besides being direct caregivers, APNs perform other professional activities, such as collaborating and consulting with other healthcare professionals; educating patients and other nurses; collecting data for clinical research projects; and participating in the development and implementation of total quality management programs, critical pathways, case management, and standards of care (Grossman, 1995).

Both CNSs and NPs work in hospitals, primary care, and other settings. Examples of CNS functions in an acute care hospital include taking the patient's social and clinical history at the time of admission, conducting the physical assessment after the patient's admission, adjusting IV infusion rates, managing pain, managing resuscitation orders, removing intracardiac catheters, and ordering routine laboratory tests and radiographic examinations. CNSs generally do not have the legal authority to prescribe drugs. In contrast, NPs may prescribe drugs in most states. CRNAs are trained to manage anesthesia during surgery and CNMs deliver babies and manage the care of mothers and healthy newborns before, during, and after delivery. The requirements for becoming an APN vary greatly from state to state. In general, the APN must have a graduate degree in nursing or certification in an advanced practice specialty area.

Nonphysician Providers

Nonphysician providers (NPPs) are clinical professionals who practice in many areas similar to those in which physicians practice but who do not have an MD or a DO degree. NPPs receive less advanced training than physicians but more training than RNs. NPPs, in many instances, can substitute for physicians. Nevertheless, they do not engage in the entire range of primary care or deal with complex cases requiring the expertise of a physician (Cooper et al., 1998). Efforts to formally establish the NPP role began in the late 1960s, in recognition of the fact that they could improve access to primary care, especially in rural areas.

NPPs include physician assistants (PAs), NPs, and CNMs. In the future, the expansion of health insurance coverage and the growth of the U.S. population will continue to drive the demand for NPPs (Jacobson and Jazowski, 2011). As of 2014, the supply of new NPs was increasing at 6.9% per capita compared to a growth rate of 3.4% for the supply of physicians (NCHS, 2016). Approximately 20,000 NPs and PAs graduated in 2015, up from 11,200 in 2006 (AHA, 2016). At least 11,000 PAs graduated in 2021 and more than 39,000 NPs graduated in 2022 (https://www.ajmc.com/view/physician-assistants-associates-at-6-decades).

Roles for these skilled NPPs are expanding as the physician workforce shrinks, the population of seniors expands, and health care becomes accessible to more Americans. NPs, in particular, are assuming a pivotal role in health care. NPPs are capable of providing a large proportion of the primary-care services provided by physicians. A substantial body of research evaluating the quality of primary care provided by NPPs shows that these providers perform as well as physicians on important clinical outcome measures, such as mortality, preventable hospitalizations, improvement of patient health status, and other quality of care measures (Agarwal et al., 2009; Evangelista et al., 2012; Kuo et al., 2015; Kurtzman and Barnow, 2017; Laurant et al., 2009; Zwilling et al., 2023; Asadi-Aliabadi, et al., 2022; Mirhoseiny, et al., 2019). In addition, patients report high levels of satisfaction with the care provided by NPPs (Evangelista et al., 2012; Golden, 2014).

Nurse Practitioners

The American Nurses Association (ANA) defines **nurse practitioners (NPs)** as individuals who have completed a program of study leading to competence as RNs in an expanded role. NPs constitute the largest group of NPPs. As of 2022, the United States had approximately 258,230 NPs (U.S. Bureau of Labor Statistics, 2023). Training for NPs covers topics of health promotion, disease prevention, health education, counseling, and disease management. These professionals take health histories, provide physical exams and health assessments, and diagnose, treat, and manage patients with acute and chronic health conditions (AACN, 2014).

More than 36,000 new NPs completed their academic programs from 2020 to 2021 (AANP, 2022) in approximately 400 academic institutions across the United States and more than 39,000 NPs graduated in 2022 (AANP, 2022). The training of NPs may be a certificate program (at least 9 months in duration) or a master's degree program (2 years of full-time study). States vary with regard to licensure and accreditation requirements for these roles. Most NPs are now trained in graduate or postgraduate nursing programs. In addition, they must complete clinical training in direct patient care. Certification examinations are offered by the American Nurses Credentialing Center, the American Academy of Nurse Practitioners, and specialty nursing organizations.

One major difference between the training and practice orientation of NPs and PAs is that NPs are oriented toward health promotion and education, whereas PAs are oriented more toward a medical model that focuses on disease (Hooker and McCaig, 2001). NPs spend extra time with patients to help them understand the need to take responsibility for their own health. NP specialties include pediatric, family, adult, psychiatric, and geriatric programs. NPs have statutory prescribing authority in almost all states, and they may serve as independent providers without supervision. These healthcare professionals can also receive direct reimbursement as providers under the Medicaid and Medicare programs.

Physician Assistants

The American Academy of Physician Assistants (1986) defines **physician assistants (PAs)** as "part of the healthcare team . . . [who] work in a dependent relationship with a supervising physician to provide comprehensive care." In 2022, there were approximately 140,910 jobs available for PAs in the United States (U.S. Bureau of Labor Statistics, 2023). PAs are licensed to perform medical procedures only under the supervision of a physician, who may be either on site or off site. Major services provided by PAs include evaluation, monitoring, diagnostics, therapeutics, counseling, and referral (Fitzgerald et al., 1995). In most states, they have the authority to prescribe medications.

As of 2023, 303 accredited PA training programs were operating in the United States, with a steady growth in enrollment (Accreditation Review Commission on Education for the Physician Assistant, 2023). PA programs award bachelor's degrees, certificates, associate degrees, master's degrees, or doctoral degrees. The mean length of the program is 26 months (Hooker and Berlin, 2002). PAs are certified by the National Commission on Certification of Physician Assistants.

Certified Nurse-Midwives

Certified nurse-midwives (CNMs) are RNs with additional training from a nurse-midwifery program in areas such as maternal and fetal procedures, maternity and child nursing, and patient assessment (Endicott, 1976). CNMs deliver babies, provide family planning education, manage gynecologic and obstetric care, and can substitute for obstetricians/gynecologists in prenatal and postnatal care. They are certified by the American College of Nurse-Midwives (ACNM) to provide care for normal expectant mothers. CNMs refer patients with high risk to obstetricians or jointly manage the care of such patients. Approximately 39 ACNM-accredited nurse-midwifery education programs are available in the United States (ACNM, 2017).

Midwifery has never assumed the central role in the management of pregnancies in the United States that it has in Europe (Wagner, 1991). Physicians, mainly obstetricians, attend most deliveries in the United States, but some evidence indicates that for low-risk pregnancies, CNMs are much less likely to use available technical tools to monitor or modify the course of labor. Patients of CNMs are less likely to be electronically monitored, induce labor, or receive epidural anesthesia. These differences are associated with lower cesarean section rates and less use of resources, such as hospital stays, operating room costs, and use of anesthesia staff (Rosenblatt et al., 1997).

Allied Health Professionals

The term **allied health** is used loosely to categorize several types of professionals in a vast number of health-related technical areas. Among these professionals are technicians, assistants, therapists, and technologists. These professionals receive specialized training, and their clinical interventions complement the work of physicians and nurses. Certain professionals, however, are allowed to practice independently, depending on state law.

In the early part of the 20th century, the healthcare provider workforce consisted of physicians, nurses, pharmacists, and optometrists. As knowledge in health sciences expanded and medical care became more complex, physicians found it difficult to spend the necessary time with their patients. Time constraints as well as the limitations in learning new skills created a need to train other professionals who could serve as adjuncts to or as substitutes for physicians and nurses.

Section 701 of the Public Health Service Act defines an **allied health professional** as someone who has received a certificate; associate's, bachelor's, or master's degree; doctoral-level preparation; or post-baccalaureate training in a science related to health care and has responsibility for the delivery of health or related services. These services may include those associated with the identification, evaluation, and prevention of diseases and disorders, dietary and nutritional services, rehabilitation, and health system management. Allied health professionals can be classified into two broad categories: technicians/assistants and therapists/technologists. **Exhibit 4-2** lists the main allied health professions in the United States.

Exhibit 4-2 Examples of Allied Health Professionals

Activities coordinator	Optician
Audiology technician	Pharmacist
Cardiovascular technician	Physical therapist
Cytotechnologist	Physical therapy assistant
Dental assistant	Physician assistant
Dietary food service manager	Radiology technician
Exercise physiologist	Recreation therapist
Histologic technician	Registered dietitian
Laboratory technician	Registered records administrator
Legal services	Respiratory therapist
Medical records technician	Respiratory therapy technician
Medical technologist	Social services coordinator
Mental health worker	Social worker
Nuclear medicine	Speech therapist
Occupational therapist	Speech therapy assistant
Occupational therapy assistant	

As noted earlier, formal requirements for these professionals range from certificates gained in postsecondary educational programs to postgraduate degrees for some professions. Typically, technicians and assistants receive less than 2 years of postsecondary education. They require supervision from therapists or technologists to ensure that treatment plans are followed. Technicians and assistants include physical therapy assistants (PTAs), certified occupational therapy assistants (COTAs), medical laboratory technicians, radiologic technicians, and respiratory therapy technicians.

Technologists and therapists receive more advanced training. They evaluate patients, diagnose problems, and develop treatment plans. Many technologists and therapists have independent practices. For example, physical therapy can be practiced in most U.S. states without a prescription or referral from a physician. Many states also allow occupational therapists and speech therapists to serve patients without referral from a physician.

Therapists

Physical therapists (PTs) provide care for patients with movement dysfunction. Educational programs in physical therapy are accredited by the Commission on Accreditation of Physical Therapy Education (CAPTE). As of 2023, there were 301 physical therapy education programs in the United States (https://ptcasdirectory.apta.org/39/List-of-PTCAS-Programs). In 1996, CAPTA increased the educational requirements for all physical therapy programs to a three-year doctorate (https://centennial.apta.org/timeline/the-clinical-doctorate-or-dpt-becomes-the-only-degree-conferred-by-capte-accredited-educational-institutions/). To obtain a license, PTs must also pass the National Physical Therapy Examination or a similar state-administered exam (Commission on Accreditation in Physical Therapy Education, 2017). CAPTE has required that a doctorate-level education must be successfully completed before taking the national physical therapy licensure examination.

Occupational therapists (OTs) help people of all ages improve their ability to perform tasks in their daily living and working environments. They work with individuals who have conditions that are mentally, physically, developmentally, or emotionally disabling. A master's degree in occupational therapy is the typical minimum requirement for entry into the field. In 2023, 171 master's degree programs or combined bachelor's and master's degree programs were accredited, and 90 doctoral degree programs were accredited by the Accreditation Council for Occupational Therapy Education (ACOTE, 2023). Speech-language pathologists treat patients with speech and language problems. Audiologists treat patients with hearing problems. The American Speech-Language-Hearing Association is the credentialing association for both audiologists and speech-language pathologists.

Other Allied Health Professionals

Medical dietetics include dietitians, nutritionists, and dietetic technicians. Registered dietitian nutritionists (RDNs) screen and assess patients using nutrition-focused physical exams to develop interventions for nutrition-related complications. RDNs play a key role in selecting and administering parenteral and enteral nutrition. They are also uniquely able to provide medical nutrition therapy (MNT)—an in-depth, evidence-based, and individually tailored approach to nutrition in the treatment of conditions across the spectrum of care, including diabetes, cancer, and eating disorders. In addition, RDNs delegate tasks to and supervise the work of nutrition and dietetics technicians, registered NDTRs, and other personnel who have direct involvement in the administration of patient nutrition care (Academy of Nutrition and Dietetics, 2018).

Registration of dietitians is carried out by the Commission on Dietetic Registration of the Academy of Nutrition and Dietetics.

Dispensing opticians fit eyeglasses and contact lenses. They are certified by the American Board of Opticianry and the National Contact Lens Examiners.

Social workers help patients and families cope with problems resulting from long-term illness, injury, and rehabilitation. The Council on Social Work Education accredits baccalaureate and master's degree programs in social work in the United States.

Many programs are accredited by the Committee on Allied Health Education and Accreditation under the American Medical Association, including those for the following professionals:

- Anesthesiologist assistants
- Cardiovascular technologists
- Cytotechnologists: study changes in body cells under a microscope
- Diagnostic medical sonographers: work with ultrasound diagnostic procedures
- Electroneurodiagnostic technologists: work with procedures related to the electrical activity of the brain and nervous system
- Emergency medical technicians and paramedics: provide medical emergent care to acutely ill or injured persons in prehospital settings
- Histologic technicians/technologists: analyze blood, tissue, and fluids
- Medical assistants: perform a number of administrative and clinical duties in physicians' offices
- Medical illustrators
- Medical laboratory technicians
- Medical record administrators: direct the medical records department
- Medical record technicians: organize and file medical records
- Medical technologists: perform clinical laboratory testing
- Nuclear medicine technologists: operate diagnostic imaging equipment and use radioactive drugs to assist in the diagnosis of illness
- Ophthalmic medical technicians
- Perfusionists: operate life support respiratory and circulatory equipment
- Radiologic technologists: perform diagnostic imaging exams, such as X-rays, computed tomography, magnetic resonance imaging, and mammography
- Respiratory therapists and technicians: treat patients with breathing disorders
- Specialists in blood bank technology
- Surgeon's assistants
- Surgical technologists: prepare operating rooms and patients for surgery

Certain healthcare workers are not required to be licensed, and they usually learn their skills on the job; however, their roles are limited to assisting other professionals in the provision of services. Examples include dietetic assistants, who assist dietitians or dietetic technicians in the provision of nutritional care; electroencephalogram technologists or technicians, who operate electroencephalographs; electrocardiogram (ECG) technicians, who operate electrocardiographs; paraoptometrics, including optometric technicians and assistants, who perform basic tasks related to vision care; health educators, who provide individuals and groups with facts on health, illness, and prevention; psychiatric/mental health technicians, who provide care to patients with mental illness or developmental disabilities; and sanitarians, who collect samples for laboratory analysis and inspect facilities for compliance with public health regulations. Increasingly, these practitioners are seeking their credentials through certifications, registrations, and training programs.

As the number of older people in the United States continues to increase, and as new developments allow for the treatment of more medical conditions, more allied health professionals will be needed. For example, home health aides will be needed as more individuals seek care outside of traditional institutional settings. Jobs for LPNs/LVNs and pharmacy technicians are also expected to increase significantly, to roughly 117,300 and 34,700 positions, respectively, by the end of 2024 (U.S. Bureau of Labor Statistics, 2015).

Allied health professionals represent an important part of the patient care system. They specialize in areas directly related to prevention, wellness, and management of acute and chronic diseases as well as behavioral health problems. These professionals have a critical role in the healthcare system and provide comprehensive, patient-centered care to millions of individuals. Studies have affirmed their positive influence on healthcare services: allied health professionals improve patient access to care, patient volume, and service efficiency as well as reduce costs of care (American Association of Community Colleges, 2014; Beazoglou, et al., 2012; Post and Stoltenberg, 2014; Griffiths et al., 2023; Blair et al., 2023).

Health Services Administrators

Health services administrators are employed at the top, middle, and entry levels of various types of organizations that deliver health services. Top-level administrators provide leadership and strategic direction, work closely with the governing boards , and are responsible for an organization's long-term success. They are responsible for the operational, clinical, and financial outcomes of their entire organization. Middle-level administrators may have leadership roles for major service centers, such as outpatient, surgical, and nursing services, or they may be departmental managers in charge of single departments, such as diagnostics, dietary, rehabilitation, social services, environmental services, or medical records. Their jobs involve major planning and coordinating functions, organizing human and physical resources, directing and supervising, operational and financial controls, and decision-making. They often have direct responsibility for implementing changes, creating efficiencies, and developing new procedures with respect to changes in the healthcare delivery system. Entry-level administrators may function as assistants to middle-level managers. They may supervise a small number of operatives. For example, their main function may be to supervise and assist with operations critical to the efficient operation of a departmental unit.

Today's medical centers and integrated delivery organizations are highly complex organizations to manage. Leaders in healthcare delivery face some unique challenges, including changes in financing and payment structures, as well as having to work with reduced levels of reimbursement. Other challenges include pressures to provide uncompensated care, greater responsibility for quality, accountability for community health, separate contingencies imposed by public and private payers, uncertainties created by new policy developments, changing configurations in the competitive environment, and maintaining the integrity of an organization through the highest level of ethical standards. As the health services administration field adapts to new expectations within the healthcare realm and new demands that have arisen from the COVID-19 pandemic, educational programs that train the next generation of health services administration professionals need to be competency-based and data-driven. Curricula should emphasize the importance of collaboration, both between the public and private sectors as well as between healthcare and non healthcare entities in developing sustainable, long-lasting solutions to current healthcare challenges. Technology should also be a major point of focus as its various forms become more and more prevalent in organizing, supporting, and administering the delivery of care (Comellas et al., 2020).

Health services administration is taught at the bachelor's and master's levels in a variety of settings, and programs may lead to several different degrees. The settings for such academic programs include schools of medicine, public health, public administration, business administration, and allied health sciences. Bachelor's degrees prepare students for entry-level positions. Mid- and senior-level positions require a graduate degree. The most common degrees are the Master of Health Administration (MHA) or Master of Health Services Administration (MHSA), Master of Business Administration (MBA, with a healthcare management emphasis), Master of Public Health (MPH), or Master of Public Administration (or Affairs; MPA). The schools of public health that are accredited by the Council on Education for Public Health (CEPH) play a key role in training health services administrators in their MHA (or MHSA) and MPH programs (CEPH, 2017). In 2023, there were approximately 115 MPH programs accredited by the Commission on Accreditation of Healthcare Management Education (CAHME) across the U.S. (https://cahme.org/advance/SELECT.php). Compared with the MPH programs, however, the MHA programs have more course requirements and are designed to furnish skills in business management (both theory and applied management) and quantitative/analytical areas, which are considered crucial for managing today's health services organizations. This disparity has been viewed as a source of concern that the schools of public health need to address (Singh et al., 1996).

Educational preparation of nursing home administrators is a notable exception to the MHA model. The training of nursing home administrators has largely been influenced by government licensing regulations. Even though licensure of nursing home administrators dates back to the mid-1960s, regulations favoring a formal postsecondary academic degree are more recent. Passing a national examination administered by the National Association of Boards of Examiners of Long-Term Care Administrators (NAB) is a standard requirement. However, the educational qualifications needed to obtain a license vary significantly from one state to another. Although approximately one-third of the states still require less than a bachelor's degree as the minimum academic preparation, an increasing number of practicing nursing home administrators have at least a bachelor's degree. The problem is that most state regulations call for only general levels of education rather than specialized preparation in long-term care administration. General education does not furnish adequate skills in all the domains of practice relevant to nursing home management (Singh et al., 1997). However, various colleges and universities offer specialized programs in nursing home administration.

Evolving Trends in the Healthcare Workforce

In a field with so many different occupations and distinct roles, it comes as no surprise that the healthcare workforce is constantly evolving in response to the anticipated needs of a changing population landscape. In this section, we highlight some of the trends that are currently shaping the workforce and the conceptualization of health care.

The advent and increased utilization of technologies such as telemedicine have placed a spotlight on the concept of virtual care. More and more, providers are recognizing the value of being able to deliver care through video chat, phone, and other remote methods. These methods allow clinicians to care for more individuals by optimizing the amount of time spent on each patient and facilitating access to care in hard-to-reach areas (Schwartz et al., 2018). The move away from on-site care and toward less costly methods of treatment can also help increase access to care for those who previously found it financially prohibitive to seek out such services (Schrader et al., 2018). In the wake of the COVID-19 pandemic, the Center for Medicare & Medicaid Services (CMS) expanded its coverage of telemedicine services, with several private insurers following suit. To support the broader implementation of virtual care, this expanded coverage should be maintained in the long term to promote more widespread adoption of telemedicine. Likewise, the workforce should embrace these new technologies as not just a substitute for traditional medicine, but as a legitimate and normal way to deliver care (Huckman, 2020).

Similar to the changes in regard to *where* health care can be delivered, changes in *who* can deliver care are occurring. Healthcare workforce shortages are placing a severe strain on providers' abilities to meet patient needs. This trend is accompanied by the increasing recognition that many previously physician-only functions can be completed just as well by other professions. Indeed, NPs, PAs, and CRNAs all have the capabilities to help alleviate physician workloads and make up for the discrepancy between the supply and demand for care (Huckman, 2020). New ways of delivering care have also opened up space for new roles that were previously not known of or less common in the healthcare industry. The demand for home health aides, community health workers, nutritionists, and more will surely expand as medical care moves out of the office and into the community. According to one study, more than 50% of the healthcare workforce of the future can expect to have roles significantly different from today's professionals (Schrader et al., 2018).

Another impetus for change in the healthcare workforce is technological innovation. Beyond the use of telemedicine and virtual care, technologies such as artificial intelligence (AI), robotics, big data and analytics, blockchain, and automation are being employed to come up with better business solutions, expand operational capacity, and improve clinical outcomes (AHA, 2020). This opens up a whole new realm of professional roles that must be added to support the implementation and maintenance of such technologies. Health care is poised to undergo dramatic changes as these technologies create a new "normal" in care delivery. Current progress in adopting these technologies is steady, but slow; healthcare leaders recognize their value but are risk averse and accustomed to familiar workflows. However, learning how to use these technologies is imperative for augmenting the current workforce and reducing workforce shortages (Schwartz et al., 2018). As technological innovation continues to develop and expand, its influence on healthcare delivery will continue to spread. Below, we summarize the key development and top trends in healthcare workforce.

Workforce Shortages

The US healthcare workforce has been significantly impacted by the COVID-19 pandemic due to shifts in the operation and financial aspects of healthcare practitioner offices and facilities, heightened health-related risks, exhaustion stemming from the increased workload due to patients, and disruptions in childcare (Cantor et al., 2022). There is presently a shortage of physicians in numerous states nationwide, and this shortage is expected to grow in the next decade. This could have adverse repercussions on healthcare delivery and potentially lead to negative impacts on patient outcomes. By 2030, the West is forecasted to have the greatest physician shortage ratio (69 physician jobs per 100 000 people), while the Northeast will have a surplus of 50 jobs per 100,000 people (Zhang et al., 2020).

Aging Workforce

The healthcare workforce, particularly nurses and physicians, is aging. As older healthcare professionals retire, there's a growing need to replace them with younger talent. This demographic shift also brings concerns about maintaining experience and expertise (Szabo et al., 2020).

Impact of Health Technology

The integration of technology into health care, such as telemedicine, electronic health records (EHRs), and AI-powered diagnostics, is changing the roles and skill sets required from healthcare workers (Ye, 2020). With the assistance of health information technology (HIT), major hospitals, along with designated hospitals, can provide services such as remote consultation and prevention and control guidance. Internet diagnosis provides online rediagnosis of some common and chronic diseases, drug distribution services, and reduction of the risk of cross-infection of patients' offline visits (Ye, 2020).

AI's ability to thoroughly analyze and handle vast amounts of data has been harnessed for detecting and forecasting virus spread during pandemics (Vaishya et al., 2020). This has been achieved through the creation of intelligent monitoring systems and the development of sophisticated algorithms, including neural networks, the susceptible-exposed-infectious-removed (SEIR) model, and long short-term memory (LSTM) networks (Yang et al., 2020).

Telemedicine has been leveraging telecommunications technologies to make use of HIT and medical information such as video imaging, thus allowing healthcare providers to work remotely (Ye, 2020). Telehealth incorporates the functions of telemedicine and a variety of nonclinical services like telepharmacy and telenursing (Ye, 2020).

5G supports real-time health data exchanging so that healthcare professionals can get access to patients' diagnosis records, medical history, and lab results without delay and information transmission barriers (Ye, 2020). With the implementation of 5G, the traditional medical workflow will be improved dramatically, and the unnecessary contact between healthcare providers and patients may be reduced (Ye, 2020).

Patient-generated health data (PGHD) through mobile health apps are becoming more and more important in health care, especially in the COVID-19 pandemic (Ye, 2020). Coronavirus tracking apps on smartphones are playing critical roles as a mobile technology to collect, gather, and share PGHD during the pandemic. Users can check whether they have had contact with patients who are infected by entering personal information (Ye, 2020). **Exhibit 4-3** provides examples of strategies that can be used to address healthcare professional shortages.

Healthcare Teams

In line with the expansion of professional roles that can play a more direct role in the provision of care, a shift from physician-centric care toward team-based care is taking place. This model of care calls for healthcare workers from various disciplines and with differing levels of expertise to come together to deliver comprehensive, coordinated care and work at the top of their respective licenses (AHA, 2020). According to the National Academy of Medicine, a healthcare team can be thought of as "a group of individuals who coordinate their actions for a common purpose, which in health care is the prevention or treatment of disease and the promotion of health. A team-based model of care strives to meet patient needs and preferences by actively engaging patients as full participants in their care, while encouraging all healthcare professionals to function to the full extent of their education, certification, and experience" (Smith et al., 2018).

Healthcare teams comprise professionals from various disciplines who enter a collaborative relationship with the patient to deliver coordinated, high-value, and patient-centered health care (Martin et al., 2022). Education for health professionals, patients or families, community outreach, and advocacy to prevent abuse are some examples of healthcare team goals.

Some healthcare teams are continuous, meaning that the teams are responsible for following up with patients throughout the entire intervention and providing care such as diagnosis, goal setting, evaluation, follow-up, and modification of patients' goals. Examples of such teams include psychiatric care teams, child development teams, and rehabilitation teams. Other healthcare teams are formed based on an event, such as a disaster plan team. Some teams perform one function, such as discharge planning. Some teams are

Exhibit 4.3 Strategies to Address Healthcare Professional Shortages

1. **Telemedicine and Telehealth**
   - Telemedicine helps connect healthcare professionals with patients in remote areas and reduces the need for physical presence (Guthrie and Snyder, 2023). Telemedicine use expanded rapidly during the COVID-19 pandemic, giving patients access to quality care while greatly reducing the spread of infection (Guthrie and Snyder, 2023).
   - The integration of health information technology and digital health tools, including home/remote monitoring, patient portal, health information exchange, electronic health records, prescription drug monitoring program, wearable devices, and mobile applications, have played a crucial role in enhancing healthcare accessibility, particularly for individuals residing in rural, underserved, and underrepresented communities (Blount et al., 2023).

2. **Medical Education and Distribution**
   - Medical education presents an opportunity to influence physicians toward meeting the healthcare needs of underserved communities when establishing their practice (Elma et al., 2022). Selecting students from underserved or rural areas, requiring them to attend rural campuses, and/or participating in rural clerkships or rotations are influential in distributing physicians in underserved or rural locations (Elma et al., 2022).

3. **Infrastructure Development**
   - Establishing clinics, hospitals, and healthcare centers in underserved areas is another strategy to create employment opportunities and attract healthcare professionals (Kaye et al., 2023; Obubu et al., 2023). There is a need for increased funding in specific regions to enhance accessibility to advanced healthcare facilities and make the most of the private sector's capabilities (Obubu et al., 2023).

4. **Policies and Regulations**
   - Policies and regulations, including relaxing licensing requirements such as streamlining licensing processes to make it easier for foreign-trained healthcare professionals to practice in underserved areas and expanding the scope of practice for non-physician healthcare providers, such as nurse practitioners and physician assistants, to help meet the demand for care and help address healthcare professional shortages (Tan et al., 2023).

5. **Medical Cooperation**
   - **Allied healthcare workers:** Evidence indicates that allied healthcare professionals like pharmacists and nurses have the potential to assume significantly broader responsibilities in assisting primary care physicians in addressing evolving healthcare service needs (Leong et al., 2021). These responsibilities encompass delivering patient care, engaging in independent prescribing of medications, and offering counseling and education, all while maintaining a similar level of healthcare quality (Leong et al., 2021).
   - **Recruit and train Community Health Workers (CHWs):** CHWs are effective at reaching several groups that experience barriers to accessing conventional health services, including rural dwellers, women and girls, people with limited financial resources, and those with limited literacy/education (Ahmed et al., 2022).

Data from Guthrie, J. D., & Snyder, J. A. (2023). Improving access to care for underserved communities through telemedicine. JAAPA: Official Journal of the American Academy of Physician Assistants, 36(9), 41-44; Blount, M. A., Douglas, M. D., Li, C., Walston, D. T., Nelms, P. L., Hughes, C. L., ... & Mack, D. H. (2023). Opportunities and Challenges to Advance Health Equity Using Digital Health Tools in Underserved Communities in Southeast US: A Mixed Methods Study. Journal of Primary Care & Community Health, 14, 21501319231184789; Elma et al., 2022; Kaye et al., 2023; Obubu, M., Chuku, N., Ananaba, A., Sadiq, F. U., Sambo, E., Kolade, O., Oyekanmi, T., Olaosebikan, K., & Serrano, O. (2023). Evaluation of healthcare facilities and personnel distribution in Lagos State: implications on universal health coverage. Hospital practice (1995), 51(2), 64–75; Tan, M. M., Oke, S., Ellison, D., Huard, C., & Veluz-Wilkins, A. (2023). Addressing Tobacco Use in Underserved Communities Outside of Primary Care: The Need to Tailor Tobacco Cessation Training for Community Health Workers. International journal of environmental research and public health, 20(8), 5574; Leong, S. L., Teoh, S. L., Fun, W. H., & Lee, S. W. H. (2021). Task shifting in primary care to tackle healthcare worker shortages: An umbrella review. The European journal of general practice, 27(1), 198–210; Ahmed, S., Chase, L. E., Wagnild, J., Akhter, N., Sturridge, S., Clarke, A., Chowdhary, P., Mukami, D., Kasim, A., & Hampshire, K. (2022). Community health workers and health equity in low- and middle-income countries: systematic review and recommendations for policy and practice. International journal for equity in health, 21(1), 49.

interdisciplinary, whereas others are multidisciplinary (Heinemann, 2002; Teams, 2020).

For both patients and providers, the healthcare team model has significant benefits. On the provider side, working as part of a team is thought to reduce levels of emotional exhaustion and improve feelings of job satisfaction. A team-based approach to patient care is seen as a way to establish and maintain employee morale, improve the status of specific occupational roles (e.g., nurses and allied health may collaborate with doctors instead of working under the leadership of doctors), and improve the efficiency of the organization (Rosen et al., 2018). Studies have found positive effects from team-based care resulting from higher job engagement, better relationships with colleagues, more involvement with patients, and a greater sense of control (Sheridan et al., 2018; Smith et al., 2018). A positive team climate and good teamwork can also help mitigate some of the detrimental effects of heavy work demands and burnout (Smith et al., 2018).

On the patient side, healthcare teams have been found to improve clinical outcomes. The patient-centered medical home (PCMH) is one of the most well-known examples of team-based care. According to the Agency for Healthcare Research and Quality (AHRQ, n.d.), the PCMH has five core functions and attributes: comprehensive care, patient-centered care, coordinated care, accessible services, and quality and safety. PCMHs have been associated with reductions in emergency department visits, 30-day readmissions, and hospital utilization, among other indicators (Green et al., 2018; Hawes et al., 2018; Smith et al., 2018). Broader research on team-based care has found similar benefits from the use of interprofessional care teams in intensive care units (ICUs), outpatient care, emergency departments, nursing homes, and in treating patients with two or more chronic conditions (Donovan et al., 2018; Meyers et al., 2019; Smith et al., 2018).

One published review used an Integrated Team Effectiveness Model (ITEM) to summarize literature findings from 1985 to 2004 on healthcare teams and evaluate these teams' effectiveness (Lemieux-Charles and McGuire, 2006). The researchers compared team-based versus non team-based intervention studies and found evidence that team-based care can bring better clinical results and patient satisfaction than improperly set up or poorly coordinated sequential care. They suggested that the more diverse the types and clinical expertise (experience) involved in team decision-making, the better the patient care and the greater the organizational effectiveness that can be provided. Staff satisfaction and team efficiency can be improved through collaboration, conflict resolution, cooperation, and cohesion.

In addition, the use of healthcare teams has been linked to improvements in patient perceptions and access to care. A study of team-based care in family practice found that patients who were cared for by a team felt that they had improved knowledge about their medical conditions (67.4%), received better care (65.0%), and had improved access to care (51.1%). Some patients also reported better overall health (51.1%), felt that they played a more active role in their own care (44.1%), and were better able to carry out self-care (48.9%) and maintain their independence (43.7%) (Szafran et al., 2018). Another study seeking to understand the relationship between team-based care and access to care among female veterans found that high ratings in care coordination and communication were positively associated with ratings of access to routine and urgent care (Brunner et al., 2018). These findings underscore the benefits of using healthcare teams to improve patients' experiences and access to care. Refer to **Exhibit 4-4** for a summary of the potential benefits for the team-based approach to health care.

Global Health Workforce Challenges

A 2006 report issued by the World Health Organization (WHO) identified 57 countries that were facing a health workforce crisis,

Exhibit 4-4 Summary of the Potential Benefits for the Team-Based Approach to Health Care

---

1. **Comprehensive Care:**
   - Healthcare teams typically consist of professionals with diverse skills and expertise, such as physicians, nurses, pharmacists, physical therapists, social workers, and more (Weiss et al., 2023). Each team member contributes unique knowledge and skills to address various aspects of a patient's health, leading to a more holistic and comprehensive approach to care (Weiss et al., 2023).
2. **Improved Patient Care:**
   - Healthcare teams prioritize patient needs and preferences and they involve patients in decision-making processes (Erjavec and Bedenčič, 2022). The quality of communication among healthcare professionals is an important aspect to improve patient care. Effective communication between physicians, nurses, and patients not only improves the quality of care but also enhances patient satisfaction and engagement in their own health care (Erjavec and Bedenčič, 2022).
3. **Specialization and Efficiency:**
   - Healthcare teams allow for specialization, ensuring that patients receive the most appropriate and effective care for their specific needs (Martin et al., 2022). For example, a physician will comprehensively assess patients' condition and recommend the treatment choices they believe will be most effective in managing their illness. Physicians will supervise patients' progress during the treatment to ensure their condition improves (Martin et al., 2022). However, a registered nurse is responsible for any questions or concerns patients have about their treatment, symptoms, side effects, or anything else (Martin et al., 2022). Registered nurses communicate all information they gather with the rest of the healthcare team and act as the patients' voice. It is their job to not only be responsible for the delivery of patients' care, but to also ensure they are well informed, able to access their own treatment, and be emotionally equipped to deal with their disease (Martin et al., 2022).
   - Collaboration among healthcare team members can simplify the care procedure (Rux, 2020). Through efficient communication and shared roles, responsibilities can be assigned to the most suitable team member, thereby reducing delays and enhancing the effectiveness of care provisions (Rux, 2020).
4. **Improved Health Outcomes:**
   - Healthcare team communication is a key driver of patient outcomes, including safety and quality measures (Preis et al., 2022). Effective communication can help prevent unanticipated adverse events measures (Preis et al., 2022).
   - Effective collaboration among healthcare professionals can result in improved patient results (Hathaway et al., 2023). When team members combine their skills, they can collaboratively recognize possible hazards, provide precise diagnoses, and formulate holistic treatment strategies that consider every facet of a patient's well-being (Hathaway et al., 2023).
5. **Extended Accessibility:**
   - By distributing responsibilities among team members, healthcare teams can extend access to care in underserved areas or for populations with limited access to healthcare resources (Traylor et al., 2021).
   - Physicians can utilize virtual communication with patients in the form of telemedicine (Elkbuli and McKenney, 2021). Those in isolation can communicate with the healthcare team, reducing the times a team member has to cross into the isolation

(continues)

Exhibit 4-4 Summary of the Potential Benefits for the Team-Based Approach to Health Care *(continued)*

zone (Elkbuli and McKenney, 2021). Telemedicine has the potential to be efficiently utilized for obstetric monitoring and delivering maternal care while minimizing the risk of exposure (Elkbuli and McKenney, 2021).

Data from Weiss, D., Tilin, F., & Morgan, M. J. (2023). The interprofessional health care team: Leadership and development. Jones & Bartlett Learning; Erjavec, K., Knavs, N., & Bedenčič, K. (2022). Communication in interprofessional health care teams from the perspective of patients and staff. Journal of Health Sciences, 12(1), 29-37; Martin, A. K., Green, T. L., McCarthy, A. L., Sowa, P. M., & Laakso, E. L. (2022). Healthcare Teams: Terminology, Confusion, and Ramifications. Journal of multidisciplinary healthcare, 15, 765–772; Rux, S. (2020). Utilizing improvisation as a strategy to promote Interprofessional collaboration within healthcare teams. Clinical Nurse Specialist, 34(5), 234-236; Preis, H., Dobias, M., Cohen, K., Bojsza, E., Whitney, C., & Pati, S. (2022). A mixed-methods program evaluation of the Alda Healthcare Experience-a program to improve healthcare team communication. BMC Medical Education, 22(1), 897; Hathaway, J. R., Tarini, B. A., Banerjee, S., Smolkin, C. O., Koos, J. A., & Pati, S. (2023). Healthcare team communication training in the United States: A scoping review. Health Communication, 38(9), 1821-1846; Traylor, A. M., Tannenbaum, S. I., Thomas, E. J., & Salas, E. (2021). Helping healthcare teams save lives during COVID-19: Insights and countermeasures from team science. American psychologist, 76(1), 1; Elkbuli, A., Ehrlich, H., & McKenney, M. (2021). The effective use of telemedicine to save lives and maintain structure in a healthcare system: current response to COVID-19. The American journal of emergency medicine, 44, 468.

meaning that the country had fewer than 23 health workers per 10,000 people. Most of these countries are economically weak, and they are predominantly located in sub-Saharan Africa. The report also pointed out a provider shortage of 4.3 million doctors, midwives, nurses, and support workers (WHO, 2006). A 2017 Global Burden of Disease Study further elaborated on this shortage, estimating that only half of all countries have the capacity to provide quality health care. Countries in sub-Saharan Africa, Southeast and South Asia, and some Oceania countries face the most severe shortages (GBD 2017, 2017). The uneven distribution of healthcare professionals within countries has further exacerbated this shortage. According to the WHO (2015), half of the world's population lives in rural areas, but only 23% of the world's healthcare workers, 38% of nursing staff, and 24% of doctors provide services for these underserved populations.

Another WHO (2005) publication emphasized that the shift from acute to chronic health problems is placing different demands on the healthcare workforce, as addressing chronic diseases requires different resources and skill sets. The increased prevalence of chronic conditions around the globe requires this workforce to adopt a patient-centered approach, improve communication skills, ensure safety and quality of patient care, monitor patients across time, use available technology, and consider care from a population perspective (WHO, 2005).

A WHO report released in 2014 noted that the aging health workforce is creating an ongoing dilemma in the healthcare sector. Staff retiring or leaving for better-paying jobs are not being replaced, and not enough young people are entering the profession or being adequately trained to replace them. Moreover, internal and international migration of health workers is exacerbating regional imbalances (WHO, 2014a).

In Europe, while the number of physicians per capita is increasing, that growth appears to be insufficient to accommodate the expanding needs of an aging population (Lang, 2011). In addition, far more specialists than generalists have entered the healthcare sector in recent years; shortages of nurses, physiotherapists, and occupational therapists are predicted to occur in the future (Lang, 2011).

The situation is similar in the United States, where the number of older adults is expected to double between 2005 and 2030 (Institute of Medicine, 2008). This trend will undoubtedly lead to an aging health workforce. The United States is hoping to add new people to the geriatric care-oriented workforce as well as retaining the services of existing geriatric specialists to alleviate some of the strains (Institute of Medicine, 2008). However, projected physician shortages of more than 100,000 by 2030 and even greater shortages in other healthcare roles (e.g., more than 400,000 home health aides by 2025) suggest that the U.S. healthcare field will be severely understaffed in the near future (AAMC, 2019b; Schrader et al., 2018). Along with an aging workforce and increased prevalence of chronic disease, an aging population and the limited capacity of educational programs to produce more workers are contributing to the widening gap between supply and demand for care (A Closer Look, 2020). The U.S. healthcare workforce is also characterized by high rates of burnout, estimated at 35%–54% for nurses and physicians (AHA, 2020). An excessive workload, administrative burden, and inability to find meaning and purpose in work have all been singled out as factors contributing to burnout (AHA, 2020). These high burnout rates provide further evidence of the difficulties faced by U.S. providers as they seek to meet the demands of a growing patient population.

Growth in the number of nonphysician providers may address these shortages to some extent (Riegel et al., 2012). Evidence supporting the involvement of NPPs in the prevention and management of chronic health problems continues to grow. For example, integrating NPPs into multidisciplinary healthcare teams has emerged as an effective strategy for improving the control of hypertension among high-risk populations (Brownstein et al., 2007; Fleming et al., 2015; Sookaneknun et al., 2004; Walsh et al., 2006). NPPs are effective in providing care for patients with chronic conditions, with their care resulting in improvements in patients' ability to keep appointments, better compliance with prescribed regimens, increased risk reduction, and greater engagement of patients in self-monitoring and adherence to medications (Roark et al., 2011). The supply of these providers, such as PAs and APRNs, is expected to continue to grow (AAMC, 2019b).

Community-based healthcare workers (CHWs) have also proved to be valuable in expanding access to healthcare services, particularly in developing countries. These workers serve as physician assistants by providing preventive medical services, monitoring community health, identifying high-risk patients, and even providing basic treatment services. Studies have shown that CHWs can provide excellent care for people with HIV/AIDS, manage communicable diseases such as malaria and tuberculosis, promote immunization uptake and breastfeeding practices, improve tuberculosis treatment outcomes, and reduce child morbidity and mortality (Bangdiwala et al., 2010; Lehmann et al., 2008).

Strong government frameworks can play a role in developing and sustaining a sufficient healthcare workforce. These influence and help guide medical education, health employment, international exchanges of health services, worker migration patterns, and innovative partnership models, among other aspects (Kamineni, 2019; Stilwell et al., 2004). For example, medical education can be reconceptualized so that it is shorter, less burdensome, or more targeted to the actual work in which students will engage when they graduate (Al-Shamsi, 2017). Cross-country collaborations and the development of exchange programs for healthcare workers and medical education can be encouraged as well (Kamineni, 2019). Incentives can be instituted to encourage healthcare workers to work in rural or underserved areas, thereby help address discrepancies in access to care (MacGregor et al., 2018). Tools that can be used for this purpose include recruiting medical and health science students of rural origin, financial support in the form of scholarships and salary bonuses, and development of personal and professional support networks in these areas (MacGregor et al., 2018; Raffoul et al., 2019; Safi et al., 2018). Promotion of diversity and gender equity should ideally lead to a more balanced healthcare workforce that can care for the complex and varied needs of the patient population (Kamineni, 2019; Raffoul et al., 2019). Such measures are crucial to delivering a comprehensive targeted care and are particularly important in countries and cultures where a lack of female healthcare workers has historically restricted the ability of women to seek out care (Safi et al., 2018).

The healthcare industry could also make full use of technology to augment healthcare resources, such as utilizing e-health and e-learning, AI, and virtual-reality simulations to train and empower health workers. Likewise, the adoption of personalized wearable devices for home-based care and telemedicine strategies might potentially transform healthcare delivery. New care models should be developed, as the health system focuses on preventive care and encourages a holistic approach that covers all socioeconomic determinants of health.

A growing public health concern across the globe is the migration of health professionals from developing countries to the United States, United Kingdom, Canada, and Australia. For example, IMGs make up 25% of the U.S. physician population, which includes U.S. citizens who go to medical schools abroad (Educational Commission for Foreign Medical Graduates, 2015). To address this migration, WHO developed the Global Code of Practice on the International Recruitment of Health Personnel, which establishes principles and voluntary standards for countries to consider in workforce development and recruitment. This code includes the following components (WHO, 2014b):

- Greater commitment to assist countries facing critical health worker shortages with their efforts to improve and support their health workforce
- Joint investment in research and information systems to monitor the international migration of health workers and develop evidence-based policies
- Commitment of member states to meet their health personnel needs with their own human resources as far as possible, including taking measures to educate, retain, and sustain their health workforces
- Enshrinement of migrant workers' rights and ensuring they are equal to the rights of domestically trained health workers

The migration of healthcare workers is counterbalanced by another growing trend: medical tourism. The medical tourism industry has undergone significant growth in recent decades, drawing patients from all over the world to medical facilities located in every global region. Medical tourism in the United States has grown steadily, with exports (i.e., travelers coming to the United States) having doubled and imports (U.S. travelers going abroad) having increased almost ninefold from a low base in the early 2000s (Chambers, 2015). Approximately 0.5% of all air travelers entering the United States annually—between 100,000 and 200,000 people—list health treatment as a reason for visiting (Chambers, 2015). Foreign patients most often cite access to advanced medical care as their reason for traveling to the United States for treatment. The three largest source markets for foreign travelers visiting the United States for health treatment in 2011 were the Caribbean, Europe, and Central America—accounting for 44%, 24%, and 10% of arrivals, respectively (U.S. Department of Commerce, 2011). U.S. outbound medical tourists are thought to make up approximately 10% of the worldwide total of medical tourists. From 2007 to 2017, the number of Americans who sought medical treatment abroad rose from 750,000 to 1.7 million (Dalen and Alpert, 2019). Americans cite cost savings as the most common reason to go outside the United States for health treatment.

The market for medical tourism appears poised for further growth, with potentially far-reaching economic impacts on both the source and destination countries. Opportunities for financial benefits from medical tourism include potentially exerting competitive pressure on systems importing health care, which may help drive down the costs of healthcare services offered in domestic systems. Moreover, medical tourism can be an important source of foreign exchanges, with income being generated both for the health sector in particular and through general increases in tourist income. Some health systems within source countries might even develop relations with off-shore medical tourism facilities in an effort to alleviate their own excessive waiting lists and to lower healthcare costs (Lunt et al., 2011).

Summary

Health services professionals in the United States constitute the largest labor force within the country. The development of these professionals is influenced by demographic trends, advances in research and technology, disease and illness trends, and the changing environment of healthcare financing and delivery.

Physicians play a leading role in the delivery of health services in the United States, though the country has a maldistribution of physicians both by specialty and geography. The current shortages in the healthcare workforce, especially of PCPs, are likely to continue into the future, given the aging population, the growing burden of chronic diseases, and increases in the number of patients who are insured. Various policies and programs have been used or proposed to address both physician imbalance and maldistribution, including regulation of healthcare professions, reimbursement initiatives targeting suitable incentives, targeted programs for underserved areas, changes in medical school curricula, changes in the financing of medical training, and a more rational referral system.

In addition to physicians, many other health services professionals contribute significantly to the delivery of health care, including nurses, dentists, pharmacists, optometrists, psychologists, podiatrists, chiropractors, non-physician providers, and other allied health professionals. These professionals, who require different levels of training, work in a variety of healthcare settings as complements to or substitutes for physicians.

Health services administrators face new challenges in the leadership of healthcare organizations. Meeting these challenges will require reforms in the educational programs designed to train adequate managers for the various sectors of the healthcare industry.

TEST YOUR UNDERSTANDING

Terminology

advanced practice nurse (APN)
allied health
allied health professional
allopathic medicine
certified nurse-midwives (CNMs)
chiropractors
comorbidity
dental assistants
dental hygienists
dentists
doctoral nursing degrees
generalists
hospitalists
licensed practical nurses (LPNs)
maldistribution
nurse practitioners (NPs)
occupational therapists (OTs)
optometrists
osteopathic medicine

pharmaceutical care
pharmacists
physical therapists (PTs)
physician assistants (PAs)
podiatrists
primary care
psychologists
registered nurses (RNs)
residency
specialists
specialty care

Review Questions

1. Describe the major types of health services professionals (physicians, nurses, dentists, pharmacists, physician assistants, nurse practitioners, certified nurse-midwives), including their roles, training, practice requirements, and practice settings.
2. Which factors are associated with the development of health services professionals in the United States?
3. What are the major distinctions between primary care and specialty care?
4. Why is there a geographic maldistribution of the physician labor force in the United States?
5. Why is there an imbalance between primary care and specialty care in the United States?
6. Which measures have been, or can be, employed to overcome problems related to physician maldistribution and imbalance?
7. Who are nonphysician providers? What are their roles in the delivery of health care?
8. In general, who are allied health professionals? What role do they play in the delivery of health services?
9. Provide a brief description of the roles and responsibilities of health services administrators.
10. What are the major trends in healthcare workforce development?

References

Abid, M. H., D. J. Lucier, M. K. Hidrue, and B. P. Geisler. 2022. The effect of standardized hospitalist information cards on the patient experience: A Quasi-Experimental Prospective Cohort Study. *Journal of General Internal Medicine* 37: 3931–3936.

Academy of Nutrition and Dietetics. 2018. Academy of Nutrition and Dietetics: Revised 2017 Scope of practice for the registered dietitian nutritionist. *Journal of the Academy of Nutrition and Dietetics* 118: 141–165. Available at: https://doi.org/10.1016/j.jand.2017.10.002

Accreditation Council for Occupational Therapy Education (ACOTE). 2023. School. Accessed October 2023. Available at: https://acoteonline.org/all-schools/?_gl=1*hrfdqs*_ga*MTgyMDQ3NDU2LjE2OTY1Mzg4Mzc.*_ga_3CVRFYYS90*MTY5NjUzODgzNy4xLjEuMTY5NjUzOTE3Mi4zLjAuMA

Accreditation Review Commission on Education for the Physician Assistant. 2023. Accredited programs. Accessed October 2023. Available at: https://www.arc-pa.org/accreditation/accredited-programs/

Agarwal, A., W. Zhang, Y. F. Kuo, and G. Sharma. 2009. Process and outcome measures among COPD patients with a hospitalization cared for by an advance practice provider or primary care physician. *PLoS One* 24: e0148522.

Agency for Healthcare Research and Quality (AHRQ). n.d. *Defining the PCMH*. Accessed May 2020. Available at: https://pcmh.ahrq.gov/page/defining-pcmh

Ahmed, S., L. E. Chase, J. Wagnild, et al. 2022. Community health workers and health equity in low- and middle-income countries: Systematic review and recommendations for policy and practice. *International Journal for Equity in Health* 21: 49.

Al-Shamsi, M. 2017. Addressing the physicians' shortage in developing countries by accelerating and reforming the medical education: Is it possible? *Journal of Advances in Medical Education & Professionalism* 5: 210–219.

America Osteopathic Association. 2022. Osteopathic Medical Profession Report. Accessed October 2023. Available at: https://osteopathic.org/index.php?aam-media=/wp-content/uploads/2022-AOA-OMP-Report.pdf

American Academy of Physician Assistants. 1986. *PA Fact Sheet*. Arlington, VA: American Academy of Physician Assistants.

American Association of Colleges of Nursing (AACN). 2014. Your guide to graduate nursing programs. Accessed July 2016. Available at: http://www.aacn.nche.edu/publications/brochures/GradStudentsBrochure.pdf

American Association of Community Colleges. 2014. Facts about allied health professionals. Accessed February 2021. Available at: https://info.nhanow.com/blog/10-surprising-facts-about-the-allied-health-workforce

American Association of Nurse Practitioners (AANP). 2022. NP facts. Accessed October 2023. Available at: https://storage.aanp.org/www/documents/NPFacts__111022.pdf

American Association of Nurse Practitioners (AANP). 2022. Planning your nurse practitioner (NP) education. Accessed October 2023. Available at: https://www.aanp.org/student-resources-old/planning-your-np-education

American College of Nurse-Midwives (ACNM). 2017. *Midwifery education programs.* Accessed April 2017. Available at: http://www.midwife.org/Education-ProgramsDirectory

American Council on Pharmaceutical Education (ACPE). 1992. *The Proposed Revision of Accreditation Standards and Guidelines.* Chicago, IL: National Association of Boards on Pharmacy.

American Hospital Association (AHA). 2016. *Trendwatch chartbook 2016.* Accessed February 2017. Available at: http://www.aha.org/research/reports/tw/chartbook/2016/table5-5.pdf

American Hospital Association (AHA). 2020. *Trendwatch: Hospital and health system workforce strategic planning.* Accessed May 2020. Available at: https://www.aha.org/system/files/media/file/2020/01/aha-trendwatch-hospital-and-health-system-workforce-strategic-planning2_0.pdf

Asadi-Aliabadi, M., S. M. Karimi, A. Tehrani-Banihashemi, F. Mirbaha-Hashemi, L. Janani, E. Babaee, and M. Moradi-Lakeh. 2022. Effectiveness of pay for performance to non-physician health care providers: A systematic review. *Health Policy* 126: 592–602.

Association of American Medical Colleges (AAMC). 2014. *Graduate medical education: Training tomorrow's physician workforce.* Accessed February 2021. Available at: https://aamc-black.global.ssl.fastly.net/production/media/filer_public/98/7b/987b00be-2ca9-4466-89cd-0892d233f63d/gme_training_tomorrows_physician_workforce.pdf

Association of American Medical Colleges (AAMC). 2019a. *New findings confirm predictions on physician shortage.* Accessed January 2020. Available at: https://www.aamc.org/news-insights/press-releases/new-findings-confirm-predictions-physician-shortage

Association of American Medical Colleges (AAMC). 2019b. *The complexities of physician supply and demand: Projections from 2017 to 2032.* Accessed May 2020. Available at: https://www.aamc.org/system/files/c/2/31-2019_update_-_the_complexities_of_physician_supply_and_demand_-_projections_from_2017-2032.pdf

Association of American Medical College (AAMC). 2021. Active Physicians Who Are International Medical Graduates (IMGs) by Specialty, 2021. Accessed October 2023. Available at: https://www.aamc.org/data-reports/workforce/data/active-physicians-international-medical-graduates-imgs-specialty-2021

Bangdiwala, S. I., S. Fonn, O. Okoye, and S. Tollman. 2010. Workforce resources for health in developing countries. *Public Health Reviews* 32: 296–318.

Basu, S., S. A. Berkowitz, R. L. Phillips, et al. 2019. Association of primary care physician supply with population mortality in the United States, 2005–2015. *JAMA Internal Medicine* 179: 506–514.

Basu, S. S. A. Berkowitz, R. L. Phillips, et al. 2019. Association of primary care physician supply with population mortality in the United States, 2005-2015. *JAMA Internal Medicine* 179: 506–514. doi:10.1001/jamainternmed.2018.7624

Beazoglou, T. J., L. Chen, V. F. Lazar, et al. 2012. Expanded function allied dental personnel and dental practice productivity and efficiency. *Journal of Dental Education* 76: 1054–1060.

Blair, C., R. Leonard, M. Linden, T. Teggart, and S. Mooney. 2023. Allied health professional support for children and young adults living in and leaving care: A systematic scoping review. *Child: Care, Health and Development* 50: e13140.

Blount, M. A., M. D. Douglas, C. Li, et al. 2023. Opportunities and challenges to advance health equity using digital health tools in underserved communities in southeast US: A mixed methods study. *Journal of Primary Care & Community Health* 14. doi:10.1177/21501319231184789

Boulet, J. R., J. J. Norcini, G. P. Whelan, and J. A. Hallock. 2006. The international medical graduate pipeline: Recent trends in certification and residency training. *Health Affairs* 25: 469–477.

Brownstein, J. N., F. M. Chowdhury, S. L. Norris, et al. 2007. Effectiveness of community health workers in the care of people with hypertension. *American Journal of Preventive Medicine* 32: 435–447.

Brunner, J., E. Chuang, D. L. Washington, et al. 2018. Patient-rated access to needed care: Patient-centered medical home principles intertwined. *Women's Health Issues* 28: 165–171. Available from https://doi.org/10.1016/j.whi.2017.12.001

Bylsma, W. H., G. K. Arnold, G. S. Fortna, and R. S. Lipner. 2010. Where have all the general internists gone? *Journal of General Internal Medicine* 25: 1020–1023.

Cantor, J., C. Whaley, K. Simon, and T. Nguyen. 2022. US health care workforce changes during the first and second years of the COVID-19 pandemic. *JAMA Health Forum* 3: e215217-e215217). American Medical Association.

Carter, S. R., R. Moles, L. White, and T. F. Chen. 2012. Patients' willingness to use a pharmacist-provided medication management service: The influence of outcome expectancies and communication efficacy. *Research in Social and Administrative Pharmacy* 8: 487–498.

Center for Health Workforce Studies. 2018. *Health care employment projections, 2016-2026: An analysis of Bureau of Labor Statistics projections by setting and occupation.* Accessed February 2020. Available at: http://www.chwsny.org/wp-content/uploads/2018/02/BLS-Projections-2_26_18.pdf

Centers for Medicare and Medicaid Services (CMS). 2019. *HHS news: HHS to deliver value-based transformation in primary care.* Accessed February 2020. Available at: https://www.cms.gov/newsroom/press-releases/hhs-news-hhs-deliver-value-based-transformation-primary-care

Chambers, A. 2015. *Trends in U.S. health travel services trade.* USITC Executive Briefing on Trade. Accessed February 2017. Available at: https://www.usitc.gov/publications/332/executive_briefings/chambers_health-related_travel_final.pdf

Chen, L. M., J. D. Birkmeyer, S. Saint, and A. K. Jha. 2013. Hospitalist staffing and patient satisfaction in the national Medicare population. *Journal of Hospital Medicine* 8: 126–131.

Coffman, J., and T. G. Rundall. 2005. The impact of hospitalists on the cost and quality of inpatient care in the United States: A research synthesis. *Medical Care Research and Review* 62: 379–406.

Coleman, K., B. T. Austin, C. Brach, and E. H. Wagner. 2009. Evidence on the chronic care model in the new millennium. *Health Affairs* 28: 75–85.

Comellas, M., T. Yeung, C. Young-Whiting, et al. 2020. Health services administration educational programs in the United States: An assessment of past, present, and future perspectives. *Journal of Health Administration Education* 37: 171–180.

Commission on Accreditation in Physical Therapy Education. 2017. *Developing PT programs.* Accessed April 2017. Available at: http://www.capteonline.org/Programs/Developing/PT/

Congressional Research Service. 2017. *Discretionary spending under the Affordable Care Act (ACA).* Accessed February 2017. Available at: https://fas.org/sgp/crs/misc/R41390.pdf

Cooper, R. A., P. Laud, and C. L. Dietrich. 1998. Current and projected workforce of nonphysician clinicians. *Journal of the American Medical Association* 280: 788–794.

Council on Education for Public Health (CEPH). 2017. *ASPH graduate training programs.* Available at: https://ceph.org/about/org-info/who-we-accredit/accredited/

Dalen, J. E., and J. S. Alpert. 2019. Medical tourists: Incoming and outgoing. *American Journal of Medicine* 132: 9–10. Available at: https://doi.org/10.1016/j.amjmed.2018.06.022

Donovan, A. L., J. M. Aldrich, A. K. Gross, et al. 2018. Interprofessional care and teamwork in the ICU. *Critical Care Medicine* 46: 980–990. doi:10.1097/CCM.0000000000003067

Educational Commission for Foreign Medical Graduates. 2015. *IMG performance in the 2015 match.* Accessed February 2017. Available at: http://www.ecfmg.org/news/2015/03/27/img-performance-in-the-2015-match/

Educational Commission for Foreign Medical Graduates. 2019. *IMGs continue to show gains in 2019 match.* Accessed January 2020. Available at: https://www.ecfmg.org/news/2019/03/15/imgs-continue-to-show-gains-in-2019-match/

Elkbuli, A., H. Ehrlich, and M. McKenney, 2021. The effective use of telemedicine to save lives and maintain structure in a healthcare system: current response to COVID-19. *The American Journal of Emergency Medicine* 44: 468.

Endicott, K. M. 1976. Health and health manpower. In: *Health in America: 1776–1976.* Health Resources Administration, U.S. Public Health Service. DHEW Pub. No. 76616. Washington, DC: U.S. Department of Health, Education, and Welfare. 138–165.

Ericksen K. 2016. *Nursing credentials 101: From LPN & LVN to BSN & DNP.* Accessed July 2016. Available at: http://www.rasmussen.edu/degrees/nursing/blog/nursing-credentials-101-from-lpn-lvn-bsn-dnp/

Erjavec, K., N. Knavs, and K. Bedenčič. 2022. Communication in interprofessional health care teams from the perspective of patients and staff. *Journal of Health Sciences* 12: 29–37.

Evangelista, J. K., J. A. Connor, C. Pintz, et al. 2012. Pediatric nurse practitioner managed cardiology clinics: Patient satisfaction and appointment access. *Journal of Advanced Nursing* 68: 2165–2174.

Fitzgerald, M. A., P. E. Jones, B. Lazar, M. McHugh, and C. Wang. 1995. The midlevel provider: Colleague or competitor? *Patient Care* 29: 20.

Fleming, S, H. Atherton, D. McCartney, et al. 2015. Self-screening and non-physician screening for hypertension in communities: A systematic review. *American Journal of Hypertension* 28: 1316–1324.

Freed, D. H. 2004. Hospitalists: Evolution, evidence, and eventualities. *Health Care Manager* 23: 238–256.

Garber, A. M. 2005. Evidence-based guidelines as a foundation for performance incentives. *Health Affairs* 24: 174–179.

GBD. 2017: A fragile world. 2018. *Lancet* 392. Accessed May 2020. Available at: https://www.thelancet.com/action/showPdf?pii=S0140-6736%2818%2932858-7

Ginzberg, E. 1994. Improving health care for the poor. *Journal of the American Medical Association* 271: 464–467.

Golden, J. R. 2014. A nurse practitioner patient care team: Implications for pediatric oncology. *Journal of Pediatric Oncology Nursing* 31: 350–356.

Goodwin, J. S., Y. L. Lin, S. Singh, and Y. F. Kuo. 2013. Variation in length of stay and outcomes among hospitalized patients attributable to hospitals and hospitalists. *Journal of General Internal Medicine* 28: 370–376.

Green, L. A., H. C. Chang, A. R. Markovitz, and M. L. Paustian. 2018. The reduction in ED and hospital admissions in medical home practices is specific to primary care-sensitive chronic conditions. *Health Services Research* 53: 1163–1179. Available at: https://doi.org/10.1111/1475-6773.12674

Greenfield, S., E. C. Nelson, and M. Zubkoff. 1992. Variation in resource utilization among medical specialties and systems of care. *Journal of the American Medical Association* 267: 1624–1630.

Griffiths, A., R. Brooks, and R. Haythorne, et al. 2023. The impact of Allied Health Professionals on the primary and secondary prevention of obesity in young children: A scoping review. *Clinical Obesity* 13: e12571.

Grossman, D. 1995. APNs: Pioneers in patient care. *American Journal of Nursing* 95: 54–56.

Guthrie, J. D., and J. A. Snyder. 2023. Improving access to care for underserved communities through telemedicine. *JAAPA: Official Journal of the American Academy of Physician Assistants* 36: 41–44.

Hawes, E. M., J. N. Smith, N. R. Pinelli, et al. 2018. Accountable care in transitions (ACTion): A team-based approach to reducing hospital utilization in a patient-centered medical home. *Journal of Pharmacy Practice* 31: 175–182. Available at: https://doi.org/10.1177/0897190017707118

Hathaway, J. R., B. A. Tarini, S. Banerjee, C. O. Smolkin, J. A. Koos, and S. Pati. 2023. Healthcare team communication training in the United States: A scoping review. *Health Communication* 38: 1821–1846.

Health Resources and Services Administration (HRSA). 2008. *The physician workforce: Projections and research into current issues affecting supply and demand.* Accessed February 2020. Available at: https://bhw.hrsa.gov/sites/default/files/bureau-health-workforce/data-research/physiciansupplyissues.pdf

Heinemann, G. D. 2002. Teams in health care settings. In: *Team performance in health care.* G. D. Heinemann and A. M. Zeiss, eds. New York: Kluwer. 3–18.

Helper, C., and L. Strand. 1990. Opportunities and responsibilities in pharmaceutical care. *American Journal of Hospital Pharmacy* 47: 533–543.

Hooker, R. S., and L. E. Berlin. 2002. Trends in the supply of physician assistants and nurse practitioners in the United States. *Health Affairs* 21: 174–181.

Hooker, R. S., and L. F. McCaig. 2001. Use of physician assistants and nurse practitioners in primary care, 1995–1999. *Health Affairs* 20: 231–238.

Huckman, R. S. 2020. What will U.S. healthcare look like after the pandemic? *Harvard Business Review.* Accessed May 2020. Available at: https://hbr.org/2020/04/what-will-u-s-health-care-look-like-after-the-pandemic

Institute of Medicine. 2008. *Retooling for an aging America: Building the health care workforce.* Accessed April 2017. Available at: http://www.nationalacademies.org/hmd/reports/2008/retooling-for-an-aging-america-building-the-health-care-workforce.aspx

Jacobson, P. D., and S. A. Jazowski. 2011. Physicians, the Affordable Care Act, and primary care: Disruptive change or business as usual? *Journal of General Internal Medicine* 26: 934–937.

Juraschek, S. P., X. Zhang, V. W. Lin, et al. 2012. United States registered nurse workforce report card and shortage forecast. *American Journal of Medical Quality* 27: 241–249.

Kaiser Family Foundation. 2018. *Health care employment as a percent of total employment.* Accessed February 2020. Available at: https://www.kff.org/other/state-indicator/health-care-employment-as-total/?currentTimeframe=0&sortModel=%7B%22colId%22:%22Locat ion%22,%22sort%22:%22asc%22%7D

Kaiser Family Foundation. 2023. Professionally active physicians. Accessed October 2023. Available at: https://www.kff.org/other/state-indicator/total-active-physicians/?currentTimeframe=0&selectedDistributions=primary-care-physicians--specialist-physicians--total&selectedRows=%7B%22wrapups%22:%7B%22united-states%22:%7B%7D%7D%7D&sortModel=%7B%22colId%22:%

Kamineni, S. 2019. *5 ways to bridge the global health worker shortage. World Economic Forum.* Accessed May 2020. Available at: https://www.weforum.org/agenda/2019/07/5-ways-to-bridge-the-global-health-worker-shortage/

Knight, V. 2019. *American medical students less likely to choose to become primary care doctors.* Accessed January 2020. Available at: https://khn.org/news/american-medical-students-less-likely-to-choose-to-become-primary-care-doctors/

Kozakowski, S. M., G. T. Schmittling, A. L. McGaha, and N. B. Kahn, 2016. Entry of US medical school graduates into family medicine residencies: 2015-2016. *Family Medicine* 48: 688–695.

Kuo, Y. F., N. W. Chen, J. Baillargeon, M. A. Raji, and J. S. Goodwin. 2015. Potentially preventable hospitalizations in Medicare patients with diabetes: A comparison of primary care provided by nurse practitioners versus physicians. *Medical Care* 53: 776–783.

Kurtzman, E., and B. S. Barnow. 2017. A comparison of nurse practitioners, physician assistants, and primary care physicians' patterns of practice and quality of care in health centers. *Medical Care* 55: 615–622. doi: 10.1097/MLR.0000000000000689

Lang, R. 2011. *Future challenges to the provision of health care in the 21st century*. University College London. Accessed December 2013. Available at: http://www.ucl.ac.uk/lc-ccr/downloads/presentations/R_LANG_COHEHRE_LISBON_PRESENTATION.pdf

Laurant M., M. Harmsen, H. Wollersheim, R. Grol, M. Faber, and B. Sibbald. 2009. The impact of nonphysician clinicians: Do they improve the quality and cost-effectiveness of health care services? *Medical Care Research and Review* 66: 36S–89S. doi:10.1177/1077558709346277. PMID: 19880672

Lapps, J., B. Flansbaum, L. K. Leykum, H. Bischoff, and E. Howell. 2022. Growth trends of the adult hospitalist workforce between 2012 and 2019. *Journal of Hospital Medicine* 17: 888–892.

Lee, D. C., H. Liang, and L. Shi. 2016. Insurance-related disparities in primary care quality among U.S. type 2 diabetes patients. *International Journal for Equity in Health* 15: 124.

Lehmann, U., M. Dieleman, and T. Martineau. 2008. Staffing remote rural areas in middle- and low-income countries: A literature review of attraction and retention. *BMC Health Services Research* 8: 19.

Lemieux-Charles, L., and W. L. McGuire. 2006. What do we know about health care team effectiveness? A review of the literature. *Medical Care Research and Review* 63: 263–300. Available at: https://doi.org/10.1177/1077558706287003

Leong, S. L., S. L. Teoh, W. H. Fun, and S. W. Lee, 2021. Task shifting in primary care to tackle healthcare worker shortages: An umbrella review. *The European Journal of General Practice* 27: 198–210.

Lunt, N., R. Smith, M. Exworthy, S. T. Green, D. Horsfall, and R. Mannion. 2011. *Medical tourism: Treatments, markets and health system implications: A scoping review*. Organization for Economic Cooperation and Development (OECD). Accessed April 2017. Available at: https://www.oecd.org/els/health-systems/48723982.pdf

Levine, D. M., B. E. Landon, and J. A. Linder. 2019. Quality and experience of outpatient care in the United States for adults with or without primary care. *JAMA Internal Medicine* 179: 363–372.

MacGregor, R. G., A. J. Ross, and G. Zihindulai. 2018. A rural scholarship model addressing the shortage of healthcare workers in rural areas. *South African Health Review* 2018: 51–57.

Martin, A. K., T. L. Green, A. L. McCarthy, P. M. Sowa, and E. L. Laakso. 2022. Healthcare teams: Terminology, confusion, and ramifications. *Journal of Multidisciplinary Healthcare* 15: 765–772.

Meyers, D. J., A. T. Chien, K. H, Nguyen, et al. 2019. Association of team-based primary care with health care utilization and costs among chronically ill patients. *JAMA Internal Medicine* 179: 54–61. doi: 10.1001/jamainternmed.2018.5118

Mirhoseiny, S., T. Geelvink, S. Martin, H. C. Vollmar, S. Stock, and M. Redaelli. 2019. Does task delegation to non-physician health professionals improve quality of diabetes care? Results of a scoping review. *PloS One* 1410: e0223159.

Morley, P., and L. Strand. 1989. Critical reflections of therapeutic drug monitoring. *Journal of Clinical Pharmacy* 2: 327–334.

National Center for Health Statistics (NCHS). 2016. *Health, United States, 2015*. Hyattsville, MD: U.S. Department of Health and Human Services.

National Center for Health Statistics (NCHS). 2018. *Health, United States, 2017*. Hyattsville, MD: U.S. Department of Health and Human Services.

National Center for Health Statistics (NCHS). 2022. *Health, United States, 2020-2021*. Hyattsville, MD: U.S. Department of Health and Human Services.

Obubu, M., N. Chuku, A. Ananaba, et al. 2023. Evaluation of healthcare facilities and personnel distribution in Lagos State: Implications on universal health coverage. *Hospital Practice* 51: 64–75.

Organization for Economic Cooperation and Development (OECD). 2016. *Health at a glance 2015 database*. Accessed February 2017. Available at: http://stats.oecd.org/index.aspx?DataSetCode=HEALTH_STAT

Post, J. J., and J. L. Stoltenberg. 2014. Use of restorative procedures by allied dental health professionals in Minnesota. *Journal of the American Dental Association* 145: 1044–1050.

Preis, H., M. Dobias, K. Cohen, E. Bojsza, C. Whitney, and S. Pati, 2022. A mixed-methods program evaluation of the Alda Healthcare Experience-a program to improve healthcare team communication. *BMC Medical Education* 22: 897.

Rafferty, A., S. Denslow, E. L. Michalets, et al. 2016. Pharmacist-provided medication management in interdisciplinary transitions in a community hospital (PMIT). *Annals of Pharmacotherapy* 50: 649–655.

Raffoul, M., G. Bartlett-Esquilant, and R. L. Phillips Jr. 2019. Recruiting and training a health professions workforce to meet the needs of tomorrow's health care system. *Academic Medicine* 94: 651–655. doi: 10.1097/ACM.0000000000002606

Rich, E. C., M. Wilson, J. Midtling, and J. Showstack. 1994. Preparing generalist physicians: The organizational and policy context. *Journal of General Internal Medicine* 9: S115–S122.

Riegel, B., E. Sullivan-Marx, and J. Fairman. 2012. Meeting global needs in primary care with nurse practitioners. *Lancet* 380: 449–450.

Roark, R. F., B. R. Shah, K. Udayakumar, and E. D. Peterson. 2011. The need for transformative innovation in hypertension management. *American Heart Journal* 162: 405–411.

Rosen, M. A., D. DiazGranados, A. S. Dietz, et al. 2018. Teamwork in healthcare: Key discoveries enabling safer, high-quality care. *American Psychologist* 73: 433–450. Available at: https://doi.org/10.1037/amp0000298

Rosenblatt, R. A. 1992. Specialists or generalists: On whom should we base the American health care system? *Journal of the American Medical Association* 267: 1665–1666.

Rosenblatt, R. A., and D. M. Lishner. 1991. Surplus or shortage? Unraveling the physician supply conundrum. *Western Journal of Medicine* 154: 43–50.

Rosenblatt, R. A., S. A. Dobie, L.G. Hart, et al. 1997. Interspecialty differences in the obstetric care of low-risk women. *American Journal of Public Health* 87: 344–351.

Rural Health Information Hub (RHIhub). 2021. Physicians per 10,000 people for metro and nonmetro counties, 2020. Accessed October 2023. Available at: https://www.ruralhealthinfo.org/charts/109 HRSA

Rux, S. 2020. Utilizing improvisation as a strategy to promote Interprofessional collaboration within healthcare teams. *Clinical Nurse Specialist* 34: 234–236.

Safi, N., A. Naeem, M. Khalil, P. Anwari, and G. Gedik. 2018. Addressing health workforce shortages and maldistribution in Afghanistan. *Eastern Mediterranean Health Journal* 24: 951–958. Available at: https://doi.org/10.26719/2018.24.9.951

Salsberg, E., and R. Martiniano. 2018. Health care jobs projected to continue to grow far faster than jobs in the general economy. *Health Affairs*. Accessed February 2020. Available at: https://www.healthaffairs.org/do/10.1377/hblog20180502.984593/full/

Samuels, M. E., and L. Shi. 1993. *Physician Recruitment and Retention: A Guide for Rural Medical Group Practice*. Englewood, CO: Medical Group Management Press.

Schneller, E. S. 2006. The hospitalist movement in the United States: Agency and common agency issues. *Health Care Management Review* 31: 308–316.

Schrader, C., H. Leis, and M. Stevenson. 2018. *Defining healthcare's workforce for the future: Shifting demand will change the nature of work in healthcare*. Oliver Wyman. Accessed May 2020. Available at: https://www.oliverwyman.com/content/dam/oliver-wyman/v2/publications/2018/december/health-innovation-journal/Defining%20workforce.pdf

Schroeder, S., and L. G. Sandy. 1993. Specialty distribution of U.S. physicians: The invisible driver of health care costs. *New England Journal of Medicine* 328: 961–963.

Deloitte. 2018. *Technology and the workforce of the future: The future of work in health care*. Deloitte. Accessed May 2020. Available at: https://www2.deloitte.com/us/en/pages/life-sciences-and-health-care/articles/healthcare-workforce-technology.html

Schwartz, M. 1994. Creating pharmacy's future. *American Pharmacy* NS34: 44–45, 59.

Sehgal, N. J., and R. M. Wachter. 2006. The expanding role of hospitalists in the United States. *Swiss Medical Weekly* 136: 591–596.

Sheridan, B., A. T. Chien, A. S. Peters, M. B. Rosenthal, J. V. Brooks, and S. J. Singer. 2018. Team-based primary care: The medical assistant perspective. *Health Care Management Review* 43: 115–125. doi: 10.1097/HMR.0000000000000136

Shi, L. 1992. The relation between primary care and life chances. *Journal of Health Care for the Poor and Underserved* 3: 321–335.

Shi, L. 1994. Primary care, specialty care, and life chances. *International Journal of Health Services* 24: 431–458.

Shi, L., L. A. Lebrun-Harris, C. A. Daly, et al. 2013. Reducing disparities in access to primary care and patient satisfaction with care: The role of health centers. *Journal of Health Care for the Poor and Underserved* 24: 56–66.

Singh, D. A., C. H. Stoskope, and J. R. Ciesla. 1996. A comparison of academic curricula in the MPH and the MHA-type degrees in health administration at the accredited schools of public health. *Journal of Health Administration Education* 14: 401–414.

Singh, D. A., L. Shi, M. E. Samuels, and R. L. Amidon. 1997. How well trained are nursing home administrators? *Hospital and Health Services Administration* 42: 101–115.

Smith, C. D., C. Balatbat, and S. Corbridge. 2018. Implementing optimal team-based care to reduce clinician burnout. *National Academy of Medicine* doi: 10.31478/201809c. Accessed May 2020. Available at: https://nam.edu/implementing-optimal-team-based-care-to-reduce-clinician-burnout

Sookaneknun, P., R. M. Richards, J. Sanguansermsri, et al. 2004. Pharmacist involvement in primary care improves hypertensive patient clinical outcomes. *Annals of Pharmacotherapy* 38: 2023–2028.

Stanfield, P. S., N. Cross, and H. Hui. 2012. *Introduction to the Health Professions*. 6th ed. Burlington, MA: Jones & Bartlett Learning.

Starfield, B. 1992. *Primary care: Concepts, Evaluation, and Policy*. New York, NY: Oxford University Press.

Starfield, B. 2011. Point: The changing nature of disease implications for health services. *Medical Care* 49: 971–972.

Starfield, B., and L. Simpson. 1993. Primary care as part of US health services reform. *Journal of the American Medical Association* 269: 3136–3139.

Starr, P. 1982. *The Social Transformation of American Medicine: The Rise of a Sovereign Profession and the Making of a Vast Industry*. New York: Basic Books.

Stilwell, B., K. Diallo, P. Zurn, M. Vujicic, O. Adams, and M. Dal Poz. 2004. Migration of health-care workers from developing countries: Strategic approaches to its management. *Bulletin of the World Health Organization* 82: 595–600.

Strand, L. R., R. J. Cipolle, P. C. Morley, and D. G. Perrier. 1991. Levels of pharmaceutical care: A needs-based approach. *American Journal of Hospital Pharmacy* 48: 547–550.

Szabo, S., A. Nove, Z. Matthews, et. al. 2020. Health workforce demography: A framework to improve understanding of the health workforce and support achievement of the sustainable development goals. *Human Resources for Health* 18: 1–10.

Szafran, O., S. L. Kennett, N. R. Bell, and L. Green. 2018. Patients' perceptions of team-based care in family practice: Access, benefits and team roles. *Journal of Primary Health Care* 10: 248–257. Available at: https://doi.org/10.1071/HC18018

Tan, M. M., S. Oke, D. Ellison, C. Huard, and A. Veluz-Wilkins. 2023. Addressing tobacco use in underserved communities outside of primary care: The need to tailor tobacco cessation training for community health workers. *International Journal of Environmental Research and Public Health* 20: 5574.

Encyclopedia.com. *Teams, Healthcare*. 2020. Accessed June 2020. Available at: https://www.encyclopedia.com/science/encyclopedias-almanacs-transcripts-and-maps/teams-healthcare

Traylor, A. M., S. I. Tannenbaum, E. J. Thomas, and E. Salas. 2021. Helping healthcare teams save lives during COVID-19: Insights and countermeasures from team science. *American Psychologist* 76: 1.

U.S. Bureau of Labor Statistics. 2023. Occupational employment and wages—May 2022. Accessed October 2023. Available at: https://www.bls.gov/news.release/pdf/ocwage.pdf

U.S. Department of Commerce, Office of Travel and Tourism Industries. 2011. Survey of International Air Travelers Program. Accessed February 2017. Available at: http://travel.trade.gov/research/programs/ifs/index.html

U.S. Department of Health and Human Services (DHHS). 2013. *HHS awards $12 million to help teaching health centers train primary care providers.* Accessed April 2017. Available at: http://www.businesswire.com/news/home/20130719005676/en/HHS-awards-12-million-Teaching-Health-Centers

U.S. Department of Health and Human Services (DHHS). 2019. *HHS awards over $85 million to help health centers expand access to oral health care.* Accessed January 2020. Available at: https://www.hhs.gov/about/news/2019/09/18/hhs-awards-over-85-million-help-health-centers-expand-access-oral-healthcare.html

U.S. Department of Health and Human Services (DHHS). 2023. Health Workforce Shortage Areas. Accessed October 2023. Available at: https://data.hrsa.gov/topics/health-workforce/shortage-areas

Vaishya, R., M. Javaid, I. H. Khan, and A. Haleem, 2020. Artificial Intelligence (AI) applications for COVID-19 pandemic. *Diabetes & Metabolic Syndrome: Clinical Research & Reviews* 14: 337–339.

Wachter, R. M. 2004. Hospitalists in the United States: Mission accomplished or work in progress? *New England Journal of Medicine* 350: 1935–1936.

Wagner, M. 1991. Maternal and child health services in the United States. *Journal of Public Health Policy* 12: 443–449.

Walsh, E., K. M. McDonald, K. G. Shojania, et al. 2006. Quality improvement strategies for hypertension management: A systematic review. *Medical Care* 44: 646–657.

Weiss, D., F. Tilin, and M. J. Morgan, 2023. *The Interprofessional Health Care Team: Leadership and Development*. Burlington, MA: Jones & Bartlett Learning.

Wennberg, J. E., D. C. Goodman, R. F. Nease, and R. B. Keller. 1993. Finding equilibrium in U.S. physician supply. *Health Affairs* 12: 89–103.

West, C. P., and D. M. Dupras. 2012. General medicine vs subspecialty career plans among internal medicine residents. *Journal of the American Medical Association* 308: 2241–2247.

White, H. L., and R. H. Glazier. 2011. Do hospitalist physicians improve the quality of inpatient care delivery? A systematic review of process, efficiency and outcome measures. *BMC Medicine* 9: 58.

World Health Organization (WHO). 2005. *Preparing a health care workforce for the 21st century: The challenge of chronic conditions.* Accessed December 2013. Available at: https://www.who.int/chp/knowledge/publications/workforce_report.pdf

World Health Organization (WHO). 2006. *The world health report 2006: Working together for health.* Accessed December 2013. Available at: https://www.who.int/whr/2006/en/index.html

World Health Organization (WHO). 2014a. *A universal truth: No health without a workforce.* Accessed February 2017. Available at: https://www.who.int/workforcealliance/knowledge/resources/GHWA-a_universal_truth_report.pdf?ua=1

World Health Organization (WHO). 2014b. *Migration of health workers.* Accessed April 2014. Available at: https://www.who.int/hrh/migration/14075_MigrationofHealth_Workers.pdf

World Health Organization (WHO). 2015. *Increasing access to health workers in remote and rural areas through improved retention: Global policy recommendations.* Accessed June 2015. Available at: https://apps.who.int/iris/bitstream/handle/10665/44369/9789241564014_eng.pdf;jsessionid=7149E3889B1933C0E20DBABB87F4B27A?sequence=1

World Bank. 2020. Current health expenditure (% of GDP). Accessed October 2023. Available at: https://data.worldbank.org/indicator/SH.XPD.CHEX.GD.ZS?locations=US

Yan, Y. 2022. Hospitalist System under the Covid-19 Pandemic: The perspective of value co-creation. *European Journal of Public Health* 32: ckac131–289.

Yang, Z., Z. Zeng, K. Wang, et al. 2020. Modified SEIR and AI prediction of the epidemics trend of COVID-19 in

China under public health interventions. *Journal of Thoracic Disease* 12: 165.

Ye, J. 2020. The role of health technology and informatics in a global public health emergency: practices and implications from the COVID-19 pandemic. *JMIR Medical Informatics* 8: e19866.

Zhang, X., D. Lin, H. Pforsich, and V. W. Lin. 2020. Physician workforce in the United States of America: forecasting nationwide shortages. *Human Resources for Health* 18: 1–9.

Zwilling, J., B. Wise, C. Pintz, et al. 2023. US primary care provider needs: An analysis of workforce projections and policy implications. *Policy, Politics, & Nursing Practice* 24: 231–238. doi:10.1177/15271544231190606

CHAPTER 5

Medical Technology

LEARNING OBJECTIVES

- Understand the meaning and role of medical technology in healthcare delivery.
- Appreciate the growing applications of information technology and informatics in the delivery of health care.
- Explore the different aspects of telemedicine and telehealth.
- Survey the factors that drive the innovation, dissemination, and use of technology.
- Discuss the government's role in technology diffusion.
- Examine the impact of technology on various aspects of domestic and global delivery of health care.
- Study the various facets of health technology assessment and its current and future directions.

"This must be high technology."

Introduction

Medical technology has been referred to as the "boon and bane of medicine" (Drake et al., 1993) and as a "two-edged sword" because it offers new and better treatments to a wider range of people and, at the same time, is a major driver of increasing costs in health systems (Haas et al., 2010). Medical technology has played a pivotal role in advancing health care and improving patient outcomes. Sophisticated diagnostic procedures have reduced complications and disability, new medical cures have increased longevity, and new drugs have helped stabilize chronic conditions. However, most new technology comes at a price that society must ultimately pay. A tremendous amount of costly research is necessary to produce most modern breakthroughs. Once technology is developed and put into use, even more costs are generated. Yet, importantly, technological innovation has become an ongoing effort to combat new health challenges and to make transformational changes in the current paradigm of patient care.

Historically, developments in science and technology were instrumental in transforming the nature of healthcare delivery during the postindustrial era in the United States. Since then, the ever-increasing proliferation of new technology has continued to profoundly alter many facets of healthcare delivery. Besides its role in medical cost inflation, technology has triggered other changes:

- Technology has created consumer perceptions that the latest is also the best. These perceptions have led to increased demand for and utilization of new technology once it becomes available.
- Technology has changed the organization of medical services. Many specialized services that previously could be offered only in hospitals are now available in outpatient settings and patients' homes.
- Technology has driven the scope and content of medical training and the practice of medicine, fueling specialization in medicine.
- Technology has influenced the way status is associated with various health professionals. Specialization is held in higher regard than primary care and public health.
- The assessment of medical technology has become critical in evaluating new innovations for safety and effectiveness.
- The growing complexity of innovation and medical-care delivery has necessitated the formation of organizations, such as the Consortia for Improving Medicine with Innovation and Technology (CIMIT), to promote interdisciplinary collaboration among world-class experts in medicine, science, and engineering, in concert with industry and government.
- Technology has raised complex social and ethical concerns that defy straightforward answers.

Globalization has also enveloped biomedical knowledge and technology. In both developed and developing nations, physicians have access to the same scientific knowledge through medical journals that can be accessed online. Most drugs and medical devices available in the United States are also available in almost all parts of the world. However, depending on the extent of supply-side rationing, the adoption of new technology often differs widely from one country to another. Thus, even in developed nations, everyone does not have access to the latest high-tech therapies. Conversely, in almost all parts of the world, people who possess adequate means can gain access to the latest and best in medicine regardless of the type of healthcare delivery system in their country.

This chapter discusses medical technology from multiple perspectives. Where appropriate, highlights from other countries are incorporated for comparative purposes.

What Is Medical Technology?

At a fundamental level, **medical technology** is the practical application of the scientific body of knowledge for the purpose of improving health and creating efficiencies in the delivery of health care. Medical science has greatly benefited from rapid developments in other applied sciences, such as chemistry, physics, engineering, and even space technology. For example, applications of physics are found in widely used medical technologies such as X-ray technology, mammography, ultrasound, lasers, and magnetic resonance imaging (MRI). Chemistry plays a critical role in the development of pharmaceuticals. Bioengineering is employed in developing robotic systems used in surgery and advanced prostheses. Advanced telemedicine is linked to aerospace medicine, supporting remote diagnosis and treatments based on the application of satellite technology (Cinelli and Brown, 2018).

Nanomedicine is an emerging area that involves the application of nanotechnology for medical use. Nanotechnology seeks to manipulate materials on the atomic and molecular level—one nanometer is one-billionth of a meter (Taub, 2011). Nanoparticles can be used to greatly enhance the delivery and effectiveness of drugs to targeted regions of the body (Sun and Sen Gupta, 2019). Nanotechnology is not confined to a single field, but rather requires an intense collaboration between disciplines to realize its benefits.

Scientific advances have also enabled **precision medicine** (also called personalized medicine)—the customization of disease treatment based on genetic, environmental, and lifestyle factors of individual patients. The result is tailored medical decisions and treatments (Calabretta et al., 2020). Precision medicine has the potential to revolutionize how we diagnose, treat, and prevent diseases (Sisodiya, 2021). Precision medicine, empowered by genetics, has produced important benefits, and holds much promise for future medical treatment advances (Sisodiya, 2021). Scientists have increasingly recognized that differences between individuals, including biological differences between males and females, have implications for health and disease. Technologies such as artificial intelligence are being investigated to enable the identification of biomedically relevant information to facilitate the delivery of precision medicine (Cirillo et al., 2020).

Precision medicine often involves the use of genomic data to understand a patient's genetic makeup and how it influences health (Denny and Collins, 2021). This information can help in the development of targeted therapies and personalized treatment plans (Denny and Collins, 2021). Performing genome sequencing at an early stage can resolve diagnostic challenges and reveal previously undetected Mendelian diseases, such as mysterious kidney conditions, unusual cases of diabetes, or unexplained developmental delays (Turro et al., 2020). Precision medicine also enables the identification of specific molecular targets in diseases like cancer (Manzari et al., 2021). Drugs and therapies can be designed to target these specific molecular markers, leading to more effective and less toxic treatments (Manzari et al., 2021).

Medical technology involves many facets of healthcare delivery. **Table 5-1** gives examples of some of the main applications of medical technology.

Information Technology and Informatics

Information technology (IT) deals with the transformation of data into useful information. IT encompasses numerous processes—determining data needs, gathering appropriate data, storing and analyzing the data, and

Table 5-1 Examples of Medical Technologies

Type	Examples
Diagnostic	Computed tomography (CT) scan
	Fetal monitor
	Computerized electrocardiography
	Magnetic resonance imaging (MRI)
	Positron emission tomography (PET)
	Single-photon emission computed tomography (SPECT)
Survival (life saving)	Intensive care unit (ICU)
	Cardiopulmonary resuscitation (CPR)
	Bone marrow transplant
	Liver transplant
	Autologous bone marrow transplant
Illness management	Renal dialysis
	Pacemaker
	Percutaneous transluminal coronary angioplasty (PTCA)
	Stereotactic cingulotomy (psychosurgery)
Cure	Pharmaceuticals
	Hip joint replacement
	Organ transplant
	Lithotripter
Prevention	Implantable automatic cardioverter–defibrillator
	Pediatric orthopedic repair
	Diet control for phenylketonuria
	Vaccines
Monitoring (body functions, vital signs)	Wearable biosensors
Prosthetics	Electromechanical limbs
	Artificial heart valves
	Artificial kidneys
	Dental implants
Enabling (to assist or extend physical capabilities of medical professionals)	Robotic surgery
	Cyberknife surgery[1]
	Nanoknife procedure[2]
	Laser therapy
Adjunctive therapies	Certain complementary treatments
Customized treatments	Precision medicine

Type	Examples
System management	Health information systems Telemedicine
Facilities and clinical settings	Hospital satellite centers Clinical laboratories Subacute care units Modern home health care
Organizational delivery structure	Managed care Integrated delivery networks

[1]A procedure in which high doses of radiation are used with pinpoint accuracy to destroy tumors.
[2]A minimally invasive procedure that uses electric currents to destroy tumors.

Data from Rosenthal, G. 1979. Anticipating the costs and benefits of new technology: A typology for policy. In: *Medical technology: The culprit behind health care costs?* S. Altman and R. Blendon, eds. Washington, DC: US Government Printing Office. pp. 77–87.

---

reporting the information in the format desired by its end users. Different types of information are made available for specific uses to healthcare professionals, managers, payers, patients, researchers, and the government. IT departments and managers handle the continually increasing flow of information in healthcare organizations. They also play a critical role in decisions to adopt new information technologies to improve healthcare delivery. The goal is to increase organizational efficiency, and to comply with various laws and regulations.

Healthcare IT includes medical records systems to collect, transcribe, and store clinical data; radiology and clinical laboratory reporting systems; pharmacy data systems to monitor medication use and avoid errors, adverse reactions, and drug interactions; scheduling systems for patients, space (such as surgery suites), and personnel; and financial systems for billing and collections, materials management, and many other aspects of organizational management (Cohen, 2004a). In healthcare organizations, IT applications fall into three general categories (Austin, 1992):

1. **Clinical information systems** support patient care delivery. Electronic medical records, for example, provide quick and reliable information necessary to guide clinical decision making and produce timely reports on quality of care delivered. Computerized provider order entry (CPOE) enables clinicians to electronically transmit orders to a recipient—for example, from a physician's office to a pharmacy. Such systems increase efficiency and reduce errors.

2. **Administrative information systems** assist healthcare staff in carrying out financial and administrative support activities, such as payroll, patient accounting, billing, materials management, budgeting and cost control, and office automation. In medical clinics, CPOE technology may be set up to interface with the billing system to minimize claims rejections by pinpointing errors in billing codes.

3. **Decision support systems** provide information and analytical tools to support managerial and clinical decision-making. *Managerial* decision support systems can be used to forecast patient volume, project staffing requirements, and schedule patients to optimize utilization of patient care and surgical facilities. Budgeting, revenue, and cost data help monitor and improve operational efficiencies. *Clinical*

decision support systems (CDSSs) are designed to improve clinical decision-making. A patient's unique clinical data are matched to a computerized knowledge base, and software algorithms generate patient-specific treatment protocols and recommendations (Haynes and Wilczynski, 2010). CDSS tools have applications in many areas, such as diagnosis, treatment, care coordination, and prevention.

Health informatics is broadly defined as the application of information science to improve the efficiency, accuracy, and reliability of healthcare services. Health informatics requires the use of IT but goes beyond IT by emphasizing the improvement of healthcare delivery. For example, designing and evaluating the effectiveness of CDSSs are tasks that fall within the domain of health informatics. Applications of informatics are also found in electronic health records, telemedicine, and use of artificial intelligence in health care (Savoy et al. 2023). **Artificial intelligence (AI)** refers to the ability of computers to perform tasks that are generally performed by humans. AI is rapidly reshaping cancer research and personalized clinical care (Bonkhoff & Grefkes, 2022). These applications span a wide spectrum, encompassing tasks such as identifying and categorizing cancer, characterizing tumors and their surrounding microenvironment at the molecular level, exploring new drug possibilities and reusing existing ones, and forecasting treatment results for patients care (Bhinder et al., 2021). The collaboration between AI and precision medicine aligns with the overarching objective of preventing and detecting diseases in individuals at an early stage (Johnson et al., 2021). This, in turn, has the potential to reduce the overall disease burden on society, consequently lowering the expenses associated with preventable health care for everyone (Johnson et al., 2021). Exhibit 5-1 summarizes the role of AI in medicine.

Exhibit 5-1 The Role of Artificial Intelligence in Medicine

- **Predictive Medicine:** The integration of AI-driven machine learning has the potential to revolutionize the field of medicine by enabling the development of predictive models for medications and examinations that provide lifelong patient monitoring (Secinaro et al., 2021).
- **Precision Medicine:** AI promises personalized treatment with precision medicines because AI models not only learn but also remember personal preferences and are available round the clock (Grech et al., 2023).
- **Disease Diagnostics:** AI techniques can make a difference in rehabilitation therapy and surgery (Reddy, 2022). Rehabilitation robots provide physical assistance and guidance, such as assisting a patient's limb during motor therapy (Reddy, 2022). For surgery, AI holds significant potential for revolutionizing surgical robotics by enabling devices to carry out semi-automated surgical procedures with growing precision (Reddy, 2022).
- **Drug Production:** Three-dimensional Printing (3DP) is a technology that partly employs AI technology during its processes (Liu et al., 2021). 3DP in pharmaceutical manufacturing offers personalized features for patients and allows for the customization of drug size, shape, and the combination of various pharmaceutical components, potentially enhancing convenience for clinical use (Awad et al., 2020).
- **Health Service Management:** AI applications allow hospitals and all health services to work more efficiently (Secinaro et al., 2021). For instance, clinicians can access data immediately when they need it, nurses can ensure better patient safety while administering medication, and patients can stay informed and engaged in their care by communicating with their medical teams during hospital stays (Secinaro et al., 2021).

- **Clinical Decision Making:** Algorithms can enhance clinical decision-making by expediting the process and the quantity of care offered, thereby having a positive influence on the cost of healthcare services (Secinaro et al., 2021).
- **GPT-4 and Medicine:** GPT-4 holds promise in contributing to medical advancement by assisting with tasks like generating patient discharge summaries, condensing recent clinical trial findings, offering insights into ethical guidelines, and more (Waisberg et al., 2023).

Data from Secinaro, S., Calandra, D., Secinaro, A., Muthurangu, V., & Biancone, P. (2021). The role of artificial intelligence in healthcare: a structured literature review. BMC medical informatics and decision making, 21(1), 125; Grech, V., Cuschieri, S., & Eldawlatly, A. A. (2023). Artificial intelligence in medicine and research - the good, the bad, and the ugly. Saudi journal of anaesthesia, 17(3), 401–406; Reddy S. (2022). Explainability and artificial intelligence in medicine. The Lancet. Digital health, 4(4), e214–e215; Liu, P. R., Lu, L., Zhang, J. Y., Huo, T. T., Liu, S. X., & Ye, Z. W. (2021). Application of Artificial Intelligence in Medicine: An Overview. Current medical science, 41(6), 1105–1115; Awad, A., Fina, F., Goyanes, A., Gaisford, S., & Basit, A. W. (2020). 3D printing: Principles and pharmaceutical applications of selective laser sintering. International journal of pharmaceutics, 586, 119594; Waisberg, E., Ong, J., Masalkhi, M., Kamran, S. A., Zaman, N., Sarker, P., Lee, A. G., & Tavakkoli, A. (2023). GPT-4: a new era of artificial intelligence in medicine. Irish journal of medical science, 10.1007/s11845-023-03377-8

Electronic Health Records and Systems

Electronic health records (EHRs) are IT applications that enable the processing of any electronically stored information pertaining to individual patients for the purpose of delivering healthcare services (Murphy et al., 1999). EHRs replace traditional paper medical records, which document a patient's demographic information, problems and diagnoses, plan of care, progress notes, medications, vital signs, and past medical history, among other items. An EHR system with basic features should incorporate the ability to update patient-related information, view test results, maintain problem lists, and manage prescription ordering (Decker et al., 2012). According to the Institute of Medicine (2003), a fully developed EHR system includes four key components:

- Collection and storage of health information of individual patients over time
- Immediate electronic access to person- and population-level information by authorized users
- Availability of knowledge and decision support that enhances the quality, safety, and efficiency of patient care
- Support of efficient processes for healthcare delivery

The Role and Impact of Government Policy on the Adoption of Electronic Health Records

In a comparative study of six nations (China, England, India, Scotland, Switzerland, and the United States), Payne and colleagues (2019) noted that government policy that includes economic incentives to healthcare providers is critical to successfully achieving the goals of health information exchange, for which EHRs are a prerequisite. Mainly in response to policy incentives, the United States has reached near universal adoption of EHR systems (Colicchio et al., 2019).

On 18 April 2023, the Office of the National Coordinator for Health Information Technology (ONC) of the Department of Health and Human Services (HHS) opened a consultation on a proposed rule entitled "Health Data, Technology, and Interoperability: Certification Program Updates, Algorithm Transparency, and Information Sharing (HTI-1)" until 20 June 2023. The proposed rule primarily aims to promote interoperability, increase transparency, and facilitate the accessibility, sharing, and utilization of electronic health data (Office of the National Coordinator for Health Information Technology, 2023). Key provisions of the proposed rule include

(Office of the National Coordinator for Health Information Technology, September 18):

- Implementing the Electronic Health Record Reporting Program as new Condition and Maintenance of Certification requirements (Insights Condition) for developers of certified health information technology (health IT) under the Certification Program.
- Modifying and expanding exceptions in the information blocking regulations to support information sharing and certainty for regulated actors.
- Revising several Certification Program certification criteria, including existing criteria for clinical decision support (CDS), patient demographics and observations, electronic case reporting, and application programming interfaces for patient and population services.
- Raising the baseline version of the United States Core Data for Interoperability (USCDI) from Version 1 to Version 3.
- Updating standards adopted under the Certification Program to advance interoperability, support enhanced health IT functionality, and reduce burden and costs.

Benefits and Drawbacks of EHRs

When properly implemented, EHR systems can improve the quality of health care, promote time efficiency, support adherence to clinical practice guidelines, and reduce the risks of medication errors and adverse drug effects (Campanella et al., 2015; Woldemariam and Jimma, 2023; Sheikhtaheri et al., 2022). EHRs can also facilitate access to, retrievability of, and portability of patient data.

Critics argue that EHRs have changed the emphasis in health care from patient-centeredness to institutional priorities, serving institutional interests (rather than patient interests) through the documentation process—for example, reimbursement, risk management, quality and work efficiency, and regulatory compliance (de Ruiter et al., 2016). EHRs were also implemented by many practices and facilities before widely known problems were fixed. Evidence also shows that the push for EHRs, coinciding with mandates of the Affordable Care Act (ACA), has contributed to physician burnout, as the time spent on electronic documentation may amount to twice as much as the time spent on patient contact (Arndt et al., 2017). Also, the massive amount of data makes it difficult to find relevant information needed for optimal patient care. Not surprisingly, clinician satisfaction with EHRs has remained low (Lite et al., 2020). **Exhibit 5-2** summarizes the potential pros and cons of EHRs.

EHRs and Quality of Care

Services delivered independently of patients' primary EHR can lead to fragmented care, poor provider communication, privacy concerns, and billing challenges (Kim et al., 2020). However, quality improvement requires more than just implementation of EHRs. More effective and reliable systems of care and workflows, guided by information contained in the EHR, are required for sustainable performance improvement. Only when established standards of care and clinical protocols are encoded into the system software does the EHR truly support the clinical team's efforts to optimize the structure, process, efficiency, effectiveness, and outcome of care (Janett et al., 2020).

Interoperability

Interoperability makes it possible to access individual records online from many separate, automated systems within an electronic network, eliminating the need for older methods, such as letters and faxes for sharing a patient's clinical information among providers. Physicians, for example, need timely information on test results. As a patient transitions from one clinical setting to another, coordination of the patient's care becomes essential.

Exhibit 5-2 The Effects of Electronic Health Records (EHRs) on Healthcare Delivery

Positive Effects
- **Improved accessibility and efficiency:** EHRs have made patient information readily accessible to authorized healthcare providers, improving coordination and streamlining care delivery. Physicians can access patient records instantly, reducing the need for physical file retrieval and minimizing delays in diagnosis and treatment (Lintvedt et al., 2023).
- **Improved data accuracy and quality:** EHRs enable the capture of detailed data and improved documentation quality being reported (Kao, 2022).
- **Enhanced patient care:** EHRs enable real-time access to patient data, leading to better-informed clinical decisions. Healthcare providers can view a patient's medical history, lab results, and medication records, facilitating accurate diagnoses and personalized treatment plans (Tsai et al., 2020).
- **Increased patient engagement:** Patients can access their own EHRs, promoting engagement and empowerment in their health care. They can view their medical records, test results, and communicate with their providers through secure messaging platforms (Shapiro & Kamal, 2022).

Negative Effects
- **Data security concerns:** EHRs store sensitive patient information electronically, making them susceptible to data breaches and cybersecurity threats (Barbalho et al., 2022).
- **Interoperability and integration challenges:** Poor interoperability and integration between systems hindered both the implementation and the adoption/use of EHRs (Shapiro & Kamal, 2022).
- **Insufficient support for users:** The lack of knowledge on EHR functions, the paucity of user involvement during the planning, development, and implementation phases of the system life cycle of EHRs, and the users' insufficient skills in typing and health literacy levels are challenges faced while using EHRs (Tsai et al., 2020).

Data from Lintvedt, O., Marco-Ruiz, L., & Pedersen, R. (2023). User Satisfaction with Recently Deployed Electronic Health Records. Studies in health technology and informatics, 302, 192–196; Kao D. P. (2022). Electronic Health Records and Heart Failure. Heart failure clinics, 18(2), 201–211; Tsai, C. H., Eghdam, A., Davoody, N., Wright, G., Flowerday, S., & Koch, S. (2020). Effects of Electronic Health Record Implementation and Barriers to Adoption and Use: A Scoping Review and Qualitative Analysis of the Content. Life (Basel, Switzerland), 10(12), 327; Shapiro, L. M., & Kamal, R. N. (2022). Implementation of Electronic Health Records During Global Outreach: A Necessary Next Step in Measuring and Improving Quality of Care. The Journal of hand surgery, 47(3), 279–283; Barbalho, I. M. P., Fernandes, F., Barros, D. M. S., Paiva, J. C., Henriques, J., Morais, A. H. F., Coutinho, K. D., Coelho Neto, G. C., Chioro, A., & Valentim, R. A. M. (2022). Electronic health records in Brazil: Prospects and technological challenges. Frontiers in public health, 10, 963841.

Health Information Organizations

A **health information organization (HIO)** is an independent organization that brings together healthcare stakeholders within a defined geographic area and facilitates electronic information exchange among these stakeholders with the objective of improving the delivery of health care in the community. Such stakeholders often include not only healthcare providers, but also payers, laboratories, and sometimes public health departments. The HIO is managed by a board of directors, which is composed of representatives from the various stakeholder organizations.

Hospital participation in HIOs has been growing. In one nationwide study, 45% of hospitals were found to participate in a community HIO (Brown-Podgorski et al., 2018). In 2021, more than 6 in 10 hospitals engaged in key aspects of electronically sharing health information (send, receive, query) and integrating summary of care records into EHRs, a 51% increase since 2017 (Office of the National Coordinator for Health Information Technology, 2023). Many states have passed laws that govern health information exchange

> **Exhibit 5-3** The Benefits of Hospitals Participating in HIO
>
> - **Interoperability and Data Sharing:** Participation in HIOs allows hospitals to share data seamlessly with other healthcare providers, such as primary-care physicians, specialists, and long-term care facilities. This interoperability improves patient care by ensuring that essential information is readily available to authorized caregivers (Bloomrosen & Berner, 2022). A smart grid framework aligns demand for and access to generated electricity, organized into three interoperability categories: (1) the availability of electricity by ensuring basic connectivity, network interoperability, and syntactic interoperability; (2) ensuring that electricity meets specific needs by providing semantic understanding and business context; and (3) the local oversight and delivery of electricity to meet the demands of business procedures, business objectives, and economic and regulatory policies (Sarkar, 2023).
> - **Care Coordination:** HIOs promote care coordination by providing a centralized platform for healthcare professionals to access and update patient records. This helps create a more holistic view of a patient's medical history, ensuring that all involved providers are on the same page regarding diagnoses, medications, and treatment plans (Walker, 2018).
> - **Increased Productivity:** The combination of electronic health records (EHRs), health information exchange (HIE), and telehealth holds a high potential for an overall increased productivity (Poba-Nzaou et al., 2021).
> - **Patient Empowerment:** Hospitals' involvement in HIOs can also empower patients to take control of their health care. For instance, patients can query for data about themselves, know when their data are queried and shared, and configure what is shared about them (Mandel et al., 2022).
>
> Data from Bloomrosen, M., & Berner, E. S. (2022). Findings from the 2022 Yearbook Section on Health Information Exchange. Yearbook of medical informatics, 31(1), 215–218; Sarkar I. N. 2023. Health Information Exchange as a Global Utility. Chest, 163(5), 1023–1025; Walker D. M. (2018). Does participation in health information exchange improve hospital efficiency? Health care management science, 21(3), 426–438; Poba-Nzaou, P., Uwizeyemungu, S., Dakouo, M., Tchibozo, A., & Mboup, B. (2021). Patterns of health information exchange strategies underlying health information technologies capabilities building. Health systems (Basingstoke, England), 11(3), 211–231; Mandel, J. C., Pollak, J. P., & Mandl, K. D. (2022). The Patient Role in a Federal National-Scale Health Information Exchange. Journal of medical Internet research, 24(11), e41750.

even though federal legislation in this area had already existed. Such state laws may have a bearing on the extent to which hospitals participate in HIOs. **Exhibit 5-3** summarizes the benefits for hospitals to participate in HIO.

Financial Incentives Under the HITECH Act

The Health Information Technology for Economic and Clinical Health (HITECH) Act, which became part of the American Recovery and Reinvestment Act (ARRA) of 2009, was the major policy legislation that provided financial incentives for hospitals and physician offices/clinics to adopt EHRs. Beginning in 2011, Medicare and Medicaid started offering financial incentives of up to $44,000 for Medicare providers and $63,750 for Medicaid providers for "meaningful use" of health information technology (Centers for Disease Control and Prevention [CDC], 2012). To demonstrate "meaningful use," healthcare providers had to meet a range of metrics in areas such as quality, safety, efficiency, reduction of health disparities, patient engagement, care coordination, and security of health information (Halamka, 2010) (Refer to **Exhibit 5-4** for indicators of meaningful use). However, questions remain about the actual return on investment from the $36 billions of taxpayer money allocated to this initiative. Although a few recent studies have shown evidence of some positive impact of EHR (Kariotis et al., 2022; Colicchio et al., 2019), empirical evidence on the impacts of the EHR adoption program has been relatively

Exhibit 5-4 Stages of Meaningful Use of Information Technology

Stage 1
Data capture and sharing
Key clinical conditions captured
Standardized format
Information sharing
Reporting

Stage 2
Advanced clinical processes
E-prescribing
Lab reports
Shared patient care summaries
Patient-controlled data

Stage 3
Improved patient outcomes
Quality
Safety
Efficiency
Decision support
Self-management
Improved health outcome
Population health

weak, with reports indicating that many current EHR systems reduce physicians' productivity and lack data-sharing capabilities (Mennemeyer et al., 2016). David Blumenthal, President Barack Obama's national coordinator for health information technology and one of the architects of the EHR initiative, has acknowledged that electronic health records "have not fulfilled their potential. I think few would argue they have" (Schulte and Fry, 2019). This effort serves as an example of how agenda-driven policies that are based on intuition rather than robust research can become misdirected and wasteful.

Confidentiality Under HIPAA

To alleviate the concerns of both patients and providers about the confidentiality of patient information, the Health Insurance Portability and Accountability Act (HIPAA) of 1996 makes it illegal to gain access to a patient's personal health information (PHI) for reasons other than healthcare delivery, operations, and reimbursement. The HIPAA legislation mandated strict controls on the transfer of personally identifiable health data between two entities, provisions for disclosure of protected information, and penalties for violation (Clayton, 2001). In January 2013, the U.S. Department of Health and Human Services (DHHS) issued revisions to HIPAA in conjunction with the HITECH Act. More stringent rules now apply to disclosure of breaches of confidential PHI, inclusion of vendors and subcontractors as "business associates" that must comply with HIPAA requirements, restrictions on the use of PHI for marketing purposes, patient authorization related to the use of PHI for research purposes, and the use of genetic information for underwriting purposes by health insurance companies. Under the Individual Rights provision, patients have the right to receive a notice of privacy practices, request additional privacy protections, access their PHI and receive a paper or electronic copy of their PHI, request amendment of their PHI, and receive an accounting of disclosures of their PHI (Tovino, 2019).

E-Health, M-Health, E-Therapy, and E-Visits

With the growth of the Internet and the proliferation of mobile devices that offer online access, many patients are taking charge of their own health. A number of websites offer physician consultations, and others sell prescription medications. Patients are also forming online support communities to help themselves through discussion groups and bulletin boards. Alternative medicine, using supplements and other home treatments, is a popular topic for online searches (Bach and Wenz, 2020). Information empowers patients so that they become more active participants in their own health care, but it can also affect the traditional patient-physician dynamics. The vast majority of patients rely on and trust their physicians or other healthcare professionals for information, care, or support (Fox and Duggan, 2013). However, the Internet is often the first source of information—used by as many as 93% of American adults—that patients consult for specific health conditions (Pew Research Center, 2021).

Depending on the source, the online information that they find may not be reliable or accurate. Unfortunately, information available on trustworthy medical sites is often difficult to understand because of the medical jargon and terminology used, especially for those users with lower education levels and a low socioeconomic status (Oh and Song, 2017).

E-Health and M-Health

"**E-health** refers to all forms of electronic health care delivered over the Internet, ranging from informational, educational, and commercial 'products' to direct services offered by professionals, nonprofessionals, businesses, or consumers themselves" (Maheu et al., 2001). The use of e-health has grown as many providers have created secure Internet portals to enable patients to access their EHRs, engage in patient-provider email messaging, and use mobile apps for smartphones and tablets (Ricciardi et al., 2013).

The term "mobile health," or **m-health**, refers to "the use of wireless communication devices to support public health and clinical practice" (Kahn et al., 2010). These devices facilitate communication among researchers, clinicians, and patients. In addition, thanks to the proliferation of mobile devices and apps, along with fitness trackers or "wearables," many people are able to track their own health and fitness and even modify their own behaviors (Bach and Wenz, 2020).

E-Therapy

E-therapy is an alternative to face-to-face therapy for behavioral health support and counseling (Skinner and Latchford, 2006). Also referred to as online therapy, e-counseling, teletherapy, or cyber-counseling, **e-therapy** refers to any type of professional therapeutic interaction that makes use of the Internet to connect qualified mental health professionals and their clients (Rochlen et al., 2004). Internet-based psychological treatments have been found to be effective for many common mental health conditions, and they are also cost-effective for both the practitioner and the patient. Both therapist-led and self-directed online therapies can lead to significant alleviation of disorder-related symptomatology (Ybarra and Eaton, 2005). E-therapy has the potential of reaching a significant number of clients who need mental health services yet do not receive them (Wodarski and Frimpong, 2013).

E-Visits

E-visits, also known as virtual physician visits, are online clinical encounters between a patient and a physician or other clinician. Beyond traditional doctor-patient consultations, e-visits expanded to include various healthcare services, such as mental health counseling, prescription refills, and monitoring of chronic conditions (de Oliveira et al., 2023). E-visits benefited from ongoing advancements in technology. Improved video conferencing platforms, mobile apps, and electronic health records (EHR) integration made it easier for healthcare providers and patients to conduct virtual visits (Eslami & Ayatollahi, 2023).

For many health conditions, e-visits can be quite effective and provide levels of care that are equivalent to face-to-face encounters. For example, in one study, e-visits were effective in improving markers for 76% of the patients with uncontrolled diabetes (Robinson et al., 2016). Diagnostic accuracy for low-acuity illnesses has also been found to be equivalent between e-visits and face-to-face visits (Hertzog et al.,

2019). In 2015, approximately 16% of U.S. physicians provided e-visits (Hong et al., 2019). According to a survey carried out in the United States in 2021, three quarters of physicians had used telehealth to provide primary-care visits, while 72% had carried out appointments for chronic care via telehealth (Statista, 2023). Furthermore, over a third of physicians reported to have used virtual care to provide mental health support.

The use of this technology grew remarkably during the COVID-19 pandemic of 2020–2021, as the high risks associated with the contagion kept patients homebound. Telemedicine health care has grown in the United States since the beginning of the COVID-19 pandemic and will remain an integral part of medical care (Shaver, 2022). The number of teleconsultations skyrocketed in the early months of the pandemic, offsetting to some extent the reduction in in-person healthcare services (Hao et al., 2023). The number of Medicare fee-for-service beneficiary telehealth visits in the United States increased 63-fold in 2020, to nearly 52.7 million (OECD, 2023). Among respondents to multiple waves of McKinsey Surveys conducted in 2020 and 2021, two-thirds of physicians and 60% of patients agreed that virtual health is more convenient than in-person care for patients (OECD, 2023). Among individuals utilizing e-mental health services, a remarkable 74% of users affirmed that remote care had effectively assisted them in coping with a distressing situation that could have otherwise led to physical harm or suicide (Asbury, 2023). E-visits are a type of telemedicine practice, described in more detail in the next section.

Telemedicine, Telehealth, and Remote Monitoring

The terms "telemedicine" and "telehealth" are often used interchangeably. Both employ telecommunication systems for the purpose of promoting health, but there is a technical difference between the two.

Telemedicine Versus Telehealth

Telemedicine, or distance medicine, employs telecommunications technology for medical diagnosis and patient care when the provider and the client are separated by distance. Similar to an e-visit, this technology eliminates the need for face-to-face contact between the clinician and the patient. Unlike virtual visits, however, telemedicine has applications in the delivery of specialized medical services. Examples include teleradiology, the transmission of radiographic images and scans; telepathology, the viewing of tissue specimens via video-microscopy; telesurgery, controlling robots from a distance to perform surgical procedures; and clinical consultation provided by a wide range of specialists.

The term **telehealth** is broader in scope than telemedicine. It encompasses telemedicine, as traditionally known; educational, research, and administrative uses; and clinical applications that involve a variety of caregivers, such as physicians, nurses, psychologists, and pharmacists (Field and Grigsby, 2002).

Characteristics of Telemedicine

Telemedicine can be synchronous or asynchronous. **Synchronous technology** allows telecommunication to occur in real time. For example, interactive video conferencing allows two or more professionals to converse with each other and even share documents in real time. The technology allows a specialist located at a distance to directly interview and examine a patient. By comparison, **asynchronous technology** employs store-and-forward technology that allows users to review the information later. Interpretation of scans in teleradiology is one example where asynchronous technology is employed.

The use and applications of telemedicine have been expanding. Examples include its use for treating the prison population (Teichert, 2016), and the delivery of medical services in remote locations, such as high-altitude mountain telemedicine to treat pulmonary and cerebral edema and other acute mountain sicknesses (Martinelli et al., 2020). Other clinical applications of telemedicine are found in emergency departments (EDs). For example, in 2016, 58% of U.S. EDs used telemedicine, especially for stroke/neurology and psychiatry cases (Zachrison et al., 2020). Other potential uses of telemedicine include disaster response, both as a resource for responders and as a direct link to patients (Tedeschi, 2020), and medical consultations by travelers in remote areas (Rochat and Genton, 2018).

Distance can be a major impediment to receiving healthcare services—and one that telemedicine has helped overcome. For example, in Canada, the Interior Health Thoracic Surgical Group (IHTSG) uses telemedicine, through Virtual Thoracic Surgical Clinics (VTSC), to provide specialized services to a population of 1.01 million people over an area of 807,538 km² (approximately 311,800 square miles) in the interior and northern regions of British Columbia. In addition to the vast geographic distances, severe winter weather conditions and treacherous mountain passes increase the challenge of accessing health care in rural British Columbia. Between 2003 and 2015, IHTSG conducted more than 15,000 telemedicine patient encounters via videoconferencing at 63 geographic sites. On average, this application of telemedicine saved a travel distance of 766 km (475 miles) per patient (Humer and Campling, 2017).

Newer applications of telemedicine include in-home monitoring of patients. Vital signs, blood pressure, and blood glucose levels can be monitored remotely using video technology—a methodology that has been shown to be effective, well received by patients, capable of maintaining quality of care, and associated with the potential for cost savings (Johnston et al., 2000). Remote monitoring of cardiac implantable electronic devices, such as pacemakers and implantable cardioverter-defibrillators, has been gaining acceptance in the United States and Europe. This technology has been found to be highly effective in managing clinical events, such as arrhythmias, cardiovascular disease progression, and device malfunction, with remarkably few human interventions and low resource use (Ricci et al., 2013; Slotwiner and Wilkoff, 2013; Varma et al., 2023; Hillmann et al., 2023).

Despite the growing interest in telemedicine, its utilization in the United States remains limited. Some of the barriers to expanded use include lack of institutional support, cost of implementation, time constraints, interstate licensing/credentialing issues, uncertain reimbursement policies, and liability and legal concerns (Olson et al., 2019). Such issues have been largely eliminated in the Veterans Health Administration (VHA) system, with results from the VHA demonstrating substantial cost savings and patient satisfaction with care delivered through telemedicine (Kahn et al., 2016).

Tele-ICU

Telemedicine has also become a subspecialty of critical care practice (tele-intensive care unit, or tele-ICU). Also referred to as tele-critical care, tele-ICU involves a centralized or remotely based critical care team that is networked with the bedside ICU team and patients via advanced audiovisual communication and computer systems. The ICU environment is characterized by numerous distractions and interruptions; while addressing the needs of one patient, the nurse or physician may not be aware of a change in a second patient's status that may call for immediate attention. Tele-ICU provides a backup system that can avoid these problems. It operates with the goal of providing additional surveillance and support to hospital-based critical care staff, and ultimately enhancing outcomes for patients who are critically ill (Goran, 2010). Implementation of telemedicine in one surgical ICU was associated with a profound reduction in severity-adjusted ICU length of stay and ICU mortality (Kohl et al., 2012).

Innovation, Diffusion, and Utilization of Medical Technology

In the context of medical technology, innovation is the creation of a product, technique, or service perceived to be new by members of a society. The spread of technology into society once it is developed is referred to as **technology diffusion** (Luce, 1993). Rapid diffusion of a technology occurs when the innovation is perceived to be of benefit that can be evaluated or measured, is compatible with the adopter's values and needs, and is covered through third-party payment. Once technology is acquired, its use is almost ensured. Hence, the diffusion and utilization of technology are closely intertwined. The desire to have state-of-the-art technology available and to use it despite its cost or established health benefit is called the **technological imperative**.

High-tech procedures are more readily available in the United States than in most other countries, and little is done to limit the expansion of new medical technology. In addition, the United States has more high-tech equipment, such as MRI scanners, available to its population than most other countries (**Table 5-2**). However, the geographic variations in the diffusion of new medical technologies—that is, disparities—suggest that the utilization of new technologies may also be uneven, resulting in underutilization in some areas and overutilization in others (Karaca-Mandic et al., 2017).

Other nations have tried to limit—mainly through central planning—the diffusion and utilization of high-tech procedures to control medical costs. The U.K. government, for

Table 5-2 MRI Units Available per 1,000,000 Population in Selected Countries, 2019

Japan	55.21
United States	40.44
Germany	34.71
Italy	28.73
Australia	14.78
France	14.43
Canada	10.35

Data from Stewart C. (2022). Number of Magnetic Resonance Imaging (MRI) Units in Selected Countries as of 2019. Statista, https://www.statista.com/statistics/282401/density-of-magnetic-resonance-imaging-units-by-country/

instance, established the National Institute for Health and Clinical Excellence (NICE) in 1999 to decide whether the National Health Service should make select health technologies available (Milewa, 2006). Hence, MRI and computed tomography (CT) scanners are less widely available in the United Kingdom than in most OECD nations. Conversely, in many other European countries, technology diffusion has grown at a rapid pace.

Factors That Drive Innovation and Diffusion

The rate and pattern by which a technology diffuses are often governed by multiple forces (Cohen, 2004b). Public and private financing of research and development (R&D) can either promote or inhibit innovation (American Association for the Advancement of Science, 2022). Similarly, government regulations, such as the U.S. Food and Drug Administration (FDA) approval process for pharmaceuticals, biological agents, and biomedical devices, can either promote or hinder the availability of new drugs and devices. Recently, the onslaught of the COVID-19 pandemic pushed the U.S.

government to find both a cure and a vaccine for the disease in record time: Operation Warp Speed included partnerships between several federal agencies and private firms. Marketing and promotion by manufacturers can also influence the decisions of both providers and consumers about the adoption and use of technology. Some of the main forces that shape the innovation, diffusion, and utilization of technology in the United States are addressed in the following subsections:

- Anthro-cultural beliefs and values
- Medical specialization
- Payment and cost
- Technology-driven competition
- Expenditures on research and development
- Supply-side controls
- Government policy

Anthro-Cultural Beliefs and Values

Medical systems operate within the cultural context of the people whom they serve. Also, the ease with which medical information can be accessed influences people's expectations. Such influences, both old and new, affect the medical treatments that people desire. For example, 91% of Americans indicated that their ability to get the most advanced tests, drugs, medical equipment, and procedures was very important to improving the quality of health care (Schur and Berk, 2008).

As a case in point, in 2007, the Centers for Medicare and Medicaid Services (CMS) proposed sharply restricting payments for CT angiography for patients who are Medicare insured. Even though this newer imaging technology had not been shown to offer any remarkable improvements in diagnosing heart disease, the CMS faced a barrage of criticism over the proposal from radiologists and cardiologists, technology development firms such as General Electric, and 79 members of the U.S. House of Representatives. Ultimately, the CMS announced that it would not impose its proposed determination despite continued uncertainty about the test's usefulness (Appleby, 2008).

The primacy of technology in the U.S. healthcare system can also be traced to reliance on the medical model, which is reinforced by American beliefs and values. The emphasis on specialty care in this model, rather than primary care and preventive services, raises the expectations of both physicians and patients that all available technology will be used in every case.

Medical Specialization

Evidence of the technological imperative is most apparent in acute-care hospitals, especially those affiliated with medical schools, because they are the main centers for the specialty residency training programs in which physicians are trained to use the latest medical advances. Broad exposure to technology early in training affects not only clinical preferences, but also future professional behavior and practice patterns (Cohen, 2004c). Evidence also suggests that a greater consolidation of specialists in a given market can accelerate technology diffusion, increasing patients' access to the latest medical technology (Karaca-Mandic et al., 2017).

Financing and Payment

When society demands the latest high-tech care, insurers tend to reimburse for it more generously. Neonatal intensive care units (NICUs) provide one example where the high costs of saving the lives of prematurely born infants are mitigated by high insurance payments that also help subsidize less profitable hospital services. There is almost a circular relationship between technology and insurance payments: Technology drives costs, insurance makes them easier to pay, and the types of care for which insurance reimburses generously garner greater investment and experience faster growth (Frankt, 2014). Conversely, payment disincentives may be at the heart of any decisions to stop new investments in medical technology (Haas et al., 2010).

Restrictions in insurance coverage have the opposite effect. For example, customized, individually made knee implants have the potential to deliver high-quality care while decreasing overall healthcare costs by reducing hospitalizations and revision surgery, but their adoption requires the expansion of current insurance coverage (Namin et al., 2019).

Health insurance promotes the phenomenon referred to as moral hazard and provider-induced demand in the absence of mechanisms to limit utilization of high-cost services. Insurance coverage insulates both patients and providers from personal accountability for the utilization of high-cost services. Generally, both patients and physicians want to use everything that medical science has to offer as long as out-of-pocket costs are negligible to the insured.

Insurers, hospitals, and other stakeholders are now increasingly weighing price against performance in their decisions to purchase and use new medical technologies. This approach will tend to affect biomedical innovation adversely by reducing the revenues available for R&D. Conversely, a more constrained funding environment may have positive impacts by forcing medical technology firms to innovate based on **value**—that is, benefits in relation to costs (Robinson, 2015).

Technology-Driven Competition

Medical technology diffuses faster in more competitive geographic areas (Karaca-Mandic et al., 2017). Hospitals, as well as outpatient centers, compete to attract patients who are insured. Patients who are well-insured prefer quality, and institutions create perceptions of higher quality by acquiring and advertising state-of-the-art technology. Specialists have also been responsible for stimulating competition. Many physicians, for example, have opened their own specialty hospitals, diagnostic imaging facilities equipped with next-generation scanners, and same-day surgery centers that offer hotel-like facilities—and these developments have fueled a de facto "medical arms race." In response, hospitals have added new service lines—such as cancer, heart, and brain centers—and acquired costly CT scanners and high-field MRI machines (Kher, 2006), fueling more technology-based competition. To recruit specialists, medical centers often have to obtain new technology and offer high-tech procedures. When hospitals develop new services and invest heavily in modernization programs, other hospitals in the area are often forced to do the same to remain competitive. Such practices result in a tremendous duplication of services and equipment.

Self-Referral and Stark Laws. Investment interests by physicians in various types of facilities prompted Congress to pass legislation curtailing the practice of physician **self-referral**. These laws prohibit physicians from sending patients to facilities in which the referring physician or a family member has an ownership interest or some kind of compensation arrangement. Prohibition of self-referrals is based on the theory of provider-induced demand, which could create overutilization and result in increased healthcare costs.

The Ethics in Patient Referrals Act of 1989 (commonly known as Stark I after Representative Pete Stark, author of the original bill) prohibited the referral of Medicare patients to laboratories in which the referring physician had an ownership interest. The provisions of this law were subsequently expanded under the Omnibus Budget Reconciliation Act (OBRA) of 1993. Commonly referred to as Stark II, this statute covers both Medicare and Medicaid referrals. It also expanded the categories of services to include clinical laboratory services, rehabilitation services, radiology services, durable medical equipment and supplies, home health services, and inpatient and outpatient hospitalization services, among others. Nearly half of all states also have self-referral prohibitions that apply to patients who are privately insured (Mitchell, 2007).

Some exceptions to these bans do exist, such as in-office ancillary services, which allow physicians to own or lease imaging equipment for their office-based practices. Hence, a significant amount of self-referral still exists (Mitchell, 2007).

After receiving much criticism, the CMS is revising the Stark Law regulations. The main impetus for the changes is the new healthcare environment in which care coordination, accountable care organizations, and value-based arrangements between organizations are becoming common. **Exhibit 5-5** provides additional reasons for the revisions of Stark Law regulation.

Expenditures on Research and Development (R & D)

Medical research in the United States remains the primary source of new discoveries related to drugs, devices, and clinical procedures for the world. In 2020, the total investment in U.S. medical and health R&D was estimated at $245.1 billion—a little less than 5% of total U.S. health spending (**Table 5-3**). Of the $37.6 billion spent by the federal government on such R&D, 81% was attributed to the National Institutes of Health (NIH), the primary agency in the United States that both conducts and supports basic and applied biomedical research.

Exhibit 5-5 Reasons Behind the Revisions of Stark Law Regulation

- **Encouraging Value-Based Care:** To promote value-based care and care coordination, Stark Law revisions include exceptions or safe harbors that allow for greater flexibility in arrangements between healthcare providers. These changes are designed to support efforts to improve patient outcomes and reduce costs (Dorsey and Whitney, 2021; Shaker, et al., 2023).
- **Covering Office Space and Equipment Lease:** CMS revised the fair market value exception to permit parties to protect arrangements for the rental or lease of office space (adding the prohibition on percentage and per-click leases) (Kolarik, 2021).
- **Addressing Technology Advances:** CMS made the EHR exception permanent because of the continuing need with new entrants, aging EHR technology at existing practices and emerging and improved technology (Arentfox, 2021).
- **Addressing Stark Law Penalties:** Penalties for Stark Law violations can be severe, including financial penalties, exclusion from federal healthcare programs, and even criminal charges in some cases. Revisions may adjust penalty structures to provide more reasonable consequences for inadvertent or technical violations (Hodgson Russ, 2021).
- **Impacting "Commercially Reasonable" Considerations:** The three requirements applicable to many of the Stark Law exceptions are: compensation for the applicable arrangement must be at fair market value, the arrangements must be commercially reasonable, and no arrangement may consider the volume or value of referrals (or other business generated) between the parties. CMS stated that the determination as to whether an arrangement is "commercially reasonable" will depend on "whether the arrangement makes sense to accomplish the parties' goals," and such determination does not depend only on the compensation terms (Shenoy et al., 2022).

Data from Dorsey & Whitney. (April 30, 2021). Stark regulatory changes effective January 1, 2022 require modifying certain group practice compensation methodologies. Dorsey & Whitney Publications. https://www.dorsey.com/newsresources/publications/client-alerts/2021/04/stark-regulatory-changes; Shaker, M., Mauger, D., & Fuhlbrigge, A. L. 2023. Value-based, cost-effective care: the role of the allergist- mmunologist. The Journal of Allergy and Clinical Immunology: In Practice, 11(1), 132–139; Kolarik, J. (January 22, 2021). Key takeaways from the revised and clarified stark law regulations – part 2. Foley & Lardner LLP; Arentfox. (2021). 2021 Stark & Anti-Kickback Statute Final Rules. Health Care Counsel. https://www.afslaw.com/sites/default/files/2021-02/%202021%20Stark%20&%20Anti-Kickback%20Statute-Final-Rules-FINALPDF.pdf; Hodgson Russ. (January 19, 2021). Key takeaways from the Stark Law final rule. Hodgson Russ Healthcare Alert. https://www.hodgsonruss.com/newsroom-publications-13028.html#:~:text=The%20intent%20of%20the%20regulatory,for%20a%20target%20patient%20population; Shenoy, A., Shenoy, G. N., & Shenoy, G. G. (2022). The Stark law, from inception to COVID-19 blanket waivers: a review. Patient safety in surgery, 16(1), 19.

Table 5-3 U.S. Biomedical R&D Investment in 2020

	Total Investment (billions of dollars)	Share of Total Investment
Total U.S. investment	245.1	100.0%
Private industry	161.8	66.0%
Federal government	61.5	25.1%
Other institutions[1]	12.5	6.9%
Other	5.8	2.1%
Foundations	3.0	1.2%
State and local governments	2.1	0.8%

[1] Academic and research institutions.

Data from Research America. 2022. *U.S. Investments in Medical and Health Research and Development: 2016–2020.*

Global R&D performance is concentrated in a few countries. The United States, China, Japan, Germany, South Korea, France, India, and the United Kingdom jointly accounted for about 75% of global R&D performance in 2019. The global concentration of R&D performance continues to shift from the United States and Europe to East-Southeast and South Asia (National Center for Science and Engineering, 2022). International comparative data show that the growth in biomedical R&D investment in the United States has been declining compared to Asian countries, particularly China. Whereas the growth rate for R&D investment in the United States was 6% annually between 1994 and 2004, it declined to 0.8% annually between 2004 and 2012. Asian countries (China, India, South Korea, and Singapore), by comparison, increased their investments by 9.4% annually over the same period (Moses et al., 2015).

However, the three years leading to 2020 saw increases of $50.6 billion (2017–18), $61.8 billion (2018–19) and $50.8 billion (2019–20), averaging a 7.7% rate for 2015-20 in the U.S. (National Center for Science and Engineering Statistics, 2023). Yet, since 2000, Chinese R&D investment has increased by 14.2% a year on average, a growth rate nearly double that achieved by South Korea, and over four times that of the U.S. (National Center for Science and Engineering Statistics, 2023). As a result of this growth, Chinese R&D reached $563 billion in 2020, $101 billion behind the United States, closing the gap somewhat from 2019. Given global trends, the United States will relinquish its historical position in medical innovation unless measures are undertaken to reverse the drop in investments.

Supply-Side Controls

In the United States, supply-side controls (i.e., explicit rationing) have met with stiff resistance, even though such rationing may be based on well-defined criteria. In contrast, other countries have used government policy to control the diffusion of medical technology (refer to Table 5-2 for an example), which is one way to ration health care. In Europe, research has suggested that even higher levels of reimbursement do not always promote technology diffusion there (Cappellaro et al., 2011). This discrepancy with the U.S. experience arises mainly because European national healthcare programs have the means to suppress unintended diffusion of technology through central planning. To some extent, the United States also engages in technology rationing through the FDA's drug and device approval system (discussed later in this chapter).

Rationing curtails costs, but it also restricts access to critically needed care (Qeska et al., 2023). Canada, which restricts specialist services and limits expensive medical equipment to control healthcare spending, is a case in point. For several years, the Fraser Institute has researched issues related to access to care in Canada. According to its research, in 2019, patients in that country could expect to wait 10.1 weeks to consult a specialist after referral by a general practitioner, and 10.8 weeks for treatment after consulting a specialist. Canadians could also expect to wait 9.3 weeks for an MRI scan (Barua and Moir, 2019). Several studies have reported deaths resulting from delayed heart surgery due to lengthy waiting times in Canada, even in cases classified as nonurgent (Sobolev et al., 2013).

Although a full discussion of rationing is beyond the scope of this text, Alexander Friedman (2011) has observed that as we devote more resources to health care, something else of value always emerges. Our resources are limited, however, and health care is not the only vital public endeavor. Hence, many experts think that rationing is inevitable, because no modern society has found a way to deliver all the health care that people may desire (refer, for example, to Churchill, 2011).

Government Policy

Government policy in the United States plays a significant role in deciding which drugs, devices, and biologics are made available to Americans. The U.S. government also provides significant funding for biomedical research. By controlling the amount of funding, public policy indirectly influences medical innovation.

The Government's Role in Technology Diffusion

The growth of technology has been accompanied by issues of cost, safety, benefits, and risks. The government plays only a minor role in healthcare organizations' decisions to acquire new technology. As previously indicated, though, the government is an important source of funding for biomedical R&D (refer to Table 5-3). The Agency for Healthcare Research and Quality (AHRQ), a division of the DHHS, is the lead federal agency charged with supporting research that focuses on improving the quality of health care, reducing healthcare costs, and improving access to essential services. The federal government is almost single-handedly responsible for ensuring the safety and effectiveness of technologies used in healthcare delivery. This section discusses federal legislation, the role of the FDA, and states' efforts aimed at controlling the growth of healthcare facilities and technology.

Regulation of Drugs, Devices, and Biologics

The FDA, an agency under the DHHS, is responsible for ensuring that drugs and medical devices are safe and effective for their intended use. It also controls access to drugs by deciding whether a certain drug will be available by prescription only or as an over-the-counter (OTC) purchase. In addition, the FDA may stipulate how certain OTC products may be purchased and sold. For example, under the Combat Methamphetamine Epidemic Act of 2005 (incorporated into the USA PATRIOT Act and signed by President George W. Bush in March 2006), certain cold and allergy medicines containing pseudoephedrine are required to be kept behind pharmacy counters and sold in only limited quantities to consumers, who must present photo identification and sign a logbook when purchasing these items. This action was taken because pseudoephedrine is used in making methamphetamine—a highly addictive drug—in home laboratories. The FDA has also recalled personal care products because of unapproved components, labeling issues, and adverse effects (Janetos et al., 2019).

Regulation of Drugs and Evolution of the Approval Processes

The FDA's regulatory functions have evolved over time (**Table 5-4**). The first piece of drug legislation passed in the United States was the Pure Food and Drug Act of 1906, which was intended to prevent the manufacture, sale, or transportation of adulterated, misbranded, poisonous, or deleterious foods, drugs, medicines, and liquors. It was assumed that the manufacturer would conduct safety tests before marketing the product. It authorized the Bureau of Chemistry (the predecessor of the FDA) to take action only after drugs had been marketed to consumers. If innocent consumers were harmed, however, the Bureau of Chemistry could act only after such harm had been done (Bronzino et al., 1990).

Federal law governing drugs was subsequently strengthened by the passage of

Table 5-4 Summary of FDA Legislation

1906	**Pure Food and Drug Act** The FDA was authorized to take action only after drugs sold to consumers caused harm.
1938	**Food, Drug, and Cosmetic Act** Required premarket notification to the FDA so the agency could assess the safety of a new drug or device.
1962	**Kefauver-Harris Amendments** Premarket notification was inadequate. The FDA took charge of reviewing the efficacy and safety of new drugs, which could be marketed only once approval was granted.
1976	**Medical Devices Amendments** Authorized premarket review of medical devices and classified devices into three classes.
1983	**Orphan Drug Act** Drug manufacturers were given incentives to produce new drugs for rare diseases.
1990	**Safe Medical Devices Act** Healthcare facilities must report serious or potentially serious device-related injuries, illness, or death of patients and employees.
1992	**Prescription Drug User Fee Act** The FDA received authority to collect application fees from drug companies to provide additional resources to shorten the drug-approval process.
1997	**Food and Drug Administration Modernization Act** Provides for fast-track approvals for life-saving drugs when their expected benefits exceed those of current therapies.
2012	**Food and Drug Administration Safety and Innovation Act** Allows the FDA to use markers that are thought to predict or that are reasonably likely to predict clinical benefit to qualify a drug for accelerated approval if the drug is indicated for a serious condition and fills an unmet medical need.

(continues)

Table 5-4 Summary of FDA Legislation *(continued)*

Year	Legislation
2013	**Drug Quality and Security Act (renamed as Drug Supply Chain Security Act)** Aimed at the verification, detection, and recall of drugs using an electronic system. A primary goal is to identify counterfeit, unapproved, and potentially dangerous products and to prevent their use.
2016	**21st Century Cures Act** Provides funds to the FDA to shorten the approval time for new drugs and devices.
2018	**Right to Try Act** Makes investigational treatments available to people with life-threatening illnesses.
2020	**Emergency Use Authorization** Allows the FDA to help strengthen the nation's public health protections against chemical, biological, radiological, and nuclear (CBRN) threats, including infectious diseases, by facilitating the availability and use of medical countermeasures (MCMs) needed during public health emergencies.
2023	**Food Safety Modernization Act (FSMA)** Improves capacity to prevent, detect, and respond to food safety problems, and improves safety of imported foods.

the Food, Drug, and Cosmetic Act (FD&C Act) of 1938. This legislation was enacted in response to the infamous Elixir Sulfanilamide disaster, in which almost 100 people died in Tennessee due to poisoning from a toxic solvent used in this liquid's preparation (Flannery, 1986). According to the revised law, a new drug could not be marketed without first notifying the FDA and allowing the agency time to assess the drug's safety (Merrill, 1994).

The drug approval system was further transformed by the drug amendments of 1962 (Kefauver-Harris Drug Amendments), after thalidomide (a sleeping pill that was distributed in the United States as an experimental drug but had been widely marketed in Europe) was shown to cause birth defects (Flannery, 1986). The 1962 amendments essentially stated that premarket notification of drug-related risks was inadequate. They put a premarket approval system in force, giving the FDA authority to review the effectiveness and safety of a new drug before it could be marketed. Its consumer protection role enabled the FDA to prevent harm before it occurred. However, the drug approval process was criticized for slowing down the introduction of new drugs and, consequently, denying patients early benefits from the latest treatments. Drug manufacturers essentially "became prisoners of the agency's [FDA's] indecision, its preoccupation with other issues, or its lack of resources" (Merrill, 1994).

The Orphan Drug Act of 1983 and subsequent amendments were passed to give pharmaceutical firms incentives to develop new drugs for rare diseases and conditions. Incentives, such as grant funding to defray the expenses of clinical testing and exclusive marketing rights for 7 years, were necessary because a relatively small number of people are afflicted by rare conditions, creating a relatively small market for drugs treating those conditions. As a result of the Orphan Drug Act, certain new drug therapies, called **orphan drugs**, have become available for conditions that affect fewer than 200,000 people in the United States.

In the late 1980s, pressure on the FDA from those wanting rapid access to new drugs for the treatment of human immunodeficiency virus (HIV) infection called for a reconsideration of the drug review process (Rakich et al., 1992). For example, saquinavir—a protease inhibitor indicated for patients with advanced HIV infection—received accelerated approval in late 1995; however, its manufacturer, Roche Laboratories, was subsequently required to show that the drug prolonged survival or slowed clinical progression of HIV.

In 1992, Congress passed the Prescription Drug User Fee Act, which authorized the FDA to collect fees from biotechnology and pharmaceutical companies to review their drug applications. The additional funds provided needed resources. This, along with subsequent amendments, such as that implementing user fees for applicants seeking to market generic drugs, allowed the FDA to approve new drugs more quickly, thereby enabling them to reach the market in less time.

In 1997, Congress passed the Food and Drug Administration Modernization Act. This law provides for increased patient access to experimental drugs and medical devices. "Fast-track" approvals are permitted when the potential benefits of new drugs for serious or life-threatening conditions are considered significantly greater than the benefits of current therapies. In addition, the law provides for an expanded database on clinical trials, which is accessible by the public. Under a separate provision, when a manufacturer plans to discontinue a drug, patients who are heavily dependent on the drug receive advance notice.

The Food and Drug Administration Safety and Innovation Act of 2012 allows the FDA, in its assessments of new drugs' effectiveness, to use either a marker that is thought to predict clinical benefit (surrogate endpoint) or a marker that is considered reasonably likely to predict clinical benefit (intermediate clinical endpoint). These markers allow for faster approval of drugs.

For example, the FDA may approve a drug based on evidence that the drug shrinks tumors, because tumor shrinkage is considered reasonably likely to predict a real clinical benefit (FDA, 2018a).

Since 1992, when the Prescription Drug User Fee Act was passed, the regulatory focus has been on faster review of new drugs by the FDA. There is no doubt that faster reviews have allowed new drugs to become available more quickly than before this legislation was enacted. Nevertheless, there have been lingering safety concerns, mainly because several years of public use of a drug may elapse before safety problems may emerge. When safety issues do arise, the FDA may issue a "black box warning" that must appear on a prescription drug's label, alerting the user to serious or life-threatening risks. In rare cases, the FDA may rescind its approval decision and order that a drug be withdrawn from the U.S. market. Recent studies have shown that safety risks are often recognized only after the FDA has given approval to market certain drugs. For example, Frank and colleagues (2014) demonstrated that half of all new black box warnings appeared after a drug had been on the market for 12 years; drugs that were withdrawn from the market had been sold for 5 years or longer.

Despite such concerns, the push for faster approvals for drugs and devices does not seem to have changed. The 21st Century Cures Act of 2016 provides funds for the FDA to change its drug and device approval processes with the aim of shortening the period for approving new drugs and devices, especially for life-threatening diseases. Clearly, providing for faster approval of new medical technology while simultaneously ensuring its safety will remain a delicate balancing act.

The Right to Try Act of 2018 is a U.S. federal law that was signed into law on May 30, 2018. The primary purpose of this legislation is to provide patients who are terminally ill with access to experimental drugs and treatments that have not yet received full approval from the U.S. Food and Drug Administration (FDA). The law aims to give patients who have exhausted all other treatment options the opportunity to try experimental treatments in the hope of prolonging their lives or improving their quality of life. (U.S. Food and Drug Administration, 2018). This treatment avenue is available provided the patient, physician, and manufacturer are all in agreement regarding the off-study use of an eligible investigational agent (Agarwal and Saltz, 2020). Refer to **Exhibit 5-6** for summary of pros and cons of this act.

Drugs from Overseas

Drug manufacturing is a global business. Hence, the use of foreign-made drug products in the United States has greatly increased. The reason? Economics. The U.S. imports approximately 40% of finished drugs and 80% of active ingredients for drugs (FDA, 2018b). As a safeguard, all drugs approved in the United States must comply with the FD&C Act, regardless of where they are manufactured. To ensure that foreign-made drugs meet this standard, the

---

Exhibit 5-6 Pros and Cons of Right to Try Act 2018

Pros
- **Experimental Drugs May Extend Life:** Given a setting of compassionate use, even unsuccessful treatment may help strengthen patients' trust in healthcare systems due to potentially positive health outcomes (Brown et al., 2018). For instance, widely untested therapeutic vaccines were given to people living with Ebola in hopes of improving their condition (Rid and Emanuel, 2014).
- **In Line with Expanded Access:** The Right to Try legislation is similar to the Expanded Access program in that it recognizes that a streamlined process is necessary if experimental drugs are to reach patients who may not have any other options (Agarwal and Saltz, 2020).
- **Gives Patients More Options:** Right to Try laws allow patients to work directly with doctors to acquire nonclinical tested drugs, bypass the FDA, and provide multiple options for all patients who are terminally ill to acquire potentially life-extending drugs (Brown et al., 2018).

Cons
- **Lowered Trust in the FDA:** Right to Try laws are hypocritical because they rely on the FDA process of determining the toxicity and possible side effects of products in phase 1 testing, but this argument ignores the fact that drugs need to be rigorously tested to be deemed safe for widespread use (Carrieri et al., 2018).
- **Safety Consequences:** There is an inherent safety risk that may potentially cause more harm to the patient or even death than the benefit because the experimental drug did not undergo rigorous testing (Gabay, 2018).
- **Financial Burdens:** There is potentially a considerable financial burden for the patient or the patient's family because payors currently do not provide coverage and deny hospice care (Mahant, 2020).
- **Limited Patient Understanding:** The patient in most cases has limited understanding of the informed consent due to complexity and confusion of the medical terminology used in the consent form (Mahant, 2020).

Data from Brown, B., Ortiz, C., & Dubé, K. (2018). Assessment of the right-to-try law: the pros and the cons. Journal of Nuclear Medicine, 59(10), 1492–1493; Rid, A., & Emanuel, E. J. 2014. Ethical considerations of experimental interventions in the Ebola outbreak. The Lancet, 384(9957), 1896–1899; Agarwal, R., & Saltz, L. B. (2020). Understanding the Right to Try Act. Clinical cancer research: an official journal of the American Association for Cancer Research, 26(2), 340–343; Carrieri, D., Peccatori, F. A., & Boniolo, G. (2018). The ethical plausibility of the 'Right To Try' laws. Critical Reviews in Oncology/Hematology, 122, 64–71; Gabay, M. (2018). RxLegal: A Rapid Review of Right-To-Try. Hospital pharmacy, 53(4), 234–235; Mahant, V. (2020). "Right-to-Try" experimental drugs: an overview. Journal of Translational Medicine, 18(1), 253.

FDA performs routine inspections. With the passage of the Food and Drug Administration Safety and Innovation Act of 2012, the FDA's inspection program shifted from one focused heavily on U.S.-based facilities to one that conducts more foreign than domestic inspections (FDA, 2019a).

The U.S. government has taken steps to secure the integrity of the pharmaceutical supply chain, which can be threatened by medication counterfeiting, importation of unapproved and substandard drugs, and grey markets. Such illegal operations often distribute drug products with the potential for serious harm (Brechtelsbauer et al., 2016). The Drug Quality and Security Act of 2013 (later renamed the Drug Supply Chain Security Act) was passed to curtail the distribution of unauthorized drug products.

Despite the FDA's best efforts to protect American patients against harmful drugs coming from abroad, mishaps do occur. In 2018, a Chinese-made blood pressure medication was found to be contaminated with a cancer-causing chemical, triggering recalls in the United States and around the world (U.S.-China Economic and Security Review Commission [USCC], 2019). Concerns about quality control and data integrity have focused on numerous companies in India and China, where increasingly more drugs and active ingredients used in medicines for the United States are being made (Edney, 2019).

The USCC has recommended that all federally funded health systems, such as Medicare and VHA, should purchase their pharmaceuticals only from U.S. production facilities or from facilities that have been certified by the FDA to be in compliance with U.S. health and safety standards. It has also recommended that Congress should evaluate the productive capacity of the U.S. pharmaceutical industry. Most likely, pharmaceutical companies will face ongoing pressure to bring the manufacturing of drugs to the United States. The irony is that even U.S.-made drugs are not immune from the same forces that have led to corner-cutting overseas. For example, in 2016, FDA inspectors found Mylan (Morgantown, WV), the second largest generic drug maker in the United States, to be in serious violation of quality standards and data integrity (Edney, 2019). The FDA advises that medications approved in other countries may not be guaranteed to be safe, effective, or manufactured properly (U.S. Food and Drug Administration, 2023). Refer to **Exhibit 5-7** for dos and don'ts when attempting to bring drugs from overseas.

Drug Shortages

Drug shortages in the United States have been a persistent and concerning issue for several years (U.S. Food and Drug Administration, 2023). Between 2013 and 2017, shortages in the United States were identified for 163 drugs. Between 2019 and 2020, the number of US drug shortages increased by 37% (Cameron and Bushell, 2021). Moreover, the number of ongoing drug shortages has been increasing, and shortages have been lasting longer, in some cases more than eight years. The heavy dependence on foreign drug manufacturers came to light during the COVID-19 pandemic in 2020 when, barring a proven cure, certain drugs that had the potential to help the patients were held back by foreign sources. The uncertainty of COVID-19 caused anticipatory purchasing of medications around the world, driving demand to an unprecedented high (Bookwalter, 2021).

Drug shortages can have significant impacts on patients, healthcare providers, and the healthcare system (Cameron and Bushell, 2021). Shortages can worsen patients' health outcomes by causing delays in treatment or changes in treatment regimens, such as substituting less effective therapies when a drug of choice is not available. Even when alternatives to the preferred drug are available, a patient's care may be compromised. Like patients themselves,

Exhibit 5-7 Dos and Don'ts When Bringing Drugs from Overseas

- Carry no more medication than needed for a 90-day supply.
- Travelers and visitors to the United States with medications must comply with FDA, U.S. Customs and Border Protection (CBP), and Transportation Security Administration (TSA) regulations.
- One should have a valid prescription or doctor's note in English and the medication in its original container with instructions.
- If one does not have the original container, he/she should bring a copy of prescription or a letter from the doctor.
- Carry no more medication than needed for a 90-day supply.
- For stays longer than 90 days, you can have additional medication sent with proper documentation.
- FDA does not allow personal importation of unapproved foreign versions of FDA-approved drugs.
- Foreign travelers needing prescriptions filled in the United States should visit a healthcare provider.
- Shipping or mailing prescription medication to the United States is generally illegal due to FDA regulations.
- Exceptions can be made if the drug is for a serious condition with no U.S. treatment, there is no marketing to U.S. residents, and there is no unreasonable health risk.
- A letter from a doctor and other documentation is required if importing a foreign drug.
- Medication sent through the mail may be detained by Customs for inspection, while using a courier service is recommended for faster processing.

---

hospitals have faced enormous challenges dealing with shortages. About 80% of hospitals found it quite challenging to obtain drugs in short supply—even some of the commonly prescribed drugs—adding to the cost of care.

There are various reasons behind drug shortages in the United States:

- **Manufacturing Problems:** Pharmaceutical companies may encounter issues with the production of drugs, such as quality control problems, equipment breakdowns, or contamination. Manufacturers also often use the same manufacturing equipment for many drug products, so it is difficult to increase production of one product without causing manufacturing shortages and delays for another (Burry et al., 2020).
- **Supply and Demand Issues:** Sometimes, an unexpected surge in demand for a particular drug, such as during COVID-19 or other public health emergencies, can strain the supply chain and lead to shortages (Shukar et al., 2021).
- **Raw Material Shortages:** Disruptions in the supply of raw or bulk materials are frequently responsible for drug shortages (Romano et al., 2022). These shortages become particularly challenging when a key or exclusive supplier of such materials experiences production delays or ceases production altogether, impacting numerous pharmaceutical manufacturers (Romano et al., 2022).
- **Regulatory Challenges:** The FDA plays a crucial role in ensuring the safety and efficacy of drugs, and sometimes, regulatory actions like recalls, warnings, or inspections can disrupt the supply of certain medications (Tucker et al., 2020).
- **FDA Approval Delays:** Delays in the FDA approval process for new drugs or generic versions of existing drugs can create shortages. This can occur when there is limited competition for a specific drug, and any delay in bringing new suppliers to the market can exacerbate shortages (Tucker et al., 2020).
- **COVID-19 Pandemic:** The spread of COVID-19 to the level of a global

pandemic impacted the acquisition of raw materials and caused manufacturing shutdowns around the world (Badreldin and Atallah, 2021). For instance, China plays a significant role in the global pharmaceutical supply chain, providing active pharmaceutical ingredients, finished drugs, and raw materials (Bookwalter, 2021). During the COVID-19 pandemic, approximately 37 pharmaceutical factories in China that produced active ingredients for U.S. drugs had to close temporarily (Bookwalter, 2021). This led to a reliance on existing stockpiles and the search for alternative supply options by manufacturers in other regions (Bookwalter, 2021).

The FDA concluded that about half of the shortage drugs may have had inadequate financial incentives to market the product or invest in manufacturing capabilities prior to the shortage. From January 2010 to the time they went into shortage, these drugs were characterized by declining revenues and prices. For generic drugs, regulatory requirements are not seen as a deterrent to production because manufacturers are often approved to market drugs that are in shortage but make business decisions not to market them (FDA, 2019b). The FDA's authority to address shortages is limited because it has no oversight over drug purchasing. Hence, purchasers and payers, who bear the costs of drug shortages, may have to work together to alter the financial incentives of manufacturers and health systems (Hernandez et al., 2020).

Regulation of Medical Devices and Equipment

The FDA first received jurisdiction over medical devices under the FD&C Act of 1938. However, such jurisdiction was confined to the sale of products believed to be unsafe or that made misleading claims of effectiveness (Merrill, 1994).

In the 1970s, several deaths and miscarriages were attributed to the Dalkon Shield, which had been marketed as a safe and effective contraceptive device (Flannery, 1986). In 1976, the Medical Device Amendments extended the FDA's authority to include premarket review of medical devices, which were categorized into three classes. Devices in Class I pose the lowest risk (such as enema kits and elastic bandages). They are subject to general controls regarding misbranding—that is, fraudulent claims regarding their therapeutic effects. Class II devices (such as powered wheelchairs and pregnancy test kits) are subject to special requirements for labeling, performance standards, and post-market surveillance. The most stringent requirements for premarket approval regarding safety and effectiveness apply to Class III devices, which are defined as those that support life, prevent health impairment, or present an unreasonable risk of illness or injury. For most Class III devices (such as implantable pacemakers and breast implants), premarket approval is required to ensure their safety and effectiveness.

The Safe Medical Devices Act of 1990 strengthened the FDA's hand in controlling the entry of new biomedical devices into the market and in monitoring the use of marketed products (Merrill, 1994). Under this act, healthcare facilities must report serious or potentially serious device-related injuries or illness of patients and employees to the manufacturer of the device and, if death is involved, to the FDA as well. In essence, this law is intended to serve as an "early warning" system through which the FDA can obtain important information on device problems.

As the vast market for medical devices continues to grow, new challenges may emerge. Many medical devices now incorporate wireless, Internet, or regional network technology—and, therefore, must be maintained against the ongoing threat of cyberattacks. On another front, the global manufacturing enterprise of medical devices has required efforts to harmonize the regulatory differences between countries to improve safety. In response, the International Medical Device Regulators Forum was established in 2011; the United States is among its 10 members. For its part, the FDA is establishing the National Evaluation System for Health Technology (NEST) through collaborations with medical device stakeholders, with the aim of generating better evidence, more efficiently, for medical device evaluation and regulatory decision-making (FDA, 2019c).

Regulation of Biologics

Biologics, or biological products, are isolated from a variety of natural sources—human, animal, or microorganism. In contrast to most drugs, which are chemically synthesized and have a known chemical structure, biologics tend to be complex mixtures that are not easily identified or characterized (FDA, 2018c). Examples of biologics include vaccines, blood and blood components, allergenics, somatic cells, gene therapy, tissues, and recombinant therapeutic proteins, particularly when they are used for prevention or treatment of a disease or health condition.

The FDA regulates biologics under the FD&C Act of 1938 and the Public Health Service Act of 1944, which call for the FDA to ensure the safety of biologics by requiring licensing of these products. The Biologics Price Competition and Innovation Act of 2009 was incorporated into the ACA to allow the FDA to approve "biosimilars" under a process similar to the approval of generic drugs. Because of biologics' complexity, the term "generic" cannot apply to biologics; hence, the term "biosimilar" was created to apply to products that are highly similar to, or interchangeable with, an already approved biological product (referred to as the reference product). Moreover, the Biosimilar User Fee Act of 2012 (also part of the ACA) authorized the FDA to charge biopharmaceutical firms a user fee to pay for the FDA's review of applications for biosimilar products before these products could be marketed. Consumers and policymakers view the introduction of biosimilars as an important step because they are likely to result in reduced costs (Epstein et al., 2014).

Certificate of Need

The National Health Planning and Resources Development Act of 1974 required states to enact certificate of need (CON) laws so that they could obtain federal funds to carry out planning functions that would restrict the diffusion of technology and curtail rising costs. CON laws required hospitals and nursing homes to seek state approval before acquiring major equipment or embarking on new construction or modernization projects (Iglehart, 1982).

Effective January 1, 1987, the federal law was repealed largely due to changing payment environment and potential harm of CON. The payment environment has changed drastically since the federal law mandating CON programs was enacted. Instead of paying for volume of services, federal, state, and private payers now make fixed payments for each category of service, with those payments often being tied to certain quality markers. Hence, it has been argued that the fear of costs rising because of market failure no longer exists (Tinajero, 2017), making regulatory control unnecessary.

Certificate-of-need laws may also harm patients by reducing healthcare quality and reducing access to care (State Policy Network, 2021). For instance, a study by the Mercatus Center at George Mason University found the presence of a CON program is associated with 30% fewer hospitals per 100,000 residents across the entire state (State Policy Network, 2021). Under CON, patients and taxpayers may also face higher healthcare costs and fewer options (State Policy Network, 2021). The Kaiser Family Foundation found states with CON laws had 11% higher healthcare costs than states without those laws (State Policy Network, 2021).

However, most states still retain CON laws to regulate large capital outlays, limit the growth of healthcare facilities, and prevent unnecessary duplication of technology. The expectation is that these measures will contain overall healthcare costs, a large portion of which are borne by the Medicaid program. Nevertheless, conclusive evidence is lacking that CON laws have been successful in controlling rising healthcare costs.

In the past several years, many states, including Michigan, Montana, New York, North Carolina, Tennessee and Washington DC, have introduced or enacted legislation to modify their CON programs in 2021 (National Conference of State Legislature, 2023). Changes range from fully repealing an existing CON program to creating a new CON program. However, most state legislation makes targeted changes to CON oversight, such as excluding specific facilities from CON review.

As of May 2021, 35 states and the District of Columbia required providers to obtain a Certificate of Need (CON) before offering at least one healthcare service (Mitchell, 2021). CON requires certain healthcare providers to obtain a certification of their economic necessity from a state board before opening or undertaking a major expansion (Conover and Bailey, 2020). The debate over CON regulations continued to be a subject of discussion among policymakers, healthcare providers, and consumer advocacy groups (State Policy Network, 2021). Those in favor of CON regulations argue that they are essential to controlling healthcare costs and ensuring equitable access to care, while opponents argue that they stifle competition and can limit access to healthcare services (State Policy Network, 2021).

In the wake of the COVID-19 pandemic, 24 states that have CON laws on the books have suspended some portion of them or enabled emergency provisions to facilitate the rapid expansion of healthcare facilities and services during the pandemic (Erickson, 2021). As of 2022, 12 states have fully repealed their CON programs or allowed the program to expire. New Hampshire was the most recent state to repeal its CON program in 2016. Arizona, Minnesota and Wisconsin do not officially operate a CON program, but they maintain several approval processes that function similarly to CON. At least 13 states have a moratorium on certain healthcare activities and capital expenditures, meaning they will not grant CON or state approval for a specific activity. Moratoria are most common for long-term care related activities, such as expanding the number of long-term care beds in a facility.

The Impact of Medical Technology

The deployment of scientific knowledge has had far-reaching and pervasive effects, as the examples in Table 5-1 suggest. Indeed, the effects of technology often overlap, making it difficult to pinpoint technology's impact in a single area of healthcare delivery. This section discusses several areas in which the impact of medical technology has been noted.

Impact on Quality of Care

When advanced techniques can provide for more precise medical diagnoses than are possible with existing technologies, offer quicker and more complete cures than previously available, or reduce risks in a cost-effective manner, the result is improved quality. Technology can also provide new remedies where none existed before. More effective, less invasive, and safer therapeutic and preventive remedies can increase longevity and decrease morbidity. Safety is another important component of quality. The risks associated with anesthetic care during surgery, for example, have been dramatically reduced through technological advancement and automation (Majeed, 2018).

Numerous examples illustrate the role of technology in enhancing the quality of care (Gomes et al. 2023; Poalelungi et al., 2023). For instance, coronary angioplasty is now commonly performed to open blocked or narrowed coronary arteries. Before this treatment became available, patients suffering a heart attack were prescribed prolonged bed rest and treated with morphine and nitroglycerin (Congressional Budget Office [CBO], 2008). Angioplasty has reduced the need for open-heart bypass surgery. The total artificial heart (TAH), approved by the FDA in 2005 for implantation in patients with end-stage heart failure, can be a life-saving medical device for those awaiting heart transplantation. Implantable cardioverter-defibrillators prolong the lives of people who have life-threatening irregular heartbeats.

Laser technology reduces trauma in patients undergoing surgery and shortens the period for postsurgical recovery. These devices are also widely used in medical specialties for both medical and cosmetic procedures. For example, advanced laser procedures are available for high-precision eye surgery.

Robot-assisted surgery has gained significant momentum in several surgical applications. For example, this technology enables minimally invasive techniques to be used for the surgical removal of the prostate, and to surgically treat cancers of the kidney, lung, and thyroid. The robotic approach allows for improved dexterity and precision of the instruments.

Advanced bioimaging methods have created new ways to understand the body's inner workings while minimizing invasive procedures. Modern imaging technologies include MRI, positron emission tomography (PET), single-photon emission computed tomography (SPECT), CT scan, and 3-D fluorescence imaging. PET has important applications in cardiology, neurology, and oncology. For example, it can spot tumors and other problems that may not be detectable with traditional MRI or CT scans. SPECT is of great value in imaging the brain. This type of imaging could also reduce inappropriate use of invasive procedures through a more accurate diagnosis of coronary artery disease (Shaw et al., 2000). Echocardiography and Doppler ultrasound are advanced imaging techniques to study heart function and detect problems. These and other advanced imaging technologies also allow surgeons to perform minimally invasive procedures more precisely (Comaniciu et al., 2016).

Advances in molecular and cell biology have opened a new era in clinical medicine. Screening for genetic disorders, gene therapy, and the introduction of powerful new drugs for cancer and heart disease promise to radically improve the quality of medical care. Regenerative medicine and tissue engineering hold promise as means of creating other biological and bioartificial substitutes that can restore and maintain normal function in a variety of diseased and injured tissues. Products such as bioartificial kidneys, artificial implantable livers, and insulin-producing cells to replace damaged pancreatic cells are examples of what biomedical science might be able to accomplish. Treatment of disease using stem cells is another example of regenerative medicine.

Amidst the vast enthusiasm that these emerging technologies might generate, some degree of caution is warranted. Experience shows that greater proliferation of technology may not always equate to higher quality. Unless the effect of each individual technology is appropriately assessed, some innovations may be wasteful and others may be harmful.

Impact on Quality of Life

Thanks to new scientific developments, thousands of people can live normal and quality lives, which otherwise would not have been possible (Winterdijk et al., 2023; Yang et al., 2023). Many people with disabling conditions have been able to overcome their limitations in speech, hearing, vision, and movement through prosthetic devices and therapies. Long-term maintenance therapies have enabled people with conditions such as diabetes and end-stage renal disease (ESRD) to engage in activities that they otherwise would not be able to do. Major pharmaceutical breakthroughs have given people with heart disease, cancer, HIV/AIDS, and preterm birth a much longer life expectancy and improved health (Kleinke, 2001). Technological innovation has enabled many older adults to stay in their own homes instead of incurring lengthy stays in hospitals and nursing homes.

Modern technology has also been instrumental in relieving pain and suffering; in fact, pain management has been recognized as a new subspecialty in medicine. For example, in cancer pain management, new opioids have been developed for transdermal, nasal, and nebulized administration, which allow for needleless means of controlling pain (Davis, 2006). The technology underlying patient-controlled analgesia allows patients to determine when and how much medication they receive, which gives patients more independence and control.

Development of a substitute for injectable insulin could greatly enhance the quality of life for patients with diabetes—particularly older patients, who often require assistance with insulin injections. Uncontrolled diabetes can lead to complications such as heart disease, stroke, kidney failure, and blindness. An inhaled insulin powder product, Afrezza, is now available on the U.S. market, and there is ongoing research on oral administration of insulin.

Impact on Healthcare Costs

Technological innovations have been the single most important factor in medical cost inflation. Specifically, during the past several decades, they have accounted for roughly half of the total rise in real (after eliminating the effects of general inflation) healthcare spending (CBO, 2008; Sorenson et al., 2013). Nevertheless, the impacts of technology on costs differ across technologies: Some—such as cancer drugs and invasive medical devices—have significant cost implications, whereas others are cost-neutral or cost-saving (Sorenson et al., 2013; Zaleski et al., 2023; Devi et al., 2023). Four main cost drivers are associated with the adoption of medical technology:

- The cost of acquiring the new technology and equipment
- The need for specially trained physicians and technicians to operate the equipment and to analyze the results, which often leads to increases in labor costs
- Any special housing and setting requirements for the technology, which result in facility costs (McGregor, 1989)
- Higher payments from insurers to cover the cost of care associated with new technology (Wu et al., 2014)

Hence, widespread adoption of technology has a multiplier effect, as costs increase in these four main areas.

A second set of cost drivers is associated with use. Once technology is adopted by hospitals and physicians, a certain volume of use must be maintained to recover the investment. Ultimately, the technology's purchase price has a minimal effect on system-wide healthcare costs (Littell and Strongin, 1996); instead, the costs associated with use of the technology, once it is adopted, become more important. For example, the addition of an MRI unit in a facility leads to approximately 733 more MRI procedures (Baker et al., 2008). Also, many of the most notable medical advances in recent decades involve ongoing treatments for the management of chronic conditions, such as diabetes and coronary artery disease (CBO, 2008), where costs continue to aggregate over time.

Although many technologies do increase costs, others have been found to actually reduce costs. For example, the combination PET/CT imaging technique has shown significant promise for reducing the cost of cancer management by improving the accuracy of both diagnosis and staging, thereby helping to avoid expensive, futile treatments and associated side effects. Thus, PET/CT has the potential to increase a patient's quality-adjusted life years (explained later in the chapter) (Fischer et al., 2016). Technology is also credited with driving the overall reduction in the average length of inpatient hospital stays in the United States. Minimally invasive procedures using ultrasound, radio waves, or lasers can be performed in outpatient clinics, thereby reducing the need for hospitalizations.

Whereas many new technologies may increase labor costs, some actually produce labor cost savings. For example, when Northwestern University Medical Center in Chicago automated its lab, the number of human handling steps decreased from 14 to 1.5, and the turnaround time declined from 8 hours to 90 minutes. Largely because of a significant drop in labor costs, 30% in cost savings were realized through the lab automation. Not only that, but the error rate dropped to zero after the system was installed (Flower, 2006).

Economic Value of Technology

Instead of focusing solely on the excessive costs that new technologies may produce, attention is now being given to the value or worth of the advances in medical care. In a groundbreaking study, Cutler and colleagues (2006) addressed this issue by examining how medical spending has translated into additional years of life saved, based on the assumption that 50% of the improvements in life expectancy have resulted from medical care. These researchers concluded that the increases in medical spending over the 1960–2000 period, in terms of increased life expectancy, have yielded reasonable value for the money spent. For example, for a 45-year-old American who has a remaining life expectancy of 30 years, the value of remaining life is more than $200,000 per year (Murphy and Topel, 2003). For this 45-year-old person, the average annual spending in health care for each year of life gained was $53,700 (Cutler et al., 2006).

Chambers and colleagues (2014) evaluated the value offered by the specialty drugs that are produced with advanced biotechnology. Such drugs are available to treat a range of conditions, such as cancer, hepatitis C, and multiple sclerosis, but come at a high cost. The researchers concluded that despite their higher price tags relative to traditional drugs, the specialty drugs confer greater benefits and hence may offer reasonable value for the money. Indeed, new drugs may be credited to a greater extent than innovations in diagnostics, devices, and surgery for the improvements in health outcomes achieved over the years (Wamble et al., 2019). Even though medical technology innovations have been cost-effective in improving population health, the distribution of these gains has been uneven.

Impact on Access

Geography is an important factor that influences access to technology (Sahoo et al., 2023; Bonnechère et al., 2023). If a technology is not physically available to a patient population living in remote areas, access to it is limited. Geographic access to many technologies can be improved by providing mobile equipment or by employing new communications technologies to allow remote access to centralized equipment and specialized personnel. For example, use of global positioning system (GPS) technology can significantly improve emergency medical services' response time to the scenes of motor vehicle crashes and other emergencies (Gonzalez et al., 2009).

Mobile equipment can be transported to rural and remote sites, making it accessible to those populations. Mobile cardiac catheterization laboratories, for example, can provide high technology in rural settings. Cardiac catheterizations can be performed safely in a mobile laboratory at rural hospitals, provided immediate transfer is available for those patients in need of urgent intervention or revascularization (Peterson and Peterson, 2004). As discussed earlier, access to specialized medical care for rural and other hard-to-reach populations has been transformed through innovations in telemedicine.

Impact on the Structure and Processes of Healthcare Delivery

Medical technology has transformed large urban hospitals into medical centers, where the latest diagnostic and therapeutic remedies are offered. Growth of services offered in alternative settings, such as home health and outpatient surgery centers, has also been made possible primarily by technology. For example, numerous surgical procedures are now performed in same-day outpatient settings. In earlier times, many of these patients would have required hospital stays. Extensive home health services have brought many hospital and nursing home services to the patient's home, reducing the need for institutionalization. Apart from telehealth, home care technology includes kidney dialyzers, feeding pumps, ultrasound, ventilators, and pulse oximeters.

The growth of managed care, integrated delivery systems, and emerging accountable care organizations all depend on robust IT systems and information exchange capabilities. The ubiquitous bar-coding system has found several new applications in hospitals, including automation of drug dispensing, which drastically reduces medication errors (Thompson et al., 2018). Scanning of information on nurses' badges, patients' wristbands, and drugs administered ensures that the right drug is given in the right dose to the right patient (Nicol and Huminski, 2006). Barcode labeling of specimens sent to laboratories for testing has also significantly contributed to decreases in testing errors. Radio-frequency identification (RFID) technology offers several benefits over bar coding, including automated reading at a distance, reduced susceptibility to defacement, and batch processing. Although upfront capital costs are still considerable, the cost of RFID is more than offset by workflow enhancements and mitigated losses through improved patient safety (Norgan et al., 2020).

Telecommunications technology, such as videoconferencing, is used not only in telemedicine but also in diverse areas such as continuing medical education, language interpretation for patients, demonstration of new products by vendors, and collection of qualitative data for research. Such applications can often eliminate travel-related costs, such as airfares and hotel expenses.

Impact on Global Medical Practice

Technology developed in the United States has significantly impacted the practice of medicine worldwide. More than half of the world's leading medical device companies, for example, are based in the United States. In fact, the medical device industry is one of the few American manufacturing industries that consistently exports more than it imports (Holtzman, 2012). Many nations wait for the United States to develop new technologies, which can then be introduced into their systems in a more controlled and manageable fashion. This process gives them access to high-technology medical care with less national investment. Although the United States is expected to continue to maintain its lead in technological innovation, Europe, Japan, and, more recently, developing nations are also focusing their attention and resources on advances in medical technology (Tripp et al., 2012).

Impact on Bioethics

Increasingly, technological change is raising serious ethical and moral issues. For example, how can medical technology benefit everyone in society? Who should have access to costly new technology? Gene mapping of humans, genetic cloning, stem cell research, and other areas of growing interest to scientists may hold potential benefits, but they also present serious ethical dilemmas. Life support technology raises serious ethical issues, especially in medical decisions regarding continuation or cessation of mechanical support, particularly when a patient exists in a permanent vegetative state. Likewise, attention to ethical issues is critical in medical research involving human subjects and in the evaluation of experimental technologies, such as nanomedicine. In addition, ethical questions arise about whether society should bear the cost of infertility treatments, genetic tests, and lifestyle remedies that do not affect people's health and longevity.

The Assessment of Medical Technology

Technology assessment—or more specifically, **health technology assessment (HTA)**—refers to "any process of examining and reporting properties of a medical technology used in health care, such as safety, effectiveness, feasibility, and indications for use, cost, and cost-effectiveness, as well as social, economic, and ethical consequences, whether intended or unintended" (Institute of Medicine, 1985). HTA seeks to contribute to clinical decision-making and allocation of resources by providing evidence about the appropriateness of medical technologies. Value assessments of technology, based on improved outcomes, fewer complications, and affordability, require HTA methods (Lopez et al., 2020). Such assessments can be instrumental in overcoming the dilemma in medical practice that was posited by the Institute of Medicine (2011): "care that is important is often not delivered [and] care that is delivered is often not important."

Efficacy and safety are the basic starting points in evaluating the overall utility of medical technology. Cost-effectiveness and cost-benefit analyses go a step further in evaluating the safety and efficacy in relation to the cost of using the technology. Efficacy and safety are evaluated through clinical trials.

A **clinical trial** is a carefully designed research study in which human subjects participate under controlled observations. Clinical trials are carried out over three or four phases, starting with a small number of subjects to evaluate the safety, dosage range, and side effects of new treatments. Subsequent studies using larger groups of people are carried out to confirm the intervention's effectiveness and to further evaluate safety. Compliance with rigid standards is required under HIPAA to protect the rights of study participants and to ensure that the experimentation protocols are ethical. Every institution that conducts or supports biomedical or behavioral research involving human subjects must establish an institutional review board (IRB), which initially approves and periodically reviews the research.

In contrast to many developed countries, the United States does not have a national HTA program to broadly evaluate health technologies and guide coverage and pricing decisions (Schaeffer, 2020). The lack of a single national HTA organization or process reflects the current U.S. political landscape—including our preference for market-oriented solutions—as well as our decentralized insurance system, under which each private and public payer makes its own coverage decisions and conducts its own price negotiations. While U.S. payers frequently use internal processes that incorporate elements of HTA to inform their coverage decisions, these processes lack transparency and involve duplicated efforts across organizations. At the same time, shifting to a single national approach to HTA would be challenging in the United States given differences in covered populations across payers.

Efficacy

Efficacy or effectiveness is defined simply as the health benefit derived from the use of technology. If a product or service actually produces some health benefit, it can be considered efficacious or effective. Decisions about efficacy require that one ask the right questions. For example, are the current diagnostic capabilities satisfactory? What is the likelihood that the new procedure would result in a better diagnosis? If the problem is more accurately diagnosed, what is the likelihood of a better cure?

The question of evaluating health benefits is not as simple as it may seem. Significant challenges arise in defining and measuring health outcomes. Standardization of the selection of outcomes and outcome measurement instruments is still needed, without which it is difficult to compare the effectiveness of a new technology against an existing one.

It is also recommended that clinical trials include some measure of health-related quality of life (HRQL). HRQL is patients' own subjective perception of the effects of illness and medical intervention on their physical, mental, social, and emotional functioning. For some diseases, such as asthma and psoriasis, survival is not the main issue, but improvement in HRQL is very important. The difficult question is, however, how to measure HRQL (Cleemput and Neyt, 2015). People are also likely to have different opinions about which is better—longer survival time or higher quality of life. Moreover, people's own lifestyle factors—such as smoking and drinking, sleep, exercise, and leisure—play a significant role in determining HRQL (Zhang et al., 2018).

Safety

The assessment of safety is designed to protect patients against unnecessary harm from technology. As a primary benchmark, benefits must outweigh any negative consequences; however, negative consequences cannot always be predicted. Hence, clinical trials involving patients who may stand to gain the most from a technology are employed to obtain a reasonable consensus on safety. Subsequently, outcomes from wider use of technology are closely monitored to identify any problems related to safety.

Value Analysis

Value analysis is an essential process in medical technology assessment, which helps healthcare organizations, professionals, and decision-makers evaluate the cost-effectiveness and overall value of medical technologies (Onwudiwe et al., 2017). Value analysis involves a systematic approach to assessing medical technologies, considering their clinical efficacy, safety, cost, and other relevant factors (Onwudiwe et al., 2017). Refer to **Exhibit 5-8** for a process of conducting value analysis.

In view of the limited resources available for delivering health care, technology adoption should be guided by evaluating costs and benefits. **Cost-efficiency** (or cost-effectiveness) goes a step beyond the determination of efficacy. Whereas efficacy is concerned only with the benefit derived from the technology, cost-effectiveness evaluates the additional (marginal) benefits derived in relation to the additional (marginal) costs incurred. Even though weighing of benefits against costs has been difficult in actual practice, progress continues to be made in the area of economic analysis.

The health production function provides a simple theoretical model of cost-efficiency. Medical treatments and technology use are highly cost-effective when medical interventions are initiated. Past that point, additional inputs of medical care tend to decrease the benefits in relation to the costs, which continue to rise. Hence, intensive medical care may produce diminishing returns. At some point in the production of health benefits that are attributable to medical care, the marginal benefits equal the marginal costs. Economists have labeled this point the **flat of the curve**. From this point onward, it is highly unlikely that additional technological interventions will result in benefits equal to or in excess of the additional costs. As costs continue to increase, they eventually far exceed the additional health benefit. It has been suggested that a considerable number of medical

Exhibit 5-8 Process of Conducting Value Analysis

1. **Defining the Problem:** The first step in value analysis is defining the problem or clinical need that a medical technology aims to address, which involves consulting with clinicians, patients, and other stakeholders to identify areas where technology can make a difference (Onwudiwe et al., 2017).
2. **Identifying Alternatives:** Value analysis considers various alternatives, including existing technologies, new innovations, or non-technological solutions to address the defined problem. For example, if the problem is managing chronic diseases, alternatives might include different types of monitoring devices, medications, lifestyle interventions, or telemedicine solutions (Onwudiwe et al., 2017).
3. **Safety and Quality:** Evaluating the safety and quality of medical technologies includes considering adverse effects, potential complications, and how well the technology aligns with established healthcare quality standards (Caro et al., 2019).
4. **Cost Analysis:** Assessing the cost-effectiveness of medical technologies involves not only the direct acquisition costs of the technology but also the long-term operational costs, including maintenance, training, and potential cost savings through improved patient outcomes (Caro et al., 2019).
5. **Comparative Analysis:** Value analysis involves comparing different technologies and their costs and benefits. This helps decision-makers understand which technology offers the most value for a given clinical need (Ming et al., 2022).
6. **Ethical and Legal Considerations:** Legal and ethical aspects are reviewed to ensure compliance with regulations and ethical guidelines (Caro et al., 2019).

Data from Onwudiwe, N. C., Baker, A. M., Belinson, S., & Gingles, B. (2017). Assessing the value of medical devices-choosing the best path forward: where do we go from here. Value Outcomes Spotlight, 4, 15–17; Caro, J. J., Brazier, J. E., Karnon, J., Kolominsky-Rabas, P., McGuire, A. J., Nord, E., & Schlander, M. (2019). Determining Value in Health Technology Assessment: Stay the Course or Tack Away?. PharmacoEconomics, 37(3), 293–299; Ming, J., He, Y., Yang, Y., Hu, M., Zhao, X., Liu, J., Xie, Y., Wei, Y., & Chen, Y. (2022). Health technology assessment of medical devices: current landscape, challenges, and a way forward. Cost effectiveness and resource allocation: C/E, 20(1), 54. https://doi.org/10.1186/s12962-022-00389-6

interventions in the United States reach the flat of the curve, referring to a level of intensity of treatment that provides no incremental health benefit (Fuchs, 2004). Hence, continuation of high-intensity care when benefits have subsided is considered wasteful.

Some experts have argued that flat-of-the-curve medicine is not necessarily wasteful, at least at the aggregate level. For example, increased pharmaceutical consumption in developed countries has helped improve mortality outcomes, especially for middle aged people and older (Miller and Frech, 2000). In other areas, flat-of-the-curve medicine may not be improving physical health outcomes, but it may bring improved mental health (by reducing anxiety and depression, for example), better health maintenance, improved HRQL, or stability in health status, such as reduced variability of age at death (Schoder and Zweifel, 2011).

Although there are technical differences between cost-effectiveness analysis, cost-utility analysis, and cost-benefit analysis, these terms are often used interchangeably in the medical literature. Analytical techniques require both costs and benefits to be expressed in monetary terms. For example, resource inputs, such as the direct cost of treatment, staff time, increased cost of staff shortages, and training costs, should be brought into the analysis.

Benefits or health outcomes can be thought of in terms of efficacy of treatment, prognosis or expected outcomes, number of cases of a certain disease averted, years of life saved, increase in life expectancy, hospitalization and sick days avoided, early return to work, patient satisfaction, and so on. However, these gains are not always easy to quantify. Hence, the use of **quality-adjusted life year (QALY)**—a measure that includes both life expectancy and quality of life or morbidity—has become widely accepted. QALY is defined as the value of 1 year of high-quality life. When QALY is used as a measure of benefit, the analysis is technically referred to as **cost-utility analysis** (Neumann and Weinstein, 2010).

Cutler and McClellan (2001) assigned a value of $100,000 per QALY and demonstrated that, at least in four conditions (i.e., heart attacks, low-birth-weight infants, depression, and cataracts), the estimated benefit of technology was much greater than the cost. The value of $100,000 per QALY is arbitrary and highly debatable, however, and there is no standard method for the calculation of QALY. Many cost-effectiveness studies are based on a value of $50,000 per QALY, which is considered too low (Nwachukwu and Bozic, 2015). However, placement of a dollar value on human life has been challenged on ethical grounds.

Use of Cost-Benefit Analyses in the United States

In the United States, the Patient-Centered Outcomes Research Institute (PCORI), a nonprofit semi-private institution, was established under the ACA. PCORI funds research and disseminates evidence-based information to users. The ACA prohibits the use of cost-effectiveness analysis and QALY thresholds, instead specifying that comparative effectiveness research be the methodology used. **Comparative effectiveness research (CER)** is designed to compare the relative benefits and risks of alternative technologies to prevent, diagnose, treat, and monitor a clinical condition. Its aim is to provide scientific evidence on how well a given clinical intervention will work compared to other available interventions, but it leaves both cost and QALY out of the equation.

Other countries continue to make policy and clinical decisions about technologies based on cost-effectiveness research. For example, the National Institute for Health and Clinical Excellence (NICE) in the United Kingdom uses QALY in its cost-effectiveness research. Similarly, QALY thresholds are used in many other countries. Indeed, research studies now commonly use cost-effectiveness analyses that cannot be utilized in the United States because of the ACA legislation. Nwachukwu and Bozic (2015) have argued that U.S. policy disregards escalating costs and strained resources and, hence, is an outdated perspective likely rooted in an illogical fear of rationing.

Achieving a balance between efficacy and cost-effectiveness will require a change in the American mindset, which will not be forthcoming in the near future. In the United States, healthcare organizations face an ever-present fear that they will be sued if they deny access to treatments that are known to be medically effective even when their cost-effectiveness is questionable (Bryan et al., 2009). Without malpractice reform, overuse of technology will continue to drive up healthcare costs. Almost all observers realize that the United States will ultimately have to deal with the parameters of cost and value in an explicit way (Luce and Cohen, 2009). Indeed, the explicit use of cost-effectiveness ratios may become routine at some point in medical decision-making (Aby et al., 2023; Haque et al., 2023). Already, medical and surgical specialty societies in the United States are employing criteria from cost-effectiveness analyses in developing their clinical guidelines to be used in medical practice (Nwachukwu and Bozic, 2015).

Summary

Medical technology has produced many benefits by making positive changes in the quality of medical care delivered to patients, who often end up enjoying a better quality of life owing to their improved care. Medical technology can be credited with bringing increased longevity and decreased mortality to people around the world. Much of this technology has been developed through the application of scientific knowledge that was discovered in fields other than medicine. For example, applications of computer science and telecommunications have been adapted for use in the delivery of medical services. The application of information technology and informatics has become indispensable in efficient delivery of care and in the effective management of modern healthcare organizations. The fields of e-health, m-health, e-therapy, telemedicine, and telehealth will continue to expand. Nanotechnology is a cutting-edge advancement within the science and engineering fields that is beginning to find applications in health care on an experimental basis.

On the downside, the development and diffusion of technology are closely intertwined with its use. Although cost-saving technology is widely used, the uncontrolled use of most medical technology has prompted deep concerns about rising costs. Unlike other countries, the United States has not found a way to limit the use of high-cost medical technology. However, health policy in the United States does play a role in managing these costs—specifically, through the FDA's drug and device approval process and government funding for biomedical research. Uncontrolled use of technology also raises bioethical concerns because human lives are involved.

Given the costs and risks associated with the use of technology, its assessment has become an area of growing interest. In the United States, the focus of health technology assessment has traditionally been on safety and efficacy. By comparison, cost-effectiveness is widely used in other countries as a criterion for making coverage decisions. Decisions based on economic worth have not received the same level of support in the United States. As escalating healthcare expenditures approach a critical point, the appropriateness of medical treatments may be determined based on their incremental health value at a given cost.

TEST YOUR UNDERSTANDING

Terminology

administrative information systems
artificial intelligence (AI)
asynchronous technology
biologics
clinical information systems
clinical trial
comparative effectiveness research (CER)
cost-efficiency
cost-utility analysis
decision support systems
effectiveness
efficacy
e-health
electronic health records (EHRs)
e-therapy
e-visit
flat of the curve
health informatics
health information organization (HIO)
health technology assessment (HTA)
information technology (IT)
medical technology
m-health
nanomedicine
orphan drugs
precision medicine
quality-adjusted life year (QALY)
self-referral
synchronous technology
technological imperative
technology diffusion
telehealth
telemedicine
value

Review Questions

1. Medical technology encompasses more than just sophisticated equipment. Discuss.
2. What role does an IT department play in a modern healthcare organization?
3. Provide brief descriptions of clinical information systems, administrative information systems, and decision support systems in healthcare delivery.
4. Distinguish between information technology (IT) and health informatics.
5. According to the Institute of Medicine, what are the four main components of a fully developed electronic health record (EHR) system?
6. What are the main provisions of HIPAA with regard to the protection of personal health information? Which provisions were added to HIPAA under the HITECH Act?
7. What is telemedicine? How do the synchronous and asynchronous forms of telemedicine differ in their applications?
8. Which factors have been responsible for the low diffusion and low use of telemedicine?
9. Generally speaking, why is medical technology more readily available and used in the United States than in other countries?
10. How does technology-driven competition lead to greater levels of technology diffusion? How does technological diffusion, in turn, lead to greater competition? How does technology-driven competition lead to duplication of services?
11. Summarize the government's role in technology diffusion.
12. Provide a brief overview of how technology influences the quality of medical care and quality of life.
13. Discuss the relationship between technological innovation and healthcare expenditures.
14. How has technology affected access to medical care?
15. Discuss the roles of efficacy, safety, and cost-effectiveness in the context of health technology assessment.
16. Why is it important to achieve a balance between clinical efficacy and economic worth (cost-effectiveness) of medical treatments?
17. What are some of the ethical issues surrounding the development and use of medical technology?

References

Aby, E. S., A. Kaplan, and N. N. Ufere, 2023. Cost and Value in Liver Disease Guidelines: 2011-2022. *Hepatology Communications* 7.

Agarwal, R., and L. B. Saltz, 2020. Understanding the Right to Try Act. *Clinical Cancer Research* 26: 340–343.

American Association for the Advancement of Science. 2022. U.S. R&D and Innovation in a Global Context: 2022 Data Update. Accessed October 2023. Available at: https://www.aaas.org/sites/default/files/2022-05/AAAS%20Global%20R%26D%20Update%20May%202022.pdf

Appleby, J. 2008. The case of CT angiography: How Americans View and Embrace New Technology. *Health Affairs* 27: 1515–1521.

Arentfox. 2021. 2021 Stark & Anti-Kickback Statute Final Rules. *Health Care Counsel*. Available at: https://www.afslaw.com/sites/default/files/2021-02/%202021%20Stark%20&%20Anti-Kickback%20Statute-Final-Rules-FINALPDF.pdf

Arndt, B. G., J. W. Beasley, and M. D. Watkinson, et al. 2017. Tethered to the EHR: Primary Care Physician Workload Assessment Using EHR Event Log Data and Time-Motion Observations. *Annals of Family Medicine* 15: 419–426.

Asbury, E. T. 2023. Telehealth and the COVID-19 Pandemic: Making the Pivot from Offline to Online Therapeutic Interventions. *Cyberpsychology, Behavior and Social Networking* 26: 686–689.

Austin, C. J. 1992. *Information Systems for Health Services Administration*. 4th ed. Ann Arbor, MI: AUPHA Press/Health Administration Press.

Awad, A., F. Fina, A. Goyanes, S. Gaisford, and A. W. Basit, -2020. 3D printing: Principles and Pharmaceutical

Applications of Selective Laser Sintering. *International Journal of Pharmaceutics* 586: 119594.

Bach, R. L., and A. Wenz. 2020. Studying Health-Related Internet and Mobile Device Use Using Web Logs and Smartphone Records. *PLoS One* 15: e0234663. Available at: https://doi.org/10.1371/journal.pone.0234663

Badreldin, H. A., and B. Atallah. 2021. Global Drug Shortages Due to COVID-19: Impact on Patient Care and Mitigation Strategies. *Research in Social and Administrative Pharmacy* 17: 1946–1949.

Baker, L. C., S. W. Atlas, and C. C. Afendulis. 2008. Expanded Use of Imaging Technology and the Challenge of Measuring Value. *Health Affairs* 27: 1467–1478.

Barbalho, I., M. P., F. Fernandes, D. M. Barros, et al. 2022. Electronic Health Records in Brazil: Prospects and Technological Challenges. *Frontiers in Public Health* 10: 963841.

Barua, B., and M. Moir. 2019. *Waiting Your Turn: Wait Times for Health Care in Canada, 2019 Report.* Fraser Institute. Accessed June 2020. Available at: https://www.fraserinstitute.org/sites/default/files/waiting-your-turn-2019-rev17dec.pdf

Bhinder, B., C. Gilvary, N. S. Madhukar, and O. Elemento, 2021. Artificial Intelligence in Cancer Research and Precision Medicine. *Cancer Discovery* 11: 900–915.

Bloomrosen, M., and E. S. Berner. 2022. Findings from the 2022 Yearbook Section on Health Information Exchange. *Yearbook of Medical Informatics* 31: 215–218.

Bonkhoff, A. K., and C. Grefkes, 2022. Precision Medicine in Stroke: Towards Personalized Outcome Predictions Using Artificial Intelligence. *Brain* 145: 457–475.

Bonnechère, B., O. Kossi, J. Mapinduzi, et al. 2023. Mobile Health Solutions: An Opportunity for Rehabilitation in Low- and Middle Income Countries? *Frontiers in Public Health* 10: 1072322.

Bookwalter, C. M. 2021. Drug Shortages Amid the COVID-19 Pandemic. *Us Pharm* 46: 25–28.

Brechtelsbauer, E. D., B. Pennell, M. Durham, et al. 2016. Review of the 2015 Drug Supply Chain Security Act. *Hospital Pharmacy* 51: 493–500.

Bronzino, J. D., V. H. Smith, and M. L. Wade. 1990. *Medical Technology and Society: An Interdisciplinary Perspective.* Cambridge, MA: MIT Press.

Brown, B., C. Ortiz, and K. Dubé. (2018). Assessment of the Right-to-Try Law: the Pros and the Cons. *Journal of Nuclear Medicine* 59: 1492–1493.

Brown-Podgorski, B. L., K. E. Hilts, B. A. Kash, C. D. Schmit, and J. R. Vest. 2018. The Association Between State-Level Health Information Exchange Laws and Hospital Participation in Community Health Information Organizations. In: *AMIA Annual Symposium Proceedings* 313–320.

Bryan, S., S. Sofaer, T. Siegelberg, and M. Gold. 2009. Has the Time Come for Cost-Effectiveness Analysis in U.S. Health Care? *Health Economics, Policy, and Law* 4: 425–443.

Burry, L. D., J. F. Barletta, D. Williamson, et al. 2020. It Takes a Village…: Contending with Drug Shortages During Disasters. *Chest* 158: 2414–2424.

Calabretta, M. M., M. Zangheri, A. Lopreside, et al. 2020. Precision Medicine, Bioanalytics and Nanomaterials: Toward a New Generation of Personalized Portable Diagnostics. *Analyst* 145: 2841–2853.

Cameron, E. E., and M. J. Bushell, 2021. Analysis of Drug Shortages Across Two Countries During Pre-Pandemic and Pandemic Times. *Research in Social and Administrative Pharmacy* 17: 1570–1573.

Campanella, P., E. Lovato, C. Marone, et al. 2015. The Impact of Electronic Health Records on Healthcare Quality: A Systematic Review and Meta-Analysis. *European Journal of Public Health* 26: 60–64.

Cappellaro, G., S. Ghislandi, and E. Anessi-Pessina. 2011. Diffusion of Medical Technology: The Role of Financing. *Health Policy* 100: 51–59.

Caro, J. J., J. E. Brazier, J. Karnon, et al. 2019. Determining Value in Health Technology Assessment: Stay the Course or Tack Away? *PharmacoEconomics* 37: 293–299.

Carrieri, D., F. A. Peccatori, and Boniolo, G. 2018. The Ethical Plausibility of the 'Right To Try' laws. *Critical Reviews in Oncology/Hematology* 122: 64–71.

Centers for Disease Control and Prevention (CDC). 2012. Meaningful Use. Accessed November 2020. Available at: https://www.cdc.gov/ehrmeaningfuluse/introduction.html

Chambers, J. D., T. Thorat, J. Pyo, M. Chenoweth, and P. J. Neumann. 2014. Despite Higher Costs, Specialty Drugs May Offer Value for Money Comparable to that of Traditional Drugs. *Health Affairs* 33: 1751–1760.

China Economic and Security Review Commission (USCC) U.S.– 2019. 2019 Report to Congress of the U.S.-China Economic and Security Review Commission. Accessed June 2020, from https://www.uscc.gov/sites/default/files/2019-11/2019%20Executive%20Summary.pdf.

Churchill, L. R. 2011. Rationing, Rightness, and Distinctively Human Goods. *American Journal of Bioethics* 11: 15–31.

Cinelli, I., and L. Brown. 2018. Innovation in Medical Technology Driven by Advances in Aerospace. In: *Conference Proceedings: Annual International Conference of the IEEE Engineering in Medicine and Biology Society.* 941–944.

Cirillo, D., S. Catuara-Solarz, C. Morey, et al. 2020. Sex and Gender Differences and Biases in Artificial Intelligence for Biomedicine and Healthcare. *NPJ Digital Medicine 3.* Date of Electronic Publication: 2020 Jun 01. Print Publication: 2020.

Clayton, P. D. 2001. Confidentiality and Medical Information. *Annals of Emergency Medicine* 38: 312–316.

Cleemput, I., and M. Neyt. 2015. Which Quality of Life Measures Fit Your Relative Effectiveness Assessment? *International Journal of Technology Assessment in Health Care* 31: 147–153.

Cohen, A. B. 2004a. The Adoption and Use of Medical Technology in Health Care Organizations. In: *Technology in American Health Care: Policy Directions for Effective Evaluation and Management*. A. B. Cohen, and R. S. Hanft, eds. Ann Arbor, MI: University of Michigan Press. 105–147.

Cohen, A. B. 2004b. Critical Questions Regarding Medical Technology and its Effects. In: *Technology in American Health Care: Policy Directions for Effective Evaluation and Management*. Cohen, A. B., and R. S. Hanft, eds. Ann Arbor, MI: University of Michigan Press. 15–42.

Cohen, A. B. 2004c. The Diffusion of New Medical Technology. In: *Technology in American Health Care: Policy Directions for Effective Evaluation and Management*. A. B. Cohen, and R. S. Hanft, eds. Ann Arbor, MI: University of Michigan Press. 79–104.

Colicchio, T. K., J. J. Cimino, and G. Del Fiol. 2019. Unintended Consequences of Nationwide Electronic Health Record Adoption: Challenges and Opportunities in the Post-Meaningful Use Era. *Journal of Medical Internet Research* 21: e13313.

Comaniciu, D., K. Engel, B. Georgescu, and T. Mansi. 2016. Shaping the Future Through Innovations: From Medical Imaging to Precision Medicine. *Medical Image Analysis* 33: 19–26.

Congressional Budget Office (CBO). 2008. Technological Change and the Growth of Health Care Spending. Washington, DC: CBO.

Conover, C. J., and Bailey, J. 2020. Certificate of Need Laws: A Systematic Review and Cost-Effectiveness Analysis. *BMC Health Services Research* 20: 1–29.

Cutler, D. M., and M. McClellan. 2001. Is Technological Change in Medicine Worth it? *Health Affairs* 20: 11–29.

Cutler, D. M., A. B. Rosen, and S. Vijan. 2006. The Value of Medical Spending in the United States, 1960–2000. *New England Journal of Medicine* 355: 920–927.

Davis, M. P. 2006. Management of Cancer Pain: Focus on New Opioid Analgesic Formulations. *American Journal of Cancer* 5: 171–182.

de Oliveira, C. R., A. P. da Silva Etges, M. S. Marcolino, et al. 2023. COVID-19 Telehealth Service Can Increase Access to the Health Care System and Become a Cost-Saving Strategy. *Telemedicine Journal and E-Health: The Official Journal of the American Telemedicine Association* 29: 1043–1050.

de Ruiter, H., J. Liaschenko, and J. Angus. 2016. Problems with the Electronic Health Record. *Nursing Philosophy* 17: 49–58.

Decker, S. L., E. W. Jamoom, and J. E. Sisk. 2012. Physicians in Nonprimary Care and Small Practices and Those Age 55 and Older Lag in Adopting Electronic Health Record Systems. *Health Affairs* 31: 1108–1114.

Denny, J. C., and Collins, F. S. 2021. Precision Medicine in 2030—Seven Ways to Transform Healthcare. *Cell* 184: 1415–1419.

Devi, D. H., K. Duraisamy, A. Armghan, et al. 2023. 5g Technology in Healthcare and Wearable Devices: A Review. *Sensors* 23: 2519.

Dorsey & Whitney. 2021. Stark Regulatory Changes Effective January 1, 2022 Require Modifying Certain Group Practice Compensation Methodologies. *Dorsey & Whitney Publications*. Available at: https://www.dorsey.com/newsresources/publications/client-alerts/2021/04/stark-regulatory-changes

Drake, D., S. Fitzgerald, and M. Jaffe. 1993. *Hard Choices: Health Care at What Cost?* Kansas City, MO: Andrews and McMeel.

Edney, A. 2019. America's Love Affair with Cheap Drugs Has a Hidden Cost. Bloomberg. Accessed June 2020, from https://www.bloomberg.com/news/features/2019-01-29/america-s-love-affair-with-cheap-drugs-has-a-hidden-cost

Epstein, M. S., E. D. Ehrenpreis, and P. M. Kulkarni. 2014. Biosimilars: The Need, the Challenge, the Future: The FDA Perspective. *American Journal of Gastroenterology* 109: 1856–1859.

Erickson, A. C. 2021. States are Suspending Certificate of Need Laws in the Wake of COVID-19 but the Damage Might Already Be Done. *Pacific Legal Foundation (blog)*.

Eslami Jahromi, M., and H. Ayatollahi, 2023. Utilization of Telehealth to Manage the Covid-19 Pandemic in Low- and Middle-Income Countries: A Scoping Review. *Journal of the American Medical Informatics Association* 30: 738–751.

Field, M. J., and J. Grigsby. 2002. Telemedicine and Remote Patient Monitoring. *Journal of the American Medical Association* 288: 423–425.

Fischer, B. M., B. A. Siegel, W. A. Weber, K. von Bremen, T. Beyer, and A. Kalemis. 2016. PET/CT Is a Cost-Effective Tool Against Cancer: Synergy Supersedes Singularity. *European Journal of Nuclear Medicine and Molecular Imaging* 43: 1749–1752.

Flannery, E. J. 1986. Should it Be Easier or Harder to Use Unapproved Drugs and Devices? *Hastings Center Report* 16: 17–23.

Flower, J. 2006. Imagining the Future of Health Care. *Physician Executive* 32: 64–66.

Food and Drug Administration (FDA) U.S. 2023. 5 Tips for Traveling to the U.S. With Medications. Available at: https://www.fda.gov/consumers/consumer-updates/5-tips-traveling-us-medications#:~:text=A%3A%20FDA%20does%20not%20permit,as%20the%20FDA%2Dapproved%20versions

Food and Drug Administration (FDA) U.S. 2023. Drug Shortages. Available at: https://www.fda.gov/drugs/drug-safety-and-availability/drug-shortages

Food and Drug Administration (FDA), U.S. 2018. Right to Try. Available at: https://www.fda.gov/patients/learn-about-expanded-access-and-other-treatment-options/right-try

Food and Drug Administration (FDA). 2018a. Accelerated Approval. Accessed November 2020. Available at: https://www.fda.gov/patients/fast-track-breakthrough-therapy-accelerated-approval-priority-review/accelerated-approval

Food and Drug Administration (FDA). 2018b. Food and Drug Administration Safety and Innovation Act (FDASIA). Accessed June 2020, from https://www.fda.gov/regulatory-information/selected-amendments-fdc-act/food-and-drug-administration-safety-and-innovation-act-fdasia#supplychain

Food and Drug Administration (FDA). 2018c. What Are "Biologics" Questions and Answers. Accessed November 2020, from https://www.fda.gov/about-fda/center-biologics-evaluation-and-research-cber/what-are-biologics-questions-and-answers

Food and Drug Administration (FDA). 2019a. Securing the U.S. Drug Supply Chain: Oversight of FDA's Foreign Inspection Program. Accessed November 2020, from https://www.fda.gov/news-events/congressional-testimony/securing-us-drug-supply-chain-oversight-fdas-foreign-inspection-program-12102019#ftn4

Food and Drug Administration (FDA). 2019b. Drug Shortages: Root Causes and Potential Solutions. Accessed June 2020, from https://www.fda.gov/media/131130/download

Food and Drug Administration (FDA). 2019c. National Evaluation System for Health Technology (NEST). Accessed June 2020, from https://www.fda.gov/about-fda/cdrh-reports/national-evaluation-system-health-technology-nest

Fox, S., and M. Duggan. 2013. Health Online 2013. *Pew Research Center*. Accessed November 2020, from http://www.pewinternet.org/2013/01/15/health-online-2013/

Frank, C., D. U. Himmelstein, S. Woolhandler, et al. 2014. Era of Faster FDA Drug Approval Has Also Seen Increased Black-Box Warnings and Market Withdrawals. *Health Affairs* 33: 1453–1459.

Frankt, A. 2014. High-Tech Care Can Save Lives—but it Also May Create Incentives that Result in Lives Lost. *Journal of the American Medical Association* 312: 2081.

Friedman, A. 2011. Rationing and Social Value Judgments. *Journal of Bioethics* 11: 28–29.

Fuchs. 2004. More Variation in Use of Care, V. R. More Flat-of-the-Curve Medicine. *Health Affairs* 23 (Variations Suppl): 104–107.

Gabay, M. (2018). RxLegal: A Rapid Review of Right-to-Try. *Hospital Pharmacy* 53: 234–235.

Gomes, M. A., J. L. Kovaleski, R. N. Pagani, V. L. da Silva, and T. C. Pasquini. 2023. Transforming Healthcare with Big Data Analytics: Technologies, Techniques and Prospects. *Journal of Medical Engineering & Technology* 47: 1–11.

Gonzalez, R. P., G. R. Cummings, M. S. Mulekar, S. M. Harlan, and C. B. Rodning. 2009. Improving Rural Emergency Medical Service Response Time with Global Positioning System Navigation. *Journal of Trauma* 67: 899–902.

Goran, S. F. 2010. A Second Set of Eyes: An Introduction to Tele-ICU. *Critical Care Nurse* 30: 46–55.

Grech, V., S. Cuschieri, and A. A. Eldawlatly, 2023. Artificial Intelligence in Medicine and Research - the Good, the Bad, and the Ugly. *Saudi Journal of Anaesthesia* 17: 401–406.

Haas, M., J. Hall, R. Viney, and G. Gallego. 2010. Breaking up Is Hard to Do: Why Disinvestment in Medical Technology is Harder than Investment. *Australian Health Review* 36: 148–152.

Halamka, J. D. 2010. Making the Most of Federal Health Information Technology Regulations. *Health Affairs* 29: 596–600.

Hao, X., Y. Qin, M. Lv, X. Zhao, S. Wu, and K. Li, 2023. Effectiveness of Telehealth Interventions on Psychological Outcomes and Quality of Life in Community Adults During the COVID-19 Pandemic: A Systematic Review and Meta-Analysis. *International Journal of Mental Health Nursing*, 32: 979–1007.

Haque, A., M. N. Chowdhury, and Soliman, H. 2023. Transforming Chronic Disease Management with Chatbots: Key Use Cases for Personalized and Cost-Effective Care. In *2023 Sixth International Symposium on Computer, Consumer and Control (IS3C)* 367–370. IEEE.

Haynes, R. B., and N. L. Wilczynski. 2010. Effects of Computerized Clinical Decision Support Systems on Practitioner Performance and Patient Outcomes: Methods of a Decision-Maker–Researcher Partnership Systematic Review. *Implementation Science* 5: 12.

Hernandez, I., T. B. Hershey, and J. M. Donohue. 2020. Drug Shortages in the United States: Are Some Prices too Low? *Journal of the American Medical Association* 323: 819–820.

Hertzog, R., J. Johnson, J. Smith, et al. 2019. Diagnostic Accuracy in Primary Care E-Visits: Evaluation of a Large Integrated Health Care Delivery System's Experience. *Mayo Clinic Proceedings* 94: 976–984.

Hillmann, H. A., C. Hansen, O. Przibille, and D. Duncker, 2023. The Patient Perspective on Remote Monitoring of Implantable Cardiac Devices. *Frontiers in Cardiovascular Medicine*, 10: 1123848.

Hodgson Russ. 2021. Key Takeaways from the Stark Law Final Rule. *Hodgson Russ Healthcare Alert*. Available at: https://www.hodgsonruss.com/newsroom-publications-13028.html#:~:text=The%20intent%20of%20the%20regulatory,for%20a%20target%20patient%20population

Holtzman, Y. 2012. The U.S. Medical Device Industry in 2012: Challenges at Home and Abroad. Accessed November 2020. Available at: https://www.mddionline.com/news/us-medical-device-industry-2012-challenges-home-and-abroad

Hong, Y. R., K. Turner, S. Yadav, J. Huo, and A. G. Mainous III. 2019. Trends in E-Visit Adoption Among U.S. Office-Based Physicians: Evidence from the 2011-2015 NAMCS. *International Journal of Medical Informatics* 129: 260–266.

Humer, M. F., and B. G. Campling. 2017. The Role of Telemedicine in Providing Thoracic Oncology Care to Remote Areas of British Columbia. *Current Oncology Reports* 19: 52.

Iglehart, J. K. 1982. The Cost and Regulation of Medical Technology: Future Policy Directions. In: *Technology and the Future of Health Care*. J. B. McKinlay, ed. Cambridge, MA: MIT Press. 69–103.

Institute of Medicine. 1985. *Assessing Medical Technologies*. Washington, DC: National Academies Press.

Institute of Medicine. 2003. *Key Capabilities of an Electronic Health Records System*. Washington, DC: National Academies Press.

Institute of Medicine. 2011. *Learning What Works: Infrastructure Required for Comparative Effectiveness Research: Workshop Summary*. Washington, DC: National Academies Press.

Janetos, T. M., L. Akintilo, and S. Xu. 2019. Overview of High-Risk Food and Drug Administration Recalls for Cosmetics and Personal Care Products from 2002–2016. *Journal of Cosmetic Dermatology* 19: 1361–1365.

Janett, R. S., and P. P. Yeracaris. 2020. Electronic Medical Records in the American Health System: Challenges and Lessons Learned. *Ciencia & Saude Coletiva* 25: 1293–1304.

Johnson, K. B., W. Q. Wei, D. Weeraratne, et al. 2021. Precision Medicine, AI, and the Future of Personalized Health Care. *Clinical and Translational Science* 14: 86–93.

Johnston, B., L. Weeler, J. Deuser, and K. H. Sousa. 2000. Outcomes of the Kaiser Permanente Tele-Home Health Research Project. *Archives of Family Medicine* 9: 40–45.

Kahn, E. N., F. La Marca, and C. A. Mazzola. 2016. Neurosurgery and Telemedicine in the United States: Assessment of the Risks and Opportunities. *World Neurosurgery* 89: 133–138.

Kahn, J. G., J. S. Yang, and J. S. Kahn. 2010. "Mobile" Health Needs and Opportunities in Developing Countries. *Health Affairs* 29: 252–258.

Kao D. P. (2022). Electronic Health Records and Heart Failure. *Heart Failure Clinics* 18: 201–211.

Karaca-Mandic, P., R. J. Town, and A. Wilcock. 2017. The Effect of Physician and Hospital Market Structure on Medical Technology Diffusion. *Health Services Research* 52: 579–598.

Kariotis, T. C., M. Prictor, S. Chang, and K. Gray. 2022. Impact of Electronic Health Records on Information Practices in Mental Health Contexts: Scoping Review. *Journal of Medical Internet Research* 24: e30405.

Kher, U. 2006. The Hospital Wars. *Time* 168: 64–68.

Kim, G. E., O. K. Afanasiev, C. O'Dell, Sharp, C., and Ko, J. M. 2020. Implementation and Evaluation of Stanford Health Care Store-and-Forward Teledermatology Consultation Workflow Built Within an Existing Electronic Health Record System. *Journal of Telemedicine & Telecare* 26: 125–131.

Kleinke, J. D. 2001. The Price of Progress: Prescription Drugs in the Health Care Market. *Health Affairs* 20: 43–60.

Kohl, B. A., M. Fortino-Mullen, A. Praestgaard, and C. W. Hanson. 2012. The Effect of ICU Telemedicine on Mortality and Length of Stay. *Journal of Telemedicine and Telecare* 18: 282–286.

Kolarik, J. 2021. Key Takeaways from the Revised and Clarified Stark Law Regulations – Part 2. *Foley & Lardner LLP*. Available at: https://www.foley.com/en/insights/publications/2021/01/key-takeaways-clarified-stark-law-part-2

Leonard, D. Schaeffer Center for Health Policy & Economics, 2020. *Health Technology Assessment for the U.S. Healthcare System*. Accessed October 2023. Available at: https://healthpolicy.usc.edu/research/health-technology-assessment-for-the-u-s-healthcare-system/

Lintvedt, O., Marco-Ruiz, L., and Pedersen, R. 2023. User Satisfaction with Recently Deployed Electronic Health Records. *Studies in Health Technology and Informatics*, 302: 192–196.

Lite, S., W. J. Gordon, and A. D. Stern. 2020. Association of the Meaningful Use Electronic Health Record Incentive Program with Health Information Technology Venture Capital Funding. *JAMA Network Open* 3: e201402.

Littell, C. L., and R. J. Strongin. 1996. The Truth about Technology and Health Care Costs. *IEEE Technology and Society Magazine* 15: 10–14.

Liu, P. R., L. Lu, J. Y. Zhang, T. T. Huo, S. X. Liu, and Z. W. Ye, (2021). Application of Artificial Intelligence in Medicine: An Overview. *Current Medical Science*, 41: 1105–1115.

Lopez, M. H., G. W. Daniel, N. C. Fiore, A. Higgins, and M. B. McClellan. 2020. Paying for Value from Costly Medical Technologies: A Framework for Applying Value-Based Payment Reforms. *Health Affairs* 39: 1018–1025.

Luce, B., and R. S. Cohen. 2009. Health Technology Assessment in the United States. *International Journal of Technology Assessment in Health Care* 25 (Suppl 1): 33–41.

Luce, B. R. 1993. Medical Technology and Its Assessment. In: *Introduction to Health Services*. 4th ed. S. J. Williams, and P. R. Torrens, eds. Albany, NY: Delmar Publishers. 245–268.

Mahant, V. 2020. "Right-to-try" Experimental Drugs: An Overview. *Journal of Translational Medicine*, 18: 253.

Maheu, M. M., P. Whitten, and A. Allen. 2001. *E-health, Telehealth, and Telemedicine: A Guide to Start-up and Success*. San Francisco, CA: Jossey-Bass.

Majeed, A. 2018. Technology and the Future of Anesthesiology. *Anaesthesia, Pain & Intensive Care* 22: 1–4.

Mandel, J. C., J. P. Pollak, and K. D. Mandl, 2022. The Patient Role in a Federal National-Scale Health Information Exchange. *Journal of Medical Internet Research*, 24: e41750.

Manzari, M. T., Y. Shamay, H. Kiguchi, N. Rosen, M. Scaltriti, and D. A. Heller, 2021. Targeted Drug Delivery Strategies for Precision Medicines. *Nature Reviews Materials* 6: 351–370.

Marrie, R. A., A. R. Salter, T. Tyry, R. J. Fox, and G. R. Cutter. 2013. Preferred Sources of Health Information in Persons with Multiple Sclerosis: Degree of Trust and Information Sought. *Journal of Medical Internet Research* 15: e67.

Martinelli, M., D. Moroni, L. Bastiani, S. Mrakic-Sposta, G. Giardini, and L. Pratali. 2020. High-Altitude Mountain Telemedicine. *Journal of Telemedicine and Telecare*. 1357633X20921020.

McGregor, M. 1989. Technology and the Allocation of Resources. *New England Journal of Medicine* 320: 118–120.

Mennemeyer, S. T., N. Menachemi, S. Rahurkar, and E. W. Ford. 2016. Impact of HITECH Act on Physicians' Adoption of Electronic Health Records. *Journal of the American Medical Informatics Association* 23: 375–379.

Milewa, T. 2006. Health Technology Adoption and the Politics of Governance in the UK. *Social Science and Medicine* 63: 3102–3112.

Miller, R. D. Jr., and H. E. III Frech. 2000. Is There a Link Between Pharmaceutical Consumption and Improved Health in OECD Countries? *Pharmacoeconomics* 18 (Suppl 1): 33–45.

Ming, J., Y. He, Y. Yang, et al. 2022. Health Technology Assessment of Medical Devices: Current Landscape, Challenges, and a Way Forward. *Cost Effectiveness and Resource Allocation: C/E*, 20: 54. Available at: https://doi.org/10.1186/s12962-022-00389-6

Mitchell, J. M. 2007. The Prevalence of Physician Self-Referral Arrangements after Stark II: Evidence from Advanced Diagnostic Imaging. *Health Affairs* 26: w415–w424.

Mitchell, M. D. 2021. Certificate-of-Need Laws: How They Affect Healthcare Access, Quality, and Cost. *Mercatus Center*. Available at: https://www.mercatus.org/economic-insights/features/certificate-need-laws-how-they-affect-healthcare-access-quality-and-cost

Moses, H., D. H. Matheson, S. Cairns-Smith, et al. 2015. The Anatomy of Medical Research: US and International Comparisons. *Journal of the American Medical Association* 313: 174–189.

Murphy, G. F., M. A. Hanken, and M. Amatayakul. 1999. EHR Vision, Definition, and Characteristics. In: *Electronic health records: Changing the Vision*. G. F. Murphy et al., eds. Philadelphia, PA: Saunders. 3–26.

Murphy, K. M., and R. H. Topel. 2003. The Economic Value of Medical Research. In: *Measuring the Gains from Medical Research: An Economic Approach*. K. M. Murphy, and R. H. Topel, eds. Chicago, IL: University of Chicago Press. 41–73.

Namin, A. L., M. S. Jalali, V. Vahdat, et al. 2019. Adoption of New Medical Technologies: The Case of Customized Individually Made Knee Implants. *Value in Health: Journal of the International Society for Pharmacoeconomics and Outcomes Research* 22: 423–430.

National Center for Science and Engineering, 2022, *Research and Development: U.S. Trends and International Comparisons*. Accessed October 2023, from https://ncses.nsf.gov/pubs/nsb20225

National Center for Science and Engineering Statistics, 2023, *U.S. R&D Increased by $51 Billion in 2020 to $717 Billion; Estimate for 2021 Indicates Further Increase to $792 Billion*. Accessed October 2023. Available at: https://ncses.nsf.gov/pubs/nsf23320

National Conference of State Legislature. 2023. *Certificate of Need State Laws*. Accessed October 2023. Available at: https://www.ncsl.org/health/certificate-of-need-state-laws#:~:text=Currently%2C%2035%20states%20and%20D.C.%20maintain%20some%20form,state%20to%20repeal%20its%20CON%20program%20in%202016

Neumann, P. J., and M. C. Weinstein. 2010. Legislation Against Use of Cost-Effectiveness Information. *New England Journal of Medicine* 363: 1495–1497.

Nicol, N., and L. Huminski. 2006. How We Cut Drug Errors. *Modern Healthcare* 36: 38.

Norgan, A. P., K. E. Simon, and B. A. Feehan, et al. 2020. Radio-Frequency Identification Specimen Tracking to Improve Quality in Anatomic Pathology. *Archives of Pathology & Laboratory Medicine* 144: 189–195.

Nwachukwu, B. U., and K. J. Bozic. 2015. Updating Cost Effectiveness Analyses in Orthopedic Surgery: Resilience of the $50,000 per QALY Threshold. *Journal of Arthroplasty* 30: 1118–1120.

OECD. 2023. The Future of Telemedicine after COVID-19. *OECD Policy Responses to Coronavirus (COVID-19)*. Available at: https://www.oecd.org/coronavirus/policy-responses/the-future-of-telemedicine-after-covid-19-d46e9a02/

Office of the National Coordinator for Health Information Technology (ONC). 2023. Health Data, Technology, and Interoperability: Certification Program Updates, Algorithm Transparency, and Information Sharing. *Federal Register*, 88: 23746–23917.

Office of the National Coordinator for Health Information Technology (ONC) 2023. Health Data, Technology, and Interoperability: Certification Program Updates, Algorithm Transparency, and Information Sharing (HTI-1) Proposed Rule. *HealthIT.gov*. Available at: https://

www.healthit.gov/topic/laws-regulation-and-policy/health-data-technology-and-interoperability-certification-program

Office of the National Coordinator for Health Information Technology. 2023. Interoperability and Methods of Exchange Among Hospitals in 2021. Accessed October 2023, from https://www.healthit.gov/data/data-briefs/interoperability-and-methods-exchange-among-hospitals-2021

Oh, Y. S., and N. K. Song. 2017. Investigating Relationships Between Health-Related Problems and Online Health Information Seeking. *Computers, Informatics, Nursing* 35: 29–35.

Olson, D., A. Hakim, C. Gaviria-Agudelo, et al. 2019. Telehealth Practices, Barriers, and Future Interest Among Pediatric Infectious Disease Clinicians in the United States: Results from the 2019 Pediatric Infectious Diseases Society (PIDS) Telehealth Working Group survey. *Open Forum Infectious Diseases* 6 (Suppl): S341.

Onwudiwe, N. C., A. M. Baker, S. Belinson, and B. Gingles, (2017). Assessing the Value of Medical Devices-Choosing the Best Path Forward: Where Do We Go from Here. *Value Outcomes Spotlight* 4: 15–17.

Payne, T. H., C. Lovis, C. Gutteridge, et al. 2019. Status of Health Information Exchange: A Comparison of Six Countries. *Journal of Global Health* 9. doi: 10.7189/jogh.09.020427.

Peterson, L. F., and L. R. Peterson. 2004. The Safety of Performing Diagnostic Cardiac Catheterizations in a Mobile Catheterization Laboratory at Primary Care Hospitals. *Angiology* 55: 499–506.

Poalelungi, D. G., C. L. Musat, A. Fulga, et al. 2023. Advancing Patient Care: How Artificial Intelligence Is Transforming Healthcare. *Journal of Personalized Medicine* 13: 1214.

Poba-Nzaou, P., S. Uwizeyemungu, M. Dakouo, A. Tchibozo, and B. Mboup, 2021. Patterns of Health Information Exchange Strategies Underlying Health Information Technologies Capabilities Building. *Health Systems (Basingstoke, England)* 11: 211–231.

Qeska, D., S. M. Singh, F. Qiu, et al. 2023. Variation and Clinical Consequences of Wait-Times for Atrial Fibrillation Ablation: Population Level Study in Ontario, Canada. *Europace* 25: euad074.

Rakich, J. S., B. Beaufort, Jr., and K. D. Longest. 1992. *Managing Health Services Organizations*. Baltimore, MD: Health Professions Press.

Reddy S. 2022. Explainability and Artificial Intelligence in Medicine. *The Lancet Digital Health* 4: e214–e215.

Ricci, R. P., L. Morichelli, A. D'Onofrio, et al. 2013. Effectiveness of Remote Monitoring of CIEDs in Detection and Treatment of Clinical and Device-Related Cardiovascular Events in Daily Practice: The Homeguide Registry. *Europace* 15: 970–977.

Ricciardi, L., F. Mostashari, J. Murphy, J. G. Daniel, and E. P. Siminerio. 2013. A National Action Plan to Support Consumer Engagement via E-Health. *Health Affairs* 32: 376–384.

Rid, A., and E. J. Emanuel, 2014. Ethical Considerations of Experimental Interventions in the Ebola Outbreak. *The Lancet* 384: 1896–1899.

Robinson, J. C. 2015. Biomedical Innovation in the Era of Health Care Spending Constraints. *Health Affairs* 34: 203–209.

Robinson, M. D., A. R. Branham, A. Locklear, S. Robertson, and T. Gridley. 2016. Measuring Satisfaction and Usability of Facetime for Virtual Visits in Patients with Uncontrolled Diabetes. *Telemedicine & e-Health* 22: 138143.

Rochat, L., and B. Genton. 2018. Telemedicine for Health Issues While abroad: Interest and Willingness to Pay among Travellers Prior to Departure. *Journal of Travel Medicine* 25.

Rochlen, A. B., J. S. Zack, and C. Speyer. 2004. Online therapy: Review of Relevant Definitions, Debates, and Current Empirical Support. *Journal of Clinical Psychology* 60: 269–283.

Romano, S., J. P. Guerreiroand, and A. T. Rodrigues, 2022. Drug Shortages in Community Pharmacies: Impact on Patients and on the Health System. *Journal of the American Pharmacists Association* 62: 791–799.

Sahoo, S., J. Sahoo, S. Kumar, W. M. Lim, and N. Ameen, 2023. Distance is No Longer a Barrier to Healthcare Services: Current State and Future Trends of Telehealth Research. *Internet Research* 33: 890–944.

Sarkar I. N. 2023. Health Information Exchange as a Global Utility. *Chest* 163: 1023–1025.

Savoy, A., H. Patel, D. R. Murphy, A. N. Meyer, J. Herout, and H. Singh, 2023. Electronic Health Records' Support for Primary Care Physicians' Situation Awareness: A Metanarrative Review. *Human Factors* 65: 237–259.

Schoder, J., and P. Zweifel. 2011. Flat-of-the-Curve Medicine: A New Perspective on the Production of Health. *Health Economics Review* 1: 1–10.

Schulte, F., and E. Fry. 2019. Death by 1,000 Clicks: Where Electronic Health Records Went Wrong. *Kaiser Health News*. Accessed June 2020. Available at: https://khn.org/news/death-by-a-thousand-clicks/

Schur, C. L., and M. L. Berk. 2008. Views on Health Care Technology: Americans Consider the Risks and Sources of Information. *Health Affairs* 27: 1654–1664.

Secinaro, S., D. Calandra, A. Secinaro, V. Muthurangu, and P. Biancone. 2021. The Role of Artificial Intelligence in Healthcare: A Structured Literature Review. *BMC Medical Informatics and Decision Making* 21: 125.

Shaker, M., D. Mauger, and A. L. Fuhlbrigge, 2023. Value-Based, Cost-Effective Care: The Role of the Allergist-Immunologist. *The Journal of Allergy and Clinical Immunology: In Practice* 11: 132–139.

Shapiro, L. M., & Kamal, R. N. (2022). Implementation of Electronic Health Records During Global Outreach:

A Necessary Next Step in Measuring and Improving Quality of Care. *The Journal of Hand Surgery* 47: 279–283.

Shaver J. 2022. The State of Telehealth Before and After the COVID-19 Pandemic. *Primary Care*, 49: 517–530.

Shaw, L. J., D. D. Miller, D. S. Berman, and R. Hachamovitch. 2000. Clinical and Economic Outcomes Assessment in Nuclear Cardiology. *Quarterly Journal of Nuclear Medicine* 44: 138–152.

Sheikhtaheri, A., S. M. Tabatabaee Jabali, E. Bitaraf, A. TehraniYazdi, and A. Kabir, 2022. A Near Real-Time Electronic Health Record-Based COVID-19 Surveillance System: An Experience from a Developing Country. *Health Information Management Journal*: 18333583221104213.

Shenoy, A., G. N. Shenoy, and G. G. Shenoy, 2022. The Stark Law, from Inception to COVID-19 Blanket Waivers: A Review. *Patient Safety in Surgery* 16: 19.

Shukar, S., F. Zahoor, K. Hayat, et al. 2021. Drug Shortage: Causes, Impact, and Mitigation Strategies. *Frontiers in Pharmacology* 12: 693426.

Sisodiya, S. M. 2021. Precision Medicine and Therapies of the Future. *Epilepsia* 62: S90–S105.

Skinner, A. E., and G. Latchford. 2006. Attitudes to Counselling via the Internet: A Comparison Between In-Person Counselling Client and Internet Support Group Users. *Counseling and Psychotherapy Research* 6: 92–97.

Slotwiner, D., and B. Wilkoff. 2013. Cost Efficiency and Reimbursement of Remote Monitoring: A US Perspective. *Europace* 15 (Suppl 1): i54–i58.

Sobolev, B. G., G. Fradet, L. Kuramoto, and B. Rogula. 2013. The Occurrence of Adverse Events in Relation to Time after Registration for Coronary Artery Bypass Surgery: A Population-Based Observational Study. *Journal of Cardiothoracic Surgery* 8 (Special Section): 1–14.

Sorenson, C., M. Drummond, and B. Bhuiyan Khan. 2013. Medical Technology as a Key Driver of Rising Health Expenditures: Disentangling the Relationship. *ClinicoEconomics and Outcomes Research* 5: 223–234.

State Policy Network. 2021. Certificate-of-Need Laws: Why They Exist and Who They Hurt. *State Policy Network*. Available at: https://spn.org/articles/certificate-of-need-laws/

Statista. 2023. Share of Physicians Who Have Provided the Following Types of Care Through Telehealth in the United States as of 2021. Accessed October 2023, from https://www.statista.com/statistics/1300433/common-types-of-telehealth-visits-in-the-united-states/.

Sun, M., and A. Sen Gupta. 2019. Vascular Nanomedicine: Current Status, Opportunities, and Challenges. *Seminars in Thrombosis and Hemostasis*. 46: 524–544.

Taub, J. 2011. The Smallest Revolution: 5 Recent Breakthroughs in Nanomedicine. *Scientific American*. Accessed November 2020, from https://blogs.scientificamerican.com/guest-blog/the-smallest-revolution-five-recent-breakthroughs-in-nanomedicine/

Tedeschi, C. 2020. Social, Legal and Ethical Challenges in the Development and Implementation of Disaster Telemedicine. *Disaster Medicine and Public Health Preparedness*: 1–26.

Teichert, E. 2016. Putting Telemedicine Behind Bars. *Modern Healthcare* 46: 22.

Thompson, K. M., K. M. Swanson, D. L. Cox, et al. 2018. Implementation of Bar-Code Medication Administration to Reduce Patient Harm. *Mayo Clinic Proceedings. Innovations, Quality & Outcomes* 2: 342–351.

Tinajero, J. 2017. The Need to Repeal Certificate of Need Laws to Improve America's Health Care System: A Dormant Commerce Clause Analysis. *Journal of Legal Medicine* 37: 597–612.

Tovino, S. A. 2019. A Timely Right to Privacy. *Iowa Law Review* 104: 1361–1420.

Tripp, S., M. Grueber, and R. Helwig. 2012. *The Economic Impact of the U.S. Advanced Medical Technology Industry*. Cleveland, OH: Battelle Technology Partnership Practice.

Tsai, C. H., A. Eghdam, N. Davoody, G. Wright, S. Flowerday, and S. Koch, 2020. Effects of Electronic Health Record Implementation and Barriers to Adoption and Use: A Scoping Review and Qualitative Analysis of the Content. *Life (Basel, Switzerland)* 10: 327.

Tucker, E. L., Y. Cao, E. R. Fox, and B. V. Sweet, 2020. The Drug Shortage Era: A Scoping Review of the Literature 2001-2019. *Clinical Pharmacology & Therapeutics* 108: 1150–1155.

Turro, E., W. J. Astle, K. Megy, et al. 2020. Whole-Genome Sequencing of Patients with Rare Diseases in a National Health System. *Nature* 583: 96–102.

Varma, N., F. Braunschweig, H. Burri, et al. 2023. Remote Monitoring of Cardiac Implantable Electronic Devices and Disease Management. *Europace* 25: euad233.

Waisberg, E., J. Ong, M. Masalkhi, et al. 2023. GPT-4: A New Era of Artificial Intelligence in Medicine. *Irish Journal of Medical Science* 10.1007/s11845-023-03377-8.

Walker D. M. 2018. Does Participation in Health Information Exchange Improve Hospital Efficiency? *Health Care Management Science* 21: 426–438.

Wamble, D. E., M. Ciarametaro, and R. Dubois. 2019. The Effect of Medical Technology Innovations on Patient Outcomes, 1990–2015: Results of a Physician Survey. *Journal of Managed Care & Specialty Pharmacy* 25: 66–71.

Winterdijk, P., H. J. Aanstoot, and G. Nefs, 2023. The Impact of Real-Time Sensor Technology on Quality of Life for Adults with Type 1 Diabetes: A Dutch

National Survey. *Diabetes Research and Clinical Practice* 203: 110886.

Wodarski, J., and J. Frimpong. 2013. Application of E-Therapy Programs to the Social Work Practice. *Journal of Human Behavior in the Social Environment* 23: 29–36.

Woldemariam, M. T., and W. Jimma, 2023. Adoption of Electronic Health Record Systems to Enhance the Quality of Healthcare in Low-Income Countries: A Systematic Review. *BMJ Health & Care Informatics* 30.

Wu, V. Y., Y. C. Shen, M. S. Yun, and G. Melnick. 2014. Decomposition of the Drivers of the U.S. Hospital Spending Growth, 2001-2009. *Health Services Research* 14: 237–252.

Yang, Y., S. Li, Y. Cai, et al. 2023. Effectiveness of Telehealth-Based Exercise Interventions on Pain, Physical Function and Quality of Life in Patients with Knee Osteoarthritis: A Meta-Analysis. *Journal of Clinical Nursing* 32: 2505–2520.

Ybarra, M. L., and W. W. Eaton. 2005. Internet-Based Mental Health Interventions. *Mental Health Services Research* 7: 75–87.

Zachrison, K. S., K. M. Boggs, E. M. Hayden, et al. 2020. A National Survey of Telemedicine Use by US Emergency Departments. *Journal of Telemedicine and Telecare* 26: 278–284.

Zaleski, A., B. Sigler, A. Leggitt, et al. 2023. The Influence of a Wearable-Based Reward Program on Health Care Costs: Retrospective, Propensity Score–Matched Cohort Study. *Journal of Medical Internet Research* 25: e45064.

Zhang, X., R. Xia, S. Wang, et al. 2018. Relative Contributions of Different Lifestyle Factors to Health-Related Quality of Life in Older Adults. *International Journal of Environmental Research and Public Health* 15.

CHAPTER 6

Health Services Financing

LEARNING OBJECTIVES

- Study the role of healthcare financing and its impact on the delivery of health care.
- Understand the basic concept of insurance and how general insurance terminology applies to health insurance.
- Differentiate among group insurance, self-insurance, individual health insurance, managed care, high-deductible plans, and Medigap plans.
- Discuss private health insurance under the Affordable Care Act.
- Explore trends in employer-based health insurance.
- Examine the distinctive features of public insurance programs, such as Medicare, Medicaid, the Children's Health Insurance Program, the Department of Defense's programs, the Veterans Health Administration, and the Indian Health Service.
- Understand the various methods of reimbursement and the current focus on value-based reimbursement models.
- Discuss national health care and personal healthcare expenditures and trends in private and public financing.
- Explore the effects of the COVID-19 pandemic on financing and insurance.

"I have comprehensive insurance."

Introduction

Complexity of financing is one of the primary characteristics of medical care delivery in the United States. The single-payer systems implemented in countries such as Australia, Canada, and the United Kingdom simplify healthcare financing: Taxes are raised by the government to provide health insurance to the citizens, and private financing plays a minor role for those who want more extensive coverage than what the government offers. In the United States, both public and private financing play substantial roles. In the public sector, the government has created a multitude of tax-financed programs; each program serves a defined category of citizens provided they meet the established qualifications. Insurance overlap is also relatively common. For example, a significant number of Medicare beneficiaries either qualify for Medicaid or have purchased private supplementary insurance to pay for expenses not covered by Medicare. In the private sector, financing for health insurance is shared between the employer and the employee with large employers providing the bulk of financing. Self-employed people purchase health insurance in the open market. For the unemployed, the underemployed (those working part-time who do not qualify for employer-sponsored health insurance), and those who lost their private insurance due to the original formulation of the Affordable Care Act (ACA; colloquially known as Obamacare), the government attempted to facilitate the purchase of health insurance starting in 2014.

The actual payments to providers of care are handled in numerous ways. Patients generally pay a portion of the costs directly, but the bulk of these costs is paid through the insurance plans. The government and some large employers use the services of third-party administrators to process payment claims from providers.

In this chapter, financing is discussed in broad terms that include the concepts of financing, insurance, and payment. This does not mean, however, that these three functions are structurally integrated. For example, government-financed programs, such as Medicare and Medicaid, integrate the functions of financing and insurance, but contracted third-party administrators take over the payment function. Traditional insurance plans integrate the functions of insurance and payment, whereas both employers and employees provide the financing. Managed care has gone one step further in integrating all four functions of healthcare system—financing, insurance, delivery, and payment.

This chapter focuses on financing for both private and public health insurance, points out trends, discusses healthcare expenditures, and explains various payment methods to reimburse providers. The chapter concludes by exploring the effects of the COVID-19 pandemic on health insurance and financing.

The Role and Scope of Health Services Financing

As its central role, health services financing pays for health insurance premiums. Providers generally rely on their patients' insurance to get paid for the services they deliver. The various methods used to determine how much providers should be paid (i.e., reimbursement) for their services are also closely intertwined with the broad financing function.

To a large extent, financing determines who has access to health care and who does not. The distinction between insurance and access is an important one. Health insurance is a financial mechanism for paying for health care, while **access** refers to the process of actually obtaining that health care (Manchikanti et al., 2017). For instance, many uninsured people have access to charitable care, and charity is likely to continue to play a noteworthy role for a sector of the population in the United States. For example, free clinics continue to play a key role in providing health care to the uninsured (Kennedy et al., 2020). Charity care also benefits illegal immigrants, young healthy individuals who choose not to buy insurance, and individuals who do not qualify for Medicaid based on income.

Health insurance increases the demand for covered services; the demand would be less if patients paid for those same services out of pocket. Increased demand means greater use of health services, given adequate supply. According to economic theory, insurance lowers the out-of-pocket cost of medical care to consumers; hence, they will consume more medical services than if they had to pay the entire price out of their own pockets. Consumer behavior that leads to a higher use of healthcare services when the services are covered by insurance is referred to as **moral hazard** (Feldstein, 1993).

Financing also exerts powerful influences on supply-side factors, such as how much health care is produced in the private sector. Healthcare services and technology proliferate when services are covered by insurance. Even new services and technologies may start emerging, and new models of organization may form. Conversely, when reimbursement is cut, supply of healthcare services may also be curtailed.

Issues pertaining to reimbursement for services are critical in health services managers' decision making. Demand-side factors, including reimbursement, typically guide health services managers in evaluating and determining the type and extent of services that their organizations will offer. The amount of reimbursement needed to recoup capital costs over time also heavily influences decisions such as acquisition of new equipment, renovation or expansion of facilities, and launching of new services.

Similarly, financing can influence the supply and distribution of healthcare professionals. As an example, employer financing for dental insurance spawned growth in the number of dentists and dental hygienists. Mechanisms for reimbursing physicians, such as the resource-based relative value scale (RBRVS) used by Medicare, directly affect physicians' income. One of the main goals of RBRVS, implemented in 1992, was to entice more medical residents into general practice by increasing the reimbursement for services provided by generalists. Due to other factors, however, the imbalance between generalists and specialists has continued to persist.

Financing eventually affects—both directly and indirectly—the total healthcare expenditures incurred by a healthcare delivery system. The next section discusses the relationship between financing and healthcare expenditures and provides a general framework for controlling healthcare costs.

Financing and Cost Control

Healthcare financing and cost control are closely intertwined. **Figure 6-1** presents a conceptual model of cost control. In the U.S. healthcare delivery system, insurance is the main factor that determines the level of demand for medical services. Restricting financing for health insurance—as occurs with demand-side rationing—eventually controls total healthcare expenditures. Conversely, extension of health insurance to the uninsured, without supply-side rationing, increases total healthcare expenditures (E). Apart from the extent of insurance coverage, the cost of health insurance affects system-wide healthcare expenditures.

Insurance, along with payment (price = P), influences the supply or availability of health + services. Reducing reimbursement for providers has a direct influence on E, as well as an indirect influence through shrinkage in supply. Cuts in reimbursement have been used in the United States, as well as in other countries, as a primary strategy to contain the growth of healthcare expenditures.

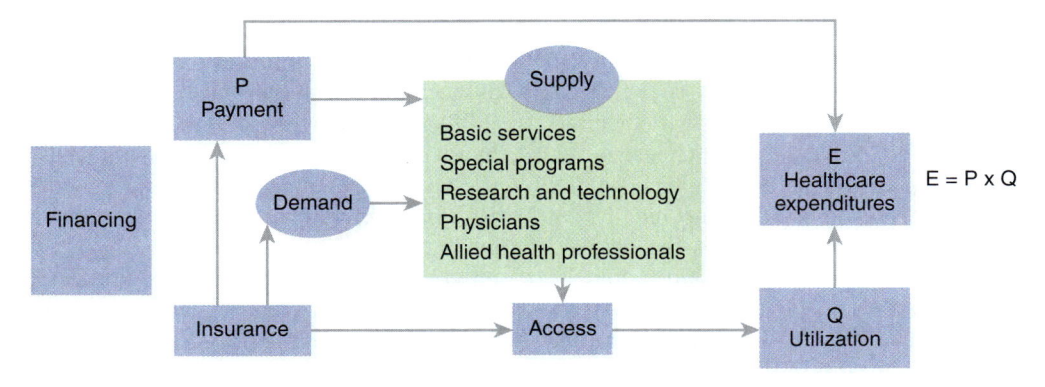

Figure 6-1 Influence of financing on the delivery of health services.

Diffusion of technology and other types of services can be directly restricted through central planning—an approach commonly used in countries that have national health insurance. When supply of technology is rationed, people may be insured but do not have free access to those services. Their reduced use of expensive technology results in direct savings. Countries that have national health care also achieve indirect savings by having fewer specialist physicians and specialized technicians and by spending less on research and development (R&D).

Insurance and supply of healthcare services together determine access and, ultimately, the use of services (quantity of services consumed = Q). Use can also be directly controlled. For example, private health insurance, as well as Medicare and Medicaid, tries to exert some limits on use by specifying which services are not covered, how often certain covered services may be received, and how much of the cost the insured may have to pay out of pocket.

Because $E = P \times Q$, rising healthcare costs can be controlled by managing the numerous factors that influence P and Q. Many of these factors are external to the healthcare delivery system. The P component, for example, includes general economy-wide inflation, as well as medical inflation that exceeds general inflation. In addition to being influenced by the intrinsic factors discussed in this section, the Q component is a function of changes in the size and demographic composition (i.e., age, sex, and racial mix) of the population (Levitt et al., 1994).

The Insurance Function

Insurance is a mechanism for protection against risk; this is its primary purpose. In this context, **risk** refers to the possibility of a substantial financial loss from an event whose probability of occurrence is relatively small (at least in a given individual's case). For example, even though auto accidents are common in the United States, the likelihood is quite small that a specific individual will have an auto accident in a given year. Even when the risk is small, people buy insurance to protect their assets against catastrophic loss.

The insuring agency that assumes risk is called the **insurer**, or underwriter. **Underwriting** is a systematic technique for evaluating, selecting (or rejecting), classifying, and rating risks. Medical underwriting, for example, takes into account the health status of people to be insured. Medical underwriting is no longer applicable to health insurance in the United States, mainly because the ACA has made it illegal to charge more or to refuse coverage for people who have **preexisting**

conditions, such as diabetes, cancer, heart disease, and HIV/AIDS. Even though charging more or refusing insurance to people with poor health status can be criticized on equity grounds, a disregard of insurance underwriting principles makes premiums increase for everyone, so that healthy people end up subsidizing health insurance for the unhealthy.

Four fundamental principles underlie the concept of insurance (Health Insurance Institute, 1969; Vaughn and Elliott, 1987):

- Risk is unpredictable for the individual insured.
- Risk can be predicted with a reasonable degree of accuracy for a large group or a population.
- Insurance provides a mechanism for transferring or shifting risk from the individual to the group through the pooling of resources.
- All members of the insured group share actual losses on some equitable basis.

Technically, healthcare services for all Americans 65 and older (the older adult population) are provided through Medicare. For those younger than age 65, private insurance—either employment-based or self-financed—is the predominant avenue for receiving health care. Medicaid and the Children's Health Insurance Program (CHIP) cover many individuals with low income, including children in low-income households. Other public programs cover defined groups of people, such as the insurance program offered by the Department of Veterans Affairs (VA) and the military health system. The remainder of the population, who lack any coverage, are the uninsured.

Because of some overlap in coverage, it is almost impossible to neatly fit people into categories based on specific types of health insurance. **Figure 6-2** provides broad approximations of the proportion of the U.S. population covered through private and public sources of health insurance in 2022. Between 2013 and 2016, the proportion of uninsured dropped from 15.1% to 9% (Wiltshire et al., 2020), shortly after the ACA was implemented in 2014.

Health insurance, particularly private health insurance, comes in the form of a **plan**, which specifies, among other details, information pertaining to costs, covered services,

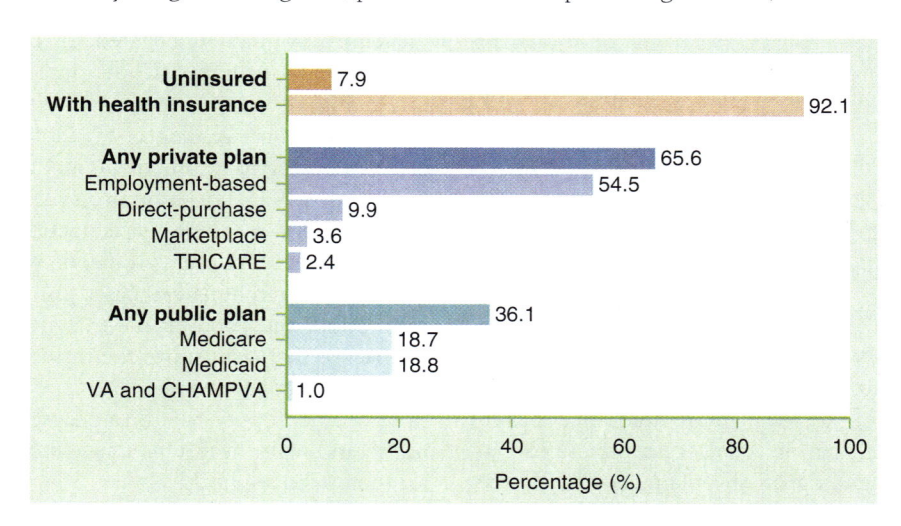

Figure 6-2 Percentage of people by type of health insurance coverage 2022 (Population as of March of the following year).

Modified from U.S. Census Bureau. Current Population Survey. 2022 and 2023 Annual Social and Economic Supplements (CPS ASEC). https://www.census.gov/content/dam/Census/library/visualizations/2023/demo/p60-281/figure1.pdf and ways to obtain health care when needed. Numerous plans are available. Anyone covered by health insurance is called the **insured** or a **beneficiary**. Two types of employer-sponsored plans are single coverage plans and family coverage plans; the latter cover the spouse and dependent children of the working employee. Medicare and Medicaid plans recognize only individual beneficiaries. In the case of married couples, for instance, Medicare and Medicaid recognize each spouse as an independent beneficiary.

Private Health Insurance

Private health insurance has also been called "voluntary health insurance." Most private health insurance is employment based, but workers are not mandated to buy it. Private insurance includes many different types of health plan providers, such as commercial insurance companies (e.g., United Health Group, Well Point, Cigna, and Aetna), Blue Cross/Blue Shield, and managed care organizations (MCOs). The nonprofit Blue Cross and Blue Shield Associations are similar to private health insurance companies, and almost all insurers operate their own MCOs. Many businesses are self-insured, using insurance companies for stop-loss coverage.

Basic Health Insurance Terminology

Premiums

A **premium** is the amount charged by the insurer to insure against specified risks. An employer may offer more than one health insurance plan, in which case premiums can vary depending on the plan selected by the employee. Employment-based health insurance is heavily subsidized by the employer, and the employee is asked to share in the cost of premiums.

Risk Rating

Premiums are determined by the actuarial assessment of risk, or **risk rating**, that adjusts premiums to reflect health status. Three different methods have been used to determine premiums: experience rating, community rating, and adjusted community rating.

Experience rating is based on a group's own medical claims experience. Under this method, premiums differ from group to group because different groups have different risks. For example, people working in various industries are exposed to various levels and types of hazards, people in certain occupations are more susceptible to certain illnesses or injuries, and older groups represent higher risks than younger groups. High-risk groups are expected to incur high use of medical care services, so these groups are charged higher premiums compared to preferred or favorable risk groups. The main issue with experience rating is that it makes premiums unaffordable for high-risk groups.

Community rating spreads the risk among members of a larger population. Premiums are based on the user experience of the entire population covered by the same type of health insurance. Under pure community rating, the same rate applies to everyone regardless of age, gender, occupation, or any other indicator of health risk (Goodman and Musgrave, 1992). For example, a person who is employed in a hazardous occupation would pay the same premium as someone who does not. When premiums are based on community rating, the good risks—that is, healthy people—actually subsidize the insurance cost for the poor risks. In other words, costs shift from people in poor health to people in good health and make health insurance more costly for those who are healthy.

Adjusted community rating, also known as modified community rating, is a middle-of-the road approach that overcomes the main drawbacks of experience rating and pure community rating. Under this method, price differences take into account demographic factors such as age, gender, geography, and family composition while ignoring other risk factors. The ACA requires the use of adjusted community rating to determine premiums for individuals and small groups.

Cost Sharing

In addition to paying a share of the cost of premiums through payroll deductions, insured individuals pay a portion of the actual cost of medical services out of their own pockets. These out-of-pocket expenses take the form of deductibles and copayments and are incurred only if and when medical services are used. A **deductible** is the amount the insured must first pay each year before any benefits are payable by the plan. For example, suppose a plan requires the insured to pay a $1,000 deductible. When the insured receives medical care, the plan starts paying only after the cost of medical services received by the insured has exceeded $1,000 in a given year. Many plans now allow the insured to use primary care and wellness services without having to pay a deductible.

The second type of cost sharing is a copayment, or coinsurance for some services. A **copayment** is a flat amount that the insured must pay each time health services are received—for example, $25 each time the patient consults a primary-care physician. **Coinsurance** is a set proportion of the medical costs that the insured must pay out of pocket. For example, an 80/20 coinsurance means that the plan pays 80% of the costs for a certain product or service; the insured pays the remaining 20%.

In case of a catastrophic illness or injury, the deductible and copayment/coinsurance amounts can add up to a substantial sum. Hence, health plans generally have an annual maximum limit on out-of-pocket cost sharing. Once the maximum cost sharing amount has been reached, the plan pays 100% of any additional expenses.

The rationale for cost sharing is to control use of healthcare services. Since insurance creates moral hazard by insulating the insured against the cost of health care, making the insured share in the cost promotes more responsible behavior in healthcare use. A comprehensive study employing a controlled experimental design conducted in the 1970s, commonly referred to as the Rand Health Insurance Experiment, demonstrated that cost sharing had a material impact in lowering use, without any significant negative health consequences. Experts now generally agree that cost sharing reduces use. Nevertheless, even though moral hazard does exist and results in frivolous and inefficient services, the expensive healthcare procedures needed in case of serious illness become affordable only with insurance (Nyman and Trenz, 2016).

Covered Services

The services covered by an insurance plan are referred to as **benefits**. Each health insurance plan spells out in a contract both covered and noncovered services. A typical disclaimer included in most contracts states that only "medically necessary" services are covered, regardless of whether such services are provided by a physician. The ACA mandated that all health plans must include certain "essential health benefits" (refer to **Exhibit 6-1** for a summary of ACA mandated benefits). Services such as eyeglasses and dental care are generally not covered by health insurance; vision and dental insurance plans can be purchased separately. The services most commonly excluded are those not ordered by a physician, such as self-care and over-the-counter products. Other services commonly excluded from health insurance coverage include cosmetic and reconstructive surgery, work-related illness and injury (covered under worker's compensation), rest cures, genetic counseling, and the like.

> **Exhibit 6-1** Essential Health Benefits Under ACA
>
> Ambulatory patient services
> Emergent services
> Hospitalization (surgery, maternal and newborn care)
> Mental health and substance-use disorder services
> Prescription medicine
> Rehabilitative and habilitative services and devices
> Laboratory services
> Preventive and wellness services
> Chronic disease management
> Pediatric services
>
> CMS (2019). Health Insurance Marketplaces. https://www.cms.gov/data-research/statistics-trends-and-reports/marketplace-products

Types of Private Insurance

Group Insurance

Group insurance can be obtained through an employer, a union, or a professional organization. A **group insurance** program anticipates that a substantial number of people in the group will purchase insurance through its sponsor. Because risk is spread out among the many insured, group insurance provides the advantage of lower costs than if the same type of coverage was purchased in the individual insurance market.

Unlike monetary wages, health insurance benefits provided through an employer are not subject to income tax. Consequently, a dollar of health insurance received from the employer is worth more than the same amount received in taxable wages or an after-tax dollar spent out of pocket for medical care. In this way, the U.S. government's tax policy provides an incentive to obtain health insurance as a benefit that is largely paid by the employer.

Starting in the 1950s, major medical insurance became widely available in the United States. This type of insurance was designed to cover catastrophic situations that could subject families to substantial financial hardships, such as hospitalization, extended illness, and expensive surgery. Since the 1970s, health insurance plans have become comprehensive in coverage and include basic and routine physician office visits and diagnostic services. The ACA required the inclusion of preventive and wellness services as part of the essential health benefits (Exhibit 6-1). Hence, health insurance today is an anomaly to the fundamental purpose of insurance. Comprehensive coverage has also increased the cost of health insurance.

Self-Insurance

In a **self-insured plan** (also called self-funded plan), the employer acts as its own insurer instead of obtaining insurance through an insurance company. Rather than pay insurers a dividend to bear the risk, many employers simply assume the risk by budgeting a certain amount to pay the medical claims incurred by their employees. In 2021, 64% of covered workers are in plans that are either fully or partially self-funded plans, including 82% of covered workers at large companies (KFF, 2021).

Self-insured employers can protect themselves against any potential risk of high losses by purchasing **reinsurance**, also called stop-loss coverage, from a private insurance company. Being self-insured gives employers a greater degree of control than purchasing regular insurance. The business can contract with an experienced insurance company as the third-party administrator to manage costs and pay claims.

The movement toward self-insurance was spurred by government policies. Self-insured private employers are exempt from a premium tax that insurance companies must pay, the cost of which is passed on to customers through higher premiums. Further, the Employee Retirement Income Security Act (ERISA) of 1974 exempts private self-insured plans from certain mandatory benefits that regular health insurance plans are required to provide in many states. Self-insured plans also avoid other types of state insurance regulations, such as reserve requirements and consumer protection requirements. Because of these plans' many advantages, employers that are large enough to make it feasible for themselves have viewed self-insurance as a better economic alternative. Notably, the ACA did not affect self-insured plans, so they have remained immune from certain ACA mandates, such as the one requiring health plans to include essential health benefits.

Individual Private Health Insurance

Individually purchased private health insurance (nongroup plans) has been a relatively small but important source of coverage for some Americans. In 2022, 9.9% of the covered U.S. population had direct-purchase coverage (Katherine, Lisa and Rachel, 2023). The family farmer, the early retiree, the self-employed person, and the employee of a business that does not offer health insurance—all of these people tend to rely on individual health insurance. In the past, for underwriting purposes, the risk indicated by each individual's health status and demographics was taken into account. Consequently, individuals with high-risk were unable to obtain privately purchased health insurance. This barrier was eliminated by provisions in the ACA.

Managed Care Plans

MCOs, such as health maintenance organizations (HMOs) and preferred provider organizations (PPOs), emerged in the 1980s in response to the rapid escalation of healthcare costs. At first, managed care plans differed from, and were less expensive than, the plans offered by traditional insurance companies. However, several factors over time converged around MCOs, and traditional insurance companies eventually began offering managed care plans. Today, the vast majority of health insurance takes the form of managed care plans. In 2022, among businesses that offered health insurance to their workers, 68% offered PPO plans and 19% offered HMO plans (KFF, 2022a).

High-Deductible Health Plans and Savings Options

High-deductible health plans (HDHPs) combine a savings option with a health insurance plan that carries a high deductible. In 2022, the average annual deductible for a single HDHP plan was $2,539, compared with $1,451 for an HMO plan (KFF, 2022). In 2022, HDHPs covered 29% of all workers in employment-based plans (KFF, 2022), up from just 4% in 2006. Because of their high deductibles, premiums for HDHPs are lower than those for other types of health plans. Savings options give consumers greater control over how to use the funds. Hence, these plans are also referred to as **consumer-directed health plans**. There are two main types of HDHPs/savings options, which are subject to different guidelines under U.S. tax law: health reimbursement arrangements (HRAs) and health savings accounts (HSAs) (**Exhibit 6-2**).

Short-Term COBRA Coverage

When people change jobs and move to a different employer, they may encounter a waiting period before their new health insurance starts. This waiting period is limited to 90 days or less under the ACA. Other individuals may face temporary unemployment after separating from a job. Some people leave the workforce before age 65, so they do not qualify for Medicare. To address these kinds of short-term coverage gaps, Congress passed the Consolidated Omnibus Budget Reconciliation Act (COBRA) of 1985, which allows workers to keep their employer's group coverage for 18 months after leaving a job. The individuals are required to pay the full cost of insurance plus a 2% administrative fee, which many people cannot afford. Extended coverage beyond

Exhibit 6-2 Key Differences Between a Health Reimbursement Arrangement and a Health Savings Account[1]

Health Reimbursement Arrangement (HRA)	Health Savings Account (HSA)
Established solely by the employer. Individuals who are self-employed cannot establish an HRA. The account is owned by the employer.	Established by the individual. The employer can assist in establishing an HSA. The account is owned by the employee.
Having an HDHP is not mandatory. Employers may offer HRAs in addition to or in place of health insurance, which may include an HDHP. Funds are used for deductibles, copayments, insurance premiums, and other medical and related expenses authorized by the Internal Revenue Service.	The individual must have a "qualified health plan" that meets federal standards and is an HDHP. The minimum annual deductible for 2021 was $1,400 for a single plan ($2,800 for a family plan). For 2021, the maximum annual out-of-pocket expenses for deductibles and copayments were capped at $7,000 for a single plan ($14,000 for a family plan). Funds cannot be used for HDHP premiums.
Funded solely by the employer; employees are not allowed to contribute. There is no limit on the amount of contribution. Contributions are tax free.	The individual must fund the HSA. Employers may contribute but are not required to do so. The maximum contribution for 2021, which is fully tax deductible, was $3,600 for a single plan ($7,200 for a family plan). Enrollees who are 55 years and older can contribute an extra $1,000 to either plan.
An employer may offer an HRA to a retiree even after age 65, or allow a retiree or terminated employee to keep an existing HRA. Conversely, an employer may terminate the account.	The individual must be younger than age 65 and not have any other health insurance (dental, vision, and long-term care insurance do not count). When a person becomes eligible for Medicare at age 65, the remaining balance in an HSA can be used, but no funds can be added.

[1] An employer may offer an HRA and an HSA. In this case, funds from the HRA can be used to pay the premiums for an HDHP, which is required with the HSA.

Data from Mengle, R. 2020. HSA contribution limits and other requirements. Available at: https://www.kiplinger.com/personal-finance/insurance/health-insurance/health-savings-accounts/601415/hsa-limits-and-minimums. Accessed November 2020.

18 months is available for someone who becomes disabled—but again affordability becomes an issue for many.

Medigap

Medigap, also called Medicare Supplement Insurance, is private health insurance that can be purchased only by those enrolled in the original Medicare program—a program that has high out-of-pocket costs (discussed later in the "Medicare" section), especially when a beneficiary is hospitalized or receives care in a skilled nursing facility. Medigap plans cover all or a portion of Medicare deductibles and copayments/coinsurance. Federal law requires that only standardized plans be sold, with each containing uniform benefits to help consumers decide which plan best suits their needs. Ten federally approved standard plans exist, but not all states have all the plans available.

Medigap plans do not cover extended long-term care, vision care, dental care, hearing aids, or private-duty nursing. Premiums vary according to the plan selected and the insurance company selling the plan.

Private Insurance Under the Affordable Care Act

Under the ACA, health insurance was expanded through three primary avenues:

- Effective September 2010, insurers were mandated to enroll young adults until the age of 26 under their parents' plans. This part of the law helped mainly nonpoor young adults gain insurance coverage (Berger, 2015; Han et al., 2016).
- The government established state-based health insurance exchanges (also called "marketplaces") through which individuals could purchase private insurance meeting the ACA criteria. These plans are called "qualified health plans." The Web-based exchanges were meant to create competition among insurers offering ACA-compliant plans. Premium subsidies, in the form of tax credits, were made available to people with incomes between 100% and 400% of the federal poverty level (FPL),[1] provided they did not qualify for Medicaid or employment-based coverage. These subsidies played a critical role in the public's embrace of the ACA. People with incomes up to 250% of FPL also became eligible for reductions in cost sharing (deductibles and copayments) if they purchased a silver plan.[2] The cost-sharing reductions were passed on to the insurers in the form of subsidies.
- The federal government offered monetary incentives to the states to expand the state-based Medicaid programs.

By 2016, an estimated 20 million uninsured adults had gained health insurance coverage because of the ACA from all three sources just described; this figure stayed stable at least through 2018 (McMorrow, et al., 2020). Much less publicized, however, was the fact that 6 million people lost the insurance they previously had (Manchikanti et al., 2017). In 2016, 12.7 million individuals were enrolled in plans sold through the exchanges (Uberoi et al., 2016). These figures—gains in insurance as well as exchange enrollments—fell far short of projections by the Congressional Budget Office (CBO) that there would be a total coverage gain of 32 million, out of which 21 million people would be enrolled in the exchanges in 2016 (CBO, 2010). Overall, exchange premium subsidies have produced 40% of the coverage gains, with expansion of states' Medicaid programs leading to the other 60% (Frean et al., 2017).

Overall, the individual market has continued its recent trajectory of increased participation by insurers and consumers since ACA launched in 2014. Pricing has largely stabilized in the past several years, and consumer access has grown as newer, tech-enabled insurers bring greater choice to the market. But uncertainty remains, in part because the enhanced premium subsidies created by the American Rescue Plan Act were due to expire at the end of 2022.

The ACA's employer mandate for providing job-based health insurance went into effect in 2015. This mandate applied to employers with 50 or more full-time equivalent (FTE) workers. Often referred to as a **play-or-pay** mandate, it required employers to either provide their employees with health insurance (play) or pay a penalty for not doing so. The mandate was intended to prevent employers

---

1 The 100% FPL was an annual income of $26,200 for a family of four in 2020 (higher in Alaska and Hawaii).

2 Based on their actuarial value, four tiers of plans (bronze, silver, gold, and platinum) are specified in the ACA. The silver plan theoretically covers 70% of the cost of medical care.

from dropping health insurance coverage for their workers. The ACA employer mandate remained in effect in 2021 and beyond (Tax professionals, 2021; Health Insurance Organization, 2023).

The ACA also included an individual mandate that required all legal residents of the United States to have health insurance, or else pay a penalty tax. This mandate was aimed primarily at pushing people—especially healthy individuals—into buying coverage through the exchanges if they did not qualify for any other health insurance. The purpose was to balance high users of healthcare services with those who would use much less. In any event, the individual mandate did not have a notable effect on coverage gains (Frean et al., 2017). In subsequent health reform efforts under the Trump administration, most Americans supported the idea of eliminating the individual mandate (Kirzinger et al., 2017). Effective 2019, the penalty was eliminated.

Economic events, such as the recession of 2008 and job losses because of business interruptions during the COVID-19 crisis in 2020, can affect the stability of insurance coverage (Gai and Jones, 2020). The ACA did not address the issue of short-term insurance interruptions. In the first 10 years after the passage of the ACA, 25% of the U.S. population experienced at least one uninsured spell in a given two-year period. Gai and Jones (2020) also observed an increased probability of reduced access to care and a decrease in the use of preventive services among people with insurance gaps. Nevertheless, such interruptions did not seem to affect people's health status and health behavior, such as weight control.

Private Insurance Under Trump's Healthcare Reform

In 2017, the Republican-controlled Congress failed to carry out President Trump's campaign promise to "repeal and replace Obamacare." Then, in 2018, the Democrats gained control of the U.S. House of Representatives, which dampened any prospects that Congress might work with the Trump administration to reform the ACA (which the Democrats had helped create). In the remainder of his term, Trump made some progress on this front by offering alternative solutions to some of the burdensome rules in the ACA.

Small businesses had found it particularly difficult to offer health insurance to their employees. In 2018, the administration loosened certain requirements in association health plans (AHPs). The new rules would allow any group of people, such as small businesses and the self-employed, to enroll in an AHP. The rules crafted by the U.S. Department of Labor (DOL) were designed to make health insurance more affordable by eliminating certain ACA rules, such as those pertaining to "essential health benefits." The CBO estimated that millions of people would switch their coverage to more affordable and more flexible AHP plans and save thousands of dollars in premiums. It also estimated that 400,000 previously uninsured people would gain coverage under AHPs (DOL, 2018). In March 2019, a federal judge struck down the program just before it was ready to go into effect, indicating that it violated the ACA.

In 2018, the Trump administration wrote new rules that would allow people to enroll in affordable short-term health plans for up to 36 months. This type of coverage is exempt from the definition of individual health insurance under the ACA; hence, the ACA mandates do not apply. This offering was also tested in the courts, and a federal judge as well as an appellate court ruled in favor of the administration.

Cost-sharing subsidies to insurers were eliminated effective 2018 because they were not explicitly appropriated by the ACA legislation. Even after the Trump administration cut the subsidy payments, insurers remained legally obligated to pay them to qualifying enrollees in silver plans. To compensate for the additional costs to the insurers, many states allowed them to place the entire cost of subsidies onto the silver plans, a practice known as silver loading (Drake and Anderson, 2020), which made the premiums go up for silver plans only. This made zero-dollar premium plans (essentially free plans after premium tax credits) more attractive to qualified consumers. Such was the case in the least expensive bronze plans. The rush to zero-dollar premium plans caused a 14.1% increase (200,000 enrollees) in marketplace enrollment among individuals with incomes of 151% to 200% of the Federal Poverty Line (FPL). These plans will be a feature of the marketplaces indefinitely (Drake and Anderson, 2020).

In January of 2020, the individual coverage HRAs took effect. Under the new rule, employers can pay as much as they want toward workers' individual plans on a pre-tax basis. Employees must enroll in an ACA-compliant individual plan or Medicare to receive the funds. The federal government projected that 800,000 employers would offer individual coverage HRAs to more than 11 million employees in the subsequent 5 years (Livingston, 2020a).

The Biden Administration, which took office in 2020, restored most of the restrictions placed on ACA by the Trump Administration.

Effects of the Affordable Care Act

The ACA has not only reduced the rate of uninsurance but also improved affordability of coverage, especially for low- to middle-income people. Some evidence also suggests that among those individuals who gained insurance through the ACA, there is a greater likelihood of having a usual source of care (Blumenthal et al., 2020). Access to health care has been uneven, however, with access for Medicaid beneficiaries being hampered by the relatively small networks of providers who take this insurance. Those who obtain insurance via the exchanges or who have employer benefits have faced high out-of-pocket costs. This is because of increased regulations and other costs faced by insurers who must cover services called "essential" that not everyone needs.

Enrollment shortfalls in the exchanges have also limited insurer participation in low-enrollment geographic areas. Consequently, the expectation of competition was not quite realized. As a result, marketplace premiums were 50% ($180) higher, on average, in areas with monopolist insurers, compared to those with more than two insurers (Parys, 2018). Changes in insurer participation and plan availability also negatively affected the marketplaces' ability to provide a stable source of health care (McKillop et al., 2018). The effects of the Affordable Care Act on insurance, access, and cost are summarized below.

Insurance Coverage

- **Expansion of Medicaid:** The Affordable Care Act protected millions of unemployed people and their families from losing coverage (Agarwal and Sommers, 2020). In the 36 states that opted to expand their Medicaid programs, expansion removed asset tests and categorical eligibility requirements (for example, policies that required enrollees to be disabled, pregnant, or parents of dependent children) and extended eligibility to all U.S. citizens and qualifying documented immigrants with incomes below 138% of the federal poverty level (Agarwal and Sommers, 2020).
- **Marketplace subsidies:** People with incomes of 100–400% of poverty who were not eligible for Medicaid or employer-sponsored coverage qualified for income-based Advance Premium Tax Credits for plans offered through new Marketplaces (Glied et al., 2020). Federal subsidies also provided greater out-of-pocket spending protection to people with incomes under 250% of poverty, including lower cost sharing and a reduced out-of-pocket spending limit (Glied et al., 2020).

- **Employer-based coverage provisions:** Beginning in 2010 all insurers and employers offering coverage were required to allow young adults up to age twenty-six to remain on their parents' policies (Glied et al., 2020). In addition, employers with more than fifty employees were required to offer minimal essential insurance to their employees and family members or face a penalty if an employee became eligible for a Marketplace tax credit because of the lack of employer-based coverage (Glied et al., 2020).
- **Insurance market reforms:** The ACA imposed several regulations on the insurance industry, including the requirement to spend a certain percentage of premium revenue on health care (the medical loss ratio) and the prohibition of rescissions (cancellations) of policies except in cases of fraud (Glied et al., 2020).
- **Dependent coverage for young adults:** Many studies have examined the effects of the ACA's dependent coverage provisions as mentioned above, generally by comparing trends among eligible young adults (those ages 19–25) and slightly older noneligible adults (those ages 26–30) (Breslau et al., 2018). Such studies found that young adult coverage increased, with estimates of the improvement ranging from 4.6% to 7.4% (Breslau et al., 2018).

Healthcare Access

- **Increased access through expanded insurance coverage:** Based on enrollment data from 2022 and early 2023, over 40 million people are currently enrolled in Marketplace or Medicaid expansion coverage related to provisions of the ACA, the highest total on record (The Assistant Secretary for Planning and Evaluation, 2023).
- **More comprehensive and accessible health plans:** According to the Biden Administration, starting in 2023, ACA insurance plans are required to have a foundation in clinical considerations and should not show bias concerning age, anticipated lifespan, existing or anticipated disabilities, level of medical reliance, well-being, or other medical factors (Policy Center for Maternal Mental Health, 2022).
- **Impact on health disparities:** The ACA aimed to reduce healthcare disparities by improving access for minority and low-income populations (Buchmueller & Levy, 2020). Early research on the ACA found that insurance coverage increased more for Black and Hispanic adults than for White adults, which slightly reduced disparities in coverage (Buchmueller & Levy, 2020).

Healthcare Costs

- **Decreased healthcare costs on the healthcare marketplaces:** The affordability of health insurance coverage in the Marketplace has reached unprecedented levels. As a result, 80% of individuals were able to discover a monthly plan for $10 or even less. Moreover, during the 2022 Open Enrollment Period, 28% of all enrollees opted for coverage priced at $10 or less after benefiting from ACA subsidies (Centers for Medicare & Medicaid Services, 2022).
- **Health insurance premiums:** The ACA brought about changes in the health insurance market. While it made insurance more affordable for many through subsidies, it also led to premium increases for some, especially for those who didn't qualify for subsidies (Hoagland and Shafer, 2021). This mixed impact on premiums sparked debate about whether the ACA truly made health care more affordable for everyone (Hoagland and Shafer, 2021).
- **Reduced out-of-pocket costs:** The ACA introduced cost-sharing reductions and out-of-pocket expense caps for low- and middle-income individuals and families. These measures aimed to limit the financial

burden on patients, making health care more affordable for those with insurance coverage (Hoagland and Shafer, 2021).
- **Preventive services:** The ACA mandated that insurance plans cover a range of preventive services without co-pays or deductibles (Hoagland and Shafer, 2021). This eliminated cost barriers for essential preventive care, which, in the long run, can reduce overall healthcare costs by catching and treating diseases early (Hoagland and Shafer, 2021).
- **Accountable Care Organizations (ACOs):** ACOs, encouraged by the ACA, aimed to improve care coordination and quality, potentially reducing unnecessary costs associated with fragmented care (Wilson et al., 2020). Wilson et al. (2020) also identified one recent systematic review and 59 primary studies and pointed out ACOs help reduce costs, including outpatient expenses and the delivery of low-value services.
- **Cost-sharing subsidies:** The ACA provided subsidies to low- and middle-income individuals to help with cost-sharing requirements like co-pays and deductibles, further reducing out-of-pocket expenses for many enrollees (Hoagland and Shafer, 2021).

Private Insurance and the COVID-19 Pandemic

The onset of COVID-19 pandemic was accompanied by an unprecedentedly large, swift decline in employment, with the unemployment rate peaking at 14.7% in April 2020 and steadily declining to 6.7% in December 2020 (Bundorf et al., 2021). Because employer-sponsored insurance (ESI) is the primary source of coverage for working-age adults, losing a job not only leads to loss of income but may also lead to loss of health insurance (Bundorf et al., 2021). Job loss was associated with a 2.2 percentage point increase in the likelihood of loss of health insurance overall, and with a 4.4 percentage point increase in the likelihood of loss of ESI coverage (Mandal et al., 2022). There was a statistically significant increase in Medicaid enrollment in expansion states, by 3.2 percentage points (Mandal et al., 2022).

Frenier et al. (2020) compiled Medicaid enrollment reports covering the period from March 1 through June 1, 2020, for twenty-six states and found that in these twenty-six states, Medicaid covered more than 1.7 million additional Americans in roughly a three-month period.

Under the Coronavirus Aid, Relief, and Economic Security (CARES) Act, the federal government reimbursed providers at Medicare rates for treating patients who are uninsured (King, 2020). The major U.S. health insurers joined Medicare and Medicaid in waiving all copayments to treat COVID-19-related illness, even though this gesture was not required by any legislation. Also, telemedicine was covered for medical consultations between patients and their doctors.

COVID-19 has forced the insurance provider to bring major process level changes such as adapting to work from remote locations, providing training and equipping staff members to work under social distancing regulations, improve the cybersecurity protocols, and simplify claims/premium processing using online payment channels (Babuna et al., 2020). Health insurance providers need to devise insurance policies incorporating the features of home health, telemedicine, and income protection features (Dutta and Singh, 2021).

Trends in Employment-Based Health Insurance

Employers are the main source of health insurance in the United States; they provide health benefits for about 153 million people, or approximately 46% of the U.S.

population. Most employees are offered health coverage at work, and most them who are offered coverage take it. Some employees may not be covered by their own employer for any of several reasons. Their employer may not offer coverage, they may not be eligible for the benefits offered by their firm, they may elect to receive coverage through their spouse's employer, or they may refuse coverage from their employers (Claxton et al., 2019, p. 65).

Table 6-1 shows, by employer size, the percentage of U.S. employers that offered health insurance and the percentage of employees who were covered from 2005 to 2022. Over the span included in the table, fewer small employers offered coverage, and a smaller proportion of their employees were covered. For large employers, a slight uptick in the offer rates was noted, yet the proportion of employees covered declined. The exact reasons for these trends are not quite clear, although one report has suggested that more than 5.7 million small-business employees or self-employed workers are enrolled in the ACA marketplaces and that more than half of all ACA marketplace enrollees are small-business owners, self-employed individuals, or small-business employees (Chase and Arensmeyer, 2018). In small businesses, 70% of employees prefer higher wages instead of health insurance. In addition, the percentage of employees who take advantage of health insurance when it is offered is lower among lower-wage earners, younger employees, and those employed in for-profit businesses (Claxton et al., 2019, pp. 63, 69). Furthermore, those who qualify for Medicaid have little or no incentives to take up employer-based insurance (Capatina, 2020).

Premium Costs in Employment-Based Plans

The cost of family plans has increased more rapidly than the cost of single-insured plans. Employers have passed on slightly more of the costs to their employees for family plans, but not for single plans (**Table 6-2**). Between 2010 and 2022, the increase in premiums far exceeded the rise in the Consumer Price Index (a measure of inflation), which was 17.5% (U.S. Bureau of Labor Statistics, 2020).

Table 6-1 Trends in Employment-Based Health Insurance, Selected Years

	Workforce Size	2005	2010	2015	2019	2020	2021	2022
Percentage of employers offering health insurance	Small employers (<200 workers)	59	68	56	56		56	47
	Large employers (200+ workers)	97	99	98	99		99	98
	All employers	60	69	57	57			
Percentage of workers covered	Small employers (<200 workers)	65	63	61	60	42	45	49
	Large employers (200+ workers)	67	63	63	61	20	22	25
	All employers	68	63	63	61	26	29	32

Data from Kaiser Family Foundation. 2022. *Employer health benefits: 2022 annual survey.* San Francisco, CA: Author.

Table 6-2 Trends in Premium Costs, Selected Years

		2005	2010	2015	2019	Percent Increase, 2010–2019	2022	Percent Increase, 2017–2022
Total annual premiums costs (dollars)	Single plan	4,024	5,049	6,251	7,188	42.4	7,911	20
	Family plan	10,880	13,770	17,545	20,576	49.4	22,463	20
Employer contribution (% of total cost)	Single plan	84.8	82.2	82.9	82.7	43.3		20
	Family plan	75.1	71	71.8	70.8	49		20
Employee contribution (% of total cost)	Single plan	15.2	17.8	17.1	17.3	38.2		20

Data from Kaiser Family Foundation. 2022. *Employer health benefits: 2022 annual survey.* San Francisco, CA: Author.

Cost Sharing in Employment-Based Plans

The most common forms of cost sharing are deductibles and copayments (or coinsurance) that enrollees must pay when using healthcare services. In 2022, for workers with single coverage in a plan with a general annual deductible, the average annual deductible is $1,763, specifically, $1,451 in HMOs, $1,322 in PPOs, and $2,539 in HDHP/SOs (KFF, 2022). For family plans, the deductibles ranged between $3,124 for HMO plans and $4,766 for HDHPs. The average copayment was $27 for primary care physician office visits and $44 for specialty physician office visits (KFF, 2022).

As of 2023, the employer mandate penalties are as follows: for a large employer that doesn't offer coverage at all: $2,880 multiplied by 30 less than the total number of full-time employees; for a large employer that offers coverage that isn't considered affordable and/or doesn't provide minimum value: $4,320 multiplied by the number of full-time employees who receive a premium tax credit in the marketplace (but this penalty will not exceed the amount of the other penalty, so that will be used instead if it's less) (Health Insurance Organization, 2023).

Public Health Insurance

Since 1965, government financing has played a significant role in expanding healthcare services, mainly to those who otherwise would not be able to afford them. Today, a significant proportion of healthcare services in the United States are supported through public programs; they cover more than one-third of the U.S. population (refer to Figure 6-2). This section discusses the financing, eligibility requirements, and services covered under the various public health insurance programs and the effects of the ACA on these services.

Public financing supports **categorical programs**, each of which is designed to benefit a certain category of people. Examples are Medicare for older adults and certain individuals with disabilities, Medicaid for the indigent, Department of Defense programs for active service members and their families, and VA health care for war veterans. Even though the government finances public insurance, for the most part, healthcare services are obtained through the private sector. An exception is the VA program, in which the financing, insurance, delivery, and payment functions are largely integrated.

Medicare

The Medicare program, also referred to as Title 18 of the Social Security Act, finances medical care for three groups of people: (1) persons 65 years and older, (2) individuals with disabilities who are entitled to Social Security benefits, and (3) people who have end-stage renal disease (ESRD—permanent kidney failure, requiring dialysis or a kidney transplant). People in these three categories can enroll regardless of their income status.

Shortly after its creation in 1967, the Medicare program had 19.5 million beneficiaries (National Center for Health Statistics [NCHS], 1996, p. 263). In March 2023, Medicare covered more than 65.7 million beneficiaries—a more than threefold increase in 55 years. The number of beneficiaries has continued to increase mainly because of the aging of the U.S. population, but also because of the two additional categories of people that were added after the program had been created for older adults. In 2022, approximately 12% of the beneficiaries were younger individuals with disabilities (Centers for Medicare and Medicaid Services [CMS], 2023a).

Medicare is a federal program operated under the administrative oversight of the Centers for Medicare and Medicaid Services, a branch of the Department of Health and Human Services (DHHS). Because it is a federal program, eligibility criteria and benefits are consistent throughout the United States.

The Balanced Budget Act (BBA) of 1997 established an independent federal agency, the Medicare Payment Advisory Commission (MedPAC), to advise the U.S. Congress on various issues affecting the Medicare program. MedPAC's statutory mandate includes analysis of payments to healthcare providers participating in Medicare, access to care, and quality of care.

For almost 30 years after its inception, Medicare had a dual structure comprising two separate insurance programs referred to as Part A and Part B. It has since become a four-part program.

Part A: Hospital Insurance

Part A, the Hospital Insurance (HI) portion of Medicare, is a true **entitlement** program. Throughout their working lives, people contribute to Medicare through special payroll taxes; hence, they are entitled to Part A benefits regardless of the amount of income and assets they may have at age 65. The employer and the employee share equally in financing the HI trust fund. All working individuals, including those who are self-employed, pay the mandatory taxes. Since 1994, all earnings have been subject to Medicare tax.

To qualify for Part A, a person or the person's spouse must have worked, earned a minimum specified amount, and paid Medicare taxes for at least 40 quarters (10 years) to earn at least 40 credits. People who have earned less than 40 credits can get Part A by paying a monthly premium.

Part A covers inpatient services for acute-care hospitals, psychiatric hospitals, inpatient rehabilitation facilities, skilled nursing facility (SNF) services, home health visits, and hospice care. Following is an overview of the type of benefits provided under Part A:

1. A maximum of 90 days of inpatient hospital care is allowed per benefit period. Once the 90 days are exhausted, a lifetime reserve of 60 additional hospital inpatient days remains. A **benefit period** is a spell of illness beginning with hospitalization and ending when a beneficiary has not been an inpatient in a hospital or an SNF for 60 consecutive days. The number of benefit periods is unlimited. These rules apply to acute-care hospitals and inpatient rehabilitation facilities.
2. A total of 90 days of care per spell of illness is allowed for treatment in a psychiatric inpatient facility, with a 60-day lifetime

reserve. Lifetime use is limited to 190 days of treatment.
3. Medicare pays for up to 100 days of care in a Medicare-certified SNF, subsequent to inpatient hospitalization for at least 3 consecutive days, not including the day of discharge. Admission to the SNF must occur within 30 days of hospital discharge.
4. Medicare pays for home health care obtained from a Medicare-certified home health agency when a person is homebound and requires intermittent or part-time skilled nursing care or rehabilitation. Medicare defines "intermittent" as skilled nursing care that is needed or given either for fewer than 7 days a week, or daily for less than 8 hours each day for up to 21 days (CMS, 2017).
5. For patients who are terminally ill, Medicare pays for care provided by a Medicare-certified hospice.

A deductible applies to each benefit period (except to home health and hospice), and copayments are based on the duration of services (except for home health). **Exhibit 6-3** gives specific details on the Part A program for 2020.

Exhibit 6-3 Medicare Part A Financing, Benefits, Deductible, and Copayments for 2020

Financing

The Hospital Insurance trust fund is financed by a payroll tax of 1.45% from the employee and 1.45% from the employer on all income. Self-employed individuals must pay the full 2.9%. As of 2013, single taxpayers earning $200,000 or more and married couples earning $250,000 or more have been required to pay an additional 0.9%, as mandated by the ACA.

Premiums: None (Those who do not qualify for premium-free coverage can buy coverage at a monthly premium of up to $458.)

Deductible: $1,408 per benefit period

Benefits	Copayments
Inpatient hospital (room, meals, nursing care, operating room services, blood transfusions, special care units, drugs and medical supplies, laboratory tests, rehabilitation therapies, and medical social services)	None for the first 60 days (benefit period) $352 per day for days 61–90 (benefit period or spell of illness in psychiatric facilities) $704 per day for days 91–150 (nonrenewable lifetime reserve days) 100% of costs after 150 days
Skilled nursing facility (after a 3-day hospital stay)	None for the first 20 days in a benefit period $176 per day for days 21–100 in a benefit period
Home health services (part-time skilled nursing care, home health aide, rehabilitation therapies, medical equipment, social services, and medical supplies)	None for home health visits 20% of approved amount for medical equipment
Hospice care	A small copayment for drugs
Inpatient psychiatric care (190-day lifetime limit)	Same as for inpatient hospital

(continues)

Exhibit 6-3 Medicare Part A Financing, Benefits, Deductible, and Copayments for 2020 *(continued)*

Noncovered Services

Long-term care
Custodial services
Personal convenience services (televisions, telephones, private-duty nurses, private rooms when not medically necessary)

Data from Centers for Medicare and Medicaid Services. Medicare costs at a glance. Available at: https://www.medicare.gov/your-medicarecosts/medicare-costs-at-a-glance. Accessed July 2020; Centers for Medicare and Medicaid Services (CMS). 2020a. *2020 annual report of the boards of trustees of the federal hospital insurance and federal supplementary medical insurance trust funds*. Available at: https://www.cms.gov/files/document/2020-medicare-trustees-report.pdf. Accessed July 2020.

Part B: Supplementary Medical Insurance

Part B, the supplementary medical insurance (SMI) portion of Medicare, is a voluntary program financed partly by general tax revenues and partly by required premium contributions. Beneficiaries bear approximately 27% of the cost of premiums (CMS, 2020a); this share has increased from 25% in 2015. Since 2007, Part B premiums have been income-based, as required by the Medicare Prescription Drug, Improvement, and Modernization Act (MMA) of 2003. Those beneficiaries whose incomes exceed a threshold amount pay a higher premium, known as the Income-Related Monthly Adjustment Amount (IRMAA). In 2023, the income threshold that triggered IRMAA was $97,000 per year ($194,000 per couple). The intent of the MMA legislation was to reduce tax-financed premium subsidies for higher-income individuals. Hence, for example, an individual earning more than $500,000 in 2023 paid $560.50 in monthly premiums, whereas someone earning less than or equal to $97,000 paid $164.90 (CMS, 2023b). Almost all persons entitled to HI also choose to enroll in SMI (92% in 2019) because they cannot get similar coverage at the same price from private insurers. The main services covered by SMI are listed in **Exhibit 6-4**. Part B also covers limited home health services under certain conditions.

Exhibit 6-4 Medicare Part B Financing, Benefits, Deductible, and Coinsurance for 2023

Financing

The general tax revenues of the federal government (approximately 73%) and monthly premiums paid by persons enrolled in Part B (approximately 27%).

Standard premium:	$164.90 per month
Income-adjusted premium[1]:	$230.80 to $560.50 per month
Deductible:	$226 annually
Coinsurance:	80/20

Main Benefits

Physician services
Emergency department services

Outpatient surgery
Diagnostic tests and laboratory services
Outpatient physical therapy, occupational therapy, and speech therapy
Outpatient mental health services
Limited home health care under certain conditions
Ambulance
Renal dialysis
Artificial limbs and braces
Blood transfusions and blood components
Organ transplants
Medical equipment and supplies
Rural health clinic services
Annual physical exam

- Wellness exam
- Preventive services (as medically needed): alcohol misuse screening and counseling, bone mass measurement, mammography, cardiovascular screening, Pap smears, colorectal cancer screening, depression screening, diabetes screening, glaucoma tests, HIV screening, nutritional counseling for diabetes and renal disease, obesity screening and counseling, prostate cancer screening, sexually transmitted infections screening, shots (flu, pneumococcal, hepatitis B), and tobacco use cessation counseling

Noncovered Services
Dental services
Hearing aids
Eyeglasses (except after cataract surgery)
Services not related to treatment or injury

[1] For single beneficiaries whose annual incomes exceed $87,000.

Data from Centers for Medicare and Medicaid Services. 2023 Medicare Part A & B Premiums and Deductibles. 2023 Medicare Part D Income-related Monthly Adjustment Amounts.

Effective January 2011, the ACA provided for an annual physical exam (called a wellness exam) for all Part B enrollees, without any cost sharing. The main purpose of the wellness exam is to do a risk assessment and develop an individualized prevention plan.

Part C: Medicare Advantage

Part C is, in reality, not a new benefit program because it does not add specifically defined new services. Instead, it provides some additional choices of health plans, with the objective of channeling a greater number of beneficiaries into managed care. The BBA of 1997 authorized the Medicare+Choice program, which took effect on January 1, 1998. Medicare+Choice was renamed Medicare Advantage (MA) under the MMA of 2003. Beneficiaries have the option to remain in the original Medicare fee-for-service program, and if the CMS has contracted with an MCO that serves a beneficiary's geographic area, the beneficiary has the option to join the Medicare Advantage plan. If they join the plan, the beneficiaries receive both Part A and Part B services through the MCO. Prescription drugs under Part D are also included if offered by the MCO.

The proportion of Medicare beneficiaries covered by MA plans has risen rapidly. In 2004, 12.8% of beneficiaries were enrolled in such plans. The enrollment rate was 37.5% in 2019 and was expected to reach 40% in 2020 (CMS, 2020a). The rising enrollments are reflected in the share of Medicare expenditures devoted to MA plans (refer to Figure 6-4 later in this chapter), which were up from 27% in 2015 to 34% in 2020.

Premiums for MA plans are in addition to those paid to Medicare for Part B coverage, but some MA plans offer zero-dollar premium plans. As an incentive to enroll, beneficiaries get additional benefits that are not available in the original Medicare plan, and there is no need to purchase Medigap coverage (i.e., separate private insurance to cover costs or services not covered by traditional Medicare). MA plans may offer dental and vision coverage, for example. Part C enrollees also have lower out-of-pocket costs. Hence, Part C is a cost-effective option for many beneficiaries. Although beneficiaries enrolled in MA plans might appear to be receiving fewer postacute services than those in traditional Medicare (Skopec et al., 2020), MA enrollees actually experience shorter lengths of stay and better outcomes for postacute care than those in traditional Medicare (Cao et al., 2020). Similarly, compared with traditional Medicare beneficiaries, MA beneficiaries have lower healthcare use without any compromise in their care satisfaction and health status. Hence, MA plans may be delivering health care more efficiently (Park et al., 2020).

MA plans receive prospective, capitated payments (i.e., based on enrollments) from the HI and SMI Part B trust fund accounts. Payments are based on benchmarks that range from 95% to 115% of local fee-for-service Medicare costs, with bonus amounts payable to plans meeting high quality-of-care standards (CMS, 2020a).

The MMA of 2003 required that Medicare Advantage include special needs plans. These plans were first offered in 2005 to meet the special needs of people who were institutionalized (e.g., in nursing homes), enrolled in both Medicare and Medicaid, or had chronic or disabling conditions. Medicare Advantage Special Needs Plans (MA-SNP) are available in limited areas, and not all plans cover all special needs situations.

In 2023, 30.8 million people are enrolled in a Medicare Advantage plan, accounting for more than half (51%) of the eligible Medicare population and $454 billion (54%) of total federal Medicare spending (net of premiums). The average Medicare beneficiary in 2023 has access to 43 Medicare Advantage plans, the largest number of options ever (Ochieng et al., 2023).

The share of Medicare beneficiaries enrolled in Medicare Advantage varies widely across counties. In 2023, nearly one third (31%) of Medicare beneficiaries live in a county where at least 60% of all Medicare beneficiaries are enrolled in Medicare Advantage plans, while 10% live in a county where less than one third of all Medicare beneficiaries are enrolled in Medicare Advantage plans. The wide variation in county enrollment rates could reflect several factors, such as differences in firm strategy, urbanicity of the county, Medicare payment rates, number of Medicare beneficiaries, healthcare use patterns, and historical Medicare Advantage market penetration (Ochieng et al., 2023).

Medicare Advantage enrollment is highly concentrated among a small number of firms. UnitedHealthcare and Humana account for nearly half (47%) of all Medicare Advantage enrollees nationwide, and in nearly a third of counties (32%; or 1,013 counties), these two firms account for at least 75% of Medicare Advantage enrollment (Ochieng et al., 2023). Refer to **Exhibit 6-5** for pros and cons regarding the plan.

Part D: Prescription Drug Coverage

Part D was added to the existing Medicare program under the MMA of 2003 and was fully implemented in 2006. Part D is available to anyone who has coverage under Part A or Part B.

Exhibit 6-5 Pros and Cons Regarding Medicare Advantage

Pros
- **Lower or no monthly costs:** Medicare Advantage plans often charge little or nothing in monthly premiums (Eisenberg, 2023). Medicare Advantage plans are usually a good choice for those who have routine healthcare needs and don't need complex or expensive treatments (Deventer, 2023).
- **Bundled coverage:** Medicare Advantage plans bundle Medicare Part A and Medicare Part B, which cover inpatient and outpatient medical care (Deventer, 2023). They also usually include Part D prescription drug coverage (Deventer, 2023).
- **Extra benefits:** Medicare Advantage plans provide extra coverage that's not available with traditional Medicare, which includes vision, hearing, and dental services, gym memberships, preventive chiropractic care, and allowances for over-the-counter supplements (Deventer, 2023).

Cons
- **Limited provider networks:** Some Medicare Advantage plans limit the doctors and hospitals that you can use if you want your medical bills covered (Deventer, 2023). In contrast, Original Medicare lets you go to any doctor that accepts Medicare, and more than 90% of primary-care physicians take Medicare (Deventer, 2023).
- **Higher costs if you have extensive medical needs:** Medicare Advantage plans can be more expensive if you need a lot of medical care or complex medical care (Deventer, 2023).

Data from Eisenberg, R. (2023, August 9). The pros and cons of Medicare Advantage plans. FortuneWell. https://fortune.com/well/2023/08/09/pros-cons-of-medicare-advantage-plans/; Deventer, C. (2023, October 13). Top Advantages & Disadvantages of Medicare Advantage. Value Penguin. https://www.valuepenguin.com/advantages-disadvantages-medicare-advantage

---

This prescription drug program requires payment of a monthly premium to Medicare, which is in addition to the premium paid for Part B. Certain low-income beneficiaries are automatically enrolled without having to pay a premium. The ACA imposed an IRMAA, such that people in certain income categories pay higher premiums.

Coverage is offered through two types of private plans approved by Medicare. Stand-alone prescription drug plans (PDPs) that offer only drug coverage are used mainly by those who want to stay in the original Medicare fee-for-service program. In contrast, Medicare Advantage Prescription Drug plans (MA-PDs) are available to those persons who are enrolled in Part C if the MCO provides prescription drug coverage—and most do.

The premiums for Part D are established by each plan; the additional income-based IRMAA, if applicable, is established by and paid directly to Medicare. For 2020, the monthly IRMAA ranged between $12.20 and $76.40. The Part D program also requires payment of a deductible, following which a basic level of coverage becomes available. After that, a coverage gap, or "doughnut hole," requires the beneficiary to pay the cost of drugs until a specific level of spending is reached. This gap is then followed by a catastrophic level of coverage (**Exhibit 6-6**). Special provisions in the program are designed to help low-income enrollees by keeping their out-of-pocket costs to a minimum. Under the ACA, all Part D drugs must be covered under a manufacturer discount agreement with the CMS. The beneficiaries receive discounts on drugs while in the coverage gap.

Medicare Out-of-Pocket Costs

Medicare carries relatively high deductibles, copayments, and premiums. Eyeglasses, dental care, and many long-term care services are not covered, and there is no limit

Exhibit 6-6 Medicare Part D Benefits and Individual Out-of-Pocket Costs for 2023

Premiums	Established by the plan, plus IRMAA (if applicable)
Deductible	$505 annually
Three levels of benefits and out-of-pocket costs beyond the $435 deductible:	
Initial coverage	Copayments/coinsurance are paid by the beneficiary. After total payments by the plan and the beneficiary have reached $4,020, the coverage gap (also called the "doughnut hole") kicks in.
Coverage gap	Beneficiary pays no more than 25% of the cost of drugs.
	Coverage gap ends when the beneficiary has spent $6,350 out of pocket (for brand-name drugs, the manufacturer's discount also counts toward out-of-pocket spending).
Catastrophic level	Beneficiary pays a small coinsurance (about 5%) or copayment.

The Extra Help Program
A special part of the Medicare drug coverage program called Extra Help is designed to serve people who have low incomes and savings. This group of beneficiaries includes those who receive Medicaid or Supplemental Security Income. For those who qualify, the out-of-pocket costs are minimal.

Data from Centers for Medicare and Medicaid Services. 2023 Medicare Part A & B Premiums and Deductibles. 2023 Medicare Part D Income-related Monthly Adjustment Amounts.

on out-of-pocket expenses, except that all MA plans have cost-sharing limits ($6,700 when in-network providers are used). The traditional Medicare program has no out-of-pocket maximums. Hence, most Medicare beneficiaries are left with high out-of-pocket costs, which represent an important share of their incomes. Medicaid (provided the beneficiary qualifies), employer retirement benefits, and purchase of Medigap plans (discussed previously) are some of the ways that individuals may pay for most of these out-of-pocket costs.

Medicare Enrolled Population and Total Expenditures

Medicare consumes more than one-fifth of the United States' national health expenditures. Data on enrolled population and expenditures appear in **Table 6-3**. During the 2010–2019 period, Medicare expenditures grew at an annual rate of 4.8% (further declined to 2.1% between 2009 and 2021), a vast improvement over the 9% growth rate during the 2000–2010 decade. Over the same period, total national health expenditures grew by 4.4% annually. Policies driven by the ACA have been largely credited with this improvement.

Medicare Financing and Spending for Services

Data on Medicare financing and spending appear in **Figure 6-3** and **Figure 6-4**. General taxes fund most of the Medicare expenditures, followed by payroll taxes. Since 2017, expenditures for MA plans have exceeded the payments to hospitals.

Public Health Insurance 261

Table 6-3 Medicare: Enrolled Population and Expenditures in Selected Years

1970	1980	1990	2000	2010	2019	2021
Population Covered (in Millions)							
20.4	28.4	34.3	39.7	47.7	61.2	
Expenditures (in Billions)							
$7.50	$36.80	$111.00	$221.80	$522.90	$796.20	$4,255.10
Proportion of Total U.S. Healthcare Expenditures							
10.00%	14.50%	15.50%	16.40%	20.20%	20.9%[1]	18.30%
Average Annual Increase in Expenditures from the Previous Year Shown							
	17%	12%	7%	9%	4.80%	2.70%

[1]Projected total national healthcare expenditures for 2019: $3,814.6 billion.

Data from National Center for Health Statistics (NCHS). 2012. *Health, United States, 2012.* Hyattsville, MD: U.S. Department of Health and Human Services. pp. 323, 356; Centers for Medicare and Medicaid Services (CMS, 2020a). *2020 annual report of the boards of trustees of the federal hospital insurance and federal supplementary medical insurance trust funds.* p. 10. Available at: https://www.cms.gov/files/document/2020-medicare-trustees-report.pdf. Accessed July 2020. 2021 Data: Centers for Medicare and Medicaid Services (2023). NHE Tables.

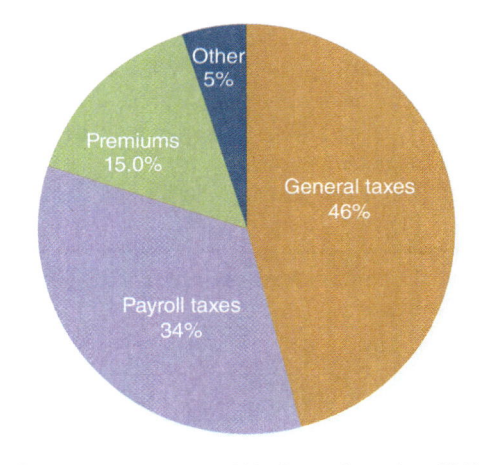

Figure 6-3 Sources of Medicare financing, 2021.

Data from Centers for Medicare and Medicaid Services (CMS). 2023. 2022 Annual report of the boards of trustees of the federal hospital insurance and federal supplementary medical insurance trust funds.

- General taxes 46%
- Payroll taxes 34%
- Premiums 15.0%
- Other 5%

Medicare Trust Funds

The Medicare program consists of two trust funds: the Hospital Insurance (HI) Trust Fund, which covers Part A, and the Supplementary Medical Insurance (SMI) Trust Fund, which covers Part B and Part D (Antos & Capretta, 2020). Each trust fund accounts for its own incomes and expenditures. Taxes, premiums, and other revenues are credited to the respective trust funds, and payments for services to Medicare recipients and administrative costs are the only purposes for which disbursements from the funds can be made.

Table 6-4 compares the trust fund results for 2015 and 2022. Despite COVID-19, Medicare trust funds showed significant improvement, as demonstrated in the surplus of HI and SMI funds between 2015 and 2022. Numerous factors affect the solvency of these trust funds. For example, future Medicare expenditures depend on the size of the population eligible for benefits, changes in the volume and intensity of services, and medical price inflation. The future HI trust fund income depends on the size of the workforce and the level of workers' earnings. These factors depend, in turn, on future birth rates, death rates, labor force participation rates,

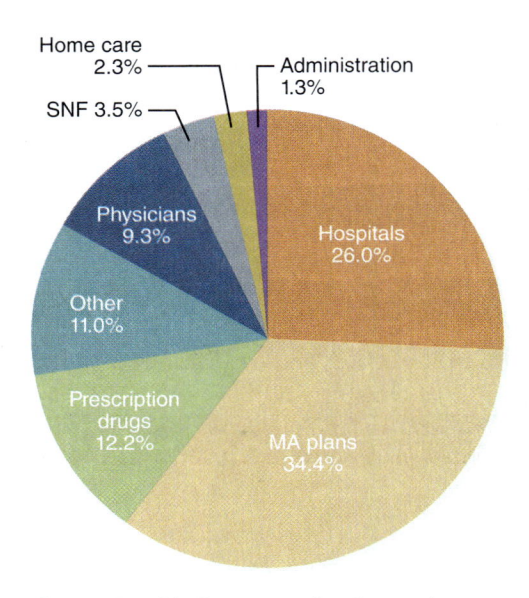

Figure 6-4 Medicare spending for services.

Data from Centers for Medicare and Medicaid Services (CMS). 2020a. *2020 Annual report of the boards of trustees of the federal hospital insurance and federal supplementary medical insurance trust funds.* Available at: https://www.cms.gov/files/document/2020-medicare-trustees-report.pdf. Accessed July 2020.

Pie chart values: Hospitals 26.0%, MA plans 34.4%, Prescription drugs 12.2%, Other 11.0%, Physicians 9.3%, SNF 3.5%, Home care 2.3%, Administration 1.3%.

services, including hospital care, skilled nursing facilities, home health care, and hospice care. COVID-19 caused the Medicare Part A program and the Hospital Insurance (HI) Trust Fund to contend with large reductions in revenues due to increased unemployment, reductions in salaries, shifts to part-time employment from full time, and a reduction in labor force participation. In addition to revenue declines, there was a 20% increase in payments to hospitals for COVID-19-related care and elimination of cost sharing associated with treatment of COVID-19. Furthermore, a part of the hospital relief effort, the Advance Payment Program, is adding to claims made against the Part A program (Cutlere et al., 2020).

The SMI Trust Fund covers physician services, outpatient care, and prescription drug coverage (Antos & Capretta, 2020). COVID-19 pandemic led to increased spending on Part B due to telehealth services and the vaccination effort. However, Part D (prescription drug) costs are driven more by the prices and use of drugs than by specific pandemic-related factors (Frank & Neuman, 2021). The SMI Trust Fund is designed to respond flexibly to changes in spending, so it has not faced the same long-term solvency issues as the HI Trust Fund (Frank & Neuman, 2021).

wage increases, and many other economic and demographic factors affecting Medicare (CMS, 2020a).

As mentioned earlier, Medicare HI trust fund provides the money pool for Part A

Table 6-4 Status of Hospital Insurance (HI) and Supplementary Medical Insurance (SMI) Trust Funds, 2015–2022 (Billions of Dollars)

	HI 2015	HI 2022	SMI 2015	SMI 2022
Assets at the beginning of year	$197.3	$142.7	$369.0	$183
Revenues	275.4	396.6	369.0	591.9
Expenditures	278.9	342.7	368.8	562.4
Difference between revenues and expenditures	−3.5	53.9	0.2	29.5
Assets at the end of year	193.8	196.6	69.5	212.5

Data from Centers for Medicare and Medicaid Services (CMS). 2017. *2016 Annual report of the boards of trustees of the federal hospital insurance and federal supplementary medical insurance trust funds.* Centers for Medicare and Medicaid Services (CMS). 2023. *2022 Annual report of the boards of trustees of the federal hospital insurance and federal supplementary medical insurance trust funds.*

Medicaid

Medicaid, also referred to as Title 19 of the Social Security Act, was originally designed to finance healthcare services for the indigent. Hence, Medicaid is almost entirely a taxpayer-financed program and is the largest source of health insurance for the low-income population in the United States. Since its inception, Medicaid has been a **means-tested program**, meaning that eligibility depends on people's financial resources. Each state administers its own Medicaid program under federal guidelines.

Medicaid is jointly financed by the federal and state governments. The federal government provides matching funds to the states based on the per capita income in each state. By law, federal matching—known as the Federal Medical Assistance Percentage (FMAP)—cannot be less than 50% of total state Medicaid program costs. Wealthier states have a smaller share of their costs reimbursed by the federal government and vice versa.

Rules for Medicaid Eligibility

Three main categories of people are automatically eligible for Medicaid: (1) families with children receiving support under the Temporary Assistance for Needy Families (TANF) program; (2) people receiving Supplemental Security Income (SSI), which includes many older adults, people who are blind, and individuals with disabilities who have low incomes; and (3) children and pregnant women whose family income is at or below 133% of the FPL. States, at their discretion, have defined other "medically needy" categories based on people's income and assets. The most important of these groups are individuals who are institutionalized in nursing or psychiatric facilities and individuals who are receiving community-based services but would otherwise be eligible for Medicaid if institutionalized. All of these people have to qualify based on income and assets, which must be below the threshold levels established by each state.

Dually Eligible Beneficiaries

Approximately 9 million people are dually eligible beneficiaries—that is, low-income older adults and young adults with disabilities who are entitled to Medicare, but also become eligible for some level of assistance under Medicaid. Medicare pays covered dually eligible beneficiaries' medical services first, because Medicaid is generally the payer of last resort. Medicaid may cover medical costs that Medicare does not cover or covers only partially. Coverage for dually eligible beneficiaries varies by state. Each year, the CMS releases eligibility standards for dually eligible beneficiaries (CMS, 2020b).

Medicaid Under the ACA

The primary goal of the ACA is to increase access to affordable health insurance for the uninsured and to make health insurance more affordable for those already covered. The ACA Medicaid expansion is one of the major insurance coverage provisions included in the law (Congressional Research Service, 2021). The ACA Medicaid expansion expanded Medicaid coverage to nearly all adults with incomes up to 138% of the Federal Poverty Level ($20,120 for an individual in 2023) and provided states with an enhanced federal matching rate (FMAP) for their expansion populations (KFF, 2023). In 2012, the U.S. Supreme Court struck down this mandate, giving states the option to either expand or not expand their Medicaid programs without any penalty from the federal government. By 2023, 41 states (including DC) have adopted the Medicaid expansion and 10 states have not adopted the expansion (KFF, 2023).

The ACA Medicaid expansion has significantly increased Medicaid enrollment and federal Medicaid expenditures. Overall, more than 14 million people gained insurance through Medicaid under the ACA (Medicaid and CHIP Payment and Access Commission [MACPAC], 2020). Medicaid has now become the second largest source of insurance coverage in the United States, after employer-based coverage (refer to Figure 6-2). As expected, between 2013 and 2018, total Medicaid costs in expansion states grew by 24% compared to nonexpansion states; most of the increased costs were paid by the federal government (Gruber and Sommers, 2020). In FY2018, an estimated 12.2 million individuals were newly eligible for Medicaid through the ACA Medicaid expansion (i.e., expansion adults) and total Medicaid expenditures for the expansion adults were an estimated $74.2 billion (Congressional Research Service, 2021).

Regarding access to care, an analysis of nationally representative data suggested that Medicaid expansion was associated with a modest improvement in access to primary care without an increase in emergency department (ED) use (Gotanda et al., 2020). However, another national study concluded that following full implementation of the ACA, there was a significant increase in ED patients, and this increase appeared to be primarily associated with expansion of Medicaid (Orgel et al., 2019). One goal of the ACA was to reduce use of costly ED visits.

Community health centers (CHCs) have played an important role in ensuring access to health care for patients with Medicaid because the ACA provided increased payments to CHCs. Because CHCs are not evenly distributed, a few studies have found evidence consistent with provider capacity constraints (McMorrow et al., 2020). Apart from issues with geographic distribution, CHCs face increasing difficulty in acquiring the necessary primary-care workforce; as a result, many cannot accommodate more patients (Rieselbach et al., 2019).

Some evidence suggests that beneficiaries in Medicaid-expansion states had an increased likelihood of having a doctor and a decreased likelihood of having difficulty affording medical care. However, there is no evidence of changes in self-reported well-being (Kobayashi et al., 2019). Improvements in mental health have been evident, but similar improvements in physical self-reported health among low-income Americans have not been confirmed (Griffith and Bor, 2020).

The expansion of Medicaid was linked to a more significant rise in overall survival rates over a two-year period (Ji et al, 2023). This increase was particularly noticeable among non-Hispanic Black individuals and in rural regions, underscoring the impact of Medicaid expansion in reducing healthcare disparities (Han et al., 2022). Medicaid expansion—particularly early expansion—was associated with increased rates of colorectal cancer screening among Black patients (Dee et al., 2022).

Issues with Medicaid

The main problem with Medicaid is the paltry reimbursement for providers. In consequence, some physicians and other providers do not serve Medicaid-covered patients. Medicaid reimbursement is a fraction of what is paid by Medicare and private insurers. Despite this discrepancy, the U.S. Supreme Court ruled in *Armstrong v. Exceptional Child Center, Inc.* that Medicaid providers do not have the right to seek relief in federal courts to force states to pay higher reimbursement (Huberfeld, 2015). Under the ACA, payments to Medicaid providers were brought up to Medicare levels, but only temporarily. Hence, the issue of physician participation is an ongoing challenge for this program.

Another critical issue with Medicaid is **churning**—that is, the constant exit and reentry of beneficiaries in this system as their eligibility changes. Churning occurs because many beneficiaries have incomes that may fluctuate from one month to another. Some evidence indicates that such coverage disruptions declined in states that expanded Medicaid under the ACA (Goldman and Sommers, 2020).

Medicaid Enrollment and Spending

Because of the churning phenomenon discussed in the previous section, the enrollment figures for Medicaid do not remain stable. Hence, the CMS furnishes quarterly reports on enrollments. By June 2023, Medicaid enrollment had grown to 85.6 million (CMS, 2023c), representing 55% growth in the number of enrollees since December 2013 (55.4 million), just before the ACA Medicaid policy went into effect (Snyder and Rudowitz, 2014). Total Medicaid spending between 2013 and 2018 increased by 34.2%. In 2018, total Medicaid spending amounted to $597.4 billion, of which 62% was paid by the federal government and the rest by state governments (CMS, 2019b). **Figure 6-5** summarizes the spending on the various Medicaid-covered services.

Children's Health Insurance Program

CHIP, codified as Title 21 of the Social Security Act, was initiated under the BBA of 1997 in response to the plight of uninsured children whose families' incomes exceeded the Medicaid threshold levels, which made them ineligible for Medicaid coverage. These children were estimated to number 10.1 million—nearly one-fourth of all uninsured persons—in 1996.

CHIP offers federal funds in the form of set block grants to states. To cover children up to 19 years of age, a state can expand its existing Medicaid program, establish a separate program for children, or use a combined approach. Federal law requires that ineligibility for Medicaid be established before approval for CHIP coverage. Each state establishes its own eligibility criteria for CHIP, which must comply with the federal guidelines. Income eligibility levels range from 170% to 400% of FPL meaning family whose income level is at or below the eligibility level is eligible for CHIP coverage for the child(ren). Thus, children in many families that do not qualify for Medicaid can be enrolled in CHIP. CHIP does not cover parents or adults, except for certain low-income pregnant women. Enrollment in 2018 was 9.6 million.

Similar to the case with Medicaid, CHIP financing is shared between the federal and

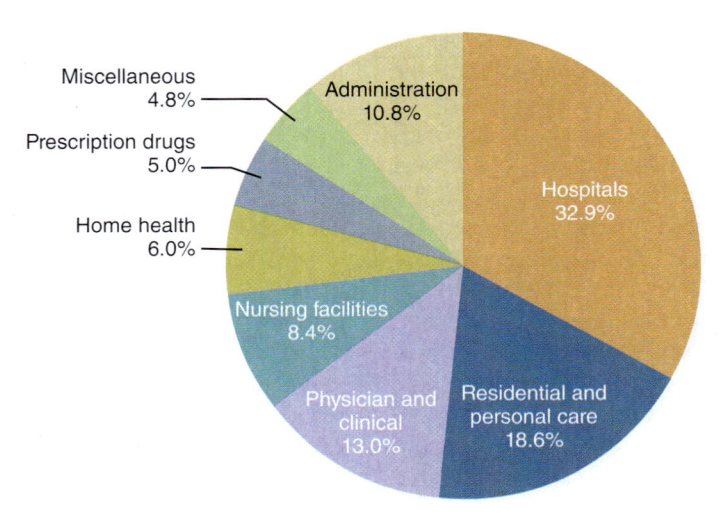

Figure 6-5 Medicaid spending for services, 2021.

Data from Centers for Medicare and Medicaid Services (CMS). 2023. Medicaid Health Expenditures 2021.

state governments. To keep the program financially strong, federal matching funds are 15 percentage points higher than what they are for Medicaid.

Although CHIP has had a significant impact in reducing the number of uninsured children, approximately 3.9 million (5%) children under the age of 19 still did not have any health insurance coverage in 2021 (Katherine and Lisa, 2022). The uninsured rate was not statistically different for children under the age of 19 between 2021 and 2022. (Katherine, Lisa, and Rachel, 2023). Growth in the overall economy is believed to be the main factor that improved families' economic condition and made people ineligible for public assistance.

Health Care for the Military

The U.S. Department of Defense (DOD) operates a large and complex healthcare program, known as the Military Health System (MHS), that provides medical services to active-duty and retired members of the armed forces, their dependents, survivors, and former spouses. This program has also been extended to National Guard/Reserve members. The system is managed by the Defense Health Agency. The Uniformed Services University of the Health Sciences not only educates and develops health professionals, scientists, and leaders for the MHS but also provides operational support to medical units around the world. Changes have been proposed to the current system that will require military healthcare facilities to focus on providing medical care to active-duty personnel only, but their implementation was postponed because of the COVID-19 pandemic. These changes will move non-uniformed beneficiaries to the TRICARE network, which will result in outsourcing health care for at least 200,000 patients (Kime, 2020).

TRICARE is the healthcare program for uniformed service members, retirees, and their families around the world. Beneficiaries may obtain health care either through DOD's medical facilities or through services purchased from civilian providers. TRICARE offers several different health insurance plans, including dental plans, and different options depending on whether the eligible beneficiaries live in the United States or overseas. For retirees age 65 and older, TRICARE offers a plan that works in conjunction with Medicare. Service members who separate from service due to a service-connected injury or illness may be eligible for VA benefits and certain TRICARE benefits. TRICARE- and VA-eligible beneficiaries can choose to use either their TRICARE or VA benefits for each separate episode of care.

Veterans Health Administration

The Veterans Health Administration (VHA), the health services branch of the U.S. Department of Veterans Affairs (VA), operates the largest integrated health services system in the United States. This system encompasses more than 1,250 healthcare facilities, including hospitals, outpatient clinics, community living centers (nursing homes), and various other facilities (VHA, 2020). In 2022, VHA had a budget of about $336 billion (VA, 2023), employed almost 402,876 full-time equivalent staff, and provided medical services to 16.2 million veterans (VA, 2022). Its Office of Research and Development focuses its research activities on health issues that affect veterans. The system actively engages in medical education through affiliations with academic health systems.

The VA MISSION Act (VA Maintaining Systems and Strengthening Integrated Outside Networks Act) of 2018 was passed to give U.S. veterans greater access to both VHA-operated healthcare facilities and community-based health care and to provide assistance to family caregivers. Investment in this program will surpass $21 billion, signaling a commitment to increase and streamline non-VHA care provided through the VHA (Kelley et al., 2020). The objective is to reduce wait times and improve overall access to health care for veterans.

The organizational units within the VA system comprise 18 geographically distributed Veterans Integrated Service Networks (VISNs). Each VISN is responsible for coordinating the activities of the hospitals, outpatient clinics, nursing homes, and other facilities located within its jurisdiction. A report by the Government Accountability Office (GAO, 2019) found that the VHA needed to improve its oversight of the performance of each VISN. At a very basic level, VHA also lacked a comprehensive policy that defined VISN roles and responsibilities.

The VHA also operates the Civilian Health and Medical Program of the Department of Veterans Affairs (CHAMPVA), which covers dependents of veterans with permanently and totally disabled. The VHA shares the cost of covered healthcare services and supplies with eligible beneficiaries.

The VA MISSION Act is a significant piece of legislation that has had a profound impact on veterans' access to health care within the United States Department of Veterans Affairs (VA) system (Massarweh et al., 2020). This law was signed into effect on June 6, 2018, and it represents a major reform of the VA healthcare system (Massarweh et al., 2020). The VA MISSION Act has been lauded for its efforts to improve access to health care for veterans by increasing their options, reducing wait times, and providing more convenient care options (Massarweh et al., 2020).

The VA MISSION Act of 2018 required states to allow out-of-state clinicians to practice telemedicine within the VA system (Mehrotra et al., 2021). This allowed veterans to access health care remotely, making it more convenient for those who may have mobility or geographical barriers (Greenstone et al., 2019).

The Expanded Choice Program within the Act allows veterans to seek care from non-VA providers if they face long wait times or live a significant distance from a VA facility (Massarweh et al., 2020). This expansion broadened the criteria for when veterans can access care in the community and increased the available funding for such care (Massarweh et al., 2020). For example, a veteran may choose to receive primary care and mental health care from a VA facility because VA clinicians typically can spend more time with patients during office visits and have more expertise in treating military-related conditions (Kullgren et al., 2020). At the same time, a veteran may choose to receive physical therapy from a local community facility when it is timelier and more convenient (Kullgren et al., 2020).

Indian Health Service

The federal program administered by the Indian Health Service (IHS), a division of the DHHS, provides comprehensive healthcare services directly to members of federally recognized American Indian and Alaska Native (AIAN) tribes and their descendants. AIANs, as citizens of the United States, are eligible to participate in all public, private, and state health programs available to the general population. However, for many Indians, IHS-supported programs are the only source of health care, especially in isolated areas. The IHS provides healthcare services through its own hospitals, health centers, and health stations as well as through services purchased from private providers. IHS services are administered through a system of 12 area offices and 170 IHS and tribally managed service units. The latter are operated under the Indian Self-Determination and Education Assistance Act of 1975, which provides tribes with the option of exercising their right to self-determination by assuming control and management of programs previously administered by the federal government (IHS, 2020).

The Payment Function

In the healthcare context, insurance companies, MCOs, Blue Cross/Blue Shield, and the government (for Medicare and Medicaid) are referred to as **third-party payers**, with the other two parties being the patient and the provider. The payment function has two main facets: (1) determination of the methods and amounts of reimbursement for the delivery of services and (2) actual payment after services have been rendered. The set fee for each type of service is commonly referred to as a charge or rate. Technically, a **charge** is a fee set by the provider, which is akin to a price in general commerce. A **rate** is a price set by a third-party payer. An index of charges listing individual fees for each type of service is referred to as a **fee schedule**. In general, to receive payment for services rendered, the provider must file a **claim** with the third-party payer. For the sake of simplicity, in this section, we refer to the determination of rates as "reimbursement" and to the payment of claims as "disbursement."

Historically, providers have preferred the fee-for-service method, but it has now largely fallen out of favor with payers because it leads to cost escalations. The Medicare program, in particular, has been at the forefront of devising innovative reimbursement methods; private payers often follow suit. Today, numerous reimbursement methods exist and are used for different types of services. Physicians, dentists, optometrists, therapists, hospitals, nursing facilities, and so on may be paid according to different reimbursement mechanisms. Trends in reimbursement have shifted toward **value-based payments** that reimburse providers for quality of care and cost-efficiency. The emergence of innovative payment models will be driven by value of health care to patients and payers, based on reducing adverse events, adopting evidence-based care standards to improve outcomes, improving patient experience, and increasing transparency of care (CMS, 2020d).

Fee for Service

Fee for service is the oldest method of reimbursement and is still in existence, although its use has been greatly reduced. This payment method is based on the assumption that health care is provided in a set of identifiable and individually distinct units of services, such as examination, x-ray, urinalysis, and a tetanus shot, in the case of physician services. For surgery, such individual services may include an admission kit, numerous medical supplies (each accounted for separately), surgeon's fees, anesthesia, anesthesiologist's fees, recovery room charges, and so forth. Each of these services is separately itemized on one bill, and there can be more than one bill. For example, the hospital, the surgeon, the pathologist, and the anesthesiologist may bill for their services separately.

Initially, providers established their own fee-for-service charges and insurers passively paid the claims. Later, insurers started to limit reimbursement to a usual, customary, and reasonable (UCR) amount. Each insurer determined on its own what the UCR charge should be through community or statewide surveys of what providers were charging. If the actual charges exceeded the UCR amount, then reimbursement from insurers was limited to the UCR amount. Providers would then **balance bill**—that is, ask the patients to pay the difference between the actual charges and the payments received from third-party payers.

The main problem under fee-for-service arrangements is that providers have an incentive to deliver additional services that are not always essential. Providers can increase their incomes by increasing the volume of services. However, dentists, therapists, and some physicians continue to receive payment according to the fee-for-service model.

Bundled Payments

Fee for service essentially pays for unbundled services. A bundled fee, also referred to as package pricing, includes several related services in one price. For example, optometrists sometimes advertise package prices that include the charges for eye exams, frames for eyeglasses, and corrective lenses. The various prospective payment methods of reimbursement are also examples of bundled payments. Package pricing reduces the incentive for providing nonessential services, thereby reducing provider-induced demand. Some evidence indicates that bundled payment methods, especially when they are prospectively set, are effective in reducing healthcare spending without significantly affecting quality of care (Hussey et al., 2012).

Medicare has pioneered a bundled payment mechanism that pays providers a single sum for a given episode. Some episodic models are still being explored, but the most extensive one includes all services during hospitalization and subsequent delivery of postacute services, such as rehabilitation and nursing home care. Incentives to share cost savings with Medicare are also incorporated (Tanenbaum, 2017). The theory behind episodic payments is that various providers collaborating to deliver services to a patient through an entire episode will result in coordinated care, improved quality, and lower cost.

Resource-Based Relative Value Scale

Under the Omnibus Budget Reconciliation Act (OBRA) of 1989, Medicare developed a reimbursement mechanism to pay physicians according to a "relative value" assigned to each physician service. The resource-based relative value scale (RBRVS) was implemented in 1992. Subsequently, third-party payers adopted the RBRVS system.

RBRVS incorporates **relative value units (RVUs)** based on the time, skill, and intensity (physician work) it takes to provide a service. Hence, RVUs reflect the resource inputs—time, effort, and expertise—needed to deliver a service. RVUs are established for different types of services that are identified by codes. The Healthcare Common Procedures Coding System (HCPCS) includes the Current Procedural Terminology (CPT) codes (Level I) as well as Level II codes for services, such as supplies, equipment, and devices.

In addition to RVUs associated with physician work, separate RVUs are included for the cost of practice (overhead costs), malpractice insurance, and geographic cost variations. A conversion factor (CF) is then used to establish a **Medicare Physician Fee Schedule (MPFS)**—a price list for physician services, based on which individual payments are made when physicians file their claims. To attract more physicians to health professional shortage areas (HPSAs), a 10% bonus is added for physicians practicing in the shortage areas (MedPAC, 2019h).

In the past, the main issue with the RBRVS system was that it continued to incentivize volume rather than quality. To address this problem, the RBRVS payment rates are adjusted further under the quality payment program (QPP).

Quality Payment Program

Under the Medicare Access and CHIP Reauthorization Act (MACRA) of 2015, Medicare implemented a QPP. MACRA payment adjustments are designed to give providers added incentives for delivering high-quality, cost-efficient care. Clinicians can opt to participate in one of two different pathways. The first option is the advanced alternative payment models (A-APMs) for qualifying participants. The criteria for participation are determined by the CMS. From 2019 through 2024, clinicians who qualify for A-APMs receive incentive payments of 5% for each year that they qualify. Clinicians who do not qualify for A-APMs follow the path of the Merit-based Incentive Payment System (MIPS). Under MIPS, annual payment increases or decreases apply based on the clinician's performance in four categories: quality, cost, clinical practice, and improvement activities.

Medicare Shared Savings Program

Under the ACA, a Medicare Shared Savings Program (MSSP) was created by the CMS just for accountable care organizations (ACOs) as a value-based payment model to incentivize ACOs to improve the quality of care for Medicare beneficiaries while reducing healthcare costs (Centers for Medicare & Medicaid Services, 2023). ACOs are groups of providers, such as physicians and hospitals, that have agreed to be held accountable for the cost and quality of health care for a group of beneficiaries. Under the ACA, any cost savings achieved through these arrangements are shared in the form of bonuses between participating ACOs and Medicare. Beneficiaries do not enroll in ACOs but rather are assigned to them by Medicare. The beneficiaries are free to obtain services outside the ACO, but if they choose to go outside the ACO, the ACO remains responsible for the spending. This provides an incentive to the ACO providers to keep their enrollees satisfied so they will stay with the ACO providers.

For the first year of the MSSP, CMS has identified 33 quality measures that are organized into four categories referred to as "domains (Centers for Medicare & Medicaid Services, 2023). The domains include: patient/caregiver experience, care coordination/patient safety, preventive health, and at-risk population. The 33 measures are intended to do the following: improve individual health and the health of populations; address quality aims such as prevention, care of chronic illness, high prevalence conditions, patient safety, patient and caregiver engagement and care coordination; support the Shared Savings Program goals of better care, better health; and lower growth in expenditures. Of the 33 measures, 12 are within the domain for "at-risk population" and relate to major cost drivers such as diabetes treatment, heart failure, and coronary artery disease (Centers for Medicare & Medicaid Services, 2023).

MSSP has demonstrated modest success in cost savings and quality improvement. ACO quality is evaluated in four domains: patient/caregiver experience, care coordination/patient safety, preventive health, and clinical care for at-risk populations. Demonstration projects are under way for a second ACO reimbursement program, called Next Generation (NextGen), which started in 2016 (MedPAC, 2019a).

Managed Care Approaches

MCOs have concentrated on three main approaches to payment. The first is the preferred-provider approach, which may be regarded as a variation of fee for service. The main distinction is that an MCO contracts with certain "preferred providers" and negotiates discounts off the charges to establish fee schedules.

In the second approach, which is called **capitation**, the provider is paid a set monthly fee per enrollee, which is sometimes referred to as a per member per month (PMPM) rate. The fixed monthly fee (PMPM rate × number of enrollees) is paid to the provider regardless of how often the enrollees receive medical services from the provider. Capitation removes the incentive for providers to increase the volume of services to generate additional revenues. It also makes providers prudent in providing only necessary services.

Fixed salary, combined with productivity-related bonuses, is the third payment method used by some MCOs that employ their own physicians.

Cost-Plus Reimbursement

Cost-plus reimbursement was the traditional method used by Medicare and Medicaid to establish per diem (daily) rates for inpatient stays in hospitals, nursing homes, and other institutions. Under the cost-plus method, reimbursement rates for institutions are based on the total costs incurred in operating the institution. The institution is required to submit a cost report to the third-party payer. Complex formulas are developed, designating certain costs as "nonallowable" and placing cost ceilings in other areas. These formulas are used to calculate the per diem reimbursement rate, also referred to as a per patient-day (PPD) rate. The payment method is called cost-plus because, in addition to the total operating costs, the reimbursement formula takes a portion of the organization's capital costs into account in arriving at the PPD rate. Because the reimbursement methodology sets rates after evaluating the costs retrospectively this mechanism is broadly referred to as **retrospective reimbursement**.

Under the cost-plus system, total reimbursement is directly related to length of stay, services rendered, and cost of providing the services. Providers have an incentive to provide services indiscriminately, which in turn drives up costs. There is little motivation for efficiency and cost containment in the delivery of services. Paradoxically, healthcare institutions can increase their profits by increasing costs under such a system.

Because of the perverse financial incentives inherent in retrospective cost-based reimbursement, this approach has been largely replaced by various prospective reimbursement methods. Nevertheless, critical access hospitals located in certain rural areas and Medicare-certified hospices are still reimbursed under the cost-plus payment system.

Prospective Reimbursement

In contrast to retrospective reimbursement, in which historical costs are used to determine the amount to be paid, **prospective reimbursement** is forward-thinking and uses certain established criteria to determine the amount of reimbursement in advance, before services are delivered. Prospective reimbursement not only minimizes some of the abuses inherent in cost-plus approaches but also enables providers, such as Medicare, to better predict future healthcare spending. In addition, it provides strong incentives to healthcare organizations to reduce costs. The organization makes a profit only if it can keep its costs below the prospective reimbursement amount. Inability to control costs jeopardizes the organization's financial health.

Medicare has been using the prospective payment system (PPS) to reimburse inpatient hospital acute-care services under Medicare Part A since 1983. Subsequently, the BBA of 1997 mandated implementation of a PPS for hospital outpatient services and postacute-care providers, such as SNFs, home health agencies, and inpatient rehabilitation facilities. The prospective reimbursement methodologies can differ rather substantially according to the type of service that an organization provides.

Payments to Inpatient Rehabilitation Facilities (IRFs)

Payments to Inpatient Rehabilitation Facilities (IRFs) in the United States are primarily made through the Medicare program, which is administered by the CMS. IRFs are healthcare facilities that provide specialized, intensive rehabilitation services to patients who require inpatient care due to severe medical conditions, injuries, or disabilities (Centers for Medicare & Medicaid Services, 2023).

Medicare uses a prospective payment system (PPS) to reimburse IRFs for the care provided to Medicare beneficiaries. The IRF PPS will use information from a patient assessment instrument (IRF PAI) to classify patients into distinct groups based on clinical characteristics and expected resource needs (Centers for Medicare & Medicaid Services, 2023). The classification is primarily determined by the patient's impairment, functional status, and comorbidities. These groups are referred to as "case-mix groups" (CMGs) needs (Centers for Medicare & Medicaid Services, 2023).

Separate payments are calculated for each group, including the application of case and facility level adjustments. IRFs are required to comply with various Medicare regulations and quality reporting requirements to be eligible for payment. IRF payments are typically made on a per-diem (daily) basis, but the total payment for an episode of care is based on the estimated length of stay for each patient's CMG (Centers for Medicare & Medicaid Services, 2023). Medicare covers rehabilitation services in IRFs for beneficiaries who meet certain criteria. Patients must have specific medical conditions, require intensive rehabilitation, and be able to participate in the rehabilitation program (Centers for Medicare & Medicaid Services, 2023).

Payment for Outpatient Rehabilitation Under the Healthcare Common Procedure Coding System

The Healthcare Common Procedure Coding System (HCPCS) is a standardized coding system used in the United States for the billing and documentation of healthcare services and procedures (Centers for Medicare & Medicaid Services, n.d.). It includes codes for a wide range of medical services and supplies, including those provided in outpatient rehabilitation settings (Centers for Medicare & Medicaid Services, n.d.). Payment for outpatient rehabilitation services under HCPCS typically involves the use of specific codes that represent the services provided. **Exhibit 6-7** shows how payment for outpatient rehabilitation works under HCPCS provided (Centers for Medicare & Medicaid Services, n.d.):

Case-Mix–Based Reimbursement

Case mix is an aggregate of the severity of conditions requiring clinical intervention. Case-mix categories are mutually exclusive and differentiate patients according to their extent of resource use. On a case-mix index, higher score categories include patients who have more severe conditions than those in lower score categories. A comprehensive assessment of each patient's condition determines the case mix for an organization. Patients who require similar levels of services are then categorized into groups that are relatively uniform according to resource consumption. To a large extent, case mix is reflected in MS-DRGs and MS-LTC-DRGs, which are discussed later in this chapter. Reimbursements to SNFs, inpatient rehabilitation facilities, and home health agencies are based primarily on case mix.

Acute-Care Hospital Payment System

Overview of DRG-Based Reimbursement. The PPS for acute-care hospital inpatient reimbursement was enacted under the Social Security Amendments of 1983. The predetermined reimbursement amount is set according to diagnosis-related groups (DRGs). Each DRG consolidates principal diagnoses that are expected to require similar amounts of hospital resources in the delivery of care.

The primary factor governing the amount of reimbursement is the type of case (a DRG classification), but other factors are also taken into account, such as geographic differences (e.g., wage levels in various areas, location of the hospital in an urban versus rural area), whether the institution is a teaching hospital (i.e., has residency programs for medical graduates), and whether the hospital treats a disproportionate share of patients with low income. The last provision was authorized by Congress to give extra financial support to "safety net" hospitals (called disproportionate share hospitals), which are mainly located in inner cities and rural areas, and serve a large number of people with limited socioeconomic status. Additional payments are also made for cases that involve extremely long hospital stays or are extremely expensive, which are referred to as **outliers**.

Exhibit 6-7 How Payment for Outpatient Rehabilitation Works Under HCPCS

1. **Evaluation and Assessment**: The process begins with an initial evaluation and assessment by a qualified healthcare provider, such as a physical therapist, occupational therapist, or speech therapist. The provider will use specific HCPCS codes to document this evaluation. These codes often reflect the type of evaluation and the complexity of the patient's condition.
2. **Treatment Services**: Once the evaluation is complete, the therapist or healthcare provider will develop a treatment plan tailored to the patient's needs. They will use HCPCS codes to document the specific therapeutic services provided during each session. These services can include physical therapy exercises, occupational therapy interventions, speech therapy sessions, and more.
3. **Timed Codes**: Many rehabilitation services are billed using timed codes, which represent the amount of time spent providing the service. For example, a physical therapy session may be billed using a timed code that corresponds to the duration of the therapy session (e.g., 15 minutes, 30 minutes, or 60 minutes).
4. **Modifiers**: HCPCS codes may be supplemented with modifiers to provide additional information about the service or the patient's condition. For example, a modifier may indicate that the service was provided in a specific setting, such as a clinic or a patient's home.
5. **Documentation and Medical Necessity**: Accurate and thorough documentation of the services provided is essential for reimbursement. Healthcare providers must demonstrate that the services are medically necessary and meet specific criteria for reimbursement.
6. **Billing and Reimbursement**: After the services are provided, the healthcare provider submits a claim to the patient's insurance company or Medicare/Medicaid using the appropriate HCPCS codes. The insurance company or payer will then process the claim and reimburse the provider based on the codes, modifiers, and the patient's insurance coverage.
7. **Coverage and Payment Rules**: The coverage and payment rules for outpatient rehabilitation services can vary depending on the patient's insurance plan and the specific rehabilitation services provided. Some services may have a limited number of covered sessions, while others may require pre-authorization or medical necessity review.

The hospital receives a predetermined fixed rate per discharge (i.e., per case) based on the patient's DRG classification and the adjustment factors just mentioned. The bundle of services consists of whatever medical care the patient requires for a given principal diagnosis. The fixed payment rates give providers financial incentives to reduce costs.

Refined Medicare Severity DRGs. In 2007, the CMS adopted a refined DRG-based PPS method that includes patient severity to better reflect hospital resource use. The new system has 335 base DRGs, most of which are further split into two or three Medicare severity diagnosis-related groups (MS-DRGs) based on comorbidities (secondary conditions) or complications (developed during hospital stay). This new payment system had 759 MS-DRGs in use in 2020. Each MS-DRG carries a relative weight that reflects how costly it is expected to be to care for a patient in a given MS-DRG category relative to other categories. Final per-discharge payments are derived through a series of adjustments, such as for use of new technology that results in substantial clinical improvement, and value-based incentives for certain outcome measures, such as patient experience, safety, and efficiency. Also added to the reimbursement is 65% of bad debts resulting from patients' nonpayment of deductibles and copayments (MedPAC, 2019b).

Because DRG-based payments furnish a financial incentive for hospitals to keep the length of stay as short as possible, the ACA required reductions in payments to hospitals that incurred excessive readmissions of patients covered by Medicare for selected conditions. The objective is to prevent facilities from discharging patients too soon. An unplanned readmission to an acute-care hospital within 30 days of discharge is the standard applied. In addition, there is a penalty for having patients who develop hospital-acquired preventable medical conditions (MedPAC, 2019b). To date, the success of these two ACA initiatives in achieving the expected results is uncertain (Blumenthal and Abrams, 2020).

Readmission rates and hospital-acquired conditions are part of a broader value-based purchasing/payment (VBP) program that was started in 2013. This program created quality-based adjustments of up to 1% to Medicare reimbursement for acute-care hospitals. Initial research shows that the VBP program did not improve measures of clinical process or patient experience, nor was it associated with significant reductions in mortality (Figueroa et al., 2016; Ryan et al., 2017). Hence, VBP programs present unforeseen challenges, which are likely to be overcome as both payers and providers gain more experience with what works and what does not work.

Over time, the CMS has gradually expanded inpatient fee-for-value programs, including the Hospital Value-Based Purchasing (HVBP) Program (Kocakulah et al., 2021). The Hospital VBP Program rewards acute-care hospitals with incentive payments for the quality of care provided in the inpatient hospital setting (Centers for Medicare & Medicaid Services, 2023). According to CMS (2023), the HVBP Program is designed to make the quality of care better for hospital patients and the hospital stays a better experience for patients. Also, the HVBP Program encourages hospitals to improve the quality, efficiency, patient experience and safety of care that Medicare beneficiaries receive during acute-care inpatient stays by eliminating or reducing adverse events (healthcare errors resulting in patient harm), adopting evidence-based care standards and protocols to obtain the best outcomes for patients with Medicare insurance, incentivizing hospitals to improve patient experience, increasing the transparency of care quality for consumers, clinicians, and others, and recognizing hospitals that provide high-quality care at a lower cost to Medicare. Hospitals are scored on measures such as mortality and complications, healthcare-associated infections, patient safety, patient experience, and efficiency and cost reduction.

Lee et al. (2020) examined whether and how the HVBP penalties affected aggregate operating outcomes of healthcare providers in hospitals. Using secondary data, they found empirical evidence that hospitals with prior-year HVBP penalties exhibited positive associations between the penalty magnitude and certain current-year care process improvements. Additionally, they observed that bonus-receiving hospitals were less apt to exhibit subsequent performance improvements for these same metrics.

Hong et al. (2020) reviewed and summarized studies that evaluated the HVBP program's impact on clinical processes, patient satisfaction, costs and outcomes, and suggested that the current HVBP did not lead to meaningful improvements in quality of care or patient outcomes and could negatively affect safety-net hospitals.

Revere et al. (2021) explored variation in overall and individual-hospital total performance score (TPS) during 2014–2018 and concluded that TPS scores were positively skewed while the distribution of domain scores varied with patient experience, (clinical) outcome, and efficiency domains having a large number of (positive) outliers. Therefore, they pointed out that it might be time for CMS to redesign the HVBP incentive program to assure the measures accurately demonstrate sustained improvement, the domain weights appropriately reflect the level of importance, and the TPS comparative ranking methodology does not discourage lower-performing hospitals from actively improving the care they deliver and achieving top ranks.

Inpatient Psychiatric DRG-Based Payment

Inpatient psychiatric facilities are either freestanding hospitals or specialized units within acute-care hospitals. On average, Medicare beneficiaries account for approximately one-fourth of discharges in inpatient psychiatric facilities. These facilities are paid a per diem rate rather than a case-specific rate, based on one of 17 psychiatric MS-DRGs. Base rates are established by using national average daily costs for routine, ancillary, and capital costs, updated for inflation. The base rates are adjusted for certain factors that also apply to acute-care hospitals (MedPAC, 2019c).

Long-Term Care Hospital Payment System

Long-term care hospitals (LTCHs) are paid in three different ways.

1. For postacute care following stay in an intensive care unit (ICU) and for patients on ventilator support, Medicare uses a PPS system, just as it does for hospitals.
2. Per-discharge payment rates are set according to Medicare severity long-term care diagnosis-related groups (MS-LTC-DRGs).
3. For discharges that do not meet the preceding criteria, the reimbursement is the lower of either the acute-care rate under the hospital PPS or the cost of caring for the patient.

Patients are assigned to MS-LTC-DRGs based on their principal diagnosis, secondary diagnoses, procedures, age, sex, and discharge status (MedPAC, 2019e).

Outpatient Services Payment Systems

Hospital-Based Outpatient Services.

In August 2000, Medicare's Outpatient Prospective Payment System (OPPS) was implemented to pay for services provided by hospital outpatient departments. The ambulatory payment classification (APC) divides all outpatient services into groups based on clinical and cost similarities. With few exceptions, all services within an APC have the same payment rate. In addition, the CMS has created new technology APCs to cover emerging technologies. Expensive drugs and biologics are paid separately. The reimbursement rates are adjusted for factors such as geographic variations in wages as well as for outpatient services delivered by certain cancer centers and children's hospitals. APC reimbursement takes the form of a bundled rate that includes services such as anesthesia, certain drugs, supplies, and recovery room charges in a packaged price established by Medicare (MedPAC, 2019f). Outpatient surgeries, such as those performed in ambulatory surgery centers, are also paid according to APC groups.

Payment for Outpatient Rehabilitation.

Outpatient therapy is performed in various settings, such as nursing homes, hospital outpatient departments, outpatient rehabilitation facilities, and home health care. The unit of payment is each individual outpatient therapy service. All services are classified according to the Healthcare Common Procedure Coding System (HCPCS). Most physical therapy and occupational therapy HCPCS codes are defined in 15-minute increments; speech therapy is an exception. Each HCPCS code is associated with RVUs, as discussed previously. To determine the rate paid to the provider, the sum of RVUs is multiplied by a dollar-amount conversion factor. When annual per-beneficiary spending exceeds a certain amount, therapy providers must certify to Medicare that the therapy services are medically necessary (MedPAC, 2019g).

Skilled Nursing Facility Payment System

First implemented in 1998, the PPS provides for a per diem prospective rate based on the intensity of care needed by patients in an SNF. More recently, the PPS underwent some major revisions that were implemented in October 2019. The new payment system is called the Patient Driven Payment Model (PDPM) because it incorporates many aspects of a patient's condition in establishing payments. The revised methodology essentially removes the incentive to provide extensive rehabilitation services that have been found to be of questionable value and to put more emphasis on nontherapy ancillary products, such as drugs, ventilator devices, and the like. Thus, resource allocation is shifted to medically complex patients based on patient clinical characteristics (Prusynski et al., 2021). Six components—nursing, physical therapy, occupational therapy, speech-language pathology, nontherapy ancillaries, and room and board—are summed to establish the daily rate (MedPAC, 2020).

The Minimum Data Set (MDS) is the instrument used to perform a comprehensive assessment of each resident admitted to an SNF. It consists of a core set of screening elements that assess the resident's clinical, functional, and psychosocial needs. The resident is then classified into a resident group for each of the five case-mix-adjusted components (room and board is not adjusted). Additional adjustment are made for geographic differences in labor costs (Acumen, 2018).

After PDPM implementation, SNFs significantly reduced their therapy staff hours (McGarry et al., 2021). Physical therapist and occupational therapist staffing levels were reduced by 5–6% during October–December 2019 relative to pre-PDPM levels, and physical therapy assistant and occupational therapist assistant levels were reduced by about 10% (McGarry et al., 2021). There was also a significant reduction in individual OT and PT use and a smaller increase in group OT and PT use (Zhang et al., 2022).

Rahman et al. (2022) observed a significant reduction in therapy volume and suggested that the PDPM did have its intended effect of altering financial incentives for SNFs related to therapy provision. Rahman et al. (2023) did another study to evaluate the spillover effect of the PDPM on Medicare Advantage (MA) enrollees, despite it being designed for Traditional Medicare (TM) beneficiaries. They found out that the PDPM had directionally similar effects on therapy use for both TM and MA enrollees, but the magnitudes were smaller for MA beneficiaries (Rahman et al., 2023).

Payments to Inpatient Rehabilitation Facilities

Since 2002, inpatient rehabilitation facilities—that is, rehabilitation hospitals and distinctly certified rehabilitation units in general hospitals—have been reimbursed according to case-mix groups (CMGs). Under this system, the patient is assigned to a CMG based on the primary reason for rehabilitation, age, functional status, cognitive status, and comorbidities. Medicare rules require that no less than 60% of the total patient population in such units have one of 13 specified conditions that require intensive rehabilitation, such as stroke, amputation, burns, or hip fracture (MedPAC, 2019d).

Payment for Home Health Services

PPS for home health agencies was adopted in 2000. Until 2020, Medicare had paid a predetermined rate for each 60-day episode of home health care. Since 2020, a 30-day unit of payment has been implemented under a patient-driven groupings model (PDGM), as required by the Bipartisan Budget Act of 2018. The PDGM model replaced the previous Prospective Payment System for home health care and brought several key changes to the reimbursement structure, aiming to promote more patient-centered care and improve accuracy in payment (Centers for Medicare & Medicaid

Services, 2023). Medicare no longer includes the number of therapy visits provided in an episode as a payment factor, under the theory that therapy services were overdelivered when that model was used for reimbursement. Instead, the PDGM system assigns 30-day periods of care to one of 432 case-mix groups. Case-mix assignment is based on five factors: early or late period of care, whether the patient enters home health care from an acute or postacute source or from the community, principal diagnosis, functional impairment, and comorbidity (CMS, 2020c).

Disbursement of Funds

After services have been delivered, some agency must perform the administrative task of verifying and paying the claims received from the providers. Disbursement of funds (claims processing) is carried out in accordance with the reimbursement policy adopted by the particular program. Commercial insurance companies and MCOs may either have their own claims departments to process payments to providers or outsource this function. Self-insured employers typically contract with a **third-party administrator (TPA)** to process and pay claims. The TPA may also monitor use and perform other oversight functions. The government contracts with third parties in the private sector to process Medicare claims; these so-called Medicare Administrative Contractors are private insurers. For Medicaid, each state has established billing codes and claim submission procedures.

National Health Expenditures

In 2021, national health expenditures (NHE)—also referred to as healthcare spending—in the United States amounted to a little more than $4.255 trillion, or an average per capita spending of $12,914 for each American (**Table 6-5**). NHE represented 18.3% of the U.S. **gross domestic product (GDP)**, where

Table 6-5 U.S. National Health Expenditures and Growth (Selected Years)

Year	NHE Amount (in Billions)	Percentage of GDP	Amount per Capita	Average Annual Percent Growth from Previous Year NHE	GDP
1960	$27.2	5.0	$146		
1970	74.6	6.9	355	10.6	7.1
1980	255.3	8.9	1,108	13.1	10.3
1990	721.4	12.1	2,843	11.0	7.6
2000	1,369.7	13.3	4,857	6.6	5.6
2010	2,596.4	17.4	8,404	6.6	3.8
2020	4,014.2	18.7	12,490	4.9	4.4
2021	4,255.1	18.3	12,914	2.7	10.7

Data from Centers for Medicare and Medicaid Services (CMS). 2020e. *National health expenditure data, historical. NHE summary, including share of GDP, CY 1960–2018 (ZIP).* Available at: https://ww+M197w.cms.gov/Research-Statistics-Data-and-Systems/Statistics-Trends-and-Reports/NationalHealthExpendData /NationalHealthAccountsHistorical. Accessed July 2020; Centers for Medicare and Medicaid Services (CMS). 2020g. *National health expenditure data, projected.* Available at: https://www.cms.gov/Research-Statistics-Data-and-Systems/Statistics-Trends-and-Reports/NationalHealthExpendData /NationalHealthAccountsProjected. Accessed July 2020. 2021 Data from Centers for Medicare and Medicaid Services (2023). NHE Tables.

the GDP is the total value of goods and services produced in the United States and is an indicator of total economic production, or total consumption. Hence, 18.3% of GDP refers to the share of the total economic output consumed by healthcare products and services in 2021.

Table 6-5 also provides NHE data and comparisons with GDP for other selected years. Over the decades, growth in both NHE and GDP has moderated, but NHE have continued to outpace the growth in GDP. The slower growth of NHE in recent years compared to previous decades undoubtedly reflects cost-containment efforts undertaken by various payers, notably the federal government for Medicare spending, which represents more than one-fifth of NHE.

The cost to the federal government of Medicaid expansion and ACA-driven marketplace subsidies and reforms was $128 billion in 2019—considerably less than the $172 originally projected by the CBO. This is a result of lower growth in healthcare costs generally, lower premiums in the marketplaces, and lower enrollment in the marketplaces (Blumenthal et al., 2020).

Three factors are major contributors to the growth in healthcare expenditures: (1) general population growth and aging; (2) intensity of service use, including moral hazard; and (3) prices for products and services. Increasing prices may account for more than 50% of the rise in healthcare expenditures (**Figure 6-6**). **Exhibit 6-8** breaks down the growth in expenditure per major categories (Centers for Medicare & Medicaid Services, 2023).

Differences Between National and Personal Health Expenditures

National health expenditures are an aggregate of the amount a nation spends for all health services and supplies, public health services, health-related research, administrative costs, and investment in structures and

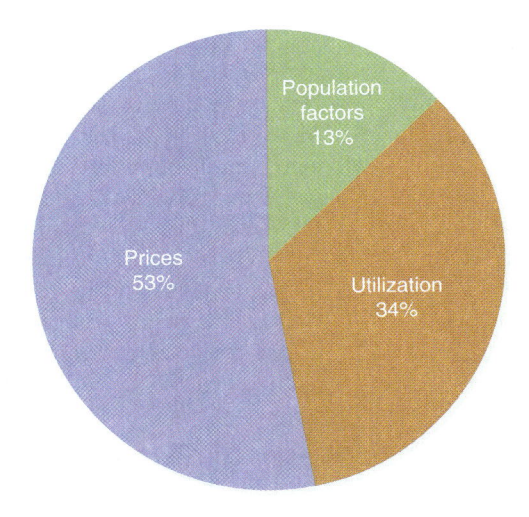

Figure 6-6 Contributors to the growth in healthcare spending.

Data from Bindman, A. B. 2020. Rising prices and health care "empires." JAMA 323, no. 9: 815–816.

Exhibit 6-8 The Growth in Healthcare Expenditures by Major Categories

National Health Expenditure (NHE) grew 2.7% to $4.3 trillion in 2021, or $12,914 per person, and accounted for 18.3% of Gross Domestic Product (GDP).

- **Medicare spending** grew 8.4% to $900.8 billion in 2021, or 21 percent of total NHE.
- **Medicaid spending** grew 9.2% to $734.0 billion in 2021, or 17 percent of total NHE.
- **Private health insurance spending** grew 5.8% to $1,211.4 billion in 2021, or 28 percent of total NHE.
- **Out-of-pocket spending** grew 10.4% to $433.2 billion in 2021, or 10 percent of total NHE.
- **Hospital expenditures** grew 4.4% to $1,323.9 billion in 2021, slower than the 6.2% growth in 2020.
- **Physician and clinical services expenditures** grew 5.6% to $864.6 billion in 2021, slower growth than the 6.6% in 2020.
- **Prescription drug spending** increased 7.8% to $378.0 billion in 2021, faster than the 3.7% growth in 2020.

equipment during a calendar year. The proportional distribution of NHE into the various categories of health services in the United States appears in **Table 6-6**.

Table 6-6 Percentage Distribution of U.S. National Health Expenditures, 2010 and 2021

	2010	2021
NHE	100.0	100.0
Personal health care	84.5	83.5
Hospital care	31.7	31.1
Physician and clinical services	19.8	20.3
Dental services	4.0	3.8
Nursing home care	5.4	4.3
Other professional services	2.7	3.1
Home health	2.7	2.9
Prescription drugs	9.7	8.9
Other personal health care	5.0	5.3
Medical products and equipment	3.5	3.9
Government administration and net cost of private health insurance	7.1	7.2
Government public health activities	2.9	4.4
Investment	5.5	4.9
Noncommercial research	1.9	1.4
Structures and equipment	3.6	3.4
Total NHE (billions)	$2,596.4	$4,255.1
Personal health expenditures (billions)	$2,194.6	$3,553.4

Data from Centers for Medicare and Medicaid Services (CMS). 2023. National health expenditure data. NHE tables (historical).

Personal health expenditures, which are a component of national health expenditures, comprise the total spending for services and goods related directly to patient care. Personal health expenditures constitute the amount remaining after subtracting from NHE all of the spending for research, structures (e.g., construction, additions, alterations) and capital equipment, administrative expenses incurred in private and public health insurance programs, and costs of government public health activities. Between 2010 and 2018, there were notable increases in the share of total spending for hospitals and government administration and net cost of private health insurance. The latter reflects the administrative costs of health insurance under the ACA. During the same period, notable decreases occurred in expenditures for dental services; nursing home care; prescription drugs; and investment in research, structures, and capital equipment. In 2021, approximately 51% of the money spent on the delivery of healthcare services was attributed to private sources, and 49% to public sources (CMS, 2022).

The Nation's Healthcare Dollar

Figure 6-7 provides a comprehensive picture of where U.S. national healthcare dollars come from (revenues), including both private and public sources, and how they are spent (expenditures). For sources of funding, there were small increases in Medicare and private health insurance payments, and corresponding decreases in Medicaid and out-of-pocket payments. Payments for hospital care increased slightly, with a corresponding decrease in expenditures for prescription drugs. These changes generally reflect post-ACA healthcare delivery operations.

COVID-19 and Healthcare Financing

Although the COVID-19 pandemic originated in China in 2019, the United States was hit hard by this highly infectious disease

280 Chapter 6 Health Services Financing

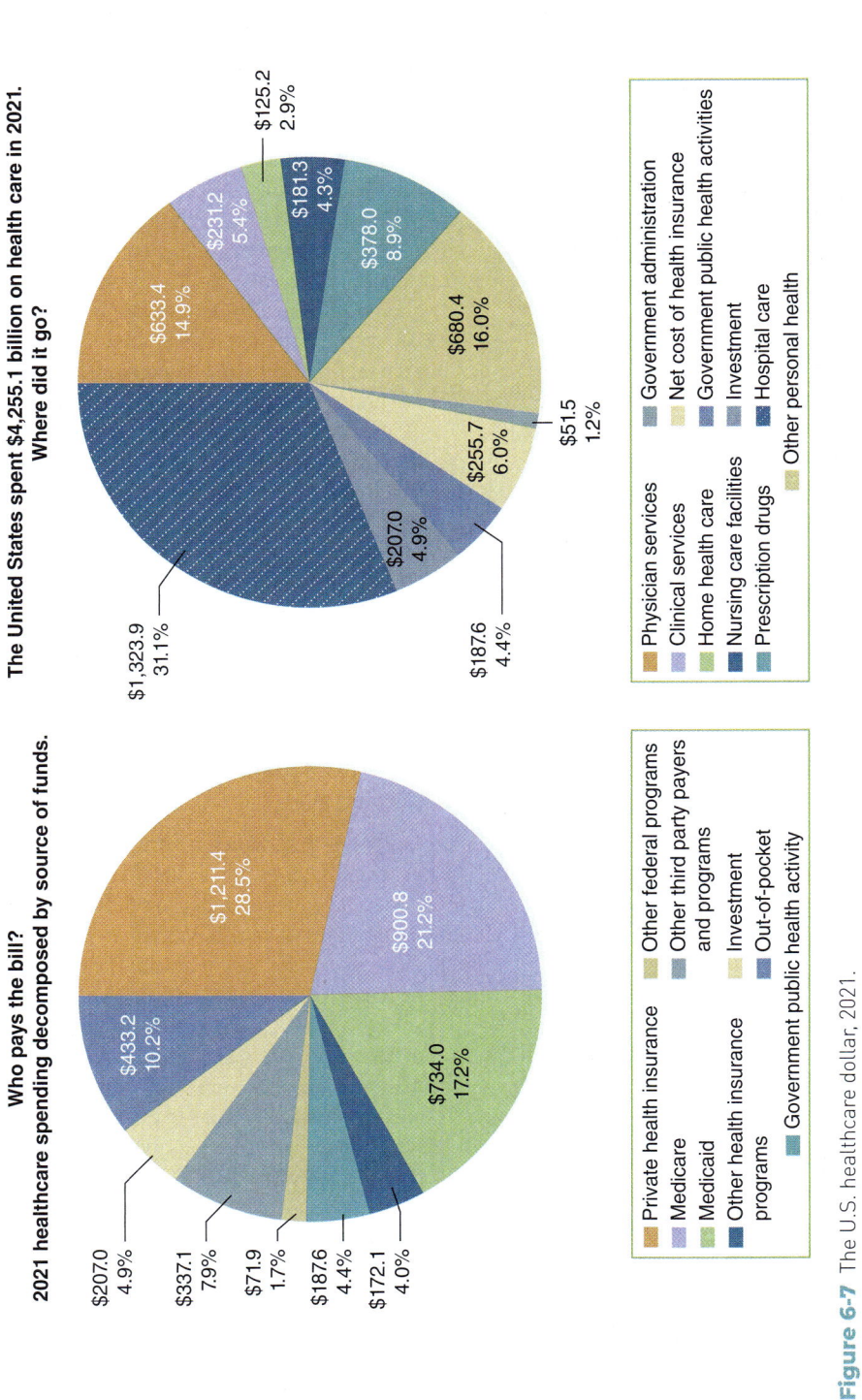

Who pays the bill?
2021 healthcare spending decomposed by source of funds.

- $1,211.4 — 28.5%
- $900.8 — 21.2%
- $734.0 — 17.2%
- $433.2 — 10.2%
- $207.0 — 4.9%
- $337.1 — 7.9%
- $71.9 — 1.7%
- $187.6 — 4.4%
- $172.1 — 4.0%

Legend:
- Private health insurance
- Medicare
- Medicaid
- Other health insurance programs
- Other federal programs
- Other third party payers and programs
- Investment
- Out-of-pocket
- Government public health activity

The United States spent $4,255.1 billion on health care in 2021. Where did it go?

- $1,323.9 — 31.1%
- $633.4 — 14.9%
- $231.2 — 5.4%
- $125.2 — 2.9%
- $181.3 — 4.3%
- $378.0 — 8.9%
- $680.4 — 16.0%
- $51.5 — 1.2%
- $255.7 — 6.0%
- $207.0 — 4.9%
- $187.6 — 4.4%

Legend:
- Physician services
- Clinical services
- Home health care
- Nursing care facilities
- Prescription drugs
- Government administration
- Net cost of health insurance
- Government public health activities
- Investment
- Hospital care
- Other personal health

Figure 6-7 The U.S. healthcare dollar, 2021.

Data from Centers for Medicare and Medicaid Services (CMS). 2023. National health expenditure data. NHE tables (historical). Available at: https://www.cms.gov/Research-Statistics-Data-and-Systems/Statistics-Trends-and-Reports/NationalHealthExpendData/NationalHealthAccountsHistorical in 2020. The pandemic claimed thousands of lives in the United States, especially among older adults and people with chronic conditions. Even after recovery from COVID-19, patients remain at risk for lung disease, heart disease, frailty, and mental health disorders that may require long-term treatments (Jiang and McCoy, 2020). Moreover, early cost estimates do not account for mass vaccination of the U.S. population.

Indirect healthcare costs are also associated with the government-mandated shutdowns imposed in an effort to control the spread of the coronavirus and with the ensuing economic crisis. Adverse health consequences of these events are also a reality. For example, social isolation is associated with mental disorders, and co-occurring mental health problems are risk factors for opioid overdose (Ataiants et al., 2020). Notably, the opioid epidemic cost the United States $2.5 trillion in the four-year period from 2015 to 2018 (American Presidency Project, 2019), so exacerbation of this crisis carries its own costs. Likewise, the job losses, financial uncertainty, closures of mom-and-pop businesses, and riots in many cities in 2020 were certain to have both economic and health consequences.

Job losses translate into not only the loss of personal income but also the loss of health insurance for many people. Most of the newly uninsured may be eligible for Medicaid, CHIP, or subsidies under the ACA. However, about 5.7 million people likely will not qualify for subsidized insurance (Livingston, 2020b). For these individuals, buying health insurance may be unaffordable.

In March 2020, President Trump signed the Families First Coronavirus Response Act. This law mandated that all insurance plans—private or public—cover the cost of a coronavirus test and any related out-of-pocket costs for medical services. Third-party payers across the nation stepped up to alleviate patients' financial burden.

A sudden mandate on March 14, 2020, from the U.S. Surgeon General urged a widespread cessation of all elective surgery across the country under a likely scenario that hospitals would be overwhelmed with patients suffering from COVID-19. The expected scenario did not materialize, but the mandate has left many hospitals and physician practices under severe financial strains.

In 2021, the Biden-Harris Administration issued guidance explaining that State Medicaid and Children's Health Insurance Program (CHIP) programs must cover all types of FDA-authorized COVID-19 tests without cost sharing under CMS's interpretation of the American Rescue Plan Act of 2019 (ARP). Medicare pays for COVID-19 diagnostic tests performed by a laboratory, such as PCR and antigen tests, with no beneficiary cost sharing when the test is ordered by a physician, non-physician practitioner, pharmacist, or other authorized healthcare professional (U.S. Department of Health and Human Services, 2022). In January 2022, insurance companies and group health plans were required by the Biden-Harris Administration to cover the cost of over-the-counter, at-home COVID-19 tests authorized, cleared, or approved by the U.S. Food and Drug Administration (FDA).

The effects of COVID-19 on healthcare financing are summarized as follows.

- **Increased healthcare spending:** The most immediate impact of COVID-19 was the surge in healthcare spending to respond to the pandemic (Béland et al., 2021). This included the development and distribution of vaccines, the expansion of testing and contact tracing, and the treatment of patients suffering from COVID-19 (Béland et al., 2021). Hospitals and healthcare systems faced substantial financial burdens as they invested in additional resources, personnel, and infrastructure to manage the influx of patients with COVID-19 (Béland et al., 2021).
- **Revenue loss for non-COVID-19 care:** Many healthcare facilities experienced a significant reduction in revenue as

non-urgent elective procedures and routine medical appointments were postponed or canceled to prioritize COVID-19 care (Li et al., 2023).
1. At the pandemic's peak, hospitals canceled not only elective surgeries but also cancer screenings, outpatient specialist visits, and even primary-care visits (Barnett et al., 2020).
2. Hospital admissions declined drastically at the start of the pandemic, mainly because hospitals restricted the number of elective surgeries and nonemergency medical services (Birkmeyer et al., 2020).
3. Hospital admissions from acute medical illnesses for non-COVID-19 patients dropped (Birkmeyer et al., 2020).
4. The cancelation of elective procedures threatened hospital solvency, given that those admissions make up almost one third of inpatient revenues—orthopedic and cardiac procedures specifically are primary revenue sources for hospitals (Khullar et al., 2020).
5. The financial impact of postponements and cancelations was significant: non-elective care declined by almost 50% during the first year of the pandemic (Cutler et al., 2020).

- **Changes in insurance coverage:** Many health insurers temporarily waived co-pays and deductibles for COVID-19 testing and treatment to reduce financial barriers to care (Graves et al., 2021). Some individuals may have lost employer-sponsored health insurance due to job losses or business closures, leading to an increase in Medicaid and marketplace enrollments (Gaffney et al., 2020).

Summary

Financing is the lifeblood of any healthcare delivery system. At its most fundamental level, it determines who pays for healthcare services and for whom. At a secondary level, financing determines who produces which types of healthcare services. Hence, financing affects both the demand and supply sides of the healthcare equation.

A significant amount of financing is attributed to the government, mainly to provide health insurance or direct services to defined categories of people. Because most publicly financed services are obtained in the private sector, the government has a sizable interest in setting (and limiting) the amount of reimbursement to providers.

The ACA significantly reduced the number of uninsured Americans, mainly through the expansion of Medicaid programs (even though some states did not implement it) and, to a lesser extent, by facilitating the creation of health insurance marketplaces, known as exchanges, for the private purchase of health insurance. Federal subsidies were made available to people with incomes between 100% and 400% of the FPL. Even so, the largest source of health insurance in the United States remains employer-based programs, which did not show any growth in coverage under the ACA.

The financial stability of Medicare trust funds has improved somewhat, but they are still headed toward insolvency unless the trend can be reversed. In an effort to reduce costs and improve quality of care under the Medicare system, the ACA implemented value-based reimbursement programs. These programs have not achieved the expected savings.

There were notable increases in the share of total spending that went to hospitals and government administration and the net cost of private health insurance. Decreases in expenditures occurred in dental services; nursing home care; prescription drugs; and investment in research, structures, and capital equipment.

The COVID-19 pandemic has had serious economic and health consequences. Job losses have increased the size of the uninsured population. Serious after-effects for healthcare expenditures, financial constraints for providers, and social costs can be expected.

TEST YOUR UNDERSTANDING

Terminology

access
adjusted community rating
balance bill
beneficiary
benefit period
benefits
capitation
case mix
categorical programs
charge
churning
claim
coinsurance
community rating
consumer-directed health plans
copayment
cost-plus reimbursement
deductible
entitlement
experience rating
fee schedule
gross domestic product (GDP)
group insurance
high-deductible health plans (HDHPs)
insurance
insured
insurer
means-tested program
Medicare Physician Fee Schedule (MPFS)
Medigap
moral hazard
national health expenditures
outliers
personal health expenditures
plan
play-or-pay
preexisting condition
premium
prospective reimbursement
rate
reinsurance
relative value units (RVUs)
retrospective reimbursement
risk
risk rating
self-insured plan
third-party administrator (TPA)
third-party payers
underwriting
value-based payments

Review Questions

1. What is meant by healthcare financing in its broad sense? How does financing affect the healthcare delivery system?
2. Discuss the general concept of insurance and its general principles. Describe the various types of private health insurance options, pointing out the differences among them.
3. Discuss how the concepts of premium, covered services, and cost sharing apply to health insurance.
4. What is the difference between experience rating and community rating?
5. What is Medicare Part A? Discuss the financing and cost-sharing features of Medicare Part A. Which benefits does Part A cover? Which benefits are not covered?
6. What is Medicare Part B? Discuss the financing and cost-sharing features of Medicare Part B. Which main benefits are covered under Part B? Which services are not covered?
7. Briefly describe the Medicare Advantage program.
8. Briefly explain the prescription drug program under Medicare Part D.
9. What are Medicare trust funds? Discuss the current state and the future challenges faced by the Medicare trust funds.
10. How did the Supreme Court's ruling on the ACA affect Medicaid? How did the ACA affect the Medicaid program in terms of coverage and cost?

11. What provisions has the federal government made for providing health care to military personnel and to veterans of the U.S. armed forces?
12. What are the major methods of reimbursement for outpatient services?
13. What are the differences between the retrospective and prospective methods of reimbursement?
14. Discuss the concept of value-based payments.
15. Discuss the prospective payment system under DRGs.
16. Distinguish between national health expenditures and personal health expenditures.
17. What are the effects of COVID-19 on health insurance and financing?

References

Agarwal, S. D., and B. D. Sommers, (2020). Insurance Coverage after Job Loss—The Importance of the ACA During the Covid-Associated Recession. *New England Journal of Medicine* 383: 1603–1606.

American Presidency Project. 2019. Press Release—The Full Cost of the Opioid Crisis: $2.5 Trillion over Four Years. Accessed February 2021. Available at: https://www.presidency.ucsb.edu/documents/press-release-the-full-cost-the-opioid-crisis-25-trillion-over-four-years

Antos, J., and J. C. Capretta. 2020. *COVID-19 and the Medicare Trust Funds*. American Enterprise Institute. Available at: http://www.jstor.org/stable/resrep25356

Ataiants, J., A. M. Roth, S. Mazzella, and S. E. Lankenau. 2020. Circumstances of Overdose among Street-Involved, Opioid-Injecting Women: Drug, Set, and Setting. *International Journal on Drug Policy* 78: 102691.

Babuna, P., X. Yang, A. Gyilbag, D. A. Awudi, D. Ngmenbelle, and D. Bian. 2020. The Impact of Covid-19 on the Insurance Industry. *International Journal of Environmental Research and Public Health* 17: 5766.

Barnett, M. L., A. Mehrotra, and B. E. Landon. 2020. Covid-19 and the Upcoming Financial Crisis in Health Care. *NEJM Catalyst Innovations in Care Delivery* 1.

Bartsch, S. M., M. C. Ferguson, J. A. McKinnell, et al. 2020. The Potential Health Care Costs and Resource Use Associated with COVID-19 in the United States. *Health Affairs* 39: 927–935.

Béland, D., G. P. Marchildon, A. Medrano, and P. Rocco. 2021. COVID-19, Federalism, and Health Care Financing in Canada, the United States, and Mexico. *Journal of Comparative Policy Analysis: Research and Practice* 23: 143–156.

Berger, A. 2015. Did the Affordable Care Act Affect Insurance Coverage for Young Adults? Data Brief No. 2. IHIS Project at the Minnesota Population Center, University of Minnesota. Accessed November 14, 2020. Available at: https://nhis.ipums.org/nhis/resources/IHIS_Data_Brief_No_2.pdf

Birkmeyer, J. D., A. Barnato, N. Birkmeyer, R. Bessler, and J. Skinner. 2020. The Impact of the COVID-19 Pandemic on Hospital Admissions in the United States: Study Examines Trends in US Hospital Admissions During the COVID-19 Pandemic. *Health Affairs* 39: 2010–2017.

Blumenthal, D., and M. Abrams. 2020. The Affordable Care Act at 10 years: Payment and Delivery System Reforms. *New England Journal of Medicine* 382: 1057–1063.

Blumenthal, D., S. R. Collins, and E. J. Fowler. 2020. The Affordable Care Act at 10 years: Its Coverage and Access Provisions. *New England Journal of Medicine* 382: 963–969.

Breslau, J., B. D. Stein, B. Han, S. Shelton, and H. Yu. 2018. Impact of the Affordable Care Act's Dependent Coverage Expansion on the Health Care and Health Status of Young Adults: What Do We Know So Far? *Medical Care Research and Review* 75: 131–152.

Buchmueller, T. C., and H. G. Levy. 2020. The ACA's Impact on Racial and Ethnic Disparities in Health Insurance Coverage and Access to Care: An Examination of How the Insurance Coverage Expansions of the Affordable Care Act Have Affected Disparities Related to Race and Ethnicity. *Health Affairs* 39: 395–402.

Bundorf, M. K., S. Gupta, and C. Kim. 2021. Trends in US Health Insurance Coverage During the COVID-19 Pandemic. *JAMA Health Forum* 2: e212487.

Bureau of Labor Statistics, U.S. 2020. Archived Consumer Price Index Supplemental Files. Accessed July 2020. Available at: https://www.bls.gov/cpi/tables/supplemental-files/home.htm

Cao, Y., J. Nie, S. A. Sisto, et al. 2020. Assessment of Differences in Inpatient Rehabilitation Services for Length of Stay and Health Outcomes Between US Medicare Advantage and Traditional Medicare Beneficiaries. *JAMA Network Open* 3: e201204.

Capatina, E. 2020. Selection in Employer Sponsored Health Insurance. *Journal of Health Economics* 71: 102305.

Centers for Medicare & Medicaid Services 2022. The State of the ACA report. Available at: https://www.cms.gov/files/document/state-anniversary.pdf

Centers for Medicare & Medicaid Services (CMS). 2023. Fact Sheet: 2023 Medicare Parts A & B Premiums and Deductibles 2023 Medicare Part D Income-Related Monthly Adjustment Amounts. Accessed October 11, 2023. Available at: https://www.cms.gov/newsroom/fact-sheets/2023-medicare-parts-b-premiums-and-deductibles-2023-medicare-part-d-income-related-monthly

Centers for Medicare & Medicaid Services (CMS). 2023. 2023 Medicaid & CHIP Enrollment Data Highlights. Accessed October 10, 2023. Available at: https://www.medicaid.gov/medicaid/program-information/medicaid-and-chip-enrollment-data/report-highlights/index.html

Centers for Medicare & Medicaid Services. 2023. Inpatient Rehabilitation Facility PPS. Available at: https://www.cms.gov/medicare/payment/prospective-payment-systems/inpatient-rehabilitation

Centers for Medicare & Medicaid Services. 2023. Patient Driven Payment Model. Available at: https://www.cms.gov/medicare/payment/prospective-payment-systems/skilled-nursing-facility-snf/patient-driven-model

Centers for Medicare & Medicaid Services. 2023. Home Health Patient-Driven Groupings Model. Available at: https://www.cms.gov/medicare/payment/prospective-payment-systems/home-health/home-health-patient-driven-groupings-model#:~:text=CMS%20finalized%20a%20new%20case,care%20into%20meaningful%20payment%20categories

Centers for Medicare & Medicaid Services. 2023. Medicare Shared Savings Program. Available at: https://www.cms.gov/medicare/payment/fee-for-service-providers/shared-savings-program-ssp-acos

Centers for Medicare & Medicaid Services. 2023. NHE Fact Sheet. Available at: https://www.cms.gov/data-research/statistics-trends-and-reports/national-health-expenditure-data/nhe-fact-sheet

Centers for Medicare & Medicaid Services. 2023. The Hospital Value-Based Purchasing (VBP) Program. Available at: https://www.cms.gov/medicare/quality/value-based-programs/hospital-purchasing

Centers for Medicare & Medicaid Services. n.d. Medicare Claims Processing Manual Chapter 5 - Part B Outpatient Rehabilitation and CORF/OPT Services. Available at: https://www.cms.gov/regulations-and-guidance/guidance/manuals/downloads/clm104c05.pdf

Centers for Medicare and Medicaid Services (CMS). 2017. Medicare and Home Health Care. Accessed July 14, 2020. Available at: https://www.medicare.gov/Pubs/pdf/10969-medicare-and-home-health-care.pdf

Centers for Medicare and Medicaid Services (CMS). 2020b. Dually Eligible Beneficiaries Under Medicare and Medicaid. Accessed July 2020. Available at: https://www.cms.gov/Outreach-and-Education/Medicare-Learning-Network-MLN/MLNProducts/Downloads/Medicare_Beneficiaries_Dual_Eligibles_At_a_Glance.pdf

Centers for Medicare and Medicaid Services (CMS). 2020c. Home Health Patient-Driven Groupings Model (PDGM): Split Implementation. Accessed July 2020. Available at: https://www.cms.gov/Outreach-and-Education/Medicare-Learning-Network-MLN/MLNMattersArticles/Downloads/MM11081.pdf

Centers for Medicare and Medicaid Services (CMS). 2020d. The Hospital Value-Based Purchasing (VBP) Program. Accessed July 2020. Available at: https://www.cms.gov/Medicare/Quality-Initiatives-Patient-Assessment-Instruments/Value-Based-Programs/HVBP/Hospital-Value-Based-Purchasing

Centers for Medicare and Medicaid Services (CMS). 2020e. National Health Expenditure Data, Historical. NHE Summary, Including Share of GDP, CY 1960-2018 (ZIP). Accessed July 2020. Available at: https://www.cms.gov/Research-Statistics-Data-and-Systems/Statistics-Trends-and-Reports/NationalHealthExpendData/NationalHealthAccountsHistorical

Centers for Medicare and Medicaid Services (CMS). 2022. National Health Expenditure Data. NHE Tables (historical). Accessed October 2023. Available at: https://www.cms.gov/data-research/statistics-trends-and-reports/national-health-expenditure-data/historical

Centers for Medicare and Medicaid Services (CMS). 2023a. 2023 Annual Report of the Boards of Trustees of the Federal Hospital Insurance and Federal Supplementary Medical Insurance Trust Funds. Accessed October 2023. Available at: https://www.cms.gov/oact/tr/2023.

Chase, D., and J. Arensmeyer. 2018. *The Affordable Care Act's Impact on Small Business*. New York: Commonwealth Fund.

Congressional Budget Office (CBO). 2010. Letter to the Honorable Nancy Pelosi, Speaker, U.S. House of Representatives, March 20. Accessed July 2020. Available at: https://www.cbo.gov/sites/default/files/111th-congress-2009-2010/costestimate/amendreconprop.pdf

Congressional Research Service (CRS). 2021. Overview of the ACA Medicaid Expansion. *CRS Report*. Available at: https://crsreports.congress.gov/product/pdf/IF/IF10399

Cutler, D. M., R. G. Frank, J. Gruber, and J. P. Newhouse. 2020. Strengthening the Medicare Trust Fund in the Era of COVID-19. *Health Affairs Forefront*. Available at: https://www.healthaffairs.org/content/forefront/strengthening-medicare-trust-fund-era-covid-19

Cutler, D. M., S. Nikpay, and R. S. Huckman. 2020. The business of medicine in the era of COVID-19. *JAMA* 323: 2003–2004.

Dee, E. C., L. J., Pierce, K. M. Winkfield, and M. B. Lam. 2022. In pursuit of equity in cancer care: Moving beyond the Affordable Care Act. *Cancer* 128: 3278–3283.

Department of Health and Human Services, U.S. 2022. Biden-Harris Administration Requires Insurance Companies and Group Health Plans to Cover the Cost of at-Home COVID-19 Tests, Increasing Access to Free Tests. Accessed October 2023. Available at: https://www.hhs.gov/about/news/2022/01/10/biden-harris-administration-requires-insurance-companies-group-health-plans-to-cover-cost-at-home-covid-19-tests-increasing-access-free-tests.html

Department of Labor (DOL), U.S. 2018. News Release: President Donald J. Trump Helps Millions of Americans Employed by Small Businesses Gain Access to Quality, Affordable Health Coverage. Accessed July 5, 2020. Available at: https://www.dol.gov/newsroom/releases/osec/osec20180619

Department of Veterans Affairs (VA). 2022. Annual Report on the Steps Taken to Achieve Full Staffing Capacity. Accessed October 9, 2023. Available at: https://www.va.gov/EMPLOYEE/docs/Section-505-Annual-Report-2022.pdf

Department of Veterans Affairs (VA). 2023. FY 2023 Summary. Accessed October 6, 2023. Available at: https://www.usaspending.gov/agency/department-of-veterans-affairs?fy=2023

Deventer, C. 2023. Top Advantages & Disadvantages of Medicare Advantage. Value Penguin. Available at: https://www.valuepenguin.com/advantages-disadvantages-medicare-advantage

Drake, C., and D. M. Anderson. 2020. Terminating Cost-Sharing Reduction Subsidy Payments: The Impact of Marketplace Zero-Dollar Premium Plans on Enrollment. *Health Affairs* 39: 41–49.

Dutta, A., and A. Singh, 2021. Consumer Preferences for Health Insurance, in the Wake of COVID-19: Ranked Features and Customer Segments. *Health Marketing Quarterly* 38: 188–204.

Eisenberg, R. 2023. The Pros and Cons of Medicare Advantage Plans. FortuneWell. Available at: https://fortune.com/well/2023/08/09/pros-cons-of-medicare-advantage-plans/

Feldstein, P. J. 1993. *Health Care Economics*. 4th ed. New York: Delmar Publishers.

Figueroa, J. F., Y. Tsugawa, J. Zheng, E. J. Orav, and A. K. Jha. 2016. Association Between the Value-Based Purchasing Pay for Performance Program and Patient Mortality in US Hospitals: Observational Study. *BMJ (Clinical research ed.)* 353: i2214.

Frank, R. G., and T. Neuman, 2021. Addressing the Risk of Medicare Trust Fund Insolvency. *JAMA* 325: 341–342.

Frean, M., J. Gruber, and B. D. Sommers. 2017. Premium Subsidies, the Mandate, and Medicaid Expansion: Coverage Effects of the Affordable Care Act. *Journal of Health Economics* 53: 72–86.

Frenier, C., S. S. Nikpay, and E. Golberstein. 2020. COVID-19 Has Increased Medicaid Enrollment, but Short-Term Enrollment Changes Are Unrelated to Job Losses: Study examines Influence COVID-19 May Have Had on Medicaid Enrollment Covering the Period of March 1 Through June 1, 2020 for 26 States. *Health Affairs* 39: 1822–1831.

Gaffney, A., D. U. Himmelstein, and S. Woolhandler, 2020. COVID-19 and US Health Financing: Perils and Possibilities. *International Journal of Health Services*, 50: 396–407.

Gai, Y., and K. Jones. 2020. Insurance Patterns and Instability from 2006 to 2016. *BMC Health Services Research* 20: 334.

Glied, S. A., S. R. Collins, and S. Lin, 2020. Did the ACA Lower Americans' Financial Barriers to Health Care? A Review of Evidence to Determine Whether the Affordable Care Act Was Effective in Lowering Cost Barriers to Health Insurance Coverage and Health Care. *Health Affairs* 39: 379–386.

Goldman, A. L., and B. D. Sommers. 2020. Among Low-Income Adults Enrolled in Medicaid, Churning Decreased after the Affordable Care Act. *Health Affairs* 39: 85–93.

Goodman, J. C., and G. L. Musgrave. 1992. *Patient Power: Solving America's Health Care Crisis*. Washington, DC: Cato Institute.

Gotanda, H., G. Kominski, Y. Tsugawa. 2020. Association Between the ACA Medicaid Expansions and Primary Care and Emergency Department Use during the First 3 years. *Journal of General Internal Medicine* 35: 711–718.

Government Accountability Office (GAO). 2019. *Veterans Health Administration: Regional Networks Need Improved Oversight and Clearly Defined Roles and Responsibilities*. Accessed July 2020. Available at: https://www.gao.gov/assets/700/699829.pdf

Graves, J. A., K. Baig, and M. Buntin. 2021. The Financial Effects and Consequences of COVID-19: A Gathering Storm. *JAMA* 326: 1909–1910.

Greenstone, C. L., J. Peppiatt, K. Cunningham, et al. 2019. Standardizing Care Coordination within the Department of Veterans Affairs. *Journal of General Internal Medicine* 34: 4–6.

Griffith, K. N., and J. H. Bor. 2020. Changes in Health Care Access, Behaviors, and Self-Reported Health among Low-Income US Adults through the Fourth Year of the Affordable Care Act. *Medical Care* 58: 574–578.

Gruber, J., and B. D. Sommers. 2020. Paying for Medicaid: State Budgets and the Case for Expansion in the Time of Coronavirus. *New England Journal of Medicine* 382: 2280–2282.

Han, X., S. Zhu, and A. Jemal. 2016. Characteristics of Young Adults Enrolled through the Affordable Care Act Dependent Coverage Expansion. *Journal of Adolescent Health* 59: 648–653.

Han, X., J. Zhao, K. R. Yabroff, C. J. Johnson, and A. Jemal. 2022. Association Between Medicaid Expansion under the Affordable Care Act and Survival among Newly

Diagnosed Cancer Patients. *Journal of the National Cancer Institute* 114: 1176–1185.

Health Insurance Institute. 1969. *Modern Health Insurance*. New York: Author.

Health Insurance Organization. 2023. What Is the Employer Mandate? Accessed October 15, 2023. Available at: https://www.healthinsurance.org/glossary/employer-mandate/#:~:text=The%20Affordable%20Care%20Act%20requires%20employers%20with%2050,sets%20a%20minimum%20baseline%20of%20coverage%20and%20affordability

Hoagland, A., and P. Shafer, 2021. Out-of-Pocket Costs for Preventive Care Persist Almost a Decade after the Affordable Care Act. *Preventive Medicine*, 150: 106690.

Hong, Y. R., O. Nguyen, S. Yadav, et al. 2020. Early Performance of Hospital Value-Based Purchasing Program in Medicare: A Systematic Review. *Medical Care* 58: 734–743.

Huberfeld, N. 2015. The Supreme Court Ruling that Blocked Providers from Seeking Higher Medicaid Payments also Undercut the Entire Program. *Health Affairs* 34: 1156–1161.

Hussey, P. S., A. W. Mulcahy, C. Schnyer, and E. C. Schneider. 2012. *Bundled Payment: Effects on Health Care Spending and Quality*. Rockville, MD: Agency for Healthcare Research and Quality.

Indian Health Service. 2020. *IHS profile*. Accessed July 20, 2020. Available at: https://www.ihs.gov/sites/newsroom/themes/responsive2017/display_objects/documents/factsheets/IHSProfile.pdf

Ji, X., K. S. Shi, A. C. Mertens, et al. 2023. Survival in Young Adults with Cancer is Associated with Medicaid Expansion through the Affordable Care Act. *Journal of Clinical Oncology* 41: 1909–1920.

Jiang, D. H., and R. G. McCoy. 2020. Planning for the Post-COVID Syndrome: How Payers Can Mitigate Long-Term Complications of the Pandemic. *Journal of General Internal Medicine* 35: 3036–3039.

Kaiser Family Foundation (KFF). 2021. Employer Health Benefits 2021 Annual Survey. Accessed October 21, 2023. Available at: https://files.kff.org/attachment/Report-Employer-Health-Benefits-2021-Annual-Survey.pdf

Kaiser Family Foundation (KFF). 2022a. 2022 Employer Health Benefits Survey. Accessed October 17, 2023. Available at: https://www.kff.org/report-section/ehbs-2022-section-4-types-of-plans-offered/

Kaiser Family Foundation (KFF). 2022b. 2022 Employer Health Benefits Survey. Accessed October 9, 2023. Available at: https://www.kff.org/report-section/ehbs-2022-section-7-employee-cost-sharing/

Kaiser Family Foundation (KFF). 2023. Status of State Medicaid Expansion Decisions: Interactive Map. Accessed October 4, 2023. Available at: https://www.kff.org/medicaid/issue-brief/status-of-state-medicaid-expansion-decisions-interactive-map/

Keisler-Starkey, K., and L. N. Bunch. 2022. Health Insurance Coverage in the United States: 2021. U.S. Census Bureau. Accessed October 8, 2023. Available at: https://www.census.gov/content/dam/Census/library/publications/2022/demo/p60-278.pdf

Keisler-Starkey, K., L. N. Bunch, and R. A. Lindstrom. 2023. *Health Insurance Coverage in the United States: 2022*. U.S. Census Bureau. Accessed October 1, 2023. Available at: https://www.census.gov/content/dam/Census/library/publications/2023/demo/p60-281.pdf

Kelley, A. T., C. L. Greenstone, and S. R. Kirsh. 2020. Defining Access and the Role of Community Care in the Veterans Health Administration. *Journal of General Internal Medicine* 35: 1584–1585.

Kennedy, A. J., V. Bakalov, L. Reyes-Uribe, et al. 2020. Free Clinic Patients' Perceptions and Barriers to Applying for Health Insurance after Implementation of the Affordable Care Act. *Journal of Community Health* 45: 492–500.

KFF 2023. Status of State Medicaid Expansion Decisions: Interactive Map. Available at: https://www.kff.org/medicaid/issue-brief/status-of-state-medicaid-expansion-decisions-interactive-

Khullar, D., A. M. Bond, and W. L. Schpero. 2020. COVID-19 and the Financial Health of US Hospitals. *JAMA* 323: 2127–2128.

Kime, P. 2020. Big Changes to Military Health System Will Be Delayed, Top Health Official Says. Military.com. Accessed July 2020. Available at: https://www.military.com/daily-news/2020/06/12/big-changes-military-health-system-will-be-delayed-top-health-official-says.html

King, J. S. 2020. Covid-19 and the Need for Health Care Reform. *New England Journal of Medicine* 382: e104.

Kirzinger, A., B. DiJulio, C. Muñana, and M. Brodie. 2017. Kaiser Health Tracking Poll—November 2017: The Role of Health Care in the Republican Tax Plan. *Kaiser Family Foundation*. Accessed July 24, 2020. Available at: https://www.kff.org/health-reform/poll-finding/kaiser-health-tracking-poll-november-2017-the-role-of-health-care-in-the-republican-tax-plan

Kobayashi, L. C., O. Altindag, Y. Truskinovsky, and L. F. Berkman. 2019. Effects of the Affordable Care Act Medicaid Expansion on Subjective Well-Being in the US Adult Population, 2010–2016. *American Journal of Public Health* 109: 1236–1242.

Kocakulah, M. C., Austill, D., and Henderson, E. 2021. Medicare Cost Reduction in the US: A Case Study of Hospital Readmissions and Value-Based Purchasing. *International Journal of Healthcare Management* 14: 203–218.

Kullgren, J. T., A. Fagerlin, and E. A. Kerr, 2020. Completing the MISSION: A Blueprint for Helping Veterans Make the Most of New Choices. *Journal of General Internal Medicine* 35: 1567–1570.

Lee, S. J., S. Venkataraman, G. R. Heim, A. V., Roth, and J. Chilingerian. 2020. Impact of the Value-Based Purchasing Program on Hospital Operations Outcomes: An Econometric Analysis. *Journal of Operations Management* 66: 151–175.

Levitt, K. R., C. A. Cowan, H. C. Lazenby, et al. 1994. National Health Spending Trends, 1960-1993. *Health Affairs* 13: 14–31.

Li, K., M. Al-Amin, and M. D. Rosko. 2023. Early Financial Impact of the COVID-19 Pandemic on U.S. Hospitals. *Journal of Healthcare Management / American College of Healthcare Executives* 68: 268–283.

Livingston, S. 2020a. Just the beginning: New Form of Employer Health Insurance Growing Slower than Planned. *Modern Healthcare* 50: 28.

LLC Acumen. 2018. *Skilled Nursing Facilities Patient-Driven Payment Model—Technical Report.* Accessed July 1, 2020. Available at: https://www.cms.gov/Medicare/Medicare-Fee-for-Service-Payment/SNFPPS/Downloads/PDPM_Technical_Report_508.pdf

Manchikanti, L., S. Helm II, R. M. Benyamin, and J. A. Hirsch. 2017. A Critical Analysis of Obamacare: Affordable Care or Insurance for Many and Coverage for Few? *Pain Physician* 20: 111–138.

Mandal, B., N. Porto, D. E. Kiss, S. H. Cho, and L. S. Head, 2022. Health Insurance Coverage during the COVID-19 Pandemic: The Role of Medicaid Expansion. *The Journal of Consumer Affairs* doi: 10.1111/joca.12500

Massarweh, N. N., K. M. Itani, and M. S. Morris, 2020. The VA MISSION Act and the Future of Veterans' Access to Quality Health Care. *JAMA* 324: 343–344.

McGarry, B. E., E. M. White, L. J. Resnik, M. Rahman, and D. C. Grabowski, . 2021. Medicare's New Patient Driven Payment Model Resulted in Reductions in Therapy Staffing in Skilled Nursing Facilities: Study Examines the Effect of Medicare's Patient Driven Payment Model on Therapy and Nursing Staff Hours at Skilled Nursing Facilities. *Health Affairs* 40: 392–399.

McKillop, C. N., T. M. Waters, C. M. Kaplan, E. K. Kaplan, M. P. Thompson, and I. Graetz. 2018. Three Years in: Changing Plan Features in the U.S. Health Insurance Marketplace. *BMC Health Services Research* 18: 450.

McMorrow, S., L. J. Blumberg, and J. Holahan. 2020. Ten Years Later: Reflections on Critics' Worst-Case Scenarios for the Affordable Care Act. *Journal of Health Politics, Policy and Law* 45 no. 4: 465–483.

Medicaid and CHIP Payment and Access Commission (MACPAC). 2020. Medicaid Enrollment Changes Following the ACA. Accessed July 11, 2020. Available at: https://www.macpac.gov/subtopic/medicaid-enrollment-changes-following-the-aca

Medicare Payment Advisory Commission (MedPAC). 2019a. Accountable Care Organization Payment Systems. Accessed July 17, 2020. Available at: http://medpac.gov/docs/default-source/payment-basics/medpac_payment_basics_19_aco_final_sec.pdf?sfvrsn=0

Medicare Payment Advisory Commission (MedPAC). 2019b. Hospital Acute Inpatient Services Payment System. Accessed July 3, 2020. Available at: http://medpac.gov/docs/default-source/payment-basics/medpac_payment_basics_19_hospital_final_v2_sec.pdf?sfvrsn=0

Medicare Payment Advisory Commission (MedPAC). 2019c. Inpatient Psychiatric Facility Services Payment System. Accessed July 8, 2020. Available at: http://medpac.gov/docs/default-source/payment-basics/medpac_payment_basics_19_psych_final_sec.pdf?sfvrsn=0

Medicare Payment Advisory Commission (MedPAC). 2019d. Inpatient Rehabilitation Facilities Payment System. Accessed July 23, 2020. Available at: http://medpac.gov/docs/default-source/payment-basics/medpac_payment_basics_19_irf_final_sec.pdf?sfvrsn=0

Medicare Payment Advisory Commission (MedPAC). 2019e. Long-Term Care Hospitals Payment System. Accessed July 29, 2020. Available at: http://medpac.gov/docs/default-source/payment-basics/medpac_payment_basics_19_ltch_final_v2_sec.pdf?sfvrsn=0

Medicare Payment Advisory Commission (MedPAC). 2019f. Outpatient Hospital Services Payment System. Accessed July 11, 2020. Available at: http://medpac.gov/docs/default-source/payment-basics/medpac_payment_basics_19_opd_final_sec.pdf?sfvrsn=0

Medicare Payment Advisory Commission (MedPAC). 2019g. Outpatient Therapy Services Payment System. Accessed July 9, 2020. Available at: medpac.gov/docs/default-source/payment-basics/medpac_payment_basics_19_opt_final_sec.pdf?sfvrsn=0

Medicare Payment Advisory Commission (MedPAC). 2019h. Physician and Other Professional Payment System. Accessed July 11, 2020. Available at: medpac.gov/docs/default-source/payment-basics/medpac_payment_basics_19_physician_final_sec.pdf?sfvrsn=0

Medicare Payment Advisory Commission (MedPAC). 2020. Report to the Congress: Medicare Payment Policy. Accessed July 3, 2020. Available at: http://medpac.gov/docs/default-source/reports/mar20_entirereport_sec.pdf?sfvrsn=0

Mehrotra, A., A. Nimgaonkar, and B. Richman, 2021. Telemedicine and Medical Licensure—Potential Paths for Reform. *New England Journal of Medicine* 384: 687–690.

National Center for Health Statistics (NCHS). 1996. *Health, United States, 1995.* Hyattsville, MD: U.S. Department of Health and Human Services.

Nyman, J. A., and H. M. Trenz. 2016. Affordability of the Health Expenditures of Insured Americans Before the Affordable Care Act. *American Journal of Public Health* 106: 264–266.

Ochieng, N., J. F. Biniek, M. Freed, A. Damico, and T. Neuman, 2023. Medicare Advantage in 2023: Enrollment Update and Key Trends. *KFF* Available at: https://www.kff.org/medicare/issue-brief/medicare-advantage-in-2023-enrollment-update-and-key-trends/

Ochieng, N., J. F. Biniek, M. Freed, A. Damico, and T. Neuman. 2023. Medicare Advantage in 2023: Premiums, Out-of-Pocket Limits, Cost Sharing, Supplemental Benefits, Prior Authorization, and Star Ratings. *KFF* Available at: https://www.kff.org/medicare/issue-brief/medicare-advantage-in-2023-premiums-out-of-pocket-limits-cost-sharing-supplemental-benefits-prior-authorization-and-star-ratings/

Orgel, G. S., R. A. Weston, C. Ziebell, and L. H. Brown. 2019. Emergency Department Patient Payer Status after Implementation of the Affordable Care Act: A Nationwide Analysis Using NHAMCS Data. *American Journal of Emergency Medicine* 37: 1729–1733.

Park, S., L. White, P. Fishman, E. B. Larson, and N. B. Coe. 2020. Health Care Utilization, Care Satisfaction, and Health Status for Medicare Advantage and Traditional Medicare Beneficiaries with and without Alzheimer disease and Related Dementias. *JAMA Network Open* 3: e201809.

Parys, J. V. 2018. ACA Marketplace Premiums Grew More Rapidly in Areas with Monopoly Insurers than in Areas with More Competition. *Health Affairs* 37: 1243–1251.

Policy Center for Maternal Mental Health (2022). *Updates to ACA Insurance Plans for 2023 and the Upcoming Expiration of Subsidies.*

Prusynski, R. A., N. E. Leland, B. K. Frogner, C. Leibbrand, and T. M. Mroz. 2021. Therapy Staffing in Skilled Nursing Facilities Declined after Implementation of the Patient-Driven Payment Model. *Journal of the American Medical Directors Association* 22: 2201–2206.

Rahman, M., D. Meyers, E. M. White, et al. 2023. Spillover Effect of the Patient Drive Payment Model on Skilled Nursing Facility Therapy Delivery among Medicare Advantage Enrollees. *Health Economics.*

Rahman, M., E. M. White, B. E. McGarry, et al. 2022. Association Between the Patient Driven Payment Model and Therapy Utilization and Patient Outcomes in US Skilled Nursing Facilities. In *JAMA Health Forum*: e214366–e214366. American Medical Association.

Revere, L., B. Langland-Orban, J. Large, and Y. Yang,. 2021. Evaluating the Robustness of the CMS Hospital Value-Based Purchasing Measurement System. *Health Services Research* 56: 464–473.

Rieselbach, R., T. Epperly, E. McConnell, J. Noren, G. Nycz, and P. Shin. 2019. Community Health Centers: A Key Partner to Achieve Medicaid Expansion. *Journal of General Internal Medicine* 34: 2268–2272.

Ryan, A. M., S. Krinsky, K. A. Maurer, and J. B. Dimick. 2017. Changes in Hospital Quality Associated with Hospital Value-Based Purchasing. *New England Journal of Medicine* 376: 2358–2366.

Skopec, L., P. J. Huckfeldt, D. Wissoker, et al. 2020. Home Health and Postacute Care Use in Medicare Advantage and Traditional Medicare. *Health Affairs* 39: 837–842.

Snyder, L., and R. Rudowitz. 2014. Medicaid Enrollment Snapshot: December 2013. *Kaiser Commission on Medicaid and the Uninsured.* Accessed July 10, 2020. Available at: http://files.kff.org/attachment/medicaid-enrollment-snapshot-december-2013-issue-brief-download

Tanenbaum, S. J. 2017. Can Payment Reform Be Social Reform? The Lure and Liabilities of the "Triple Aim." *Journal of Health Politics, Policy and Law* 42: 53–71.

Tax Professionals. 2021. The Current State of the ACA Employer's Mandate. Accessed October 18, 2023. Available at: https://www.taxprofessionals.com/articles/the-current-state-of-the-aca-employer-s-mandate

The Assistant Secretary for Planning and Evaluation 2023. Health Coverage under the Affordable Care Act: Current Enrollment Trends and State Estimates. Available at: https://aspe.hhs.gov/reports/current-health-coverage-under-affordable-care-act

Uberoi, N. et al. 2016. Health Insurance Coverage and the Affordable Care Act, 2010-2016. Issue Brief, Office of the Assistant Secretary for Planning and Evaluation, Department of Health and Human Services. Accessed July 7, 2020. Available at: https://collections.nlm.nih.gov/catalog/nlm:nlmuid-101701796-pdf

Vaughn, E. J., and C. M. Elliott. 1987. *Fundamentals of Risk and Insurance.* New York: John Wiley & Sons.

Veterans Health Administration (VHA). 2020. About VA. Accessed July 17, 2020. Available at: https://www.va.gov/ABOUT_VA/index.asp

Wilson, M., A. Guta, K. Waddell, J. Lavis, R. Reid, and C. Evans, 2020. The Impacts of Accountable Care Organizations on Patient Experience, Health Outcomes and Costs: A Rapid Review. *Journal of Health Services Research & Policy* 25: 130–138.

Wiltshire, J. C., K. R. Enard, E. G. Colato, and B. L. Orban. 2020. Problems Paying Medical Bills and Mental Health Symptoms Post-Affordable Care Act. *AIMS Public Health* 7: 274–286.

Zhang, W., J. Luck, V. Patil, C. A. Mendez-Luck, and A. Kaiser, 2022. Changes in Therapy Utilization at Skilled Nursing Facilities under Medicare's Patient Driven Payment Model. *Journal of the American Medical Directors Association* 23: 1765–1771.

PART 3

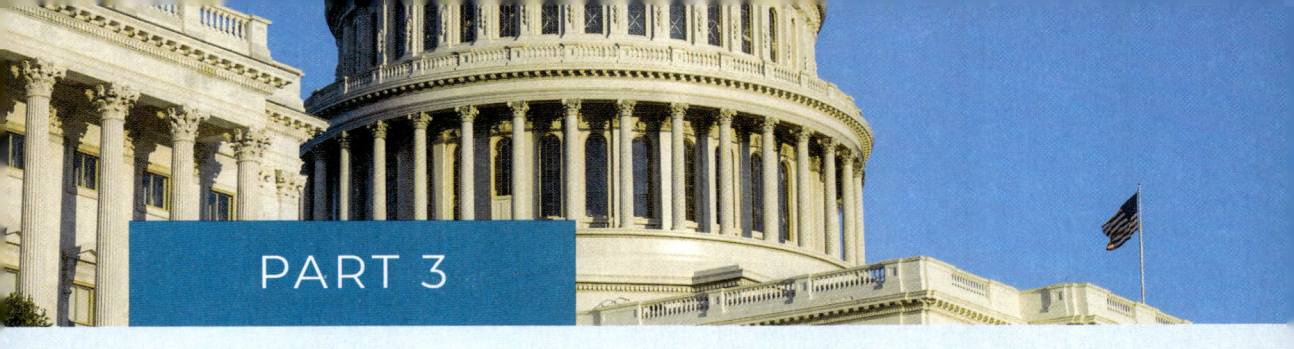

System Processes

CHAPTER 7	Outpatient and Primary Care Services	293
CHAPTER 8	Inpatient Facilities and Services	347
CHAPTER 9	Managed Care and Integrated Organizations	387
CHAPTER 10	Long-Term Care	429
CHAPTER 11	Health Services for Special Populations	461

CHAPTER 7

Outpatient and Primary Care Services

LEARNING OBJECTIVES

- Understand the meanings of outpatient, ambulatory, and primary care.
- Explore the main principles behind patient-centered medical homes and community-based primary care.
- Identify the reasons for the dramatic growth in outpatient services.
- Survey the various types of outpatient settings and services.
- Describe the role of complementary and alternative medicine in health care.
- Illustrate primary care delivery in selected countries.
- Demonstrate the role of primary care under COVID-19.
- Assess the impact of the Affordable Care Act on primary care.

"I suppose a system based on primary care is more robust."

Introduction

The terms "outpatient" and "ambulatory" have often been used interchangeably. Historically, outpatient care has been independent from services provided in healthcare institutions. In earlier days, physicians saw patients in their clinics, and most physicians also made home visits to treat patients within the limitations of medical science that was prevalent in those days. Institutions for inpatient care, such as hospitals and nursing homes, developed later. With advances in medical science, the locus of healthcare delivery coalesced around the institutional setting of community hospitals. As the range of services that could be provided on an outpatient basis continued to expand, hospitals gradually became the dominant players in providing the vast majority of outpatient care, with the exception of basic diagnostic care provided in physicians' offices (Barr and Breindel, 2004). Hospitals were better equipped to provide outpatient services because they had the resources necessary to capitalize on technological innovation. For example, hospital laboratories and diagnostic units were better equipped to perform most tests and diagnostic procedures than were independent providers. In comparison, independent providers faced greater capital constraints and competitive pressures in the healthcare marketplace.

Later, healthcare delivery increasingly grew beyond expensive acute-care hospitals to various alternative outpatient settings. Although basic primary care has traditionally been the foundation of outpatient services, some intensive procedures are increasingly being performed on an outpatient basis. Additionally, consumer demand has fueled the growth of complementary and alternative medicine.

Today, a large variety of outpatient services are available in the United States, yet many Americans do not have adequate access to health care because of maldistribution or shortages of providers and services. Hospital emergency care and community health centers constitute the main safety net for primary-care services, particularly for individuals who are uninsured. Delivery of outpatient care by public agencies has been limited in scope and detached from the dominant private system of health-service delivery. State and local government agencies sponsor limited outpatient services such as child immunizations, maternal and infant care, health screenings in public schools, monitoring of certain contagious diseases (e.g., tuberculosis), family planning, and prevention of sexually transmitted diseases. The Affordable Care Act includes provisions to address some of the issues of access for low-income and vulnerable populations.

What Is Outpatient Care?

Outpatient services do not require an overnight inpatient stay in an institution of healthcare delivery, such as a hospital or long-term care facility. Many hospitals, in addition to admitting patients for overnight or longer stays, have emergency departments (EDs) and other outpatient service centers, such as outpatient surgery, rehabilitation, and specialized clinics.

Outpatient services are also referred to as **ambulatory care**. Strictly speaking, ambulatory care constitutes diagnostic and therapeutic services and treatments provided to the "walking" (ambulatory) patient. Hence, in a restricted sense, the term "ambulatory care" refers to care rendered to patients who come to physicians' offices, hospital outpatient departments, and health centers to receive care. This term is also used synonymously with "community medicine" (Wilson and Neuhauser, 1985) because the geographic location of ambulatory services is intended to serve the surrounding community, providing convenience and easy accessibility to healthcare services for the members of that community.

However, patients do not always walk or drive their personal vehicles to the service centers to receive ambulatory care. For example, in a hospital ED, patients may arrive by land or air ambulance. EDs, in most cases, are equipped to provide secondary- and tertiary-care services rather than primary care. In other instances, such as with mobile diagnostic units and home health care, services are transported to the patient, instead of the patient coming to receive the services. Hence, the terms "outpatient" and "inpatient" are more precise, with the term **outpatient services** referring to any healthcare services that are not provided on the basis of an overnight stay in which room and board are incurred.

The Scope of Outpatient Services

Since the 1980s, extraordinary growth has occurred in the volume and variety of outpatient services, and new settings have emerged for delivering outpatient services. **Table 7-1** provides some examples. Hospital-based

Table 7-1 Owners, Providers, and Settings for Ambulatory Care Services

Past	Present
Owners/Providers	
■ Independent physician practitioners ■ Hospitals ■ Community health agencies ■ Home health agencies	■ Independent physician practitioners ■ Hospitals ■ Community health agencies ■ Managed care organizations ■ Insurance companies ■ Corporate employers ■ Group practices ■ National physician chains ■ Home health companies ■ National diversified healthcare companies
Service Settings	
■ Hospital outpatient departments ■ Physicians' offices ■ Outpatient surgery centers ■ Hospital emergency departments ■ Home health agencies ■ Neighborhood health centers	■ Physicians' offices ■ Walk-in clinics/urgent care centers ■ Retail clinics ■ Outpatient surgery centers ■ Chemotherapy and radiation therapy centers ■ Dialysis centers ■ Community health centers ■ Diagnostic imaging centers ■ Mobile imaging centers ■ Fitness/wellness centers ■ Occupational health centers ■ Psychiatric outpatient centers ■ Rehabilitation centers ■ Sports medicine clinics ■ Hand injury rehabilitation clinics ■ Women's health clinics ■ Wound care centers

Data from Barr, K. W., and C. L. Breindel. 2004. Ambulatory care. In: Health care administration: Planning, implementing, and managing organized delivery systems. L. F. Wolper, ed. 4th ed. Burlington, MA: Jones & Bartlett Learning. pp. 507–546.

medical systems and integrated delivery organizations now offer a range of healthcare services that include a variety of outpatient services. In some areas, the growth of nonhospital-based ambulatory services has intensified the competition between hospitals and community-based providers over patients seeking outpatient care. Examples of such competitors in the outpatient services market include home health care, freestanding clinics for routine and urgent care, retail clinics, outpatient rehabilitation, and freestanding imaging centers. Other services, such as dental-care and optometric services, remain independent of other types of healthcare services. Financing is the main reason for their independent nature: medical insurance plans are generally separate from dental- and vision-care plans. Philosophical and technical differences account for other variations. Chiropractic care, for instance, is generally covered by most health plans but remains isolated from the mainstream practice of medicine. Complementary and alternative therapies as well as self-care are not covered by insurance, yet the products and services in these categories continue to experience remarkable growth.

Primary care is the foundation of ambulatory health services, but not all ambulatory care is primary care. For example, hospital ED services are not intended to be primary in nature. Conversely, services other than primary care have now become an integral part of outpatient services. Thanks to technological advances in medicine, many advanced treatments are now provided in ambulatory-care settings. Examples include conditions requiring urgent treatment, outpatient surgery, renal dialysis, and chemotherapy.

Primary Care

Primary care plays a central role in a healthcare delivery system. Other essential levels of care include secondary and tertiary care (which are distinct from the primary, secondary, and tertiary prevention discussed in the *Beliefs,* *Values, and Health* chapter). Compared with primary care, secondary- and tertiary-care services are more complex and specialized.

Primary care is distinguished from secondary and tertiary care according to its duration, frequency, and level of intensity. **Secondary care** is usually short term, involving sporadic consultation from a specialist to provide expert opinion and surgical or other advanced interventions that primary-care physicians (PCPs) are not equipped to perform. It includes hospitalization, routine surgery, specialty consultation, and rehabilitation.

Tertiary care, the most complex level of care, is provided for relatively uncommon conditions. Typically, such care is institution based, highly specialized, and technology driven. Much of tertiary care is rendered in large teaching hospitals, such as university hospitals. Examples include trauma care, burn treatment, neonatal intensive care, tissue transplants, and open heart surgery. In some instances, tertiary treatment may be extended, and the tertiary-care physician may assume long-term responsibility for the bulk of the patient's care.

It has been estimated that 75% to 85% of people in the general population require only primary-care services in a given year, 10% to 12% require referrals to short-term secondary-care services, and 5% to 10% use tertiary-care specialists (Starfield, 1994). These proportions vary in populations with special healthcare needs.

Definitions of primary care often focus on the type or level of services, such as prevention, diagnostic and therapeutic services, health education and counseling, and minor surgery. Although primary care specifically emphasizes these services, many specialists also provide the same spectrum of services. For example, the practice of most ophthalmologists has a large element of prevention in addition to diagnosis, treatment, follow-up, and minor surgery. Similarly, most cardiologists are engaged in health education and counseling. Hence, primary care should be more appropriately viewed as an approach to providing health care rather than as a set of specific services (Starfield, 1994).

World Health Organization Definition

Traditionally, primary care has been the cornerstone of ambulatory-care services. The World Health Organization (WHO, 1978) describes **primary health care** as follows:

> Essential health care based on practical, scientifically sound, and socially acceptable methods and technology made universally accessible to individuals and families in the community by means acceptable to them and at a cost that the community and the country can afford to maintain at every stage of their development in a spirit of self-reliance and self-determination. It forms an integral part of both the country's health system of which it is the central function and the main focus of the overall social and economic development of the community. It is the first level of contact of individuals, the family, and the community with the national health system, bringing health care as close as possible to where people live and work and constitutes the first element of a continuing healthcare process.

Three elements in this definition are particularly noteworthy for an understanding of primary care: point of entry, coordination of care, and essential care.

Point of Entry

Primary care is the point of entry into a health-services system in which healthcare delivery is organized around primary care (Starfield, 1992). Primary care is the first contact a patient makes with the healthcare delivery system. This first contact feature is closely associated with the "gatekeeper" role of the primary-care practitioner. **Gatekeeping** implies that patients do not visit specialists and are not admitted to a hospital without first being referred by their PCPs. The interposition of primary care protects patients from undergoing unnecessary procedures and overtreatment (Franks et al., 1992).

The United Kingdom's National Health Service (NHS) is an example of a healthcare delivery system founded on the principles of gatekeeping. In the NHS, primary care is the single portal of entry to secondary care and acts as a filter so that 90% of care is provided outside of hospitals in ambulatory-care settings (Orton, 1994). General practitioners (GPs) are primary-care gatekeepers in the U.K. system. In the United States, under certain managed care, such as most Kaiser Health Plans, patients initiate care with their PCPs and obtain authorization when specialized services are needed.

Coordination of Care

One of the main functions of primary care is to coordinate the delivery of health services between the patient and the myriad of delivery components of the system. Hence, in addition to providing basic services, primary-care professionals serve as patient advisors and advocates. Coordination of an individual's total healthcare needs is meant to ensure continuity and comprehensiveness. These desirable goals of primary care are best achieved when the patient and the provider have formed a close mutual relationship over time. Thus, primary care can be regarded as the hub of the healthcare delivery system wheel. The various components of the healthcare delivery system are located around the rim of this wheel, and the spokes signify the coordination of continuous and comprehensive care (**Figure 7-1**).

Countries whose health systems are oriented more toward primary care achieve better health levels, higher satisfaction with health services among their citizens, and

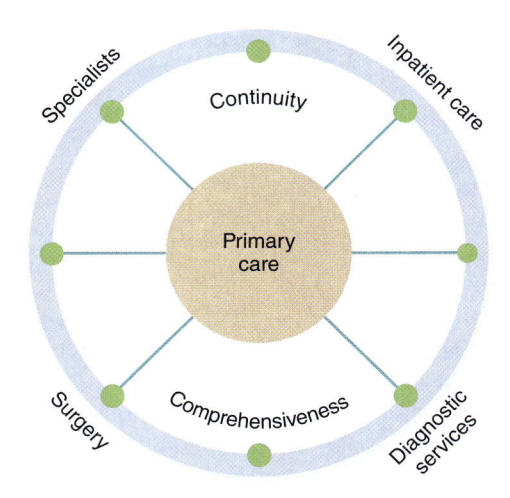

Figure 7-1 The coordination role of primary care in healthcare delivery.

lower expenditures on the overall delivery of health care (Basu et al., 2019; Levine et al., 2019; Starfield, 1994, 1998; Ferreira-Batista et al., 2023; Landa et al., 2023). Even in the United States, better health outcomes are achieved in states with higher ratios of PCPs and better availability of primary care (Shi, 1994; Shi and Starfield, 2000, 2001; Shi et al., 2002). Likewise, higher ratios of family and general physicians in the population are associated with lower hospitalization rates for conditions that can be successfully treated with good primary care (Chang et al., 2011; Parchman and Culler, 1994). Having a regular source of primary care also leads to fewer ED visits and inappropriate specialty consults. The primary-care setting is the ideal place to manage chronic conditions so individuals can stay healthier over time (Rubin et al., 2015; Sepulveda et al., 2008). Notably, adults who have PCPs as their regular source of care experience lower mortality (Franks et al., 1998; Jerant et al., 2012). In addition, research has presented that primary care may play an important role in mitigating the adverse health effects of income inequality (Jones et al., 2013; Shi et al., 1999). A higher proportion of PCPs in a given area has been known to lead to lower spending on health care (Chernew et al., 2009).

Coordination of health care has definite advantages. Studies have revealed that both the appropriateness and the outcomes of healthcare interventions are better when PCPs refer patients to specialists, as opposed to patients self-referring to specialists (Bakwin, 1945; Roos, 1979; Khatri et al., 2023; Fjellså et al., 2023).

Essential Care

Primary health care is regarded as essential health care. The goal of the healthcare delivery system is to optimize population health, not just the health of individuals who have the means to access health services. Achieving this goal requires that disparities across population subgroups be minimized to ensure equal access. Because financing of health care is a key element in determining access, universal access to primary-care services is better achieved under a national healthcare program.

Institute of Medicine Definition

The Institute of Medicine's (IOM) Committee on the Future of Primary Care recommends that primary care be the usual and preferred—though not the only—route of entry into the healthcare system. To emphasize this point, the IOM has defined primary care as "the provision of integrated, accessible healthcare services by clinicians who are accountable for addressing a large majority of personal healthcare needs, developing a sustained partnership with patients, and practicing in the context of family and community" (Vanselow et al., 1995, p. 192).

The term "integrated" in this definition embodies the concepts of comprehensive, coordinated, and continuous services that provide a seamless process of care. Primary care is *comprehensive* because it addresses any health problem at any given stage of a patient's life cycle. *Coordination* ensures the provision of a combination of health services to best meet the patient's needs. *Continuity* refers to care administered over time by a single provider or a team of healthcare professionals.

The IOM definition also emphasizes accessibility and accountability as key characteristics of primary care. *Accessibility* refers to the ease with which a patient can initiate an interaction with a clinician for any health problem. It includes efforts to eliminate barriers, such as those posed by geography, financing, culture, race, and language. Both clinicians and patients have **accountability**. The clinical system is accountable for providing quality care, producing patient satisfaction, using resources efficiently, and behaving in an ethical manner. Patients are responsible for their own health to the extent that they can influence it, as well for judicious use of resources when they need health care. The partnership between a patient and a clinician is based on mutual trust, respect, and responsibility.

Various countries have established policies that hold primary-care practices accountable for managing chronic conditions and meeting clinical standards. These policies tend to include financial incentives and primary-care practice redesign, with an emphasis on use of information technology (IT) and interdisciplinary teams to support effective, safe, patient-centered, coordinated, and efficient care.

The IOM definition of primary care recognizes that primary-care clinicians must consider the influence of the family on a patient's health status and be aware of the patient's living conditions, family dynamics, and cultural background. In addition, exemplary primary care requires an understanding of and a responsibility for the community's health (Vanselow et al., 1995).

Primary-Care Providers

Physicians in general family practice are most commonly the providers of primary care in Europe. In the United States, primary-care practitioners are not only restricted to physicians trained in general and family practice but also include physicians trained in internal medicine, pediatrics, and obstetrics and gynecology. One cannot assume, however, that these various types of practitioners are equally skilled in rendering primary-care services (Starfield, 1994). Unless a medical training program is dedicated to providing instruction in primary care, significant differences are likely to exist between its graduates and other PCPs. In fact, some controversy and competition have arisen among practitioners as to which specialists should be providing primary care. The specialty of family practice, in particular, represents a challenge to internal medicine in providing adult primary care and to pediatrics in providing child primary care.

Nonphysician providers (NPPs) are also playing a larger role in the delivery of primary care in the United States. In light of the increasing emphasis on healthcare cost containment, NPPs—who include nurse practitioners (NPs), physician assistants (PAs), and certified nurse-midwives (CNMs), among others—are in great demand in primary-care delivery settings, particularly in medically underserved areas (MUAs). Data from Medicaid managed care organizations (MCOs) demonstrate that patients receiving care from NPs at nurse-managed health centers experience significantly fewer ED visits, hospital inpatient days, and specialist visits, and female patients are at a significantly lower risk of giving birth to low-birth-weight infants, compared with patients in conventional health care (National Nursing Centers Consortium, 2003).

A retrospective cross-sectional analysis of national administrative data from Veterans Health Administration (VHA) primary-care encounters showed that NPs and PAs attended approximately 30% of all VHA primary-care encounters, and that NPs, PAs, and physicians fill similar roles in VHA primary care (Morgan et al., 2012). Similar results were also found in a study conducted in community health centers, with NPs and PAs providing 21% and 10%, respectively, of care for vulnerable populations (Morgan et al., 2015). Nevertheless, PCPs continue to fill an expert role that NPPs cannot match.

Primary Care and Public Health Integration

Because of primary-care's gatekeeping role for the healthcare system, it is increasingly recognized as a core component of integrated care. Integrated care, as mentioned earlier, emphasizes coordinated delivery and is concerned with providing people-centered care (Peckham, 2017; WHO, 2016). Primary care forms the basis of this model by acting as the point of first contact for patients and their families as they enter and move through the system (Loewenson and Simpson, 2017; Peckham, 2017). Shifting the focus toward prevention and early detection also helps promote general health and well-being in an aging and expanding population (WHO, 2018).

Significant attention has been devoted in recent years to strengthening primary-care's foundational role through integration with public health under what is now commonly referred to as "primary health care" (WHO, 2018). Primary health care consists of three main elements: (1) primary care and essential public health functions as the core of integrated services, (2) multisectoral policy and action, and (3) empowered people and communities (WHO, 2018). The integration of primary care with public health is grounded in the overlap of many of their functions and the prospect of better, more proactive care provision that addresses both individual- and population-level concerns. According to a 2012 IOM report, five principles are essential to the integration of primary care and public health:

1. A shared goal of population health improvement
2. Community engagement in defining and addressing population health needs
3. Aligned leadership
4. Sustainability
5. Sharing and collaborative use of data and analysis

Building on these principles, many different approaches can be taken to integrate primary-care and public-health services. One popular approach has been to integrate public-health professionals into the primary-care infrastructure. Although such a model does not constitute a full integration of the two fields, it has been implemented to various degrees in countries such as Iran, Brazil, and the United States (WHO, 2018). Another method is to build incentives into primary care to achieve certain public-health goals, as has long been done in the United Kingdom; yet another is to deliver routine public-health training to primary-care staff so that they can develop the skills needed to provide effective public-helath services (WHO, 2018). These methods represent some of the many ways integration can be achieved.

Although documentation remains limited, the available evidence shows positive effects in terms of access, utilization, and cost for primary-care systems that have incorporated public-health strategies. For example, countries that have adopted primary-care models with a population-health perspective have experienced improvements in costs, complications, and mortality. Providing access to a holistic range of health and social services also increase enrollment of vulnerable individuals and reduce hospital admission costs (Loewenson and Simpson, 2017; Stock et al., 2010). It appears that expanding primary-care's reach to tackle broader issues related to health allows it to operate more effectively as a preventive service focused on overall well-being, rather than consigning it to the role of a reactive system focused on disease. Taking on these issues at not just an individual level but also a population level provides better opportunities to detect and prevent health problems and reduce disease burden.

When seeking to achieve these goals through the successful integration of primary care and public health, both enabling and hindering factors come into play. Systemic factors, which encompass environmental factors outside of the actual organization engaging in integration, include government involvement as well as funding and resource factors. Organizational factors, which involve issues such as having a common agenda, knowledge, and resource limitations, and management and accountability, can also either facilitate or hinder progress. Interpersonal factors, including having a shared purpose and beliefs, positive relationships, and effective communication, affect the mutual understanding, enthusiasm, and trust between collaborators (Rechel, 2020). Any approach to integration must be mindful of these factors and the context in which the collaborative model is being implemented. Practitioners must also recognize that the experiences of previously successful models will not necessarily have the same impact in a different setting (Rechel, 2020).

The COVID-19 crisis demonstrates the importance of placing primary health care at the core of health systems, both to manage an unexpected surge of demand and to maintain continuity of care for all. Strong primary health care, organized in multidisciplinary teams and with innovative roles for health professionals, integrated with community health services, equipped with digital technology, and working with well-designed incentives helps deliver a successful health system response. The innovations introduced in response to the pandemic need to be maintained to make health systems more resilient against future public health emergencies and able to meet the challenges of aging societies and the growing burden of chronic conditions (OECD, 2021).

Primary Care and the Affordable Care Act

The Affordable Care Act (ACA) included four major provisions related to primary care:

- Increased Medicare and Medicaid payments to primary-care providers
- New incentives such as funding for scholarships and loan repayment for primary-care providers working in underserved areas
- Expansion of the health center program and strengthening of health center capacity
- Creation of additional training programs, such as 11 Teaching Health Centers to train primary-care providers

These measures were aimed at enhancing the primary-care workforce and strengthening the primary-care system, especially in underserved areas (Ku et al., 2011). On the surface, these measures appear to be steps in the right direction. Unfortunately, given the critical shortages in primary care (refer to the *Health Services Professionals* chapter), building a workforce cannot be accomplished in a short period of time. Current and prospective physicians also evaluate factors other than the proposed incentives when determining whether they will become PCPs or specialists. For example, physicians may feel burdened and frustrated by new regulatory demands if they have to spend a large share of their time complying with onerous regulations instead of treating patients. In addition, because the increased reimbursement for PCPs under the ACA was temporary, it may not turn out to be a significant factor in providers' decisions to leave or stay in practice or in influencing medical students to enter primary care. As the income gap between PCPs and specialists is one of the biggest discouraging factors for entering primary care, this issue must be seriously addressed if PCP shortages are to be alleviated (Steinwald et al., 2018).

As a result of the ACA, the primary-care system in the United States is expected to experience an influx of newly insured patients. However, if PCPs become overburdened, many of the goals of primary care may remain unrealized for a large segment of the U.S. population.

The ACA also eliminated out-of-pocket costs for preventive services such as immunizations, certain cancer screenings, contraception, reproductive counseling, obesity screening, and behavioral assessments for children. This coverage is guaranteed for more than 137 million Americans, including 55 million women. Approximately 39 million Medicare beneficiaries have received preventive services such as cancer screenings, bone-mass measurements, annual physical examinations, and smoking cessation assistance due to the elimination of out-of-pocket costs for this care.

On another front, the ACA allocated $1.5 billion to the National Health Service Corps, a training program, which for decades has offered scholarships and loan forgiveness to young primary-care clinicians who volunteer to practice in underserved areas. As of September 30, 2015, there were 9,600 Corps clinicians providing primary-care services, more than twice the number of these clinicians in 2008 (White House, 2016). Under the Trump administration, however, these achievements were significantly scaled back.

However, President Biden's FY23 budget invested $700 million in programs–like the National Health Service Corps, Behavioral Health Workforce Education and Training Program, and the Minority Fellowship Program—that provide training, access to scholarships, and loan repayment to mental health and substance use disorder clinicians committed to practicing in rural and other underserved communities (The White House, 2022). These major new investments will expand the pipeline of behavioral health providers and improve their geographic distribution to target areas with the greatest unmet need.

New Directions in Primary Care

Patient-Centered Medical Homes

The term "medical home" was first coined in 1967 to describe the team-oriented approaches developed for special-needs children whose healthcare needs require constant coordination. A **medical home** consists of an interdisciplinary team of physicians and allied health professionals who partner with patients and their families, taking responsibility for ongoing patient care using a team approach, technology, and evidence-based protocols to deliver and coordinate care. PCPs serve as advocates for patients to help them access a wide variety of healthcare services, ensuring that the patient's values, wishes, and directives are honored (Caudill et al., 2011).

The patient-centered medical home (PCMH) has emerged as a promising solution to address the significant fragmentation, poor quality, and high costs that afflict the U.S. healthcare system. With regard to PCMH and service utilization, evaluations of appropriate care have typically focused on greater use of preventive services, immunizations, and well-care visits, whereas evaluations of inappropriate use of services have examined outcomes such as ED visits, rates of hospitalization for preventable ambulatory conditions, and use of high-cost or inefficient procedures. Findings from these evaluations provide considerable support for the value of PCMHs, as they promote appropriate care and reduce inappropriate care or disparities in care (Christensen et al., 2013; Ferrante et al., 2010; Rosenthal et al., 2015; Shi et al., 2015; Shi et al., 2016; Swietek et al., 2020; Burton et al., 2020).

In terms of the impact of a PCMH on the patient's experience and quality of care, studies suggest that both adult patients and parents of pediatric patients who go to a PCMH-designated primary-care practice are satisfied with the care that they and their children receive and are likely to perceive these healthcare interactions as positive experiences (Christensen et al., 2013; Rosenthal et al., 2015); however, evidence for the associations between PCMH and some other quality indicators remains mixed (Christensen et al., 2013; Rosenthal et al., 2015; Stevens et al., 2010). Likewise, findings regarding PCMH and healthcare costs are inconsistent (Christensen et al., 2013; Crits-Cristoph et al., 2018;

Gao et al., 2016; Gilfillan et al., 2010; Reid et al., 2009; Burton et al., 2020).

In terms of the impact of PCMHs and clinical outcomes, several studies have demonstrated a positive impact of PCMHs on clinical measures at the practice level (Gao et al., 2016; Hu et al., 2018; Shi et al., 2015; Shi et al., 2016; Veet et al., 2020), but insufficient evidence is available to determine the effect of PCMH implementation at the patient level. More rigorous evaluations and standardization of key outcomes are needed to strengthen the empirical basis for the medical home concept and to assess the viability of its implementation (Mulvihill et al., 2007).

A number of tools are used to assess important aspects of the PCMH. For example, the National Committee for Quality Assurance's (NCQA) Physician Practice Connections—Patient-Centered Medical Home (PPC-PCMH) tool is a practice self-report measure that has become the de facto standard used to judge "medical homeness." It assesses nine standards: access and communication, patient tracking and registries, care management, patient self-management support, electronic prescribing, test tracking, referral tracking, performance reporting and improvement, and advanced electronic communications. The three-level scoring system implicitly acknowledges that, for most practices, meeting these reporting standards will be a staged process (NCQA, 2008). NCQA's PCMH Recognition program is the most widely adopted PCMH evaluation program in the United States. More than 10,000 practices (with 50,000+clinicians) are recognized by NCQA (2023). More than 95 organizations support NCQA Recognition by providing financial incentives, transformation support, care management, learning collaboratives, or MOC credit.

Unlike the NCQA, the Accreditation Association for Ambulatory Health Care (AAAHC) conducts mandatory site visits to all applicants for its PCMH recognition program. AAAHC's recognition program involves the largest number of survey items by far (238 items), and AAAHC is unique in that it allows applicants to apply for either "accreditation" (which involves obtaining the base AAAHC accreditation in addition to meeting the organization's medical home standards) or a less burdensome option called "certification" (which does not require the base AAAHC accreditation). The AAAHC's Medical Home tool measures a practice's performance with regard to patient rights and responsibilities; organizational governance and administration; the patient–care team relationship; comprehensiveness, continuity, and accessibility of care; clinical records and health information; and quality of care (AAAHC, 2009).

Other PCMH assessment tools include the Joint Commission's Primary Care Medical Home Designation Standards (Joint Commission, 2011), URAC's Patient-Centered Health Care Home (PCHCH) Program Toolkit, TransforMED's Medical Home Implementation Quotient, and the Center for Medical Home Improvement's Medical Home Index. State-level tools are also available, including Blue Cross Blue Shield of Michigan's PCMH Designation standards, Minnesota's statewide multipayer Health Care Home Certification standards, and Oklahoma's SoonerCare (Medicaid) PCMH standards, among others (Burton et al., 2012).

Most of the PCMH assessment tools cover several key content domains: access to care, comprehensiveness of care, continuity of care, culturally competent communication, patient engagement and self-management, coordination of care, care plan, population management, team-based care, evidence-based care, quality measurement and improvement, community resources, medical records, health IT, standardized care, adherence to current law, and congruence between practice and patient (Burton et al., 2012).

Primary-Care Assessment Tools

Beyond the PCMH, many tools have been developed over the years to measure primary-care performance at various scales and settings.

The Primary Care Assessment Tools (PCAT) instrument, developed by the Johns Hopkins Primary Care Policy Center under the leadership of Dr. Barbara Starfield and Dr. Leiyu Shi, has emerged as a leading method for conducting such measurements. PCAT is a set of instruments developed to assess and measure the performance and quality of primary-care services at multiple levels within the healthcare system. The tools are developed based on a theoretical framework of primary-care domains and characteristics. The PCAT measure the presence and extent of four cardinal domains and three related domains of primary care and user affiliation with the care source. These tools are designed to evaluate primary care from the perspectives of patients, healthcare providers, healthcare facilities, and the healthcare system as a whole. An important characteristic of the PCAT is that it allows for assessment of both structure-related components of primary care (related to the capacity to provide services) and process-related components (related to the provision of services when needed). PCAT includes questions to assess four core domains—first-contact care, ongoing care, coordinated care, and comprehensive care—and three related domains of primary care—family-centeredness, community orientation, and cultural competence (Johns Hopkins Primary Care Policy Center, n.d.). Here's an overview of the PCAT and how they measure primary-care performance at various levels.

- **Patient level**
  PCAT-Patient-Centered Medical Home (PCMH): This tool assesses the extent to which primary-care practices function as patient-centered medical homes (Stange et al., 2010). It evaluates the patient's experience of care, including access, continuity, comprehensiveness, and coordination of services (Stange et al., 2010). The PCMH is being promoted as the future of primary-care practice that will help reform the U.S. healthcare system into one that is more accessible, effective, efficient, safe, and economical (Ferrante et al., 2010).

- **Provider level**
  PCAT-Provider: This tool collects data from healthcare providers and professionals to assess their perceptions of the primary-care services they offer. It measures aspects such as the provider's scope of practice, job satisfaction, and collaboration within the primary-care team (Shi et al., 2001).

- **Facility level**
  PCAT-Adult: This tool is designed to assess the quality and performance of primary-care facilities or practices from the perspective of adult patients (Shi et al., 2001). It covers dimensions such as accessibility, continuity, comprehensiveness, coordination, and the overall experience of care (Shi et al., 2001).
  PCAT-Child: Similar to PCAT-Adult, this tool is tailored to assess the quality of primary care for children. It focuses on pediatric health care, ensuring that primary care for children meets specific requirements and standards (Agency for healthcare research and quality, 2014).

- **System level**
  PCAT-Systems: This instrument is designed to assess the broader primary-care system, evaluating its capacity, organization, and performance (Shi et al., 2001). It helps policymakers and researchers understand how well the primary-care system is functioning within a specific region or healthcare system (Shi et al., 2001).

The PCAT has been widely developed and used around the world, with multiple international versions currently in circulation. Countries where the PCAT has been used include Brazil, Canada, China, Japan, South Korea, South Africa, and more (Aoki et al., 2016; Bresick et al., 2016; D'Avila et al., 2017; Jeon, 2011; Mei et al., 2016; Wang and Haggerty, 2019; Pesse-Sorensen et al., 2019; Pinto et al., 2021a; Pinto et al., 2021b). **Table 7-2** provides

Table 7-2 Examples of Questions in the Primary Care Assessment Tools (PCATs)

Primary Care Domains	Adult Patient	Child Patient	Provider	Facility
First contact (utilization)	When you have a new health problem, do you go to your PCP before going somewhere else?	When your child needs a regular general checkup, do you go to your PCP before going somewhere else?	NA	NA
First contact (accessibility)	When your PCP is open, can you get advice quickly over the phone if you need it?	When your PCP is open and your child gets sick, would someone from there care for them the same day?	When your office is open and patients get sick, would someone from your office care for them that day?	When your facility is open and patients get sick, would someone from your facility care for them that day?
Ongoing care	If you have a question, can you call and talk to the doctor or nurse who knows you best?	When you take your child to your PCP's office, are they taken care of by the same doctor or nurse each time?	At your office, do patients meet with the same clinician each time they make a visit?	If patients have a question, can they call and talk to the doctor or nurse who knows them best?
Coordination	For your specialist appointment, did your PCP or someone working with your PCP help you make the appointment for that visit?	After your child went to the specialist or special service, did your PCP talk with you and your child about what happened at the visit?	When patients need a referral, do you discuss different places the family might go to get help with their problem?	When patients are referred, do the clinicians give them any written information to take to the specialist?
Coordination (information systems)	When you go to your PCP, do you bring any of your own medical records, such as shot records or reports of medical care you had in the past?	Could you go through your child's medical record if you wanted to?	Are patients expected to bring their medical records, such as immunizations or medical care they received in the past?	Would your facility allow patients to examine their medical records if they wanted to?

Table 7-2 Examples of Questions in the Primary Care Assessment Tools (PCATs)

Primary Care Domains	Adult Patient	Child Patient	Provider	Facility
Comprehensiveness (services available)	Following is a list of services that you or your family might need at some time. For each one, please indicate whether it is available at your PCP's office. (i.e., immunizations, family planning)	Following is a list of services that your child or family might need at some time. For each one, please indicate whether it is available at your PCP's office. (i.e., immunizations, birth control)	If patients need any of the following services, would they be able to get them on site at your office? (i.e., immunizations, family planning)	If patients need any of the following services, would they be able to get them on site at your facility? (i.e., immunizations, family planning)
Comprehensive (services provided)	In visits to your PCP, are any of the following subjects discussed with you? (i.e., nutrition, home safety)	In visits to your child's PCP, are any of the following subjects discussed with you and your child? (i.e., nutrition, home safety)	Are the following subjects discussed with patients? (i.e., nutrition, exercise)	Are the following subjects discussed with patients? (i.e., nutrition, exercise)
Family-centeredness	Has your PCP asked about illnesses or problems that might run in your family?	Does your PCP ask you about your ideas and opinions when planning treatment and care for your child?	Does your office ask patients about their ideas and opinions when planning treatment and care for the patient or family member?	Do the doctors and nurses at your facility ask about illnesses or problems that might run in the patients' families?
Community orientation	Does your PCP know about the important health problems of your neighborhood?	Does anyone at your PCP's office ever make home visits?	Does your office make home visits?	Do you think the clinicians at your facility have adequate knowledge about the health problems of the communities you serve?
Cultural competence	Would you recommend your PCP to a friend or relative?	Would you recommend your child's PCP to someone who does not speak English well?	Can your office communicate with people who do not speak English well?	If needed, does your facility take into account a family's special beliefs about health care or use of folk medicine, such as herbs/homemade medicines?

some examples of questions from the surveys that are used to assess individual domains of primary care. PCAT instruments have been widely used in research, policy development, and quality improvement initiatives to enhance primary-care services and outcomes.

Community-Oriented Primary Care

Current thoughts about primary-care delivery have extended beyond the traditional biomedical paradigm, which focuses on medical care for the individual in an encounter-based system. The broader biopsychosocial paradigm integrates the health of the population as well as that of the individual. **Community-oriented primary care (COPC)** emphasizes the relations between the population and community, on the one hand, and personal health care, on the other hand (van Weel et al., 2008). COPC incorporates the elements of good primary-care delivery and adds a population-based approach to identifying and addressing community health problems. The main challenge has been bringing together individual health needs in the larger context of community health needs.

COPC incorporates the ideals espoused by both the WHO and IOM in the delivery of primary care. The 1978 International Conference on Primary Health Care (held at Alma-Ata in the former Soviet Union, under the auspices of the WHO) declared a philosophical vision of an affordable community-based primary healthcare system (WHO, 1978). More recently, the WHO (2010) has offered additional guidelines that encompass five key elements: (1) reducing exclusion and social disparities in health through universal coverage reforms, (2) organizing health services around people's needs and expectations, (3) integrating health into all sectors, (4) pursuing collaborative models of policy dialogue, and (5) increasing stakeholder participation. IOM (2012) has endorsed COPC as a dynamic, interdisciplinary model that integrates primary care and public health to create significant improvements in primary-care delivery.

The application and adoption of COPC principles in actual practice, however, have not materialized in the United States. One fundamental problem is a lack of consensus on what a "community" is or should be. Assuming that consensus on the definition of a community can be reached, technological advances have reached a stage of development at which they can adequately reflect a community's health. Information technology can also assist in prioritizing and developing a course of action. Perhaps the biggest hurdles to COPC in the United States are workforce shortages and financial incentives. COPC requires a major transformation of the current system and faces the same implementation problems as medical homes.

Primary Care and Pandemics

In the face of a global disease pandemic, primary care plays a critical role in alleviating strain on the healthcare system and in managing patients. It is often the first line of contact with patients and suspected cases, taking on a crucial triage role as primary-care providers perform initial assessments and determine whether patients need more medical attention or can self-monitor at home. By filtering out and managing uncomplicated cases, primary-care practices clear up space and free up resources in hospitals to treat patients with more severe disease (Vasan, 2017). Clinics located in underserved communities also act as a safety net for vulnerable populations who otherwise would not be able to afford or access care (Lewis, 2018). For these groups, who have historically borne the worst burden in pandemics, access to care is crucial.

Having a strong primary-care system can also prevent an onslaught of severe cases and reduce the risk of further transmission. One of its important attributes is continuity, as primary-care providers build long-term relationships with patients. These long-term relationships help foster trust with patients and encourage them to seek out care and follow medical advice (Vasan, 2017). This increases the likelihood that those patients who have been exposed or become ill are properly treated and aware of guidelines they must follow to quarantine, isolate, and prevent further transmission of disease. Additionally, primary-care's emphasis on preventive care helps reduce the burden of chronic disease and comorbidities, which are risk factors for more severe illness (Damian, 2020; Vasan, 2017). By having a high-functioning, well-funded primary-care system in place, these health problems can be more effectively managed and prevented.

The essential nature of a high-functioning primary-care system during public health crises was no better exemplified than during the 2020–2022 COVID-19 pandemic, which overwhelmed the U.S. healthcare system and disproportionately affected vulnerable populations (Centers for Disease Control and Prevention [CDC], 2020; Martin, 2020). The high case rate in the United States and the disease's disproportionate impact on people of color happened at a time when both the number of primary-care visits and the number of Americans with a usual source of primary care had declined in recent years. Public trust in physicians also ranks low in the United States—a sentiment and a problem that have likely been exacerbated in communities of color by consistent underinvestment in those communities (Damian, 2020; Lewis et al., 2020). As COVID-19 spread across the United States, there were strong calls to reorganize the nation's primary-care system. This effort would include increasing funding and investment, restructuring the payment system, and giving more support to family and community-based care (Koller, 2020; Tritter and Schwarz, 2020). Primary-care systems that are community-focused, comprehensive, and well-resourced have been in the best positions to successfully respond to and mitigate COVID-19 (Tritter and Schwarz, 2020; Urquiza, 2020; Elliott et al., 2023; Aoki et al., 2023; Chami et al., 2023). As policymakers consider how to strengthen the United States' future pandemic response, the field of primary care deserves renewed focus and attention. Below are summaries of the role of primary care during COVID-19.

- **Surveillance:** Primary-care physicians are a key component of surveillance systems, with the responsibility to report to public health when they identify communicable diseases of significance (Kinder et al., 2021). For example, as a patient's first point-of-contact, primary care tends to identify a spike in seasonal influenza earlier than emergency departments and can serve as a reliable indicator of underlying trends in community transmission (Kearon & Risdon, 2020).
- **Triage and treatment of illness in the community:** The majority of the patients with COVID-19 will be treated first and solely by primary care because the majority of infected individuals experience only mild to moderate symptoms (Kearon & Risdon, 2020). A model based on pandemic influenza and SARS found that a higher concentration of hospitals is linked to greater spread and mortality, while a higher concentration of community-based primary-care clinics to triage, diagnose, and treat the pandemic illness was associated with reduced transmission and mortality (Kearon & Risdon, 2020).
- **Prevention of spread among vulnerable populations:** Certain populations will be at a higher risk of contracting communicable diseases, such as those who are unstably housed or living in congregate settings (Kearon & Risdon, 2020). By proactively reaching out to the most vulnerable patients, family physicians can provide education and support to prevent spread to these individuals (Kearon & Risdon, 2020).
- **Vaccination:** Primary-care providers are typically responsible for administering vaccines, including those developed to

prevent the spread of the pathogen causing the pandemic (Kearon & Risdon, 2020). Primary-care clinicians, more than other groups of clinicians, scientists, government officials, media, etc., have the greatest chance for instilling confidence about the vaccine to their patients, including the most vulnerable and the most distrusting (Katzman & Katzman, 2021). They also help establish vaccination schedules and prioritize high-risk groups (Mitchell et al., 2020).

- **Postpandemic recovery:** In the post-peak period, family physicians will have a large role in caring for these patients with increased needs (Lal & Schwalbe, 2023). Following the relaxation of physical-distancing measures, there will likely be an increase in demand of counseling and mental health services, higher volume of preventive care, and a higher acuity of medical complaints (Lal & Schwalbe, 2023).
- **Pandemic planning:** A core component of pandemic recovery is to assess lessons learned and begin to prepare and plan for another pandemic (Kearon & Risdon, 2020). COVID-19 highlights the importance of having primary-care representatives in the creation of pandemic preparedness plans (Kearon & Risdon, 2020).
- **Improve share of individual and population data and knowledge:** Integration of primary care and public health, with a person-centered focus rather than an orientation toward diseases, can improve the health of an entire community (Kinder et al., 2021). For example, at drive-through test centers, the test results must be communicated to primary-care clinicians, which enables the family doctor to follow up with the patient on treatment and isolation, as well as proactively assess the family's situation and contact trace (Kinder et al., 2021).
- **Communication and education:** Primary-care providers are essential in educating patients and communities about preventive measures, symptoms, and the importance of vaccination (Mitchell et al., 2020). They play a significant role in dispelling misinformation, ensuring that patients have accurate information about the pandemic, and promoting health protective behaviors, psychological well-being, and business continuity (Desborough et al., 2021).

Primary Care and Integrated Care System

Primary care plays a significant role in an integrated care delivery system as illustrated below.

- **Chronic disease management:** Primary-care providers are at the forefront of managing chronic conditions (National Academies of Sciences, Engineering, and Medicine, 2021). They work closely with patients to develop care plans, monitor progress, and adjust treatments to optimize outcomes. By doing so, they help reduce hospitalizations and emergency department visits (National Academies of Sciences, Engineering, and Medicine, 2021).
- **Coordinated care management:** Interprofessional primary-care (IPC) teams provide comprehensive and coordinated care and are ideally equipped to support those populations most at risk of adverse health outcomes, including older adults, and patients with chronic physical and mental health conditions (Donnelly et al., 2021). A practice team tailored to the whole-person primary care including health coaches, care coordinators, and community health workers facilitates communication between different specialists and services and ensures that patients receive the right care at the right time (Donnelly et al., 2021).
- **Preventive and health promotion health services:** Primary care focuses on preventive care, wellness, and health

promotion (National Academies of Sciences, Engineering, and Medicine, 2021). Primary-care providers engage in patient education and encourage lifestyle modifications, helping to prevent or manage chronic conditions and reduce the need for acute care (National Academies of Sciences, Engineering, and Medicine, 2021).
- **Behavioral health integration:** Primary-care practices often integrate behavioral health specialists to provide timely assessment, counseling, and treatment, addressing both physical and mental health needs (National Academies of Sciences, Engineering, and Medicine, 2021). Integrated models of primary care and behavioral health can improve normative and process integration; studies have revealed that mental and behavioral health team integration produces better health outcomes and lower costs for adults and improved outcomes for children and adolescents (National Academies of Sciences, Engineering, and Medicine, 2021).
- **Pharmacist integration:** Primary-care teams increasingly involve pharmacists in medication management and reconciliation (National Academies of Sciences, Engineering, and Medicine, 2021). This collaboration helps ensure medication adherence, reduce adverse drug interactions, and improve overall medication safety (National Academies of Sciences, Engineering, and Medicine, 2021).
- **Public health integration:** Primary-care capabilities to respond to the immediate and long-term health consequences of the pandemic, including economic, mental, and social health complications, requires a high level of integration between public health agencies and primary-care practices (Vahidy et al., 2020). Public health and primary-care integration has many benefits beyond crisis situations such as COVID-19. A close partnership can improve the treatment of chronic conditions and increase the effectiveness and enhance dissemination of prevention and health promotion (Azar et al., 2020). Integration also increases the capacity of primary care to influence public health, by bringing a larger focus to the health of a community through connected healing and trusted relationships, thereby reaching individuals and their families who otherwise may not access primary-care services (Azar et al., 2020).
- **Telehealth and remote monitoring:** Digital technology with data system integration is a key facilitator of integrated care delivery and foundational to achieving accessible high-quality primary care (National Academies of Sciences, Engineering, and Medicine, 2021). Primary-care providers use telehealth to expand access to care and monitor patients remotely, which is especially valuable for patients with chronic conditions, allowing for regular check-ins and early intervention when issues arise (National Academies of Sciences, Engineering, and Medicine, 2021).

Growth in Outpatient Services

In the United States, the proportion of total surgeries performed in outpatient departments of community hospitals increased from 16.3% in 1980 to 49% in 2018 (**Figure 7-2**). This decline in inpatient procedures has actually been outpaced by the growth of ambulatory procedures. Notably, for patients older than 65 years, the rate of inpatient surgeries has not decreased (Kozak et al., 1999; National Center for Health Statistics [NCHS], 2010). In a study performed by Wier et al. (2015), the 10 most common ambulatory surgeries performed in community hospitals in 28 states were lens and cataract procedures (9.3% of all ambulatory surgeries), other therapeutic procedures on muscles and tendons (5.8%), other operating room therapeutic procedures on joints

Growth in Outpatient Services

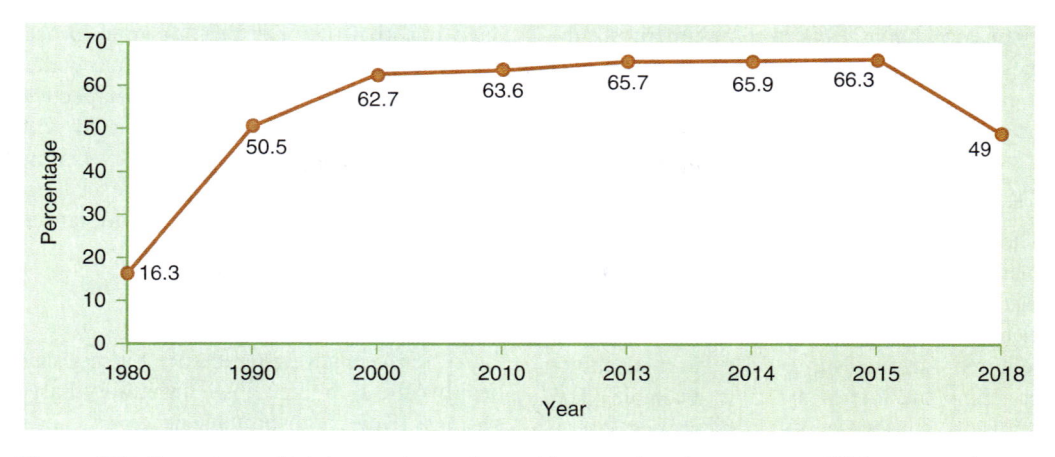

Figure 7-2 Percentage of total surgeries performed in outpatient departments of U.S. community hospitals, 1980–2015.

Data from National Center for Health Statistics. 2018. Health, United States, 2017. Hyattsville, MD: U.S. Department of Health and Human Services. Table 82. 2018 data from: McDermott, KW, Liang L. (2006). Overview of major ambulatory surgeries performed in hospital-owned facilities, 2019 Statistical Brief #287. Healthcare Cost and Utilization (HCUP) Statistical Briefs.

(4.5%), cholecystectomy and common duct exploration (4.0%), excision of semilunar cartilage of the knee (3.6%), inguinal and femoral hernia repair (2.8%), other operating room therapeutic procedures on the skin and breast (2.5%), lumpectomy and quadrantectomy of the breast (2.4%), decompression peripheral nerve (2.4%), and other hernia repair (2.3%).

Factors Influencing the Growth of Outpatient Services

Over the years, several noteworthy changes have been instrumental in shifting the delivery of health care from inpatient to outpatient settings. These changes can be broadly classified as reimbursement, technological factors, utilization control factors, physician practice factors, and social factors.

Reimbursement

Until the 1980s, health insurance coverage was usually more generous for inpatient services than for outpatient services. For years, many interventions that could have been performed safely and effectively on an outpatient basis remained inpatient procedures because third-party reimbursement for outpatient care was limited. These payment policies began to change during the 1980s. In response, hospitals aggressively developed outpatient services to offset their declining revenues from inpatient care.

In the mid-1980s, Medicare substituted a prospective payment system (PPS) for its traditional cost-plus system to reimburse inpatient hospital services (refer to the *Health Services Financing* chapter). PPS reimbursement, which is based on diagnosis-related groups (DRGs), provides fixed case-based payments to hospitals. In contrast, the outpatient sector was not subject to payment restrictions. Therefore, hospitals had a strong incentive to minimize inpatient lengths of stay and to provide continued treatment in outpatient settings—which led to mushrooming costs in the outpatient sector. In 2000, Medicare implemented prospective reimbursement mechanisms in an effort to contain these costs, such as the Medicare Outpatient Prospective Payment System (OPPS) for services provided in hospital outpatient departments and home health resource groups (HHRGs) for home health care (refer to the *Health Services*

Financing chapter). Cost-containment strategies adopted by managed care also stress lower inpatient use, with a corresponding emphasis on outpatient services.

Technological Factors

The development of new diagnostic and treatment procedures and less-invasive surgical methods has made it possible to provide services in outpatient settings that previously required hospital stays. For example, shorter-acting anesthetics are now available. The diffusion of arthroscopes, laparoscopes, lasers, and other minimally invasive technologies has also made many surgical procedures less traumatic. These modern procedures have dramatically curtailed recuperation time, which has made same-day surgical procedures very common. Many office-based physicians have also expanded their capacity to perform outpatient diagnostic, treatment, and surgical services as acquisition of technology has become more feasible and cost-effective.

Utilization Control Factors

To discourage lengthy hospital stays, payers have instituted prior authorization policies for inpatient admission as well as close monitoring during hospitalization. The *Managed Care and Integrated Organizations* chapter discusses the most widely adopted utilization control methods.

Physician Practice Factors

The growth of managed care and the consolidation trend associated with large hospital-centered institutions weakened physician autonomy and professional control over the delivery of medical care. Physicians also lost income. To counter these forces, an increasing number of physicians have broken their ties with hospitals and started their own specialized care centers, such as ambulatory surgery centers and cardiac care centers. In these kinds of specialized ambulatory care centers, physicians often find that they can perform more procedures in less time and earn higher incomes (Jackson, 2002). From patients' perspective, higher volumes may also be associated with better-quality care. Such factors may be behind the growth in specialized centers of excellence for cataract and hernia surgeries and cardiac procedures.

Social Factors

Patients have a strong preference for receiving health care in home- and community-based settings. Unless absolutely necessary, most patients do not want to be institutionalized. Staying in their own homes gives people a strong sense of independence and control over their lives—elements considered important for a better quality of life.

Large hospitals have traditionally been located in congested urban centers, but increasing numbers of suburbanites now perceive these locations as inconvenient. Hence, many freestanding outpatient centers and satellite clinics operated by inner-city hospitals are now located in the suburbs.

Types of Outpatient Care Settings and Methods of Delivery

The services described in this section are not always operated independently of each other. For example, a hospital may operate physician clinics in addition to some of the freestanding facilities described here. Also, in a constantly evolving system, new settings and methods are likely to emerge. However, in general, the various settings for outpatient service delivery found in the U.S. healthcare delivery system can be grouped as follows:

- Private practice
- Hospital-based services
- Freestanding facilities
- Retail clinics
- Mobile medical, diagnostic, and screening services

- Home health care
- Hospice services
- Ambulatory long-term care services
- Public health services
- Community health centers
- Free clinics
- Telephone access
- Complementary and alternative medicine

Private Practice

Physicians, as office-based practitioners, are the backbone of ambulatory care and provide the vast majority of primary-care services. Most visits entail relatively limited examination and testing, and encounters with the physician are generally brief. Office waiting time is typically longer than the actual time spent with the physician.

In the past, the solo practice of medicine and small partnerships attracted large numbers of practitioners. Self-employment offered a degree of independence not generally available in large organizational settings. Today, however; most physicians are affiliated with group practices or institutions, such as hospitals and MCOs. Several factors account for this shift: uncertainties created by rapid changes in the healthcare delivery system, contracting by MCOs with consolidated organizations rather than solo entities, competition from large healthcare delivery organizations, the high cost of operating a solo practice, complexity of billings and collections in a multipayer system, and increased external demands, such as the necessity of having up-to-date IT systems. Group practice and other organizational arrangements offer the benefits of a patient referral network, negotiated leverage with MCOs, sharing of overhead expenses, ease of obtaining coverage from colleagues for personal time off, and attractive starting salaries with benefits and profit-sharing plans.

Group practice of medicine in the United States has experienced a sharp increase in recent years (see **Figure 7-3**). An estimated 59.3% of physicians are now in solo or single-specialty group practices, whereas 24.7% are in multispecialty group practices (American Medical Association, 2015). According to the Physicians

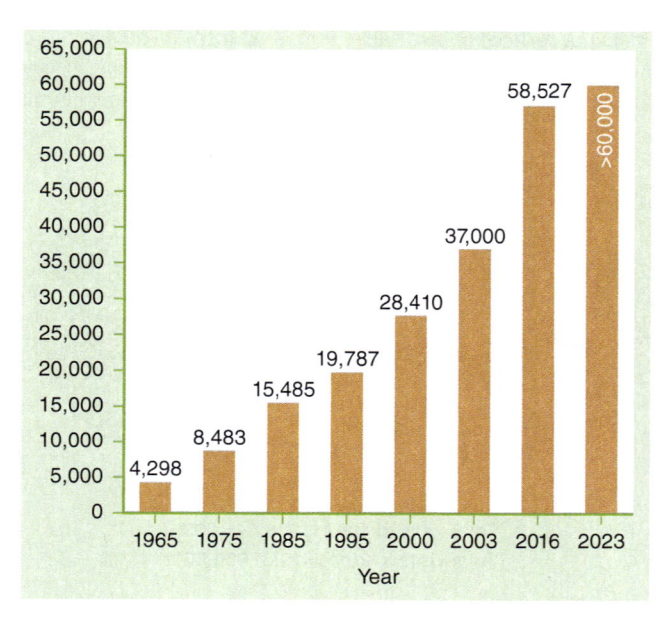

Figure 7-3 Growth in the number of medical group practices in the United States.
Data from Medical Group Management Association. 2023. Medical Group Fast Facts.

Foundation (2018), 23.3% of group practices have two to five physicians, 14.7% have six to 10 physicians, 16.6% have 11 to 30 physicians, 11.1% have 31 to 100 physicians, and 16.4% have 101 or more physicians.

Group practice clinics also offer important advantages to patients. In many instances, patients can receive up-to-date diagnostic, treatment, pharmaceutical, and certain surgical services in the same location. All but the most advanced secondary and tertiary procedures can be performed within these large clinics. Patients also often consult cross-referrals among partner physicians located near each other as an added convenience.

Apart from physicians, other private practitioners often work in solo or group practice settings. For example, dentists, optometrists, podiatrists, psychologists, and physical, occupational, and speech therapists typically work under this practice model.

Figure 7-4 shows the distribution of total ambulatory visits among physicians' offices, hospital-based outpatient departments, and hospital EDs in the United States. In 2011, approximately 79% of all ambulatory care visits occurred in physicians' offices. Hospitals have made substantial strides in gaining market share through their outpatient services.

Hospital-Based Outpatient Services

A few years ago, hospital administrators regarded the outpatient departments of urban hospitals with a certain level of contempt. The outpatient department was often viewed as the "stepchild" of the institution and the least popular area of the hospital in which to work. Even today, some hospital outpatient clinics in inner-city areas may function as the community's safety net, providing primary care to medically indigent and uninsured populations. For the most part; however, outpatient services are now a key source of profit for hospitals. Consequently, hospitals have expanded their outpatient departments, and use of these services has grown (refer to Figure 7-4). This trend is the result of fierce competition in the healthcare industry; as MCOs emphasize preventive and outpatient care, there has been a relentless drive to cut costs. To compensate for the steady erosion in inpatient revenues stemming from MCO frugality, hospitals have begun sprucing up and expanding their outpatient services.

A hospital-developed continuum of inpatient and outpatient service offers opportunities for cross-referrals among services that

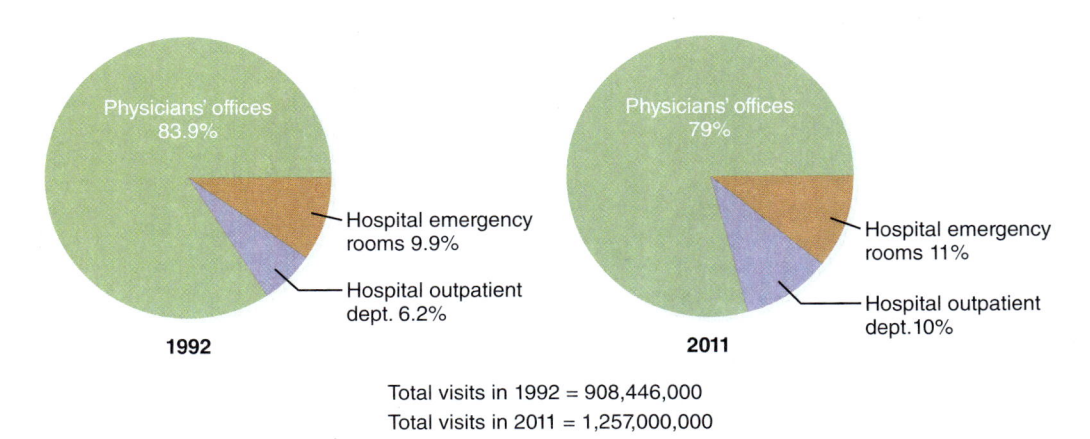

1992
- Physicians' offices 83.9%
- Hospital emergency rooms 9.9%
- Hospital outpatient dept. 6.2%

2011
- Physicians' offices 79%
- Hospital emergency rooms 11%
- Hospital outpatient dept. 10%

Total visits in 1992 = 908,446,000
Total visits in 2011 = 1,257,000,000

Figure 7-4 Ambulatory care visits in the United States.

Data from National Center for Health Statistics. 1996. Health, United States, 1995. Hyattsville, MD: U.S. Department of Health and Human Services. pg. 193; National Center for Health Statistics. 2018. Health, United States, 2017. Hyattsville, MD: U.S. Department of Health and Human Services. Table 76.

keep patients within the same delivery system. For example, a hospital that provides both inpatient and outpatient services can enhance its revenues by referring postsurgical cases to its affiliated units for rehabilitation and homecare follow-up. Patients receiving various types of outpatient services constitute an important source of referrals back to hospitals for inpatient care. By offering both inpatient and outpatient services, hospitals can also expand their patient base.

Prior to 1985, outpatient care accounted for less than 15% of the total gross patient revenues for all U.S. hospitals. This share has grown to 48% (American Hospital Association, 2016, 2018). As part of the growing competition in delivery of outpatient services, hospitals and hospital systems have launched specialized services, such as sports medicine, women's health, and renal dialysis. Many hospitals have also developed health promotion/disease prevention and health fitness programs as outreach efforts to the communities they serve.

Most hospital-based outpatient services can be broadly classified into five main types: clinical, surgical, emergency, home health, and women's health.

Clinical Services. The acquisition of group practices has enabled hospitals to increase their market share for outpatient clinical care. Referrals for inpatient, surgical, and other specialized services have generated additional revenues for these hospitals. Both public and private nonprofit hospitals located in inner-city locations provide uncompensated clinical services through their outpatient settings to patients who do not have access to private practitioner offices for routine care. Teaching hospitals operate various clinics, offering highly specialized, research-based services.

Surgical Services. Hospital-based ambulatory surgery centers provide same-day surgical care; patients are sent home after a few hours of recovery time following surgery. Follow-up care

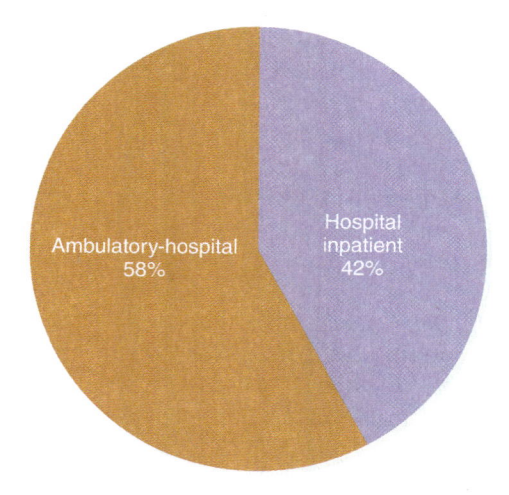

Figure 7-5 Medical procedures by location.
Data from Steiner, C.A., et al. 2017. Surgeries in hospital-based ambulatory surgery and hospital inpatient settings, 2014. Available at: https://www.hcup-us.ahrq.gov/reports/statbriefs/sb223-Ambulatory-Inpatient-Surgeries-2014.pdf. Accessed January 2020.

generally continues in the physician's office. In outpatient medical procedures, hospitals have the upper hand over freestanding centers due to their advances in medical technology, pain management, and prompt responses to emergent conditions (**Figure 7-5**).

Emergency Services. The ED has long been a vital outpatient component of many community hospitals. The main purpose of this department is to have services available around the clock for patients who are acutely ill or injured, particularly those with serious or life-threatening conditions requiring immediate attention. When deemed medically appropriate, prompt hospitalization can occur directly from the ED. This department has various specialists on call and is commonly staffed by physicians who have specialized training in emergency medicine. In small hospitals, the staff may be members of the regular medical staff in rotation. Another option is to contract ED staffing to physician groups specializing in emergency medicine.

Weinerman and colleagues (1966) defined three categories of conditions for which patients present themselves to the ED:

- **Emergent conditions** are critical and require immediate medical attention; time delay is harmful to the patient, and the disorder is acute and potentially threatening to life or function.
- **Urgent conditions** require medical attention within a few hours; a longer delay presents possible danger to the patient, and the disorder is acute but not severe enough to be life threatening.
- **Nonurgent conditions** do not require the resources of an emergency service, and the disorder is nonacute or minor in severity.

As has been well documented, in the United States, EDs are overused for nonurgent or routine care that could be more appropriately addressed in a primary-care setting. Of the 138.9 million ED patient visits reported to the National Ambulatory Medical Care Survey in 2017, for example, 0.9% were triaged as needing immediate attention, 9.9% as emergent, 33.9% as urgent, 24.0% as semi-urgent, and 3.9% as nonurgent (NCHS, 2017). Reasons for nonurgent use of ED include unavailability of primary care, erroneous self-assessment of the severity of the ailment or injury, the 24-hour open-door policy, convenience, socioeconomic stress, psychiatric comorbidities, and a lack of social support (Greenwood-Ericksen, 2019; Hummel et al., 2014; Liggins, 1993; Padgett and Brodsky, 1992; Tabriz et al., 2023; Fernández Chávez et al., 2023; Montoro-Pérez et al., 2023). Moreover, because the Emergency Medical Treatment and Active Labor Act (EMTALA) of 1986 requires screening and evaluation of every patient, necessary stabilizing treatment, and admission to the hospital when necessary regardless of ability to pay, EDs often function as a public "safety net" for the uninsured.

The uninsured and people covered by the Medicaid program use disproportionately more ED services than people who have private insurance coverage (Capp et al., 2015; McCaig and Burt, 2002; Meisel et al., 2011). Many private physicians do not provide services to Medicaid enrollees because of Medicaid's low reimbursement rates, which often leave people on Medicaid without a regular source of primary care (Hing et al., 2015; McNamara et al., 1993).

Crowding in EDs has also been exacerbated by hospital and ED closings nationwide. In 1992, approximately 6,000 hospitals had EDs; fewer than 5,000 remain today (Morganti et al., 2013). Yet, the demand for ED visits has increased considerably, as reflected by the growth in the annual number of ED visits—up from 93.4 million to 130.4 million between 1994 and 2013 (McCaig and Newar, 2006; NCHS, 2013). Because of overcrowding, EDs must use triage mechanisms to screen patients according to their level of severity.

Because EDs require high-tech facilities, necessitate highly trained personnel, and must be accessible 24 hours a day, their costs are high and their services are not designed for nonurgent care. Inappropriate use of emergency services wastes precious resources. One estimate places the financial costs at $32 billion per year as a result of privately insured patients seeking out emergency services when they could just as well be treated in lower-cost primary-care settings (United Health Group, 2019). Hence, alternatives to the ED for nonurgent and routine care are critically needed—a problem that can be traced back to the United States' inadequate primary-care infrastructure. Precisely for this reason, the ACA did not have any material impact on the overuse of EDs for nonurgent conditions (Searing and Cantlin, 2016).

Home Health Care. Many hospitals have opened separate home health departments, which provide mainly post-acute care and rehabilitation therapies. Hospitals have entered the home health business to keep discharged patients within the hospital system. Hospitals operate approximately 7.4% of all Medicare-certified home health agencies in the United States (Centers for Medicare and Medicaid Services [CMS], 2016). Home health care is discussed in detail later in this chapter.

Women's Health Centers. Emerging recognition in the 1980s of the prominence of women as a major health market led medical institutions to develop specialized women's health centers in hospital-based and/or hospital-affiliated settings. The following are some of the reasons behind the growth of women's centers:

- Recognition that women are the major users of health care. They seek health care more often than men do (Bertakis, 2000). Morbidity is greater among women than among men, even after adjusting data for childbearing-related conditions.
- A change in philosophy in American culture toward women, as the idea of gender equality has become more accepted.
- Recognition that the female majority in the United States will continue to grow, as the aging population includes more females.

Hospital-sponsored women's health centers rely on a variety of service delivery models. These models exist on a continuum that includes telephone information and referral, educational programs, health screening and diagnostics, comprehensive primary care for women, and mental health services. In addition to services in obstetrics, gynecology, and primary care, women's health centers offer mammography, ultrasound, osteoporosis screening, and other health screenings. Women's health is discussed in greater detail in the *Health Services for Special Populations* chapter.

Freestanding Facilities

Freestanding medical clinics include walk-in clinics, urgent care centers, surgicenters, and other outpatient facilities, such as outpatient rehabilitation centers, optometric centers, and dental clinics. These clinics, which are often owned or controlled by private corporations, commonly employ practitioners on salary.

Walk-in clinics provide ambulatory services, ranging from basic primary care to urgent care, but they are used on a nonroutine, episodic basis. The main advantages of these clinics are convenience of location, evening and weekend hours, and availability of services on a "walk-in" (no appointment) basis.

Urgent care centers offer extended hours; many are open 24 hours a day, 7 days a week, and accept patients with no appointments. These centers offer a wide range of routine services for basic and acute conditions on a first-come, first-served basis, but they are not comparable to hospital EDs.

Surgicenters are freestanding ambulatory surgery centers independent of hospitals. They usually provide a full range of services for the types of surgeries that can be performed on an outpatient basis and do not require overnight hospitalization.

Outpatient rehabilitation centers provide physical therapy, occupational therapy, and speech pathology services. In the past, generous Medicare reimbursement attracted various operators to open outpatient rehabilitation centers, but caps were instituted under the Balanced Budget Act of 1997. The therapy reimbursement caps are determined on a calendar-year basis. For physical therapy and speech–language pathology services combined, the annual cap per patient was $2,330 for 2023 (U.S. Department of Health & Human Services.2020). For occupational therapy services, the cap was $2,230 for 2023. Deductible and coinsurance amounts applied to therapy services count toward the amount accrued before a cap is reached.

In recent years, neighborhood optical centers providing vision services have replaced many office-based opticians. Other freestanding facilities include audiology clinics, dental centers, hemodialysis centers, pharmacies, and suppliers of **durable medical equipment (DME)**. DME suppliers furnish ostomy supplies, hospital beds, oxygen tanks, walkers, wheelchairs, and many other types of supplies and equipment. A growing number of the various types of freestanding facilities are part of large regional and nationwide chains, which are opening new facilities at an unprecedented rate in new geographic locations.

Retail Clinics

The introduction of small clinics, staffed mostly by NPPs, in shopping malls and large retail stores, has been a relatively recent phenomenon. Once viewed as a threat to PCPs, retail clinics are now increasingly viewed as complementary services that are conveniently available to people for minor ailments. Because of their low cost of operation, even most people who are uninsured can pay for their services out of pocket. In turn, payers have started to establish contracts with retail clinics. There were 1,801 active retail clinics in 44 states as of March of 2023 (Definitive Health Care, 2023). Most retail clinics in the United States are in the Southeast (34.1%) and the Midwest (27.7%). The West (9.5%) has the fewest retail clinics.

Mobile Medical, Diagnostic, and Screening Services

Ambulance service and first aid treatment provided to the victims of severe illness, accidents, and disasters by trained emergency medical technicians (EMTs) are the most commonly encountered mobile medical services. Such services are also referred to as prehospital medicine.

Early attention following traumatic injury is often life saving. EMTs are specially trained to provide such attention at the site and in transit to the hospital. Most ambulance personnel have a basic EMT rating, but advanced training can lead to EMT-Paramedic certification. Paramedics are trained to administer emergency drugs and provide advanced life support (ALS) emergency medical services. Examples include intravenous administration of fluids and drugs, treatment for shock, electrocardiograms (ECGs), electrical interventions to support cardiac function, and endotracheal intubation (insertion of a tube as an air passage through the trachea).

To provide a speedy response to emergencies, most urban centers have developed formal emergency medical systems that incorporate all area hospital EDs, along with transportation and communication systems. These communities typically establish 911 emergency phone lines to provide immediate access to services for those persons needing emergency care. When the system receives a 911 call, an ambulance is dispatched by a central communications center, which also identifies and alerts the hospital most appropriately equipped to deal with the type of emergency and located closest to the site where the emergency has occurred. Specialized ambulance services or advanced life support ambulances include mobile coronary care units, shock-trauma vans, and disaster relief vans, all of which are staffed by paramedics and EMTs who have advanced training.

Mobile medical services also constitute an efficient and convenient way to provide certain types of routine health services. Mobile eye care, podiatric care, and dental care units, for example, can be brought to a nursing home or retirement center where they can efficiently serve many patients residing in the facility. They are a convenient service for patients, many of whom include people who are frail and older adults. Such mobile services allow patients to avoid an often difficult and tiring trip to a regular clinic.

Mobile diagnostic services include mammography and magnetic resonance imaging (MRI). Such mobile units take advanced diagnostic services to small towns and rural communities. They offer the advantages of convenience to patients and cost-efficiency in the delivery of diagnostic care.

Health screening vans, staffed by volunteers who are trained professionals and operated by various nonprofit organizations, are often seen at malls and fair sites. The personnel in the vans commonly offer various types of health education and health promotion services and perform screening checks, such as blood pressure and cholesterol screening, for anyone who walks in.

Home Health Care

Home health care brings certain types of services to patients in their own homes. Without home services, the only alternative for most such patients would be institutionalization in a hospital or nursing home. Home health is consistent with the philosophy of maintaining people in the least restrictive environment possible.

Home health care encompasses a wide range of services and supplies that a person receives at home under a plan of care established by a doctor. It can include skilled nursing and home health aide services, physical therapy, occupational therapy, speech–language pathology services, medical social services, DME (e.g., wheelchairs, hospital beds, oxygen, and walkers), medical supplies, and other services provided in the individual's home (National Council on Aging, 2016). Home health is delivered in the United States by a combination of large and small home health providers, both for-profit and nonprofit. The number of home health agencies in the United States has been decreasing since the peak in 2013 with 12,459 agencies recorded. As of 2021, 11,353 home health agencies serve patients across the United States, with approximately 11,474 of those agencies being certified to treat patients with Medicare coverage (CMS, 2021a; CMS, 2021b). In total, more than 1.46 million individuals are employed in the home health care services industry (U.S. Bureau of Labor Statistics, 2023).

Growth in expenditures going to freestanding home healthcare agencies (additional home healthcare services are provided in hospital-based facilities and are considered hospital care) accelerated from 2014 to 2015, with this spending increasing 6.3% to reach $88.8 billion in 2015; by comparison, the growth rate was 4.5% from 2013 to 2014. Stronger growth in spending by both Medicare (2.6%) and Medicaid (6.0%)—the two largest payers, which collectively accounted for 76% of U.S. home health spending—along with faster growth in private health insurance and out-of-pocket spending drove the overall acceleration of home health expenditures in 2015 (CMS, 2016). Home health expenditures are projected to continue growing from $102.2 billion in 2018 to $201.3 billion in 2028 (Keehan et al., 2020).

According to publicly available data published in 2020 by "Home Health Compare," patient outcomes improve with delivery of home healthcare services. These data show that, after patients received home health care, 91% of wounds improved or healed after an operation, 78% of patients had less pain when moving around, 77% got better at bathing, and 77% had improved breathing (Alliance for Home Health Quality and Innovation, 2019; CMS, 2020). Home health care immediately following hospitalization is generally the least costly setting in which to deliver care for newly discharged patients, compared with discharging patients to skilled nursing facilities, inpatient rehabilitation facilities, or long-term, acute-care hospitals as the first setting postdischarge. For example, Medicare expenditures for a patient treated in the home after hospital discharge average $20,345, compared with an average of $28,294 for postdischarge care across all settings (Dobson et al., 2012).

Home health providers often leverage technology to enable the provision of care at home. To varying degrees, these providers use a diverse array of technologies ranging from remote monitoring, including phone calls (including the growing array of mobile technologies and applications), to health information technology, to in-home therapeutic and diagnostic technologies. Such technologies are often key tools that enable home health providers to improve quality and reduce the

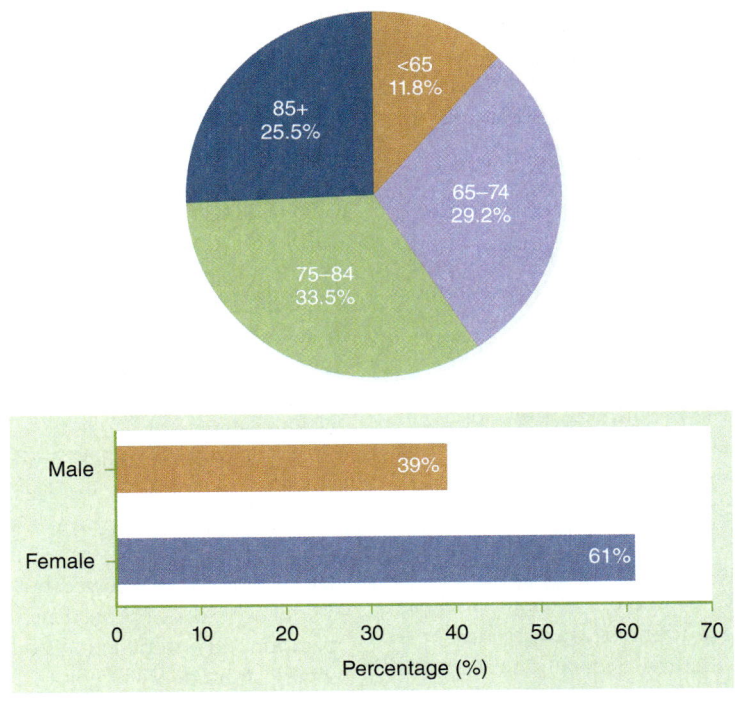

Figure 7-6 Demographic characteristics of U.S. home health patients, 2018.
Data from Alliance for Home Health Quality and Innovation. 2021. Home health chartbook 2021.

cost of care delivered to patients (Alliance for Home Health Quality and Innovation, 2014).

Figure 7-6 shows the demographic characteristics of patients who received home health care in 2018. According to the Alliance for Home Health Quality and Innovation (2019), home healthcare patients tended to be age 65 or older (87.9%), female (62.5%), and White (80.8%).

Because of variations in data sources, national expenditures for home health care are difficult to calculate. The CMS (2018) estimates that total expenditures for home health amounted to $108.8 billion in 2019. By 2027, this number is expected to rise to $186.8 billion. Medicare and Medicaid account for 76% of home health spending (CMS, 2018). After payments to home health agencies were sharply cut under the Balanced Budget Act of 1997, home health expenditures by Medicare declined significantly: They accounted for only 2.6% of total Medicare spending in 2015, compared with 9% in 1997 (CMS, 2015b; National Association for Home Care and Hospice, 2010).

Figure 7-7 shows revenue sources for home healthcare providers and the average distribution of revenues from these sources. **Table 7-3** and **Table 7-4** provide additional statistics on home health.

Hospice Services

The term **hospice** refers to a cluster of comprehensive services for terminally ill persons with a medically determined life expectancy of 6 months or fewer. Hospice programs provide services that address the special needs of dying persons and their families. More than half of all patients in hospice programs are diagnosed with cancer upon admission.

Hospice is a method of care, not a location, and services are taken to patients and

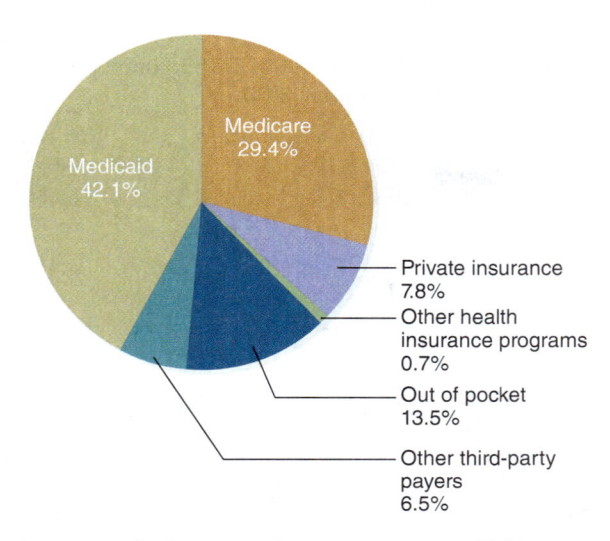

Figure 7-7 Estimated payments for home care by payment source, 2017.
Data from CMS. 2021. CRS Analysis of National Health Expenditure Account (NHEA).

Pie chart values:
- Medicaid 42.1%
- Medicare 29.4%
- Private insurance 7.8%
- Other health insurance programs 0.7%
- Out of pocket 13.5%
- Other third-party payers 6.5%

Table 7-3 Selected Organizational Characteristics of U.S. Home Health and Hospice Care Agencies in the United States, 2018

Characteristic	Home Health Care[1]	Hospice Care[1]
	Number	
All agencies[2]	11,500	4,700
	Percentage Distributions	
All agencies[2]	100.0	100.0
Ownership		
For profit	82.0	60.4
Nonprofit	14.3	21.3
Government and other	3.7	12.3
Medicare Certification Status		
Certified as home healthcare agency	78.9	NA
Certified as hospice care agency	NA	NA
Medicaid Certification Status		
Certified as home healthcare agency	78.4 (0.4)	NA
Certified as hospice care agency	NA	NA

Table 7-3 Selected Organizational Characteristics of U.S. Home Health and Hospice Care Agencies in the United States, 2018

Characteristic	Home Health Care[1]	Hospice Care[1]
Geographic Region		
Northeast	9.1	9.3
Midwest	26.8	20.3
South	43.9	37.4
West	20.3	32.9
Location		
Metropolitan statistical area (MSA)[3]	85.4	81.1
Micropolitan statistical area[4]	8.1	11.5
Neither	6.5	7.4

[1]Include agencies that provide both home health and hospice care services (mixed).
[2]Include agencies that provide home healthcare services, hospice care services, or both types of services and currently or recently served patients in home health and/or hospice care. Agencies that provided only homemaker services or housekeeping services, assistance with instrumental activities of daily living (IADLs), or durable medical equipment and supplies were excluded from the survey.
[3]A metropolitan statistical area is a county or group of contiguous counties that contains at least one urbanized area of 50,000 or more population. It may also contain other counties that are economically and socially integrated with the central county as measured by commuting.
[4]A micropolitan statistical area is a nonmetropolitan county or group of contiguous nonmetropolitan counties that contains an urban cluster of 10,000 to 49,999 persons. It may include surrounding counties if there are strong economic ties among the counties, based on commuting patterns.

Note: Numbers may not add to totals because of rounding and/or because estimates and percentage distributions include a category of unknowns not reported in the table. Percentages are based on the unrounded numbers.

Data from Sengupta M, et al. 2022. Post-acute and long-term care providers and services users in the United States, 2017-2018. National Center for Health Statistics. Vital Health Statistics, 3, no. 47. DOI: https://dx.doi.org/10.15620/cdc:115346.

Table 7-4 Patients in Home Health and Hospice Care Served at the Time of the Interview, by Agency Type and Number of Patients in the United States, 2007

Number of Patients	Home Health Care Only	Home Health and Hospice Care (Mixed)
	Mean (Standard Error)	
Number of patients in home health care	109.0 (9.2)	177.7 (17.7)
	Percentage Distributions (Standard Error)	
Total	100.0	100.0
0–25	16.0 (4.3)[1]	9.8 (2.4)[1]
26–50	21.3 (4.2)[1]	25.1 (6.4)[1]
51–100	29.0 (4.0)	18.4 (3.1)

Number of Patients	Home Health Care Only	Home Health and Hospice Care (Mixed)
101–150	10.8 (2.3)[1]	9.4 (1.9)[1]
151 or more	23.0 (3.5)	37.4 (4.8)
Mean (Standard Error)		
Number of patients in hospice care	78.1 (6.4)	39.1 (5.7)
Percentage Distributions (Standard Error)		
Total	100.0	100.0
0–25	29.5 (5.4)	57.6 (5.6)
26–50	22.1 (4.9)	24.5 (5.9)
51–100	21.2 (4.0)	6.3 (1.4)[1]
101–150	9.9 (2.5)[1]	2
151 or more	11.6 (2.3)[1]	2

[1] Estimate does not meet standards of reliability or precision because the sample size is between 30 and 59 or the sample size is greater than 59 but has a relative standard error of 30% or more.

[2] Estimate does not meet standards of reliability or precision because the sample size is fewer than 30.

Note: Unknowns are excluded when calculating estimates. There was one (unweighted) case with an unknown number of patients in home health care and 19 (unweighted) cases with an unknown number of hospice care patients. Percentages are based on the unrounded numbers.

Reproduced from Park-Lee E. Y., and F. H. Decker. 2010. Comparison of home and hospice care agencies by organizational characteristics and services provided: United States, 2007. National Health Statistics Reports no. 30: 1–23.

their families wherever they are located. Thus, hospice can be a part of home health care when the services are provided in the patient's home. In other instances, hospice services are taken to patients in nursing homes, retirement centers, or hospitals. Services can be organized out of a hospital, nursing home, freestanding hospice facility, or home health agency (**Figure 7-8**).

Hospice regards the patient and family as the unit of care. This special kind of care includes the following considerations:

- Meeting the patient's physical needs, with an emphasis on pain management and comfort
- Meeting the patient's and family's emotional and spiritual needs
- Providing support for the family members before and after the patient's death
- Focusing on maintaining quality of life rather than prolonging life (Miller, 1996)

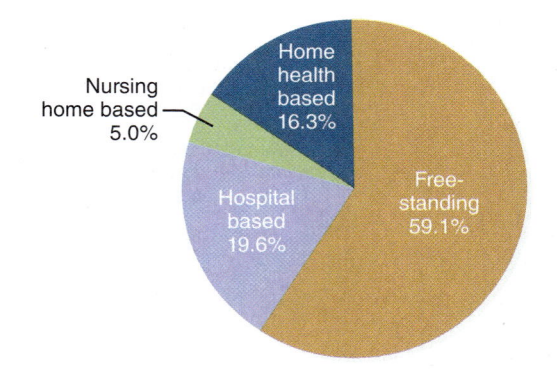

Figure 7-8 Types of hospice agencies, 2014.

Data from National Hospice and Palliative Care Organization. 2015. NHPCO facts and figures: Hospice care in America. Available at: http://www.nhpco.org/sites/default/files/public/Statistics_Research/2015_Facts_Figures.pdf. Accessed March 2021. p. 8.

The two primary areas of emphasis in hospice care are (1) pain and symptom management, which is referred to as **palliation**, and (2) psychosocial and spiritual support according to the holistic model of care (refer to the *Beliefs, Values, and Health* chapter). Counseling and spiritual help are made available to relieve anguish and help the patient deal with their death. Social services include help with arranging final affairs. Apart from medical, nursing, and social services staff, hospice organizations rely heavily on volunteers.

The idea of providing comprehensive care to patients who are terminally ill was first promoted by Dame Cicely Saunders in the 1960s in England. In the United States, the first hospice was established in 1974 by Sylvia Lack in New Haven, Connecticut (Beresford, 1989). Hospice organizations expanded after Medicare extended hospice benefits in 1983. Hospice is a cost-effective option for both private and public payers. It is estimated that for every $1 spent on hospice, Medicare saves $1.52 in Part A and Part B expenditures (National Hospice Organization, 1995). Hospice enrollment has been found to save money for Medicare to improve care quality for patients across a number of different lengths of service, primarily those patients who do not need medically intensive care (Kelley et al., 2013). It has also been associated with more than $13,000 in cost reductions per patient (Fiala et al., 2020). Many states now provide hospice benefits under Medicaid. **Figure 7-9** shows the sources of coverage for hospice services.

To receive Medicare certification, a hospice must meet these basic conditions:

- Provide physician certification that the patient's prognosis is for a life expectancy of 6 months or fewer
- Make nursing services, physician services, and drugs and biologics available on a 24-hour basis
- Provide nursing services under the supervision of a registered nurse
- Make arrangements for inpatient care when necessary
- Provide social services by a qualified social worker under the direction of a physician

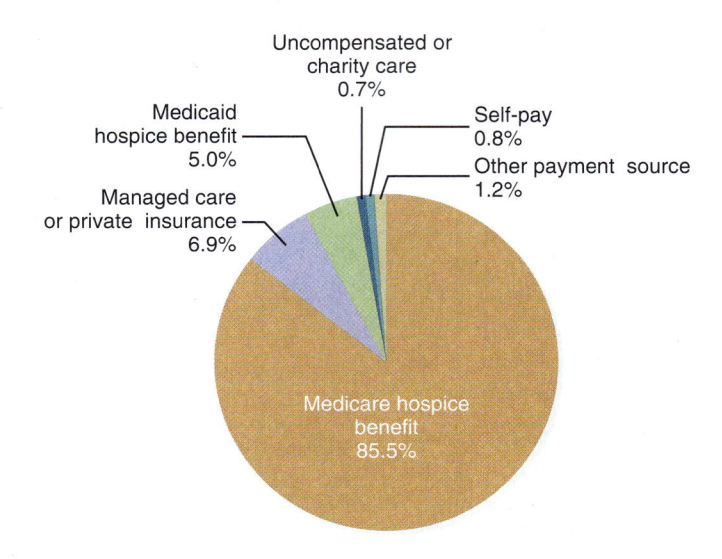

Figure 7-9 Coverage of patients for hospice care at the time of admission, 2014.

Data from the National Hospice and Palliative Care Organization. 2015. NHPCO facts and figures: Hospice care in America. Available at: http://www.nhpco.org/sites/default/files/public/Statistics_Research/2015_Facts_Figures.pdf. Accessed March 2021. p. 10.

- Make counseling services available to both the patient and the family, including bereavement support after the patient's death
- Provide needed medications, medical supplies, and equipment for pain management and palliation
- Provide physical, occupational, and speech therapy services when necessary
- Provide home health aide and housekeeping services when needed

In 2020, 1.72 million Medicare beneficiaries in the United States received hospice services; the average length of service was 97 days (National Hospice and Palliative Care Organization [NHPCO], 2022). The majority of hospice patients were 80 years or older (64.2%), female (58.4%), and White (82.5%). The top diagnoses were cancer (30.1%), circulatory/heart (17.6%), dementia (15.6%), and respiratory (11.0%). There are approximately 5,058 Medicare-certified hospice programs in the United States (NHPCO, 2022). The majority of these programs are for-profit (72%), followed by nonprofit (24%), while just under 3% were government-owned.

Medicare is the largest source of financing for hospice. In terms of levels of hospice care, the Medicare Hospice Benefit affords patients four levels of care to meet their needs: routine home care, continuous home care, inpatient respite care, and general inpatient care. In 2017, 98.2% of care was provided at the routine home care level (NHPCO, 2018). Tables 7-3 and 7-4 provide additional statistics on hospice care.

The U.S. hospice movement was founded by volunteers, and there is a continued commitment to volunteer service in this movement. In fact, hospice is unique in that it is the only type of provider program whose Medicare conditions of participation requires volunteers to provide at least 5% of total patient-care hours. In 2014, approximately 430,000 hospice volunteers provided 19 million hours of service (NHPCO, 2015).

Ambulatory Long-Term Care Services

Long-term care has typically been associated with inpatient care provided in nursing homes, but providers in two main types of settings—case management and adult daycare—deliver outpatient services. **Case management** provides for coordination and referral among a variety of healthcare services. The objective is to find the most appropriate setting to meet a patient's healthcare needs. **Adult daycare** complements informal care provided at home by family members with professional services available in adult daycare centers during the normal workday. The *Long-Term Care* chapter discusses both of these services in more detail.

Public Health Services

Public health services in the United States are typically provided by local health departments, and the range of services offered varies greatly by locality. Generally, public health services are limited to well-baby care, sexually transmitted disease clinics, family planning services, screening and treatment for tuberculosis, and ambulatory mental health. Inner-city, low income and uninsured populations are the main beneficiaries of these services. Health programs delivered in public schools fall under the public health domain but are limited to vision and hearing screening and assistance with dysfunctions that impede learning. Ambulatory clinics in prisons also fall in the public health domain.

The public school setting is a growing area of practice for physical therapists, occupational therapists, and speech–language pathologists. These professionals help children with special physical and emotional dysfunctions. The Individuals with Disabilities Education Act (IDEA) of 1975 (which is subject to reauthorization every 3 years) has been instrumental in enabling children with special needs to receive services in public schools so that they can obtain optimal access to education.

Community Health Centers

Creation of community health centers (CHCs)—formerly called neighborhood health centers (NHCs)—was authorized during the 1960s as part of the Lyndon B. Johnson administration's War on Poverty campaign, mainly to address healthcare needs in medically underserved regions of the United States. The federal government's application of the **medically underserved** designation signals that a community has a dearth of primary-care providers and delivery settings, as well as poor-health indicators for the populace. Such areas are often characterized by economic, geographic, or cultural barriers that limit access to primary health care for a large segment of the population. CHCs are required by law to locate in MUAs and provide services to anyone seeking care, regardless of insurance status or ability to pay. Hence, CHCs are a primary-care safety net for the nation's low income and uninsured population in both inner-city and rural areas.

Although CHCs are private, nonprofit organizations, they operate under the auspices of the federal government. Section 330 of the Public Health Service Act provides federal grant funding for CHCs. These centers also heavily depend on funding through the Medicaid program. Private-pay patients are charged on sliding-fee scales, determined by the patient's income.

CHCs tailor their services to family-oriented primary and preventive health care and dental services (Shi et al., 2007). These centers have developed considerable expertise in managing the healthcare needs of underserved populations. Many have established systems of care that include outreach programs, case management, transportation, translation services, alcohol and drug abuse screening and treatment, mental health services, health education, and social services.

In 2022, CHCs served 31.5 million patients in the United States, who collectively made more than 127 million patient visits. Most patients who use CHCs are members of vulnerable populations—90% of the patients had incomes below 200% of the federal poverty level and 19% were uninsured in 2022 (National Association of Community Health Centers, 2023). Among special populations, approximately 1.4 million homeless individuals and nearly 1 million agricultural workers received services under this program (Health Resources and Services Administration [HRSA], 2023). Between 2000 and 2022, the number of patients served at HRSA-funded health centers more than tripled, from 9.6 million to 30.5 million. One in nine individuals in the United States relies on a health center for affordable, accessible primary care (HRSA, 2023).

Despite these centers serving a population that is often sicker and at greater risk for poor health outcomes than the general population, the quality of care provided at CHCs is equivalent and often surpasses care provided by other primary-care providers. More than 93% of HRSA-funded health centers met or exceeded at least one *Healthy People 2020* goal for clinical performance in 2015. More than 68% of these centers are recognized by national accrediting organizations as patient-centered medical homes. In addition, more than 92% of CHCs have electronic health records (EHRs) installed and in use at all sites and for all providers (HRSA, 2016).

Health centers also meet or exceed nationally accepted practice standards for treatment of chronic conditions. In fact, the IOM and the Government Accountability Office have recognized health centers as models for screening, diagnosing, and managing chronic conditions such as diabetes, cardiovascular disease, asthma, depression, cancer, and human immunodeficiency virus (HIV). Health centers perform better on ambulatory care quality measures compared with private physicians and have been found to save the healthcare system $24 billion annually (National Association of Community Health Centers [NACHC], 2019).

Studies indicate that CHCs provide accessible, cost-effective, and quality care (NACHC, 2015, 2016a, 2016b; Rieselbach et al., 2019; Saloner et al., 2020). Because the majority of the patients they serve are members of vulnerable groups (i.e., low income, minorities, homeless), CHCs play an important role in reducing health disparities among these populations (NACHC, 2013). CHCs are also key partners for Medicaid, as Medicaid seeks to accelerate practice innovations that drive savings while also improving outcomes (NACHC, 2016c).

A unique quality of health center programs is the emphasis placed on both primary-care services and enabling services—that is, nonclinical services intended to eliminate geographic, linguistic, cultural, and socioeconomic barriers to care, such as transportation, interpretation, case management, and health education, among others. To care for the diverse nonclinical needs of their patients, health centers have increased their enabling services staff by 40% since 2010 (HRSA, 2014). Enabling services staff made up almost 10% of all CHC personnel in 2018 (HRSA, 2018).

In 2011, the ACA provided $1 billion to CHCs to expand primary care to nearly 11 million underserved Americans who did not have a regular source of care. Under the ACA, access to health center services increased, particularly for patients insured under Medicaid. Moreover, increased direct investment in health centers led to expanded primary-care capacity (Kaiser Family Foundation, 2017).

Free Clinics

Modeled after the 19th-century dispensary, the **free clinic** is a general ambulatory care center, primarily serving people with low incomes, people who are homeless, and the uninsured. Free clinics have three main characteristics:

- Services are provided at no charge or at a very nominal charge.
- The clinic is not directly supported or operated by a government agency or health department.
- Services are delivered mainly by trained volunteer staff.

Free clinics focus on the delivery of primary care. Other services offered by these facilities vary, depending on the number and training of their volunteer staff. The number of free clinics has continued to grow nationally and is estimated at more than 1,400 across the United States (National Association of Free and Charitable Clinics [NAFC], 2023). Although mainly a voluntary effort, care delivery through free clinics has taken on the form of an organized movement. The NAFC focuses on the issues and needs of the free clinics and the people they serve in the United States.

Other Clinics

Federal funding is used to operate migrant health centers that serve transient farmworkers in agricultural communities and rural health centers that serve populations in isolated, underserved rural areas. The Community Mental Health Center program was established to provide ambulatory mental health services in underserved areas.

Telephone Access

Telephone access is a means of bringing expert opinion and advice to the patient, especially during the hours when physicians' offices are closed. Referred to as **telephone triage**, this type of access has expanded under managed care.

The Park Nicollet Clinic of the Minneapolis, Minnesota, Health System illustrates how such a system functions. Its telephone call-in system operates 7 days a week, 24 hours a day (McVay and Cooke, 2006). The system is staffed by specially trained nurses who receive patients' calls. Using a computer-based clinical decision support system (refer to the *Medical Technology* chapter), the nurse can access the patient's medical history and view the most recent radiology and laboratory test results. The decision support system enables the nurse to give instructions on how to deal with the patient's problem. Consultation with a primary-care physician is done when necessary (Appleby, 1995). The nurse can direct patients to appropriate medical services, such as an ED or a physician's office.

Complementary and Alternative Medicine

Because of the tremendous growth of this part of the healthcare spectrum, the role of complementary and alternative medicine (CAM)—also referred to as "nonconventional therapies" or "natural medicine"—in the delivery of health care cannot be ignored. Although the terms "complementary medicine" and "alternative medicine" are often used synonymously, technically, there is a distinction between the two: complementary treatments are used *together with* conventional medicine, whereas **alternative medicine** is used *instead of* conventional medicine (Barnes et al., 2008).

In the United States, the dominant healthcare practice is biomedicine-based allopathic medicine, also referred to as conventional medicine. CAM refers to the broad domain of all healthcare resources other than those intrinsic to biomedicine (CAM Research Methodology Conference, 1997); it covers a heterogeneous spectrum of ancient to new approaches that purport to prevent or treat disease (Barnes et al., 2008).

CAM therapies include a wide range of treatments, such as homeopathy, herbal formulas, use of other natural products as preventive and treatment agents, acupuncture, meditation, yoga exercises, biofeedback, and spiritual guidance or prayer. Chiropractic is also largely regarded as a CAM treatment.

CAM treatments are not associated with any particular settings for healthcare delivery. With few exceptions, most therapies are self-administered or at least require active patient participation. The types of trained and licensed healthcare professionals discussed in the *Health Services Professionals* chapter are rarely involved in the delivery of unconventional care. A Doctor of Naturopathic Medicine (ND) degree and Diplomate of the Homeopathic Academy of Naturopathic Physicians (DHANP) are offered in the United States. Also, natural medicine–based private clinics are emerging across the United States.

Even though the efficacy of most CAM treatments has not been scientifically established, their use has exploded. CAM's growth has happened mainly for the following reasons:

- Most people who seek CAM therapies believe that they have already explored conventional Western treatments but have not been helped by these measures. These patients typically have chronic disorders, such as persistent pain, for which Western medicine can usually offer only symptomatic relief rather than definitive treatment.
- People who want to avoid or delay certain complex surgeries or toxic allopathic treatments are persuaded that at least there is no harm in trying alternative treatments first.
- Most people feel empowered by having access to the vast amount of medical and health-related information available through the Internet and feel in control to pursue what they think is best for their own health.
- Many patients report that they seek alternative therapies and individuals who practice them because they want practitioners to take the time to listen to them, understand them, and deal with their personal life as well as their pathology. They believe that alternative practitioners will meet those needs (Gordon, 1996).

According to the 2017 National Health Interview Survey (NHIS), the percentage of adults in the United States age 18 years and older who used yoga rose from 9.5% to 14.3% between 2012 and 2017. The percentage of adults who used meditation rose from 4.1% to 14.2% over the same period (National Center for Complementary and Integrative Health [NCCIH], 2018). Similarly, the percentage of children ages 4 to 17 who used yoga rose from 3.1% in 2012 to 8.4% in 2017, and the percentage who practiced meditation rose from 0.6% to 5.4%. Although people of all backgrounds use CAM, its use among adults is greater among women and those with higher levels of education and higher incomes (NCCIH, 2016a). In a 2010 survey of people aged 50 years and older, conducted by the NCCIH and AARP, 33% of respondents reported that they had discussed CAM with a healthcare provider (NCCIH, 2016b). People use CAM for a wide array of diseases and conditions. American adults are most likely to use CAM for musculoskeletal problems such as back, neck, or joint pain (NCCIH, 2016a).

Effective coordination of conventional medical services and CAM has the potential to save money and improve healthcare quality because, for some chronic problems, conventional medicine offers few proven benefits. Examples include psychosomatic ailments and cases in which patients have recurring complaints of unexplained painful symptoms or spells of dizziness. Such nagging complaints can cause the patient to rack up high medical costs and compromise the individual's quality of life. Lower-cost therapies, such as stress management and meditation classes, can save numerous trips to physicians and costly diagnostic tests.

One study found median expenditures to be $39 for CAM care, compared with $74.40 for conventional outpatient care (Lafferty et al., 2006). In 2012, Americans spent $30.2 billion out-of-pocket on complementary health approaches—$28.3 billion for adults and $1.9 billion for children—during the 12 months prior to the survey. This equates to 1.1% of total healthcare expenditures in the United States ($2.82 trillion) and to 9.2% of total out-of-pocket healthcare spending ($328.8 billion). Americans spent $14.7 billion out-of-pocket on visits to complementary practitioners, which is almost 30% of what they spent out-of-pocket on services received from conventional physicians ($49.6 billion). They spent $12.8 billion out-of-pocket on natural product supplements, which was approximately one-fourth of what they spent out-of-pocket on prescription drugs ($54.1 billion) (Nahin et al., 2016; NCCIH, 2016a).

CAM also appears to be popular in Europe, Canada, and other industrialized countries. Even though most of these countries provide universal access to medical care, a significant number of people try alternative treatments.

Given the growing public demand for complementary medicine and its claims for health promotion, disease prevention benefits, and promise for certain chronic conditions, mainstream medicine has shown a growing interest in better understanding the value of alternative treatments. Even so, skepticism about CAM therapies is justifiable because alternative medicine is predominantly unregulated. Also, the efficacy of most treatments and the safety of some have not been scientifically evaluated. Some study findings suggest that cranberry juice cocktails have no effect on preventing recurrent urinary tract infections (Barbosa-Cesnik et al., 2011) and Echinacea does not reduce the duration and severity of the common cold (Barrett et al., 2010), but white tea extract has potential anticancer benefits (Mao et al., 2010). Only rigorous scientific inquiry and research-based evidence will bring about a genuine integration of alternative therapies into the conventional practice of medicine. A 2013 article in the *Natural Medicine Journal* noted that published research studies have revealed that CAM therapies are cost-effective and may offer cost savings, but more research is necessary on individual treatments (Tais and Zoberg, 2013).

Nevertheless, some developments are noteworthy. In 1993, Congress established the

Office of Alternative Medicine (OAM), which became the National Center for Complementary and Alternative Medicine (NCCAM) in 1998. Budget allocations for the center increased from $2 million in 1993 to $128.3 million in 2012 (NCCAM, 2013). In December of 2014, Congress renamed NCCAM as the National Center for Complementary and Integrative Health (NCCIH) (National Institutes of Health [NIH], 2019). The center received $146 million in funding for fiscal year 2019 (NCCIH, 2019). Its objectives are to advance fundamental science and methods development, improve care for hard-to-manage symptoms, foster health promotion and disease prevention, enhance the complementary and integrative health research workforce, and disseminate objective evidence-based information on complementary and integrative health interventions (NIH, 2019). A few U.S. medical schools now include instruction in alternative medicine.

Utilization of Outpatient Services

In 2019, Americans made approximately 883,725 million visits to office-based physicians (**Table 7-5**). Physicians in general and family practice accounted for the largest share of these visits (22.9%), followed by physicians in pediatrics (15.4%), internal medicine (9.2%), and obstetrics and gynecology (8.3%). Doctors of osteopathy accounted for 6.7% of the visits. The South led the United States in the proportion of physician visits (36.0%), followed by the West (22.0%), the Midwest (21.2%), and the Northeast (20.8%). Most physician office visits (92.7%) took place in metropolitan areas.

Table 7-6 presents the most frequently mentioned principal reasons for visiting a physician in 2019. The top 10 reasons were progress visit, general medical examination,

Table 7-5 U.S. Physician Characteristics, 2019

Physician Characteristics	Number of Visits (in Thousands)
All visits	1,036,484
Professional Degree	
Doctor of medicine	980,280
Doctor of osteopathy	56,204
Specialty Type	
Primary care	521,466
Medical specialty	300,186
Surgical specialty	214,832
Metropolitan Status	
Metropolitan statistical area	972,700
Nonmetropolitan statistical area	63,785

Note: Numbers may not add to totals because of rounding.
Modified from Centers for Disease Control and Prevention (CDC). Santo L, Kong K. 2019. National Ambulatory Medical Care Survey: 2019 National Summary Tables.

Table 7-6 Principal Reason for Visiting a Physician, 2019

Principal Reason for Visit	Number of Visits (in thousands)
All visits	1,036,484
Progress visit, not otherwise specified	221,258
General medical examination	60,352
Postoperative visit	28,479
Gynecologic examination	25,218
Counseling, not otherwise specified	22,685
Medication, other and unspecified kinds	18,491
Hypertension	15,194
Well-baby examination	15,141
Cough	15,048
Diabetes mellitus	13,393
Prenatal examination, routine	12,565
For other and unspecified test results	12,465
Knee symptoms	10,370
Skin rash	10,295
Preoperative visit for specified and unspecified types of surgery	9,328
Other special examination	9,939
All other reasons	488,995

Note: Numbers may not add to totals because of rounding.
Modified from Centers for Disease Control and Prevention (CDC). Santo L, Kong K. 2019. National Ambulatory Medical Care Survey: 2019 National Summary Tables.

postoperative visit, gynecologic examination, counseling, medication, hypertension, well-baby examination, cough, and diabetes mellitus. **Table 7-7** shows the most frequent principal diagnoses cared for by office-based physicians.

Primary Care in Other Countries

More than half of the world's population is still not covered by essential health services mostly provided by primary-care doctors. Two billion people face severe financial hardship due to healthcare costs. PHC ensures good quality, more affordable and equitable access to essential health services, and is the most inclusive, effective, and efficient path to UHC (World Health Organization, 2023). Radically scaling up PHC in countries could save over 60 million lives. It can also deliver 75% of the projected health gains from the Sustainable Development Goals.

Implementing PHC requires enhanced collaboration to improve political commitment, governance, financing, and engagement.

Table 7-7 Primary Diagnosis Group, 2019

Primary Diagnosis Group[1]	Number of Visits	Percentage Distribution
All visits	1,036,484	100.0
Diseases of the respiratory system	52,376	5.1
Diseases of the musculoskeletal and connective tissue	77,476	7.5
Diseases of the circulatory system	106,381	10.3
Symptoms, signs, and abnormal clinical and laboratory findings, not elsewhere classified	85,356	8.2
Mental, behavioral, and neurodevelopmental disorders	57,171	5.5
Diseases of the skin and subcutaneous tissue	47,478	4.6
Endocrine, nutritional, and metabolic disease	71,892	6.9
Diseases of the eye and adnexa	47,584	4.6
Diseases of the genitourinary system	42,425	4.1
Neoplasms	59,000	5.7
Injury, poisoning, and certain other consequences of external causes	59,407	5.7
Diseases of the nervous system	27,614	2.7
Diseases of the digestive system	35,354	3.4
Diseases of the ear and mastoid process	18,893	1.8
Certain infectious and parasitic diseases	10,150	1.0
Pregnancy, childbirth, and the puerperium	5,788	0.6
Diseases of the blood and blood-forming organs and certain disorders involving the immune mechanism	15,243	1.5
All other diagnoses[2]	212,937	20.5

[1]Based on International Classification of Diseases, 10th Revision, Clinical Modification (ICD-10-CM). Certain codes are combined to better describe utilization of ambulatory care services.
[2]Includes certain conditions originating in the perinatal period (P00–P96), congenital malformations, deformations and chromosomal abnormalities (Q00–Q99), external causes of morbidity (V00–Y99), and factors influencing health status and contact with health services (Z00–Z99).
*Estimate does not meet NCHS standards of reliability.

Note: Numbers may not add to totals because of rounding.

Modified from Centers for Disease Control and Prevention (CDC). Santo L, Kong K. 2019. National Ambulatory Medical Care Survey: 2019 National Summary Tables.

It also requires a paradigm shift, from building health systems that focus on treating diseases to co-creating systems that tend to the totality of the health and well-being of people so that communities can be healthier and better protected from diseases. Around the world, there is little consistency in how primary-care services are accessed and how physicians get paid. In the United Kingdom, the Netherlands, and New Zealand, patients register with a primary-care doctor. In Australia, the Netherlands, New Zealand, Norway, Sweden, Iceland, Italy, Denmark, and the United Kingdom, patients go through primary care for referrals to specialists and are often required to register with primary-care practices (except in Australia). Canada, France, and Germany use financial incentives to encourage registration with primary-care practices and coordinated referrals (Schoen et al., 2012; Thomson et al., 2012). The German "sickness funds" (insurance plans) offer an enrollment option.

In improving primary care in the United States, many approaches from around the world can be referred to as models. Although individual countries institute primary care in the context of their own populations and societies, relevant takeaways can still be gleaned from how they have chosen to build their systems. In the following section, some characteristics of these strong primary-care models are discussed, along with how they relate to primary care in the United States.

Many countries, such as Australia, Canada, Spain, and the United Kingdom, organize their healthcare systems around a primary-care model that plays gatekeeper to the rest of the system; in fact, the United Kingdom even requires registry with a GP, as do the Netherlands and New Zealand (European Observatory on Health Systems and Policies, 2015; Roland et al., 2012; Starfield, 2010; Tikkanen et al., 2020a, 2020b). Having primary care play a gatekeeping role facilitates coordination of care and control of healthcare utilization and costs (European Observatory on Health Systems and Policies, 2015; Kaneko et al., 2019). Primary care systems that play a gatekeeping role demonstrate greater efficiency—for example, the primary-care system in Spain handles 94% of all patient encounters (European Observatory on Health Systems and Policies, 2015).

The importance of delivering multidisciplinary and team-based care is also widely acknowledged in many countries. In Australia, for example, the government has established primary-health networks and funds large multidisciplinary super clinics (Tikkanen et al., 2020a). The National Health Service (NHS) in the United Kingdom has also explicitly outlined goals to scale up multidisciplinary care, and general practices are undergoing changes in this direction (Tikkanen et al., 2020c). The reorganization of the Spanish healthcare system under the General Health Act of 1986 identified multidisciplinary teams as one of the main pillars of primary care (European Observatory on Health Systems and Policies, 2015). Many of these countries are also introducing or ramping up involvement of nurses, pharmacists, mental health counselors, and other types of providers to enhance coordination and continuity of patient care (Organization for Economic Cooperation and Development [OECD], 2020). Such efforts help address the broad spectrum of patient needs in the population and reduce fragmentation.

To reduce financial barriers to accessing services, many countries have made conscious efforts to make primary care more cost-accessible. Both Canada and the United Kingdom have no cost sharing for primary-care services, meaning that patients can access primary care without having to pay any out-of-pocket fees—although this does not necessarily extend to pharmaceuticals (Starfield, 2010). Citizens and residents in Spain also have free access to the public health system, with the exception of copayments for outpatient pharmaceuticals for those persons younger than age 65 (European Observatory on Health Systems and Policies, 2015). Such policies make health care more financially affordable for individuals who otherwise might be unable to seek out care, which can reduce ED use and promote early treatment (Rice et al., 2013). These countries' universal coverage policies contribute to their abilities to achieve better health outcomes at a lower cost (Starfield, 2010).

Use of a gatekeeping model for primary care, in conjunction with emphasis on multidisciplinary care and low cost sharing, represent ways in which the aforementioned countries attempt to provide accessible, comprehensive, and coordinated care without expending significant costs. Although the United States has made progress in supporting models of multidisciplinary care, it has yet to provide a solid foundation for primary care to play a gatekeeping role in its healthcare system (Tikkanen et al., 2020d). Healthcare expenses for the average patient are also significantly higher in the United States, which creates a major financial barrier to care (Rice et al., 2013). Building off the successes of other countries, instituting a gatekeeping model and reducing out-of-pocket expenses for patients may help improve access to primary care and cut down on healthcare expenditures in the United States. Doubling down on policy efforts and governmental support for multidisciplinary, team-based care could also improve coordination and reduce the high levels of fragmentation seen across the U.S. healthcare system.

Models of Primary-Care Practice

Below, we illustrate some "best-practice" models of primary care around the world.

- **The United Kingdom: The National Health Service (NHS) Model.** The NHS provides universal access to healthcare services and focuses on delivering primary care through general practitioners (GPs) (NHS England, n.d.). It places a strong emphasis on preventive care and population health, aiming to reduce health inequalities (NHS England, n.d.). Patients can register with a GP, and services are free at the point of use (NHS England, n.d.). Primary care includes general practice, community pharmacy, dental, and optometry (eye health) services (NHS England, n.d.). The NHS were better equipped to provide mental health and well-being support to staff as a result of the COVID-19 pandemic (Barr-Keenan et al., 2021).

- **Norway: Telemedicine and E-health.** Norway has a well-regarded helathcare system that provides comprehensive primary-care services to its residents (Rolf, 2020). Norway has been a pioneer in the use of telemedicine and e-health solutions to improve access to primary care, particularly in remote and underserved areas (Rolf, 2020). Patients can consult with healthcare providers through video calls, phone calls, and online platforms (Rolf, 2020). Rolf (2020) found that there has been a marked change in Norway, with an extreme increase in video consultations, especially in primary care and in the mental health field. The government also released an app for tracking the illness, which so far has been downloaded by approximately ¼ of the population (Rolf, 2020).

Australia: The Collaboratives Program. Primary Health Care (PHC) in Australia, which has evolved through major reforms, has been adapting to the complex healthcare needs of the socio-culturally diversified nation and has achieved many of the PC attributes, including service diversity, accessibility, acceptability, and quality of care (Mengistu et al., 2023). The PHC system has developed several implementation strategies to increase service diversity, accessibility, acceptability, and quality of care (Mengistu et al., 2023). Australia has adopted a collaborative-care approach that involves general practitioners, nurses, and allied health professionals working together to provide holistic care, which aims to address the physical, mental, and social aspects of health (Knight et al., 2012).

Switzerland: Universal Healthcare Coverage. According to the Organization for Economic Cooperation and Development, the Swiss healthcare system is one of the most effective in the world (Cohidon et al., 2015). Switzerland provides universal healthcare coverage for its residents (Cohidon et al., 2015). Every Swiss citizen and resident is required to have basic health insurance, which covers a wide range of medical services, including primary care (Cohidon et al., 2015). This ensures that virtually everyone in the country has access to primary-care services (Cohidon et al., 2015). Switzerland has an integrated healthcare system where primary-care providers often work closely with specialists and hospitals (Cohidon et al., 2015). This coordination of care helps ensure that patients receive appropriate and timely referrals to specialists when needed (Cohidon et al., 2015).

Canada: Medicare and Canada Health Act. Canada has a healthcare system known as Medicare, which provides universal access to healthcare services for all Canadian residents (Government of Canada, 2023). The provincial and territorial governments are responsible for the management, organization, and delivery of healthcare services for their residents (Government of Canada, 2023). For example, the federal government is responsible for setting and administering national standards for the healthcare system through the Canada Health Act, providing funding support for provincial and territorial healthcare services, and supporting the delivery for healthcare services to specific groups (Government of Canada, 2023). The Canada Health Act (1984) defines the following standards to which provincial health insurance programs must conform in exchange for federal funding: universality (coverage of the whole population on uniform terms and conditions), portability of coverage among provinces, public administration, accessibility (first-dollar coverage for physician and hospital services), and comprehensiveness (defined as medically necessary health services provided by hospitals and physicians) (Hutchison et al., 2011). In practice, medical necessity is broadly defined, covering most physicians' services (Hutchison et al., 2011). Canadians are entitled to choose their own family physician, and because the Canada Health Act prohibits user charges for insured services, medically necessary physicians' services are free at the point of care (Hutchison et al., 2011).

Summary

In the history of healthcare delivery, the main settings for ambulatory services have come full circle. First came a shift from outpatient settings to hospitals. Now, ambulatory services delivered outside of the hospital have mushroomed. The reasons for this shift are mainly economic, social, and technological. Many physicians have broken their ties with hospitals and started their own specialized care centers, such as ambulatory surgery centers and cardiac care centers. A variety of general medical and surgical interventions are now provided in ambulatory-care settings. Thus, ambulatory services now transcend basic and routine primary-care services.

Conversely, primary care has become more "specialized." Primary care is no longer concerned simply with the treatment of simple ailments; primary-care physicians must coordinate a plethora of services to maintain the long-term viability of their patients' health. Application of principles to establish patient-centered medical homes and delivery of community-based primary care is slow in taking shape.

In response to the changing economic incentives within the healthcare delivery system, numerous types of outpatient services have emerged, and a variety of settings for the delivery of services have developed. The growing interest in complementary and alternative medicine is largely consumer driven. Compared with the conventional Western medicine found in the United States, alternative medicine, with its emphasis on self-care, is an area where many patients feel more in control of their own destiny.

TEST YOUR UNDERSTANDING

Terminology

accountability
adult daycare
alternative medicine
ambulatory care
case management
community-oriented primary care (COPC)
durable medical equipment (DME)
emergent conditions
free clinic
gatekeeping
home health care
hospice
medical home
medically underserved
nonurgent conditions
outpatient services
palliation
primary health care
secondary care
surgicenters
telephone triage
tertiary care
urgent care centers
urgent conditions
walk-in clinics

Review Questions

1. Describe how some of the changes in the health-services delivery system have led to a decline in hospital inpatient days and a growth in ambulatory services.
2. What implications has the decline in hospital occupancy rates had for hospital management?
3. All primary care is ambulatory, but not all ambulatory services represent primary care. Discuss.
4. What are the main characteristics of primary care?
5. Critique the gatekeeping role of primary care.
6. Discuss how the patient-centered medical home advances primary care.
7. What is community-oriented primary care? Explain.
8. Discuss the two main factors that determine what should be an adequate mix of generalists and specialists.
9. What are some of the reasons why solo practitioners are joining group practices?
10. Why is it important for hospital administrators to regard outpatient care as a key component of their overall business strategy?
11. Discuss the main hospital-based outpatient services.
12. What are some of the social changes that led to the creation of specialized health centers for women?
13. Why do patients sometimes use the hospital emergency department for nonurgent conditions? What are the consequences?

14. What are mobile healthcare services? Discuss the various types of mobile services.
15. What is the basic philosophy of home health care? Describe the services it provides.
16. What are the conditions of eligibility for receiving home health services under Medicare?
17. Explain the concept of hospice care and the types of services a hospice provides.
18. What are some of the main requirements for Medicare certification of a hospice program?
19. Describe the scope of public health ambulatory services in the United States.
20. Describe the main public and voluntary outpatient clinics and the main problems they face.
21. What is complementary and alternative medicine? What role does it play in the delivery of health care?
22. Briefly explain how a telephone triage system functions.
23. What role can primary care play in pandemics such as the COVID-19 pandemic of 2020–2021?
24. Discuss the global trends in primary care.
25. What is a primary care-oriented healthcare system?

References

Chang, C. H., T. A., Stukel, A. B. Flood, et al. 2011. Primary Care Physician Workforce and Medicare Beneficiaries' Health Outcomes. *Journal of the American Medical Association* 2520: 2096–2104.

Accreditation Association for Ambulatory Health Care (AAAHC). 2009. *AAAHC Standards*. Accessed March 2021. Available at: https://www.mgma.com/about/organization

Agency for Healthcare Research and Quality. 2014. Care Coordination Accountability Measures for Primary Care Practice. Available at: https://www.ahrq.gov/research/findings/final-reports/pcpaccountability/pcpacc1.html

Alliance for Home Health Quality and Innovation. 2014. *The Future of Home Health Care project*. Accessed February 2017. Available at: http://www.ahhqi.org/images/pdf/future-whitepaper.pdf

American Hospital Association. 2016. *TrendWatch Chartbook*. Accessed January 12, 2020. Available at: https://www.aha.org/system/files/2018-01/2016-chartbook.pdf

American Hospital Association. 2018. *TrendWatch Chartbook*. Accessed 2, January 2020. https://www.aha.org/system/files/2018-07/2018-aha-chartbook.pdf

American Medical Association. 2015. *Updated Data on Physician Practice Arrangements: Inching Toward Hospital Ownership*. Accessed January 2017. Available at: https://www.ama-assn.org/sites/default/files/media-browser/premium/health-policy/prp-practice-arrangement-2015.pdf

Aoki, T., M. Inoue, and T. Nakayama. 2016. Development and Validation of the Japanese Version of Primary Care Assessment Tool. *Family Practice* 33: 112–117. Available at: https://doi.org/10.1093/fampra/cmv087

Aoki, T., Y. Sugiyama, R. Mutai, and M. Matsushima. 2023. Impact of Primary Care Attributes on Hospitalization during the COVID-19 Pandemic: A Nationwide Prospective Cohort Study in Japan. *The Annals of Family Medicine* 21: 27–32.

Appleby, C. Boxed in? *Hospitals and Health Networks* 69: 28–34.

Azar, K., M. Z. Shen, R. J. Romanelli, et al. 2020. Disparities in Outcomes among COVID-19 Patients in a Large Health Care System in California. *Health Affairs (Project Hope)* 39: 1253–1262. Available at: https://doi.org/10.1377/hlthaff.2020.00598

Bakwin, H. 1945. Pseudodoxia Pediatrica. *New England Journal of Medicine* 232: 691–697. doi: 10.1056/NEJM194506142322401

Barbosa-Cesnik, C., M. B. Brown, M. Buxton, et al. Cranberry Juice Fails to Prevent Recurrent Urinary Tract Infection: Results from a Randomized Placebo-Controlled Trial. *Clinical Infectious Diseases* 52: 23–30.

Barnes, P. M., B. Bloom, and R. L. Nahin. 2008. Complementary and Alternative Medicine among Adults and Children: United States, 2007. Hyattsville, MD: National Center for Health Statistics. 2008.

Barr, K. W., and C. L. Breindel. 2004. Ambulatory Care. In: *Health Care Administration: Planning, Implementing, and Managing Organized Delivery Systems*. L. F. Wolper, ed. 4th ed. Sudbury, MA; Jones & Bartlett Publishers. pp. 507–546.

Barrett, B., R. Brown, Rakel, D., et al. 2010. Echinacea for Treating the Common Cold. *Annals of Internal Medicine* 153: 769–777.

Barr-Keenan, R., T. Fay, A. Radulovic, and S. Shetty. 2021. Identifying Positive Change Within the NHS as a Result of the COVID-19 Pandemic. *Future Healthcare Journal* 8: e671–e675.

Basu, S., S. A. Berkowitz, R. L. Phillips, et al. 2019. Association of Primary Care Physician Supply with Population Mortality in the United States, 2005–2015. *JAMA Internal Medicine* 179: 506–514. doi:10.1001/jamainternmed.2018.7624

Beresford, L., and S. R. Connor. History of the National Hospice Organization. Arlington, VA: National Hospice Organization.

Bertakis, K. D., A. Rahman, L. J. Helms, E. J. Callahan, and J. A. Robbins. 2000. Gender Differences in the Utilization of Health Care Services. *Journal of Family Practice* 49: 147–152.

Bresick, G. F., A-R. Sayed, C. le Grange, S. Bhagwan, N. Mange, and D. Hellenberg. 2016. Western Cape Primary Care Assessment Tool (PCAT) Study: Measuring Primary Care Organisation and Performance in the Western Cape Province, South Africa (2013). *African Journal of Primary Health Care & Family Medicine* 8: e1–e12. Available at: https://doi.org/10.4102/phcfm.v8i1.1057

Bureau of Labor Statistics. U.S. 2023. Employed Persons by Detailed Industry, Sex, Race, and Hispanic or Latino ethnicity. Accessed November 2023. Available at: https://www.bls.gov/cps/cpsaat18.htm

Burton, R. A., K. J. Devers, and R. A. Berenson. 2012. Patient-Centered Medical Home Recognition Tools: A Comparison of Ten Surveys' Content and Operational Details. Accessed February 2017. Available at: http://web.pdx.edu/~nwallace/CRHSP/PCMHTools.pdf

Burton, R. A., K. J. Devers, R. A. Berenson, S. Zuckerman, S. G. Haber, and V. Keyes, 2020. Patient-centered Medical Home Activities Associated with Low Medicare Spending and Utilization. *The Annals of Family Medicine* 18: 503–510.

CAM Research Methodology Conference. 1997. Defining and Describing Complementary and Alternative Medicine. *Alternative Therapies* 3: 49–56.

Capp, R., D. R. West, K. Doran, et al. 2015. Characteristics of Medicaid-covered Emergency Department Visits Made by Nonelderly Adults: A National Study. *Journal of Emergency Medicine* 49: 984–989.

Caudill, T. S., R. Lofgren, C. Darrell Jennings, and M. Karpf. Health Care Reform and Primary Care: Training Physicians for Tomorrow's Challenges. *Academic Medicine* 86: 158–160.

Centers for Disease Control and Prevention (CDC). 2020. COVID-19: Health Equity Considerations and Racial and Ethnic Minority Groups. Accessed May 2020. Available at: https://www.cdc.gov/coronavirus/2019-ncov/community/health-equity/race-ethnicity.html?CDC_AA_refVal=https%3A%2F%2Fwww.cdc.gov%2Fcoronavirus%2F2019-ncov%2Fneed-extra-precautions%2Fracial-ethnic-minorities.html

Centers for Medicare & Medicaid Services (CMS). 2021a. CMS Program Statistics - Medicare Providers. Accessed November 2023. Available at: https://data.cms.gov/summary-statistics-on-provider-enrollment/medicare-provider-type-reports/cms-program-statistics-medicare-providers

Centers for Medicare & Medicaid Services (CMS). 2021b. Home Health Quality Reporting Program. Accessed November 2023. Available at: https://www.cms.gov/medicare/quality/home-health#:~:text=In%202021%2C%20there%20were%2011%2C474%20Medicare-certified%20home%20health,Service%20%28FFS%29%20beneficiaries%20using%20the%20home%20health%20care

Centers for Medicare and Medicaid Services (CMS). 2015b. National Health Expenditures 2015 Highlights. Accessed March 20, 2021. Available at: https://www.cms.gov/newsroom/press-releases/cms-releases-2015-nation

Centers for Medicare and Medicaid Services (CMS). 2016. Home Health Compare Datasets. Accessed March 10, 2021. Available at: https://healthdata.gov/dataset/home-health-compare-data

Centers for Medicare and Medicaid Services (CMS). 2018. *NHE Projections 2018–2027*: Tables. Accessed January 2020. Available at: https://www.cms.gov/Research-Statistics-Data-and-Systems/Statistics-Trends-and-Reports/NationalHealthExpendData/NHE-Fact-Sheet

Centers for Medicare and Medicaid Services (CMS). 2019. Therapy Services. Accessed January 2020. Available at: https://www.cms.gov/Medicare/Billing/TherapyServices

Centers for Medicare and Medicaid Services (CMS). 2020. Home Health Compare Datasets. Accessed February 2020. Available at: https://data.medicare.gov/data/home-health-compare

Chami, N., H. A. Shah, S. Nastos, et al. Association Between Virtual Primary Care and Emergency Department Use During the First Year of the COVID-19 Pandemic in Ontario, Canada. *CMAJ* 195: E108–E114.

Chernew, M. E., L. Sabik, A. Chandra, and J. P. Newhouse. 2009. Would Having More Primary Care Doctors Cut Health Spending Growth? *Health Affairs* 28: 1327–1335.

Christensen, E. W., K. A. Dorrance, S. Ramchandani, et al. 2013. Impact of a Patient-centered Medical Home on Access, Quality, and Cost. *Military Medicine* 178: 135–141.

Cohidon, C., J. Cornuz, and N. Senn. 2015. Primary Care in Switzerland: Evolution of Physicians' Profile and Activities in Twenty Years (1993–2012). *BMC Family Practice* 16: 1–9.

Crits-Christoph, P., R. Gallop, E. Noll, et al. 2018. Impact of a Medical Home Model on Costs and Utilization Among Comorbid HIV-positive Medicaid Patients. *American Journal of Managed Care* 24: 368–375.

D'Avila, O. P., L. F. da Silva Pinto, L. Hauser, et al. 2017. O Uso Do Primary Care Assessment Tool (PCAT): Uma Revisão Integrativa e Proposta de Atualização. [The

Use of the Primary Care Assessment Tool (PCAT): An Integrative Review and Proposed Update.] *Ciencia & Saude Coletiva* 22: 855–865. Available at: https://doi.org/10.1590/1413-81232017223.03312016

Damian, A. J., B. H. Johnson, D. V. Moyer, I. Tong, and M. Tuggy. 2020. Approaching Primary Care's Role in Responding To COVID-19 Through A Health Equity Lens [PowerPoint slides]. *Primary Care Collaborative* Accessed June 2020. Available at: https://www.pcpcc.org/webinar/pcc-webinar-primary-care%E2%80%99s-role-responding-covid-19

Definitive Healthcare, 2023. How Many Retail Clinics Are in the U.S. Accessed November 2023. Available at: https://www.definitivehc.com/resources/healthcare-insights/retail-clinics-us

Department of Health & Human Services. U.S. 2020. Therapy Services: Guidance for CY 2019 Therapy Services Updates. Accessed November 2023. Available at: https://www.hhs.gov/guidance/document/therapy-services

Desborough, J., S. H. Dykgraaf, C. Phillips, et al. 2021. Lessons for the Global Primary Care Response to COVID-19: A Rapid Review of Evidence from Past Epidemics. *Family Practice* 38: 811–825.

Dobson, A. et al. 2012. Improving Health Care Quality and Efficiency: Clinically Appropriate and Cost-Effective Placement (CACEP) Project. Accessed February 2017. Available at: https://www.dobsondavanzo.com/clientuploads/Publications/Bundling%20and%20Episodic%20Payment/CACEP_2012.pdf

Donnelly, C., R. Ashcroft, N. Bobbette, et al. 2021. Interprofessional Primary Care During COVID-19: A Survey of the Provider Perspective. *BMC Family Practice* 22: 1–12.

Elliott, J., C. Tong, S. Gregg,, et al. 2023. Policy and Practices in Primary Care That Supported the Provision and Receipt of Care for Older Persons During the COVID-19 Pandemic: A Qualitative Case Study in Three Canadian Provinces. *BMC Primary Care* 24: 199.

European Observatory on Health Systems and Policies. 2015. Building Primary Care in a Changing Europe: Case Studies. World Health Organization. 2015. Available at: https://www.euro.who.int/__data/assets/pdf_file/0011/277940/Building-primary-care-changing-Europe-case-studies.pdf?ua=1

Fernández Chávez, A. C., J. M. Aranaz-Andrés, M. Roncal-Redin, et al. 2023. Impact of the COVID-19 Pandemic on Inappropriate Use of the Emergency Department. *Microorganisms* 11: 423.

Ferrante, J. M., B. A. Balasubramanian, S. V. Hudson, and B. F. Crabtree. 2010. Principles of the Patient-Centered Medical Home and Preventive Services Delivery. *Annals of Family Medicine* 8: 108–116.

Ferreira-Batista, N. N., A. D. Teixeira, M. D. Diaz, et al. Is Primary Health Care Worth It in the Long Run? Evidence from Brazil. *Health Economics* 32: 1504–1524.

Fiala, M. A., T. Gettinger, C. L. Wallace, R. Vij, and T. M. Wildes. Cost Differential Associated with Hospice Use among Older Patients with Multiple Myeloma. *Journal of Geriatric Oncology* 11: 88–92.

Fjellså, H. M., A. M. Lunde Husebø, H. Braut, A. Mikkelsen, and M. Storm. 2023. Older Adults' Experiences with Participation and eHealth in Care Coordination: Qualitative Interview Study in a Primary Care Setting. *Journal of Participatory Medicine* 15: e47550.

Franks, P., and C. M. Clancy. Gatekeeping Revisited: Protecting Patients from Overtreatment. *New England Journal of Medicine* 327: 424–429.

Franks, P., and K. Fiscella. 1998. Primary Care Physicians and Specialists as Personal Physicians: Health Care Expenditures and Mortality Experience. *Journal of Family Practice* 47: 105–109.

Yue Gao, Y., R. S. Nocon, K. E. Gunter, et al. 2016. Characteristics Associated with Patient-Centered Medical Home Capability in Health Centers: a Cross-Sectional Analysis. *Journal of General Internal Medicine* 31: 1041–1051.

Gilfillan, R. J., J. Tomcavage, M. B. Rosenthal, et al. 2010. Value and the Medical Home: Effects of Transformed Primary Care. *American Journal of Managed Care* 16: 607–614.

J. S. Gordon. 1996. Alternative Medicine and the Family Practitioner. *American Family Physician* 54: 2205–2212.

Government of Canada. 2023. Canada's Health Care System. Available at: https://www.canada.ca/en/health-canada/services/canada-health-care-system.html

Greenwood-Ericksen, M. B., and K. Kocher. 2019. Trends in Emergency Department Use by Rural and Urban Populations in the United States. *JAMA Network Open* 2: e191919. doi: 10.1001/jamanetworkopen.2019.1919

Health Resources and Services Administration (HRSA). 2014. Uniform Data System. Accessed May 17, 2017. Available at: https://data.hrsa.gov/tools/data-reporting/program-data/national

Health Resources and Services Administration (HRSA). 2016. Health Center Program: Impact and Growth. Accessed February 14, 2017. Available at: https://bphc.hrsa.gov/about/healthcenterprogram/index.html

Health Resources and Services Administration (HRSA). 2023. Health Center Program: Impact and Growth. Accessed November 2023. Available at: https://bphc.hrsa.gov/about-health-centers/health-center-program-impact-growth

Hing, E., S. L. Decker, and E. Jamoom. Acceptance of New Patients with Public and Private Insurance by Office-Based Physicians: United States, 2013. *NCHS Data Brief* 195: 1–8.

Hu, R., L. Shi, A. Sripipatana, et al. The Association of Patient-Centered Medical Home Designation with Quality of Care of HRSA-Funded Health Centers. *Medical Care* 56: 130–138. doi: 10.1097/MLR.0000000000000862

Hummel, K., M. J. Mohler, C. J. Clemens, and Burris Duncan. Why Parents Use the Emergency Department During Evening Hours for Nonemergent Pediatric Care. *Clinical Pediatrics* 53: 1055–1061.

Hutchison, B., J. F. Levesque, Strumpf, E., and N. Coyle. Primary Health Care in Canada: Systems in Motion. *The Milbank Quarterly* 89: 256–288.

Institute of Medicine (IOM). 2012. Primary Care and Public Health: Exploring Integration to Improve Population Health. Washington, DC: National Academies Press.

Jackson, C. 2002. Cutting into the Market: Rise of Ambulatory Surgery Centers. *American Medical News*. Accessed March 9, 2021. Available at: https://www.globenewswire.com/news-release/2020/08/28/2085256/0/en/1-89-Billion-Ambulatory-Surgery-Centers-Market-and-Competitive-Outlook-2026.html

Ki-Yeob J. Cross-Cultural Adaptation of the US Consumer Form of the Short Primary Care Assessment Tool (PCAT): The Korean Consumer Form of the Short PCAT (KC PCAT) and the Korean Standard Form of the Short PCAT (KS PCAT). *Quality in Primary Care* 19: 85–103.

Jerant, A., J. J. Fenton, and P. Franks. 2012. Primary Care Attributes and Mortality: A National Person-Level Study. *Annals of Family Medicine* 10: 34–41.

Johns Hopkins Primary Care Policy Center. n.d. Primary Care Assessment Tools. Johns Hopkins Bloomberg School of Public Health. Available at: https://www.jhsph.edu/research/centers-and-institutes/johns-hopkins-primary-care-policy-center/pca_tools.html

Joint Commission. 2011. Optional Self-Assessment for Primary Care Medical Home (PCMH) Certification for Ambulatory Health Care Centers. 2011. Accessed February 2, 2017. Available at: http://www.jointcommission.org/assets/1/18/AHC_PCMH_SAT.pdf

Jones, E., L. Shi, A. Seiji, R. Sharma, C. Daly, and Q. Ngo-Metzger. Access to Oral Health Care: The Role of Federally Qualified Health Centers in Addressing Disparities and Expanding Access *American Journal of Public Health* 103: 488–493.

Kaiser Family Foundation. 2017. Community Health Centers: Recent Growth and the Role of the ACA. Accessed February 12, 2017. Available at: http://files.kff.org/attachment/Issue-Brief-Community-Health-Centers-Recent-Growth-and-the-Role-of-the-ACA

Kaneko, M., K. Motomura, H. Mori, et al. 2019. Gatekeeping Function of Primary Care Physicians Under Japan's Free-Access System: A Prospective Open Cohort Study Involving 14 Isolated Islands. *Family Practice* 36: 452–459. Available at: https://doi.org/10.1093/fampra/cmy084

Katzman, J. G., and J. W. Katzman. 2021. Primary Care Clinicians as COVID-19 Vaccine Ambassadors. *Journal of Primary Care & Community Health* 12: 21501327211007026

Kearon J., and C. Risdon. The Role of Primary Care in a Pandemic: Reflections During the Covid-19 Pandemic in Canada. *Journal of Primary Care & Community Health* 11: 2150132720962871.

Keehan, S. P., G. A. Cuckler, J. A. Poisal, et al. 2020. National Health Expenditure Projections, 2019–28: Expected Rebound in Prices Drives Rising Spending Growth. *Health Affairs* 39.

Kelley, A. S., D. Parth, Q. Du, M. D. Aldridge Carlson, and R. S. Morrison. 2013. Hospice Enrollment Saves Money for Medicare and Improves Care Quality across a Number of Different Lengths-of-Stay. *Health Affairs (Millwood)* 32: 552–561.

Khatri, R., A. Endalamaw, D. Erku, et al. Continuity and Care Coordination of Primary Health Care: A Scoping Review. *BMC Health Services Research* 23: 750.

Kinder, K., A. Bazemore, M. Taylor, et al. 2021 Integrating Primary Care and Public Health to Enhance Response to a Pandemic. *Primary Health Care Research & Development* 22: e27.

Knight, A. W., C. Caesar, D. Ford, A. Coughlin, and C. Frick. 2012. Improving Primary Care in Australia through the Australian Primary Care Collaboratives Program: A Quality Improvement Report. *BMJ Quality & Safety* 21: 948–955.

Koller, C. F. 2020. Don't Rebuild the Health System, Reorient It. *Milbank Memorial Fund*. 2020. Accessed June 2020. Available at: https://www.milbank.org/2020/05/dont-rebuild-the-health-system-reorient-it/

Kozak, L. J., E. McCarthy, and R. Pokras. 1999. Changing Patterns of Surgical Care in the United States, 1980–1995. *Health Care Financing Review* 21: 3149.

Ku, L., K. Jones, P. Shin, B. Bruen, and K. Hayes. 2011. The States' Next Challenge: Securing Primary Care for Expanded Medicaid Populations. *New England Journal of Medicine* 364: 493–495.

Lafferty, W. E., P. T. Tyree, and A. S. Bellas, et al. 2006. Insurance Coverage and Subsequent Utilization of Complementary and Alternative Medicine Providers." *American Journal of Managed Care* 12: 397–404.

Lal, L. and N. Schwalbe. 2023 Primary Health Care: A Cornerstone of Pandemic Prevention, Preparedness, Response, and Recovery. *Lancet* 401: 1847.

Landa, P., J-D. Lalonde, F. Bergeron, et al. Impact of Primary Health Care Reforms in Quebec Health Care System: A Systematic Literature Review Protocol. *BMJ Open* 13: e068666.

Levine, D., B. E. Landon, and J. A. Linder. 2019. Quality and Experience of Outpatient Care in the United States for Adults with or without Primary Care. *JAMA Internal Medicine* 179: 363–372. doi: 10.1001/jamainternmed.2018.6716

Lewis, C., S. Seervai, T. Shah, M. K. Abrams, and L. C. Zephyrin. 2020. Primary Care and the COVID-19 Pandemic. *Commonwealth Fund*. Available at: https://www.commonwealthfund.org/blog/2020/primary-care-and-covid-19-pandemic

Lewis V. A. 2018. Protecting America's Care Safety Net. *Health Affairs Blog* Accessed June 10, 2020. Available at: https://www.healthaffairs.org/do/10.1377/hblog20180216.403478/full/

Liggins, K. 1993. Inappropriate Attendance at Accident and Emergency Departments: A Literature Review. *Journal of Advanced Nursing* 18: 1141–1145.

Loewenson, R. and S. Simpson. 2017. Strengthening Integrated Care through Population-Focused Primary Care Services: International Experiences Outside the United States. *Annual Review of Public Health* 38: 413–429.

Mao, J. T., W-X. Nie, I-H. Tsu, et al. 2010. White Tea Extract Induces Apoptosis in Non-Small Cell Lung Cancer Cells: The Role of PPAR-γ and 15-Lipoxygenases. *Cancer Prevention Research* 3: 1132–1140.

Martin, R. (Host). 2020. How COVID-19 Patients Are Affected by Health and Other Disparities. In *Morning Edition*. NPR. Accessed June 2020. Available at: https://www.npr.org/2020/04/15/834746342/how-covid-19-patients-are-affected-by-health-and-other-disparities?fbclid=IwAR2wyaqfPf5uXGBfCIgMVAgFcvd1KwHgw-Bekx6Xp7VPbQPiINh_HGpOmt8

McCaig L. F., and C. W. Burt. 2002. National Hospital Ambulatory Medical Care Survey: 1999 Emergency Department Summary. Atlanta, GA: Centers for Disease Control and Prevention, National Center for Health Statistics.

McCaig L. F., and E. W. Newar. 2006. National Hospital Ambulatory Medical Care Survey: 2004 Department Summary. Atlanta, GA: Centers for Disease Control and Prevention, National Center for Health Statistics.

McNamara, P., and W. R. Koning. 1993. Pathwork Access: Primary Care in EDs on the Rise. *Hospitals* 67: 44–46.

McVay G. J., and D. J. Cooke. 2006. Beyond Budgeting in an IDS: The Park Nicollet Experience: Is the Traditional Budgeting Process Worth All the Time and Effort That it Requires? "There's a better way," Was the Conclusion of One Large Midwestern Integrated Delivery System. *Healthcare Financial Management* 60: 100–107.

Mei, J., Y. Liang, L.Yu Shi, J-Ge., Zhao, Y-T. Want, and L. Kuang. 2016. The Development and Validation of a Rapid Assessment Tool of Primary Care in China. *BioMed Research International* 2016: 6019603.

Meisel, Z. F., J. M. Pines, D. Polsky, J. P. Metlay, M. D. Neuman, and C. C. Branas. 2011. Variations in Ambulance Use in the United States: The Role of Health Insurance. *Academic Emergency Medicine* 18: 1036–1044.

Mengistu, T. S., R. Khatri, D. Erku, and Y. Assefa. 2023. Successes and Challenges of Primary Health Care in Australia: A Scoping Review and Comparative Analysis. *Journal of Global Health* 13: 04043.

Miller, G. 1996. Hospice. In: *The Continuum of Long-Term Care: An Integrated Systems Approach*. C. J. Evashwick, ed. (Albany: Delmar Publishers, 98–108.

Mitchell, S., V. Maynard, V. Lyons, N. Jones, and C. Gardiner. 2020. The Role and Response of Primary Healthcare Services in the Delivery of Palliative Care in Epidemics and Pandemics: A Rapid Review to Inform Practice and Service Delivery during the COVID-19 Pandemic. *Palliative Medicine* 34: 1182–1192.

Montoro-Pérez, N., M. Richart-Martínez, and R. Montejano-Lozoya. 2023. Factors Associated with the Inappropriate Use of the Pediatric Emergency Department. A Systematic Review. *Journal of Pediatric Nursing* 69: 38–46.

Morgan, P., D. H. Abbott, R. B. McNeil, and D. A. Fisher. 2012. Characteristics of Primary Care Office Visits to Nurse Practitioners, Physician Assistants and Physicians in United States Veterans Health Administration Facilities, 2005 to 2010: A Retrospective Cross-Sectional Analysis. *Human Resources for Health* 13: 42. doi: 10.1186/1478-4491-10-42

Morgan, P., C. Everett, and E. Hing. 2015. Nurse Practitioners, Physician Assistants, and Physicians in Community Health Centers, 2006–2010. *Healthcare* 3: 102–107.

Morganti, K. G., S. Bauhoff, J. C. Blanchard, et al. 2013. The Evolving Role of Emergency Departments in the United States. *RAND Health*. 2013. Accessed February 2017. Available at: http://www.rand.org/content/dam/rand/pubs/research_reports/RR200/RR280/RAND_RR280.pdf

Mulvihill, B. A., M. Altarac, S. Swaminthan, R. S. Kirby, A. Kulczycki, and D. E. Ellis. 2007. Does Access to a Medical Home Differ According to Child and Family Characteristics, Including Special-Health-Care-Needs Status, among Children in Alabama? *Pediatrics* 119: 107–113.

Nahin, R. L., P. M. Barnes, and B. J. Stussman. 2016. Expenditures on Complementary Health Approaches: United States, 2012. *National Health Statistics Reports*. Hyattsville, MD: National Center for Health Statistics.

National Academies of Sciences, Engineering, and Medicine. 2021. Implementing High-Quality Primary Care: Rebuilding the Foundation of Health Care.

National Association for Home Care and Hospice. 2010. Basic Statistics About Home Care. Accessed March 18, 2021. Available at: http://www.nahc.org/wp-content/uploads/2017/10/10hc_stats.pdf

National Association of Community Health Centers (NACHC). 2013. Studies On Health Centers and Disparities. Accessed March 2021. Available at: https://www.nachc.org/wp-content/uploads/2016/12/NACHC_50th-Report.pdf

National Association of Community Health Centers (NACHC). 2015. Studies on Health Centers Improving Access to Care. Accessed February 2017. Available at: http://nachc.org/wp-content/uploads/2015/06/HC_Access_0415.pdf

National Association of Community Health Centers (NACHC). 2016a. Studies of Health Center Cost Effectiveness. Accessed February 2017. Available at: http://nachc.org/wp-content/uploads/2016/06/HC_CE_06.16.pdf

National Association of Community Health Centers (NACHC). 2016b. Studies of Health Center Quality of Care. Accessed February 10, 2017. Available at: http://nachc.org/wp-content/uploads/2016/06/HC_Quality_06.16.pdf

National Association of Community Health Centers (NACHC). 2016c. Health Centers and Medicaid. Accessed February 10, 2017. Available at: http://nachc.org/wp-content/uploads/2016/12/Medicaid-FS_12.16.pdf

National Association of Community Health Centers (NACHC). 2019. America's Health Centers. Accessed February 4, 2020. Available at: http://www.nachc.org/wp-content/uploads/2019/09/Americas-Health-Centers-Updated-Sept-2019.pdf

National Association of Community Health Centers. 2023. America's Health Centers: By the Numbers. Accessed November 24, 2023. Available at: https://www.nachc.org/wp-content/uploads/2023/08/Americas-Health-Centers-2023.pdf

National Association of Free & Charitable Clinics. 2024. 2024 Patient Fact Sheet Free & Charitable Clinics and Pharmacies. Accessed August 2024, from https://nafcclinics.org/infographics-reports/

National Center for Complementary and Alternative Medicine (NCCAM). 2013. Appropriations History. Accessed March 2021. Available at: https://www.nccih.nih.gov/about/budget/nccih-funding-appropriations-hist

National Center for Complementary and Integrative Health (NCCIH). 2016a. 2016 Strategic Plan. Accessed February 1, 2017. Available at: https://nccih.nih.gov/sites/nccam.nih.gov/files/NCCIH_2016_Strategic_Plan.pdf

National Center for Complementary and Integrative Health (NCCIH). 2016b. Complementary and Alternative Medicine: What People Aged 50 and Older Discuss with Their Health Care Providers. Accessed February 2017. Available at: https://nccih.nih.gov/sites/nccam.nih.gov/files/news/camstats/2010/NCCAM_aarp_survey.pdf

National Center for Complementary and Integrative Health (NCCIH). 2018. National Health Interview Survey 2017. Accessed February 2020. Available at: https://nccih.nih.gov/research/statistics/NHIS/2017

National Center for Complementary and Integrative Health (NCCIH). 2019. About NCCIH. Accessed February 2, 2020. Available at: https://nccih.nih.gov/about

National Center for Health Statistics (NCHS). 2010. National Hospital Discharge Survey. Accessed January 2, 2017. Available at: https://www.cdc.gov/nchs/nhds/nhds_publications.htm

National Center for Health Statistics (NCHS). 2013. National Hospital Ambulatory Medical Care Survey: 2013 Emergency Department Summary Tables. Accessed February 2017. Available at: https://www.cdc.gov/nchs/data/ahcd/nhamcs_emergency/2013_ed_web_tables.pdf

National Center for Health Statistics (NCHS). 2017. National Hospital Ambulatory Medical Care Survey: 2017 Emergency Department Summary Tables. Accessed January 3, 2020. Available at: https://www.cdc.gov/nchs/data/nhamcs/web_tables/2017_ed_web_tables-508.pdf

National Committee for Quality Assurance (NCQA). 2008. Physician Practice Connections: Patient-Centered Medical Home. Accessed March 13, 2021. Available at: https://www.ncqa.org/programs/health-care-providers-practices/patient-centered-medical-home-pcmh/

National Committee for Quality Assurance (NCQA). 2023. Patient-Centered Medical Home (PCMH). Accessed November 15, 2023. Available at: https://www.ncqa.org/programs/health-care-providers-practices/patient-centered-medical-home-pcmh/

National Hospice and Palliative Care Organization (NHPCO). 2015. NHPCO Facts and Figures: Hospice Care in America. Accessed March 2021. Available at: https://www.nhpco.org/factsfigures/

National Hospice and Palliative Care Organization (NHPCO). 2022. NHPCO Facts and Figures: 2022 Edition. Accessed November 15, 2023. Available at: https://www.nhpco.org/wp-content/uploads/NHPCO-Facts-Figures-2022.pdf

National Hospice Organization. 1995. An Analysis of the Cost Savings of the Medicare Hospice Benefit (National Hospice Organization Item Code 712901). (Miami, FL: Lewin-VHI Inc).

National Institutes of Health (NIH). 2019. The NIH Almanac: National Center for Complementary and Integrative Health (NCCIH). Accessed February 2020. Available at: https://www.nih.gov/about-nih/what-we-do/nih-almanac/national-center-complementary-integrative-health-nccih

National Nursing Centers Consortium. 2003. Accessed March 7, 2021. Available at: https://campaignforaction.org/resource/nurse-managed-health-centers-nmhcs/.

NHS England. n.d. Primary Care Services. Available at: https://www.england.nhs.uk/get-involved/get-involved/how/primarycare/

The Organisation for Economic Co-operation and Development (OECD). 2021. Strengthening the Frontline: How Primary Health Care Helps Health Systems Adapt during the COVID-19 Pandemic. Accessed November 2023. Available at: https://www.oecd-ilibrary.org/social-issues-migration-health/strengthening-the-frontline-how-primary-health-care-helps-health-systems-adapt-during-the-covid-19-pandemic_9a5ae6da-en

Organization for Economic Cooperation and Development (OECD). 2020. Realising the Potential of Primary Care. Accessed June 2020. Available at: https://www.oecd-ilibrary.org/sites/a92adee4-en/1/3/1/index.html?itemId=/content/publication/a92adee4-en&_csp_=11e8b4af7aae0212bc3f99670160b6f2&itemIGO=oecd&itemContentType=book#section-d1e3658

Orton, P. 1994. Shared Care. *Lancet* 344: 1413–1415.

Deborah K., D. K. Padgett, and B. Brodsky. 1992. Psychosocial Factors Influencing Non-Urgent Use of the Emergency Room: A Review of the Literature and Recommendations for Research and Improved Service Delivery. *Social Science & Medicine* 35: 1189–1197.

Parchman M., and S. Culler. 1994. Primary Care Physicians and Avoidable Hospitalization. *Journal of Family Practice* 39: 123–128.

Peckham, S. 2017. Integrated Primary Care May Be the Answer But Do We Really Know What It Is? *Primary Health Care Research & Development* 18: 301–302.

Pesse-Sorensen, K., A. Fuentes-García, and J. Ilabaca. Primary Care Assessment Tool Applied to Primary Health Care Workers from Conchalí, Santiago. *Revista Medica de Chile* 147: 305–313.

Physicians Foundation. 2018. *2018 Survey of America's Physicians: Practice Patterns & Perspectives*. Accessed January 7, 2020. Available at: https://physiciansfoundation.org/wp-content/uploads/2018/09/physicians-survey-results-final-2018.pdf

Pinto, L.F., E. Harzheim, O. P. D'Avila L. Hauser, L.,V. Baron, V., and D. Ponka. 2021a. Ten Years of the Primary Care Assessment Tool in *Canadian Family Physician*: What Is Next? Contributions from the Brazilian National Health Survey and the Canadian Community Health Survey. 67: 479–480. doi: https://doi.org/10.46747/cfp.6707479

Pinto, L. F., L. A. Quesada, O. P. D'Avila, et al. Primary Care Assessment Tool: Regional Differences Based on the National Health Survey from Instituto Brasileiro de Geografia e Estatística. *Ciência & Saúde Coletiva*. 26: 3965–3979.

Rechel, B. 2020. How to Enhance the Integration of Primary Care and Public Health? Approaches, Facilitating Factors and Policy Options. World Health Organization. Accessed June 11, 2020. Available at: https://www.euro.who.int/en/about-us/partners/observatory/publications/policy-briefs-and-summaries/how-to-enhance-the-integration-of-primary-care-and-public-health-approaches,-facilitating-factors-and-policy-options-2020

Reid, R. J., P. A. Fishman, O. Yu, et al. 2009. Patient-Centered Medical Home Demonstration: A Prospective, Quasi-Experimental, before and after Evaluation. *American Journal of Managed Care* 27: 362–367.

Rice, T., P. Rosenau, L. Unruh, et al. 2013. United States of America: Health System Review. *Health Systems in Transition* 15: 1–431.

Rieselbach, R., T. Epperly, E. McConnell, J. Noren, G. Nycz, and P. Shin. 2019. Community Health Centers: A Key Partner to Achieve Medicaid Expansion. *Journal of General Internal Medicine* 34: 2268–2272.

Roland, M., B. Guthrie, and D. C. Thomé. 2012. Primary Medical Care in the United Kingdom. *Journal of the American Board of Family Medicine* 25: S6–S11.

Rolf W. 2020. E-health in Norway Before and During the Initial Phase of the Covid-19 Pandemic. *Studies in Health Technology Informatics* 272: 9–12.

Roos, N. 1979. Who Should Do the Surgery? Tonsillectomy and Adenoidectomy in One Canadian Province. *Inquiry* 16: 73–83.

Rosenthal, M. B., A. D. Sinaiko, D. Eastman, B. Chapman, and G. Partridge. 2015. Impact of the Rochester Medical Home Initiative on Primary Care Practices, Quality, Utilization, and Costs. *Medical Care* 53: 967–973.

Rubin, G., A. Berendsen, and S. M. Crawford, et al. 2015. The Expanding Role of Primary Care in Cancer Control. *Lancet Oncology* 16: 1231–1272.

Saloner, B., A. S. Wilk, and J. Levin. 2020. Community Health Centers and Access to Care Among Underserved Populations: A Synthesis Review. *Medical Care Research and Review* 77: 3–18.

Searing, L. M., and K. A. Cantlin. 2016. Nonurgent Emergency Department Visits by Insured and Uninsured Adults. *Public Health Nursing* 33: 93–98.

Sepulveda, M.-J., T. Bodenheimer, and P. Grundy. 2008. Primary Care: Can It Solve Employers' Health Care Dilemma? *Health Affairs* 27: 151–158.

Shi, L. 1994. Primary Care, Specialty Care, and Life Chances. *International Journal of Health Services* 24: 431–458.

Shi L., and B. Starfield. 2000. Primary Care, Income Inequality, and Self-Related Health in the US: Mixed-Level Analysis. *International Journal of Health Services* 30: 541–555.

Shi, L., and B. Starfield. 2001. Primary Care Physician Supply, Income Inequality, and Racial Mortality in US Metropolitan Areas. *American Journal of Public Health* 91: 1246–1250.

Shi, L., B. Starfield, B. Kennedy, and I. Kawachi. 1999. Income Inequality, Primary Care, and Health Indicators. *Journal of Family Practice* 48: 275–284.

Shi, L., B. Starfield, R. Politzer, and J. Regan. 2002. Primary Care, Self-Rated Health Care, and Reduction in Social Disparities in Health. *Health Services Research* 37: 529–550.

Shi, L., P. Collins, K. Felix Aaron, V. Watters, and L. Greenblat Shah. 2007. Health Center Financial Performance: National Trends and State Variation, 1998–2004. *Journal of Public Health Management and Practice* 13: 133–150.

Shi, L., D. C. Lock, D-C. Lee, et al. 2015. Patient-Centered Medical Home Capability and Clinical Performance in HRSA-Supported Health Centers. *Medical Care* 53: 389–395.

Shi, L., D-C. Lee, M. Chung, H. Liang, D. Lock, and A. Sripipatana. 2016. Patient-Centered Medical Home Recognition and Clinical Performance in U.S. Community Health Centers. *Health Service Research*. doi: 10.1111/1475-6773.12523.

Shi, L., B. Starfield, and J. Xu. Primary Care Assessment tool—Adult Edition. *The Journal of Family Practice* Available at: https://doi.org/10.1037/t77102-000

Stange, K. C., P. A. Nutting, W. L. Miller, et al. (2010). Defining and Measuring the Patient-Centered Medical Home. *Journal of General Internal Medicine* 25: 601–612.

Starfield, B. 1992. *Primary Care: Concept, Evaluation, and Policy*. (New York: Oxford University Press, 1992).

Starfield, B. 1994. Is Primary Care Essential? *Lancet* 344: 1129–1133.

Starfield, B. 1998. *Primary Care: Balancing Health Needs, Services and Technology*. (New York: Oxford University Press,.)

Starfield, B. 2010. Reinventing Care: Lessons from Canada for the United States. *Health Affairs* 29.

Steinwald, B., P. B. Ginsburg, C. Brandt, S. Lee, and K. Patel. 2018. Medical Graduate Medical Education Funding Is Not Addressing the Primary Care Shortage: We Need a Radically Different Approach. Accessed January 2020. Available at: https://www.brookings.edu/research/medicare-graduate-medical-education-funding-is-not-addressing-the-primary-care-shortage-we-need-a-radically-different-approach/

Stevens, G. D., M. Seid, T. A. Pickering, and K-Y. Tsai. 2010. National Disparities in the Quality of a Medical Home for Children. *Maternal Child Health* 14: 580–589.

Stock, S., A. Drabik, G. Büscher, et al. 2010. German Diabetes Management Programs Improve Quality of Care and Curb Costs. *Health Affairs* 29. Available at: https://doi.org/10.1377/hlthaff.2009.0799

Swietek, K. E., B. N. Gaynes, G. L. Jackson, M. Weinberger, and E. Domino. Effect of the Patient-Centered Medical Home on Racial Disparities in Quality of Care. *Journal of General Internal Medicine* 35: 2304–2313.

Tabriz, A. A., K. Turner, Y. R. Hong, S. Gheytasvand, B. D. Powers, and J. E. Lafata. 2023. Trends and Characteristics of Potentially Preventable Emergency Department Visits Among Patients with Cancer in the US. *JAMA Network Open* 6: e2250423–e2250423.

Tais S., and E. Zoberg. 2013. The Economic Evaluation of Complementary and Alternative Medicine. *Natural Medicine Journal* 5. Accessed May 2017. Available at: http://www.naturalmedicinejournal.com/journal/2013-02/economic-evaluation-complementary-and-alternative-medicine

The White House. 2022. FACT SHEET: President Biden to announce strategy to address our national mental health crisis, as part of unity agenda in his first State of the Union. Accessed November 2023. Available at:https://www.whitehouse.gov/briefing-room/statements-releases/2022/03/01/fact-sheet-president-biden-to-announce-strategy-to-address-our-national-mental-health-crisis-as-part-of-unity-agenda-in-his-first-state-of-the-union/

Tikkanen, R., R. Osborn, E. Mossialos, A. Djordjevic, and G. A. Wharton. 2020a. International Health Care System Profiles: Australia. *Commonwealth Fund*. Accessed June 2020. Available at: https://www.commonwealthfund.org/international-health-policy-center/countries/Australia

Tikkanen, R., R. Osborn, E. Mossialos, A. Djordjevic, and G. A. Wharton. 2020b. International Health Care System Profiles: Canada. *Commonwealth Fund*. Accessed June 2020. Available at: https://www.commonwealthfund.org/international-health-policy-center/countries/Canada

Tikkanen, R., R. Osborn, E. Mossialos, A. Djordjevic, and G. A. Wharton. 2020c. International Health Care System Profiles: England. *Commonwealth Fund*. Accessed June 2020. Available at: https://www.commonwealthfund.org/international-health-policy-center/countries/England

Tikkanen, R., R. Osborn, E. Mossialos, A. Djordjevic, and G. A. Wharton. 2020d. International Health Care System Profiles: United States. *Commonwealth Fund*. Accessed June 2020. Available at: https://www.commonwealthfund.org/international-health-policy-center/countries/united-states

Tritter, B., and D. Schwarz. 2020. As COVID-19 Spreads, It's Time to Diagnose and Treat Our Broken PHC Systems. *Primary Health Care Performance Initiative*. Accessed June 2020. Available at: https://improvingphc.org/blog/2020/03/24/covid-19-spreads-its-time-diagnose-treat-our-broken-phc-systems

United Health Group. 2019. 18 Million Avoidable Hospital Emergency Department Visits Add $32 Billion in Costs to the Health Care System Each Year. Accessed January 10, 2020. Available at: https://www.unitedhealthgroup.com/content/dam/UHG/PDF/2019/UHG-Avoidable-ED-Visits.pdf

Urquiza, R. 2020. Early Focus on PHC Improves COVID-19 Response in San Luis, Argentina. *Primary Health Care Performance Initiative*. 2020. Accessed June 2020. Available at: https://improvingphc.org/blog/2020/05/21/early-focus-phc-improves-covid-19-response-san-luis-argentina

Vahidy F. S., J.C. Nicolas, J. R. Meeks, et al. 2020. Racial and Ethnic Disparities in SARS-CoV-2 Pandemic: Analysis of a COVID-19 Observational Registry for a Diverse US Metropolitan Population. *BMJ Open* 10: e039849.

van Weel, C., J. De Maeseneer, and R. Roberts. 2008. Integration of personal and community health care. *Lancet* 372: 871–872.

Vanselow, N. A., M. S. Donaldson, and K. D. Yordy. 1995. From the Institute of Medicine. *Journal of the American Medical Association* 273: 192.

Vasan, A. 2017. To Prepare for Epidemics, Strengthen Primary Care. *U.S. News & World Report*. Accessed June 12, 2020. Available at: https://www.usnews.com/news/healthcare-of-tomorrow/articles/2017-02-15/to-prepare-for-epidemics-strengthen-primary-care

Veet, C. A., T. R. Radomski, C. D'Avella, et al. 2020. Impact of Healthcare Delivery System Type on Clinical, Utilization, and Cost Outcomes of Patient-centered Medical Homes: A Systematic Review. *Journal of General Internal Medicine* 35: 1276–1284.

Wang, W., and J. Haggerty. 2019. Development of Primary Care Assessment Tool–Adult Version in Tibet: Implication for Low- and Middle-Income Countries. *Primary Health Care Research & Development* 20: e94.

Weinerman, E. R., R. S. Ratner, A. Robbins, and M. A. Lavenhar. 1966. Yale Studies in Ambulatory Medical Care. V. Determinants of Use of Hospital Emergency Services. *American Journal of Public Health* 56: 1037–1056.

White House. *Fact Sheet: Health Care Accomplishments*. 2016. Accessed January 2017. Available at: https://obamawhitehouse.archives.gov/the-press-office/2016/03/22/fact-sheet-health-care-accomplishments

Lauren M., L. M. Wier, , C. A. Steiner, and P. L. Owens. 2015. Surgeries in Hospital-Owned Outpatient Facilities, 2012. Accessed January 2017. Available at: https://www.hcup-us.ahrq.gov/reports/statbriefs/sb188-Surgeries-Hospital-Outpatient-Facilities-2012.pdf

Wilson, F. A., and D. Neuhauser. 1985. *Health Services in the United States*. 2nd ed. Cambridge, MA: Ballinger Publishing.

World Health Organization (WHO). 1978. *Primary Health Care*. Geneva, Switzerland: WHO.

World Health Organization (WHO). 2010. *Primary Health Care*. Geneva, Switzerland: WHO.

World Health Organization (WHO). 2016. *Integrated Care Models: An Overview*. Accessed June 2020. Available at: https://www.euro.who.int/__data/assets/pdf_file/0005/322475/Integrated-care-models-overview.pdf

World Health Organization (WHO). 2018. *Primary Health Care: Closing the Gap Between Public Health and Primary Care Through Integration*. Accessed June 2020. Available at: http://www.imperialwhocc.org/wp-content/uploads/2019/01/WHO-Integrating-PH-ito-PC-24th-October-20184.pdf

World Health Organization (WHO). 2023. *Seventy countries convene to step up primary health care*. Accessed November 2023. Available at: https://www.who.int/news/item/23-10-2023-seventy-countries-convene-to-step-up-primary-health-care

CHAPTER 8

Inpatient Facilities and Services

LEARNING OBJECTIVES

- Get a functional perspective on the evolution of hospitals.
- Survey the factors that contributed to the growth of hospitals prior to the 1980s.
- Understand the reasons for the subsequent decline of hospitals and their use.
- Describe some key measures pertaining to hospital operations and inpatient use.
- Compare useful measures in U.S. hospitals to those in other countries.
- Differentiate among various types of hospitals.
- Evaluate the controversy surrounding physician-owned specialty hospitals.
- Comprehend some basic concepts in hospital governance.
- Understand and differentiate between licensure, certification, and accreditation and the Magnet Recognition Program of the American Nurses Credentialing Center.
- Get a perspective on some key ethical issues.

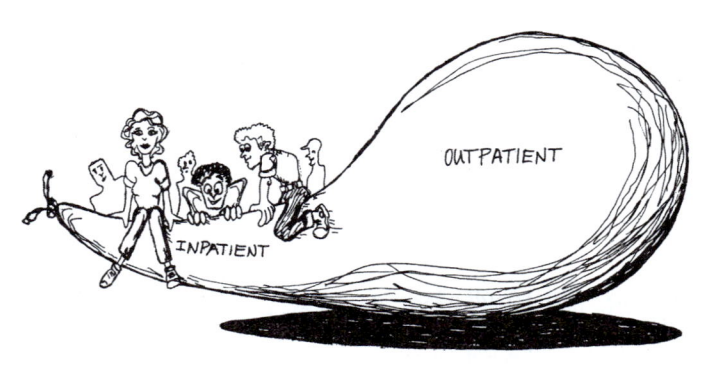

"We have the inpatient sector under control."

Introduction

The term **inpatient** is used in conjunction with an overnight stay in a healthcare facility, such as a hospital, whereas *outpatient* refers to services provided while the patient is not lodged in a healthcare facility. Although the primary function of hospitals is to deliver inpatient acute-care services, many hospitals have expanded their scope of services to include nonacute and outpatient care.

According to the American Hospital Association (AHA), a **hospital** is an institution with at least six beds whose primary function is "to deliver patient services, diagnostic and therapeutic, for particular or general medical conditions" (AHA, 1994). In addition, a hospital must be licensed, have an organized physician staff, and provide continuous nursing services under the supervision of registered nurses (RNs). Other characteristics of a hospital include an identifiable governing body that is legally responsible for the conduct of the hospital, a chief executive with continuous responsibility for the operation of the hospital, maintenance of medical records on each patient, pharmacy services maintained in the institution and supervised by a registered pharmacist, and food service operations that meet the nutritional and therapeutic requirements of the patients (Health Forum, 2001). The construction and operation of the modern hospital are governed by federal laws; state health department regulations; city ordinances; standards of the Joint Commission; and national codes for building, fire protection, and sanitation.

In the past 200 years or so, hospitals have gradually evolved from ordinary institutions of refuge for people who are homeless and with low incomes to ultramodern facilities that provide technologically advanced services to the critically ill and injured. The term "medical center" is used by some hospitals, reflecting their high level of specialization and wide scope of services, which may include teaching and research. The growth of multi-hospital chains, especially those providing a variety of healthcare services in addition to acute-care, has also introduced the nomenclature "hospital system" or "health system."

This chapter describes institutional care delivery with specific reference to acute-care—mostly characterized by secondary and tertiary levels of care—in community hospitals. It also discusses various ways to classify hospitals and points out important trends and critical issues that will continue to shape the delivery of inpatient services.

Hospital Transformation in the United States

From about 1840 to 1900, hospitals underwent a drastic change in purpose, function, and number. From supplying merely food, shelter, and meager medical care to people with limited financial resources who are sick, armies, persons infected with contagious diseases, mental health conditions, and individuals requiring emergency treatment, they began to provide skilled medical and surgical attention and nursing care to all people (Raffel, 1980). Subsequently, hospitals became centers of medical training and research. More recent transformations have been mainly organizational in nature, as hospitals have consolidated into medical systems, delivering a broad range of healthcare services. These transformations can be neatly categorized according to five significant functions in the evolution of hospitals:

1. Primitive institutions of social welfare
2. Distinct institutions of care for the sick
3. Organized institutions of medical practice
4. Advanced institutions of medical training and research
5. Consolidated systems of health services delivery

Primitive Institutions of Social Welfare

Except for a few hospitals that were located in some of the major U.S. cities, during the 1800s, most regions in the country had municipal almshouses (or poorhouses) and pesthouses. Financed through charitable gifts and local government funds, these institutions essentially performed a social welfare function. Almshouses served primarily the destitute of society who needed food and shelter. They also took care of the sick, who received limited nursing care as needed. People generally stayed in these institutions for months rather than days. Pesthouses were used to quarantine people who were sick with contagious diseases, such as smallpox and yellow fever, so the rest of the community would be protected.

Distinct Institutions of Care for the Sick

Not until the late 1800s did infirmaries or hospital departments of city poorhouses break away to become independent medical care institutions. These were the first public (government) hospitals (Haglund and Dowling, 1993), in this case operated by local governments. For example, the Kings County Almshouse and Infirmary, organized in Brooklyn in 1830, later became the Kings County Hospital (Raffel, 1980). Nevertheless, these first public hospitals still served mainly the indigent. Hospitals at this stage often had poor hygiene, inadequate ventilation, and care provided by untrained nurses.

In Europe, the first hospitals were established predominantly by religious orders. Nurses, who were primarily monks and nuns, attended to both the physical and spiritual needs of the patients. Later, many of these hospitals became tax-financed public institutions as less church money became available for hospitals and monasteries. In England, private donations and taxes supported the "royal hospitals." Other British hospitals were nonprofit (or voluntary) hospitals, which served as a model for such hospitals in the United States (Raffel and Raffel, 1994). Later, creation of the National Health Service in 1948 brought the British nonprofit hospitals under government ownership.

In the United States, the founding of **voluntary hospitals**—nonprofit community hospitals financed through local philanthropy as opposed to taxes—was often inspired by influential physicians, with the financial backing of local donors and philanthropists. These hospitals accepted both indigent and paying patients, but to cover their operating expenses, they required charitable contributions from private citizens.

The first voluntary hospital in the United States established specifically to care for the sick was the Pennsylvania Hospital in Philadelphia, which opened in 1752. At the time, the city already had an almshouse. However, Dr. Thomas Bond, a London-trained physician, brought to prominence the need for a hospital to care for the ill and low income of the city. Benjamin Franklin, who was a friend and advisor of Dr. Bond, was instrumental in promoting the idea and in raising voluntary contributions to finance the hospital. According to the Pennsylvania Hospital's charter, the contributors had the right to make all laws and regulations relating to the hospital's operation. The contributors also elected members to form the governing board, or the board of trustees. Thus, the control of voluntary hospitals was in the hands of influential community laypeople rather than physicians (Raffel and Raffel, 1994).

Other prominent voluntary hospitals included the New York Hospital in New York, which was completed in 1775 but, due to the Revolutionary War, was not opened to civilian patients until 1791. The Massachusetts General Hospital in Boston was incorporated in 1812 and opened in 1821. During this period, the almshouses continued to serve an important function by receiving overflow patients who could not be admitted to the hospitals because of the unavailability of beds or who had to be discharged from hospitals because they were declared incurable (Raffel and Raffel, 1994). Later hospitals in the United States were modeled after the Pennsylvania, New York, and Massachusetts General hospitals.

Organized Institutions of Medical Practice

Social and demographic change, but above all advances in medical science and technology, transformed hospitals into institutions of medical practice. Beginning in the latter half of the 19th century, new medical technology, facilities, and personnel training all became centered in the hospital.

Over time, improvements in hygiene, advanced medical care, and surgical services made hospitals more acceptable to the middle and upper classes. Indeed, hospitals began to attract affluent patients who could afford to pay privately. Thus, the hospital was transformed from a charitable institution into one that could generate a profit. In many instances, physicians started opening small hospitals, financed by wealthy and influential sponsors. These facilities were the first proprietary (for-profit) hospitals.

In the early 20th century, the field of hospital administration became a discipline in its own right. Hospitals needed administrators with expertise in financial management and organizational skills to manage them. The administrative structure of the hospital was organized into departments, such as food service, pharmacy, x-ray, and laboratory. In turn, it became necessary to employ professional staff to manage the delivery of services. Efficiency began to emerge as an important element in the management of hospitals. This early emphasis on efficiency foreshadowed two main issues that continue to affect health policy and hospital management: the pressure on hospitals to introduce new technology while containing costs and the assumption that hospitals should operate like businesses (Arndt and Bigelow, 2006). Pressure to control costs, along with the availability of advanced medical care in outpatient settings, forced hospitals to limit care to more acute periods of illness rather than the full course of a disease.

Hospital accreditation was another notable development in the early 20th century. The American College of Surgeons (ACS) began inspecting hospitals in 1918 and developed standards for hospital equipment and hospital wards. Until 1951, the ACS singlehandedly took responsibility for improving hospital-based medical practice. In 1951, this effort evolved into the Joint Commission on Accreditation of Hospitals, a private nonprofit body formed through the joint efforts of the ACS, the American College of Physicians, the AHA, and the American Medical Association (AMA). The organization changed its name in 1987 to the Joint Commission on Accreditation of Healthcare Organizations, which more accurately describes the variety of health facilities it accredits. Since 2007, its official name has been the Joint Commission.

Advanced Institutions of Medical Training and Research

Advances in biomedical knowledge made it necessary for physicians to receive most of their training in hospitals, which in turn led to collaborations between hospitals and universities. Pennsylvania Hospital, for example, taught courses required by the College of Philadelphia's medical school, which later became the University of Pennsylvania School of Medicine. Similarly, New York Hospital served as a teaching hospital for medical students of Columbia Medical School, and Massachusetts General Hospital provided practical clinical instruction for students of Harvard Medical School (Raffel and Raffel, 1994). To complete physicians' medical training, internships and residencies became necessary.

The Johns Hopkins Hospital (opened in 1889), with its adjoining medical school (opened in 1893), inaugurated a new era during which teaching was combined with clinical practice and scientific inquiry in medicine. In affiliation with university-based medical schools, many hospitals became centers of medical research. The vast number of clinical records and large array of medical conditions among hospital patients provided a wealth of data that informed investigative studies to advance medical knowledge. Even today, large hospitals play an important role in clinical studies. To a lesser extent, some aspects of medical training have shifted to other settings, such as nursing homes, hospices, and community health centers.

Consolidated Systems of Health Services Delivery

Hospitals have been the major cost centers in the healthcare delivery system. During the 1980s and 1990s, concerns over rising costs prompted the introduction of prospective and capitated payment methods and aggressive use of review practices that brought about drastic reductions in the length of inpatient stays. The declining use of acute-care beds had left most hospitals with excess capacity in the form of empty beds. As the acute-inpatient care sector of healthcare delivery became less profitable, hospitals adopted a number of consolidation strategies. Multihospital systems formed through mergers and acquisitions; hospital systems diversified into nonacute services, such as outpatient centers, home health care, long-term care, and subacute care; and some hospitals affiliated with networks through contractual arrangements.

Intense consolidation in certain hospital markets diluted competition, which benefited hospitals. Research suggests that hospital consolidation in the 1990s raised prices by at least 5% as competition eroded (Vogt and Town, 2006).

The Expansion Phase: Late 1800s to Mid-1980s

Hospitals grew in numbers when they became a necessary local adjunct of medical practice. Growth in medical technology increased the volume of surgical procedures, almost all of which were performed in hospitals. The number of U.S. hospitals grew from 178 (35,604 beds) in 1872 to 4,359 (421,065 beds) in 1909. By 1929, 6,665 hospitals provided 907,133 beds in the United States (Haglund and Dowling, 1993). As new beds were built, their availability almost ensured that they would be used. This phenomenon led Milton Roemer (1916–2001) to proclaim, "a built bed is a filled bed"—an affirmation known popularly as Roemer's law (Roemer, 1961).

Haglund and Dowling (1993) identified six significant factors in the growth of hospitals: advances in medical science, development of specialized technology, advances in medical education, development of professional nursing, growth of health insurance, and the role of government. The first three factors were discussed in the previous section; this section covers the last three.

Development of Professional Nursing

During the latter half of the 19th century, Florence Nightingale was instrumental in transforming nursing into a recognized profession in Great Britain. Following the founding of the Nightingale School of Nursing in England, nursing schools in the United States were established at Bellevue Hospital (New York City), New Haven Hospital (New Haven, Connecticut), and Massachusetts General Hospital (Boston). The benefits of having trained nurses in hospitals became apparent as the increased efficacy of treatment and hygiene associated with such care improved patient recovery (Haglund and Dowling, 1993). Thus, professional nursing was instrumental in transforming hospitals, which to an increasing extent came to be regarded as places of healing, and found acceptance with the middle and upper classes.

Growth of Private Health Insurance

Private health insurance in the United States first began as a hospital insurance plan to protect both patients and hospitals against financial instability. During and after the Great Depression of the 1930s, many hospitals were forced to close, and the financial solvency of many more was threatened. Consequently, the number of hospitals in the United States dropped from 6,852 in 1928 to 6,189 in 1937. The growth of private health insurance subsequently became a vehicle for enabling people to pay for hospital services, and the flow of insurance money helped revive the financial stability of hospitals. Historically, insurance plans provided generous coverage for inpatient care, placing few restrictions on patients and physicians (Feldstein, 1971).

Role of Government

Government funding for hospital construction perhaps played the most important role in the expansion of hospitals in the 20th century. Subsequently, Medicare and Medicaid provided indirect funding to the hospital industry by vastly expanding public-sector health insurance.

The Hill-Burton Act

Relatively little hospital construction took place during the Great Depression and World War II, so, by the end of the war, there was a severe shortage of hospital beds in the United States. The Hospital Survey and Construction Act of 1946, commonly referred to as the Hill-Burton Act, provided federal grants to states for the construction of new community hospitals (nonfederal, short-stay hospitals) that would be operated on a nonprofit basis. This legislation required that each state develop and upgrade, annually, a plan for health facility construction based on bed-to-population ratios, which became the basis for the allocation of federal construction grants to the states (Raffel, 1980).

In 1946, after World War II ended, 3.2 community hospital beds were available per 1,000 civilian population in the United States. The objective of the Hill-Burton Act was to reach 4.5 beds per 1,000 population (Teisberg et al., 1991). The Hill-Burton program assisted in the construction of nearly 40% of the beds in the nation's short-stay general hospitals and was the single greatest factor that increased the U.S. bed supply during the 1950s and 1960s (Haglund and Dowling, 1993). Indeed, the Hill-Burton Act made it possible for even small, remote communities to have their own hospitals (Wolfson and Hopes, 1994). By 1980, the United States had reached its goal of 4.5 community hospital beds per 1,000 civilian population (National Center for Health Statistics [NCHS], 2002) even though the Hill-Burton program ended in 1974.

Thanks to the Hill-Burton Act, nonprofit community hospitals in the United States far outnumber all other types of hospitals even today. Competition from the new hospitals led to the closure of many smaller proprietary, for-profit hospitals.

Public Health Insurance

The creation of the Medicare and Medicaid programs in 1965 also had a significant—albeit indirect—impact on the increased number of hospital beds and their use (Feldstein, 1993), as government-funded health insurance became available to a large number of older adults and Americans with low income. Between 1965 and 1980, the number of community hospitals in the United States increased from 5,736 (741,000 beds) to 5,830 (988,000 beds); total admissions per 1,000 population increased from 130 to 154; and total inpatient

The Downsizing Phase: Mid-1980s Onward

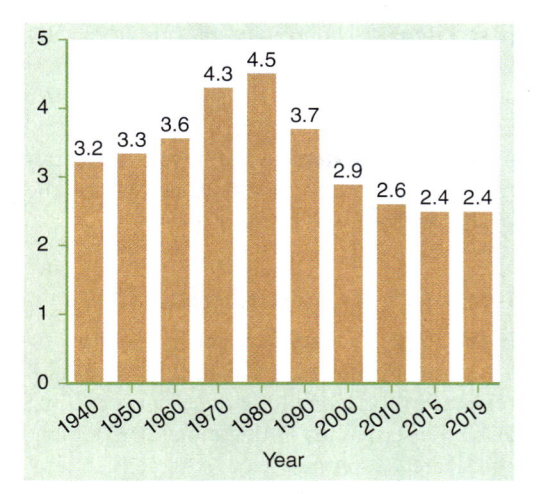

Figure 8-1 Trends in the number of U.S. community hospital beds per 1,000 resident population.

Data from National Center for Health Statistics. 2021. *Health, United States, 2020-21*. Hyattsville, MD: U.S. Department of Health and Human Services. National Center for Health Statistics. 2018. *Health, United States, 2017*. Hyattsville, MD: U.S. Department of Health and Human Services.

days per 1,000 population increased from 1,007 to 1,159. The percentage of occupied beds also remained relatively stable at around 76% (AHA, 1990). **Figure 8-1** shows trends from 1940 to 2015 in the number of beds per 1,000 resident population.

The Downsizing Phase: Mid-1980s Onward

The mid-1980s marked a turning point in the growth and use of hospital beds. After a sharp decline in 1985, the number of community hospitals and the total number of beds continued to decline until 2005 (**Figure 8-2**). The main reasons for the decline in hospital capacity and use were a shift from inpatient to outpatient care driven by changes in reimbursement and the impact of managed care. Consequently, a number of hospitals had to either close down or repurpose the use of acute-care beds for other types of services, such as nursing home care.

In 2015, the average occupancy rate (percentage of beds occupied) in community hospitals was 63.6%, and the average length of stay was 5.5 days (NCHS, 2018). Hospital

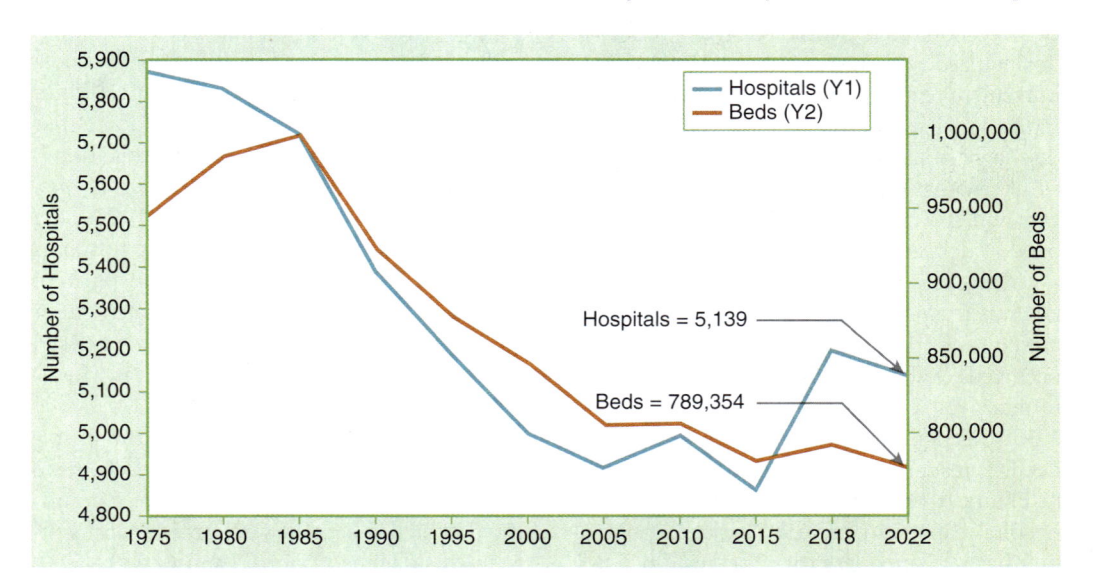

Figure 8-2 The decline in the number of U.S. community hospitals and beds.

Data from National Center for Health Statistics. 2002. *Health, United States, 2002*. Hyattsville, MD: U.S. Department of Health and Human Services. p. 279; *Health, United States, 2017*, Table 89; Health Forum. 2020. Fast facts on U.S. hospitals. Available at: https://www.aha.org/statistics/fast-facts-us-hospitals. Accessed August 2020. 2022 data from American Hospital Association. 2022. Fast Facts on U.S. Hospitals, 2022.

utilization has remained relatively stable in recent years. The COVID-19 pandemic that hit the United States in 2020, however, had a significant effect on hospital use resulting in the increase of the average length of stay to 5.7 days.

Changes in Reimbursement

The Tax Equity and Fiscal Responsibility Act (TEFRA) of 1982 required the conversion of hospital Medicare reimbursement from cost-plus to a prospective payment system (PPS) based on diagnosis-related groups (DRGs). Under PPS, hospitals are paid a fixed amount per admission according to the patient's principal diagnosis, regardless of how long the patient stays in the hospital. To make a profit, the hospital must keep its costs below the fixed reimbursement amount, which creates an incentive to minimize the patient's length of stay. Following Medicare's lead, other payers soon adopted prospective methods to reimburse hospitals. Private insurers also resorted to competitive pricing and discounted fees and closely monitored when patients would be hospitalized and for how long. As PPS reimbursement exerted pressure on hospitals to reduce the length of stay after admission, early discharge from hospitals became practical only as alternative services, such as home health care and subacute long-term care, were developed to deliver post acute continuity of care.

The effect of PPS reimbursement on hospitals was dramatic. In the 1980s, 550 hospitals closed and 159 mergers and acquisitions occurred (Balotsky, 2005). Since then, the number of community hospital beds per 1,000 resident population has continued to decline, reaching 2.4 per 1,000 in 2015 (refer to Figure 8-1). Notably, since 1998, the U.S. hospital capacity per 1,000 resident population has remained less than the level in 1946, when the Hill-Burton Act was passed. In those days, the additional hospital bed capacity may have been necessary because the settings for post discharge continuity of care were not well developed. Subsequently, technological advances enabled the development and use of these alternative delivery settings. Hence, technology has played a major role in the tremendous advances in efficiency within the healthcare system.

Impact of Managed Care

In the 1990s, managed care became a growing force that transformed the delivery of health services in the United States (Heaton & Tadi, 2023; Kaiser Family Foundation, 2023). Managed care has emphasized cost containment and the efficient delivery of services by stressing the use of alternative delivery settings whenever appropriate. Notably, greater market penetration by health maintenance organizations (HMOs) played a significant role in lowering hospital use and profitability (Clement and Grazier, 2001).

Hospital Closures

Between 1990 and 2000, more than 200 rural hospitals (8% of all rural hospitals) and nearly 300 urban hospitals (11% of all urban hospitals) closed for economic reasons (Office of Inspector General, 2003). Declining use was the main factor underlying this trend. Overall, the total number of community hospitals declined by 9% during the 1990s; the total number of beds in community hospitals declined by 11% (NCHS, 2013). Hospitals of all sizes throughout the United States either closed entire wings or converted those beds to alternative uses, such as outpatient care, long-term care, or rehabilitation services.

Since 2000, many government-run hospitals, at both the federal and local levels, have closed. For example, the number of community hospitals operated by state and local governments declined from 1,163 in 2000 to 944 in 2023 (AHA, 2023; NCHS, 2016) because those facilities could not compete with private community hospitals.

Some Key Utilization Measures and Operational Concepts

Discharges

The total number of patient discharges per 1,000 population (hospitalization rate) is one indicator of access to hospital inpatient services and of the extent of use. Because babies born in the hospital are not included in admissions, discharges provide a more accurate count of inpatients served by a hospital. **Discharge** data for a hospital indicate the total number of patients discharged from the hospital's acute-care beds during a given period. Deaths in hospitals are counted as discharges.

In general, hospitalization rates and lengths of stay increase with age (except for infants). Females have a higher rate of hospitalization compared to males but incur shorter lengths of stay. This holds true even when data are adjusted to account for pregnancy-related hospitalizations. Other details on hospitalizations in the United States are given in **Table 8-1**.

In 2016, Medicare paid for the largest number of hospitalizations, followed by private insurance and Medicaid. More than 6 million inpatient days were attributed to patients without insurance. Relative to the U.S. population, the East South Central area (Mississippi, Alabama, Tennessee, and Kentucky) had a disproportionately higher share of hospital stays; the Pacific and Mountain divisions in the western United States had a disproportionately lower share of hospital stays (Freeman et al., 2018).

People living in low-income communities—a proxy for socioeconomic status—have higher hospitalization rates and longer lengths of stay compared to those living in higher-income communities. Low-income population groups are generally in poorer health and have less access to routine primary care. These patients

Table 8-1 Discharges, Average Length of Stay, and Average Cost per Stay in U.S. Community Hospitals, 2016

Characteristics	Hospital Stays (in Thousands)	Stays per 1,000 Population (Hospitalization Rates)	Average Length of Stay (Days)	Average Cost per Stay ($)
Total	35,700	104.2	4.6	11,700
Age				
< 1 year	4,200	210.8	3.9	5,900
1–17 years	1,300	17.1	4.2	12,500
18–44 years	8,700	75.4	3.8	8,600
45–64 years	8,800	104.3	5.1	14,500
65–84 years	9,900	232.5	5.2	14,500
≥ 85 years	2,800	455.7	5.1	11,300
Gender				
Male	15,400	91.3	5.0	13,300
Female	20,200	116.6	4.3	10,500

(continues)

Table 8-1 Discharges, Average Length of Stay, and Average Cost per Stay in U.S. Community Hospitals, 2016 *(continued)*

Characteristics	Hospital Stays (in Thousands)	Stays per 1,000 Population (Hospitalization Rates)	Average Length of Stay (Days)	Average Cost per Stay ($)
Primary Payer				
Medicare	14,100	—	5.3	13,600
Medicaid	8,200	—	4.6	9,800
Private insurance	10,700	—	3.9	10,900
Uninsured	1,500	—	4.1	9,300
Community Income in the Area of Residence				
Lowest	10,800	122.7	4.8	11,000
Highest	7,000	82.5	4.5	12,900

Reproduced from Weiss, A. J., and A. Elixhauser. 2014. *Overview of hospital stays in the United States, 2012 (Statistical Brief #180)*. Rockville, MD: Agency for Healthcare Research and Quality. Available at: http://www.hcup-us.ahrq.gov/reports/statbriefs/sb180-Hospitalizations-United-States-2012.pdf. Accessed May 2017.

also have higher levels of trust in the technical quality of hospital services compared to primary care (Kangovi et al., 2013).

Inpatient Days

An **inpatient day** (also called a patient day) is a night spent in the hospital by a patient. The cumulative number of patient days over a certain period is known as **days of care**. Days of care per 1,000 population over the course of one year reflect the use of inpatient services.

Average Length of Stay

Average length of stay (ALOS) is calculated by dividing the total days of care by the total number of discharges. ALOS measures the number of days a patient, on average, spends in the hospital. Hence, this measure, when applied to individuals or specific groups of patients, is an indicator of the severity of illness and resource use. In addition, ALOS has cost implications. Other things being equal, short hospital stays reduce the cost per discharge. **Figure 8-3** illustrates ALOS trends in community hospitals.

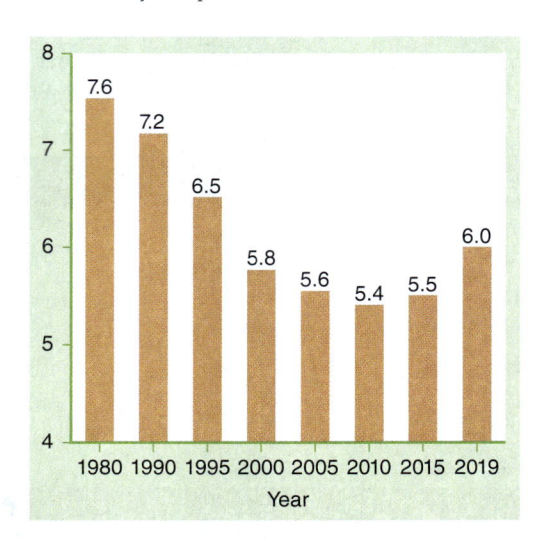

Figure 8-3 Trends in average length of stay in nonfederal short-stay hospitals, selected years.

Data from National Center for Health Statistics. 2018. *Health, United States, 2017.* Hyattsville, MD: Department of Health and Human Services. Table 82. 2019 data from American Hospital Association (AHA). 2023. Annual Survey of Hospitals. Hospital Statistics 2021 edition.

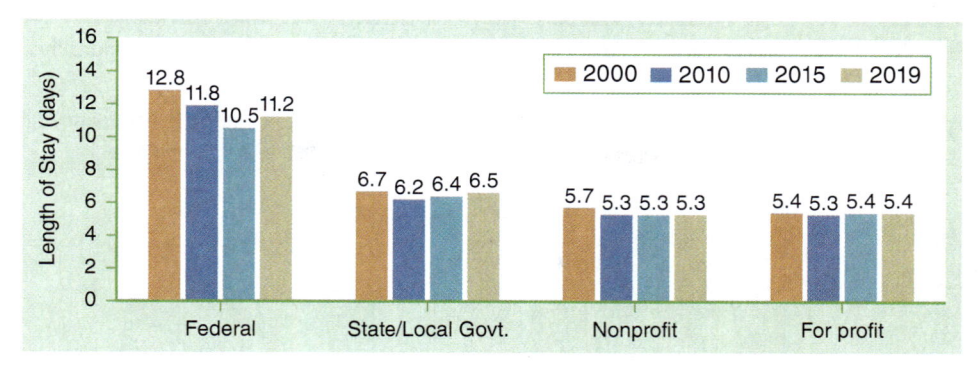

Some Key Utilization Measures and Operational Concepts

Figure 8-4 Average lengths of stay by U.S. hospital ownership, selected years.

Data from National Center for Health Statistics. 2018. *Health, United States, 2017.* Hyattsville, MD: Department of Health and Human Services. Table 82. 2019 data from American Hospital Association (AHA). 2023. Annual Survey of Hospitals. Hospital Statistics 2021 edition.

Figure 8-4 shows trends in ALOS by type of hospital ownership. Government-owned hospitals have longer lengths of stay compared to private hospitals. Federal hospitals mainly include those in the Veterans Health Administration system, which serve an aging population. State and local government hospitals disproportionately serve the low income and uninsured.

Hospital Access and Utilization: Comparative Data

There has been increasing interest in comparing the U.S. health system to the health systems of other countries. For this purpose, the Organization for Economic Cooperation and Development (OECD) is a reliable source of comparative healthcare data. **Table 8-2** provides hospital user data for selected OECD members. Note that the data for the United States in this table include all hospitals, not just community hospitals (as in Table 8-1).

Japan is clearly an outlier in hospital capacity and use. Because a greater supply of hospital beds generally leads to higher use (Roemer's law), policymakers around the world have adopted the policy of reducing the number of hospital beds. Since 2000, the number of beds per capita has decreased in nearly all OECD countries. Part of the decrease can be attributed to advances in medical technology. Between 2000 and 2017, the number of discharges fell in the majority of OECD countries, with some of the largest reductions observed in countries where there were also large decreases in the number of beds. High occupancy rates of curative- (acute-) care beds can be symptomatic of a health system under pressure and may lead to bed shortages and higher rates of infection (OECD, 2019). The number of discharges fell between 2009 and 2019 in the majority of OECD countries, with some of the largest reductions in countries where there were also large decreases in the number of beds (as in Estonia, Finland, Iceland, Luxembourg and Sweden) (OECD, 2021).

Capacity

The number of beds set up and staffed for inpatient use determines the size or capacity of a hospital. Among all community hospitals in the United States, 86% have fewer than 300 beds (**Figure 8-5**). The average size of a community hospital was approximately 161 beds in 2015. Between 2000 and 2010, the number of hospitals with fewer than 50 beds increased by 33% (from 1,198 to 1,591) (NCHS, 2018), primarily because of a dramatic rise in the number of

Table 8-2 Inpatient Hospital Utilization: Comparative Data for Selected OECD Countries, 2021

	Hospital Beds per 1,000 Population	Discharges per 1,000 Population	Average Length of Stay (Days)	Occupancy Rate (%)
Australia	NA	174[1]	4.7	NA
Canada	2.5	72[1,2]	7.7	91.6
France	5.7	161[1]	5.5	78.9
Germany	7.8	219	7.4	79.1
Japan	12.6	123	16.4	76.1
United Kingdom	2.3	129	6.2	NA
United States	2.8	NA	5.4	64.3

[1] Newborns are not included.
[2] Data are not comparable to other countries.

Data from Organization for Economic Cooperation and Development (OECD). 2023. *Health at a glance, 2023: OECD indicators.*

physician-owned specialty hospitals (discussed later in the section "Specialty Hospitals"). However, regulations under the Affordable Care Act (ACA) put a squeeze on the growth of these hospitals. Consequently, between 2010 and 2015, the growth trickled down to 3.4% (NCHS, 2018).

Total number of community hospitals = 6,090

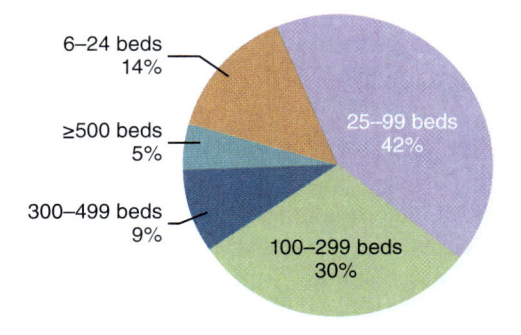

- 6–24 beds: 14%
- 25–99 beds: 42%
- 100–299 beds: 30%
- 300–499 beds: 9%
- ≥500 beds: 5%

Figure 8-5 Breakdown of U.S. community hospitals by size, 2019.

Data from Michas F. 2022. Number of registered hospitals in the U.S. in 2019 by number of beds. https://www.statista.com/statistics/459779/total-hospital-numbers-in-the-us-by-number-of-beds/

Average Daily Census

The average number of inpatients receiving care each day in a hospital is called the **average daily census**. This measure is often used to define occupancy of inpatient beds in hospitals and other inpatient facilities. The total inpatient days during a given period (days of care) is divided by the number of days in that period to arrive at the average daily census. For example, if the number of total inpatient days for July is 3,162, then the average daily census for July is 102 (3,162/31).

Occupancy Rate

The **occupancy rate** for a given period is derived by dividing the average daily census for that period by the average number of beds (capacity). The resulting fraction is then expressed as a percentage (percent of beds occupied); it indicates the proportion of a hospital's total inpatient capacity actually used. Occupancy rates are also calculated for other types of inpatient facilities, such as nursing

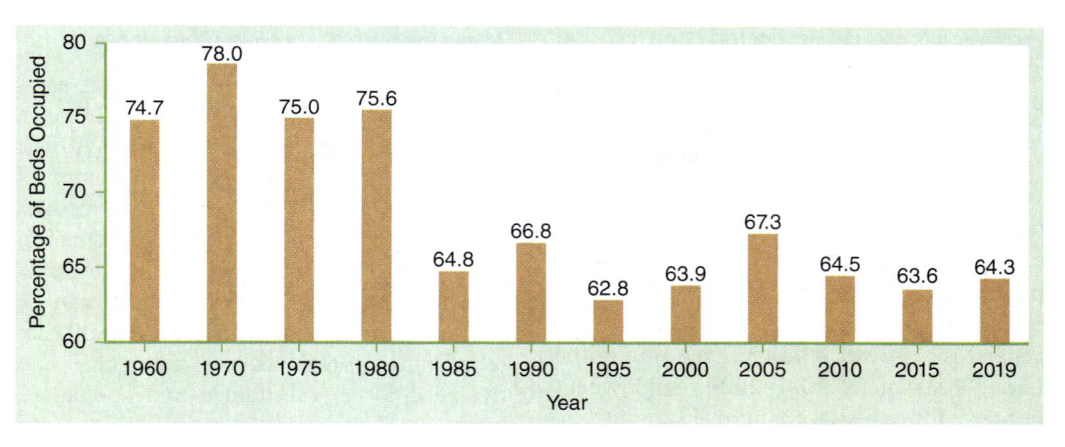

Figure 8-6 Change in occupancy rates in U.S. community hospitals, 1960–2019 (selected years).

Data from National Center for Health Statistics. 2019. *Health, United States, 2019*. Hyattsville, MD: U.S. Department of Health and Human Services.

homes, and often used as a measure of performance when compared with competitors or with statewide or nationwide data.

Figure 8-6 shows the change in aggregate occupancy rates for U.S. community hospitals from 1960 to 2019. Individual hospitals can compare their own occupancy rates against industry benchmarks. In a competitive environment, facilities with higher occupancy rates are considered more successful than those with lower occupancy rates.

Hospital Demand, Employment, Expenditures, and Profitability

Hospital demand refers to the need for healthcare services and the use of hospital facilities by patients (Feldstein, 1977). Increases in demand for hospital services and expenditures are driven by demographic trends such as aging of the population and overall population growth; advances in medical technology; health insurance status of the population; health status of the population, such as the prevalence of diseases, especially chronic conditions (Feldstein, 1977); accidents and emergencies; and overall healthcare awareness (van Oostveen et al., 2015). Hospital demand can vary regionally and is often impacted by government policies and health insurance coverage (van Oostveen et al., 2015). The COVID-19 pandemic, however, was an outlier. As the nation was gripped by the pandemic, the number of hospitalizations mounted, but many routine as well as critical services were cancelled. Projecting the demand for intensive care became a major challenge because the forecasting models turned out to be misleading (Chin et al., 2020).

Pharmaceutical care in hospitals by clinical pharmacists who can address medication-related issues can shorten hospital stays (Lin et al., 2020). Similarly, pharmaceutical care delivered by community pharmacists can prevent hospitalizations (Pai et al., 2009). Hospital use is also significantly reduced for patients with human immunodeficiency virus (HIV)/acquired immunodeficiency syndrome (AIDS) who adhere to their antiretroviral therapy regimens (Nachega et al., 2010).

Hospital employment refers to the number of persons employed (head counts) and the number of full-time equivalent (FTE) persons employed in general and specialty hospitals, including self-employed workers (OECD, 2023). Hospitals offer a wide range of job opportunities, including healthcare professionals (such as doctors, nurses, and allied health staff), administrative and support staff (such as receptionists, janitors, and IT professionals), and management and leadership roles (OECD, 2023). Demand for services is the most important factor that affects hospital employment. Hospitals are the largest employers in the healthcare industry, and hospitals and medical systems are among the largest employers in several states. Health care in general is a growth industry. Even during the Great Recession of 2007–2009, employment in the healthcare sector continued to increase even when the rate of unemployment had reached 10% in the general economy (U.S. Bureau of Labor Statistics, 2018).

Other factors have had a downward influence on hospital demand and jobs. For example, a shift away from treatment on an inpatient basis and toward treatment in outpatient settings has increased demand for outpatient services. Along with the growth of outpatient centers, employment in the outpatient sector has more than doubled since 2003 (Kacik, 2018a). This trend is expected to continue in the future.

Hospital Expenditures

Hospital expenditures refer to the costs associated with operating and maintaining a healthcare facility (Redelmeier & Fuchs, 1993). These expenses encompass a wide range of items, including physicians' services, medical equipment and supplies, facility maintenance, utilities, and administrative costs (Redelmeier & Fuchs, 1993). Hospital expenditures can be substantial due to the high cost of healthcare services, advanced medical technology, and the need for a well-trained and specialized workforce (Redelmeier & Fuchs, 1993). Along with the shift in utilization of hospital services, the share of personal health expenditures for hospital care had declined until 2005, but it has slowly crept up since then (**Table 8-3**).

Inpatient hospital services constitute the largest share (about one-third) of total healthcare expenditures in the United States. **Figure 8-7** shows the aggregate costs and hospital stays by payer type. Most of the hospital use is incurred by Medicare and Medicaid beneficiaries; hence, most of the inpatient expenditures are borne by the government. Even though Medicare is the single largest

Table 8-3 Share of Personal Health Expenditures Used for Hospital Care

	Personal Health Expenditures[1]	Hospital Expenditures[1]	Percentage Share
1980	217.0	100.5	46.3%
1990	615.3	250.4	40.7%
2000	1,161.5	415.5	35.8%
2005	1,695.7	608.6	35.9%
2010	2,191.4	822.3	37.5%
2015	2,710.2	1,034.6	38.2%
2018	3,075.5	1,191.8	38.8%
2019	3,207.0	1,192.0	37.2%

[1]Expenditures are in billions of dollars.

Data from Centers for Medicare and Medicaid Services (CMS). 2019. *National health expenditure data. NHE tables (historical)*.

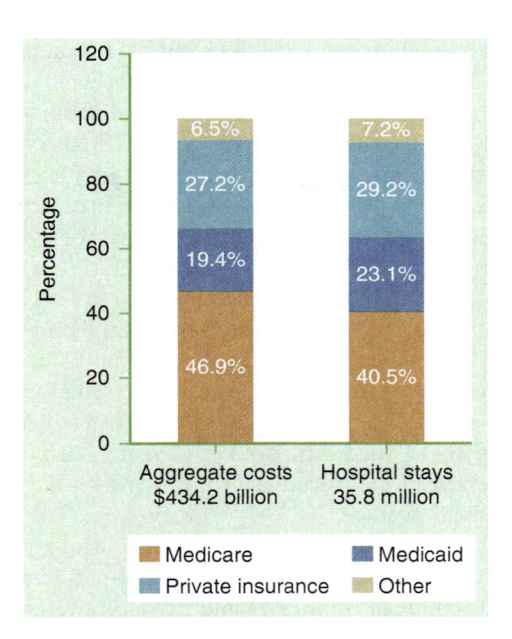

Figure 8-7 Aggregate hospital costs and hospital stays by payer type, 2017.

Data from Liang, L., et al., 2020. *National inpatient hospital costs: The most expensive conditions by payer, 2017.* Statistical Brief #261. Agency for Healthcare Research and Quality. Available at: https://hcup-us.ahrq.gov/reports/statbriefs/sb261-Most-Expensive-Hospital-Conditions-2017.jsp. Accessed August 2020.

payer for hospital services, the program's inpatient costs as a proportion of total costs actually declined from 36.9% in 2007 to 32.6% in 2017 (Sanofi-Aventis/Forte Information Resources, 2019). Overall, hospital expenditures have risen faster than total personal healthcare expenditures (Table 8-3), so the year-to-year rise in hospital-related expenses remains a central concern among policymakers (Liang et al., 2020).

Profitability

The profitability of hospitals can vary widely depending on factors like location, size, ownership, patient demographics, and the mix of services provided (Bai & Anderson, 2016). Hospitals can be classified into various ownership models, such as non-profit, for-profit, and government-run facilities, and each type has different financial goals (Bai & Anderson, 2016). Non-profit hospitals aim to reinvest any surplus funds into improving healthcare services, while for-profit hospitals seek to generate profits for their shareholders (Bai & Anderson, 2016). Government-run hospitals may have varying financial objectives based on policy goals (Bai & Anderson, 2016).

Research shows that hospital revenues are declining as expenses keep rising, thus squeezing hospital operating margins (profitability). Between 2015 and 2016, expenses for nonprofit hospitals grew by 7.5% while revenue grew by 6.6% (Burrill and Kane, 2017). The transition from volume-based reimbursement to value-based payments has presented a major challenge to hospitals' profitability, along with the shift from inpatient to outpatient care.

Even as hospital admissions have fallen, overall hospital employment has risen. Labor is the largest single component of hospital costs, accounting for roughly 50% of most hospitals' total operating costs (Burrill and Kane, 2017).

Profitability has implications for hospital survival. Hospitals with a higher ratio of RNs per bed (which translates into improved quality of care), a higher operating margin, lower percentage of revenues from Medicare and Medicaid, and lower competition are less likely to suffer adverse financial consequences (Pai et al., 2017). It is also noteworthy that hospitals located in states that implemented Medicaid expansion (an option left up to each state after the 2012 Supreme Court decision on the ACA) have significantly increased Medicaid revenues, decreased uncompensated care costs, and improvements in profit margins compared with hospitals located in states that did not expand their Medicaid programs (Blavin, 2016).

International Cost Comparisons

Variations in per capita health spending can be the result of differences in prices for healthcare goods and services, and in the quantity of care that individuals are using ("volume") (OECD, 2020). To better understand the impact of volume and prices on health spending across countries, data expressed in national currencies are converted into a common currency using Purchasing Power Parities (PPP) (OECD, 2020). PPPs are conversion rates that show the ratio of prices for a basket of goods in one currency to the same goods in another (OECD, 2020). When PPPs are used to convert expenditure to a common unit means, the results are valued at a uniform price level and the comparison of expenditures across countries reflects only the differences in the volume of goods and services consumed (OECD, 2020). PPPs are calculated by first gathering price information for a representative basket of products and services and averaging them within groups (OECD, 2020). These product group prices are converted to price relativities, which are then weighted and averaged for each aggregation level (for example hospitals, health care, or GDP) (OECD, 2020).

To compare the relative price differences in various national currencies, the OECD converts the prices into a common currency using Purchasing Power Parities (PPP). Hence, PPPs measure differences in price levels between countries. **Figure 8-8** shows uniform hospital prices in selected countries. In 2017, hospital services in Switzerland were priced at 213% (more than twice) of the OECD average. In the United States, the same services cost 37% more than the OECD average. In the United Kingdom, the same hospital services were priced at 71% (29% less) of the OECD average.

Hospital expenditure typically accounts for around a third of overall health spending in OECD countries and therefore weighs heavily in the overall health price level calculations. However, the variation in prices of hospital services and procedures is even

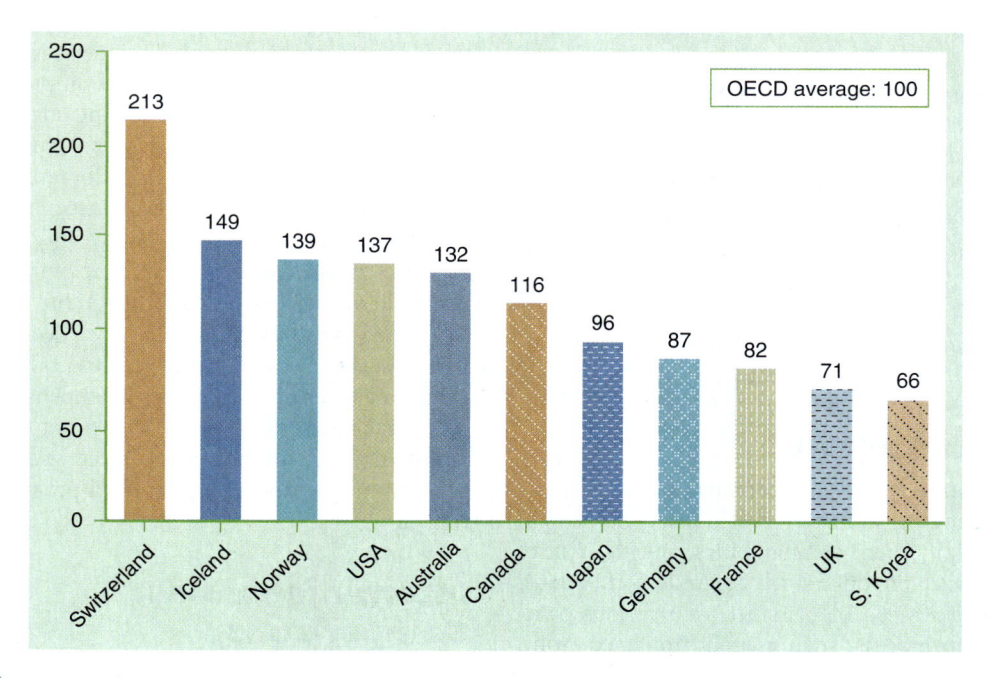

Figure 8-8 International comparative hospital prices, 2017.

Data from Organization for Economic Cooperation and Development (OECD). 2020. *Focus on health care prices.* Available at: http://www.oecd.org/health/health-systems/Health-Care-Prices-Brief-May-2020.pdf. Accessed August 2020.

greater across OECD countries than in the health sector as a whole. The average price for a caesarean section in Norway, Iceland and Switzerland is around 8,000 Euros—around twice the level in France, the Netherlands and Belgium, and seven times the price in Estonia and Portugal. Similarly, at 12,000 Euros, the typical price of a hip replacement in Luxembourg or Norway is seven times that reported for Turkey, Latvia and Lithuania (OECD, 2020).

Estimates for 2017 suggest that average hospital prices in Switzerland are more than double the average level calculated across OECD countries, whereas prices in Turkey are only around an eighth of the OECD average (OECD, 2020). More labor intensive than the health sector as a whole (typically 60-70% of hospital spending is staff costs), service prices in hospitals are heavily determined by local (national) wage levels, but may also be influenced by hospital financing mechanisms and funding arrangements, the structure of service provision, as well as the market structure and competition among payers and among providers, and the way prices are set (Barber et al., 2019).

Types of Hospitals

The U.S. hospital market includes a variety of institutional forms, including both private and government-owned hospitals. Most hospitals are private, nonprofit, short-stay, community hospitals (**Figure 8-9**). Private, for-profit (investor-owned) community hospitals are next in predominance; then come the state and local government-owned community hospitals and, finally, federal hospitals, which are not community hospitals.

The endless variations in hospital characteristics defy any simple classification. The classification arrangements described in this section have been commonly used to differentiate among the various types of hospitals. Keep in mind, however, that these classifications are not mutually exclusive.

Classification by Ownership

Public Hospitals

Public hospitals are owned by agencies of federal, state, or local governments. Note that the word "public" does not have its ordinary

- Other* 2%
- Psychiatric (nonfederal) 11%
- Federal 3%
- State and local government 15%
- Private for profit 20%
- Private nonprofit 49%

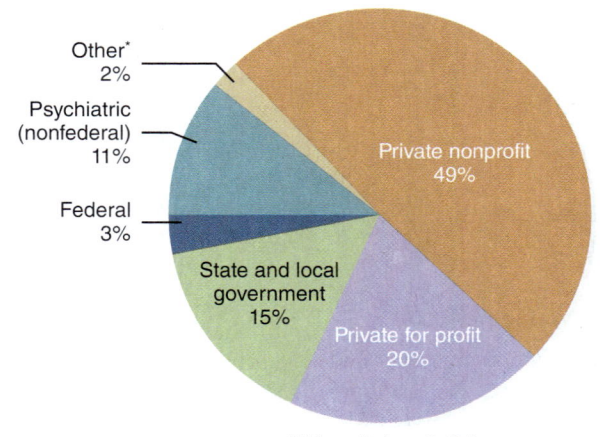

All hospitals = 6,129

*Long-term hospitals and hospital units in institutions such as prisons, college campuses, etc.

Figure 8-9 Proportion of total U.S. hospitals by type of hospitals, 2023.

Data from Health Forum. 2023. FY2023 fast facts on US hospitals. AHA hospital statistics, 2023 edition.

meaning in this context. A public hospital, for instance, is not necessarily a hospital that is open to the general public. For example, federal hospitals serve special groups of federal beneficiaries, such as Native Americans, military personnel, and veterans, rather than the general population. Veterans Affairs (VA) hospitals constitute the largest group among federal hospitals.

Local governments, such as counties and cities, operate hospitals to serve the general population. Many of these hospitals are located in large urban areas, where they function as an important safety net for the inner-city indigent and disadvantaged populations. Hence, Medicare, Medicaid, and state and local tax dollars pay for a large portion of the services these hospitals provide. Because of increasing financial pressures, many public hospitals have had to privatize or close in recent years. Out of the 1,444 state and local government-owned community hospitals operating in the United States in 1990, only 944 remained in operation in 2023 (Health Forum, 2020; AHA, 2023).

Most hospitals operated by city and county governments are small to moderate in size. Some large public hospitals are affiliated with medical schools; they play a significant role in training physicians and other healthcare professionals. Compared with private hospitals, public hospitals incur higher use, at least in terms of ALOS (refer to Figure 8-4). ALOS is the highest in federal hospitals and veterans are the biggest users of these hospitals.

Private Nonprofit Hospitals

Nonprofit hospitals are owned and operated by community associations or other nongovernment organizations. Their primary mission is to benefit the community in which they are located. Patient fees, third-party reimbursement, donations, and endowments cover their operating expenses. The private nonprofit sector constitutes the largest group of hospitals (refer to Figure 8-9), accounting for 48% of all U.S. hospitals. In a managed care environment, nonprofit hospitals have been found to be more efficient than for-profit hospitals. Efficiency is determined by the amount of inputs (e.g., medical supplies, labor) utilized to generate hospital outputs (e.g., discharges, visits, medical training) (Keon-Hyung et al., 2009).

Private For-Profit Hospitals

For-profit **proprietary hospitals**—also referred to as **investor-owned hospitals**—are owned by individuals, partnerships, or corporations. They are operated for the financial benefit of the entity that owns the institution; in other words, they are accountable to their stockholders.

At the beginning of the 20th century, more than half of all U.S. hospitals were proprietary institutions. Most of these hospitals were small and were established by physicians who wanted to hospitalize their own patients (Stewart, 1973). Later, most of these institutions were closed or acquired by community organizations or hospital corporations due to population shifts, increased costs, and the necessities of modern clinical practice (Raffel and Raffel, 1994).

Even though nonprofit hospitals have maintained their overall dominance in the U.S. hospital market, closures have reduced the number of these hospitals and their bed numbers. Conversely, the numbers of for-profit hospitals and beds have increased quite substantially (**Table 8-4**). The greater increase in the number of hospitals compared to the number of beds and the significant reduction in the average size of U.S. hospitals reflect the growth of physician-owned specialty hospitals (discussed later in the section "Specialty Hospitals"), which are smaller in size than other community hospitals. However, private nonprofit hospitals continue to boast higher occupancy rates than for-profit hospitals.

Table 8-4 Changes in Number of U.S. Hospitals, Beds, Average Size, and Occupancy Rates

	2000	2015	Change
Private Nonprofit			
Number of hospitals	3,003	2,845	−5.3%
Number of beds	582,988	530,579	−9.0%
Average size	194	186.5	−3.9%
Occupancy rate	65.5%	65.3%	−0.2%
Private For-Profit			
Number of hospitals	749	1,034	38.1%
Number of beds	109,883	135,569	23.4%
Average size	147	131.1	−10.8%
Occupancy rate	55.9%	57.5%	1.6%

Data from National Center for Health Statistics. 2018. *Health, United States, 2017.* Hyattsville, MD: U.S. Department of Health and Human Services. Table 89.

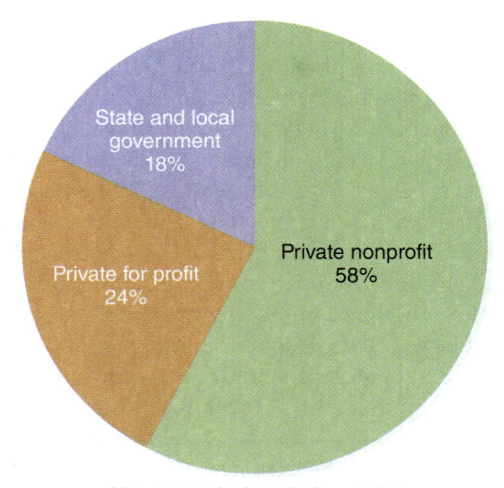

Figure 8-10 Breakdown of U.S. community hospitals by type of ownership, 2023.

All community hospitals = 5,157

- State and local government 18%
- Private for profit 24%
- Private nonprofit 58%

Data from Health Forum. 2023. FY2023 fast facts on US hospitals. AHA hospital statistics, 2023 edition.

Classification by Public Access

Almost 85% of all U.S. hospitals are classified as community hospitals (Health Forum, 2020). A **community hospital** is a nonfederal, short-stay hospital whose primary mission is to serve the general community. It may be a private for-profit facility or a private nonprofit facility, or it may be owned by the state or local government, but not by the federal government (**Figure 8-10**). A community hospital can also be a general hospital or a specialty hospital. Noncommunity hospitals include hospitals operated by the federal government, such as VA hospitals to serve veterans; hospital units of institutions, such as prisons and infirmaries in colleges and universities; and long-stay hospitals.

Classification by Multiunit Affiliation

Hospitals are considered to be part of a multihospital chain—also referred to as a **multihospital system (MHS)**—when two or more hospitals are owned, leased, sponsored, or contractually managed by a central organization (Health Forum, 2020). MHSs are predominant in the private sector—including both nonprofit and for-profit institutions. In the public sector, the Veterans Health Administration (VHA) operates the single largest MHS in the United States, with more than 172 medical centers operated by the federal government (Veterans Health Administration. 2023).

The number of hospitals in MHSs has grown annually since 2004, and the pace of consolidation that contributes to their formation has accelerated and is likely to continue. In 2023, 3,514 community hospitals (68% of all community hospitals) were affiliated with MHSs or a diversified single hospital system (AHA, 2023). The pace of consolidation (i.e., hospitals acquiring physician clinics, and hospitals in turn merging into larger systems) has been accelerating for some time. Not only have hospitals and physicians been joining MHSs, but the systems themselves have been merging to form even larger systems (Burns et al., 2015).

It is generally believed that larger health systems create better efficiencies, but this does not appear to be happening on a widespread scale. To the contrary, health system consolidation has been found to limit competition, which results in higher prices (Bindman, 2020). This outcome occurs despite the fact that the vast majority of these consolidated health systems are nonprofit entities (**Table 8-5**).

Table 8-5 The Largest U.S. Multihospital Chains, 2019

Name of Hospital System (Location)	Number of Hospitals
Nonprofit Chains	
Ascension Health (St. Louis, MO)	139
CommonSpirit Health (Chicago, IL)	140
Trinity Health (Livonia, MI)	88
Providence St. Joseph Health (Renton, WA)	52
AdventHealth (Altamonte Springs, FL)	46
Atrium Health (Charlotte, NC)	50
Providence Health and Services (Renton, WA)	26
For-Profit Chains	
HCA (Nashville, TN)	182
Community Health Systems (Franklin, TN)	79
LifePoint Health (Brentwood, TN)	84
Tenet Health System (Dallas, TX)	61
Vibra Healthcare (Mechanicsburg, PA)	65

Data from Falvey, A. 2023. 100 of the largest hospitals and health systems in America in 2023. *Becker's Hospital Review.*

Classification by Type of Service

General Hospitals

A **general hospital** provides a variety of services, including general and specialized medicine, general and specialized surgery, and obstetrics, to meet almost all medical needs of the community it serves. It provides diagnostic, treatment, and surgical services for patients with a variety of medical conditions. Most hospitals in the United States are general hospitals.

The term "general hospital" does not imply that these hospitals are less specialized or that their care is inferior to that of specialty hospitals. The difference lies in the nature of services, not their quality. General hospitals provide a broader range of services for a larger variety of conditions, whereas specialty hospitals provide a narrow range of services for specific medical conditions or patient populations.

Specialty Hospitals

According to the North American Industry Classification System developed by the U.S. Census Bureau, **specialty hospitals** are establishments that primarily engage in providing diagnostic and medical treatment to inpatients with a specific type of disease or medical condition (but not services for psychiatric care or substance abuse). Specialty hospitals forge their own distinct service niches. Traditionally, the two most common types of specialty hospitals have been rehabilitation hospitals and children's hospitals. With increasing competition, however, other types of specialty hospitals have emerged to provide treatments that are also available in many general hospitals. Examples include orthopedic hospitals, cardiac hospitals, cancer (oncology) hospitals, and women's hospitals.

Physicians find such specialized hospitals more efficient, and in many instances, physicians are full or part owners of these hospitals.

Affiliation with such hospitals gives physicians control over hospital operations, flexibility with their time, and an opportunity to enhance their incomes.

Physician-Owned Specialty Hospitals.

Physician-owned specialty hospitals are medical facilities that are primarily owned and operated by a group of physicians who specialize in a particular area of medicine, such as cardiology, orthopedics, or gastroenterology (Swanson, 2021). These hospitals are often smaller in size and focus on providing specialized care for specific medical conditions (Swanson, 2021).

In the past, critics of physician-owned hospitals (POHs) have argued that physicians' ownership stakes in hospitals create a conflict of interest that could lead to increased use and healthcare costs (Hollingsworth et al., 2010). In a report to Congress, the Medicare Payment Advisory Commission (MedPAC, 2006) pointed out that POHs (1) have lower proportions of Medicaid-covered patients than community general hospitals in the same markets; (2) admit less severe, more profitable cases; (3) draw patients away from community general hospitals, although general hospitals are typically able to compensate for the revenue loss; and (4) do not have lower costs per severity-adjusted discharge than competing general hospitals in the same markets. Hence, administrators of general hospitals have argued that specialty hospitals engage in "cream-skimming" insured patients, thereby leaving costly emergency and uncompensated cases to general hospitals. Despite such allegations, however, the presence of specialty hospitals in the acute-care markets do not financially harm general hospitals (Schneider et al., 2007). Nevertheless, the ACA closed the door on future physician-owned hospitals effective January 1, 2011, by mandating that hospitals could not be owned by physicians if those facilities wanted to receive Medicare payments. Existing POHs also faced restrictions on their expansion, except for facilities that treat large numbers of patients in the Medicaid program. The ACA-mandated limitations have remained controversial.

The previously mentioned concerns arose based on studies that included only a small number of hospitals. A more recent large study found that POHs performed only 1.2% of all procedures done in U.S. hospitals. More specifically, concerns about over use of surgeries at POHs may be unfounded (Chen et al., 2017; Schroeder et al., 2018). However, there appears to be over-selection of profitable and less disadvantaged patients by POHs. On the plus side, patient outcomes are generally superior at POHs compared to other hospitals after adjusting for patient demographics and case complexity. POHs achieve shorter lengths of stay, fewer complications, and lower readmission rates at a lower cost (Bae et al., 2020). Although some concerns remain, the quality benefits afforded by such facilities should not be ignored (Refer to **Exhibit 8-1** for a list of benefits).

Psychiatric Hospitals

The primary function of a psychiatric inpatient facility is to provide diagnostic and treatment services for a variety of severe mental conditions, such as bipolar disorder, schizophrenia, severe depression, dual diagnosis (mental illness compounded by chemical dependency), and serious emotional disturbances in children and adolescents. The main services offered in such a hospital include psychiatric, psychological, and social work programs. A psychiatric hospital must also have a written agreement with a general hospital for the transfer of patients who may require medical, obstetric, or surgical services (Health Forum, 2001). Inpatient psychiatric facilities can be either freestanding hospitals or specialized psychiatric units in a general hospital. In 2020, there were 668 psychiatric hospitals in the United States, 46.7% of which were private for-profit facilities, and 205 were operated by public agencies (Statista, 2023).

Exhibit 8-1 Quality Benefits Noted in Physician-owned Specialty Hospitals

- **Expertise and focus:** Physician-owned specialty hospitals are typically founded and operated by doctors who are experts in their respective fields (Miller, 2021). This specialization allows for a higher level of expertise on specific medical conditions, leading to better outcomes and patient care (Miller, 2021).
- **Enhanced quality of care:** The physician-owned specialty hospitals often have a well-defined scope of practice, which allows for a concentrated approach to treating specific medical conditions (Trybou, 2014). This specialization can lead to improved patient outcomes and a higher quality of care (Trybou, 2014).
- **Personalized care:** Physician-owned hospitals are much smaller than traditional hospitals and tend to have a lower nurse-to-patient ratio (Trybou, 2014). Patients can receive care in a more intimate and less stressful environment (Trybou, 2014). With more personalized attention from doctors, nurses, and other staff, patients are more satisfied with the care they receive (Trybou, 2014).
- **Relatively lower costs:** Contrary to prior concerns, physician-owned hospitals providing cardiac or orthopedic care were found to provide higher-quality care at lower or comparable cost (Miller, 2021). This can make high-quality care more accessible to patients (Miller, 2021).

Data from Miller, B. 2021. Cost and Quality of Care in Physician-Owned Hospitals: A Systematic Review. Mercatus Special Study; Trybou, J., De Regge, M., Gemmel, P., Duyck, P., & Annemans, L. (2014). Effects of physician-owned specialized facilities in health care: a systematic review. Health Policy, 118(3), 316–340.

State Mental Health Institutions. At one time, mental health institutions operated by state governments played a primary role in treating people with mental health conditions. Over time, various policy efforts focused on deinstitutionalizing people whose needs could be adequately met in community-based settings. Consequently, many of these institutions were closed or some of their beds were taken out of service. The length of hospitalizations and the number of inpatient stays has decreased, however. According to one national study, the ALOS in these hospitals is 106 days, indicating the patients admitted tend to have complex psychiatric/behavioral conditions. Nevertheless, the number of readmissions after discharge have increased, indicating that many patients may be prematurely discharged (Ortiz, 2019).

Rehabilitation Hospitals

Rehabilitation hospitals specialize in therapeutic services to restore the maximum level of functioning in patients who have suffered recent disability due to an episode of illness or an accident. According to Medicare rules, to be classified as a rehabilitation hospital, at least 60% of the hospital's inpatients must require intensive rehabilitation for one or more of 13 specified conditions, such as stroke, spinal cord injury, major multiple trauma, and brain injury (Centers for Medicare and Medicaid Services [CMS], 2018). Intensive rehabilitation refers to provision of at least 3 hours of therapy per day. Rehabilitation hospitals also serve amputees, victims of accident or sports injuries, and individuals needing intensive cardiac rehabilitation. Facilities and staff are available to provide physical therapy, occupational therapy, and speech–language pathology. Most rehabilitation hospitals have special arrangements for psychological, social work, and vocational services and are required to have written arrangements with a general hospital for the transfer of patients who need medical, obstetric, or surgical care not available at the institution (Health Forum, 2001).

Inpatient rehabilitation facilities (IRFs) can be either freestanding hospitals or specialized rehabilitation units in a general hospital. In 2017, approximately 1,180 IRFs were Medicare certified (MedPAC, 2019c).

Children's Hospitals

Children's hospitals are community hospitals that typically have specialized facilities to deal mainly with complex, severe, or chronic illnesses among children. Nearly all children's hospitals provide neonatal intensive care units, pediatric intensive care units, trauma centers, and transplant services. Thus, these hospitals provide a wide range of high-intensity services for children, such as pediatric surgery, cardiology, orthopedic surgery, cancer treatment, HIV/AIDS treatment, and rehabilitation services (DelliFraine, 2006). Some specialize in services such as orthopedics or cancer treatment.

Children's hospitals can be freestanding or they can be pediatric centers located in major hospitals. Most pediatric intensive care units are found in large hospitals identified as tertiary centers or academic centers. These hospitals (a total of 63 in 2016) house almost half of all U.S. pediatric intensive care beds (Horak et al., 2019). In most communities, no specialty children's hospitals exist; hence, general acute-care hospitals serve as de facto children's hospitals (DelliFraine, 2006).

Classification by Length of Stay

Short-Stay Hospitals

A **short-stay hospital** is one in which the average length of stay is 25 days or less. Most hospitals fall into this category. Patients admitted to these hospitals suffer from acute conditions. Hospitals with average stays of more than 25 days are considered long-stay hospitals; they include psychiatric hospitals, long-term care hospitals providing subacute care, and chronic disease hospitals.

Long-Term Care Hospitals

The majority of long-stay hospitals in the United States are **long-term care hospitals (LTCHs)**. A long-term care hospital is a special type of long-stay hospital described in section 1886(d)(1)(B)(iv) of the Social Security Act. LTCHs must meet Medicare's conditions of participation for acute-care hospitals and must have an ALOS greater than 25 days. LTCHs serve patients who need post acute care, but have complex medical needs and may have multiple chronic problems requiring long-term hospitalization. Many patients are admitted to LTCHs from short-stay hospital intensive care units with respiratory/ventilator-dependent or other complex medical conditions. Reflecting the higher patient complexity in these facilities, in 2017, the LTCH average length of stay was 26.2 days (AHA, 2019).

Classification by Location

Hospitals can be classified based on their location—that is, they can be either urban or rural. **Urban hospitals** are located in a county that is part of a metropolitan statistical area (MSA). The U.S. Census Bureau has defined an MSA as a geographic area that includes at least (1) one city with a population of 50,000 or more or (2) an urbanized area of at least 50,000 inhabitants and a total MSA population of at least 100,000. **Rural hospitals** are located in a county that is not part of an MSA. In 2018, 35% of all U.S. community hospitals were located in rural areas (Health Forum, 2020).

Rural hospitals provide care to approximately 60 million people in the United States (Weil, 2020) but face several challenges. They disproportionately rely on government payments because they serve a higher proportion of patients who are older and from low socioeconomic status compared to urban hospitals. Government payments—for example, Medicaid reimbursement—do not cover the full cost of services. The financial viability of these hospitals is further put at risk because of their communities' low population density, which tends to keep hospital size small and patient volume low (AHA, 2011). Rural hospitals also face a sustained workforce shortage. The continued urbanization of American surgery—referring to growing surgeon shortages—is a bad omen for rural hospitals and is expected to lead to additional closures and worsen the issue of access (Ellison et al., 2020).

Swing Bed Hospitals

The swing bed program for rural hospitals was authorized under the Omnibus Reconciliation Act of 1980. A hospital **swing bed** can be used for acute care or skilled nursing care as needed. The swing bed program enabled many rural hospitals to survive during a period of declining occupancy rates. It also enabled rural residents to access post acute nursing care services, which were not otherwise available in many rural communities.

Under Medicare, the swing bed program operates under two distinct payment systems, for acute hospital stays and skilled nursing facility (SNF) stays, which complicates financial management. To overcome this drawback, many rural hospitals have switched to critical access hospital status.

Critical Access Hospitals

In an attempt to save some of the very small rural hospitals, the Balanced Budget Act of 1997 created the Medicare Rural Hospital Flexibility Program (MRHFP). Under this program, a rural hospital, upon meeting certain conditions, can file an application with Medicare to be classified as a **critical access hospital (CAH)**. To qualify as a CAH, the hospital should have no more than 25 acute-care and/or swing beds and must provide 24-hour emergency medical services. It must also meet a distance test in relation to other hospitals.

CAHs are not subject to the prospective payment systems applicable to other healthcare providers; they receive cost-plus reimbursement for inpatient, outpatient, laboratory, therapy, and most post acute services in swing beds. Total payment to the hospital is fixed at 101% of reasonable costs. Because of their many financial advantages, the number of CAHs has jumped from 850 in 2003 (Mantone, 2005) to more than 1,362 today, representing 76% of all rural hospitals (Rural Health Information Hub. 2023).

Other Rural Designations

To improve access in some remote locations, Congress created two additional rural hospital designations: sole community hospital and Medicare-dependent hospital.

Sole Community Hospitals. If, because of its remote location, a rural hospital is the sole source of hospital services in a wide geographic area, it may qualify for sole community hospital (SCH) status. SCHs are important safety net providers. Approximately 17% of rural hospitals are classified as SCHs (MedPAC, 2019a). These hospitals benefit from certain payment adjustments from Medicare.

Medicare-Dependent Hospitals. Small rural hospitals that may not qualify for the SCH designation may be classified as Medicare-dependent hospitals (MDHs) if at least 60% of their discharges are Medicare beneficiaries. In addition to PPS reimbursement, these hospitals receive payments that are partially based on their costs. Approximately 6% of rural hospitals are classified as MDHs (MedPAC, 2019a).

Classification by Size

There is no standard way to classify hospitals by size. According to one classification scheme, hospitals with fewer than 100 beds would be classified as small, those with 100 to 500 beds as medium, and those with 500-plus beds as large. Others may classify by size a little differently. Fewer than half (47%)

of all community hospitals in the United States have 100 beds or more (refer to Figure 8-5).

Experience in the manufacturing and retail sectors of the economy suggests that large enterprises can often realize economies of scale. This benefit arises because of their purchasing power for resource inputs and their ability to spread overhead costs over a larger volume of sales. In the hospital industry, several factors influence economic efficiency. For example, cost structures differ according to services offered (e.g., specialty care, emergency services), academic and teaching activities, and location (rural versus urban). Hence, it is not always feasible to assess economies of scale for hospitals. Nevertheless, in a comprehensive review of the literature, Giancotti and colleagues (2017) found consistent evidence of economies of scale for hospitals with 200–300 beds; diseconomies of scale could be expected to occur with fewer than 200 beds and more than 600 beds.

Other Types of Hospitals

Teaching Hospitals

To be designated as a **teaching hospital**, a hospital must have one or more graduate residency programs approved by the AMA. The mere presence of nursing programs or training affiliations for other health professionals, such as therapists and dietitians, does not make an institution a teaching hospital.

The term **academic medical center** is commonly used when one or more hospitals, with or without affiliated outpatient clinics, are organized around a medical school. Apart from the training of physicians, research activities and clinical investigations become an important undertaking in such a center.

Among the largest and most prestigious teaching hospitals are the members of the Council of Teaching Hospitals and Health Systems (COTH), which has approximately 400 members in the United States (including 62 VA medical centers) and Canada (Association of American Medical Colleges [AAMC], n.d.). These hospitals usually have substantial teaching and research programs and are affiliated with the medical schools of large universities.

Three main traits separate teaching and nonteaching hospitals. First, teaching hospitals provide medical training to physicians, research opportunities to health services researchers, and specialized care to patients. These hospitals receive add-on payments from Medicare to reflect the additional costs of patient care associated with resident training, based on the number of residents per inpatient bed. Medicare also pays separately for the direct costs of operating approved training programs for medical, osteopathic, dental, or podiatric residents (MedPAC, 2019b).

Second, teaching hospitals have a broader and more complex scope of services than nonteaching hospitals. These hospitals often operate several intensive care units, possess the latest medical technologies, and attract a diverse group of physicians representing most specialties and many subspecialties. Major teaching hospitals also offer many unique tertiary care services not generally found in other institutions, such as burn care, trauma care, and organ transplantation. Hence, teaching hospitals attract patients who frequently have more complicated diagnoses or need more complex procedures. Because of the greater case-mix complexity of teaching hospitals, greater resources are required for the treatment of their patients.

Third, many of the major teaching hospitals are located in economically depressed, older inner-city areas and are owned by state or local governments. Consequently, these hospitals provide a significant amount of charity care to patients who are uninsured.

Church-Affiliated Hospitals

During the latter half of the 19th century and the early 20th century, various churches established their own hospitals. For example,

Catholic sisterhoods established the first church-sponsored hospitals in the United States. Later, Protestant denominations organized hospitals in accord with their missions of service, and Jewish philanthropic organizations opened hospitals so that Jewish patients could observe their dietary laws more faithfully and Jewish physicians could more easily find sites for training and work opportunities (Raffel, 1980).

Most church-affiliated hospitals are community general hospitals. They may be large or small, teaching or nonteaching. Affiliation with a medical school may also vary. Church-affiliated hospitals do not discriminate in rendering care, but they are generally sensitive to the sponsoring denomination's special spiritual and/or dietary emphasis (Raffel and Raffel, 1994).

Osteopathic Hospitals

In 1970, osteopathic hospitals became eligible to apply for registration with the AHA (1994). For many years after osteopathy was established as a separate branch of medicine in 1874, osteopaths had to develop their own hospitals because of the antagonism from the established allopathic medical practitioners. Since then, both groups have inspected each other's medical schools and satisfied themselves that each is worth associating with and that each could serve on the other's faculties and practice side by side in the same hospitals (Raffel and Raffel, 1994).

Many osteopathic hospitals today are part of hospital systems and maintain their osteopathic identity within the context of these larger systems. An independent osteopathic hospital is no longer a necessity and seems to be economically out of place in today's market (Hilsenrath, 2006). Also, the operation of osteopathic hospitals has been found to be more costly and less productive in comparison to their counterparts (Sinay, 2005). Consequently, a number of these hospitals have closed.

Expectations for Nonprofit Hospitals

Laypeople often assume that nonprofit (sometimes called not-for-profit) healthcare corporations do not make a profit. In fact, every corporation—regardless of whether it is for profit or nonprofit—must make a profit (surplus of revenues over expenses) if it is to survive over the long term. No business can survive for long if it continually spends more than it takes in. That rule of economics holds true for both the nonprofit and for-profit sectors (Nudelman and Andrews, 1996).

The Internal Revenue Code, Section 501(c)(3), grants tax-exempt status to nonprofit organizations. As such, these institutions are exempt from federal, state, and local taxes, such as income taxes, sales taxes, and property taxes. In general, nonprofit organizations must (1) provide some defined public good, such as service, education, or community welfare; and (2) not distribute profits to any individuals. In contrast, a major goal for a for-profit corporation is to provide its shareholders with a return on their investment, although it achieves this goal primarily by excelling at its basic mission. For any health services provider, the basic mission is to deliver the highest-quality care at the most reasonable price possible.

Since 1969, a community-benefit standard has been applied to nonprofit hospitals. It broadly refers to services that the government would otherwise have to undertake (Owens, 2005). In 1983, this standard was modified to include specific criteria that hospitals must meet to qualify for tax exemption: a 24-hour emergency department, policy guidelines for treating the uninsured, and health promotion in the community (Alexander et al., 2009).

The ACA included four new requirements related to community benefits, which were promulgated by adding section 501(r) to the Internal Revenue Code. Nonprofit hospitals must (1) establish written financial assistance and emergency care policies,

(2) limit charges for individuals who are eligible for assistance under the hospital's financial assistance policy, (3) limit certain billing and collection actions against those who fall within the guidelines of financial assistance, and (4) conduct a community health needs assessment and adopt an implementation strategy at least once every 3 years. Hospitals that fail to comply with the community health needs assessment mandate are subject to an excise tax (Betbeze, 2011; Internal Revenue Service [IRS], 2016).

Section 4958 of the IRS code prohibits executive compensation that may be deemed unreasonable for tax-exempt organizations. Nonprofit hospitals must be prepared to demonstrate not only that they are paying salaries within some reasonable range of industry standards but also that executives are bringing measurable value in key areas of operations, including community benefits (Appleby, 2004).

In many communities, nonprofit hospitals compete head-to-head with for-profit hospitals. For example, nonprofit hospitals frequently engage in the same kinds of aggressive marketplace behaviors that for-profit hospitals pursue. Generally, nonprofit hospitals operate in locations with higher average incomes, lower poverty rates, and lower rates of uninsurance than for-profit hospitals (Congressional Budget Office [CBO], 2006). In 2013, 7 of the 10 most profitable hospitals in the United States were nonprofit organizations (Bai and Anderson, 2016).

Institutional theory actually predicts such behavior. When for-profit and nonprofit organizations face similar regulatory, legal, and professional constraints, they often imitate each other (O'Connell and Brown, 2003). In the hospital industry, competition commonly occurs in the same communities for the same patients, with revenues coming from the same public and private third-party sources, and often involving the same physician providers who have admitting privileges at more than one hospital.

Recent studies show that vague regulatory language, extensive restrictions, and burdensome documentation requirements for reporting financial assistance contribute to significant variations in how hospitals deliver charity care (Goodman et al., 2020). Hence, significant gaps exist in the delivery of community benefit services by nonprofit hospitals (Worthy et al., 2016). A Modern Healthcare analysis of about 100 Illinois hospitals' tax forms revealed that measuring community benefit spending can provide an inconsistent or distorted view of a hospital's level of charity care (Kacik, 2018b). Furthermore, hospitals routinely report different amounts of charity care to the IRS and CMS (Gaskin et al., 2019).

As just discussed, legislation over time and reporting by hospitals have tainted the evaluation of what constitutes charity or community benefit. In turn, the measurement of these constructs has proved challenging. Even though for-profit hospitals in the United States have been known to deliver services to those who cannot afford to pay, an objective comparison of the charitable services provided by for-profit hospitals versus those provided by nonprofit hospitals has not been forthcoming. Hence, the debate continues over what is and what is not a community benefit, and whether giving tax-exempt status to certain hospitals has created an unequal and unfair system.

Some Management Concepts

From a management standpoint, hospitals are complex organizations. Compared to other business enterprises of similar size, both the external and internal environments of hospitals are more complex. A hospital is responsible to numerous stakeholders in its external environment, including the community, the government, insurers, managed care organizations (MCOs), and accreditation agencies. A hospital's organizational structure also differs substantially from that of other large organizations in the business world.

Hospital Governance

Hospital governance has traditionally assumed a tripartite structure, in which the three major sources of authority are the chief executive officer (CEO), the board of trustees, and the chief of staff (**Figure 8-11**). In earlier periods, when physicians operated their own hospitals, trustees dominated the hospitals. Trustees were often the source of capital investment, and their influence in the community brought prestige to the hospital. Later, as voluntary hospitals increased in number, the balance of power shifted, with physicians gaining the upper hand because they played a critical role in bringing patients to the hospitals. As changes in the healthcare environment made the management of hospitals more complex, considerable power then passed from physicians to senior managers.

The medical staff constitute a separate organizational structure that operates in parallel to the administrative structure. Such a dual structure is rarely seen in other businesses and presents numerous opportunities for conflicts to arise between the CEO and the medical staff. Physicians account for approximately 85% of hospital spending without necessarily being employees (Burns et al., 2020). Matters become even more complicated when the lines of authority cross between the two structures. For example, nursing services, pharmacists, diagnostic technicians, and dietitians are administratively accountable to the CEO (via the vertical chain of command) but professionally accountable to the medical staff (Raffel and Raffel, 1994). Although most of the medical staff are not paid employees of the hospital, physicians' interest in employment has been growing as they seek ways to stabilize their incomes and achieve a better work-life balance in a changing healthcare landscape (Shoger, 2011).

Regardless of whether the physicians are independent practitioners or contracted employees of the hospital, they play a significant role in the hospital's success. It requires special skills on the part of the CEO to manage the dual structure to achieve the organization's overall objectives.

Board of Trustees

The **board of trustees** (also referred to as the governing body or board of directors) of a hospital consists of influential business and community leaders. The board is legally responsible for the hospital's operations. It has specific responsibilities for defining the hospital's mission and long-range direction. The board is also responsible for evaluating, from a strategic standpoint, major decisions such as incurring capital expenditures for building and equipment, approving annual budgets, and monitoring performance against plans and budgets. The CEO is a member of the board, and one or more physicians also sit on the board as voting members.

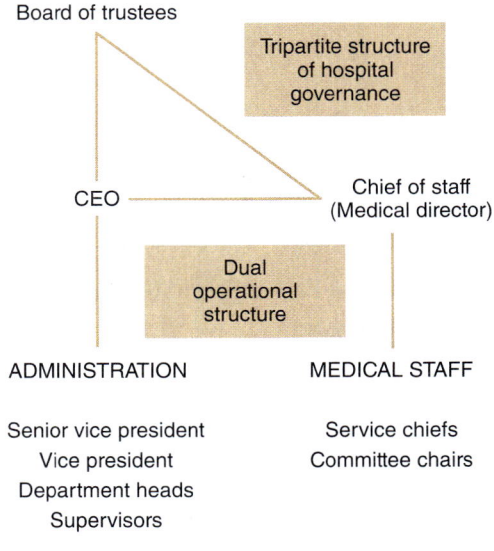

Figure 8-11 Hospital governance and operational structures.

One of the most important responsibilities of the board is to appoint the CEO, evaluate their performance, and remove the CEO if necessary. The CEO is charged with providing the board with timely reports on the institution's progress toward achieving its mission and objectives. In most hospitals, the board also approves the appointment of physicians and other professionals to the hospital's medical staff.

Boards often function through committees. Standing committees usually include executive, medical staff, human resources, finance, planning, quality improvement, and ethics. Special, or ad hoc, committees are established as needed. The two most important committees, from a governance standpoint, are the executive committee and the medical staff committee. The **executive committee** has continuing monitoring responsibility and authority over the hospital. Usually, it receives reports from other committees, monitors policy implementation, and makes recommendations. The **medical staff committee** is charged with managing medical staff relations. For example, this committee reviews admitting privileges and the performance of the medical staff and must take into account the legal and ethical obligations of the hospital regarding patient safety, quality improvement, and patient satisfaction.

Chief Executive Officer

In the past, the titles of "superintendent" and later "administrator" were commonly used for a hospital's chief executive. Today, the most commonly encountered titles are "chief executive officer" and "president." The CEO's job is to accomplish the organization's mission and objectives by exhibiting leadership within the organization. The CEO has the ultimate responsibility for the hospital's day-to-day operations.

The CEO receives delegated authority from the board and is responsible for managing the organization with the help of senior managers. In large hospitals, these senior managers often carry the title of senior vice president or vice president for various key service areas, such as nursing services, rehabilitation services, human resources, and finance.

Medical Staff

The hospital's medical staff is an organized body of physicians who provide medical services to the hospital's patients and perform related clinical duties. Most physicians are in private practice outside the hospital. The hospital grants them admitting privileges, which enable the physicians to admit and care for their patients in the hospital. Other clinicians, such as dentists and podiatrists, may also be granted admitting privileges. Appointment to the medical staff is a formal process outlined in the hospital's medical staff bylaws. The medical staff use a framework of self-governance, which upholds the strong tradition of physician independence but are formally accountable to the board of trustees. Lines of communication to the CEO and the board are established through various committee representations.

A medical director, or **chief of staff**, heads the medical staff. In all but the smallest hospitals, the medical staff are organizationally divided by major specialties into departments, such as anesthesiology, internal medicine, obstetrics and gynecology, orthopedic surgery, pathology, cardiology, and radiology. A **chief of service**, such as chief of cardiology, heads each specialty.

The medical staff generally has their own executive committee that sets general policies and serves as the main decision-making body in medical matters. Most hospitals have additional committees. The **credentials committee** grants and reviews admitting privileges for those already credentialed and for new doctors whose skills are yet untested. The **medical records committee** ensures that accurate documentation is maintained on the entire regimen of care given to each patient. This committee also manages confidentiality issues related to medical records. The **utilization review committee** performs routine checks to ensure that inpatient placements, as well as the lengths of stay, are clinically appropriate. The **infection control committee** reviews policies and procedures for minimizing infections in the hospital. The **quality improvement committee** supervises the program for continual quality improvement.

Licensure, Certification, and Accreditation

A license to operate a certain number of hospital beds is a basic regulatory requirement. State governments manage the **licensure** of healthcare facilities, and each state sets its own standards for licensure. The state's department of health has licensure-related responsibilities. State licensure standards strongly emphasize the physical plant's compliance with building codes, fire safety, climate control, space allocations, and sanitation. Minimum standards are also established for equipment and personnel. State licensure, however, is not directly tied to the quality of care that a healthcare facility actually delivers.

All facilities are legally required to be licensed to operate, but they do not have to be certified or accredited. **Certification** gives a hospital the authority to participate in the Medicare and Medicaid programs. The U.S. Department of Health and Human Services (DHHS) has developed a body of health, safety, and quality standards referred to as **conditions of participation** and has the authority to enforce those standards for hospitals that participate in the Medicare or Medicaid program. The currently defined conditions focus primarily on the actual quality of care furnished to patients and the outcomes of that care. Each state's department of health verifies the actual compliance with the standards through periodic inspections.

In contrast to licensure and certification, which are government regulatory mechanisms, **accreditation** is a private undertaking designed to assure that accredited healthcare facilities meet certain basic standards. Seeking accreditation is voluntary, but the passage of Medicare in 1965 specified that accredited facilities were eligible for purposes of Medicare reimbursement. Accreditation of a hospital by the Joint Commission confers **deemed status** on the hospital, meaning the hospital is deemed to have met Medicare and Medicaid certification standards. Thus, an accredited hospital does not need to go through the certification process. Private organizations that have been approved by the CMS to confer deemed status are said to have "deeming authority." In addition to the Joint Commission, the American Osteopathic Association has deeming authority to accredit hospitals.

The Joint Commission also sets standards for and accredits long-term care facilities, psychiatric hospitals, substance abuse programs, outpatient surgery centers, urgent care clinics, group practices, community health centers, hospices, and home health agencies. Different sets of standards apply to each category of healthcare organization. Some facilities, such as nursing homes, do not receive deemed status as a result of accreditation and must also be certified by DHHS to receive Medicare and Medicaid reimbursement. Over the years, the Joint Commission has refined its accreditation standards and process of verifying compliance. Since 2006, this organization has moved from scheduled to unannounced inspections, with the intention that hospitals should attempt to comply with all the standards all the time. Refer to **Exhibit 8-2** for key hospital metrics.

Exhibit 8-2 Key Hospital Metrics

Ambulatory Care Sensitive Hospitalization
Average daily census
Average inpatient days
Average length of stay
Occupancy rate

Magnet Recognition Program[1]

Magnet hospital is a special designation conferred by the American Nurses Credentialing Center, an affiliate of the American Nurses Association, that recognizes quality patient care, nursing excellence, and innovations in professional nursing practice in hospitals. This designation was created after a study of 163 hospitals was undertaken in 1983 by the American Academy of Nursing's Task Force on Nursing Practice in Hospitals. The study found that 41 of these hospitals had an environment that attracted and retained well-qualified nurses and promoted quality patient care. These hospitals were labeled "Magnet hospitals" because of their ability to attract and retain professional nurses. The characteristics that seemed to distinguish "Magnet" organizations from others became known as the Forces of Magnetism. The Forces of Magnetism have since been incorporated into quality indicators and standards of nursing practice as defined in *ANA Nursing Administration: Scope & Standards of Practice*. The Magnet designation is granted after a thorough and lengthy process that includes review of data on quality indicators.

Magnet recognition has been shown to be associated with better job satisfaction, nursing empowerment, and less turnover, but also with better outcomes for patients, more research and evidence-based practice, a superior reputation for the organization, and an easier time recruiting for the organization (Harolds and Miller, 2020). Notably, Magnet and non-Magnet hospitals do not appear to show any meaningful differences in staffing levels (de Cordova et al., 2020). There were 591 Magnet hospitals (about 10% of hospitals) in the US as of October 2023 (American Nurses Credentialing Center, 2023).

Ethical and Legal Issues in Patient Care

Ethical issues arise in all types of health services organizations, but the most significant ones occur in acute-care hospitals. Increasing levels of technology create situations requiring decision-making under complex circumstances. For example, life-sustaining therapies in intensive care and dealing with life and death issues commonly raise ethical concerns. Likewise, ethical issues arise in healthcare research and in experimental medicine. The Joint Commission requires accredited institutions to establish mechanisms that allow patients, families, and employees to obtain resolution of ethical issues or issues that may present a conflict of interest (Hamric and Wocial, 2016).

Principles of Ethics

Ethics requires judgment. Because clear-cut rules are often not available in the healthcare environment, medical practitioners and managers must rely on certain well-established principles as guides to ethical decision-making. Four important principles of ethics are respect for others, beneficence, nonmaleficence, and justice.

The principle of respect for others has four elements: autonomy, truth-telling, confidentiality, and fidelity. Autonomy allows people to govern themselves by choosing and pursuing a course of action without external coercion. In healthcare delivery, it refers to patient empowerment, which undergirds the philosophy of patient-centered care. Autonomy is ensured by obtaining consent for treatment, explaining the various treatment alternatives, allowing patients and their families to participate in decision-making and selection of treatment options, and treating patients with respect and dignity. Constant tension exists between autonomy and paternalism,

---

[1]The Magnet Recognition Program is a registered trademark of the American Nurses Credentialing Center.

the view that someone else must decide what the patient will undergo without the patient's involvement. Truth-telling requires a caregiver to be honest. This principle often needs to be balanced with nonmaleficence because a tension is created when truth-telling could result in harm to the patient. The principle of confidentiality sometimes becomes a source of conflict when the legal system requires disclosure of patient information. Fidelity means performing one's duty, keeping one's word, and keeping promises.

The principle of beneficence means that hospitals and caregivers have a moral obligation to benefit others. A health services organization is ethically obligated to do all it can to alleviate suffering caused by ill health and injury. This obligation includes providing a certain amount of charity care to the financially needy.

The principle of nonmaleficence means that medical professionals have a moral obligation not to harm others. Many healthcare interventions, including certain preventive measures such as immunization, carry risks. Hence, in health care, nonmaleficence requires that the potential benefits from medical treatment sufficiently outweigh the potential harm.

The principle of justice encompasses fairness and equality. It denounces discrimination in the delivery of health care.

Legal Rights

Legal issues often arise in the areas of patient competency and the patient's right to refuse treatment. Although the right of patients who are mentally competent to refuse medical care is well established, the desires of patients who are incapable or comatose present ethical challenges. Unless such patients have expressed their wishes in advance, family members or legal guardians may end up making decisions regarding sustained medical treatment, or state laws may govern such decisions. Medical and legal experts and family members may differ on the controversial issue of withdrawing nutrition and other life support means for patients who are dying. However, certain legal mechanisms have been established to deal with the issues of patients' rights.

Bill of Rights and Informed Consent

The Patient Self-Determination Act of 1990 applies to all healthcare facilities participating in Medicare or Medicaid. This law requires hospitals and other facilities to provide all patients, upon admission, with information on patients' rights. Most hospitals and other inpatient institutions have developed a **patient's bill of rights**—a document that reflects the law concerning issues such as confidentiality and consent. Other patient rights include the right to make decisions regarding medical care, be informed about diagnosis and treatment, refuse treatment, and formulate advance directives.

Based on the principle of autonomy, **informed consent** refers to the patient's right to make an informed choice regarding medical treatment. The current climate in medical ethics supports honest and complete disclosure of medical information. In 1972, the Board of Trustees of the AHA affirmed the document known as the Patient's Bill of Rights, which states that patients have the right to obtain from their physicians complete current information concerning their diagnosis, treatment, and prognosis in terms that the patients can be reasonably expected to understand (Rosner, 2004). Informed consent is customarily obtained via a signature on preprinted forms and becomes part of the patient's medical record.

Certain principles governing patients' rights are being incorporated into provider mindsets and organizational culture within the **patient-centered care** model. Involving patients in their own treatment, grounding treatment decisions in patients' preferences, and creating a caregiving environment in which staff solicit patients' input and meet their needs for information and education collectively promote patient-centered care (Cross, 2004).

Advance Directives

Advance directives specify the patient's wishes regarding continuation or withdrawal of treatment when the patient lacks decision-making capacity. Advance directives are intended to ensure that the patient's end-of-life wishes are carried out. Three types of advance directives are in common use: do-not-resuscitate orders, living wills, and durable powers of attorney.

- A **do-not-resuscitate order** directs medical caregivers not to administer any artificial means to resuscitate the person when their heart or breathing stops. It is based on the theory that a patient may prefer to die rather than live when strong odds are against a good quality of life after cardiopulmonary resuscitation because severe disabilities would likely remain.
- A **living will** communicates a patient's wishes regarding medical treatment when they are unable to make decisions due to terminal illness or incapacitation. The main drawback of a living will is that it is general in nature and does not cover all possible situations.
- A **durable power of attorney** for health care is a written legal document in which the patient appoints another individual to act as the patient's agent for purposes of healthcare decision making in the event that the patient is unable or unwilling to make such decisions. Although a durable power of attorney can cover most circumstances, its main drawback is that the appointed person may not act in the same manner in which the patient would have acted had they remained competent.

Mechanisms for Ethical Decision Making

Many healthcare organizations, especially large acute-care hospitals, have **ethics committees** charged with developing guidelines and standards for ethical decision-making in the delivery of health care (Paris, 1995). Ethics committees are also responsible for resolving issues related to medical ethics. Such committees are multidisciplinary, including physicians, nurses, clergy, social workers, legal experts, ethicists, and administrators. In some states, such as Texas, ethics committees have decision-making authority to overrule the patient's or their representative's desire to continue life-sustaining treatment when, based on medical judgment, the treatment is not appropriate (Berlin, 2020).

Although physicians and other caregivers have moral responsibilities on the clinical side, the healthcare executive who leads the health services organization must also assume the role of a moral agent. As a **moral agent**, the manager morally affects and is morally affected by actions taken. Although executives are entrusted with the fiduciary responsibility to act prudently in managing the affairs of the organization, their responsibilities to patients must take precedence.

In governing the affairs of an organization, healthcare executives must recognize that ethics entails much more than simply obeying the law. The law represents only the minimum standard of morality established by society. Similarly, healthcare professionals must recognize that, even though they are bound by the law, they also have a higher calling—one that includes numerous positive duties to patients, to society, and to each other (Darr, 1991).

Summary

Hospitals are institutions that engage primarily in the delivery of inpatient acute-care services, although many have branched out to provide post acute and outpatient services. In the United States, almshouses and pesthouses first evolved into public hospitals to serve the poor. Subsequently, voluntary hospitals were established to serve all classes of people. Over time, advances in medical science, improvements in hygiene, and evolution of nursing care transformed hospitals into institutions of medical practice, many of which then became important centers of medical training and research. Since the 1980s, economic pressures have led many hospitals to consolidate. Health systems that offer a full continuum of healthcare services now exist in many locations.

Hospitals in the United States went through an expansion phase in the mid-20th century that lasted until the mid-1980s. The Hill-Burton Act of 1946 was the single greatest factor contributing to the increase in the nation's bed supply. The federal government later played an equally important role in reducing inpatient use by establishing the prospective payment system. Some of the key measures of inpatient use are discharges, inpatient days, average length of stay, capacity, average daily census, and occupancy rates. The growth of managed care has also been significant in reducing inpatient use. Despite these accomplishments, hospital costs have not abated, and U.S. hospitals are among the most expensive in the world.

Hospitals can be classified in numerous ways, and the various classification schemes help differentiate one hospital from another. Performance statistics by hospital type can help executives compare their hospital to others in the same category. Although most U.S. hospitals are general community hospitals, various specialty hospitals treat specific types of patients or conditions. Roughly half of all U.S. community hospitals are nonprofit organizations. In response to controversies surrounding physician-owned specialty hospitals, the Affordable Care Act placed restrictions on their expansion. Yet, these hospitals offer many benefits to patients, especially better quality of care over other hospitals.

Most public and voluntary hospitals are nonprofit organizations; as such, these institutions enjoy some tax advantages. They are expected to provide community benefits that are equivalent in value to the tax subsidies received; however, many nonprofit hospitals emulate the behavior of their for-profit counterparts. Moreover, evaluation and reporting of community benefits have been inconsistent.

Hospitals are among the most complex organizations to manage; they must satisfy numerous external stakeholders and manage a complex internal governance structure. A hospital cannot legally operate unless it is licensed by the state in which it is located. To participate in the Medicare and Medicaid programs, a hospital can voluntarily apply for accreditation by the Joint Commission. Magnet hospitals are recognized for their ability to recruit and retain qualified nurses and to deliver high-quality patient care.

Ethical decision making has been a special area of concern for hospitals. From a medical standpoint, ethical issues often pertain to patient privacy, confidentiality, informed consent, and end-of-life treatment. The patient's bill of rights and advance directives are two of the legal means to address these issues. Active ethics committees develop policies and standards and deal with ethical issues as they arise.

TEST YOUR UNDERSTANDING

Terminology

academic medical center
accreditation
advance directives
average daily census
average length of stay (ALOS)
board of trustees
certification
chief of service

chief of staff
community
community hospital
conditions of participation
credentials committee
critical access hospital (CAH)
days of care
deemed status
discharge
do-not-resuscitate order
durable power of attorney
ethics committees
executive committee
general hospital
hospital
infection control committee
informed consent
inpatient
inpatient day
investor-owned hospitals
licensure
living will
long-term care hospitals (LTCHs)
Magnet hospital
medical records committee
medical staff committee
moral agent
multihospital system (MHS)
occupancy rate
patient-centered care
patient's bill of rights
proprietary hospitals
public hospitals
quality improvement committee
rehabilitation hospitals
rural hospitals
short-stay hospital
specialty hospitals
swing bed
teaching hospital
urban hospitals
utilization review committee
voluntary hospitals

Review Questions

1. What is the difference between inpatient and outpatient services?
2. As hospitals evolved from rudimentary custodial and quarantine facilities to their current state, how did their purpose and function change?
3. What were the main factors responsible for the growth of hospitals until the latter part of the 20th century?
4. Name the main forces that were responsible for hospital downsizing. How did each of these forces affect the decline in inpatient hospital use?
5. What is a voluntary hospital? How did voluntary hospitals evolve in the United States?
6. Discuss the role of government in the growth, as well as the decline, of hospitals in the United States.
7. What are inpatient days? What is the significance of this measure?
8. How does hospital use vary according to a person's age, gender, and socioeconomic status?
9. Explain the relationship between hospital demand, employment, expenditures, and profitability.
10. Discuss the different types of public hospitals and the roles they play in the delivery of healthcare services in the United States.
11. What are some of the differences between private nonprofit and for-profit hospitals?
12. What is a long-term care hospital (LTCH)? What role does it play in healthcare delivery in the United States?
13. The table gives some operational statistics for two hospitals located in the same community. Use the table to answer the following questions.
    a. Calculate the following measures for each hospital (wherever appropriate, calculate the measure for each pay type). Discuss the meaning and significance of each measure, and point out the differences between the two hospitals.
        i. Hospital capacity
        ii. ALOS
        iii. Occupancy rate
    b. Operationally, which hospital is performing better? Why?

Calendar Year 2020	Nonprofit Community Hospital (A)	Proprietary Community Hospital (B)
Number of beds in operation	320	240
Total discharges	12,051	9,230
Medicare	5,130	3,876
Medicaid	3,565	2,118
Private insurance	3,356	3,236
Total hospital days	72,421	51,684
Medicare	36,935	26,359
Medicaid	23,175	12,921
Private insurance	12,311	12,404
Total inpatient revenues	$45,755,000	$35,800,000
Dollar value of community benefits	$5,000,000	$3,500,000

    c. Do you think the nonprofit hospital is meeting its community benefit obligations in exchange for its tax-exempt status? Explain.

    d. Do you think the hospitals have a problem with excess capacity? If so, what would you recommend?

14. Why have physicians developed their own specialty hospitals? What are the main criticisms that these hospitals have faced?

15. What criteria does Medicare use to classify a hospital as a rehabilitation hospital?

16. How do you differentiate between a community hospital and a noncommunity hospital?

17. What is a critical access hospital (CAH)? Why was this designation created?

18. What are some of the main differences between teaching and nonteaching hospitals?

19. Discuss some of the issues relative to the tax-exempt status of nonprofit hospitals.

20. Discuss the governance of a modern hospital.

21. In the context of hospitals, what are the differences between licensure, certification, and accreditation?

22. What can a hospital do to address some of the difficult ethical problems relative to end-of-life treatment?

References

Alexander, J. A., G. J. Young, B. J. Weiner, and L. R. Hearld. 2009. How Do System-Affiliated Hospitals Fare in Providing Community Benefit? *Inquiry* 46: 72–91.

American Hospital Association (AHA). 1990. *Hospital Statistics 1990–1991 Edition*. Chicago, IL: Author.

American Hospital Association (AHA). 1994. *AHA Guide to the Health Care Field: 1994 edition*. Chicago, IL: Author.

American Hospital Association (AHA). 2011. *The Opportunities and Challenges for Rural Hospitals in an Era of Health Reform*. Washington, DC: AHA and Avalere Health.

American Hospital Association (AHA). 2023. *Fast Facts on U.S. Hospitals*, 2023. Accessed November 2023. Available at: https://www.aha.org/system/files/media/file/2023/05/Fast-Facts-on-US-Hospitals-2023.pdf

American Hospital Association (AHA). 2023. *Fast Facts on U.S. Hospitals*, 2023. Accessed November 2023. Available at: https://www.aha.org/system/files/media file/2023/05/Fast-Facts-on-US-Hospitals-2023.pdf

American Nurses Credentialing Center (ANCC). 2023. *Find a Magnet Organization*. Accessed November 2023. Available at: https://www.nursingworld.org/organizational-programs/magnet/find-a-magnet-organization/

Appleby, J. 2004. IRS Looking Closely at What Non-Profits Pay. *USA Today*. 02b.

Arndt, M., and B. Bigelow. 2006. Toward the Creation of an Institutional Logic for the Management of Hospitals: Efficiency in the Early Nineteen Hundreds. *Medical Care Research and Review* 63: 369–394.

Association of American Medical Colleges (AAMC). n.d. *Council of Teaching Hospitals and Health Systems (COTH): Member Services and Benefits*. Accessed August 2020. Available at: https://aamc-orange.global.ssl.fastly.net/production/media/filer_public/f6/a8/f6a875e5-acf5-442a-87e1-f91f24c0f3d1/cothmemberservices.pdf

Bae, J., J. M. Hyer, A. Z. Paredes, et al. 2020. Evaluation of Costs and Outcomes of Physician-Owned Hospitals Across Common Surgical Procedures. *American Journal of Surgery* 220: 120–126.

Bai, G., and G. F. Anderson, 2016. A More Detailed Understanding of Factors Associated with Hospital Profitability. *Health Affairs* 35: 889–897.

Balotsky, E. R. 2005. Is It Resources, Habit or Both: Interpreting Twenty Years of Hospital Strategic Response to Prospective Payment. *Health Care Management Review* 30: 337–346.

Barber, S. L., L. Lorenzoni, and P. Ong, 2019. *Price Setting and Price Regulation in Health Care: Lessons for Advancing Universal Health Coverage* (No. WHO/WKC-OECD/K18014). World Health Organization.

Berlin, J. 2020. Preserving Do No Harm: Supreme Court Tosses Challenge to Medical Ethics Committee Law. *Texas Medicine* 116: 22–23.

Betbeze, P. 2011. Reassessing Community Benefit. *Health Leaders Magazine* 14: 50.

Bindman, A. B. 2020. Rising Prices and Health Care "Empires." *Journal of the American Medical Association* 323: 815–816.

Blavin, F. 2016. Association Between the 2014 Medicaid Expansion and US Hospital Finances. *Journal of the American Medical Association* 316: 1475–1483.

Bureau of Labor Statistics. U.S. 2018. *Healthcare Jobs and the Great Recession*. Accessed August 2020. Available at: https://www.bls.gov/opub/mlr/2018/article/healthcare-jobs-and-the-great-recession.htm

Burns, L. R., J. S. McCullough, D. R. Wholey, G. Kruse, P. Kralovec, and R. Muller. 2015. Is the System Really the Solution? Operating Costs in Hospital Systems. *Medical Care Research and Review* 72: 247–272.

Burns, L. R., J. A. Alexander, and R. M. Andersen. 2020. How Different Governance Models May Impact Physician–Hospital Alignment. *Health Care Management Review* 2: 173–184.

Burrill, S., and A. Kane. 2017. *Chapter 3: Hospital Profit Margins: Hospital CEO Survey Series*. Deloitte Development LLC. Accessed August 2020. Available at: https://www2.deloitte.com/us/en/pages/life-sciences-and-health-care/articles/improve-hospital-profit-margins.html

Centers for Medicare and Medicaid Services (CMS). 2018. *IRF Classification Criteria*. Accessed August 2020. Available at: https://www.cms.gov/Medicare/Medicare-Fee-for-Service-Payment/InpatientRehabFacPPS/Criteria

Chen, A. F., E. Pflug, D. O'Brien, M. G. Maltenfort, and J. Parvizi. 2017. Utilization of Total Joint Arthroplasty in Physician-Owned Specialty Hospitals vs Acute Care Facilities. *Journal of Arthroplasty* 32: 2060–2064.

Chin, V., N. I. Samia, R. Marchant, O. Rosen, J. P. Ioannidis, M. A. Tanner, and S. Cripps. 2020. A Case Study in Model Failure? COVID-19 Daily Deaths and ICU Bed Utilisation Predictions in New York State. *European Journal of Epidemiology*. 35: 733–742.

Clement, J. P., and K. L. Grazier. 2001. HMO Penetration: Has it Hurt Public Hospitals? *Journal of Health Care Finance* 28: 25–38.

Congressional Budget Office (CBO). 2006. Nonprofit Hospitals and the Provision of Community Benefits. Accessed August 2020. Available at: https://www.cbo.gov/sites/default/files/109th-congress-2005-2006/reports/12-06-nonprofit.pdf

Cross, G. M. 2004. What Does Patient-Centered Care Mean for the VA? *Forum, Academy Health* 1–2, 8.

Darr, K. 1991. *Ethics in Health Services Management*. 2nd ed. Baltimore, MD: Health Professions Press.

de Cordova, P. B., T. Jones, K. A. Riman, J. Rogowski, and M. D. McHugh. 2020. Staffing Trends in Magnet and Non-Magnet Hospitals after State Legislation. *Journal of Nursing Care Quality* 35: 323–328.

DelliFraine, J. L. 2006. Communities with and without Children's Hospitals: Where Do the Sickest Children Receive Care? *Hospital Topics* 84: 19–28.

Ellison, E. C., B. Satiani, D. P. Way, W. M. Oslock, H. Santry, and T. E. Williams. 2020. The Continued Urbanization of American Surgery: A Threat to Rural Hospitals. *Surgery* 169: 543–549.

Feldstein, M. 1977. Quality Change and the Demand for Hospital Care. *Econometrica: Journal of the Econometric Society* 1681–1702.

Feldstein, M. 1971. *The Rising Cost of Hospital Care*. Washington, DC: Information Resource Press.

Feldstein, P. J. 1993. *Health Care Economics*. 4th ed. Albany, NY: Delmar Publishers.

Freeman, W. J., A. J. Weiss, and K. C. Heslin. 2018. *Overview of U.S. Hospital Stays in 2016: Variation by Geographic Region, 2012*. Statistical Brief #246. Rockville, MD: Agency for Healthcare Research and Quality. Accessed August 2020. Available at: https://www.hcup-us.ahrq.gov/reports/statbriefs/sb246-Geographic-Variation-Hospital-Stays.pdf

Gaskin, D. J., B. Herring, H. Zare, and G. Anderson. 2019. Measuring Nonprofit Hospitals' Provision of Charity Care Using IRS and CMS Data. *Journal of Healthcare Management* 64: 293–314.

Giancotti, M., A. Guglielmo, and M. Mauro. 2017. Efficiency and Optimal Size of Hospitals: Results of a Systematic Search. *PLoS One* 12: 1–40.

Goodman, C. W., A. Flanigan, J. C. Probst, and A. S. Brett. 2020. Charity Care Characteristics and Expenditures among US Tax-Exempt Hospitals in 2016. *American Journal of Public Health* 110: 492–498.

Haglund, C. L., and W. L. Dowling. 1993. The Hospital. In: *Introduction to Health Services*. 4th ed. S. J. Williams and P. R. Torrens, eds. Albany, NY: Delmar Publishers. 135–176.

Hamric, A. B., and L. D. Wocial. 2016. Institutional Ethics Resources: Creating Moral Spaces. *Hastings Center Report* 46 (suppl): S22–S27.

Harolds, J. A., and L. B. Miller. 2020. Quality and Safety in Healthcare, Part LXXVI: The Value of Magnet® Hospital Recognition. *Clinical Nuclear Medicine*. 1536–0229, 2020. Publisher: Lippincott; PMID: 32796251.

Health Forum. 2001. *AHA Guide to the Health Care Field: 2001–2002 edition*. Chicago, IL: Author.

Health Forum. 2020. *Fast Facts on US Hospitals. AHA Hospital Statistics, 2020 edition*. Accessed August 2020. Available at: https://www.aha.org/system/files/media/file/2020/01/2020-aha-hospital-fast-facts-new-Jan-2020.pdf

Heaton, J., and P. Tadi. 2023. Managed Care Organization. In *StatPearls*. StatPearls Publishing.

Hilsenrath, P. E. 2006. Osteopathic Medicine in Transition: Postmortem of the Osteopathic Medical Center of Texas. *Journal of the American Osteopathic Association* 106: 558–561.

Hollingsworth, J. M., Z. Ye, S. A. Strope, S. L. Krein, A. T. Hollenbeck, and B. K. Hollenbeck. 2010. Physician Ownership of Ambulatory Surgery Centers Linked to Higher Volume of Surgeries. *Health Affairs* 29: 683.

Horak, R. V., J. F. Griffin, A. M. Brown, et al. 2019. Growth and Changing Characteristics of Pediatric Intensive Care 2001–2016. *Critical Care Medicine* 47: 1135–1142.

Internal Revenue Service (IRS). 2016. New Requirements for 501(c)(3) Hospitals under the Affordable Care Act. Accessed February 2021. Available at: http://www.ir.gov/Charities-Non-Profits/Charitable-Organizations/New-Requirements-for-501c3-Hospitals-Under-the-Affordable-Care-Act

Kacik, A. 2018a. Number of Outpatient Facilities Surges as Industry Values More Convenient, Affordable Care. *Modern Healthcare*. Accessed August 2020. Available at: https://www.modernhealthcare.com/article/20181220/NEWS/181229992/number-of-outpatient-facilities-surges-as-industry-values-more-convenient-affordable-care

Kacik, A. 2018b. Flaws in Reporting Create Knowledge Vacuum Regarding Community Benefits. *Modern Healthcare* 48: 20.

Kaiser Family Foundation (KFF). 2023. 10 things to Know about Medicaid Managed Care. Accessed November 2023. Available at: https://www.kff.org/medicaid/issue-brief/10-things-to-know-about-medicaid-managed-care/

Kangovi, S., F. K. Barg, T. Carter, J. A. Long, R. Shannon, and D. Grande. 2013. Understanding Why Patients of Low Socioeconomic Status Prefer Hospitals over Ambulatory Care. *Health Affairs* 32: 1196–1203.

Keon-Hyung, L., S. B. Yang, and M. Choi. 2009. The Association Between Hospital Ownership and Technical Efficiency in a Managed Care Environment. *Journal of Medical Systems* 33: 307–315.

Liang, L., B. Moore, and A. Soni. 2020. *National Inpatient Hospital Costs: The Most Expensive Conditions by Payer, 2017*. Statistical Brief #261. Agency for Healthcare Research and Quality. Accessed August 2020. Available at: https://hcup-us.ahrq.gov/reports/statbriefs/sb261-Most-Expensive-Hospital-Conditions-2017.jsp

Lin, G., R. Huang, J. Zhang, G. Li, L. Chen, and X. Xi, et al. 2020. Clinical and Economic Outcomes of Hospital Pharmaceutical Care: A Systematic Review and Meta-Analysis. *BMC Health Services Research* 20: 487.

Mantone, J. 2005. Critical Time at Rural Hospitals. *Modern Healthcare* 35: 22.

Medicare Payment Advisory Commission (MedPAC). 2006. *Report to the Congress: Physician-Owned Specialty Hospitals Revisited*. Washington, DC: Author.

Medicare Payment Advisory Commission (MedPAC). 2019a. *Critical Access Hospital Payment System*. Washington, DC: Author.

Medicare Payment Advisory Commission (MedPAC). 2019b. *Hospital Acute Inpatient Services Payment System*. Washington, DC: Author.

Medicare Payment Advisory Commission (MedPAC). 2019c. *Inpatient Rehabilitation Facilities Payment System*. Washington, DC: Author.

Miller, B. 2021. Cost and Quality of Care in Physician-Owned Hospitals: A Systematic Review. *Mercatus Special Study*.

Nachega, J. B., R. Leisegang, D. Bishai, et al. 2010. Association of Antiretroviral Therapy Adherence and Health Care Costs. *Annals of Internal Medicine* 152: 18–25.

National Center for Health Statistics (NCHS). 2002. *Health, United States, 2002*. Hyattsville, MD: Department of Health and Human Services.

National Center for Health Statistics (NCHS). 2013. *Health, United States, 2012*. Hyattsville, MD: Department of Health and Human Services.

National Center for Health Statistics (NCHS). 2018. *Health, United States, 2017*. Hyattsville, MD: Department of Health and Human Services.

Nudelman, P. M., and L. M. Andrews. 1996. The "Value Added" of Not-for-Profit Health Plans. *New England Journal of Medicine* 334: 1057–1059.

O'Connell, L., and S. L. Brown. 2003. Do Nonprofit HMOs Eliminate Racial Disparities in Cardiac Care? *Journal of Healthcare Finance* 30: 84–94.

OECD. 2020. *Healthcare Prices and Purchasing Power Parities*. Available at: https://www.oecd.org/health/health-purchasing-power-parities.htm

OECD. 2023. *Hospital Employment*. OECD Health Statistics 2023. Available at: file:///Users/yulingli/Downloads/HEALTH_REAC_11_Hospital%20employment%20(1).pdf

Office of Inspector General. 2003. *Trends in Urban Hospital Closure: 1990–2000*. Accessed August 2020. Available at: http://oig.hhs.gov/oei/reports/oei-04-02-00611.pdf

Organization for Economic Cooperation and Development (OECD). 2019. *Health at a Glance, 2019: OECD Indicators*. Accessed August 2020. Available at: https://www.oecd-ilibrary.org/docserver/4dd50c09-en.pdf?expires=1597784317&id=id&accname=guest&checksum=17A0C45135450B10B4E8B807410CC683

Organization for Economic Cooperation and Development (OECD). 2021. Health at a Glance, 2021: OECD Indicators. Accessed November 2023. Available at: https://www.oecd-ilibrary.org/docserver/ae3016b9-en.pdf?expires=1699139539&id=id&accname=guest&checksum=3C2EE721E0BB431A2E115153420A3A6D

Ortiz, G. 2019. Predictors of 30-day Postdischarge Readmission to a Multistate National Sample of State Psychiatric Hospitals. *Journal for Healthcare Quality* 41: 228–236.

Owens, B. 2005. The Plight of the Not-for-Profit. *Journal of Healthcare Management* 50: 237–250.

Pai, A. B., A. Boyd, J. Depczynski, I. M. Chavez, N. Khan, and H. Manley. 2009. Reduced Drug Use and Hospitalization Rates in Patients Undergoing Hemodialysis Who Received Pharmaceutical Care: A 2-year, Randomized, Controlled Study. *Pharmacotherapy* 29: 1433–1440.

Pai, D. R., H. Hosseini, and R. S. Brown. 2017. Does Efficiency and Quality of Care Affect Hospital Closures? *Health Systems* 8: 17–30.

Paris, M. 1995. The Medical Staff. In: *Health Care Administration: Principles, Practices, Structure, and Delivery*. 2nd ed. L. F. Wolper, ed. Gaithersburg, MD: Aspen Publishers. 32–46.

Raffel, M., W. 1980. *The US Health System: Origins and Functions*. New York: John Wiley and Sons.

Raffel, M. W., and N. K. Raffel. 1994. *The US Health System: Origins and Functions*. 4th ed. Albany, NY: Delmar Publishers.

Redelmeier, D. A., and V. R. Fuchs, (1993). Hospital Expenditures in the United States and Canada. *New England Journal of Medicine* 328: 772–778.

Roemer, M. I. 1961. Bed Supply and Hospital Utilization: A Natural Experiment. *Hospitals* 35: 36–42.

Rosner, F. 2004. Informing the Patient about a Fatal Disease: From Paternalism to Autonomy: The Jewish View. *Cancer Investigation* 22: 949–953.

Rural Health Information Hub. 2023. Critical Access Hospitals (CAHs). Accessed November 23, 2023. Available at: https://www.ruralhealthinfo.org/topics/critical-access-hospitals

Sanofi-Aventis/Forte Information Resources. 2019. *Public Payer Digest: Trends in Chronic Disease Management. Managed Care Digest Series*. Bridgewater, NJ: Author.

Schneider, J. E., R. L. Ohsfeldt, M. A. Morrisey, P. Li, T. R. Miller, and B. A. Zelner. 2007. Effects of Specialty Hospitals on the Financial Performance of General Hospitals, 1997–2004. *Inquiry* 44: 321–334.

Schroeder, G. D., M. F. Kurd, C. K. Kepler, et al. 2018. The Effect of Hospital Ownership on Health Care Utilization in Orthopedic Surgery. *Clinical Spine Surgery* 31: 73–79.

Shoger, T. R. 2011. Commonsense Contracts. *Trustees* 64: 6–7.

Sinay, T. 2005. Cost Structure of Osteopathic Hospitals and Their Local Counterparts in the USA: Are They Any Different? *Social Science and Medicine* 60: 1805–1814.

Statista. 2023. Number of Psychiatric Hospitals in the U.S. in 2020, by Operation Type. Accessed November 12, 2023. Available at: https://www.statista.com/statistics/712645/psychiatric-hospitals-number-in-the-us-by-operation-type/

Stewart, D. A. 1973. *The History and Status of Proprietary Hospitals. Blue Cross Reports—Research Series 9*. Chicago, IL: Blue Cross Association.

Swanson, A. 2021. Physician Investment in Hospitals: Specialization, Selection, and Quality in Cardiac Care. *Journal of Health Economics* 80: 102519.

Teisberg, E. D. et al. 1991. *The Hospital Sector in 1992*. Boston, MA: Harvard Business School.

Trybou, J., M. De Regge, P. Gemmel, P. Duyck, and L. Annemans 2014. Effects of Physician-owned

Specialized Facilities in Health Care: A Systematic Review. *Health Policy* 118: 316–340.

van Oostveen, C. J., D. J. Gouma, P. J. Bakker, and D. T. Ubbink. 2015. Quantifying the Demand for Hospital Care Services: A Time and Motion Study. *BMC Health Services Research* 15: 15.

Veterans Health Administration. 2023. About VHA. Accessed November 12, 2023. Available at: https://www.va.gov/health/aboutvha.asp.

Vogt, W. B., and R. Town. 2006. *How Has Hospital Consolidation Affected the Price and Quality of Hospital Care?* Princeton, NJ: Robert Wood Johnson Foundation.

Weil, A. R. 2020. Rural Health, Behavioral Health, and More. *Health Affairs* 39: 919–920.

Wolfson, J., and S. L. Hopes. 1994. What Makes Tax-Exempt Hospitals Special? *Healthcare Financial Management* 4: 56–60.

Worthy, J. C., and C. L. Anderson. 2016. Analysis of the Community Benefit Standard in Texas Hospitals. *Journal of Healthcare Management* 61: 94–102.

CHAPTER 9

Managed Care and Integrated Organizations

LEARNING OBJECTIVES

- Review the link between the development of managed care and earlier organizational forms in the U.S. healthcare delivery system.
- Grasp the basic concepts of managed care and how managed care organizations achieve cost savings.
- Distinguish between the main types of managed care organizations.
- Examine the different models of health maintenance organizations and explain the advantages and disadvantages of each model.
- Describe why managed care did not achieve its cost-control objectives.
- Discuss managed care enrollments in employer-based health insurance, Medicaid, and Medicare.
- Discuss the driving forces behind organizational integration and strategies commonly used to achieve integration.
- Describe highly integrated healthcare systems namely, integrated delivery systems and accountable care organizations.

"The many forms of managed care."

Introduction

Managed care has been the single most dominant force in fundamentally transforming the delivery of health care in the United States since the 1990s. Even the Affordable Care Act (ACA) of 2010—the most sweeping healthcare reform initiative in recent history—did not attempt to obliterate managed care and had to work within its parameters. So entrenched has managed care become in the U.S. healthcare system that it has almost completely replaced traditional fee-for-service insurance.

Although the nature of managed care may vary across plans and countries, there are common elements of managed care in countries such as Switzerland, Great Britain, the Netherlands, Germany, China, and Latin America (Ehlert and Oberschachtsiek, 2014; Zhang et al., 2023; Hennrich, 2022; Espinosa et al., 2022). Germany, the Netherlands, and Switzerland have taken steps toward incorporating the concept of managed care into their health insurance markets, with the aim of enhancing efficiency (Duijmelinck and van de Ven, 2016). Even prior to these transitions, general practitioners in several European countries had regulated patients' access to specialists and assumed responsibility for a per capita annual budget (Deom et al., 2010). In this chapter, however, managed care is discussed in the U.S. context.

In the United States, the transition to managed care became necessary as employers grappled with the unaffordable excesses associated with unrestrained delivery of services, which had led to spiraling health insurance premiums. In the traditional insurance system (also referred to as fee-for-service or indemnity insurance) that prevailed prior to managed care, insurance companies had no incentive to manage how services were delivered and how the providers were paid. With no controls over delivery and payment, costs got out of hand. The only way to control the runaway costs was to integrate delivery and payment with the functions of financing and insurance. This integration of functions was accomplished through managed care.

As employers increasingly abandoned traditional insurance and switched to managed care as a defense against rising insurance costs, managed care started wielding enormous buying power over both physicians and hospitals. Perhaps not surprisingly, providers saw this dominance as a threat to their independence and earnings. For their part, the insureds who had previously been able to seek any provider of their choice now had some restrictions placed on that freedom. The result was a "managed care backlash." As a result of opposition from physicians and consumers and regulation from policymakers in the 1990s, managed care organizations (MCOs) were forced to relax their tight controls over healthcare utilization and payments to providers. Some diversification within the industry also occurred, as different types of managed care plans were designed. Consequently, managed care evolved into something quite different from what it was originally intended to be and, eventually, had limited success in controlling healthcare costs.

The balancing of power on the demand and supply sides of the healthcare market led to organizational integration. To counter the erosion of their marketplace power, providers began forming integrated organizations, led by hospitals. The larger systems formed through such consolidation, however, did not quite achieve the dual goals of quality and cost. Later, the ACA triggered the growth of accountable care organizations (ACOs) with the expectation that, by incorporating financial incentives in reimbursement systems, these organizations could be held accountable for quality and cost through collaborative delivery of care to the beneficiaries of public insurance programs.

What Is Managed Care?

Managed care is an organized approach to delivering a comprehensive array of healthcare services to a group of enrolled members through efficient management of services needed by the members and negotiation of prices or payment arrangements with providers. It is an approach to financing and delivering health care that seeks to control costs and ensure or improve quality of care through a variety of methods, including provider network management and utilization management and quality assurance (Sturm et al., 1998).

Managed care is generally discussed in two different contexts. First, and more commonly, it refers to an approach for providing healthcare services that has two main features: (1) integration of the financing, insurance, delivery, and payment functions within one organizational setting (**Figure 9-1**) and (2) formal control over utilization. Second, the term "managed care" can refer to an MCO, which can take a variety of forms. In this context, managed care is an organization that delivers healthcare services using the approach just discussed.

Cost containment is not the only objective that managed care seeks to achieve, although the potential for cost containment has been the driving force behind the phenomenal growth of managed care. MCOs are also involved in initiatives that improve health and wellness, disease management, enrollee satisfaction, quality of care, and overall organizational performance.

Financing

In a managed care system, premiums are based on negotiated contracts between employers and the MCO. A fixed premium per enrollee includes all healthcare services provided for in the contract, and premiums cannot be raised during the term of the contract.

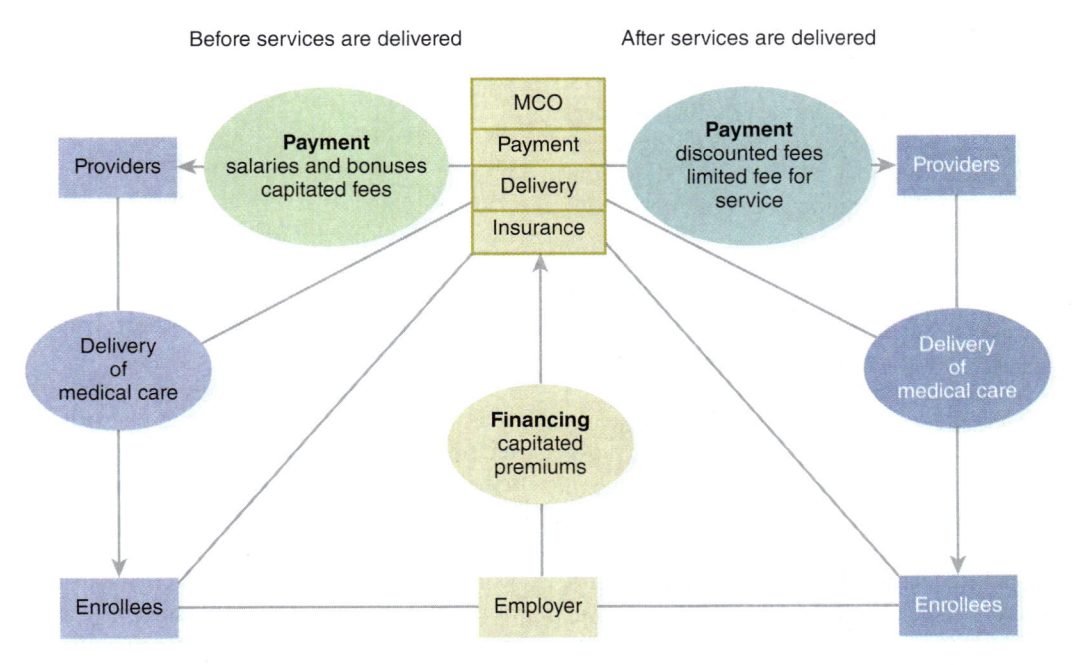

Figure 9-1 Integration of healthcare delivery functions through managed care.

Insurance

The MCO functions like an insurance company by assuming all risk. In other words, the MCO takes financial responsibility if the total cost of services provided exceeds the revenue from fixed premiums.

Delivery

In an ideal scenario, an MCO would operate its own hospitals and outpatient clinics and employ its own physicians. Some large MCOs actually do employ their own physicians on salary. Others have concluded mergers with hospitals and/or group practices. Most MCOs, however, arrange for the delivery of medical services through contracts with physicians, clinics, and hospitals that operate independently.

Payment

MCOs use three main types of payment arrangements with providers: capitation, discounted fees, and salaries. All three methods incorporate risk sharing, albeit in varying degrees, between the MCO and the providers. Risk sharing puts the burden on the providers to be cost-conscious and to curtail unnecessary utilization Sometimes, a limited amount of fee-for-service reimbursement is used for specialized services.

Capitation refers to the payment of a fixed monthly fee per member to a healthcare provider. All healthcare services are included in the one set fee, so that risk shifts from the MCO to the provider.

Discounted fee arrangements can be regarded as a modified form of fee for service. After the delivery of services, the provider can bill the MCO for each service separately but is paid according to a pre-negotiated schedule called a **fee schedule**. In this case, risk is borne by the MCO, but the MCO can lower its costs by paying discounted rates. Providers agree to discount their regular fees in exchange for the volume of business that the MCO brings them.

A third method of payment is salaries for physicians employed by the MCO. Under this arrangement, physicians are paid fixed salaries. Then, at the end of the year, a pool of money is distributed among the physicians in the form of bonuses based on various performance measures. Hence, with this method of payment, some risk shifts from the MCO to the physicians. Research demonstrates that financial incentives for providers result in higher performance on care effectiveness measures (Borenstein et al., 2004). Financial incentives have also been shown to have a modest positive effect on quality, particularly in staff- and group-model health maintenance organizations (HMOs) (Tisnado et al., 2008).

Evolution of Managed Care

The concept of managed care is not new, even though the widespread application of the concept is a more recent phenomenon. The principles on which managed care is based have been around for nearly a century. For example, the first private health insurance arrangement for hospital services (known as the Baylor Plan) in the United States was based on capitation (**Exhibit 9-1**). In 1929, this plan started enrolling teachers for a fixed monthly fee per enrollee that was paid to Baylor Hospital; no insurance company was involved in the arrangement.

The idea of managed care evolved from what the medical establishment pejoratively referred to as the corporate practice of medicine. Even before private health insurance became widespread, these practices were used sporadically as cost-effective means of providing healthcare services to certain groups of people. Contract practice takes the idea of capitation a step further by incorporating a defined group of enrollees. Here, the employer is the financier that contracts with one or more providers to furnish health care to a group of

Exhibit 9-1 The Evolution of Managed Care: Capitation

Health insurance	Capitation Bearing of Risk by Providers
Initially, health insurance combined the insurance, delivery, and payment functions of health care, as mentioned in the Baylor Plan, but further evolution of this initial concept was thwarted by organized medicine. Contract practice moved toward the integration of these functions, bypassing the insurance companies.	
Contract practice	Defined group of enrollees Capitation or salary Bearing of risk by providers ↓
Prepaid group practice	Comprehensive services Defined group of enrollees Capitation Bearing of risk by providers ↓
Managed care	Utilization controls Comprehensive services Defined group of enrollees Capitation, discounted fees, or salary Limited fee for service Limits on choice of providers Sharing of risk with providers Financial incentives to providers Accountability for plan performance

enrollees—the employees—at a predetermined fee per enrollee.

Prepaid group practice goes another step further. First, it preserves the principles of capitation, bearing of risk by the provider, and a defined group of enrollees whose healthcare contract is financed by their employer. It then adds the delivery of comprehensive services. Prepaid practice, which gave rise to HMOs in the mid-1970s, was well established in the form of plans such as the Kaiser Foundation Health Plan (Oakland, California, 1942), the Group Health Cooperative of Puget Sound (Seattle, Washington, 1947), and the Health Insurance Plan of Greater New York (1947).

Managed care has incorporated a variety of cost-control features, such as utilization management to control inefficient use of healthcare services, discounted fees and salaries as alternative methods of payment to providers, limits on the choice of providers from whom enrollees can obtain services, and accountability to the stakeholders by evaluating performance on certain quantifiable measures. Certain efforts—such as emphasis on preventive services, chronic disease management, and maternity care—are directed at not only cost containment but also improving the health of the enrolled population.

Accreditation of Managed Care Organizations

The National Committee for Quality Assurance (NCQA), a private nonprofit organization, began accrediting MCOs in 1991. Accreditation emerged in response to the demand for standardized, objective information about the quality of MCOs. Participation in the accreditation program is voluntary. To be accredited, MCOs must comply with NCQA standards. Plans receiving high accreditation ratings show higher patient satisfaction ratings and greater degree of involvement in monitoring and prevention activities (Richter and Beauvais, 2018).

NCQA ratings are based on three types of quality measures: measures of clinical quality from NCQA's Healthcare Effectiveness Data and Information Set (HEDIS) and Health Outcomes Survey (HOS); measures of patient experience using the Consumer Assessment of Healthcare Providers and Systems (CAHPS); and results from NCQA's review of a health plan's health quality processes (NCQA Accreditation) (NCQA, 2022). NCQA rates health plans that choose to report measures publicly.

Quality Assessment in Managed Care

Developed by the NCQA, the HEDIS performance measures date back to 1989. Originally designed for private employers' needs as purchasers of health insurance, HEDIS has been adapted for use by the general public, public insurers, and regulators. Over two-thirds of all U.S. health plans use HEDIS measures (Ng et al., 2015) to evaluate performance on important dimensions of clinical care and service. These measures have also been used quite extensively to compare the quality of care in health plans. HEDIS 2020/2021 includes measures that cover the following domains (NCQA, 2020): HEDIS 2023 includes measures that cover the following domains (NCQA, 2023):

- Effectiveness of care (e.g., immunizations, screenings, management of chronic conditions)
- Access and availability of care (e.g., access to preventive services, treatment for alcohol and drug dependency, prenatal and postpartum care)
- Experience of care (e.g., the CAHPS Health Plan Survey, which is used to collect standardized information on enrollees' experiences with health plans and their services)
- Utilization and Risk Adjusted Utilization (e.g., appropriate frequency of visits, inpatient utilization, mental health utilization)
- Health plan descriptive information, which includes board certification of physicians, enrollments, and race/ethnic diversity of the enrolled population, among other details
- Measures reported using electronic clinical data systems (e.g., use of electronic health records)

Historical Growth of Managed Care

As previously mentioned, the main impetus for managed care's growth was rapid cost escalations during the 1970s and 1980s under the dominant fee-for-service system. Employers, who in many instances paid the entire cost of health insurance premiums on their employees' behalf, began switching to managed care only after they experienced notable escalations in premium costs. The Health Maintenance Organization Act of 1973 provided some federal support for the creation of HMOs and generated widespread awareness of this alternative to fee-for-service medicine.

Flaws in the Fee-for-Service Model

Traditional fee-for-service health insurance is also referred to as **indemnity insurance**. An indemnity plan allows the insured to obtain healthcare services anywhere and from any physician or hospital. Indemnity insurance and fee-for-service reimbursement to providers are closely intertwined.

Uncontrolled Utilization

In the fee-for-service practice of medicine, moral hazard was omnipresent. In a system dominated by specialists and an absence of primary-care gatekeeping, patients were free to go to any provider. Care received from specialists and utilization of sophisticated technology gave patients the impression of high quality. In turn, competition was driven by such impressions rather than by cost or assessed quality. Physicians and hospitals competed for patients by offering the most up-to-date technologies and the most attractive practice settings (Wilkerson et al., 1997).

Despite research conducted to study this issue over the years, both in the United States and elsewhere, the validity of **provider-induced demand** has been controversial in some circles. Nevertheless, ample evidence exists that providers had an incentive to promote higher utilization in pursuit of higher revenues when controls over utilization were inadequate (Nguyen and Derrick, 1997; Rice and Labelle, 1989; Yip, 1998). This was found to be particularly true in the fee-for-service environment (Nguyen et al., 2017). A 10% reduction in fees, for example, would not necessarily translate into a 10% reduction in total expenditures on physician services because physicians generated demand in response to real fee reductions (Rice and Labelle, 1989).

Uncontrolled Prices and Payment

In traditional indemnity insurance, the insurance company exercised little control over providers' charges or patients' utilization of services. Providers set charges at an artificially high level and billed insurance by submitting item-by-item claims. The insurance company was merely a passive payer of claims—it paid what the providers billed, limited only by what the insurer deemed to be usual, customary, and reasonable charges. The insurance company had little incentive to control costs because it could simply increase the premiums the following year based on utilization during the previous year.

Focus on Illness Rather Than Wellness

Indemnity insurance paid for services only when a specific medical diagnosis was reported on the insurance claim; thus, visits for preventive checkups were not covered. The fee-for-service system also presented a second, even bigger problem: Indemnity insurance provided more thorough coverage when a person was hospitalized, and the physician was paid for daily hospital visits when the patient was being treated in the hospital. Thus, costly hospitalization of patients was lucrative for both physicians and hospitals.

Employers' Response to Rise in Premiums

When it first appeared, the concept of managed care was designed to compete against fee-for-service medicine. Until the 1980s, HMOs were the predominant form of managed care. The price-based competition from HMOs was often referred to as "shadow pricing," because HMOs typically offered more benefits and somewhat lower premiums than indemnity plans (Zelman, 1996). At this stage, however,

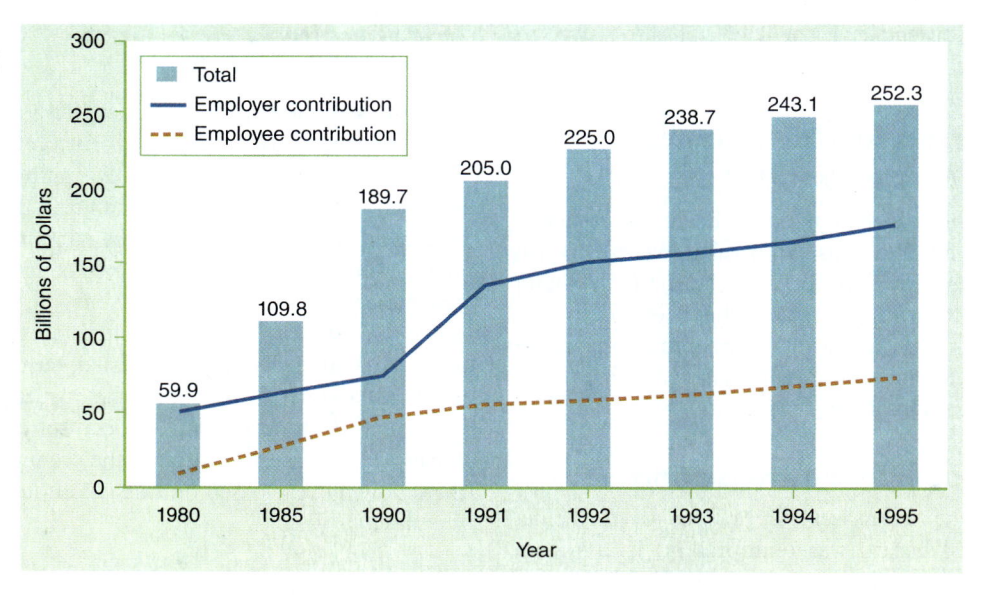

Figure 9-2 Growth in the cost of U.S. health insurance (private employers), 1980–1995.
Data from National Center for Health Statistics. 1998. Health, United States, 1998. Hyattsville, MD: U.S. Department of Health and Human Services. p. 348.

managed care plans had limited appeal. Individuals covered by indemnity insurance saw little benefit in joining a plan that would restrict their choice of providers. Most providers also saw little benefit in contracting with HMOs that might restrict their potential income or alter their style of practice (Wilkerson et al., 1997). For the most part, employers remained passive.

Between 1980 and 1990, the total cost of private health insurance increased at an average annual rate of more than 12% (**Figure 9-2**). Economic realities forced employers to make the transition from indemnity plans to managed care. Among the U.S. population with employer-based health insurance, the proportion of those enrolled in various managed care plans jumped from 27% in 1988 to 86% in 1998, and then to 99% in 2022 (**Figure 9-3**). The latest figures of health insurance premium contributions are captured in **Table 9-1**. Between 2011 and 2021, total annual health insurance premium increased from $15,073 to $22,221. Employer's contribution held around 70% (70.9%–73.1%).

Weakened Economic Position of Providers

Indirectly, excess capacity in the healthcare delivery system may have contributed to the growth of managed care (McGuire, 1994). The Medicare prospective payment system, which was introduced in the mid-1980s, had a marked impact on hospital economics. Left with significant unused capacity in the form of empty beds, hospitals had substantially weakened bargaining power in relation to the growing economic power of managed care, which was being pushed by employers' intent on containing their own costs. Thus, with the growth of managed care, the balance of power in the medical marketplace swung toward the demand side of the economic equation. On the supply side, physicians, for example, initially showed great resistance to managed care. However, as the financing of health care quickly shifted toward managed care, physicians were left with the stark choice of participating or being left out.

Efficiencies and Inefficiencies in Managed Care **395**

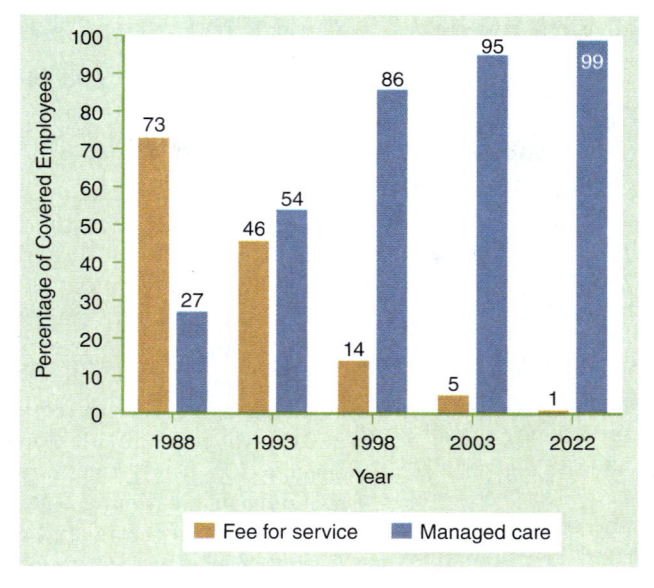

Figure 9-3 Percentage of worker enrollment in health plans, selected years.

Data from Kaiser Family Foundation and Health Research and Educational Trust (Kaiser/HRET). 2003. Employer health benefits: 2003 annual survey. Menlo Park, CA: Author; Kaiser Family Foundation and Health Research and Educational Trust (Kaiser/HRET). 2016. Employer health benefits: 2016 annual survey. Menlo Park, CA: Author. 2022 data from: KFF Employer Health Benefits Survey, 2021; Kaiser/HRET Survey of Employer-Sponsored Health Benefits, 2011, 2016, and 2021. https:///www.kff.org/report-section/ehbs-2021-summary-of-findings/

Table 9-1 Mean Annual Worker and Employer Health Insurance Premium Contributions for Family Coverage in Selected Years

Year	2011	2016	2021
Total premium	$15073	$18142	$22221
Employer contribution	$10944 (72.6%)	$12865 (70.9%)	$16253 (73.1%)
Worker contribution	$4129 (27.4%)	$5277 (29.1%)	$5969 (26.9%)

Data from: KFF Employer Health Benefits Survey, 2021; Kaiser/HRET Survey of Employer-Sponsored Health Benefits, 2011, 2016, and 2021. https:///www.kff.org/report-section/ehbs-2021-summary-of-findings/

Efficiencies and Inefficiencies in Managed Care

Efficiency can be determined by the number of inputs (e.g., medical supplies, labor) utilized to generate certain outputs (e.g., discharges, visits, medical training). In a managed care environment, hospitals have been found to be more efficient (Keon-Hyung et al., 2009).

Managed care achieves efficiencies in several ways. First, by integrating the four functions of healthcare delivery (financing, insurance, delivery, and payment), MCOs eliminate insurance and payer intermediaries and realize some savings. Second, MCOs control costs by sharing risk with providers or by extracting discounts from providers. Risk sharing promotes economically prudent delivery of health care. It is an indirect method of utilization control because it largely eliminates provider-induced demand. Third, cost savings are achieved by coordinating a broad range of patient services and by monitoring care to determine whether services are appropriate and delivered in the most cost-effective settings. For example, by emphasizing outpatient services, MCOs achieve lower rates of hospital utilization. Some evidence also suggests that HMO plans incur lower utilization of costly procedures compared to non-HMO plans (Miller and Luft, 1997). Fourth, gatekeeping reduces moral hazard. Finally, a focus on wellness and preventive services saves money through illness prevention, as well as through early detection and treatment of more serious illnesses.

Although many of the cost-control measures adopted by managed care have been applauded, other results have not been so commendable. The complexity that arises when providers have to deal with numerous plans does not add value to the delivery of health care. For example, administrative inefficiencies are created for providers, who must deal with differences in each plan's protocols and procedures. Another problem is that many contracts with providers exclude some services. For example, carving out laboratory testing services for outpatients has been a common practice. Many MCOs rely on one of the large national lab chains, such as Quest Diagnostics or Roche Diagnostics, to provide these services, which may create inconveniences for both patients and providers. A third area of inefficiency is the lengthy appeals process that patients and providers must sometimes navigate when an MCO denies services. Finally, less utilization is not necessarily more efficient care. One recent study found that Medicaid populations in managed care may encounter significantly more fragmented care than their counterparts who are covered by fee-for-service plans (Kern et al., 2020). In short, managed care does not always create the well-coordinated, seamless system that patients and providers would like to have (Southwick, 1997).

Cost Control Methods in Managed Care

MCOs use various methods to promote efficient delivery of health care. Effective management of healthcare delivery becomes necessary because, in the United States, approximately 20% of patients—typically those with comorbidities, frail older individuals, and those with complex medical conditions, sometimes referred to as high-need, high-cost patients—account for 80% of overall healthcare spending (Berk and Monheit, 2001; Joynt et al., 2013). Moreover, estimates suggest that nearly one-third of healthcare spending in the United States is a result of unnecessary care (Levine and Mulligan, 2015). Utilization management of institutional inpatient services takes priority because the cost of hospital care represents nearly 50% of the total costs that health plans pay for medical services (Melnick et al., 2011).

American consumers often favor specialty care over primary care, but more expensive healthcare services do not always equate to better health. Except in primary care, most of the increase in healthcare spending has not produced improved clinical outcomes (Kravitz, 2008). In addition, U.S. consumers, who are bombarded by advertisements for expensive new pharmaceuticals, often expect their physicians to prescribe the latest drugs even when an older and cheaper drug may be quite satisfactory in obtaining expected results. Following is some of the common methods used for utilization management:

- Choice restriction
- Care coordination
- Disease management
- Pharmaceutical management
- Utilization review
- Practice profiling

Not all MCOs use all of these mechanisms. Traditionally, HMOs have employed tighter utilization controls than other managed care plans.

Choice Restriction

Traditional indemnity insurance gave the insured open access to any provider, whether generalist or specialist. This freedom led to overutilization of services, as studies have pointed out. In contrast, most managed care plans impose some restrictions on where and from whom the patient can obtain medical care. Patients still have a choice of physicians, but the choice is limited to physicians who are either employees of the MCO or have established contracts with the MCO. A physician who has a formal affiliation with an MCO is said to be on the **panel** of the MCO. In a **closed-panel** (or closed-access or in-network) plan, services obtained from providers outside the panel are not covered by the plan. By contrast, an **open-panel** (or open-access or out-of-network option) plan allows access to providers outside the panel, but enrollees almost always have to pay higher out-of-pocket costs.

Because the MCO has greater control over the providers who are on its panel, use is better managed under closed-panel plans compared to those that allow access outside the panel. From the enrollees' standpoint, the restricted choice of providers is a trade-off for lower out-of-pocket costs.

Care Coordination

Care delivery can be fragmented when patients must move between and across care settings because of diverse health issues that need to be addressed by different care providers. Fragmented care often results in patients not receiving appropriate therapies, which results in poor outcomes, and even worse overall survival. Hence, both direct and indirect costs are associated with fragmented care. Care coordination is a means to achieve integrated, interdisciplinary services while overcoming discontinuities in care delivery. The concept of care coordination has also been fused with the notion of accountable care and has given rise to new models of care delivery (discussed in the section "Highly Integrated Healthcare Systems").

Gatekeeping

Certain MCOs require that their enrollees must have a primary-care physician (PCP) who coordinates all healthcare services—a mechanism referred to as "gatekeeping." This practice emphasizes preventive care, health screenings, routine physical examinations, and other primary-care services. When gatekeeping is used, secondary-level services (**Figure 9-4**) are obtained only on referral from the primary-care physician. Gatekeeping strategies have been shown to result in modest cost savings (Pati et al., 2005), although one Swiss study showed savings of 15% to 19% per person for individuals enrolled in a gatekeeping plan compared to those enrolled in a fee-for-service plan (Schwenkglenks et al., 2006).

Case Management

Case management is an advanced level of care coordination that uses a client-centered approach for evaluating and coordinating care, particularly for patients who have complex, potentially costly problems that require a variety of services from multiple providers over

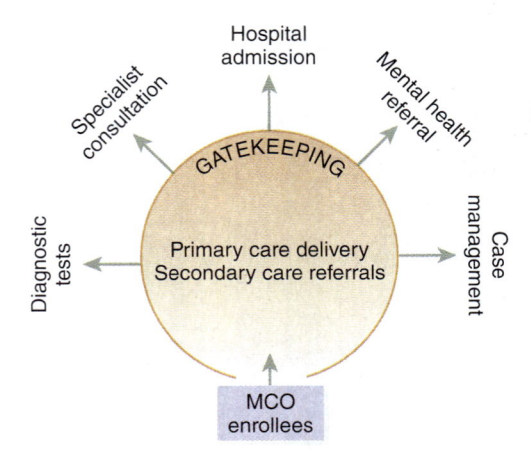

Figure 9-4 Care coordination and utilization control through gatekeeping.

an extended period. Examples of conditions managed through this model include acquired immunodeficiency syndrome (AIDS), spinal cord injury, bone marrow transplant, lupus, cystic fibrosis, and severe workplace injuries. Patients with these conditions need expensive secondary- and tertiary-care services more often than they need primary care. Multiple comorbidities often require extensive care coordination to simultaneously address several health issues. In such circumstances, a primary-care gatekeeper cannot adequately coordinate all of the patient's needs, as these needs may change quite frequently.

In the case management model, an experienced healthcare professional, such as a nurse practitioner, with knowledge of available healthcare resources coordinates an individual's total health care in consultation with primary- and secondary-care providers. Based on the patient's needs, which change over time, services are arranged so that they are delivered in the most appropriate and cost-effective settings (**Figure 9-5**).

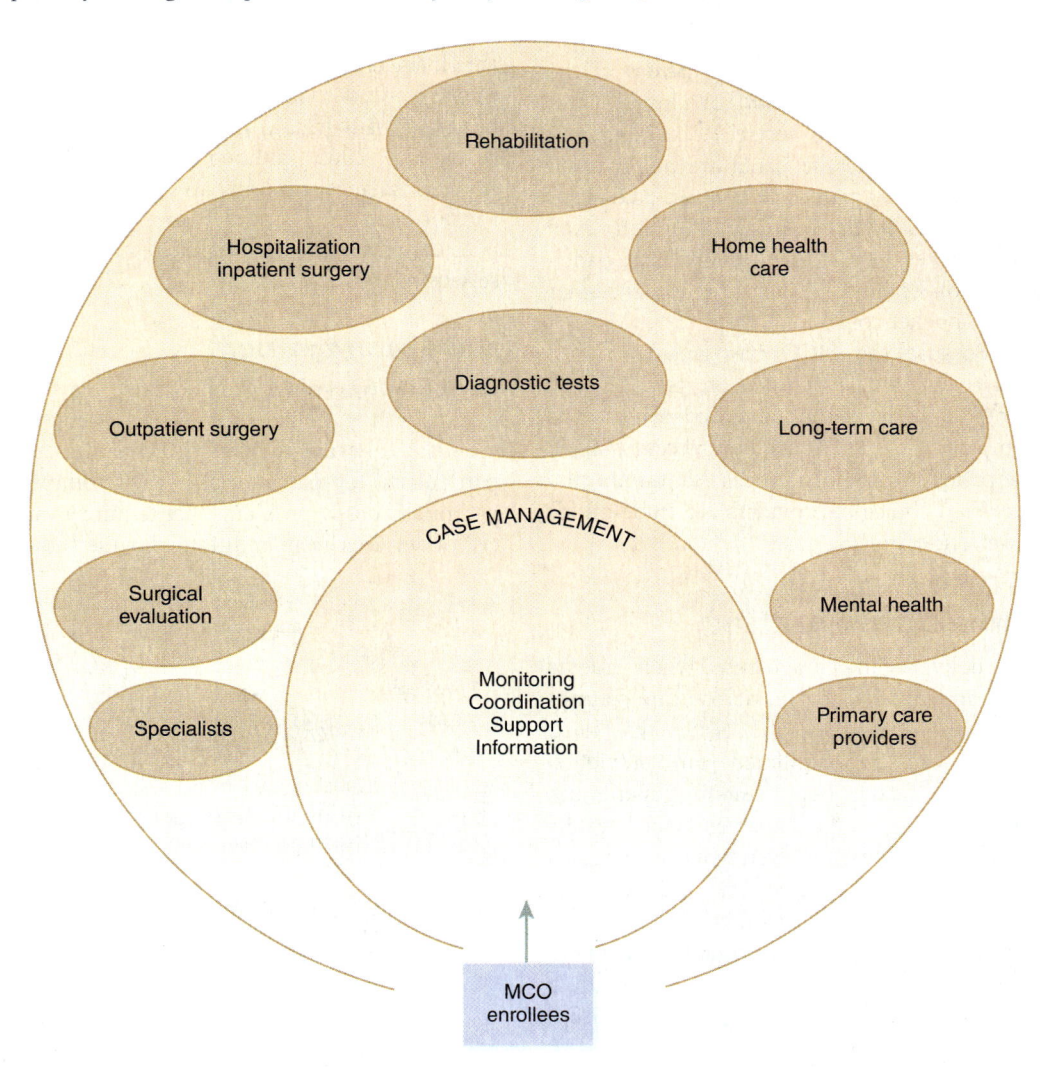

Figure 9-5 Case management function in care coordination.

In one study, advanced case management strategies used for high-risk populations in five states resulted in reduced costs for health care while improving the delivery of services (Lattimer, 2005). Physician practices, however, often do not have the resources to carry out case management functions. By comparison, MCOs that have a large number of high-need, high-cost enrollees, such as Medicare and/or Medicaid beneficiaries, are in a better position to undertake care coordination functions. For example, UnitedHealthcare (UHC), one of the nation's largest MCOs, launched a program targeted to the Medicaid population, known as Accountable Care Communities (Moin et al., 2020). This experimental model aimed at bridging the gap between medical and social services. To date, only a few states have implemented this model for their Medicaid populations (Yorkery, 2017).

Disease Management

Whereas case management is typically highly individualized and focused on coordinating the care of patients who are at high risk with multiple or complex medical conditions (Short et al., 2003), **disease management** is a population-oriented strategy for people with chronic conditions, such as diabetes, asthma, depression, and coronary artery disease. After subgroups among all the enrollees in a health plan have been identified according to their specific chronic conditions, disease management focuses on patient education, training in self-management, ongoing monitoring of the disease process, and follow-up to ensure that people are complying with their medical regimens. In a nutshell, disease management can be referred to as "self-care with professional support," with the patient assuming significant responsibility for their own health. The goal of disease management is to prevent or delay comorbidities and complications arising from uncontrolled chronic conditions.

Substantial evidence from the United States and overseas indicates that disease management improves quality of care and disease control. It may also add to a person's quality of life, at least for certain complex chronic conditions, such as multiple sclerosis (Ng et al., 2013) and chronic obstructive pulmonary disease (Ferrone et al., 2019). The cost-saving potential of disease management, however, is not clearly established.

Pharmaceutical Management

Since 2000, U.S. expenditures on prescription drugs increased more rapidly than total personal healthcare expenditures. To manage these rising costs, health plans use three main strategies:

- *Drug formularies.* A **formulary** is a list of prescription drugs approved by a health plan. Drugs not listed on the formulary are not covered by the plan.
- *Tiered cost sharing.* Out-of-pocket co-payments are stratified into tiers for generic drugs, preferred brand drugs, nonpreferred brand drugs, and drugs in specialty tiers (Brill, 2007). The lowest cost sharing applies to generic drugs. Specialty drugs include biologics and other pharmaceuticals that are not only expensive but may also need to be injected or infused or may require special handling. Examples of specialty pharmaceuticals include drugs for oncology, rheumatology, hepatitis C, and multiple sclerosis. Medicare defines specialty drugs as those costing $670 or more per month (in 2019).
- *Pharmacy benefits managers (PBMs).* Because of their size and purchasing power, PBMs are able to extract discounts from pharmaceutical manufacturers. These companies also handle drug utilization review (discussed in the next section).

Utilization Review

Utilization review (UR) is the process of evaluating the appropriateness of services provided. It is sometimes misunderstood as a mechanism for denying services, but its main objective is to ensure that appropriate levels of services are delivered, care is cost-efficient, and subsequent care is planned. Hence, quality of care has become an important component of UR. Drug UR practices have also become common because of ongoing increases in the use and cost of prescription drugs. Misuse of certain drugs can not only waste resources but also harm patients. Three main types of UR are distinguished based on when the review is undertaken: prospective, concurrent, and retrospective. All three also apply to pharmaceutical management.

Prospective Utilization Review

Prospective utilization review determines the appropriateness of utilization before the care is actually delivered. An example of prospective UR is the decision by a primary-care gatekeeper to refer or not refer a patient to a specialist. However, not all managed care plans use gatekeepers. Some plans require the enrollee or the provider to call the plan administrators for preauthorization (also called precertification) of services for hospital admissions as well as surgical and other high-cost procedures, such as magnetic resonance imaging (MRI). In case of an emergency admission to an inpatient facility, plans generally require notification within 24 hours. Plans use preestablished clinical guidelines to authorize hospitalization and assign an initial length of stay.

In drug UR, formularies are the first step in prospective review. Subsequently, the PBM can require preauthorization for certain drugs and biologics. In inpatient care, one objective of prospective UR is to prevent unnecessary or inappropriate institutionalization; however, it also serves other functions. The prospective review system notifies the concurrent review system of a new case so that the length of stay can be monitored and additional days of care be authorized when necessary.

Concurrent Utilization Review

Concurrent utilization review determines, on a daily basis, the length of stay necessary in a hospital. It also monitors the use of ancillary services and ensures that the selected medical treatment is appropriate and necessary. Concurrent UR is a critical undertaking when hospitals receive prospective reimbursement because the length of stay determines the profitability, or lack thereof, in a given case. Optimal drug therapy and management have been shown to reduce length of stay in hospitals in addition to reducing drug use and cost (Chen et al., 2009).

Concurrent UR is closely linked to **discharge planning**, which focuses on ensuring post-discharge continuity of care. For example, if a patient is admitted with a hip fracture, it is important to determine whether a rehabilitation hospital or a skilled nursing facility (SNF) would be more appropriate for the patient's convalescent care. If the patient requires care in an SNF, discharge planners must find out whether the appropriate level of rehabilitation services will be available in the SNF and how long the plan will pay for rehabilitation therapies in a long-term care setting. For a patient who will be discharged home, subsequent home health services and durable medical equipment (DME) may be necessary. The objective of discharge planning is "to get all the ducks in a row" to provide seamless services at the lowest cost and in the best interest of the patient.

Retrospective Utilization Review

Retrospective utilization review refers to the review of utilization after services have been delivered. A close examination of medical records is undertaken to assess the appropriateness of care. Retrospective review may also involve an analysis of utilization data to determine patterns of overutilization or underutilization. It allows monitoring of billing accuracy and compilation of provider-specific practice patterns, with feedback then being given to physicians. Such statistical data can be helpful for taking corrective action and for monitoring subsequent progress.

Retrospective drug review can help reduce inappropriate use of controlled substances, among other things (Daubresse et al., 2013). It enables clinical pharmacists to intervene with the prescribing physician to emphasize therapeutic appropriateness and drug interactions that can affect future prescribing habits (Angalakuditi and Gomes, 2011; Starner et al., 2009).

Practice Profiling

Practice profiling refers to the monitoring of physician-specific practice patterns and the comparison of individual practice patterns to some norm. It may incorporate results of patient satisfaction surveys and compliance with clinical practice guidelines. Profiling can be used to decide which providers have the right fit with the plan's managed care philosophy and goals. The profile reports are also used to give feedback to physicians so they can modify their own behavior of medical practice. Profiling may be combined with financial incentives to boost compliance with standard practice patterns.

As a case in point, opioid abuse and related deaths have been recognized as a public health crisis in the United States and Canada. Studies show that high- or low-intensity prescribing patterns for opioids influence long-term opioid use by patients (Delaney et al., 2020; Lee et al., 2020). One way to influence physician prescribing practices is through feedback on the prescribing profiles of other physicians (Kane et al., 2018).

Types of Managed Care Organizations

HMOs were the most common type of MCO until, in the late 1970s, commercial insurance companies developed preferred provider organizations (PPOs) to compete with HMOs. Today, many health insurance companies in the United States offer different types of managed care plans. For example, the largest health insurers in the United States, such as United-Healthcare, Blue Cross/Blue Shield, Humana, and Aetna, operate both HMOs and PPOs. Moreover, many HMOs offer **triple-option plans**, which combine the features of indemnity insurance, HMO, and PPO; the insured has the flexibility to choose which feature to use when seeking out healthcare services. The three main types of managed care arrangements discussed in this section are HMOs, PPOs, and point-of-service (POS) plans.

Health Maintenance Organization

A **health maintenance organization (HMO)** is distinguished from other types of plans by the following main characteristics:

- Traditionally, indemnity insurance paid for medical care only when a person was ill, whereas an HMO not only provided medical care during illness but also offered a variety of services to help people maintain their health. The ACA removed this distinction, as almost all health plans are required to provide preventive services.
- The enrollee is generally required to choose a PCP from the panel of physicians. The PCP delivers services in accordance with the gatekeeping model, discussed previously.
- The provider receives a capitated fee regardless of whether the enrollee uses healthcare services and regardless of the quantity of services used.
- All health care must be obtained from in-network hospitals, physicians, and other healthcare providers. Hybrid plans that have an HMO component, such as POS and triple-option plans, allow out-of-network use at a higher out-of-pocket cost.

- Specialty services, such as mental health and substance abuse treatment, are frequently carved out. A **carve-out** is a special contract outside regular capitation that HMO funds separately—for example, a contract with a managed behavioral healthcare organization (MBHO) for mental health services.
- The HMO is responsible for ensuring that services comply with certain established standards of quality.

In the employer-based health insurance market, HMO enrollment grew rapidly in the first half of the 1990s, peaking in 1996 (**Figure 9-6**). Subsequently, PPO and POS plans became more popular. HMOs fell into disfavor with enrollees because these plans were the most restrictive regarding choice of providers and utilization controls. Lately, however, HMO enrollment has been rising, albeit at a slow pace. The reason for the rise is very likely lower out-of-pocket costs compared with other plans, but perhaps also the fact that many HMOs have eliminated the gatekeeping requirement to access specialists. Conversely, the majority of Medicaid beneficiaries have been enrolled in HMO plans (discussed in the section "Medicaid Enrollment").

Four HMO models are commonly used: staff, group, network, and independent practice association (IPA). These models differ primarily in their arrangements with participating physicians. Some HMOs cannot be categorized neatly into any one of the four models because they may use a hybrid arrangement, referred to as a **mixed model**. An example of a mixed model is an HMO that is partially organized as a staff model, employing its own physicians, and partially relying on the group model by contracting with a group practice.

Staff Model

A **staff model** HMO employs its own salaried physicians. Based on the physician's productivity and the HMO's performance, bonuses may be added to the physician's salary. Staff model HMOs must employ physicians in all the common specialties to provide for the range of healthcare needs of their members. Contracts with selected subspecialties are established for infrequently needed services. The HMO operates one or more ambulatory care facilities that contain physicians' offices; employs support staff; and may have ancillary support facilities, such as laboratory and radiology departments. Inpatient services are often contracted out by the HMO.

Compared with other HMO models, staff model HMOs can exercise a greater degree of control over the practice patterns of their physicians. These HMOs also offer the convenience of "one-stop shopping" for their enrollees

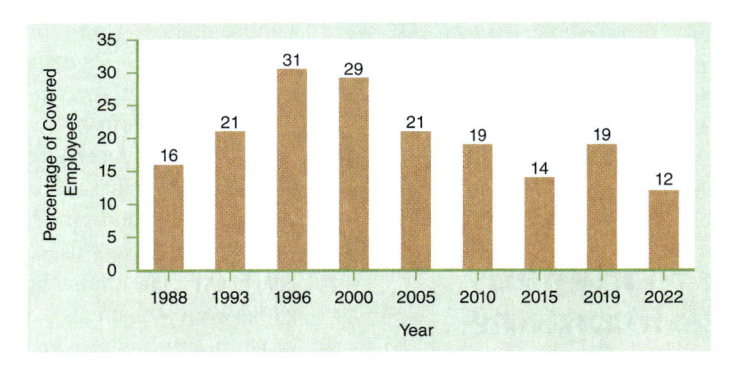

Figure 9-6 Percentage of covered employees enrolled in HMO plans, selected years.

Data from Claxton, G., et al. 2019. Employer health benefits: 2019 annual survey. Henry J. Kaiser Family Foundation. Menlo Park, CA: Author. 2022 data from: KFF Employer Health Benefits Survey, 2021; Kaiser/HRET Survey of Employer-Sponsored Health Benefits, 2011, 2016, and 2021. https://www.kff.org/report-section/ehbs-2021-summary-of-findings/

because most routinely needed services are located in the same clinic (Wagner, 1995).

Staff model HMOs also present several disadvantages. The fixed salary expense can be high, requiring these HMOs to have a large number of enrollees to cover their operating expenses. Enrollees may also have a limited choice of physicians. When expanding into new markets, a staff model HMO requires heavy capital outlays (Wagner, 1995). Because of such disadvantages, the staff model has been the least popular of the four models.

Group Model

A **group model** HMO contracts with a single multispecialty group practice and contracts separately with one or more hospitals to provide comprehensive services to its members. The group practice employs the physicians rather than the HMO. The HMO pays an all-inclusive capitation fee to the group practice to provide physician services to its members, but the group practice may have contracts with other MCOs as well.

Large groups are usually attractive to HMOs because they deliver a large block of physicians with one contract. However, a large group contract can also be a downside for the HMO. If the contract is lost, the HMO will have difficulty meeting its service obligations to the enrollees.

Another advantage is that the group model HMO is able to avoid large expenditures in fixed salaries and facilities. Affiliation with a reputable multispecialty group practice lends the HMO prestige and creates a perception of quality among its enrollees. On the downside, enrollees may find the choice of physicians too limited.

Network Model

Under the **network model**, the HMO contracts with more than one medical group practice. This model is especially adaptable to large metropolitan areas and widespread geographic regions where group practices are located. Each group is paid a capitation fee based on the number of enrollees and is responsible for providing all physician services to those individuals. The network model can offer a wider choice of physicians than either the staff or group model. Its main disadvantage is the dilution of utilization control.

Independent Practice Association Model

In 1954, a variant of the prepaid group practice plan was established by the San Joaquin County Foundation for Medical Care in Stockton, California. This plan, which was a prototype of the **IPA model**, was initiated by the San Joaquin County Medical Society (MacColl, 1966). As a result of political pressures from organized medicine, this form of HMO was specifically included in the HMO Act of 1973 (Mackie and Decker, 1981).

An **independent practice association (IPA)** is a legal entity separate from the HMO. The IPA contracts with both independent solo practitioners and group practices. The HMO then contracts with the IPA instead of contracting with individual physicians or group practices (**Figure 9-7**). Hence, the IPA is an intermediary representing a large number of physicians. The HMO pays a capitation amount to the IPA, but the IPA retains administrative control over how it pays its physicians. For example, it may reimburse physicians through capitation, or it may use some other means, such as a modified fee-for-service arrangement.

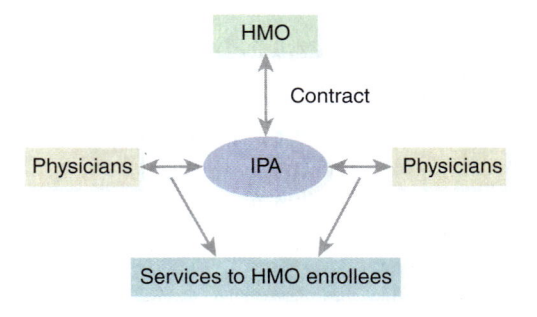

Figure 9-7 The IPA-HMO model.

The IPA often shares risk with the physicians and assumes the responsibility for utilization management and quality assessment.

Under the IPA model, the HMO is still responsible for providing healthcare services to its enrollees, but the logistics of arranging physician services shift to the IPA. This approach relieves the HMO of the administrative burden of establishing contracts with numerous providers and managing utilization. Financial risk also transfers to the IPA. The IPA model provides an expanded choice of providers to enrollees. IPAs can grow rapidly without the cost of purchasing physician practices, and they allow the physicians to remain independent (Casalino and Chenven, 2017). A major advantage for small- or medium-size physician practices is the sharing of care management and information technology resources with other practices through the IPA (Casalino et al., 2013).

A major disadvantage of the IPA model is that, if a contract is lost, the HMO loses a large number of participating physicians. The IPA acts as a buffer between the HMO and physicians. Hence, the IPA does not have as much leverage in changing physician behavior as a staff or a group model HMO would have.

Of the four HMO models, the IPA model has been the most successful in terms of the share of all enrollments over time. Its success likely reflects the wider choice of physicians that the enrollees have and the buffer an IPA creates between the HMO and its practicing physicians.

Preferred Provider Organization

A **preferred provider organization (PPO)** is distinguished from other types of managed care plans by the following main characteristics:

- The PPO establishes contracts with a select group of physicians and hospitals. These providers on the PPO's panel are referred to as "preferred providers."
- Generally, the PPO includes an open-panel option, in which the enrollee can use out-of-network providers but incurs higher cost sharing for doing so. The additional out-of-pocket expenses serve as a deterrent to going outside the panel. If a PPO does not provide an out-of-network option, it is referred to as an **exclusive provider plan**.
- Instead of using capitation as a method of payment, PPOs make discounted fee arrangements with providers. The discounts can be 35% or more of the providers' established charges. Negotiated payment arrangements with hospitals can be based on diagnosis-related groups (DRGs), bundled charges for certain services, or discounts. Hence, no direct risk sharing with providers is involved.
- PPOs apply fewer restrictions to the care-seeking behavior of enrollees. In most instances, no primary-care gatekeeping is implemented. Prior authorization (retrospective UR) is generally employed only for hospitalization and high-cost outpatient procedures (Robinson, 2002).

Insurance companies (including Blue Cross/Blue Shield), independent investors, and hospital alliances own most PPOs. Other PPOs are owned by HMOs, and some are jointly sponsored by a hospital and physicians (refer to **Exhibit 9-2** for characteristics of provider-sponsored health plans). As a less stringent choice of managed care for both enrollees and providers, PPOs have enjoyed remarkable success. After reaching their peak enrollment of 61% of covered employees in 2005 (**Figure 9-8**), enrollment in PPOs has declined as high-deductible health plans (HDHPs) have gained popularity in recent years.

Point-of-Service Plans

A **point-of-service (POS) plan** combines features of classic HMOs with some of the characteristics of patient choice found in

Exhibit 9-2 Characteristics of Provider-sponsored Health Plans

Provider-sponsored health plans (PSHPs) are health plans owned by a hospital or integrated health system licensed by the appropriate state regulatory agency/department that contract with employers, individuals, or Medicare and Medicaid (Keckley et al., 2015).

Quality

- **High quality of care:** Provider-sponsored health plans in the health insurance marketplaces are associated with higher-quality care, as measured by CMS clinical quality measures (Cai et al., 2022).
- **Enhanced patient relationships:** Members of a PSHP are the same patients that health system clinicians assist every day in their offices. This relationship facilitates trust and collaboration with members (Johns Hopkins Medicine, 2023). By affiliation with a local health system, the PSHP benefits from established familiarity, enhancing members' adherence, self-care and better health outcomes.

Effectiveness

- **More integrated approach:** Using care coordination and care management strategies, PSHP can more deftly assist with communication between primary-care providers and specialists, and improve information sharing (Johns Hopkins Medicine, 2023). This enhanced integration can improve the quality of the care and reduce costs, while providing an optimal experience to members and patients.
- **Inherent value-based care:** PSHPs break the constraints of fee-for-service payment models with an inherent value-based structure, incentivizing care to be delivered efficiently and effectively, including using virtual and team-based care (Johns Hopkins Medicine, 2023). PSP payment incentives are better aligned for investing in preventive care and quality improvement. This can encourage cost-effective care delivery and better patient outcomes.

Cost

- **Cost Savings:** Some PSHPs claim to offer cost savings by reducing administrative expenses and eliminating the need for a third-party insurer (Breon, 2016). Lower overhead costs may translate to lower premiums for plan members.
- **Potential for Higher Costs:** On the other hand, if the provider network is limited to a specific health system, it may limit choices for patients and could potentially lead to higher costs if out-of-network care is needed (O'Connor, 2018).

Data from Keckley, P. H., Karp, M., & Nugent, M. (2015). The Performance of Provider-Sponsored Health Plans: Key Findings, Strategic Implications. Navigant Center for Healthcare Research and Policy Analysis, 2018-11; Cai, S. T., Anderson, D., Drake, C., & Abraham, J. M. (2022). Association Between Provider-Sponsored Health Plan Ownership and Health Insurance Marketplace Plan Quality. Journal of general internal medicine, 37(14), 3603-3610; Johns Hopkins Medicine. (2023, July 10). Three Critical Advantages of Provider-Sponsored Health Plans. Johns Hopkins Health Plans. https://www.hopkinsmedicine.org/johns-hopkins-health-plans/news/three-critical-advantages-provider-sponsored-health-plans; Breon R. C. (2016). Provider-Sponsored Health Plans: Lessons Learned over Three Decades. Frontiers of health services management, 33(1), 3–15; O'Connor, S. J. (2018). Provider Sponsored Insurance: A Scoping Review. Journal of Accounting and Finance, 18(2), 175.

PPOs. Hence, these plans are a type of hybrid plan, also referred to as open-ended HMOs. When first brought on the market, these plans had a two-pronged objective: (1) retain the benefits of tight utilization management found in HMOs but (2) offer an alternative to their unpopular feature of restricted provider choice. The features borrowed from HMOs were capitation or other risk-sharing payment arrangements with providers and the gatekeeping method of utilization control. The feature borrowed from PPOs was the patient's ability to choose between an in-network or out-of-network provider at the point (time)

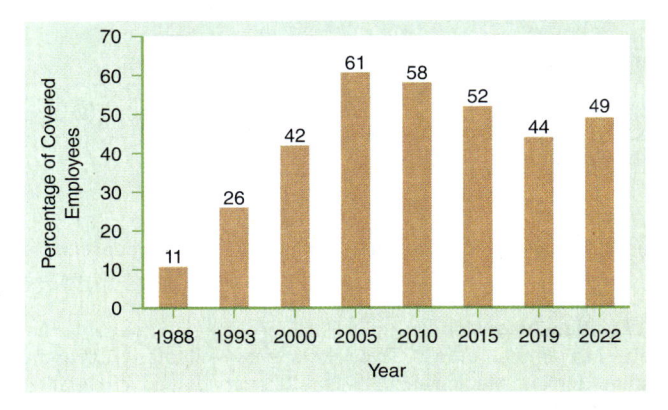

Figure 9-8 Percentage of covered employees enrolled in PPO plans, selected years.

Data from Claxton, G., et al. 2019. Employer health benefits: 2019 annual survey. Henry J. Kaiser Family Foundation. Menlo Park, CA: Author. 2022 data from: KFF Employer Health Benefits Survey, 2021; Kaiser/HRET Survey of Employer-Sponsored Health Benefits, 2011, 2016, and 2021. https:///www.kff.org/report-section/ehbs-2021-summary-of-findings/

of receiving services—hence, the name "point of service." Triple-option plans are also, in essence, point-of-service plans.

POS plans grew in popularity soon after they first emerged in 1988. Over time, as HMOs relaxed some of their utilization control practices and as PPOs, which already offered a choice of providers, proliferated, the need for a hybrid plan became less important to consumers. After reaching its peak in 1999, employee enrollment in POS plans declined sharply (**Figure 9-9**).

Trends in Managed Care

Managed care is now a mature industry in the United States. In the employment-based health insurance market, indemnity insurance has almost entirely disappeared. In the public sector, states have increasingly enrolled Medicaid beneficiaries in managed care plans. Medicare beneficiaries have also found value for their premium dollars by enrolling in Medicare Advantage (MA) plans.

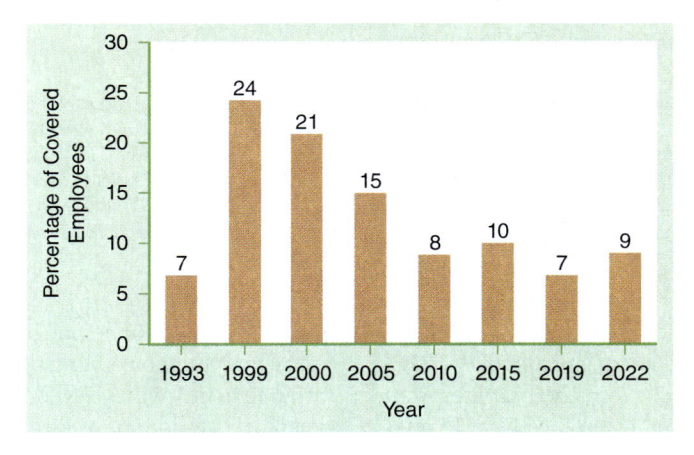

Figure 9-9 Percentage of covered employees enrolled in POS plans, selected years.

Data from Claxton, G., et al. 2019. Employer health benefits: 2019 annual survey. Henry J. Kaiser Family Foundation. Menlo Park, CA: Author. 2022 data from: KFF Employer Health Benefits Survey, 2021; Kaiser/HRET Survey of Employer-Sponsored Health Benefits, 2011, 2016, and 2021. https:///www.kff.org/report-section/ehbs-2021-summary-of-findings/

Employment-Based Health Insurance Enrollment

PPOs continue to dominate employment-based health insurance enrollments (**Figure 9-10**). HDHPs continue to gain momentum and are particularly attractive for young, healthy individuals and families. An HDHP can be a managed care plan but carries higher deductibles than other plans.

Medicaid Enrollment

Waivers under the Social Security Act, particularly sections 1115 and 1915(b), first allowed states to enroll their Medicaid recipients in managed care plans. Subsequently, the Balanced Budget Act of 1997 gave states the authority to implement mandatory managed care programs without requiring federal waivers (Moscovice et al., 1998). As a result, enrollment of Medicaid beneficiaries in HMOs has grown rapidly, from 56% of all Medicaid beneficiaries in 2000 to almost 88% in 2017 (Sanofi-Aventis, 2013; Sanofi-Aventis/Forte Information Resources, 2019). The influx of new individuals covered by Medicaid into the U.S. healthcare market under the ACA is responsible for much of the increase in recent years (Sabik et al., 2020). The managed care penetration rate for Medicaid was 77% in 2010 and 2011 (Sanofi-Aventis/Forte Information Resources, 2019), before the ACA became effective. Medicaid enrollment in comprehensive managed care organizations (MCOs) increased by 15.4 percent – from 58.5 million in 2020 to 67.6 million in 2021. Many states suggested that the increases in enrollment at least partly resulted from the temporary enrollment continuity provisions put in place in response to the COVID-19 Public Health Emergency (PHE) (CMS, 2023).

Many states have implemented a different model of managing healthcare delivery, particularly in rural areas where managed care has not flourished. Medicaid **primary-care case management (PCCM)** is a model in which state Medicaid agencies contract with PCPs to provide and coordinate all needed care for Medicaid beneficiaries who select them or are assigned to them by the state. The PCP is paid a monthly case management fee in addition to regular fee-for-service payments, unlike in risk-based managed care, where payments are based on capitation (Henry J. Kaiser Family Foundation, 2015). PCCM appears to play an important role in determining whether enrollees receive preventive screenings, such as mammograms (Sabik et al., 2020). For Medicaid recipients, care coordination is also higher in PCCM than in HMO plans (Gilchrist-Scott et al., 2017).

Medicare Enrollment

Medicare beneficiaries have the option to enroll in Medicare Advantage (MA; Part C of Medicare) or remain in the original fee-for-service program. The MA alternative gives

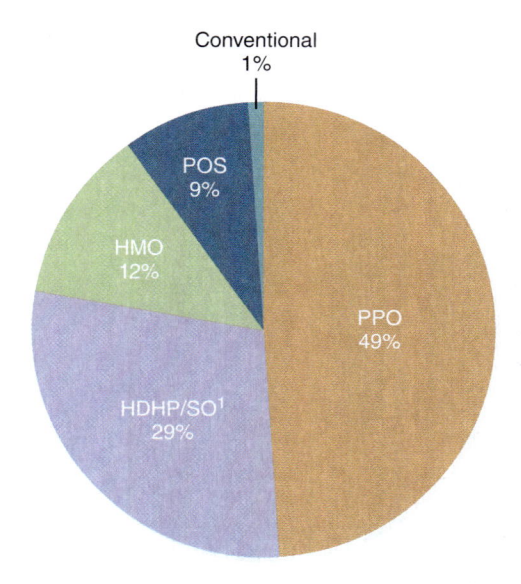

Figure 9-10 Share of managed care enrollments in employer-based health plans.

Conventional 1%
POS 9%
HMO 12%
PPO 49%
HDHP/SO[1] 29%

Data from Claxton, G., et al. 2019. Employer health benefits: 2019 annual survey. Henry J. Kaiser Family Foundation. Menlo Park, CA: Author. 2022 data from: KFF Employer Health Benefits Survey, 2021; Kaiser/HRET Survey of Employer-Sponsored Health Benefits, 2011, 2016, and 2021. https:/// www.kff.org/report-section/ehbs-2021-summary-of-findings/

Medicare beneficiaries the choice of enrolling in a managed care plan.

Over the years, enrollments in Part C have fluctuated according to capitation payments by Medicare to participating MCOs. Payment policies have shifted alongside political persuasions, competition and choice, bargaining power of private plans, quality improvement, and cost containment (Adrion, 2020). Nevertheless, enrollment in MA plans has grown steadily; it more than doubled between 2008 and 2018. In 2020, 36% of all Medicare beneficiaries were enrolled in Part C (**Figure 9-11**).

Impact on Cost, Access, and Quality

The growth of managed care in both the private and public health insurance sectors provides ample testimony to the widely held belief that managed care provides cost savings and better value for money than traditional indemnity insurance. Even as managed care has become the primary vehicle for providing health insurance through employers and to a large extent through Medicaid, Medicare has remained an open field for studying differences between managed care and indemnity insurance.

Influence on Cost Containment

Managed care has been widely credited with slowing the rate of growth in healthcare expenditures during the 1990s. In the insurance sector, growth rates for premiums slowed during the first half of the 1990s, and by 1996 they had fallen below the rate of inflation (Morrisey and Ohsfeldt, 2003). In the provider sector, Shen and colleagues (2010) reported that higher HMO penetration was associated with significant reductions in both costs and revenues for hospitals. However, subsequent to 2000, the relationship appeared to become weaker, which also coincided with the weakening power of managed care.

Eventually, a backlash from both enrollees and providers prompted MCOs to back away from aggressive cost-control measures. Hence, the full cost-containment potential of managed care was never realized. For example, the "any willing provider" laws and patient protection

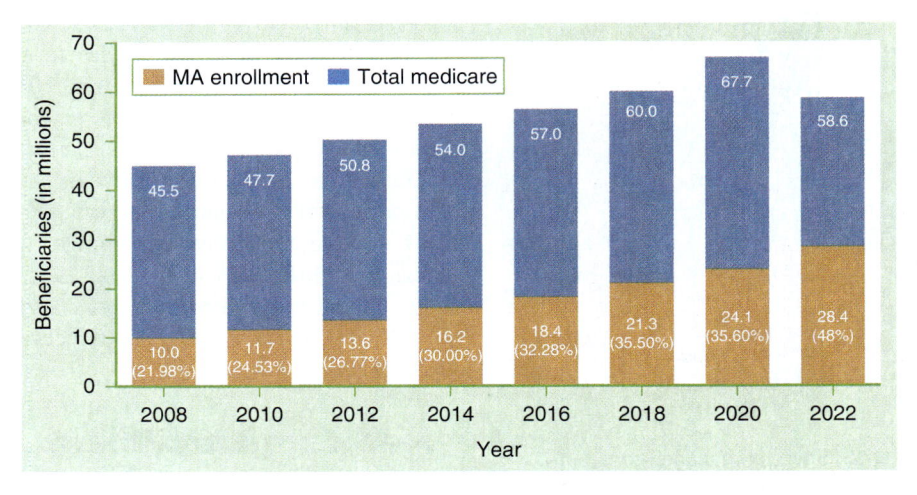

Figure 9-11 Beneficiaries (in millions) in Medicare Advantage Plans, Selected Years.

Data from Sanofi-Aventis/Forte Information Resources. 2019. Public payer digest: Trends in chronic disease management. Managed digest series, 2019. Bridgewater, NJ: Author. 2020 data are from Freed, M., et al. 2020. A dozen facts about Medicare Advantage in 2020. Kaiser Family Foundation. Available at: https://www.kff.org/medicare/issue-brief/a-dozen-facts-about-medicare-advantage-in-2020. Accessed August 2020. 2022 data from KFF Analysis of CMS Medicare Advantage Enrollment Files, 2010-2022; Medicare Choice Conditions (CCW) Data Warehouse from 5% of beneficiaries, 2010-2017; CCW data from 20% of beneficiaries.

laws (discussed in the section "Historical Managed Care Backlash and the Aftermath") passed by many states caused premiums to rise and reversed any gains in cost containment made by MCOs (Dugan, 2015). More recently, the phenomenal growth in the number of Medicaid beneficiaries enrolled in HMOs has resulted in cost savings. Perez (2018) estimated that a 10% increase of managed care enrollment reduces state Medicaid spending by almost 3%, or approximately $55 million.

The cost-containment effects of MA programs have remained controversial. Nevertheless, some evidence indicate that increased enrollment in MA plans may have a role in moderating fee-for-service Medicare costs—a spillover effect of managed care into the fee-for-service realm. It is believed that the same providers treat both categories of patients, and the pressure on providers in MA plans to change physicians' care patterns may transfer over to all Medicare patients (Johnson et al., 2016). Baicker and Robbins (2015) have also reported on the spillover effects of managed care. They found that in areas with greater enrollment of Medicare beneficiaries in managed care, the non-managed care beneficiaries had fewer days in the hospital but more outpatient visits, which is consistent with a substitution of less expensive outpatient care for more expensive inpatient care.

Impact on Access

Managed care enrollees have good access to primary and preventive care. Baker and colleagues (2004) found that timely breast cancer and cervical cancer screening was twice as likely to occur among women receiving services in geographic areas with a greater HMO market share, compared to women in areas with low managed care penetration. Studies have also reported similar findings on health screenings and diabetes care (Ayanian et al., 2013; Hung et al., 2016; Hinto et al., 2022; Ludomirsky et al., 2022). In MA plans, better access to primary care may have been responsible for lowering the risk of preventable hospitalizations. This effect has been particularly beneficial for ethnic/minority groups (Basu, 2012). For some minority groups, disparities in diabetes care are also found to be smaller in MA plans compared to fee-for-service Medicare (Mahmoudi et al., 2016).

In the ACA era, the influx of new patients covered by Medicaid into the managed care market has resulted in limited access to certain healthcare services. For example, Yan (2020) reported limited access to some high-tech obstetric services and high-quality hospital services by women needing obstetric care. Patients on Medicaid also faced barriers to obtaining specialty care because few specialists in MCO networks were accepting new patients and because of MCO administrative requirements for obtaining specialist consults (Timbie et al., 2019).

For mental health care, according to one study (Benson et al., 2020), participation of psychiatrists in health plans varied greatly—93% participated in commercial plans versus only 33% in Medicaid managed care plans. Conversely, one study suggested that Medicaid expansion had actually increased the availability of services for Medicaid recipients who had severe mental illness (Blunt et al., 2020). In addition, Medicaid expansion under the ACA has had a limited but positive impact on the utilization of mental health services by low-income Americans, although it may also have increased racial/ethnic disparities in this area (Breslau et al., 2020). It is possible that the increased access is associated with the substantial rise in emergency department use for mental health conditions by people who are on Medicaid (Theriault et al., 2020). The majority of mental health services are provided in primary-care settings, for which the evidence on access is mixed.

Overall, it appears that Medicaid managed care recipients have faced uneven access to primary-care services, particularly in areas where community health centers were not available (Melnikow et al., 2020). **Exhibit 9-3**

Exhibit 9-3 Access to Mental Health Services Under Managed Care

Benefits
- **Network of Providers:** MCOs typically have a network of healthcare providers, including mental health professionals like psychiatrists, psychologists, social workers, and counselors (Zhu et al., 2021). Access to mental health services is often limited to these in-network providers. Patients can usually find a list of these providers through the MCOs' website or customer service (Zhu et al., 2021).
- **Improved quality of care:** MCOs often emphasize care coordination, which can be beneficial for individuals with complex mental health needs (Schamess, 1996). This involves collaboration among various providers to ensure comprehensive care.
- **Reduced costs:** Many managed care plans require patients to make co-payments, which are fixed, out-of-pocket payments for each visit or service (Stadhouders et al., 2019). Consulting an in-network mental health provider typically results in lower out-of-pocket costs (Stadhouders et al., 2019). MCOs often negotiate discounted rates with their in-network providers. If a patient chooses to visit an out-of-network provider, the cost-sharing can be higher, and reimbursement rates may be lower. The co-payment for mental health services may differ from those of other medical services. Deductibles, on the other hand, represent the amount a patient must pay before their insurance coverage kicks in. High deductibles can be a barrier to accessing mental health care (Stadhouders et al., 2019).
- **Telehealth services:** Flexibility of network adequacy standards may also present opportunities to adapt to new mental healthcare delivery modalities, such as telehealth (Zhu et al., 2021). In light of the COVID-19 pandemic, state Medicaid programs have expanded coverage for telehealth and lifted restrictions on reimbursement for telehealth visits (Zhu et al., 2021). This allows patients to consult with mental health professionals remotely, improving access in underserved areas or for individuals who have difficulty accessing in-person care.

Challenges
- **Limited network:** One concern with managed care is the availability of mental health providers within the network (Madonna, 2020). If there are limited providers in a specific area, it can create barriers to access (Madonna, 2020). Some states have regulations to ensure that there are an adequate number of mental health providers in managed care networks (Madonna, 2020).

Data from Zhu, J. M., Breslau, J., & McConnell, K. J. (2021, May). Medicaid managed care network adequacy standards for mental health care access: balancing flexibility and accountability. In JAMA Health Forum (Vol. 2, No. 5, pp. e210280-e210280). American Medical Association; Schamess, G. (1996). Introduction: Who profits and who benefits from managed mental health care?; Stadhouders, N., Kruse, F., Tanke, M., Koolman, X., & Jeurissen, P. (2019). Effective healthcare cost-containment policies: a systematic review. Health Policy, 123(1), 71-79; Madonna, 2020.

summarizes access to mental health services under managed care.

Influence on Quality of Care

It is not surprising that quality varies across health plans; however, the overall quality of care in managed care plans has been found to be at least equivalent to that in traditional fee-for-service plans. Despite anecdotal evidence, individual perceptions, and isolated stories propagated by the news media during the 1990s, no comprehensive research has clearly demonstrated that managed care's growth came at the expense of quality in health care (Dugan 2020; Hinton et al., 2022). In fact, the evidence points mostly in the opposite direction. A comprehensive review of the literature by Miller and Luft (2002) concluded that HMO and non-HMO plans provided roughly equal quality of care, as measured for a wide range of conditions, diseases, and interventions. At the same time, HMOs were found to decrease the use of hospitals and other expensive resources. Hence, managed care plans have been cost-effective without the erosion of quality.

Higher managed care penetration has been associated with increased quality in hospitals based on indicators such as inappropriate utilization, wound infections, and iatrogenic complications (Sari, 2002). Studies comparing quality of care in Medicare fee-for-service and MA plans have shown that the level of quality, as evaluated by breast cancer screening, quality of diabetes care, cholesterol screening, testing for cardiovascular disease, and various HEDIS measures, is significantly higher in MA plans (Ayanian et al., 2013; Brennan and Shepard, 2010). MA plans are also associated with a reduction in preventable hospitalizations—for example, for urinary tract infections that can be detected early and treated with medications (Nicholas, 2013). Expansion of Medicaid eligibility under the ACA has had no observable negative impact on Medicaid managed care plans' reported quality on widely used performance indicators. Nonetheless, there remains considerable variation in the quality of care delivered to Medicaid managed care recipients (Ndumele et al., 2018).

One troubling note is the mental/behavioral health disparities in quality that have been noted across racial/ethnic groups in MA plans (Breslau et al., 2018). Research on the quality of mental health services delivered to Medicaid recipients is largely lacking, however. According to clinicians who specialize in treating patients with human immunodeficiency virus (HIV), quality of care for these patients covered by Medicaid may have improved, although barriers remain (McManus et al., 2020).

Historical Managed Care Backlash and the Aftermath

The large-scale transition of healthcare delivery to managed care in the 1990s was met with widespread criticism, which turned into a backlash from consumers, physicians, and legislators across the United States. Three main reasons were behind the discontentment, and the ensuing widespread media frenzy which further shaped unsympathetic public opinion toward managed care.

First, a large number of employees experienced at least some loss of freedom to choose their providers after the employers dropped the traditional indemnity plans that had allowed enrollees to choose any physician or hospital.

Second, the insured did not experience a reduction in their own share of the premium costs or a drop in their out-of-pocket expenses under managed care.

Third, when faced with tight utilization management from MCOs, physicians became openly hostile toward managed care. In national surveys, managed care penetration was found to be negatively correlated with physicians' satisfaction (Landon et al., 2003). Much of this discontent stemmed from the pressure to change the way physicians had traditionally practiced medicine, which had not included any accountability for appropriateness of utilization and costs. Physicians' vocal discontent no doubt also influenced patients' views about managed care.

Ultimately, as the momentum continued to shift toward enrollment in managed care, physicians had little choice except to contract with managed care or face the prospect of losing patients. Employees had little choice except to enroll in managed care plans, personally bear significantly higher premium costs, or go without health insurance altogether. As this drama unfolded, employers largely remained passive, as their main objective of reducing their own premium costs had been attained.

In response to widespread complaints and negative publicity about managed care, numerous "patient protection laws" were passed, mainly by the states. Naturally, the laws were not uniform throughout the nation. They differed in complexity and presented an administrative nightmare for insurers who sought to manage plans across the states. In general, however, it has been argued that laws were directly responsible for forcing MCOs to abandon or scale back their practices related to gatekeeping restrictions, financial incentives for physicians, and stringent utilization review that often questioned the medical necessity of certain services (Hall, 2005). The majority of MCO executives, however, did not believe that these laws had any remarkable effect on their practices. Instead, MCOs made certain accommodations in their practices from a business standpoint to gain market share. Moreover, certain practices could not be sustained because they did not achieve the anticipated savings (Hall, 2005). In the end, both regulatory and market forces may have had a combined effect on changing some of the managed care's behaviors and practices.

In addition to regulations that were designed to loosen up some of the restrictions for the enrollees, one group of laws in particular favored physicians. Known as "any willing provider laws," they require admission of any provider into a network as long as that provider can abide by the terms and conditions of network membership. A little more than half of all states have such statutes (Noble, 2014). Proponents of such laws argue that they broaden the choice of providers for consumers; opponents contend they raise costs and eliminate price competition. The latter charge arises because the laws weaken MCOs' ability to select providers on the basis of obtaining reduced prices in exchange for the volume of business the MCOs would bring to the providers.

In the aftermath of the backlash and anti-managed care laws, physicians and hospitals found bargaining power shifting in their direction, mainly through organizational integration. Many providers were able to push back on MCOs by terminating contracts or negotiating more favorable payment arrangements (Short et al., 2001; Strunk et al., 2001).

The balance achieved between the bargaining powers of MCOs on the one hand and providers on the other has left consumers in the middle. Employers have been forced to absorb the lion's share of rising premiums; they, in turn, have passed some of those costs on to their employees through higher cost sharing.

Organizational Integration

The term organizational integration refers to various strategies that healthcare organizations employ to achieve economies of operation, diversify their existing operations by offering new products or services, or gain market share. In the United States, the integration movement began with hospital mergers and acquisitions during the 1990s and early 2000s—a phenomenon that was national in scope. Since then, the integration movement has accelerated.

Numerous factors can drive hospital consolidation, such as technology, effects of reimbursement, and growth of services in alternative delivery settings, but the role of managed care cannot be underestimated. For instance, some evidence indicate that hospitals gained increased pricing power over MCOs subsequent to consolidations (Capps and Dranove, 2004). Ginsburg (2005) reached the same conclusion: "Hospitals correctly perceived that by merging with others in the same community, they would increase their leverage with health plans" (p. 1514). Physician groups also sought to align themselves with hospitals to maintain their autonomy and find refuge from the growing influence of managed care.

More recently, the move toward alternative reimbursement models such as value-based payments, aimed at promoting accountability of organizations for both cost and quality, has been cited as a driver for organizational integration (Ouayogodé et al., 2020). For example, changes in payment models, along with penalties for readmissions after patients are initially discharged, may incentivize hospitals to vertically integrate into subacute-care services (Hogan et al., 2019). Such a strategy is referred to as **diversification**, which is the addition of new services that the organization had not offered before.

The highly integrated Kaiser Permanente model, which has been in use in California since the 1940s, has long been known for its cost-effective care and delivery of high-quality services to its enrollees. This model has even influenced the mindsets and policy development within many European healthcare systems (Strandberg-Larsen et al., 2007).

Integration Strategies

Various integration strategies are illustrated in **Figure 9-12**. Three strategies are especially popular: (1) outright ownership, such as through a merger or acquisition; (2) joining hands with another organization in the common ownership of an entity; or (3) having a stake in an organization without owning it.

Mergers and Acquisitions

Mergers and acquisitions involve integration of existing assets. **Acquisition** refers to the purchase of one organization by another.

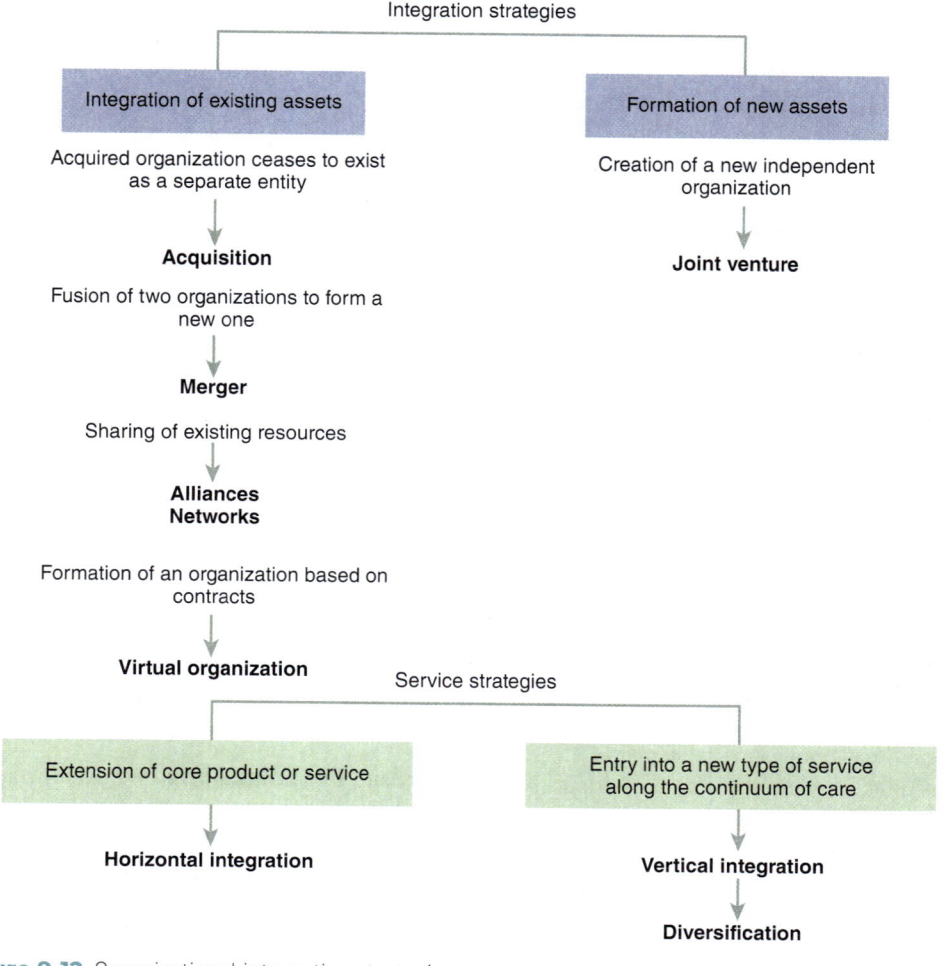

Figure 9-12 Organizational integration strategies.

The acquired company ceases to exist as a separate entity and is absorbed into the purchasing corporation. A **merger** involves a mutual agreement to unify two or more organizations into a single entity. The separate assets of two organizations are consolidated, typically under a new name. Both entities cease to exist, and a new corporation forms. A merger requires the willingness of all parties after they have assessed the advantages and disadvantages of merging their organizations.

Small hospitals may merge to gain efficiencies by eliminating duplication of services. A large hospital may acquire smaller hospitals to serve as satellites in a major metropolitan area with sprawling suburbs. A regional health system may form after a large hospital has acquired smaller hospitals and certain providers of long-term care, outpatient care, and rehabilitation to diversify its services. Multifacility nursing home chains and home health firms often acquire other facilities as a means to enter new geographic markets.

Joint Ventures

A **joint venture** is formed when two or more institutions share resources to create a new organization to pursue a common purpose (Pelfrey and Theisen, 1989). Each partner in a joint venture continues to conduct business independently. The new company created by the partners also remains independent.

Joint ventures are often used as a diversification strategy when the new service can benefit all the partners and when competing against each other for that service would be undesirable. For example, hospitals in a given region may engage in a joint venture to form a home health agency that benefits all partners. An acute-care hospital, a multispecialty physician group practice, a skilled nursing facility, and an insurer may join hands to offer a managed care plan (Carson et al., 1995). In this case, each of the participants continues to operate its own business, but they all have a common stake in the new MCO.

Alliances

In one respect, the healthcare industry is unique in that organizations often develop cooperative arrangements with rival providers. Cooperation instead of competition, in some situations, eliminates duplication of services while ensuring that all the health needs of the community are fulfilled (Carson et al., 1995). An **alliance** is an agreement between two or more organizations to share their existing resources without joint ownership of assets.

The main advantages of alliances are threefold:

- Alliances are relatively simple to form.
- Alliances provide the opportunity to evaluate the financial and legal ramifications of the arrangement before a potential "marriage" takes place. In essence, forming an alliance gives organizations the opportunity to evaluate the advantages of an eventual merger.
- Alliances require little financial commitment and can be easily dissolved, similar to an engagement prior to a marriage.

Even when a merger is not contemplated, alliance members can reap the benefits of consolidation while maintaining their independence (Butcher, 2016).

Networks. A network is formed through alliances with numerous providers. It is built around a core organization, such as an MCO, a hospital, or a large group practice. An IPA is also a type of network in which physicians are brought under the umbrella of a nonphysician organization.

Virtual Organizations. When contractual arrangements between organizations form a new organization, the result is referred to as a virtual organization or an organization without walls. The formation of networks based on contractual arrangements is called **virtual integration**. IPAs are a prime example of virtual organizations. These organizations bring together scattered entities under one mutually cooperative arrangement. Little or no capital is necessary to form such an organization.

Service Strategies

Horizontal Integration

Horizontal integration is a growth strategy in which a healthcare delivery organization extends its core product or service. Commonly, the new services are similar to or substitutes for existing services. Horizontal integration may be achieved through internal development, acquisition, or merger. Horizontally linked organizations may be closely coupled through ownership or loosely coupled through alliances. The main objective of horizontal integration is to control the geographic distribution of a certain type of healthcare service. For example, multihospital chains, nursing facility chains, or a chain of drugstores, under the same management, with member facilities offering the same core services or products, are horizontally integrated. Diversification into new products and/or services is not achieved through horizontal integration.

Vertical Integration

Vertical integration links services at different stages in the production process of health care—for example, integration of primary-care, acute-care, postacute services, and a hospital. The main objective of vertical integration is to increase the comprehensiveness and continuity of care across a continuum of healthcare services. Hence, vertical integration is a diversification strategy.

Vertical integration may be achieved through acquisitions, mergers, joint ventures, or alliances. Formation of networks and virtual organizations can also involve vertical integration. Vertically integrated regional health systems may be the best-positioned organizations to become the providers of choice for managed care or for direct contracting with self-insured employers (Brown, 1996).

Basic Forms of Integration

The major participants in organizational integration have traditionally been physicians and hospitals. However, other entities may also be involved.

Management Services Organizations

In a complex healthcare landscape, a **management services organization (MSO)** can supply management expertise, administrative tools, and information technology to physician practices and small or independent hospitals. Certain MSOs operate mainly to acquire existing clinical organizations. Other MSOs simply provide business expertise without taking ownership of the clinic or hospital, generally under a long-term contract (Hernandez and Salber, 2020).

Physician–Hospital Organizations

A **physician-hospital organization (PHO)** is a legal entity that forms an alliance between a hospital and local physicians. In addition to contracting with MCOs, if a PHO is large enough, it can contract its services directly to employers while engaging a third-party administrator to process claims. PHOs are also in a prime position to function as ACOs.

Today, hospitals seem to be in the driver's seat, as physicians are increasingly turning to hospitals for financial support. There has been a significant and consistent growth in the number of physicians employed by hospitals. Between 2012 and 2018, physician employment by hospitals increased by 70% in all regions of the United States. In January 2018, 44% of all physicians (almost 170,000) were employed by hospitals, mainly through acquisition of physician practices (Physicians Advocacy Institute, 2019). Empirical evidence suggests that hospital-owned PHOs incur higher costs compared with physician practices without any demonstrable improvement in quality (Ho et al., 2020; Post et al., 2018).

Provider-Sponsored Organizations

A **provider-sponsored organization (PSO)** is a risk-bearing entity that incorporates the insurance function into integrated clinical care delivery. PSOs may be sponsored by physicians, by hospitals, or jointly by physicians and hospitals, and offer provider-sponsored health plans (PSHPs) directly to employers and public payers. Thus, they compete with regular MCOs.

PSOs attracted national attention in 1996 when Congress proposed that PSOs could legitimately participate in Medicare risk contracts. Later, the Balanced Budget Act of 1997 opened up the Medicare market to PSOs as an option to HMOs under the Medicare+Choice program (the precursor to MA). The Balanced Budget Act also required these entities to carry adequate coverage for risk protection.

The initial appeal of PSOs was their promise to deal with patients directly rather than through contracted arrangements, as an HMO would. However, after they suffered financial losses, PSOs failed in large numbers. In many instances, larger HMOs acquired PSOs. One major reason for PSO failures has been their lack of experience with risk management (the insurance function).

More recently, provider organizations have again begun seeking to sponsor their own health plans. As of 2016, there were approximately 270 PSHPs, a 25% increase over the previous five years (Bechtel and Greenwald, 2018). Notable provider-sponsored plans are operated by Kaiser Permanente in California, Geisinger Health in Pennsylvania, and HealthPartners in Minnesota (Winfield, 2018). Research shows that receipt of care within a PSHP may be associated with improved quality, effectiveness, and patient satisfaction, as well as lower procedure rates (Parekh et al., 2018).

Highly Integrated Healthcare Systems

Highly integrated systems are vertically integrated systems that generally include a hospital, a physician component that often includes multiple specialties, and at least one system-wide contract with a payer, such as Medicare, Medicaid, or an MCO. The payers may stipulate some responsibility for quality and cost.

The pace of organizational integration in the U.S. healthcare system has continued to intensify. The primary reasons for the drive toward integration include the ongoing evolution of the overall healthcare delivery system in the United States toward value-based payment models, collaborative care (also referred to as coordinated care, multidisciplinary care, or integrated care), and accountability for population health. This changing landscape necessitates some form of organizational integration, either through ownership or partnerships with other providers in a vertically integrated fashion, and linked through electronic health records (EHRs) and telemedicine when necessary.

Today's integrated delivery systems represent a step beyond managed care. MCOs may or may not be partners in this arrangement. Typically, MCOs have arranged to provide physical, mental/behavioral, and dental health services separately without coordination. In general, however, fragmentation of care results in higher costs and poorer outcomes. As an example, interhospital fragmented care, in which the same patient is admitted to different hospitals, is associated with increased mortality, longer length of stay, and increased risk of rehospitalization (Snow et al., 2020). In the ambulatory care setting, patients with cancer who receive services from multiple providers are less likely to undergo curative therapy when they are diagnosed at an early stage and have worse overall survival than those patients who receive coordinated services (Hester et al., 2019).

Integrated Delivery Systems

An **integrated delivery system (IDS)**, also called an "integrated delivery network," is a network of organizations that provides or arranges to provide a coordinated continuum of services to a defined population and is willing to be held clinically and fiscally accountable for the outcomes and health status of the population serviced (Shortell et al., 1993). An IDS encompasses various forms of ownership and other strategic linkages among hospitals, physicians, and insurers.

The U.S. integrated delivery network market size was valued at USD 1,309.1 billion in 2022 and is anticipated to grow at a CAGR of 10.1% over the forecast period from 2023 to 2030 (Grand View Research, 2023). IDSs were initially formed to vertically integrate healthcare services along the continuum of care, with the aim of offering one-stop shopping to MCOs. In an evolving healthcare system, they are now held clinically and fiscally accountable for the health status and outcomes for the population served. To achieve this goal, they need systems to manage and to improve clinical outcomes. Patient-centered care, collaborative care delivery, evidence-based protocols, disease management, and EHRs are at the heart of clinical management. IDSs may also include pharmaceutical management and telemedicine (Maeda et al., 2014). Although these factors may produce better care, vertical integration has been shown to result in higher prices and higher health insurance premiums (Scheffler et al., 2018). In some cases, IDSs have lowered healthcare utilization, but the anticipated cost savings have not materialized (Hwang et al., 2013). In other cases, IDSs may actually increase costs without any gains in quality (Kralewski et al., 2014).

Apart from their low socioeconomic status, people on Medicaid tend to have complex medical conditions (physical and developmental disabilities and/or multiple comorbid physical and behavioral health conditions) and often experience mixed results under Medicaid managed care, as previously discussed. One study reported on the experiences of patients covered by Medicaid in a large IDS that operates its own MCO. Using efficient care coordination, disease management, and case management strategies, Geisinger Health System (the largest IDS in central Pennsylvania, covering more than 170,000 Medicaid members) achieved lower inpatient and professional costs and reduced utilization of emergency department and urgent care sites (Maeng et al., 2016). In general, higher-quality organizations incorporate greater levels of care coordination, which is also associated with greater cost savings (Parasrampuria et al., 2018).

More recent studies have shown that the development of a more integrated, people-centered care system has the potential to bring significant benefits to health and the provision of health care for all, including improved access to care, enhanced ownership and clinical outcomes, improved health literacy and self-care, increased satisfaction with care services, increased job satisfaction among healthcare workers, improved service efficiency, and an overall cost reduction (Feng et al., 2021). Patients benefit from consistent care through integrated delivery systems (Sathian et al., 2022). They can receive care from primary-care providers, specialists, and other healthcare professionals within the same system, ensuring continuity and a holistic approach to their health needs (Sathian et al., 2022).

In response to COVID-19, especially in less affluent nations, low and middle-income countries predominantly embraced an integrated healthcare delivery system characterized by organized horizontal integration, driven by specific policy actions (Sathian et al., 2022). The principal facilitator of these integrated healthcare systems was effective government oversight, coupled with decentralized decision-making capabilities of local institutions and collaborative efforts across various sectors (Sathian et al., 2022).

Integrated delivery systems can also optimize resource utilization and eliminate redundant administrative costs (Hwang et al., 2013). IDSs were associated with lower cost of care (Hwang et al., 2013). Two studies found that clinical service integration in various forms of Accountable Care Organizations and large multispecialty group practices would lower cost of care (Veet et al., 2020).

Accountable Care Organizations

In a general sense, an **accountable care organization (ACO)** is an integrated group of providers who are willing and able to take responsibility for improving the overall health status, care efficiency, and satisfaction with care for a defined population (DeVore and Champion, 2011). **Exhibit 9-4** illustrates how providers may coordinate patient care.

Given that IDSs in their existing form did not quite achieve certain expected results, mainly in the area of cost savings, a need has arisen to arrange incentives geared toward achieving organizational, clinical, and financial integration. Such an arrangement was adopted in the ACA of 2010 for the purpose of delivering coordinated services to Medicare populations, but within the framework of value-based payments. A two-pronged approach was designed. First, financial incentives would bring together various providers—physicians, hospitals, and other clinicians—to form a virtual organization, called an ACO, in which the providers would collaborate to deliver care to a defined population of patients. To this end, a shared savings program was implemented in 2013 that authorized Medicare to pay bonuses to providers if an ACO achieved targeted cost savings while meeting defined quality objectives. Second, Medicare would assign patients not already covered by managed care to an ACO from which they would receive all needed services.

Exhibit 9-4 How Providers Coordinate Patient Care

- **Use of electronic health records:** Doctors can use the same platform for their electronic health records so that each provider can refer to and update a patient's medical history and communicate with the patient through an electronic app (Weiss et al., 2021).
- **Join an Accountable Care Organization (ACO):** Groups of doctors, hospitals, and other health care professionals join and work together in an ACO to give patients high-quality, coordinated service and health care, improve health outcomes, and manage costs (Centers for Medicare & Medicaid Services, n.d.). ACOs may be in a specific geographic area and/or focused on patients who have a specific condition, like chronic kidney disease. ACOs often help facilitate greater communication between primary-care doctors and specialists and may connect patients with social services.
- **Take part in a program or model:** Providers may take part in a CMS Innovation Center model, Medicare Shared Savings Program, or another program that supports care coordination (Centers for Medicare & Medicaid Services, n.d.). These programs may help advise on how doctors can work together and reward successful coordination that promotes better patient health.

Data from Weiss, E. F., Malik, R., Santos, T., Ceide, M., Cohen, J., Verghese, J., & Zwerling, J. L. (2021). Telehealth for the cognitively impaired older adult and their caregivers: lessons from a coordinated approach. Neurodegenerative disease management, 11(1), 83-89; Centers for Medicare & Medicaid Services. (n.d.). Care coordination. https://www.cms.gov/medicare/payment/fee-for-service-providers/shared-savings-program-ssp-acos/about

More recently, some states have started to experiment with alternative payment models and care delivery through ACOs to the states' Medicaid populations with the objectives of improving health outcomes and reducing expenditures. Early results appear promising (Rutledge et al., 2019). Some other countries have also introduced integrated, accountable care initiatives to tackle historical organizational and financial fragmentation (Pimperl et al., 2017).

Early evidence suggests that ACOs have achieved higher quality and lower costs (Kanter et al., 2019). Cost savings among high achievers have been driven by a reduced number of admissions to hospitals and skilled nursing facilities (Schulz et al., 2018). Overall, however, only modest savings have been achieved, and some of these savings have been returned to providers through shared savings bonuses (Chernew et al., 2020). Medicare bonus payments per ACO increased from $1.4 million in 2013 to $1.8 million in 2018; this represents an increase of almost 23%, compared to an increase of a little more than 10% in the number of Medicare members over the same period (Sanofi-Aventis/Forte Information Resources, 2020). Some evidence also suggests that ACOs with MCO contracts in the private market produce better value. They have higher quality scores at lower benchmark expenditures, compared with ACOs that have only public contracts with Medicare and Medicaid (Peiris et al., 2016).

Since 2012, the state of Oregon has formed a series of Coordinated Care Organizations—networks of providers that collaboratively deliver medical care, mental/behavioral health services, and dental care to the state's Medicaid population. This program resembles traditional Medicaid managed care in some ways, yet is different in other respects. Some of its key features include greater accountability, improved care coordination, community governance, global budgets that include all services, and incentives for improved outcomes (Howard et al., 2015). To date, the Oregon program has led to decreased opioid prescriptions compared with other states' Medicaid programs (Abraham, 2020), reduced infant mortality (Bui et al., 2019), and better access and quality as reported by members (Wright et al., 2019).

There were more than 1,600 active ACOs across the United States in 2023 (Definitive Healthcare, 2023). Today, ACOs remain in their infancy. Their eventual success or failure will depend on their ability to consistently deliver value and reduce the cost of health care. In certain markets, ACOs may also present antitrust concerns. **Antitrust** policy consists of federal and state laws that prohibit or regulate certain types of business practices that may stifle competition. The largest physician practices in most markets potentially remain at risk for antitrust review (Kleiner et al., 2017). This threat could limit ACOs' size and geographic reach and their ability to achieve economies of scale (Bacher et al., 2013).

Medicare Shared Savings Program

Medicare Shared Savings Program (Shared Savings Program) ACOs are groups of doctors, hospitals, and other healthcare providers who collaborate to give coordinated high-quality care to people with Medicare, focusing on delivering the right care at the right time while avoiding unnecessary services and medical errors (Centers for Medicare & Medicaid Service, 2023).

The Medicare Shared Savings Program (MSSP) was associated with modest reductions in Medicare spending, reduced inpatient utilization, reduced readmissions, improved preventive care, and improved patient experience (Huang et al., 2023). An increasing number of hospitals are participating in MSSP ACOs (Huang et al., 2023). MSSP participation was associated with differential increases in net patient revenue, Medicare revenue, inpatient revenue share, and Medicare revenue share, and a differential reduction in allowance and discount rate (Huang et al., 2023). Participation in MSSP ACOs was also associated with small savings for beneficiaries with serious mental illness (–$233 per person per year) in total healthcare spending, primarily related to savings from chronic medical conditions (excluding mental health; –$227 per person per year) and not from savings related to mental health services (–$6 per person per year) (Figueroa et al., 2022). Savings were driven by reductions in acute and postacute care for medical conditions (Figueroa et al., 2022).

Summary

Managed care evolved through the integration of the insurance function with the concepts of contract practice and prepaid group practice during the late 19th and early 20th centuries. Even though managed care has since become the dominant medium through which the vast majority of Americans obtain healthcare services, its full potential to achieve cost-effectiveness has often been thwarted by opposition from providers, consumers, and policymakers. Participation in the HEDIS program, however, has improved the quality of services provided by MCOs.

The growing power of managed care was one major factor that triggered integration among healthcare providers. The pace of integration between physicians, hospitals, and other providers has continued to accelerate in recent years. Highly integrated organizations are held accountable for achieving specific objectives related to costs, quality, and consumer satisfaction. Nevertheless, integrated delivery systems have not quite achieved the dual objectives of accountability and cost containment. The growth of accountable care organizations was triggered by the Affordable Care Act of 2010. Financial incentives removed the fragmentation that had existed between vertically integrated organizations for the purpose of delivering collaborative care. To date, these organizations have achieved modest cost savings and improvements in quality of care.

TEST YOUR UNDERSTANDING

Terminology

accountable care organization (ACO)
acquisition
alliance
antitrust
carve-out
case management
closed-panel
concurrent utilization review
discharge planning
disease management
diversification
efficiency
exclusive provider plan
fee schedule
formulary
group model
health maintenance organization (HMO)
horizontal integration
indemnity insurance
independent practice association (IPA)
integrated delivery system (IDS)
IPA model
joint venture
management services organization (MSO)
merger
mixed model
network model
open-panel
panel
physician-hospital organization (PHO)
point-of-service (POS) plan
practice profiling
preferred provider organization (PPO)

primary-care case management (PCCM)
prospective utilization review
provider-induced demand
provider-sponsored organization (PSO)
retrospective utilization review
staff model
triple-option plans
utilization review (UR)
vertical integration
virtual integration

Review Questions

1. What are some of the key differences between traditional indemnity insurance and managed care?
2. What are the three main payment mechanisms used in managed care? With each mechanism, who bears the risk?
3. Explain how the fee-for-service practice of medicine led to uncontrolled utilization.
4. How do MCOs achieve cost-efficiencies by integrating the quad functions, risk sharing with providers, and care coordination? What are some of the inefficiencies created by managed care?
5. Discuss the concept of utilization monitoring and control.
6. How does case management achieve efficiencies in the delivery of health care? How does case management differ from disease management?
7. Explain how MCOs engage in pharmaceutical management. How does utilization review apply to drug management?
8. Describe the three utilization review methods, giving appropriate examples. Discuss the benefits of each type of utilization review.
9. What is an HMO? How does it differ from a PPO?
10. Briefly explain the four main models for organizing an HMO. Discuss the advantages and disadvantages of each model.
11. What is a point-of-service plan? Why did it initially grow in popularity? What caused its subsequent decline?
12. To what extent has managed care been successful in containing healthcare costs?
13. Has the quality of health care declined as a result of managed care? Explain.
14. What is organizational integration? Why did healthcare organizations integrate?
15. What is the difference between a merger and an acquisition? What is the purpose of these organizational consolidations? Give examples.
16. When would a joint venture be considered a preferable integration strategy?
17. What is the main advantage of two organizations forming an alliance?
18. State the main strategic objectives of horizontal and vertical integration.
19. What is an accountable care organization? Describe its current status in U.S. healthcare delivery.

References

Abraham, A. J. 2020. Inappropriate Opioid Prescribing in Oregon's Coordinated Care Organizations. *Journal of Addiction Medicine* 14: 293–299.

Adrion, E. R. 2020. Politics and Policymaking in Medicare Part C. *Medical Care* 58: 285–292.

Angalakuditi, M., and J. Gomes. 2011. Retrospective Drug Utilization Review: Impact of Pharmacist Interventions on Physician Prescribing. *Clinicoeconomics and Outcomes Research* 3: 105–108.

Ayanian, J. Z., B. E. Landon, A. M. Zaslavsky, R. C. Saunders, L. G. Pawlson, and J. P. Newhouse. 2013. Medicare Beneficiaries More Likely to Receive Appropriate Ambulatory Services in HMOs Than in Traditional Medicare. *Health Affairs* 32: 1228–1235.

Bacher, G. E., M. E. Chernew, D. P. Kessler, and S.M. Weiner. 2013. Regulatory Neutrality Is Essential to Establishing a Level Playing Field for Accountable Care Organizations. *Health Affairs* 32: 1426–1432.

Baicker, K., and J. Robbins. 2015. Medicare Payments and System-Level Health-Care Use: The Spillover Effects of Medicare Managed Care. *American Journal of Health Economics* 1: 399–443.

Baker, L., K. A. Phillips, J. S. Haas, S.Y. Liang, and D. Sonneborn. 2004. The Effect of Area HMO Market Share on Cancer Screening. *Health Services Research* 39: 1751–1772.

Basu, J. 2012. Medicare Managed Care and Primary Care Quality: Examining Racial/Ethnic Effects across States. *Health Care Management Science* 15: 15–28.

Bechtel, A., and M. Greenwald. 2018. The Five Steps to Successfully Implementing a Provider- Sponsored Health Plan. *Health Management Technology* 39: 24.

Benson, N. M., C. Myong, J. P. Newhouse, V. Fung, and J. Hsu. 2020. Psychiatrist Participation in Private Health Insurance Markets: Paucity in the Land of Plenty. *Psychiatric Services* 71: 1232–1238.

Berk, M. L., and A. C. Monheit. 2001. The Concentration of Health Expenditures Revisited. *Health Affairs* 20: 9–18.

Blunt, E. O., J. C. Maclean, I. Popovici, and S. C. Marcus. 2020. Public Insurance Expansions and Mental Health Care Availability. *Health Services Research* 55: 615–625.

Borenstein, J., E. Badamgarav, J. M., Henning, A. D. Gano Jr, and S. S. Weingarten. 2004. The Association between Quality Improvement Activities Performed by Managed Care Organizations and Quality of Care. *American Journal of Medicine* 117: 297–304.

Brennan, N., and M. Shepard. 2010. Comparing Quality of Care in the Medicare Program. *American Journal of Managed Care* 16: 841–848.

Breon R. C. (2016). Provider-Sponsored Health Plans: Lessons Learned over Three Decades. *Frontiers of Health Services Management*, 33: 3–15.

Breslau, J., M. N. Elliott, A. M. Haviland, et al. 2018. Racial and Ethnic Differences in the Attainment of Behavioral Health Quality Measures in Medicare Advantage Plans. *Health Affairs* 37: 1685–1692.

Breslau, J., B. Han, J. Lai, and H. Yu . 2020. Impact of the Affordable Care Act Medicaid Expansion on Utilization of Mental Health Care. *Medical Care* 58: 757–762.

Brill, J. V. 2007. Trends in Prescription Drug Plans Delivering the Medicare Part D Prescription Drug Benefit. *American Journal of Health-System Pharmacy* 64: S3–S6.

Brown, M. 1996. Mergers, Networking, and Vertical Integration: Managed Care and Investor-Owned Hospitals. *Health Care Management Review* 21: 29–37.

Bui, L. N., J. Yoon, S. M. Harvey, and J. Luck. 2019. Coordinated Care Organizations and Mortality among Low-Income Infants in Oregon. *Health Services Research* 54: 1193–1202.

Butcher L. 2016. Building Alliances to Stay Independent. *Hospitals & Health Networks* 90: 46–52.

Cai, S. T., Anderson, D., Drake, C., and Abraham, J. M. 2022. Association between Provider-Sponsored Health Plan Ownership and Health Insurance Marketplace Plan Quality. *Journal of General Internal Medicine* 37: 3603–3610.

Capps, C., and D. Dranove. 2004. Hospital Consolidation and Negotiated PPO Prices. *Health Affairs* 23: 175–181.

Carson, K. D., P. P. Carson, and C. W. Roe. 1995. *Management of Healthcare Organizations*. Cincinnati, OH: South-Western College Publishing.

Casalino, L. P., and N. Chenven. 2017. Independent Practice Associations: Advantages and Disadvantages of an Alternative Form of Physician Practice Organization. *Healthcare (Amsterdam, Netherlands)* 5: 46–52.

Casalino, L. P., F. M. Wu, A. M. Ryan, et al. 2013. Independent Practice Associations and Physician-Hospital Organizations Can Improve Care Management for Smaller Practices. *Health Affairs* 32: 1376–1382.

Centers for Medicare & Medicaid Services (CMS). 2023. Medicaid Managed Care Enrollment and Program Characteristics, 2021. Accessed November 2023. Available at: https://www.medicaid.gov/sites/default/files/2023-07/2021-medicaid-managed-care-enrollment-report.pdf

Centers for Medicare & Medicaid Services. 2023. Shared Savings Program (SSP)/ACOs. Available at: https://www.cms.gov/medicare/payment/fee-for-service-providers/shared-savings-program-ssp-acos/about

Centers for Medicare & Medicaid Services. n.d. Care Coordination. Available at: https://www.cms.gov/medicare/payment/fee-for-service-providers/shared-savings-program-ssp-acos/about

Chen, C., D. McNeese-Smith, M. Cowan, V. Upenieks, and A. Afifi. 2009. Evaluation of a Nurse Practitioner–Led Care Management Model in Reducing Inpatient Drug Utilization and Cost. *Nursing Economics* 27: 160–168.

Daubresse, M., P. P. Gleason, Y. Peng, N. D. Shah, S. T. Ritter, and G. C. Alexander. 2013. Impact of a Drug Utilization Review Program on High-Risk Use of Prescription-Controlled Substances. *Pharmacoepidemiology and Drug Safety* 23: 419–427.

Definitive Healthcare. 2023. How Many Accountable Care Organizations (ACOs) Are in Each State? Accessed November 2023. Available at: https://www.definitivehc.com/resources/healthcare-insights/accountable-care-organizations-by-state

Delaney, L. D., V. Gunaseelan, H. Rieck, J. M. Dupree IV, B. R. Hallstrom, and J. F. Waljee. 2020. High-Risk

Prescribing Increases Rates of New Persistent Opioid Use in Total Hip Arthroplasty Patients. *Journal of Arthroplasty* 35: 2472–2479.

Deom, M., T. Agoritsas, P. A. Bovier, and T.V. Perneger 2010. What Doctors Think about the Impact of Managed Care Tools on Quality of Care, Costs, Autonomy, and Relations with Patients. *BMC Health Services Research* 10: 2–8.

DeVore, S., and R. W. Champion. 2011. Driving Population Health through Accountable Care Organizations. *Health Affairs* 30: 41–50.

Dugan, J. 2015. Trends in Managed Care Cost Containment: An Analysis of the Managed Care Backlash. *Health Economics* 24: 1604–1618.

Dugan, J. A. 2020. Fixed Effects Analysis of the Incidence of Cardiovascular Outcomes under Managed Care Following the Managed Care Backlash. *Medicine* 99.

Duijmelinck, D., and W. van de Ven. 2016. What Can Europe Learn from the Managed Care Backlash in the United States? *Health Policy (Amsterdam, Netherlands)* 120: 509–518.

Ehlert, A., and D. Oberschachtsiek. 2014. Does Managed Care Reduce Health Care Expenditure? Evidence from Spatial Panel Data. *International Journal of Health Care Finance & Economics* 14: 207–227.

Espinosa, O., P. Rodríguez-Lesmes, L. Orozco, et al. 2022. Estimating Cost-Effectiveness Thresholds under a Managed Healthcare System: Experiences from Colombia. *Health Policy and Planning* 37: 359–368.

Feng, W., X. Feng, P. Shen, et al. 2021. Influence of the Integrated Delivery System on the Medical Serviceability of Primary Hospitals. *Journal of Healthcare Engineering* 2021. 9950163.

Ferrone, M., M. G. Masciantonio, N. Malus, et al. 2019. The Impact of Integrated Disease Management in High-Risk COPD Patients in Primary Care. *NPJ Primary Care Respiratory Medicine* 29.

Figueroa, J. F., J. Phelan, H. Newton, E. J. Orav, and E. R. Meara, 2022. ACO Participation Associated with Decreased Spending for Medicare Beneficiaries with Serious Mental Illness. *Health Affairs* 41: 1182–1190.

Gilchrist-Scott, D. H., J. A. Feinstein, and R. Agrawal. 2017. Medicaid Managed Care Structures and Care Coordination. *Pediatrics* 140.

Ginsburg, P. B. 2005. Competition in Health Care: Its Evolution over the Past Decade. *Health Affairs* 24: 1512–1522.

Grand View Research. 2023. U.S. Integrated Delivery Network Market Size, Share & Trends Analysis Report, By Integration Model (Vertical, Horizontal), By Service Type (Acute Care/Hospitals, Primary Care, Long-term Health, Specialty Clinics), And Segment Forecasts, 2023 – 2030. Accessed November 2023. Available at: https://www.grandviewresearch.com/industry-analysis/us-integrated-delivery-network-market

Hall, M. A. 2005. The Death of Managed Care: A Regulatory Autopsy. *Journal of Health Politics, Policy and Law* 30: 427–452.

Hennrich, P. 2022. Implementation of a Managed Care Programme in Germany Using the Example of the Baden-Wuerttemberg Contract on Care in the Field of Cardiology. *International Journal of Integrated Care*, 22.

Henry, J. Kaiser Family Foundation. 2015. *Medicaid Delivery System and Payment Reform: A Guide to Key Terms and Concepts*. Accessed August 2020. Available at: https://www.kff.org/medicaid/fact-sheet/medicaid-delivery-system-and-payment-reform-a-guide-to-key-terms-and-concepts/#:~:text=Medicaid%20Delivery%20System%20and%20Payment%20Reform%3A%20A%20Guide,statute.%202%20Payment%20Models.%20...%203%20Appendix.%20

Hernandez, N., and P. Salber. 2020. Is a Management Services Organization (MSO) Right for Your Practice? Accessed September 2020. Available at: https://thedoctorweighsin.com/management-services-organization-mso

Hester, C. A., N. Karbhari, N. E. Rich, et al. 2019. Effect of Fragmentation of Cancer Care on Treatment Use and Survival in Hepatocellular Carcinoma. *Cancer* 125: 3428–3436.

Hinton, E., R. Rudowitz, L. Stolyar, and N. Singer. 2022. 10 Things to Know about Medicaid Managed Care. *Kaiser Family Foundation Issue Brief*. Accessed July, 12, 2022.

Ho, V., L. Metcalfe, L. Vu, M. Short, and R. Morrow. 2020. Annual Spending Per Patient and Quality in Hospital-Owned Versus Physician-Owned Organizations: An Observational Study. *Journal of General Internal Medicine* 35: 649–655.

Hogan, T. H., C. H. Lemak, L. R. Hearld, et al. 2019. Market and Organizational Factors Associated with Hospital Vertical Integration into Sub-Acute Care. *Health Care Management Review* 44: 137–147.

Howard, S. W., S. L. Bernell, J. Yoon, J. Luck, and C. M. Ranit. 2015. Oregon's Experiment in Health Care Delivery and Payment Reform: Coordinated Care Organizations Replacing Managed Care. *Journal of Health Politics, Policy and Law* 40: 245–255.

Huang, H., X. Zhu, F. Ullrich, A. C. MacKinney, and K. Mueller. 2023. The Impact of Medicare Shared Savings Program Participation on Hospital Financial Performance: An Event-Study Analysis. *Health Services Research* 58: 116–127.

Hung, A., B. Stuart, and I. Harris. 2016. The Effect of Medicare Advantage Enrollment on Mammographic Screening. *American Journal of Managed Care* 22: e53–e59.

Hwang, W., J. Chang, M. LaClair, and H. Paz. 2013. Effects of Integrated Delivery System on Cost and Quality. *American Journal of Managed Care* 19: e175–e184.

Hwang, W., J. Chang, M. LaClair, and H. Paz. 2013. Effects of Integrated Delivery System on Cost and Quality. *Am J Manag Care* 19: e175–e184.

Johns Hopkins Medicine. 2023. Three Critical Advantages of Provider-Sponsored Health Plans. *Johns Hopkins Health Plans*. Available at: https://www.hopkinsmedicine.org/johns-hopkins-health-plans/news/three-critical-advantages-provider-sponsored-health-plans

Johnson, G., J. F. Figueroa, X. Zhou, E. J. Orav, and A. K. Jha. 2016. Recent Growth in Medicare Advantage Enrollment Associated with Decreased Fee-for-Service Spending in Certain US Counties. *Health Affairs* 35: 1707–1715.

Joynt, K. E., A. A. Gawande, E. J. Orav, and A. K. Jha. 2013. Contribution of Preventable Acute Care Spending to Total Spending for High-Cost Medicare Patients. *Journal of the American Medical Association* 309: 2572–2578.

Kane, N. A., N. L. Ashworth, E. H. Jess, and K. A. Mazurek. 2018. Opioids, Benzodiazepines and Z-Drugs: Alberta Physicians' Attitudes and Opinions upon Receipt of Their Personalized Prescribing Profile. *Journal of Medical Regulation* 104: 8–13.

Kanter, G. P., D. Polsky, and R. M. Werner. 2019. Changes in Physician Consolidation with the Spread of Accountable Care Organizations. *Health Affairs* 38: 1936–1943.

Keckley, P. H., M. Karp, and M. Nugent. 2015. The Performance of Provider-Sponsored Health Plans: Key Findings, Strategic Implications. *Navigant Center for Healthcare Research and Policy Analysis* 2018:11.

Keon-Hyung, L., S. B. Yang, and M. Choi. 2009. The Association Between Hospital Ownership and Technical Efficiency in a Managed Care Environment. *Journal of Medical Systems* 33: 307–315. https://pubmed.ncbi.nlm.nih.gov/19697697/

Kern, L. M., M. Rajan, H. A. Pincus, L. P. Casalino, and S. S. Stuard. 2020. Health Care Fragmentation in Medicaid Managed Care vs. Fee for Service. *Population Health Management* 23: 53–58.

Kleiner, S. A., D. Ludwinski, and W. D. White. 2017. Antitrust and Accountable Care Organizations: Observations for the Physician Market. *Medical Care Research and Review* 74: 97–108.

Kratewski, J., B. Dowd, M. Savage, and J. Tong. 2014. Do Integrated Health Care Systems Provide Lower-Cost, Higher-Quality Care? *Physician Executive* 40: 14–18.

Kravitz, R. 2008. Beyond Gatekeeping: Enlisting Patients as Agents for Quality and Cost-Containment. *Journal of General Internal Medicine* 23: 1722–1723.

Landon, B. E., J. Reschovsky, and D. Blumenthal. 2003. Changes in Career Satisfaction among Primary Care and Specialist Physicians, 1997–2001. *Journal of the American Medical Association* 289: 442–449.

Lattimer, C. 2005. Advanced Care Management Strategies Reduce Costs and Improve Patient Health in High-Risk Insurance Pools. *Lippincott's Case Management* 10: 261–263.

Lee, Y. C., B. Lu, H. Guan, J. D. Greenberg, J. Kremer, and D. H. Solomon. 2020. Physician Prescribing Patterns and Risk of Future Long-Term Opioid Use Among Patients with Rheumatoid Arthritis: A Prospective Observational Cohort Study. *Arthritis & Rheumatology* 72: 1082–1090.

Levine, D., and J. Mulligan. 2015. Overutilization, Overutilized. *Journal of Health Politics, Policy & Law* 40: 421–437.

Ludomirsky, A. B., W. L. Schpero, J. Wallace, et al. 2022. In Medicaid Managed Care Networks, Care is Highly Concentrated among a Small Percentage of Physicians: Study Examines the Availability of Physicians in Medicaid Managed Care Networks. *Health Affairs* 41: 760–768.

MacColl, W. A. 1966. *Group Practice and Prepayment of Medical Care*. Washington, DC: Public Affairs Press.

Mackie, D. L., and D. K. Decker. 1981. *Group and IPA HMOs*. Gaithersburg, MD: Aspen Publishers.

Maeda, J. L., K. M. Lee, and M. Horberg. 2014. Comparative Health Systems Research Among Kaiser Permanente and Other Integrated Delivery Systems: A Systematic Literature Review. *Permanente Journal* 18: 66–77.

Maeng, D. D., S. R. Snyder, C. Baumgart, A. L. Minnich, J. F. Tomcavage, and T. R. Graf. 2016. Medicaid Managed Care in an Integrated Health Care Delivery System: Lessons from Geisinger's Early Experience. *Population Health Management* 19: 257–263.

Mahmoudi, E., W. Tarraf, B. L. Maroukis, and H. G. Levy. 2016. Does Medicare Managed Care Reduce Racial/Ethnic Disparities in Diabetes Prevention Care and Healthcare Expenditure? *American Journal of Managed Care* 22: e360–e367.

McGuire, J. P. 1994. The Growth of Managed Care. *Health Care Financial Management* 48: 10.

McManus, K. A., J. Ferey, E. Farrell, R. Dillingham, et al. 2020. National Survey of US HIV Clinicians: Knowledge and Attitudes About the Affordable Care Act and Opinions of Its Impact on Quality of Care and Barriers to Care. *Open Forum Infectious Diseases* 7.

Melnick, G. A., Y. C. Shen, and V. Y. Wu. 2011. The Increased Concentration of Health Plan Markets Can Benefit Consumers Through Lower Hospital Prices. *Health Affairs* 30: 1728–1733.

Melnikow, J., E. Evans, G. Xing, et al. 2020. Primary Care Access to New Patient Appointments for California Medicaid Enrollees: A Simulated Patient Study. *Annals of Family Medicine* 18: 210–217.

Miller, R. H., and H. S. Luft. 1997. Does Managed Care Lead to Better or Worse Quality of Care? *Health Affairs* 16: 7–26.

Miller, R. H., and H. S. Luft. 2002. HMO Plan Performance Update: An Analysis of the Literature, 1997–2001. *Health Affairs* 21: 63–86.

Moin, T., J. M. Harwood, C. M. Mangione, et al. 2020. Trends in Costs of Care and Utilization for Medicaid Patients with Diabetes in Accountable Care Communities. *Medical Care* 58: S40–S45.

Morrisey, M. A., and R. L. Ohsfeldt. 2003. Do "Any Willing Provider" and "Freedom of Choice" Laws Affect HMO Market Share? *Inquiry* 40: 362–374.

Moscovice, I., M. Casey, and S. Krein. 1998. Expanding Rural Managed Care: Enrollment Patterns and Prospects. *Health Affairs* 17: 172–179.

National Committee for Quality Assurance (NCQA). 2023. HEDIS Measurement Year 2023 Volume 1 Summary Table of Measures, Product Lines and Changes. Accessed November 2023. Available at: https://www.ncqa.org/wp-content/uploads/2022/08/MY-2023-Summary-Table-of-Measures-Product-Lines-Changes.pdf

Ndumele, C. D, W. L. Schpero, and A. N. Trivedi. 2018. Medicaid Expansion and Health Plan Quality in Medicaid Managed Care. *Health Services Research* 53 (suppl 1): 2821–2838.

Ng, A., P. Kennedy, and B. Hutchinson. 2013. Self-Efficacy and Health Status Improve After a Wellness Program in Persons with Multiple Sclerosis. *Disability & Rehabilitation* 35: 1039–1044.

Ng, J., F. Ye, L. Roth, et al. 2015. Human Papillomavirus Vaccination Coverage among Female Adolescents in Managed Care Plans—United States, 2013. *Morbidity and Mortality Weekly Report* 64: 1185–1189.

Nguyen, L. L., A. D. Smith, R. E. Scully, et al. 2017. Provider-Induced Demand in the Treatment of Carotid Artery Stenosis: Variation in Treatment Decisions between Private Sector Fee-for-Service vs Salary-Based Military Physicians. *JAMA Surgery* 152: 565–572.

Nguyen, N. X., and F. W. Derrick. 1997. Physician Behavioral Response to a Medicare Price Reduction. *Health Services Research* 32: 283–298.

Nicholas L. H. 2013. Better Quality of Care or Healthier Patients? Hospital Utilization by Medicare Advantage and Fee-for-Service Enrollees. *Forum for Health Economics & Policy* 16: 137–161.

Noble, A. 2014. *Any Willing or Authorized Providers*. National Conference of State Legislatures. Accessed December 2020. Available at: https://www.ncsl.org/research/health/any-willing-or-authorized-providers.aspx

O'Connor, S. J. 2018. Provider Sponsored Insurance: A Scoping Review. *Journal of Accounting and Finance* 18: 175.

Ouayogodé, M. H., T. Fraze, E. C. Rich, and C. H. Colla. 2020. Association of Organizational Factors and Physician Practices' Participation in Alternative Payment Models. *JAMA Network Open* 3.

Parasrampuria, S., A. H. Oakes, S. S. Wu, M. A. Parikh, and W. V. Padula . 2018. Value and Performance of Accountable Care Organizations: A Cost-Minimization Analysis. *International Journal of Technology Assessment in Health Care* 34: 388–392.

Parekh, N., I. Hernandez, T. R. Radomski, and W. H. Shrank. 2018. Relationships between Provider-Led Health Plans and Quality, Utilization, and Satisfaction. *American Journal of Managed Care* 24: 628–632.

Pati, S., S. Shea, D. Rabinowitz, and O. Carrasquillo. 2005. Health Expenditures for Privately Insured Adults Enrolled in Managed Care Gatekeeping vs Indemnity Plans. *American Journal of Public Health* 95: 286–291.

Peiris, D., M. C. Phipps-Taylor, C. A. Stachowski, et al. 2016. ACOs Holding Commercial Contracts are Larger and More Efficient Than Noncommercial ACOs. *Health Affairs* 35: 1849–1856.

Pelfrey, S., and B. A. Theisen. 1989. Joint Venture in Health Care. *Journal of Nursing Administration* 19: 39–42.

Perez, V. 2018. Effect of Privatized Managed Care on Public Insurance Spending and Generosity: Evidence from Medicaid. *Health Economics* 27: 557–575.

Physicians Advocacy Institute. 2019. *Updated Physician Practice Advocacy Study: National and Regional Changes in Physician Employment 2012–2018*. Accessed September 2020. Available at: http://www.physiciansadvocacyinstitute.org/Portals/0/assets/docs/021919-Avalere-PAI-Physician-Employment-Trends-Study-2018-Update.pdf?ver=2019-02-19-162735-117

Pimperl, A., O Groene, J. Mousquès, D. Peiris, and H. Hildebrandt. 2017. What Can We Learn from the US Experiences on Accountable Care Organizations? Reflections from Germany, the UK, France and Australia. *International Journal of Integrated Care* 17: 1–8.

Post, B., T. Buchmueller, and A. M. Ryan. 2018. Vertical Integration of Hospitals and Physicians: Economic Theory and Empirical Evidence on Spending and Quality. *Medical Care Research and Review* 75: 399–433.

Rice, T. H., and R. J. Labelle. 1989. Do Physicians Induce Demand for Medical Services? *Journal of Health Politics, Policy and Law* 14: 587–600.

Richter, J. P., and B. Beauvais. 2018. Quality Indicators Associated with the Level of NCQA Accreditation. *American Journal of Medical Quality* 33: 43–49.

Robinson, J. C. 2002. Renewed Emphasis on Consumer Cost Sharing in Health Insurance Benefit Design. *Health Affairs Web Exclusives* 2002: W139–W154.

Rutledge, R. I., M. A. Romaire, C. L. Hersey, W. J. Parish, S. M. Kissam, and J. T. Lloyd. 2019. Medicaid Accountable Care Organizations in Four States: Implementation and Early Impacts. *Milbank Quarterly* 97: 583–619.

Sabik, L. M., B. Dahman, A. Vichare, and C. J. Bradley. 2020. Breast and Cervical Cancer Screening Among Medicaid Beneficiaries: The Role of Physician

Payment and Managed Care. *Medical Care Research and Review* 77: 34–45.

Sanofi-Aventis. 2013. *Managed Care Digest Series, 2013: Public Payer Digest.* Bridgewater, NJ: Author.

Sanofi-Aventis/Forte Information Resources. 2019. *Public Payer Digest: Trends in Chronic Disease Management. Managed Care Digest Series, 2019.* Bridgewater, NJ: Author.

Sari, N. 2002. Do Competition and Managed Care Improve Quality? *Health Economics* 11: 571–584.

Sathian, B., E. van Teijlingen, and P. Simkhada. (2022). Editorial: Integrated Health Service Delivery and COVID-19. *Frontiers in Public Health* 10: 1008777.

Schamess, G. (1996). Introduction: Who Profits and Who Benefits from Managed Mental Health Care? Smith College Studies in Social Work, 66(3), 209–220. https://doi.org/10.1080/00377319609517461

Scheffler, R. M., D. R. Arnold, and C. M. Whaley. 2018. Consolidation Trends in California's Health Care System: Impacts on ACA Premiums and Outpatient Visit Prices. *Health Affairs* 37: 1409–1416.

Schulz, J., M. DeCamp, and S. A. Berkowitz. 2018. Spending Patterns Among Medicare ACOs That Have Reduced Costs. *Journal of Healthcare Management* 63: 374–381.

Schwenkglenks, M., G. Preiswerk, R. Lehner, F. Weber, and T. D. Szucs. 2006. Economic Efficiency of Gatekeeping Compared with Fee for Service Plans: A Swiss Example. *Journal of Epidemiology and Community Health* 60: 24–30.

Shen, Y., V. Y. Wu, and G. Melnick. 2010. Trends in Hospital Cost and Revenue, 1994–2005: How Are They Related to HMO Penetration, Concentration, and For-Profit Ownership? *Health Services Research* 45: 42–61.

Short, A. C., G. P. Mays, and T. K. Lake. 2001. Provider Network Instability: Implications for Choice, Costs, and Continuity of Care. Community Tracking Study Issue Brief No. 39. Washington, DC: Center for Studying Health System Change.

Short, A. C., G. Mays, and J. Mittler. 2003, October. Disease Management: A Leap of Faith to Lower-Cost, Higher-Quality Health Care. Issue Brief No. 69. Washington, DC: Center for Studying Health System Change.

Shortell, S. M., R. R. Gillies, D. A. Anderson, J. B. Mitchell, and K. L. Morgan. Creating Organized Delivery Systems: The Barriers and Facilitators. *Hospital and Health Services Administration* 38: 447–466.

Snow, K., K. Galaviz, and S. Turbow. 2020. Patient Outcomes Following Interhospital Care Fragmentation: A Systematic Review. *Journal of General Internal Medicine* 35: 1550–1558.

Southwick, K. 1997. Case study: How United HealthCare and Two Contracting Hospitals Address Cost and Quality in Era of Hyper-Competition. *Strategies for Healthcare Excellence* (COR Healthcare Resources): 1–9.

Stadhouders, N., F. Kruse, M. Tanke, X. Koolman, and P. Jeurissen, 2019. Effective Healthcare Cost-Containment Policies: A Systematic Review. *Health Policy* 123: 71–79.

Starner, C. I., S. A. Norman, R. G. Reynolds, and P. P. Gleason. 2009. Effect of Retrospective Drug Utilization Review on Potentially Inappropriate Prescribing in the Elderly. *American Journal of Geriatric Pharmacotherapy* 7: 11–19.

Strandberg-Larsen, M., M. L. Schiøtz, and A. Frølich. 2007. Kaiser Permanente revisited: Can European Health Care Systems Learn? *Eurohealth* 13: 24–26.

Strunk, B. C., P. B. Ginsburg, and J. R. Gabel. 2001. Tracking Health Care Costs. *Health Affairs Suppl. Web Exclusives*: W39–W50.

Sturm, R., W. Goldman, and J. McCulloch, 1998. *How Does Managed Care Affect the Cost of Mental Health Services?* Accessed November 25, 2024. Available at https://www.rand.org/pubs/research_briefs/RB4515.html

The National Committee for Quality Assurance (NCQA). 2022. 2022 Health Plan Ratings Methodology. Accessed November 2023. Available at:https://www.ncqa.org/wp-content/uploads/2022/07/2022-HPR-Methodology_Updated_7.29.2022.pdf

Theriault, K. M., R. A. Rosenheck, and T. G. Rhee. 2020. Increasing Emergency Department Visits for Mental Health Conditions in the United States. *Journal of Clinical Psychiatry* 81.

Timbie, J. W., A. M. Kranz, A. Mahmud, and C. L. Damberg. 2019. Specialty Care Access for Medicaid Enrollees in Expansion States. *American Journal of Managed Care* 25: e83–e87.

Tisnado, D. M., D. E. Rose-Ash, J. L. Malin, J. L. Adams, P. A. Ganz, and K. L. Kahn. 2008. Financial Incentives for Quality in Breast Cancer Care. *American Journal of Managed Care* 14: 457–466.

Veet, C. A., T. R. Radomski, C. D'Avella, et al. 2020. Impact of Healthcare Delivery System Type on Clinical, Utilization, and Cost Outcomes of Patient-Centered Medical Homes: A Systematic Review. *Journal of General Internal Medicine* 35: 1276–1284.

Wagner, E. R. 1995. Types of Managed Care Organizations. In: *Essentials of Managed Health Care*. P. R. Kongstvedt, ed. Gaithersburg, MD: Aspen Publishers: 24–34.

Weiss, E. F., R. Malik, T. Santos, M. Ceide, et al. 2021. Telehealth for the Cognitively Impaired Older Adult and Their Caregivers: Lessons from a Coordinated Approach. *Neurodegenerative Disease Management* 11: 83–89.

Wilkerson, J. D., K. J. Devers, and R. S. Given. 1997. The Emerging Competitive Managed Care Marketplace. In: *Competitive Managed Care: The Emerging Health*

Care System. J. D. Wilkerson et al., eds. San Francisco, CA: Jossey-Bass Publishers.

Winfield, L. 2018. *Provider-Sponsored Health Plans: Cautions and Opportunities. Healthcare Financial Management Association*. Accessed September 2020. Available at: https://www.hfma.org/topics/hfm/2018/april/60249.html

Wright, B. J., N. Royal, L. Broffman, H. F. Li, and K. Dulacki. 2019. Oregon's Coordinated Care Organization Experiment: Are Members' Experiences of Care Actually Changing? *Journal for Healthcare Quality* 41: e38–e46.

Yan, J. 2020. The Impact of Medicaid Managed Care on Obstetrical Care and Birth Outcomes: A Case Study. *Journal of Women's Health* 29: 167–176.

Yip, W. C. 1998. Physician Response to Medicare Fee Reductions: Changes in the Volume of Coronary Artery Bypass Graft (CABG) Surgeries in the Medicare and Private Sectors. *Journal of Health Economics* 17: 675–699.

Yorkery, B. 2017. Accountable Care Communities: Moving from Health Care Delivery Systems to Systems of Health. *North Carolina Medical Journal* 78: 242–244.

Zelman, W. A. 1996. *The Changing Health Care Marketplace*. San Francisco, CA: Jossey-Bass Publishers.

Zhang, J., P. Ye, M. Yang, et al. 2023. Development of a Conceptual Framework to Scale Up Co-Managed Care for Older Patients with Hip Fracture in China: A Qualitative Study. *BMC Health Services Research* 23: 898.

Zhu, J. M., J. Breslau, and K. J. McConnell. 2021. Medicaid Managed Care Network Adequacy Standards for Mental Health Care access: Balancing Flexibility and Accountability. In *JAMA Health Forum* 2: e210280–e210280). American Medical Association.

CHAPTER 10

Long-Term Care

LEARNING OBJECTIVES

- Describe long-term care (LTC) and why it is needed.
- Understand the interactions between age, gender, multimorbidity, and functional deficits.
- Describe the main characteristics of LTC.
- Understand the various services incorporated in LTC delivery.
- Identify the users of LTC services and their unique needs.
- Explore the continuum of LTC and why it is necessary.
- Identify the home- and community-based LTC services and who pays for them.
- Describe LTC institutions and the levels of services they provide.
- Discuss specialized LTC facilities and continuing care retirement communities.
- Explore institutional trends, utilization, and expenditures.
- Understand the barriers to private LTC insurance.

"Now, honey, where are we supposed to go from here?"

Introduction

Long-term care (LTC) is a complex subsystem within the larger, even more complex U.S. healthcare delivery system. Encompassing numerous services, it defies a simple definition. In addition to healthcare professionals, family and friends play an important role in the delivery of LTC.

Several different sources of financing are associated with the various LTC services. Regular health insurance does not cover LTC; if it does, the coverage is limited. Private insurance just for LTC has made limited headway. Hence, payment for LTC services falls largely under the purview of government healthcare programs. These sources of public financing, however, have their own eligibility criteria, so not everyone qualifies.

Even though not all older adults need LTC services, advancing age is often accompanied by chronic conditions, comorbidity, and disability. When a person is no longer able to carry out certain essential tasks of daily living, the need for LTC is triggered.

LTC is not synonymous with nursing homes. Surveys over time have shown that the vast majority of older Americans wish to stay in their own homes indefinitely. Indeed, community-based services are not only preferred by most older people but are also more economical. Hence, these services have grown more rapidly than LTC institutions. To reflect this shift, the term "long-term services and supports" (LTSS) has been suggested to refer to a broad spectrum of LTC options (Reinhard et al., 2011).

This chapter provides an overview of LTC, its main users, various types of community-based and institutional services, and financing of these services. LTC services form a continuum from basic help to more advanced care to address the varied needs of a heterogeneous population. Even older adults, who are the predominant users of LTC services, are not a homogeneous group; thus, they need a variety of services to meet their LTC needs.

Age, Functional Deficits, and Long-Term Care

Age and the need for LTC are highly correlated; the need for such care increases with advancing age. For example, only 8% of people in the 65–74 age group need LTC services. The percentage of those needing LTC increases to 17% in the 75–84 age group, and to 42% in the 85-plus age group (Hado and Komisar, 2019). Although older adults constitute the majority of LTC users, some young adults and even children may need LTC.

In 2017, a person who attained the age of 65 could expect to live for another 19 years (National Center for Health Statistics, 2019). By 2030, 20% of the total U.S. population is projected to be older, up from 15% in 2016. The number of people 85 years and older (the oldest old) is expected to nearly double by 2035, from 6.5 million to 11.8 million, and to nearly triple by 2060, to 19 million people (Vespa et al., 2020). An increase in the number of people who are older adults will be accompanied by issues related to chronic conditions, disability, and the need for LTC services.

The rest of the developed world, as well as many developing countries, also face aging-related problems and challenges in providing adequate LTC services to their populations. Indeed, the older people as a proportion of the total population is already higher in other developed countries, such as Japan, Germany, France, and the United Kingdom, than it is in the United States.

Of course, age by itself does not suggest the need for LTC. In 2018, 45% of noninstitutionalized older persons in the United States assessed their own health as excellent or very good, compared to 65% for persons ages 18–64 (Administration on Aging [AOA], 2020). A growing number of non-White older people are in poorer health, however, and they are likely to face a greater need for LTC services later in life. For example, compared to Whites, a greater proportion of Black and Hispanic people have hypertension, asthma, diabetes, and functional disabilities (Federal Interagency Forum on Aging-Related Statistics, 2016). Social and cultural factors pertaining to minority groups will present new challenges in the delivery of LTC services.

Two common indicators used to assess functional limitations are the activities of daily living (ADLs) scale and instrumental activities of daily living (IADLs). As examples, ADLs include a person's ability to bathe, dress, and eat; IADLs include a person's ability to prepare meals, do housework, and manage medication use. Limitations in ADLs indicate a more severe decline in a person's functional status than limitations in IADLs do.

Among older Americans, 80% have multiple chronic conditions (Gerteis et al., 2014). In addition to age, the prevalence of disability and functional limitations rises dramatically among persons who have multiple chronic conditions (multimorbidity), and women suffer more disabling conditions than men (**Table 10-1**). Serious illness or injury can also lead to a rapid decline in a person's health. With certain types of disabilities, many people can maintain their independence by using adaptive devices (e.g., walkers, wheelchairs, adaptive eating utensils) to overcome their deficits and may not require any LTC services. Over time, however, the individual may no longer be able to perform certain common tasks of daily living because of functional decline; LTC services are then needed.

Cognitive impairment may also lead to functional decline. **Cognitive impairment** is a mental disorder that is indicated by a person having difficulty remembering, learning new things, concentrating, or making decisions that affect the individual's everyday life. Such impairment ranges from mild to severe and may lead to disturbing behaviors. Cognitive impairment with or without dementia contributes to neuropsychiatric symptoms and increased disability (Tabert et al., 2002).

Table 10-1 Association Between Age, Gender, Multimorbidity, and ADL/IADL Limitations

Number of Chronic Conditions	Mean Number of ADL and IADL Limitations			
	Age 65–74		Age ≥75	
	Men	Women	Men	Women
0	0.3	0.3	0.5	0.5
1	0.4	0.4	0.7	0.7
2	0.6	0.7	0.9	1.0
3	0.9	1.1	1.2	1.5
4	1.2	1.6	1.6	2.2
5	1.7	2.5	2.2	3.1
6	2.4	3.8	2.9	4.6
7	3.5	7.5	4.2	6.8
8	4.2	8.8	8.1	10.1

Note: ADL/IADL figures have been rounded.

Data from Jindai, K., et al. 2016. *Multimorbidity and functional limitations among adults 65 or older*, NHANES 2005–2012. Centers for Medicare and Medicaid Services. Available at: https://www.cdc.gov/pcd/issues/2016/16_0174.htm#:~:text=Disease%2C%20functional%20limitation%2C%20and%20disability%20should%20not%20be,develop%20interventions%20for%20high-risk%20adults%2065%20or%20older.

People receiving care in nursing homes have a greater degree of ADL decline compared to people who can live at home or in community housing that offers some support services (**Figure 10-1**).

The Nature of Long-Term Care

Long-term care (LTC) can be defined as a variety of individualized, well-coordinated services that promote the maximum possible independence for people with functional limitations and are provided over an

Chapter 10 Long-Term Care

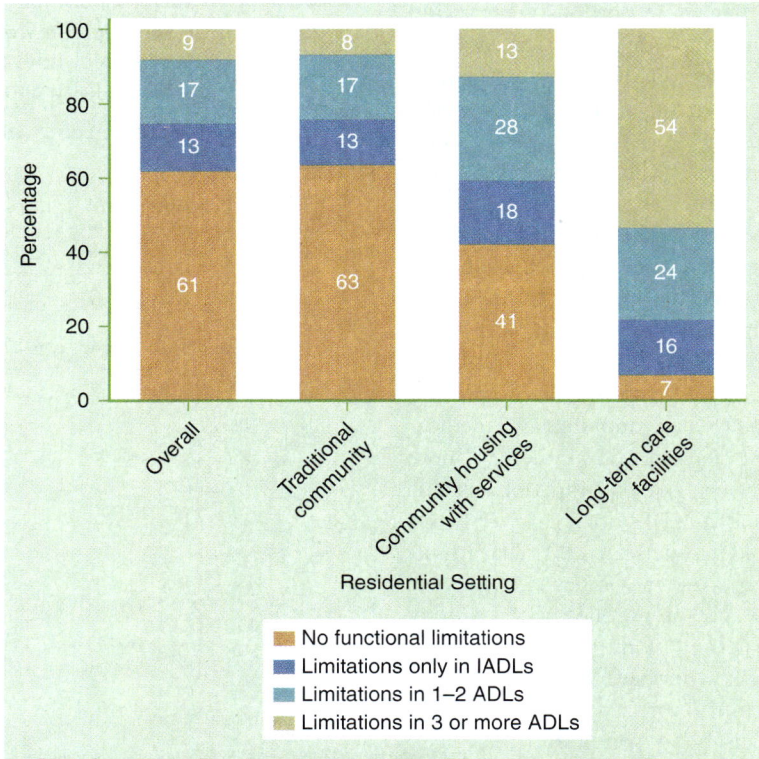

NOTE: Community housing with services appiles to respondents who reported they lived in retirement communities or apartments, senior citizen housing, continuing care retirement facilities, assisted living facilities, staged living communities, board and care facilities/homes, and similar situations, and who reported they had access to one or more of the following services through their place of residence: meal preparation, cleaning or housekeeping services, laundry services, or help with medications. Respondents were asked about access to these services, but not whether they actually used the services. A residence (or unit) is considered a long-term care facility if it is certified by Medicare or Medicaid; or has 3 or more beds, is licensed as a nursing home or other long-term care facility, and provides at least one personal care service; or provides 24-hour, 7-day-a-week supervision by a nonfamily, paid caregiver. Long-term care facility residents with no limitations may include individuals with limitations in performing certain IADLs, such as doing light or heavy housework or meal preparation. These questions were not asked of facility residents.
Reference population: These data refer to Medicare beneficiaries who were continuously enrolled during the calendar year.

Figure 10-1 Percentage distribution of Medicare beneficiaries age 65 and over with limitations performing activities of daily living (ADLs) and instrumental activities of daily living (IADLs), by residential setting, 2017.

Reproduced from Federal Interagency Forum on Aging-Related Statistics. 2020. Older Americans 2020: Key indicators of well-being. Washington, DC: US Government Printing Office. p. 55.

extended period of time in accordance with a holistic approach, while maximizing the care recipients' quality of life. To the extent possible, the delivery of LTC should employ appropriate current technology and available evidence-based practices. LTC is unique in healthcare delivery and is multidimensional.

Variety of Services

A variety of LTC services are necessary because individual needs, as determined by health status, finances, and other factors, vary greatly among people who require these services. Hence, services should (1) fit the needs of different individuals, (2) address their changing needs over time, and (3) suit their personal preferences.

Individualized Services

LTC services are tailored to the needs of the individual as determined by an assessment of the individual's physical, mental, and emotional condition. Other factors incorporated into the assessment include a history of the person's medical and psychosocial conditions; a social history of family relationships, former occupation, and leisure activities; and cultural factors, such as racial and ethnic background, language, and religious practices. The information obtained from a comprehensive assessment is used to develop an individualized plan of care that addresses each type of need through customized interventions.

Well-Coordinated Total Care

LTC providers are responsible for managing the total healthcare needs of an individual client. **Total care** requires that any healthcare need is recognized, evaluated, and addressed by appropriate clinical professionals (Singh, 2016). Hence, interface between the LTC system and the rest of the healthcare system is necessary to provide an easy transition among the various types of healthcare settings and services, both LTC and non-LTC (**Figure 10-2**). The main non-LTC services include primary-care, mental health services, acute- care hospitals, and various outpatient services, such as those provided by specialist physicians, dentists, optometrists, podiatrists, diagnostic labs, and imaging centers.

For most people, managing the myriads of healthcare services, eligibility requirements, and financing is an overwhelming challenge. Hence, case management (discussed later in the "Case Management" section) becomes an important service for many people. One key role of case management is to match the client's specific needs with the available services that are likely to best address those needs, regardless of whether they are obtained within the LTC sector or from the non-LTC sector.

Maintenance of Residual Function

Loss of the ability to independently perform certain IADL and/or ADL functions creates dependency. Caregiver assistance becomes necessary when a person is either unable or unwilling to perform the tasks of daily living. However, recovery from functional impairments is often not possible. In that case, LTC has two main goals: (1) to maintain residual function—that is, whatever ability to function a person still has; and (2) to prevent further decline. These goals are accomplished by letting the person do as much as possible for himself or herself. Some individuals—such as a comatose patient in a persistent vegetative state, for example—may be totally dependent on a caregiver.

Extended Period of Care

For most LTC clients, the delivery of various services extends over a relatively long period because the underlying causes of functional decline are often irreversible. In other cases, rehabilitation therapies or postacute convalescence may be needed for a relatively short

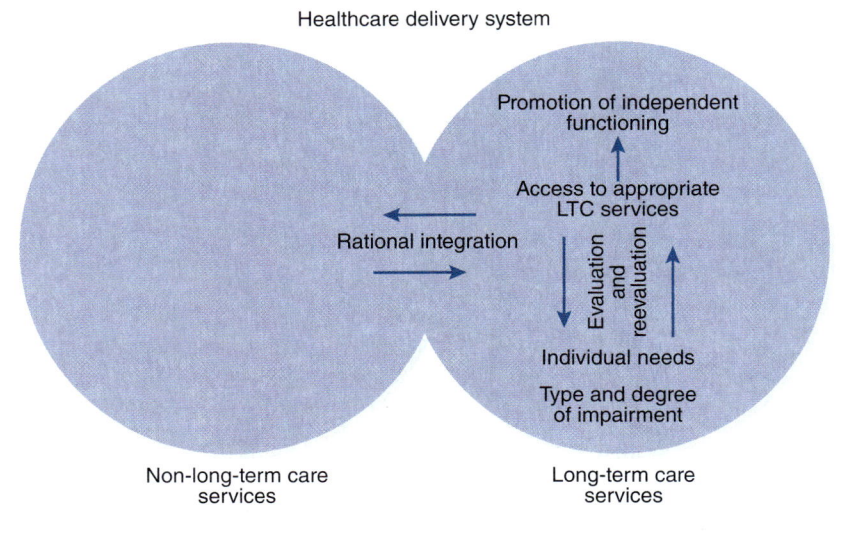

Figure 10-2

Healthcare delivery system

- Promotion of independent functioning
- Access to appropriate LTC services
- Rational integration
- Evaluation and reevaluation
- Individual needs
- Type and degree of impairment

Non-long-term care services | Long-term care services

Key characteristics

1. The LTC system is rationally integrated with the rest of the healthcare delivery system. This rational integration facilitates easy access to services between the two components of the healthcare delivery system.
2. Appropriate placement of the patient within the LTC system is based on an assessment of individual needs. For example, individual needs determine whether and when institutionalization may be necessary.
3. The LTC system accommodates changes in individual needs by providing access to appropriate LTC services as determined by a reevaluation of needs.
4. LTC services are designed to compensate for existing impairment and have the objective of promoting independence to the extent possible.

Figure 10-2 Key characteristics of a well-designed long-term care system.

---

duration, generally less than 90 days, with the patient subsequently returning to independent living. People receiving community-based LTC services generally need them for a long duration to prevent institutionalization. A smaller number of LTC recipients need institutional care for an extended period, or even indefinitely. Examples include people with severe dementia, incontinence of bowel and bladder, severe psychiatric or behavioral issues, unstable postacute conditions, and those in a comatose/vegetative state.

Holistic Care

A holistic approach to healthcare delivery focuses on every aspect of what makes a person whole and complete. A person's needs and preferences are incorporated into medical care delivery and all aspects of daily living. Physical aspects of care include medical exams, nursing care, medications, and rehabilitation treatments. The individual's mental and emotional well-being are addressed, for example, by minimizing stress and anxiety. Opportunities are created for socializing with family, friends, and volunteers. Pursuit of spirituality and religious faith is encouraged.

Quality of Life

A sense of satisfaction, fulfillment, and self-worth are regarded as critical patient outcomes in any healthcare delivery setting. They take on added significance in LTC, however, because (1) a loss of self-worth often accompanies disability and dependency, and (2) patients remain in LTC settings for relatively long periods, with little hope of full recovery in most instances.

Quality of life is a multifaceted concept that encompasses at least five factors: lifestyle pursuits, living environment, clinical palliation, human factors, and personal choices.

- Lifestyle factors are associated with personal enrichment and making one's life meaningful through activities one enjoys. Many older people still enjoy pursuing their former leisure activities, such as woodworking, crocheting, knitting, gardening, and fishing. Even those whose function has declined to a vegetative or comatose state must be engaged in something that promotes sensory awakening through visual, auditory, olfactory, and tactile stimulation.
- The living environment must be comfortable, safe, and appealing to the senses. Cleanliness, décor, furnishings, and other aesthetic features are important.
- Clinical **palliation** should be available for relief from unpleasant symptoms, such as pain or nausea—for instance, when a patient is undergoing chemotherapy.
- Human factors refer to caregiver attitudes and practices that emphasize caring, compassion, respect, and preservation of human dignity for the patient. Institutionalized residents find it disconcerting to have lost their autonomy and independence. Quality of life is enhanced when residents in an LTC facility have some latitude to govern their own lives and have adequate privacy. **Person-centered care** has emerged as an important concept in LTC: It emphasizes the centrality of the recipient of care, whereas economic efficiencies of the organization were often assigned a higher priority in the past.
- Being able to make personal choices is important to most people. In nursing facilities, for example, food is often the primary area of discontentment, which can be addressed by offering a selection of menu choices. Also, the ability to set one's own schedule is important to most people. Many older people resent being awakened early in the morning when caregivers begin their responsibilities to care for residents' hygiene, bathing, and grooming.

Use of Current Technology

Technology offers one avenue for at least mitigating the impending challenges of the growing need for LTC. In addition, technology can improve overall safety and quality of care. For example, a **personal emergency response system (PERS)** enables an at-risk older adult living alone at home to summon help in an emergency at any time during the day or night. A fall detector can be used either at home or in an institution. Electronic medication dispensers are programmed to dispense pills and sound an alarm as reminders for a person to take prescribed medications. Technology also enables remote monitoring of people who live independently. Examples of technology used in institutional settings include global positioning systems (GPS) to monitor a resident who may wander away, sensor technology to prevent and heal pressure ulcers by detecting moisture levels and length of time spent in one position, use of robotic pets, and pedometers to measure daily activity levels (Morley, 2012).

Use of Evidence-Based Practices

Evidence-based care incorporates the use of best practices that have been evaluated for effectiveness and safety through clinical research. Best practices are often detailed in clinical practice guidelines, which provide directions and protocols for treatment interventions for specific health conditions.

The American Medical Directors Association (AMDA), for example, publishes clinical practice guidelines on important topics related to the treatment of clinical conditions commonly encountered in LTC settings. Evidence-based protocols are meant to be used for staff training and in caregiving routines to improve the quality of care. Studies show that the use of evidence-based practices in nursing homes can reduce falls (Teresi et al., 2013), prevent pressure ulcers (Niederhauser et al., 2012; Riordan and Voegeli, 2009), and increase satisfaction among nurses (Barba et al., 2012).

Long-Term Care Services

The large array of LTC services can include a combination of different types of services depending on an individual's assessed needs at a given point in time, as new needs arise, and as needs change over time. Potential services include the following:

- Medical care, nursing, and rehabilitation
- Mental health services and dementia care
- Social support
- Preventive and therapeutic LTC
- Informal and formal care
- Respite care
- Community-based and institutional services
- Housing
- End-of-life care

Medical Care, Nursing, and Rehabilitation

Medical care, nursing, and rehabilitation services focus on three main areas: (1) postacute continuity of care, (2) clinical management of chronic illness and comorbidity, and (3) restoration or maintenance of physical function. LTC often becomes necessary after the treatment of an acute episode in a hospital. However, patients in LTC settings may also experience new acute episodes, such as pneumonia, bone fracture, or stroke, and require admission to a general hospital. Older adults are more prone to hospitalization compared to younger age groups; that is, younger patients are more likely to be treated as outpatients, whereas older patients tend to be admitted as inpatients for the same medical conditions.

Nurses, rehabilitation therapists, nutritionists, and other professionals typically provide clinical care in LTC settings under the direction of a physician. Preventing complications from chronic conditions (tertiary prevention) is an important aspect of LTC. Rehabilitation involves short-term therapy treatments to help a person regain or improve physical function. It is provided immediately after the onset of a disability. Examples of cases requiring rehabilitation include orthopedic surgery, stroke, limb amputation, and prolonged illness.

Mental Health Services and Dementia Care

Despite widely held beliefs, mental disorders are not a normal part of aging. Nevertheless, an estimated 25% of older adults have depression, anxiety disorders, or other significant psychiatric conditions, and mental health disorders are frequently comorbid in older adults, occurring in conjunction with common chronic illnesses such as diabetes, cardiac disease, and arthritis (Robinson, 2010). Psychiatric symptoms and cognitive decline are particularly common among nursing home residents. Mental disorders range in severity from problematic to disabling to fatal.

Major barriers must be overcome to ensure delivery of mental health care to all persons who need it. In general, assessing psychiatric illness in geriatric patients can be difficult, especially since comorbidity may obscure the diagnosis (Refer to **Box 10-1** for the correlations between age, gender, multimorbidity, and functional limitations). For example, patients with multiple chronic illnesses may

> **Box 10-1** The Correlations Between Age, Gender, Multimorbidity, and Functional Limitations

Multimorbidity is defined as the co-occurrence of two or more chronic conditions (Navickas et al., 2016). Functional limitation is defined as the presence of any of 14 activities of daily living (ADLs) or instrumental activities of daily living (IADLs) (Navickas et al., 2016).

- Jiao et al. (2021) used data collected by self-reported questionnaires from adults aged 65 years and older living in a rural area in Japan in 2017 and found out that older persons with multimorbidity have a high risk of functional limitation if they are aged 65 years and older living in a rural area, and social relationships altered the association between multimorbidity and function status.
- Zhao et al. (2021) used random-effects logistic regression models to examine the association of multimorbidity with ADL limitation, IADL limitation, and mental disease. The results show that the burden of multimorbidity is high in China, particularly amongst the older population (Zhao et al., 2021). Multimorbidity is associated with higher levels of functional limitations and depression (Zhao et al., 2021).
- Fisher et al. (2021) used a population-based, cross-sectional analysis of data from The Canadian Longitudinal Study on Aging, including 51,338 participants with a similar proportion of men and women (49% versus 51%) and 42% age 65 years or older to examine the association between functional limitation and multimorbidity. The study found higher odds of functional limitation for those with multimorbidity that included versus excluded mental health conditions, at all levels of multimorbidity (Fisher et al., 2021).
- Landré et al. (2022) examined change in prevalence of ADL and IADL between 2008 and 2015 among adults of 60–94 years and the role of age, sex, and multimorbidity. The findings include:
  1. The decline in ADL was primarily evident in those with multimorbidity.
  2. The decline in ADL was evident in those with one to 2 limitations but less pronounced in those with three of more limitations.
  3. A temporal trend of decline in ADL limitations between 2008 and 2015 was observed, this was particularly true among adults older than 75 years with the largest improvements evident at age 90.
  4. The prevalence of ADL or IADL limitations and multimorbidity was higher in women and change in limitations was not similar in men and women. The most notable difference was observed in IADL limitations where men but not women aged 60–65 showed an increase in 2015 compared to 2008.

Data from Navickas, R., Petric, V. K., Feigl, A. B., & Seychell, M. (2016). Multimorbidity: What do we know? What should we do?. Journal of comorbidity, 6(1), 4–11; Jiao, D., Watanabe, K., Sawada, Y., Tanaka, E., Watanabe, T., Tomisaki, E., ... & Anme, T. (2021). Multimorbidity and functional limitation: the role of social relationships. Archives of Gerontology and Geriatrics, 92, 104249; Zhao, Y. W., Haregu, T. N., He, L., Lu, S., Katar, A., Wang, H., ... & Zhang, L. (2021). The effect of multimorbidity on functional limitations and depression amongst middle-aged and older population in China: a nationwide longitudinal study. Age and ageing, 50(1), 190-197; Fisher, K., Griffith, L. E., Gruneir, A., Kanters, D., Markle-Reid, M., & Ploeg, J. (2021). Functional limitations in people with multimorbidity and the association with mental health conditions: Baseline data from the Canadian Longitudinal Study on Aging (CLSA). PLoS One, 16(8), e0255907; Landré, B., Gil-Salcedo, A., Jacob, L., Schnitzler, A., Dugravot, A., Sabia, S., & Singh-Manoux, A. (2022). The role of age, sex, and multimorbidity in 7-year change in prevalence of limitations in adults 60–94 years. Scientific Reports, 12(1), 18270.

display symptoms of either dementia or depression that are attributed to their primary medical condition rather than to an underlying psychiatric illness (Tune, 2001). Hence, older adults with mental disorders are less likely than younger adults to receive correct diagnoses and needed mental health care.

With the growing prevalence of dementia in the United States and around the world, caring for patients with dementia has become a major focus in LTC. **Dementia** is a general term for progressive and irreversible decline in cognition, thinking, and memory. Approximately 15% of people older than 70 years of age have dementia (Hurd et al., 2013), the majority of whom have **Alzheimer's disease**—a progressive degenerative disease of the brain that produces memory loss, confusion, irritability, and severe functional decline. An estimated 5.8 million Americans age 65 and older are living with Alzheimer's dementia, 80% of whom are age 75 or older (Alzheimer's Association, 2020). People with mild dementia may receive home-based care. By comparison, 48% of nursing home residents have some form of dementia (Harris-Kojetin et al., 2019).

Social Support

LTC clients need social and emotional support to help them cope with life events and changes that may cause stress, frustration, anger, fear, grief, or other emotional imbalances. Adaptation to new surroundings and new people becomes necessary when a person leaves their own home and moves to supportive housing or a nursing home. Social support is also needed when problems and issues arise in the interactions among people within social systems. For example, conflicts may arise between what a patient wants for himself or herself and what the family thinks is best for the patient. Conflicts may also arise between patients and caregivers.

Social services are also necessary to facilitate the coordination of total care needs. Examples include transportation services, information, counseling, recreation, and spiritual support. For residents in LTC facilities, remaining connected with the community and the outside world is an important aspect of social support.

Preventive and Therapeutic LTC

In the context of LTC, prevention generally refers to preventing or delaying institutionalization. Various community-based LTC services perform a preventive function by providing good nutrition and access to services, such as vaccinations, flu shots, and routine medical care. Therapeutic services, such as nursing care, rehabilitation, and therapeutic diets, are specified in a plan of care and administered as directed by a physician.

Informal and Formal Care

Among the older adults who receive LTC services in the United States, 80% live in private homes (Congressional Budget Office [CBO], 2013). Contrary to popular belief, most LTC services in the United States are provided informally by family, friends, and surrogates such as neighbors and members from church or other community organizations. It is estimated that 41 million family caregivers in the United States provided an estimated 34 billion hours of care to adults with limitations in daily activities. The estimated economic value of their unpaid contributions was approximately $470 billion in 2017 (Reinhard et al., 2019). Family members also play an important role in supporting their loved ones who are receiving institutional care.

Informal care reduces the use of formal home health care and delays nursing home entry (Van Houtven and Norton, 2004). In a population of older people with disabilities, insufficient informal care is associated with overall discontinuation of living at home, all-cause mortality, hospitalization, and institutionalization (Kuzuya et al., 2011).

The pool of informal caregivers in the United States, in relation to the increasing number of older adults needing LTC, is expected to shrink rather dramatically in the future. Various reports suggest that the number of older people who are divorced, unmarried, or without children is increasing. Such people may have to depend on paid LTC services, although it remains unclear how those services will be financed. If the government ends up filling the financing gaps, the burden will fall on future taxpayers.

Respite Care

Negative feelings, such as anger, dissatisfaction, guilt, frustration, tension, and family conflict, are some common issues faced by family caregivers. Under such pressures, caregivers may experience stress and burnout. **Respite care** is the most frequently suggested intervention to address family caregivers' feelings of stress and burnout. Its objective is to provide relief or assistance to caregivers for limited periods, thereby allowing them some free time without subjecting the patient to neglect. Respite care can include any kind of LTC service, such as adult day care, which allows people to work during the day, or temporary institutionalization, which allows families to take some time off.

Community-Based and Institutional Services

For many people who need LTC, the availability of community-based services provided by formal agencies becomes an important factor in living independently. Such services are brought to the person's home or delivered in a community-based location; hence, these services are collectively referred to as home- and community-based services (HCBS). HCBS have a fourfold objective: (1) to deliver LTC in the most economical and least restrictive setting whenever appropriate, (2) to supplement informal caregiving when advanced services are needed or to substitute informal services when a person lacks a social network that might provide informal care, (3) to provide temporary respite to informal caregivers, and (4) to delay or prevent institutionalization.

Institutionalization can be for a long-term or short-term duration. Functional deficits in three or more ADLs dramatically increase the probability that an individual will need institutional care. The main goals for institutional care are (1) to deliver therapeutic services in accordance with the plan of care, (2) to provide professional help for ADL functions that the resident cannot perform, (3) to implement measures to prevent further loss of remaining function, and (4) to coordinate services with non-LTC providers to address the resident's total care needs.

Figure 10-3 illustrates the various types of HCBS and institutional LTC settings. For many patients, there are complex interlinkages between the services that are brought to the patients and the services that they obtain by being physically transferred to receive them.

Housing

In the LTC context, housing refers to noninstitutional housing other than a person's own home. It includes independent living facilities and retirement living centers/communities—both private and public—that may or may not provide support services, such as meals, housekeeping, transportation, and scheduled recreational activities. In such housing arrangements, residents have their own self-contained apartments or individual cottages that allow maximum privacy, and they can come and go as they please. Occasional needs for LTC services are met by obtaining home health care through an outside agency. Institutions, in contrast, are distinguished by services that go beyond basic support services to include therapeutic services delivered in accordance with a plan of care.

Housing that supports independent living for older adults and for persons with disabilities must take into account physical function and safety issues. Examples of supportive features include safety pull-cords to summon help in an emergency, grab bars in bathrooms to prevent falls, kitchenettes that allow the preparation of meals or snacks, railings in hallways to assist in mobility, and easy means of access to the outdoors.

Private Housing

Upscale retirement centers abound in which the residents can expect to pay a fairly substantial entrance fee plus a monthly rental or maintenance fee. These complexes feature

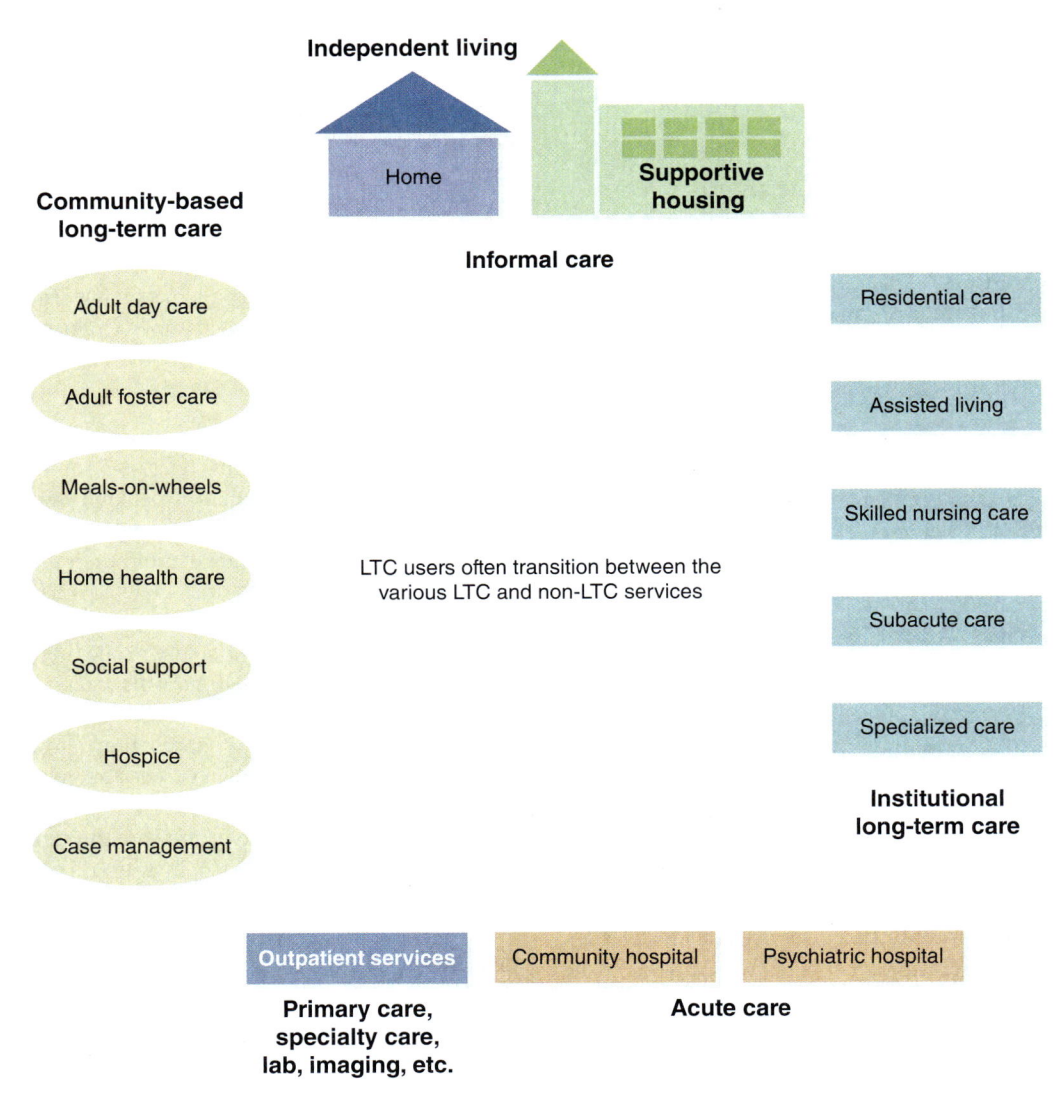

Figure 10-3 Range of services for individuals in need of long-term care.
Data from Singh, D. A. 1997. *Nursing home administrators: Their influence on quality of care.* New York: Garland Publishing. p. 15.

various types of recreational facilities and social programs. The fees often include the evening meal. Housekeeping services and transportation may be included as well.

Public Housing

More modest housing complexes provide government-assisted, subsidized housing for low-income people. The U.S. Department of Housing and Urban Development (HUD) administers three main kinds of rent subsidy programs: (1) federal aid to local housing agencies, which allows them to offer reduced rent to low-income tenants; (2) vouchers that a tenant can apply toward renting housing of their choice; and (3) public housing operated by the government (less commonly available). HUD also provides federal funds to nonprofit sponsors to help them construct rental housing that may include certain support services.

End-of-Life Care

Dealing with death and dying is very much a part of LTC. End-of-life care focuses on preventing needless pain and distress for terminally ill patients and their families. It also places a high emphasis on maintaining patient dignity and comfort.

Almost three-fourths of all deaths in the United States occur in people who are 65 years or older. Among older adults, the five most common causes of death are heart disease (25% of deaths), various cancers (21% of deaths), chronic lower respiratory diseases (7% of deaths), cerebrovascular diseases (6% of deaths), and Alzheimer's disease (6% of deaths) (National Center for Health Statistics, 2019).

Care professionals seem to be well positioned to provide end-of-life care in some LTC settings. In others, terminal patients are referred to hospice services; patients are either transferred to a freestanding hospice or the services are brought to the patient wherever the patient resides.

Users of Long-Term Care

In 2018, 14 million adults in the United States needed LTC services, of whom 56% were age 65 and older, and 44% were ages 18 to 64 (Hado and Komisar, 2019). Someone turning age 65 today has almost a 70% chance of needing some type of long-term care services and supports in their remaining years (Administration for Community Living, 2022). Twenty percent of them will need it for longer than 5 years. Research shows that a little more than half of the Americans who are turning age 65 will develop a disability serious enough to require LTC services (Favreault and Dey, 2016). 7.5 million Americans have some form of long-term care insurance as of January 1, 2020 (American Association for Long-Term Care Insurance. 2020).

Many children need LTC services because of disability arising from congenital disorders such as cerebral palsy, autism, spina bifida, and epilepsy. The term **developmental disability (DD)** describes the general physical incapacity that such children may face at a very early age. Those who acquire such dysfunctions are referred to as having developmental disabilities. **Intellectual disability (ID)**—that is, below-average intellectual capacity, which can be caused by a disorder such as Down syndrome—also leads to DD status in most cases. The close association between the two is reflected in the term intellectual/developmental disability (IDD). Approximately 14% of children in the 3–17 age group have developmental disabilities; boys are almost twice as likely as girls to have this kind of disability (Boyle et al., 2011). Those with severe ID and/or DD are also likely to have disturbing behavioral issues and usually require institutional care in specialized facilities that provide special programming. Advances in health care have greatly increased the life expectancy for people with IDD, so that many now live well into adulthood. Even so, adults with IDD typically experience premature aging, as they exhibit age-related declines in health and functioning earlier than in the general population (Ouellette-Kuntz et al., 2018).

Other young adults have permanent disabilities stemming from neurodegenerative disease, such as multiple sclerosis (Hauser and Cree, 2020); other degenerative conditions, such as dementia; traumatic injuries, such as those stemming from vehicle crashes, sports mishaps, or industrial accidents; or surgical complications. Subsequent to receiving acute care, these patients often must spend years in an LTC institution.

In recent years, use of highly active antiretroviral therapy in treating human immunodeficiency virus (HIV)/acquired immunodeficiency syndrome (AIDS) has increased the life span of individuals with this disease. Those surviving to older ages with HIV/AIDS, however, often face the prospect of accelerated aging accompanied by increased comorbidity and decline in health and function, leading to premature disablement—both physical and cognitive (Leveille and Thapa, 2017). In LTC settings, people with HIV/AIDS are often younger than other populations, male, and unmarried (Foebel et al., 2015). They may be disconnected from traditional informal support networks and rely heavily on formal care providers (Shippy and Karpiak, 2005).

Patients with HIV/AIDS have a variety of medical and social needs that may evolve over time. Those changing needs may require transitions between community-based services, nursing homes, and hospitals. Effective care coordination for these patients results in fewer unmet needs for supportive services and often better utilization of services (Vargas and Cunningham, 2006).

Level of Care Continuum

The importance of providing different levels of services to a heterogeneous population has given rise to a continuum of clinical categories, ranging from basic personal care to subacute care and specialized services.

Personal Care

Personal care refers to light assistance with basic ADLs. Delivery of these services is largely the domain of **paraprofessionals**—personnel who provide basic ADL services, such as personal care attendants, certified nursing assistants (CNAs), and therapy aides. Personal care can be provided by informal caregivers, home health agencies, adult day care, adult foster care, and residential and assisted living facilities. Higher levels of care often include a component of personal care.

Custodial Care

Custodial care is nonmedical care provided to support and maintain the patient's condition. It requires no active medical or nursing treatments. Services provided are designed to maintain rather than restore functioning, with an emphasis on preventing further deterioration. Examples are personal care with basic ADLs, range-of-motion exercises, bowel and bladder training, and assisted walking. Custodial services are rendered by paraprofessionals, such as aides, rather than by licensed nurses or therapists. The settings in which custodial care is provided resemble those in which personal care is offered.

Restorative Care

In its strictest sense, **restorative care** or rehabilitation refers to restoration of lost function. It involves short-term therapy treatments to help a person regain or improve physical function. Such care is provided immediately after the onset of a disability. Examples of cases requiring short-term restorative therapy include orthopedic surgery, stroke, limb amputation, and prolonged illness. Treatments are rendered by physical therapists, occupational therapists, and speech-language pathologists. Restorative care can be provided by home health agencies, rehabilitation hospitals, outpatient rehabilitation clinics, adult day care centers, and assisted living and skilled nursing facilities.

Skilled Nursing Care

Skilled nursing care is medically oriented care provided mainly by a licensed nurse under the overall direction of a physician in accordance with a plan of care. Delivery of care includes assessment and reassessment to determine the patient's care needs, monitoring of acute and unstable chronic conditions, and a variety of treatments that may include wound care, tube care management, intravenous (IV) therapy, oncology care, HIV/AIDS care, and management of neurologic conditions. Rehabilitation therapies often form an important component of skilled nursing care. Home health agencies and skilled nursing facilities provide skilled nursing care.

Subacute Care

The term **subacute care** describes postacute services for people who remain critically ill during the postacute phase of illness or injury or who have complex conditions that require ongoing monitoring and treatment or intensive rehabilitation. In the past, this level of care was available only in acute-care hospitals. Conditions frequently requiring subacute care upon acute care discharge include respiratory failure, stroke, joint replacement, cardiac surgery, heart failure, and pneumonia (Sultana et al., 2019).

Home- and Community-Based Services

Financing for formal HCBS comes from a variety of sources: private out-of-pocket payments, private long-term care insurance, Medicaid, Medicare, and other public sources. Public policy has been the main impetus behind the growth of HCBS, which has considerably reduced the need for institutionalization.

Under the Older Americans Act of 1965, federal funds are granted to states to support a variety of community-based services, such as nutrition programs for older adults, case management, housekeeping services, and transportation services. These services are available to Americans age 60 years and older, particularly those with social or economic need. The federal Administration on Aging manages the program. LTC programs across the United States are carried out primarily through an administrative network of state agencies on aging, area agencies on aging, and Native American tribal organizations.

In 1981, the HCBS waiver program was enacted under Section 1915(c) of the Social Security Act. The 1915(c) waivers allow states to expand the community-based LTC services delivered through the Medicaid program. Services are available to those Medicaid beneficiaries who would otherwise require institutional care. Today, waiver programs are the largest providers of LTC services for people with IDD (Friedman and Feldner, 2018). Although nearly all states provide HCBS to Medicaid beneficiaries, the eligibility criteria, scope and extent of services offered, and spending per recipient of services vary considerably across states (Segelman et al., 2017). Research also demonstrates that waivers for older adults are primarily focused on supporting individuals in their own homes, allowing them to age in place. In general, though, HCBS waivers are an underutilized mechanism for funding LTC services (Friedman et al., 2019). Some federal funding available to the states under Title XX Social Services Block Grants from the U.S. Department of Health and Human Services (DHHS) may also be used for community-based LTC services when such services can prevent or reduce inappropriate institutionalization. Some states also provide limited assistance with ADLs in a person's home under the Medicaid Personal Care Services program.

A 1999 decision by the U.S. Supreme Court (*Olmstead v. L.C.*) directed states to provide community-based services for persons with disabilities—including persons with IDD, physical disabilities, and mental illness—when such services are determined to be appropriate by healthcare professionals. Also, states must develop a comprehensive working plan to place qualified people with IDD in less restrictive settings. Most adults with IDD now live in community housing with support services.

Even though Medicaid recipients have been the main beneficiaries of policies that promote HCBS, approximately one-fifth of community-dwelling Medicare recipients have serious physical or cognitive limitations, and three-fourths have three or more chronic conditions. Only one-fourth of these Medicare recipients qualify for Medicaid (Davis et al., 2016). Hence, there are serious gaps in their ability to receive LTC services on a continuous basis.

Home Health Care

The organizational setup for home health care commonly involves a community- or hospital-based home health agency that sends healthcare professionals and paraprofessionals to patients' homes to deliver services approved by a physician. Skilled nursing care is the service most often received by home health patients (**Figure 10-4**).

Of the 12,200 home health agencies in the United States, the majority are private for-profit organizations, and almost all are certified by Medicare (Harris-Kojetin et al., 2019). Medicare is the single largest payer for home health services in the country, though Medicaid is not far behind (**Figure 10-5**).

Preliminary evidence indicates that a properly structured home care program may actually reduce disability among older adults, thereby having a strong preventive effect. In a demonstration project funded by the Centers for Medicare and Medicaid Services (CMS), 75% of the older adult participants showed improved performance of ADLs after receiving 5 months of home-based services from an interprofessional team. The average number of ADLs with which the participants had difficulty declined from 3.9 to 2.0 after the 5-month program (Szanton et al., 2016).

Adult Daycare

Adult daycare (ADC) is a daytime group program designed to meet the needs of functionally and/or cognitively impaired adults and to provide partial respite to family caregivers so they can work during the day or pursue other responsibilities of life. ADC is designed for people who live with their families but cannot safely remain alone during the day. As of 2020, there were an estimated 5,500 adult day services centers in the United States serving 237,400 participants, with a total allowable

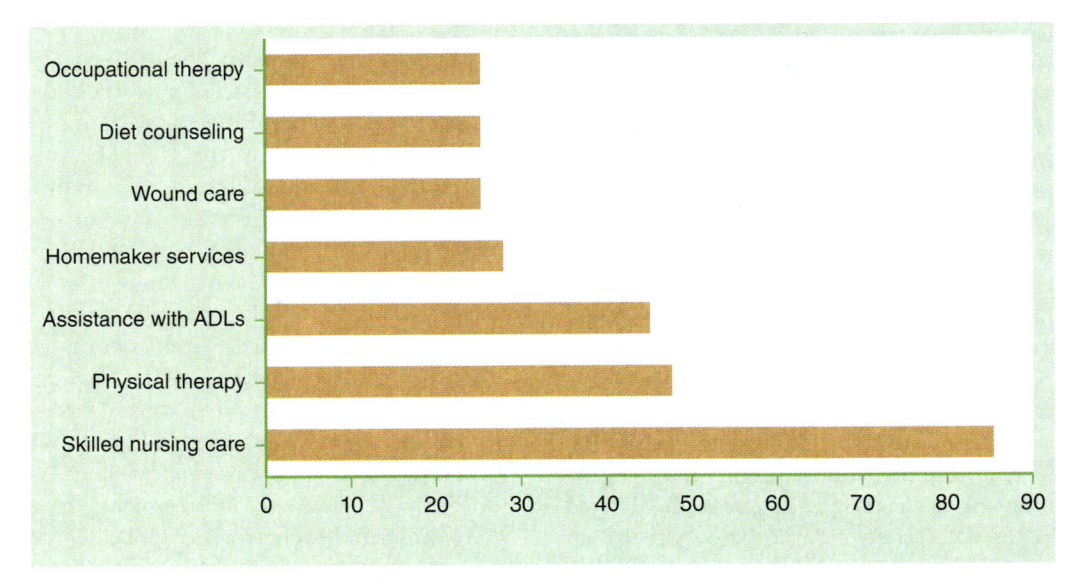

Figure 10-4 Most frequently provided services to home health patients.

Data from Jones, A. L., et al. 2012. Characteristics and use of home health care by men and women aged 65 and over. National health statistics reports, no. 52. Hyattsville, MD: National Center for Health Statistics.

Figure 10-5 Sources of payment for home health care, 2017.

Data from National Center for Health Statistics. 2019. *Health, United States, 2018.* Hyattsville, MD: U.S. Department of Health and Human Services. Table 44.

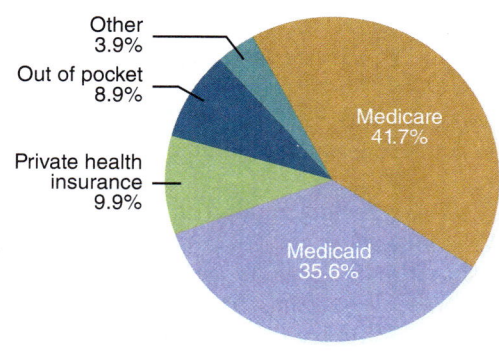

- Medicare 41.7%
- Medicaid 35.6%
- Private health insurance 9.9%
- Out of pocket 8.9%
- Other 3.9%

Total expenditures = $83.2 billion

capacity of 294,000 participants (National Center for Health Statistics. 2020).

These centers operate programs during normal business hours 5 days per week, although some offer evening and weekend services as well. Half of all ADCs in the United States predominantly serve racial/ethnic minorities (Lendon et al., 2020), and ADC populations are more ethnically diverse than those found in nursing homes and assisted living facilities (Harris-Kojetin et al., 2019).

Most ADC services are highly focused on prevention and health maintenance, with the objective of preventing or delaying institutionalization, but they also incorporate nursing care, psychosocial therapies, and rehabilitation. As such, ADC services, in many instances, have become alternatives to home health care and assisted living, or serve as a transitional step before placement in an LTC institution.

Not all ADC centers provide the same level of services. Almost 65% of these programs provide nursing care, 68% offer dietary and nutritional services, about half offer rehabilitation and social services, and approximately one-third offer mental health (including dementia care) and pharmacy services (Harris-Kojetin et al., 2019). Group socialization, therapeutic recreational activities, and meals are included.

Medicaid provides funding for ADC services under Section 1915(c) waivers; almost 66% of the users have Medicaid as the source of funding (Harris-Kojetin et al., 2019). Medicare does not pay for ADC services but may cover rehabilitation services under Part B.

Adult Foster Care

Adult foster care (AFC) is a service characterized by small, family-run homes that provide room, board, and varying levels of supervision, oversight, and personal care to nonrelated adults who are unable to care for themselves ("AARP Studies Adult Foster Care for the Elderly," 1996). The foster care setting comprises a community-based private home for people who do not require skilled nursing care. Participants in such programs are older adults or individuals with disabilities who have a medical diagnosis, a psychiatric diagnosis, or a need for personal care. Typically, the caregiving family resides in part of the home. To maintain the family environment, most states license fewer than 10 beds per family unit.

This type of program differs widely from state to state and goes by several names, including adult family care, community residential care, and domiciliary care. Each state has established its own standards for the licensing of AFCs. Funding for AFCs may come from Medicaid, private insurance, or personal sources. Medicare does not pay for AFC services but may cover rehabilitation services under Part B.

The Veterans Health Administration (VHA) established a medical foster home (MFH) program in 2008. It combines the typical foster care consisting of supervision and personal assistance with comprehensive medical care through its home-based primary-care (HBPC) program. The veterans pay out of pocket for room, board, and support, and the VHA pays for and provides medical care. This program provides an alternative to typical nursing home care (Levy et al., 2019).

Senior Centers

Senior centers are local community centers for older adults where seniors can congregate and socialize. Nearly 11,000 senior centers serve more than 1 million older adults every day in the United States (National Council on Aging, 2015). Many centers offer one or more meals daily. Others sponsor wellness programs, health education, counseling services, recreational activities, information and referrals, and limited healthcare services, including health screening, especially for glaucoma and hypertension. Funding comes from a variety of sources—for example, federal, state, and local governments; fundraising events; public and private grants; businesses; bequests; and participant contributions (National Council on Aging, 2015).

Home-Delivered and Congregate Meals

The Elderly Nutrition Program (ENP) is the nation's oldest framework for providing community- and home-based preventive nutrition in the United States. This program has been in operation since 1972 for congregate meals, and since 1978 for home-delivered meals. The ENP program was authorized under the Older Americans Act, which also provides the majority of its funding. Additional funds are provided through Title XX block grants, 1915(c) waivers, and private donations.

The ENP provides a hot noon meal 5 days per week to Americans 60 years and older (and their spouses) who cannot prepare a nutritionally balanced noon meal for themselves. Home-delivered meals for homebound persons are commonly referred to as **meals-on-wheels**. Ambulatory clients are encouraged to get their meals at senior centers or other congregate settings, where they also have the opportunity to socialize.

ENP services successfully meet the needs of the community-dwelling vulnerable older people. For example, participants in the meals-on-wheels program are more than twice as likely as the general population to be in poor or fair health, more than half live alone, more than one-third are age 85 or older, and more than one-third have difficulty with three or more ADLs (Kowlessar et al., 2015).

It is a common practice for local-area Agencies on Aging to contract out the preparation of ENP meals to local nursing homes, hospitals, or religious organizations. Volunteers then carry the meals to homebound participants. Congregate meals may be served on the premises of participating facilities, such as hospitals and nursing homes, or at local senior centers or religious establishments.

Housekeeping Services

Depending on availability of funds, states may provide limited housekeeping and chore services—such as essential shopping, light cleaning, meal preparation, and minor home repairs—to low-income people. Such homemaker programs may be staffed largely or entirely by volunteers. The Medicaid program may pay for some housekeeping services, or these services may be funded through the local seniors programs under Title XX Social Services Block Grants or the Older Americans Act. Besides the limited public funding options that help a relatively small number of people, private housekeeping service agencies have sprung up across the nation.

Continuing Care at Home

Continuing care at home (CCAH) is a new model of home-based care that has only recently emerged. Its growth has been slow because of regulatory issues at the state government level. CCAH programs represent an extension of the continuing care retirement center (CCRC) model that has been in existence for a number of years. As discussed later in this chapter, CCRCs provide a continuum of housing and institutional LTC services on one campus. Thus, CCRCs are also at the forefront of developing these home-based programs.

To participate in the CCAH program, clients are required to pay an initial lump-sum fee and a monthly fee under a contract that guarantees a person's future LTC. To qualify, a person must be in good health and not need LTC services at the time of enrollment. CCAH services typically include care coordination, routine home maintenance, home health care, transportation, meals, and social and wellness programs (Spellman and Brod, 2014). Most services are provided at the client's home, with the objective of delaying institutionalization. When institutional services are needed, the client receives them at the CCRC's assisted living and/or skilled nursing care facilities or at subcontracted local facilities.

Case Management

Case management involves evaluating a patient's physical, medical, and psychosocial needs; preparing a plan to address those needs and identifying the services that would be most appropriate, including LTC; determining eligibility for services and how those services would be financed; making referrals to those services; coordinating the delivery of services; and reevaluating the patient's needs as circumstances change over time. Two main case management models are widely used today: the brokerage model and the managed care/integrated model.

Brokerage Model

In the **brokerage model**, once the patient's needs have been independently assessed, case managers arrange services through other providers. The case manager is usually a freestanding agent who is mainly responsible for linking the patient with other organizations, agencies, and service providers, but has no formal administrative or financial relationship with these entities. The main functions of case management carried out in this model are needs assessment, development of a service plan, and making referrals. There is minimal coordination and monitoring of services.

In the public domain, preadmission screening is a type of the brokerage model. The purpose of such screening is to determine whether a Medicaid beneficiary's needs can be better met in a nursing facility or through HCBS. In addition, federal regulations require an evaluation of a patient for mental illness and/or ID before such a patient can be admitted to a Medicaid-certified nursing facility (refer to the discussion of nursing facility certification under "Skilled Nursing Facilities"); this process is called **Preadmission Screening and Resident Review (PASRR)**.

Managed Care/Integrated Model

The managed care/integrated model of case management has two main features: (1) capitation as a method of payment and (2) all-inclusive services provided within the fixed capitation fee. For Medicaid recipients, an increasing number of states have contracted with health maintenance organizations (HMOs) to provide integrated LTC services that include care coordination, various community-based services, and nursing home placement when indicated. As would be expected in state-run programs, access to services and care coordination varies depending on the state of residence (Williamson et al., 2016).

Another integrated model is the **Program of All-Inclusive Care for the Elderly (PACE)**. PACE programs receive capitated funding from Medicare and Medicaid to cover all services and are responsible for meeting the full spectrum of their enrollees' healthcare needs (Segelman et al., 2014). This program is available in most states to people 55 years and older. It focuses on frail older adults who have already been certified for nursing home placement under Medicare and/or Medicaid. PACE's main purpose is to prevent the progression of disability and to keep the participants out of nursing homes. At the core of the program are ADC services, augmented by home care and meals-on-wheels (Gross et al., 2004).

PACE was authorized under the Balanced Budget Act of 1997 after the On Lok project in San Francisco demonstrated that, in many instances, institutionalization could be prevented through appropriate case management. Under this program, all medical care and social services are coordinated by a PACE team. PACE has no deductibles or copayments—which is an incentive for qualified individuals to participate. Studies have consistently shown that the rates of hospitalization and readmission are substantially lower for PACE enrollees than for comparable populations (Segelman et al., 2014). Consequently, this approach offers substantial cost savings over alternative models of LTC delivery (Wieland et al., 2013).

Recent Policies Related to Community-Based Services

The two main policies discussed here simply add to the patchwork of options that benefit mainly Medicaid recipients while leaving many of the Medicare recipients with unmet LTC needs.

Money Follows the Person

The **Money Follows the Person (MFP)** demonstration program was codified in the Deficit Reduction Act (DRA) of 2005 to provide adequate federal funding to states for the sole purpose of moving qualified people whose care is funded by Medicaid from nursing homes back into community-based settings. The precursors to the MFP program were demonstration projects in most states, launched between 1998 and 2002 through federal grants, that showed many nursing home residents could successfully transition back to their communities. Under the MFP program, funds that had previously been used by the state to pay for nursing home care are applied toward HCBS. This program enables Medicaid beneficiaries residing in an inpatient facility for 90 days or more to move to a qualified residence in the community. Participants are eligible for MFP services for 365 days after they have made the move (Liao and Peebles, 2019).

The MFP program has shown slow but steady progress in transitioning people out of nursing homes. Declines in Medicaid and Medicare expenditures after transition of all target populations have been noted (Irvin, 2015). However, several barriers to community discharge persist, including the need for rehabilitation or personal assistance services, lack of caregiver support, finances, housing, and transportation. Some of these barriers can result from an extended period of institutionalization (Mills et al., 2013).

Community First Choice

The Affordable Care Act (ACA) created financial incentives for states to establish "attendant services and supports" to deliver personal care to individuals who require an institutional level of care. To qualify for the Community First Choice (CFC) program, which supplies such care, the individual must be eligible for Medicaid and have an income that does not exceed 150% of the federal poverty level. To date, only a few states have implemented this program. The need to maintain existing programs alongside CFC was mentioned by several states as influencing their decision not to implement this program (DHHS, 2015).

Institutional Long-Term Care Continuum

Institutional LTC is appropriate for patients whose needs cannot be adequately met in a community-based setting. Apart from the patient's clinical condition, factors such as inability to live alone or lack of social support may suggest a need for the individual to be in an institution. The institutional sector of LTC offers a continuum of services (refer to Figure 10-3), from institutions that offer only basic personal and custodial care to those that provide skilled nursing, subacute care, or specialized services. However, the distinction between some of the institutional categories is not always clear-cut. It is a common practice to refer to people residing in LTC institutions as "residents" rather than as "patients."

For institutions at the lower end of the services continuum, and even in independent living and supportive housing, the concept of **aging-in-place** has become important, particularly from the viewpoint of consumer choice. This concept refers to people's preference and expectation to stay in one place for as long as possible and to delay or avoid transfer to an institution where the acuity level of residents is higher. In residential care facilities, management often faces the dilemma of how to continue to house residents who have escalating needs for care—for example, when patients develop incontinence of bladder or bowel.

Most care in LTC institutions is provided by nonphysician staff, such as nurses, CNAs, dietitians, social workers, and therapists. Residents have the right to be treated by a physician of their choice, who makes periodic rounds to monitor the care being delivered. A transfer agreement with a local hospital facilitates transition between the acute care and LTC facilities. At the onset of an acute episode, such as pneumonia or injury from a fall, the resident is transferred to a hospital.

Residential and Personal Care Facilities

Residential and personal care facilities are also known as "domiciliary care facilities," "board-and-care homes," or "sheltered care facilities." Sometimes AFC homes and even assisted living facilities are combined together with this category. For example, the report by Harris-Kojetin et al. (2019) lumps together "assisted living and similar residential care communities" in one category, even though the two types of facilities are quite distinct in terms of the services they provide.

Residential and personal care facilities provide physically supportive dwelling units, monitoring and/or assistance with medications, oversight, and personal or custodial care. No nursing or medical services are provided. To maintain a residential rather than an institutional environment, many such facilities limit the admission of residents with severe disabilities, but some may take patients with mild levels of mental dysfunction. Services are provided by paraprofessionals rather than by licensed personnel. Minimal staffing is provided 24 hours a day for supervision and assistive purposes. More advanced services can be arranged through an external home health agency when needed.

In terms of the level of comfort, these kinds of facilities can range from spartan to deluxe. The latter are often private-pay facilities. For people who have limited incomes, Supplemental Security Income (SSI) can be used along with other types of government assistance funds to pay for housing. Services include meals, housekeeping and laundry services, and social and recreational activities.

Assisted Living Facilities

An **assisted living facility (ALF)** provides some nursing and rehabilitation services in addition to personal care, 24-hour supervision, social services, and recreational activities. These facilities are appropriate for people who cannot function independently but do not require skilled nursing care. Some ALFs, however, now offer Alzheimer's/dementia care (Hoban, 2013). ALFs operate predominantly on a private-pay basis. To maintain the desired residential environment, these facilities generally have private accommodations rather than the semi-private accommodations commonly found in skilled nursing facilities.

All states now require ALFs to be licensed. In the absence of federal standards, however, regulations vary from state to state. These regulations continue to evolve in response to the rising acuity levels of residents. More than half of the residents in ALFs have considerable healthcare needs, such as needs for nursing care and assistance with transfers, medications, eating, and dressing. Yet, in one research study, fewer than half of the facilities were found to have registered nurses or licensed practical nurses on staff (Han et al., 2016). Because of the lack of regulatory oversight, evaluations of quality in ALFs are practically nonexistent.

Skilled Nursing Facilities

A **skilled nursing facility (SNF)** is a typical nursing home at the higher end of the institutional continuum. Patients are generally transferred from a hospital to the SNF after an acute episode. Over time, the care needs of the residents in SNFs have become increasingly more complex, requiring much higher levels of staffing compared to ALFs. Although many nursing home residents stay for a long period of time (sometimes for years), short-term stays for convalescence and rehabilitation under Medicare coverage have become common.

Alzheimer's disease and depression are the most common diagnoses among nursing home residents, more than in any other type of LTC setting. Residents in nursing homes and those using home health services in community settings have approximately the same level of needs in regard to assistance with ADLs; one main exception is toileting, for which the need for assistance is higher among nursing home residents (Harris-Kojetin et al., 2019). Nursing home residents, however, require higher levels of nursing care and medical oversight.

The nursing home environment is generally more institutional and clinical than the residential environment emphasized in ALFs. In recent years, a movement, loosely referred to as "culture change," has sought to transform the existing facilities into more homelike and vibrant living environments. Newer facilities are being built with innovative designs that offer a sense of community living, a greater degree of privacy, and enriched environments that promote physical and psychological well-being and reduce boredom and stress (refer to Singh, 2016, Chapter 7).

SNFs are heavily regulated through licensure and certification requirements. All facilities in a particular state must be licensed, though licensing regulations differ considerably from state to state. Most licensing regulations establish the minimum qualifications required for administrators and other staff, prescribe minimum staffing levels, establish standards for building construction, and require compliance with the national fire and safety codes. To admit residents covered under the Medicaid and/or Medicare programs, nursing homes must also be certified and must demonstrate compliance with the federal certification standards enforced by the CMS. These standards are quite stringent and are often regarded as minimum standards of quality. Compliance is verified through periodic inspections.

The Nursing Home Reform Act, passed in 1987, created two categories for certification purposes. A nursing home certified to admit Medicare residents is called an SNF. This facility can be freestanding or a **distinct part**—that is, a section of a nursing home that is distinctly separate and distinguishable from the rest of the facility. When SNF certification applies to a distinct part, Medicare residents can be admitted only to that section. A nursing home certified for Medicaid only (but not for Medicare) is called a **nursing facility (NF)**. Most nursing homes have opted for **dual certification** as both an SNF and an NF, which allows them to admit Medicare- and/or Medicaid-insured residents. The federal certification standards governing SNFs and NFs are essentially the same. Medicare- and Medicaid-insured residents do not receive two different levels of services; rather, the SNF and NF categories have been created to account for the two distinct sources of public financing.

The term "facility" does not necessarily refer to a separate physical structure in this context. Instead, this term can be used for the facility as a whole or, within the context of licensure and certification, it may apply more specifically to different sections or units of a building (distinct parts) with different certifications or no certification (**Figure 10-6**).

A small proportion of facilities have elected not to participate in the Medicaid and/or Medicare programs. They can admit only residents who can pay privately, either out of pocket or through private LTC insurance. These facilities are described as **noncertified**; however, they must be licensed under the state licensure regulations. **Private-pay residents**—those not covered by either Medicare or Medicaid for nursing home care—are not restricted to noncertified facilities; that is, these residents also may be admitted to SNF- or NF-certified beds. Thus, the restriction applies only to Medicare- and Medicaid-insured residents, who cannot be admitted to noncertified facilities.

The ACA requires that to participate in the Medicare and/or Medicaid programs, nursing facilities must institute effective compliance and ethics programs (Farhat, 2013). The ACA also mandates that nursing facilities implement the Quality Assurance Performance Improvement (QAPI) program, which was developed by the CMS. QAPI's goal is not only to correct quality lapses once they are identified but also to continuously improve quality performance.

The CMS provides Web-accessible information on nursing homes' compliance and quality for consumers through a program called Nursing Home Compare. The information provided includes five-star quality ratings that incorporate performance on certification inspections, quality measures, and staff hours per resident.

Subacute Care Facilities

The three main institutional locations for subacute care—long-term care hospitals (LTCHs), hospital transitional care units/extended care units (HTCUs/ECUs) certified as SNFs, and freestanding nursing homes—vary in terms of availability, cost, and quality. Selection of

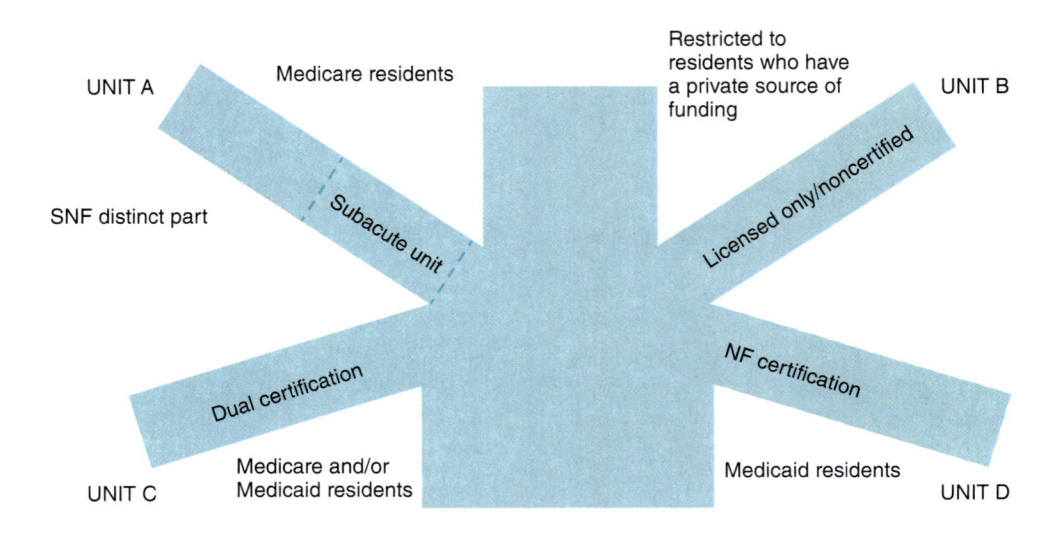

Figure 10-6 Distinctly certified units in a nursing home.

the most appropriate setting for a specific patient is governed by numerous factors, both clinical and nonclinical. The main nonclinical factor is the availability of subacute care services in a given location (Buntin et al., 2005).

In terms of costs, LTCHs are the most expensive. In some cases, nursing homes are a more cost-effective alternative to LTCHs. Because of their high cost, LTCHs are appropriate for medically stable, post–intensive care unit patients (Medicare Payment Advisory Commission [MedPAC], 2016).

Postacute needs can vary widely among patients, but there is no uniform system of clinical assessment and payment for subacute care. Medicare uses different payment methodologies for the different settings.

Specialized Care Facilities

Specialized facilities provide services for individuals with distinct medical needs. For example, some nursing homes and subacute care facilities have specialized units for residents requiring ventilator care, wound care, intensive rehabilitation, closed head trauma care, or Alzheimer's/dementia care. Specialized facilities also exist for IDD patients who require active treatment.

Intermediate Care Facilities for Individuals with Intellectual Disabilities

In 1971, Section 1905(d) of the Social Security Act authorized Medicaid coverage for the care of IDD residents in specialized facilities. Most of these residents have other disabilities in addition to ID. For example, many (1) are nonambulatory; (2) have seizure disorders, behavioral problems, mental illness, or visual or hearing impairments; or (3) have a combination of these conditions. For the care of these residents, federal regulations have provided a separate certification category for LTC facilities classified as intermediate care facilities for individuals with intellectual disabilities (ICF/IIDs). The primary purpose of ICF/IIDs is to furnish nursing and rehabilitative services that involve "active treatment." Active treatment entails aggressive and consistent specialized programs that include skill training to help the residents function as independently as possible.

Alzheimer's Facilities

Informal caregivers, ADC centers, and ALFs can all play a role in the care of people living with dementia, but specialized Alzheimer's facilities are often needed for patients who have severe dementia or when comorbid conditions are present. Modern Alzheimer's facilities are characterized by small-group living arrangements, copious use of natural lighting, pastel colors, pleasant surroundings, protected pathways for wandering, and special programming. All these features are integrated to provide an environment that helps minimize agitation, anxiety, disruptiveness, and combativeness.

Continuing Care Retirement Communities

A **continuing care retirement community (CCRC)** integrates and coordinates independent living and institutional components of the LTC continuum. As a convenience factor, different levels of services are all located on the same campus. CCRCs also guarantee delivery of higher-level services when future needs arise. Services include independent living in cottages or apartments with or without support services, and medical and nursing care, rehabilitation, and social services in an ALF or

SNF. Residents enter these communities when they are still relatively healthy.

CCRCs, for the most part, require private financing, with the exception of services delivered in a Medicare-certified SNF. Three types of CCRC contracts are common in the industry:

- A life care or extended contract comprises a complete package of services that includes a commitment to provide unlimited future LTC services without an increase in the monthly fee.
- A modified contract provides for support services in independent living and includes a limited number of days of care in assisted living and SNF without an increase in the monthly fee.
- A fee-for-service contract includes only support services in independent living; higher levels of services must be paid for out of pocket at the prevailing rates.

There is a wide variation in entrance and monthly fees for CCRCs based on amenities and the type of contract. In the state of New York, for example, entrance fees begin at approximately $115,000 for a single-person independent living unit; monthly fees begin at approximately $2,100 (New York Department of Health, 2022). There are currently more than 2,000 CCRCs in the United States.

Institutional Trends, Utilization, and Expenditures

With the emphasis in government policy placed on community-based care, the institutional LTC sector has undergone significant changes over time. For example, the number of nursing home beds per 1,000 population age 65 and older has steadily declined, decreasing from 49.7 beds in 2000 to a low of 35.1 beds in 2015 (Sanofi-Aventis, 2016). The total number of assisted living facility beds, in contrast, increased from 779,700 beds in 2011 to 789,800 beds in 2015 (Sanofi-Aventis, 2016). Over time, community-based services and assisted living have absorbed much of the care that was previously delivered by nursing homes. Consequently, nursing homes have experienced a gradual decline in occupancy rates.

Table 10-2 presents trends in nursing home capacity, utilization, and expenditures for nursing homes. Medicaid is the single largest payer for nursing home services (**Figure 10-7**). Although spending for nursing homes has risen rather dramatically (as shown in Table 10-2), as a proportion of the total national healthcare expenditures, spending

Table 10-2 Trends in Nursing Home Capacity, Utilization, and Expenditures, Selected Years

		2000	2005	2016	Change 2000–2016
Capacity	Number of facilities	16,886	15,995	15,647	−7.3%
	Number of beds	1,795,388	1,724,582	1,690,304	−5.9%
Utilization	Number of residents	1,480,076	1,436,442	1,346,941	−9.0%
	Occupancy	82.4%	83.3%	79.7%	−2.7%-age points
Expenditures	Total expenditures (millions of $)	85,045	111,436	163,029	+91.7%

Data from Health, United States, 2007, Table 117; Health, United States, 2017, Table 92. National Center for Health Statistics. Hyattsville, MD: U.S. Department of Health and Human Services. Centers for Medicare and Medicaid Services. National health expenditure data. NHE tables (historical).

454 Chapter 10 Long-Term Care

Figure 10-7 Sources of Payment for nursing home care, 2018.

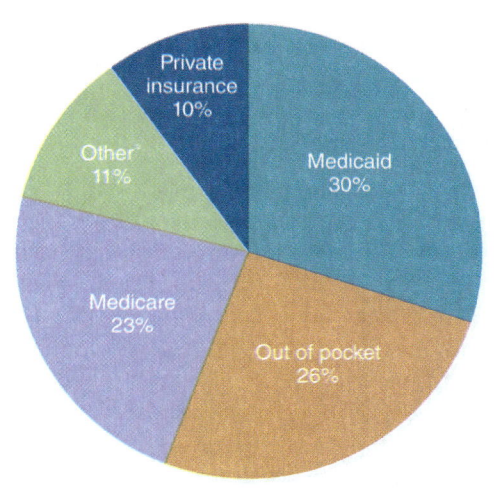

Medicaid 30%
Out of pocket 26%
Medicare 23%
Other* 11%
Private insurance 10%

Total expenditures: $168.5 billion

*VA, state and local programs, other private revenues

Data from Centers for Medicare and Medicaid Services (CMS). 2019c. *National health expenditure data. NHE tables (historical)*. Available at: https://www.cms.gov/Research-Statistics-Data-and-Systems/Statistics-Trends-and-Reports/NationalHealthExpendData/NationalHealthAccountsHistorical. Accessed October 2020.

for nursing homes has decreased from 5.4% in 2010 to 4.6% in 2018 (CMS, 2019).

The number of SNFs sharing providers with hospitals decreased from 6,966 in 2008 to 4,773 in 2016, whereas the mean number of partnering hospitals per SNF increased modestly from 1.26 in 2008 to 1.35 in 2016 (White et al., 2020). As of 2021, the number of skilled nursing facilities had decreased to 14,908, the lowest it has been since 2005 when there were 15,006 skilled nursing facilities (Statista, 2023). The statistic represents the total number of Medicare skilled nursing facilities in the United States from 1967 to 2021. Medicare regulations and changes in reimbursement are the likely causes of this decline. Some of the hospital-based SNFs may have been converted to LTCHs, which have undergone an increase in their numbers over time.

ALFs and other residential/personal care facilities continue to serve a larger number of residents. For example, the number of users of these facilities increased by 14% between 2012 and 2016 (National Center for Health Statistics, 2019). Nursing home services are used mostly by people in the 65–84 age group. However, the oldest old are the predominant users of ALFs and other residential/personal care facilities (**Table 10-3**).

Insurance for Long-Term Care

Private LTC insurance is separate from regular health insurance, as the latter generally does not cover LTC costs. Medicare, which is the major health insurance program for older Americans, also does not cover most LTC services. Medicaid requires spending down most of one's assets to poverty levels to qualify for LTC coverage. As the cost of LTC continues to rise, most people are likely to have few options for paying for such care. Moreover, most are unprepared to cope with the high risk of needing LTC in their retirement years, a period when incomes for most people also dwindle.

Table 10-3 Use of Nursing Home and ALF/Residential/Personal Care Facilities by Age Groups, 2016

	<65 Years	65–84 Years	85+ Years
Nursing homes	16.5%	44.9%	38.6%
ALF/residential/personal care facilities	6.6%	41.3%	52.1%

Reproduced from National Center for Health Statistics. 2019. *Health, United States, 2018*. Hyattsville, MD: U.S. Department of Health and Human Services.

LTC expenditures may potentially eat into the income and savings of a large portion of middle-class retirees, jeopardizing their standard of living (Ameriks et al., 2016).

After experiencing rapid growth until 2006, the number of people carrying LTC insurance has leveled off. One area of growth comprises combination or hybrid products that combine LTC benefits with either life insurance or an annuity. These products can pay out if LTC is needed, but if not needed, they provide a death benefit or annuity payout (Ameriks et al., 2016).

As people continue to live longer, claims paid by LTC insurers have risen sharply. Consequently, premiums have become unaffordable for most middle-income people. Also, a large number of LTC insurers have left the market altogether. Insurers have faced challenges in anticipating future costs and the ability to spread the risk over a large number of people because of leveling sales of LTC policies. For several years, the ratio of actual to expected losses from claim payments has exceeded 100%. In fact, between 2010 and 2014, the LTC insurance industry experienced deterioration in its financial performance because the underlying morbidity assumptions used in the initial pricing of premiums were too low (Ameriks et al., 2016).

Public policy has created few incentives to spur the growth of LTC insurance. The DRA of 2005 created the Long-Term Care Insurance Partnership Program, which allows individuals who purchase private LTC insurance to shield part of their financial assets when they become eligible to receive Medicaid benefits for LTC. This policy seems to have had some effect in spurring the purchase of LTC insurance. By 2015, slightly more than two out of every five new LTC policies sold were Partnership policies. More than half the states provide tax incentives for the purchase of LTC insurance, but there is little evidence that such incentives have played a noticeable role in persuading consumers to purchase LTC insurance (Ameriks et al., 2016).

The ACA did little to address the impending dilemma of how to provide LTC—a dilemma that many people will face as they age. The impending burden on Medicaid and Medicare will be unsustainable. Hence, LTC financing is at a critical juncture.

Summary

The need for long-term care arises when an individual is no longer able to perform ADL and/or IADL functions because of a severe chronic condition, multiple illnesses, or cognitive impairment. Such individuals may need both LTC and non-LTC services on an ongoing basis. LTC is unique within the healthcare delivery arena and is a multidimensional concept.

LTC encompasses medical care, nursing, rehabilitation, social support, mental health care, housing alternatives, and end-of-life care. LTC services often complement what people with impaired functioning can do for themselves. Informal caregivers provide the bulk of LTC services in the United States. Respite care can provide family members with temporary relief from the burden of caregiving. When the required intensity of care exceeds the capabilities of informal caregivers, alternatives include professional community-based services to supplement informal care.

Institutional services vary from basic personal assistance to more complex skilled nursing care and subacute care. Institutional care can be of long or short duration. People with severe dementia, incontinence, severe psychiatric or behavioral issues, or unstable postacute conditions, and those in a comatose/vegetative state may need nursing home care for a long time. Other patients may require short-term postacute convalescence and restorative care. A continuing care retirement community offers independent living and institution-based LTC services. Specialized institutions exist for people with Alzheimer's disease or severe intellectual or developmental disability.

Nursing homes must have federal SNF certification to admit patients with Medicare insurance as well as NF certification for patient admittance. Most facility beds in the United States are dually certified as both SNFs and NFs. Medicaid is the most common source of funding for nursing home care.

The LTC industry has become more competitive as services offered by community-based and institutional options have started to overlap. Within the institutional sector, the number of nursing homes and beds has been declining; this trend is especially pronounced for hospital-based SNFs. Conversely, ALFs have experienced remarkable growth.

Although costs for LTC provided in the public sector continue to rise, few people have purchased private LTC insurance. Better government policies are needed to spur growth in private insurance, as Medicaid and Medicare expenditures for LTC will be unsustainable in the long term.

TEST YOUR UNDERSTANDING

Terminology

adult daycare (ADC)
adult foster care (AFC)
aging-in-place
Alzheimer's disease
assisted living facility (ALF)
brokerage model
case management
cognitive impairment
continuing care retirement community (CCRC)
custodial care
dementia
developmental disability (DD)
distinct part
dual certification
evidence-based care
intellectual disability (ID)
long-term care (LTC)
meals-on-wheels
Money Follows the Person (MFP)
noncertified
nursing facility (NF)
palliation
paraprofessionals
personal care
personal emergency response system (PERS)
person-centered care
Preadmission Screening and Resident Review (PASRR)
private-pay residents
Program of All-Inclusive Care for the Elderly (PACE)
quality of life
respite care
restorative care
senior centers
skilled nursing care
skilled nursing facility (SNF)
subacute care
total care

Review Questions

1. Long-term care services must be individualized, integrated, and coordinated. Elaborate on this statement, pointing out why these elements are essential in the delivery of LTC.
2. Age is not the primary determinant for long-term care. Comment on this statement, explaining why this is or is not true.
3. What is meant by "quality of life"? Briefly discuss the five main features of this multifaceted concept.
4. What are some of the challenges in the delivery of mental health services for older people?

5. Discuss the preventive and therapeutic aspects of long-term care.
6. How do formal long-term care and informal long-term care differ? What is the importance of informal care in LTC delivery?
7. What are the main goals of community-based and institution-based LTC services?
8. What is respite care? Why is it needed?
9. Distinguish between supportive housing and institutional long-term care.
10. Why do some children and adolescents need long-term care?
11. Why has long-term care become an important service for people with HIV/AIDS?
12. Briefly discuss the brokerage model of case management and the PACE program.
13. What is meant by the continuum of institutional long-term care? Discuss the clinical services delivered by residential/personal care facilities, assisted living facilities, and skilled nursing facilities.
14. What is the difference between licensure and certification? What are the two types of certifications? What purpose does each serve from (a) a clinical standpoint and (b) a financial standpoint?
15. Describe a continuing care retirement community. Include in your response the financing and contractual arrangements.
16. Discuss the main issues with private long-term care insurance. Briefly explain the Long-Term Care Insurance Partnership Program.

References

Administration for Community Living. 2022. AARP Studies Adult Foster Care for the Elderly. 1996. *Public Health Reports* 111: 295.

Long-TermCare.gov. n.d. How Much Care Will You Need? Accessed October 2024. Available at: https://acl.gov/ltc/basic-needs/how-much-care-will-you-need

Administration on Aging (AoA). 2020. 2019 Profile of Older Americans. Accessed September 2020. Available at: https://acl.gov/sites/default/files/Aging%20and%20Disability%20in%20America/2019ProfileOlderAmericans508.pdf

Alzheimer's Association. 2020. 2020 Alzheimer's Disease Facts and Figures. Accessed September 2020. Available at: https://www.alz.org/media/Documents/alzheimers-facts-and-figures_1.pdf

American Association for Long-Term Care Insurance. 2020. Long-Term Care Insurance Facts Data–Statistics–2020 Reports. Accessed November 2023. Available at: https://www.aaltci.org/long-term-care-insurance/learning-center/ltcfacts-2020.php#2020total

Ameriks, J., V. Bodnar, J. Briggs, et al. 2016. The State of Long-Term Care Insurance: The Market, Challenges, and Future Innovations. Kansas City, MO: National Association of Insurance Commissioners.

Barba, B. E., J. Hu, and J. Efird. 2012. Quality Geriatric Care as Perceived by Nurses in Long-term and Acute Care Settings. *Journal of Clinical Nursing* 21: 833–840.

Boyle, C. A., S. Boulet, L. A. Schieve, et al. 2011. Trends in the Prevalence of Developmental Disabilities in US Children, 1997–2008. *Pediatrics* 127: 1034–1042.

Buntin, M. B., A. D. Garten, S. Paddock, D. Saliba, M. Totten, and J. J. Escarce. 2005. How Much is Postacute Care Use Affected by Its Availability? *Health Services Research* 40: 413–434.

Centers for Medicare and Medicaid Services (CMS). 2019. National Health Expenditure Data. NHE Tables (Historical). Accessed October 2020. Available at: https://www.cms.gov/Research-Statistics-Data-and-Systems/Statistics-Trends-and-Reports/NationalHealthExpendData/NationalHealthAccountsHistorical

Congressional Budget Office (CBO). 2013. Rising Demand for Long-Term Services and Supports for Elderly People. Accessed December 2020. Available at: https://www.cbo.gov/sites/default/files/113th-congress-2013-2014/reports/44363-ltc.pdf

Davis, K., A. Willink, and C. Schoen. 2016. Medicare Help at Home. Health Affairs Blog. Accessed October 2020. Available at: https://www.healthaffairs.org/do/10.1377/hblog20160413.054429/full/

Department of Health and Human Services, U.S. (DHHS). 2015. Community First Choice: Final Report to Congress. Accessed October 2020. Available at: https://www.medicaid.gov/sites/default/files/2019-12/cfc-final-report-to-congress.pdf

Farhat, T. 2013. Compliance Clock Ticks. *McKnight's Long-Term Care News* 34: 30–31.

Favreault, M., and J. Dey. 2016. Long-Term Services and Supports for Older Americans: Risks and Financing. U.S. Department of Health and Human Services. Accessed September 2020. Available at: https://aspe.hhs.gov/system/files/pdf/106211/ElderLTCrb-rev.pdf

Federal Interagency Forum on Aging-Related Statistics. 2016. Older Americans 2016: Key Indicators of Well-Being. Washington, DC: US Government Printing Office.

Fisher, K., L. E. Griffith, A. Gruneir, D. Kanters, M. Markle-Reid, and L. Ploeg. 2021. Functional Limitations in People with Multimorbidity and the Association with Mental Health Conditions: Baseline Data from the Canadian Longitudinal Study on Aging (CLSA). *PLoS One* 16: e0255907.

Foebel, A. D., J. P. Hirdes, R. Lemick, and J. W. Y. Tai. 2015. Comparing the Characteristics of People Living with and Without HIV in Long-Term Care and Home Care in Ontario, Canada. *AIDS Care* 27: 1343–1353.

Friedman, C., and H. A. Feldner. 2018. Physical Therapy Services for People with Intellectual and Developmental Disabilities: The Role of Medicaid Home- and Community-Based Service Waivers. *Physical Therapy* 98: 844–854.

Friedman, C., J. Caldwell, A. Rapp Kennedy, and M. C. Rizzolo. 2019. Aging in Place: A National Analysis of Home- and Community-Based Medicaid Services for Older Adults. *Journal of Disability Policy Studies* 29: 245–256.

Gerteis, J., D. Izrael, D. Deitz, L. LeRoy, R. Ricciardi, R. Miller, and J. Basu. 2014. Multiple Chronic Conditions Chartbook: 2010 Medical Expenditure Panel Survey Data. Rockville, MD: Agency for Healthcare Research and Quality.

Gross, D. L., H. Temkin-Greener, S. Kunitz, and D. B. Mukamel. 2004. The Growing Pains of Integrated Health Care for the Elderly: Lessons from the Expansion of PACE. *Milbank Quarterly* 82: 257–282.

Hado, E., and H. Komisar. 2019. Long-Term Care Services and Supports. AARP Public Policy Institute. Accessed September 2020. Available at: https://www.aarp.org/content/dam/aarp/ppi/2019/08/long-term-services-and-supports.doi.10.26419-2Fppi.00079.001.pdf

Han, K., A. M. Trinkoff, C. L. Storr, N. Lerner, and B. K. Yang. 2016. Variations across U.S. Assisted Living Facilities: Admissions, Resident Care Needs, and Staffing. *Journal of Nursing Scholarship* 49: 24–32.

Hauser, S. L., and B. A. Cree. 2020. Treatment of Multiple Sclerosis: A Review. *American Journal of Medicine* 133: 1380–1390.

Hoban, S. 2013. Assisted living 2013: On the Upswing. *Long-Term Living: For the Continuing Care Professional* 62: 28–30.

Hurd, M. D., P. Martorell, A. Delavande, K. J. Mullen, and K. M. Langa. 2013. Monetary Costs of Dementia in the United States. *New England Journal of Medicine* 368: 1326–1334.

Irvin, C. V. 2015. Money Follows the Person 2014 Annual Evaluation Report. Cambridge, MA: Mathematica Policy Research.

Jiao, D., K. Watanabe, Y. Sawada, et al. 2021. Multimorbidity and Functional Limitation: The Role of Social Relationships. *Archives of Gerontology and Geriatrics* 92:104249.

Kowlessar, N., K. Robinson, and C. Schur. 2015. Older Americans Benefit from Older Americans Act Nutrition Programs. Research Brief Number 8. Administration on Aging. Accessed October 2020. Available at: https://nutritionandaging.org/wp-content/uploads/2015/10/2015_0928_AoA_Brief_September.pdf

Kuzuya, M., J. Hasegawa, Y. Hirakawa, et al. 2011. Impact of Informal Care Levels on Discontinuation of Living at Home in Community-Dwelling Dependent Elderly Using Various Community-Based Services. *Archives of Gerontology & Geriatrics* 52: 127–132.

Landré, B., Gil-Salcedo, A., Jacob, L., et al. 2022. The Role of Age, Sex, and Multimorbidity in 7-Year Change in Prevalence of Limitations in Adults 60–94 Years. *Scientific Reports* 12: 18270.

Lendon, J. P., V. Rome, and M. Sengupta. 2020. Variations Between Adult Day Services Centers in the United States by the Racial and Ethnic Case-Mix of Center Participants. *Journal of Applied Gerontology*: 733464820934996.

Leveille, S. G., and S. Thapa. 2017. Disability Among Persons Aging with HIV/AIDS. *Interdisciplinary Topics in Gerontology and Geriatrics* 42: 101–118.

Levy, C., E. A. Whitfield, and R. Gutman. 2019. Medical Foster Home is Less Costly than Traditional Nursing Home Care. *Health Services Research* 54: 1346–1356.

Liao, K., and Peebles V. 2019. Money Follows the Person: State Transitions as of December 31, 2019. Mathematica, Under Contract with the CMS. Accessed October 2020. Available at: https://www.medicaid.gov/medicaid/long-term-services-supports/downloads/mfp-2019-transitions-brief.pdf

Medicare Payment Advisory Commission (MedPAC). 2016. Long-Term Care Hospital Services: Assessing Payment Adequacy and Updating Payments. Report to Congress. Washington, DC: Author.

Mills, W. L., A. L. Snow, N. L. Wilson, A. D. Naik, and M. E. Kunik. 2013. Conceptualization of a Toolkit to Evaluate Everyday Competence in Planning Transitions from Nursing Homes to the Community. *Journal of the American Medical Directors Association* 4: 626.e1–626.e7.

Morley, J. E. 2012. High Technology Coming to a Nursing Home near You. *Journal of the American Medical Directors Association* 13: 409–412.

National Center for Health Statistics. 2019. *Health, United States, 2018.* Hyattsville, MD: U.S. Department of Health and Human Services.

National Center for Health Statistics. 2020. Long-Term Care Providers and Services Users in the United States, Adult Day Services Center Component: National Post-Acute and Long-term Care Study, 2020. Accessed November 2023. Availableat: https://www.cdc.gov/nchs/data/npals/2020-NPALS-ADSC-Weighted-Estimates-508.pdf

National Council on Aging. 2015. Senior Centers: Fact Sheet. Accessed October 2020. Available at: https://d2mkcg26uvg1cz.cloudfront.net/wp-content/uploads/FactSheet_SeniorCenters.pdf

Navickas, R., V. K. Petric, A. B. Feigl, and M. Seychell, (2016). Multimorbidity: What Do We Know? What Should We Do? *Journal of Comorbidity* 6: 4–11.

New York Department of Health. 2022. Continuing Care Retirement Communities & Fee-for-Service Continuing Care Retirement Communities. Accessed November 2023. Available at: https://www.health.ny.gov/facilities/long_term_care/retirement_communities/continuing_care/#:~:text=Continuing%2520Care%2520Retirement%2520Communities%2520%2526%2520Fee-For-Service%2520Continuing%2520Care,%2520%2520716-929-5817%2520%252010%2520more%2520r

Niederhauser, A., C. V. Lukas, V. Parker, et al. 2012. Comprehensive Programs for Preventing Pressure Ulcers: A Review of the Literature. *Advances in Skin & Wound Care* 25: 167–188.

Ouellette-Kuntz, H., E. Stankiewicz, M. McIsaac, and L. Martin. 2018. Improving Prediction of Risk of Admission to Long-Term Care or Mortality among Home Care Users with IDD. *Canadian Geriatrics Journal* 21: 303–306.

Reinhard, S. C., E. Kassner, A. Houser et al. 2011. How the Affordable Care Act Can Help Move States toward a High-Performing System of Long-Term Services and Supports. *Health Affairs* 30: 447–453.

Reinhard, S. C., L. F. Feinberg, A. Houser, R. Choula, and M. Evans. 2019. Valuing the Invaluable: 2019 Update. AARP Public Policy Institute. Accessed August 2020. Available at: https://www.aarp.org/content/dam/aarp/ppi/2019/11/valuing-the-invaluable-2019-update-charting-a-path-forward.doi.10.26419-2Fppi.00082.001.pdf

Riordan, J., and D. Voegeli. 2009. Prevention and Treatment of Pressure Ulcers. *British Journal of Nursing* 18: S20–S27.

Robinson, K. M. 2010. Policy Issues in Mental Health among the Elderly. *Nursing Clinics of North America* 45: 627–634.

Segelman, M., J. Szydlowski, B. Kinosian, et al. 2014. Hospitalizations in the Program of All-Inclusive Care for the Elderly. *Journal of the American Geriatric Society* 62: 320–324.

Segelman, M., O. Intrator, Y. Li, D. Mukamel, P. Veazie, and H. Temkin-Greener. 2017. HCBS Spending and Nursing Home Admissions for 1915(c) Waiver Enrollees. *Journal of Aging & Social Policy* 29: 395–412.

Shippy, R. A., and S. E. Karpiak. 2005. Perceptions of Support among Older Adults with HIV. *Research on Aging* 27: 290–306.

Singh D. A. 2016. *Effective Management of Long-Term Care Facilities.* 3rd ed. Burlington, MA: Jones & Bartlett Learning.

Spellman, S., and K. Brod. 2014. Continuing Care at Home. *Senior Housing & Care Journal* 22: 112–118.

Statista. 2023. Number of Medicare Skilled Nursing Facilities in the U.S. from 1967 to 2021. Accessed November 2023. Available at: https://www.statista.com/statistics/195317/number-of-medicare-skilled-nursing-facilities-in-the-us/

Sultana, I., M. Erraguntla, H. C. Kum, D. Delen, and M. Lawley. 2019. Post-Acute Care Referral in United States of America: A Multiregional Study of Factors Associated with Referral Destination in a Cohort of Patients with Coronary Artery Bypass Graft or Valve Replacement. *BMC Medical Informatics and Decision-Making 19*: 223.

Szanton, S. L., B. Leff, J. L. Wolff, L. Roberts, and L. N. Gitlin. 2016. Home-Based Care Program Reduces Disability and Promotes Aging in Place. *Health Affairs* 35: 1558–1563.

Tabert, M. H., S. M. Albert, L. Borukhova-Milov, et al. 2002. Functional Deficits in Patients with Mild Cognitive Impairments: Prediction of AD. *Neurology* 58: 758–764.

Teresi, J. A., M. Ramirez, D. Remler, et al. 2013. Comparative Effectiveness of Implementing Evidence-Based Education and Best Practices in Nursing Homes: Effects on Falls, Quality-of-Life and Societal Costs. *International Journal of Nursing Studies* 50: 448–463.

Tune, L. 2001. Assessing Psychiatric Illness in Geriatric Patients. *Clinical Cornerstone* 3: 23–36.

Van Houtven, C. H., and E. Norton. 2004. Informal Care and Health Care Use of Older Adults. *Journal of Health Economics* 23: 1159–1180.

Vargas, R. B., and W. E. Cunningham. 2006. Evolving Trends in Medical Care-Coordination for Patients with HIV and AIDS. *Current HIV/AIDS Reports* 3: 149–153.

Vespa, J., D. M. Armstrong, and L. Medina. 2020. Demographic Turning Points for the United States: Population Projections for 2020 to 2060. U.S. Census Bureau. Accessed October 2024. Available at: https://www.census.gov/content/dam/Census/library/publications/2020/demo/p25-1144.pdf

White, E. M., C. M. Kosar, M. Rahman, and V. Mor, 2020. Trends in Hospitals and Skilled Nursing Facilities

Sharing Medical Providers, 2008–16: Study Examines the Extent to which Hospitals and Nursing Homes Share Physicians and Advanced Practice Clinicians. *Health Affairs* 39: 1312–1320.

Wieland, D., B. Kinosian, E. Stallard, and R. Boland. 2013. Does Medicaid Pay More to a Program of All-Inclusive Care for the Elderly (PACE) than for Fee-for-Service Long-Term Care? *Journal of Gerontology: Series A, Biological Sciences and Medical Sciences* 68: 47–55.

Williamson, H. J., E. A. Perkins, A. Acosta, M. Fitzgerald, J. Agrawal, and O. T. Massey. 2016. Family Caregivers of Individuals with Intellectual and Developmental Disabilities: Experiences with Medicaid Managed Care Long-Term Services and Supports in the United States. *Journal of Policy & Practice in Intellectual Disabilities* 13: 287–296.

Zhao, Y. W., T. N. Haregu, L. He, et al. (2021). The Effect of Multimorbidity on Functional Limitations and Depression amongst Middle-Aged and Older Population in China: A Nationwide Longitudinal Study. *Age and Ageing* 50: 190–197.

CHAPTER 11

Health Services for Special Populations

LEARNING OBJECTIVES

- Describe population groups facing greater challenges and barriers in accessing healthcare services.
- Identify racial and ethnic disparities in health status.
- Discuss the health concerns of United States children and the health services available to them.
- Discuss the health concerns of U.S. women and the health services available to them.
- Describe rural health challenges and measures taken to improve access to care in rural populations.
- Describe the characteristics and health concerns of homeless populations and migrant workers.
- Describe the U.S. mental health system.
- Summarize the AIDS epidemic in the United States, the population groups affected by it, and the services available to patients with HIV/AIDS.
- Identify the benefits of the Affordable Care Act for certain vulnerable groups.

"They all have something in common."

Introduction

Certain population groups in the United States face greater challenges than the general population in accessing timely and needed healthcare services (Shortell et al., 1996). As a consequence, members of these groups are at greater risk of poor physical, psychological, and/or social health (Aday, 1993). Various terms are used to describe these populations, such as "underserved populations," "medically underserved," "medically disadvantaged," "underprivileged," and "American underclasses." The causes of their vulnerability are largely attributable to unequal social, economic, health, and geographic conditions. These population groups consist of racial and ethnic minorities, children who are uninsured, women, persons living in rural areas, individuals and families who are unhoused, people with mental health conditions, the chronically ill or those who have disabilities, and persons with **human immunodeficiency virus (HIV)/acquired immunodeficiency syndrome (AIDS)**. They are more vulnerable than the general population and experience greater barriers in access to care, financing of care, and racial or cultural acceptance.

After presenting a conceptual framework to study vulnerable populations, this chapter defines these special population groups, describes their health needs, summarizes the major challenges they face, and highlights strategies to resolve disparities. The potential impact of the Affordable Care Act (ACA) and COVID-19 pandemic on vulnerable populations is also discussed.

Framework to Study Vulnerable Populations

The vulnerability framework (**Exhibit 11-1**) is an integrated approach to studying vulnerability (Shi and Stevens, 2010). From a health perspective, vulnerability refers to the

Exhibit 11-1 The Vulnerability Framework

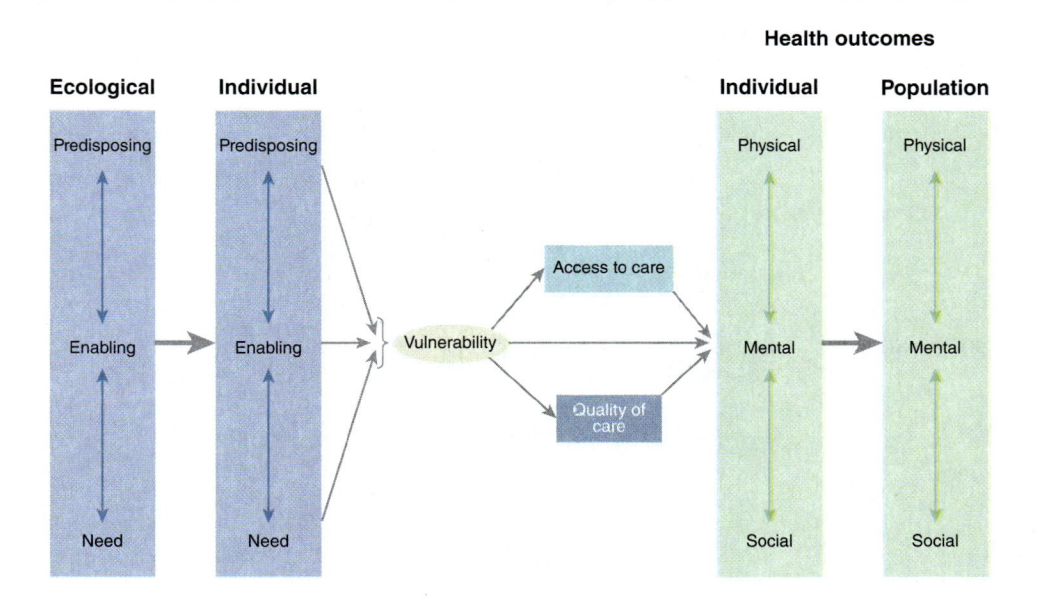

likelihood of experiencing poor health or illness. Poor health can be manifested physically, psychologically, and socially. Because poor health along one dimension is likely to be compounded by poor health along other dimensions, the health needs are greater for those persons with problems along multiple dimensions compared to those persons with problems along a single dimension.

According to the framework, vulnerability is determined by a convergence of (1) predisposing, (2) enabling, and (3) need characteristics at both the individual and ecological (contextual) levels (**Exhibit 11-2**). Not only do these predisposing, enabling, and need characteristics converge and determine individuals' access to health care, they also ultimately influence individuals' risk of contracting illness or, for those already sick, recovering from illness. Individuals with multiple risks (i.e., a combination of two or more vulnerability traits) typically experience worse access to care, care of lesser quality, and inferior health status than do those with fewer vulnerability traits.

Understanding vulnerability as a combination or convergence of disparate factors is preferred over studying individual factors separately because vulnerability, when defined as a convergence of risks, best captures reality. This approach not only reflects the co-occurrence of risk factors but also underscores the belief that it is difficult to address disparities related to one risk factor without addressing the others.

This vulnerability model has a number of distinctive characteristics. First, it is a comprehensive model, including both individual and ecological attributes of risk. Second, it is a general model, focusing on the attributes of vulnerability for the total population rather than vulnerable traits of subpopulations. Although there are individual differences in exposure to risks, some common, cross-cutting traits affect all vulnerable populations. Third, a major distinction of the model is its emphasis on the convergence of vulnerability. In other words, the effects of experiencing multiple vulnerable traits may lead to cumulative vulnerability that is additive or even multiplicative.

Racial/Ethnic Minorities

The 2020 U.S. census questionnaire listed 15 racial categories, as well as places to write in specific races not listed on the form (U.S. Census Bureau, 2020a). These racial categories were White, Black, American Indian or Alaska Native, Chinese, Filipino, Asian Indian, Vietnamese, Korean, Japanese, Other Asian, Native Hawaiian, Samoan, Chamorro, Other Pacific Islander, or some other race. Respondents could choose more than one race.

The U.S. Census Bureau (2022a) estimated that, in 2022, more than 23.5% of the U.S. population was made up of minorities: Black or African American people (13.6%), Hispanic or Latino people (19.1%), Asian people (6.3%), Native Hawaiian and Other Pacific Islander people (0.3%), and American Indian and Alaska Native people (1.3%). In addition, 2.9% of all Americans self-identified as being two or more races (U.S. Census Bureau, 2023).

Significant differences exist across the various racial/ethnic groups on health-related lifestyles and health status. For example, in 2016, the percentage of live births in which

---

Exhibit 11-2 Predisposing, Enabling, and Need Characteristics of Vulnerability

Predisposing characteristics:
- Racial/ethnic characteristics
- Gender and age (women and children)
- Geographic location (rural health)

Enabling characteristics:
- Insurance status (uninsured)
- Homelessness

Need characteristics:
- Mental health
- Chronic illness/disability
- HIV/AIDS

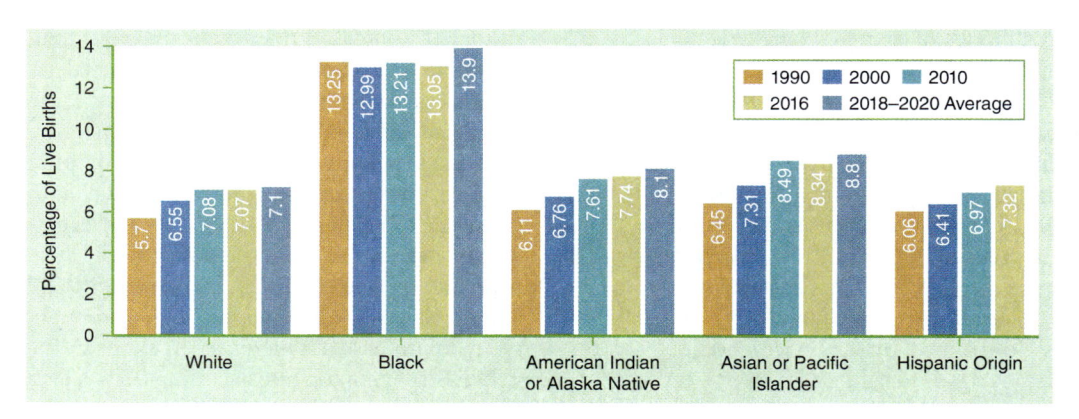

Figure 11-1 Percentage of U.S. live births weighing less than 2,500 grams by mother's detailed race.
Data from National Center for Health Statistics (NCHS). 2023. *Health, United States, 2023.* Hyattsville, MD: U.S. Department of Health and Human Services.

the neonate weighed less than 2,500 grams (low birth weight) was greatest among Black people, followed by Asian or Pacific Islander people, American Indian people or Native American people, Hispanic people, and White people (**Figure 11-1**). White people were most likely to begin prenatal care during their first trimester, followed by the Asian, Hispanic, Black, American Indian or Alaska Native, and Pacific Islander populations (**Table 11-1**). Mothers of Hispanic and Asian and Pacific Islander origin were least likely to smoke cigarettes during pregnancy, followed by the Black, White, and American Indian or Alaska Native populations (**Figure 11-2**). The White adult population

Table 11-1 Characteristics of U.S. Mothers by Race/Ethnicity

Item	1970	1980	1990	2000	2016[1]
Prenatal Care Began During First Trimester					
All mothers	68.0	76.3	75.8	83.2	77.1
White	72.3	79.2	79.2	85.0	82.3
Black	44.2	62.4	60.6	74.3	66.5
American Indian or Alaskan Native	38.2	55.8	57.9	69.3	63.0
Asian or Pacific Islander	—	73.7	75.1	84.0	80.6 (Asian), 51.9 (Pacific Islander)
Hispanic origin	—	60.2	60.2	74.4	72.0
Education of Mother 16 Years or More					
All mothers	8.6	14.0	17.5	24.7	All females aged 25+	21.0
White	9.6	15.5	19.3	26.3	White	21.3
Black	2.8	6.2	7.2	11.7	Black	15.3

Item	1970	1980	1990	2000	2016[1]	
American Indian or Alaska Native	2.7	3.5	4.4	7.8	American Indian or Alaska Native	—
Asian or Pacific Islander	—	30.8	31.0	42.8	Asian	32.1
Hispanic origin	—	4.2	5.1	7.6	Hispanic origin	11.6
Low Birth Weight (Less Than 2,500 Grams)[2]						
All mothers	7.93	6.84	6.97	7.57	8.17	
White	6.85	5.72	5.70	6.55	7.07	
Black	13.90	12.69	13.25	12.99	13.05	
American Indian or Alaska Native	7.97	6.44	6.11	6.76	7.74	
Asian or Pacific Islander	—	6.68	6.45	7.31	8.34	
Hispanic origin[3]	—	6.12	6.06	6.41	7.32	

[1] 2016 data for education refer to total population estimates of females aged 25 and over, not just mothers.
[2] Excludes live births with unknown birth weight. Percentage based on live births with known birth weight.
[3] Prior to 1993, data from states that did not report Hispanic origin on the birth certificate were excluded. Data for non-Hispanic White and non-Hispanic Black women for years prior to 1989 are not nationally representative and are provided solely for comparison with Hispanic data.

Data from National Center for Health Statistics (NCHS). 2010. *Health, United States, 2009.* Hyattsville, MD: U.S. Department of Health and Human Services. pp. 159, 163; National Center for Health Statistics (NCHS). 2018. *Health, United States, 2017.* Hyattsville, MD: U.S. Department of Health and Human Services. Table 5; U.S. Department of Health and Human Services (HHS). 2018. Timing and adequacy of prenatal care in the United States, 2016. *National Vital Statistics Reports* 67, no. 3; U.S. Census Bureau. 2017. *Educational attainment in the United States: 2016.* Available at: https://www.census.gov/data/tables/2016/demo/education-attainment/cps-detailed-tables.html. Accessed February 2020.

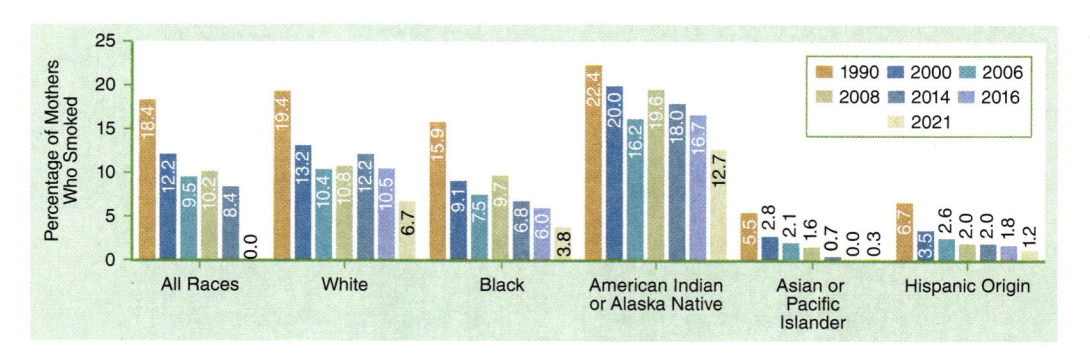

Figure 11-2 Percentage of U.S. mothers who smoked cigarettes during pregnancy according to mother's race.

Data from National Center for Health Statistics (NCHS). 2011. *Health, United States, 2010.* Hyattsville, MD: U.S. Department of Health and Human Services. Table 119; National Center for Health Statistics (NCHS). 2012. *Health, United States, 2011.* Hyattsville, MD: U.S. Department of Health and Human Services. Table 84; Centers for Disease Control and Prevention (CDC). 2016. Smoking prevalence and cessation before and during pregnancy: Data from the birth certificate, 2014. *National Vital Statistics Reports* 65. Available at: https://www.cdc.gov/nchs/data/nvsr/nvsr65/nvsr65_01.pdf. Accessed July 2017; Data from Centers for Disease Control and Prevention (CDC). 2018. *Cigarette smoking during pregnancy: United States, 2016.* NCHS Data Brief, no. 305. Available at: https://www.cdc.gov/nchs/data/databriefs/db305.pdf. Accessed January 2020. 2021 data from Martin J, Osterman M, Driscoll A. Declines in cigarette smoking during pregnancy in the United States, 2016-2021. *NCHS Data Brief, no. 458.* Hyattsville, MD: National Center for Health Statistics, 2023.

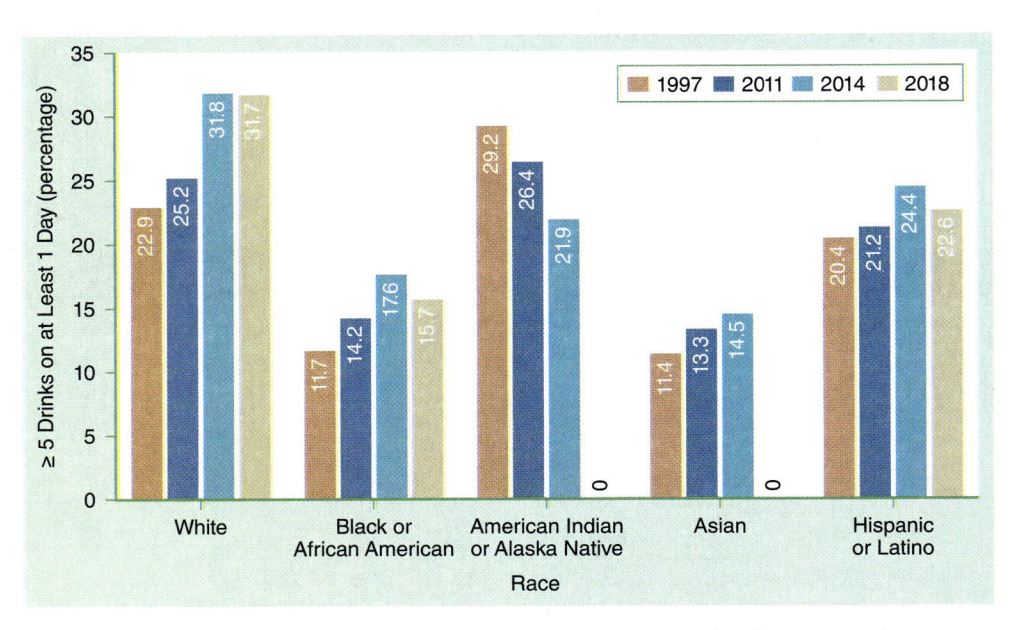

Figure 11-3 Alcohol consumption by persons 18 years of age and older (age/sex adjusted).

Data from National Center for Health Statistics (NCHS). 2014. *National Health Interview Survey*. Available at: https://www.cdc.gov/nchs/nhis/. Accessed March 2017; National Center for Health Statistics (NCHS). 2019. Figure 9.3: Age-sex-adjusted percentage of adults aged 18 and over who had at least 1 heavy drinking day in the past year, by race and ethnicity: United States, 2018. Available at: https://public.tableau.com/profile/nhis6957#!/vizhome/FIGURE9_3/Dashboard9_3. Accessed January 2020.

were more likely to consume alcohol than other races (**Figure 11-3**). Among women 40 years of age and older, utilization of mammography was highest among Black women and lowest among Hispanic women (**Figure 11-4**).

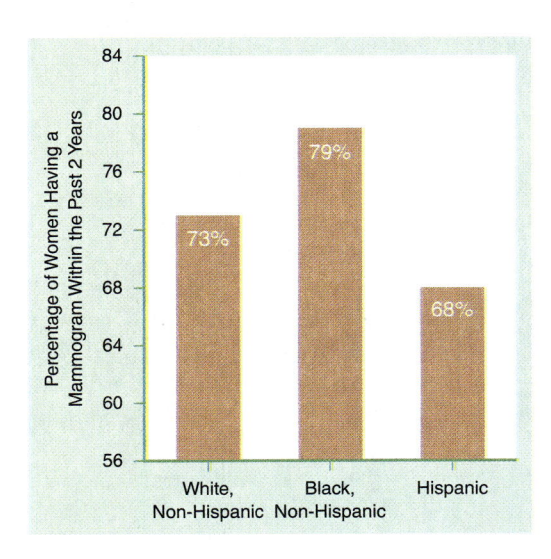

Figure 11-4 Use of mammography by women 40 years of age and older.

Data from Kaiser Family Foundation. 2023. Analysis of the Center for Disease Control and Prevention (CDC)'s Behavioral Risk Factor Surveillance System (BRFSS) 2020 Survey Results.

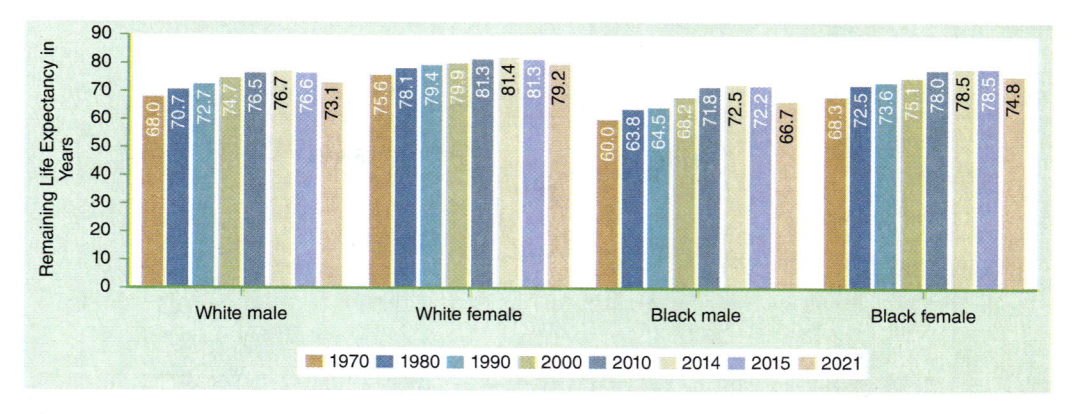

Figure 11-5 U.S. life expectancy at birth.

Data from National Center for Health Statistics (NCHS). 2019. *Health, United States, 2018*. Hyattsville, MD: U.S. Department of Health and Human Services. Table 4. 2021 data from Arias, E., Tejada-Vera, B., Ahmad, F., Kochanek, K.D. (2022). Provisional life expectancy estimates for 2021. https://www.cdc.gov/nchs/data/vsrr/vsrr023.pdf

Black Americans

Black Americans are more likely to be economically disadvantaged than Whites. They also fall behind in health status, despite progress made during the past few decades. Black people have shorter life expectancies than White people (**Figure 11-5**); higher age-adjusted death rates for a majority of leading causes of death (**Table 11-2**); higher age-adjusted death rates (**Figure 11-6**); and higher infant, neonatal, and postneonatal mortality rates (**Table 11-3**). On self-reported measures of health status, Black people are more likely to report fair or poor health status compared to White people (**Figure 11-7**). In terms of behavioral risks, Black males are slightly more likely to smoke cigarettes than White males (18.5% versus 16.0%), but White females are more

Table 11-2 Age-Adjusted Death Rates for Selected Causes of Death, 1970–2018

Race and Cause of Death	1970	1980	1990	2000	2010	2018
All Persons: Deaths per 100,000 Standard Population						
All causes	1,222.6	1,039.1	938.7	869.0	747.0	723.6
Diseases of the heart	492.7	412.1	321.8	257.6	179.1	163.6
Ischemic heart disease	—	345.2	249.6	186.8	113.6	90.9
Cerebrovascular diseases	147.7	96.2	65.3	60.9	39.1	37.1
Malignant neoplasms	198.6	207.9	216.0	199.6	172.8	149.1
Chronic lower respiratory diseases	21.3	28.3	37.2	44.2	42.2	39.7
Influenza and pneumonia	41.7	31.4	36.8	23.7	15.1	14.9
Chronic liver disease and cirrhosis	17.8	15.1	11.1	9.5	9.4	11.1
Diabetes mellitus	24.3	18.1	20.7	25.0	20.8	21.4

(continues)

Table 11-2 Age-Adjusted Death Rates for Selected Causes of Death, 1970–2018 *(continued)*

Race and Cause of Death	1970	1980	1990	2000	2010	2018
Human immunodeficiency virus (HIV) disease	—	—	10.2	5.2	2.6	1.5
Unintentional injuries	60.1	46.4	36.3	34.9	38.0	48.0
Motor vehicle-related injuries	27.6	22.3	18.5	15.4	11.3	11.7
Suicide	13.1	12.2	12.5	10.4	12.1	14.2
Homicide	8.8	10.4	9.4	5.9	5.3	5.9
White						
All causes	1,193.3	1,012.7	909.8	849.8	741.8	728.3
Diseases of the heart	492.2	409.4	317.0	253.4	176.9	163.3
Ischemic heart disease	—	347.6	249.7	185.6	113.5	91.8
Cerebrovascular diseases	143.5	93.2	62.8	58.8	37.7	35.9
Malignant neoplasms	196.7	204.2	211.6	197.2	172.4	151.0
Chronic lower respiratory diseases	21.8	29.3	38.3	46.0	44.6	42.0
Influenza and pneumonia	39.8	30.9	36.4	23.5	14.9	14.9
Chronic liver disease and cirrhosis	16.6	13.9	10.5	9.6	9.9	12.0
Diabetes mellitus	22.9	16.7	18.8	22.8	19.0	19.6
Human immunodeficiency virus (HIV) disease	—	—	8.3	2.8	1.4	0.9
Unintentional injuries	57.8	45.3	35.5	35.1	40.3	50.9
Motor vehicle-related injuries	27.1	22.6	18.5	15.6	11.7	11.9
Suicide	13.8	13.0	13.4	11.3	13.6	16.2
Homicide	4.7	6.7	5.5	3.6	3.3	3.4
Black						
All causes	1,518.1	1,314.8	1,250.3	1,121.4	898.2	867.8
Diseases of the heart	512.0	455.3	391.5	324.8	224.9	206.9
Ischemic heart disease	—	334.5	267.0	218.3	131.2	104.8
Cerebrovascular diseases	197.1	129.1	91.6	81.9	53.0	51.6
Malignant neoplasms	225.3	256.4	279.5	248.5	203.8	171.2
Chronic lower respiratory diseases	16.2	19.2	28.1	31.6	29.0	30.0

Race and Cause of Death	1970	1980	1990	2000	2010	2018
Influenza and pneumonia	57.2	34.4	39.4	25.6	16.8	16.0
Chronic liver disease and cirrhosis	28.1	25.0	16.5	9.4	6.7	7.2
Diabetes mellitus	38.8	32.7	40.5	49.5	38.7	38.2
Human immunodeficiency virus (HIV) disease	—	—	26.7	23.3	11.6	6.2
Unintentional injuries	78.3	57.6	43.8	37.7	31.3	47.5
Motor vehicle-related injuries	31.1	20.2	18.8	15.7	10.9	14.0
Suicide	6.2	6.5	7.1	5.5	5.2	67.1
Homicide	44.0	39.0	36.3	20.5	17.7	21.4

Reproduced from National Center for Health Statistics (NCHS). 2019. *Health, United States, 2018*. Hyattsville, MD: U.S. Department of Health and Human Services. Table 5. 2018 data from National Center for Health Statistics (NCHS) 2021. Table 5. Age-adjusted death rates for selected causes of death, by sex, race, and Hispanic origin: United States, selected years 1950-2018. Available from: https://www.ncbi.nlm.nih.gov/books/NBK569311/table/ch3.tab5/. 2019.

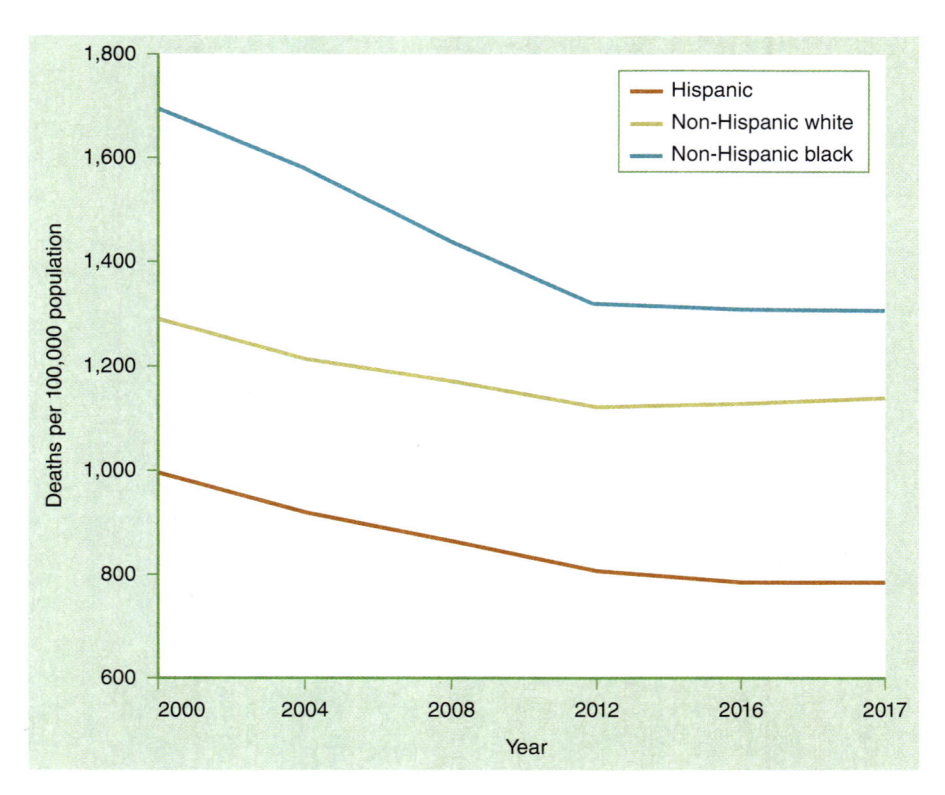

Figure 11-6 Age-adjusted death rates for persons aged 25 and over.

Data from Curtin, S. C., and E. Arias. 2019. *Mortality trends by race and ethnicity among adults aged 25 and over, 2000–2017*. NCHS Data Brief, no 342. Hyattsville, MD: National Center for Health Statistics.

Table 11-3 Infant, Neonatal, and Postneonatal Mortality Rates by Mother's Race (per 1,000 Live Births)

Race of Mother	Infant Deaths					Neonatal Deaths					Postneonatal Deaths				
	1983	1990	2000	2010	2020	1983	1990	2000	2010	2020	1983	1990	2000	2010	2020
All mothers	10.9	8.9	6.9	6.1	3.4	7.1	5.7	4.6	4.0	3.6	3.8	3.2	2.3	2.1	1.9
White	9.3	7.3	5.7	5.2	4.4	6.1	4.6	3.8	3.5	2.9	3.2	2.7	1.9	1.8	1.5
Black	19.2	16.9	13.5	11.2	10.4	12.5	11.1	9.1	7.3	6.6	6.7	5.9	4.3	3.9	3.8
American Indian or Alaska Native	15.2	13.1	8.3	8.3	7.7	7.5	6.1	4.4	4.3	3.8	7.7	7.0	3.9	4.0	3.9
Asian or Pacific Islander	8.3	6.6	4.9	4.3	3.1	5.2	3.9	3.4	3.0	2.3	3.1	2.7	1.4	1.3	0.8
Hispanic origin (selected states)	9.5	7.5	5.6	5.3	4.7	6.2	4.8	3.8	3.6	3.3	3.3	2.9	1.8	1.7	1.4

Data from Ely, DM & Driscoll, AK (2022). Infant mortality in the United States, 2020: data from the period linked birth/infant death file. *National Vital Statistics Reports: From the Centers for Disease Control and Prevention, National Center for Health Statistics, National Vital Statistics System, 71*(5), 1-18.

Racial/Ethnic Minorities

stroke deaths are highest among the non-Hispanic Black population, as are rates of hypertension. Non-Hispanic Black women are likely to lose more expected years of life due to breast cancer compared to non-Hispanic White people (Hung et al., 2016). The prevalence of diabetes is highest among the Hispanic and non-Hispanic Black population compared to the non-Hispanic White population (National Center for Health Statistics [NCHS], 2019c).

Hispanic Americans

The Hispanic American population grew 23% from 2010 to 2020 (UASFACTS, 2022b), compared to a 7.7% increase for the total U.S. population (UASFACTS, 2022c). In 2022, the U.S. Hispanic population numbered nearly 63.7 million (U.S. Census Bureau, 2023a), more than four times higher than the Hispanic population of 15 million in 1980; it is projected to reach 111 million by 2060 (U.S. Census Bureau, 2018).

In 2022, the median age of the Hispanic population was 30.7 (U.S. Census Bureau, 2023a), compared to 40.8 years for non-Hispanic Whites. Also, 7.7% of Hispanics

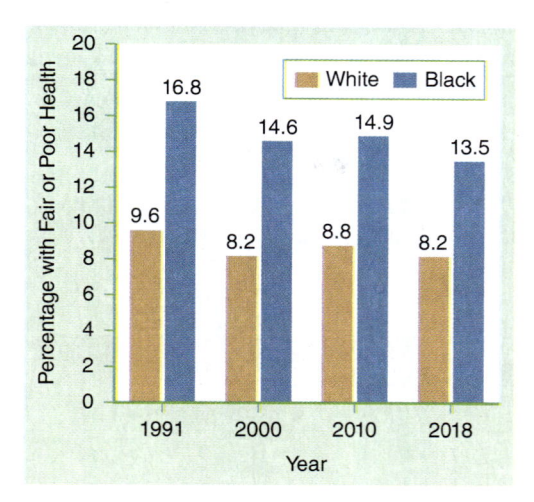

Figure 11-7 Respondent-assessed health status.

Data from National Center for Health Statistics (NCHS). 1996. *Health, United States, 1995*. Hyattsville, MD: U.S. Department of Health and Human Services. p. 172; National Center for Health Statistics (NCHS). 2013. *Health, United States, 2012*. Hyattsville, MD: U.S. Department of Health and Human Services. p. 168; National Center for Health Statistics (NCHS). 2019. *Health, United States, 2018*. Hyattsville, MD: U.S. Department of Health and Human Services. Table 16. National Center for Health Statistics (NCHS). 2021. *Health, United States, 2019*. Hyattsville, MD: U.S. Department of Health and Human Services. Table 16.

likely to smoke than Black females (13.0% versus 11.5%) (**Figure 11-8**). Black people have lower levels of serum cholesterol than White people (**Table 11-4**). Rates of heart disease and

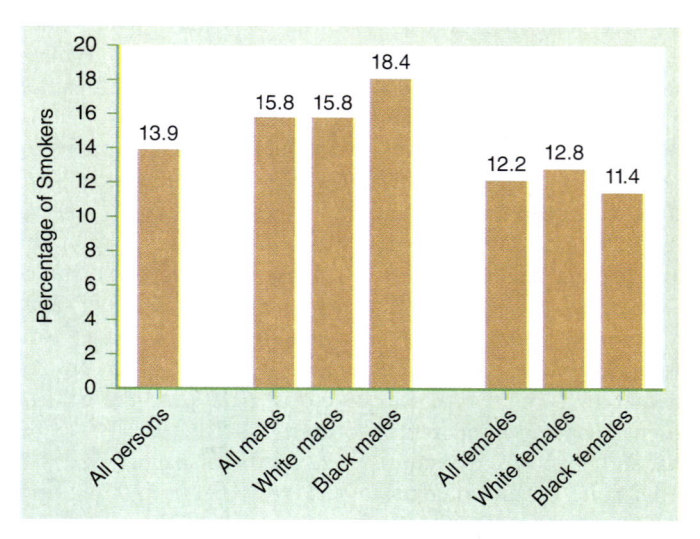

Figure 11-8 Current cigarette smoking by persons 18 years of age and older, age-adjusted, 2018.

Data from National Center for Health Statistics (NCHS). 2021. *Health, United States, 2019*. Hyattsville, MD: U.S. Department of Health and Human Services. Table 17.

Table 11-4 Selected Health Risks Among Persons 20 Years and Older, 2013–2016

Sex and Race[1]	Percentage with Hypertension	Percentage with Cholesterol Level ≥ 240 mg/dL	Percentage Who Are Overweight
Both sexes	55.4	27.1	70.9
White			
Male	57.5	30.0	75.3
Female	37.1	26.1	64.6
Black			
Male	65.3	25.0	70.6
Female	57.7	23.7	80.6

[1] 20–74 years, age adjusted.

Data from National Center for Health Statistics (NCHS). 2019. *Health, United States, 2018*. Hyattsville, MD: U.S. Department of Health and Human Services. Table 26.

were younger than age 5, compared to 5.1% of non-Hispanic Whites (U.S. Census Bureau, 2023b). One in every four children, 25.7% (18.8 million), in the United States were of Hispanic origin in 2020, up from 23.1% (17.1 million) in 2010 (U.S. Census Bureau, 2023c).

Many Hispanic Americans experience significant barriers in accessing medical care. This represents a greater problem for those from Central America (39% foreign born) than those from South America (25.6% foreign born) and Mexico (29% foreign born) (Pew Research Center. 2023). Hispanic Americans face a number of challenges when it comes to access to health care and medical treatments. Overall, Hispanic adults are less likely than other Americans to have health insurance and to receive preventative medical care. Language and cultural barriers, as well as factors such as higher levels of poverty, particularly among recent Hispanic immigrants, are among the social and economic dynamics that contribute to disparate health outcomes for Hispanic Americans. The COVID-19 pandemic is a stark illustration of health disparities: Hispanic Americans are far more likely than White Americans to have been hospitalized or died because of the coronavirus (Pew Research Center, 2022).

In 2020, 17% of Hispanic persons lived below the federal poverty level (FPL), compared to 8.2% of non-Hispanic White persons (U.S. Census Bureau, 2021a). Because of their relatively low education levels, Hispanic Americans have higher unemployment rates than non-Hispanic Whites (4.6% versus 3.4% in 2023; U.S. Bureau of Labor Statistics, 2023d) and are more likely to be employed in semiskilled, nonprofessional occupations (U.S. Census Bureau, 2023e).

Hispanic people (20%) are more likely than White people (8%) to be uninsured, and to face increased social and economic barriers that impact health (KFF, 2021). For example, 13% of adult Hispanic Americans reported food insecurity, while only 6% of the Whites did in 2019. And the percentage among children was 16% and 7% respectively. In 2019, 22.5% of Hispanic persons younger than age 65 were uninsured, compared to 8.8% of non-Hispanic White persons and 11.2% of the non-Hispanic Black or African American populations; Hispanic (15.6%) adults aged

18–64 delayed or did not receive needed medical care due to cost more often than non-Hispanic White adults (11.2%) (NCHS, 2023).

Hispanic Americans are less likely to take advantage of preventive care than non-Hispanic Whites and members of certain other races. Hispanic women 40 years or older were least likely to use mammography (60.9% versus 65.8% for non-Hispanic White women and 69.7% for non-Hispanic Black women; refer to Figure 11-4). In 2016, fewer Hispanic mothers began their prenatal care during the first trimester than the U.S. average (72.0% of Hispanic mothers versus 77.1% as the U.S. average; refer to Table 11-1). Among the Hispanic population 2 years of age and older in 2017, 63.1% had at least one dental visit during a year, compared to 71.5% for non-Hispanic White people (NCHS, 2019c).

People of Hispanic origin also experience greater behavioral risks than White people and members of certain other racial/ethnic groups. For example, among individuals 18 years and older in 2014, a higher proportion of Hispanic people drank five or more alcoholic drinks per day than people of other ethnic origins (24.4% for the Hispanic population versus 17.6% for Black people and 14.5% for Asian people; refer to Figure 11-3). In contrast, fewer Hispanic individuals smoked compared to people from other ethnic groups. From 2015 to 2017, 13.2% of Hispanic males 18 years and older identified themselves as "current smokers," compared to 17.8% of non-Hispanic White males and 20.0% of non-Hispanic Black males (NCHS, 2019c). Among female adults, 7.1% of Hispanic people smoked during 2015–2017, compared to 16.0% of non-Hispanic White people and 12.7% of non-Hispanic Black people (NCHS, 2019c).

Asian Americans

Minority health epidemiology has typically focused on the Black, Hispanic, and American Indian or Alaska Native populations because Asian American people represent a relatively small proportion of the U.S. population. In 2022, Asian people accounted for only 6.3% of the U.S. population, with this subpopulation including 21 million individuals (U.S. Census Bureau, 2022a). To include the diversity of Asian American people, the NCHS has expanded the race codes it uses into nine categories for them: White, Black, Native American, Chinese, Japanese, Hawaiian, Filipino, Other Asian/Pacific Islanders, and other races. Nevertheless, even the category of "Other Asian/Pacific Islander" people is extremely heterogeneous, encompassing 21 subgroups with different health profiles.

Asian American persons constitute one of the fastest-growing population segments in the United States. The nation's Asian population rose to 11.9 million by 2000 and then nearly doubled to 22.4 million by 2019 – an 88% increase within two decades (Pew Research Center, 2021), compared to 16% for the U.S. population as a whole (UASFACTS, 2022c). The Asian American populations' numbers are projected to surpass 46 million by 2060, nearly four times their current total (Pew Research Center, 2021). By 2055, it is projected that Asian American people will become the biggest minority group in the United States (Lopez et al., 2017).

In terms of education, income, and health, the Asian American and Pacific Islander populations (AA/PIs) are very diverse. In 2021, 92.9% of AA/PIs 25 years of age or older had at least graduated from high school, compared with 95.1% of non-Hispanic White people; in addition, the percentage of AA/PIs 25 and older with a bachelor's degree or higher was 61%, compared to 41.9% for non-Hispanic White people (U.S. Census Bureau, 2022b). More than half of Asian individuals age 25 and older (54%) had a bachelor's degree or more education, compared with 33% of the U.S. population in the same age range (Pew Research Center, 2021). Educational attainment varies greatly among the subgroups, however. For example, in 2016, the percentages of Asian Indian (74%), Korean (56%), and Chinese (55%) adults who had earned at least a bachelor's degree were higher than the average of 54% for all Asian adults, while the percentage for Laotian and Vietnamese was 18% and 29%, respectively (National Center for Education Statistics, 2019).

In 2019, the median annual household income of households headed by Asian people was $85,800, compared with $61,800 among all U.S. households (Pew Research Center, 2021). In addition, a smaller percentage of Asian people (8.6%) lived below the FPL, compared to Black people (17.1%) and Hispanic people (16.9%) (U.S. Census Bureau, 2023f).

One study found that Chinese, Asian Indian, Filipino, and other AA/PI children were more likely to be without contact with a health professional, compared to non-Hispanic White children. Citizenship/nativity status, maternal education attainment, and poverty status were all significant independent risk factors for healthcare access and utilization (Yu et al., 2004). In addition, cultural practices and attitudes may prevent AA/PI women from receiving adequate preventive care, such as Pap smears and breast cancer screening. Pap testing behaviors differed significantly between racial groups each year. In 2014, 2016, and 2018, White people reported the highest rates of Pap testing (range: 91.44%–92.49%), and Asian people (range: 67.56%–71.07%) consistently screened the lowest (McDaniel et al., 2021).

Failure to recognize the heterogeneity of this minority population sometimes contributes to the myth that the entire AA/PI population is both healthy and economically successful. In fact, the heterogeneity of the AA/PI population is reflected in the various indicators of health status. For instance, people of Vietnamese descent are more likely to assess their own health status as fair or poor, compared to people of Korean, Chinese, Filipino, Asian Indian, and Japanese descent (NCHS, 2014b). The incidence of overweight and obesity varies greatly, with Filipino adults being 70% more likely to be affected by obesity than the rest of the AA/PI population. In terms of the total U.S. population, overall smoking rates are the lowest among AA/PIs. Nevertheless, 20% of Korean persons smoke cigarettes—a rate higher than that for both Black adults (14.6%) and Hispanic adults (16.6%). Compared with White people, Asian Indian people are more than twice as likely to have diabetes (Centers for Disease Control and Prevention [CDC], 2019a, 2019b, 2019f).

American Indians and Alaska Natives

More than three-fourths of the American Indian and Alaska Native (AIAN) population resides in rural and urban areas outside of reservations or on off-reservation trust lands (U.S. Census Bureau, 2011d). According to the Census Bureau (2011d), the AIAN population is growing at a rate of 26.7% per year. In 2020, there were 9.7 million AIAN people (alone or in combination), comprising 2.9% of the total U.S. population of 329.5 million (U.S. Census Bureau, 2021b). This is an increase of 86.5% from the last Census in 2010 (National Council on Aging, 2023).

Concomitantly, demand for expanded healthcare services within this population has been increasing for several decades and is becoming more acute. The incidence and prevalence of certain diseases and conditions—such as diabetes, hypertension, infant mortality and morbidity, chemical dependency, and AIDS- and HIV-related morbidity—in the AIAN population are all high enough to be matters of prime concern. Compared to the general U.S. population, Native American individuals also have much higher mortality rates from unintentional injuries, diabetes, alcoholism, liver disease, homicide, and suicide (Indian Health Service [IHS], 2019a).

It is also no secret that Native American people continue to occupy the bottom of the socioeconomic strata in the United States. AIANs are approximately twice as likely to be low income and unemployed as other Americans (U.S. Census Bureau, 2011d). Nevertheless, the health status of American Indian people appears to be improving. For example, the mortality rate among Native American expectant mothers dropped from 28.5 deaths per 100,000 live births in 1972–1974 to 8.3 deaths per 100,000 live births in 2007–2009 (IHS, 2014); infant mortality declined from 8.3 deaths per 1,000 births in 2000 to 7.6 deaths per 1,000 births in 2013 (NCHS, 2016b). Even with these gains, Native American people continue to experience significant health disparities compared to the general U.S. population. The life expectancy of Native American individuals is 5.5 years less than that for the U.S. population as a whole (IHS, 2019a). Notably, Native American people die at higher rates than other American populations from alcohol abuse (558% higher), diabetes (217% higher), unintentional injuries (147% higher), homicide (111% higher), and suicide (69% higher) (IHS, 2019a).

The provision of health services to American Indian persons by the federal government was first negotiated in 1832, as partial compensation for land cessions. Subsequent laws have expanded the scope of services and allowed American Indian people greater autonomy in planning, developing, and administering their own healthcare programs. These laws explicitly permit the practice of traditional as well as Western medicine.

Indian Health Care Improvement Act

The Indian Health Care Improvement Act of 1976 (IHCIA), which was amended in 1980, outlined a 7-year effort to help bring AIAN health to a level of parity with the general population. Although this goal of health parity remains unmet, the IHCIA has at least been successful in minimizing prejudice, building trust, and putting responsibility back into the hands of AIANs. The Affordable Care Act has included the permanent reauthorization of the IHCIA.

Indian Health Service

The goal of the federal program administered by the IHS is to ensure that comprehensive and culturally acceptable health services are available to AIANs (IHS, 2013). The IHS (2010, 2019b) serves the members and descendants of more than 573 federally recognized AIAN tribes. The healthcare needs of a rapidly expanding American Indian population have grown faster than medical care resources, however, and most of these communities continue to be medically underserved.

IHS is divided into 12 area offices, each of which is responsible for program operations in a particular geographic area. Each area office is composed of branches dealing with various administrative and health-related services. Delivery of health services is the responsibility of 170 IHS and tribally managed service units operating at the local level (IHS, 2010, 2019b). The IHS mandate has been made particularly difficult because the locations of Indian reservation communities are among the least geographically accessible in the United States (Burks, 1992).

Besides rendering primary and preventive care, special initiatives focus on areas such as injury control, alcoholism, diabetes, mental health, maternal and child health, Indian youth and children, care for older adults, and HIV/AIDS (IHS, 1999b). Additional areas of focus include domestic violence and child abuse, oral health, and sanitation (IHS, 1999a). Even with the limitations in the IHS's scope of service, many American Indian people do not avail themselves of the system's services. In particular, more than half of low-income uninsured Indian people do not have access to the IHS. Among the low-income population, Indian people with IHS access tend to fare better than uninsured Indian people (Zuckerman et al., 2004).

Racial Disparities Since COVID-19

The COVID-19 pandemic has highlighted stark health disparities among Black, Hispanic, Native American, and Native Hawaiian/Pacific Islander populations in several areas, including infections, hospitalizations, death rates, and vaccination rates (Simmons et al., 2021). Several factors contribute to COVID-19 disparities, most stemming from long-standing systemic inequalities and structural racism (Simmons et al., 2021). Underlying health and social inequities put many racial and ethnic populations at increased risk of getting sick, having more severe illness, and dying from COVID-19 (Simmons et al., 2021). For instance, disparities in employment can influence the likelihood of being exposed to COVID-19 in a workplace, while disparities in income might restrict access to secure housing, transportation, or medical services, which could impact the risk of COVID-19 exposure (Simmons et al., 2021). An analysis of county-level data for 3,142 U.S. counties showed the majority of observed racial disparities in COVID-19 deaths persisted even after controlling for 2019 mortality rates and COVID-19 cases per 100,000 people, which suggests socioeconomic factors play a key role in these disparities (Khanijahani, 2021). Differences in quality of care across nursing homes, which serve people with disabilities and older adults, and which have been particularly hard hit by the pandemic, are another key factor (Grabowski & Mor, 2020).

Healthcare access disparities were visible, with Black and Hispanic respondents reporting significantly lower levels of access to a provider for COVID-19-related services, general medical services, and telehealth for mental health services (Ruprecht et al., 2021). Sexual minority respondents reported significantly lower rates of using telehealth for mental health services, and gender minority respondents reported significantly lower levels of primary-care provider access (Ruprecht et al., 2021). There were evident COVID-19 disparities experienced in Chicago, especially for Black and Hispanic people, sexual minority, and gender minority groups (Ruprecht et al., 2021). A greater focus must be paid to health equity, including providing increased resources and supplies for affected groups, adapting to inequities in the built environment, and ensuring adequate access to healthcare services to ameliorate the burden of COVID-19 on these marginalized populations (Ruprecht et al., 2021).

Wetzler & Cobb (2022) pointed out that variations in health outcomes, behaviors, and healthcare usage among adults of the same race and ethnicity were notably larger when comparing different socioeconomic groups. More recently, Karmouta and colleagues (2022) found higher rates and severity of retinopathy of prematurity (ROP) in Hispanic neonates compared to non-Hispanic White neonates. However, the link between race and ethnicity and ROP was primarily influenced by disparities in gestational age, a factor largely explained by the income levels in the neighborhood.

Buder et al. (2023) explored the creation and evaluation of a socioeconomic status (SES) index using data from the Bureau of Justice Statistics. They classified SES into low, middle, and high categories and applied this classification to four national datasets (Buder et al., 2023). Through weighted descriptive statistics and logistic regression, the study found similarities in SES classifications, especially regarding race/ethnicity (Buder et al., 2023). The SES index, capturing cumulative structural determinants, was highlighted as advantageous over single-variable indicators like education and income (Buder et al., 2023). The composite index allowed for uniform comparisons across datasets, controlling for various SES factors (Buder et al., 2023). The findings emphasized the importance of considering both SES and race/ethnicity in health disparities research (Buder et al., 2023).

Zarei et al. (2023) used data from 2016 to 2019 National Survey of Children's Health to examine the associations between race and ethnicity (Asian, Black, Hispanic, White, Other-race); mental health outcomes (depression, anxiety, and behavior/conduct problems) stratified by household generation; and between household generation and outcomes stratified by race and ethnicity, adjusting for demographics (age, sex, family income to poverty ratio, parental education), and an adverse childhood experience (ACE) score (Zarei et al., 2023). When categorizing by household generation, children from racial and ethnic minority backgrounds typically exhibited odds of outcomes like or lower than those of White children (Zarei et al., 2023). The only exception was higher odds of behavior/conduct problems in third-generation or later Black children (Zarei et al., 2023). When considering race and ethnicity, third-generation or later children showed increased odds of depression compared to their first-generation counterparts (Zarei et al., 2023). Additionally, third-generation or later, racial, and ethnic minority children had heightened odds of anxiety and behavior/conduct problems compared with their first-generation counterparts (Zarei et al., 2023). These associations generally remained significant even after adjusting for the ACE score (Zarei et al., 2023). The lower odds of common mental health conditions in minority children may be influenced by factors like differential reporting, which could be attributed to factors such as discrimination, systemic racism, and other generational variations that warrant further investigation to promote health equity (Zarei et al., 2023).

The Uninsured

The *Health Services Financing* chapter discussed the number of uninsured people in the United States and the reasons why so many Americans lack health insurance. Although the rate of uninsurance among adults has increased, recent national survey data show that the uninsured rate among children (ages 0–17) fell from 6.4% in 2020 to 4.5% in 2022 (Assistant Secretary for Planning and Evaluation, 2023).

Ethnic minorities are more likely than White people to lack health insurance. The U.S. Census Bureau (2022c) estimated that, in 2021, 17.7% of Hispanic residents were uninsured, compared to 9.6% of Black residents, 5.8% of Asian American residents, and 5.7% of White residents; most of this uninsured population comprises working-age adults aged 19 to 64. Lack of coverage is also more prevalent in the southern and western regions of the United States and among individuals who lack a college degree.

Generally, persons who are uninsured are in poorer health than the general population (NCHS, 2016a). Studies have also shown that the uninsured use fewer health services compared to the insured (CDC, 2010b). In 2018, 52% of uninsured people reported having no regular source of health care (Kaiser Family Foundation, 2019a). Decreased utilization of lower-cost preventive services—a characteristic of the uninsured population—can ultimately result in an increased need for more expensive emergency health care. Kesici & Yilmaz (2023) used an exploratory qualitative method based on in-depth interviews with 12 breast cancer patients to explore variations in treatment pathways based on the type of health insurance. They found that patients with private insurance reported easy access to timely and comprehensive treatment. Those without, however, had to navigate complicated routes to treatment; they generally had to resort to seeking treatment from more than one hospital (Kesici & Yilmaz, 2023).

Even when the uninsured can access health care, they often have serious problems paying their medical bills. In 2018, 19% of uninsured adults younger than age 65 postponed obtaining needed prescription drugs because of cost concerns, compared to 13%

of those with public insurance and 6% of privately insured individuals (Kaiser Family Foundation, 2019a).

The plight of the uninsured affects those who have insurance as well. Medical expenditures for uncompensated care to the uninsured were estimated to total $85 billion in 2013 (Kaiser Family Foundation, 2014b). Much of this cost was absorbed by Medicaid, federal grants to nonprofit hospitals, and charitable organizations. The ACA did make sizable progress in reducing the number of uninsured in the United States. It is not clear how future legislation or ACA reform will address the ongoing problem of uninsurance (Wallender et al., 2023; Chang et al., 2023; Liddell and Lilly, 2022; Lee et al., 2022).

Children

In 2022, there were approximately 72 million children younger than 18 years living in the United States, representing 21.7% of the total population (U.S. Census Bureau, 2022a). Approximately 13 million children (18%) lived in households with incomes below the U.S. Census Bureau's poverty threshold (U.S. Census Bureau, 2019b). The racial and ethnic diversity of U.S. children continues to increase; notably, Hispanic children accounted for more than 25% of all U.S. children in 2015, up from 8.8% in 1980.

Nearly 20% of U.S. children younger than 18 years have a special healthcare need, defined as having a chronic medical, behavioral, or developmental condition lasting 12 months or longer and experiencing a service-related or functional consequence (Federal Interagency Forum on Child and Family Statistics, 2016). In 2017, 11% of children ages 5–17 were identified as having activity limitation resulting from one or more chronic conditions (Federal Interagency Forum on Child and Family Statistics, 2019).

The National Survey of Children's Health (NSCH) used a validated 5-item screener that asks parents/caregivers if their child has any of the following service needs or limitations due to a health condition that has lasted or is expected to last 12 months or longer: (1) Need or use of prescription medication(s); (2) Elevated need or use of medical care, mental health, or education services; (3) Functional limitation(s) (that limit daily activity); (4) Need or use of special therapies (e.g. physical, occupation, or speech therapy); (5) Emotional, developmental, or behavioral problem for which treatment or counseling is needed.

In 2019–2020, nearly 1 in 5 children (19.4%, 14.1 million) in the United States had a special healthcare need. More than 1 in 4 households with children (28.6%) had at least one such need. Special healthcare needs were slightly more common among non-Hispanic Black children (23.3%) and children living in poverty (22.8%). In 2019–2020, 1 in 4 children (25.5%) experienced functional limitations either alone or in combination with some other healthcare need.

Excess body weight in children is associated with both excess morbidity during childhood and excess body weight in adulthood. Among youth aged 2 to 19 years, the prevalence of obesity increased from 16.9% in 2011 to 2012 to 19.7% in 2017 to 2020 (Hu et. al, 2022). For children and adolescents aged 2–19 years in 2017–2020, the prevalence of obesity was 19.7% and affected about 14.7 million children and adolescents. Obesity prevalence was 26.2% among Hispanic children, 24.8% among non-Hispanic Black children, 16.6% among non-Hispanic White children, and 9.0% among non-Hispanic Asian children (CDC, 2022).

Children living in rural areas were more likely to be overweight than their urban counterparts. In addition, children with lower household incomes were significantly more likely to be overweight or overweight than those living in households with higher incomes. The rate of overweight and obesity among children in households with incomes below 100% of the FPL was approximately twice that of children with household incomes of 400% or more of the FPL (Health Resources and Services Administration [HRSA], 2015).

Health insurance is a major determinant of access to and utilization of health care. From 1993 to 2021, the percentage of children without insurance decreased from 14% to 5% (Federal Interagency Forum on Child and Family Statistics, 2019; Assistant Secretary for Planning and Evaluation, 2023), but the coverage rates varied across races and ethnicities. Hispanic children were more likely to be uninsured (7.8%) than White, non-Hispanic children (2.7%) and Black, non-Hispanic children (3%). White, non-Hispanic children were more likely to have private insurance (73.1%) compared to Hispanic children (42.6%) and Black, non-Hispanic children (43%) (U.S. Census Bureau, 2022c).

In urban and large rural areas, children living in households with the lowest incomes were less likely to have health insurance than their peers living in households in the highest income categories. For instance, 95.3% of children in large rural areas with household incomes below 100% of the FPL had current health insurance, compared to 98.2% of those with household incomes of 400% or more of the FPL. Among children living in households with incomes below 100% of the FPL, children in small and large rural areas were significantly more likely to have health insurance than those in urban areas—94.7% and 95.3% versus 91.2%, respectively (HRSA, 2015).

Child unintentional injury death rates decreased 11% from 2010 to 2019, but injury is still the leading cause of death for children and teens in the United States—and some are at higher risk. More than 7,000 children and teens age 0–19 died because of unintentional injuries in 2019, about 20 deaths each day. Leading causes of child unintentional injury include motor vehicle crashes, suffocation, drowning, poisoning, fires, and falls (CDC, 2021a).

Asthma is one of the most common childhood chronic diseases. The prevalence of asthma among U.S. children doubled from 1980 to 1995 but then increased more slowly during the 2000s. Approximately 4.7 million U.S. children younger than age 18 (6.5%) currently have asthma (CDC, 2021b). In 2021, 11.6% of Black, non-Hispanic children were reported to currently have asthma, compared to 5.5% of White, non-Hispanic children; 5.9% of Hispanic children; and 3.3% of Asian, non-Hispanic children (CDC, 2021b).

Depression has a significant impact on adolescent development and well-being. In 2023, approximately 16.39% of youths ages 12–17 reported suffering from at least one major depressive episode (MDE) during the past year—a higher prevalence than was reported in 2017 (13%) (Mental Health America, 2023). Nearly 60% of youth with MDE in the past year did not receive treatment for depression in 2021 (Childstatas, 2023).

Vaccination rates for children for selected diseases differ by race, poverty status, and area of residence (**Table 11-5**). White children have higher vaccination rates for diphtheria/tetanus/pertussis (DTP), polio, measles, *Haemophilus influenzae* serotype b (Hib), and combined series compared to Black children. Children who come from families with incomes below the FPL have lower vaccination rates than other children. Those who live in inner cities have higher vaccination rates.

Children's health has certain unique aspects in terms of delivery of health care. Among these factors influencing pediatric health care are children's developmental vulnerability, dependency, and differential patterns of morbidity and mortality. **Developmental vulnerability** refers to the rapid and cumulative physical and emotional changes that characterize childhood and the potential impacts that illness, injury, or disruptive family and social circumstances can have on a child's life-course trajectory. **Dependency** refers to children's special circumstances that require

Table 11-5 Vaccinations of Children 19–35 Months of Age for Selected Diseases According to Race, Poverty Status, and Residence in a Metropolitan Statistical Area (MSA), 2017 (%)

Vaccination	Race Total	Race White	Race Black	Below Poverty Level	At or Above Poverty Level	Inner City	Remaining Areas
DTP[1]	83	83	80	79	85	85	83
Polio[2]	93	92	92	91	93	93	93
Measles-containing vaccines or measles/mumps/rubella[3]	92	91	90	89	93	93	91
HIB[4]	81	84	77	75	83	82	81
Combined series[5]	70	72	67	63	74	72	70

[1] Diphtheria/tetanus/pertussis, four doses or more.
[2] Three doses or more.
[3] Respondents were asked about measles-containing or measles/mumps/rubella (MMR) vaccines.
[4] *Haemophilus influenzae* type b, three doses or more.
[5] The combined series consists of four doses of DTP vaccine, three doses of polio vaccine, and one dose of measles-containing vaccine (4 : 3 : 1 : 3 : 3 : 1).

Data from National Center for Health Statistics (NCHS). 2019. *Health, United States, 2018*. Hyattsville, MD: U.S. Department of Health and Human Services. Table 31.

adults—parents, school officials, caregivers, and sometimes neighbors—to recognize and respond to their health needs, seek healthcare services on their behalf, authorize treatment, and comply with recommended treatment regimens. These dependency relationships can be complex, change over time, and affect utilization of health services by children.

Children and the U.S. Healthcare System

The various programs that serve children's healthcare needs in the United States have distinct eligibility, administrative, and funding criteria that can present barriers to access. The patchwork of disconnected programs also makes it difficult to obtain health care in an integrated and coordinated fashion. These programs can be categorized into three broad sectors: the personal medical and preventive services sector, the population-based community health services sector, and the health-related support services sector.

Personal medical and preventive health services include primary and specialty medical services, which may be delivered in private and public medical offices, health centers, and hospitals. Personal medical services are principally funded by private health insurance, Medicaid, and out-of-pocket payments.

Population-based community health services include community-wide health promotion and disease prevention services. Examples are immunization delivery and monitoring programs, lead screening and abatement programs, and child abuse and neglect prevention. Other health services include special child abuse treatment programs and rehabilitative services for children with complex congenital conditions or other chronic and debilitating diseases. Community-based programs also perform assurance and coordination functions, such as case management and referral programs, for children with chronic diseases and early interventions and monitoring for infants at risk for developmental disabilities. Funding for this sector comes from federal programs, such as Medicaid's Early Periodic Screening, Diagnosis, and Treatment (EPSDT) program; Title V (Maternal and Child Health) of the Social Security Act; and other categorical programs.

Health-related support services include nutrition education, early intervention, rehabilitation, and family support programs, among other services. An example of a rehabilitation service is education and psychotherapy for children with HIV. Family support services include parent education and skill building in families with infants at risk for developmental delays because of physiological or social conditions, such as low birth weight or very low income. Funding for these services comes from diverse agencies, such as the U.S. Department of Agriculture, which funds the Special Supplemental Nutrition Program for Women, Infants, and Children (WIC), and the U.S. Department of Education, which funds the Individuals with Disabilities Education Act (IDEA).

Women

In 2022, the U.S. population was estimated to include more than 333 million individuals, with females accounting for 50.4% of the total population (U.S. Census Bureau, 2022a). Women are playing an increasingly important role in the delivery of health care. Not only do women remain the leading providers of care in the nursing profession, but they are also well represented in various other health professions, including allopathic and osteopathic medicine, dentistry, podiatry, and optometry (**Figure 11-9**). According to the American Medical Association, female-dominated physician specialties include obstetrics/gynecology (83.4%), allergy and immunology (73.5%), pediatrics (72.1%), medical genetics and genomics (66.7%), hospice and palliative medicine (66.3%), and dermatology (60.8%)

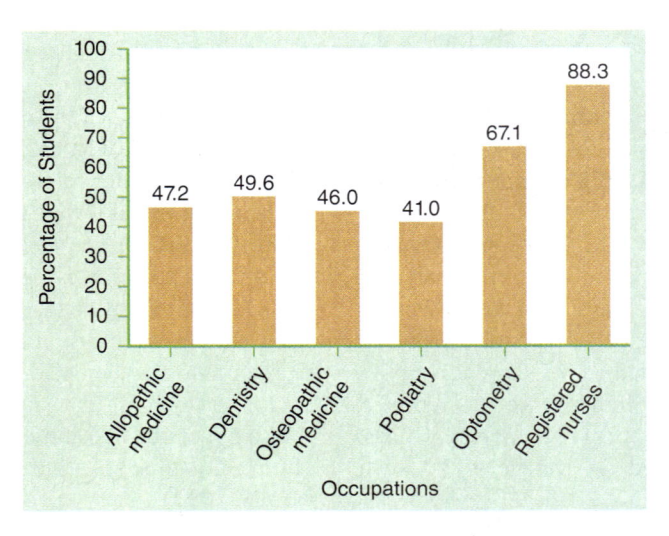

Figure 11-9 Percentage of female students of total enrollment in schools for selected health occupations, 2013–2014.

Data from Association of American Medical Colleges (AAMC). 2017. *The state of women in academic medicine: The pipeline and pathways to leadership, 2013–2014.* Available at: https://www.aamc.org/members/gwims/statistics/#bench. Accessed March 2021.

(Murphy, 2019). In contrast, women are severely underrepresented in several surgical specialties, radiology, and pain medicine.

Women in the United States can expect to live about 5 years longer than men (NCHS, 2019c), but they suffer greater morbidity and poorer health outcomes. Morbidity is greater among women than among men, even after childbearing-related conditions are factored out. For instance, nearly 38% of women report having chronic conditions that require ongoing medical treatment, compared to 30% of men (Salganicoff et al., 2005). Women also have a higher prevalence of certain health problems than men over the course of their lifetimes (Sechzer et al., 1996). Heart disease and stroke account for a higher percentage of deaths among women than among men at all stages of life. Approximately 42% of women who have heart attacks die within a year, compared to 24% of men who have heart attacks (Misra, 2001). Research has also demonstrated that women are more likely to experience functional limitations due to health than men (NCHS, 2019c).

Among respondents to the 2018 National Health Interview Survey, 65.5% of women reported being in excellent or very good health, while 24.1% reported being in good health and 10.4% reported being in fair or poor health (NCHS, 2019a). Self-reported health status was similar among men and women but varied greatly with age and educational attainment (NCHS, 2016a). Overall, though, women reported more physically and mentally unhealthy days than men. Women reported an average of 4.2 days of poor physical health, compared to 3.5 days per month for men in 2014. Similarly, women reported an average of 4.2 mentally unhealthy days, while men reported an average of 3.1 such days per month (CDC, 2014a).

The CDC defines binge drinking as consuming four or more drinks on a single occasion for women and five or more drinks on a single occasion for men. In 2018, men were more likely than women to report at least one day of heavy drinking (30.9% versus 19.8%, respectively) in the past year. However, among women, the incidence of heavy drinking increased from 12.1% in 2006 to 19.8% in 2018 (NCHS, 2019a). An estimated 10% of women 18 years and older currently smoke cigarettes, with this rate having declined in recent years (CDC, 2023).

Overweight and obesity are associated with an increased risk of numerous diseases and conditions. In 2017–2020, no differences in obesity prevalence were observed between men and women overall (41.8% each). However, obesity has increased significantly over the past decade for non-Hispanic Black and Mexican American women, contributing to widening health disparities. The rates of obesity among females in 2013–2016 were 37.9% in non-Hispanic White women, 56.0% in non-Hispanic Black women, and 48.9% in Hispanic women (NCHS, 2019c).

In 2019, 1,381,015 women died in the United States. Of these deaths, nearly half were attributable to heart disease and malignant neoplasms—responsible for 21.8% and 20.5% of deaths, respectively. Compared to men, women also had a greater relative burden of mortality from cerebrovascular diseases (6.2%), which was the third leading cause of death for women but the fifth leading cause for men. After cerebrovascular diseases, Alzheimer's disease was the fourth leading cause of death for women; by comparison, it ranked seventh as a cause of death for men (NCHS, 2023). Between 2014 and 2019, three causes of death increased in relative burden among women: diabetes (from 2.7% to 2.8% of deaths), Alzheimer's disease (from 5% to 6% of deaths), and unintentional injury (from 3.9% to 4.4% of deaths) (CDC, 2015b; NCHS, 2023).

In terms of health insurance coverage, 89% of the 97.3 million women ages 19 to 64 residing in the United States had some form of coverage in 2021 (Kaiser Family

Foundation, 2022). Approximately 58.6 million of these women (60%) received their health coverage from employer-sponsored insurance (Kaiser Family Foundation, 2020). However, gaps in private-sector and publicly funded programs and lack of affordability left a little more than one in ten women uninsured. Considerable state-level variation in uninsured rates is noted across the United States, with these rates ranging from 23% of women in Texas to 3% of women in Washington, DC and Massachusetts (Kaiser Family Foundation, 2020). Women who have lower incomes, women of color, and women who are immigrants were also at greater risk of being uninsured (Kaiser Family Foundation, 2020).

Office on Women's Health

The Public Health Service's Office on Women's Health (OWH) is dedicated to the achievement of a series of specific goals that span the spectrum of disease and disability. These goals range across the life cycle and address cultural and ethnic differences among women. OWH promotes, coordinates, and implements a comprehensive women's health agenda on research, service delivery, and education across various government agencies.

OWH was responsible for implementing the National Action Plan on Breast Cancer (NAPBC), a major public–private partnership dedicated to improving the diagnosis, treatment, and prevention of breast cancer through research, service delivery, and education. OWH also worked to implement measures to prevent physical and sexual abuse against women, as delineated in the Violence Against Women Act of 1994. This agency is currently active in projects promoting breastfeeding, women's health education and research, girl and adolescent health, and heart health.

Within the Substance Abuse and Mental Health Services Administration (SAMHSA), the Advisory Committee for Women's Services has targeted six areas for special attention: physical and sexual abuse of women; women as caregivers; women with mental and addictive disorders; women with HIV/AIDS, sexually transmitted diseases, and/or tuberculosis; older women; and women detained in the criminal justice system.

The Women's Health Initiative (WHI), supported by the National Institutes of Health (NIH), was the largest clinical trial conducted in U.S. history, involving more than 161,000 women (NIH, 2002). It focused on diseases that are the major causes of death and disability among women—heart disease, cancer, and osteoporosis. In 2002, the Women's Health Initiative published a groundbreaking study, finding detrimental effects of postmenopausal hormone therapy on women's development of invasive breast cancer, coronary heart disease, stroke, and pulmonary embolism (NIH, 2002).

Since 2005, the WHI has continued as Extension Studies, which are annual collections of health updates and outcomes in active participants (https://www.whi.org/about-whi. The second Extension Study enrolled 93,500 women in 2010 and follow-up of these women continues annually. The current extension study is collecting annual health information from consenting WHI participants through 2020 (https://www.nhlbi.nih.gov/science/womens-health-initiative-whi). While WHI continues to focus on strategies to prevent the major causes of death, disability, and frailty in older women, the breadth and richness of the WHI data allow for the exploration and investigation of many more research questions on women's health and aging. WHI ancillary studies are separate research projects that enroll WHI participants. Examples include the Women's Health Initiative Strong and Healthy Study (WHISH), the Objective Physical Activity and Cardiovascular Health Study (OPACH) and the Women's Health Initiative Sleep Hypoxia Effects on Resilience (WHISPER).

Women and the U.S. Healthcare System

Women face a distinct disadvantage in obtaining employer-based health insurance coverage because they are more likely than men to work part-time, receive lower wages, and have interruptions in their work histories. Hence, women who are married are more likely to be covered as dependents under their spouse's plans and are at a higher risk of being uninsured. Women also rely on Medicaid for their healthcare coverage to a greater extent compared to men. In 2022, 57.3% of adult women under age 65 were covered by Medicaid, versus 42.7% of men (KFF, 2022).

Women are more likely than men to use contraceptives (**Figure 11-10**), but contraceptives have long been among the most poorly covered reproductive healthcare service in the United States. As of February 2020, 29 states required insurers that cover prescription drugs to provide coverage of FDA-approved prescription contraceptive drugs and devices (Guttmacher Institute, 2020).

When it was passed in 2010, the ACA required private insurance to cover, with no cost sharing, a wide variety of preventive services and additional services for women, including Food and Drug Administration (FDA)–approved prescription contraceptives (although this specific regulation has been contested through the years and now includes certain exceptions; Rovner, 2020), domestic violence screening, breastfeeding supports, and human papillomavirus (HPV) testing. Although such services are not required under Medicaid, several states have started to cover all preventive services important for women with or without cost-sharing (Kaiser Family Foundation, 2013).

Rural Health

For rural citizens, access to health care may be affected by poverty, long distances to service providers, rural topography, weather conditions, lack of transportation, and being uninsured. Consequently, residents of rural areas are less likely to utilize health services, and they have poorer health outcomes than their counterparts in more urban areas. A greater percentage of persons residing in a rural area report being in fair or poor health compared to those in urban areas (National Rural Health Association, 2016). In addition, residents of rural areas are more likely to report health

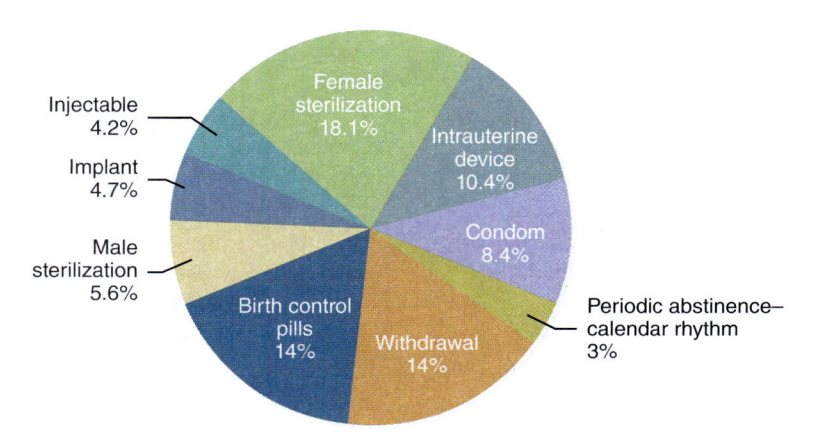

Injectable 4.2%
Implant 4.7%
Male sterilization 5.6%
Female sterilization 18.1%
Intrauterine device 10.4%
Condom 8.4%
Periodic abstinence–calendar rhythm 3%
Withdrawal 14%
Birth control pills 14%

Percentage of women using contraception is 61.6%.

Figure 11-10 Contraceptive use in the past month among women 15–49 years old, 2017–19.

Data from Daniels K, Abma JC. Current contraceptive status among women aged 15-49: United States, 2017-19. NCHS Data Brief, no. 388. Hyattsville, MD: National Center for Health Statistics, 2020.

problems, such as headaches and back and neck pain, than residents of urban areas—17.2% versus 14.7%, respectively (CDC, 2012a, 2012d).

People in rural areas are more likely than urban residents to forgo or delay care due to cost—15% versus 13%, respectively (Carter et al., 2021). Across all races and ethnicities, rural residents have lower levels of insurance coverage. Among Hispanic rural residents, 45.3% do not have health insurance, compared to 40.9% of urban Hispanic residents. Among White residents, 21.3% of rural residents are uninsured, compared to 13.1% of urban residents (U.S. Census Bureau, 2014; Ziller, 2014). In addition, the uninsured often do not have a usual source of care (Larson and Fleishman, 2003).

Geographic maldistribution that creates a shortage of healthcare professionals in rural settings results in barriers in access to care. As of February 2020, there were approximately 6,800 designated primary-care health professional shortage areas (HPSAs), 6,100 dental HPSAs, and 5,300 mental health HPSAs in the United States (HRSA, 2020). Nearly 24% of the U.S. population resides in areas where primary-care health professionals are in short supply (HRSA, 2020); more than 33 million Americans live in a nonmetropolitan federally designated health professional shortage area (HRSA, Bureau of Health Professions, 2013). The scarcity of healthcare providers encompasses a broad spectrum of professionals, including pediatricians, obstetricians, internists, dentists, nurses, and allied health professionals (Patton and Puskin, 1990). Rural hospitals often face financial strains, which results in these facilities generally being smaller hospitals that provide fewer services than urban hospitals.

Various steps have been taken to improve access to health care in rural America, including the promotion of the National Health Service Corps (NHSC), the designation of HPSAs and medically underserved areas (MUAs), the development of community and migrant health centers (C/MHCs), and the enactment of the Rural Health Clinics Act. In 2018, there were 4,528 certified rural health clinics throughout the United States (Kaiser Family Foundation, 2019c). In addition, the Office of Rural Health Policy, which is part of the Health Resources and Services Administration of the U.S. Department of Health and Human Services (DHHS), was established in 1987 to promote better health care in rural America (HRSA, Office of Rural Health Policy, 2015). Several measures and enhanced funding have been initiated to improve rural emergency medical services, to bolster the rural health workforce, and to develop behavioral health capacity in rural areas (National Conference of State Legislatures, 2013).

National Health Service Corps (NHSC)

NHSC was created in 1970 under the Emergency Health Personnel Act, with the intention being to recruit and retain physicians to provide needed services in areas with physician shortages. A 1972 amendment created a scholarship program targeting HPSAs. The scholarship and loan repayment program applies to doctors, dentists, nurse practitioners, midwives, and mental health professionals who serve a minimum of 2 years in underserved areas. Since 1972, more than 50,000 health professionals have been placed in medically underserved communities in hospitals and clinics (HRSA, Bureau of Health Professions, 2020). Currently, more than 18,000 health professionals are providing services under NHSC (https://nhsc.hrsa.gov/)

Health Professional Shortage Areas

The Health Professions Educational Assistance Act of 1976 outlined the criteria used to designate health manpower shortage areas, later renamed health professional shortage areas (HRSA, Bureau of Health Professions, 2007).

The act provided that three different types of HPSAs could be designated: geographic areas, population groups, and medical facilities. A geographic area must meet the following three criteria for designation as a primary-care HPSA:

1. The geographic area involved must be rational for the delivery of health services.
2. One of the following conditions must prevail in the area:
   - The area has a population to full-time equivalent primary-care physician (PCP) ratio of at least 3,500:1.
   - The area has a population to full-time equivalent PCP ratio of less than 3,500:1 but greater than 3,000:1, and has unusually high needs for primary-care services or insufficient capacity of existing primary-care providers.
3. Primary-care professionals in contiguous areas are overutilized, excessively distant, or inaccessible to the population of the area under consideration (HRSA, Bureau of Health Professions, 2007).

A population group can be designated as an HPSA for primary care if it can be demonstrated that barriers to access prevent members of the group from using local healthcare providers. Likewise, medium- and maximum-security federal and state correctional institutions and public or nonprofit private residential facilities can be designated as facility-based HPSAs. HPSAs are classified on a scale of 1 to 4, with scores of 1 and 2 signifying the areas of greatest need.

Medically Underserved Areas (MUA)

The primary purpose of the MUA designation, which was established in the HMO Act of 1973, was to support community health center and rural health clinic programs. The 1973 statute required that several factors be considered when designating MUAs, such as available health resources in relation to the sizes of the geographic area and the population, health indices, and care and demographic factors affecting the need for care. To meet this mandate, the Index of Medical Underservice was developed, which comprises four variables (refer to the following information below). The index yields a single numerical value on a scale from 0 to 100; any area with a value less than 62 (the median of all counties) is designated as an MUA.

- Percentage of the population below the poverty income level
- Percentage of the population 65 years of age and older
- Infant mortality rates
- Number of primary-care practitioners per 1,000 population

Migrant Workers

Migrant workers are farm workers who travel long distances from their primary residence or lack a primary residence entirely, due to either seasonal crop changes or work availability. While their exact number is difficult to assess due to citizenship issues and the transient nature of this population, it is widely accepted that there are at least 3 million migrant workers in the United States (Larson and Plascencia, 1993; Migrant Health Promotion, 2013; National Center for Farmworker Health, 2012; Rust, 1990). The migrant population is largely composed of racial and ethnic minorities. As of 2022, 70% of migrant workers in the United States were foreign-born and 68% were born in Mexico or Central America (NCFH, 2022).

In 2009, the average annual income of a family in which at least one member was a migrant worker was between $17,500 and $19,999. An estimated 52% of migrant worker families have incomes that fall below the poverty level (U.S. Department of Labor, 2018). However, only 43% of workers are currently receiving any public assistance (U.S. Department of Labor, 2011).

As of 2015–2016, approximately 66% of migrant workers lacked health insurance (U.S. Department of Labor, 2018). Furthermore, approximately 30% of female migrant workers who became pregnant did not have their first prenatal visit until their second trimester, and approximately 14% did not have their first visit until their third trimester (Bircher, 2009). In addition to the occupational health risks to which this population is exposed, their lack of access to and utilization of health services translates into poor health outcomes.

The rate of obesity among migrant workers has risen to 81% of males and 76% of females (Villarejo et al., 2000). These rates are not found among migrant workers during their first year in the United States, so dietary changes in later years likely account for the high rates of obesity. In addition to higher rates of chronic conditions, migrant populations are at greater risk for developing infectious diseases. The rate of HIV/AIDS is considerably higher in the migrant worker population than in the general population, with observed rates ranging between 5% and 26% (National Center for Farmworker Health, 2011).

To address the growing health needs of this population, services have been provided to migrant workers and their families through state programs and through HRSA's Migrant Health Program, as discussed in the following sections.

Community and Migrant Health Centers (C/MHC)

C/MHCs provide healthcare services to low-income populations on a sliding-fee scale, thereby addressing both geographic and financial barriers to access. Whereas community health centers must be located in areas designated as MUAs, migrant health centers must be located in "high-impact" areas, defined as areas that serve at least 4,000 migrant and/or seasonal farm workers for at least 2 months per year. For more than 5 decades, C/MHCs have provided primary care and preventive health services to populations in designated MUAs. Because of a shortage of physicians, C/MHCs heavily rely on nonphysician providers (NPPs) to deliver care. In 2015, C/MHCs served approximately 995,232 migrants and seasonal farm workers (HRSA, 2018).

Rural Health Clinics Act

The Rural Health Clinics Act was developed in 1977 to respond to the concern that isolated rural communities could not generate sufficient revenues to support the services of a physician. In many cases, the only sources of primary care or emergency services in these areas were NPPs, who were ineligible at that time for Medicare or Medicaid reimbursement. The Rural Health Clinics Act permitted physician assistants (PAs), nurse practitioners (NPs), and certified nurse-midwives (CNMs) associated with rural clinics to practice without the direct supervision of a physician; enabled rural health clinics to be reimbursed by Medicare and Medicaid for their services; and tied the level of Medicaid payment to the level established by Medicare.

To be designated as a rural health clinic, a public- or private-sector physician practice, clinic, or hospital must meet several criteria, including location in an MUA, a geographic HPSA, or a population-based HPSA. More than 4,500 rural health clinics currently provide primary-care services to more than 8 million people in 50 states (Centers for Medicare and Medicaid Services [CMS], 2019; HRSA, 2015).

People Who Experience Homelessness

Although their exact number is unknown, an estimated 3.5 million people (1.35 million of whom are children) are likely to experience homelessness in a given year (National Law Center on Homelessness and Poverty, 2015). According to the January 2022 PIT Count, 582,462 people were experiencing homelessness across America. This amounts to roughly 18 out of every 10,000 people. The vast majority (72%) were individual adults, but a notable share (28%) were people living as families which include children (NAEH, 2023). Although most persons who are homeless live in major urban areas, 41% live in suburban and rural areas (HUD, 2020).

The adult population experiencing homelessness is composed of 68% men or boys and 38.3% women or girls (NAEH, 2023). An estimated 19% of all people who are homeless are children younger than the age of 18, and 30% are families with children (HUD, 2020). Approximately 5.7% of all adults who are homeless are veterans (NAEH, 2023).

Women in particular who experience homelessness face major difficulties: economic and housing needs and special gender-related issues that include pregnancy, childcare responsibilities, family violence, fragmented family support, job discrimination, and wage discrepancies. The economic standing of women is often more unstable than that of men, and women are more likely to live in poverty than men. In 2018, 15.5 million women were living in poverty in the United States, of whom 46% were in extreme poverty (National Women's Law Center, 2019). The low wages and extreme poverty faced by women increase their risk for becoming homeless. In addition, domestic violence is a factor that contributes to family homelessness, with 18% of families citing this issue as the main cause of their status (U.S. Conference of Mayors, 2011). Among all women who are homeless, 1 in 4 state that their experience was a direct result of violence committed against them (Jasinski, 2005). Women experiencing homelessness, regardless of their parenting status, should be linked with social services, family support, self-help, and housing resources. Women with mental illness caring for children need additional services, with an emphasis on parenting skills and special services for children. Thus, homelessness is a multifaceted problem related to personal, social, and economic factors.

The economic picture for persons who are homeless is dismal and suggests that persons experiencing homelessness are severely in need of the financial and educational resources necessary to access health care. A majority (60%) of mothers living in poverty who have ever been homeless did not complete high school (Institute for Children, Poverty, and Homelessness, 2011). In addition, approximately 38% of the homeless population is unsheltered, living in the streets or outdoors (National Alliance to End Homelessness, 2012). Receipt of public benefits among people who are homeless is low. For example, a survey revealed that among more than 9,000 clients served by Maryland's Health Care for the Homeless, 75% were uninsured (Health Care for the Homeless, 2012). The number of individuals experiencing homelessness who receive public benefits remains low because of federal restrictions that prohibit giving federal help to persons without a physical street address.

A shortage of adequate low-income housing across the United States is the major precipitating factor for homelessness. Unemployment, personal or family life crises, rent increases that are out of proportion to inflation, and reduction in public benefits can also directly result in the loss of a home. Illness, by comparison, tends to result in the loss of a home in a more indirect way. Another indirect cause of homelessness is deinstitutionalization of individuals from public mental hospitals, substance abuse programs, and overcrowded prisons and jails.

Community-based residential alternatives for individuals with mental illnesses vary from independent apartments to group homes staffed by paid caregivers. Independent living may involve either separate apartments or single-room occupancy units in large hotels, whereas group homes are staffed during at least a portion of the day and traditionally provide some on-site mental health services (Schutt and Goldfinger, 1996).

The homeless population—both adults and children—has a high prevalence of untreated acute and chronic medical, mental health, and substance abuse problems. The reasons for this increased prevalence are debatable. Some argue that people may become homeless because of a physical or mental illness. Others argue that homelessness itself may lead to the development of physical and mental disability because homelessness is associated with specific risk factors such as excessive use of alcohol; illegal drugs; cigarettes; sleeping in an upright position, which results in venous stasis and its consequences; extensive walking in poorly fitting shoes; and grossly inadequate nutrition. While there might not be a consensus on the reasons for the generally poorer health of the homeless population, the outcomes are easily seen. Homeless adults typically have eight to nine medical conditions or illnesses (Breakey et al., 1989). Homeless children have a risk of mortality nearly double that of housed children (Kerker et al., 2011).

Persons who are homeless are also at a greater risk of assault and victimization regardless of whether they live in a shelter or outdoors. Many are exposed to extreme heat, cold, and other weather conditions. They are also exposed to illness because of overcrowding in shelters and overexposure to weather. Homelessness has been on the rise from 2017 to 2022, experiencing an overall increase of 6%. In 2022, counts of individuals (421,392 people) and chronically homeless individuals (127,768) reached record highs in the history of data collection. It rose by a modest 0.3 percent from 2020 to 2022, a period marked by both pandemic-related economic disruptions and robust investments of federal resources into human services (NAEH, 2023).

Barriers to Health Care

The homeless population face barriers to obtaining ambulatory services but incur high rates of hospitalization. A high use of inpatient services in this manner amounts to the substitution of inpatient care for outpatient services. Both individual factors (competing needs, substance dependence, and mental illness) and system factors (availability, cost, convenience, and appropriateness of care) account for the barriers to adequate ambulatory services.

Other barriers to accessing health care include lack of transportation to medical-care providers and competing needs for basic food, shelter, and income, which often take precedence over obtaining health services or following through with a prescribed treatment plan. Homeless individuals who experience psychological distress and disabling mental illness may be in the greatest need of health services yet be the least able to obtain them. This inability to obtain health care may be attributable to such individual traits of mental illness as paranoia, disorientation, unconventional health beliefs, lack of social support, lack of organizational skills to gain access to needed services, and fear of authority figures and institutions resulting from previous institutionalization. The social conditions of street life also affect compliance with medical care, as unsheltered persons often lack proper sanitation and a stable place to store medications. In addition, they lack resources to obtain proper food for the medically indicated diets necessary for conditions such as diabetes or hypertension.

Federal efforts to provide medical services to the homeless population are delivered primarily through the Health Care for the Homeless (HCH) program. CHCs supported by the 1985 Robert Wood Johnson Foundation/Pew Memorial Trust HCH program (subsequently covered by the 1987 McKinney Homeless Assistance Act) have addressed many of the access and quality-of-care issues faced by the homeless population. In 2018, U.S. CHCs served approximately 1.4 million homeless patients (HRSA, 2018). A walk-in appointment system reduces access barriers at these medical facilities. Medical care, routine laboratory tests, substance abuse counseling, and some medications are provided free of charge to eliminate financial barriers.

The Mental Health Services for the Homeless Block Grant program sets aside funds for states to implement services for persons with mental disorders who are homeless. These services include outreach services; community mental health services; rehabilitation; referrals to inpatient treatment, primary care, and substance abuse services; case management services; and supportive services in residential settings.

Services for veterans experiencing homelessness are provided through the U.S. Department of Veterans Affairs (VA). The Homeless Chronically Mentally Ill Veterans Program provides outreach, case management services, and psychiatric residential treatment for veterans who are homeless and suffering from mental illness in community-based facilities in 45 U.S. cities. Notably, homelessness among veterans declined by almost 50% between 2009 and 2019 (HUD, 2020). The Domiciliary Care for Homeless Veterans Program addresses the health needs of veterans who have psychiatric illnesses or alcohol or drug abuse problems; it offers more than 2,000 beds at 43 sites across the United States (VA, 2012).

The Salvation Army also provides a variety of social, rehabilitation, and support services for persons who are homeless. Its centers include adult rehabilitation and food programs and permanent and transitional housing.

Mental Health

Mental disorders are common psychiatric illnesses affecting adults and present a serious public health problem in the United States. Mental disorders are among the leading cause of disability for the U.S. population (CDC, 2014b). Mental illness is a risk factor for death from suicide, cardiovascular disease, and cancer. In recent years, suicide has been the ninth leading cause of death in the United States and the second leading cause of death among persons aged 10–34 (CDC, 2019c). Non-Hispanic White men 85 years or older have one of the highest rates of suicide—approximately 50 suicide deaths per 100,000 population (Population Reference Bureau, 2006). AIAN males are at higher risk for suicides as well; their mortality rate from this cause is approximately 33.5 suicide deaths per 100,000 population (CDC, 2019c).

Mental health disorders can be either psychological or biological in nature. Many mental health diseases—including mental retardation (MR), developmental disabilities (DD), and schizophrenia—are now known to be biological in origin. Other behaviors, including those related to personality disorders and neurotic behaviors, are still subject to interpretation and professional judgment.

National studies have concluded that the most common mental disorders are phobias; substance abuse, including alcohol and drug dependence; and affective disorders, including depression. Schizophrenia is considerably less common, affecting an estimated 0.6% of the U.S. population (Reeves et al., 2011).

More than one in five adults experience a mental disorder every year. 22.8% (57.8 million) and 5.5% (14.1 million) of U.S. adults experienced mental illness or severe mental illness in 2021, with 47.2% and 65.4% of them receiving treatment respectively in 2021 (NAMI, 2023). The prevalence of SMI was higher among females (7.0%), individuals in the 18–25 age group (11.4%), AI/AN adults (9.3%), and persons reporting themselves as being two or more races (8.2%) (NIMH, 2021).

The mental health of children has drawn increasing attention in recent years. More than 1 in 5 children has a mental disorder—a higher rate than that for adults; approximately 4 million children or adolescents have SMI (NIMH, 2015). The lifetime prevalence of any mental disorder in adolescents aged 13–18 is 49.5% (NIMH, 2019). Over 60% of those with major depression do not receive any mental health treatment; even in states with the greatest access, nearly 1 in 3 are going without treatment (NHA, 2022). If left untreated, mental health problems in children can lead to more severe and/or co-occurring mental illness (Kessler et al., 1997).

Most mental health services are provided in the general medical sector—a concept first described by Regier and colleagues. (1988) as the de facto mental health service system—rather than through formal mental health specialist services. The de facto system combines specialty mental health services with general counseling services, such as those provided in primary-care settings, nursing homes, and community health centers by ministers, counselors, self-help groups, families, and friends. Specifically, mental health services are provided through public and private resources in both inpatient and outpatient facilities. These facilities include state and county mental hospitals, private psychiatric hospitals, nonfederal general hospital psychiatric services, VA psychiatric services, residential treatment centers, and freestanding psychiatric outpatient clinics (**Table 11-6**).

Total expenditures for mental disorders have increased dramatically in the past few decades, from $31 billion in 1986 to $172 billion in 2009 (SAMHSA, 2014). Nevertheless, only 37.9% of all individuals with mental illness received mental health services in 2010, and only 48.5% of such individuals covered under Medicaid/CHIP received care in that year (SAMHSA, 2012a, 2012b). The U.S. **mental health system** essentially consists of two subsystems: one primarily for individuals with insurance coverage or private funds, and the other for those persons without private coverage.

Table 11-6 Mental Health Organizations, 2020

Service/Organization	Number of Mental Health Organizations
All organizations	12,275
Psychiatric hospitals	608
General hospitals	1,066
Outpatient mental health facilities	4,941
Residential treatment centers for children	580
All other	5,080

Data from Michas, F. (2022). Number of mental health treatment facilities in the U.S. in 2020 by service setting. http://www.statista.com/statistics/450277/mental-health-facilities-in-the-us-by-service-type/.

Barriers to Mental Health Care

Two major barriers to accessing mental health care are commonly experienced across the United States: prohibitive costs of services and a shortage of available mental health professionals. In 2013, among young adults who delayed or did not seek needed mental health care, 50.1% stated that their failure to seek care was due to the prohibitive cost of treatment (SAMHSA, 2015). In addition to being unable to cover the high costs of care, many individuals currently reside in a mental health HPSA. A mental health HPSA is defined as an area in which the population to mental health professional ratio equals 30,000 people to 1 mental health professional and 30,000 people to 1 psychiatrist (Kaiser Family Foundation, 2019b). As of 2019, more than 6,000 mental health HPSAs were found across the United States (Kaiser Family Foundation, 2019b). This shortage translates into services being available to meet only 27% of the need for mental health services, leaving other patients without needed care (Kaiser Family Foundation, 2019b).

The Uninsured and Mental Health

Patients without insurance coverage or personal financial resources are treated in state and county mental health hospitals and in community mental health clinics. Care is also provided in short-term, acute-care hospitals and emergency departments. Local governments are the providers of last resort, with the ultimate responsibility to provide somatic and mental health services for all citizens regardless of ability to pay.

The Insured and Mental Health

For patients who have insurance coverage or the ability to pay, availability of both inpatient and ambulatory mental health care has expanded tremendously in recent decades. Inpatient mental health services for patients with insurance are usually provided through private psychiatric hospitals. These hospitals may operate on either a nonprofit or a for-profit basis. Notably, national chains of for-profit mental health hospitals have experienced significant growth.

Patients with insurance coverage are also more likely to receive care through the offices of private psychiatrists, clinical psychologists, and licensed social workers. Some mental health services are provided by the VA and by the military healthcare system as well; however, access to these services is limited based on eligibility.

Managed Care and Mental Health

Managed care providers have expanded their services to include delivery of mental health care. Many state and local governments have also contracted with managed care organizations (MCOs) to manage their full healthcare benefits packages, which include mental health and substance abuse services for their Medicaid enrollees.

Many health maintenance organizations (HMOs) contract with specialized companies that provide managed behavioral health care, an arrangement called carve-out; such carve-outs are implemented mainly because HMOs typically lack the in-house capacity to provide treatment (McConnell et al., 2023; Friedman et al., 2019). Using case managers and reviewers, most of whom are psychiatric nurses, social workers, and psychologists, these specialized companies manage and authorize the use of mental health and substance abuse services. The case reviewers, using clinical protocols to guide them, assign patients to the least expensive appropriate treatment, emphasizing outpatient alternatives over inpatient care. Working with computerized databases, a reviewer studies a patient's particular problem and then authorizes an appointment with an appropriate provider in the company's selective network. On average, psychiatrists constitute approximately 4.5% of any given provider network, psychologists 18%, counselors 17%, and psychiatric social workers 65% (NIMH, 2015).

Mental Health Professionals

A variety of professionals provide mental health services (**Table 11-7**), including psychiatrists, psychologists, social workers, nurses, counselors, and therapists.

Psychiatrists are physicians who specialize in the diagnosis and treatment of mental disorders. They receive postgraduate specialty training in mental health after completing medical school. Psychiatric residencies cover medical—as well as behavioral—diagnosis and treatments. A relatively small proportion of the total mental health workforce consists of psychiatrists, but they exercise disproportionate influence in the system by virtue of their authority to prescribe drugs and admit patients to hospitals.

Table 11-7 Mental Health Providers by Discipline, Selected Years

Staff Discipline	Number	Year
Psychiatrists	33,727	2009
Child and adolescent psychiatrists	6,398	2009
Psychologists	95,545	2011
Clinical social workers	193,038	2011
Psychiatric nurses	13,701	2008
Substance abuse counselors	48,080	2011
Counselors	144,567	2011
Marriage and family therapists	62,316	2011

Reproduced from Substance Abuse and Mental Health Services Administration (SAMHSA). 2013. *Behavioral health, United States, 2012.* Available at: http://www.samhsa.gov/data/sites/default/files/2012-BHUS.pdf.

Psychologists usually hold a doctoral degree, although some have master's degrees. These professionals are trained in interpreting and changing the behavior of people. Psychologists cannot prescribe drugs, but they provide a wide range of services to patients with neurotic and behavioral problems. Psychologists use such techniques as psychotherapy and counseling, which psychiatrists typically do not engage in. Psychoanalysis is a subspecialty in mental health that involves the use of intensive treatment by both psychiatrists and psychologists.

Social workers receive training in various aspects of mental health services, particularly counseling. These professionals are trained at the master's degree level. They also compete with psychologists for patients.

Nurses are involved in mental health care through the subspecialty of psychiatric nursing. This kind of specialty training for nurses dates back to the latter part of the 1800s. Today, nurses provide a wide range of mental health services.

Many other healthcare professionals contribute to the array of available services, including marriage and family counselors, recreational therapists, and vocational counselors. Numerous people work in related areas, such as adult daycare (ADC) and alcohol/drug abuse counseling, and as psychiatric aides in institutional settings.

The Chronically Ill Population

Chronic diseases are now the leading cause of death in the United States, leading to 7 out of 10 deaths each year (CDC, 2016a). Collectively, heart disease, cancer, and stroke account for almost 50% of all U.S. deaths each year (CDC, 2019a). Heart disease is the number one cause of death in the United States, with a mortality rate of 209.6. deaths per 100,000 persons (CDC, 2022). One person dies every 33 seconds from cardiovascular disease. The age-adjusted prevalence of heart disease in adults aged 18 and over decreased from 6.2% in 2009 to 5.5% in 2018; in 2019, 5.5% of adults reported that they had been diagnosed with heart disease (NCHS, 2023).

Chronic disease results in adverse consequences such as limitations on daily life activities. Among adults who have a weight within normal range with one or more chronic illnesses, the number of sick or unhealthy days they experience each month leads to loss of productivity that costs more than $15 billion per year (Witters and Agrawal, 2011). For adults who are overweight with one or more chronic illnesses, this loss is more than double—an estimated $32 billion annually. Overall, the total loss of productivity due to overweight or other chronic illnesses is estimated at more than $153 billion each year.

The loss in human potential and workdays notwithstanding, chronic disease is expensive and places a huge economic demand on the country. Treatment of people with chronic diseases accounts for 86% of total U.S. healthcare costs, which amounted to $2.9 trillion in 2013 (CDC, 2015a). The total estimated cost of diagnosed diabetes in 2017 was $327 billion, including $237 billion in direct medical costs and $90 billion in decreased productivity (ADA, 2018). Smoking-related illnesses cost the United States more than $300 billion a year (CDC, 2019e).

Much of the burden of chronic diseases results from four modifiable risk behaviors: physical activity, nutrition, smoking, and alcohol use (CDC, 2010a). In 2018, almost half (45.8%) of adults did not meet the CDC's recommendations for aerobic physical activity. In addition, 72.4% did not meet the recommendations for muscle-strengthening physical activity (CDC, 2019i). There has also been a decline in participation in physical education classes among high school students, from 42% in 1991 to 31% in 2011. In addition, the U.S. population as a whole suffers from poor nutrition. More detailed coverage on chronic diseases can be found in the *Beliefs, Values, and Health* chapter.

Disability

As of 2021, more than 1 in 4 (27%) adults in the United States have some type of disability (CDC, 2023). 46% of Americans ages 75 and older and 24% of those ages 65 to 74 report having a disability, according to estimates from the Census Bureau's 2021 American Community Survey (ACS), compared to 12% of adults ages 35 to 64 and 8% of adults under 35 (Pew Research Center, 2023).

The chronic conditions most responsible for disabilities are arthritis, heart disease, back problems, asthma, and diabetes (Kraus et al., 1996). Individuals with disabilities tend to be covered by public insurance (30% by Medicare and 10% by Medicaid), whereas those who have no disabilities are more likely to have private health insurance (U.S. Census Bureau, 2011a). In addition, Medicaid is the primary payer (40%) for long-term services and supports for individuals with disabilities, including nursing facility stays and home- and community-based services (Kaiser Family Foundation, 2014b).

Disability can be categorized as mental, physical, or social. Physical disability usually relates to a person's mobility and other basic activities performed in daily life; mental disability involves both the cognitive and emotional states; and social disability is considered the most severe disability because management of social roles requires both physical and mental well-being (Ostir et al., 1999).

Two commonly used measures of disability—activities of daily living (ADLs) and instrumental activities of daily living (IADLs)—are covered in the *Beliefs, Values, and Health* chapter. Another tool for assessing disability is the Survey of Income and Program Participation (SIPP), which measures disability by asking participants about functional limitations—that is, difficulty in performing activities such as seeing, hearing, walking, and having one's speech understood. The ADL and IADL scales are more widely used than the SIPP.

Despite the availability of community-based and institutional long-term care services for people with functional limitations, many of these individuals do not get help with the basic tasks of personal care. Indeed, approximately one in five persons with an ADL limitation does not receive needed assistance (Newcomer et al., 2005). Furthermore, racial minorities are more likely to experience unmet personal assistance needs (Newcomer et al., 2005).

HIV/AIDS

Figure 11-11 illustrates trends in HIV reporting. The number of cases reported increased between 1985 and 1993, decreased between 1994 and 2000, increased between 2001 and 2003, and has decreased since 2005.

In the United States, the death rates among people with HIV decreased by about 37%

HIV/AIDS 495

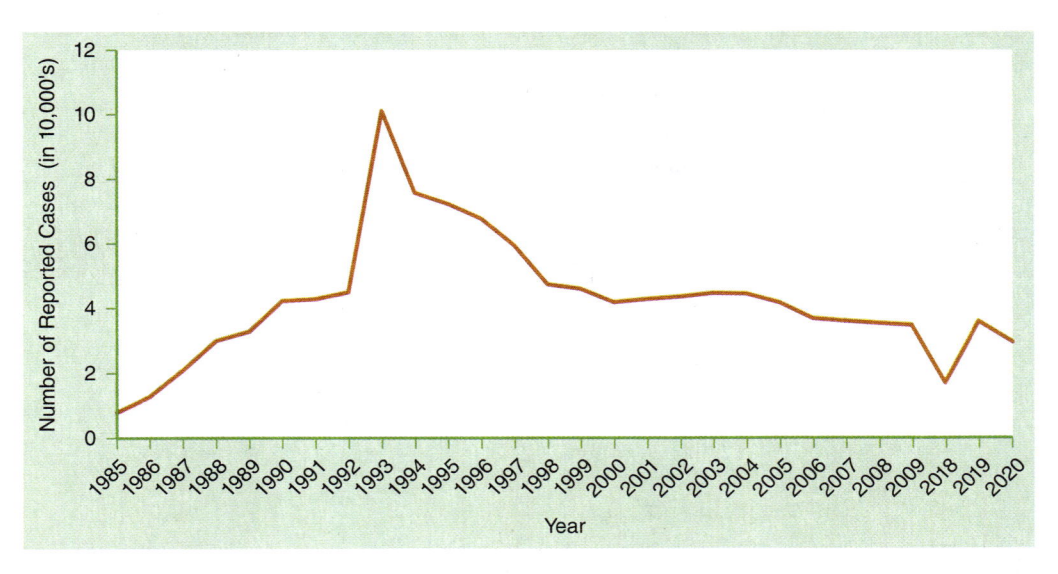

Figure 11-11 AIDS cases reported in the United States.

Data from U.S. Census Bureau, *Statistical abstract of the United States, 1993*, p. 134; *Statistical abstract of the United States, 1994*, p. 139; *Statistical abstract of the United States, 1995*, p. 140; *Statistical abstract of the United States, 1996*, p. 142; *Statistical abstract of the United States, 1998*, p. 147; *Statistical abstract of the United States, 1999*, p. 148; *Statistical abstract of the United States, 2000*, p. 138; *Statistical abstract of the United States, 2001*, p. 120; *Statistical abstract of the United States, 2003*, p. 132; *Statistical abstract of the United States, 2004–2005*, p. 121; *Statistical abstract of the United States, 2006*, p. 125; *Statistical abstract of the United States, 2007*, p. 120; *Statistical abstract of the United States, 2008*, p. 121; *Statistical abstract of the United States, 2012*, p. 126; Centers for Disease Control and Prevention (CDC). 2019. *HIV surveillance report: Statistics overview*. Available at: https://www.cdc.gov/hiv/pdf/library/reports/surveillance/cdc-hiv-surveillance-report-2018-updated-vol-32.pdf. Accessed January 2020. 2019 and 2020 data from CDC. HIV Surveillance Report 2020; Vol. 33. https://stacks.cdc.gov/view/cdc/121127/cdc_121127_DS1.pdf. Published May 2022.

from 2010 to 2018 (CDC, 2020). Declines in reported AIDS cases are attributed to new treatments; decreasing death rates may reflect the fact that benefits from new treatments are being fully realized. Consequently, the number of people living with AIDS has continued to increase. About 1.2 million people were living with HIV in the United States in 2021 (HIV.gov, 2023); by comparison, that figure was 341,332 in 2001 (CDC, 2011). Among women who are Black, Hispanic, or minority, AIDS/HIV is still a major public health concern. Males and Black people continued to have significantly higher rates of HIV than females and White people (**Table 11-8**).

HIV Infection in Rural Communities

In 2018, 37,377 people were diagnosed with HIV infection in the United States, and 17,032 people were diagnosed with AIDS. Since the HIV/AIDS epidemic began in the early 1980s, a total of 1,254,576 people have been diagnosed with AIDS in the United States (CDC, 2019h).

Rural persons with HIV and AIDS are more likely to be young, non-White, and female and to have acquired their infection through heterosexual contact. Additionally, a growing number of these persons who are HIV-infected, live in the rural South, a region historically characterized by a disproportionate number of persons who have lower incomes and belong to a minority group, strong religious beliefs and sanctions, and less access to comprehensive health services (CDC, 1995). Trends in new cases of HIV and AIDS in rural areas indicate that poor and non-White residents are disproportionately affected by these diseases.

HIV in Children

In the absence of specific therapy to interrupt transmission of HIV, an HIV-infected woman has a 20% chance of having a child born with

Table 11-8 Diagnoses of HIV infection, by Year of Diagnosis and Selected Characteristics, 2016–2020—United States

	2016 No.	2016 Rate[a]	2017 No.	2017 Rate[a]	2018 No.	2018 Rate[a]	2019 No.	2019 Rate[a]	2020 (COVID-19 Pandemic) No.	2020 (COVID-19 Pandemic) Rate[a]
Gender										
Male	31,332	—	30,461	—	29,730	—	28,948	—	24,269	—
Female	7,512	—	7,300	—	7,084	—	6,917	—	5,439	—
Transgender woman/girl[b]	675	—	612	—	627	—	652	—	638	—
Transgender man/boy[b]	22	—	33	—	48	—	45	—	40	—
Additional gender identity[c]	11	—	15	—	15	—	23	—	17	—
Total					36,901		35,922		29,765	
Child (<13 yrs at diagnosis)										
Perinatal	107	—	88	—	68	—	46	—	44	—
Other	23	—	17	—	19	—	11	—	13	—
Subtotal	130	0.2	105	0.2	87	0.2	57	0.1	57	0.1
Race/ethnicity										
American Indian/Alaska Native	216	9.1	200	8.3	173	7.2	205	8.5	201	8.3
Asian	931	5.2	930	5.1	868	4.6	739	3.9	637	3.3
Black/African American	16,799	41.7	16,279	40.1	15,786	38.6	15,503	37.6	12,856	31.0
Hispanic/Latino[d]	10,101	17.6	9,941	17.0	9,956	16.7	9,896	16.4	8,008	13.1
Native Hawaiian/other Pacific Islander	38	6.7	51	8.8	61	10.3	66	10.9	66	10.8
White	9,885	5.0	9,643	4.9	9,448	4.8	9,070	4.6	7,843	4.0
Multiracial	1,582	23.2	1,377	19.7	1,212	16.9	1,106	15.0	792	10.5

Modified from Centers for Disease Control and Prevention. *HIV Surveillance Report, 2020*; Vol. 33. https://stacks.cdc.gov/view/cdc/121127/cdc_121127_DS1.pdf. Published May 2022. Accessed May 23, 2023.

HIV (Cooper et al., 2000). Building on previous success with zidovudine monotherapy in the 1990s, clinical studies established the efficacy of antiretroviral therapy in reducing the mother-to-child transmission rate when administered prenatally (Cooper et al., 2000). Today, use of this therapy has resulted in a decrease of the rate of mother-to-child transmission to only 2% (Cooper et al., 2000). Guidelines on the use of antiretroviral drugs in pregnant HIV/AIDS-infected women have now been established (NIH, 2012; World Health Organization, 2004). The importance of preventing perinatal transmission is underscored by the fact that 68% of all AIDS cases among U.S. children are caused by mother-to-child transmission in pregnancy, labor, delivery, or breastfeeding (CDC, 2016b).

Children born with AIDS suffer from failure to thrive, leaving them unable to grow and develop as healthy children. Without intervention, failure to thrive may lead to developmental delays that can have negative lifetime consequences for the child and their family.

HIV in Women

Women account for a rapidly growing proportion of the population with HIV/AIDS. In 2016, women represented 52% of HIV cases worldwide (UN Women, 2018). For Black U.S. women ages 15 to 44 and Hispanic women ages 25 to 44, HIV/AIDS was among the top 10 causes of death in 2010 (CDC, 2013a).

For women in general, injection drug use (IDU) is the most common cause of HIV exposure, followed by heterosexual contact (CDC, 2019h). Aside from the inherent risks of IDU, drug use contributes to a higher risk of contracting HIV if heterosexual sex with an IDU user occurs or when sex is traded for drugs or money (CDC, 2013b). Black and Hispanic minority women are at particular risk for these modes of exposure. Despite accounting for less than one-fourth of the total U.S. female population, Black and Hispanic women represent more than three-fourths (76%) of all AIDS cases in women (CDC, 2020). In 2018, 57% of all new HIV diagnoses in the United States were made in Black women (CDC, 2020).

HIV/AIDS-Related Issues

Need for Research

Much of the current HIV-related research focuses on the development of a vaccine to prevent HIV-negative people from acquiring HIV. Researchers are also seeking to develop a therapeutic vaccine to prevent HIV-positive people from developing symptoms of AIDS.

People with HIV/AIDS cover a broad spectrum of social classes, races, ethnicities, sexual orientations, and genders. Therefore, behavioral intervention research should focus on the particular subpopulations that are most vulnerable to HIV infection and are in urgent need of preventive interventions. These groups include gay youth and young adults, especially those who are Black and Hispanic; disenfranchised and impoverished women; heterosexual men, especially those who are Black and Hispanic; inner-city youth; and out-of-treatment substance abusers and their sexual partners. Research should address not only prevention and therapy in individuals, but also the impact of broader interventions (e.g., among drug users or those involved in sexual networks or community-wide groups) that might change behavioral norms and, consequently, affect individual behavior (Merson, 1996).

Public Health Concerns

Trends related to AIDS underscore the synergy between poverty and intravenous drug use. Further, control of the HIV epidemic among the poor is hampered by this population's preoccupation with other problems related to survival, such as homelessness, crime, and lack of access to adequate health care.

Additionally, a relationship exists between the tuberculosis epidemic and HIV. Indeed, tuberculosis, which is classified as an **opportunistic infection (OI)** in the HIV/AIDS setting, is the leading cause of death among HIV-infected people on a worldwide basis. Tuberculosis in people with HIV is also a particular public health concern because people with HIV are at greater risk of developing multidrug-resistant tuberculosis—a variant that is understandably difficult to treat and can be fatal (CDC, 1999a, 1999b).

Reducing the spread of AIDS requires understanding of a variety of sexual issues, ranging from the concept that even heterosexual men may engage in anonymous homosexual intercourse to the difficulty that adolescents may have in controlling their sexual urges. Prejudice against individuals who are gay or lesbian is manifested as **homophobia**, a fear and/or hatred of these individuals. Homophobia explains the initially slow policy-related response to the HIV epidemic.

Unfortunately, testing for HIV may not limit the virus's spread because many people who learn their HIV status do not change the behaviors that contribute to its spread. HIV infection has no cure, and the current treatments do not affect the transmissibility of the virus.

In some cases, criminal law has been used to contain the spread of HIV and to protect public health (CDC, 2019g). For example, some U.S. laws require that persons convicted of sex offenses be tested for HIV. Most of these laws, however, are disproportionately enforced against prostitutes. These laws suggest that persons who test positive for HIV may receive longer prison sentences; however, it is questionable whether this type of punishment actually reduces the spread of HIV.

Health promotion efforts, including those used to reduce the transmission of HIV, are often hamstrung by psychosocial and other factors. For example, humans generally have difficulty changing their behaviors. Further, much human behavior is associated with functional needs (e.g., unsafe sex might fulfill a need for intimacy). Social learning theory explains that behavior change first requires knowledge, followed by a change of attitude or perspective.

Discrimination

HIV-positive people may experience discrimination in access to health care. Unfortunately, some policies of various government agencies intended to help persons in need have also had a discriminatory impact on people with HIV/AIDS. For example, the Social Security Administration has not historically considered many of the HIV-related symptoms of women and IDUs in adjudicating disability claims. Although the Department of Defense provides adequate medical care to individuals who acquire HIV in the military, recruits who test positive for HIV cannot join the military (Congressional Research Service, 2019).

Provider Training

Increased knowledge about HIV and personal contact with people who have HIV have improved the attitudes of many healthcare providers toward individuals with HIV and contributed to their willingness to care for people with HIV. Training of healthcare professionals should encompass not only medical and treatment-related information but also a range of competencies related to interpersonal skills.

In the area of psychosocial skills, the following characteristics are essential in an effectively trained provider: good communication skills (ability to establish rapport, ask questions, and listen), positive attitudes (respect, empowerment, and trust), and an approach that incorporates principles of holistic care. In the area of cultural competence, essential elements include understanding and respecting the person's specific culture; understanding that racial and ethnic minorities have important and multiple subdivisions or functional units; acknowledging the issues of gender and sexual orientation within the context of cultural competence; and respecting the customs, including modes of communication, of the person's culture. In the area of substance abuse, the following elements are essential for primary-care providers: understanding the complex medical picture presented by a person who suffers from both HIV and addiction; understanding the complicated psychosocial, ethical, and legal issues related to care of addicted persons; and being aware of personal attitudes about addiction that may impair providers' ability to give care objectively and nonjudgmentally (e.g., in the administration of pain medication; Gross and Larkin, 1996).

Cost of HIV/AIDS

Medical care for patients with HIV/AIDS is extremely expensive. Pharmaceutical companies claim that the high prices they charge for AIDS therapies reflect their extensive investment in the research and development of these drugs. Currently, Medicaid covers more than 282,000 people with HIV (Kaiser Family Foundation, 2019b). In fiscal year (FY) 2019, combined federal and state Medicaid spending on persons with HIV totaled $10.1 billion, making it the second largest source of public financing for HIV/AIDS care in the United States, after Medicare. Of this amount, the federal share was $6.3 billion, or 30% of federal HIV care spending (Kaiser Family Foundation, 2019b). Lack of insurance and underinsurance represent formidable financial barriers to HIV/AIDS care.

The U.S. government also invests substantial amounts of money in research and development through research supported at the NIH and CDC. Government funding is directed toward several areas related to HIV (**Figure 11-12**): 73% on antiretroviral medications, 13% on inpatient care, 9% on outpatient care, and 5% on other HIV-related medications and laboratory costs. For patients who initiate highly active antiretroviral therapy (HAART) when their CD4 cell count is 200/L, their projected life expectancy is 22.5 years, their discounted lifetime cost is $354,100, and their undiscounted cost is $567,000

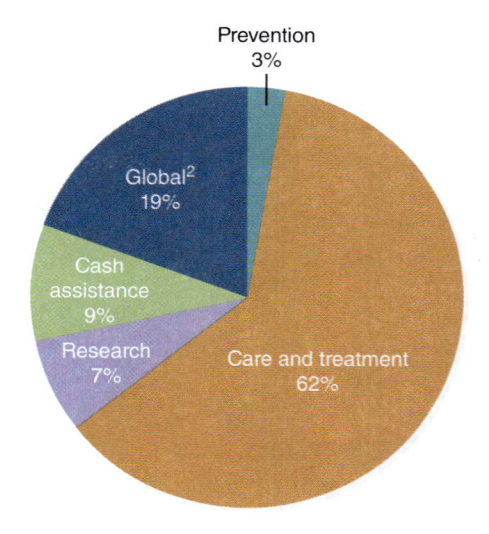

Figure 11-12 Federal spending for HIV/AIDS by category,[1] FY 2019.

[1]Categories may include funding across multiple agencies/programs.
[2]The "global" category includes international HIV research at NIH.

Data from Kaiser Family Foundation. 2016b. *U.S. federal funding for HIV/AIDS: Trends over time.* Available at: http://kff.org/global-health-policy/fact-sheet/u-s-federal-funding-for-hivaids-trends-over-time/. Accessed March 2017.

(Schackman et al., 2006). Indirect costs attributable to HIV/AIDS include lost productivity, largely because of worker morbidity and mortality. However, other factors affect cost projections associated with the HIV/AIDS epidemic, including the level of employment of HIV-positive people; regional differences in the cost of care, including the lack of subacute care in many parts of the country; and the rate at which HIV spreads.

Containment of escalating medical costs, including the coordination of medical care, is the objective of two HIV-specific efforts: the Medicaid waiver program and the Ryan White Comprehensive AIDS Resources Emergency (CARE) Act. Through the **Medicaid waiver program**, states may design packages of services to specific populations, such as older adults, persons with disabilities, and persons who test HIV positive.

The passage of the Ryan White CARE Act in 1990 provided federal funds to develop treatment and care options for persons with HIV/AIDS (Summer, 1991). Title II of this legislation is administered by states and has been used to establish HIV clinics and related services in areas lacking the resources needed to offer this specialty care. Some public health systems have used Ryan White CARE Act money to provide HIV/AIDS services in rural communities in which people with limited financial resources or who are medically underserved lack access to adequate care. Federal spending attributable to the Ryan White CARE Act totaled an estimated $2.3 billion in 2019 (Kaiser Family Foundation, 2019e).

AIDS and the U.S. Healthcare System

The course of AIDS is characterized by a gradual decline in the patient's physical, cognitive, and emotional function and well-being. Such a comprehensive decline requires a continuum of care, including emergency care, primary care, housing and supervised living, mental health and social support, nonmedical services, and hospice care. This continuum can encompass elements such as outreach and case finding, preventive services, outpatient and inpatient care, and coordination of private and public insurance benefits.

As HIV disease progresses, many persons become disabled and rely on public entitlement or private disability programs for income and healthcare benefits. These programs include Social Security Disability Income and Supplemental Security Income, both of which are administered by the Social Security Administration. Medicare and Medicaid frequently become primary payers for affected individuals' health care because of the onset of disability and depletion of personal funds. Approximately 70,000 previously uninsured people with HIV/AIDS were expected to gain coverage under the ACA. Most of them would have gained insurance through Medicaid expansion (Kaiser Family Foundation, 2014a). Preliminary data showed that about half of uninsured individuals with HIV/AIDS were able to gain coverage in Medicaid expansion states, whereas the number without coverage in nonexpansion states stayed relatively the same (Berry et al., 2016).

Addressing Disparities Across Subpopulations

Extensive efforts have been made to address and eliminate the pervasive disparities experienced by vulnerable populations in the United States. As social determinants of health play a major, well-recognized role in shaping those disparities, many interventions target structural aspects such as the environment, neighborhood conditions, nutritional food access, and more. However, not all efforts are made equal, and some interventions have been found to be more effective than others. Brown et al. (2019), for example, highlighted some important features of health disparities interventions that were common to successful programs. In particular, community engagement and taking a generalized approach that focuses on common risk factors instead of specific diseases were identified as key factors. Thornton et al. (2016) also presented evidence indicating that early childhood and education, urban planning and community development, housing, income enhancements and supplements, and employment are proven areas of focus where interventions can effectively target upstream societal determinants that have significant and wide-ranging impacts on health disparities.

The role of health systems and collaboration has also been emphasized in the design and implementation of strategies targeting health disparities. Although health systems have traditionally seen their role as ensuring the equitable provision of health care to all people who come into contact with the system, this narrow focus fails to account for external barriers that might lead to inequitable access and rules out taking a preventive approach to health (Wesson et al., 2019). Health systems on their own, however, do not necessarily have the resources or expertise to address those barriers and the other social determinants that factor into health and well-being. Building trust within the community and engaging in collaboration with other entities in a broader social context can allow them to leverage their capabilities to lead health disparities interventions (Wesson et al., 2019).

One example of a successful health system collaboration is the Community Asthma Initiative (CAI) undertaken by Boston Children's Hospital (Woods et al., 2016). In this program, families living in Boston neighborhoods with high rates of poverty and asthma were assigned community health workers who provided case management and home visiting services. These services included assessment of eligibility for federal assistance, asthma education, home environmental assessments, and working with landlords, property managers, and the public housing authority to resolve housing code violations. Additionally, partnerships with local after-school programs, public health agencies, community health centers, the YMCA, and more helped the initiative expand its reach in targeting the social determinants of health that impact asthma morbidity. Through the CAI, asthma-related hospitalizations in children were reduced by 79% and asthma-related emergency department visits were reduced by 56% (Woods et al., 2016). This initiative's success highlights the potential for health systems to coordinate effective collaborations between various organizations and stakeholders to reduce existing health disparities and improve population health.

Beyond local initiatives, many efforts are ongoing at the state and federal levels to address health disparities. State and federal action can tackle these disparities on a broader scale that regional initiatives are too localized to address, thus making their efforts critical to systemic change. For example, some states have created programs to attract or support young students from underrepresented backgrounds to pursue a career in health care (National Conference of State Legislatures, 2017). Other efforts have sought to glean better understandings of the disparities present within each state and to come up with more effective strategies and recommendations for addressing them. Legislation passed in Minnesota in 2015, for example, created a task force with duties that included identifying possible opportunities for reducing health disparities through healthcare financing. The legislation also allocated funds for decreasing infant mortality rate disparities (National Conference of State Legislatures, 2017).

At the federal level, relevant entities include the Agency for Healthcare Research and Quality, which publishes annual reports on healthcare quality disparities; the Office of Minority Health, which develops policies for addressing racial and ethnic disparities; and the Health Resources and Services Administration, which provides funding for the care of vulnerable populations (Tikkanen et al., 2020). The ACA also includes provisions for increased funding of community health centers and support of cultural competency training (Artiga et al., 2020).

The extent of, and variation in, health disparities across the United States makes it difficult to devise any single intervention that could address all concerns. Like so many other things, disparities result from a myriad of factors and, therefore, require complex, multifaceted, and evidence-based approaches to resolve. Certain intervention features and areas of focus have shown promise in addressing inequities. Collaborations are also essential, especially when taking into account the individual capabilities of those involved and the unique characteristics and problems of each community. Federal and state support in the form of funding, policy initiatives, and more are crucial to tackling these disparities with more force on a larger scale. In time, it is hoped these efforts will make more concrete progress toward completely eliminating health disparities in the United States. Selected recent examples of strategies to address disparities across subpopulations are provided below.

Focus on social determinants of health. Xiao and Lindsey (2021) pointed to the need to improve the long-term effect of mental health treatment with greater attention to the social determinants of health, especially in early adolescence and in the transition to adulthood, especially regarding the mental health treatment experiences of Black people.

Engage diversity and inclusion. Integrating mental health into primary-care settings and school mental health programs, as well as providing mandatory suicidal risk screening in schools, could facilitate better monitoring of at-risk subpopulations and provision of timely interventions (Gadomski et al., 2015). Reducing the stigma of mental health help-seeking, particularly for minority individuals from culturally diverse backgrounds, could significantly increase public awareness and help-seeking behaviors among vulnerable populations (Batterham et al., 2013).

Utilize multilevel intervention approaches. Combining broad public health campaigns using mass media and gatekeeper training could improve the effectiveness of suicide prevention initiatives (Li et al., 2021; Niederkrotenthaler et al., 2014; Xiao et al., 2021). Additionally, for sexual minority youth, peer gatekeeping programs through social networks, such as the Trevor Project, are encouraged (Gould et al. 2012).

Maximize communication and collaboration. Take COVID-19 vaccine hesitancy, for instance. To address this problem and to mitigate the disparities in minority groups, it will require making available data on vaccinations that can be broken down by multiple dimensions of inequity, including race-ethnicity, socioeconomic status, and geography, among others (Strully et al., 2021). States and localities should work to maximize communication and collaboration between equity task forces and other related task forces, such as those working on vaccine distribution and implementation, so equity goals can be centered through all parts of vaccine campaigns (Strully et al., 2021). Additionally, states and localities should build on COVID-19 related task forces to develop sustainable infrastructure for health equity and justice (Strully et al., 2021). For example, the Michigan gubernatorial administration has used momentum around COVID-19 disparities to convene a Black Leadership Advisory Council to advise the governor on legislation that promotes race equality and support for Black arts and community groups and on a Poverty Task Force to develop an anti-poverty agenda for the state (Strully et al., 2021).

Community engagement and empowerment. States and localities should support community organizations with needed funds and resources so they can expand their work to address vaccine equity (Strully et al., 2021). The importance of community engagement and building on existing community structures has been widely recognized at both the federal and state/local levels (Strully et al., 2021). Michigan has again been cited as a promising example as their vaccine equity task force has solicited applications to rapidly fund promising initiatives from community organizations (Strully et al., 2021).

Racism in Health Care

An issue that has yet to be properly addressed in the field of health care is the enduring presence of racism. Racism is not only an issue of societal institutions that deal with economic and social well-being; it is distinctly palpable within the healthcare system as well. As a system dedicated to improving the health of the individuals and communities that it serves, health care must not only acknowledge the deep connection between health and racism as experienced in everyday life but also address its own role in perpetuating that same racism within its own walls.

Racism in health care does not typically surface in a blatant, overt way but rather tends to take the form of racial microaggressions or underrepresentation of people of color in the healthcare workforce (Evans et al., 2020; Snyder et al., 2018). Examples of microaggressions include experiences in which the provider makes assumptions about the patient's race, seems to hold low expectations for the patient due to their race, or ignores the context of race on health (Snyder et al., 2018). Racism also surfaces in the significant variations in the way providers approach nonminority and minority patients. Recent studies have found evidence of poorer-quality care and physician dismissal or downplaying of condition severity in minority patients (Carroll, 2020; Russell, 2020; Stepanikova, 2012). For example, Black patients are less likely to receive physician referrals and to be left out of certain medical discussions (LaVeist et al., 2002; Peterson et al., 2020; Russell, 2020).

Historic underrepresentation of certain racial groups in health care also reflects the institutionalized racism present within this sector. In 2018, only 5% of all active physicians in the United States identified as Black or African American, and a mere 5.8% identified as Hispanic (AAMC, 2019), both of which were disproportional to the actual makeup of the U.S. population. Reducing imbalances in the workforce could lead to significant improvements in the delivery of culturally competent care and increase patient trust (Evans et al., 2020).

In creating more targeted, focused efforts to address racism and underrepresentation in health care, many areas need to undergo change. Supporting the entry of more racial minorities into the healthcare workforce represents a major avenue for change. Greater emphasis on cultural competency training and the importance of avoiding racial bias is also vital (Carroll, 2020). Additionally, the field of academia must acknowledge the role it plays in centering public discussion and influencing opinions on certain topics, including racism. Academic publications on health disparities between racial groups rarely place enough emphasis on racism, particularly in its systemic and institutionalized forms, as a driver of inequity (Boyd et al., 2020). Instead of proposing unfounded underlying genetic or biological differences as the cause of disparities, or suggesting that patient behaviors and mistrust of the healthcare system are the root cause of the problem, a more direct and explicit focus on racism and how its presence in the healthcare system has fueled that mistrust over the years should be promulgated (Boyd et al., 2020). Academic journals should regularly review their publication guidelines to ensure they reflect such considerations (Boyd et al., 2020).

The disparities between racial groups in terms of healthcare access, quality, and outcomes have been clearly evidenced and documented in academic literature. However, less frequently discussed is how strongly these disparities are rooted in the systemic and institutionalized racism that permeates modern American society. This type of racism, tacit and inconspicuous, extends into the healthcare system as well. Stronger and more explicit efforts must be taken to address and eliminate the presence of racism in health care and guarantee health equity for all. Refer to **Box 11-1** for further examples of racism in health care.

Box 11-1 Racism in Health Care

- Racialized minorities experience inadequate health care (Hamed et al., 2022). Experiences of racism are associated with lack of trust and delay in seeking health care (Hamed et al., 2022). Racialized minority healthcare staff experience racism in their workplace from healthcare users and colleagues and lack of organizational support in managing racism (Hamed et al., 2022).

(continues)

> **Box 11-1 Racism in Health Care** *(continued)*
>
> Research on implicit racial bias illustrates that healthcare staff exhibit racial bias in favor of majority group (Hamed et al., 2022). Studies examining healthcare staff's reflections on racism and antiracist training show that healthcare staff tend to construct health care as impartial and that healthcare staff do not readily discuss racism in their workplace (Hamed et al., 2022).
>
> - Black women find themselves at the crossroads of both racism and sexism (Dill & Duffy, 2022). Within the healthcare sector, Black women exhibit higher representation than any other demographic, predominantly occupying lower-paying positions in long-term care and hospital settings (Dill & Duffy, 2022). By directing focused investments into the care infrastructure for Black women, there is an opportunity to dismantle certain structural obstacles that have historically marginalized and undervalued their contributions (Dill & Duffy, 2022).
> - Structural racism refers to historical and contemporary policies, practices, and norms that create and maintain White supremacy by segregating racial and ethnic communities from access to opportunity and upward mobility by making it more difficult to secure high-quality education, jobs, housing, health care, and equal treatment in the criminal justice system (Zambrana & Williams, 2022).
> - Structural racism in coverage and financing has created a two-tier system of racially segregated care in which minority people receive poorer-quality care (Yearby et al., 2022). Ample evidence suggests that Black and Latino people receive lower-quality care compared to White people, even after insurance coverage and income are adjusted for (Yearby et al., 2022). For example, compared with White patients, racial and ethnic minority patients are less likely to receive evidence-based cardiovascular care, kidney transplants when indicated, age-appropriate diagnostic screening for breast and colon cancer, timely treatment related to cancer and stroke, appropriate mental health treatment, and adequate treatment when presenting suffering from pain (Yearby et al., 2022).
>
> Data from Hamed, S., Bradby, H., Ahlberg, B. M., & Thapar-Björkert, S. (2022). Racism in healthcare: a scoping review. BMC Public Health, 22(1), 988; Dill & Duffy, 2022; Zambrana, R. E., & Williams, D. R. (2022). The Intellectual Roots of Current Knowledge on Racism and Health: Relevance to Policy and the National Equity Discourse: Article examines the roots of current knowledge on racism and health and relevance to policy and the national equity discourse. Health Affairs, 41(2), 163–170; Yearby, R., Clark, B., & Figueroa, J. F. (2022). Structural Racism in Historical and Modern US Health Care Policy: Study examines structural racism in historical and modern US health care policy. Health Affairs, 41(2), 187–194.

The Effects of COVID-19

Ensuring the safety and well-being of vulnerable populations during the COVID-19 pandemic has presented a major challenge. These groups include people with lower incomes, people with disabilities, refugees, minorities, the uninsured, and other marginalized communities that have historically paid the greatest price in terms of health and welfare during infectious disease epidemics. They face significant challenges in gaining access to equitable care and staying economically and socially stable during the pandemic. Because of their higher rates of chronic disease, they are also at higher risk of developing severe symptoms if they contract the virus. Many vulnerable individuals do not receive paid sick leave or any type of paid leave that would make caring for a sick family member or a child home from school economically viable. Others may have lost their jobs as a consequence of the pandemic, making it more difficult to access high-quality, nutritional food and safe, affordable housing (Benfer and Wiley, 2020).

COVID-19 cases skyrocketed among vulnerable populations. In Chicago, for instance, Black and African American people accounted for more than 50% of all cases. The infection rate in predominantly Black counties in the United States was also more than three times that in predominantly White counties (Yancy, 2020). The Native American population was also put at severe risk—at one point, the Navajo Nation had more per capita cases of COVID-19 than any state in the country. Given the high rates of chronic disease, shortages of medical personnel, and poor access to basic necessities such as running water among this population, Doctors Without Borders dispatched a team to help mitigate the unfolding Navajo health crisis. This international humanitarian organization, which typically works in war-torn regions around the world, had never sent teams to the United States prior to the COVID-19 pandemic (Capatides, 2020).

Additionally, the U.S. homeless population faced major barriers in access to health care and an elevated risk of community transmission of COVID-19 (Tsai and Wilson, 2020). Likewise, the uninsured faced significant barriers in accessing care because they do not have established provider-patient relationships or healthcare networks. Another challenge was safeguarding the health of the 2.3 million prisoners in the United States. Correctional facilities do not have the medical capabilities to treat those who fall seriously ill from COVID-19; prison healthcare systems are generally understaffed and ill equipped to handle a surge in patients (Williams et al., 2020). A high prevalence of chronic disease and the elevated risk of transmission inherent in such close, enclosed quarters made these facilities high-risk breeding grounds for virus transmission (Berwick et al., 2020; Liu et al., 2023; Tan et al., 2023).

Summary

This chapter has examined the major characteristics of certain U.S. population groups that face challenges and barriers in accessing healthcare services—namely, racial/ethnic minorities, children and women, persons living in rural areas, persons experiencing homelessness, migrants, individuals with mental illnesses, and persons with HIV/AIDS. The health needs of these population groups vary, as do the services available to them. The gaps that currently exist between these population groups and the rest of the population indicate that the United States must make significant efforts to address the unique health concerns of its most vulnerable subpopulations.

TEST YOUR UNDERSTANDING

Terminology

acquired immunodeficiency syndrome (AIDS)
chronic
dependency
developmental vulnerability
disability
homophobia
human immunodeficiency virus (HIV)
Medicaid waiver program
mental health system
opportunistic infection (OI)
psychiatrists
psychologists

Review Questions

1. How can the framework of vulnerability be used to study vulnerable populations in the United States?

2. What are the racial/ethnic minority categories distinguished in the United States?

3. What health challenges do White Americans face, compared with those faced by minorities?
4. Who are the AA/PIs?
5. What is the Indian Health Service?
6. What are the health concerns of children?
7. Which childhood characteristics have important implications for health system design?
8. Which health services are currently available for children?
9. What are the health concerns of women?
10. What are the roles of the Office on Women's Health?
11. What are the challenges faced in rural health?
12. Which measures have been taken to improve access to care in rural areas of the United States?
13. What are the characteristics and health concerns of the homeless population?
14. How are mental health services provided in the United States?
15. Who are the major mental health professionals?
16. How does AIDS affect different population groups in the United States?
17. Which services and policies currently combat AIDS in the United States?
18. What is the impact of the ACA on vulnerable populations?

References

L. A. Aday. 1993. *At Risk in America: The Health and Health Care Needs of Vulnerable Populations in the United States*. San Francisco, CA: Jossey-Bass Publishers.

American Diabetes Association (ADA). 2018. Economic Costs of Diabetes in the U.S. in 2017. *Diabetes Care* Accessed October 2024. Available at: https://doi.org/10.2337/dci18-0007

Artiga, S., K. Orgera, and O. Pham. 2020. *Disparities in Health and Health Care: Five Key Questions and Answers*. Kaiser Family Foundation. Accessed July 2020. Available at: https://www.kff.org/disparities-policy/issue-brief/disparities-in-health-and-health-care-five-key-questions-and-answers/

Assistant Secretary for Planning and Evaluation. 2023. Children's Health Coverage Trends: Gains in 2020-2022 Reverse Previous Coverage Losses. Accessed November 2023. Available at: https://aspe.hhs.gov/sites/default/files/documents/77d7cc41648a371e0b5128f0dec2470e/aspe-childrens-health-coverage.pdf

Association of American Medical Colleges (AAMC). 2019. *Diversity in Medicine: Facts and Figures 2019*. Accessed July 2020. Available at: https://www.aamc.org/data-reports/workforce/interactive-data/figure-18-percentage-all-active-physicians-race/ethnicity-2018

Batterham, P. J., A. L. Calear, and H. Christensen. 2013. Correlates of Suicide Stigma and Suicide Literacy in the Community. *Suicide and Life-Threatening Behavior* 43: 406–417.

Benfer E. A., and L. F. Wiley. 2020. Health Justice Strategies to Combat COVID-19: Protecting Vulnerable Communities During a Pandemic. *Health Affairs*. doi: 10.1377/hblog20200319.757883

Berry, S. A., J. A. Fleishman, and B. R. Yehia, et al. 2016. Healthcare Coverage for HIV Provider Visits Before and after Implementation of the Affordable Care Act. *Clinical Infectious Diseases* 63: 387–395. Accessed October 2024. Available at: doi: 10.1093/cid/ciw278

Bircher H. 2009. Prenatal Care Disparities and the Migrant Farm Worker Community. *MCN American Journal of Maternal–Child Nursing* 34: 303–307.

Boyd R. W., E. G. Lindo, L. D. Weeks, and M. R. McLemore. 2020. On Racism: A New Standard for Publishing on Racial Health Inequities. *Health Affairs Blog*. doi: 10.1377/hblog20200630.939347

Breakey W. R., P. J. Fischer, M. Kramer, et al. 1989. Health and Mental Health Problems of Homeless Men and Women in Baltimore. *Journal of the American Medical Association* 262: 1352–1357.

Brown A. F., G. X. Ma, J. Miranda, et al. 2019. Structural Interventions to Reduce and Eliminate Health Disparities. *American Journal of Public Health* 109: S72–S78. Available at: https://doi.org/10.2105/AJPH.2018.304844

Buder, I., J. Jennings, D. H. Kim, and N. Waitzman. 2023. Socioeconomic Status & Health Disparities: Utilizing a Composite Index across Health Datasets. In *Forum for Social Economics*: 1–19. London, UK: Routledge.

Burks L. J. 1992. Community Health Representatives: The Vital Link in Native American Health Care. *IHS Primary Care Provider* 16: 186–190.

Capatides C. 2020. *Doctors Without Borders Dispatches Team to the Navajo Nation*. CBS News. Accessed June 2020. Available at: https://www.cbsnews.com/news/doctors-without-borders-navajo-nation-coronavirus/

References

Carroll A. E. 2020. Health Disparities Among Black Persons in the US and Addressing Racism in the Health Care System. *JAMA Health Forum*. Accessed July 2020. Available at: https://jamanetwork.com/channels/health-forum/fullarticle/2767595

Carter, B., and O. Dean. 2021. Rural-Urban Health Disparities Among US Adults Ages 50 and Older. Washington, DC: AARP Public Policy Institute.

Centers for Disease Control and Prevention (CDC). 1995. *Facts About Women and HIV/AIDS*. Atlanta, GA: CDC.

Centers for Disease Control and Prevention (CDC). 1999a. *CDC fact sheet: Recent HIV/AIDS treatment advances and the implications for prevention*. Accessed December 2010. Available at: http://www.cdc.gov/nchstp/hiv_aids/pubs/facts.htm

Centers for Disease Control and Prevention (CDC). 1999b. *CDC Fact Sheet: The Deadly Intersection Between TB and HIV*. Accessed December 2010. Available at: http://www.cdc.gov/nchstp/hiv_aids/pubs/facts.htm

Centers for Disease Control and Prevention (CDC). 2010a. *The Power of Prevention: Chronic Disease: The Public Health Challenge of the 21st Century*. Accessed January 2011. Available at: https://www.cdc.gov/chronicdisease/pdf/2009-Power-of-Prevention.pdf

Centers for Disease Control and Prevention (CDC). 2010b. Vital signs: Health Insurance Coverage and Health Care Utilization, United States, 2006–2009 and January–March 2010. *Morbidity and Mortality Weekly Report* 59: 1–7.

Centers for Disease Control and Prevention (CDC). 2011. *HIV Surveillance Report: Diagnoses of HIV Infection and AIDS in the United States and Dependent Areas, 2011*. 23. Atlanta, GA: U.S. Department of Health and Human Services.

Centers for Disease Control and Prevention (CDC). 2012a. Deaths: Leading Causes for 2009. *National Vital Statistics Reports* 61.

Centers for Disease Control and Prevention (CDC). 2012b. Youth risk behavior surveillance—United States, 2011. *Morbidity and Mortality Weekly Report* 61: SS–4.

Centers for Disease Control and Prevention (CDC). 2013a. *HIV among Women*. Accessed March 2021. Available at: http://action.naacp.org/page/-/Health%20Documents/HIV_among_Women_Fact_Sheet.pdf

Centers for Disease Control and Prevention (CDC). 2013b. HIV Infection Among Heterosexuals at Increased Risk—United States, 2010. *Morbidity and Mortality Weekly Report* 6210: 183–188.

Centers for Disease Control and Prevention (CDC). 2014a. *Behavioral Risk Factor Surveillance System, 2014*. Accessed March 2017. Available at: https://www.americashealthrankings.org/explore/2015-annual-report/measure/PhysicalHealth/state/ALL

Centers for Disease Control and Prevention (CDC). 2014b. *Web-Based Injury Statistics Query and Reporting System (WISQARS)*. Accessed March 2021. Available at: http://www.cdc.gov/ncipc/wisqars

Centers for Disease Control and Prevention (CDC). 2015a. *At a Glance 2015: National Center for Chronic Disease Prevention and Health Promotion*. Accessed March 2017. Available at: https://www.cdc.gov/chronicdisease/resources/publications/aag/pdf/2015/nccdphp-aag.pdf

Centers for Disease Control and Prevention (CDC). 2015b. *Deaths: Leading Causes for 2014*. Accessed March 2017. Available at: https://www.cdc.gov/nchs/data/nvsr/nvsr65/nvsr65_05.pdf

Centers for Disease Control and Prevention (CDC). 2016a. *Chronic Disease Overview*. Accessed March 2021. Available at: https://www.cdc.gov/chronicdisease/overview/

Centers for Disease Control and Prevention (CDC). 2016b. *HIV in the United States and Dependent Areas*. Accessed March 2021. Available at: https://www.cdc.gov/hiv/statistics/overview/ataglance.html

Centers for Disease Control and Prevention (CDC). 2019a. *African Americans and Tobacco Use*. Accessed February 2020. Available at: https://www.cdc.gov/tobacco/disparities/african-americans/index.htm

Centers for Disease Control and Prevention (CDC). 2019b. *Asian Americans, Native Hawaiians, or Pacific Islanders and Tobacco Use*. Accessed February 2020. Available at: https://www.cdc.gov/tobacco/disparities/asian-americans/index.htm

Centers for Disease Control and Prevention (CDC). 2019c. Deaths: Leading Causes for 2017. *National Vital Statistics Reports* 68. Available at: https://www.cdc.gov/nchs/data/nvsr/nvsr68/nvsr68_06-508.pdf

Centers for Disease Control and Prevention (CDC). 2019e. *Economic Trends in Tobacco*. Accessed February 2020. Available at: https://www.cdc.gov/tobacco/data_statistics/fact_sheets/economics/econ_facts/index.htm

Centers for Disease Control and Prevention (CDC). 2019f. *Hispanics/Latinos and Tobacco Use*. Accessed February 2020. Available at: https://www.cdc.gov/tobacco/disparities/hispanics-latinos/index.htm

Centers for Disease Control and Prevention (CDC). 2019g. *HIV and STD Criminalization Laws*. Accessed February 2020. Available at: https://www.cdc.gov/hiv/policies/law/states/exposure.html

Centers for Disease Control and Prevention (CDC). 2019h. *HIV Surveillance Report, Vol. 30: Diagnoses of HIV Infection in the United States and Dependent Areas, 2018 (preliminary)*. Accessed February 2020. Available at: https://www.cdc.gov/hiv/pdf/library/reports/surveillance/cdc-hiv-surveillance-report-2018-preliminary-vol-30.pdf

Centers for Disease Control and Prevention (CDC). 2019i. *2008 Physical Activity Guidelines for Americans: Trends in Meeting the 2008 Physical Activity Guidelines, 2008–2018*. Accessed February 2020. Available at: https://www.cdc.gov/physicalactivity/downloads/trends-in-the-prevalence-of-physical-activity-508.pdf

Centers for Disease Control and Prevention (CDC). 2020. *HIV and Women*. Accessed July 2020. Available at: https://www.cdc.gov/hiv/group/gender/women/index.html

Centers for Disease Control and Prevention (CDC). 2015b. *Deaths: Leading Causes for 2014*. Accessed November 2023. Available at: https://www.cdc.gov/nchs/data/nvsr/nvsr65/nvsr65_05.pdf

Centers for Disease Control and Prevention (CDC). 2020. *Diagnose and Treat to Save Lives: Decreasing Deaths Among People with HIV.* Accessed November 2023. Available at: https://www.cdc.gov/hiv/statistics/deaths/index.html

Centers for Disease Control and Prevention (CDC). 2021. *Injuries Among Children and Teens*. Accessed November 2023. Available at: https://www.cdc.gov/injury/features/child-injury/index.html#:~:text=Child%20unintentional%20injury%20death%20rates%20decreased%2011%25%20from,2019.%20That%20is%20about%2020%20deaths%20each%20day

Centers for Disease Control and Prevention (CDC). 2021b. *Most Recent National Asthma Data*. Accessed November 2023. Available at: https://www.cdc.gov/asthma/most_recent_national_asthma_data.htm

Centers for Disease Control and Prevention (CDC). 2022. *Childhood Obesity Facts*. Accessed November 2023. Available at: https://www.cdc.gov/obesity/data/childhood.html

Centers for Disease Control and Prevention (CDC). 2023. *Current Cigarette Smoking Among Adults in the United States*. Accessed November 2023. Available at: https://www.cdc.gov/tobacco/data_statistics/fact_sheets/adult_data/cig_smoking/index.htm

Centers for Disease Control and Prevention (CDC). 2023. *Disability Impacts All of Us*. Accessed November 2023. Available at: https://www.cdc.gov/ncbddd/disabilityandhealth/infographic-disability-impacts-all.html

Centers for Disease Control and Prevention. 2020. *Prevalence of Multiple Chronic Conditions Among US Adults, 2018*. Accessed November 2023. Available at: https://www.cdc.gov/pcd/issues/2020/20_0130.htm

Centers for Disease Control and Prevention. 2022. *Heart Disease*. Accessed November 2023. Available at: https://www.cdc.gov/nchs/fastats/heart-disease.htm

Centers for Medicare and Medicaid Services (CMS). 2019. *Rural Health Clinic*. Accessed February 2020. Available at: https://www.cms.gov/Outreach-and-Education/Medicare-Learning-Network-MLN/MLNProducts/Downloads/RuralHlthClinfctsht.pdf

ChildStats.gov. 2018. *POP1 Child Population: Number of Children (in Millions) Ages 0–17 in the United States by Age, 1950–2018 and Projected 2019–2050*. Accessed February 2020. Available at: https://www.childstats.gov/americaschildren/tables/pop1.asp

Chang, B., I. H. Cheng, and H. G. Hong. 2023. The Fundamental Role of Uninsured Depositors in the Regional Banking Crisis. Available at SSRN 4507551.

Childstats. 2023. *America's Children: Key National Indicators of Well-Being, 2023*. Accessed November 2023. Available at: https://www.childstats.gov/americaschildren/health4.asp

Congressional Research Service. 2019. *HIV/AIDS in the Military*. Accessed February 2020. Available at: https://fas.org/sgp/crs/natsec/IF11238.pdf

Cooper, E. R., M. Charurat, L. Mofenson, et al. 2000. Combination Antiretroviral Strategies for the Treatment of Pregnant HIV-1–Infected Women and Prevention of Perinatal HIV-1 Transmission. *Journal of Acquired Immune Deficiency Syndromes* 29: 484–494.

Evans M. K., L. Rosenbaum, D. Malina, S. Morrissey, and E. J. Rubin. 2020. Diagnosing and Treating Systemic Racism. *New England Journal of Medicine* 383: 274–276. doi: 10.1056/NEJMe2021693

Federal Interagency Forum on Child and Family Statistics. 2016. *America's Children in Brief: Key National Indicators of Well-Being, 2016*. Accessed March 2017. Available at: https://www.childstats.gov/pdf/ac2016/ac_16.pdf

Federal Interagency Forum on Child and Family Statistics. 2019. *America's Children: Key National Indicators of Well-Being*, 2019. Accessed February 2020. Available at: https://www.childstats.gov/pdf/ac2019/ac_19.pdf

Friedman, S. A., S. L. Ettner, E. Chuang, et al. 2019. The Effects of Three Kinds of Insurance Benefit Design Features on Specialty Mental Health Care Use in Managed Care. *The Journal of Mental Health Policy and Economics* 22: 43.

Gadomski, A. M., K. E. Fothergill, S. Larson, et al. 2015. Integrating Mental Health into Adolescent Annual Visits: Impact of Previsit Comprehensive Screening on Within-Visit Processes. *Journal of Adolescent Health* 56: 267–273.

Gould, M. S., J. L. Munfakh, M. Kleinman, and A. M. Lake. 2012. National Suicide Prevention Lifeline: Enhancing Mental Health Care for Suicidal Individuals and Other People in Crisis. *Suicide and Life-Threatening Behavior* 42: 22–35.

Grabowski, D. C., and V. Mor. 2020. Nursing Home Care In Crisis In The Wake of COVID-19. *JAMA* 324: 23–24.

Gross, E. J., and M. H. Larkin. 1996. The Child with HIV in Day Care and School. *Nursing Clinics of North America* 31: 231–241.

Guttmacher Institute. 2020. *Insurance Coverage of Contraceptives*. Accessed February 2020. Available at: https://www.guttmacher.org/state-policy/explore/insurance-coverage-contraceptives

Hamed, S., H. Bradby, B. M. Ahlberg, and S. Thapar-Björkert. 2022. Racism in Healthcare: A Scoping Review. *BMC Public Health* 22: 988.

Health Care for the Homeless. 2012. *Who We Help*. Accessed September 2013. Available at: https://www.hchmd.org/who-we-help

Health Resources and Services Administration (HRSA). 2015a. *2015 Health Center Data*. Accessed March 2017. Available at: https://bphc.hrsa.gov/uds/datacenter.aspx

Health Resources and Services Administration (HRSA). 2018. *2018 Health Center Data*. Accessed March 2021. Available at: https://bphc.hrsa.gov/uds/datacenter.aspx?q=tall&year=2018&state=

Health Resources and Services Administration (HRSA). 2020a. *Shortage Areas*. Accessed February 2020. Available at: https://data.hrsa.gov/topics/health-workforce/shortage-areas

Health Resources and Services Administration (HRSA), Bureau of Health Professions. 2007. *What is Shortage Designation?* Accessed December 2008. Available at: https://bhw.hrsa.gov/shortage-designation

Health Resources and Services Administration (HRSA), Bureau of Health Professions. 2013. *National Health Service Corps*. Accessed September 2013. Available at: http://nhsc.hrsa.gov/corpsexperience/aboutus/index.html

Health Resources and Services Administration (HRSA), Bureau of Health Professions. 2020b. *National Health Service Corps*. Accessed February 2020. Available at: https://bhw.hrsa.gov/loans-scholarships/nhsc

Health Resources and Services Administration (HRSA), Office of Rural Health Policy. 2015b. *About FORHP*. Accessed May 2017. Available at: https://www.hrsa.gov/ruralhealth/aboutus/index.html

HIV.gov. 2023. *U.S. Statistics, Fast Facts*. Accessed November 2023. Available at: https://www.hiv.gov/hiv-basics/overview/data-and-trends/statistics/

Hu, K., and A. E. Staiano. 2022. Trends in Obesity Prevalence Among Children and Adolescents Aged 2 to 19 Years in the US from 2011 to 2020. *JAMA Pediatrics* 176: 1037–1039.

M. C. Hung, D. U. Ekwueme, S. H. Rim, and A. White. 2016. Racial/Ethnicity Disparities in Invasive Breast Cancer Among Younger and Older Women: An Analysis Using Multiple Measures of Population Health. *Cancer Epidemiology* 45: 112–118.

Indian Health Service (IHS). 1999a. *A Quick Look*. Washington, D.C.: Public Health Service.

Indian Health Service (IHS). 1999b. *Fact Sheet: Comprehensive Health Care Program for American Indians and Alaskan Natives*. Washington, DC: Public Health Service.

Indian Health Service (IHS). 2010. *IHS Year 2010 Profile: IHS Fact Sheet*. Washington, DC: Public Health Service.

Indian Health Service (IHS). 2013. *Agency Overview*. Accessed September 2013. Available at: http://www.ihs.gov/aboutihs/overview/

Indian Health Service (IHS). 2014. *Trends in Indian Health: 2014 Edition*. Assessed March 2021. Available at: https://www.ihs.gov/dps/includes/themes/newihstheme/display_objects/documents/Trends2014Book508.pdf

Indian Health Service (IHS). 2019a. *Disparities*. Accessed February 2020. Available at: https://www.ihs.gov/newsroom/factsheets/disparities/

Indian Health Service (IHS). 2019b. *IHS Profile*. Accessed February 2020. Available at: https://www.ihs.gov/newsroom/factsheets/ihsprofile/

Institute for Children, Poverty and Homelessness. 2011. *Profiles of Risk: Education*. Research Brief No. 2. Accessed May 2017. Available at: https://www.onefamilyinc.org/Blog/wp-content/uploads/2011/10/icph_familiesatrisk_no-2.pdf

Jasinski J. L. 2005. *The Experience of Violence in the Lives of Homeless Women: A Research Report*. Accessed January 2014. Available at: https://www.ncjrs.gov/pdffiles1/nij/grants/211976.pdf

Kaiser Family Foundation. 2013. *Health Reform: Implications for Women's Access to Coverage and Care*. Accessed September 2013. Available at: https://www.kff.org/report-section/health-reform-implications-for-womens-access-to-coverage-and-care-issue-brief/

Kaiser Family Foundation. 2014a. *Assessing the Impact of the Affordable Care Act on Health Insurance Coverage of People with HIV*. Accessed May 2017. Available at: http://kff.org/hivaids/issue-brief/assessing-the-impact-of-the-affordable-care-act-on-health-insurance-coverage-of-people-with-hiv/

Kaiser Family Foundation. 2014b. *The Affordable Care Act's Impact on Medicaid Eligibility, Enrollment, and Benefits for People with Disabilities*. Accessed March 2017. Available at: http://kff.org/health-reform/issue-brief/the-affordable-care-acts-impact-on-medicaid-eligibility-enrollment-and-benefits-for-people-with-disabilities/

Kaiser Family Foundation. 2019a. *Key Facts About the Uninsured Population*. Accessed February 2020. Available at: https://www.kff.org/uninsured/issue-brief/key-facts-about-the-uninsured-population/

Kaiser Family Foundation. 2019b. *Mental Health Care Health Professional Shortage Areas (HPSAs)*. Accessed February 2020. Available at: https://www.kff.org/other/state-indicator/mental-health-care-health-professional-shortage-areas-hpsas/?currentTimeframe=0&sortModel=%7B%22colId%22:%22Location%22,%22sort%22:%22asc%22%7D

Kaiser Family Foundation. 2019c. *Number of Medicare Certified Rural Health Clinics*. Accessed February

2020. Available at: https://www.kff.org/other/state-indicator/total-rural-health-clinics/?currentTimeframe=0&sortModel=%7B%22colId%22:%22Location%22,%22sort%22:%22asc%22%7D

Kaiser Family Foundation. 2019d. *U.S. Federal Funding for HIV/AIDS: Trends over Time*. Accessed February 2020. Available at: https://www.kff.org/hivaids/fact-sheet/u-s-federal-funding-for-hivaids-trends-over-time/

Kaiser Family Foundation. 2020. *Women's Health Insurance Coverage*. Accessed February 2020. Available at: https://www.kff.org/womens-health-policy/fact-sheet/womens-health-insurance-coverage-fact-sheet/

Kaiser Family Foundation. 2022. *Distribution of Nonelderly Adults with Medicaid by Sex*. Accessed November 2023. Available at:https://www.kff.org/medicaid/state-indicator/medicaid-distribution-nonelderly-adults-by-sex/?currentTimeframe=0&selectedRows=%7B%22wrapups%22:%7B%22united-states%22:%7B%7D%7D%7D&sortModel=%7B%22colId%22:%22Location%22,%22sort%22:%22asc%22%7D

Kaiser Family Foundation. 2022. *Women's Health Insurance Coverage*. Accessed November 2023. Available at: https://www.kff.org/womens-health-policy/fact-sheet/womens-health-insurance-coverage/

Kaiser Family Foundation. 2022. *Health and Health Care for Hispanic People, 2021*. Accessed November 2023. Available at: https://www.kff.org/racial-equity-and-health-policy/slide/health-and-health-care-for-hispanic-people/

Karmouta, R., M. Altendahl, T. Romero, et al. 2022. Association Between Social Determinants of Health and Retinopathy of Prematurity Outcomes. *JAMA Ophthalmology* 140: 496–502.

Kerker, B. D., J. Bainbridge, J. Kennedy, et al. 2011. A Population-Based Assessment of the Health of Homeless Families in New York City, 2001–2003. *American Journal of Public Health* 101: 546–553.

Kesici, Z., and V. Yilmaz. 2023. Insurance-Based Disparities in Breast Cancer Treatment Pathways in a Universal Healthcare System: A qualitative study. *BMC Health Services Research* 23: 112.

Kessler R. C., C. G. Davis, and K. S. Kendler. 1997. Childhood Adversity and Adult Psychiatric Disorder in the US National Comorbidity Survey. *Psychological Medicine* 27: 1101–1119.

Khanijahani, A. 2021. Racial, Ethnic, and Socioeconomic Disparities in Confirmed COVID-19 Cases and Deaths in the United States: A County-Level Analysis as of November 2020. *Ethnicity & Health* 26: 22–35.

Kraus, L. E. 1996. *Chartbook on Disability in the United States, 1996. An InfoUse Report*. Washington, DC: U.S. National Institute on Disability and Rehabilitation Research.

Larson, A., and L. Plascencia. 1993. *Migrant Enumeration Study*. Washington, DC: Office of Minority Health.

Larson S. L., and J. A. Fleishman. 2003. Rural–Urban Differences in Usual Source of Care and Ambulatory Service Use: Analyses of National Data Using Urban Influence Codes. *Medical Care* III65–III74.

LaVeist, T. A., A. Morgan, M. Arthur, S. Plantholt, and M. Rubinstein. 2002. Physician Referral Patterns and Race Differences in Receipt of Coronary Angiography. *Health Services Research* 37: 949–962. Available at: https://doi.org/10.1034/j.1600-0560.2002.60.x

Lee, A., J. Ruhter, C. Peters, N. De Lew, and B. D. Sommers. 2022. National Uninsured Rate Reaches All-Time Low in Early 2022. U.S. Department of Health and Human Services Office of the Assistant Secretary for Planning and Evaluation.

Li, H., Y. Han, Y. Xiao, X. Liu, A. Li, and T. Zhu. 2021. Suicidal Ideation Risk and Socio-Cultural Factors in China: A Longitudinal Study on Social Media from 2010 to 2018. *International Journal of Environmental Research and Public Health* 18: 1098.

Liddell, J. L., and J. M. Lilly. 2022. Healthcare Experiences of Uninsured and Under-Insured American Indian Women in the United States. *Global Health Research and Policy* 7: 5.

Liu, E., C. A. Dean, and K. Elder. 2023. The Impact of COVID-19 on Vulnerable Populations. *Frontiers in Public Health* 11: 1267723.

Lopez G., N. G. Ruiz, and E. Patton. 2017. *Key Facts About Asian Americans, a Diverse and Growing Population*. Pew Research Center. Accessed January 2020. Available at: https://scholar.google.com/scholar?hl=en&as_sdt=0%2C31&q=Key+facts+about+Asian+Americans%2C+a+diverse+and+growing+population%2C+Lopez&btnG=

McConnell, K. J., S. Edelstein, J. Hall, et al. 2023. The Effects of Behavioral Health Integration in Medicaid Managed Care on Access to Mental Health and Primary Care Services—Evidence from Early Adopters. *Health Services Research* 58: 622–633.

McDaniel, C. C., H. H. Hallam, T. Cadwallader, H. Y. Lee, and C. Chou. 2021. Persistent Racial Disparities in Cervical Cancer Screening with Pap Test. *Preventive Medicine Reports* 24: 101652.

Mental Health America (NHA). 2022. *The State of Mental Health in America*. Accessed November 2023. Available at: https://mhanational.org/sites/default/files/2022%20State%20of%20Mental%20Health%20in%20America.pdf

Mental Health America. 2023. *The State of Mental Health in America: 2023 Key Findings*. Access November 2023. Available at: https://mhanational.org/issues/state-mental-health-america

Merson M. H. 1996. Returning Home: Reflections on the USA's Response to the HIV/AIDS Epidemic. *Lancet* 347: 1673–1676.

Migrant Health Promotion. 2013. *Farmworkers in the United States*. Accessed September 2013. Available at: http://www.migranthealth.org/index.php?option=com_content&view=article&id=38&Itemid=30

Misra, D., C. Cassady, K. Rothert, V. Poole, ed. 2001. *Women's Health Data Book: A Profile of Women's Health in the United States*. 3rd ed. Washington, DC: Jacobs Institute of Women's Health and Henry J. Kaiser Family Foundation.

Murphy B. 2019. *These Medical Specialties Have the Biggest Gender Imbalances*. American Medical Association. Accessed January 2020. Available at: https://www.ama-assn.org/residents-students/specialty-profiles/these-medical-specialties-have-biggest-gender-imbalances

National Alliance to End Homelessness. 2012. *The State of Homelessness in America 2012*. Homelessness Research Institute. Accessed March 2021. Available at: http://www.endhomelessness.org/page/-/files/file_FINAL_The_State_of_Homelessness_in_America_2012

National Alliance on Mental Illness (NAMI). 2023. Mental Health by the Numbers. Accessed November 2023. Available at: https://www.nami.org/mhstats

National Alliance to End Homelessness (NAEH). 2023. State of Homelessness: 2023 edition. Accessed November 2023. Available at: https://endhomelessness.org/homelessness-in-america/homelessness-statistics`/state-of-homelessness/#homelessness-in-2022

National Center for Education Statistics. 2019. Status and Trends in the Education of Racial and Ethnic Groups. Accessed November 2023. Available at: https://nces.ed.gov/programs/raceindicators/indicator_rfas.asp

National Center for Farmworker Health. 2011. *HIV/AIDS Agricultural Worker Factsheet*. Accessed March 2017. Available at: http://www.ncfh.org/uploads/3/8/6/8/38685499/fs-hiv_aids.pdf

National Center for Farmworker Health. 2012. *Facts About Farmworkers*. Available at: http://www.ncfh.org/uploads/3/8/6/8/38685499/fs-facts_about_farmworkers.pdf. Accessed May 2017.

National Center for Health Statistics. 2023. Health, United States, 2020–2021: Annual Perspective. Hyattsville, MD.

National Center for Health Statistics (NCHS). 2014b. *National Health Interview Survey*. Accessed March 2017. Available at: https://www.cdc.gov/nchs/nhis/.

National Center for Health Statistics (NCHS). 2016a. *Early Release of Selected Estimates Based on Data from the National Health Interview Survey, January–June 2016*. Accessed May 2017. Available at: https://www.cdc.gov/nchs/data/nhis/earlyrelease/earlyrelease201611_01.pdf

National Center for Health Statistics (NCHS). 2016b. *Health, United States, 2015*. Hyattsville, MD: U.S. Department of Health and Human Services.

National Center for Health Statistics (NCHS). 2019a. *Early Release of Selected Estimates Based on Data from the 2018 National Health Interview Survey*. Accessed February 2020. Available at: https://www.cdc.gov/nchs/nhis/releases/released201905.htm#11

National Center for Health Statistics (NCHS). 2019b. *Health Insurance Coverage: Early Release of Estimates from the National Health Interview Survey, 2018*. Accessed February 2020. Available at: https://www.cdc.gov/nchs/data/nhis/earlyrelease/insur201905.pdf

National Center for Health Statistics (NCHS). 2019c. *Health, United States, 2018*. Hyattsville, MD: U.S. Department of Health and Human Services.

National Center for Health Statistics. *Health, United States, 2020–2021: Annual Perspective*. Hyattsville, MD. 2023.

National Conference of State Legislatures (NCSL). 2013. *Improving Rural Health: State Policy Options*. Accessed March 2017. Available at: http://www.ncsl.org/documents/health/RuralHealth_PolicyOptions_1113.pdf

National Conference of State Legislatures (NCSL). 2017. *Health Care*. Accessed March 2021. Available at: https://www.ncsl.org/Portals/1/Documents/Health/HealthDisparities_2017_31448.pdf

National Council on Aging. 2023. American Indians and Alaska Natives: Key Demographics and Characteristics. Accessed November 2023. Available at: https://www.ncoa.org/article/american-indians-and-alaska-natives-key-demographics-and-characteristics

National Institute of Mental Health (NIMH). 2015. *Any Mental Illness (AMI) Among U.S. Adults*. Accessed March 2017. Available at: https://www.nimh.nih.gov/health/statistics/prevalence/any-mental-illness-ami-among-us-adults.shtml

National Institute of Mental Health (NIMH). 2019. *Mental Illness*. Accessed February 2020. Available at: https://www.nimh.nih.gov/health/statistics/mental-illness.shtml

National Institute of Mental Health (NIMH). 2021. *Mental Illness*. Accessed November 2023. Available at: https://www.nimh.nih.gov/health/statistics/mental-illness

National Institutes of Health (NIH). 2002. *News Release: NHLBI Stops Trial of Estrogen Plus Progestin Due to Increased Breast Cancer Risk, Lack of Overall Benefit*. Accessed March 2021. Available at: http://www.nhlbi.nih.gov/new/press/02-07-09.htm

National Institutes of Health (NIH). 2012. *Guidelines for the Use of Antiretroviral Agents in HIV-1–Infected Adults and Adolescents*. U.S. Department of Health and Human Services. Accessed March 2021. Available at: http://aidsinfo.nih.gov/contentfiles/lvguidelines/AdultandAdolescentGL.pdf

National Law Center on Homelessness and Poverty. 2015. *Homelessness in America: Overview of Data and Causes*. Accessed May 2017. Available at: https://www.nlchp.org/documents/Homeless_Stats_Fact_Sheet

National Rural Health Association. 2016. *About Rural Health Care.* Accessed March 2017. Available at: https://www.ruralhealthweb.org/about-nrha/about-rural-health-care

National Women's Law Center. 2019. *National Snapshot: Poverty Among Women & Families,* 2019. Accessed February 2020. Available at: https://nwlc-ciw49tixgw5lbab.stackpathdns.com/wp-content/uploads/2019/10/PovertySnapshot2019.pdf

Newcomer, R., T. Kang, M. LaPlante, and S. Kaye. 2005. Living Quarters and Unmet Need for Personal Care Assistance Among Adults with Disabilities. *Journals of Gerontology Series B: Psychological Sciences and Social Sciences* 9: S205–S213.

Niederkrotenthaler, T., D. J. Reidenberg, B. Till, and M. S. Gould. (2014). Increasing Help-Seeking and Referrals for Individuals at Risk for Suicide by Decreasing Stigma: The Role of Mass Media. *American Journal of Preventive Medicine* 47: S235–S243.

Ostir, G. V., J. E. Carlson, S. A. Black, L. Rudkin, J. S. Goodwin, and K. S. Markides. 1999. Disability in Older Adults 1: Prevalence, Causes, and Consequences. *Behavioral Medicine* 24: 147–156.

Patton L., and D. Puskin. 1990. *Ensuring access to health care services in rural areas: A half century of federal policy.* Washington, D.C.: Essential Health Care Services Conference Center at Georgetown University Conference Center.

Peterson J. M., A. Pepin, R. Thomas, et al. 2020. Racial Disparities in Breast Cancer Hereditary Risk Assessment Referrals. *Journal of Genetic Counseling.* Advance online publication. https://doi.org/10.1002/jgc4.1250

Pew Research Center. 2021. Key Facts about Asian Americans, a Diverse and Growing Population. Accessed November 2023. Available at: https://www.pewresearch.org/short-reads/2021/04/29/key-facts-about-asian-americans/

Pew Research Center. 2022. Hispanic Americans' Experiences with Health Care. Accessed November 2023. Available at: https://www.pewresearch.org/science/2022/06/14/hispanic-americans-experiences-with-health-care/

Pew Research Center. 2023. 8 Facts about Americans with Disabilities. Accessed November 2023. Available at: https://www.pewresearch.org/short-reads/2023/07/24/8-facts-about-americans-with-disabilities/

Pew Research Center. 2023. 11 Facts about Hispanic Origin Groups in the U.S. Accessed November 2023. Available at https://www.pewresearch.org/short-reads/2023/08/16/11-facts-about-hispanic-origin-groups-in-the-us/

Population Reference Bureau. 2006. *Elderly White Men Afflicted by High Suicide Rates.* Accessed May 2017. Available at: http://www.prb.org/Publications/Articles/2006/ElderlyWhiteMenAfflictedbyHighSuicideRates.aspx

Planning and Evaluation. 2023. *Children's Health Coverage Trends: Gains in 2020-2022 Reverse Previous Coverage Losses.* Accessed November 2023. Available at: https://aspe.hhs.gov/sites/default/files/documents77d7cc41648a371e0b5128f0dec2470e/aspe-childrens-health-coverage.pdf

Reeves, W. C., T. W. Strine, L. A. Pratt, et al. 2011. *Mental Illness Surveillance Among Adults in the United States.* Accessed March 2017. Available at: https://www.cdc.gov/mmwr/preview/mmwrhtml/su6003a1.htm

Regier, D. A., J. H. Boyd, J. D. Burke, et al. 1988. One Month Prevalence of Mental Disorders in the United States: Based on Five Epidemiologic Catchment Area Sites. *Archives of General Psychiatry* 45: 977–986.

Rovner J. 2020. High Court Allows Employers to Opt out of ACA's Mandate on Birth Control Coverage. Accessed March 2021. Available at: https://khn.org/news/high-court-allows-employers-to-opt-out-of-acas-mandate-on-birth-control-coverage/

Ruprecht, M. M., X. Wang, A. K. Johnson, et al. 2021. Evidence of Social and Structural COVID-19 Disparities by Sexual Orientation, Gender Identity, and Race/Ethnicity in an Urban Environment. *Journal of Urban Health* 98: 27–40.

Russell, T. 2020. Racism in Care Leads to Health Disparities, Doctors and Other Experts Say as They Push for Change. *The Washington Post.* Accessed July 2020. Available at: https://www.washingtonpost.com/health/racism-in-care-leads-to-health-disparities-doctors-and-other-experts-say-as-they-push-for-change/2020/07/10/a1a1e40a-bb9e-11ea-80b9-40ece9a701dc_story.html

Rust G. S. 1990. Health Status of Migrant Farmworkers: A Literature Review and Commentary. *American Journal of Public Health* 80: 1213–1217.

Salganicoff, A., U. R. Ranji, and R. Wyn. 2005. *Women and Health Care: A National Profile.* Menlo Park, CA: Henry J. Kaiser Family Foundation.

Schackman, B. R., K. A. Gebo, R. P. Walensky, et al. 2006. The Lifetime Cost of Current Human Immunodeficiency Virus Care in the United States. *Medical Care* 44: 990–997.

Schutt, R. K., and S. M. Goldfinger. 1996. Housing Preferences and Perceptions of Health and Functioning Among Homeless Mentally Ill Persons. *Psychiatric Services* 47: 381–386.

Sechzer, J. A., et al. 1996. *Women and Mental Health.* New York: Academy of Sciences.

Simmons, A., A. Chappel, A. R. Kolbe, L. Bush, and B. D. Sommers. 2021. Health Disparities by Race and Ethnicity During the Covid-19 Pandemic: Current Evidence and Policy Approaches. Washington, DC: Office of the Assistant Secretary for Planning and Evaluation, U.S. Department of Health & Human Services, 1–11.

Shi, L., and G. Stevens. 2010. *Vulnerable Populations in the United States*. 2nd ed. San Francisco, CA: Jossey-Bass Publishers.

Shortell, S. M., R. R. Gillies, D. A. Anderson, K. M. Erickson, and J. B. Mitchell. 1996. *Remaking Health Care in America*. San Francisco, CA: Jossey-Bass Publishers.

Snyder, C. R., P. Z. Wang, and A. R. Truitt. 2018. Multiracial Patient Experiences with Racial Microaggressions in Health Care Settings. *Journal of Patient-Centered Research and Reviews* 5: 229–238. https://doi.org/10.17294/2330-0698.1626

Stepanikova, I. 2012. Racial-Ethnic Biases, Time Pressure, and Medical Decisions. *Journal of Health and Social Behavior* 53: 329–343. Available at: https://doi.org/10.1177/0022146512445807

Strully, K. W., T. M. Harrison, T. A. Pardo, and J. Carleo-Evangelist. 2021. Strategies to Address COVID-19 Vaccine Hesitancy and Mitigate Health Disparities In Minority Populations. *Frontiers in Public Health* 9: 645268.

Substance Abuse and Mental Health Services Administration (SAMHSA). 2012a. *Mental Health, United States, 2010*. HHS Publication No. (SMA) 12-4681. Rockville, MD: Author.

Substance Abuse and Mental Health Services Administration (SAMHSA). 2012b. *Results from the 2011 National Survey on Drug Use and Health: Mental Health Findings*. NSDUH Series H-45, HHS Publication No. (SMA) 12-4725. Rockville, MD: Author.

Substance Abuse and Mental Health Services Administration (SAMHSA). 2013. *Behavioral Health, United States, 2012*. Available at: http://archive.samhsa.gov/data/2012Behavioral HealthUS/2012-BHUS.pdf

Substance Abuse and Mental Health Services Administration (SAMHSA). 2014. *National Mental Health Services Survey (N-MHSS): 2010. Data on Mental Health Treatment Facilities*. BHSIS Series S-69, HHS Publication No. (SMA) 14-4837. Rockville, MD: Author. Accessed May 2017. Available at: https://www.samhsa.gov/data/sites/default/files/NMHSS2010_Web/NMHSS2010_Web/NMHSS2010_Web.pdf

Substance Abuse and Mental Health Services Administration (SAMHSA). 2014. *Projections of National Expenditures for Treatment of Mental and Substance Use Disorders, 2010–2020*. HHS Publication No. SMA-14-4883. Rockville, MD: Author.

Substance Abuse and Mental Health Services Administration (SAMHSA). 2015. *1.5 Million Young Adults Do Not Receive Needed Mental Health Services*. Rockville, MD: Author. Accessed May 2017. Available at: https://www.samhsa.gov/data/sites/default/files/report_1975/Spotlight-1975.html

Summer L. 1991. *Limited Access: Health Care for the Rural Poor*. Washington, D.C.: Center on Budget and Policy Priorities.

Tan, S. Y., C. De Foo, M. Verma, et al. 2023. Mitigating the Impacts of The COVID-19 Pandemic on Vulnerable Populations: Lessons for Improving Health and Social Equity. *Social Science & Medicine* 116007.

Thornton, R. L., C. M. Glover, C. W. Cené, D. C. Glik, J. A. Henderson, and D. R. Williams. 2016. Evaluating Strategies for Reducing Health Disparities by Addressing the Social Determinants of Health. *Health Affairs* 35: 1416–1423. Available at: https://doi.org/10.1377/hlthaff.2015.1357

Tikkanen, R., R. Osborn, E. Mossialos, A. Djordjevic, and G. A. Wharton. 2020. *International Health Care System Profiles: United States*. Commonwealth Fund. Accessed July 2020. Available at: https://www.commonwealthfund.org/international-health-policy-center/countries/united-states

Tsai J., and M. Wilson. 2020. COVID-19: A Potential Public Health Problem for Homeless Populations. *Lancet* 5: e186–e187. https://doi.org/10.1016/S2468-2667(20)30053-0

UN Women. 2018. *Facts and Figures: HIV and AIDS*. Accessed February 2020. Available at: https://www.unwomen.org/en/what-we-do/hiv-and-aids/facts-and-figures

U.S. Census Bureau. 2011a. *American Community Survey, American FactFinder*, Table B18135. Accessed March 2021. Available at: http://factfinder2.census.gov

U.S. Census Bureau. 2011b. *The American Indian and Alaska Native Population: 2010*. 2010 Census Briefs. Washington, DC: Government Printing Office.

U.S. Census Bureau. 2014. *Health Insurance Coverage in the United States: 2013*. Washington, DC: Government Printing Office.

U.S. Census Bureau. 2018. *Hispanic Population to Reach 111 Million by 2060*. Accessed January 2020.U.S. Census Bureau. Available at: https://www.census.gov/library/visualizations/2018/comm/hispanic-projected-pop.html 2019a. *Health Insurance Coverage in the United States: 2018*. Washington, DC: Government Printing Office.

U.S. Census Bureau. 2019b. *QuickFacts: United States*. Accessed January 2020. Available at: https://www.census.gov/quickfacts/fact/table/US/IPE120218

U.S. Census Bureau. 2020a. *Questions Asked on the Form*. Accessed March 2021. Available at: https://2020census.gov/en/about-questions.html

U.S. Census Bureau. 2021b. 2020 *Census Illuminates Racial and Ethnic Composition of the Country*. Accessed November 2023. Available at:https://www.census.gov/library/stories/2021/08/improved-race-ethnicity-measures-reveal-united-states-population-much-more-multiracial.html#:~:text=population%20grew%2088.7%25.-,American%20Indian%20and%20Alaska%20Native%20Population,-From%202010%20to

U.S. Census Bureau. 2021a. *The Hispanic Population in the United States: 2021*. Accessed November 2023.

Available at: https://www.census.gov/data/tables/2021/demo/hispanic-origin/2021-cps.html

U.S. Census Bureau. 2022a. *QuickFacts: United States.* Accessed November 2023. Available at: https://www.census.gov/quickfacts/fact/table/US/IPE120218

U.S. Census Bureau. 2022b. *Census Bureau Releases New Educational Attainment Data.* Accessed November 2023. Available at: https://www.census.gov/newsroom/press-releases/2022/educational-attainment.html

U.S. Census Bureau. 2022c. *Health Insurance Coverage by Race and Hispanic Origin: 2021.* Accessed November 2023. Available at: https://www.census.gov/content/dam/Census/library/publications/2022/acs/acsbr-012.pdf

U.S. Census Bureau. 2023. *Poverty in the United States: 2022.* Accessed November 2023. Available at: https://www.census.gov/content/dam/Census/library/publications/2023/demo/p60-280.pdf

U.S. Census Bureau. 2023a. *Hispanic Heritage Month: 2023.* Accessed November 2023. Available at: https://www.census.gov/newsroom/facts-for-features/2023/hispanic-heritage-month.html

U.S. Census Bureau. 2023b. *National Population by Characteristics: 2020-2022.* Accessed November 2023. Available at: https://www.census.gov/data/tables/time-series/demo/popest/2020s-national-detail.html

U.S. Census Bureau. 2023c. *One in Every Four Children in the United States Were of Hispanic Origin in 2020.* Accessed November 2023. Available at: https://www.census.gov/library/stories/2023/05/hispanic-population-younger-but-aging-faster.html

U.S. Census Bureau, 2023e. *Labor Force Characteristics by Race and Ethnicity, 2021.* Accessed November 2023. Available at: https://www.bls.gov/opub/reports/race-and-ethnicity/2021/home.htm

U.S. Census Bureau. 2023f. *Poverty in the United States: 2022.* Available at: https://www.census.gov/content/dam/Census/library/publications/2023/demo/p60-280.pdf

U.S. Conference of Mayors. 2011. *Hunger and Homelessness Survey.* Accessed March 2021. Available at: http://www.ncdsv.org/images/USCM_Hunger-homelessness-Survey-in-America's-Cities_12%202011.pdf

U.S. Department of Housing and Urban Development (HUD). 2020. *The 2019 Annual Homeless Assessment Report (AHAR) to Congress.* Accessed February 2020. Available at: https://files.hudexchange.info/resources/documents/2019-AHAR-Part-1.pdf

U.S. Department of Labor. 2011. *Changing Characteristics of U.S. Farm Workers: 21 Years of Findings from the National Agricultural Workers Survey.* Accessed September 2013. Available at: http://migrationfiles.ucdavis.edu/uploads/cf/files/2011-may/carroll-changing-characteristics.pdf

U.S. Department of Labor. 2018. *Findings from the National Agricultural Workers Survey (NAWS) 2015–2016: A Demographic and Employment Profile of United States Farmworkers.* U.S. Department of Labor. Accessed July 2020. Available at: https://www.dol.gov/sites/dolgov/files/ETA/naws/pdfs/NAWS_Research_Report_13.pdf

U.S. Department of Veterans Affairs (VA). 2012. *Homeless Incidence and Risk Factors for Becoming Homeless in Veterans.* Accessed March 2017. Available at: https://www.va.gov/oig/pubs/VAOIG-11-03428-173.pdf

UASFACTS. 2022b. *The Hispanic Population Has Quadrupled in the Past Four Decades. It Is Also Becoming More Diverse.* Accessed November 2023. Available at:https://usafacts.org/articles/demographics-hispanic-americans/?utm_source=google&utm_medium=cpc&utm_campaign=ND-Immigration&gclid=CjwKCAiAsIGrBhAAEiwAEzMlCwhlXMw8Ky0zKLIaDy8l_4rRFbX_VXT6_0Cb6bkIY8Qf_tV189WOpxoCT5QQAvD_BwE

UASFACTS. 2022c. *How has the Population Changed in the US?* Accessed November 2023. Available at: https://usafacts.org/data/topics/people-society/population-and-demographics/our-changing-population/

Villarejo, D., A. Souter, R. Mines, et al. 2000. *Suffering in Silence: A Report on the Health of California's Agricultural Workers.* Davis, CA: California Institute for Rural Studies.

Wallender, E., G. Peacock, M. Wharton, and R. P. Walensky. 2023. Uninsured and Not Immune—Closing the Vaccine-Coverage Gap for Adults. *New England Journal of Medicine.*

Wesson, D. E., C. R. Lucey, and L. A. Cooper. 2019. Building Trust in Health Systems to Eliminate Health Disparities. *Journal of the American Medical Association* 322: 111–112. doi: 10.1001/jama.2019.1924

Wetzler, H., and H. Cobb. 2022. Income and Race-Ethnicity Disparities in Medical Care Utilization and Expenditures in the United States, 2017–2019. *MedRxiv:* 2022–2205.

Williams B., C. Ahalt, D. Cloud, D. Augustine, L. Rorvig, and D. Sears. 2020. Correctional Facilities in the Shadow of COVID-19: Unique Challenges and Proposed Solutions. *Health Affairs.* doi: 10.1377/hblog20200324.784502

Witters, D., and S. Agrawal. 2011. *Unhealthy U.S. Workers' Absenteeism Costs $153 billion.* Accessed January 2014. Available at: http://www.gallup.com/poll/150026/unhealthy-workers-absenteeism-costs-153-billion.aspx

Woods, E. R., U. Bhaumik, S. J. Sommer, et al. 2016. Community Asthma Initiative to Improve Health Outcomes and Reduce Disparities Among Children with Asthma. *Morbidity and Mortality Weekly Report Supplements* 65: 11–20.

World Health Organization. 2004. *Antiretroviral Drugs for Treating Pregnant Women and Preventing HIV Infection in Infants: Guidelines on Care, Treatment and*

Support for Women Living with HIV/AIDS and Their Children in Resource-Constrained Settings. Accessed May 2017. Available at: http://www.who.int/hiv/pub/mtct/en/arvdrugsguidelines.pdf

Yancy C. W. 2020. COVID-19 and African Americans. *Journal of the American Medical Association.* doi: 10.1001/jama.2020.6548

Yearby, R., B. Clark, and J. F. Figuero. 2022. Structural Racism In Historical And Modern US Health Care Policy: Study Examines Structural Racism in Historical and Modern US Health Care Policy. *Health Affairs* 41: 187–194.

Yu, S. M., Z. J. Huang, and G. K. Singh. 2004. Health Status and Health Services Utilization Among US Chinese, Asian Indian, Filipino, and Other Asian/Pacific Islander Children. *Pediatrics* 113: 101–107.

Zambrana, R. E., and D. R. Williams. 2022. The Intellectual Roots of Current Knowledge on Racism and health: Relevance to Policy and The National Equity Discourse. *Health Affairs* 41: 163–170.

Zarei, K., L. Kahle, D. W. Buckman, et al. 2023. Parent-Child Nativity, Race, Ethnicity, and Common Mental Health Conditions Among United States Children and Adolescents. *The Journal of Pediatrics* 263: 113618.

Ziller, E. C. 2014. *Access to Medical Care IN Rural America.* New York: Springer Publishing.

Zuckerman, S., J. Haley, Y. Roubideaux, and M. Lillie-Blanton. 2004. Health Service Access, Use, and Insurance Coverage Among American Indians/Alaska Natives and Whites: What Role Does the Indian Health Service Play? *American Journal of Public Health* 94: 53–59.

PART 4

System Outcomes

CHAPTER 12	Cost, Access, and Quality	519
CHAPTER 13	Health Policy	573

CHAPTER 12

Cost, Access, and Quality

LEARNING OBJECTIVES

- Identify the meaning of healthcare costs and review recent trends.
- Examine the factors that have led to cost escalations in the past.
- Describe regulatory and market-oriented approaches to contain costs.
- Explain why some regulatory cost-containment approaches were unsuccessful.
- Discuss the access to care framework and various dimensions of access to care.
- Understand the use of technology such as telemedicine and HEREHR to improve access to care.
- Describe access indicators and measurements.
- Explain the nature, scope, and dimensions of quality.
- Differentiate between quality assurance and quality assessment.
- Appreciate new initiatives related to quality in health care such as the Accountable Care
- Organizations and Value-based Payment.
- Discuss the implications of the Affordable Care Act for healthcare costs, access, and quality.

The healthcare sector of the economy is like a monster with a voracious appetite that needs to be controlled.

Introduction

Cost, access, and quality are the three major cornerstones of healthcare delivery. For many years, employers and third-party payers in the United States have been preoccupied with controlling the growth of healthcare expenditures. Cost and access go hand in hand: Expansion of access will increase healthcare expenditures. Their intertwined nature is a major reason that attempts to implement universal coverage in the United States have failed in the past and why it remains difficult to achieve this goal even in the post-Affordable Care Act (ACA) era. Although cost and access remain the primary concerns within the U.S. healthcare delivery system, quality of health care has joined them at center stage in recent decades. Cost, access, and quality are interrelated in complex ways.

From a macro perspective, costs of health care are commonly viewed in terms of national health expenditures (NHE). A widely used measure of NHE is the proportion of its gross domestic product (GDP) that a country spends on the delivery of healthcare services. From a micro perspective, healthcare expenditures refer to costs incurred by employers to purchase health insurance and out-of-pocket costs incurred by individuals when they receive healthcare services. Improving access to health care and ensuring equal access to quality health care are contingent on expenditures at both the macro and micro levels.

Sustainable high-quality care should also be cost-effective. Hence, cost is an important factor in the evaluation of quality. In addition, quality is achieved by having up-to-date capabilities, using evidence-based processes, and measuring **outcomes**. Quality goals are accomplished when the system capabilities and practices employed in the delivery of health care achieve desirable outcomes for individuals and populations.

This chapter discusses the major reasons for the dramatic rise in healthcare expenditures. Costs in the United States are compared to those in other countries, and the impact of cost-containment measures is examined. Dimensions of access are presented as well. Finally, quality of care and its measurement are discussed.

Cost of Health Care

The term "cost" can carry different meanings in the delivery of health care, depending on whose perspective is considered:

- When consumers and financiers speak of the "cost" of health care, they usually mean the "price" of health care. This could refer to the physician's bill, the price of a prescription, or the cost of health insurance premiums.
- From a national perspective, healthcare costs refer to how much a nation spends on health care—that is, NHE or healthcare spending. Since expenditures (E) equal price (P) times quantity (Q), growth in healthcare spending can be accounted for by increases in the prices charged by the providers of health services and by increases in the utilization of services.
- From the perspective of providers, the notion of cost refers to the cost of producing healthcare services. Inputs such as staff salaries, capital costs for buildings and equipment, rental of space, and purchase of supplies are included in the cost of production.

Trends in National Health Expenditures

The *Health Services Financing* chapter provided an overview of national and personal health expenditures, their composition, and the proportional share between the private and public sectors. Healthcare spending spiraled upward at double-digit rates during the 1970s, right after the Medicare and Medicaid programs created a massive growth in access

Cost of Health Care

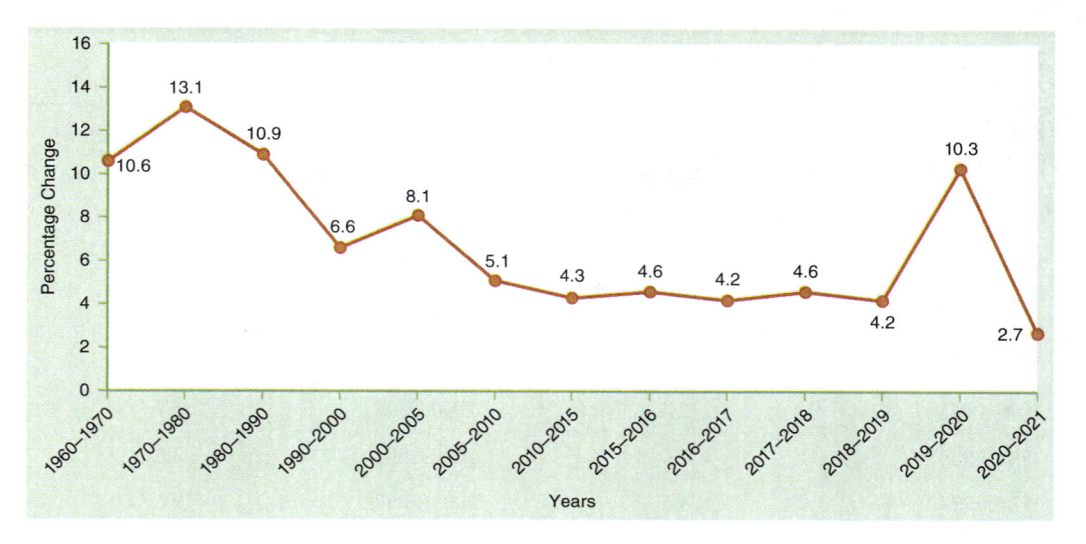

Figure 12-1 Average annual percentage growth in U.S. national healthcare spending.

Data from Centers for Medicare and Medicaid Services (CMS). 2019. *National health expenditure data: Historical.* Available at: https://www.cms.gov/Research-Statistics-Data-and-Systems/Statistics-Trends-and-Reports/NationalHealthExpendData/NationalHealthAccountsHistorical. Accessed January 2020; National Center for Health Statistics (NCHS). 2013. *Health, United States, 2012*, Hyattsville, MD: U.S. Department of Health and Human Services. p. 323; National Center for Health Statistics (NCHS). 2019. *Health, United States, 2018.* Hyattsville, MD: U.S. Department of Health and Human Services. Table 42.

in 1965. Between 1965 and 1970, government expenditures for healthcare services and supplies had grown by 140%, from $7.9 billion to $18.9 billion (U.S. Department of Health and Human Services [DHHS], 1996). During much of the 1980s, average annual growth in national health spending continued in the double digits, but the rate of increase slowed considerably (**Figure 12-1**). In the 1990s, medical inflation was finally brought under control at a single-digit rate of growth, mainly due to control exerted over payment and utilization through managed care (**Table 12-1**). In 2022, the United States spent $4.5 trillion on health and health care, which amounts to $12,555 per person.

Table 12-1 Average Annual Percentage Increase in U.S. National Healthcare Spending, 1975–2018

Periods	Increase (%)	Periods	Increase (%)
1975–1980	13.6	1990–1995	7.3
1975–1976	14.7	1990–1991	9.2
1976–1977	13.7	1991–1992	9.5
1977–1978	11.9	1992–1993	6.9
1978–1979	12.9	1993–1994	5.1
1979–1980	14.8	1994–1995	4.9
1980–1985	11.6	1995–2000	5.9

(continues)

Table 12-1 Average Annual Percentage Increase in U.S. National Healthcare Spending, 1975–2018 *(continued)*

Periods	Increase (%)	Periods	Increase (%)
1980–1981	16.1	1995–1996	4.6
1981–1982	12.5	1996–1997	4.7
1982–1983	10.0	1997–1998	5.4
1983–1984	9.7	1998–1999	5.7
1984–1985	9.9	1999–2000	6.9
1985–1990	*10.2*	*2000–2005*	*8.1*
1985–1986	7.6	2000–2001	8.5
1986–1987	8.5	2001–2002	9.6
1987–1988	11.9	2002–2003	8.5
1988–1989	11.2	2003–2004	7.2
1989–1990	12.1	2004–2005	6.8
2005–2010	*5.1*	*2010–2015*	*4.3*
2005–2006	6.5	2010–2011	3.4
2006–2007	6.4	2011–2012	4.0
2007–2008	4.5	2012–2013	3.0
2008–2009	4.0	2013–2014	5.2
2009–2010	4.1	2014–2015	5.8
2015–2018	*4.5*		
2015–2016	4.6		
2016–2017	4.2		
2017–2018	4.6		

Data from National Center for Health Statistics (NCHS). [Hyattsville, MD: U.S. Department of Health and Human Services.] 1996. *Health, United States, 1995*, p. 243; 1998. *Health, United States, 1996–97*, p. 249; 2000. *Health, United States, 1999*, p. 284; 2001. *Health, United States, 2000*, p. 322; 2003. *Health, United States, 2002*, p. 288; 2007. *Health, United States, 2006*, p. 377; 2013. *Health, United States, 2012*, p. 323; 2014. *Health, United States, 2013*, p. 327; 2016. *Health, United States, 2015*, p. 293; 2017. *Health, United States, 2016*, p. 314; 2019. *Health, United States, 2018*, Table 42; Levit, K., et al. 2003. Trends in U.S. health care spending, 2001. *Health Affairs 22*, no. 1: 154–164; Centers for Medicare and Medicaid Services (CMS). 2019. *National health expenditure data: Historical.* Available at: https://www.cms.gov/Research-Statistics-Data-and-Systems/Statistics-Trends-and-Reports/NationalHealthExpendData/NationalHealthAccountsHistorical. Accessed January 2020.

Trends in NHE are commonly evaluated in three ways. The first method compares medical inflation to general inflation in the economy, which is measured by annual changes in the consumer price index (CPI). Except for a brief period between 1978 and

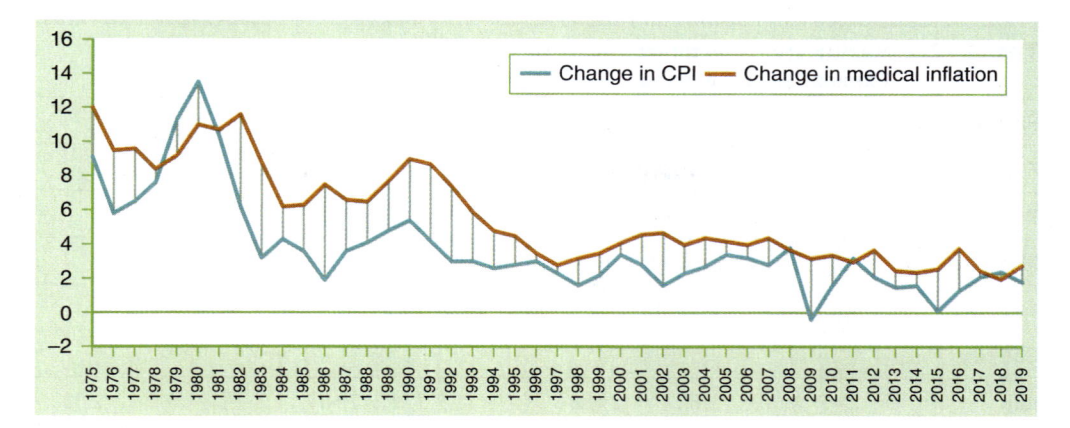

Figure 12-2 Annual percentage change in CPI and medical inflation, 1975–2019.

Data from Bureau of Labor Statistics. 2020. Databases, tables, and calculators by subject: CPI for all urban consumers (CPI-U). Available at: https://data.bls.gov/cgi-bin/surveymost?cu. Accessed January 2020.

1981, when the U.S. economy was experiencing hyperinflation, as well as a few isolated cases, the rates of change in medical inflation have remained consistently above the rates of change in the CPI (**Figure 12-2**). The second method compares changes in NHE to those in the GDP. With only isolated exceptions, healthcare spending growth rates have consistently surpassed growth rates in the general economy (**Figure 12-3**). When spending on health care grows at a faster rate than GDP, it means that healthcare consumes a larger share of the total economic output. Put another way, a growing share of total economic resources is devoted to the delivery of health care.

The third method is based on international comparisons. Compared to other nations, the United States devotes a larger share of its economic resources to health care (**Table 12-2**). In addition, U.S. growth in healthcare spending has outpaced the growth in healthcare spending in other countries

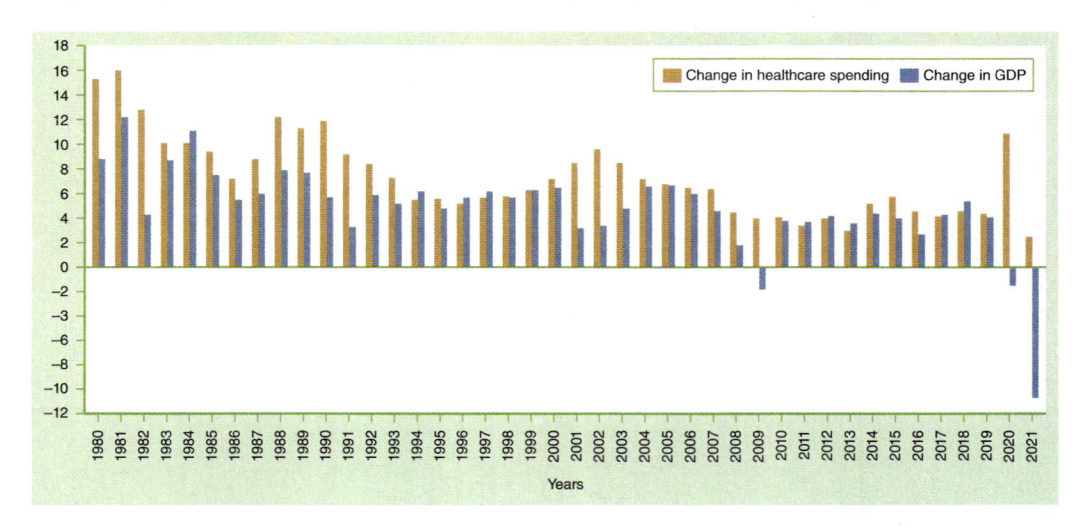

Figure 12-3 Annual percentage change in U.S. national healthcare expenditures and GDP, 1980–2021.

Data from Centers for Medicare and Medicaid Services (CMS). 2019. National health expenditure data: Historical. Available at: https://www.cms.gov/Research-Statistics-Data-and-Systems/Statistics-Trends-and-Reports/NationalHealthExpendData/NationalHealthAccountsHistorical. Accessed January 2020.

Table 12-2 Healthcare Expenditures as a Proportion of GDP and per Capita Healthcare Expenditures (Selected Years, Selected OECD Countries, 2019–2021

Financing scheme	All financing schemes								
Function	Current expenditure on health (all functions)								
Provider	All providers								
Measure	Per capita, current prices								
Year	2019			2020			2021		
Country									
Italy	(B)	8.7	2,603.8		9.6	2,685.6	(P)	9.5	2,833.7
United Kingdom		9.9	3,334.1		12.0	3,839.6	(P)	11.9	4,107.4
France		11.1	4,014.6		12.2	4,159.5	(P)	12.4	4,549.2
Austria		10.5	4,689.3		11.5	4,881.1	(P)	12.2	5,488.2
Germany		11.7	4,889.1		12.8	5,192.4	(P)	12.8	5,498.5
Netherlands		10.1	4,753.4		11.1	5,108.4	(P)	11.2	5,521.9
Canada		11.0	6,730.9	(DP)	12.9	7,507.1	(DP)	11.7	7,613.0
United States		16.7	10,855.5		18.8	11,859.2	(E)	17.8	12,318.1
Denmark		10.1	40,351.1		10.5	42,058.5	(P)	10.8	46,368.4
Sweden		10.8	53,214.6	(P)	11.5	55,380.8	(P)	11.4	59,306.1
Finland		9.2	3,984.1		9.6	4,137.7			
Belgium		10.7	4,438.8		11.1	4,379.7			
Australia		10.2	7,988.7	(E)	10.6	8,564.5			
Japan		11.0	485,093.2	(P)	11.1	474,988.9			

Data extracted on 31 May 2023 18:58 UTC (GMT) from OECD.Stat
Legend:
B: Break
P: Provisional value
D: Difference in methodology
E: Estimated value

Data from: OECD (2023). Total U.S. Healthcare Expenditures as a Proportion of GDP and per Capita Health Care Expenditures (Selected Years, Selected OECD Countries; per Capita Expenditures in U.S. Dollars). https://stats.oecd.org/index.aspx?DataSetCode=SHA#

(**Figure 12-4**). Numerous reasons have been given for the growth of healthcare expenditures, and several initiatives have been employed over the years to prevent out-of-control spending. These topics are discussed later in this chapter.

The rate of growth in health spending decreased to its lowest level in four decades

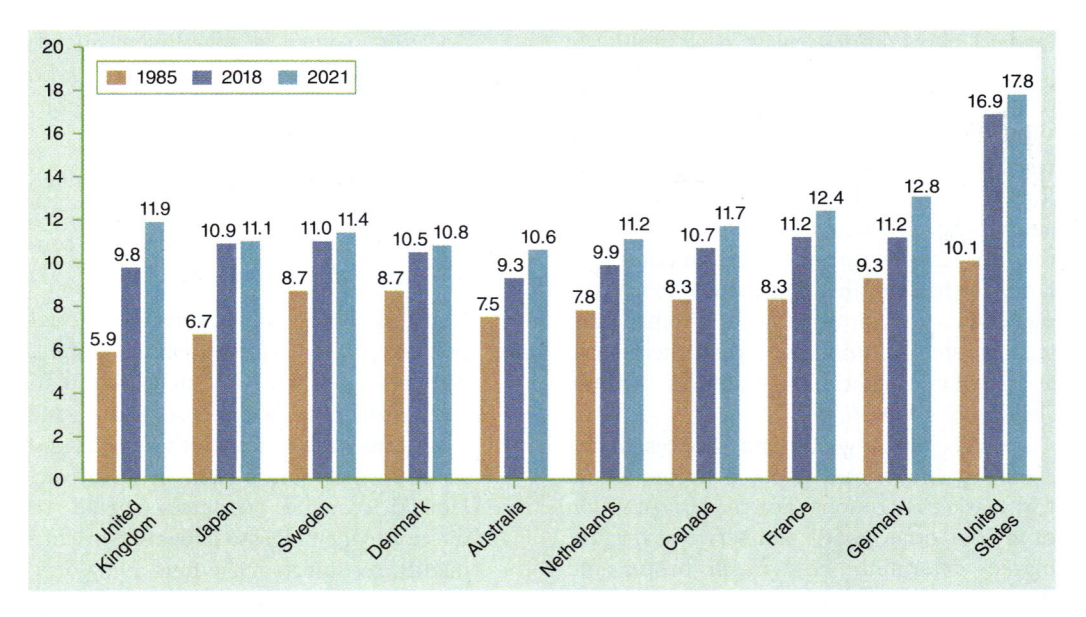

Figure 12-4 U.S. healthcare spending as a percentage of GDP for selected OECD countries, 1985, 2018, and 2021.

Data from National Center for Health Statistics (NCHS). 2002. Health, United States, 2002. Hyattsville, MD: U.S. Department of Health and Human Services; Organization for Economic Cooperation and Development (OECD). 2020. Health spending. Available at: https://data.oecd.org/healthres/health-spending.htm. Accessed January 2020.

(5.7% average annual growth) between 1993 and 2000 as managed care proliferated, but the good news ended in 2002—a year that recorded the fastest annual growth in NHE (9.3%) since 1992. Since then, the rate of growth has slowed down considerably, hovering around 5% the past few years (refer to Table 12-1). In 2009, the rate of growth decreased to 3.9%, a decline largely attributable to the most severe recession the United States had experienced since 1933. As a result of the recession, personal healthcare expenditures paid mostly by private sources increased just 2.8%, the lowest rate since the 1990s, when managed care implemented tight cost control measures (Hartman et al., 2011).

Implementation of the ACA will be a major factor in determining the future growth of healthcare expenditures. Higher utilization of healthcare services will undoubtedly lead to medical care cost inflation unless measures are employed to slow down the rise in the price and quantity factors. A 2016 Commonwealth Fund publication suggested that ACA reforms have likely contributed to slower healthcare spending growth due to the tightening of payment rates and implementation of incentives to reduce costs (Schoen, 2016). Multiple other reports have also linked the ACA to reductions in growth rates for healthcare spending (Martin et al., 2018; Rama, 2018; Van de Water, 2019).

According to the CMS, Office of the Actuary, healthcare spending is projected to account for 19.4% of GDP by 2027 (CMS, 2019d). In 2007, the Congressional Budget Office estimated that health care would consume 37% of GDP by 2050 and 49% by 2082. These forecasts portend that the healthcare sector will remain one of the fastest-growing components of the U.S. economy.

Should Healthcare Costs Be Contained?

Americans view growth in expenditures in other sectors of the economy, such as manufacturing, much more favorably than they do expenditures on medical care. Increased medical expenditures create new healthcare jobs, do not pollute the air, save rather than destroy lives, and alleviate pain and suffering. Why shouldn't society be pleased that more resources are flowing into a sector that cares for the aged and the sick? It would seem to be a more appropriate use of a society's resources than spending those same funds on faster cars, fancy clothes, or other consumable items. Yet, increased expenditures for these other consumable items do not cause the concern that arises when medical expenditures increase (Feldstein, 1994).

Unlike other goods and services in the economy, health care is not delivered under free market conditions. For the consumption of various other goods and services, the free market determines how much people and the nation should spend, depending on their economic capabilities. In the United States, the private sector and the government share roughly equally in the financing of health care. In a quasi-market, such as health care in the United States, it would be almost impossible to determine how much the nation should spend. Hence, in the United States, three main sources are used to assess whether too much is spent on health care:

- The first source, international comparisons (refer to Table 12-2), is actually not an unbiased tool. In countries other than the United States, the government decides how much should be spent on health care, with various rationing measures—such as supply-side controls, comparatively little spending on developing new technology, and price controls (for pharmaceuticals, for example)—being used to maintain certain levels of predetermined spending.
- The second source is the rise in health insurance premiums in the private sector. This factor triggered private employers to abandon traditional fee-for-service insurance plans, especially during the 1980s, and to seek employee coverage through health maintenance organization (HMO) plans.
- The third source is government spending on health care for beneficiaries who receive health care through various public insurance programs.

Experts generally agree that the United States spends too much on health care and, therefore, call for expenditures to be controlled. The main reasons are as follows:

- Rising healthcare costs consume greater portions of the total economic output. Because economic resources are limited, rising healthcare cost means that Americans have to forgo other goods and services when more is spent on health care.
- Limited economic resources should be directed to their highest-value uses. In a free market, consumers make purchasing decisions based on their perception of value, knowing that an expenditure on one good means forgoing purchases of other goods and services (Feldstein, 1994). In healthcare delivery, comprehensive health insurance creates a moral hazard and provider-induced demand, both of which fuel inefficiencies in the consumption of resources.
- U.S. businesses argue that rising insurance premium costs must be passed on to consumers in the form of higher prices, which may interfere with businesses' ability to stay globally competitive. For example, health insurance premiums have consistently increased faster than inflation in the general economy or workers' wages in recent years. Between 2006 and 2016, the cumulative growth in health insurance premiums was 58%, whereas cumulative inflation was 19% and cumulative wage growth was 33% (Bureau of Labor Statistics, 2017a, b; Kaiser Family Foundation, 2016). Insurance premiums have increased 22% since 2014 (Kaiser Family Foundation, 2019).
- Rising premium costs limit the ability of many employers—especially small businesses—to offer health benefits. Even when those benefits are offered, employers

may limit the ability of some employees to contribute toward the purchase of employer-sponsored insurance coverage (Kaiser Family Foundation, Health Research and Education Trust, 2010).
- Rising healthcare costs take a toll on average- and low-income Americans. The 2016 Commonwealth Fund International Health Policy Survey pointed out that affordability of health care was one of the biggest economic problems for many Americans (Commonwealth Fund, 2016). One-third of Americans went without recommended care, did not visit a doctor when sick, or failed to fill a prescription because of costs, compared to 7% of survey respondents in the United Kingdom and Germany, and 8% in the Netherlands and Sweden.
- The government has only limited ability to raise people's taxes, given that most American taxpayers believe that they already pay more than their fair share of taxes. Paradoxically, half of Americans, many of whom use tax-financed health care, pay no federal income taxes (*USA Today*, 2010).

Reasons for Cost Escalation

Numerous factors contribute to rising healthcare expenditures, and they interact in complex ways. Hence, one cannot point to just one or two main causes of this cost escalation. General inflation in the economy is a more visible cause of healthcare spending because it affects the cost of producing healthcare services through such factors as higher wages and cost of supplies. Some of the other factors mentioned in this section are also discussed in other chapters of this text. They are included here, along with additional pertinent details, to provide a comprehensive picture of the reasons underlying medical cost inflation:

- Third-party payment
- Imperfect market
- Growth of technology
- Increase in the population of older adults and of chronic conditions
- Medical model of healthcare delivery
- Multipayer system and administrative costs
- Defensive medicine
- Waste and abuse
- Practice variations

Third-Party Payment

Health care is among the few services for which a third party—not the consumer—pays for most services used. Whether payment is made by the government or by a private insurance company, individual out-of-pocket expenses are far lower than the actual cost of the service (Altman and Wallack, 1996). Hence, patients are generally insensitive to the cost of care. Introduction of prospective payment methods and capitation has, to a large extent, minimized provider-induced demand. However, the backlash against managed care from consumers and providers alike has, in a sense, kept the door open to the overuse of high-cost technologies and other services. Also, fee-for-service reimbursement and its discounted fee variation are still widely used in the outpatient sector of healthcare delivery. Hence, provider-induced demand has not been expunged from the system.

Imperfect Market

Prices charged by providers for healthcare services are likely to be much closer to the cost of producing the services in a highly regulated or highly competitive market (Altman and Wallack, 1996). Because the U.S. healthcare delivery system follows neither the highly regulated single-payer model nor a free market model, utilization remains largely unchecked; prices charged for healthcare services remain higher than the true economic costs of production (Altman and Wallack, 1996). A quasi-market results in increased healthcare expenditures because both the quantity and price factors remain unchecked.

Growth of Technology

The United States has been characterized as following an early start/fast growth pattern in the adoption and diffusion of intensive procedures (TECH Research Network, 2001).

As an example of this trend, the use of advanced imaging and scanning during visits to physician offices and outpatient departments more than tripled from 1996 to 2007 (National Center for Health Statistics [NCHS], 2010). Medicare Part B spending for imaging services under the physician fee schedule more than doubled between 2000 and 2006, from $6.9 billion to $14.1 billion (U.S. Government Accountability Office, 2008). However, following cuts to imaging reimbursements, this growth slowed (American Association of Physicists in Medicine, 2011).

New technology is expensive to develop, and costs incurred in research and development (R&D) are included in total healthcare expenditures. One reason that Canada and European nations, compared to the United States, have incurred lower healthcare costs is that they have proportionally invested far less in healthcare R&D.

Increase in the Number of Older Adults

Since the early part of the 20th century, life expectancy in the United States has consistently increased (save for a 1-year decline in 2020 due to the COVID-19 pandemic; Arias et al., 2021) (**Figure 12-5**). Life expectancy at birth has been extended by more than 30 years in the United States, from 47.3 years in

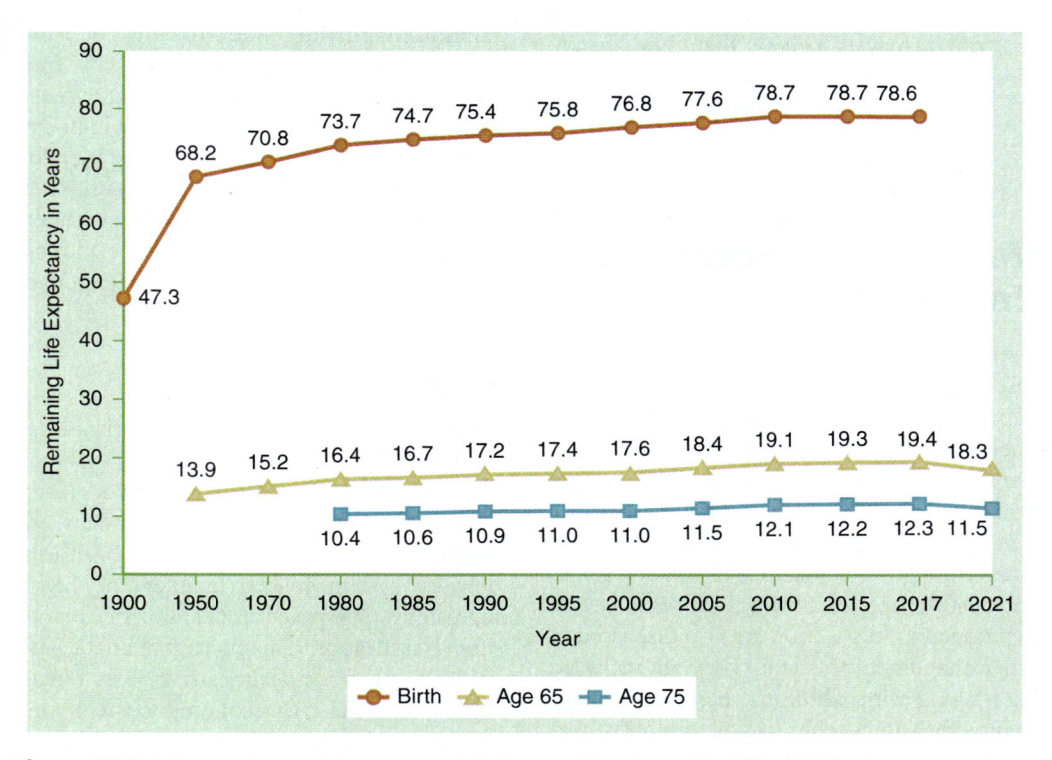

Figure 12-5 Life expectancy of Americans at birth, age 65, and age 75, 1900–2021 (selected years).

Data from National Center for Health Statistics (NCHS). 2002. Health, United States, 2002. Hyattsville, MD: U.S. Department of Health and Human Services. p. 116; National Center for Health Statistics (NCHS). 2019. Health, United States, 2018. Hyattsville, MD: U.S. Department of Health and Human Services. Table 4.

Reasons for Cost Escalation

1900 to 78.6 years in 2017 (NCHS, 2019b). Consequently, the United States—along with other industrialized nations—is experiencing an aging boom. Growth in the number of U.S. older adults has outpaced growth in the younger population since 1900. **Figure 12-6** shows changes in the demographic makeup of the U.S. population from 1970 to 2010. Most remarkable is the growth in the 85-and-older group, whereas the youngest age group is shrinking (in a relative sense). Growth in the number of older adults is projected to continue through the middle of the 21st century.

Between 2000 and 2030, the proportion of the U.S. population 65 years and older is expected to increase from 12.4% to 20.6%; that is, 1 in 5 Americans will be older adults in 2030 (U.S. Census Bureau, 2018). The number in the 85-and-older category is projected to more than double.

Older adults consume more health care than younger people, largely due to a higher prevalence of chronic conditions. Take diabetes (one of the most common chronic conditions) as an example. The American Diabetes Association released data on March 22, 2018,

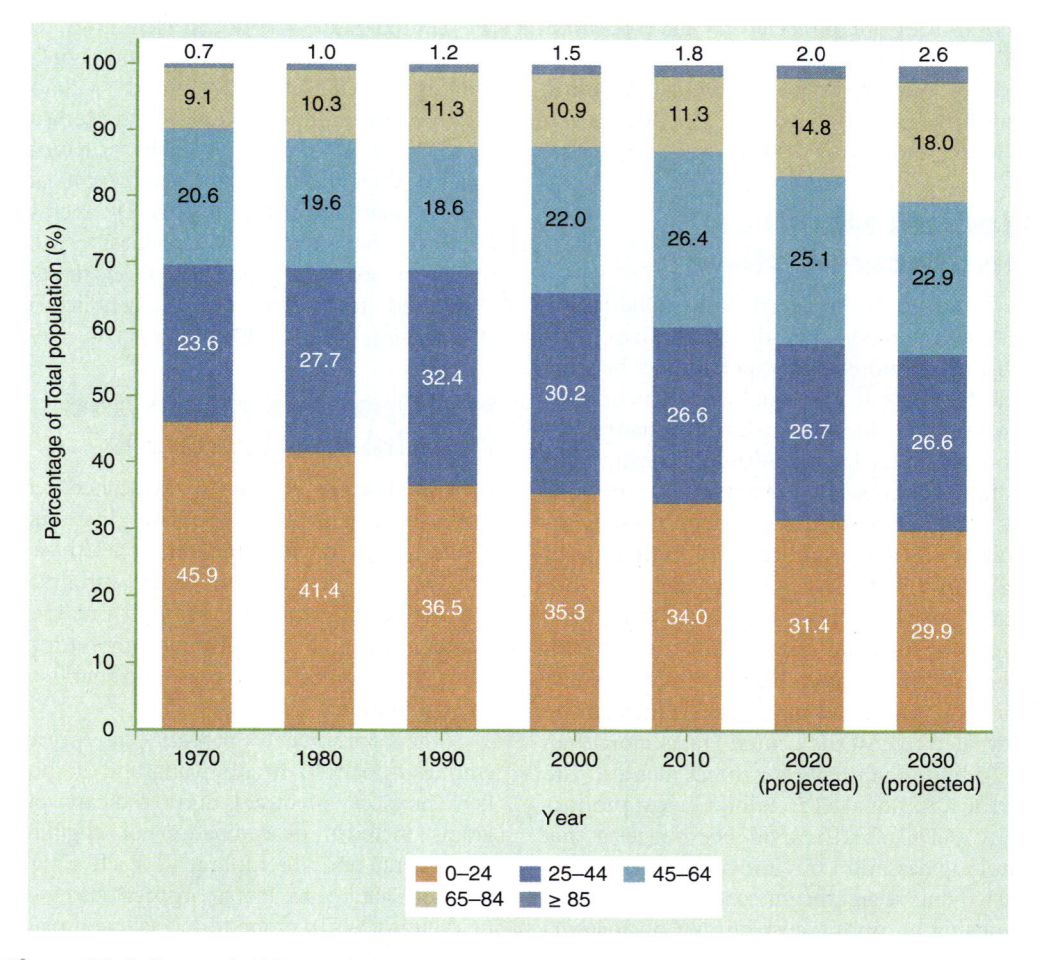

Year	≥85	65–84	45–64	25–44	0–24
1970	0.7	9.1	20.6	23.6	45.9
1980	1.0	10.3	19.6	27.7	41.4
1990	1.2	11.3	18.6	32.4	36.5
2000	1.5	10.9	22.0	30.2	35.3
2010	1.8	11.3	26.4	26.6	34.0
2020 (projected)	2.0	14.8	25.1	26.7	31.4
2030 (projected)	2.6	18.0	22.9	26.6	29.9

Figure 12-6 Change in U.S. population mix between 1970 and 2010, and projections for 2020 and 2030.

Data from National Center for Health Statistics (NCHS). 2013. Health, United States, 2012. Hyattsville, MD: U.S. Department of Health and Human Services. p. 45; U.S. Census Bureau. 2018. 2017 National population projection tables. Available at: https://www.census.gov/data/tables/2017/demo/popproj/2017-summary-tables.html. Accessed January 2020.

estimating that the total costs of diagnosed diabetes rose from $245 billion in 2012 to $327 billion in 2017 (American Diabetes Association 2020). This figure represents a 26% increase over the five-year period.

In 2020, the average personal healthcare spending for people 65 and older was $22,356 per person, over 5 times higher than spending per child ($4,217) and almost 2.5 times the spending per working-age person ($9,154) (CMS, 2021). Given this fact, healthcare expenditures are sure to rise as the U.S. population continues to age unless drastic steps are taken to curtail spending. Total Medicare expenditures are projected to increase from 2.7% of GDP in 2005 to 9% of GDP in 2050, and to average 7.4% in annual spending growth from 2018 to 2027 (CMS, 2019a; Van de Water and Lavery, 2006).

Medical Model of Healthcare Delivery

As discussed in the *Beliefs, Values, and Health* chapter, the medical model emphasizes medical interventions after a person has become sick. It does not put equal emphasis on prevention and lifestyle behavior changes to promote better health. Although health promotion and disease prevention are not the answer to every health problem, these principles have not been accorded their rightful place in the U.S. healthcare delivery system. Consequently, more costly healthcare resources must be deployed to treat health problems that could have been prevented. For example, smoking-related illnesses are estimated to cost the United States more than $170 billion annually for direct medical care and an additional $156 billion in lost productivity (CDC, 2019). Evidence suggests that smoking cessation programs have the potential to achieve significant cost savings without imposing an undue cost burden on insurers and employers (Levy, 2006). Although the prevalence of cigarette smoking has been slowly declining, 13% of U.S. adult males and 10% of U.S. adult females still smoked in 2021 (Cornelius et al., 2023).

Overweight and obesity rates have shown alarming increases in the United States and in many other developed nations in recent decades. Nearly 30.7% of adults are overweight, more than 42.4% of adults have high BMI and 9.2% of adults have extreme high BMI (NIH, 2021).

Overweight and obesity substantially elevate a person's risk of developing heart disease, diabetes, some types of cancers, musculoskeletal disorders, and gallbladder problems. Of the total medical spending in the United States, 10% ($147 billion) can be attributed to overweight and obesity, rivaling the spending attributed to smoking (Finkelstein et al., 2009). Both Medicare and Medicaid expend a disproportionate share of their funds to treat overweight- and obesity-related health problems. On average, Medicare beneficiaries with obesity incur $600 per beneficiary per year in extra costs compared to normal-weight beneficiaries (Finkelstein et al., 2009).

Multipayer System and Administrative Costs

Administrative costs are associated with the management of the financing, insurance, delivery, and payment functions of health care. They include management of the enrollment process, setting up contracts with providers, claims processing, utilization monitoring, denials and appeals of claims, and marketing and promotional expenses.

The enrollment process in private, employer-financed health plans and in publicly financed Medicaid and Medicare programs includes determination of eligibility, enrollment, and disenrollment. Each activity has associated costs. Private insurers also incur marketing costs to promote and sell their plans.

Providers must deal with numerous healthcare plans in which the extent of benefits and reimbursement is not standardized.

It is difficult and costly to remain current with the numerous and changing rules and regulations.

Denials of payment result in rebilling and follow-up. Denials of services result in appeals and incur costs for the insurer to review the appeals and for the provider to furnish justifications for the delivery of services. Utilization review and authorization of care lead to additional costs for both payers and providers.

It is estimated that administrative costs of insurance (15%) and providers (15%) account for 30% of U.S. health spending (The Commonwealth fund, 2023). The ACA requires health plans to standardize electronic data exchange to reduce administrative costs, although it does not provide any specific guidelines on how information must be transferred (Blanchfield et al., 2010). Nevertheless, the ACA addresses only a minute portion of the total administrative costs; hence, its likely effects in reducing these costs are negligible.

Defensive Medicine

The U.S. healthcare delivery system is characterized by litigation risks for providers. Fear of legal liability is one of the main reasons for carrying out unnecessary cesarean sections, for example, because it makes it easier to defend a potential birth injury case. A report by the National Bureau of Economic Research found evidence suggesting that defensive medicine raised inpatient spending by 5% (Frakes and Gruber, 2018). Unrestrained malpractice awards by the courts and increased malpractice insurance premiums for physicians also significantly add to the cost of health care.

Fraud and Abuse

Fraud and (system) abuse (concepts introduced in the *Health Services Financing* chapter) are another type of waste in health care. **Fraud**, defined as a knowing disregard of the truth, has been identified as a major problem in the Medicare and Medicaid programs. Fraud occurs when billing claims or cost reports are intentionally falsified. It may also occur when more services are provided than are medically necessary or when services not provided are billed. In **upcoding**, another fraudulent practice, the provider bills for a higher-priced service but actually delivers a lower-priced service. These practices are illegal under the False Claims Act.

Under the anti-kickback statute (Medicare and Medicaid Patient Protection Act of 1987), it is illegal to provide any remuneration to any individual or entity in exchange for a referral for services to be paid by the Medicare or Medicaid program. Knowingly providing such financial inducements amounts to a federal crime, which is punishable by imprisonment. The Stark Laws prohibit physician self-referral for laboratory or other designated health services. The General Accounting Office estimates that healthcare fraud, waste and abuse may account for as much as 10% of all healthcare expenditures in the United States (Department of Justice Archives, 2020).

Practice Variations

The work of John Wennberg and others brought to the fore a disturbing aspect of physician behavior, which accounts for wide variations in treatment patterns for similar patients. Numerous studies in the United States and abroad have documented notable differences in utilization rates for hospital admissions and surgical procedures among different communities, as well as for the same specialties (Feldstein, 1993). These practice variations are referred to as **small area variations (SAVs)** because the differences in practice patterns have been associated with only certain geographic areas of the country. For example, in earlier studies, variations in the rate of tonsillectomies in New England counties could not be explained by differences in the demographics or other characteristics of the populations studied (Wennberg and Gittelsohn, 1973). Similarly, the overall inpatient hospital utilization by an aged population in East Boston, Massachusetts, was higher than that by an equivalent population in New Haven, Connecticut (Wennberg et al., 1987). More recent investigations of regional differences in Medicare spending demonstrated that higher rates of inpatient-based care and specialist services were associated with higher costs but not with improved quality of care, health outcomes, access to services, or satisfaction with care (Fisher et al., 2003a, 2003b). This variation, which can be as great as twofold, cannot be explained by age, gender, race, pricing variations, or health status (Baucus and Fowler, 2002).

A 2016 study found that 40% to 50% of all geographic variations in utilization can be attributed to demand-side factors, including health and preferences, while the remainder may be due to place-specific supply factors (Finkelstein et al., 2016). Such geographic variations produce gross inefficiencies in the U.S. healthcare delivery system because they increase costs without yielding appreciably better outcomes. They are also unfair because workers and Medicare beneficiaries in low-cost, more-efficient regions subsidize the care of those in high-cost regions (Wennberg, 2002).

SAVs cannot be explained by demand inducement. For example, no incentives exist for physicians to induce demand in Canada or Britain, yet variations similar to those in the United States have also been found in those countries. SAVs indicate that patients in some parts of the country are receiving too much treatment, whereas others may be receiving too little. Medical opinions often differ on the appropriateness of clinical interventions because physicians use different criteria for hospital admissions and surgical interventions (Gittelsohn and Powe, 1995; Badinski et al., 2023; Kosaraju et al., 2023; Townsend et al., 2023).

Cost Containment: Regulatory Approaches

Although many attempts to control healthcare spending have been undertaken in the United States, most of them have been met with only limited success—mainly because system-wide cost controls are almost impossible to implement in a quasi-market system. Cost-containment measures in the United States have been piecemeal efforts, affecting only certain targeted sectors of the healthcare delivery system at a time. For instance, when prices have been regulated, utilization has been left untouched; similarly, when capital expenditures have required preapprovals, operating costs of production have been exempted.

Single-payer systems in other industrialized countries have created national regulatory mechanisms to keep their healthcare spending in line with their GDPs. Many of these countries enforce **top-down control** over total expenditures. In such a system, the country's government establishes budgets for entire sectors of the healthcare delivery system. Funds are distributed to providers in accordance with these global budgets, so total spending remains within established budget limits. The downside to this approach is that, under fixed budgets, providers are not as responsive to patient needs and the system provides little incentive to be efficient in the delivery of services. Once budget allocations are used up, providers are forced to cut back services, particularly for illnesses that are not life threatening and that do not represent an emergency.

This top-down approach stands in sharp contrast to the "bottom-up" approach used in the United States, where each provider and managed care organization (MCO) establishes its own fees or premiums (Altman and Wallack, 1996). Competition, created by employers shopping for the best premium rates and by MCOs contracting with providers who agree to favorable fee arrangements, determines what the total expenditures will be. To some extent, the United States also uses regulatory cost control, although it is not as comprehensive as the schemes used in countries with national healthcare programs.

Cost-control efforts in the United States are characterized by a combination of government regulation and market-based competition. A fragmented approach to cost control allows providers to shift costs, mainly from low payers to higher payers or from one delivery sector to another. For example, when regulatory controls are employed to squeeze costs out of the inpatient sector, providers experience reduced revenues from inpatient services. To make up for the lost revenues, they may increase utilization of outpatient services if that sector is free of controls. In another scenario, when the government implements cost-control measures, providers may start charging higher prices to private payers. This practice is very common in the nursing home industry, in which reimbursement is restricted under Medicaid rate-setting criteria. In this case, nursing home administrators make a conscious attempt to make up for lost revenues by admitting more private-pay residents and by establishing higher private-pay charges.

Regulatory approaches to cost containment, in the United States and elsewhere, typically control healthcare supply, prices, and utilization (**Exhibit 12-1**). Supply-side controls (health planning) enable policymakers to limit the number of hospital beds and diffusion of costly technology, but regulatory limits on the healthcare system's capacity inevitably create monopolies on the supply side. To ensure that these artificially created monopolies do not exploit their economic power, health planning is always coupled with stiff price and budgetary controls (Reinhardt, 1994).

Health Planning

Health planning refers to a government undertaking steps to align and distribute healthcare resources so that—at least in the eyes of government officials—the system will achieve the desired health outcomes for all people. The planning function becomes critical in a centrally controlled national healthcare program to ensure that the basic healthcare needs of the population are met and that expenditures are maintained at predetermined levels.

The central planning function does not fit well in the U.S. system—a system in which more than half of healthcare financing is in private hands and there is no central administrative agency to monitor the system as a whole. Instead, the types of healthcare services, their geographic distribution, access to these services, and the prices charged by providers develop independently of any preformulated plans. Levels of expenditures cannot be predetermined, and such a system is not conducive to achieving broad social objectives. Nevertheless, the United States has tried some forms of health planning on voluntary or mandated bases, although these efforts have been met with only limited success.

Health Planning Experiments in the United States

Some of the early efforts to control healthcare costs in the United States took the form of voluntary health planning, with the goal of minimizing duplication of services. In the 1930s and 1940s, community-wide voluntary organizations, called hospital councils, were established by hospitals in some of the largest cities. Hospitals agreed to share or consolidate services, or they traded the closing of a service in one hospital for the expansion of another service (Williams, 1995). Voluntary planning worked only on a limited basis and only in instances where participating hospitals could gain an advantage through cooperative planning. Consequently, voluntary planning did little to increase the overall efficiency of the health system (Gottlieb, 1974).

The federal government got involved in health planning after the passage of legislation

Exhibit 12.1 Regulation-Based and Competition-Based Cost-Containment Strategies

Regulation-Based Cost-Containment Strategies

Supply-side controls
Restrictions on capital expenditures (new construction, renovations, and technology diffusion)
Example: Certificate of need
Restrictions on supply of physicians
Example: Entry barriers for foreign medical graduates

Price controls
Artificially determined prices
Examples: Reimbursement formulas
Prospective payment systems
Diagnosis-related groups
Resource utilization groups
Global budgets

Utilization controls
Peer review organizations

Competition-Based Cost-Containment Strategies

Demand-side incentives
Cost sharing
Sharing of premium costs
Deductibles and copayments

Supply-side regulation
Antitrust regulation

Payer-driven competition
Competition among insurers
Competition among providers

Utilization controls
Managed care

---

enacting Medicare and Medicaid in the 1960s. Soon after these programs were established, Congress, recognizing the increasing dollars the federal government was putting into health care, concluded that it had the right to control escalating costs (Williams, 1995). The comprehensive health planning legislation of the mid-1960s mandated the establishment of local and state health planning agencies, which assessed local healthcare needs and advocated for better coordination and distribution of resources. However, these agencies had little or no actual regulatory power and were largely ineffective (Williams, 1995). When their work was evaluated, planned and unplanned areas were found to have the same amount of duplication of facilities and services and their rates of increase in hospital costs were the same (May, 1974).

Certificate-of-Need Statutes

State-enacted statutes of **certificate of need (CON)** represented a legislative attempt to control capital expenditures by health facilities. The CON process required prior approval from a state government agency for the construction of new facilities, expansion of existing facilities, or acquisition of expensive new technology. Approvals were based on the demonstration of a community need for additional services. Although the CON legislation was justified based on the promise of better planning of resources and greater control over increasing expenditures, its adoption proved easier in states that had greater competition among hospitals (Wendling and Werner, 1980). Essentially, this pattern indicated that hospitals supported CON legislation when it was to their own benefit—these hospitals did not want additional capital spending on new construction and equipment by their competitors. CON laws did not seem to lower hospital expenditures on a per patient-day basis.

CON statutes also represented a conservative approach to containing rising hospital costs because they did not address reimbursement and provided no incentives to change utilization behavior among either patients or physicians (Feldstein, 1993). In the case of nursing homes, however, CON regulations have been used to contain Medicaid costs. In the face of a growing demand for nursing home beds, CON regulations have restricted the supply of nursing home beds that otherwise would have been utilized. More recently, the Home and Community-Based Services (HCBS) waiver program—also referred to as 1915(c) waivers—has been used to curtail nursing home utilization and costs. As of 2023, 35 states had established some type of CON program (National Conference of State Legislatures, 2023).

Price Controls

Perhaps the most important effort to control the costs of inpatient hospital care was the conversion of hospital Medicare reimbursement from a cost-plus payment scheme to a prospective payment system (PPS) based on diagnosis-related groups (DRGs) authorized under the Social Security Amendments of 1983. The DRG-based reimbursement significantly reduced growth in inpatient hospital spending but had little effect on total per capita Medicare cost inflation because costs were merely shifted from the inpatient to the outpatient sector (**Figure 12-7**).

Medicare has implemented other price-control measures through multiple reimbursement methods that apply to physicians, home health care, and various inpatient service providers. These programs seem to have been

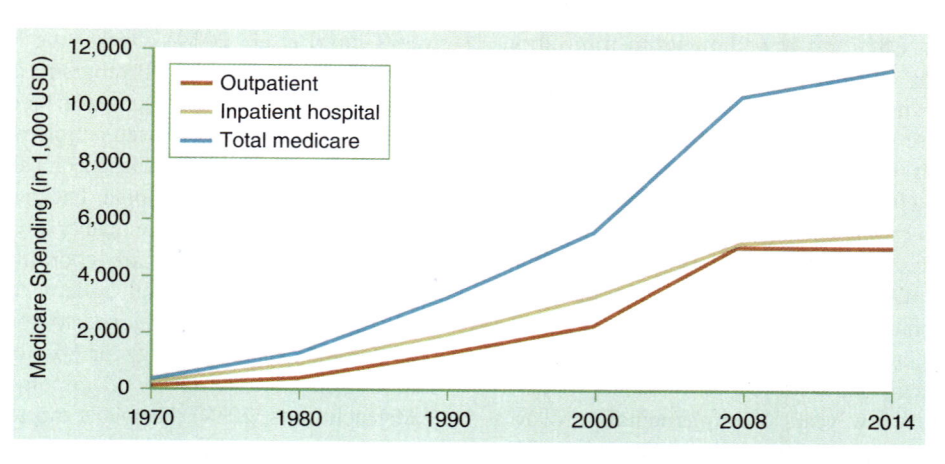

Figure 12-7 Increase in U.S. per capita Medicare spending, 1970–2016 (selected years).
Data from National Center for Health Statistics (NCHS). 2018. Health, United States, 2017. Hyattsville, MD: U.S. Department of Health and Human Services. Table 107.

successful. For example, before the implementation of the resource-based relative value scale (RBRVS) for physician payments, per capita Medicare spending for physician services had increased at an average annual rate of 11.7% between 1980 and 1990. After the introduction of RBRVS, per capita Medicare spending for physician services increased by only 5% annually between 1995 and 2005, based on CMS data.

A 2016 MACPAC brief noted that state Medicaid programs can use relative value units and conversion factors established by Medicare or apply their own conversion factors and update them when appropriate. States have also sought to control their Medicaid expenditures by employing complex formulas that produce arbitrary reimbursement rates and payment ceilings.

Later proposals have aimed to align Medicare payments with quality of care. In 2003, as part of the Medicare Prescription Drug, Improvement, and Modernization Act, the U.S. Congress asked the Institute of Medicine (IOM) to assess the potential for implementing pay-for-performance (P4P) methods in the Medicare program (IOM, 2004). IOM found mixed evidence regarding the effectiveness of P4P payments and noted that unintended adverse consequences of P4P could include decreased access to care, increased disparities in care, and impediments to innovation. On the one hand, IOM concluded that careful monitoring of P4P could minimize these adverse consequences. On the other hand, it argued that if Medicare payment structures were left unchanged, they would pose a barrier to improved quality of care.

Research has not yet shown that P4P significantly improves outcomes or controls costs (Eijkenaar et al., 2013; Kruse et al., 2012; Ryan, 2009; Shih et al., 2014). Over the longer term, gains from improvements made in the first few years of implementation of this payment system tend to fade (Jha et al., 2012; Werner et al., 2011). Also, little evidence supports the contention that hospitals would respond to P4P incentives (Nicholas et al., 2011). On the contrary, if P4P were to result in revenue losses for providers or cost increases for payers, it would have negative repercussions (Kruse et al., 2012).

Despite the controversies over such price controls, the ACA directed CMS to establish a Value-Based Purchasing (VBP) Program for Medicare payments to hospitals. The law also directed CMS to expand VBP to other areas of healthcare delivery, such as home health agencies and skilled nursing facilities (Darden et al., 2023; Cheng et al., 2023; Grabowski et al., 2023). In 2017, the Hospital VBP Program was funded by reducing participating hospitals' base fiscal year (FY) 2017 operating Medicare severity diagnosis-related group (MS-DRG) payments by 2%. Leftover funds were then redistributed to hospitals based on their total performance scores (CMS, 2017). States are also adopting VBP for Medicaid to avoid wasteful spending and to improve population health. Over two-thirds of all Medicaid programs have at least one initiative to improve health outcomes and reduce cost growth (Missouri Foundation for Health, 2019).

The Medicare program is not alone in considering P4P strategies. As of 2019, 25 out of the 40 states with comprehensive risk-based managed care organizations had instituted P4P in their Medicaid managed care quality initiatives (Gifford et al., 2019). One of the largest efforts is the MassHealth P4P program, implemented in 2008 by the Massachusetts Medicaid Program. In 2008, Massachusetts implemented a P4P program for all hospitals, specifically for surgical infection and pneumonia. The program has since expanded to include quality measures related to perinatal care, care coordination, health disparities, safety, and patient experience. The metrics were developed to complement the state's quality strategy for Accountable Care Organizations (ACOs) (Commonwealth of Massachusetts, 2019). Hospitals can receive bonus payments based on their performance metrics for each condition and can be penalized for preventable readmissions.

Researchers did not find a statistically significant improvement in quality after the first two years of MassHealth's program. Similar to the case for P4P in Medicare, evaluation of this program found only a limited effect on quality improvement (Ryan and Blustein, 2011). Experts have raised several potential reasons that P4P programs can have limited results, including the number of financial incentives (Ryan and Blustein, 2011), confusion with reporting and payout requirements, as well as delays in the receipt of bonus payments (Delbanco et al., 2018), and diminishing returns for good quality performance provided (Ryan and Blustein, 2011).

The California Integrated Healthcare Association's (IHA's) statewide Value-Based P4P program, which has been in operation since 2003, is so far the largest and longest-running private-sector P4P experiment in the United States (James, 2012). IHA has worked in partnership with the National Committee for Quality Assurance (NCQA) since the program's inception. The VBP4P program was refined in 2018 when the program name was changed to "Align. Measure. Perform." (AMP). The overall objectives of the AMP program are to drive improvements in clinical quality and patient experience while also controlling healthcare costs and utilization rates (Paula Gallagher. 2021).

When the revised AMP program was launched, it included new compliance requirements intended to make progress on the path towards the AMP objectives by demonstrating performance through reporting specific and uniform quality metric calculations. Organizations participating in the California AMP program receive annual incentive payments for controlling costs and utilization rates measured against benchmarks and that payment is increased or decreased based on the quality metrics scores (Paula Gallagher, 2021). However, despite the investment by healthcare organizations, especially in information technology (IT) adoption and data collection, no "breakthrough quality improvements" were achieved and no evidence of "any savings or moderation in cost trends" was found (Damberg et al., 2009).

Peer Review

The term **peer review** refers to the general process of medical review of utilization and quality when it is carried out directly by or under the supervision of physicians (Wilson and Neuhauser, 1985). To foster application of this concept, the Social Security Amendments of 1972 required the establishment of professional standards review organizations (PSROs). These associations of physicians reviewed professional and institutional services provided under Medicare and Medicaid. The stated purpose of these peer reviews was monitoring and control of both cost and quality. When Congress evaluated the performance of PSROs for their cost-control effectiveness, however, the findings showed that the program had not produced any net savings.

Because of their questionable effectiveness, the PSROs were replaced in 1984 by a new system of peer review organizations (PROs), now called **quality improvement organizations (QIOs)**. QIOs are private organizations composed of practicing physicians and other healthcare professionals in each state who are paid by the CMS under contract to review the care provided to Medicare beneficiaries. To control utilization, QIOs determine whether care is reasonable, necessary, and provided in the most appropriate setting.

Cost Containment: Competitive Approaches

Competition refers to rivalry among sellers for customers (Dranove, 1993). In healthcare delivery, it means that providers of healthcare services try to attract patients who can choose among several different providers. Although competition more commonly refers to price competition, it may also be based on technical quality, amenities, access, or other factors (Dranove, 1993). Because competition is an essential element for the operation of free markets, competitive approaches are also referred to as market-oriented approaches. Competitive strategies fall into four broad categories: demand-side incentives, supply-side regulation, payer-driven price competition, and utilization controls (refer to Exhibit 12-1).

Demand-Side Incentives

The underlying notion of cost sharing is that if consumers pay out of pocket for a larger share of the cost of healthcare services they use, they will consume services more judiciously. In essence, cost sharing encourages consumers to ration their own health care. For example, cost sharing leads people to forgo professional services for minor ailments but not for serious problems (Wong et al., 2001).

Cost sharing—which is now a common feature of almost all health plans—became popular after the Rand Health Insurance Experiment empirically demonstrated the effects of cost sharing. The most comprehensive study of its type, this experiment ran from 1974 through 1981. It enrolled more than 7,000 people into 1 of 14 different health plans, which included a free plan carrying no deductible or copayments and three other plans with varying degrees of cost sharing. The researchers found that cost sharing resulted in lower costs compared to the free plan. Coinsurance rates of 25% resulted in a 19% decline in expenditures because out-of-pocket costs reduced healthcare utilization. Increasing the coinsurance rates resulted in further declines in utilization and expenditures. Another important finding of the Rand Experiment was that lower utilization due to cost-sharing did not affect most measures of health status. People enrolled in the free plan did better in three areas—vision, blood pressure, and dental health—but the average appraised mortality risk for people on the free plan was close to the risk for those whose plans included cost-sharing (Feldstein, 1993).

Supply-Side Regulation

U.S. antitrust laws prohibit business practices that stifle competition among providers. Such practices include price fixing, price discrimination, exclusive contracting arrangements, and mergers that the Department of Justice deems anticompetitive. The purpose of antitrust policy is to ensure competitiveness and, in turn, the efficiency of economic markets. In a competitive environment, MCOs, hospitals, and other healthcare organizations have to be cost-efficient to survive.

Payer-Driven Price Competition

Generally speaking, consumers drive competition. However, healthcare markets are imperfect because patients are not typical consumers in the marketplace—insured patients lack the incentive to be good shoppers. Patients also face information barriers that prevent them from being efficient shoppers. Despite the information boom that characterizes the Internet age, it remains extremely difficult for individual patients or their surrogates to obtain needed information on cost and quality.

Payer-driven competition in the form of managed care has overcome the drawbacks of patient-driven competition (Dranove, 1993). Payer-driven competition occurs at two different points. First, employers shop for the best value in terms of the cost of premiums and the benefits package (competition among insurers). Second, MCOs shop for the best value from providers of health services (competition among providers).

Utilization Controls

Managed care also helps overcome some of the other inefficiencies of an imperfect healthcare market. The utilization controls established by managed care have cut through some of the unnecessary or inappropriate services provided to consumers. Managed care is designed to intervene in the decisions made by care providers to ensure that they deliver only appropriate and necessary services and that they provide these services efficiently. MCOs base this intervention on information that is not generally available to consumers. In this way, MCOs act on the consumer's behalf (Dranove, 1993).

Cost Containment Under Health Reform

To keep costs from spiraling upward in an unsustainable manner, some cost-control measures are essential. The main cost-control measures under the ACA have taken the form of Medicare payment cuts to providers. Initially, it was believed that competition among health plans through the exchanges would also help control the cost of health insurance premiums, yet various mandates imposed on health plans actually increased premium costs. It is not clear whether expansion of the prescription drug benefit under Medicare Part D, by phasing out the coverage gap, is cost neutral. Another major impact on costs comes from the various new taxes imposed under the ACA.

To assess the ACA's impact on healthcare costs is difficult, as it is unclear how the government will report healthcare expenditures. For example, will the government subsidies paid to millions of Americans to purchase health insurance be fully captured as healthcare costs? What about the costs associated with the expansion of the Internal Revenue Service necessary to collect the various taxes and penalties specified by the ACA?

Some advocates of the ACA have asserted that this act would control rising healthcare costs (Kaiser Family Foundation, 2013; Zuckerman and Holahan, 2012). According to the Commonwealth Fund, ACA reforms have contributed to the slowdown in healthcare spending growth by tightening provider payment rates and providing incentives to reduce costs. Under the ACA, Medicare alone was projected to spend $1 trillion less by 2020 (Schoen, 2016).

Access to Care

Access refers to the ability of a person to obtain healthcare services when needed. More broadly, access to care is the ability to obtain needed, affordable, convenient, acceptable, and effective personal health services in a timely manner. It may also refer to whether an individual has a usual source of care (such as a primary-care physician), indicate the ability to use healthcare services (based on availability, convenience, referral, or some other criterion), or reflect the acceptability of particular services (according to an individual's preferences and values). Access has several key implications for health and healthcare delivery:

- Access to medical care is one of the key determinants of health, along with environment, lifestyle, and heredity factors.
- Access is a significant benchmark in assessing the effectiveness of the medical-care delivery system. For example, access can be used to evaluate national trends against specific goals, such as those proposed in *Healthy People 2010, 2020,* and *2030.*
- Measures of access reflect whether the delivery of healthcare is equitable.
- Access is linked to quality of care and the efficient use of needed services.

Framework of Access

The conceptualization of access to care can be traced to Andersen (1968) and was later refined by Aday and Andersen (1975) and Aday and colleagues (1980). Andersen (1968) believed that, in addition to need, predisposing and enabling conditions prompt some people to use more medical services than others. Predisposing conditions include an individual's sociodemographic characteristics, such as age, sex, education, marital status, family size, race and ethnicity, and religious preference. These factors indicate a person's propensity to use medical care. For example, holding everything else constant, older adults are more likely to use medical care than young people. Enabling conditions include income, socioeconomic status, price of medical services, financing of medical services, and occupation. These factors focus on the individual's means, which support that person's ability to use medical care. For example, holding everything else constant, individuals with high incomes are more likely to use medical care than individuals with low incomes, particularly in countries that do not provide national health insurance.

The distinction between predisposing and enabling conditions can be applied to assess the equity of a healthcare system (Aday et al., 1993). To the extent that significant differences in medical-care utilization can be explained by need and certain predisposing characteristics (e.g., age, gender), the delivery of medical care is considered equitable. When enabling characteristics create significant differences in medical-care utilization, the delivery of medical care is considered inequitable.

This access to care model has been expanded to include characteristics of health policy and the healthcare delivery system (Aday et al., 1980). Examples of health policy include major healthcare financing initiatives (Medicare, Medicaid, the Children's Health Insurance Program [CHIP], and the ACA) and organization of health services delivery (Medicaid managed care, community health centers, ACO). Characteristics of the healthcare delivery system include availability (volume and distribution of services) and organization (mechanisms of entry into and movement within the system). Both health policy and the healthcare delivery system are aggregate components, in contrast to the individual components of predisposing, enabling, and need characteristics. The expanded access to care model recognizes the importance of systemic and structural barriers to access and is useful in comparing access to care among countries with different health policies and healthcare delivery systems.

Because of managed care's dominance in U.S. healthcare delivery, the revised version of the access framework was updated by Docteur and colleagues (1996) (**Figure 12-8**). According to this model, access to care is a two-stage process in a managed care environment. In the first stage, individuals select among the health plans available to them, with those choices being constrained by structural, financial, and personal characteristics. In the second stage, individuals seek medical care while being constrained by both plan-specific and nonplan factors. The access to care framework accounts for people enrolling and staying with the plan or disenrolling, and it links actual utilization with clinical and policy outcomes. Although comprehensive models are useful in conceptualizing access to care, they are difficult to test because of the range of variables and the differing levels of analysis they require.

Dimensions of Access

Penchansky and Thomas (1981) described access to care as consisting of five dimensions: availability, accessibility, accommodation, affordability, and acceptability. *Availability* refers to the fit between service capacity and individuals' requirements. Availability-related issues include whether primary and preventive services are available to patients; whether enabling services, such as transportation, language, and social services, are made available by the provider; whether the health plan has sufficient specialists to care for patients' needs; and whether access to primary-care services is provided 24 hours a day, 7 days a week.

Accessibility refers to the fit between the locations of providers and patients.

Access to Care 541

Determinants of Plan Selection

Structural
- Available plan choices and characteristic reputation
- Associated characteristics of provider networks/reputation
- Extent/nature of active marketing and information available on choices/plan characteristics
- Market characteristics (e.g., percentage HMO penetration, managed care maturity)

Financial
- Beneficiary premium/supplemental benefits
- Beneficiary preexisting supplemental coverage through self/spouse and any external subsidy
- Income and liquid financial needs

Personal
- Beneficiary knowledge/assumptions about managed care and requirements
- Previous experience with managed care and existing attitudes
- Existing physician relationship/care-seeking behavior
- Demographics and socioeconomic characteristics
- Health/disability status and any special needs
- Other special needs (e.g., geographic mobility)

Associated Health Plan Delivery System
- Hours and location of service
- Provider micro/network size/walking time
- Gatekeeper and referral rules
- Utilization management and quality oversight
- Active outreach/education of new, existing members
- Transportation/cultural acceptability
- Administrative accessibility

Determinants Of Continuity Of Enrollment
- Patient satisfaction
- Provider satisfaction/stability of network turnover
- Stability of plan/plan participation
- Stability of service area/patient location
- Stability of health plan choices
- Changing patient needs and status
- Death

Health plan choice/environment

Use of services
- Visits
- Procedures

Mediators
- Appropriateness
- Efficiency of treatment
- Quality of providers
- Patient adherence
- Timeliness of initial treatment re: fitness
- Complicating patient condition/factors
- Continuity of care

Clinical And Policy Outcomes

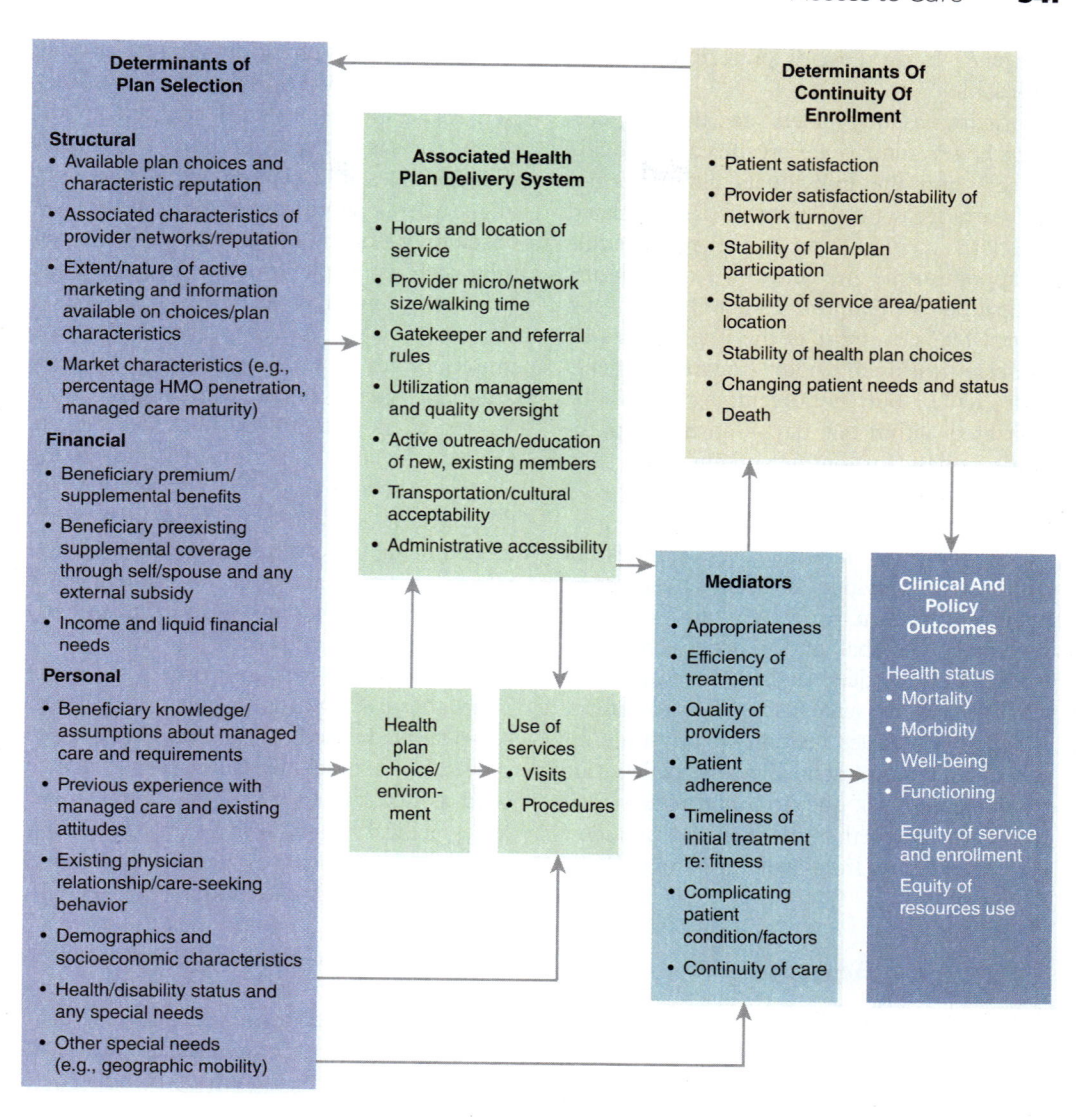

Health status
- Mortality
- Morbidity
- Well-being
- Functioning

Equity of service and enrollment

Equity of resources use

Figure 12-8 Framework for access in the managed care context.

Reproduced from Docteur, E. R., et al. 1996. Shifting the paradigm: monitoring access in Medicare managed care. *Health Care Financing Review* 17, no. 4: 5–21.

Individuals with different enabling conditions (e.g., transportation) are likely to have different perceptions of accessibility. Accessibility-related issues include convenience (Can the provider be reached by public or private transportation?), design (Is the provider site designed for convenient use by older adults or patients with disabilities?), and payment options (Will the provider accept patients regardless of payment source [e.g., Medicare, Medicaid]?).

Affordability refers to individuals' ability to pay. Even individuals with insurance often have to consider deductibles and copayments prior to utilization. Affordability-related questions include: Are insurance premiums too high? Are deductibles and copayments reasonable for the services covered under the plan? Is the cost of prescription drugs affordable?

Accommodation refers to the fit between how resources are organized to provide services and the individual's ability to use the arrangement. Accommodation-related questions include: Can a patient schedule an appointment? Are scheduled office hours compatible with most patients' work and way of life? Can most of the urgent cases be addressed within one hour? Can most patients with acute, but nonurgent, problems be addressed within one day? Can most appropriate requests for routine appointments, such as preventive exams, be met within one week? Does the plan permit walk-in services?

Acceptability reflects the attitudes of patients and providers and refers to the compatibility between patients' attitudes toward providers' personal and practice characteristics and providers' attitudes toward their clients' personal characteristics and values. Acceptability issues include waiting time for scheduled appointments; whether patients are encouraged to ask questions and review their records; and whether patients and providers are accepted regardless of race, religion, or ethnic origin.

Types of Access

Andersen (1997) described four main types of access: potential access, realized access, equitable or inequitable access, and effective and efficient access. *Potential access* refers to both healthcare system characteristics and enabling characteristics. Examples of healthcare system characteristics include capacity (e.g., physician–population ratio), organization (e.g., managed care penetration), and financing mechanisms (e.g., health insurance coverage). Enabling characteristics include personal (e.g., income) and community resources (e.g., public transportation).

Realized access refers to the type, site, and purpose of health services (Aday, 1993). The type of utilization refers to the category of services rendered: physician, dentist, or other practitioner; hospital or long-term care admission; prescriptions; medical equipment; and so on. The site of utilization refers to the place where services are received (e.g., inpatient setting, such as short-stay hospital, psychiatric hospital, or nursing home; or ambulatory setting, such as hospital outpatient department, emergency department (ED), physician's office, staff-model HMO, public health clinic, community health center, freestanding emergency center, or patient's home). The purpose of utilization refers to the reason that medical care was sought: for health maintenance in the absence of symptoms (primary prevention), for the diagnosis or treatment of illness to return to well-being (secondary prevention or illness related), or for rehabilitation or maintenance in the case of a chronic health problem (tertiary prevention or custodial care).

Equitable access refers to the distribution of healthcare services according to the patient's self-perceived need (e.g., symptoms, pain, physical and functional status) or evaluated need as determined by a health professional (e.g., medical history, test results). *Inequitable access* refers to services distributed according to enabling characteristics (e.g., income, insurance status).

Effective and efficient access links realized access to health outcomes (IOM, 1993). For example, does adequate prenatal care lead to successful birth outcomes as measured by birth weight? Is immunization related to reduction of vaccine-preventable childhood diseases, such as diphtheria, measles, mumps, pertussis, polio, rubella, and tetanus? Are preventive services related to the early detection and diagnosis of treatable diseases? The concepts of effectiveness and efficiency link access to quality of care.

Measurement of Access

Using the conceptual models, access can be measured at three different levels: individual, health plan, and delivery system. Access indicators at the individual level include (1) measures of medical services utilization relative to enabling and predisposing factors, while controlling for need for care (Aday and Andersen, 1975), and (2) the patient's assessment of the interaction with the provider. Examples include differences in physician visits by race/ethnicity, gender, age, income, and insurance. Patients' perceived level of access is closely related to patient satisfaction with care and is part of the access to care framework (Aday et al., 1984).

At the health plan level, there are three types of indicators:

- Plan characteristics that affect enrollment, such as the costs of premiums, deductibles, copayments, coverage for preventive care, authorization of new and expensive procedures, physician referral incentives, and out-of-plan use
- Plan practices that affect access, such as travel time to a usual source of care and waiting time to consult a physician (accessibility); whether an appointment is necessary, hours of operation, language, and other enabling services (accommodation); and the content of provider–patient encounters, including tests ordered and done, and referral to specialists (contact)
- Plan quality as measured by the Healthcare Effectiveness Data and Information Set (HEDIS) and patient satisfaction surveys

Indicators of access at the level of the healthcare delivery system comprise ecological measures that affect populations rather than individuals. System indicators help researchers study access in an environmental context—that is, how context affects the access of persons and groups. Examples of system access indicators include health policies or programs related to access, physician–population ratios, hospital beds per 1,000 population, percentage of population with insurance coverage, median household income, state-per-capita spending on welfare and preventive care, and percentage of population without access to primary-care physicians.

Population-based surveys supported by federal statistical agencies are the major sources of data for conducting access-to-care analyses. Large national surveys, such as the National Health Interview Survey, the Medical Expenditure Panel Survey (MEPS), and the Community Tracking Survey, are the major data sources used to monitor access trends and other issues of interest. Other well-known national surveys include the Current Population Survey, the National Hospital Discharge Survey, the Ambulatory Medical Care Survey, the National Nursing Home Survey, and the National Home and Hospice Care Survey. In addition, the federal government periodically collects data on special topics, such as human immunodeficiency virus (HIV)/acquired immunodeficiency syndrome (AIDS); mental health; healthcare utilization by veterans, military staff, and their dependents; patient satisfaction; and community health centers.

States, professional associations, and research institutions also regularly collect data on healthcare topics of interest to them. Examples of state-based initiatives include state health services utilization data (all-payer hospital discharge data systems), state managed care data (managed care encounter data), and state Medicaid enrollee satisfaction data (Medicaid enrollee satisfaction surveys). Examples of association-based initiatives include data on physicians (the American Medical Association's Physician Masterfile and the Periodic Survey of Physicians, which was first conducted in 1969 and is still performed today) and hospitals (the American Hospital Association's Annual Survey of Hospitals, which was first conducted in 1946 and continues to be performed today). Examples of research institution-based initiatives include collection of data on the healthcare delivery system (Center for Evaluative Clinical Sciences: Dartmouth Atlas of Health Care in the United States), women's health (Kaiser Family Foundation:

Women's Health Survey), minority health (Commonwealth Fund: Minority Health Survey), family health (Urban Institute: National Survey of America's Families), health insurance (Commonwealth Fund: Biennial Health Insurance Survey), and access to care (Robert Wood Johnson Foundation [RWJF]: National Access Surveys).

Current Status of Access

In the United States, barriers to access still exist at both the individual and system levels. Many of these barriers are experienced by vulnerable population groups. Access is best predicted by race, income, and occupation, and these three factors are interrelated: That is, people belonging to minority groups tend to be of low socioeconomic status, not well educated, and more likely to work in jobs that pose greater health risks.

Table 12-3 and **Table 12-4** summarize physician contacts by categories of age, sex, race, income, and geographic location (also see **Figure 12-9** for selected updates). **Table 12-5** summarizes dental visits (also see **Figure 12-10** and **12-11** for selected updates). However, these results are not adjusted for health need, so they are not true indicators of access. Instead, they provide utilization measures as a proxy for access.

The Affordable Care Act and Access to Care

Overall insurance coverage and access to health care have increased under the ACA. For example, the proportion of the U.S. population without a regular source of care decreased from 29.8% in 2013 to 26% in 2014 (Karpman et al., 2015). By March 2015, 73.9% of patients who are older adults reported having a usual source of care, an increase of 3.4% from September 2013 (Shartzer et al., 2016). This change was even more pronounced among low-income adults targeted by the Medicaid expansion: The proportion with a usual source of care increased by 5.2 percentage points in this population (Shartzer et al., 2016). Approximately 87.6% of all individuals in the United States currently have a usual source of care (NCHS, 2022).

The ACA also led to a significant decline in the proportion of adults who reported difficulty finding a doctor or other provider

Table 12-3 Visits to Office-Based Physicians, 2015

Characteristic	Number of Visits (Millions)	Percentage Distribution	Visits per 100 Persons/Year
All visits	990.8	100.0	297
Age			
Younger than 18 years	149.6	15.1	203
18–44 years	230.5	23.3	204
45–64 years	305.1	30.8	366
65–74 years	159.8	16.1	585
75 years and older	145.9	14.7	762

Data from National Center for Health Statistics (NCHS). 2018. *Health, United States, 2017*. Hyattsville, MD: U.S. Department of Health and Human Services. Table 76.

Table 12-4 Number of Healthcare Visits According to Selected Patient Characteristics, 2017

Characteristic	None	1–3 Visits	4–9 Visits	≥ 10 Visits
Total	14.0%	50.4%	23.2%	12.4%
Sex				
Male	17.6%	51.9%	20.9%	9.7%
Female	10.5%	49.0%	25.6%	15.0%
Race				
White	13.9%	49.2%	24.0%	12.9%
Black	13.9%	53.5%	21.4%	11.3%
Income as a Percentage of the Federal Poverty Level				
Below 100%	17.1%	43.3%	23.2%	16.4%
Characteristic	None	1–3 Visits	4–9 Visits	≥ 10 Visits
100–199%	17.7%	46.7%	22.2%	13.4%
200–399%	15.6%	50.5%	22.3%	11.5%
400% or more	10.0%	53.8%	24.5%	11.7%
Geographic Region				
Northeast	10.2%	51.8%	24.2%	13.8%
Midwest	13.1%	51.8%	22.8%	12.2%
South	15.7%	49.4%	23.2%	11.7%
West	15.0%	49.7%	22.8%	12.5%
Location of Residence				
Within metropolitan statistical area	13.5%	50.9%	23.3%	12.3%
Outside metropolitan statistical area	17.4%	46.6%	22.8%	13.2%

Data from National Center for Health Statistics (NCHS). 2019. *Health, United States, 2018*. Hyattsville, MD: U.S. Department of Health and Human Services. Table 30.

(Karpman et al., 2015). Fewer people are reporting problems with medical bills and financial barriers to obtaining care (Collins et al., 2015). In addition, the ACA has been associated with improved trends in self-reported coverage and access to primary care (Courtemanche et al., 2018). Thus, compared to pre-ACA trends, the proportions of Americans reporting that they lack a personal physician, lack easy access to medicine, and are unable to afford care have all decreased significantly (Sommers et al., 2015).

Despite the welcome progress made, gaps persist in regard to access to and affordability of health care, particularly for low-income adults. Moreover, the newly insured face challenges such as changing their care-seeking patterns

546 Chapter 12 Cost, Access, and Quality

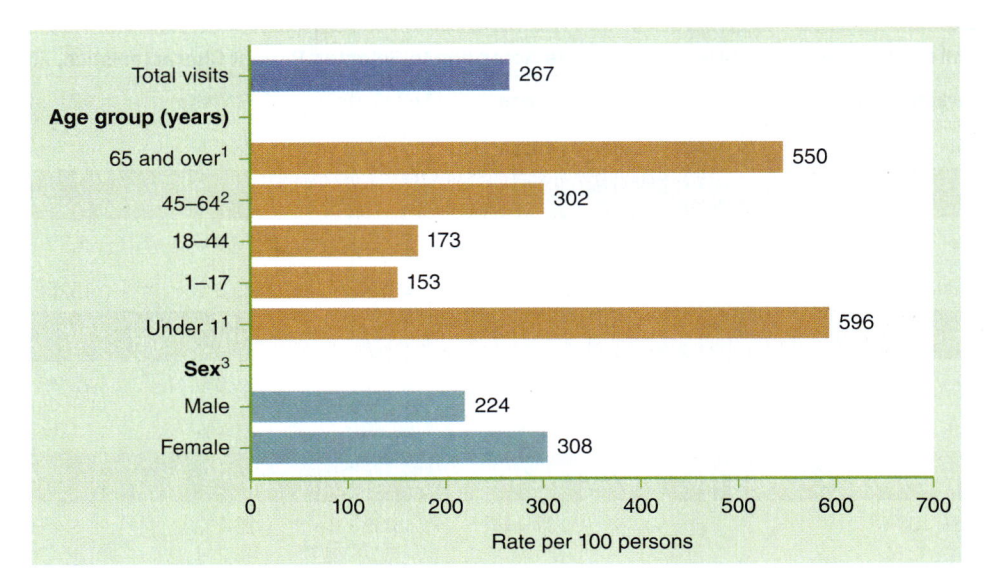

Figure 12-9 Visit rates, by selected demographics, United States, 2018.

Characteristic	Rate per 100 persons
Total visits	267
Age group (years)	
65 and over[1]	550
45–64[2]	302
18–44	173
1–17	153
Under 1[1]	596
Sex[3]	
Male	224
Female	308

Reproduced from Ashman, J. J., Rui, P., & Okeyode, T. (2021). Characteristics of office-based physician visits, 2018. https://www.cdc.gov/nchs/data/databriefs/db408-H.pdf

Table 12-5 Dental Visits in the Past Year Among Persons 18–64 Years of Age, 2017

Characteristic	Percentage of Population
All persons	64.0
Income as a Percentage of the Federal Poverty Level	
Below 100%	48.2
100–199%	47.4
200–399%	59.9
400% or more	77.6
Race and Hispanic Origin	
White, non-Hispanic	68.1
Black, non-Hispanic	59.9
Hispanic	54.0
Sex	
Male	61.1
Female	66.8

Data from National Center for Health Statistics. 2019. *Health, United States, 2018*. Hyattsville, MD: U.S. Department of Health and Human Services. Table 37.

The Affordable Care Act and Access to Care

[Bar chart showing percentage of adults aged 18–64 with a dental visit in the past 12 months, by survey year and sex: United States, 2019 and 2020.

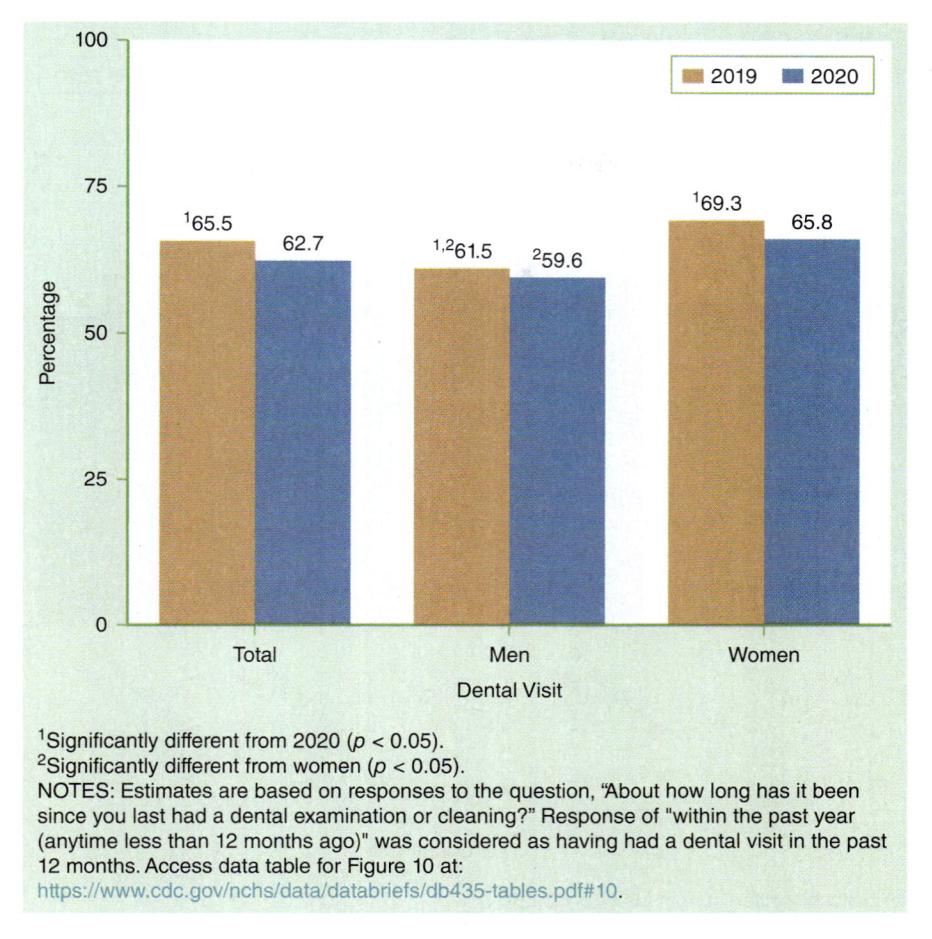

- Total: 2019 = 65.5[1], 2020 = 62.7
- Men: 2019 = 61.5[1,2], 2020 = 59.6[2]
- Women: 2019 = 69.3[1], 2020 = 65.8]

[1]Significantly different from 2020 ($p < 0.05$).
[2]Significantly different from women ($p < 0.05$).
NOTES: Estimates are based on responses to the question, "About how long has it been since you last had a dental examination or cleaning?" Response of "within the past year (anytime less than 12 months ago)" was considered as having had a dental visit in the past 12 months. Access data table for Figure 10 at:
https://www.cdc.gov/nchs/data/databriefs/db435-tables.pdf#10.

Figure 12-10 Percentage of adults aged 18-64 with a dental visit in the past 12 months, by survey year and sex: United States, 2019 and 2020.
Reproduced from Cha, A. E., & Cohen, R. A. (2022). Dental care utilization among adults aged 18-64: United States, 2019 and 2020. https://www.cdc.gov/nchs/data/databriefs/db435.pdf

and behaviors, and some may run into provider capacity issues. More than 25% of people who are not older adults report having no source of usual care; among those who have reported access problems, more than one-third could not find a doctor who would treat them; and almost 70% delayed care because they could not get an appointment. These adults were more likely to be younger, male, Hispanic, and low income compared to those persons who had a usual source of care (Shartzer et al., 2016).

The ACA also improved access to certain services for people who already had health insurance coverage. The federal HHS Assistant Secretary for Planning and Evaluation (ASPE) estimated that in 2020, approximately 151.6 million people (58 million women, 57 million men, and 37 million children) currently are enrolled in non-grandfathered private health insurance plans that cover preventive services (KFF, 2023). Under the ACA, preventive services covered without cost sharing have expanded to include more services, such as wellness visits, contraception, and breastfeeding comprehensive support and counseling.

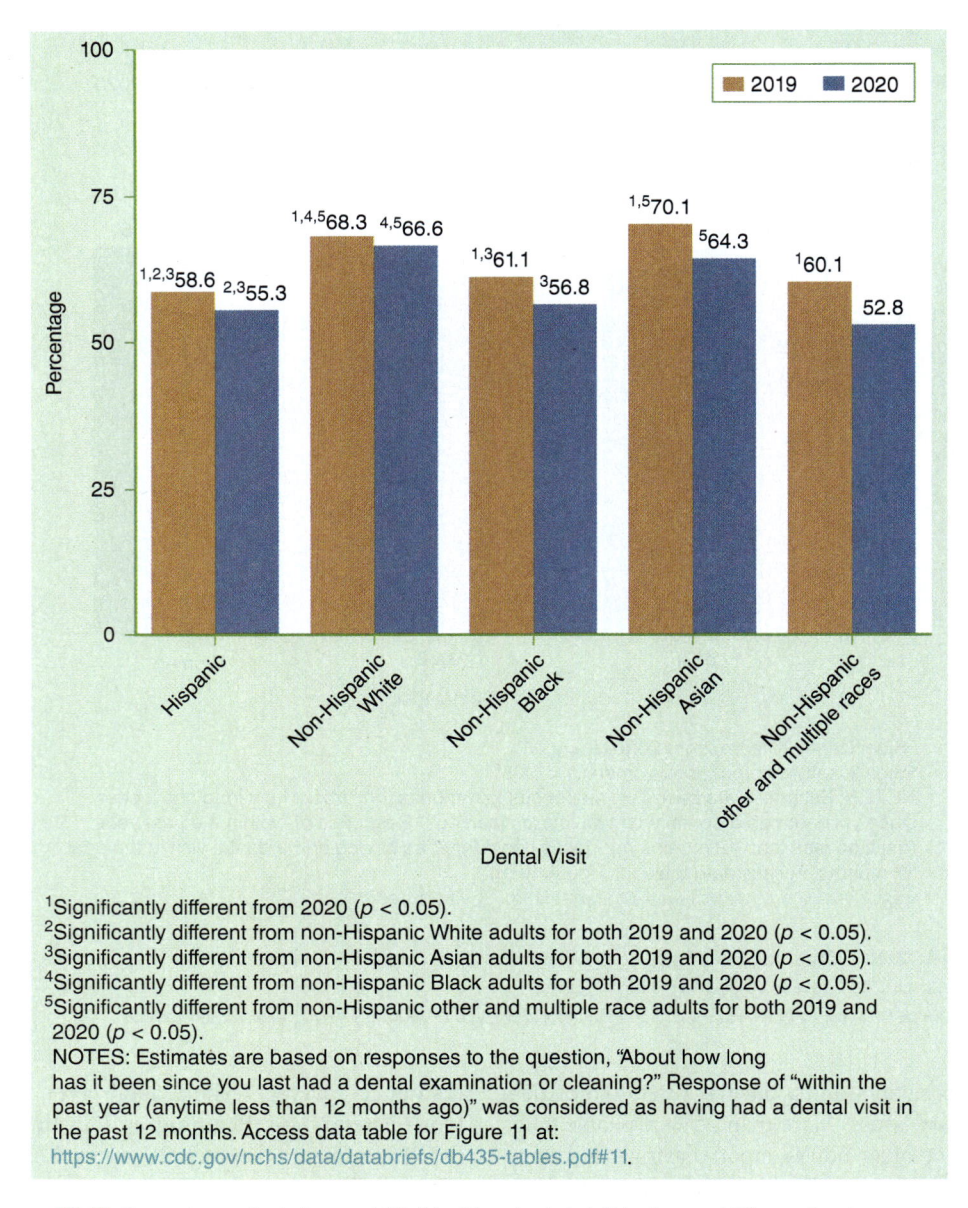

Figure 12-11 Percentage of adults aged 18-64 with a dental visit in the past 12 months, by survey year and race and ethnicity: United States, 2019 and 2020.

[1] Significantly different from 2020 ($p < 0.05$).
[2] Significantly different from non-Hispanic White adults for both 2019 and 2020 ($p < 0.05$).
[3] Significantly different from non-Hispanic Asian adults for both 2019 and 2020 ($p < 0.05$).
[4] Significantly different from non-Hispanic Black adults for both 2019 and 2020 ($p < 0.05$).
[5] Significantly different from non-Hispanic other and multiple race adults for both 2019 and 2020 ($p < 0.05$).

NOTES: Estimates are based on responses to the question, "About how long has it been since you last had a dental examination or cleaning?" Response of "within the past year (anytime less than 12 months ago)" was considered as having had a dental visit in the past 12 months. Access data table for Figure 11 at: https://www.cdc.gov/nchs/data/databriefs/db435-tables.pdf#11.

Group	2019	2020
Hispanic	58.6 [1,2,3]	55.3 [2,3]
Non-Hispanic White	68.3 [1,4,5]	66.6 [4,5]
Non-Hispanic Black	61.1 [1,3]	56.8 [3]
Non-Hispanic Asian	70.1 [1,5]	64.3 [5]
Non-Hispanic other and multiple races	60.1 [1]	52.8

Reproduced from Cha, A. E., & Cohen, R. A. (2022). Dental care utilization among adults aged 18-64: United States, 2019 and 2020. https://www.cdc.gov/nchs/data/databriefs/db435.pdf

Telemedicine and Access

As one component of improving access to care, technological services such as telehealth are becoming more widely utilized as part of everyday care. Telehealth, broadly defined, refers to "the use of electronic information and telecommunication technologies to support long-distance clinical health care, patient and professional health-related education, public health, and health administration" (HRSA, 2019). Fully embracing what telehealth has to offer not only allows for improvements in patient access to care but also creates increased capacity for providers to treat more patients.

Telehealth is an enormous asset in terms of access and efficiency. It increases the ease of communication between patient and provider by allowing for "virtual visits" and remote consultations (Weigel et al., 2020). Additional functions include remote patient monitoring and health education (National Conference of State Legislatures, 2019). These abilities increase the convenience of care provision on the patient side by reducing travel time and the likelihood of conflict with work or other obligations. Individuals who previously found it difficult to access care due to geographic concerns can also more easily access medical care when needed. The ability of telehealth to broaden access to care was demonstrated in a study conducted by Ashwood et al. (2017), which examined utilization patterns of a California HMO. They found that approximately 88% of the telehealth visits analyzed represented new utilization, indicating that the vast majority of patients had not previously sought out care. These results indicate telehealth's ability to expand access to care, although—as noted in the study—health spending may subsequently rise as well.

On the provider side, telehealth can make care delivery more productive by facilitating coordination and consultation with other providers, thereby streamlining the process of care and reducing the likelihood of redundancy (Young and Nesbitt, 2016). As evidence of its advantages, a study by Thielke and King (2020) examined electronic consultation platforms (eConsult) that facilitate direct communication between primary-care clinicians and specialists. They found that use of such a platform was safe and associated with improved access to specialty care, higher efficiency, higher patient and clinician satisfaction, and lower cost. Increased deployment of such technologies could help remediate the long-standing issues with efficiency and access that afflict the U.S. healthcare system.

Mann et al. (2020) provided data on the feasibility and impact of video-enabled telemedicine use among patients and providers and its impact on urgent and nonurgent healthcare delivery from one large health system (NYU Langone Health) during COVID-19. Between March 2nd and April 14th 2020, telemedicine visits increased from 102.4 daily to 801.6 daily. There was also a reported 683% increase in urgent care after the system-wide expansion of virtual urgent care staff in response to COVID-19 (Mann et al., 2020). Telemedicine usage was highest by patients 20 to 44 years of age, particularly for urgent care (Mann et al., 2020).

Patients of all ages have quickly become used to sharing biometric data via their patient portal and answering screeners on their phones before their video visits (Mann et al., 2020). Pregnant individuals with hyperglycemia or hypertension now routinely sync their home monitoring devices to their providers through the EHR and are having expedited postpartum hospital stays enabled by telemedicine and remote monitoring (Mann et al., 2020).

To expand the use of telehealth, however, many concerns must be addressed to ensure that its implementation can be carried out successfully. One of the biggest concerns is the issue of reimbursement. Telehealth reimbursement is governed by a complex network of regulations stemming from the federal government, states, and private payers. These regulations can make the issue of who or what gets covered confusing for both patients and providers. Telehealth coverage has traditionally varied across payers and may be contingent on how service is delivered, where it is being delivered, and to whom it is delivered (Weigel et al., 2020). Although the federal government and many states and private payers relaxed their regulations to expand telehealth reimbursement during the COVID-19 pandemic, whether these temporary relaxations will translate into long-term policies remains an issue (Weigel et al., 2020).

Beyond reimbursement concerns, the actual implementation of telehealth services presents challenges, including high start-up costs and the need to reconfigure workflows (Weigel et al., 2020). Introducing this new method of care also necessitates that clinicians, nurses, and all other relevant workers undergo training on how to use the new technologies smoothly and securely (Weigel et al., 2020). Privacy and Health Insurance Portability and Accountability Act (HIPAA)–related concerns must be addressed as well, considering that information may not be as secure when transferred over third-party platforms (Weigel et al., 2020). On the patient side, concerns with using telehealth may encompass issues pertaining to quality, necessitating the need to consider safeguards to ensure that the quality of care delivered is on par with the quality that would be delivered via an in-person visit.

The aforementioned concerns represent only a few of the many challenges that must be considered in expanding telehealth's role in U.S. healthcare systems. Although telehealth has great potential to expand access and increase capacity, many hurdles must be overcome that may make providers less willing to make the transition. The COVID-19 pandemic, however, has shown that telehealth is no longer a form of care delivery that should be ignored. As we continue to seek out ways to improve equity in access and efficiency, telehealth should be considered as one method to help close that gap.

Electronic Health Records and Access

The digitization of health records improves information sharing among healthcare providers, leading to more coordinated and efficient care (Acholonu & Raphael, 2022). Access to the EHR can facilitate shared clinical decision-making and improved communication with patients, families, and among healthcare providers (Acholonu & Raphael, 2022).

EHRs have a variety of applications in the healthcare system in clinical care, administration, clinical research, and finance (Tebeje & Klein, 2021). Judson et al. (2020) deployed a digital self-triage and self-scheduling tool with coronavirus symptom checker prepared from an EHR. The tool was used by all primary-care patients in a large academic health system at the University of California, San Francisco (UCSF), to address the COVID-19 pandemic (Judson et al., 2020). The tool has high sensitivity (87.5%) for identifying the emergency-level illness of COVID-19 and the high specificity (89.5%) to suggest self-care and minimize the time of triage (Judson et al., 2020).

Robotics and Health Care

Robots are being utilized in healthcare settings for tasks such as surgery, rehabilitation, and medication delivery (Kyrarini et al., 2021). Rehabilitation robots are a special robot type designed primarily for aiding humans with physical impairments during the process of rehabilitation (Kyrarini et al., 2021). Recently, the industry has shown a growing interest in developing robots to assist nurses in hospitals and clinics (Kyrarini et al., 2021). The robotic nursing assistants are designed to function under the direct control of nurses (Kyrarini et al., 2021). A robotic nursing assistant will act as a teammate, helping nurses by performing non-critical tasks, such as fetching supplies, giving nurses more time to focus on critical tasks, such as caring for patients (Kyrarini et al., 2021). One example is Moxi developed by Diligent Robotics, which retrieves and brings supplies to hospital rooms and nursing stations, delivers samples to laboratories, and removes soiled linen bags (Kyrarini et al., 2021). Moxi is able to navigate fully autonomously and safely by avoiding static and dynamic obstacles (Kyrarini et al., 2021). The trials at the Texas hospitals showed that Moxi was accepted not only by the nurses and the clinical staff but also by the patients and their families (Kyrarini et al., 2021).

Quality of Care

One reason the pursuit of quality in health care has trailed behind the emphasis on cost and access is the difficulty of defining and measuring quality. Since the 1990s, healthcare cost inflation has slowed after several years of rapidly rising. Intuitively, cost control may negatively impact quality. In spite of the progress made, there is still a long road ahead in deciding what constitutes good quality in medical care, how to ensure it for patients, and how to reward providers and health plans whose outcomes indicate successes in quality improvement. One challenge in achieving this goal is that patients, providers, and payers all define quality differently, which translates into different expectations of the healthcare delivery system and, in turn, differing evaluations of its quality (McGlynn, 1997).

Quality measures are defined by the United States Centers for Medicare & Medicaid Services (CMS) as "tools that help us measure or quantify healthcare processes, outcomes, patient perceptions, and organizational structure and/or systems that are associated with the ability to provide high-quality health care and/or that relate to one or more quality goals for health care" (Centers for Medicare & Medicaid Services, 2023).

The IOM has defined **quality** as "the degree to which health services for individuals and populations increase the likelihood of desired health outcomes and are consistent with current professional knowledge" (McGlynn, 1997). This definition has several implications:

- Quality performance occurs on a continuum, theoretically ranging from unacceptable to excellent.
- The focus is on services provided by the healthcare delivery system, as opposed to individual behaviors.
- Quality may be evaluated from the perspective of individuals and populations or communities.
- The emphasis is on desired health outcomes, and scientific research must identify the services that improve health outcomes.

For example, Blum's model of health and wellness clearly points to more significant factors—other than medical care—in determining the health and well-being of individuals and populations. Therefore, more healthcare expenditures will not necessarily produce better health, and high-quality care must also be cost-effective. The observation that most medical care is delivered at the flat of the curve clearly points to a greater need to incorporate the cost of care into the assessment of quality.

Dimensions of Quality

There are different types of quality measures, and they are usually categorized into four categories: process, outcome, structural, and balancing measures (Centers for Medicare & Medicaid Services, 2023).

Process measures reflect compliance with actions implemented to achieve the goals of a QI project (Jazieh, 2020). For example, administering thrombolytic therapy within 90 minutes from onset of symptoms or giving aspirin before arriving at the hospital are processes that can be measured within the scope of a QI project for acute MI (Jazieh, 2020).

Outcome measures are the patient's health status. As such, these measures are usually the most pertinent (Jazieh, 2020). Examples of outcome measures include post-MI 30-day mortality, pre-hospital mortality, or incidence of severe chronic heart failure (Jazieh, 2020).

Structural measures reflect the capacity of the organization, including systems and processes (e.g., number of board-certified cardiologists, patient-to-emergency nurse ratio, or availability of cardiac catheterization laboratory 24 hours a day) (Jazieh, 2020).

Balancing measures refer to the consequences of implementing a QI project that were not necessarily intended (Jazieh, 2020). These consequences can have a negative impact, such as staff overload, dissatisfaction, or additional financial cost, or have a positive impact, such as cost savings or improved patient satisfaction (Jazieh, 2020).

Quality may also be viewed from both micro and macro perspectives. The micro view focuses on services at the point of delivery and their subsequent effects. It is associated with the performance of individual caregivers and healthcare organizations. In contrast, the macro view assesses quality from the standpoint of populations. It reflects the performance of the entire healthcare delivery system by evaluating indicators such as life expectancy, mortality rates, incidence and prevalence of certain health conditions, and so on.

Micro View

The micro dimension of healthcare quality encompasses the clinical aspects of care delivery, the interpersonal aspects of care delivery, and quality of life.

Clinical Aspects

Clinical aspects of care deal with technical quality, such as the facilities where care is delivered, the qualifications and skills of caregivers, the processes and interventions used, the cost-efficiency of care, and the results or effects on patients' health.

One example of lack of clinical quality is medical errors. According to the IOM (2000), 44,000 to 98,000 patients die in U.S. hospitals each year because of medical errors. A 2016 study suggested that medical errors are the third leading cause of death in the United States, behind heart disease and cancer (Makary and Daniel, 2016). The Agency for Healthcare Research and Quality (AHRQ, 2000) has identified four types of medical errors:

- Medication errors, or adverse drug events (ADEs), are errors in prescribing and administering medicines to patients.
- Surgical errors are errors in performing surgical operations.
- Diagnostic inaccuracies may lead to incorrect treatment or unnecessary testing.
- Systemic factors, such as organization of healthcare delivery and distribution of resources, may contribute to preventable adverse events.

Interpersonal Aspects

When quality is viewed from the patient's perspective, interpersonal aspects of care become essential. Patients lack technical expertise, so they often judge the quality of technical care indirectly based on their perceptions of the practitioner's interest, concern, and demeanor during clinical encounters (Donabedian, 1985). Interpersonal relations and satisfaction become even more important when placed within the holistic context of healthcare delivery. Positive interactions between patients and practitioners are major contributors to treatment success through greater patient compliance and return for care (Svarstad, 1986). Expressions of love, hope, and compassion can enhance the healing effects of medical treatments.

Interpersonal aspects of quality are also important from the standpoint of organizational management. Consumers—that is, patients and their surrogates—gain lasting impressions of organizational quality from the way they are treated by an organization's employees. Such employee-customer interactions include encounters not just with the direct caregivers but also with a variety of other employees associated with the healthcare organization, such as receptionists, cafeteria workers, housekeeping employees, and billing clerks.

To measure interpersonal aspects of quality, patient satisfaction surveys have been widely used by various types of healthcare organizations. Ratings by consumers provide the most appropriate method for evaluating interpersonal quality (McGlynn and Brook, 1996). Satisfaction surveys have been used to give physicians feedback on important dimensions of interpersonal communication and service quality.

Quality of Life

The concept of quality of life has drawn greater attention in recent years because patients with chronic and debilitating diseases are now living longer, albeit in a declining state of health. Chronic problems often impose serious limitations on patients' functional status (physical, social, and mental functioning), access to community resources and opportunities, and sense of well-being (Lehman, 1995).

In a composite sense, during or subsequent to disease, a person's own perception of health, ability to function, role limitations stemming from physical or emotional problems, and personal happiness are referred to as **health-related quality of life (HRQL)**. General HRQL refers to the essential or common components of overall well-being that are more broadly applicable to almost everyone. Disease-specific HRQL focuses entirely on impairments that are caused by a specific disorder and the effects and side effects of treatments for that disorder. For example, arthritis quality of life is concerned with joint pain and mobility and the side effects of anti-inflammatory agents; depression quality of life deals with the symptoms of depression, such as suicidal thoughts, and medication side effects, such as blurred vision, dry mouth, constipation, and impotence (Bergner, 1989); and cancer-specific HRQL may include anxiety about cancer recurrence (Ganz and Litwin, 1996) and pain management.

Institution-related quality of life is another important attribute of quality in addition to the clinical and interpersonal aspects. It refers to a patient's quality of life while confined in an institution as an inpatient. Factors contributing to institutional quality of life can be classified into three main groups: environmental comfort, self-governance, and human factors. Cleanliness, safety, noise levels, odors, lighting, air circulation, environmental temperature, and furnishings are some of the key comfort factors that are particularly relevant to the physical aspects of institutional living. Self-governance means autonomy to make decisions, freedom to air grievances without fear of reprisal, and reasonable accommodation of personal likes and dislikes. Human factors are associated with caregiver attitudes and practices; they include privacy and confidentiality, treatment from staff in a manner that maintains respect and dignity, and freedom from physical and/or emotional abuse.

Quality Assessment and Assurance

The terms "quality assessment" and "quality assurance" are often encountered in the literature on healthcare quality, though they are not always well defined or differentiated. **Quality assessment** refers to the measurement of quality against an established standard. It includes the process of defining how quality is to be determined, identification of specific variables or indicators to be measured, collection of appropriate data to make the measurement possible, statistical analysis, and interpretation of the results of the assessment (Williams and Brook, 1978). **Quality assurance** is synonymous with quality improvement. It is the process of institutionalizing quality through ongoing assessment and using the results of assessment for continuous quality improvement (CQI) (Williams and Torrens, 1993). Quality assurance goes a step beyond quality assessment: it is a system-wide or organization-wide commitment to engage in the improvement of quality on an ongoing basis.

Although the two activities of quality assessment and quality assurance are related, quality assurance cannot occur without quality assessment. That is, quality assessment is an integral part of the process of quality assurance. Conversely, it is possible to conduct quality assessment without engaging in quality assurance.

In the past, quality assurance focused on observing deviations from established standards by using inspection techniques and was applied in conjunction with punitive actions for noncompliance. The nursing home industry presents a typical case. Standards of patient care in nursing homes and the system for evaluating performance were developed mainly in conjunction with the certification of facilities for Medicare and Medicaid. Federal regulations developed by the CMS are viewed as minimum standards or baseline criteria for defining the quality of resident care in certified facilities. Compliance with the standards is monitored through periodic inspections of these facilities, and serious noncompliance is punishable by monetary fines and threats of expulsion from the Medicare and Medicaid reimbursement programs.

Quality assurance is based on the principles of **total quality management (TQM)**, also referred to as CQI. The philosophy of TQM was developed and used in other industries before it was adapted for healthcare delivery. The adoption of TQM by many hospitals and health systems has streamlined administration, reduced lengths of stay, improved clinical outcomes, and produced higher levels of patient satisfaction (HCIA Inc. and Deloitte & Touche, 1997).

The Donabedian Model

In his well-known model to help define and measure quality in healthcare organizations, Donabedian (1985) proposed three domains in which healthcare quality could be examined: structure, process, and outcomes. These three domains are both closely linked and hierarchical (**Figure 12-12**). Structure is the

Outcome
Final Results

Patient satisfaction
Health status
Recovery
Improvement
Nosocomial infections
Iatrogenic illnesses (injuries)
Rehospitalization
Mortality
Incidence and prevalence of disease

Process
Actual Delivery of Health Care

Technical aspects of care
- Diagnosis
- Treatment procedures
- Correct prescriptions
- Accurate drug administration
- Pharmaceutical care
- Waiting time
- Cost

Interpersonal aspects of care
- Communication
- Dignity and respect
- Compassion and concern

Structure
Resource Inputs

Facilities
- Licensing
- Accreditation

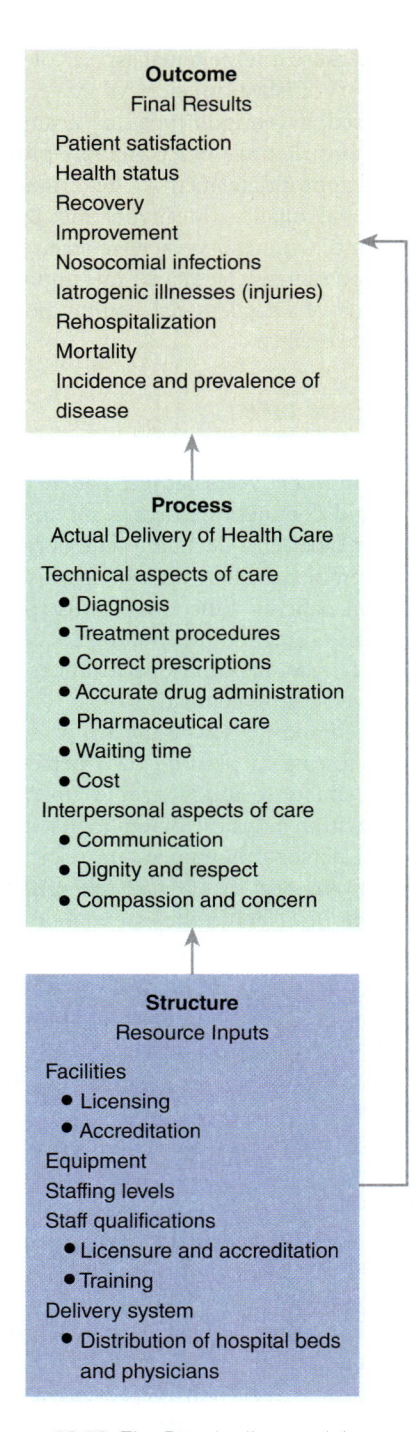

Equipment
Staffing levels
Staff qualifications
- Licensure and accreditation
- Training

Delivery system
- Distribution of hospital beds and physicians

Figure 12-12 The Donabedian model.

foundation of the quality of health care. Good processes require a good structure; in other words, deficiencies in structure have a negative effect on the processes of healthcare delivery. Structure and process together influence quality outcomes. Structure primarily influences process; it has only a secondary direct influence on outcome. For improvement of quality, outcomes must be measured and compared against pre-established benchmarks. When desired outcomes are not achieved, one must examine the processes and structures to identify and correct deficiencies.

The quality of a healthcare provider's structures and processes determine the quality of outcomes. Some significant initiatives toward process improvement have been undertaken, including those based on clinical practice guidelines, cost-efficiency measures, critical pathways, and risk management.

Processes That Improve Quality

Clinical Practice Guidelines

Clinical practice guidelines (also called medical practice guidelines) are explicit descriptions representing preferred clinical processes for specified conditions. Hence, clinical practice guidelines are scientifically-based protocols to guide clinical decisions. The goal is to assist practitioners in adopting a "best practice" approach in delivering care for a given health condition (Ramsey, 2002). Such evidence-based guidelines provide a mechanism for standardizing the practice of medicine and improving the quality of care. Proponents believe that these guidelines simultaneously promote lower costs and induce better outcomes; critics view them as an administrative mechanism to reduce utilization.

One of the primary mandates of AHRQ is to build a scientific base that shows which healthcare practices work and which do not work. As part of this effort, AHRQ has established a National Guideline Clearinghouse (NGC) in partnership with the American Medical Association (AMA) and America's Health Insurance Plans. The NGC is a comprehensive database of evidence-based clinical practice guidelines and related documents. It facilitates access to information produced by different organizations by making all of the data available at one site. This Internet-based resource enables healthcare professionals to compare clinical recommendations. Guidelines have been catalogued in the areas of diseases; chemicals and drugs; analytical, diagnostic, and therapeutic techniques and equipment; and behavioral disciplines and activities.

Cost-Efficiency

Also referred to as cost-effectiveness, **cost-efficiency** is an important concept in quality assessment. A service is cost-efficient when the benefit received is greater than the cost incurred to provide the service. Medical care delivered at the flat of the curve is not cost-effective.

Overutilization (overuse) occurs when the costs or risks of a treatment outweigh its benefits, but additional care is still delivered. When health care is overused, its value is diluted because resources are wasted. Hence, inefficiency can also be regarded as unethical because it deprives someone else of the potential benefits of health care. **Underutilization** (underuse) occurs when the benefits of an intervention outweigh its risks or costs, yet it is not used (Chassin, 1991). Potential adverse health outcomes related to underutilization include hospitalizations that could be avoided by providing better medical access and timely care, low birth weight due to lack of prenatal care, infant mortality due to lack of early pediatric care, and low cancer survival rates due to lack of early detection and treatment.

The principles of cost-efficiency indicate that healthcare costs can be reduced without lowering quality of care. Conversely, quality can be improved without increasing costs. Thus, a trade-off does not have to occur between cost and quality. Medicare's introduction of PPS offers an example. The discharge of patients "quicker and sicker" triggered by PPS initially raised some alarm concerning decreased quality, but studies showed that processes of care in hospitals actually improved and mortality rates were unchanged or lower (Rogers et al., 1990). Other potential negative health outcomes that can be avoided by curtailing overuse include life-threatening drug interactions, nosocomial infections, and iatrogenic illnesses.

Critical Pathways

Critical pathways are outcome-based and patient-centered case management tools that are interdisciplinary in nature, facilitating coordination of care among multiple clinical departments and caregivers. Such a timeline identifies planned medical interventions, along with expected patient outcomes, for a specific diagnosis or class of cases, often defined by a DRG. The outcomes and interventions included in the critical pathway are broadly defined. In addition to technical outcomes, pathways may measure such factors as patient satisfaction, self-reported health status, mental health, and activities of daily living (ADLs). Interventions may include treatments, medications, diagnostic tests, diet, activity regimens, consultations, discharge planning, and patient education. A critical pathway serves as a plan of action for all disciplines caring for a patient and incorporates a system for documenting and evaluating variances from the critical path plan.

Critical pathways are unique to the institutions that develop them because they are based on the particular practices of that facility and its caregivers. A pathway is also customized to the patient population being served and the available patient care resources.

Critical pathways are meant to promote interdisciplinary collaboration within the environment of the hospital and its market. The latter occurs by making patients and families active participants in the process. For these reasons, critical pathways are difficult to replicate from one organization to another. Use of critical pathways reduces costs and improves quality by reducing errors, improving coordination among interdisciplinary players, streamlining case management functions, providing systematic data with which to assess care, and reducing variations in practice patterns (Giffin and Giffin, 1994).

Risk Management

Risk management consists of proactive efforts to prevent adverse events related to clinical care and facilities operations; it especially focuses on avoiding medical malpractice (Orlikoff, 1988). Indeed, initiatives undertaken by a healthcare organization to review clinical processes and establish protocols for the specific purpose of reducing malpractice litigation can actually enhance quality. Because malpractice concerns may also result in **defensive medicine**, risk management approaches should employ the principles of cost-efficiency along with standardized practice guidelines and critical pathways.

Perhaps not surprisingly, the threat of malpractice litigation also has a downside. Notably, fear of litigation makes hospitals and physicians reluctant to disclose preventable harm and actual medical errors. In consequence, fear of litigation may actually conceal problems that may compromise patient safety (Lamb et al., 2003).

Public Reporting of Quality

Public reporting on macro levels of quality expanded in the early 2000s. This section summarizes the major public reporting initiatives.

National Quality Forum

The National Quality Forum (NQF) is an organization established in 1999 as part of a call to action to develop a more standardized set of quality measures in health care (Burstin et al., 2016). Since its creation, the NQF has been a leading figure in quality measure endorsement owing to the expertise of its membership and consensus-based approach. Many federal and state programs, such as those within CMS and AHRQ, use NQF-endorsed quality measures in their reporting (Claxton et al., 2015). CMS, in conjunction with America's Health Insurance Plans (AHIP), the NQF, and other organizations, also formed a Core Quality Measure Collaborative (CQMC) to identify core measures for use in the collection and reporting of quality. Many of these measures have already been implemented in CMS quality-reporting programs, and many private payers use NQF-endorsed measures as well (Claxton et al., 2015; CMS, 2020). NQF-endorsed quality measures are comprehensive in nature: they reflect structure-, process-, and outcome-related aspects of health care and also deal with cost/resource use and efficiency (NQF, 2020b). In addition to endorsing quality measures, the NQF provides recommendations on health policy issues related to performance measurement and program efficacy (Melillo, 2020; NQF, 2020a).

CMS Programs on Quality

CMS started launching quality initiatives in 2001 (CMS, 2013b). Quality programs specific to Medicare include the Home Health Quality Reporting Program, Hospital VBP Program, Hospice Quality Reporting Program, Inpatient Rehabilitation Facility Quality Reporting Program, Long-Term Care Hospital Quality Reporting Program, Measures Management System, Nursing Home Quality Initiative, Outcome and Assessment Information Set (OASIS), Physician Compare Initiative, End-Stage Renal Disease (ESRD) Quality Incentive Program, and Post-Acute Care Quality Initiatives (https://www.cms.gov/Medicare/Medicare.html). CMS also has initiatives to improve the quality of care provided to Medicaid and CHIP enrollees related to dental care; higher weight; maternal and infant health; home and community-based services; vaccines; health disparities; tobacco cessation; patient safety; asthma; emergency room utilization; and improving care transitions (https://www.medicaid.gov/medicaid/quality-of-care/quality-improvement-initiatives/index.html).

The following provides more details on CMS's efforts to enhance quality.

- CMS developed a public reporting program known as Hospital Compare, which provides information about the quality of care at more than 4,000 Medicare-certified hospitals across the United States (https://www.medicare.gov/care-compare). Hospital Compare has expanded beyond the 10 process measures available at the beginning of this program and now includes data on structural measures, ED throughput, compliance, and hospital outpatient facilities; hospital 30-day risk standardized mortality and readmission rates for acute myocardial infarction, heart failure, and pneumonia; patient experience and satisfaction; medical imaging usage (Medicare.gov, 2016; Ross et al., 2010); and data on the Hospital VBP Program under the ACA (CMS, 2013a).

- CMS and AHRQ jointly developed the Hospital Consumer Assessment of Healthcare Providers and Systems (CAHPS) survey, which collects uniform measures of patients' perspectives on various aspects of their inpatient care (CMS, 2005). Results are publicly reported on the CMS Hospital Compare website. Healthcare organizations, public and private purchasers, consumers, and researchers can use the CAHPS results to inform their purchasing or contracting decisions and to improve the quality of healthcare services (AHRQ, 2010). CAHPS surveys ask about experiences with health plans, clinicians, and specific

facilities, including hospitals and nursing homes (https://www.ahrq.gov/cahps).
- The Physician Quality Reporting System allows physicians and other eligible professions to participate by reporting quality measures to CMS about specific services provided to their Medicare patients with specific conditions (https://www.cms.gov/Medicare/Quality-Initiatives-Patient-Assessment-Instruments/PQRS/Downloads/PQRS_Overview FactSheet_2013_08_06.pdf). Physicians can earn incentives by reporting. In 2015, the program began applying negative payment adjustment to individuals and practices that did not adequately report data.
- Quality improvement organizations are contracted by CMS for each state to review medical care and help beneficiaries with concerns about quality of care. QIO contracts are 3 years in length. The core functions of the QIO program are to improve quality of care for beneficiaries, protect the integrity of the Medicare Trust Fund, and protect beneficiaries by addressing individual complaints (CMS, 2013b). The two types of organizations that work under the direction of CMS in support of this program are (1) beneficiary- and family-centered care QIOs, which focus on helping Medicare beneficiaries exercise their right to high-quality health care, and (2) quality innovation network QIOs, which bring beneficiaries, providers, and communities together in initiatives to increase patient safety and health (CMS, 2016c).
- Ambulatory Surgical Center Quality Reporting is a pay-for-reporting, quality-data program, in which ambulatory care centers report quality of care for standardized measures to receive the full annual update to their annual payment rates (CMS, 2013a). Measures included in payment determination are patient burns, patient falls, hospital transfers/admissions, and incidents involving the wrong site, wrong side, wrong patient, wrong procedure, or wrong implant (CMS, 2016a).

AHRQ Quality Indicators

Since 2003, AHRQ has published the annual National Healthcare Quality Report and National Healthcare Disparities Report (AHRQ, 2012, 2013b). In identifying key measures for these reports, the Federal Interagency Workgroup focused on priority areas established in *Healthy People 2010* (AHRQ, 2005). AHRQ has developed a set of quality indicators (QIs) that measure the quality of the process of care in an outpatient or inpatient setting (Farquhar, 2008). Prevention QIs identify hospital admissions that could have been avoided. Inpatient QIs and patient safety indicators both reflect quality of care inside hospitals, with the former focusing on inpatient mortality and the latter on potentially avoidable complications and iatrogenic events. Pediatric quality indicators reflect the quality of care received by children inside hospitals and identify potentially avoidable hospitalizations.

Current AHRQ QI modules include Prevention Quality Indicators, Inpatient Quality Indicators, Patient Safety Indicators, and Pediatric Quality Indicators. These measures expand upon the Healthcare Cost and Utilization Project (HCUP) QIs, and several are endorsed by the NQF. Specific information on individual quality indicators within each module can be found at https://www.qualityindicators.ahrq.gov/. Selected indicators are also used by CMS's Hospital Compare website (https://www.medicare.gov/care-compare/; AHRQ, 2013a; NQF, 2013).

An example of an ongoing AHRQ quality initiative is the AHRQ's Patient Safety Network (PSNet). PSNet is a Web-based resource that features news and resources on patient safety. The site offers updates on literature, news, tools, and meetings, and it provides browsing capability and allows for site customization (https://psnet.ahrq.gov).

States' Public Reporting of Hospital Quality

Many states also provide data on hospital outcomes of care, typically focusing on healthcare-associated infections, readmission rates, and mortality rates following hospitalization for the same clinical conditions reported by CMS (acute myocardial infarction, heart failure, and pneumonia). One of the advantages of state-based public reporting programs is that their reporting is not limited to Medicare fee-for-service beneficiaries but also includes younger adults and older adults insured through private plans and Medicaid-affiliated HMOs.

As an example, Minnesota has made significant efforts to improve the quality of health care delivered within the state. A 2008 health reform created the Minnesota Statewide Quality Reporting and Measurement System, through which clinics and hospitals publicly report quality measures. This system undergoes annual review with public comment from the community and is updated as necessary (Minnesota Department of Health, n.d.). To maintain consistency, health plans are not allowed to require data submission on quality measures not included within the state's standardized set.

The state of Maryland has taken a slightly different approach to reporting quality. Healthcare quality is monitored by the Maryland Health Care Commission (MHCC), an independent agency established in 1999 by the Maryland General Assembly (MHCC, 2020). Through the MHCC, the Center for Quality Measurement and Reporting publishes Maryland Health Care Quality Reports on its website. Data can be viewed publicly and are generally updated every three months. Healthcare settings covered include hospitals, long-term care facilities, and health insurance plans, with specific topics including flu prevention, patient safety, and surgery (MHCC, 2020; MHCC, n.d.).

While individual state efforts to maintain and improve quality are commendable and necessary, the differences in regulation and reporting reflect the wide variation that exists in the quality-reporting arena, highlighting the need for more standardization. To better assess the state of healthcare quality in the United States and reduce the burden on clinicians, who spend innumerable hours documenting and reporting on quality measures, more work needs to be done to determine which quality measures are most necessary and useful and which measures and programs can be eliminated.

The Affordable Care Act and Quality of Care

The ACA includes some provisions for improving quality of care through programs that link payment to quality outcomes in Medicare, strengthening of the quality infrastructure, and encouraging the development of new patient care models, such as patient-centered medical homes and accountable care organizations.

The ACA initiated the National Quality Strategy (NQS) to set national goals to improve the quality of health care. To date, three objectives have been established: (1) to make health care more accessible, safe, and patient centered; (2) to address environmental, social, and behavioral influences on health and health care; and (3) to make care more affordable (RWJF, 2013).

New payment models in the ACA, such as accountable care organizations (ACOs), use a value-based model in which healthcare organizations are reimbursed based on quality measures. ACOs are intended to promote integration and coordination of care for patients over the spectrum of healthcare services, such as ambulatory, inpatient, and postacute services. The value-based payment model is designed to ensure that patients receive high-quality care by evaluating organizations on numerous quality measures related to patient safety, care coordination, and patient/caregiver experience while generating financial savings (CMS, 2016b). Organizations are incentivized to provide high-quality care in two ways: (1) by being penalized for failing to report these quality measures and (2) by sharing in the savings generated due to the implementation of these quality measures. A number of achievements are identified with the implementation of ACOs, as described next

Improved coordination. ACOs promote better communication and collaboration among healthcare providers (Wilson et al., 2020). This can result in streamlined processes and reduced fragmentation of care, ultimately enhancing patient access to a more coordinated and efficient healthcare system (Wilson et al., 2020). Wilson et al. (2020) also found that as compared to low-performing ACOs, high-performing ACOs had formed collaborative relationships with local hospitals enabling improved coordination through the receipt of timely information about admissions and discharge of patients. ACOs improve the way healthcare providers coordinate and deliver care, from coordination within a single visit (e.g., improved previsit planning or team-based care) to coordination across settings and providers for complex patients (e.g., coordination between primary care, postacute care, and hospitals) (Lewis, 2022). Improved coordination is expected to reduce duplication, increase quality of care, and reduce unnecessary costs associated with fragmented care, as well as improve patients' experiences with health care (Lewis, 2022).

Health information exchange. Technology played a crucial role in facilitating integration within healthcare delivery systems (Reddy et al., 2019). According to Perloff and Sobul (2022), electronic health records (EHRs) and healthcare technologies enabled seamless sharing of patient information among different care settings, improving care coordination and continuity. Telehealth and remote monitoring technologies were increasingly adopted, supporting virtual care delivery and remote patient monitoring (Perloff & Sobul, 2022). For example, Aledade, collaborating with independent physicians, implemented an all-encompassing telehealth solution for its nationwide network of physician-led ACOs. This enabled primary-care practices to continue providing access to patients who are older adults and high risk, ensuring their safety at home and reducing the risk of virus transmission (National Association of ACOs, 2020). Atlantic Health System's ACO in New Jersey employed predictive modeling to detect patients at high risk. They also offered telehealth visits and remote patient monitoring, including monitoring oxygen levels, to prevent hospitalizations or allow patients to be discharged to their homes instead of nursing homes (National Association of ACOs, 2020).

Patient engagement. Studies examining patient engagement found that the majority of physicians in ACOs implemented some form of patient engagement, but it was found that more emphasis was needed on shared decision-making, co-development of care plans and engagement in governance and quality improvement activities (Wilson et al., 2020). Physician organizations that participated in ACOs were found to be more likely to have care-transition management practices in place, including communication between primary-care physicians and hospitals around patient admissions and discharge plans (Wilson et al., 2020).

Cost control. An increasing number of hospitals are participating in Medicare Shared Savings Program (MSSP) ACOs (Huang et al., 2023). MSSP ACOs are groups of doctors, hospitals, and other healthcare providers who collaborate to give coordinated high-quality care to people with Medicare, focusing on delivering the right care at the right time while avoiding unnecessary services and medical errors (CMS, 2023). The Medicare Shared Savings Program (MSSP) was associated with modest reductions in Medicare spending, reduced inpatient utilization, reduced readmissions, improved preventive care, and improved patient experience

(Huang et al., 2023). MSSP participation was associated with differential increases in net patient revenue, Medicare revenue, inpatient revenue share, Medicare revenue share, and a differential reduction in allowance and discount rate (Huang et al., 2023). Participation in MSSP ACOs was associated with small savings for beneficiaries with serious mental illness (−$233 per person per year) in total healthcare spending, primarily related to savings from chronic medical conditions (excluding mental health; −$227 per person per year) and not from savings related to mental health services (−$6 per person per year) (Figueroa et al., 2022). Savings were driven by reductions in acute and postacute care for medical conditions (Figueroa et al., 2022).

Shared savings. Since the passage of the ACA in 2010, the vision of "paying for the quality and outcomes of healthcare delivery" rather than "paying for the volume of services" has been realized, and the whole healthcare system has reached a milestone of paying for value (Werner et al., 2021). For instance, value-based payment models gained momentum recently, as payers and providers increasingly shifted away from fee-for-service reimbursement (van Staalduinen et al., 2022). ACOs, bundled payments, and pay-for-performance initiatives were implemented to incentivize providers to deliver high-quality, cost-effective care (Lewis, 2022).

Bravo et al. (2023) discussed a proposed model of the Medicare Shared Savings Program (MSSP) between ACOs and the CMS. The program aimed to align incentives by transferring part of the payer's risk to ACOs, encouraging them to reduce costs and improve health outcomes (Bravo et al., 2023). They introduced cost- and risk-sharing contracts, highlighting the impact of the payer's gain-sharing and loss-sharing parameters on coordination efforts. They suggested that the choice of risk-sharing track in MSSP significantly influences care coordination, emphasizing the importance of policymakers' consideration in designing risk-sharing tracks to promote effective care coordination (Bravo et al., 2023).

Based on interviews and research, McClellan et al. (2020) presented a diverse range of organizations that have effectively utilized value-based models (including rural and urban settings, safety net facilities, primary-care and specialized clinics, hospitals, and independent practices) to swiftly address the challenges posed by the COVID-19 pandemic.

In addition to ACOs, a number of value-based payment models are being explored, including pay-for-performance report cards for physicians, bundled payments for care improvement, numerous state innovation models, and initiatives to transform primary care (CMS, 2015). Most of these value-based models are still in their early phases, and evidence of their effectiveness and impact has not yet been published.

As a result of efforts to improve the quality of care, the number of patient safety and medical errors has decreased since 2010. Incidents involving patient harm fell by 17% from 2010 to 2013, which translates to approximately 50,000 fewer people dying as a result of preventable errors and infections (AHRQ, 2014). The decline in hospital-acquired conditions is estimated to have prevented more than 87,000 deaths from 2010 to 2014 (AHRQ, 2015). From 2014 to 2017, the rate of hospital-acquired conditions fell 13% and saved an estimated 20,500 lives (AHRQ, 2019). The rate of hospital readmissions among Medicare beneficiaries has also declined, from a mean of 19.1% in 2010 (Zuckerman et al., 2016) to a mean of 14.7% in 2016 (COMH, 2020) with 78% among those 65 years and older. The 30-day hospital readmissions among Medicare beneficiaries age 65 and older per 1,000 declined from 47.5 in 2012 to 31.3 in 2021 (The Commonwealth Fund, 2023).

Moreover, self-reports of timely access to care and primary physicians being informed about specialty care have significantly improved since ACO contracts came into being. Patients with chronic conditions and high predicted spending have also reported significantly improved ratings of physicians, interactions with physicians, and overall care (McWilliams et al., 2014).

The Patient-Centered Outcomes Research Institute (PCORI) was established through funding provided by the ACA. This institute is responsible for comparative effectiveness research, which studies health outcomes, clinical effectiveness, and the appropriateness of different medical treatments (Frank et al., 2014). PCORI's main mission is to improve the quality and relevance of evidence available to help patients, caregivers, clinicians, employers, and insurers make informed health decisions. The ultimate goal is to improve healthcare outcomes by providing patients with high-quality evidence they can use to make informed healthcare decisions.

Evidence of the ACA's overall impact on health outcomes is limited, but its effects may be similar to those of other healthcare provisions that have provided health insurance to a previously uninsured group. Medicaid expansions have increased self-reported overall physical and mental health and reduced mortality (Baicker et al., 2013; Broaddus and Aron-Dine, 2019; Sommers et al., 2012). Young adults covered under the ACA have an increased probability of self-reporting excellent physical and mental health (Barbaresco et al., 2015).

Although the ACA has led to a number of innovative performance-based delivery systems intended to improve the quality of care, a fair amount of work still needs to be done to fully understand how to best design and implement value-based payment programs (Damberg et al., 2014). Moreover, it is still too early to draw definite conclusions about the quality effects of the ACA. Although the preliminary data are promising, showing reductions in hospital-acquired conditions and Medicare readmissions, the causes of these trends need further investigation. More evidence and time are needed to fully assess the ACA's impact on quality of care.

Summary

Increasing costs, lack of access, and concerns about quality pose the greatest challenges to healthcare delivery in the United States. To some extent, these three issues are interrelated. Increasing costs limit the system's ability to expand access. A lack of universal coverage negatively affects the health status of uninsured groups. Despite spending the most resources on health care, the United States continues to rank in the bottom quartile among developed countries on outcome indicators such as life expectancy and infant mortality.

Nations that have national health insurance can control system-wide costs through top-down controls, mainly in the form of global budgets. This approach is not possible in the United States, which has a multi-payer system. In the United States, regulatory approaches have been used to try to constrain the supply side, but the major emphasis has been on limiting reimbursement to providers. Several competitive approaches have been used, mainly through the expansion of managed care. A move toward prospective payments and the growth of managed care can be largely credited with putting the brakes on rising healthcare spending during the 1990s.

Access to medical care is one of the key determinants of health status, along with environment, lifestyle, and hereditary factors. It is also regarded as a significant benchmark in assessing the effectiveness of the medical-care delivery system. Access is explained in terms of enabling and predisposing factors, as well as factors related to health policy and healthcare delivery. It has five dimensions: availability, accessibility, accommodation, affordability, and acceptability. Measures of access can relate to individuals, healthcare plans, and the healthcare delivery system.

Quality in health care has been difficult to define and measure, although it has received increasing emphasis in recent decades. At the micro level, healthcare quality encompasses the clinical aspects of care delivery, the interpersonal aspects of care delivery, and quality of life. Indicators of quality at the macro level are commonly associated with life expectancy, mortality, and morbidity. Quality assessment is the measurement of quality against an established standard, whereas quality assurance emphasizes improvement of quality using the principles of continual quality improvement. Donabedian proposed that quality should be assessed along three dimensions: structure, process, and outcomes. These three dimensions are complementary and should be used in a collective manner to monitor quality of care. Since 2000, several federal and state initiatives have been implemented to report on certain macro levels of quality.

TEST YOUR UNDERSTANDING

Terminology

administrative costs
certificate of need (CON)
clinical practice guidelines
competition
cost-efficiency
critical pathways
defensive medicine
fraud
health planning
health-related quality of life (HRQL)
institution-related quality of life
outcomes
overutilization
peer review
quality
quality assessment
quality assurance
quality improvement organizations (QIOs)
risk management
small area variations (SAVs)
top-down control
total quality management (TQM)
underutilization
upcoding

Review Questions

1. What is meant by the term "healthcare costs"? Describe the three meanings of the term "cost."
2. Why should the United States control the rising costs of health care?
3. How do the findings from the Rand Health Insurance Experiment reinforce the relationship between growth in third-party reimbursement and increase in healthcare costs? Explain.
4. Explain how, under imperfect market conditions, both prices and quantity of health care are higher than they would be in a highly competitive market.
5. What are some of the reasons for increased healthcare costs that are attributed to the providers of medical care?
6. What are some of the main differences between the broad cost-containment approaches used in the United States and those used in countries with national health insurance?
7. Discuss the effectiveness of CON regulation in controlling healthcare expenditures.
8. Discuss price controls and their effectiveness in controlling healthcare expenditures.

9. Discuss the role of quality improvement organizations in cost containment.
10. What are the four competition-based cost-containment strategies?
11. What are the implications of access for health and healthcare delivery?
12. What are the roles of enabling and predisposing factors in access to care?
13. Briefly describe the five dimensions of access.
14. What are the four main types of access described by Andersen?
15. Describe the measurement of access to care at the individual, health plan, and delivery system levels.
16. What are some of the implications of the definition of quality proposed by the Institute of Medicine? In which way is the definition incomplete?
17. Discuss the dimensions of quality from the micro and macro perspectives.
18. Discuss the two types of health-related quality of life.
19. Distinguish between quality assessment and quality assurance.
20. What are the basic principles of total quality management (continual quality improvement)?
21. Give a brief description of the Donabedian model of quality.
22. Discuss the main developments in process improvement that have occurred in recent years.
23. Discuss the implications of the ACA for healthcare access, cost, and quality.

References

Acholonu, R. G., and J. L. Raphael, 2022. The Influence of the Electronic Health Record on Achieving Equity and Eliminating Health Disparities for Children. *Pediatric Annals* 51: e112–e117.

Aday, L. A. 1993. Indicators and Predictors of Health Services Utilization. In: *Introduction to Health Services*. 4th ed. S. J. Williams and P. R. Torrens, eds. Albany, NY: Delmar Publishers. 46–70.

Aday, L. A., and R. Andersen. 1975. *Development of Indices of Access to Medical Care*. Ann Arbor, MI: Health Administration Press.

Aday, L. A., R. Andersen, and G. V. Fleming. 1980. *Health Care in the US: Equitable for Whom?* Newbury Park, CA: Sage.

Aday, L. A., G. V. Fleming, and R. Andersen. 1984. *Access to Medical Care in the US: Who Has It, Who Doesn't?* Research Series No. 32. Chicago, IL: Center for Health Administration Studies, University of Chicago, Pluribus Press.

Aday, L. A. et al. 1993. *Evaluating the Medical Care System: Effectiveness, Efficiency, and Equity*. Ann Arbor, MI: Health Administration Press.

Agency for Healthcare Research and Quality (AHRQ). 2000, April. *Reducing Errors in Health Care: Translating Research into Practice*. AHRQ Publication No. 00-PO58. Accessed May 2017. Available at: https://archive.ahrq.gov/qual/errors.htm

Agency for Healthcare Research and Quality (AHRQ). 2005. *National Healthcare Quality Report: Background on the measure's Development Process*. Accessed May 2017. Available at: https://archive.ahrq.gov/research/findings/nhqrdr/nhqr02/nhqrprelim.html

Agency for Healthcare Research and Quality (AHRQ). 2010. Consumer Assessment of Healthcare Providers and Systems (CAHPS). Accessed January 2011. Available at: http://www.cahps.ahrq.gov

Agency for Healthcare Research and Quality (AHRQ). 2012. *Annual Progress Report to Congress: National Strategy for Quality Improvement in Health Care*. Accessed January 2014. Available at: http://www.ahrq.gov/workingforquality/nqs/nqs2012annlrpt.pdf

Agency for Healthcare Research and Quality (AHRQ). 2013a. *AHRQ Quality Indicators*. Accessed January 2014. Available at: http://www.qualityindicators.ahrq.gov/

Agency for Healthcare Research and Quality (AHRQ). 2013b. *National Healthcare Quality and Disparities Reports*. Accessed September 2013. Available at: http://www.ahrq.gov/research/findings/nhqrdr/index.html

Agency for Healthcare Research and Quality (AHRQ). 2014. *Interim Update on 2013 Annual Hospital-Acquired Condition Rate and Estimates of Cost Savings and Deaths Averted from 2010 to 2013*. Accessed February 2017. Available at: https://www.ahrq.gov/sites/default/files/wysiwyg/professionals/quality-patient-safety/pfp/interimhacrate2013.pdf

Agency for Healthcare Research and Quality (AHRQ). 2015. *Saving Lives and Saving Money: Hospital-Acquired Conditions Update*. Accessed February 2017. Available

References

at https://www.ahrq.gov/professionals/quality-patient-safety/pfp/interimhacrate2014.html

Agency for Healthcare Research and Quality (AHRQ). 2019. *AHRQ National Scorecard on Hospital-Acquired Conditions Updated Baseline Rates and Preliminary Results 2014–2017*. Accessed February 2020. Available at: https://www.ahrq.gov/sites/default/files/wysiwyg/professionals/quality-patient- safety/pfp/hacreport-2019.pdf

Altman, S. H., and S. S. Wallack. 1996. Health Care Spending: Can the United States Control It? In: *Strategic Choices for a Changing Health Care System*. S. Altman and U. Reinhardt, eds. Chicago, IL: Health Administration Press.

American Association of Physicists in Medicine. 2011. *MedPAC Verifies Drop in Imaging Spending, Utilization*. Accessed February 2017. Available at: http://www.aapm.org/pubs/enews/documents/MedPACverifies.pdf

American Diabetes Association. 2020. *The Cost of Diabetes*. Accessed August 2020. Available at: https://www.diabetes.org/resources/statistics/cost-diabetes

Andersen, R. 1968. *A Behavioral Model of Families' Use of Health Services*. Research Series No. 25. Chicago, IL: Center for Health Administration Studies, University of Chicago.

Andersen, R. 1997. *Too Big, Too Small, Too Flat, Too Tall: Search for "Just Right" Measures of Access in the Age of Managed Care*. Chicago, IL: Paper presented at the Association for Health Services Research Annual Meeting.

Arias, E., B. Tejada-Vera, and F. Ahmad. 2021. Provisional Life Expectancy Estimates for January through June, 2020. *Vital Statistics Rapid Release* 10. Available at: https://dx.doi.org/10.15620/cdc:100392

Ashwood, J. S., A. Mehrotra, D. Cowling, and L. Uscher-Pines. 2017. Direct-to-Consumer Telehealth May Increase Access to Care but Does not Decrease Spending. *Health Affairs* 36. Available at: https://doi.org/10.1377/hlthaff.2016.1130

Badinski, I., A. Finkelstein, M. Gentzkow, and P. Hull. 2023. Geographic Variation in Healthcare Utilization: The role of Physicians (No. w31749). National Bureau of Economic Research.

Baicker, K., S. L. Taubman, H. L. Allen, et al. 2013. The Oregon Experiment: Effects of Medicaid on Clinical Outcomes. *New England Journal of Medicine* 368: 1713–1722.

Barbaresco, S., C. J. Courtemanche, and Y. Qi. 2015. Impacts of the Affordable Care Act Dependent Coverage Provision on Health-Related Outcomes of Young Adults. *Journal of Health Economics* 40: 54–68.

Baucus, M., and E. J. Fowler. 2002. Geographic Variation in Medicare Spending and the Real Focus of Medicare Reform. *Health Affairs* (Suppl Web Exclusives): W115–W117.

Bergner, M. 1989. Quality of Life, Health Status, and Clinical Research. *Medical Care* 27: S148–S156.

Blanchfield, B. B., J. L. Heffernan, B. Osgood, R. R. Sheehan, and G. S. Meyer. 2010. Saving Billions of Dollars and Physicians' Time by Streamlining Billing Practices. *Health Affairs* 29: 1248–1254.

Borza, T., M. K. Oerline, T. A., Skolarus, et al. 2019. Association Between Hospital Participation in Medicare Shared Savings Program Accountable Care Organizations and Readmission Following Major Surgery. *Annals of Surgery* 269: 873–878. Available at: https://doi.org/10.1097/SLA.0000000000002737

Bravo, F., R. Levi, G. Perakis, and G. Romero, 2023. Care Coordination for Healthcare Referrals Under a Share-Savings Program. *Production and Operations Management* 32: 189–206.

Broaddus, M., and A. Aron-Dine. 2019. *Medicaid Expansion Has Saved at Least 19,000 Lives, New Research Finds: State Decisions Not to Expand Have Led to 15,000 Premature Deaths*. Accessed February 2020. Available at: https://www.cbpp.org/sites/default/files/atoms/files/11-6-19health.pdf

Bureau of Labor Statistics. 2017a. *CPI Inflation Calculator*. Accessed February 2017. Available at: https://www.bls.gov/data/inflation_calculator.htm

Bureau of Labor Statistics. 2017b. *Current Employment Statistics: CES national*. Accessed May 2017. Available at: https://www.bls.gov/ces/

Burstin, H., S. Leatherman, and D. Goldmann. 2016. The Evolution of Health Care Quality Measurement in the United States. *Journal of Internal Medicine* 279: 154–159.

Centers for Disease Control and Prevention (CDC). 2016. *Obesity and Overweight*. Accessed February 2017. Available at: https://www.cdc.gov/nchs/fastats/obesity-overweight.htm

Centers for Disease Control and Prevention (CDC). 2019. *Economic Trends in Tobacco*. Accessed February 2020. Available at: https://www.cdc.gov/tobacco/data_statistics/fact_sheets/economics/econ_facts/index.htm

Centers for Medicare and Medicaid Services (CMS). 2005. *Costs and Benefits of HCAHPS*. Accessed January 2011. Available at: http://www.cms.gov/HospitalQualityInits/downloads/HCAHPSCostsBenefits200512.pdf

Centers for Medicare and Medicaid Services (CMS). 2013a. *ASC Quality Reporting*. Accessed January 2014. Available at: https://www.cms.gov/Medicare/Quality-Initiatives-Patient-Assessment-Instruments/ASC-Quality-Reporting/

Centers for Medicare and Medicaid Services (CMS). 2013b. *Quality Improvement Organizations*. Accessed January 2014. Available at: https://www.cms.gov/medicare/quality-initiatives-patient-assessment-instruments/qualityimprovementorgs/index.html

Centers for Medicare and Medicaid Services (CMS). 2015. *Better Care, Smarter Spending, Healthier People: Improving Our Health Care Delivery System.* Accessed March 2021. Available at: https://www.cms.gov/newsroom/fact-sheets/better-care-smarter-spending-healthier-people-improving-our-health-care-delivery-system-0

Centers for Medicare and Medicaid Services (CMS). 2016a. *ASC Quality Reporting.* Accessed February 2017. Available at: https://www.cms.gov/Medicare/Quality-Initiatives-Patient-Assessment-Instruments/ASC-Quality-Reporting/

Centers for Medicare and Medicaid Services (CMS). 2016b. *Improving Quality of Care for Medicare Patients: Accountable Care Organizations.* Medicare Learning Network. Accessed March 2021. Available at: https://www.cms.gov/newsroom/fact-sheets/improving-quality-care-medicare-patients-accountable-care-organizations-0

Centers for Medicare and Medicaid Services (CMS). 2016c. *Quality Improvement Organizations.* Accessed February 2017. Available at: https://www.cms.gov/Medicare/Quality-Initiatives-Patient-Assessment-Instruments/QualityImprovementOrgs/index.html?redirect=/QualityImprovementOrgs/

Centers for Medicare and Medicaid Services (CMS). 2017. *Hospital Value-Based Purchasing.* Accessed March 2021. Available at: https://www.cms.gov/Medicare/Quality-Initiatives-Patient-Assessment-Instruments/Value-Based-Programs/HVBP/Hospital-Value-Based-Purchasing

Centers for Medicare and Medicaid Services (CMS). 2019a. *CMS Office of the Actuary Releases 2018–2027 Projections of National Health Expenditures.* Accessed February 2020. Available at: https://www.cms.gov/newsroom/press-releases/cms-office-actuary-releases-2018-2027-projections-national-health-expenditures

Centers for Medicare and Medicaid Services (CMS). 2019b. *Historical.* Accessed February 2020. Available at: https://www.cms.gov/Research-Statistics-Data-and-Systems/Statistics-Trends-and-Reports/NationalHealthExpendData/NationalHealthAccountsHistorical

Centers for Medicare and Medicaid Services (CMS). 2019c. *NHE Fact Sheet.* Accessed February 2020. Available at: https://www.cms.gov/Research-Statistics-Data-and-Systems/Statistics-Trends-and-Reports/NationalHealthExpendData/NHE-Fact-Sheet

Centers for Medicare and Medicaid Services (CMS). 2019d. *Projected.* Accessed February 2020. Available at: https://www.cms.gov/Research-Statistics-Data-and-Systems/Statistics-Trends-and-Reports/NationalHealthExpendData/NationalHealthAccountsProjected

Centers for Medicare and Medicaid Services (CMS). 2020. *Core Measures.* Accessed August 2020. Available at: https://www.cms.gov/Medicare/Quality-Initiatives-Patient-Assessment-Instruments/QualityMeasures/Core-Measures

Centers for Medicare & Medicaid Services (CMS). 2021. *NHE fact sheet: Historical NHE, 2021.* Accessed November 2023. Available at: https://www.cms.gov/data-research/statistics-trends-and-reports/national-health-expenditure-data/nhe-fact-sheet

Centers for Medicare & Medicaid Services. 2023. *Quality Measures.* Accessed October 24, 2024. Available at: https://www.cms.gov/medicare/quality/measures

Centers for Medicare & Medicaid Services. 2023. *Shared Savings Program (SSP)/ACOs.* Accessed October 24, 2024. Available at: https://www.cms.gov/medicare/payment/fee-for-service-providers/shared-savings-program-ssp-acos/about

Chassin, M. R. 1991. Quality of Care: Time to Act. *Journal of the American Medical Association* 266: 3472–3473.

Cheng, N., Li, H., and Bang, Y. 2023. Pay-for-Performance Schemes and Hospital HIT Adoption. *Decision Support Systems* 164: 113868.

Chukmaitov, A., D. W. Harless, G. J. Bazzoli, and D. B. Muhlestein. 2019. Preventable Hospital Admissions and 30-Day All-Cause Readmissions: Does Hospital Participation in Accountable Care Organizations Improve Quality of Care? *American Journal of Medical Quality* 34: 14–22. Available at: https://doi.org/10.1177/1062860618778786

Claxton, G., C. Cox, S. Gonzales, R. Kamal, and L. Levitt. 2015. *Measuring the Quality of Healthcare in the U.S.* Peterson-KFF Health System Tracker. Accessed August 2020. Available at: https://www.healthsystemtracker.org/brief/measuring-the-quality-of-healthcare-in-the-u-s/

CMS Office of Minority Health (COMH). Impact of Hospital Readmissions Reduction Initiatives on Vulnerable Populations. Baltimore, MD: Centers for Medicare & Medicaid Services; September 2020.

Cole, A. P., A. Krasnova, A. Ramaswamy, et al. 2019. Prostate Cancer in the Medicare Shared Savings Program: Are Accountable Care Organizations Associated with Reduced Expenditures for Men with Prostate Cancer? *Prostate Cancer and Prostatic Diseases* 22: 593–599. Available at: https://doi.org/10.1038/s41391-019-0138-1

Collins, S. R., P. W. Rasmussen, M. M. Doty, and S. Beutel. 2015. *The Rise in Health Care Coverage and Affordability Since Health Reform Took Effect.* New York: Commonwealth Fund.

Commonwealth Fund. 2016. *2016 Commonwealth Fund International Health Policy Survey of Adults.* Accessed February 2017. Available at: http://www.commonwealthfund.org/interactives-and-data/surveys/international-health-policy-surveys/2016/2016-inter national-survey

Commonwealth of Massachusetts. 2019. RY2019 MassHealth Acute P4P Technical Session. Accessed December 2023. Available at: https://www.mass.gov/files/documents/2019/08/08/ry20-masshealth-acute-p4p-technical-session.pdf

Congressional Budget Office. 2007. *The Long-Term Outlook for Health Care Spending*. Accessed January 2011. Available at: http://www.cbo.gov/ftpdocs/87xx/doc8758/11-13-LT-Health.pdf

Cornelius, M. E., Loretan C. G., Jamal A., et al. 2023. Tobacco Product Use Adults—United States, 2021. *Morbidity and Mortality Weekly Report* 72: 475–483. Available at: https://www.cdc.gov/mmwr/volumes/72/wr/mm7218a1.htm

Courtemanche, C., J. Marton, B. Ukert, A. Yelowitz, and D. Zapata. 2018. Effects of the Affordable Care Act on Health Care Access and Self-Assessed Health After 3 Years. *Inquiry* 55. Available at: doi: 10.1177/0046958018796361

Damberg, C. L., K. Raube, S. S. Teleki, and E. dela Cruz. 2009. Taking Stock of Pay-for-Performance: A Candid Assessment from the Front Lines. *Health Affairs* 28: 517–525.

Damberg, C. L., M. E. Sorbero, S. L. Lovejoy, G. R. Martsolf, L. Raaen, and D. Mandel. 2014. *Measuring Success in Health Care Value-Based Purchasing Programs: Summary and Recommendations*. Accessed February 2017. Available at: http://www.rand.org/pubs/research_reports/RR306z1.html

Darden, M., I. McCarthy, and E. Barrette. 2023. Who in Pay-for-Performance? Evidence from Hospital Prices and Financial Penalties. *American Journal of Health Economics* 9: 435–460.

Delbanco, S. F., M. Lehan, and R. Murray. 2018. The Evidence on Pay-For-Performance: Not Strong Enough on Its Own? Accessed December 2023. Available at: https://www.healthaffairs.org/content/forefront/evidence-pay-for-performance-not-strong-enough-its-own

Department of Justice Archives. 2020. Health Care Fraud—Generally. Accessed November 2023. Available at: https://www.justice.gov/archives/jm/criminal-resource-manual-976-health-care-fraud-generally

Docteur, E. R., D. C. Colby, and M. Gold. 1996. Shifting the Paradigm: Monitoring Access in Medicare Managed Care. *Health Care Financing Review* 17: 5–21.

Donabedian, A. 1985. *Explorations in Quality Assessment and Monitoring: The Methods and Findings of Quality Assessment and Monitoring*. Vol. 3. Ann Arbor, MI: Health Administration Press.

Dranove, D. 1993. The Case for Competitive Reform in Health Care. In: *Competitive Approaches to Health Care Reform*. R. J. Arnould, R. F. Rich, and W. D. White, eds. Washington, DC: Urban Institute Press. 67–82.

Eijkenaar, F., M. Emmert, M. Scheppach, and O. Schöffski. 2013. Effects of Pay for Performance in Health Care: A Systematic Review of Systematic Reviews. *Health Policy* 110: 115–130.

Farquhar, M. 2008. AHRQ Quality Indicators. In *Patient Safety and Quality: An Evidence-Based Handbook for Nurses*. R. G. Hughes, ed. Rockville, MD: Agency for Healthcare Research and Quality. Accessed February 2014. Available at: https://www.ncbi.nlm.nih.gov/books/NBK2664/

Feldstein, P. J. 1993. *Health Care Economics*. 4th ed. Albany, NY: Delmar Publishers.

Feldstein, P. 1994. *Health Policy Issues: An Economic Perspective on Health Reform*. Ann Arbor, MI: AUPHA Press/Health Administration Press.

Figueroa, J. F., J. Phelan, H. Newton, E. J. Orav, and E. R. Meara. 2022. ACO Participation Associated with Decreased Spending for Medicare Beneficiaries with Serious Mental Illness. *Health Affairs* 41: 1182–1190.

Finkelstein, A., M. Gentzkow, and H. Williams. 2016. Sources of Geographic Variation in Health Care: Evidence from Patient Migration. *Quarterly Journal of Economics*, 131: 1681–1726.

Finkelstein, E. A., J. G. Trogdon, J. W. Cohen, and W. Dietz. 2009. Annual Medical Spending Attributable to Obesity: Payer- and Service-Specific Estimates. *Health Affairs* 28: W822–W831.

Fisher, E. S., D. E. Wennberg, T. A. Stukel, D. J. Gottlieb, F. L. Lucas, and E. L Pinder. 2003a. The Implications of Regional Variations in Medicare Spending. Part 1: the Content, Quality, and Accessibility of Care. *Annals of Internal Medicine* 138: 273–287.

Fisher, E. S., D. E. Wennberg, T. A. Stukel, D. J. Gottlieb, F. L. Lucas, and E. L. Pinder. 2003b. The Implications of Regional Variations in Medicare Spending. Part 2: Health Outcomes and Satisfaction with Care. *Annals of Internal Medicine* 138: 288–298.

Frakes, M. D., and J. Gruber. 2018. *Defensive Medicine: Evidence from Military Immunity*. Accessed February 2020. Available at: https://www.nber.org/papers/w24846.pdf

Frank, L., E. Basch, J. V. Selby, and For the Patient-Centered Outcomes Research Institute. 2014. The PCORI Perspective on Patient-Centered Outcomes Research. *Journal of the American Medical Association* 312: 1513–1514.

Gallagher, P. 2021. Are You Ready for Changes in the California IHA AMP Program? My 2021. Available at https://www.qrc-analytics.com/2021/11/30/are-you-ready-for-changes-in-the-california-iha-amp-program/

Ganz, P. A., and M. S. Litwin. 1996. Measuring Outcomes and Health-Related Quality of Life. In: *Changing the US Health Care System: Key Issues in Health Services, Policy, and Management*. R. M. Andersen et al., eds. San Francisco, CA: Jossey-Bass Publishers.

Giffin, M., and R. B. Giffin. 1994. Market Memo: Critical Pathways Produce Tangible Results. *Health Care Strategic Management* 12: 1–6.

Gifford, K., E. Ellis, A. Lashbrook, et al. 2019. *A View From the States: Key Medicaid Policy Changes: Results from a 50-State Medicaid Budget Survey for State Fiscal Years 2019 and 2020*. Accessed March 2021. Available at:

https://www.kff.org/report-section/a-view-from-the-states-key-medicaid-policy-changes-delivery-systems/

Gittelsohn, A., and N. R. Powe. 1995. Small Area Variation in Health Care Delivery in Maryland. *Health Services Research* 30: 295–317.

Gottlieb, S. R. 1974. A Brief History of Health Planning in the United States. In: *Regulating Health Facilities Construction*. C. C. Havighurst, ed. Washington, DC: American Enterprise Institute for Public Policy Research.

Grabowski, D. C., A. Chen, and D. Saliba. 2023. Paying for Nursing Home Quality: An Elusive But Important Goal. *Public Policy & Aging Report* 33: S22–S27.

Hartman, M., A. Martin, O. Nuccio, and A. Catlin. 2011. Health Spending Growth at a Historic Low in 2008. *Health Affairs* 29: 147–155.

HCIA Inc., and Deloitte Touche. 1997. *The Comparative Performance of US Hospitals: The Sourcebook*. Baltimore, MD: HCIA Inc.

Health Resources and Service Administration (HRSA). 2019, August. *Telehealth Programs*. Accessed August 2020. Available at: https://www.hrsa.gov/rural-health/telehealth

Huang, H., X. Zhu, F. Ullrich, A. C. MacKinney, and K. Mueller. 2023. The Impact of Medicare Shared Savings Program Participation on Hospital Financial Performance: An Event-Study Analysis. *Health Services Research* 58: 116–127.

Institute of Medicine (IOM). 1993. *Access to Health Care in America*. M. Millman, ed. Washington, DC: National Academy Press.

Institute of Medicine (IOM). 2000. *To Err is Human: Building a Safer Health System*. L. T. Kohn et al., eds. Washington, DC: National Academy Press.

Institute of Medicine (IOM). 2004. *Rewarding Provider Performance: Aligning Incentives in Medicare*. Washington, DC: National Academies Press.

James, J. 2012. Health Policy Briefs: Pay-for-Performance. *Health Affairs*. Accessed September 2013. Available at: http://www.healthaffairs.org/healthpolicybriefs/brief.php?brief_id=78

Jazieh, A. R. 2020. Quality Measures: types, Selection, and Application in Health Care Quality Improvement Projects. *Global Journal on Quality and Safety in Healthcare* 3: 144–146.

Jha, A. K., K. E. Joynt, E. J. Orav, and A.M. Epstein. 2012. The Long-Term Effect of Premier Pay for Performance on Patient Outcomes. *New England Journal of Medicine* 366: 1606–1615.

Judson, T. J., A. Y. Odisho, A. B. Neinstein, et al. 2020. Rapid Design and Implementation of an Integrated Patient Self-Triage and Self-Scheduling Tool for COVID-19. *Journal of the American Medical Informatics Association* 27: 860–866.

Kaiser Family Foundation. 2013. *Health Costs*. Accessed January 2014. Available at: http://www.kaiseredu.org/issue-modules/us-health-care-costs/background-brief.aspx

Kaiser Family Foundation. 2016. *2016 Employer Health Benefits Survey*. Accessed February 2017. Available at: http://kff.org/report-section/ehbs-2016-summary-of-findings/

Kaiser Family Foundation. 2019. *2019 Employer Health Benefits Survey*. Accessed February 2020. Available at: https://www.kff.org/report-section/ehbs-2019-section-1-cost-of-health-insurance/

Karpman, M., A. Weiss, and S. K. Long. 2015. *QuickTake: Access to Health Care Providers Improved Between September 2013 and September 2014. Health Reform Monitoring Survey 2015*. Accessed February 2017. Available at: http://hrms.urban.org/quicktakes/Access-to-Health-Care-Providers-Improved.html

Kosaraju, R. S., G. C. Fonarow, M. K. Ong, et al. 2023. Geographic Variation In The Quality Of Heart Failure Care Among US Veterans. *JACC: Heart Failure*.

Kruse, G. B., D. Polsky, E. A. Stuart, and R. M. Werner. 2012. The Impact of Hospital Pay-for-Performance on Hospital and Medicare costs. *Health Services Research* 47: 2118–2136.

Kyrarini, M., F. Lygerakis, A. Rajavenkatanarayanan, et. al. 2021. A Survey of Robots in Healthcare. *Technologies* 9: 8.

Lamb, R. M., D. M. Studdert, R. M. J. Bohmer, D. M. Berwick, and T. A. Brennan. 2003. Hospital Disclosure Practices: Results of a National Survey. *Health Affairs* 22: 73–83.

Lehman, A. F. 1995. Measuring Quality of Life in a Reformed Health System. *Health Affairs* 14: 90–101.

Levy, D. E. 2006. Employer-sponsored Insurance Coverage of Smoking Cessation Treatments. *American Journal of Managed Care* 12: 553–562.

Lewis, S. 2022. Value-Based Healthcare: Is it the Way forward?? *Future Healthcare Journal* 9: 211–215.

MACPAC. 2016. *Issue brief: Medicaid Physician Payment Policy*. Accessed March 2021. Available at: https://www.macpac.gov/publication/medicaid-physician-payment-policy/

Makary, M. A., and M. Daniel. 2016. Medical error: The Third Leading Cause of Death in the US. *BMJ* 353: i2139.

Mann, D. M., J. Chen, R. Chunara, P. A. Testa, and O. Nov. 2020. COVID-19 Transforms Health Care Through Telemedicine: Evidence from the Field. *Journal of the American Medical Informatics Association* 27: 1132–1135.

Martin, A. B., M. Hartman, B. Washington, A. Catlin, and National Health Expenditure Accounts Team. 2018. National Health Care Spending in 2017: Growth Slows to Post–Great Recession Rates; Share of GDP Stabilizes. *Health Affairs* 38. Available at: https://doi.org/10.1377/hlthaff.2018.05085

Maryland Health Care Commission (MHCC). 2020. *MHCC Overview*. Accessed August 2020. Available at: https://mhcc.maryland.gov/mhcc/pages/home/mhcc_overview/mhcc_overview.aspx

Maryland Health Care Commission (MHCC). n.d. *Hospital Quality Measures*. Accessed August 2020. Available at: https://www.marylandqmdc.org/Article/View/6596c21f-1eec-42e0-90ac-c0963ff3ae73

May, J. 1974. The planning and licensing agencies. In: *Regulating Health Facilities Constructions*. C. C. Havighurst, ed. Washington, DC: American Enterprise Institute for Public Policy Research.

McClellan, M., R. Roiland, and M. Japinga. et al. 2020. Value-Based Care in the COVID-19 Era: Enabling Health Care Response and Resilience.

McGlynn, E. A. 1997. Six Challenges in Measuring the Quality of Health Care. *Health Affairs* 16: 7–21.

McGlynn, E. A., and R. H. Brook. 1996. Ensuring Quality of Care. In: *Changing the US Health Care System: Key Issues in Health Services, Policy, and Management*. R. Andersen et al., eds. San Francisco, CA: Jossey-Bass Publishers.

McWilliams, J. M., B. E. Landon, M. E. Chernew, and A. M. Zaslavsky. 2014. Changes in Patients' Experiences in Medicare Accountable Care Organizations. *New England Journal of Medicine* 371: 1715–1724.

Medicare.gov. 2016. *Hospital Compare: Measures and Current Data Collection Periods*. Accessed March 2021. Available at: https://www.cms.gov/Medicare/Quality-Initiatives-Patient-Assessment-Instruments/HospitalQualityInits/HospitalCompare

Melillo, G. 2020. *Can Healthcare Quality Measures Benefit Patient Health?* AJMC. Accessed August 2020. Available at: https://www.ajmc.com/view/can-healthcare-quality-measures-benefit-patient-health

Minnesota Department of Health. n.d. *Health Care Quality Measures*. Accessed August 2020. Available at: https://www.health.state.mn.us/data/hcquality/index.html

Missouri Foundation for Health. 2019. Medicaid Value-Based Purchasing. Accessed December 2023. Available at: https://mffh.org/wp-content/uploads/2023/08/VBP-Factsheet.pdf

National Center for Health Statistics (NCHS). 2010. *Health, United States, 2009*. Hyattsville, MD: U.S. Department of Health and Human Services.

National Center for Health Statistics (NCHS). 2019a. *Early Release of Selected Estimates Based on Data from the 2018 National Health Interview Survey*. Accessed February 2020. Available at: https://www.cdc.gov/nchs/nhis/releases/released201905.htm#2

National Center for Health Statistics (NCHS). 2019b. *Health, United States, 2018*. Hyattsville, MD: U.S. Department of Health and Human Services. National Conference of State Legislatures. 2019. *CON: Certificate of Need State Laws*. Accessed February 2020. Available at: http://www.ncsl.org/research/health/con-certificate-of-need-state-laws.aspx

National Institute of Health (NIH). 2021. Overweight & Obesity Statistics. Accessed November 2023. Available at: https://www.niddk.nih.gov/health-information/health-statistics/overweight-obesity

National Center for Health Statistics. 2022. Access to Health Care. Accessed November 2023. Available at: https://www.cdc.gov/nchs/fastats/access-to-health-care.htm

National Conference of State Legislatures. 2023. Certificate of Need State Laws. Accessed November 2023. Available at: https://www.ncsl.org/health/certificate-of-need-state-laws

National Quality Forum (NQF). 2013. *Endorsed Individual And Composite Measures*. Accessed May 2017. Available at: https://www.qualityindicators.ahrq.gov/Downloads/Modules/V45/Module_NQF_Endorsement_V4.5.pdf

National Quality Forum (NQF). 2020a. *Measures, Reports, And Tools*. Accessed August 2020. Available at: http://www.qualityforum.org/Measures_Reports_Tools.aspx

National Quality Forum (NQF). 2020b. *What We Do*. Accessed August 2020. Available at: http://www.qualityforum.org/what_we_do.aspx

Nicholas, L. H., J. B. Dimick, and T. J. Iwashyna. 2011. Do Hospitals Alter Patient Care Effort Allocations Under Pay-For-Performance? *Health Services Research* 46: 61–81.

Orlikoff, J. E. 1988. *Malpractice Prevention and Liability Control for Hospitals*. 2nd ed. Chicago, IL: American Hospital Publishing.

Penchansky, R., and J. W. Thomas. 1981. The Concept of Access: Definition and Relationship to Consumer Satisfaction. *Medical Care* 19: 127–140.

Perloff, J., and S. Sobul 2022. Use of Electronic Health Record Systems in Accountable Care Organizations. *American Journal of Managed Care* 28: e31–e34.

Peterson Center on Healthcare and Kaiser Family Foundation. 2019. *How Has U.S. Spending on Healthcare Changed over Time?* Accessed February 2020. Available at: https://www.healthsystemtracker.org/chart-collection/u-s-spending-healthcare-changed-time/#item-start

Rama, A., 2018. *National Health Expenditures, 2016: Annual Spending Growth on the Downswing*. Accessed February 2020. Available at: https://www.ama-assn.org/sites/ama-assn.org/files/corp/media-browser/member/health-policy/prp-annual-spending-2016.pdf

Ramsey, S. D. 2002. Economic Analyses And Clinical Practice Guidelines: Why Not A Match Made In Heaven? *Journal of General Internal Medicine* 17: 235–237.

Reddy, S., J. Fox, and M. P. Purohit. 2019. Artificial Intelligence-Enabled Healthcare Delivery. *Journal of the Royal Society of Medicine* 112: 22–28.

Reinhardt, U. E. 1994. Providing access to health care and controlling costs: The Universal Dilemma. In: *The Nation's Health*. 4th ed. P. R. Lee and C. L. Estes, eds. Boston, MA: Jones & Bartlett Learning. 263–278.

Robert Wood Johnson Foundation (RWJF). 2013. *What is the National Quality Strategy?* Accessed January 2014. Available at: http://www.rwjf.org/en/research-publications/find-rwjf-research/2012/01/what-is-the-national-quality-strategy-.html

Rogers, W. H. 1990. Quality of Care Before and After Implementation of the DRG-Based Prospective

Payment System: A Summary of Effects. *Journal of the American Medical Association* 264: 1989–1994.

Ross, J. S., S. Sheth, and H. M. Krumholz. 2010. State-Sponsored Public Reporting of Hospital Quality: Results Are Hard to Find and Lack Uniformity. *Health Affairs* 29: 2317–2322.

Rutledge, R. I., M. A. Romaire, C. L. Hersey, W. J. Parish, S. M. Kissam, and J. T. Lloyd. 2019. Medicaid Accountable Care Organizations in Four States: Implementation and Early Impacts. *Milbank Quarterly* 97: 583–619. Available at: https://doi.org/10.1111/1468-0009.12386

Ryan, A. M. 2009. Effects of the Premier Hospital Quality Incentive Demonstration on Medicare Patient Mortality and Cost. *Health Services Research* 44: 821–842.

Ryan, A. M., and J. Blustein. 2011. The Effect Of The Masshealth Hospital Pay-For-Performance Program On Quality. *Health Services Research* 46: 712–728. Available at: https://doi.org/10.1111/j.1475-6773.2010.01224.x

Ryan, A. M., and J. Blustein, 2011. The Effect of the Masshealth Hospital Pay-for-Performance Program on Quality. *Health Services Research* 46: 712–728.

Schoen, C. 2016. *The Affordable Care Act and the U.S. Economy: A Five-Year Perspective.* Commonwealth Fund. Accessed February 2017. Available at: http://www.commonwealthfund.org/publications/fund-reports/2016/feb/aca-economy-five-year-perspective

Shartzer, A., S. K. Long, and N. Anderson. 2016. Access to Care and Affordability Have Improved Following Affordable Care Act Implementation; Problems Remain. *Health Affairs (Millwood)* 35: 161–168.

Shih, T., L. H. Nicholas, J. R. Thumma, J. D. Birkmeyer, and J. B. Dimick. 2014. Does Pay-for-Performance Improve Surgical Outcomes? An Evaluation of Phase 2 of the Premier Hospital Quality Incentive Demonstration. *Annals of Surgery* 259: 677.

Skopec, L., and B. D. Sommers. 2013. *Seventy-One Million Additional Americans Are Receiving Preventive Services Coverage Without Cost-Sharing Under the Affordable Care Act.* Accessed May 2017. Available at: https://aspe.hhs.gov/basic-report/seventy-one-million-additional-americans-are-receiving-preventive-services-coverage-without-cost-sharing-under-affordable-care-act

Sommers, B. D., K. Baicker, and A. M. Epstein. 2012. Mortality and Access to Care Among Adults After State Medicaid Expansions. *New England Journal of Medicine* 367: 1025–1034.

Sommers, B., D., M. Z. Gunja, K. Finegold, and T. Musco. 2015. Changes in Self-Reported Insurance Coverage, Access to Care, and Health under the Affordable Care Act. *Journal of the American Medical Association* 314: 366–374.

Svarstad, B. L. 1986. Patient–Practitioner Relationships and Compliance with Prescribed Medical Regimens. In: *Applications of Social Sciences to Clinical Medicine and Health Policy.* L. H. Aiken and D. Mechanic, eds. New Brunswick, NJ: Rutgers University Press.

Tebeje, T. H., and J. Klein. 2021. Applications of e-health to Support Person-Centered Health Care at the Time of COVID-19 Pandemic. *Telemedicine and e-Health* 27:150–158.

TECH Research Network. 2001. Technology Change Around the World: Evidence From Heart Attack Care. *Health Affairs* 20: 25–42.

The Commonwealth Fund. 2023. High U.S. Health Care Spending: Where Is It All Going? Accessed November 2023. Available at: https://www.commonwealthfund.org/publications/issue-briefs/2023/oct/high-us-health-care-spending-where-is-it-all-going

The Commonwealth Fund. 2023. Hospital 30-day Readmissions Age 65 And Older, Per 1,000 Medicare Beneficiaries. Accessed December 2023. Available at: https://www.commonwealthfund.org/datacenter/hospital-30-day-readmissions-age-65-and-older-1000-medicare-beneficiaries

Thielke, A., and V. King. 2020. *Electronic Consultations (Econsults): A Triple Win for Patients, Clinicians, and Payers.* Milbank Memorial Fund. Accessed August 2020. Available at: https://www.milbank.org/wp-content/uploads/2020/06/eConsults_Milbank_Report_v4.pdf

Townsend, P., P. Phillimore, and A. Beattie. 2023. Health and Deprivation: Inequality and the North. *Taylor & Francis* vol. 8. Available at: https://doi.org/10.4324/9781003368885

U.S. Census Bureau. 2018. *Older People Projected to Outnumber Children for the First Time in U.S. history.* Accessed February 2020. Available at: https://www.census.gov/newsroom/press-releases/2018/cb18-41-population-projections.html

U.S. Department of Health and Human Services (DHHS). 1996. *Health, United States, 1995.* Hyattsville, MD: National Center for Health Statistics.

U.S. Government Accountability Office. 2008. *Medicare Part B Imaging Services: Rapid Spending Growth and Shift to Physician Offices Indicate Need for CMS to Consider Additional Management Practices.* Accessed January 2011. Available at: http://www.gao.gov/products/GAO-08-452

USA Today. 2010. Our View on Financing Government: When 47% Don't Pay Income Tax, It's Not Healthy for USA. Accessed May 2017. Available at: https://usatoday30.usatoday.com/news/opinion/editorials/2010-04-16-editorial16_ST_N.htm

Van de Water, P. N. 2019. *More Evidence of Post-ACA Slowdown in Health Care Spending.* Accessed February 2020. Available at: https://www.cbpp.org/blog/more-evidence-of-post-aca-slowdown-in-health-care-spending

Van de Water, P. N., and J. Lavery. 2006. Medicare Finances: Findings of the 2006 Trustees Report. *Medicare Brief* 13: 1–8.

Weigel, G., A. Ramaswamy, L. Sobel, A. Salganicoff, J. Cubanski, and M. Freed. 2020. *Opportunities and Barriers for Telemedicine in the U.S. During the COVID-19 Emergency and Beyond*. Kaiser Family Foundation. Accessed August 2020. Available at: https://www.kff.org/womens-health-policy/issue-brief/opportunities-and-barriers-for-telemedicine-in-the-u-s-during-the-covid-19-emergency-and-beyond/

Wendling, W., and J. Werner. 1980. Nonprofit Firms and the Economic Theory of Regulation. *Quarterly Review of Economics and Business* 20: 6–18.

Wennberg., J. E. 2002. Unwarranted Variations in Healthcare Delivery: Implications for Academic Medical Centres. *British Medical Journal* 325: 961–964.

Wennberg, J. E., and A. Gittelsohn. 1973. Small Area Variations in Health Care Delivery. *Science* 183: 1102–1108.

Wennberg, J. E., J. L. Freeman, and W. J. Culp. 1987. Are Hospital Services Rationed in New Haven or Over-Utilized in Boston? *Lancet* 1: 1185–1189.

Werner, R. M., J. T. Kolstad, E. A. Stuart, and D. Polsky. 2011. The Effect of Pay-for-Performance in Hospitals: Lessons for Quality Improvement. *Health Affairs* 30: 690–698.

Werner, R. M., E. J. Emanuel, H. H. Pham, and A. S. Navathe. 2021. The Future of Value-Based Payment: A Road Map to 2030.

Williams, K. N., and R. H. Brook. 1978. Quality Measurement and Assurance. *Health Medical Care Services Review* 1: 3–15.

Williams, S. J. 1995. *Essentials of Health Services*. Albany, NY: Delmar Publishers.

Williams, S. J., and P. R. Torrens. 1993. Influencing, Regulating, and Monitoring the Health Care System. In: *Introduction To Health Services*. 4th ed. S. J. Williams and P. R. Torrens, eds. Albany, NY: Delmar Publishers. 377–396.

Wilson, F. A., and D. Neuhauser. 1985. *Health Services in the United States*. 2nd ed. Cambridge, MA: Ballinger Publishing.

Wilson, M., Guta, A., Waddell, K., Lavis, J., Reid, R., and Evans, C. 2020. The Impacts of Accountable Care Organizations on Patient Experience, Health Outcomes and Costs: A Rapid Review. *Journal of Health Services Research & Policy* 25: 130–138.

Wong, M. D., R. Andersen, C. D. Sherbourne, R. D. Hays, and M. F. Shapiro. 2001. Effects of Cost Sharing on Care Seeking and Health Status: Results from the Medical Outcomes Study. *American Journal of Public Health* 91: 1889–1894.

Young, H. M., and T. S. Nesbitt. 2016. Increasing the Capacity of Primary Care Through Enabling Technology. *Journal of General Internal Medicine* 32: 398–403. Available at: doi: 10.1007/s11606-016-3952-3.

Zuckerman, R. B., S. H. Sheingold, E. J. Orav, J. Ruhter, and A. M. Epstein. 2016. Readmissions, Observation, and the Hospital Readmissions Reduction Program. *New England Journal of Medicine* 374: 1543–1551.

Zuckerman, S., and J. Holahan. 2012. *Despite Criticism, The Affordable Care Act Does Much To Contain Health Care Costs*. Accessed January 2014. Available at: http://www.urban.org/UploadedPDF/412665-Despite-Criticism-The-Affordable-Care-Act-Does-Much-to-Contain-Health-Care-Cost.pdf

CHAPTER 13

Health Policy

LEARNING OBJECTIVES

- Discuss the definition, scope, and role of health policy in the United States.
- Recognize the principal features of U.S. health policy.
- Describe the process by which legislative health policy is developed.
- Identify critical health policy issues in the United States.
- Discuss the passage, implementation, repeal, and restoration of the Affordable Care Act from a political perspective.

"Ladies and gentlemen, to come up with a uniform health policy, we will now break up into 31 different groups."

Introduction

Even though the United States does not have a centrally controlled system of healthcare delivery, it does have a history of federal, state, and local government involvement in health care and health policy. Government involvement in social welfare programs can be traced back to almshouses and pesthouses, the two well-known government-run institutions of the 19th century. Perhaps the most visible policy efforts, which continue to have implications today, are the social programs created under the Social Security legislation during Franklin Roosevelt's presidency in the 1940s. Amendments to the Social Security Act later created the massive public health insurance programs Medicare and Medicaid in 1965, the Children's Health Insurance Program (CHIP) in 1997, and the recently enacted Patient Protection and Affordable Care Act (ACA).

The government's success in bringing about social change through health policy has given it a solid footing to engage in further expansion of tax-financed health care. Hence, the government continues to find new opportunities to mold healthcare delivery through health policy. This chapter defines what health policy is and explores the principal features of health policy in the United States. It describes how legislative policy is developed and provides a policy context for many past developments in healthcare delivery, including the ACA.

What Is Health Policy?

Public policies are authoritative decisions made in the legislative, executive, or judicial branch of government intended to direct or influence the actions, behaviors, or decisions of others (Longest, 2010; Shi, 2014). When public policies pertain to or influence the pursuit of health, they become health policies. **Health policy** can be defined as "the aggregate of principles, stated or unstated, that . . . characterize the distribution of resources, services, and political influences that impact on the health of the population" (Shi, 2019, p.19).

Public policies are supposed to serve the interests of the public; however, the term "public" has been interpreted differently in the political landscape. At the most general level, the term "public" refers to all Americans. "Public" can also refer to voters or likely voters in political elections. Finally, this term can refer to only those who are politically active—that is, those Americans who communicate directly with their representatives by writing or calling them, who contribute money to politicians or political groups, who attend protests or other forums on behalf of a particular interest or candidate, or who, in other ways, make their voices and policy preferences heard. People who are older, have more years of education, and have strong party identification are more likely to be politically active.

Legislators and policymakers tend to be responsive to the views or wishes of these active Americans, particularly when they are constituents from within their legislative districts. In contrast, politicians tend to strongly lean toward supporting policies that agree with their own ideologies or advance their own political agendas. Because most policymakers are also politicians, policymaking and politics are often closely intertwined. Unfortunately, policymaking often becomes highly politicized and is held hostage to the ideologies of whichever political party happens to be in power at a given time. The party in power can also exert considerable peer pressure on its own members to support policies along party lines. For most politicians, their primary concern may be getting elected or reelected. Hence, certain policies are driven by a strong desire to keep campaign promises or to please some powerful constituent groups.

This kind of policy-for-politics approach does not ask for or consider the cost-benefit trade-offs of a proposed policy. Policies driven by political considerations are likely to be near-sighted. In addition, party-line politics keep the American public deeply divided on major issues, as witnessed during the 2016 and 2020 presidential elections.

Uses of Policy
Regulatory Tools

Health policies may be used as **regulatory tools** (Longest, 2010). Such policies call on government to prescribe and control the behavior of a particular target group by monitoring the group and imposing sanctions if it fails to comply. Examples of regulatory policies abound in the healthcare system. Federally funded quality improvement organizations (QIOs; formerly called peer review organizations), for instance, develop and enforce standards concerning appropriate care under the Medicare program. State insurance departments across the country regulate insurance companies and managed care organizations in an effort to protect customers from default on coverage in case of financial failure of the insurer, excessive premiums, and mendacious practices. Since the passage of the ACA, the U.S. Department of Health and Human Services (DHHS) has been charged with the responsibility of implementing many of its provisions, whereas the U.S. Department of the Treasury, through the Internal Revenue Service (IRS), has been charged with the responsibility of regulating the employer mandate and collecting the many taxes imposed by the ACA.

Some health policies are "self-regulatory." For example, physicians set standards of medical practice, hospitals accredit one another as meeting the standards that the Joint Commission has set, and schools of public health decide which courses should be part of their graduate programs in public health. Similarly, managed care organizations (MCOs) voluntarily collect and report on quality measures, using Healthcare Effectiveness Data and Information Set (HEDIS) data, to the National Committee for Quality Assurance, which is a voluntary, nongovernmental agency.

Allocative Tools

Health policies may also be used as **allocative tools** (Longest, 2010). They involve the direct provision of income, services, or goods to certain groups of individuals or institutions. Allocative tools in the healthcare arena may be either distributive or redistributive.

Distributive policies spread benefits throughout society. Typical distributive policies include funding of medical research through the National Institutes of Health (NIH), the development of medical personnel (e.g., medical education through the National Health Service Corps), the construction of facilities (e.g., hospitals under the Hill-Burton Act program during the 1950s and 1960s), and the initiation of new institutions (e.g., health maintenance organizations [HMOs] under the Health Maintenance Organization Act of 1973).

Redistributive policies are designed to benefit only certain groups of people by taking money from one group and using it for the benefit of another. This system often creates visible beneficiaries and payers. For this reason, health policy is often most visible and politically charged when it performs redistributive functions. Redistributive policies include Medicaid—which takes tax revenue from the more affluent and spends it on the impoverished in the form of free health insurance—as well as CHIP, welfare, and public housing programs.

Redistributive policies, in particular, are believed to be essential for addressing the fundamental causes of health disparities. Expansion of health insurance for the uninsured—a key goal of the ACA—is also based on a redistributive approach.

Different Forms of Health Policies

Health policies often emerge as a by-product of social policies enacted by the government. For example, the Social Security Act of 1935 was passed mainly as a retirement income security measure for older adults, but it also contained the Old Age Assistance program, which enabled older people to pay for services in homes for older people and boarding homes. After World War II, policies that excluded fringe benefits from income or Social Security taxes and a 1948 Supreme Court ruling that employee benefits, including health insurance, could be legitimately included in the collective bargaining process had the effect of promoting employment-based private health insurance. Consequently, employer-based health benefits grew rapidly in the mid-20th century.

The extraordinary growth of medical technology in the United States can also be traced to health policies that directly support biomedical research and encourage private investments in such research. The NIH had a budget of approximately $10 million when the agency was established in the early 1930s. Following exponential growth in its funding, the fiscal year 2020 budget for the NIH was $41.68 billion (Senate Appropriations Committee, 2019). The fiscal year 2023 NIH budget was $49.183 billion, $3 billion more than enacted in 2022 (Congressional Research Service, 2023). Encouraged by policies such as patent laws that permit firms to recoup their investments in research and development, private industry is the largest financier of biomedical research and development in the United States.

Health policies affect groups or classes of individuals, such as physicians, people with low income, older adults, and children. They can also affect various types of organizations, such as medical schools, HMOs, hospitals, nursing homes, manufacturers of medical technology, and employers. Examples include licensing of physicians and nurses by states; federal certification of healthcare institutions, which enables these facilities to receive public funds to care for patients covered by the Medicare and Medicaid programs; court decisions that may prevent the merger of two hospitals on the grounds of violating federal antitrust laws; and local ordinances banning smoking in public places.

Statutes or laws, such as the statutory language contained in the 1983 Amendments to the Social Security Act that authorized the prospective payment system (PPS) for reimbursing hospitals for Medicare beneficiaries, are also considered policies. Another example is the certificate of need (CON) programs, through which many states seek to regulate capital expansion in their healthcare systems. While CON programs have changed significantly over the past 30 years, as of 2023, 35 states and Washington, DC, maintained some type of CON program, while 3 states had some variation of the program (National Conference of State Legislatures, 2023). States that maintain CON programs often target expansion of outpatient and long-term care facilities, which make up a growing segment of the healthcare market (National Conference of State Legislatures, 2019).

The scope of health policy is limited by both the political and economic systems of a country. In the United States, where pro-individual and pro-market sentiments dominate, public policies have been incremental and noncomprehensive. Even the massive ACA is regarded as a major incremental reform (Glied, 2019). National policies and programs typically reflect the notion that local communities are in the best position to identify the most desirable strategies to address their unique needs. The type of change that can be enacted at the community level is clearly limited, however, because communities are bounded by policies and regulations formulated at the national and state levels.

Principal Features of U.S. Health Policy

Several features characterize U.S. health policy, including the government's subsidiary position relative to the private sector; fragmented, incremental, and piecemeal reform; pluralistic politics associated with demanders and suppliers of policy; a decentralized role for the states; and the impact of presidential leadership. These features often act or interact to influence the development and evolution of health policies.

Government as Subsidiary to the Private Sector

In much of the developed world, national healthcare programs are built on a consensus that health care is a right of citizenship and that government should play a leading role in its delivery. In contrast, in the United States, health care has not been considered a right of citizenship or a primary responsibility of government. Instead, the private sector has played a dominant role in developing the U.S. healthcare landscape. Traditionally, Americans have been opposed to any major government interventions in healthcare financing and delivery, except for helping the underprivileged. Over the past few years, an argument has been made that health care should also be a right in the United States; this view finally prevailed and became the basis for the ACA. Because not all Americans espouse liberal views, however, the ACA has deeply divided the nation.

Americans' general mistrust of government dates back to the founding of the United States. The Declaration of Independence defined the new nation by making a great protest over government intrusion on personal liberty. It outlined the individual's right to life, liberty, and the pursuit of happiness. Later, the U.S. Constitution further limited the powers of government. The fundamental beliefs and values that most Americans still subscribe to evolved from these earlier founding documents.

Generally speaking, the government's role in U.S. health care has grown incrementally, mainly to address perceived problems and negative health consequences for the underprivileged. Also, the most credible argument for policy intervention in the nation's domestic activities begins with the identification of situations in which markets fail or do not function efficiently. In an ironic twist, even though health care in the United States functions under imperfect market conditions, problems and issues in health care are often blamed on "the market," which prompts politicians to further regulate health care through policy interventions. For example, cost escalations in the healthcare delivery system were assumed to reflect the inability of private parties to control healthcare costs, which paved the way for various prospective payment methods.

Unfortunately, certain policy interventions have also fueled the growth of healthcare expenditures, at least indirectly. The legislation passed in many states to rein in managed care organizations' initiatives to contain escalating healthcare costs is a prime example. Meanwhile, for lack of other cost-control alternatives, several states passed laws to enroll all of their Medicaid beneficiaries in managed care programs. By comparison, voluntary enrollment by Medicare enrollees in the federal Medicare Advantage (Part C) program has been less successful.

Government spending for health care has been largely confined to filling the gaps in areas where the private sector has been unwilling or unable to address certain issues. For example, court decisions such as *Duggan v. Bowen* and *Olmstead v. L.C.* were largely responsible for promoting large-scale transfers of people with mental illness and disabilities from institutions to community-based settings across the United States. Other policy interventions include various public health measures, such as environmental protection, communicable disease control, and preparedness for disasters and bioterrorism.

Fragmented Policies

Fragmentation of the government's power in the United States follows the design of the Founding Fathers, who developed a structure of "checks and balances" to limit the government's power.

Federal, state, and local governments pursue their own policies, with little coordination of purpose or programs occurring. The subsidiary role of the government and the attendant mixture of private and public approaches to the delivery of health care have also resulted in a complex and fragmented pattern of healthcare financing in which (1) the employed are predominantly covered by voluntary insurance provided through contributions that they and their employers make; (2) older people are insured through a combination of private-public financing of Medicare; (3) people with lower income are covered by Medicaid through a combination of federal and state tax revenues; and (4) special population groups—for example, veterans, American Indians, members of the armed forces, Congress, and employees of the executive branch—have coverage provided directly by the federal government.

Incremental and Piecemeal Policies

The incremental and piecemeal health policies observed in the United States have resulted from numerous compromises made to accommodate a variety of competing interests. An example is the broadening of the Medicaid program since its introduction in 1965. In 1984, the first steps were taken to mandate coverage of pregnant individuals and children in two-parent families who met income requirements and to mandate coverage for all children 5 years or younger who met Medicaid's financial requirements. In 1986, states were given the option of covering pregnant individuals and children up to 5 years of age in families with incomes less than 100% of the federal poverty level (FPL). In 1988, that option was increased to cover families with incomes less than 185% of the FPL. In 1997, under CHIP, states were allowed to use Medicaid to extend coverage to uninsured children who otherwise did not qualify for the existing Medicaid program. The Medicaid experience illustrates how a program may be reformed and/or expanded through successive legislative action achieved through compromises between the two opposite political parties.

The Medicare program was also expanded incrementally. At first, it covered only older adults under Parts A and B in 1965. Since then, Medicare has been expanded to include benefits for speech, physical, and chiropractic therapy in 1972. In the 1980s, the Medicare program added a payment option for HMOs. Over the years, Congress expanded Medicare eligibility to younger people with permanent disabilities who receive Social Security Disability Insurance payments and those who have end-stage renal disease (ESRD). In 1982, the program added hospice benefits, and in 2001, Medicare was further expanded to cover younger people with amyotrophic lateral sclerosis.

Interest Groups as Demanders of Policy

Health policy outcomes in the United States are heavily influenced by the demands of interest groups and the compromises struck to satisfy those demands. **Exhibit 13-1** summarizes the major concerns of the dominant interest groups. The powerful interest groups involved in healthcare politics have historically resisted any major changes in the existing healthcare system (Alford, 1975). Each group fights hard to protect its own best interests; however, the result for any single group is less than optimal. Well-organized interest groups are the most effective "demanders" of policies. By combining and concentrating their members' resources, such groups can dramatically change the ratio between the costs and benefits of participation in the political process for policy change. These interest groups represent a variety of individuals and entities, such as physicians in the American Medical Association (AMA); senior citizens allied with AARP (American Association of Retired Persons); institutional providers, such as hospitals belonging to the American Hospital Association (AHA); nursing homes belonging to the

Exhibit 13-1 Key Healthcare Concerns of Selected Interest Groups

Federal and State Governments
- Cost containment
- Access to care
- Quality of care

Employers
- Cost containment
- Workplace health and safety
- Minimum regulation

Consumers
- Access to care
- Quality of care
- Lower out-of-pocket costs

Insurers
- Administrative simplification
- Elimination of cost shifting

Practitioners
- Income maintenance
- Professional autonomy
- Malpractice reform

Provider Organizations
- Profitability
- Administrative simplification
- Bad debt reduction

Technology Producers
- Tax treatment
- Regulatory environment
- Research funding

American Health Care Association; and the pharmaceutical companies making up the Pharmaceutical Research and Manufacturers of America (PhRMA).

Physicians have often found it hard to lobby for their interests with a single voice because they include so many specialty groups. For example, the American Academy of Pediatrics is involved in advocacy for children's health issues. Other specialty groups include Physicians for a National Health Program, the American Society of Anesthesiologists, and the Society of Thoracic Surgeons. Sometimes, however, these groups come together on issues that threaten the interests of all physicians. For example, the various physician groups coalesced in 1992, when Medicare decided to change the reimbursement system from fee for service to a resource-based relative value scale (RBRVS). Notably, the physicians did not prevail in this case.

The policy agendas of interest groups reflect the interests of their members. For example, AARP advocates for programs to expand healthcare financing for older adults. It became a major advocate for prescription drug coverage for Medicare beneficiaries by supporting the Medicare Prescription Drug Improvement and Modernization Act of 2003. In a surprising move, AARP enthusiastically supported the ACA even though the law had proposed Medicare cuts, which were opposed by older adults. It was suggested that payment cuts to Medicare Advantage (MA) plans might trigger a withdrawal of participating insurers from MA, which would financially benefit AARP, the largest sponsor of Medigap plans (Roy, 2012). For once, this organization seemed to have abandoned its primary mission to champion the interests of its older adult members.

Other examples of interest groups include labor unions, which have become the staunchest supporters of national health insurance. The primary concerns of educational and research institutions and accrediting bodies are embedded in policies that would generate higher funding to support their educational and research activities.

Pharmaceutical and medical technology organizations are concerned with detecting changes in health policy and influencing the formulation of policies concerning approval and monitoring of drugs and devices. Three main factors drive health policy concerns about medical technology:

- Medical technology is an important contributor to rising health costs.
- Medical technology often provides health benefits.

- The utilization of medical technology provides economic benefits by creating jobs in health care and other sectors of the economy.

These factors are likely to remain important determinants of U.S. policies on medical technology. Another factor driving U.S. technology policy is policymakers' desire to develop cost-saving technology and expand access to it. The government is spending large amounts of money on outcomes studies and comparative effectiveness studies to identify the value of alternative technologies that promise better care at lower costs.

Business also is a major interest group, although it is generally split into two factions: large versus small employers. U.S. employers' health policy concerns are shaped mostly by the degree to which they provide health insurance benefits to their employees, their employees' dependents, and their retirees. Many small business owners adamantly oppose health policies requiring them to cover employees because they believe they cannot afford to provide this benefit. Employees also pay attention to health policies that affect worker health or labor-management relations. For example, employers must comply with federal and state regulations focusing on employee health and well-being and on the prevention of job-related illnesses and injuries. Employers are often inspected by regulatory agencies to ensure that they adhere to workplace health and safety policies.

Other relatively newer members of the health policy community represent consumer interests. For example, the Tea Party movement, which represents conservative Americans, actively demonstrated in Washington, DC, and around the United States during the legislative battle to pass the ACA, although they ultimately lost this fight. Consumer representation on the liberal side during the ACA debate was noticeably silent, perhaps for two main reasons: (1) It was believed that a liberal majority in Congress and a liberal president were already taking action on their behalf, and (2) the Tea Party movement was often marginalized in the news media (based largely on false reports).

Pluralistic Suppliers of Policy

In the United States, each branch and level of government can influence health policy. For example, both the executive and legislative branches at the federal, state, and local levels can establish health policies, and the judicial branch can uphold, strike down, or modify existing laws affecting health and health care at federal, state, or local levels. Perhaps the biggest factor is shifts in control of the presidency and Congress, which can either create or close down opportunities for reform (Oliver et al., 2004). Fundamental ideologies, leaning toward the left or the right, come to the fore when advocates of these ideologies seek to take policy action as control passes from one political party to the other. The dominant political party often ends up sweeping its agenda through Congress as long as there is little resistance from powerful interest groups and the American people. For either meaningful support or resistance to occur toward a proposed policy, transparency and truthful information must be made available by the policymakers, and it must be faithfully carried to the public by the news media.

All three branches of government—legislative, executive, and judicial—are suppliers of policy. Of these, the legislative branch is the most active in policymaking, as evidenced by the numerous policies that take the form of statutes or laws. Legislators play central roles in providing policies demanded by their various constituencies.

Members of the executive branch also act as suppliers of policies. Presidents, governors, and other high-level public officials routinely propose policies in the form of proposed legislation and push legislators to enact their preferred policies. Executives and administrators in charge of departments and agencies of government make policies in the form of rules and regulations used to implement statutes and programs. In this manner, they interpret congressional interest, thereby becoming intermediary suppliers of policies.

The judicial branch of government is a policy supplier as well. Whenever a court interprets an ambiguous statute, establishes judicial precedents, or interprets the Constitution, it makes policy. These activities are not conceptually different from legislators enacting statutes or members of the executive branch establishing rules and regulations for the implementation of the statutes. All three activities concur during the definition of policy, as they are authoritative decisions made within government to influence or direct the actions, behaviors, and decisions of others.

Decentralized Role of the States

In the United States, under the theory of federalism, political power is shared between the federal government and the governments in each state. Hence, individual states play a significant role in the development and implementation of health policies. An example is the state governments' dominant role in regulating managed care in the delivery of health care. Other examples of states' roles include financial support for the care and treatment of people with limited financial resources and people with chronic disabilities, oversight of healthcare practitioners and facilities through state licensure and regulation, training of health personnel (states pay most of the costs to train healthcare professionals), and authorization of health services available through local governments. **Exhibit 13-2** lists the arguments often cited in favor of decentralizing health programs at the state level.

Many of the incremental policy actions related to health care have originated in state governments. One such action by states was

Exhibit 13-2 Arguments for Enhancing States' Role in Health Policy Making

- Americans distrust centralized government in general and lack faith in the federal government as an administrator in particular.
- The federal government has grown too large, intrusive, and paternalistic.
- The federal government is too impersonal, distant, and unresponsive.
- State and local governments are closer to the people and more familiar with local needs; therefore, they are more accessible and accountable to the public and better able to develop responsive programs than federal agencies.
- National standards reduce flexibility and seriously constrain the ability of states to experiment and innovate.
- States are equipped to take on such functions (i.e., they have more full-time legislators, professional staffs, and bureaucrats).
- States are more likely to implement and enforce programs of their own making.
- States have served as important laboratories for testing different structures, approaches, and programs and for providing insight into the political and technical barriers encountered in enactment and implementation.
- States can respond to crises more quickly.
- It is easier to change a state law than a federal law.
- States are more willing to take risks.

the creation of "insurance risk pools," a type of program that helped people acquire private insurance otherwise unavailable to them because of the medical risks they posed to insurance companies. These special programs were financed by a combination of individual premiums and taxes on insurance carriers. The ACA does away with the need for state-based risk pools under the assumption that insurers cannot legally deny insurance to anyone with a preexisting medical condition, no matter how severe the condition.

Other state-initiated programs have sought to address the needs of vulnerable populations. For example, New Jersey developed a program to ensure access to care for all pregnant individuals. Florida set up a program called Healthy Kids Corporation, which linked health insurance to schools. Washington developed a special program for the low-income employees that used HMOs and preferred provider organizations (PPOs) to provide care within the state's counties. Maine established MaineCare, a program that offered HMO-based coverage at moderate prices to small businesses with 15 or fewer employees. Minnesota created the Children's Health Plan, a program designed to provide benefits to children up to 9 years of age who lived in families with incomes less than 185% of the FPL but who did not qualify for Medicaid.

Two states in particular took bold policy initiatives to expand health insurance coverage. In 1989, Oregon embarked on a controversial experiment that expanded Medicaid coverage to more than 100,000 additional people by reducing the Medicaid benefits package (Bodenheimer, 1997). In 2006, Massachusetts passed a universal health insurance program based on employer and employee mandates.

The dichotomous federal-state approach to policymaking has some distinct disadvantages. For one thing, the divergence between states and the federal government makes it difficult to coordinate a national strategy in many areas. For example, it would be difficult to plan a national disease-control program if some states do not participate or if states do not collect and report data in a uniform manner.

States may also interpret federal incentives in ways that jeopardize the policy's original intent. For example, many states took advantage of federal matching grants for Medicaid by including a number of formerly state-funded services under their "expanded" Medicaid programs. This allowed states to obtain increased federal funding while providing exactly the same level of services they had provided prior to the "expansion." This phenomenon, called Medicaid maximization, although pursued by only a few states, had an impact outside of those states and may have contributed to rising national healthcare costs in the early 1990s (Coughlin et al., 1999). Subsequent to a 2012 U.S. Supreme Court decision, states have been able to choose whether to expand their Medicaid programs, as was originally mandated by the ACA, and not risk losing federal matching funds. Under the ACA, states are promised that their additional expenses incurred as a result of Medicaid expansion will be paid by the federal government.

Impact of Presidential Leadership

To pass national policy initiatives, a strong presidential role is almost always necessary. Lyndon Johnson's role in the passage of the Medicare and Medicaid legislation, George W. Bush's role in adding prescription drug coverage to Medicare, and Barack Obama's role in the enactment of the ACA are key examples. Presidents have important opportunities to influence congressional outcomes through their efforts to bring about compromises, to engage in political maneuvering, or to take advantage of economic and political situations, particularly when policies concern their own preferred agendas.

Even under the most auspicious political circumstances, however, presidents are often thwarted from getting their agendas fully adopted by Congress. For example, while running for a U.S. Senate seat, candidate Barack Obama made it clear that he was a proponent of a single-payer healthcare system. This position was opposed by hospitals, insurance companies, and the pharmaceutical industry. Only after President Obama's administration reached compromises with this powerful industry block did the ACA become a reality.

Sometimes presidents' political agendas result, years later, in unintended and undesirable consequences. In 1946, President Harry Truman took advantage of reports that the United States had severe capacity deficits in the hospital sector and that many Americans across the country were unable to access acute-care services, using them as a stepping stone to create the Hill-Burton Act—a law passed by Congress in 1946 that gave grants and loans to hospitals, nursing homes, and other health facilities for construction and modernization. In 1965, President Lyndon Johnson dreamed of a "great society" to push his Medicare and Medicaid agenda through Congress. Both the Truman- and Johnson-advocated programs were passed through political compromises. Over time, however, overbuilding of hospitals and unrestrained use of Medicare and Medicaid funding sent healthcare costs into an uncontrolled upward spiral. Paradoxically, just when the nation achieved its goal of 4.5 community hospital beds per 1,000 population in 1980, as envisioned under the Hill-Burton Act program, the government concluded that the Medicare and Medicaid programs were no longer sustainable due to the rapid rise in healthcare costs. Subsequently, President Ronald Reagan authorized the PPS method of payment to reduce hospital utilization, which started a downward trend in inpatient stays and created a glut of unoccupied hospital beds in many parts of the United States.

Rising healthcare costs shortly after the Medicare and Medicaid programs were implemented also created an economic opportunity for President Richard Nixon to pass the Health Maintenance Organization Act in 1973. In addition, Nixon succeeded in getting the CON legislation enacted under the National Health Planning and Resources Development Act of 1974. This act represented another effort to restrain rapidly rising healthcare costs, as it required approvals for purchases of new healthcare technology and new hospital construction.

In the 1990s, even though President Bill Clinton's comprehensive healthcare reform efforts failed, his incremental initiatives did succeed in creating CHIP and enacting the Health Insurance Portability and Accountability Act (HIPAA) of 1996. Clinton's first term in office was marked by a relatively high level of public interest in healthcare reform, but his administration did not act on it quickly enough. Also, the ever-changing details of his proposal, when made public, proved too complex for most people to grasp. Moreover, Americans did not want their taxes increased to pay for healthcare reform.

Politics of the Affordable Care Act

Prior to Barack Obama's victory in the 2008 presidential election, there was much excitement among his supporters about the prospect of the first Black U.S. president, especially one whose campaign mantra was "hope and change." Anyone asking pointed questions about Obama's vision of hope and change ran the risk of the queries becoming distorted into a racial issue by the U.S. media. Hence, amid the excitement of the election, pertinent issues often went unaddressed. In regard to his healthcare initiatives, Obama simply stated that everyone would have health insurance. Perhaps by design, not even a general model of the proposed plan was ever made public. Nonetheless, Obama had overwhelming support from the members of his own party.

The enactment of the ACA became reality following a unique set of political circumstances that is perhaps unparalleled in the history of U.S. policymaking. At the time, both houses of Congress had solid Democratic majorities and strong Democratic leadership—Nancy Pelosi in the House of Representatives and Harry Reid in the Senate. The United States was then in the middle of the worst economic downturn since the Great Depression, with an unemployment rate that exceeded 10%. Obama and his Democratic colleagues blamed former President George W. Bush for the nation's various malaises. In addition, they portrayed the insurance industry as the villain responsible for rising healthcare costs.

Whereas the Clinton plan had been presented in full to the public in 1993, details of the ACA legislation were largely kept secret from the public. Democrats made little effort to make passage of the ACA a bipartisan process. Republicans, who were in the minority in both houses of Congress, made few contributions to the debate on healthcare reform. In the end, the ACA passed without a single Republican vote.

Oberlander (2010) identified other factors that contributed to the passage of the ACA. Instead of employing different reform strategies, members of the House of Representatives introduced a single health reform bill that combined three bills from three House committees, demonstrating greater agreement among Democrats. The final legislation also allowed certain exemptions from individual and employer mandates.

Oberlander (2010) also credited weak opposition to the bill from health industry stakeholders as playing a key role in its passage. Instead of waging a war against the industry, Obama and congressional Democrats were willing to compromise. By promising growth in their markets—that is, millions of newly insured people who would use health care—they received pledges from important industry stakeholders, including PhRMA and the AHA, to support healthcare reform. Even the insurance industry and the AMA endorsed the legislation, although their support faded over time.

Another key factor behind the ACA's success was the speed with which the reform was pushed through the legislative process. A notable drawback was that the general public was confused about the legislation and was not supportive (Patel and McDonough, 2010). In the end, however, that did not seem to have mattered. Today, the public remains divided on the legislation. As of May 2023, tracking polls showed that 40% hold unfavorable views of the ACA versus 59% holding favorable views (Kaiser Family Foundation, 2023).

The Development of Legislative Health Policy

The making of U.S. health policy is a complex process that involves the private and public sectors, including multiple levels of government. It reflects several unique aspects of the U.S. system of government and the U.S. populace:

- The relationship of the government to the private sector
- The distribution of authority and responsibility within a federal system of government
- The relationship between policy formulation and implementation
- A pluralistic ideology as the basis of politics
- Incrementalism as the strategy for reform

The Policy Cycle

The formation and implementation of health policy occurs in a policy cycle comprising five components: (1) issue raising, (2) policy design, (3) public support building, (4) legislative decision-making and policy support building, and (5) legislative decision-making and policy implementation. These activities are likely to be shared by Congress and interest groups to varying degrees.

Issue raising is clearly essential in the policy formation cycle. The enactment of a new policy is preceded by a variety of actions that first create a widespread sense that a problem exists and needs to be addressed. The president may form policy concepts from a variety of sources, including campaign information; recommendations from advisers, cabinet members, and agency chiefs; personal interests; expert opinions; and public opinion polls.

The second component of policymaking is the design of specific policy proposals. Presidents have substantial resources to develop new policy proposals. They may call on segments of the executive branch of government, such as the Centers for Medicare and Medicaid Services (CMS) and policy staffs within the

DHHS. An alternative—and one that was preferred by both Presidents John Kennedy and Lyndon Johnson—is to use outside task forces.

In building public support, presidents can choose from a variety of strategies, including major addresses to the nation and efforts to mobilize their administration to make public appeals and organized attempts to increase support among interest groups. To facilitate legislative decision-making and policy support building, presidents, key staff, and department officials interact closely with Congress. Presidents generally meet with legislative leaders several mornings each month to shape the coming legislative agenda and identify possible problems as bills move through various committees.

Legislative Committees and Subcommittees

The legislative branch creates health policies and allocates the resources necessary to implement them. Congress has three important powers that make it extremely influential in the health policy process.

First, the Constitution grants Congress the power to "make all laws which shall be necessary and proper for carrying into execution." The doctrine of implied powers states that Congress may use any reasonable means not directly prohibited by the Constitution to carry out the will of the people. This mandate gives it great power to enact laws influencing all manner of health policy.

Second, Congress possesses the power to tax, which allows it to influence and regulate the health behavior of individuals, organizations, and states. Taxes on cigarettes, for example, are intended to reduce individual cigarette consumption, whereas tax relief for employer benefits is designed to promote increased insurance coverage for employed people.

Third, Congress possesses the power to spend. This ability to allocate resources not only allows for direct expenditures on the public's health through federal programs, such as Medicare and the NIH, but also gives Congress the ability to induce state conformance with federal policy objectives. Congress may prescribe the terms under which it dispenses funds to the states, such as mandating the basic required elements of the jointly federal- and state-funded Medicaid program.

At least 14 committees and subcommittees in the House of Representatives, 24 committees and subcommittees in the Senate, and more than 60 other such legislative panels directly influence legislation (Falcone and Hartwig, 1991; Morone et al., 2008). The conglomeration of reform proposals that emerge from these committees face a daunting political challenge—separate consideration and passage in each chamber, negotiations in a joint conference committee to reconcile the bills passed by the two houses, and then return to each chamber for approval. In the Senate, 41 of the 100 members can thwart the whole process at any point. In some circumstances, the nuclear option can be applied, which is a parliamentary procedure that allows the Senate to override a rule or precedent by a simple majority of 51 votes.

Five committees—three in the House and two in the Senate—control most of the legislative activity in Congress (Longest, 2010). They are discussed in the following subsections.

House Committees

The Constitution provides that all bills involving taxation must originate in the House of Representatives. The organization of the House gives this authority to the Ways and Means Committee. Hence, the Ways and Means Committee is the most influential by virtue of its power to tax. This committee was the launching pad for much of the health financing legislation passed in the 1960s and early 1970s under the chairmanship of Representative Wilbur Mills (Democrat-Arkansas). Ways and Means has sole jurisdiction over Medicare Part A, Social Security, unemployment compensation, public welfare, and healthcare reform. It also shares jurisdiction over Medicare Part B with the House Energy and Commerce Committee. The latter committee has jurisdiction over Medicaid, Medicare Part B, matters of public health, mental health, health personnel, HMOs, foods and drugs, air pollution, consumer products safety, health planning, biomedical research, and health protection.

The Committee on Appropriations is responsible for funding substantive legislative provisions. Its subcommittee on Labor, Health and Human Services, Education, and Related Agencies is responsible for health appropriations. Essentially, this committee holds the power of the purse. The committee and the subcommittee are responsible for allocating and distributing federal funds for individual health programs, except for Medicare and Social Security, which are funded through their respective trust funds.

Senate Committees

The Committee on Labor and Human Resources has jurisdiction over most health bills, including the Public Health Service Act; the Food, Drug, and Cosmetic Act; HMOs; health personnel; and mental health legislation (e.g., Community Mental Health Centers Act). This committee formerly included a subcommittee on Health and Scientific Research, which was used by its then chairman, Senator Edward Kennedy (Democrat-Massachusetts), as a forum for debating whether the United States should have a national healthcare program. When the full committee came under Republican control in the 1980s, the subcommittee was abolished.

The Committee on Finance and its Subcommittee on Health, similar to the Ways and Means Committee in the House, have jurisdiction over taxes and revenues, including matters related to Social Security, Medicare, Medicaid, and Maternal and Child Health (Title V of the Social Security Act). It is responsible for many of the Medicare and Medicaid amendments, such as QIOs, PPS, and amendments controlling hospital and nursing home costs.

The Legislative Process

When a bill is introduced in the House of Representatives, the House leader (the Speaker of the House of Representatives) assigns it to an appropriate committee. The committee chair forwards the bill to an appropriate subcommittee. The subcommittee then forwards the proposed legislation to agencies that will be affected by the legislation, holds hearings ("markup") and testimonies, and may add amendments. The subcommittee and committee may recommend, not recommend, or recommend tabling the bill. Diverse interest groups, individuals, experts in the field, and business, labor, and professional associations often exert influence on the bill through campaign contributions and intense lobbying. The full House then hears the bill and may add amendments. The bill can be approved with or without amendments. The approved bill is then sent to the Senate.

In the Senate, the bill is sent to an appropriate committee and then forwarded to an appropriate subcommittee. The subcommittee may send the bill to agencies that will be affected. It also holds hearings and testimonies from all interested parties (e.g., private citizens, business, labor, agencies, and experts). The subcommittee votes on and forwards the proposed legislation with appropriate recommendations. Amendments may or may not be added. Subsequently, the full Senate hears the bill and may add amendments. If the bill and House amendments are accepted, the bill goes to the president. If the Senate adds amendments that have not been voted on by the House, the bill must go back to the House floor for a vote.

If the amendments are minor and noncontroversial, the House may vote to pass the bill. If the amendments are significant and controversial, the House may call for a conference committee to review the amendments. The conference committee consists of members from equivalent committees of the House and Senate. If the recommendations of the conference committee are not accepted, another conference committee is called.

After the bill has passed both the House and the Senate in identical form, it is forwarded to the president for signature. If the president signs the legislation, it becomes law. If the president does not sign the legislation, at the end of 10th day, it becomes law unless the president vetoes the legislation. If less than 10 days are left in the congressional session, presidential inaction results in a veto—known as a "pocket veto." The veto can be overturned by a two-thirds majority of the Congress; otherwise, the bill is dead.

Policy Implementation

Once legislation has been signed into law, it is not a fait accompli. The new law is forwarded to the appropriate agency of the executive branch, where multiple levels of federal bureaucracy must interpret and implement the legislation. Rules and regulations must be written, detailing what the entities affected by the legislation must do to comply with it. During this process, politicians, interest groups, or program beneficiaries may influence the legislation's ultimate design. Sometimes, the result can differ significantly from its sponsors' intent. The process of policymaking is complex enough; its implementation can be quite daunting as well.

The responsible agency publishes proposed regulations in the *Federal Register* and holds hearings on how the law is to be implemented. A bureaucracy, only loosely controlled by either the president or Congress, writes (publishes, gathers comments about, and rewrites) regulations. Then the program goes on to the 50 states for enabling legislation, if appropriate. There, organized interests hire local lawyers and lobbyists, and a completely new political cycle begins.

Finally, all parties may adjourn to the courts, where long rounds of litigation may shape the final outcome.

Implementation of the ACA

Since the signing of the ACA into law on March 23, 2010, several provisions have gone into effect, including 26 provisions in 2010, 18 provisions in 2011, and 10 provisions in 2012 (Kaiser Family Foundation, 2013). An additional 11 provisions went into effect with 2013 deadlines, 15 provisions with 2014 deadlines, and 3 provisions with 2015 and later deadlines (Kaiser Family Foundation, 2013).

State take-up of the ACA provisions has varied. For example, 41 states (including DC) have enacted the Medicaid expansion, and 10 states have not adopted the expansion as of December 2023 (Kaiser Family Foundation, 2023a). Only 19 states have decided to create state-based health insurance marketplaces, with another 3 opting for a state-based marketplace using the federal platform (Kaiser Family Foundation, 2023b); the remaining 29 states' health insurance marketplaces are federally facilitated.

Critical Policy Issues

Most past health policy initiatives have focused on access to care, cost of care, and quality of care. Some Americans contend that they have the right (access) to the best care (quality) at the least expense (cost) despite their level of income or social class. Legislative efforts, by comparison, have been specific to issues related to access (expanding insurance coverage, outreach programs in rural areas), cost containment (PPS, RBRVS), and quality (creating the Agency for Healthcare Research and Quality [AHRQ] and calling for clinical practice guidelines).

With the publication of the *Healthy People 2010, 2020, and 2030* initiatives, elimination of health disparities across sociodemographic subpopulations has emerged as a bold policy objective. As health disparities are caused primarily by nonmedical factors, the advancement of this goal signals a new policy direction that integrates U.S. health policy with broader social policies (Healthy People 2020, n.d.). Although it is highly unlikely that this goal will be fulfilled in the relatively near future, the promotion of this policy objective reflects a significant government commitment. The remainder of this section highlights the three areas of greatest health policy concern.

Access to Care

The underlying support for government policies to enhance access to care is the social justice principle that access to health care is a right that should be guaranteed to all American citizens. There are two variations on this argument: (1) All citizens have a right to the same level of care, and (2) all citizens have a right to some minimum level of care. Which position the United States should espouse has never been openly debated in policy circles. In the past, efforts to ensure access to comprehensive services were aimed primarily at the most needy and underserved populations, as was the case with Medicaid. Medicare, in contrast, does not incorporate the same level of access, as its coverage is limited by high deductibles and copayments and exclusion of certain services.

Providers

Policy issues include ensuring a sufficient number and desirable geographic distribution of various types of providers. The debate over the supply of physicians is an important public policy issue because policy decisions influence the number of persons entering the medical profession; that number, in turn, has implications for policies related to access and cost. The number of new entrants into the profession is influenced by government assistance programs for individual students and by government grants made directly to educational institutions. An increased supply of physicians—particularly specialists—may result in increased healthcare expenditures because of increased demand for care induced by those physicians. However, such an increased supply of physicians, particularly primary-care physicians, is also necessary to provide basic health care to the newly insured under any expansion of health insurance coverage (Klink, 2015). For example, the ACA will likely fail to achieve its access goals if the supply of primary-care physicians remain inadequate.

One goal on which both Republicans and Democrats seem to agree is preserving community health centers as a safety net for the underprivileged. Consequently, federal support for these centers has been boosted. Funding for community health centers doubled over a 5-year period during the George W. Bush administration, and this program received $2 billion in the American Recovery and Reinvestment Act of 2009. In addition, the ACA established the Community Health Center Fund, which provided $11 billion in funding over a 5-year period for the expansion of health centers across the United States (Health Resources and Services Administration [HRSA], 2013). Today, HRSA funds nearly 1,400 health centers and more than 100 Health Center Program look-alike (LAL) organizations (HRSA, 2023).

Integrated Access

Access to care continues to be a problem in many communities, partly because health policies enacted since 1983 have focused on narrowly defined elements of the delivery system. The United States has not had a unified strategy of reforming the overall system based on a policy of integrated services. Despite an increased reliance on accountable care organizations (ACOs) proposed in the ACA, and other provisions such as integration of long-term care services, it is too early to forecast whether the ACA will make significant headway in making integrated access a reality. For example, long-term care services need to be integrated not just within their own orbit of services but also with the larger healthcare delivery system.

Access and Older People

Three main concerns dominate the debate about Medicare policy: (1) Spending should be restrained to keep the program viable, (2) the program is not adequately focused on the management of chronic conditions, and (3) the program does not cover long-term nursing home care. These concerns originate from the assumption that older people need public assistance to finance their health care. The ACA's proposed Community Living Assistance Services and Supports (CLASS) provision was repealed in 2012 due to concerns about its stability and feasibility (Colello and Mulvey, 2013). While the CLASS provision will not be implemented, the requirements it established were taken into consideration by the Commission on Long-Term Care, which made recommendations to Congress in 2013 on the development and implementation of a long-term care system (American Taxpayer Relief Act of 2012, P.L. 112-240; Colello and Mulvey, 2013; Commission on Long-Term Care, 2016). Since this development, however, no major reforms have yet been put forth.

Access and Minorities

As pointed out in the *Health Services for Special Populations* chapter, minorities are more likely than Whites to face problems with accessing healthcare services. However, with the exception of Native Americans, no minority population within the United States has programs specifically designed to serve its needs. Resolving the problems confronting minority groups would require policies designed to target the special needs of minorities, encourage professional education programs sensitive to those special needs, and develop programs to expand the delivery of services to areas populated by minorities.

The Office of Minority Health was reauthorized by the ACA in 2010 to "improve the health of racial and ethnic minority populations through the development of health policies and programs that will eliminate health disparities" (DHHS, 2016). In 2011, two strategic plans were launched to reduce disparities: the HHS Action Plan to Reduce Racial and Ethnic Health Disparities and the National Stakeholder Strategy for Achieving Health Equity. In 2013, the National Standards for Culturally and Linguistically Appropriate Service in Health and Health Care (National CLAS Standards) were updated in an attempt to further improve health equity (DHHS, 2016). CMS has also established a minority research grant program to identify ways to better address health disparities (CMS, 2021).

Access in Rural Areas

Delivery of healthcare services in rural communities has always raised the question of how to bring advanced medical care to residents of sparsely settled areas. In the area of acute and long-term care, policies have been crafted in the form of the swing bed program and critical access hospitals.

In the medical care arena, purchasing high-tech equipment that will serve only a few people is not cost-efficient, and finding physicians who want to live in rural areas can be difficult. The use of telemedicine, especially as a means to increase access for patients with chronic diseases in rural areas, is expected to increase in coming years. Between 2016 and 2017, telemedicine use surged 53% (AMA, 2019). The value of the telemedicine market is set to climb from $38 billion in 2018 to more than $130 billion globally by 2025, largely fueled by U.S. adoption of this healthcare delivery approach (LaRock, 2019). As health systems face increasing pressure to deliver high-quality care within strict financial constraints, telemedicine may prove a valuable way to use healthcare resources more cost-effectively. For example, it is estimated that chronic diabetes care costs could be reduced by an average of 9% per year with the effective use of telemedicine as opposed to expensive office visits and hospitalizations (Wilson and Maeder, 2015). Furthermore, the uptake of telemedicine will most likely improve with the increasing availability of reliable wireless communication and user interface devices; these devices may allow telemedicine to be more easily used at the point of care.

A recent review of the literature concluded that there are two major drivers of telemedicine development (Wilson and Maeder, 2015). The first driver is high-volume demand for a particular service in which it is difficult to physically connect a patient and the expert needed to deal with the patient's needs. The second driver arises within high-criticality applications, in which the clinical expertise to deliver a service is needed urgently. Owing to these factors, the use of telemedicine is expanding beyond just providing care to rural areas and is increasingly used to provide cost-effective care to an increasing number of patients.

The *Health Services for Special Populations* chapter discussed various policy attempts to alleviate shortages of healthcare professionals in rural areas. They include federal designation of health professional shortage areas (HPSA) and funding for the National Health Service Corps. The latter funding covers only a limited period of time per physician, however, so it will not help remedy healthcare workforce shortages over the longer term. The ACA contains provisions to boost the healthcare workforce and funding for the National Health Service Corps.

Access and Low Income

In the United States, low-income mothers and their children are more likely to be uninsured than other groups. Many of these families also live in medically underserved areas, such as inner cities. Pregnant individuals in low-income families are far less likely to receive prenatal care than people in higher income categories. CHIP was designed to increase low-income children's access to healthcare services, but it requires periodic reauthorization, which can hamper continuity of services to those enrolled in this program. The Medicare Access and CHIP Reauthorization Act of 2015 (MACRA) extended the authorization of CHIP through September 30, 2017 (Congress.gov, 2015). In January 2018, CHIP funding was extended an additional six years through 2023 (Kaiser Family Foundation, 2018). Section 5111 of the Consolidated Appropriations Act extends federal funding for CHIP for another two years, through the end of fiscal year 2029.

Access and Persons with HIV/AIDS

People with human immunodeficiency virus (HIV)/acquired immunodeficiency syndrome (AIDS) can face significant barriers in obtaining insurance coverage, and their illness can lead to catastrophic healthcare expenditures. The ACA makes it illegal to deny insurance coverage to people with HIV/AIDS. However, because of the many legal requirements that place increased burdens on health insurers, premiums for many insureds are expected to skyrocket. If this happens, people with HIV/AIDS and other individuals with serious preexisting conditions could well end up on Medicaid rolls.

In 2003, President George W. Bush pledged $15 billion over 5 years to combat HIV/AIDS in developing countries, with a particular focus on Africa. In 2010, the White House released the National HIV/AIDS Strategy, which outlined goals for reducing infection rates, increasing access to care, and reducing the disparities experienced in receiving care (White House, 2010). To support the achievement of these goals, federal funding for domestic and global HIV/AIDS programs and policies has increased, with $34.8 billion in funding allocated for fiscal year 2019 (Kaiser Family Foundation, 2019b).

Cost of Care

No other aspect of healthcare policy has received more attention during the past 40 years than efforts to contain healthcare costs. As pointed out elsewhere in this text, the government's main weapon of cost control has been payment cuts to providers. PPS has achieved success in curtailing inpatient costs, but outpatient costs have continued to climb. Direct control over utilization has not been tried by public payers (the Medicaid program in the state of Oregon is an exception), but it became widely unpopular when HMOs tried it. Whether public policy can be used to impose explicit rationing of healthcare services in the United States remains to be determined. The fragmented multipayer system does not lend itself to a centralized policy of cost containment.

As an example, prescription drug spending has been rising rapidly over the past few years, significantly driving up overall healthcare costs. Overall spending on prescription drugs grew from $520 billion in 2016 to $603 billion in 2021, a 16% increase. This rate of growth was similar to overall national healthcare spending growth, with prescription drugs maintaining approximately an 18% share of total healthcare expenditures throughout this time period (ASPE, 2022). In contrast, the U.S. drug prescription market grew at an average annual pace of only 2% from 2003 to 2013 (Aitken et al., 2016; Tichy et al., 2020). The recent increase in drug expenditures has been driven by both brand-name entries into the market and price increases for generic drugs. More than 3,500 generic drugs at least doubled in price from 2008 to 2015, with increases up to 1,000% in the prices of some drugs (Jaret, 2015). Manufacturers cited research and development costs to justify these high pharmaceutical prices (Pharmaceutical Research and Manufacturers of America, 2016). In conjunction with this trend, several new high-value drugs obtained marketing approval from the Food and Drug Administration (FDA), and their launch into the U.S. market further drove up the overall cost of prescription drugs (PwC Health Research Institute, 2016). Growth in prescription spending is projected to continue at a pace of about 4% to 5% annually through 2027 (Kamal et al., 2019).

The increasing drug prices have drawn considerable public attention, such as the outcry over Mylan's increase of the price for its EpiPen from $100 to $600 in 2016. In 2020, then President Trump issued an executive order that calls for DHHS to implement a new model of payment in which drug companies must accept the lowest government prices paid by comparable nations around the world (Winfield Cunningham, 2020). However, no such policy has yet been implemented. In another effort to contain costs, DHHS and the U.S. Food and Drug Administration (FDA) came up with a plan to facilitate safe importation of medicines from foreign markets (FDA, 2020). Whether such a plan will have an impact on costs remains unclear. The prices of prescription drugs may well continue to rise in the upcoming years.

Recently, the Biden administration announced 10 prescription drugs where Medicare will negotiate prices with manufacturers under the Inflation Reduction act. For instance, individuals under Medicare can receive certain vaccines for free as well as obtain insulin at a maximum of $35 per product per month for almost 4 million diabetic seniors. Specifically, in August 2022, President Biden signed the Inflation Reduction Act into law to lower prescription drug prices, especially the out-of-pocket Medicare Part B drug costs. As part of the new law, manufacturers are required to pay a rebate to Medicare if a drug's price increase exceeds the rate of inflation. It also authorizes Medicare to directly negotiate drug prices for select medications. Part B drugs may be eligible to be selected for negotiation starting in 2026 for prices effective in 2028 (The White House, 2022; NHS, 2023). In August 2023, Biden administration implemented a historic law to lower health care and prescription drug costs, which could usher in a new era for American seniors. Over the next 4 years, Medicare will negotiate prices for up to 60 drugs covered under Medicare Part D and Part B, and up to an additional 20 drugs every year after that (The White House, 2023).

Quality of Care

Along with access and cost, quality of care is the third main concern of healthcare policy. In March 2001, the Institute of Medicine (IOM; now called the National Academy of Medicine) issued a comprehensive report on this topic, called *Crossing the Quality Chasm*. Building on the extensive evidence collected by the IOM committee, the report identified six areas for quality improvement (Berwick, 2002):

- Safety: Patients should be as safe in healthcare facilities as they are in their homes.
- Effectiveness: The healthcare system should avoid overuse of ineffective care and underuse of effective care.
- Patient-centeredness: Respect for the patient's choices, culture, social context, and special needs must be incorporated into the delivery of services.
- Timeliness: Waiting times and delays should be continually reduced for both patients and caregivers.
- Efficiency: Health care should engage in a never-ending pursuit to reduce total costs by curtailing waste, such as waste of supplies, equipment, space, capital, and the innovative human spirit.
- Equity: The system should seek to close racial and ethnic gaps in health status.

Research on Quality

Funding to evaluate new treatment methods and diagnostic tools has increased dramatically; so has funding for research to measure the outcomes of medical interventions and appropriateness of medical procedures. The mission of AHRQ (one of the 12 agencies within DHHS) is to improve the quality, safety, efficiency, and effectiveness of health care for all Americans. AHRQ fulfills this mission by developing and working with the healthcare system to implement information that does the following:

- Reduces the risk of harm from healthcare services by using evidence-based research and technology to promote the delivery of the best possible care
- Transforms the practice of health care to achieve wider access to effective services and reduce unnecessary healthcare costs
- Improves healthcare outcomes by encouraging providers, consumers, and patients to use evidence-based information to make informed treatment decisions

Ultimately, AHRQ seeks to achieve its goals by translating research into improved healthcare practice and policy. Healthcare providers, patients, policymakers, payers, administrators, and others use AHRQ research findings to improve healthcare quality, accessibility, and outcomes of care (AHRQ, 2013).

Comparative effectiveness research (CER) is one notable undertaking by the AHRQ. The Effective Health Care Program (EHCP) funds researchers, research centers, and academic organizations in working with AHRQ to produce effectiveness and comparative effectiveness research. This program was created as a result of the Medicare Prescription Drug, Improvement, and Modernization Act (MMA) of 2003. EHCP reviews and synthesizes published and unpublished evidence, generates new evidence and tools, and translates research findings into more helpful formats. The program produces research reviews, original research reports, and research summaries (AHRQ, 2017).

Malpractice Reform

The federal government began its actions to relieve the malpractice crisis and devote greater attention to policing the quality of medical care with the Health Care Quality Act of 1986. This legislation mandated the creation of a national database within DHHS to provide data on legal actions against healthcare providers. The database helps people recruiting physicians in one state discover actions against those physicians in other states. To date, though, comprehensive tort reform has failed to materialize, despite much talk from politicians about its desirability.

Studies have both reported an association between medical malpractice expenditures and healthcare spending (Bilimoria et al., 2016; Popescu, 2015) and suggested that there is mixed to little evidence showing that reforms are an effective method for dealing with medical malpractice (Born and Karl, 2016; Stockley, 2019). Some states have limited damage awards in malpractice cases, but as yet no uniform national policy has emerged. One main reason for the inertia in this area is opposition from trial lawyers and consumer groups, who contend that limiting lawsuit awards hurts victims of egregious medical mistakes and reduces incentives to protect patient safety.

Role of Research in Policy Development

The research community can influence health policymaking through documentation, analysis, and prescription (Longest, 2010). The first role of research in policymaking is documentation—that is, the gathering, cataloging, and correlating of facts that depict the state of the world that policymakers face. This process may help define a given public policy problem or raise its political profile.

A second way in which research informs and influences policymaking is through analysis of what does and does not work. Examples include program evaluation and outcomes research. Often taking the form of demonstration projects intended to provide a basis for determining the feasibility, efficacy, or practicality of a possible policy intervention, such analysis can help define solutions to health policy problems.

The third way in which research influences policymaking is through offering prescription. Research may demonstrate that a course of action being contemplated by policymakers may (or may not) lead to undesirable or unexpected consequences, thereby making a significant contribution to policymaking.

Future Considerations in Domestic Health Policy

With the enactment of and controversy surrounding the ACA, the landscape of health policy in the United States is undergoing significant change. While the health policy reforms after the ACA will impact access to health services, increased attention must also be given to ensuring high-quality, personalized, and effective care for each and every patient. This consideration is especially important in the area of primary and preventive health policy, which can be used as a tool to both improve health outcomes and ensure long-term cost containment. Currently, initiatives are under way to expand and evaluate primary-care delivery models, such as patient-centered medical homes, that aim to provide consistent, continuous, and high-quality care.

Current Domestic Health Policy Initiatives

In recent years, many health policy initiatives have been pushed forth at the federal and state levels, as well as in the private sector. At the federal level, Presidents Donald Trump and Joe Biden have advocated for vastly different types of initiatives to pursue, including those regarding the future status of the ACA and the handling of the COVID-19 pandemic. Trump was highly opposed to the ACA and spent his four years in office attempting to roll back its mandates (Levitt, 2020). In contrast, Biden is an advocate for expanding upon the ACA to make premiums more affordable. He also hopes to create a public health insurance option like Medicare (Levitt, 2020).

With regard to COVID-19, Trump's position was largely to delegate responsibility for dealing with the pandemic to the states. He withdrew the United States from the World Health Organization (WHO), and his stances on certain hygiene and distancing guidelines were in conflict with official guidance laid out by the Centers for Disease Control and Prevention (CDC). After taking office, Biden reinstated U.S. involvement with the WHO, promised to put scientists and experts at the helm of the pandemic response, and planned to expand the federal government's role in dealing with this crisis (Levitt, 2020).

At the state level, recent health policy initiatives have focused on issues such as the ongoing opioid crisis and the affordability of health insurance. In regard to the former topic, states have implemented various measures over the years to improve addicts' access to treatment and conduct better surveillance of opioid prescribing patterns. These efforts include expanding access to naloxone, a drug that can reverse drug overdoses, and implementing prescription drug monitoring programs (PDMPs) that use electronic databases to provide information on controlled substance prescriptions, physicians' prescribing behaviors, and patients' prescription-use behaviors (Purington, 2019). PDMPs have demonstrated effectiveness in changing prescribing behaviors and reducing substance abuse treatment admissions (CDC, 2020). A toolkit released by the National Governors Association in 2020 identified areas in which PDMPs can improve to increase their utility and impact; these include expanding the types of substances and information tracked as well as promoting interstate data sharing (National Governors Association, 2020).

With regard to health insurance affordability, states have taken various actions over the years to address the cost of purchasing insurance in the ACA's health insurance marketplaces. Because insurance premiums in these marketplaces have risen considerably in the past few years, some states have developed reinsurance programs that partially reimburse insurers for high-cost claims, promoting the lowering of premiums (Tolbert et al., 2019). Other states have expanded or are considering expanding upon the federal subsidies for premiums by implementing their own state-funded subsidies (Tolbert et al., 2019). With regard to the availability of alternative insurance plans outside of the marketplaces, states are relatively evenly divided in either limiting these plans in hopes of lowering marketplace premiums or allowing their sale in accordance with federal guidelines, which were loosened during the Trump administration (Tolbert et al., 2019). Proponents of these alternative plans tout them as more affordable options for those who find marketplace premiums too expensive (Tolbert et al., 2019). However, expanding the array of alternative insurance plans, which mainly cater to healthy individuals, is likely to drive up premiums for marketplace insurance plans, which must abide by ACA regulations that mandate the coverage of essential health benefits and individuals with preexisting conditions (Tolbert et al., 2019).

Aside from government-led health initiatives, the private sector has been active in coming up with its own innovations. Some large corporations, for example, have initiated efforts to provide employees with their own forms of health care or health insurance. These efforts, while not all successful, aim to reduce the cost of care while also promoting better quality (Blumenthal and Galvin, 2019). A high-profile example of such an initiative was the now-terminated Haven, a nonprofit organization created through a partnership between Amazon, Berkshire Hathaway, and JPMorgan Chase. The organization's vision was to simplify and make affordable the delivery of quality care through the leveraging of data and technology (Haven, n.d.). Another corporate partnership established in recent years is the Health Transformation Alliance, a coalition of 54 companies that provides employees with a variety of health programs that they can choose from (Koons, 2020).

Large corporations have also begun foraying into retail health care for public use, where they capitalize on their accessible locations, sizable employee bases, and technological capabilities to provide various healthcare services. Walmart, for example, has opened up a pilot health clinic in Georgia offering primary care, dental, counseling, and x-ray services (Huckman, 2019). CVS launched HealthHUB stores, which offer an expanded selection of healthcare services, products, and support (CVS Health, 2019). Other companies, such as Apple, are capitalizing on their technological strengths to provide various electronic health services. Apple Health Records, a component of Apple's Health app, is currently being used by various medical practices across the country as a means to allow patients to access electronic health records on their phones. This company also partnered with the White House and the CDC, as well as with Stanford Medicine, to develop COVID-19 apps during the pandemic (Adams, 2020).

As can be understood from the diversity of initiatives being pursued in the federal, state, and private realms, many aspects of the U.S. healthcare system are viewed as unsatisfactory or problematic. From cost to quality to COVID-19, health care is not operating as efficiently, effectively, or equitably as it should. The myriad of initiatives that are currently in motion, of which only a small minority are discussed here, represent admirable efforts to make improvements upon these issues. Unfortunately, the vast number and variety of initiatives may have an unintended consequence, sowing even more confusion among consumers who are trying to navigate the already fragmented healthcare system (Blumenthal and Galvin, 2019).

Better government direction and support would help increase the clarity and coordination among the sectors involved. A reevaluation of the healthcare structure could also induce the system-level changes needed to tackle problems more effectively. Currently, a good systems approach to dealing with population health is sorely lacking. From the national level to the individual level, and from homes to workplaces to neighborhoods, recognizing how these units are interconnected and influence one another allows for the creation of strategies that can better target the structures and policies that impact specific issues (Diez Roux, 2020). At the same time, a better data collection system should be established to measure population health metrics across socioeconomic and racial/ethnic groups (Diez Roux, 2020). Public health must be made more of a consistent priority in terms of both government support and integration with the rest of the healthcare system.

Government action in health care can often be incremental and slow due to partisan disagreements on how progress should be made. A report by Jones and Pagel (2020), for example, sheds light on the contrasting viewpoints held by Democrats and Republicans on the types of solutions that should be devised to tackle healthcare costs. According to the report, Democrats are more supportive of solutions that address systemic drivers of costs, while Republicans are more focused on the impact of high costs on individuals. This difference in priorities makes it hard to compromise on how to address cost issues. However, Jones and Pagel (2020) maintain that productive conversations can take place if there are a small number of individuals with more thorough knowledge of the healthcare system. As reliable, trustworthy sources of information, these individuals can guide productive discussions forward by illuminating how systemic issues and individual costs are related. Framing healthcare proposals in terms of how addressing one side benefits the other can help spur progress through recognition of common goals (Jones and Pagel, 2020). The use of common values, such as affordability and transparency, can also help bridge the partisan divide. Following are examples of the health policy initiatives under the Biden Administration.

The American Rescue Plan Act (ARPA). Signed into law in March 2021, the ARPA was a $1.9 trillion economic stimulus bill aiming to address the ongoing COVID-19 pandemic (Japinga et al., 2022). It included provisions such as funding for vaccine distribution, expanded subsidies for Affordable Care Act (ACA) health insurance plans, and financial assistance for individuals and families (Japinga et al., 2022). For example, the legislation expands subsidies for 2 years to consumers who purchase health insurance on state exchanges and caps premium payments at 8.5% of income (Japinga et al., 2022). Expanded subsidies will benefit all exchange participants, but particularly older adults with higher incomes (Japinga et al., 2022). Affordable Care Act rules previously did not allow for subsidies beyond 400% of the federal poverty level (Japinga et al., 2022). Now, under ARPA, a 60-year-old with an income of 430% of the federal poverty level would experience more than a 50% reduction in premiums for gold or silver plans (Japinga et al., 2022). The administration hopes to make these increases permanent in the pending reconciliation legislation (Japinga et al., 2022). Moreover, ARPA allocates a total of $350 billion to states for COVID-19 recovery, vaccination campaigns, and various public health and economic initiatives (Japinga et al., 2022). States have the chance to allocate these funds towards economic recovery, bolstering healthcare infrastructure, and supporting safety net programs (Japinga et al., 2022). An example of this is North Carolina, which intends to use some of the relief funds to advance health research innovation, promote health and wellness, and enhance food security programs for vulnerable residents (Japinga et al., 2022).

The Value-Based Payment Agenda. The Centers for Medicare and Medicaid Services (CMS) is moving towards patient-centered payment reforms, aligning quality measures with patient goals, advancing health equity, and improving access to community resources (Japinga et al., 2022). The Merit-based Incentive Payment System (MIPS) is highlighted as a key mechanism for specialty care actions, with proposed Value Pathways to reduce provider burden. CMS aims to prioritize alternative payment models promoting comprehensive care, potentially leading to increased coordination between primary care and specialty care (Japinga et al., 2022). Additionally, there are proposed benefit reforms, such as phasing out coinsurance requirements for colorectal cancer screening tests by 2030.

Expanding Access to Medicaid. The Biden Administration encouraged states to expand Medicaid under the ACA to provide health coverage to more low-income individuals (Rice et al., 2021). States will be able to apply for federal permission to modify their Medicaid programs only to "protect and strengthen Medicaid and the ACA"; waivers from federal Medicaid rules will only be considered if they do not "reduce coverage under or otherwise undermine coverage (Rice et al., 2021). An additional $100 million was allotted to education and outreach, and a new special open enrollment period was enacted to allow an additional opportunity for people to purchase subsidized coverage to help those economically disadvantaged by COVID-19 (Rice et al., 2021).

Telehealth and Home Care. The $1.2 trillion bipartisan Infrastructure Investment and Jobs Act signed by President Biden in November of 2021 includes $65 billion for broadband infrastructure and initiatives to increase affordability and adoption of telehealth (Japinga et al., 2022). The proposed reconciliation bill initially included $400 billion to improve home care infrastructure, increase the number of home care workers, and increase the amount of take-home pay many of them receive, but this number is expected to be much lower in the final version (Japinga et al., 2022).

Enhancing Mental Health Care. President Biden announced new actions that would improve and strengthen mental health parity requirements and ensure that more than 150 million Americans with private health insurance can better access mental health benefits under their insurance plan (The White House, 2023). Congress made changes to the Mental Health Parity and Addiction Equity Act (MHPAEA) in 2020, emphasizing the need for health plans to ensure that access to mental health and substance use benefits is no more restrictive than for medical benefits (The White House, 2023). The rule calls for evaluations of provider networks, out-of-network payment practices, and prior authorization requirements to identify and rectify disparities (The White House, 2023). It prohibits health plans from employing more restrictive practices for mental health care than for medical care and closes existing loopholes, extending compliance requirements to over 200 additional health plans (The White House, 2023).

The rule is expected to increase utilization of mental health and substance use care, ensure comparable payment for mental health professionals, and potentially attract more individuals to the mental health workforce (The White House, 2023). The Administration is also planning to issue a request for information on collaborating with states to ensure MHPAEA compliance for Medicaid beneficiaries in private Medicaid health plans (The White House, 2023). The proposed rule is part of broader efforts to address the mental health care crisis, including proposed rules for expanded access to services in Medicare, investments in crisis response, and initiatives to provide mental health services in schools (The White House, 2023).

Rural Health Transformation

In recent years, there has been a major push across the nation to address the longstanding disparities in health outcomes and access to care that exist between rural and urban regions of the United States. In general, rural Americans have less access to care, are more likely to be uninsured, have higher rates of poverty, include larger numbers of people who are older adults, and experience greater isolation compared to their urban counterparts (Hostetter and Klein, 2017). A study by Moy et al. (2017) examining mortality data for U.S. residents from 1999 to 2014 also determined that nonmetropolitan areas have higher age-adjusted death rates from the five leading causes of death compared to metropolitan areas, as well as higher percentages of potentially excess deaths. The health disparities between rural and urban regions of America emerged as a source of great concern during the COVID-19 pandemic, which put immense pressures on rural hospitals that were already struggling to stay afloat (DHHS, 2020; Stephenson, 2020). In an effort to reduce disparities and ensure that rural populations have proper access to quality care through the pandemic and beyond, many strategies have been devised at the local and national levels to transform rural healthcare delivery.

To counter workforce concerns and difficulty in recruiting physicians to rural areas, a number of strategies have been proposed. One of these suggestions is to allow other types of healthcare providers to take on certain physician responsibilities, thereby easing physicians' burden. Rusk County Memorial Hospital in Ladysmith, Wisconsin, took this approach after it lost half of its primary-care workforce. Three advanced practice nurses were hired to serve as hospitalists—a move that improved quality of care, shortened lengths of stays, and increased patient satisfaction (Hostetter and Klein, 2017). Other methods to expand and support the rural healthcare workforce include implementation of telemedicine as well as academic training programs (Greenwood-Ericksen et al., 2020).

To address mounting financial concerns, global budgets have been proposed as a way to provide rural healthcare facilities with fixed, predictable sources of income (Greenwood-Ericksen et al., 2020; Hostetter and Klein, 2017). Global budgets eliminate reliance on fee-for-service payments, which have debilitated rural hospitals as patient admissions decline. They also promote the use of preventive care and encourage hospitals to focus on improving the overall health of the communities they serve (Sharfstein, 2016). Pennsylvania is currently testing a global budget model in its rural hospitals with the aim of incentivizing hospitals to control costs and focus on population health (CMS, 2020b). Maryland also has ten rural hospitals that have been operating on global budgets since 2010, a move that has increased these hospitals' focus on care coordination, primary-care follow-up, and community health partnerships (Sharfstein, 2016). Aside from global budgets, the COVID-19 pandemic brought about increased federal funding for rural hospitals as well as an expansion of telehealth services and reimbursement. Advocates argue that such measures should be made permanent in the post-COVID world to support innovative rural health efforts that improve quality and access to care (Greenwood-Ericksen et al., 2020).

In addition to local and state efforts, various agencies at the national level are taking action to address rural health disparities. In response to an executive order issued by the Trump administration in August 2020, DHHS released a Rural Action Plan outlining a strategy to build a more sustainable and efficient method of care delivery. The report identified four points of focus to transform rural health (DHHS, 2020):

1. *Build a sustainable health and human services model for rural communities* by empowering rural providers to transform service delivery on a broad scale
2. *Leverage technology and innovation* to deliver quality care and services to rural communities more efficiently and cost-effectively
3. *Focus on preventing disease and mortality* by developing rural-specific efforts to improve health outcomes
4. *Increase rural access to care* by eliminating regulatory burdens that limit the availability of needed clinical professionals

The Rural Action Plan further elaborated on specific actions being taken by DHHS to address rural health concerns, as well as policies and programs in the Trump administration's proposed fiscal year 2021 budget that targeted rural health issues. These included an expansion of Medicare's telehealth benefit to permit rural health clinics and federally qualified health centers to provide telehealth services, as well as an expansion of telehealth access to the Indian Health Service and tribal facilities (Stephenson, 2020).

Complementing DHHS's efforts, the CMS announced its Community Health Access and Rural Transformation (CHART) Model as a new initiative to transform rural healthcare delivery into a system that is based on value rather than volume (CMS, 2020a). After lead organizations and ACOs are selected to participate, the implementation period for this model began in 2022.

The Biden-Harris Administration is taking further actions to improve the health of rural communities and help rural healthcare providers stay open (U.S. Department of Health and Human Services, 2023), as shown in the following initiatives.

- Build on the Affordable Care Act and Inflation Reduction Act to increase access to affordable health coverage and care for those living in rural communities
  - More outreach to rural Americans on ACA Marketplace enrollment

- Increasing access to the Low-income subsidy under the Medicare Part D prescription drug program
- Closing the Medicaid coverage gap
- Keep more rural hospitals open in the long run to provide critical services in their communities
    - Public consultation on Medicare policies for rural providers and beneficiaries
    - Supporting rural hospitals by helping them avoid closing their doors and instead converting to rural emergency hospitals
    - Funding rural providers to join value-based care initiatives
    - Grants to rural hospitals and communities to provide healthcare services
    - Completing vital sanitation construction projects across Indian country
    - Understanding rural health providers' cybersecurity needs
- Bolster the rural health workforce, including for primary-care and behavioral health providers
    - Increase resident training opportunities in rural hospitals
    - Expanding the workforce and recognizing the role of community health workers
    - Developing and investing in the nursing workforce
    - New Office of Rural Health to address workforce needs
    - Virtual physician supervision
    - Prioritizing rural communities in funding of community economic grant competition
    - Addressing the water and wastewater infrastructure needs of rural communities
- Support access to needed care such as behavioral health and through telehealth services
    - Expanding access to services provided via telehealth
    - Increasing access to and payment for behavioral health services
    - Improving access to treatment for opioid use disorders
    - Advancing network adequacy for behavioral health providers
    - Improving access to providers for Medicaid beneficiaries in rural areas
    - Access to care in Medicare Advantage in rural areas
    - School-based services in rural communities

Health Insurance Expansion

Under the Biden administration, an updated version of ACA is proposed with the goal of further expanding health insurance coverage. By expanding ACA premium subsidies, the Biden plan is likely to lower the cost of marketplace coverage for enrollees, including the uninsured and others currently priced out of the marketplace (Kaiser Family Foundation, 2020d).

Other health insurance reforms may also be initiated, at least on an experimental basis. For example, Wang et al. (2018) extended the idea of capitation and proposed a novel couple-oriented insurance scheme—couplitation, which is named after capitation. Different from a regular family plan of health insurance, couplitation is aimed at developing comprehensive coverage for spouse-vulnerable chronic diseases. Presence of a chronic or major disease in a spouse suggests that the partner is also at risk. Therefore, the premium charged for the partners under couplitation should be higher than that of one spouse but lower than that of two unrelated adults. Spouses with or without chronic and major illness would be differentiated under the premise of couplitation. Couplitation may improve rates of early health examination (i.e., primary-care uptake) in a manner paralleling capitation, which reimburses providers based on their patients' average costs. This novel health insurance scheme merits further attention in health sectors.

International Health Policy

Like domestic health policy efforts, international health initiatives have faced challenges in recent years as a result of continuing attempts to reduce government spending. As a result of these cost-cutting efforts, government spending on global health initiatives has remained largely stable. For example, the Global Health Initiative (2014)—the umbrella for the global health programs launched by President Obama between 2009 and 2014—dedicated more than $50 billion to achieve health goals, including $13 billion to maternal health and child survival and $39 billion to HIV/AIDS funding.

Within the current budget constraints, initiatives must attempt to address immediate health concerns and build the capacity of the United States and other countries to address evolving health issues, which in turn requires a greater emphasis on innovation in global health policy. Global public health policies often vacillate with a changing political climate. In January 2017, for example, President Donald Trump reinstated the Mexico City Policy, which bans foreign nongovernmental organizations from performing or actively promoting abortions if they want to receive U.S. global health funding. This policy was first enacted under the Reagan administration in 1984, and as of 2019, had been in place for 19 of the past 34 years (Kaiser Family Foundation, 2019a). President Joe Biden immediately reversed course on this front, rescinding the Mexico City Policy after he took office.

Health Reforms Around the World

In the wake of the global COVID-19 pandemic, nations around the world have been reevaluating their health priorities and healthcare infrastructures. Many of these countries offer important takeaways that the United States can apply to improve its own health system.

In the early days of the pandemic, patients' out-of-pocket costs skyrocketed for COVID-19 testing and treatment (Abrams, 2020). Although federal mandates and insurer guarantees eased the financial burden for many people, both insured and uninsured individuals slipped through the cracks (Fehr et al., 2020). Out-of-pocket costs had been a concern in the United States even prior to the COVID-19 pandemic. Despite being a high-income, well-resourced nation, many Americans find cost and affordability to be barriers to obtaining health care (Schneider, 2020).

Australia and Germany offer useful insights into alternative health insurance models that could increase affordability and access. Both countries operate under a model of universal public health care that can be supplemented by private health insurance. About half of all Australians have some form of private and dental insurance to cover services not provided for under public coverage, while about one-fourth of all eligible Germans opt into private health insurance, which has certain financing and other requirements that must be met (Scheffler and Wang, 2020).

From the experiences of these two countries, a notable takeaway is the importance of the individual mandate. In Australia, where private health insurance is not mandatory, this sector is shrinking as fewer people choose to purchase private insurance. Likewise, if public health insurance is implemented in the United States but not made mandatory for all Americans, its sustainability would be compromised. To encourage support for an individual mandate, public health insurance should be of high enough quality to be considered a viable alternative to private insurance. Additionally, to limit risk selection favoring healthier individuals, provider participation must be made mandatory, as it is in Germany. These teaching points from countries that have adopted a combined public-private insurance model can assist the United States in devising its own model for universal health coverage and affordability (Scheffler and Wang, 2020).

The Netherlands offers another model that can provide inspiration for the United States in post-COVID-19 health system redesign. To keep the healthcare system afloat during the pandemic, Dutch health insurers and providers agreed on a deal to maintain accessibility and quality. Broadly speaking, the terms of the deal included (1) a fixed budget for providers, (2) compensation for additional COVID-19-related costs, and (3) an additional fee to providers that serves as an incentive to catch up on delayed non-COVID-19-related care (Tanke and Ikram, 2020). The deal was intended to preserve quality, competition, and value while also promoting digital health care and collaboration. Having a fixed income allowed providers to focus on the pandemic response and refer patients to other facilities without worrying about experiencing financial hardship from the loss of these patients. Maintaining a competitive marketplace also gives patients more options to choose from while simultaneously incentivizing providers to deliver quality care (Tanke and Ikram, 2020). The Dutch method serves as an example for the United States in designing a more resilient healthcare system.

In addition to Australia, Germany, and the Netherlands, other countries and regions structured their health systems in ways that supported their responses to the pandemic and that the United States can learn from. For example, legal regulations in Norway mandate that infectious diseases posing a public health threat must be treated at no cost for patients, facilitating early testing, treatment, and quarantine. In Taiwan, a national health insurance card issued for all residents allows for the tracking of patient medical information. These data were used to call back individuals who displayed respiratory symptoms but tested negative for the flu during the pandemic so that they could be retested for COVID-19 (Tikkanen et al., 2020). This system supported COVID-19 surveillance and the contact tracing process but can also be useful in centralizing patient information to be more accessible to providers who need to coordinate care.

As the pandemic continued to disrupt American society and consume healthcare resources, the United States' abysmal response underscored the need for reform. International examples of strong health systems or useful health system traits offer evidence to draw from in making those changes. Although the models themselves are not perfect, they provide insight into how the United States can build a healthcare system that is resilient in times in crises, affordable and accessible to patients, and supportive of public health efforts.

World Health Organization Health Initiatives

As an international organization dedicated to promoting global health and well-being, the World Health Organization (WHO) has launched many initiatives over the years to target problems that have significant levels of global impact. The following discussion covers a few recent initiatives and topic areas that the WHO has chosen as targets.

Mental health's role in supporting overall health, sustainable development, and economic productivity has become increasingly acknowledged over the years as a critical component of personal, as well as population-level, well-being (WHO, 2019). According to the WHO, depression and anxiety disorders cost the global economy $1 trillion every year. Mental health disorders also contribute to higher suicide rates and are common among individuals with communicable and noncommunicable diseases (WHO, 2019). To support its vision of having all people achieve the highest standard of mental health and well-being, WHO launched the WHO Special Initiative for Mental Health (2019–2023) in 2019 with the goal of providing universal health coverage, including access to quality and affordable mental health care, to 100 million more people in 12 priority countries (WHO, 2019). In accomplishing this goal, the WHO Special Initiative has outlined two strategic actions it will take: (1) advance mental health policies, advocacy, and human rights, and (2) scale up interventions and services across community-based, general health, and specialist settings.

Another area to which the WHO has given significant attention is universal health coverage (UHC). UHC is defined as all people having access to affordable, necessary health services, when and where they need them (WHO, n.d.). Currently, approximately half the world's population does not receive needed health services, and an estimated 100 million people descend into extreme poverty annually due to healthcare costs (WHO, n.d.). As part of its quest to achieve UHC for 1 billion more people by 2023, WHO is involved in a number of collaborations seeking to promote and increase global capacity to provide UHC. One of these is UHC2030, a vast partnership among various countries and organizations to foster global and country-level health systems strengthening geared toward supporting UHC (UHC2030, n.d.). WHO also provides support for the Universal Health Coverage Partnership, a cooperative effort designed to promote policy dialogue on UHC, develop health financing strategies, and provide funding, support, and expertise to support implementation, among other aims (UHC Partnership, n.d.).

Of all the global health concerns receiving attention today, the most pressing is COVID-19. In response to the global pandemic, the WHO has been at the forefront of international efforts to contain the spread of the disease. To support individual countries and encourage global cooperation, WHO has developed many resources, including the COVID-19 Partners Platform, a collaborative tool that allows for real-time tracking to support country preparedness and response activities, and the COVID-19 Solidarity Response Fund, which receives donations from individuals, corporations, and institutions to support WHO's global response efforts. WHO has also issued pandemic response guidelines, helped form a supply chain task force to facilitate the procurement of necessary supplies, and coordinated scientific research efforts around the world (WHO, 2020). COVID-19 remained at the top of WHO's priority list as the pandemic continued and vaccine development was ongoing (WHO, 2023; World Bank, 2022).

For the WHO, 2023 marked a successful year for eliminating diseases across the globe. Azerbaijan, Tajikistan, and Belize were declared to be malaria-free, while Egypt attained a "gold tier" status on eliminating hepatitis C despite having one of the highest rates of hepatitis C in the world. Reaching the halfway mark to WHO's goal, 50 countries have eliminated at least one neglected tropical disease.

It has also been reported that as artificial intelligence technologies only gain more prominence, the WHO is ensuring the safe and confidential implementation of health care. More specifically, the WHO provided guidance regarding the regulatory considerations concerning the treatment of conditions like cancer or tuberculosis while also emphasizing the significance of ethics and privacy of data. Internationally this has meant new efforts like the Global Initiative on Digital Health hosted by the Indian government that aims to support strategies in upcoming years. Furthermore, the WHO has spearheaded a digital health partnership with the European Commission in an aim to start the development of digital approaches for better healthcare delivery (WHO, 2023).

WHO works worldwide to promote health, keep the world safe, and serve the vulnerable (World Health Organization, 2023). The goal is to ensure that a billion more people have universal health coverage, to protect a billion more people from health emergencies, and to provide a further billion people with better health and well-being (World Health Organization, 2023). Some of the new WHO initiatives include the following:

Access to COVID-19 Tools (ACT) Accelerator. Since April 2020, the ACT-Accelerator partnership, launched by WHO and partners, has supported the fastest, most coordinated, and successful global effort in history to develop tools to fight a disease.

Comprehensive Mental Health Action Plan 2013-2030. The Sixty-sixth World Health Assembly, consisting of Ministers of Health of 194 Member States, adopted the WHO's Comprehensive Mental Health Action Plan 2013-2020 in May 2013. In 2019, the action plan was extended until 2030 by the Seventy-second World Health Assembly. Then in 2021, the Seventy-fourth World Health Assembly endorsed updates to the action plan, including updates to the plan's options for implementation and indicators.

COVID-19 Technology Access Pool. In May 2020, WHO, the government of Costa Rica, and other partners launched the COVID-19 Technology Access Pool (C-TAP) to facilitate faster, equitable, and affordable access to COVID-19 health products for people in all countries.

Decade of Healthy Ageing (2021-2030). The United Nations Decade of Healthy Ageing (2021–2030) is a global collaboration, aligned with the last ten years of the Sustainable Development Goals, to improve the lives of older people, their families, and the communities in which they live. WHO was asked to lead the implementation of the Decade in collaboration with the other UN organizations and serves as the Decade Secretariat.

Global Action Plan for Healthy Lives and Well-Being for All. The Global Action Plan for Healthy Lives and Well-being for All (SDG3 GAP), established in 2019, brings together 13 multilateral health, development and humanitarian agencies. Its goal is to help countries accelerate progress on the health-related Sustainable Development Goals (SDGs) targets through a set of commitments to strengthen collaboration across the agencies to take joint action and provide more coordinated and aligned support to country-owned and led national plans and strategies.

Global Initiative on Digital Health. The Global Initiative on Digital Health (GIDH) is a WHO-managed network of stakeholders organized to facilitate the implementation of the Global Strategy on Digital Health 2020-2025 and other WHO norms and standards for Digital Health System Transformation. The Initiative will serve as a platform to enable a wide global ecosystem to work collectively to promote country capacity and strengthen international cooperation in digital health.

Framework Convention on Tobacco Control (FCTC). The WHO Framework Convention on Tobacco Control is an international treaty aimed at reducing the health and economic impact of tobacco use. It provides a framework for tobacco control measures at the national, regional, and international levels.

Healthcare Reforms Around the World

As the following examples show, nations around the world are deepening their healthcare system reform efforts.

The United States: Affordable Care Act (ACA). The Affordable Care Act (ACA), which was enacted in 2010, marked the most significant extension of healthcare coverage within the U.S. healthcare system since the establishment of Medicare and Medicaid in 1965 (The Assistant Secretary for Planning and Evaluation, 2023). This comprehensive reform law substantially broadened access to health insurance for millions of Americans by following two primary avenues:

1. It granted premium tax credits to individuals whose incomes ranged from 100% to

400% of the federal poverty level (FPL). These credits were intended to reduce the expenses associated with obtaining individual market health insurance plans through newly established state marketplaces.
2. It enlarged the eligibility criteria for Medicaid to encompass adults with incomes reaching up to 138% of the federal poverty level (FPL) in states that chose to participate.

The United Kingdom: The National Health Service (NHS) Model. The NHS provides universal access to healthcare services and focuses on delivering primary care through general practitioners (GPs) (NHS England, n.d.). It places a strong emphasis on preventive care and population health, aiming to reduce health inequalities (NHS England, n.d.). Patients can register with a GP, and services are free at the point of use. Primary care includes general practice, community pharmacy, dental, and optometry (eye health) services. The NHS were better equipped to provide mental health and wellbeing support to staff as a result of the COVID-19 pandemic (Barr-Keenan et al., 2021).

Germany: Digital Healthcare Act. Reimbursement is a key challenge for many new digital health solutions, whose importance and value have been highlighted and expanded by the current COVID-19 pandemic (Gerke et al., 2020). Germany's new Digital Healthcare Act (DVG) entitles all individuals covered by statutory health insurance to reimbursement for certain digital health applications (i.e., insurers will pay for their use) (Gerke et al., 2020). The DVG also aims to accelerate the adoption and use of telehealth. In particular, under the DVG, patients can more easily take advantage of video consultations (Gerke et al., 2020). During such a consultation, a patient can be informed about circumstances that are essential for consent to a medical measure, including its nature, scope, implementation, expected risks, and consequences (Gerke et al., 2020).

China: Universal Health Coverage. In 2009, the Chinese government launched a new round of healthcare reform towards universal health coverage, aiming to provide universal coverage of basic health care (Tao et al., 2020). The government has since quadrupled its funding for health (Yip et al., 2019). The reform's first phase (2009–11) emphasized expanding social health insurance coverage for all and strengthening infrastructure (Yip et al., 2019). The second phase (2012 onwards) prioritized reforming its healthcare delivery system through: (1) systemic reform of public hospitals by removing mark-up for drug sales, adjusting fee schedules, and reforming provider payment and governance structures; and (2) overhaul of its hospital-centric and treatment-based delivery system (Yip et al., 2019). The year of 2019 marks the 10th anniversary of China's most recent healthcare reform (Tao et al., 2020).

Switzerland: Universal Healthcare Coverage. According to the Organization for Economic Cooperation and Development, the Swiss healthcare system is one of the most effective in the world (Cohidon et al., 2015). Switzerland provides universal healthcare coverage for its residents (Cohidon et al., 2015). Every Swiss citizen and resident are required to have basic health insurance, which covers a wide range of medical services, including primary care (Cohidon et al., 2015). This ensures that virtually everyone in the country has access to primary-care services (Cohidon et al., 2015). Switzerland has an integrated healthcare system where primary-care providers often work closely with specialists and hospitals (Cohidon et al., 2015). This coordination of care helps ensure that patients receive appropriate and timely referrals to specialists when needed (Cohidon et al., 2015).

Australia: The Collaboratives Program. Primary Health Care (PHC) in Australia, which has evolved through major reforms, has been adapting to the complex healthcare needs of the socio-culturally diversified nation, and has achieved many of the PC attributes, including service diversity, accessibility, acceptability, and quality of care (Mengistu et al., 2023). The PHC system has developed several implementation strategies to increase service diversity, accessibility, acceptability, and quality of care (Mengistu et al., 2023). Australia has adopted a collaborative care approach that involves general practitioners, nurses, and allied health professionals working together to provide holistic care, which aims to address the physical, mental, and social aspects of health (Knight et al., 2012).

Canada: Medicare and Canada Health Act. Canada has a healthcare system known as Medicare, which provides universal access to healthcare services for all Canadian residents (Government of Canada, 2023). The provincial and territorial governments are responsible for the management, organization, and delivery of healthcare services for their residents (Government of Canada, 2023). For example, the federal government is responsible for setting and administering national standards for the healthcare system through the Canada Health Act, providing funding support for provincial and territorial healthcare services, and supporting the delivery for healthcare services to specific groups. The Canada Health Act (1984) defines the following standards to which provincial health insurance programs must conform in exchange for federal funding: universality (coverage of the whole population on uniform terms and conditions), portability of coverage among provinces, public administration, accessibility (first-dollar coverage for physician and hospital services), and comprehensiveness (defined as medically necessary health services provided by hospitals and physicians) (Hutchison et al., 2011). In practice, medical necessity is broadly defined, covering most physicians' services (Hutchison et al., 2011). Canadians are entitled to choose their own family physician, and because the Canada Health Act prohibits user charges for insured services, medically necessary physicians' services are free at the point of care (Hutchison et al., 2011).

Summary

The U.S. healthcare delivery system is the product of many health policies, which over the years have brought about incremental changes in this system. Health policies are developed to serve the public interests, but those public interests are quite diverse. On the one hand, interest group politics often have a remarkable influence on policymaking. On the other hand, a complex process and divided opinions may leave the public out of even major policy decisions. Although the public wants the government to control healthcare costs, it also believes that the federal government already controls too much of Americans' daily lives. Presidential leadership and party politics played a major role in the passage of the ACA, but several critical policy issues pertaining to access, cost, and quality remain unresolved. Among future challenges, cost containment will be the most daunting. Ensuring the ability to handle pandemics such as COVID-19 is another major challenge. The political feasibility of adopting a public policy to impose explicit rationing in the United States is unknown as of now.

TEST YOUR UNDERSTANDING

Terminology
allocative tools
distributive policies
health policy
public policies
redistributive policies
regulatory tools

Review Questions

1. What is health policy? How can health policies be used as regulatory or allocative tools?
2. What are the principal features of U.S. health policy? Why do these features characterize U.S. health policy?
3. Identify healthcare interest groups and their concerns.
4. Why do you think the Clinton health reform failed but the Obama health reform succeeded?
5. What is the process of legislative health policy in the United States? How is this process related to the principal features of U.S. health policy?
6. Describe the critical policy issues related to access to care, cost of care, and quality of care.
7. How might the United States learn from other countries in handling pandemics such as COVID-19?

References

Abrams, A. 2020. Total Cost of Her COVID-19 treatment: $34,927.43. *Time*. Accessed October 2020. Available at: https://time.com/5806312/coronavirus-treatment-cost/

Adams, K. 2020. *Apple Moves Further into Health Care: A Timeline of the Past Year.* Accessed September 2020. Available at: https://www.beckershospitalreview.com/healthcare-information-technology/apple-moves-further-into-healthcare-a-timeline-of-the-past-year.html

Agency for Healthcare Research and Quality (AHRQ). 2013. *AHRQ Annual Highlights, 2012.* Accessed August 2013. Available at: https://www.ahrq.gov/sites/default/files/publications/files/highlt12.pdf

Agency for Healthcare Research and Quality. 2017. *Effective Health Care Program: What is the Effective Health Care Program?* Accessed March 2021. Available at: https://effectivehealthcare.ahrq.gov

Aitken, M., E. R. Berndt, D. Cutler, M. Kleinrock, and L. Maini. 2016. Has the Era of Slow Growth for Prescription Drug Spending Ended? *Health Affairs* 35: 1595–1603.

Alford, R. R. 1975. *Health Care Politics: Ideology and Interest Group Barriers to Reform.* Chicago, IL: University of Chicago Press.

American Medical Association (AMA). 2019. *Telehealth up 53%, Growing Faster Than Any Other Place of Care.* Accessed February 2020. Available at: https://www.ama-assn.org/practice-management/digital/telehealth-53-growing-faster-any-other-place-care

American Taxpayer Relief Act of 2012 (ATRA). Pub. L. 112-240, Sec 643.

Assistant Secretary for Planning and Evaluation (ASPE). 2022. Trends in Prescription Drug Spending, 2016-2021. Accessed December 2023. Available at: https://aspe.hhs.gov/sites/default/files/documents/88c547c976e915fc31fe2c6903ac0bc9/sdp-trends-prescription-drug-spending.pdf

Barr-Keenan, R., T. Fay, A. Radulovic, and S. Shetty. 2021. Identifying Positive Change Within the NHS as a Result of the COVID-19 Pandemic. *Future Healthcare Journal* 8: e671–e675.

Berwick, D. M. 2002. A User's Manual for The IOM's "Quality Chasm" Report. *Health Affairs* 21: 80–90.

Bilimoria, K. Y., M. W. Sohn, J. W. Chung, et al. 2016. Association Between State Medical Malpractice Environment and Surgical Quality and Cost in the United States. *Annals of Surgery* 263: 1126–1132.

Blumenthal, D., and R. Galvin. 2019. *The Private Sector Takes on Health Care.* Accessed September 2020. Available at: https://www.commonwealthfund.org/blog/2019/private-sector-takes-health-care

Bodenheimer, T. 1997. The Oregon Health Plan: Lessons for the Nation. *New England Journal of Medicine* 337: 651–655.

Born, P. H., and J. B. Karl. 2016. The Effect of Tort Reform on Medical Malpractice Insurance Market Trends. *Journal of Empirical Legal Studies* 13: 718–755.

Centers for Disease Control and Prevention (CDC). 2020. *Prescription Drug Monitoring Programs (PDMPs)*. Accessed September 2020. Available at: https://www.cdc.gov/drugoverdose/pdmp/states.html

Centers for Medicare and Medicaid Services (CMS). 2020a. *Community Health Access and Rural Transformation (CHART) Model fact sheet*. Accessed October 2020. Available at: https://www.cms.gov/newsroom/fact-sheets/community-health-access-and-rural-transformation-chart-model-fact-sheet

Centers for Medicare and Medicaid Services (CMS). 2020b. *Pennsylvania Rural Health Model*. Accessed October 2020. Available at: https://innovation.cms.gov/innovation-models/pa-rural-health-model

Centers for Medicare and Medicaid Services (CMS). 2021. *Minority Research Grant Program*. Accessed March 2021. Available at: https://www.cms.gov/About-CMS/Agency-Information/OMH/equity-initiatives/advancing-health-equity/minority-research-grant-program

Cohidon, C., J. Cornuz, and N. Senn. 2015. Primary Care in Switzerland: Evolution of Physicians' Profile and Activities in Twenty Years (1993–2012). *BMC Family Practice*: 1–9.

Colello, K. J., and J. Mulvey. 2013. *Community Living Assistance Services and Supports (CLASS): Overview and Summary of Provisions*. CRS Report R40847. Washington, DC: Congressional Research Service.

Commission on Long-Term Care. 2016. *Home*. Accessed February 2017. Available at: http://www.ltccommission.org/

Congress.gov. 2015. *H.R.2: Medicare Access and CHIP Reauthorization Act of 2015*. Accessed February 2017. Available at: https://www.congress.gov/bill/114th-congress/house-bill/2

Congressional Research Service (2023). Available at: https://crsreports.congress.gov/product/pdf/R/R43341/45

T. Coughlin, S. Zuckerman, S. Wallin, and J. Holahan. 1999. A Conflict of Strategies: Medicaid Managed Care and Medicaid Maximization. *Health Services Research* 34: 281–293.

CVS Health. 2019. *CVS Health Announces Significant Expansion of Healthhub to Deliver a Differentiated, Consumer Health Experience*. Accessed September 2020. Available at: https://cvshealth.com/news-and-insights/articles/cvs-health-announces-significant-expansion-of-healthhub-to-deliver-a

Diez Roux, A.V. 2020. Population Health in the Time of COVID-19: Confirmations and Revelations. *Milbank Quarterly* 98: 629–640. https://onlinelibrary.wiley.com/doi/full/10.1111/1468-0009.12474

Falcone, D., and L. C. Hartwig. 1991. Congressional Process and Health Policy: Reform and Retrenchment. In: *Health Policies and Policy*. 2nd ed. T. Litman and L. Robins, eds. New York: John Wiley & Sons. pp. 126–144.

Fehr, R., C. Cox, K. Pollitz, J. Tolbert, J. Cubanski, and R. Rudowitz. 2020. *Five Things to Know About the Cost of COVID-19 Testing and Treatment*. Kaiser Family Foundation. Accessed October 2020. Available at: https://www.kff.org/coronavirus-covid-19/issue-brief/five-things-to-know-about-the-cost-of-covid-19-testing-and-treatment/

Gerke, S., A. D. Stern, and T. Minssen. 2020. Germany's Digital Health Reforms in the COVID-19 Era: Lessons and Opportunities for Other Countries. *NPJ Digital Medicine* 3: 94.

Glied. G. 2019. The Potential of Incremental Health Reform. *Health Affairs*. Accessed February 2020. Available at: https://www.healthaffairs.org/do/10.1377/hblog20190122.530762/full/

Global Health Initiative. 2014. *U.S. Global Health Programs*. Accessed March 2021. Available at: https://www.kff.org/global-health-policy/fact-sheet/u-s-funding-for-global-health-the-presidents-fy-2014-budget-request/

Government of Canada. 2023. *Canada's Health Care System*. Available at: https://www.canada.ca/en/health-canada/services/canada-health-care-system.html

Greenwood-Ericksen, M. B., S. D'Andrea, and S. Findley. 2020. *Transforming the Rural Health Care Paradigm*. JAMA Network. Accessed October 2020. Available at: https://jamanetwork.com/channels/health-forum/fullarticle/2770355

Havenhealthcare.com. n.d. *Vision*. Accessed September 2020. Available at: https://havenhealthcare.com/vision

Health Resources and Services Administration (HRSA). 2013. *The Affordable Care Act and Health Centers*. Accessed March 2021. Available at: https://www.hrsa.gov/about/news/press-releases/2013-08-01-hccn.html

Health Resources and Services Administration (HRSA). 2023. Health Center Program: Impact and Growth. Accessed December 2023. Available at: https://bphc.hrsa.gov/about-health-centers/health-center-program-impact-growth

Healthy People 2020. *Social Determinants of Health*. Accessed February 2020. Available at: https://www.healthypeople.gov/2020/topics-objectives/topic/social-determinants-of-health

Hostetter, M., and S. Klein. 2017. *In focus: Reimagining Rural Health Care*. Commonwealth Fund. Accessed October 2020. Available at: https://www.commonwealthfund.org/publications/newsletter-article/2017/mar/focus-reimagining-rural-health-care

Huckman, R. S. 2019. *Can Big-Box Retailers Provide Local Health Care?* Harvard Business Review. Accessed September 2020. Available at: https://hbr.org/2019/10/can-big-box-retailers-provide-local-health-care

Hutchison, B., J. F. Levesque, E. Strumpf, and N. Coyle, 2011. Primary Health Care In Canada: Systems In Motion. *The Milbank Quarterly*, 89: 256–288.

Japinga, M., A. Bartz, R. Saunders, and M. McClellan, 2022. Health Policy Priorities for the Biden Administration. *Clinical Gastroenterology and Hepatology: The Official*

Clinical Practice Journal of the American Gastroenterological Association 20: 477–480.

Jaret, P. 2015. *Prices Spike For Some Generic Drugs: Costs for Brand Names Also Increasing.* AARP. Accessed January 2017. Available at: http://www.aarp.org/health/drugs-supplements/info-2015/prices-spike-for-generic-drugs.html

Jones, D. K., and C. Pagel. 2020. *Bipartisan Approaches To Tackling Health Care Costs at the State Level.* Milbank Memorial Fund. Accessed October 2020. Available at: https://www.milbank.org/publications/bipartisan-approaches-to-tackling-health-care-costs-at-the-state-level/

Kaiser Family Foundation. 2013. *Summary of the Affordable Care Act.* Accessed June 2017. Available at: http://www.kff.org/health-reform/fact-sheet/summary-of-the-affordable-care-act/

Kaiser Family Foundation. 2018. *Summary of the 2018 CHIP Funding Extension.* Accessed February 2020. Available at: https://www.kff.org/medicaid/fact-sheet/summary-of-the-2018-chip-funding-extension/

Kaiser Family Foundation. 2019a. *The Mexico City Policy: An Explainer.* Accessed February 2020. Available at: https://www.kff.org/global-health-policy/fact-sheet/mexico-city-policy-explainer/

Kaiser Family Foundation. 2019b. *U.S. Federal Funding for HIV/AIDS: Trends over Time.* Accessed February 2020. Available at: https://www.kff.org/hivaids/fact-sheet/u-s-federal-funding-for-hivaids-trends-over-time/

Kaiser Family Foundation. 2020d. *Analysis: A Proposal Like Biden's Health Plan Would Lower the Cost of ACA Marketplace Coverage for Nearly All Potential Enrollees and Lower Premiums for Over 12 Million Workers with Employer Coverage.* Accessed November 2020. Available at: https://www.kff.org/health-reform/press-release/analysis-a-proposal-like-bidens-health-plan-would-lower-the-cost-of-aca-marketplace-coverage-for-nearly-all-potential-enrollees-and-lower-premiums-for-over-12-million-workers-with-employer-c/

Kaiser Family Foundation, 2023a. Status of State Medicaid Expansion Decisions: Interactive Map. Accessed December 2023. Available at: https://www.kff.org/medicaid/issue-brief/status-of-state-medicaid-expansion-decisions-interactive-map/.

Kaiser Family Foundation, 2023b. State Health Insurance Marketplace Types, 2024. Accessed December 2023. Available at: https://www.kff.org/health-reform/state-indicator/state-health-insurance-marketplace-types/?currentTimeframe=0&sortModel=%7B%22colId%22:%22Location%22,%22sort%22:%22asc%22%7D

Wager, E., Telesford, I., and Cox, C. 2019. *What Are the Recent and Forecasted Trends in Prescription Drug Spending?* Peterson-KFF Health System Tracker. Accessed February 2020. Available at: https://www.healthsystemtracker.org/chart-collection/recent-forecasted-trends-prescription-drug-spending/#item-start

Klink, K. 2015. Incentives for Physicians to Pursue Primary Care in the ACA era. *AMA Journal of Ethics* 17: 637–646. doi: 10.1001/journalofethics.2015.17.7.stas1-1507.

Knight, A. W., C. Caesar, D. Ford, A. Coughlin, and C. Frick. 2012. Improving Primary Care in Australia Through the Australian Primary Care Collaboratives Program: A Quality Improvement Report. *BMJ Quality & Safety*, 21: 948-955.

Koons, C. 2020. The Amazon–Berkshire–JPMorgan Health Venture Fails to Disrupt. *Bloomberg Businessweek.* Accessed September 2020. Available at: https://www.bloomberg.com/news/articles/2020-05-21/bezos-buffett-dimon-joint-venture-fails-to-disrupt-health-care

LaRock, Z. 2019. *The Telemedicine Boom Is Imminent, and It's Creating Opportunities for Providers.* Insider. Accessed February 2020. Available at: https://www.businessinsider.com/telemedicine-will-boom-but-barriers-persist-2019-3

Levitt, L. 2020. *Trump vs Biden on Health Care. JAMA Health Forum.* Accessed September 2020. Available at: https://jamanetwork.com/channels/health-forum/fullarticle/2770427?resultClick=1

Longest, B. B. 2010. *Health Policymaking in the United States.* 5th ed. Ann Arbor, MI: Health Administration Press.

Mengistu, T. S., R. Khatri, D. Erku, and Y. Assefa. 2023. Successes and Challenges Of Primary Health Care in Australia: A Scoping Review and Comparative Analysis. *Journal of Global Health* 13: 04043.

Morone, J. A., Litman, T. J., Robins, L. S. 2008. *Health Policies and Policy.* 4th ed. New York: Delmar. Available at: https://www.amazon.com/Politics-Theodor-Leonard-Learning-Hardcover/dp/B00DU85WH0

Moy, E., M. C. Garcia, B. Bastian, et al. 2017. Leading Causes of Death in Nonmetropolitan and Metropolitan Areas—United States, 1999–2014. *Morbidity and Mortality Weekly Report: Surveillance Summaries* 66: 1–8. Available at: http://dx.doi.org/10.15585/mmwr.ss6601a1

National Conference of State Legislatures. 2019. *CON: Certificate of Need State Laws.* Accessed February 2020. Available at: https://www.ncsl.org/research/health/con-certificate-of-need-state-laws.aspx

National Conference of State Legislatures. 2023. Certificate of Need State Laws. Accessed December 2023. Available at: https://www.ncsl.org/health/certificate-of-need-state-laws

National Governors Association. 2020. *State Strategies to Improve the Use of Prescription Drug Monitoring Programs to Address Opioid and Other Substance Use Disorders.* Accessed September 2020. Available at: https://www.nga.org/wp-content/uploads/2020/07/NGA_PDMP_Toolkit-July-2020.pdf

NHS England. n.d. *Primary Care Services.* Available at: https://www.england.nhs.uk/get-involved/get-involved/how/primarycare/

Oberlander, J. 2010. Long Time Coming: Why Health Reform Finally Passed. *Health Affairs* 29: 1112–1116.

Oliver, T. R., P. R Lee, and H. L. Lipton. 2004. A Political History of Medicare and Prescription Drug Coverage. *Milbank Quarterly* 82: 283–354.

Patel, K., and J. McDonough. 2010. From Massachusetts to 1600 Pennsylvania Avenue: Aboard the Health Reform Express. *Health Affairs* 29: 1106–1111.

Pharmaceutical Research and Manufacturers of America. 2016. *Prescription Medicines: Costs in Context*. Accessed January 2017. Available at: http://phrma-docs.phrma.org/sites/default/files/pdf/prescription-medicines-costs-in-context-extended.pdf

Popescu, G. H. 2015. Increased Medical Malpractice Expenditures as a Main Determinant of Growth in Health Care Spending. *American Journal of Medical Research* 2: 80.

Purington, K. 2019. *Tackling the Opioid Crisis: What State Strategies Are Working?* National Academy for State Health Policy. Accessed September 2020. Available at: https://www.nashp.org/tackling-the-opioid-crisis-what-state-strategies-are-working/

PwC Health Research Institute. 2016. *Medical Cost Trend: Behind the Numbers 2016*. Washington, DC: PwC.

Rice, T., A. J. Barnes, P. Rosenau, L. Y. Unruh, and E. van Ginneken. 2021. Health Reforms in the United States: The Outlook after Biden's first 100 Days. *Health Policy* 125: 1277–1284.

Roy, A. 2012. *How the AARP Made $2.8 Billion by Supporting Obamacare's Cuts to Medicare*. Forbes. Accessed October 2013. Available at: http://www.forbes.com/sites/aroy/2012/09/22/the-aarps-2-8-billion-reasons-for-supporting-obamacares-cuts-to-medicare

Scheffler, R. M., and T. L. Wang. 2020. The Public–Private Option in Germany and Australia: Lessons for the United States. *Milbank Quarterly Opinion*. Available at: https://doi.org/10.1599/mqop.2020.0921

Schneider, E. C. 2020. Health Care as an Ongoing Policy Project. *New England Journal of Medicine* 383: 405–408. doi: 10.1056/NEJMp2021701.

Senate Appropriations Committee. 2019. *Summary of H.R. 1865*. Accessed February 2020. Available at: https://www.appropriations.senate.gov/imo/media/doc/121619%20--%20HR1865%20Domestic%20Intl%20Asst%20Package%20Summary.pdf

Sharfstein, J. M. 2016. Global Budgets for Rural Hospitals. *Milbank Quarterly* 94: 255–259. doi: 10.1111/1468-0009.12192.

Shi, L. 2019. *Introduction to Health Policy*. 2nd ed. Chicago, IL: Health Administration Press, AUPHA.

Stephenson, J. 2020. *Federal Plan Proposes Improving Rural Health Care Through Telehealth*. JAMA Network. Accessed October 2020. Available at: https://jamanetwork.com/channels/health-forum/fullarticle/2771057

Stockley, K. 2019. *How Do Changes in Medical Malpractice Liability Laws Affect Health Care Spending and the Federal Budget?* Congressional Budget Office. Accessed February 2020. Available at: https://www.cbo.gov/system/files/2019-04/55104-Medical%20Malpractice_WP.pdf

Tanke, M., and U. Ikram. 2020. A Unique Deal in Dutch Health Care: Private Insurers And Providers Find Common Ground to Address COVID-19 Effects. *NEJM Catalyst*. Accessed October 2020. Available at: https://catalyst.nejm.org/doi/full/10.1056/CAT.20.0514

The White House. 2022. *Inflation Reduction Act Guidebook*. Accessed December 2023. Available at: https://www.whitehouse.gov/cleanenergy/inflation-reduction-act-guidebook/

The White House. 2023. *FACT SHEET: Biden-Harris Administration Announces First Ten Drugs Selected for Medicare Price Negotiation*. Accessed December 2023. Available at: https://www.whitehouse.gov/briefing-room/statements-releases/2023/08/29/fact-sheet-biden-harris-administration-announces-first-ten-drugs-selected-for-medicare-price-negotiation/

The White House. 2023. *FACT SHEET: President Biden Announces New Actions to Lower Health Care Costs and Protect Consumers from Scam Insurance Plans and Junk Fees as Part of "Bidenomics" Push*. Available at: https://www.whitehouse.gov/briefing-room/statements-releases/2023/07/07/fact-sheetpresident-biden-announces-new-actions-to-lower-health-care-costs-and-protect-consumers-from-scam-insurance-plans-and-junk-fees-as-part-of-bidenomics-push/#:~:text=Since%20the%20beginning%20of%20his,every%20sector%20of%20the%20economy

The White House. 2023. *FACT SHEET: Biden-Harris Administration Takes Action to Make it Easier to Access In-Network Mental Health Care*. Available at: https://www.whitehouse.gov/briefing-room/statements-releases/2023/07/25/fact-sheet-biden-harris-administration-takes-action-to-make-it-easier-to-access-in-network-mental-health-care/

Tichy, E. M., G. T. Schumock, and J. M. Hoffman, et al. 2020. National Trends in Prescription Drug Expenditures and Projections for 2020. *American Journal of Health-System Pharmacy* 77: 1213–1230. Available at: https://doi.org/10.1093/ajhp/zxaa116

Tikkanen, R., G. A. Wharton, A. Djordjevic, E. Mossialos, and R. D. Williams II. 2020. *The 2020 International Profiles of Health Care Systems: A Useful Resource for Interpreting Country Responses to the COVID-19 Pandemic*. Commonwealth Fund. Accessed October 2020. Available at: https://www.commonwealthfund.org/blog/2020/2020-international-profiles-useful-resource-interpreting-responses-covid-19

Tolbert, J., M. Diaz, C. Hall, and S. Mengistu. 2019. *State Actions to Improve the Affordability Of Health Insurance in the Individual Market*. Kaiser Family Foundation. Accessed September 2020. Available at: https://www.kff.org/health-reform/issue-brief/state-actions-to

-improve-the-affordability-of-health-insurance-in-the-individual-market/

Tractica. 2015. *Home Health Technologies*. Accessed March 2021. Available at: https://www.businesswire.com/news/home/20150820005008/en/Telehealth-Home-Health-Technologies-Increasingly-Attractive-Healthcare

UHC2030. n.d. *Our Mission*. Accessed October 2020. Available at: https://www.uhc2030.org/our-mission/

Universal Health Coverage (UHC) Partnership. n.d. *Why Policy Dialogue Makes It Happen: Moving Jointly Towards Universal Health Coverage*. Accessed October 2020. Available at: https://www.uhcpartnership.net/about/

U.S. Department of Health and Human Services (DHHS). 2016. *HHS Finalizes Streamlined Medicare Payment System That Rewards Clinicians for Quality Patient Care*. Accessed May 2017. Available at: https://wayback.archive-it.org/3926/20170127192642/https://www.hhs.gov/about/news/2016/10/14/hhs-finalizes-streamlined-medicare-payment-system-rewards-clinicians-quality-patient-care.html

U.S. Department of Health and Human Services (DHHS). 2020. *Rural Action Plan*. Accessed October 2020. Available at: https://www.hhs.gov/sites/default/files/hhs-rural-action-plan.pdf

U.S. Food and Drug Administration (FDA). 2020. *FDA Takes Actions to Help Lower U.S. Prescription Drug Prices*. Accessed November 2020. Available at: https://www.fda.gov/news-events/press-announcements/fda-takes-actions-help-lower-us-prescription-drug-prices

U.S. Department of Health and Human Services. 2023. *The Biden-Harris Administration Is Taking Actions to Improve the Health of Rural Communities and Help Rural Health Care Providers Stay Open*. https://www.hhs.gov/about/news/2023/11/03/department-health-human-services-actions-support-rural-america-rural-health-care-providers.html

J.-Y. Wang, Y. W. Liang, C. C. Yeh, C. S. Liu, and C. Y. Wang. 2018. Time-dependent Risks of Cancer Clustering Among Couples: A Nationwide Population-Based Cohort Study in Taiwan. *BMJ Open* 8: e018968. doi: 10.1136/bmjopen-2017-018968.

White House. 2010. *National HIV/AIDS Strategy for the United States*. Accessed March 2021. Available at: https://obamawhitehouse.archives.gov/blog/2010/07/13/announcing-national-hivaids-strategy

Wilson, L. S., and A. J. Maeder. 2015. Recent Directions in Telemedicine: Review of Trends in Research and Practice. *Healthcare Informatics Research* 21: 213–222.

Winfield Cunningham, P. 2020. The Health 202: Trump Keeps Claiming He Lowered Prescription Drug Prices. But that is largely not true. *The Washington Post*. Accessed November 2020. Available at: https://www.washingtonpost.com/politics/2020/09/18/health-202-trump-keeps-claiming-he-lowered-prescription-drug-prices-that-is-largely-not-true/

World Bank (WB). 2022. Accelerating COVID-19 Vaccine Deployment: Removing Obstacles to Increase Coverage Levels and Protect Those at High Risk. Accessed December 2023. Available at: G20-Report--Accelerating-COVID-19-Vaccine-Deployment.pdf

World Health Organization (WHO). 2019. *The WHO Special Initiative for Mental Health (2019–2023): Universal Health Coverage For Mental Health*. Accessed October 2020. Available at: https://apps.who.int/iris/bitstream/handle/10665/310981/WHO-MSD-19.1-eng.pdf?ua=1

World Health Organization (WHO). 2020. *Timeline: WHO's COVID-19 Response*. Accessed October 2020. Available at: https://www.who.int/emergencies/diseases/novel-coronavirus-2019/interactive-timeline#event-73

World Health Organization (WHO). n.d. *Universal Health Coverage*. Accessed October 2020. Available at: https://www.who.int/health-topics/universal-health-coverage#tab=tab_1

World Health Organization (WHO). 2023. Global Research and Innovation for Health Emergencies: Building the World's Resilience Against Future Outbreaks and Pandemics. Accessed December 2023. Available at:https://cdn.who.int/media/docs/default-source/documents/r-d-blueprint-meetings/global-research-and-innovation-for-health-emergencies_report-2023.pdf?sfvrsn=9341366_2

World Health Organization. 2023. *Initiatives*. https://www.who.int/initiatives

World Health Organization. 2023. *What We Do*. https://www.who.int/about/what-wedo#:~:text=WHO%20works%20worldwide%20to%20promote,better%20health%20and%20well%2Dbeing

PART 5

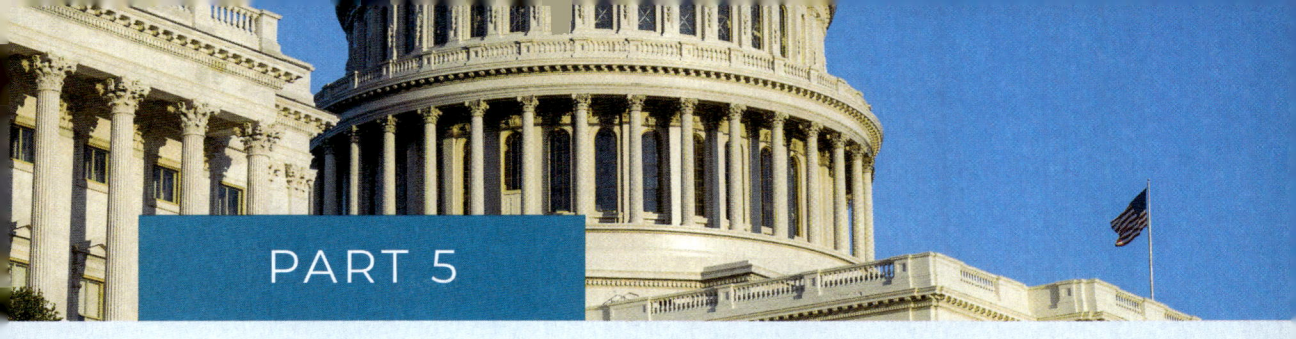

System Outlook

CHAPTER 14 The Future of Health Services Delivery..............613

CHAPTER 14

The Future of Health Services Delivery

LEARNING OBJECTIVES

- Identify the major forces of future change that affect healthcare delivery.
- Assess the options for healthcare reform in the United States.
- Discuss the evolution of the healthcare delivery infrastructure and the progress in population health.
- Describe the expert recommendations to address the future of nursing and primary care.
- Discuss the future of long-term care.
- Evaluate the status of international cooperation in dealing with global threats.
- Provide an overview of new frontiers in clinical technology.
- Survey the future of evidence-based health care.

"Will the United States have a single-payer system?"

Introduction

The outlook for healthcare delivery in the United States is predicated on major current developments and the course that these developments might take in the relatively near future. Any attempts to project the future of health care inevitably provoke more questions than answers, and the future often turns out differently than people anticipate (Kenen, 2011). Indeed, prognostication is an art that is fraught with assumptions that may not materialize and other developments that may yet come (Vitalari, 2016).

The broad healthcare delivery system is subject to several external factors that exert powerful influences to shape and mold its future direction. Forces such as demographic trends and political dynamics can be expected to follow a certain course, so that some predictions can be made on this basis. For other external factors, even short-term predictions are difficult. For instance, it is impossible to predict the global forces that may impact the health of populations in many nations.

Future change also relies on historical precedents. Certain fundamental features of U.S. healthcare delivery, such as its largely private infrastructure and the U.S. public's fundamental values, have in the past prompted resistance to any proposals for a sweeping transformation of health care. Yet, certain historical precedents have also been used as a springboard for current change, and they will no doubt influence future change as well.

Another major factor affecting the projection is related to the second term of the Trump Administration. At the time of this writing, Donald Trump has just defeated Pamela Harris by wide margin (312 vs. 226 electoral college votes) and gained control of both the Senate and Congress (although by a much smaller margin). Although with Republicans in control of both chambers, President Trump could have initiated changes in U.S. healthcare delivery, given the disagreements within the Republican party and the relative low emphasis by Trump on healthcare reform during the campaign stage, changes in U.S. healthcare landscape is likely to be incremental.

This chapter examines the future of health care within the larger national and global contexts. It also assesses the likely future course of healthcare reform, clinical technology, and new models of delivering health care.

Forces of Future Change

The framework presented here includes forces that help us understand why certain changes have occurred in the past, and that inform the direction of change that might occur in the future. This framework can be used for viewing healthcare delivery and policy from a macro perspective. In addition, it can be used by healthcare executives to craft strategies for their organizations that are aligned with the changes occurring in the broader healthcare environment.

The eight forces included in the framework are (1) social and demographic, (2) political, (3) economic, (4) technological, (5) informational, (6) ecological, (7) global, and (8) cultural-anthro. These forces often interact in complex ways, and these interactions are not always simple to interpret. For example, technological innovation and adoption of healthy lifestyles (cultural-anthro factors) can influence labor force participation and improve workforce productivity (economic factors), which in turn can provide the means to deliver better health care to a larger segment of the population. Low unemployment and the quality of immigration, through growth-oriented policies (political forces), can also rev up a nation's economic engines to provide the necessary revenues for healthcare delivery. Hence, a keen observation of the various forces can create opportunities for change.

With the passage of time, some forces become more dominant than others. For example, the ebb and flow of politics may bring about a temporary, and sometimes even a permanent, change. Passage of the Affordable Care Act (ACA) in the past and rotating control of the government by the Republican or Democrat Party are cases in point. Hence, the U.S. healthcare system will continue to evolve, but no one truly knows its ultimate destiny.

For several decades, the U.S. healthcare delivery system has not been driven by free-market forces. Over the years, the government has become a major player that controls a growing segment of healthcare financing, and it has increasingly wielded control over the private sector through its legal and regulatory powers. Yet, the government needs the private healthcare sector to serve its millions of beneficiaries in public health insurance programs. At least for the relatively near future, tension and power balancing between the private and public sectors will continue and, for better or for worse, we will encounter ongoing changes in the way Americans receive health care.

Currently, healthcare expenditures account for almost one-fifth of the U.S. economy. The ongoing ability to deliver health care is, therefore, closely tied to the nation's economic health, regardless of whether that health care is delivered through private or public insurance programs.

Social and Demographic Forces

From a demographic standpoint, the United States is getting bigger, older, and more ethnically diverse. More specifically, the global number of people older than 60 increased from 200 million in 1950 to 1 billion in 2020, and is predicted to reach 2 billion by 2050 and 3 billion by 2100 (Newman et al., 2023). Shifts in the demographic composition of the population, cultural factors, and lifestyles affect not only the need for health care, but also the means by which those needs will be met (Ecevit et al., 2023; Adanlawo and Nkomo, 2023; Lopreite et al., 2023). Research in Europe has shown that population aging may have a greater influence on future healthcare expenditures than risk factors such as obesity, smoking, and harmful alcohol use (Goryakin et al., 2020), even though the effects of lifestyle factors cannot be downplayed.

As such, increasing life expectancy means a rapidly aging global population, marking a key driver of chronic diseases and multimorbidity. Unfortunately, this has led to an increase in unmet healthcare needs among older adults, a healthcare issue that has recently been targeted with applications of artificial intelligence (Ma et al., 2023). These implementations range from technologies that serve as rehabilitation therapists, emotional supporters, social facilitators, supervisors, and cognitive promoters within older adults' health care.

Older adults, people who are vulnerable, and people with certain high-cost health conditions all present varied needs. These groups also have the highest healthcare costs, so they are essentially drivers of change in the healthcare system. For instance, when examining healthcare utilization across a life course in Canada, the per capita use of hospital admission increased with age (Tillmann et al., 2021). Vulnerable populations in the United States receive health care mainly through Medicaid and Medicare, the two largest public health insurance programs. One study found that the annual average healthcare spending per person among the high-needs population—defined as adults with three or more chronic conditions and a functional limitation. Limitations in core areas of functioning that include the physical, cognitive, emotional, and social domains is four times higher than the spending per person for the general adult U.S. population, and three times higher than the spending per person for adults with chronic conditions but no functional limitation (Hayes et al., 2016).

The expanding government programs are currently on an unsustainable financial path. Going forward, growth in Medicare, Medicaid, and Children's Health Insurance Program (CHIP) expenditures is expected to consume a greater share of the country's overall economic output—from 6.1% of the U.S. gross domestic product (GDP) in 2020 to 9.2% in 2050. The proportion of federal outlays consumed by these programs is projected to rise from 28% in 2019 to 40% in 2050 (Congressional Budget Office [CBO], 2020). That implies spending in non-healthcare areas will have to be drastically curtailed. Whether benefit cuts will be applied to Medicare and Medicaid in the future is anyone's guess.

An equally challenging factor to predict is how population shifts will affect the composition of the healthcare workforce, because healthcare delivery is a labor-intensive enterprise (Cristea et al., 2020; Singh et al., 2022; Kiplagat et al., 2022). In a free society, people choose their professions and where they work. Hence, social and demographic factors play a significant role in determining the number of healthcare professionals and their geographic distribution. Future immigration is one factor that will likely affect the supply of caregivers. Although the United States will need productive immigrants, uncontrolled immigration, particularly undocumented immigration, can bring other unpredictable problems into the country, such as disease, crime, and a strain on the nation's resources exceeding the economic contribution of the immigrants.

Moreover, an aging healthcare workforce results in safety challenges, training needs, and of the overall shortage of the labor market. This was especially magnified after COVID-19 as concerns regarding safe and effective crisis response were raised as age was established to elevate risk for severe infection or death in coronavirus 2 cases (Adams and Walls, 2020). Although there is a dearth of literature surrounding the management of an ageing health workforce, recent research has compiled strategies that target supply, demand and health workforce training, retirement planning, extending working lives, health and lifestyle, retention and sustainability, and working environments (Kurashvili et al., 2023). This ranges from the implementation of replenishing aging doctors with younger medical graduates to investing in improving lifestyle behaviors among aging healthcare workforce or focusing on the retention of rural health workers. Much value has also been placed on the context brought by COVID-19 as it affects this population in the healthcare setting.

The U.S. society's cultural mix, which also reflects the rate and nature of immigration, will continue to slowly transform the nation's healthcare delivery. Between 2018 and 2050, the effect of net immigration on the growth of the U.S. population will increase from 48% to 100%, as mortality rates are projected to surpass fertility rates (CBO, 2020).

Social and cultural factors affect exposure and vulnerability to disease, risk-taking behaviors, perceptions of and responses to health problems, and healthcare-seeking behavior. For example, emergency department (ED) use remains disproportionately higher among Black people compared to White people (National Center for Health Statistics [NCHS], 2019), even after the passage of the ACA. A large population of undocumented immigrants, estimated to number at least 11.3 million (Krogstad et al., 2017) and growing, is not covered by any health insurance program; it also taps into the nation's healthcare resources through ED use and charity care. Historically, the United States has failed to craft and pursue a well-thought-out immigration policy. In consequence, although the precise effects of immigration on the economy and on health care remain unclear, there is little doubt that healthcare resources will be further strained.

Economic Forces

Economic growth, employment, household incomes, inflation, and the national debt are major forces that will determine the availability of healthcare services, their cost, and their affordability. Household incomes, especially for middle-class families, largely determine the affordability of health care, and household incomes depend on the nation's economic health and quality of employment.

As job losses mounted during the Great Recession (2007–2009), as many as 5 million Americans lost their employer-sponsored health coverage (Holahan, 2011). One might argue that the ACA could not have become law had the Great Recession not shortly preceded its enactment. The reality of job and health insurance losses once again brought health security to the forefront of the domestic policy agenda (Sage and Westmoreland, 2020).

By 2019, the economic well-being of Americans had improved substantially since 2013. In 2020, however, the financial lives of many families were disrupted because of COVID-19 and the lockdowns implemented to limit its spread. Apart from the economic toll, the effects of these lockdowns have included serious mental health and substance abuse issues for many people. At the same time, affordability of health care has remained a challenge for many Americans. In 2019, 25% of U.S. adults went without some form of medical care, mainly dental care and visiting a doctor (Federal Reserve Board, 2020). Furthermore, a 2023 study suggests that adults with self-reported post-COVID-conditions experienced greater challenges with healthcare affordability as compared to the rest of the population (Karpman, 2023).

In 2019, the United States reached the lowest levels of unemployment since the 1960s, and it remained true that unemployment rates were lower among individuals with college degrees than those with lower levels of education. Also, the annual median income among young college graduates was $24,700 higher than for those holding a high school diploma (DeSilver, 2019). Since the onset of the COVID-19 pandemic and the shock to the economy, job losses have been consistent with roughly 6.2 million workers losing access to health insurance that they previously got through their own employer (Economic Policy Institute, 2020).

For many years, the United States has been paying for its operations through federal debt. National debt is a function of economic production, taxation, and spending policies. Debt as a percentage of GDP is a useful measure for comparing amounts of debt in different years because it shows debt in relation to the size of the economy. Using that measure, U.S. debt rose from 70% of GDP in 2012 to 119.47% at the end of 2023 and is expected to rise to 129% by the end of 2033 (Fred, 2023). To put those numbers in perspective, the debt was 35% of GDP in 2007, with the United States then being hit by a severe recession in 2007–2009. In 2020, the COVID-19 pandemic ended the longest economic expansion in U.S. history and triggered the deepest downturn in output and employment since the demobilization following World War II (CBO, 2020). A mushrooming national debt increases the risk of a fiscal crisis in the future, and the nation faces daunting challenges to overcome. To stimulate economic growth, it must curtail unproductive spending by implementing tough policies. On the flip side, if a default occurs, it will lead to unpleasant consequences for many Americans. Any default would negatively affect the economy, households, and entitlement programs such as Medicaid, Medicare, and Social Security, the very safety nets on which many vulnerable people depend.

The impact of a COVID-19 infection can linger long after symptoms dissipate (Binder Dijker Otte, 2022). Studies estimate that approximately 14% of COVID-19 survivors between the ages of 18 and 65 develop new symptoms and receive new diagnoses up to six months after their initial bout with the virus. Insurers could experience an uptick in appeals as those denied coverage for respiratory therapy and other rehabilitative treatments may appeal insurers' decisions. The emergence and proliferation of COVID-19 long haulers may cause carriers to reevaluate their definition of "medical necessity."

Inflational pressure continues to haunt the U.S. economy. Many analysts agree that higher cost-of-living, largely due to inflation, was one of the major reasons for the defeat of the democratic party's presidential bid. Given the depressive economic outlook and the uncertain trade policies around the world, inflation will remain a major concern of the new Trump Administration.

Political Forces

The history of health care in the United States and in other countries is replete with examples of major changes brought about through political will, depending on which party has the legislative majority. Party politics along ideological lines can hold up major initiatives from moving forward. Politics, however, serves a nation best when it is subservient to the people's needs and wants. Americans have remained divided over major policy issues, however, and health care is one such issue.

Recent politics in the United States have been marked with acrimony, hegemony, ideological dominance, political activism, and unilateralism. These attributes can be observed in a predominantly propagandist media, divisive rhetoric and actions from both private and public entities, high-level political corruption, and a political machinery that pushes forward predominantly a one-sided agenda. Only the future will reveal the consequences of such powerful forces on the nation's social, economic, physical, and mental health and well-being. One can surmise, however, that if allowed to continue, in the long term, such forces can only yield undesirable results.

Healthcare Reform Directions of the Second Trump Administration

Although it is not clear what the second Trump Administration will do in terms of healthcare reform efforts, we have summarized the following potential directions based on his campaign and other documents.

Alteration of Obamacare. Instead of completely repealing Obamacare (Kekatos. 2024a), Trump has proposed improvements and alternatives (Kekatos, 2024b). In March 2024, Trump wrote on Truth Social that he was "not running to terminate" the Affordable Care Act, but wanted to make it "better" and "less expensive" (Dangerfield, 2024). His campaign stated that, rather than "ending" the ACA, it aimed to reduce costs by "increasing transparency, promoting choice and competition, and expanding access to new medical and prescription drug options." Specific plans included the elimination of tax credits (Owermohle, 2024) although there was disagreement within Republicans (MTN Staff, 2024), and the elimination of additional provisions or add-ons (such as outreach funds, shortening enrollment periods, loosening regulations on insurers, and the enhanced ACA subsidies to improve plans or lower premiums) of the ACA through the American Rescue Plan Act (ARPA) (Armour, 2024; Sudborough, 2024; Weixel, 2024). Efforts to weaken the ACA could include allowing consumers to purchase health plans that don't comply with ACA consumer protections, and insurers to charge sicker people higher premiums (Armour, 2024). These potential changes could lead to healthy people avoiding insurance (Ault, 2024), and significantly higher premiums for people with chronic diseases (Owermohle, 2024).

Medicaid Cuts. During his campaign, Trump made no specific mention of Medicaid, and he also excluded Medicaid from his pledge not to cut spending on Medicare and Social Security programs (Owermohle, 2024). For this reason, it is more likely that he will push ahead with cuts to Medicaid than to Medicare. There are several ways in which Medicaid could be reduced. Some states have already begun to apply work requirements to program participants, and there is a possibility that this will be extended to other states in the future, leading to a reduction in Medicaid (Owermohle, 2024; Sudborough, 2024; MTN Staff, 2024, Ault, 2024). In addition, capping federal funding, as has been proposed by conservatives for some time, would also be an effective way to reduce the program (Armour, 2024; Weixel, 2024). Furthermore, there is also a growing possibility that applications for Medicaid waivers to implement state-specific Medicaid programs will be rejected (Sudborough, 2024).

Promotion of Medicare Advantage. Under the Trump administration, there is a possibility that Medicare Advantage, a private insurance plan, will be promoted as an alternative to the original Medicare. Conservative groups have proposed that many Medicare beneficiaries be transferred to Medicare Advantage (Ault, 2024). In addition, the Heritage Foundation, a conservative think tank, has proposed making Medicare Advantage the default option for Medicare in its policy plan "Project 2025" (Kekatos, 2024b). This initiative aims to reduce Medicare costs and improve service quality.

Price Reduction of Medicines by the IRA (Inflation Reduction Act) and the Most Favored Nation (MFN). Some Trump supporters predicted that the authority of the Medicare drug price negotiation with pharmaceutical companies under the IRA will be maintained under the Trump administration, and that efforts to reduce prices will continue (Owermohle, 2024; Armour, 2024). However, there was no mention of the intention to utilize this process in Trump's election campaign (MTN Staff, 2024). In addition, the Republican Party announced its intention to abolish this drug price negotiation model, and it is possible that Trump would support the Republican Party's position and discontinue this model (Sudborough, 2024; Ault, 2024).

During his first administration, Trump was keen to reduce the cost of prescription drugs, but due to opposition from the pharmaceutical industry, the policy known as "most favored nation" treatment was not realized (MTN Staff, 2024). It is possible that the Trump Administration would tackle cost reduction of medicine by going back to the "most favored nation" concept or similar approach (Owermohle, 2024).

Ambiguous Attitude Towards Abortion. Trump has distanced himself from the nationwide abortion restrictions sought by some conservatives (Owermohle, 2024; MTN Staff, 2024). Since his victory in the Republican primary earlier this year, he has taken the position that abortion restrictions should be left to voters in individual states (Dangerfield, 2024; Ault, 2024), and in October he reiterated this position on the social platform X (Kekatos, 2024b). He has also called for the Republican Party to change its platform to reflect this position (Sudborough, 2024). Before the election, he stated that he would not sign a national abortion ban bill, and he has also indicated that he would veto any such bill if it reached the stage where it required the president's signature (Armour, 2024; Weixel, 2024).

Reorganization of the CDC and NIH. Republican lawmakers are discussing the reorganization of two public health agencies, the Centers for Disease Control and Prevention (CDC) and the National Institutes of Health (NIH) (Owermohle, 2024). In particular, the CDC may be split into two organizations, one responsible for infectious disease control and the other for chronic disease prevention (MTN Staff, 2024). The aim of this reorganization is to improve the expertise of each organization and increase the efficiency of public health measures.

Technological Forces

It is widely believed that technological innovation in medical sciences will continue to revolutionize health care. Americans strongly favor ongoing innovation, greater availability, and wider use of new technology. One recent example of this preference is the passage of the 21st Century Cures Act of 2016, which is aimed at advancing medical innovation and ensuring quick access to new treatments. The high cost of research and development and the subsequent costs associated with unrestrained use of technology do raise questions about how long this pattern can go on, given that growth in healthcare spending will continue to surpass GDP growth. Technologies that promote a greater degree of self-reliance or achieve cost efficiencies will almost certainly receive much attention in the future. Nevertheless, the overall effect of technology is to increase costs unless it is accompanied by utilization control measures.

Informational Forces

Information technology (IT) has numerous applications in healthcare delivery (Bentahar et al., 2023; Dicuonzo et al., 2023; Vishwakarma et al., 2023). IT has also become an indispensable tool for managing today's healthcare organizations. Realization of IT's full potential is still evolving and will continue well into the future. The use of smart cards in health care, for example, can combat forgery and identity theft, thereby curtailing fraud and abuse (Horowitz, 2012). Americans have often viewed smart cards with suspicion and distrust, mainly because of fears that their personal health information could be compromised. Smart cards are already in wide use in European health systems, and it is only a matter of time before their use becomes acceptable in the United States. That use could well begin with Medicare and Medicaid beneficiaries through government mandates. Recently, healthcare organizations have started to implement cloud computing to provide high-quality treatment while managing costs and fostering better collaboration with stakeholders (Komalasari, 2023).

Ecological Forces

New diseases, natural disasters, and bioterrorism have major implications for public health, and potentially even global consequences. Communicable diseases—such as new strains of influenza and coronavirus—and diseases related to environmental agents—such as vector-borne diseases (e.g., West Nile virus and chikungunya virus)—can trigger mass hysteria, particularly in large population centers, especially when the disease remains mysterious and treatments are not readily available. For example, some cases of the deadly Ebola virus infection created widespread concern in the United States in 2014. It is yet unknown whether COVID-19 will be conquered once and for all or whether it will keep emerging every year, to be kept under control through vaccinations similar to the seasonal flu. **Zoonoses** are diseases or infections that are naturally transmittable from vertebrate animals to humans. Growth of populations around the globe will intensify interactions at the human-animal-ecosystems interface, raising the probability of engendering diseases that are as yet unknown.

When a significant number of people are affected or threatened by disease, research and technological innovation shift into high gear. For example, several vaccines against COVID-19 have been developed in record time. Technologies, such as remote sensing and geographic information systems (GIS), will find ongoing applications in public health and safety in such circumstances.

Natural disasters not only disrupt people's daily lives but also create conditions that pose serious health risks through contamination of food and water. Health problems and psychological distress often follow. The roles of the Centers for Disease Control and Prevention (CDC) and other partnering agencies will continue to evolve as new challenges emerge. On the downside, the growing need to combat new ecological threats will divert resources from the provision of routine health care to the people who most need them.

Global Forces

The economies of the world have become progressively more interdependent. Globalization has become an extremely complex phenomenon because the various forces discussed here interact as this process continues to evolve (Huynen et al., 2005). For example, Rennen and Martens (2003) define contemporary globalization in terms of an intensification of cross-national cultural, economic, political, social, and technological interactions. Hence, health and health care in various countries will continue to be affected in diverse ways through multiple pathways.

During the COVID-19 pandemic, the supply shock that started in China in February, 2020 and the demand shock that followed as the global economy shut down exposed vulnerabilities in the production strategies and supply chains of firms just about everywhere (Harvard Business Review, 2020). Manufacturers worldwide are going to be under greater political and competitive pressures to increase their domestic production, grow employment in their home countries, reduce or even eliminate their dependence on sources that are perceived as risky, and rethink their use of lean manufacturing strategies that involve minimizing the amount of inventory held in their global supply chains. The challenge for companies will be to make their supply chains more resilient without weakening their competitiveness.

Some indications suggest that the trend toward globalization in health care will intensify. Increasingly, generic drugs and medical equipment are being manufactured in Asian countries for export to Europe, Canada, and the United States. As such, the relocation of production chains in health care aims to optimize efficiency, enhance supply chains and overall access to medical supplies, allowing for more adaptable corporate responses to different public health priorities. This trend has made the products more affordable in the United States, but ensuring the drugs' safety and the integrity of foreign-made equipment, as well as securing adequate supplies to meet demand on a consistent basis, pose major challenges.

Medical tourism is likely to increase as consumers seek timely and cheaper alternatives abroad. Given the high cost of healthcare services in the United States and Europe, providers in other countries will continue to offer a wider array of lower-cost but almost identical high-quality health services, with these services often coming with greater amenities (Reeves, 2011). It is likely that at some point insurers may start paying for services that are more economically delivered overseas.

Cross-border telemedicine is a rapidly developing trend (George and Henthorne, 2009). Indeed, several U.S. hospitals have already established affiliations with hospitals in foreign countries. In the future, foreign hospitals and clinics are likely to provide a wider array of services within the United States.

Finally, universal health care seems to be emerging as a global trend. A number of developing nations, such as Indonesia, Thailand, the Philippines, and India, are either establishing or expanding government-run healthcare schemes aimed at covering all citizens. These initiatives are being undertaken even as government-run programs (Medicare and Medicaid) in the United States and the National Health System (NHS) in the United Kingdom are struggling to maintain financial sustainability. For example, the hospital trusts in the NHS had a financial deficit of £5 billion (approximately $6.5 billion) in 2018–2019 (Allen, 2019), and the Medicare hospital insurance trust fund in the United States had a deficit of almost $6 billion in 2019 (Centers for Medicare and Medicaid Services [CMS], 2020). Ongoing deficits in the future may jeopardize access to health care for millions.

Cultural-Anthro Forces

In the healthcare context, the term *cultural-anthro* refers to a society's beliefs, values, ethos, traditions, and experiences. In the United States, the dominant beliefs and values have traditionally been those espoused primarily by middle-class Americans. These beliefs and values have historically acted as a strong deterrent against attempts to initiate radical changes in the financing and delivery of health care. In a society that is becoming more culturally diverse and politically factious, however, a significantly higher proportion of Americans now say that the federal government has a responsibility to make sure that all Americans have health insurance—63% held this opinion in 2020 (Pew Research Center, 2020) compared with 47% in 2015 (Gallup, 2016). Thus, we are witnessing a gradual shift away from historical American views.

The healthcare systems in developed nations are largely focused on curative medicine. Although population-level preventive interventions improve health and reduce the need for curative interventions, personal responsibility toward one's own health will remain a key determinant of the success of disease prevention efforts.

Healthcare Reform in Transition

Passage of the ACA in 2010 was marketed as maintaining private competition (witness President Obama's oft-repeated mantra, "If you like your healthcare plan, you'll be able to keep your healthcare plan"), perhaps to disguise the heavy outlays in public spending that would be necessary to support Medicaid expansion and tax subsidies. As mentioned previously, the Great Recession of 2007–2009 may have served as a backdrop for the ACA's wider acceptance by Americans. In 2021 and beyond, the debates related to health care are likely to occur against the backdrop of the COVID-19 pandemic.

During the congressional deliberations on the ACA among the Democrats, it appeared that some legislators wanted to create a **single-payer system**—a national healthcare program in which the financing and insurance functions are taken over by the federal government, a system labeled as "socialized medicine" (Dalen et al., 2019). Because of a lack of support for this proposal from some Democrats, and to build the consensus that became essential to pass the ACA, the single-payer option was eventually dropped (Halpin and Harbage, 2010).

In 2021, the specter of healthcare reform once again came to the fore. During the Democratic presidential debates in 2020, the phrase "Medicare for all" was heavily used as part of the reform platform for the future. Others have embraced the idea of building on the ACA by expanding Medicaid and tax subsidies and including a "buy-in" option. Although the catchphrases "Medicare for all," "public option," and "buy in" remain undefined and undetailed (as the saying goes, "the devil is in the details"), they all point to an increasingly heavy-handed role of the government in the financing and delivery of health care. Indeed, one bill that was floated in Congress in 2019 would have provided coverage for all health care, including long-term care, prescription drug care, and dental care, with no premium payments, coinsurance payments, or deductibles. This is an extreme case because there is no example of such a comprehensive healthcare system anywhere in the world (Wilensky, 2019). To further confuse what the Democratic politicians may have in mind, a "Medicare for more" proposal advocated by some seeks to lower the eligibility age for Medicare from 65 to 50. As it currently stands, Medicare coverage requires both premiums and deductibles. However, how much individuals would have to pay to enroll in a Medicare buy-in option has not been specified.

Once again, the conflicting notions of universal health insurance and lower costs are packaged together, even though doing more for less has seldom, if ever, worked in any government-run program. Not considered in these debates is who might be the potential losers.

On one side of the equation, libertarian groups have predicted that any radical changes would abolish the private health insurance market and jeopardize hospital finances, forcing many hospitals to close (Perez, 2020). There is no reason to think that physicians' practices and incomes would be unaffected by such a sea change. Moreover, universal health care cannot function without choosing winners and losers based on rationing of limited resources, as the experiences in many nations have already demonstrated. Also, universal coverage can function only when it is made compulsory through higher taxes and new mandates (Crowley et al., 2020). On the other side of the equation, liberals have countered that employer-based health insurance is crumbling (because of the burden imposed by the COVID-19 pandemic), the safety nets have wide geographic variations, high-deductible insurance plans result in delayed care for people with chronic conditions, and underlying racial and geographic disparities in care continue to persist (Weisbart, 2020). Hence, their proposed remedy is to implement a single-payer system under the guise of an "improved Medicare for all." At this point, no one knows what such a system would be like, how it would affect patients and providers, and how it would create value by improving quality at a lower cost. Also lost in such arguments is the larger issue of access. Will a newly insured population be able to get timely healthcare services when needed? If so, how?

Proposal by the American College of Physicians

The American College of Physicians (ACP) has put forward a policy proposal to achieve universal coverage through either a single-payer system or a public-financed coverage option, as described by Crowley and colleagues (2020). These proposals are issued notwithstanding the fact that most Americans are pleased with their existing coverage and quality of health care, even though high costs are viewed as a problem in the current system. However, both ACP proposals would impose higher taxes on working people.

As mentioned previously, the single-payer option would be a government-insured-and-financed system in which private insurance would play only a supplemental role for those who choose to have coverage for services above and beyond what a government plan would offer. For example, in the Canadian single-payer system, people can have private insurance for prescription drugs. The system could be tailored as a federal-state partnership, similar to Medicaid. However, transforming the current pluralistic U.S. system would cause major disruptions in the healthcare industry and create winners and losers. Those costs would include a loss of autonomy for physicians and increased workloads for all clinicians. In addition, patients would have to sacrifice their choice of providers. Hence, implementing a single-payer model would be politically difficult and would strain the federal budget, which would trigger price controls for providers and rationing of care for patients.

A public option model could include expansion of financial subsidies that are currently a part of the ACA, a Medicare buy-in, or mandating employers to pay when their employees choose the public option instead of the plans offered by the employer. Because this model would function under the current multiple payer system, it would still require a more complex regulatory structure, including price controls. Clearly, such a proposal would cause disruptions in the existing system, albeit of a lesser magnitude than under a single-payer system. Refer to **Exhibit 14-1** for a critique of the single-payer system or "Medicare for all" proposal.

A Third Option

Considering the reform proposals just discussed, neither repeal and replacement of the ACA nor Medicare for all is realistic. In between these two extremes lies the reality that a large segment of the population is currently satisfied with their employer-based health insurance. Thus, a lasting reform would

Exhibit 14-1 Potential Downsides of the Single-Payer System, or "Medicare for All" Proposal

- **Large increase in government revenue (i.e., taxes)**
  Shifting nearly all private spending for health care onto the public ledger would necessitate very large increases in government spending, and thus substantially higher taxes, cuts in other federal spending, and/or further increases in the federal deficit (Blumberg & Holahan, 2019).

- **Elimination of consumer choice of insurer and other benefits of competition**
  With an entire population of consumers in the same insurance plan and private insurers prohibited as alternatives, consumers who are dissatisfied with the new government system could not "vote with their feet" and choose a new carrier (Blumberg & Holahan, 2019). This could place significant pressure on the government to meet consumer needs in aggregate; however, it might make it more challenging for subgroups of consumers to have their needs or preferences met (Blumberg & Holahan, 2019). Similarly, some potentially beneficial elements of competition and incentives would be lost; for example, differences in cost sharing would encourage patients to use more efficient providers and providers to be more efficient (Blumberg & Holahan, 2019).

- **Likely persistent inequities in access**
  Those with high incomes would likely continue to pay out of pocket to receive some care on terms they are more satisfied with than those of a uniform government healthcare system (Blumberg & Holahan, 2019). If more providers can support themselves on private-paying patients, fewer providers would provide care under the single-payer system (Blumberg & Holahan, 2019).

- **Rationing and long waiting times**
  Single-payer health insurance could lead to rationing of services and long waiting times for medical care, potentially reducing overall access to timely and efficient health care (Diamond, 2009).

- **Physician oversight and payment restrictions**
  Physicians may face unwanted and unnecessary government oversight in healthcare decisions, potentially restricting the use of beneficial therapies. Government-set prices may lead to reduced reimbursement for physicians, impacting access to care and innovation (Diamond, 2009).

- **Potential undermanagement of care in public insurance programs**
  Though the Medicare system allocates a significantly lower percentage of its total spending to administration than do private insurers, at least some experts find that the traditional Medicare program "undermanages" the delivery of medical care to its beneficiaries (Blumberg & Holahan, 2019). These analysts have concluded that quality of care and efficiency of delivery systems could be improved with more active management by the program (Blumberg & Holahan, 2019). Such considerations should be accounted for when estimating the potential savings in administrative costs achievable and desirable under a single-payer program (Blumberg & Holahan, 2019).

Data from Blumberg, L.J. & Holahan, J. (2019). The Pros and Cons of Single-Payer Health Plans. https://www.urban.org/sites/default/files/publication/99918/pros_and_cons_of_a_single-payer_plan.pdf; Diamond, M. A. (2009). Con: Single-Payer Health Care: Why It's Not the Best Answer. *American journal of respiratory and critical care medicine*, 180(10), 921–922.

---

aim for the middle, not the extremes (Antos, 2019). Even so, any meaningful reform must address several issues.

Medicaid enrollment criteria should be restructured so that this program functions as a true safety net. Under the ACA, the federal government pays for nearly the entire cost of Medicaid in some states for men whose incomes are above the poverty line, and for 50% to 70% of the costs for women and children in households with incomes below the poverty line (Antos, 2019). The ACA does not provide tax subsidies to families who find their employers' plans to be unaffordable. Hence, subsidies should be restructured to give families a choice to enroll in whatever plan best serves their needs. It is also argued that the subsidies provided under the ACA were ill designed. Younger enrollees faced higher after-subsidy premiums than older individuals, which was the likely cause of adverse selection (Graetz et al., 2017). **Adverse selection** is the phenomenon in which healthy people enroll in fewer numbers than those who utilize more healthcare services, which then causes premiums to rise for everyone. Faced with rising premiums, younger enrollees often choose to drop out of the plans. As adverse selection continues, it destabilizes the insurance market as it becomes more and more difficult to control costs. Unfortunately, adverse selection cannot be fully addressed without medical underwriting in which prices reflect the risk of healthcare utilization. Prior to the ACA, many states had managed their own **high-risk pools** to enable people with high-risk conditions to purchase health insurance at more affordable rates than was possible otherwise. Post-ACA, high-risk pools have garnered much criticism, based mainly on philosophical grounds.

Burdensome regulations must be relaxed to promote competition and create better efficiencies in the delivery of health care. One major hurdle to regulatory reform is differences in the appetite for government control between conservative and liberal states. The archaic McCarran-Ferguson Act of 1945 allows states to regulate insurers and also makes selling insurance across state lines illegal. It has created oligopolies in which a small number of insurers have captured large shares of the health insurance market. Purchase of health insurance across state lines offers a significant opportunity to reduce the number of people who are uninsured by reducing the cost of insurance (Parente et al., 2008).

Despite the criticism, consumer-directed high-deductible health plans (HDHPs), coupled with a tax-free spending account, may well have a significant role in any future healthcare reform because these plans are especially appealing to people who are young and healthy. HDHPs provide an incentive to curtail unnecessary care that other types of health insurance plans actually encourage through the phenomena of moral hazard and provider-induced demand. A multiyear study demonstrated that HDHPs do, indeed, decrease healthcare spending with long-lasting effects. Moreover, at least over a 3-year period, this study found no evidence that the decreased spending resulted in complications from foregone care (Haviland et al., 2016).

Defined contribution programs, similar to those found in employer-based retirement plans, could also be a part of healthcare reform. Under such a program, the benefit to the employee is a fixed amount paid by the employer. The employees can then decide which type of health insurance plan would be most appropriate for their individual and/or family situation.

On the delivery side, competition has been quashed through hospital mergers and use of large middlemen agents to purchase drugs and medical supplies. Competition-killing regulations include the certificate of need (CON) laws that persist in several states and the ACA's ban on new physician-owned hospitals. The concentration of economic power in the hands of a few has raised prices (Tepper, 2019). These higher medical costs, in turn, translate into higher insurance premiums. Regulatory reform that expands competition will improve access to affordable health care.

Other changes should include tort reform to mitigate the effects of malpractice lawsuits against physicians and hospitals. The costs of malpractice lawsuits are eventually passed on to consumers in the form of higher insurance premiums. Caps on court-awarded damages are associated with a decrease in defensive medicine, an increase in physician supply, and a decrease in healthcare spending (Agarwal et al., 2019).

In conclusion, ongoing healthcare reform is necessary. However, there is much room for a multipronged approach, as discussed here and pointed out in subsequent sections. The main barriers are political ideologies and a thirst for power among today's politicians.

Innovations in the Healthcare Delivery Infrastructure

Along with the paradigm shift in healthcare delivery (refer to **Exhibit 14-2**), the healthcare infrastructure will continue to evolve as some innovative models demonstrate success in providing better value for the money and improved patient outcomes (refer to **Exhibit 14-3** for components of value-based system). Models of care delivery and value-based payments that incentivize quality and efficiency go hand in hand because the whole concept of innovation in care delivery is geared toward improving quality and reducing costs while delivering services to a larger number of patients. Accountable care organizations (ACOs) and patient-centered medical homes (PCMHs) are still in their infancy, and the financial stability of these organizations is somewhat uncertain at present. Another model, referred to as the next-generation ACO model, allows certain provider groups to assume higher levels of financial risk and reap higher rewards than those available under the Medicare Shared Savings Program. These newer ACOs are at an experimental stage, and they have experienced a high level of turnover (Sanofi-Aventis/Forte Information Resources, 2020). Also, their cost-savings potential has been questioned (Castellucci, 2020). Over time, experimentation and demonstration projects will eventually determine which models of care delivery succeed in providing the best value, and how financial risks and rewards can be balanced from both the providers' and payers' perspectives.

The Center for Medicare and Medicaid Services (CMS) has also spearheaded new payment initiatives like the BPCI-Advanced Model, centered around a bundled payment that combines payments for the physician, hospital, and other provider services into one amount. Interestingly, it is also connected to quality measures and qualifies as an advanced alternative payment model. This encourages clinicians to improve the quality of care while also reducing variation from standards of care. CMS also announced the Making Care Primary Model to be established in Colorado, North Carolina, New Jersey, New Mexico, New York, Minnesota, Massachusetts and Washington in July of 2024. This aims to improve care management and allow primary clinicians to form partnerships with specialists on three domains: care management, care integration and community connection (CMS, 2023).

Having different models of care by no means suggests a dismantling of the traditional

Exhibit 14-3 Critical Components of Value Based System

Incentives for outcomes
Payments tied to achieving quality metrics
Clinical integration (alignment of providers) critical
Primary-care and prevention focused
IT meaningful use essential
Scale
Shared risk among providers

Exhibit 14-2 Paradigm Shift of Healthcare Delivery

Previous Paradigm	Future Paradigm
Treating illness	Maintaining health
Volume of service	Value of service
Acute care	Primary care
Experience-based care	Evidence-based care
Individual patient care	Patient panel care
Individual practice	Team practice
Fragmented care	Integrated care

infrastructure consisting of hospitals of different types, small and large clinics, and other existing settings for care. By taking advantage of certain incentives in the payment systems, providers can align themselves into formal and informal structures that promote the desirable goals of providing better care at reduced cost. Yet, the COVID-19 pandemic has put many providers under financial stress, particularly rural hospitals and organizations that serve lower socioeconomic-status populations. The short-term response of many organizations has been to furlough staff. In the long term, however, financial stresses could invite further mergers and consolidations, and even closures, in the healthcare industry (Moore, 2020). As already pointed out, an erosion of competition has negative effects on costs and access.

Organizational- and patient-related challenges can be addressed through astute leadership. For example, adoption of new models of care and organizational reconfigurations will require workforce realignment and stability. Providers need to ensure that reimbursement will be adequate to cover the cost of their services. Patient skepticism will need to be addressed because patients will not choose an ACO or a medical home, for instance, but rather will be assigned to one by the payer.

Care coordination, ease of navigating the system by patients, preventive care, and management of chronic conditions will continue to be critical foci as the healthcare delivery infrastructure continues to evolve. Patient activation and patient-centered care will remain the driving forces from the standpoint of individual patients. In addition, community-oriented primary care and population health will receive ongoing attention.

Continued adoption of IT, use of cost-saving technology, and evidence-based care will undergird the system to eliminate waste, improve efficiencies, and produce better patient outcomes. IT systems, for instance, will be essential for the information exchange that is necessary to ensure care coordination across several providers. Payers will hold healthcare organizations accountable for achieving the desired goals in the areas just mentioned. Collectively, these factors suggest that healthcare reform will not be a static, one-time achievement.

It may be ironic, but it took the COVID-19 pandemic to highlight the value of telemedicine. On March 17, 2020, the CMS announced coverage and payment for virtual health visits to reduce in-person contact between healthcare workers and patients (Hunt and Hooten, 2020). Private insurers followed suit by instituting similar policies and actively promoting the use of telemedicine. Hunt and Hooten (2020) predict that over time, a two-tiered healthcare system could develop where access to in-person care is rationed or associated with high copayments. The delivery system could well evolve to replace periodic in-person encounters between patients and providers with an ongoing relationship that includes remote monitoring of health status and virtual consultations (Adler et al., 2009). Large insurance companies, such as United Health, are strong proponents of this model (Japsen, 2015).

Future growth of telemedicine will have implications in several areas, such as training of physicians and nurses to perform remote clinical evaluations, remote monitoring of vital signs, and restructuring of clinical work spaces. Although much has been learned about the routine use of telemedicine in a short period, questions remain. For example, how will telemedicine impact people based on race, age, geographic location, vulnerability status, health risk status, and disability status? How will quality and payment methods be integrated into telemedicine to assess the value of such care?

The scenarios discussed in this section point to staffing challenges and ongoing cost control as major driving forces going forward. The optimal use of telemedicine for routine care will be complemented with the extensive use of home care to manage higher-risk populations. Technologies such as sensors, early warning systems, and remote monitoring will play a growing role. Many patients in need of acute care for non-life-threatening conditions, such as wounds and fractures, will go to freestanding emergent and urgent care clinics; the number of these clinics has been increasing. Nonphysician practitioners will deliver most routine health care, freeing up physicians to address the needs of the sickest patients. Similarly, nurse extender clinical aides will take over some functions currently performed by nurses. Use of mobile communication devices will provide the needed support. Clinical decision support systems combined with evidence-based treatment protocols will become indispensable.

During the COVID-19 pandemic, advancements have been achieved in the adoption of telemedicine for screening infected individuals, monitoring affected subjects, and ensuring continuous care for those with chronic illnesses (Omboni et al., 2022). However, the utilization of telemedicine varied among countries impacted by the pandemic. The lessons learned from the COVID-19 pandemic should contribute to fortifying existing solutions and formulating a more cohesive strategy to facilitate the widespread implementation of telemedicine in healthcare systems (Omboni et al., 2022). This objective is crucial for better preparation against future pandemic waves and enhancing the overall management of both COVID-19 and non-COVID-19 patients (Omboni et al., 2022). Specifically, second-line home-based telemedicine solutions, functioning as "virtual hospitals," have the potential to alleviate the burden on frontline services, especially emergency departments, and intensive care units (Omboni et al., 2022).

There is a genuine concern that telemedicine might be viewed as a direct replacement for in-person healthcare services and could be primarily promoted as a cost-cutting measure or as an unwise incentive for physicians to increase earnings through excessive services, potentially compromising patient care (Marinelli et al., 2022). Addressing this issue involves enhancing the safe use of digital devices through improved training and experience for both healthcare providers and users (Marinelli et al., 2022). Moreover, it is crucial to promote awareness regarding the true objectives of telemedicine, which are centered on improving accessibility without compromising the quality of care (Marinelli et al., 2022). To achieve this, there is a need for the development of widely accepted ethical standards in the form of best practices, guidelines, national legislation, and international collaboration for sharing information and data on all aspects related to telemedicine practices (Marinelli et al., 2022). These efforts aim to optimize and standardize telemedicine-based care for the benefit of all patients, aligning with the principles of major human rights treaties that emphasize the universal right to health (Marinelli et al., 2022). As technology continues to advance and play a pivotal role in upholding the right to health, normative standards and guidelines must evolve accordingly to guide professionals in delivering telemedicine-based care in an ethical and legally sound manner (Marinelli et al., 2022).

The 21st century is bringing greater progress, with technological advances revolutionizing the healthcare sector. The World Health Organization says innovation, particularly in the digital sphere, is taking place at unprecedented scale. **Exhibit 14-4** details five innovations that are pushing even more boundaries in health care.

Toward Population Health

To date, the integration of primary care with its focus on individual health and public health with its focus on population health has not materialized in the United States. The concepts of community-oriented

Exhibit 14-4 Examples of Innovations in Health Care

1. *Artificial intelligence (AI)*
   - AI can detect diseases early and make more accurate diagnoses more quickly than conventional means. In breast cancer, AI is enabling mammograms to be reviewed 30 times faster with almost 100% accuracy, reducing the need for biopsies.
   - A deep-learning algorithm developed by health-tech company Qure.ai is enabling the early detection of lung cancer. The firm says a study demonstrated a 17% improvement when using AI to interpret chest X-rays compared to conventional radiology readings.
2. *3D printing*
   - The technology is being used for creating dental implants, replacement joints, as well as for made-to-measure prosthetics. Research into using 3D printers for manufacturing skin tissue, organs, and even medication is also underway.
   - One of the main benefits of 3D printing is that it greatly accelerates production processes and, therefore, also reduces the cost of traditionally manufactured products. The technology has reduced the time it takes to produce hearing aids from more than one week to just one day, according to the American Hospital Association.
3. *CRISPR gene editing*
   - Clustered Regularly Interspaced Short Palindromic Repeats (CRISPR) gene-editing technology can potentially transform how diseases are treated. It could help make significant advances against killer diseases like cancer and HIV in a matter of years.
4. *Virtual reality (VR)*
   - The technology can be developed in various ways, such as performing more advanced surgery, helping with pain relief, and treating mental health conditions.
5. *Smart bandages*
   - A bandage that uses sensors to monitor wound healing has been developed by researchers in the United States. It "promotes faster closure of wounds, increases new blood flow to injured tissue, and enhances skin recovery by significantly reducing scar formation," according to the Stanford University team behind it.

primary care (COPC) and PCMHs have encountered difficulties in their large-scale implementation. For example, the issue of healthcare disparities is an ongoing concern even as the healthcare system strives toward improving population health (De Marchis et al., 2019). The Family Medicine for America's health project was launched in 2014 by several family medicine organizations. This project views PCMHs as the implementation arm that incorporates COPC, with the aim of addressing the issues of both individual and population health. Achieving such a goal will require payment reform, ongoing research into both care delivery and infrastructure, use of technology to overcome practical problems, and workforce education and development (Wilson, 2018).

Accountable Health Communities

To achieve population health improvement, an emerging model—called accountable health communities (AHCs)—has been sponsored by the CMS. The program seeks to address population health from a community perspective by integrating health care, public health, and social services. The aim is to focus on multiple drivers of health to address the health and well-being of communities while reducing costs (Lyda-McDonald, 2019). In some cases, AHCs may be able to join hands with ACOs to form community coalitions to address broad social determinants of health (Tipirneni et al., 2015) by combining health-sector efforts with efforts to mitigate social forces that negatively impact patient care and health outcomes (Chaiyachati et al., 2016). For example, inadequate nutrition and unhealthy living conditions can increase the risk of developing chronic conditions, reduce a person's ability to manage those conditions, and lead to avoidable healthcare utilization.

The Vermont Blueprint

In 2006, the state of Vermont launched the Vermont Blueprint for Health—a program designed to meet the medical and social needs of people in the state's communities. The single state-based ACO works in collaboration with PCMHs, community health teams, and other programs such as those focusing on promotion of healthy lifestyles and self-management of certain chronic conditions. Under the ACO's umbrella, an integrated network of health providers assumes responsibility and risk for the health of the population and the cost of care. Community health teams play an important role in linking patients with social and economic services that can help support healthy living (Vermont Agency of Human Services, 2020). This model has managed to deliver high-quality care while reducing expenditures from lower hospitalization rates and outpatient facility use (Jones et al., 2016).

As of November 2023, of approximately 170 Primary-Care Practices in Vermont, 131 are Active Blueprint for Health Patient Centered Medical Home (PCMH) Practices (State of Vermont Blueprint for Health, 2023). Building on the PCMH model, the Blueprint program has expanded to include the Hub and Spoke System of Care for individuals with opioid use disorder (OUD) and specifically supports primary-care practices providing medication-assisted treatment (MAT). The Blueprint also created the Women's Health Initiative to ensure access to services that support pregnancy intention (Agency of Human Services, 2023). While the program has evolved beyond the original "chronic care management plan" described in legislation, it remains true to the original vision of all-payer supported, community-directed health reform that promotes the health of all Vermonters (Agency of Human Services, 2023).

Patient Activation

Patient activation refers to a patient's skills, confidence, ability, and motivation to become actively engaged in their own health care. It differs from compliance, in which the emphasis is on getting patients to follow medical advice given by providers (Hibbard and Greene, 2013). Activation often coincides with actual changes in behavior, such as changing one's diet, engaging in physical activity, and having regular checkups. Hence, patients themselves, through their own daily actions and choices, determine to a large extent their need for care and health outcomes (Tusa et al., 2020).

Activation goes a step beyond **patient-centered care**, in which care providers allow patients to make the choices that best fit their individual circumstances (Institute of Medicine [IOM], 2001). Patient-centered care is characterized by shared decision making, as health professionals take the time to understand patients' individual needs, preferences, and values and invite patients' participation in their care. By contrast, activated patients engage in and take responsibility for their own health. Even though the two are not isolated concepts, highly activated patients are the ones who benefit the most from shared decision-making (Poon et al., 2020).

There is convincing evidence that patients who are actively engaged in their own health generally have better health outcomes and a better health-related quality of life, and they also incur lower healthcare costs (Tusa et al., 2020). Hence, promotion of patient activation can be an important tool in realizing the goals of both individual and population health. The role of health professionals is to engage patients and instill in them the knowledge and confidence needed to maintain behaviors that promote better health (Tufts University

School of Medicine, 2014). Activation can be improved over time through information, education, support, and encouragement.

Future Workforce Challenges

An adequate and well-trained workforce is a critical component of the healthcare delivery infrastructure. Workforce-related issues and challenges will continue to require attention, especially in light of the emerging models of care discussed in the previous sections. This section highlights future needs and recommendations for change.

The Nursing Profession

In 2010, the Institute of Medicine (now called the National Academy of Medicine) released its report titled *The Future of Nursing: Leading Change, Advancing Health*, which is widely regarded as the blueprint for future change in the nursing profession. The Campaign for Action has been created to put the IOM's recommendations into practice. The nursing profession will face ongoing challenges that also have implications for healthcare organizations, educational institutions, and policymakers.

Full Extent of Practice

Nurses should practice to the full extent of their education and training. Ample research suggests that the delivery of services by nurse practitioners and advanced practice registered nurses does not compromise quality of care and has the potential to reduce costs and improve access. Unfortunately, outdated federal and state laws and institutional policies create barriers to utilizing their full scope of practice. Although some states have reformed their laws, other states still need to take similar actions to enhance the delivery of primary-care services. The Veterans Health Administration has sought to craft a single set of rules concerning basic prescriptive authority, admissions, and physician supervision—rules that previously varied by state (Fauteux et al., 2017).

Higher Levels of Education

Nurses should obtain higher levels of education and training to adequately address the needs of a patient population with complex needs. Nurse competencies should include leadership, health policy, system improvement, research in evidence-based practices, teamwork and collaboration, and competency in specific content areas, including community health, public health, and geriatrics. Nurses are also being called upon to fill expanding roles and to master technological tools and information management systems while collaborating with and coordinating care across teams of health professionals. The Campaign for Action's goal was to increase the proportion of nurses with baccalaureate degrees to 80% by 2020. By 2018, 57% of all employed nurses had baccalaureate or higher degrees. Although much work needs to be done, a significant increase in the number of employed nurses with doctoral degrees should fill faculty positions in colleges and universities to increase the academic preparation of nurses (Campaign for Action, 2020).

Upon entering the profession, however, nurses experience a high turnover rate. Transition-to-practice residencies have been found to improve skills in organization, management, and communication and to lead to higher retention. Finally, there is a great need for nurses' continuing education to keep pace with the needs of an increasingly complex, team-based healthcare system (IOM, 2016).

Campaign for Action to Improve Nursing Practice

The Campaign for Action is a national initiative in the United States that aims to improve health care through nursing practice (Hassmiller et al., 2013). The campaign seeks to transform health care and build a healthier America by leveraging the expertise and influence of nurses (Hassmiller et al., 2013). The campaign is rooted in the recommendations of the Institute of Medicine's (IOM) report, "The Future of Nursing: Leading Change, Advancing Health," which identified key areas for improvement in nursing practice and education (Hassmiller et al., 2013). The Campaign for Action focuses on implementing these recommendations to enhance the role of nurses in providing high-quality, patient-centered car (Hassmiller et al., 2013). The Campaign is calling upon all nurses—from schools, workplaces, public health facilities, hospitals, and other community settings—to build a Culture of Health (Canales et al., 2020).

Campaign efforts to highlight nurses working to build healthier communities are laudable, but the lack of attention on system-level alterations to address social determinants of health (SDOH) is concerning (Canales et al., 2020). The Campaign needs to re-evaluate its tagging process and begin highlighting nursing actions aligned with RWJF definitions for the SDOH and consistent with the action framework RAND established to meet the Culture of Health goals (Canales et al., 2020). Also, the Campaign might be well-served if it partnered with organizations steeped in a history of understanding the SDOH—such as the Council of Public Health Nursing Organizations, which includes the APHA's Public Health Nursing Section, the American Nurses' Association, the Alliance of Nurses for Healthy Environments, the Association of Public Health Nurses, the Rural Nurse Organization, and the Association of Community Health Nursing Educators—so that future BHC posts better reflect SDOH activities (Canales et al., 2020).

Cultural Diversity

Achieving cultural diversity in the nursing workforce remains a challenge. Although cultural diversity among nurses has been increasing, the diversity of the nursing workforce does not yet reflect the diversity of the communities it serves (Campaign for Action, 2020). Likewise, men make up less than 10% of the registered nurse (RN) workforce (IOM, 2016). It is believed that a more diverse workforce will be better suited to delivering more culturally relevant care.

Team Collaboration

Collaboration will require all members of a team to work together to their full potential on behalf of patients. Nurses are needed in leadership positions to contribute their unique perspectives and expertise in the areas of care delivery, quality, and safety. In 2014, for example, nurses accounted for only 5% of hospital board membership, whereas physicians represented 20% (IOM, 2016). In addition, members of the nursing profession need to communicate effectively with key stakeholders and the media about the ongoing needs related to health care.

Data and Information Systems

Effective workforce planning and policy making require better data and improved information systems. Data collection and analysis should drive the systematic assessment and projection of workforce requirements by role, skill mix, region, and demographics to inform changes in nursing practice and education.

Primary-Care Physicians

The United States will need an additional 44,000 to 51,000 primary-care physicians by 2025 (Carney et al., 2020). However, despite the critical importance of primary care to support the evolving healthcare infrastructure, the interest in primary care and the number of medical graduates entering this field has continued to decline (Dalen et al., 2017). To adequately address the future primary-care needs, efforts must be directed in two main areas.

Four Pillars of Primary Care

The Council of Academic Family Medicine (CAFM), representing the family medicine academic organizations, has adopted the "Four Pillars for Primary-Care Physician Workforce" as a succinct model to identify necessary conditions to ensure the needed growth in the number of primary-care physicians (American Academy of Family Physicians, 2014). Efforts to develop an appropriate primary-care workforce include attention to each of the four pillars:

Pipeline: The pipeline process begins in the early school years as students are exposed to role model primary-care physicians in their communities and includes an educational system with robust opportunities in math and science (American Academy of Family Physicians, 2014). It then continues through college as students begin to pursue pre-health educational pathways and interact with advisors and career counselors, who can provide support and information about being a primary-care physician (American Academy of Family Physicians, 2014). Providing targeted college guidance counselors with information, resources, and materials is an example of a way to enhance the pipeline of those who may choose to become primary-care physicians (American Academy of Family Physicians, 2014).

Process of medical education: The second pillar includes the traditional focus on curriculum development throughout medical student and residency education (American Academy of Family Physicians, 2014). Family medicine organizations are recognized leaders throughout the medical education community for their focus on innovative curriculum, assessment and evaluation, and faculty development (American Academy of Family Physicians, 2014).

Practice transformation: The Patient-Centered Medical Home (PCMH) model of care provides the framework of primary-care practice for the future (American Academy of Family Physicians, 2014). This may involve community activism and changes beyond the medical practice itself (American Academy of Family Physicians, 2014). Learners must be exposed to practices that deliver this desirable and sustainable model of patient-centered care (American Academy of Family Physicians, 2014).

Payment reform: Payment reform generally refers to income of practicing physicians, but comprehensive attention to payment reform requires reform of funding for medical education (American Academy of Family Physicians, 2014). A primary-care physician workforce cannot grow without a sustainable methodology for financing the training of physicians, which includes medical student debt relief and new models for financing Graduate Medical Education (GME), particularly in ambulatory, community-based settings (American Academy of Family Physicians, 2014).

The first two pillars provide the outline for medical school deans, admissions, and curriculum committees, all experiencing more pressure to increase their numbers of primary-care graduates (American Academy of Family Physicians, 2014).

To compete in the new, value-based healthcare system, both insurance companies and larger healthcare systems need more primary-care physicians working in patient-centered medical homes (American Academy of Family Physicians, 2014). To achieve this, they must financially support the third pillar of practice transformation (American Academy of Family Physicians, 2014).

The final pillar of payment reform is clearly the most important and the most difficult to achieve (American Academy of Family Physicians, 2014). Balanced payment for primary care and specialty care is fundamental to meeting the triple aim of "better care, better health, lower costs" (American Academy of Family Physicians, 2014). The audiences include the federal and state legislators, insurers, health systems, and the public, and the partners are the AAFP, CAFM, professional colleagues, and consumer groups (American Academy of Family Physicians, 2014). The "four pillars" is a powerful vehicle for promoting the expansion of the primary-care workforce which can serve as an "elevator speech" to effectively communicate the key steps to increase the number of primary-care physicians in the United States (American Academy of Family Physicians, 2014).

Realign and Rebalance Demands

Experts point to imbalances in workloads, time allocations, expectations of both organizations and patients, and payments. These factors are no longer aligned with the transformations in the nature of primary-care practice that have occurred over the past 30 years, and this mismatch threatens the very survival of primary care. As an example, 71% of the general internal medicine primary-care faculty at the University of Michigan who have practiced more than 3 years now work part-time (McMahon et al., 2020). This trend away from full-time primary-care practice must be taken as a warning for the future.

McMahon and colleagues (2020) propose several policy and practice changes. First, health systems must redesign their practices. The so-called face-to-face clinical time must be redefined to reflect the reality of practice in today's environment. Data suggest that a full-time primary-care clinician should have 24 (rather than 32) hours of face-to-face clinical time during the typical workweek, with an associated 20 hours of virtual visits and administrative activity. Second, given the emergence of consumerism, reassessment of what constitutes reasonable expectations on the part of both patients and providers is necessary. Third, value-based payment schemes need to be redesigned to ensure that clinical outcomes are linked to performance metrics and that the measured value is under the physician's direct management control. A prime example is the extent of hospital readmissions, which have shown little change even with intensive outpatient management. The changes in practice resulting from the COVID-19 pandemic have occasioned an exponential increase in virtual-care delivery, and this trend must be part of the equation in balancing the factors discussed here.

Training in Geriatrics

Growth in the number of older adults in the United States in recent years is attributed to increases in life expectancy and aging of the baby boomer generation. By 2030, more than one-fifth of the U.S. population is projected to be 65 years or older, compared with 15% in 2016 (Vespa et al., 2020). Despite the clear need for more geriatric-care practitioners, this field has not attracted healthcare professionals in sufficient numbers. Hence, innovative programs to train primary-care practitioners in geriatrics will need ongoing support.

The Health Resources and Services Administration has created two programs to address these needs. First, the Geriatrics Academic Career Award Program was created to support the career development of junior faculty in geriatrics at accredited schools in various medical and other health-related disciplines. Second, the Geriatrics Workforce Enhancement Program is designed to educate and train the primary-care workforce in integrated geriatrics and primary-care models. One grant-funded program in this area is the Extension for

Community Healthcare Outcomes—Geriatrics (Project ECHO-Geriatrics). It consists of monthly, interactive videoconferencing sessions that connect attendees to a University of Washington interdisciplinary geriatrics specialist panel and to each other. The sessions cover the breadth of issues relevant to older adults in primary care (Bennett et al., 2018). One such initiative, labeled ECHO-AGE, includes training, mentoring, and consultations. This program has shown to improve patient outcomes, such as alleviating dementia-related behavioral problems in nursing home residents (Catic et al., 2014). The Veterans Health Administration (VHA) system has implemented its own workforce development program to enhance the geriatrics knowledge and skills of its primary-care workforce caring for older veterans, especially in rural areas (Howe et al., 2019).

The Future of Long-Term Care

In the future, significant demographic and economic trends will make long-term care (LTC) less affordable for most people in the United States and increase the already high level of dependency on Medicaid to fund such care. Several factors make it extremely difficult for individuals to plan for future LTC—namely, unpredictability of the future need for LTC (many older people will not need it), escalating costs of these services, erosion of people's ability to save for retirement, and unaffordability of LTC insurance because of high premiums. Hence, there have been calls to make LTC a national priority (Kwak and Polivka, 2014). Medicaid cannot continue to cover the increasing costs of LTC for too long without the program eventually collapsing. Proposals for direct cuts to this benefit are likely to fall victim to partisan politics. Any meaningful reform will have to review the entire welfare system—for example, by formulating programs to take people who can work off the welfare rolls.

The trend away from nursing home use (except for people with complex needs and those needing short-term postacute care) to receive LTC services in community-based settings has become firmly entrenched in the U.S. culture. At the same time, the need for both institutional skilled nursing care and assisted living care will continue to have an important place in the LTC spectrum of services.

The LTC sector is not impervious to the workforce issues discussed previously. Indeed, LTC may be affected more adversely by these issues than other areas of health care because of employee preferences to work in hospitals and clinics rather than in LTC settings. Based on current trends, the occupations anticipated to grow the most in the LTC sector include social workers, community and social services coordinators, and home health and personal care aides (Spetz et al., 2015).

New technology is expected to either replace some of these human functions or improve LTC workers' efficiency and productivity. For example, LTC requires frequent monitoring of patients—a function that can be partially replaced by sensor technology. Sensor technology can also measure blood pressure and heart rate. IT advances will facilitate transfers of patients between facilities, such as hospitals and nursing homes, freeing up some social work and nursing time. Robotic exoskeleton technology will be used to assist patients with mobility and body mechanics to compensate for disability. Similar technology will be used to prevent the worker injuries that are often sustained when moving and transferring a patient, as from bed to a wheelchair.

A number of recent innovative approaches to improve geriatric care are worth mentioning, as follows.

Technological Advancements in Care for Older Adults: Remote monitoring devices, for example, are equipped with sensors that can measure an individual's heart rate, blood pressure, and oxygen levels

(Knippenberg et al., 2021). This data is then transmitted to healthcare professionals who can assess the patient's health status and intervene if necessary (Tomorrow Bio, 2023). This technology not only provides real-time health monitoring but also offers peace of mind to older adults who can remain in the comfort of their own homes while receiving the care they need (Tomorrow Bio, 2023). In addition to remote monitoring, assistive technologies, such as smart home devices and wearable sensors, enhance safety and support independent living (Tomorrow Bio, 2023). Smart home devices can be programmed to automatically adjust lighting, temperature, and even remind older adults to take their medications (Tomorrow Bio, 2023). Wearable sensors, on the other hand, can detect falls and alert healthcare providers or family members, ensuring prompt assistance when needed (Tomorrow Bio, 2023).

Home-Based Geriatric Care Innovations: Home-based geriatric-care models bring medical services into the comfort of older adults' homes (Tomorrow Bio, 2023). These initiatives use telemedicine, remote monitoring, and home healthcare visits to provide comprehensive care, reduce hospital readmissions, and improve patient satisfaction (Tomorrow Bio, 2023).

Hospital-Based Geriatric Care Innovations: Hospital-based geriatric-care innovations focus on enhancing the hospital experience for older adults (Tomorrow Bio, 2023). These models incorporate specialized geriatric units that provide tailored care to older patients, focusing on preventing common issues like falls, delirium, and medication errors (Tomorrow Bio, 2023). The integration of geriatric-trained health care professionals and interdisciplinary teams ensures the best possible outcomes for older adults during their hospital stay (Tomorrow Bio, 2023).

Global Threats and International Cooperation

Since 1948, the World Health Organization (WHO) has been regarded as the primary agency to promote global public health. WHO has been viewed as an important arm of the global community, represented by the United Nations, to provide public health leadership, disseminate critical information, and play a major role in fostering international cooperation. WHO's efforts have been credited with the eradication of smallpox, treatment of tuberculosis, vaccinations against common infections, and combatting tobacco use. Despite its successes, however, WHO has had some major failures (Gostin et al., 2015; Wibulpolprasert and Chowdhury, 2016).

Recent Historical Context

The outbreak of severe acute respiratory syndrome (SARS) in 2003 demonstrated how globalization had accelerated the spread of infectious diseases. Scholars have disagreed about WHO's effectiveness in managing the spread of SARS around the world (Smith, 2009). Subsequent to the SARS outbreak, public health treaties, under the auspices of WHO, were regarded as the most effective means of preventing, preparing for, and controlling the spread of infectious diseases in a globalized world (Burkle, 2015). Previously, international air travel had enabled infectious diseases to spread quickly around the globe. SARS, which originated in China and spread to more than 20 countries in 2003, and the spread of the polio virus from India to northern Minnesota in 2005 (Milstein et al., 2006) had highlighted the importance of early identification of infectious threats and subsequent rapid response to prevent further spread, which is often difficult without international cooperation (Johns et al., 2011). The Chinese government, however, had covered up the initial outbreak of SARS and continued to spread false information about the outbreak for months (Smith, 2009).

Recognizing the public health threats posed by infectious diseases, 196 countries signed the International Health Regulations treaty (IHR) in 2005. This treaty was WHO's response in the aftermath of SARS. The aim of IHR was to facilitate international efforts to prevent and respond to public health risks before they could threaten the health of people worldwide. The IHR includes a code of conduct for notification of and responses to disease outbreaks with pandemic potential (Congressional Research Service, 2020).

In 2013, the world faced an outbreak of Ebola virus disease (EVD). In 2014, the United States joined other nations and international organizations in launching the Global Health Security Agenda (GHSA), with the aim of accelerating full implementation of the IHR. In 2018, 65 countries, along with international and regional organizations and more than 100 private companies, nongovernmental organizations, and academic institutions, were part of the GHSA (GHSA Steering Group, 2018). Both China and WHO have been participating members of GHSA since 2014. Moreover, for years, the CDC had partnered with China, strengthening China's ability to play an effective global health leadership role to promote global health security (CDC, 2019).

The Case of COVID-19

In 2020, COVID-19 (coronavirus disease 2019) became a major pandemic that affected almost every country in the world. This disease is caused by the highly infectious SARS-CoV-2 (severe acute respiratory syndrome coronavirus 2) virus, which was initially called the Wuhan virus in China, after the Chinese city of Wuhan where the virus originated. Its rapid, unchecked spread throughout the world is regarded as a massive failure in global surveillance and information sharing.

According to official accounts, COVID-19 began around December 2019, as WHO claims that "a cluster of cases of pneumonia" was reported by China on December 31, 2019 (WHO, 2020). It is widely believed, however, that the disease spread actually started earlier than the official date given by WHO. As was the case with the SARS epidemic, the initial reaction of Chinese officials was to cover up the information, but by mid-January 2020 the situation had become so severe that it could no longer be concealed (Forster, 2020). Doctors within China who tried to warn fellow healthcare workers were accused of "making false comments" and "disturbing the social order"; some were even detained by government authorities. While some experts in China were sounding alarms about a cover-up, WHO was praising China's response; indeed, in mid-January 2020, it informed the world that there was no evidence of human-to-human transmission (Reports on the Actions of the Chinese Government, 2020). Just a week or so later, WHO reversed its position and confirmed that human-to-human transmission was occurring (Schaefer, 2020). Despite this knowledge, in late January 2020, WHO recommended that no restrictions on international travel were necessary (Lee et al., 2020). China did not allow WHO officials to enter the country until mid-February, so that they could examine the situation firsthand (Schaefer, 2020). Even though the pandemic was quickly spreading to other nations, it was not until March 11, 2020, that WHO declared the COVID-19 outbreak to be a global pandemic. WHO's failures are a major travesty of its obligations to the nations that have continued to support the agency financially and have been good-faith signatories to its public health treaties.

The Future of International Cooperation

Going forward, there are more questions than answers about international cooperation on health issues. First, and most importantly, what future role can WHO take in facilitating cross-border measures during a pandemic after its credibility has been seriously eroded? Second, how can certain nations that are governed by despotic regimes be made more responsible and held accountable for their obligations to be transparent when incidents of serious infections occur? Not only China, but at least two other despotic regimes, Russia and Iran, orchestrated propaganda campaigns claiming that the novel coronavirus was an American bioweapon (Schaefer, 2020).

Although WHO carries what Gostin and colleagues (2015) refer to as "normative authority" (i.e., the power to shape or influence global rules and norms and to monitor compliance), the organization has functioned primarily in a technical role of making recommendations, which member nations are free to adopt or ignore. IHR, the one binding international health treaty, has failed to live up to its promise, mainly because there are no effective mechanisms to ensure accountability of both member nations and WHO itself. Member nations resist intrusions into their sovereignty, even though they expect WHO to exert a stronger leadership role. Hence, it is believed that WHO cannot succeed unless members act as shareholders, foregoing a measure of sovereignty for the global common good. For its part, WHO must be open to scrutiny and be held accountable when failures occur (Gostin et al., 2015).

BRICS is one of the largest alliances of middle-income countries, representing Brazil, Russia, India, China, and South Africa, half of the global population. Research suggests that within this health collaboration, communicable diseases, access to medicine, and universal health coverage can be considered the top health priorities. It is important to note, however, that this cooperation faces several challenges that range from declining economic growth to limited policies. Possible future steps involve enhancing BRICS countries' unified image, promoting further dialogue, encouraging connections with the private sector, broadening new areas of focus, and broadening the range of countries and actors involved through BRICS Plus (Liu et al., 2023).

There is an immediate need for an international independent organization that is brave, aggressive, and vocal in its defense of global public health (Ford and Piédagnel, 2003). Although the COVID-19 pandemic has exposed some blatant failures in international cooperation, it does not signal the end of global health threats—and it suggests that preparation for future events is more critical than ever.

There are eight crucial flash points the COVID-19 pandemic caused, exacerbated, or revealed, which are priorities in future international cooperation (Wilson Center. 2022).

One Health approach. One Health concept acknowledges that disease and illness spread through the inextricable linkages between humans, animals, and their environments. For many years leading up to COVID-19, public health professionals, veterinarians, and researchers who study this human, animal, and environment paradigm have lamented the lack of attention paid to this gap in our global health security.

Disease Surveillance. It should be noted that the world health surveillance systems suffered from critical issues with surveillance, data gathering, and testing that set public health responses back during the crucial first months of 2020.

Declaration of a PHEIC. A Public Health Emergency of International Concern (PHEIC) was declared on January 30, 2020 by WHO. Delaying the declaration of a PHEIC holds the world back from necessary action while the declaration of a PHEIC is an intensely political move whose implications must be considered and prepared for.

Travel and Trade Issues. In theory, it is required to report a newly detected virus to the correct and functioning surveillance systems set up to prepare for future outbreaks, epidemics, and pandemics. But the reporting often comes at the cost of ostracization by the international community. In the United States, there is evidence that the initial travel restrictions did slow the spread, but the time bought did not stop it and if anything provided a false sense of comfort while other public health measures were not taken to prepare for the inevitable.

WHO Enforcement Mechanisms. For an organization with the leading minds in public health, virology, science communication, and management, the WHO lacks meaningful enforcement mechanisms needed to assure compliance with directives.

Global Equity. COVID-19 facilitated a furthering of the rift between the resourced and the under-resourced. In the United States and elsewhere, COVID-19 widened the gap in wealth between the affluent and the impoverished, only exacerbating legacy issues and creating a more unequal society.

Vaccine Sharing. Unequal vaccine sharing and resulting vaccine diplomacy are, like many COVID-19 related problems, based on a lack of preparation married to an international community in crisis and division.

New Technologies. COVID-19 did provide many entry points where new technology could solve or mitigate a new problem, such as mRNA vaccine and use of surveillance apps

Future Public Health Threats

Disease and disability will continue to pose major challenges globally. Natural disasters occur without warning, causing large-scale devastation followed by disease and disability. Examples include the Haiti earthquake in January 2010; the earthquake and tsunami that killed thousands in Japan in March 2011; and industrial accidents, such as the oil rig explosion in the Gulf of Mexico in April 2010. Large-scale bioterrorism has not yet occurred, but global unrest amid the rise of extremism makes it a real possibility in the future. Such prospects necessitate ongoing preparations, rapid deployment of resources, and sufficient capacity of the healthcare infrastructure to deal with mass casualties. When major disasters strike, the need for resources is often far greater than the available supply.

Wars and terrorism in the Middle East and Africa have created failed states, displacing millions of people from their homes and communities, and magnifying health emergencies.

By May 2024, more than 120 million people were forcibly displaced worldwide as a result of persecution, conflict, violence or human rights violations including 43.4 million refugees and 63.3 million internally displaced people (UN Refugee Agency, 2024). Resources have been stretched thin as aid workers have sought to deal with these refugees' physical and emotional distress and need for medical services. Trends suggest that this situation will get worse before it gets better. Recent outbreaks and the COVID-19 pandemic also suggest that new infectious diseases and failures of rogue nations to take positive action will threaten people's health and safety in the future.

Emerging antibiotic resistance among infectious agents is another public health and security threat. Almost all of the antibiotic-resistant pathogens that exist naturally can be bioengineered through forced mutation or cloning. In addition, existing pathogens can be genetically manipulated to make them resistant to available antibiotics. Prevention of drug-resistant infections will have to go hand in hand with the development of new antimicrobial drugs.

Despite international treaties, such as the 1972 Biological and Toxin Weapons Convention (BWC), which prohibits the development, possession, acquisition, stockpiling, and transfer of biological and toxin agents, compliance with and enforcement of such bans have remained ongoing concerns. The notion that some rogue nations have biological warfare programs is not a fanciful belief.

American Academy of Arts and Sciences (2022) suggested a failure of international cooperation in effectively addressing the global challenges posed by COVID-19 by emphasizing the dominance of a state-centric approach during the early phases of the pandemic, with national governments asserting sovereign control, closing borders, and prioritizing domestic interests. It highlighted the limited success of global cooperation, citing instances like the G7 and G20 meetings that fell short of comprehensive and coordinated action (American Academy of Arts and Sciences, 2022). It also underscored the challenges posed by the lack of international consensus, export bans, and disruptions in supply chains during the pandemic (American Academy of Arts and Sciences, 2022).

Jones and Hameiri (2022) highlighted the failure of global governance during the COVID-19 pandemic, focusing on the shortcomings of the WHO and the Global Governance of Security Threats (GGST). Key points include the WHO's compromised independence due to major donors, particularly China, impacting its response to the outbreak (Jones and Hameiri, 2022). The WHO's endorsement of China's misleading information, including support for lockdowns, is criticized (Jones and Hameiri, 2022). Jones and Hameiri (2022) also criticized wealthy states for weakening the WHO by making it dependent on voluntary funding and points out their own deficiencies in pandemic preparedness, exposing the gap between perceived readiness and actual capabilities (Jones and Hameiri, 2022). The technocratic and de-democratized nature of GGST is blamed for a lack of meaningful implementation, and Jones and Hameiri (2022) concluded by noting the failure of international solidarity and underfinancing of WHO programs.

A number of recommendations are made to enhance the role of the WHO, as follows.

Enhancing Compliance with the International Health Regulations (IHR). Member states of WHO have rejected formal sanctions, and instead, the IHR focuses on incentivizing cooperation (Jones and Hameiri, 2022). Two key strategies are encouraged, which are the director-general's power to declare a Public Health Emergency of International Concern and the reliance on market forces and digital technology to encourage transparency (Jones and Hameiri, 2022). Recommendations include a new investment package for lower- and middle-income countries, material rewards tied to funding from international institutions, health security assessment programs, periodic reviews of national preparedness, stress tests, support for non-governmental monitoring, and a financial insurance scheme for states reporting disease events transparently (Jones and Hameiri, 2022).

Strengthening Global Health Governance. There is a need for a stronger and more coordinated global health governance framework (Jones and Hameiri, 2022). The WHO could play a pivotal role in facilitating collaboration and setting standards for pandemic preparedness and response (Jones and Hameiri, 2022).

Reforming Financing Mechanisms. Reforms in financing mechanisms are essential to ensure sustained funding for global health initiatives (Jones and Hameiri, 2022). A more predictable and equitable funding model can enhance the WHO's capacity to respond effectively to health crises (Jones and Hameiri, 2022).

Facilitating Equitable Access to Health Technologies. The WHO can continue to advocate for and facilitate equitable access to health technologies, including vaccines, diagnostics, and treatments (Jones and Hameiri, 2022). Addressing global health inequalities requires collaborative efforts to ensure that everyone, regardless of their economic status, has access to essential health tools (Jones and Hameiri, 2022).

New Frontiers in Clinical Technology

Despite its association with cost escalation, technological progress will continue. Increased efforts in technology assessment will go hand in hand with new innovations. To what extent clinical decisions will be influenced by the cost-effectiveness of technology, however, remains an open question. As cost-effectiveness research investigates this issue, its results will likely find their way into health policy.

Medicine is advancing on several fronts. The future seems bright owing to the promise of better cures, higher-quality care, and improved quality of life. Understanding of the human genome has paved the way for a number of new approaches to prevent and treat disease. The convergence of artificial intelligence (AI) and precision medicine promises to revolutionize health care (Johnson et al., 2021).

Genetic medicine has opened a pathway for understanding the association of genes with specific disease traits. One application of genetic medicine is **gene therapy**, which involves the use of genes to prevent or treat a wide array of diseases such as hypertension, diabetes, and cancer. Currently at an experimental stage, gene therapy may eventually allow doctors to insert a functioning gene into a patient's targeted cells to correct an inborn defect or provide the cell with a new function. This technique is expected to replace treatment with medications or surgery in some areas. The future challenge is to develop methods that deliver just enough genetic material to only the right cells. Cancer treatment is receiving much attention as a prime candidate for gene therapy since current techniques (surgery, radiation, and chemotherapy) are effective in only half of all cases and can greatly reduce a patient's quality of life. Radiogenomics is a novel research field that focuses on establishing associations between radiological features and genomic or molecular expression. The objective is to better understand the underlying disease mechanisms and allow for the delivery of personalized medicine (Trivizakis et al., 2020).

Personalized and precision medicine will drive developments in the pharmacotherapeutic arena. Personal characteristics of individual patients can vary so much that not all medications work for everyone. Hence, a one-size-fits-all approach can be both wasteful and ineffective. In **personalized medicine**, specific gene variations among patients will be matched with responses to selected medications to increase effectiveness and reduce unwanted side effects. Going a step further, **precision medicine** will take into account not only variability in genes but also the environment and lifestyle factors. AI augments and complements human intelligence and intuition so that humans become faster and smarter in making decisions. For example, AI has outperformed physicians in diagnosing certain diseases (Xu et al., 2019). *Computational medicine*—use of models that include knowledge-based and data-based approaches to make complex decisions in individual cases—is also likely to play a role in the individualization of medical care (Bukowski et al., 2021).

In the future, rational drug design will replace the trial-and-error method of discovering new drugs, which is very expensive. Rational design will utilize multidisciplinary advances in various sciences to address specific targets such as a microorganism that causes disease or a defective human body molecule that activates a disease. The objective is to shorten the drug discovery process, thereby reducing the cost of finding new drugs. Multiple-target drugs have attracted much attention as promising tools aimed at several subpathologies in the treatment of complex diseases such as Alzheimer's disease (Benek et al., 2020).

Targeted drug delivery has the potential to provide more effective treatment by using nanoparticles as drug delivery vehicles. For example, cellular uptake of nanoparticles may efficiently translocate drug molecules into cancer tumors without damaging healthy tissues (Ding and Ma, 2013). Nanotechnology also has the potential to deliver antiviral formulations to specific targeted sites and viral reservoirs in the body (Lembo and Cavalli, 2010).

Imaging technologies have accounted for some of the most dramatic advances in health care. Advances in this area have continued, with great benefits to patients. For example, infrared fluorescence can be used during live surgery for better visualization to prevent unintended injuries. Three-dimensional (3D) technology provides faster and more accurate analysis of magnetic resonance imaging (MRI) and computed tomography (CT) images.

Advances in *minimally invasive surgery* include image-guided brain surgery, minimal-access cardiac procedures, and endovascular placement of grafts for abdominal aneurysms. Robotic surgery is in its early stages, but it will likely be used in many different procedures in the future. "Liquid biopsies" involving blood tests are an emerging technology that will replace some of the traditional biopsies to diagnose cancer.

Vaccines have traditionally been used prophylactically to prevent specific infectious diseases, such as diphtheria, smallpox, and whooping cough. However, the therapeutic use of vaccines in the treatment of noninfectious diseases, such as cancer, has opened new frontiers in medicine. At the same time, development of new vaccines for emerging infectious diseases remains on the research agenda. Making vaccines safer for wide-scale preventive use against bioterrorism, in which such agents as smallpox and anthrax may be used, will also be an ongoing pursuit.

Immunotherapy is a promising field in the treatment of cancers. New technologies can genetically modify a patient's own immune system to recognize and kill cancer cells.

Blood substitutes will likely be available one day for large-scale use. Even though the safety of blood used in transfusions has been greatly enhanced, substitutes for real blood are necessary when supplies fall short, particularly in times of war and in natural disasters.

Regenerative medicine holds the promise of regenerating damaged tissues and organs in vivo (in the living body) through reparative techniques that stimulate previously irreparable organs into healing themselves. Regenerative medicine also enables scientists to grow tissues and organs in vitro (in the laboratory) and safely implant them when the body cannot be prodded into healing itself. This revolutionary technology has the potential to develop therapies for previously untreatable diseases and conditions. However, tissue regeneration is limited by factors such as tissue type and growth hormones. 3-D bioprinting is an emerging science that may one day enable the production of transplantable human organs and surgical implants (Badwaik, 2019).

Xenotransplantation, in which animal tissues are used for transplants in humans, is an evolving research area. It holds promise as a means to overcome the critical shortages of available donor organs. Organs from genetically engineered animals may one day be available for transplantation (Schneider and Seebach, 2013).

Artificial Intelligence (AI) plays a crucial role in advancing precision medicine by leveraging large-scale data, complex algorithms, and computational power to tailor medical care to individual patients. Here are some key aspects of how AI contributes to precision medicine.

Genomic Data Analysis. Precision medicine often involves the use of genomic data to understand a patient's genetic makeup and how it influences their health (Denny and Collins, 2021). Performing genome sequencing at an early stage can resolve diagnostic challenges and reveal previously undetected Mendelian diseases, such as mysterious kidney conditions, unusual cases of diabetes, or unexplained developmental delays (Turro et al., 2020).

Targeted Therapies. Precision medicine enables the identification of specific molecular targets in diseases like cancer (Manzari et al., 2021). Drugs and therapies can be designed to target these specific molecular markers, leading to more effective and less toxic treatments (Manzari et al., 2021).

Disease Prediction and Diagnosis. The advancement of investigation tools and electronic health records (EHR) enables a paradigm shift from guideline-specific therapy toward patient-specific precision medicine (Su et al., 2021). Using EHR, the AI algorithms help predict the diagnosis and outcomes of liver cirrhosis, HCC, NAFLD, portal hypertension, varices, liver transplantation, and acute liver failure (Su et al., 2021). AI helps predict severity and patterns of fibrosis, steatosis, activity of NAFLD, and survival of HCC by using pathological data (Su et al., 2021).

The Future of Evidence-Based Health Care

Evaluating the effectiveness of care is the primary goal of evidence-based medicine (EBM). The current and future focus of EBM is to show, with a sufficiently high degree of certainty, that a new practice of care is superior to the usual practice (Fischer and Ghelardi, 2016).

For quite some time, payers and policymakers have believed that incorporation of EBM into medical practice would increase the value of healthcare services. However, research itself as well as the implementation of research-based results in clinical practice have faced several problems. As a result, clinical practice guidelines are replete with recommendations that rely solely on expert opinion because needed studies are lacking. Moreover, even when high-grade clinical trial evidence is available, its reported efficacy in idealized settings may not necessarily reflect what can be achieved in actual practice (Curtis and Krumholz, 2015).

Even though the objective of EBM has been to reduce misuse and overuse of medical care and curtail waste, international studies have shown that the majority of recommendations in American and European evidence-based guidelines are not based on strong evidence (Venus and Jamrozik, 2020). Hence, many standards of care are established without rigorous prior evidence (Kirpalani et al., 2016).

Questionable research practices also abound. Results based on small sample sizes, tiny effects, invalid exploratory analyses, and flagrant conflicts of interest are just some examples of how flimsy research can mislead developers of practice guidelines (Horton, 2015). In such an environment, the evidence is not always trustworthy.

Practitioners face many constraints in evaluating the reliability of research findings. No wonder, then, that many practitioners and even patients are apprehensive about EBM. Further, significant limitations in the current body of literature have hampered the broad dissemination and uptake of evidence-based interventions. In behavioral medicine, for example, traditional research design and data collection methods have had serious limitations (Buscemi et al., 2017). One main drawback in health outcomes research is the difficulty of capturing the interrelatedness of social and medical factors. Thus, a tension may exist in employing EBM in the delivery of patient-centered care.

Comparative effectiveness research (CER) is designed to study how well a chosen intervention works compared to other available treatments. At present, however, there are no universally agreed upon standards for evaluating evidence in CER. Hence, experts often disagree about the probabilities of risks and benefits of alternative interventions (Lie et al., 2017). Such issues are not easily resolved. Another key concern revolves around which outcomes should be measured. Hence, CER remains controversial.

Going forward, some critical areas that will require close attention include the robustness of research studies, sound interpretation of their results, relevance to clinical practice, formulation of clear and specific clinical practice guidelines, performance measures, clinical decision support tools, and properly aligned financial incentives (Timbie et al., 2012). If these aims can be achieved, EBM can indeed improve the quality of patient care by decreasing the variability in the practice of medicine (Sanders et al., 2014).

Evidence-based medicine (EBM) and comparative effectiveness research (CER) are essential components of modern health care, aimed at providing clinicians and policymakers with the best available evidence to make informed decisions about patient care and resource allocation. However, like any approach in the field of medicine, EBM and CER are not without controversies. Here are some key controversies and considerations.

Bias in Research. The bias can stem from various sources, including funding sources, conflicts of interest, and methodological flaws (Murad et al., 2016). For example, industry-funded studies may be more likely to produce results favorable to the sponsor's interests (Murad et al., 2016).

Patient Preferences and Values. EBM and CER may not always fully account for individual patient preferences and values (Ratnani et al., 2023). Treatment decisions based solely on evidence may not align with what is most important to patients in terms of quality of life or personal values (Ratnani et al., 2023). Critics have suggested that EBM focuses on groups of patients and does not consider the differences between each patient, subgroup analyses, or patient values and preferences (Ratnani et al., 2023).

The Need for Further Research

More research and evaluation are needed on the following areas before large-scale adoption can be advocated.

Integration of Patient-Centered Outcomes. Future research is likely to place greater emphasis on patient-centered outcomes and incorporate patient preferences into decision-making processes, which can enhance the relevance and acceptance of evidence-based recommendations (Chalkidou et al., 2009).

Advancements in Data Science and Technology. The integration of big data, artificial intelligence, and other technological advancements may enhance the efficiency of evidence generation and synthesis (Chalkidou et al., 2009). This could lead to more personalized and precise treatment recommendations (Chalkidou et al., 2009). There is an emergent need to address the gaps at various levels to synchronize the functions of different paradigms of the practice of EBM (Ratnani et al., 2023). The gaps created in the practice of EBM by the evolving technology, integration of data science, and integration of AI in medicine are consequently impacting the physicians' learning in training (Ratnani et al., 2023).

Summary

Health care delivery in the United States and abroad will undoubtedly continue to change. The framework of future change presented in this chapter can help inform the nature and direction of that change. Regardless of which shape the healthcare delivery system might take under current and future reform efforts, major challenges related to cost, access, and quality will not simply go away. The calls for a single-payer system and "Medicare for all" are not panaceas. Any meaningful reform will need to address multiple areas.

The U.S. demographic landscape continues to change, and various models and concepts of healthcare delivery remain at an experimental stage. The future delivery system will likely incorporate several models of care to address the needs of a diverse population at both the individual and population levels. However, an infrastructure that fails to ensure primary-care delivery presents a major obstacle to achieving this goal. Recommendations have been proposed to reform nursing, primary care, and training in geriatrics. The financing and delivery of long-term care will put further strains on the U.S. healthcare system. Nevertheless, technology will play a major role in shaping the future system of health care.

International threats will continue to be an unwelcome aspect of globalization. Rapid responses in dealing with infectious diseases that can quickly spread around the world, natural disasters, and human-made threats of terrorism will increasingly require global assistance, cooperation, and joint efforts. Recent experiences have demonstrated that cooperation from despotic regimes may not be forthcoming unless stronger measures are implemented to hold them accountable.

New frontiers in clinical technology will continue to emerge. Medical treatments in the next 10 to 15 years are likely to be very different from the ones in vogue now, although proven traditional methods will not be wholly abandoned. Standardized protocols for practitioners will continue to be informed by scientific evidence, including results from comparative effectiveness research and patient-oriented research. To accomplish this, however, several obstacles must be overcome.

TEST YOUR UNDERSTANDING

Terminology

adverse selection
comparative effectiveness research (CER)
gene therapy
genetic medicine
high-risk pools
patient activation
patient-centered care
personalized medicine
precision medicine
single-payer system
xenotransplantation
zoonoses

Review Questions

1. Explain the eight main forces that will determine future change in health care.
2. What are some options for future healthcare reform in the United States?
3. Discuss the main elements of the evolving healthcare delivery infrastructure in the United States.
4. What is patient activation? What are the main challenges in activation?
5. What recommendations have been made to transform the nursing profession?
6. What recommendations can be made to address the future demand for primary-care physicians?

7. How can training in geriatrics be improved?
8. What are the main challenges faced by long-term care in the future?
9. Give an overview of what new technology might achieve in the delivery of health care.
10. What role does international cooperation play in globalization? How can it be improved?
11. What improvements are necessary for the future of evidence-based health care?

References

Adams, J.G., and Walls, R. M. 2020. Supporting the Health Care Workforce during the COVID-19 Global Epidemic. *JAMA*, 323: 1439–1440.

Adanlawo, E. F., and Nkomo, N. Y. 2023. The Implications of Population Aging on Local Health Care Expenditure: A 22-year Panel Data Analysis. *International Journal of Innovative Technologies in Social Science*, 3.

Adler, R. et al. 2009. *Healthcare 2020*. Palo Alto, CA: Institute for the Future. https://legacy.iftf.org/our-work/health-self/health-care/ Report accessed December 2012.

Agarwal, R., A. Gupta, S. Gupta et al. 2019. The Impact of Tort Reform on Defensive Medicine, Quality of Care, and Physician Supply: A Systematic Review. *Health Services Research* 54: 851–859.

Agency of Human Services. 2023. Annual Report on Blueprint for Health. Accessed December 2023. Available at: https://blueprintforhealth.vermont.gov/sites/bfh/files/doc_library/2022%20Annual%20Report%20Draft%20Jan%2031%202023%20%28006%29.pdf

Allen, S. 2019. *2020 Global Health Care Outlook: Laying a Foundation for the Future*. Deloitte Development LLC. Accessed November 2020. Available at: https://documents.deloitte.com/insights/2020globalhealthcareoutlook

American Academy of Arts and Sciences. 2022. International Cooperation Failures in the Face of the COVID-19 Pandemic. Available at: https://www.amacad.org/sites/default/files/publication/downloads/2022_Humanitarian-Health_International-Cooperation-COVID-19.pdf

American Academy of Family Physicians. 2014. The Four Pillars for Primary Care Physician Workforce Reform: A Blueprint for Future Activity. 2014. *Annals of Family Medicine* 12: 83–87.

American Academy of Family Physicians. 2020. *Four Pillars of Primary Care Physician Workforce Reform. Infographic: Four Pillars for Primary Care Workforce Development*. Accessed on November 2020. Available at: https://www.aafp.org/news/media-center/kits/four-pillars-of-primary-care.html

Antos, J. 2019. Improve Markets, Not Government Controls, for Real Health Reform. *Journal of Ambulatory Care Management* 42: 173–177.

Armour, Stephanie. 2024. "How health care could change under the new Trump administration", *npr* https://www.npr.org/sections/shots-health-news/2024/11/06/nx-s1-5181861/2024-election-trump-kennedy-health-care

Ault, Alicia. 2024. "Healthcare: What Could Change Under New Trump Administration?", *Medscape* https://www.medscape.com/viewarticle/healthcare-what-could-change-under-new-trump-administration-2024a1000kd7?form=fpf

Badwaik, R. 2019. 3D Printed Organs: The Future of Regenerative Medicine. *Journal of Clinical & Diagnostic Research* 13: 1–8.

Benek, O., J Korabecny, and O Soukup. 2020. A Perspective on Multi-Target Drugs for Alzheimer's Disease. *Trends in Pharmacological Sciences* 41: 434–445.

Bennett, K. A., T. Ong, A. M. Verrall, M. V. Vitiello, Z. A. Marcum, and E. A. Phelan. 2018. Project ECHO-Geriatrics: Training Future Primary Care Providers to Meet the Needs of Older Adults. *Journal of Graduate Medical Education* 10: 311–315.

Bentahar, O., S. Benzidia, and M. Bourlakis, 2023. A Green Supply Chain Taxonomy in Healthcare: Critical Factors for a Proactive Approach. *The International Journal of Logistics Management* 34: 60–83.

Binder Dijker Otte (BDO). 2022. How COVID-19 Changed the Health Insurance Industry. Accessed December 2023. Available at: https://www.bdo.com/insights/industries/insurance/how-covid-19-changed-the-health-insurance-industry

Blumberg, L.J., and Holahan, J. 2019. The Pros and Cons of Single-Payer Health Plans. Available at: https://www.urban.org/sites/default/files/publication/99918/pros_and_cons_of_a_single-payer_plan.pdf

Bukowski, R., K. Schulz, K. Gaither, et al. 2021. Computational Medicine, Present and the Future: Obstetrics and Gynecology Perspective. *American Journal of Obstetrics and Gynecology* 224: 16–34.

Burkle, F. M. 2015. Global Health Security Demands a Strong International Health Regulations Treaty and Leadership from a Highly Resourced World Health Organization. *Disaster Medicine and Public Health Preparedness* 9: 568–580.

Buscemi, J., E. A. Janke, K. C. Kugler, et al. 2017. Interventions in Behavioral Medicine: New Approaches

and Future Directions. *Journal of Behavioral Medicine* 40: 203–213.
Campaign for Action. 2020. *Nurse Education and Diversity on Rise, Latest Figures Show.* Accessed November 2020. Available at: https://campaignforaction.org/nurse-education-and-diversity-on-rise.
Canales, M. K., Drevdahl, D. J., and Kneipp, S. M. 2020. RWJF's Future of Nursing's Campaign for Action: A Content Analysis of Social Determinants of Health Activities. *Nursing Forum* 55: 645–653.
Carney, P. A., E. Thayer, L. Green, et al. 2020. Conditions Influencing Collaboration among the Primary Care Disciplines as They Prepare the Future Primary Care Physician Workforce. *Family Medicine* 52: 398–407.
Castellucci, M. 2020. Next Gen ACOs Aren't Saving Medicare Money. *Modern Healthcare* 50: 2.
Catic, A. G., M. L. Mattison, I. Bakaev, M. Morgan, S. M. Monti, and L. Lipsitz. 2014. ECHO-AGE: An Innovative Model of Geriatric Care for Long-Term Care Residents with Dementia and Behavioral Issues. *Journal of the American Medical Directors Association* 15: 938–942.
Caudill, T., R. Lofgren, C. D. Jennings, and M. Karpf. 2011. Health Care Reform and Primary Care: Training Physicians for Tomorrow's Challenges. *Academic Medicine* 86: 158–160.
Centers for Disease Control and Prevention (CDC). 2019. *CDC in China.* Accessed November 2020. Available at: https://www.cdc.gov/globalhealth/countries/china/pdf/china_fact-sheet.pdf
Centers for Medicare and Medicaid Services (CMS). 2020. *2020 Annual Report of the Boards of Trustees of the Federal Hospital Insurance and Federal Supplementary Medical Insurance Trust Funds.* Accessed July 2020. Available at: https://www.cms.gov/files/document/2020-medicare-trustees-report.pdf
Chaiyachati, K. H., D. T. Grande, and J. Aysola. 2016. Health Systems Tackling Social Determinants of Health: Promises, Pitfalls, and Opportunities of Current Policies. *American Journal of Managed Care* 22: e393–e394.
Chalkidou, K., Tunis, S., Lopert, R., et al. 2009. Comparative Effectiveness Research and Evidence-Based Health Policy: Experience from Four Countries. *The Milbank Quarterly* 87: 339–367.
Cristea, M., G. G. Noja, P. Stefea, and A. L. Sala, 2020. The Impact of Population Aging and Public Health Support on EU Labor Markets. *International Journal of Environmental Research and Public Health* 17: 1439.
Congressional Budget Office (CBO). 2020. *The 2020 Long-Term Budget Outlook.* Accessed November 2020. Available at: https://www.cbo.gov/system/files/2020-09/56516-LTBO.pdf
Congressional Research Service. 2020. *The Global Health Security Agenda (GHSA): 2020–2024.* Accessed November 2020. Available at: https://fas.org/sgp/crs/row/IF11461.pdf

Crowley, R., H. Daniel, T. G. Cooney, and L. S. Engel. 2020. Envisioning a Better U.S. Health Care System for All: Coverage and Cost of Care. *Annals of Internal Medicine* 172 (suppl): S7–S32.
Curtis, J. P., and H. M. Krumholz. 2015. The Predicament of Comparative Effectiveness Research Using Observational Data. *Annals of Internal Medicine* 163: 799–800.
Dangerfield, Katie. 2024. "5 ways Trump's presidential win could change U.S. health care", *GlobalNEWS* https://globalnews.ca/news/10855972/donald-trump-us-election-victory-health-care/
Dalen, J. E., K. J. Ryan, and J. S. Alpert. 2017. Where Have the Generalists Gone? They Became Specialists, Then Subspecialists. *American Journal of Medicine* 130: 766–768.
Dalen, J. E., et al. 2019. An alternative to Medicare for all. *American Journal of Medicine* 132: 665–667. https://www.amjmed.com/article/S0002-9343(19)30078-6/fulltext
De Marchis, E. H., K. Doekhie, R. Willard-Grace, and J. Nwando Olayiwola. 2019. The Impact of the Patient-Centered Medical Home on Health Care Disparities: Exploring Stakeholder Perspectives on Current Standards and Future Directions. *Population Health Management* 22: 99–107.
Denny, J. C., and Collins, F. S. 2021. Precision Medicine in 2030—Seven Ways to Transform Healthcare. *Cell* 184: 1415–1419.
DeSilver, D. 2019. *10 Facts about American Workers.* Pew Research Center. Accessed November 2020. Available at: https://www.pewresearch.org/fact-tank/2019/08/29/facts-about-american-workers
Diamond, M. A. 2009. Con: Single-Payer Health Care: Why It's Not the Best Answer. *American Journal of Respiratory and Critical Care Medicine* 180: 921–922.
Dicuonzo, G., F. Donofrio, A. Fusco, and M. Shini. 2023. Healthcare System: Moving Forward with Artificial Intelligence. *Technovation* 120: 102510.
Ding, H. M., and Y. Q. Ma. 2013. Controlling Cellular Uptake of Nanoparticles with pH-Sensitive Polymers. *Scientific Reports* 3:2804.
Ecevit, E., M. Cetin, E. Kocak, R. Dogan, and O. Yildiz. 2023. Greenhouse Gas Emissions, Economic Globalization, and Health Expenditures Nexus: Does Population Aging Matter in Emerging Market Economies? *Environmental Science and Pollution Research* 30: 29961–29975.
Economic Policy Institute. 2020. 12 million People Have Likely Lost Employer-Sponsored Health Insurance since February. Accessed December 2023. Available at: https://www.epi.org/press/12-million-people-have-likely-lost-employer-sponsored-health-insurance-since-february-policymakers-should-work-to-delink-jobs-and-access-to-insurance-coverage-by-expanding-public-options/
N. Fauteux, R. Brand, J. L. Fink, M. Frelick, and D. Werrlein. 2017. *The Case for Removing Barriers to*

APRN Practice. Robert Wood Johnson Foundation. Accessed November 2020. Available at: https://www.rwjf.org/en/library/research/2017/03/the-case-for-removing-barriers-to-aprn-practice.html

Federal Reserve Board (Board of Governors of the Federal Reserve System). 2020. *Report on the Economic Well-Being of U.S. Households in 2019 Featuring Supplemental Data from April 2020*. Accessed November 2020. Available at: https://www.federalreserve.gov/publications/files/2019-report-economic-well-being-us-households-202005.pdf

Fischer, A. J., and G. Ghelardi. 2016. The Precautionary Principle, Evidence-Based Medicine, and Decision Theory in Public Health Evaluation. *Frontiers in Public Health* 4: 107.

Ford, N., and J. M. Piédagnel. 2003. WHO Must Continue Its Work on Access to Medicines in Developing Countries. *Lancet* 361: 3.

E. Forster 2020. Behind the Mask. *History Today* 70: 40–49.

Gallup. 2016. *Gallup Review: Healthcare and the Election*. Accessed November 2020. Available at: https://news.gallup.com/opinion/polling-matters/196814/gallup-review-healthcare-election.aspx

FRED. 2023. Federal Debt: Total Public Debt As Percent of Gross Domestic Product. Available at: https://fred.stlouisfed.org/series/gfdegdq188S

George, B. P., and T. L. Henthorne. 2009. The Incorporation of Telemedicine with Medical Tourism: A Study of Consequences. *Journal of Hospitality Marketing and Management* 18: 512–522.

GHSA Steering Group. 2018. *Global Health Security Agenda (GHSA): 2024 Framework*. Accessed November 2020. Available at: https://ghsagenda.org/wp-content/uploads/2020/06/ghsa2024-framework.pdf

Y. Goryakin, S. P. Thiebaut, S. Cortaredona, et al. 2020. Assessing the Future Medical Cost Burden for the European Health Systems under Alternative Exposure-to-Risks Scenarios. *PLoS One* 15: 1–14.

Gostin, L. O., D. Sridhar, and D. Hougendobler. 2015. The Normative Authority of the World Health Organization. *Public Health* 129: 854–863.

Graetz, I., C. N. McKillop, C. M. Kaplan, and T. M. Waters. 2017. Lessons Learned from the Affordable Care Act: The Premium Subsidy Design May Promote Adverse Selection. *Medical Care Research and Review* 75: 762–772.

Halpin, H. A., and P. Harbage. 2010. The Origins and Demise of the Public Option. *Health Affairs* 29: 1117–1124.

A. M. Haviland, M. D. Eisenberg, A. Mehrotra, P. J. Huckfeldt, and N. Sood. 2016. Do "Consumer-Directed" Health Plans Bend the Cost Curve over Time? *Journal of Health Economics* 46: 33–51.

Harvard Business Review. 2020. Global Supply Chains in a Post-Pandemic World. Accessed December 2023. Available at: https://hbr.org/2020/09/global-supply-chains-in-a-post-pandemic-world

Hassmiller, S., Reinhard, S., and Brassard, A. 2013. The Future of Nursing: Campaign for Action. *Health Policy and Advanced Practice Nursing: Impact and Implications* 75.

Hayes, S. L., C. A. Salzberg, D. McCarthy, et al. 2016. *High-Need, High-Cost Patients: Who Are They and How Do They Use Health Care? A Population-Based Comparison of Demographics, Health Care Use, and Expenditures*. Issue Brief 26. Washington, DC: Commonwealth Fund. https://www.commonwealthfund.org/publications/issue-briefs/2016/aug/high-need-high-cost-patients-who-are-they-and-how-do-they-use

Hibbard, J. H., and J. Greene. 2013. What the Evidence Shows about Patient Activation: Better Health Outcomes and Care Experiences; Fewer Data on Costs. *Health Affairs* 32: 207–214.

Holahan, J. 2011. The 2007–09 Recession and Health Insurance Coverage. *Health Affairs* 30: 145–152.

Horowitz, B. T. 2012. Smart Card Use Surging in Health Care, Government. *eWeek*. 7.

Horton, R. 2015. Offline: What Is Medicine's 5 Sigma. *Lancet* 385: 1380.

Howe, J. L., J. D. Penrod, E. Gottesman, A. Bean, and B. J. Kramer. 2019. The Rural Interdisciplinary Team Training Program: A Workforce Development Workshop to Increase Geriatrics Knowledge and Skills for Rural Providers. *Gerontology & Geriatrics Education* 40: 3–15.

Hunt II, T. L., and W. M. Hooten. 2020. The Effects of COVID-19 on Telemedicine Could Outlive the Virus. *Mayo Clinic Proceedings. Innovations, Quality & Outcomes* 4: 583–585.

Huynen, M. M., P. Martens, and H. B. M. Hilderink. 2005. The Health Impacts of Globalisation: A Conceptual Framework. *Globalization and Health* 1: 1–12.

Institute of Medicine (IOM). 2001. *Crossing the Quality Chasm: A New Health System for the 21st Century*. Washington, DC: National Academies Press.

Institute of Medicine (IOM). 2010. *The Future of Nursing: Leading Change, Advancing Health*. Washington, DC: National Academy of Sciences.

Institute of Medicine (IOM). 2016. *Assessing Progress on the Institute of Medicine Report: The Future of Nursing*. Washington, DC: National Academies Press.

Japsen, B. 2015. *Doctors' Virtual Consults with Patients to Double by 2020*. Accessed November 2020. Available at: https://www.forbes.com/sites/brucejapsen/2015/08/09/as-telehealth-booms-doctor-video-consults-to-double-by-2020/?sh=5aeed6684f9b

Jones, L., and Hameiri, S. 2022. Explaining the Failure of Global Health Governance during COVID-19. *International Affairs* 98: 2057–2076.

Johns, M. C., R. L. Burke, K. G. Vest, et al. 2011. A Growing Global Network's Role in Outbreak Response: AFHSC-GEIS 2008–2009. *BMC Public Health* 11 (suppl 2): S3.

Johnson, K. B., W. Q. Wei, D. Weeraratne, et al. 2021. Precision Medicine, AI, and the Future of Personalized Health Care. *Clinical and Translational Science* 14: 86–93.

Jones, C., K. Finison, K. McGraves-Lloyd, et al. 2016. Vermont's Community-Oriented All-Payer Medical Home Model Reduces Expenditures and Utilization

While Delivering High-Quality Care. *Population Health Management* 19: 196–205.

Karpman M, Zuckerman S, and Morriss, S. 2023. Health Care Access and Affordability Among US Adults Aged 18 to 64 Years with Self-reported Post–COVID-19 Condition. *JAMA Network Open* 6: e237455. doi: 10.1001/jamanetworkopen.2023.7455

Kekatos, [4] Mary. 2024b. "What a 2nd Trump term may look like for health care issues including ACA, abortion", *ABC News* https://abcnews.go.com/Health/2nd-trump-term-health-care-issues-including-aca/story?id=115560059

Kekatos, Mary. 2024a. "What we know about Trump's health care plans after Harris says he'll roll back protections", *ABC News* https://abcnews.go.com/Health/trumps-health-care-plans-after-harris-hell-roll/story?id=115387505

Kenen, J. 2011. Dx on the Preexisting Condition Insurance Plan. *Health Affairs* 30: 379–382.

Kiplagat, J., Tran, D. N., and Barber, T. 2022. How Health Systems Can Adapt to a Population Ageing with HIV and Comorbid Disease. *The Lancet HIV* 9: e281–e292.

Kirpalani, H., W. E. Truog, C. T. D'Angio, and M. Cotten. 2016. Recent Controversies on Comparative Effectiveness Research Investigations: Challenges, Opportunities, and Pitfalls. *Seminars in Perinatology* 40: 341–347.

Knippenberg, E., Timmermans, A., Palmaers, S., and Spooren, A. 2021. Use of a Technology-Based System to Motivate Older Adults in Performing Physical Activity: A Feasibility Study. *BMC Geriatrics* 21: 1–10.

Komalasari, R. Cloud Computing's Usage in Healthcare. Recent Advancements in Smart Remote Patient Monitoring, Wearable Devices, and Diagnostics Systems, edited by F. Zeshan and A. Ahmad, IGI Global, 2023. 183–194. Available at: https://doi.org/10.4018/978-1-6684-6434-2.ch009

Krogstad, J. M., J. S. Passel, and D. V. Cohn. 2017. *5 Facts about Illegal Immigration in the U.S. Pew Research Center.* Accessed November 2020. Available at: https://www.pewresearch.org/fact-tank/2019/06/12/5-facts-about-illegal-immigration-in-the-u-s/

Kurashvili, M., Reinhold, K., and Järvis, M. 2022. Managing an Ageing Healthcare Workforce: A Systematic Literature Review. *Journal of Health Organization and Management* doi: https://doi.org/10.1108/jhom-11-2021-0411

Kwak, J., and L. J. Polivka. 2014. The Future of Long-Term Care and the Aging Network. *Generations* 38: 67–73.

Lee, K., C. Z. Worsnop, K. A. Grépin, and A. Kamradt-Scott. 2020. Global Coordination on Cross-Border Travel and Trade Measures Crucial to COVID-19. *Lancet* 395: 1593–1595.

Lembo, D., and R. Cavalli. 2010. Nanoparticulate Delivery Systems for Antiviral Drugs. *Antiviral Chemistry & Chemotherapy* 21: 53–70.

Lie, R. K., F. K. Chan, C. Grady, V. H. Ng, and D. Wendler. 2017. Comparative Effectiveness Research: What to Do When Experts Disagree about Risks. *BMC Medical Ethics* 18.

Liu, Z., Wang, Z., Xu, M., Ma, J., Sun, Y., and Huang, Y. 2023. The Priority Areas and Possible Pathways for Health Cooperation in BRICS Countries. *Glob Health Res Policy* 2023.;8:36. doi: 10.1186/s41256-023-00318-x

Lopreite, M., Misuraca, M., and Puliga, M. 2023. An Analysis of the Thematic Evolution of Ageing and Healthcare Expenditure Using Word Embedding: A Scoping Review of Policy Implications. *Socio-Economic Planning Sciences* 101600.

Lyda-McDonald, B. 2019. Partnering to Improve Health: Developing Accountable Care Communities in North Carolina. *North Carolina Medical Journal* 80: 124–127.

Ma, B., J. Yang, Wong, F. K., et al. 2022 Artificial Intelligence in Elderly Healthcare: A Scoping Review. *Ageing Research Reviews*. 101808. doi: https://doi.org/10.1016/j.arr.2022.101808

Manzari, M. T., Y. Shamay, H. Kiguchi, N. Rosen, M. Scaltriti, and D. Heller, A. 2021. Targeted Drug Delivery Strategies for Precision Medicines. *Nature Reviews Materials* 6: 351–370.

Marinelli, S., G. Basile, and S. Zaami. 2022. Telemedicine, Telepsychiatry and COVID-19 Pandemic: Future Prospects for Global Health. In *Healthcare* 10: 2085. MDPI.

McMahon, L. F., K. Rize, N. J. Irby-Johnson, and V. Chopra. 2020. Designed to Fail? The Future of Primary Care. *Journal of General Internal Medicine* 36: 515–517.

Milstein, J. B., M. Kaddar, and M. P. Kieny. 2006. The Impact of Globalization on Vaccine Development and Availability. *Health Affairs* 25: 1061–1069.

Moore, K. D. 2020. *2020 is Challenging Us to Re-Imagine Integrated Healthcare.* Healthcare Financial Management Association. Accessed November 2020. Available at: https://www.hfma.org/topics/hfm/2020/september/2020-is-challenging-us-to-re-imagine-integrated-healthcare.html

MTN Staff. 2024. "5 Ways President-Elect Trump Plans to Change Healthcare", *MoneyTalksNEWS* https://www.moneytalksnews.com/ways-president-elect-trump-plans-to-change-healthcare/

Murad, M. H., E. P. Hess, and V. M. Montori, 2016. Evidence-Based Medicine and Comparative Effectiveness Research. In: Levy, A., Sobolev, B., eds. Comparative Effectiveness Research in Health Services. *Health Services Research*. Springer, Boston, MA.

National Center for Health Statistics (NCHS). 2019. *Health, United States, 2018.* Hyattsville, MD: U.S. Department of Health and Human Services.

Newman A., Cauley J. A., and Springerlink (Online Service). The Epidemiology of Aging. Springer Netherlands; 2012.

Omboni, S., Padwal, Alessa, T., et al. (2022). The Worldwide Impact of Telemedicine during COVID-19: Current Evidence and Recommendations for the Future. *Connected Health* 1: 7.

Owermohle, Sarah. 2024. "Donald Trump returns to the presidency with big ambitions to shake up health care", *STAT* https://www.statnews.com/2024/11/06/presidential-election-trump-health-care-abortion-medicare-rfk/

Parente S. T., R. Feldman, J. Abraham, and Y. Xu. 2008. *Consumer Response to a National Marketplace for Individual Insurance.* Accessed November 2020. Available at: https://aspe.hhs.gov/system/files/pdf/75826/report.pdf

Perez, K. 2020. Elizabeth Warren's Medicare-for-All Plan: The Devil in the Details. *Healthcare Financial Management Magazine* 74: 22–23.

Pew Research Center. 2020. *Majority of Democrats Favor a Single National Government Program to Provide Health Care Coverage.* Accessed March 2021. Available at: https://www.pewresearch.org/fact-tank/2020/09/29/increasing-share-of-americans-favor-a-single-government-program-to-provide-health-care-coverage/ft_2020-09-29_healthcare_01

Poon, B. Y., S. M. Shortell, and H. P. Rodriguez. 2020. Patient Activation as a Pathway to Shared Decision-Making for Adults with Diabetes or Cardiovascular Disease. *Journal of General Internal Medicine* 35: 732–742.

Reeves, T. C. 2011. Globalizing Health Services: A Policy Imperative? *International Journal of Business and Management* 6: 44–57.

Ratnani, I., S. Fatima, M. M. Abid, Z. Surani, and S. Surani 2023. Evidence-Based Medicine: History, Review, Criticisms, and Pitfalls. *Cureus* 15: e35266.

Rennen, W., and P. Martens. 2003. The Globalisation Timeline. *Integrated Assessment* 4: 137–144.

Reports on the Actions of the Chinese Government in the Outbreak of the New Coronavirus [translated]. 2020. News Coverage on What the Chinese State Did for the COVID-19 Outbreak in China. *Modern China Studies* 27: 11–78.

Sage, W. M., and T. M. Westmoreland. 2020. Following the Money: The ACA's Fiscal–Political Economy and Lessons for Future Health Care Reform. *Journal of Law, Medicine & Ethics* 48: 434–442.

Sanders, J. O., K. J. Bozic, S. D. Glassman, D. S. Jevsevar, and K. L. Weber. 2014. Clinical Practice Guidelines: Their Use, Misuse, and Future Directions. *Journal of the American Academy of Orthopaedic Surgeons* 22: 135–144.

Sanofi-Aventis/Forte Information Resources. 2020. *Provider Digest: Trends in Chronic Disease Management. Managed Care Digest Series, 2020.* Bridgewater, NJ: Author.

Schaefer, B. D. 2020. *The World Health Organization Bows to China.* Heritage Foundation. Accessed November 2020. Available at: https://www.heritage.org/global-politics/commentary/the-world-health-organization-bows-china

Schneider, M. K., and J. D. Seebach. 2013. Xenotransplantation Literature Update, July–August 2013. *Xenotransplantation* 20: 308–310.

Singh, R., P. P. Parikh, M. Nicole, et al. 2022. Trends in the Neurosurgical Workforce and Implications in Providing for an Aging Population. *World Neurosurgery* 160: e261–e266.

Smith, F. L. 2009. WHO Governs? Limited Global Governance by the World Health Organization during the SARS Outbreak. *Social Alternatives* 28: 9–12.

Spetz, J., L. Trupin, T. Bates, and J. M. Coffman. 2015. Future Demand for Long-Term Care Workers Will Be Influenced by Demographic and Utilization Changes. *Health Affairs* 34: 936–945.

State of Vermont Blueprint for Health. 2023. Blueprint Patient Centered Medical Homes in Vermont. Accessed December 2023. Available at: https://blueprintforhealth.vermont.gov/sites/bfh/files/documents/All_PCMH_List_2023_BPOnly_0.pdf

Su, T. H., C. H. Wu, and J. H. Kao, 2021. Artificial Intelligence in Precision Medicine in Hepatology. *Journal of Gastroenterology and Hepatology* 36: 569–580.

Sudborough, Susannah. 2024. "How the cost of health care could increase after Trump's reelection", *MassLive* https://www.masslive.com/news/2024/11/how-trumps-reelection-may-result-in-americans-spending-more-on-health-care-experts-say.html

Tepper, J. 2019. Medicare for All Myths: The Latest Democratic Plan Could Become Obamacare on Steroids. *American Conservative* 18: 20–24.

Weixel, Nathaniel. 2024. "What Trump's return could mean for US health policy", *THE HILL* https://thehill.com/newsletters/health-care/4977828-what-a-second-trump-term-means-for-health-care/

Timbie, J. W., D. S. Fox, K. Van Busum, and E. C. Schneider. 2012. Five Reasons That Many Comparative Effectiveness Studies Fail to Change Patient Care and Clinical Practice. *Health Affairs* 31: 2168–2175.

Tipirneni, R., K. D. Vickery, and E. P. Ehlinger. 2015. Accountable Communities for Health: Moving from Providing Accountable Care to Creating Health. *Annals of Family Medicine* 13: 367–369.

Tomorrow Bio. 2023. Innovations in Geriatric Care: A New Era of Ageing Medicine. https://www.tomorrow.bio/post/innovations-in-geriatric-care-a-new-era-of-ageing-medicine-2023-06-4727581267-medical-advance

E. Trivizakis, G. Z. Papadakis, I. Souglakos, et al. 2020. Artificial Intelligence Radiogenomics for Advancing Precision and Effectiveness in Oncologic Care. *International Journal of Oncology* 57: 43–53.

Tufts University School of Medicine. 2014. *New Tool for Health Communicators: The Patient Activation Model.* Accessed November 2020. Available at: https://sites.tufts.edu/healthcomm/2014/04/27/new-tool-for-health-communicators-the-patient-activation-model/

Turro, E., Astle, W. J., Megy, K., et al. 2020. Whole-Genome Requencing of Patients with Rare Diseases in a National Health System. *Nature* 583: 96–102.

N. Tusa, H. Kautiainen, P. Elfving, S. Sinikallio, and P. Mäntyselkä. 2020. Relationship between Patient Activation Measurement and Self-Rated Health in Patients with Chronic Diseases. *BMC Family Practice* 21.

UN Refugee Agency. 2024. *Fact Sheet: Global Forced Displacement*. Accessed November 2024. Available at: https://www.unrefugees.org/refugee-facts/statistics/#:~:text=Global%20Trends%20At-a-Glance&text=43.4%20million%20refugees,protection%2C%20a%20majority%20from%20Venezuela

Venus, C., and E. Jamrozik. 2020. Evidence-Poor Medicine: Just How Evidence-Based Are Australian Clinical Practice Guidelines? *Internal Medicine Journal* 50 no. 1: 30–37.

Vermont Agency of Human Services. 2020. *Annual Report on the Vermont Blueprint for Health*. Accessed November 2020. Available at: https://blueprintforhealth.vermont.gov/sites/bfh/files/documents/BlueprintforHealthAnnualReport2019FINAL_1312020.pdf

J. Vespa, D. M. Armstrong, and L. Medina. 2020. *Demographic Turning Points for the United States: Population Projections for 2020 to 2060*. U.S. Census Bureau. Accessed September 2020. Available at: https://www.census.gov/content/dam/Census/library/publications/2020/demo/p25-1144.pdf

Vishwakarma, A., G. S. Dangayach, M. L. Meena, Gupta, and Luthra, S. 2023. Adoption of Blockchain Technology Enabled Healthcare Sustainable Supply Chain to Improve Healthcare Supply Chain Performance. *Management of Environmental Quality: An International Journal* 34: 1111–1128.

Vitalari, N. P. 2016. Prospects for the Future of the U.S. Healthcare Industry: A Speculative Analysis. *American Journal of Medical Research* 3: 7–52.

Weisbart, E. 2020. Would Medicare for All Be the Most Beneficial Health Care System for Family Physicians and Patients? Yes: Improved Medicare for All Would Rescue an American Health Care System in Crisis. *American Family Physician* 102: 389–391.

Wibulpolprasert, S., and Chowdhury, M. 2016. World Health Organization: Overhaul or Dismantle? *American Journal of Public Health* 106: 1910–1911.

Wilensky, G. R. 2019. Medicare for All. *Milbank Quarterly* 97: 391–394.

Wilson, S. A. 2018. Family Medicine for America's Health—4 Years Later, Heading into the Future. *Family Medicine* 50: 399–402.

Wilson Center. 2022. International Cooperation for the Future Pandemic Preparation. Accessed December 2023. Available at: https://www.wilsoncenter.org/international-cooperation-future-pandemic-preparation

World Health Organization (WHO). 2020. *Archived: WHO Timeline—COVID-19*. Accessed November 2020. Available at: https://www.who.int/news/item/27-04-2020-who-timeline---covid-19

Xu, J., P. Yang, S. Xue, et al. 2019. Translating Cancer Genomics into Precision Medicine with Artificial Intelligence: Application, Challenges and Future Perspectives. *Human Genetics* 138: 109–124.

Glossary

A

Academic medical center The organization of one or more hospitals around a medical school. Apart from the training of physicians, research activities and clinical investigations become an important undertaking in these institutions.

Access The ability of a person to obtain healthcare services when needed. More broadly, access to care is the ability to obtain needed, affordable, convenient, acceptable, and effective personal health services in a timely manner. It may also refer to whether an individual has a usual source of care (such as a primary-care physician), has indicated the ability to use healthcare services (based on availability, convenience, referral, or some other criterion), or has reflected on the acceptability of particular services (according to an individual's preferences and values).

Accountability The responsibility of clinicians and patients, respectively, for the provision and receipt of efficient and quality healthcare services.

Accountable care organization (ACO) An integrated group of providers who are willing and able to take responsibility for improving the overall health status, care efficiency, and satisfaction with care for a defined population.

Accreditation A private mechanism designed to assure that accredited healthcare facilities meet certain basic standards.

Acquired immunodeficiency syndrome (AIDS) The occurrence of immune deficiency caused by the human immunodeficiency virus (HIV).

Acquisition Purchase of one organization by another.

Activities of daily living (ADLs) The most commonly used measure of disability, which includes whether an individual needs assistance to perform basic activities, such as eating, bathing, dressing, toileting, and getting into or out of a bed or chair. Refer to functional status and instrumental activities of daily living (IADLs).

Acute condition The condition that is relatively severe, episodic (of short duration), and often treatable and subject to recovery. Refer to subacute care.

Adjusted community rating Also called modified community rating; a method of determining health insurance premiums that takes into account demographic factors such as age, gender, geography, and family composition, while ignoring other risk factors.

Administrative costs Costs that are incidental to the delivery of health services. They are associated with the management of the financing, insurance, delivery, and payment functions of health care. They include management of the enrollment process, setting up contracts with providers, claims processing, utilization monitoring, denials and appeals of claims, and marketing and promotional expenses.

Administrative information systems Systems designed to assist in carrying out financial and administrative support activities such as payroll, patient accounting, materials management, and office automation.

Adult daycare (ADC) A community-based, long-term care service that provides a wide range of health, social, and recreational services to older adults who require supervision and care while members of the family or other informal caregivers are away at work.

Adult foster care (AFC) Long-term care services provided in small, family-operated homes, located in residential communities, which provide room, board, and varying levels of supervision, oversight, and personal care to nonrelated adults.

Advance directives A patient's wishes regarding continuation or withdrawal of treatment when the patient lacks decision-making capacity.

Advanced practice nurse (APN) A general name for nurses who have education and clinical experience beyond that required of a registered nurse (RN). APNs include four areas of specialization in nursing: clinical nurse specialists (CNSs), certified registered nurse anesthetists (CRNAs), nurse practitioners (NPs), and certified nurse-midwives (CNMs).

Adverse selection A phenomenon in which individuals who are likely to use more healthcare services than other persons due to their poor health. These individuals enroll in health insurance plans in greater numbers compared to people who are healthy. Refer to favorable risk selection.

Agent One of the factors of the epidemiology triangle, which must be present for an infectious disease to occur; in other words, an infectious disease cannot occur without an agent.

Aging-in-place Older people's preference and expectation to stay in one place for as long as possible and to delay or avoid transfer to an institution where the acuity level of patients is higher.

Alliance A joint agreement between two organizations to share their resources without having joint ownership of assets.

Allied health A broad category that includes services and professionals in many health-related technical areas. Allied health professionals include technicians, assistants, therapists, and technologists.

Allied health professional Someone who has received a certificate; associate's, bachelor's, or master's degree; doctoral-level preparation; or post-baccalaureate training in a science related to health care and has responsibility for the delivery of health or related services. These services may include those associated with the identification, evaluation, and prevention of diseases and disorders, dietary and nutritional services, rehabilitation, and health system management.

Allocative tools Use of health policy in which there is a direct provision of income, services, or goods to groups of individuals who usually reap benefits from receiving them.

Allopathic medicine A philosophy of medicine that views medical treatment as active intervention to counteract the effects of disease through medical and surgical procedures that produce effects opposite those of the disease. Refer to homeopathy and osteopathic medicine.

Almshouse The common ancestor of both hospitals and nursing homes; an unspecialized institution existing during the 18th and mid-19th centuries that mainly served general welfare functions, essentially providing shelter to the individuals who were unhoused, had mental illness, were older or orphaned, had disabilities, or had illnesses with no family to care for them.

Alternative medicine Also called alternative and complementary medicine; nontraditional remedies, such as acupuncture, homeopathy, naturopathy, biofeedback, yoga exercises, chiropractic, and herbal therapy.

Alzheimer's disease A progressive degenerative disease of the brain that leads to loss of memory, confusion, irritability, severe loss of functioning, and ultimately death. The disease is named after German neurologist, Alois Alzheimer (1864–1915).

Glossary

Ambulatory care Also referred to as outpatient services. It includes (1) services rendered to patients who come to physicians' offices, outpatient departments of hospitals, and health centers to receive care; (2) outpatient services intended to serve the surrounding community (community medicine); and (3) certain services that are transported to the patient.

Antitrust Federal and state laws that make certain anticompetitive practices illegal, including price fixing, price discrimination, exclusive contracting arrangements, and mergers among competitors.

Artificial intelligence (AI) Refers to the ability of computers to perform tasks that are generally performed by humans.

Assisted living facility (ALF) A residential setting that provides personal care services, 24-hour supervision, scheduled and unscheduled assistance, social activities, and some healthcare services.

Asynchronous technology Use of store-and-forward technology that allows the user to review the information at a later time.

Average daily census Average number of hospital beds occupied daily over a given period of time; it provides an estimate of the number of inpatients receiving care each day at a hospital.

Average length of stay (ALOS) The average number of days each patient stays in the hospital. For individual or specific categories of patients, this measure indicates severity of illness and resource use.

B

Balance bill The practice in which the provider bills the patient for the leftover sum after insurance has only partially paid the charge initially billed.

Beneficiary Anyone covered under a particular health insurance plan.

Benefit period The period of illness beginning with hospitalization and ending when the beneficiary has not been an inpatient in a hospital or a skilled nursing facility for 60 consecutive days.

Benefits Services covered by an insurance plan.

Biologics Biological products such as vaccines, blood and blood components, allergenics, somatic cells, gene therapy, tissues, and recombinant therapeutic proteins.

Bioterrorism The use of chemical, biological, and nuclear agents to cause harm to relatively large civilian populations.

Board of trustees The governing body of a hospital; it is legally responsible for hospital operations and is charged with defining the mission and long-term direction of the hospital.

Brokerage model A model of long-term care case management in which patients' needs are independently assessed by a freestanding case manager, who then arranges services through other providers.

C

Capitation A reimbursement mechanism under which the provider is paid a set monthly fee per enrollee (sometimes referred to as per member per month [PMPM] rate) regardless of whether the enrollee visits the provider and how often the enrollee visits the provider.

Carve-out The assignment through contractual arrangements of specialized services to an outside organization because these services are not included in the contracts that the managed care organization (MCO) has with its providers or the MCO does not provide the services.

Case management An organized approach to evaluating and coordinating care, particularly for patients who have complex, potentially costly problems that require a variety of services from multiple providers over an extended period.

Case mix An aggregate of the severity of conditions requiring medical intervention.

Case-mix categories are mutually exclusive and differentiate patients according to the extent of resource use.

Cases People who end up acquiring a negative health condition.

Categorical programs Public healthcare programs designed to benefit only a certain category of people.

Certificate of need (CON) Control exercised by a government planning agency over expansion of medical facilities—for example, determination of whether a new facility should be opened in a certain location, whether an existing facility should be expanded, or whether a hospital should be allowed to purchase major equipment.

Certification A status conferred by the U.S. Department of Health and Human Services, which entitles a hospital to participate in Medicare and Medicaid. A necessary condition is for the hospital to comply with the conditions of participation.

Certified nurse-midwives (CNMs) Registered nurses with additional training from a nurse-midwifery program in areas such as maternal and fetal procedures, maternity and child nursing, and patient assessment. CNMs deliver babies, provide family planning education, and manage gynecologic and obstetric care. They can substitute for obstetricians/gynecologists in prenatal and postnatal care. Refer to nonphysician practitioner.

Charge The amount a provider bills for rendering a service. Refer to cost.

Chief of service A physician who is in charge of a specific medical specialty in a hospital, such as cardiology.

Chief of staff Also known as the medical director; a physician who supervises the medical staff in a hospital.

Chiropractors Licensed practitioners who have completed the doctor of chiropractic (DC) degree. Requirements for licensure include completion of an accredited program that awards a DC degree and an examination by the state chiropractic board.

Chronic Refers to diseases or health conditions that last for a significant amount of time (3 months or more) and often with no complete cure or recovery.

Chronic condition A condition that persists over time and is not severe but is generally irreversible.

Churning A phenomenon in which people gain and lose health insurance periodically.

Claim A demand for payment of covered medical expenses sent to an insurance company.

Clinical information systems Systems that provide for organized processing, storage, and retrieval of information to support patient care processes.

Clinical practice guidelines Also known as medical practice guidelines; standardized guidelines in the form of scientifically established protocols, representing preferred processes in medical practice.

Clinical trial A research study, generally based on random assignments, designed to study the effectiveness of a new drug, device, or treatment.

Closed-panel Also called closed network, in network, or closed access; a health plan that pays for services only when they are provided by physicians and hospitals within the plan's network.

Cognitive impairment A mental disorder in which a person has difficulty remembering, learning new things, concentrating, or making decisions that affect the individual's everyday life.

Coinsurance A set proportion of the medical costs that the insured must pay out of pocket when healthcare services are received. Refer to copayment.

Community hospital A nonfederal (i.e., Veterans Affairs and military hospitals are excluded), short-term, general or specialized hospital whose services are available to the public.

Community-oriented primary care (COPC) The combination of the elements of good primary-care delivery with a population-based approach to identifying and addressing community health problems.

Community rating A system in which all members of a community are charged the same insurance rate.

Comorbidity The presence of more than one health problem in an individual.

Comparative effectiveness research (CER) A concept in which a chosen medical intervention is guided by scientific evidence on how well it would work compared to other available treatments.

Competition Rivalry among sellers for the purpose of attracting customers.

Concurrent utilization review A process that determines, on a daily basis, the length of stay necessary in a hospital. It also monitors the use of ancillary services and ensures that the medical treatment provided is appropriate and necessary.

Conditions of participation Standards developed by the U.S. Department of Health and Human Services that a facility must comply with to participate in the Medicare and Medicaid programs.

Consumer-directed health plans High-deductible health plans that include a savings option to pay for routine healthcare expenses.

Continuing care retirement community (CCRC) An organization that integrates and coordinates the independent living and institutional components of the long-term care continuum. As a convenience factor, different levels of services are all located on one campus. CCRCs also guarantee delivery of higher-level services as future needs arise.

Copayment A flat amount the person with insurance must pay each time health services are received. Refer to coinsurance.

Cost-efficiency Also known as cost-effectiveness; a state in which the benefit received from a service is greater than the cost incurred to provide that service. Refer to efficiency.

Cost-plus reimbursement A payment scheme in which reimbursement to a provider is based on cost plus a factor to cover the value of capital.

Cost shifting Also known as cross-subsidization; in general, shifting of costs from one entity to another as a way of making up losses in one area by charging more in other areas. For example, when care is provided to the uninsured, the provider compensates for the costs for those services by charging more to the insured.

Cost-utility analysis Analysis that includes the use of quality-adjusted life years.

Credentials committee A committee that reviews the qualifications of clinicians so as to decide whether those clinicians should have admitting privileges.

Critical access hospital (CAH) Medicare designation for small rural hospitals with 25 or fewer beds that provide emergency medical services in addition to short-term hospitalization for patients with noncomplex healthcare needs. CAHs receive cost-plus reimbursement.

Critical pathways Outcome-based, patient-centered, interdisciplinary case management tools designed to facilitate coordination of care among multiple clinical departments and caregivers. A critical pathway identifies planned medical interventions in a given case, along with expected outcomes.

Cross-subsidization Also known as cost shifting; in general, shifting of costs from one entity to another as a way of making up losses in one area by charging more in other areas. For example, when care is provided to the uninsured, the provider compensates for the costs for those services by charging more to the insured.

Crude rates Measures referring to the total population; they are not specific to any age groups or disease categories.

Cultural authority The general acceptance of and reliance on the judgment of the members of a profession because of their superior knowledge and expertise.

Custodial care Nonmedical care provided to support and maintain the patient's condition, generally requiring no active medical or nursing treatments.

D

Days of care Cumulative number of patient days over a given period of time.

Decision support systems Computer-based information and analytical tools to support managerial decision-making in healthcare organizations.

Deductible The portion of healthcare costs that the insured must first pay (generally up to an annual limit) before insurance payments kick in. Insurance payments may be further subject to copayment.

Deemed status A designation used when a hospital, by virtue of its accreditation by the Joint Commission or the American Osteopathic Association, does not require separate certification from the Department of Health and Human Services to participate in the Medicare and Medicaid programs.

Defensive medicine Excessive medical tests and procedures performed as a protection against malpractice lawsuits, and otherwise regarded as unnecessary.

Demand The quantity of health care purchased by consumers based solely on the price of those services.

Demand-side rationing Barriers to obtaining health care faced by individuals who do not have sufficient income to pay for services or to purchase health insurance.

Dementia A general term for progressive and irreversible decline in cognition, thinking, and memory. Alzheimer's disease is one disorder that leads to severe dementia.

Dental assistants Healthcare professionals who usually work for dentists in the preparation, examination, and treatment of patients.

Dental hygienists Healthcare professionals who work under the supervision of dentists and provide preventive dental care, including cleaning teeth and educating patients on proper dental care.

Dentists Professionals who diagnose and treat dental problems related to the teeth, gums, and tissues of the mouth.

Dependency (1) A person's reliance on another for assistance with common daily functions, such as bathing and grooming. Refer to activities of daily living. (2) Children's reliance on adults, such as parents or school officials, to recognize and respond to their health needs.

Developmental disability (DD) A physical incapacity that generally accompanies intellectual disability (mental retardation) and often arises at birth or in early childhood.

Developmental vulnerability Rapid and cumulative physical and emotional changes that characterize childhood and the potential impact that illness, injury, or untoward family and social circumstances can have on a child's life-course trajectory.

Disability It can be mental, physical, or social. Physical disability usually relates to a person's mobility and other basic activities performed in daily life; mental disability involves both the cognitive and emotional states; and social disability is considered the most severe disability because management of social roles requires both physical and mental well-being.

Discharge A patient who has received inpatient services. The total number of discharges indicate access to hospital inpatient services as well as the extent of utilization.

Discharge planning Part of the overall treatment plan that is designed to facilitate discharge from an inpatient setting. It includes, for example, an estimate of how long the patient will be in the hospital, what the expected outcome is likely to be, whether any special requirements will be needed at discharge, and what needs to be facilitated to ensure postacute continuity of care.

Disease management Used primarily by health plans, a population-oriented strategy involving patient education, training in self-management, ongoing monitoring of the disease process, and follow-up aimed at people with chronic conditions, such as diabetes, asthma, depression, and coronary artery disease.

Dispensaries Outpatient clinics that are independent of hospitals provide free care to those who could not afford to pay. Urban workers and their families often depended on such charity. These private institutions were financed by bequests and voluntary subscriptions. The main function was to provide basic medical care and to dispense drugs to ambulatory patients. Young physicians and medical students desiring clinical experience staffed the dispensaries. Hence, this model served a dual purpose: It provided needed services to the poor, and it enabled both physicians and medical students to gain experience in diagnosing and treating a variety of cases. Later, many dispensaries were gradually absorbed into hospitals as outpatient departments.

Distinct part A section of a nursing home that is distinctly certified from the rest of the facility; it generally refers to a skilled nursing facility.

Distributive policies Policies intended to spread benefits throughout society. Examples are funding of medical research through the National Institutes of Health, the training of medical personnel through the National Health Services Corps, the construction of health facilities under the Hill-Burton Act program, and the initiation of new institutions (e.g., health maintenance organizations).

Diversification Addition of new services that the organization has not offered before.

Do-not-resuscitate order Advance directive telling medical professionals not to perform cardiopulmonary resuscitation. Through these orders, patients can make their wishes known regarding aggressive efforts at resuscitation.

Doctoral nursing degrees These include the Doctor of Nursing Practice (DNP), Doctor of Nursing Science (DNS), and Doctor of Philosophy in Nursing (PhD).

Dual certification Having both skilled nursing facility (SNF) and nursing facility (NF) certifications. Dual certification allows a facility to admit both patients covered by Medicaid and Medicare.

Durable medical equipment (DME) Supplies and equipment not immediately consumed, such as ostomy supplies, wheelchairs, and oxygen tanks.

Durable power of attorney A written document that provides a legal means for a patient to delegate authority to another to act on the patient's behalf, even after the patient has been incapacitated.

E

Effectiveness Also known as efficacy; the health benefits of a medical intervention.

Efficacy Refer to effectiveness.

Efficiency Provision of higher-quality and more appropriate services at a lower cost, generally measured in terms of benefits relative to costs. Refer to cost-efficiency.

E-health Healthcare information and services offered over the Internet by professionals and nonprofessionals alike.

Electronic health records (EHRs) Information technology applications that enable the processing of any electronically stored information pertaining to individual patients for the purpose of delivering healthcare services.

Emergent conditions Acute conditions that require immediate medical attention.

Emigration Migration out of a defined geographic area.

Enrollee A person enrolled in a health plan, especially a managed care plan.

Entitlement A healthcare program to which certain people are entitled by right. For example, almost everyone at 65 years of age is entitled to Medicare coverage because of contributions made through taxes.

Environment One of the factors of the epidemiology triangle, which is external to the host; it includes the physical, social, cultural, and economic aspects of the environment.

Environmental health The field that focuses on the environmental determinants of health.

Epidemic An outbreak of an infectious disease that spreads rapidly and affects many individuals within a population. Refer to pandemic.

E-therapy Any type of professional therapeutic interaction that makes use of the Internet to connect qualified mental health professionals and their clients.

Ethics committees Interdisciplinary committees that are responsible for developing guidelines and standards for ethical decision-making in the provision of health care and for resolving issues related to medical ethics.

Evidence-based care Delivery of health care that incorporates the use of best practices that have been evaluated for effectiveness and safety through clinical research. Best practices often incorporate clinical practice guidelines.

E-visits Online clinical encounters between a patient and a physician or other clinician which can be quite effective and provide levels of care that are equivalent to face-to-face encounters.

Exclusive provider plan A health plan that is very similar to those offered by preferred provider organizations, except that insureds are restricted to in-network providers.

Executive committee A committee within the governing body that has monitoring responsibility and authority over the hospital. Usually, it receives reports from other committees, monitors policy implementation, and makes recommendations. The medical staff also have a separate executive committee that establishes policy and has oversight regarding medical matters.

Experience rating Setting of insurance rates based on a group's actual healthcare expenses in a prior period, which allows healthier groups to pay less. Refer to community rating.

F

Fee for service Payment of separate fees to providers for each separate service, such as examination, administering a test, and hospitalization.

Fee schedule A list of fees charged for various healthcare services.

Fertility The capacity of a population to reproduce.

Flat of the curve Medical care that produces relatively few or no benefits for the patient because of diminishing marginal returns.

Formulary A list of prescription drugs approved by a health plan.

Fraud Defined as a knowing disregard of the truth. Intentional filing of false billing claims or cost reports and provision of services that are not medically necessary or the services not provided are billed.

Free clinic A general ambulatory care center serving primarily the poor and the homeless who may live next to affluent neighborhoods. Free clinics are staffed predominantly by trained volunteers, and care is given for free or at a nominal charge.

Free market A competitive market characterized by the unencumbered operation of the forces of supply and demand and where numerous buyers and sellers freely interact.

G

Gatekeeping The use of primary-care physicians to coordinate healthcare services needed by enrollees in a managed care plan.

Gene therapy A therapeutic technique in which a functioning gene is inserted into targeted cells to correct an inborn defect or to provide the cell with a new function.

General hospital A hospital that provides a variety of services, including general medicine, specialized medicine, general surgery, specialized surgery, and obstetrics, to meet the general medical needs of the community it serves. Such a facility provides diagnostic, treatment, and surgical services for patients with a variety of medical conditions.

Generalists Physicians in family practice, general internal medicine, or general pediatrics. Refer to specialists.

Genetic medicine In the treatment of certain diseases, the association of genes with specific disease traits.

Global budgets Allocation of pre-established total expenditures for a healthcare system or subsystem.

Global health Efforts to protect the entire global community against threats to people's health and to deliver cost-effective public health and clinical services to the world's population.

Globalization Various forms of cross-border economic activities that are driven by the global exchange of information, the production of goods and services more economically in developing countries, and increased interdependence of mature and emerging world economies.

Gross domestic product (GDP) A measure of all the goods and services produced by a nation in a given year.

Group insurance An insurance policy obtained through an entity, such as an employer, a union, or a professional organization, under the assumption that a substantial number of people in the group will participate in purchasing insurance through that entity.

Group model A health maintenance organization (HMO) model in which the HMO contracts with a multispecialty group practice and separately with one or more hospitals to provide comprehensive services to its members.

H

Healthcare reform In the U.S. context, expansion of health insurance to cover the uninsured.

Health determinants Factors that contribute to the general well-being of individuals and populations.

Health informatics The application of information science to improve the efficiency, accuracy, and reliability of healthcare services. Health informatics requires the use of information technology (IT) but goes beyond IT by emphasizing the improvement of healthcare delivery.

Health information organization (HIO) An independent organization that brings together healthcare stakeholders within a defined geographic area and governs electronic information exchange among these stakeholders, with the objective of improving the delivery of health care in the community.

Health maintenance organization (HMO) A type of managed care organization that provides comprehensive medical care for a predetermined annual fee per enrollee.

Health plan The contractual arrangement between a managed care organization and an enrollee, including the collective array of covered health services to which the enrollee is entitled.

Health planning Decisions made by governments to limit healthcare resources, such as hospital beds and diffusion of costly technology.

Health policy Public policy that pertains to or influences the pursuit of health.

Health-related quality of life (HRQL) In a composite sense, a person's own perception of health, ability to function, role limitations stemming from physical or emotional problems, and personal happiness during or subsequent to disease experience.

Health risk appraisal The evaluation of risk factors associated with host, agent, and environment and their health consequences for individuals.

Health technology assessment (HTA) Any process of examining and reporting the properties of a medical technology used in health care, such as safety, effectiveness, feasibility, and indications for use, cost, and cost-effectiveness, as well as social, economic, and ethical consequences, whether intended or unintended.

High-deductible health plans (HDHPs) Health plans that combine a savings option with a health insurance plan carrying a high deductible.

High-risk pools State-based pools, which existed before 2014, to make health insurance available to people who otherwise would have been uninsurable because of preexisting health conditions.

Holistic health The well-being of every aspect of what makes a person whole and complete.

Holistic medicine A philosophy of health care that emphasizes the well-being of every aspect of a person, including the physical, mental, social, and spiritual aspects of health.

Home health care Services such as nursing, therapy, and health-related homemaker or social services that are brought to patients in their own homes because such patients are generally unable to leave their homes safely to get the care they need.

Homophobia Prejudice against, fear of, and/or hatred of gays and lesbians.

Horizontal integration A growth strategy in which an organization extends its core product or service. Refer to vertical integration.

Hospice A cluster of special services for individuals who are dying, which blends medical, spiritual, legal, financial, and family-support services. The venue in which services are provided can vary from a specialized facility to a nursing home to the patient's own home.

Hospital A licensed institution with at least six beds, whose primary function is to deliver diagnostic and therapeutic patient services for various medical conditions. A hospital must have an organized physician staff, and it must provide continuous nursing services under the supervision of registered nurses.

Hospitalists Physicians who specialize in the care of patients who are hospitalized.

Host One of the factors of the epidemiology triangle; an organism, generally a human, who receives the agent and becomes sick.

Human immunodeficiency virus (HIV) A virus that can destroy the immune system and lead to acquired immunodeficiency syndrome (AIDS).

I

Iatrogenic illnesses Illnesses or injuries caused by the process of medical care.

Immigration Migration to a defined geographic area.

Incidence The number of new cases of a disease in a defined population within a specified period.

Indemnity insurance Also referred to as fee-for-service health insurance; a health insurance plan that allows the insured to obtain healthcare services anywhere and from any physician or hospital. Indemnity insurance and fee-for-service reimbursement to providers are closely intertwined.

Independent practice association (IPA) A legal entity that physicians in private practice can join so that the organization can represent them in the negotiation of managed care contracts.

Infection control committee A medical committee that is responsible for reviewing policies and procedures for minimizing infections in the hospital.

Information technology (IT) Technology used for the transformation of data into useful information; it focuses on determining data needs, gathering appropriate data, storing and analyzing the data, and reporting the information generated in a user-friendly format.

Informed consent A fundamental patient right to make an informed choice regarding medical treatment based on full disclosure of medical information by the providers.

Inpatient A term used in conjunction with an overnight stay in a healthcare facility, such as a hospital.

Inpatient day A night spent in the hospital by a person admitted as an inpatient; also called a patient day or a hospital day.

Institution-related quality of life A patient's quality of life while confined in an institution as an inpatient. Examples include comfort factors (e.g., cleanliness, safety, noise levels, odors, lighting, air circulation, environmental temperature, and furnishings) and factors related to emotional well-being (e.g., autonomy to make decisions, freedom to air grievances without fear of reprisal, reasonable accommodation of personal likes and dislikes, privacy and confidentiality, treatment from staff in a manner that maintains respect and dignity, freedom from physical and/or emotional abuse).

Instrumental activities of daily living (IADLs) A person's ability to perform household and social tasks, such as home maintenance, cooking, shopping, and managing money. Refer to activities of daily living (ADLs).

Insurance A mechanism for protection against risk.

Insured The individual who is covered for risk by insurance.

Insurer An insurance agency or managed care organization that offers insurance.

Intellectual disability (ID) Below-average intellectual capacity, which can be caused by a disorder such as Down syndrome.

Investor-owned hospital Also referred to as proprietary hospitals; for-profit hospitals owned by individuals, partnerships, or corporations.

IPA model The Independent Practice Association (IPA) model is a healthcare delivery model that connects independent healthcare providers to provide comprehensive healthcare to patients.

J

Joint venture Creation of a new organization in which two or more institutions share resources to pursue a common purpose.

L

Licensed practical nurses (LPNs) Also known as licensed vocational nurses (LVNs) in some states; nurses who have completed a state-approved program in practical nursing and a national written examination. LPNs often work under the supervision of registered nurses to provide patient care. Refer to registered nurses.

Licensure Licensing of a healthcare facility that an organization must obtain to operate. Licensure is conferred by each state upon compliance with its standards.

Life expectancy Actuarial determination of how long, on average, a person of a given age is likely to live.

Living will A legal document in which a patient puts into writing what their preferences are regarding treatment during terminal illness and the use of life-sustaining technology. Such a directive instructs a physician to withhold or discontinue medical treatment when the patient is terminally ill and unable to make decisions.

Long-term care (LTC) A variety of individualized, well-coordinated services that are designed to promote the maximum possible independence for people with functional limitations. These services are provided over an extended period to meet the patients' physical, mental, social, and spiritual needs, while maximizing quality of life.

Long-term care hospitals (LTCHs) These are a special type of long-stay hospital described in section 1886(d)(1)(B)(iv) of the Social Security Act. LTCHs must meet Medicare's conditions of participation for acute (short-stay) hospitals and must have an average length of stay greater than 25 days. LTCHs serve patients who have complex medical needs and may suffer from multiple chronic problems requiring long-term hospitalization.

M

Magnet hospital A special designation conferred by the American Nurses Credentialing Center, an affiliate of the American Nurses Association, that recognizes high-quality patient care, nursing excellence, and innovations in professional nursing practice in hospitals.

Maldistribution An imbalance (i.e., surplus in some but shortage in others) of the distribution of health professionals, such as physicians, needed to maintain the health status of a given population at an optimal level. Geographic maldistribution refers to the surplus in some regions (e.g., metropolitan areas) but shortage in other regions (e.g., rural and inner-city areas) of needed health professionals. Specialty maldistribution refers to the surplus in some specialties (e.g., physician specialists) but shortage in others (e.g., primary care).

Managed care A system of healthcare delivery that (1) seeks to achieve efficiencies by integrating the four functions of healthcare delivery, (2) employs mechanisms to control (manage) utilization of medical services, and (3) determines the price at which the services are purchased and, consequently, how much the providers get paid.

Management services organization (MSO) An organization that brings management expertise and, in some instances, capital for expansion to physician group practices.

Market justice A distributional principle according to which health care is most equitably distributed through the market forces of supply and demand rather than government interventions. Refer to social justice.

Meals-on-wheels A program of home-delivered meals for older people, which is administered by Area Agencies on Aging under Title VII of the Older Americans Act.

Means test A program in which eligibility depends on income.

Means-tested program A government-run health insurance program in which eligibility depends on people's financial resources.

Medicaid A joint federal–state program of health insurance for the poor.

Medicaid waiver program A program that enables states to design packages of services targeted at specific populations, such as older people, individuals with disabilities, and those who test positive for human immunodeficiency virus. The waiver is an alternative to some form of institutional care.

Medical home The quality features of primary healthcare delivery in settings such as a physician office or community health center.

Medical model Delivery of health care that places its primary emphasis on the treatment of disease and relief of symptoms instead of prevention of disease and promotion of optimum health.

Medical records committee A medical committee that is responsible for certifying complete and clinically accurate documentation of the care given to each patient.

Medical staff committee A committee within the governing body that is charged with medical staff relations in a hospital. For example, it reviews admitting privileges and the performance of the medical staff.

Medical technology Practical application of the scientific body of knowledge for the purpose of improving health and creating efficiencies in the delivery of health care.

Medical tourism Travel abroad to receive elective, nonemergency medical care.

Medically underserved A designation determined by the federal government that indicates a dearth of primary-care providers and delivery settings, as well as poor health indicators of the populace. The majority of this population group are Medicaid recipients.

Medicare A federal program of health insurance for older people, certain individuals with disabilities, and people with end-stage renal disease.

Medicare Physician Fee Schedule (MPFS) A national price list for physician services established by Medicare.

Medigap Commercial health insurance policies purchased by individuals covered by Medicare to insure the expenses not covered by Medicare.

Mental health system In the United States, there is a combination of two subsystems that provide mental healthcare services: one primarily for individuals with insurance coverage or money and one for those without. Patients without insurance coverage or personal financial resources are primarily treated in state and county mental health hospitals or in community mental health clinics. Patients with insurance coverage or the personal ability to pay receive care from both inpatient and ambulatory mental healthcare systems.

Merger Unification of two or more organizations into a single entity through mutual agreement.

M-health Mobile health; the use of wireless communication devices to support public health and clinical practice.

Migration The geographic movement of populations between defined geographic units, which involves a permanent change of residence.

Mixed model An organizational arrangement in which a health maintenance organization cannot be categorized neatly into a single model type because it features some combination of large medical group practices, small medical group practices, and independent practitioners, most of whom have contracts with a number of managed care organizations.

Money Follows the Person (MFP) A demonstration program codified in the Deficit Reduction Act of 2005 to provide adequate federal funding to states for the sole purpose of moving qualified people whose care is funded by Medicaid from nursing homes back into community-based settings.

Moral agent A person, such as a healthcare executive, who has the moral responsibility to ensure that the best interest of patients takes precedence over fiduciary responsibility toward the organization.

Moral hazard Consumer behavior that leads to a higher utilization of healthcare services because people are covered by insurance.

Morbidity Sickness.

Mortality Death.

Multihospital system (MHS) Operation of two or more hospitals owned, leased, sponsored, or contractually managed by a central organization.

N

Nanomedicine A new area, still in its infancy, which involves the application of nanotechnology for medical use. This cutting-edge advancement within science and engineering is not a single field but rather an intense collaboration between disciplines to manipulate materials on the atomic and molecular level (one nanometer is one-billionth of a meter).

Natality The birth rate.

National health expenditures Total amount spent for all health services and supplies and health-related research and construction activities consumed in a country during a calendar year.

National health insurance (NHI) A tax-supported national healthcare program in which services are financed by the government but are rendered by private providers (Canada is an example of a country that has NHI).

National health system (NHS) A tax-supported national healthcare program in which the government finances and also controls the service infrastructure (The United Kingdom is an example of a country that has an NHS).

Need Obtaining healthcare services based on individual judgment (in contrast to demand for health services). The patient makes the primary determination of the need for health care and, under most circumstances, initiates contact with the system. The physician may make a professional judgment and determine need for referral to higher-level services.

Network model An organizational arrangement in which a health maintenance organization contracts with more than one medical group practice.

Noncertified A nursing facility that cannot admit patients covered by Medicaid or Medicare.

Nonurgent conditions Conditions that do not require the resources of an emergency service, and in which the disorder is nonacute or minor in severity.

Nurse practitioners (NPs) Individuals who have completed a program of study leading to competence as registered nurses in an expanded role. NP specialties include pediatric, family, adult, psychiatric, and geriatric programs. Refer to nonphysician practitioner.

Nursing facility (NF) A nursing home (or part of a nursing home) certified to provide services to Medicaid beneficiaries. Refer to skilled nursing facility.

O

Occupancy rate The percentage of a hospital's total inpatient capacity that is actually utilized.

Occupational therapists (OTs) Healthcare professionals who help people of all ages improve their ability to perform tasks in their daily living and working environments. OTs work with individuals who have conditions that are mentally, physically, developmentally, or emotionally disabling.

Open-panel Also known as open access, a healthcare plan that allows insureds access to providers outside the panel, but some conditions apply, such as higher out-of-pocket costs.

Opportunistic infection (OI) An infection that occurs when the body's natural immune system breaks down.

Optometrists Professionals who provide vision care, which includes examination, diagnosis, and correction of vision problems. They must be licensed to practice.

Organized medicine Concerted activities of physicians, mainly to protect their own interests, through such associations as the American Medical Association.

Orphan drugs Certain new drug therapies for conditions that affect fewer than 200,000 people in the United States.

Osteopathic medicine A medical philosophy based on the holistic approach to treatment. It uses the traditional methods of medical practice, which include pharmaceuticals, laboratory tests, x-ray diagnostics, and surgery, and supplements them by advocating treatment that involves correction of the position of the joints or tissues and emphasizes diet and environment as factors that might destroy natural resistance. Refer to allopathic medicine.

Outcomes The end results of healthcare delivery; often viewed as the bottom-line measure of the effectiveness of the healthcare delivery system.

Outliers Unusual cases that call for additional reimbursement under a payment method; these atypical cases require an exceptionally long inpatient stay or incur exceptionally high costs compared to the overall distribution of cases.

Outpatient services Any healthcare services that are not provided based on an overnight stay in which room and board costs are incurred. Refer to ambulatory care.

Overutilization Also known as overuse; utilization of medical services, the cost of which exceeds the benefit to consumers or the risks of which outweigh potential benefits.

P

Package pricing Bundling of fees for an entire package of related services.

Palliation Serving to relieve or alleviate, such as pharmacologic pain management and nausea relief.

Panel Providers selected to render services to the members of a managed care plan; the plan generally refers to them as "preferred providers."

Paraprofessionals Personnel, such as certified nursing assistants and therapy aides, who provide basic assistance with activities of daily living and/or assist licensed and professional staff.

Part A The component of Medicare that provides coverage for hospital care and limited nursing home care.

Part B The federal government subsidized voluntary insurance for physician services and outpatient services.

Patient activation A person's ability to manage their own health and utilization of health care.

Patient-centered care Delivery of health care that respects and responds to patients' wants, needs, and preferences so that they can make choices about their care that best fit their individual circumstances.

Patient's bill of rights A document that reflects the law concerning the rights a patient has while confined to an institution such as a hospital. Issues addressed in the bill of rights include confidentiality, consent, and the right to make decisions regarding medical care, to be informed about diagnosis and treatment, to refuse treatment, and to formulate advance directives.

pay-for-value Refer to value-based payments.

Peer review The general process of medical review of utilization and quality when it is carried out directly or under the supervision of physicians.

Personal care Assistance with basic activities of daily living.

Person-centered care A mode of care that emphasizes the centrality of the recipient of care.

Personal emergency response system (PERS) A system that provides at-risk older persons with an effective and convenient means to summon help if an emergency occurs. Using a transmitter unit, the individual can activate an alarm that sends a medical alert to a local 24-hour response center.

Personal health expenditures The portion of national health expenditures remaining after expenditures for research and construction, administrative expenses incurred in health insurance programs, and costs of government public health activities are subtracted. These expenditures go toward services and goods related directly to patient care.

Personalized medicine A treatment approach in which gene variations among patients are matched with responses to selected medications to increase effectiveness and reduce unwanted side effects.

Pesthouse A type of facility operated by local governments during the 18th and mid-19th centuries to quarantine people who had contracted a contagious disease such as cholera, smallpox, typhoid, or yellow fever. The primary function of a pesthouse was to isolate people with contagious diseases and, hence, to protect the community from the spread of contagious disease. These institutions were the predecessors of contagious-disease and tuberculosis hospitals.

Phantom providers Practitioners who generally function in an adjunct capacity; the patient does not receive direct services from them. They bill for their services separately, and the patients often wonder why they have been billed. Examples include anesthesiologists, radiologists, and pathologists.

Pharmaceutical care A mode of pharmacy practice in which the pharmacist takes an active role on behalf of patients, which includes giving information on drugs and advice on their potential misuse and assisting prescribers in appropriate drug choices. In so doing, the pharmacist assumes direct responsibility, in collaboration with other healthcare professionals and with patients, to achieve the desired therapeutic outcomes.

Pharmacists Professionals who have graduated from an accredited pharmacy program that awards a bachelor of pharmacy or doctor of pharmacy degree and have successfully completed a state board examination and a supervised internship.

Physical therapists (PTs) Healthcare professionals who provide care for patients with movement dysfunction.

Physician assistants (PAs) Healthcare professionals who work in a dependent relationship with a supervising physician to provide comprehensive medical care to patients. The major services provided by PAs include evaluation, monitoring, diagnostics, therapeutics, counseling, and referral. Refer to nonphysician practitioner.

Physician–hospital organization (PHO) A legal entity formed between a hospital and a physician group to achieve shared market objectives and other mutual interests.

Plan The form in which health insurance, particularly private health insurance, is obtained. The plan specifies, among other details, information pertaining to costs, covered services, and how to obtain health care when needed.

Planned rationing Also called supply-side rationing; government efforts to limit the availability of healthcare services, particularly expensive technology.

Play-or-pay A type of employer mandate in which employers must choose to provide health insurance to employees ("play") or pay a penalty.

Podiatrists Healthcare professionals who treat patients with foot diseases or deformities.

Point-of-service (POS) plan A managed care plan that allows its members to decide at the time they need medical care (at the point of service) whether to go to a provider on the panel or to pay more to receive services out of network.

Population at risk All of the people in the same community or population group who are susceptible to acquiring a disease or a negative health condition.

Practice profiling Use of provider-specific practice patterns and comparing individual practice patterns to some norm.

Preadmission Screening and Resident Review (PASRR) An evaluation required under federal regulations before a patient can be admitted to a Medicaid-certified nursing facility, which determines whether a nursing facility is the best alternative for individuals with serious mental illness or intellectual disability or whether their needs can be adequately met in community-based settings.

Precision medicine A treatment approach that takes into account not only variability in genes but also the environment and lifestyle factors.

Preexisting conditions Physical and/or mental conditions that existed before the effective date of an insurance policy.

Preferred provider organization (PPO) A type of managed care organization that has a panel of preferred providers who are paid according to a discounted fee schedule. The enrollees have the option to go to out-of-network providers but incur a higher level of cost sharing for doing so.

Premium The insurer's charge for insurance coverage; the price for an insurance plan.

Premium cost sharing Employers' requirement that their employees pay a portion of the health insurance cost.

Glossary

Prepaid plan A contractual arrangement under which a provider must provide all needed services to a group of members (or enrollees) in exchange for a fixed monthly fee paid in advance to the provider on a per-member basis (called capitation).

Prevalence The number of cases of a given disease in a given population at a certain point in time.

Primary care Basic and routine health care provided in an office or clinic by a provider (physician, nurse, or other healthcare professional) who takes responsibility for coordinating all aspects of a patient's healthcare needs; an approach to healthcare delivery that is the patient's first contact with the healthcare delivery system and the first element of a continuing healthcare process.

Primary-care case management (PCCM) A managed care arrangement in which a state contracts directly with primary-care providers, who agree to be responsible for the provision and/or coordination of medical services for Medicare recipients under their care.

Primary health care Essential health care that constitutes the first level of contact by a patient with the health delivery system and the first element of a continuing healthcare process.

Primary prevention In a strict epidemiologic sense, the prevention of disease—for example, health education, immunization, and environmental control measures.

Private-pay residents U.S. residents not covered by either Medicare or Medicaid.

Program of All-Inclusive Care for the Elderly (PACE) An example of the integrated care model of long-term care case management for clients who have been certified as eligible for nursing home placement. PACE has had a high success rate of keeping clients in the community.

Proprietary hospitals Also referred to as investor-owned hospitals; for-profit hospitals owned by individuals, a partnership, or a corporation.

Prospective reimbursement A method of payment in which certain pre-established criteria are used to determine in advance the amount of reimbursement.

Prospective utilization review A process that determines the appropriateness of utilization before the care is actually delivered.

Provider Any entity that delivers healthcare services and can either independently bill for those services or is tax supported. Examples of providers include physicians, dentists, optometrists, and therapists in private practices; hospitals; diagnostic and imaging clinics; and suppliers of medical equipment (e.g., wheelchairs, walkers, ostomy supplies, oxygen).

Provider-induced demand Artificial creation of demand by providers that enables them to deliver unneeded services to boost their incomes.

Provider-sponsored organization (PSO) Also known as a provider service organization; a quasi-managed care organization that is a risk-bearing entity sponsored by physicians, by hospitals, or jointly by physicians and hospitals to compete with regular managed care organizations.

Psychiatrists Physicians who receive postgraduate specialty training in mental health after completion of medical school. These professionals treat patients with mental disorders, prescribe drugs, and admit patients to hospitals.

Psychologists Mental health professionals who must be licensed or certified to practice. These professionals are trained in interpreting and changing the behavior of people and may specialize in such areas as clinical, counseling, developmental, educational, engineering, personnel, experimental, industrial, psychometric, rehabilitation, school, and social psychology. They use such techniques as psychotherapy and counseling, which psychiatrists typically do not engage in.

Public health A wide variety of activities undertaken by state and local governments to ensure conditions that promote optimal health for society as a whole.

Public hospitals Hospitals owned by the federal, state, or local government.

Public policies Authoritative decisions made in the legislative, executive, or judicial branches of government that are intended to direct or influence the actions, behaviors, or decisions of others.

Q

Quad-function model The four key functions necessary for healthcare delivery: financing, insurance, delivery, and payment.

Quality The degree to which health services for individuals and populations increase the likelihood of desired health outcomes and are consistent with current professional knowledge.

Quality-adjusted life year (QALY) The value of 1 year of high-quality life, used as a measure of health benefit.

Quality assessment The measurement of quality against an established standard. It includes the process of defining how quality is to be determined, identification of specific variables or indicators to be measured, collection of appropriate data to make the measurement possible, statistical analysis, and interpretation of the results of the assessment.

Quality assurance The process of ongoing quality measurement and use of the results of assessment for ongoing quality improvement. Refer to total quality management.

Quality improvement committee A medical committee that is responsible for overseeing the program for continuous quality improvement.

Quality improvement organization (QIO) A private organization composed of practicing physicians and other healthcare professionals in each state that is paid by the Centers for Medicare and Medicaid Services under contract to review the care provided to Medicare beneficiaries.

Quality of life (1) Factors considered important by patients, such as environmental comfort, security, interpersonal relations, personal preferences, and autonomy in making decisions when institutionalized. (2) Overall satisfaction with life during and following a person's encounter with the healthcare delivery system.

R

Rate The price for a healthcare service set by a third-party payer.

Redistributive policies Policies that take money or power from one group and give it to another. An example is the Medicaid program, which takes tax revenue and spends it on the poor in the form of health insurance.

Registered nurses (RNs) Nurses who have completed an associate's degree (ADN), a diploma program, or a bachelor's degree (BSN) and are licensed to practice.

Regulatory tools Uses of health policy in which the government prescribes and controls the behavior of a particular target group by monitoring the group and posing sanctions if it fails to comply.

Rehabilitation hospitals Hospitals that specialize in providing restorative services to rehabilitate individuals with disabilities or who are chronically ill to a maximum level of functioning.

Reimbursement The amount insurers pay to a provider. The payment may be just a portion of the actual charge.

Reinsurance Stop-loss coverage that self-insured employers purchase to protect themselves against any potential risk of high losses.

Relative value units (RVUs) Measures based on physicians' time, skill, and intensity required to provide a service.

Residency Graduate medical education in a specialty that takes the form of paid on-the-job training, usually in a hospital.

Respite care A service that provides temporary relief to informal caregivers, such as family members.

Restorative care Short-term therapy to help a person regain or improve physical function.

Retrospective reimbursement A payment scheme in which reimbursement rates are based on costs actually incurred.

Retrospective utilization review A review of utilization after services have been delivered.

Risk The possibility of a substantial financial loss from an event for which the probability of occurrence is relatively small.

Risk factors Environmental elements, personal habits, or living conditions that increase the likelihood of developing a particular disease or negative health condition in the future.

Risk management Limiting risks against lawsuits or unexpected events.

Risk rating Insurance rating according to which high-risk individuals pay more than the average premium price, and low-risk individuals pay less than the average price.

Rural hospitals Hospitals located in counties that are not part of a metropolitan statistical area.

S

Secondary care Routine hospitalization, routine surgery, and specialized outpatient care, such as consultation with specialists and rehabilitation. Compared to primary care, these services are usually brief and more complex, involving advanced diagnostic and therapeutic procedures.

Secondary prevention Efforts to detect disease in early stages so as to provide a more effective treatment—for example, screening and periodic health examinations. The main objective is to block the progression of a disease or an injury, that is, to keep it from developing into an impairment or disability.

Self-insured plan A health plan in which a large company acts as its own insurer by collecting premiums and paying claims. Such businesses most often purchase reinsurance against unusually large claims.

Self-referral The practice in which physicians order services from laboratories or other medical facilities in which they have a direct financial interest, usually without disclosing this conflict of interest to the patient.

Senior centers Local community centers for older adults that provide opportunities to congregate and socialize. Many centers offer subsidized meals, wellness programs, health education, counseling, and referral services.

Short-stay hospital A hospital in which the average length of stay is less than 25 days.

Single-payer system A national healthcare program in which the financing and insurance functions are taken over by the federal government.

Skilled nursing care Medically oriented care provided mainly by a licensed nurse under the overall direction of a physician.

Skilled nursing facility (SNF) A nursing home (or part of a nursing home) certified to provide services under Medicare. Refer to **nursing facility**.

Small area variations (SAVs) Unexplained variations in the treatment patterns for similar patients and medical conditions.

Social contacts The number of activities a person engages in within a specified period of time. Examples include visits with friends and relatives, and attendance at social events, such as conferences, picnics, or other outings.

Social justice A distribution principle according to which health care is most equitably distributed by a government-run national healthcare program. Refer to market justice.

Social resources Social contacts that can be relied upon for support, such as family, relatives, friends, neighbors, and members of a religious congregation; they are indicative of adequacy of social relationships.

Socialized health insurance (SHI) Health care that is financed through government-mandated contributions by employers and employees and delivered by private providers (Germany, Israel, and Japan are examples of countries with SHI).

Socialized medicine Any large-scale government-sponsored expansion of health insurance or intrusion in the private practice of medicine.

Specialists Physicians who specialize in specific healthcare problems; examples include anesthesiologists, cardiologists, and oncologists. Refer to generalists.

Specialty care Care that tends to be limited to illness episodes, the organ system, or the disease process involved. Specialty care, if needed, generally follows primary care.

Specialty hospitals Hospitals that admit only certain types of patients or those with specified illnesses or conditions. Examples include rehabilitation hospitals, tuberculosis hospitals, children's hospitals, cardiac hospitals, and orthopedic hospitals.

Staff model A health maintenance organization (HMO) arrangement in which the HMO employs salaried physicians.

Standards of participation Minimum quality standards established by government regulatory agencies to certify providers for delivery of services to patients covered by Medicare and Medicaid.

Subacute care Clinically complex services that are beyond traditional skilled nursing care.

Subacute condition The condition that is a less severe phase of an acute illness. It can be a postacute condition, requiring continuity of treatment after discharge from a hospital. Examples include ventilator and head trauma care.

Supply-side rationing Also called planned rationing; government efforts to limit the availability of healthcare services, particularly expensive technology.

Surge capacity The ability of a healthcare facility or system to expand its operations to safely treat an abnormally large influx of patients.

Surgicenters Freestanding, ambulatory surgery centers that perform various types of surgical procedures on an outpatient basis.

Swing bed A hospital bed used for acute care or skilled nursing care, depending on fluctuations in demand.

Synchronous technology Technology in which telecommunications occur in real time.

System A set of interrelated and interdependent components that are logically coordinated to achieve a common goal.

T

Teaching hospital A hospital with an approved residency program for physicians.

Technological imperative The use of technology without cost considerations, especially when the benefits to be derived from the use of technology are small compared to the costs.

Technology diffusion The proliferation of technology once it is developed.

Telehealth The use of electronic information and telecommunication technologies to support long-distance clinical health care, patient and professional health-related education, public health, and health administration. It increases the ease of communication between patient and provider by allowing for "virtual visits" and remote consultations.

Telemedicine Use of telecommunications technology that enables physicians to conduct two-way, interactive video consultations or transmit digital images, such as x-rays and magnetic resonance imaging results, to other sites.

Telephone triage Telephone access to a trained nurse for expert opinion and advice, especially during the hours when physicians' offices are closed.

Tertiary care The most complex level of care, which is typically institution-based, highly specialized, and highly technological. Examples include burn treatment, transplantation, and coronary artery bypass surgery.

Tertiary prevention Interventions to prevent complications from chronic conditions and avoid further illness, injury, or disability.

Third party An intermediary between patients and providers, which carries out the functions of insurance and payment for healthcare delivery.

Third-party administrator (TPA) An administrative organization, other than the employee benefit plan or healthcare provider, that collects premiums, pays claims, and/or provides administrative services.

Third-party payers In a multipayer system, the payers for covered services—for example, insurance companies, managed care organizations, and the government. They are neither the providers nor the recipients of medical services.

Title XVIII Title XVIII (18) of the Social Security Amendment of 1965; the Medicare program.

Title XIX Title XIX (19) of the Social Security Amendment of 1965; the Medicaid program.

Top-down control Use of global budgets in a healthcare system to control total expenditures in accordance with preestablished limits. Refer to global budgets.

Total care In the context of long-term care delivery, recognition of any healthcare need that may arise, with that need then being evaluated and addressed by appropriate clinical professionals.

Total quality management (TQM) Also known as continuous quality improvement (CQI); an environment in which all aspects of health services within an organization are oriented to patient-related objectives and the production of desirable health outcomes. TQM holds the promise of not only improving quality but also increasing efficiency and productivity by identifying and implementing less costly ways to provide services; it is viewed as an ongoing effort to improve quality.

Travel ban An effective measure imposed on people to restrict travel during a pandemic to delay the spread of the disease.

Triple-option plans Health insurance plans that combine the features of indemnity insurance, a health maintenance organization, and a preferred provider organization; the insured has the flexibility to choose which feature to use when using healthcare services.

U

Underutilization Withholding of medical care services particularly when potential benefits may exceed the cost or the risks.

Underwriting A systematic technique used by an insurer for evaluating, selecting (or rejecting), classifying, and rating risks.

Uninsured People who lack health insurance coverage.

Universal access The ability of all citizens to obtain health care when needed. It is a misnomer because timely access to certain services may still be a problem because of supply-side rationing.

Universal coverage Health insurance coverage for all citizens.

Upcoding A fraudulent practice in which a higher-priced service is billed when a lower-priced service is actually delivered.

Urban hospitals Hospitals located in counties that are part of a metropolitan statistical area.

Urgent care centers Walk-in clinics that are generally open to patients after normal business hours in the evenings and weekends, and for which patients do not have to make an appointment.

Urgent conditions Conditions that require medical attention within a few hours; a longer delay presents possible danger to the patient. This kind of disorder is acute but not necessarily severe.

Utilization The consumption of healthcare services and the extent to which healthcare services are used.

Utilization review (UR) The process of evaluating the appropriateness of services provided.

Utilization review committee A process by which an insurer reviews decisions made by physicians and other providers on how much care to provide.

V

Value Provision of greater benefits or higher quality at the same or lower price levels (costs).

Value-based payments (VBP) Refer to payment methods that compensate providers based on the quality and cost of care they provide to patients.

Vertical integration Linking of services that are at different stages in the production process of health care. Examples include a hospital system that acquires a firm that produces medical supplies, and a physician group practice or a hospital that launches hospice, long-term care, or ambulatory care services. Refer to horizontal integration.

Virtual integration The formation of networks based on contractual arrangements.

Voluntary health insurance Private health insurance (in contrast to government-sponsored compulsory health insurance).

Voluntary hospitals Nonprofit hospitals.

W

Walk-in clinics Freestanding, ambulatory clinics in which patients are accepted without appointments on a first-come, first-served basis.

X

Xenotransplantation Also known as xenografting; transplanting of animal tissue into humans.

Z

Zoonoses Any disease or infection that is naturally transmittable from vertebrate animals to humans.

Index

Page numbers followed by *b, f, e,* or *t* indicate material in boxes, figures, exhibits, or tables, respectively.

A

AAAHC. *See* Accreditation Association for Ambulatory Health Care (AAAHC)
AALL. *See* American Association of Labor Legislation (AALL)
AAMC. *See* Association of American Medical Colleges (AAMC)
AARP. *See* American Association of Retired Persons (AARP)
ABHM. *See* American Board of Hospital Medicine (ABHM)
ABPS. *See* American Board of Physician Specialists (ABPS)
Abuse, fraud and, 531
ACA. *See* Affordable Care Act€(ACA)
Academic medical center, 371
Acceptability, 542
Access, defined, 238
Accessibility, 299, 540–541
Access to care, 539–544, 588–590
    ACA and, 544–545, 547–551
    current status of, 544, 544*t*–546*t*, 546*f*–548*f*
    dimensions of, 540–542
    electronic health records, 550
    framework of, 539–540, 541*f*
    integrated access, 588–589
    and low income, 590
    managed care impact on, 409–410, 410*e*
    measurement of, 542–544
    and minorities, 589

    and older people, 589
    partial aspect to, 11
    and persons with HIV/AIDS, 590
    providers, 588
    in rural areas, 589–590
    telemedicine and, 548–550
    types of, 542
    universal, 11
Accommodation, 542
Accountability, 299
Accountable care organizations (ACOs), 18–19, 270, 388, 418–419, 418*e*, 588, 598, 626
Accountable health communities (AHCs), 629–630
Accreditation, 376
Accreditation Association for Ambulatory Health Care (AAAHC), 303
Accreditation of managed care, 392
ACOs. *See* Accountable care organizations (ACOs)
ACP. *See* American College of Physicians (ACP)
Acquisition, 413–414
ACS. *See* American College of Surgeons (ACS)
Action for Mental Health, 117
Activities of daily living (ADLs), 77, 431
Acute-care hospital payment system, 272–275
    DRG-based reimbursement, overview of, 272–275
    inpatient psychiatric DRG-based payment, 275

    refined Medicare severity DRGs, 273–275
Acute condition, 53
ADA. *See* American Dental Association (ADA)
Adjusted community rating, 242–243
ADLs. *See* Activities of daily living (ADLs)
Administrative costs, 14, 530–531
Administrative information systems, 193
Adult daycare (ADC), 325, 444–445
Adult foster care (AFC), 445
Advanced institutions of medical training and research, 350–351
Advance directives, 379
Advanced practice nurse (APN), 163
Adverse selection, 625
Affordable Care Act (ACA), 7, 106, 131–132, 146, 574, 579, 580, 582, 584, 596, 615, 617, 618, 622, 623
    access to care and, 544–545, 547–551
    Court challenges, 133–134
    disease prevention, 60–61
    effects of, 249–251
    evaluation of, 134–136, 135*e*
    implementation of, 587
    Medicaid under, 263–264
    patchy legacy, 132–133
    politics of, 583–584
    primary care and, 301–302
    private insurance under, 247–248
    quality of care and, 559–562

Index

Age-adjusted death rates
  for persons aged 25 and over, 469f
  for selected causes of death, 467t–470t
Agency for Healthcare Research and Quality (AHRQ), 208, 501, 587
  Patient Safety Network (PSNet), 558
  quality indicators, 558
Agent, 53
Age-specific mortality rate, 77
Aging-in-place, 449
AHA. *See* American Hospital Association (AHA)
AHCAs. *See* Australian Health Care Agreements (AHCAs)
AHCs. *See* Accountable health communities (AHCs)
AHRQ. *See* Agency for Healthcare Research and Quality (AHRQ)
AI. *See* Artificial intelligence (AI)
AIDS, 88. *See also* HIV/AIDS
Alaska Natives, 474–475
ALF. *See* Assisted living facility (ALF)
Allen, F. C., 79
Alliance for Home Health Quality and Innovation, 319–320
Alliances, 414–415
Allied health professionals, 166–169
  defined, 166
  examples of, 166e
  other, 167–169
  therapists, 167
Allocative tools, 575
Allopathic medicine, 148
Almshouse, 109
Alternative medicine, 328–330
Alzheimer's disease, 438
Alzheimer's facilities, 452
AMA. *See* American Medical Association (AMA)
Ambulatory care, 294. *See also* Outpatient care

Ambulatory long-term care services, 325
Ambulatory Medical Care Survey, 543
Ambulatory payment classification (APC), 275
American Academy of Pediatrics, 579
American and European evidence-based guidelines, 643
American Association of Labor Legislation (AALL), 122
American Association of Retired Persons (AARP), 578, 579
American Board of Hospital Medicine (ABHM), 154
American Board of Physician Specialists (ABPS), 154
American College of Physicians (ACP), 621
American College of Surgeons (ACS), 350
American Dental Association (ADA), 160
American Health Care Association, 579
American Hospital Association (AHA), 121, 578
American Indians, 474–475
American Medical Association (AMA), 108, 350, 578
American Recovery and Reinvestment Act (ARRA), 198, 588
American Rescue Plan Act (ARPA), 596, 618
American Society of Anesthesiologists, 579
America's Health Insurance Plans, 555
Ample research, 631
ANA Nursing Administration: Scope & Standards of Practice, 377
Angioplasty, 218
Annual percentage decline in U.S. cancer mortality, 1991–2016, 59t

Anthro-cultural
  beliefs and values, 204
  forces, 621
Antibiotic-resistant pathogens, 639
Antitrust policy, 419
APN. *See* Advanced practice nurse (APN)
Armstrong v. Exceptional Child Center, Inc., 264
ARRA. *See* American Recovery and Reinvestment Act (ARRA)
Artificial intelligence (AI), 194, 194e–195e
Asian Americans, 473–474
ASPR. *See* Assistant Secretary for Preparedness and Response (ASPR)
Assessment
  efficacy, 222–223
  safety, 223
  use of cost-benefit analyses, 225
  value analysis, 223–225, 224e
Assistant Secretary for Preparedness and Response (ASPR), 67
Assisted living facility (ALF), 449–450
Association of American Medical Colleges (AAMC), 116
Asynchronous technology, 201
Australia, 23–24
Australian Health Care Agreements (AHCAs), 24
Autonomy, 377
  and organization, 115
Availability, 540
Average daily census, 358
Average length of stay (ALOS), 356–357, 356f, 357f
Avian influenza, 64

B

Balance bill, 14, 127, 268
Balanced Budget Act (BBA) of 1997, 254

Index

Baylor plan, 120–121
Behavioral medicine, 643
Behavioral risk factors, 53
  percentage of U.S. population with, 54t
Behavior modification, 56–57
Beliefs and values
  acute, subacute, and chronic conditions, 53–56
  in American culture, 81–87
  anthro-cultural, 81–87, 204
  behavioral risk factors, 53
  demographic change, 78
  determinants of health, 71–75
  equitable distribution of health care, 82–83
  global health measures, 80–81
  health concepts, 50–56
  health promotion and disease prevention, 56–61
  health-related measures, 75–81
  health services utilization measures, 79–80
  Healthy People 2020, 88–92
  Healthy People 2030, 92–93
  healthy people initiatives, 87–88
  integration of individual and population health, 86–87
  justice in U.S. health delivery system, 85–86
  managers/policymakers and, 50
  market justice, 86
  mental health measures, 78
  public health, 61–69
  quality of life, 52–53
  risk factors and disease, 53–56
  social health measures, 79
  social justice, 84–85
  spiritual health measures, 79
Beneficiary, 242
Benefit period, 254
Benefits, 243
Biden Administration, 596
Biden-Harris Administration, 598

Biden, Joe, 593, 594, 600
Bill of rights, 378
Bioethics, technology impact on, 221–222
Biological and Toxin Weapons Convention (BWC), 640
Biologics Price Competition and Innovation Act, 217
Biosimilar User Fee Act, 216
Bioterrorism, 67
Bipartisan Budget Act of 2018, 276
Black Americans, 467–471, 467t–470t, 469f, 471f, 476f
Black box warning, 211
Blood substitutes, 642
Blue Cross Blue Shield Association, 121–122
Blue Cross Blue Shield of Michigan's PCMH Designation standards, 303
Blue Cross plans, 121
Blue Shield movement, 121
Blum, H. L., 72
Board of trustees, 374–375
Breslow, L., 79
Broad healthcare delivery system, 614
Bundled payments, 268–269
Bush, George H. W., 127
Bush, George W., 67, 208, 582, 583, 588, 590
BWC. *See* Biological and Toxin Weapons Convention (BWC)
Byrnes, John W., 126

C

Campaign for Action, 631–632
Canada, 24–26
Canadian single-payer system, 623
Cancer, 54–55
Capitation, 270
Care continuum, level of, 442–443
  custodial care, 442

personal care, 442
restorative care, 442
skilled nursing care, 442–443
subacute care, 443
Care coordination, 397–399, 397f
CARES Act. *See* Coronavirus Aid, Relief, and Economic Security (CARES) Act
Carnegie Foundation, 116
Carter, Jimmy, 127
Carve-out, 402
Case management, 325, 397–399, 398f, 447–448
  brokerage model, 447
  integrated model, 447–448
  managed care model, 447–448
Case-mix-based reimbursement, 272–277
  acute-care hospital payment system, 272–275
  inpatient psychiatric DRG-based payment, 275
  outpatient services payment systems, 275
  payment for home health services, 276–277
  payments to inpatient rehabilitation facilities, 276
  Skilled nursing facility payment system, 276
Cases, incidence and prevalence of, 76
Categorical programs, 253
CBO. *See* Congressional Budget Office (CBO)
CCRC. *See* Continuing care retirement community (CCRC)
Center for Medical Home Improvement's Medical Home Index, 303
Centers for Disease Control and Prevention (CDC), 594, 619, 620, 627
Centers for Medicare and Medicaid Services (CMS), 584, 596, 621

Index

CER. *See* Comparative effectiveness research (CER)
Certificate of need (CON), 534–535
Certificate of need (CON) laws, 625
Certificate of need (CON) programs, 576
Certification, 376
Certified nurse-midwives (CNMs), 163, 165–166, 165–166, 299
Certified registered nurse anesthetists (CRNAs), 163
Charge, 268
CHART Model. *See* Community Health Access and Rural Transformation (CHART) Model
CHCs. *See* community health centers (CHCs)
Chief executive officer, 375
Chief of service, 375
Chief of staff, 375
Children
 asthma in, 479
 depression in, 479
 and healthcare system, 480–481
 health insurance, 479
 HIV/AIDS in, 495, 497
 mental health of, 490–491
 special health care need of, 480–481
 unintentional injuries in, 479
 vaccination rates for, 479–480, 480*t*
Children's Health Insurance Program (CHIP), 4, 7, 82, 127, 265–266, 574, 578, 590, 616
Children's Health Plan, 582
Children's hospitals, 369
China, 26–28
Chinese government, 637
Chiropractors, 162
Choice restriction, 397
Cholera, 118
Chronic condition, 54–56
 main reasons for, in U.S. population, 54*t*
 risk factors for, 54
Chronic Disease Management Program, 33
Chronic diseases, 19, 493–494
Church-affiliated hospitals, 371–372
Churning, 264
CIMIT. *See* Consortia for Improving Medicine with Innovation and Technology (CIMIT)
Civilian Health and Medical Program of the Department of Veterans Affairs (CHAMPVA), 267
Claim, 268
CLASS. *See* Community Living Assistance Services and Supports (CLASS)
Cleveland Clinic, 18, 130
Clinical decision support systems, 628
Clinical information systems, 193
Clinical nurse specialists (CNSs), 163
Clinical technology, new frontiers in, 641–643
Clinical trial, 222
Clinton, Bill, 125, 583
Clinton, Hillary, 125
Closed-panel, 397
CMS Primary Cares, 18
CMS programs on quality, 557–558
CNMs. *See* Certified nursemidwives (CNMs)
CNSs. *See* Clinical nurse specialists (CNSs)
COAG. *See* Council of Australian Governments (COAG)
Cognitive impairment, 431
Coinsurance, 243
Collaborative tool, 602
Commercial insurance, 122
Commission on Long-Term Care, 589
Committee on Labor and Human Resources, 586
Communicable diseases, 620
Communities Putting Prevention to Work (CPPW), 56
Community and Migrant Health Centers, 487
Community Asthma Initiative (CAI), 501
Community-based health care workers (CHWs), 177
Community-based services, 439, 440*f*
 Community First Choice, 448
 Money Follows the Person, 448
 policies related to, 448
Community First Choice, 448
Community Health Access and Rural Transformation (CHART) Model, 598
Community health assessment, 93
Community health centers (CHCs), 264, 326–327
 funding for, 588
Community hospital, 365
Community Living Assistance Services and Supports (CLASS), 589
Community Mental Health Centers Act of 1963, 117
Community-oriented primary care (COPC), 307, 628–629
Community rating, 242
Community Tracking Survey, 543
Comorbidity, 153
Comparative effectiveness research (CER), 225, 592, 643
Competition, 537
Complementary medicine, 328–330
Comprehensive Mental Health Action Plan 2013-2030, 603
Computational medicine, 641
Computed tomography (CT), 642
Concurrent utilization review, 400

Index

Conditions of participation, 376
Confidentiality under HIPAA, 199
Congressional Budget Office (CBO), 616
CON programs. *See* Certificate of need (CON) programs
Consolidated systems of health services delivery, 351
Consortia for Improving Medicine with Innovation and Technology (CIMIT), 190
Consumer Assessment of Healthcare Providers and Systems (CAHPS), 392
Consumer-directed health plans, 245
Contemporary globalization, 621
Continuing care retirement community (CCRC), 452–453
Contribution programs, 625
Copayment, 243
COPC. *See* Community-oriented primary care (COPC)
Coronary angioplasty, 218
Coronavirus Aid, Relief, and Economic Security (CARES) Act, 67, 251
Coronaviruses, 65
Coronavirus Preparedness and Response Supplemental Appropriations Act, 67
Corporate era medical care, 128–129
 early developments, 128
 HMO Act of 1973, 128–129
Corporatization of healthcare delivery, 129
Cost-benefit analyses, 225
Cost containment
 competitive approaches, 537–539
  demand-side incentives, 538
  payer-driven price competition, 538
  supply-side regulation, 538
  utilization controls, 539
 under health reform, 539
 regulatory approaches, 532–537
  health planning, 533–535
  peer review, 537
  price controls, 535–537
Cost containment, managed care influence on, 408–409
Cost-efficiency, 223
Cost of care, 591–592
Cost of HIV/AIDS, 499–500
Cost-plus reimbursement, 270–271
Cost-saving technology, 627
Cost sharing, 243
Cost shifting, 126
Costs, of health care, 520–527
 containment of, 525–527
 national health expenditure trends, 520–525
 reasons for escalation of, 527–532
  defensive medicine, 531
  elderly population, increase in, 528–530
  fraud and abuse, 531
  growth of technology, 528
  imperfect market, 527
  medical model of healthcare delivery, 530
  multipayer system and administrative costs, 530–531
  practice variations, 531–532
  third-party payment, 527
 regulation, 532–537
Cost-utility analysis, 225
Council of Academic Family Medicine (CAFM), 634
Council of Australian Governments (COAG), 24
Council on Education for Public Health (CEPH), 170
Couplitation, 599
Covered services, 243–244
COVID-19 pandemic, 50, 66–67, 130, 170, 203, 596, 597, 600, 600
 access to care and, 550
 case of, 637–638
 disease surveillance, 638
 drug shortages in, 215
 effects of, 504–505
 emergency preparation, 20–21
 e-visits during, 200–201
 global equity, 639
 healthcare financing and, 279–282
 health insurance and, 7
 health security in action and, 69–71
 impact of, 617
 new technologies, 639
 One Health approach, 638
 primary care and, 308
 private health insurance and, 251
 racial disparities, 476–477
 travel and trade issues, 639
 travel ban in, 66
 vaccine sharing, 639
COVID-19 Partners Platform, 602
COVID-19 Solidarity Response Fund, 602
COVID-19 Technology Access Pool, 603
CPPW. *See* Communities Putting Prevention to Work (CPPW)
Credentials committee, 375
Critical access hospitals (CAH), 370
Critical policy issues, 587–588
 access to care, 588–590
 cost of care, 591–592
 quality of care, 592–593
CRNAs. *See* Certified registered nurse anesthetists (CRNAs)
Cross-border telemedicine, 621
Crossing the Quality Chasm, 592
Cross-subsidization, 126
Crude measures of utilization, 80
Crude rates, 77
Cultural-anthro forces, 621–622
Cultural authority, 113
Current Population Survey, 543
Custodial care, 442

Index

D

Days of care, 356
Decade of healthy ageing, 603
Decentralized role of the states, 581–582, 581e
Decision making, mechanisms for ethical, 379
Decision support systems, 193–194
Declaration of Independence, 577
Deemed status, 376
Defense Production Act (DPA), 66
Defensive medicine, 15, 531, 556
Deficit Reduction Act (DRA), 448
Deinstitutionalization, 117
Delivery, 6
Demand, 11
Demand-side incentives, 538
Demand-side rationing, 84
Dementia care, 436–438
Democratic presidential debates in 2020, 622
Democrat Party, 615
Democrats, 595
Demographic change, 78
  births, 78
  migration, 78
Dental assistants, 170
Dental hygienists, 160
Dentists, 159–161
Dent v. West Virginia, 115
Department of Health and Human Services (DHHS), 199, 485
Dependency, 114–115, 479
Developing countries, 33–34
Developing nations, 621
Developmental disability (DD), 441
Developmental vulnerability, 479
3-D fluorescence imaging, 218
DGME. *See* Direct Graduate Medical Education (DGME)
DHANP. *See* Diplomate of the Homeopathic Academy of Naturopathic Physicians (DHANP)

DHHS. *See* Department of Health and Human Services (DHHS)
Diabetes Prevention Program (DPP), 57
Diagnosis-related groups (DRGs)
  based payment, inpatient psychiatric, 275
  based reimbursement, overview of, 272–273
  refined Medicare severity, 273–275
Diagnostic and Statistical Manual of Mental Disorders, Fifth Edition (DSM-5), 52
Diligent robotics, 550
Diplomate of the Homeopathic Academy of Naturopathic Physicians (DHANP), 328
Direct Graduate Medical Education (DGME), 155
Disabilities, 494
Disability, 77
Disaster Medical Assistance Teams (DMATs), 68
Disbursement of funds, 277
Discharge, 355, 355t
Discharge planning, 400
Discrimination, 498
Disease management, 399
Disease prevention, 56–61
  under ACA, 60–61
Dispensaries, 109
Distinct institutions of care for sick, 349–350
Distinct part, 450
Distributive policies, 575
Diversification, 413
DMATs. *See* Disaster Medical Assistance Teams (DMATs)
Doctoral nursing degrees, 162
Doctor of Dental Medicine (DMD), 159
Doctor of Dental Surgery (DDS), 159
Domestic health policy, future considerations in, 593–599

  current domestic health policy initiatives, 593–597
  health insurance expansion, 599
  rural health transformation, 597–599
Donabedian model, 554–555, 554f
Do-not-resuscitate order, 379
Doppler ultrasound, 218
DPP. *See* Diabetes Prevention Program (DPP)
Dreaded hospital, 110
Drug(s)
  from overseas, 212–213
  Pros and Cons, 212e
  regulation and approval process, 209–212, 209t–210t
  shortages, 213–215, 214e
Drug formularies, 399
Drug Quality and Security Act of 2013, 213
Drug Supply Chain Security Act, 213
DSM-5. *See Diagnostic and Statistical Manual of Mental Disorders*, Fifth Edition (DSM-5)
Dual certification, 450
Duggan v. Bowen, 577
Duke University Medical Center, 130
Durable medical equipment (DME), 317
Durable power of attorney, 379
Dutch method, 601

E

EBM. *See* Evidence-based medicine (EBM)
Ebola virus disease (EVD), 66, 637
Echocardiography, 218
Ecological forces, 620
Economic forces, 616–618
Economic value of technology, 220

Index

Educational reform, 116
Effective and efficient access, 542
Effective Health Care Program (EHCP), 592
Effectiveness, defined, 222
Efficacy, defined, 222
Efficiency, 395
EHCP. *See* Effective Health Care Program (EHCP)
E-health, 200
EHRs. *See* Electronic health records (EHRs)
Elderly population, increase in, 528–530
Electronic health records (EHRs), 20, 550
Electronic health records and systems, 195
  components of, 195
Eliot, Charles, 116
Elixir Sulfanilamide disaster, 210
Emergency department (ED), 616
Emergency Health Personnel Act, 485
Emergency Medical Treatment and Active Labor Act (EMTALA), 316
Emergency services, 315–316
Emergent conditions, 316
Emigration, 78
Employee Retirement Income Security Act (ERISA), 244
Employer-based retirement plans, 625
Employers' response to rise in premiums, 393–394, 394f, 395f, 395t
Employment-based health insurance, 122
Employment-based trends, 251–253, 252t
  cost sharing in, 253
  premium costs in, 252–253, 253t
EMTALA. *See* Emergency Medical Treatment and Active Labor Act (EMTALA)
End-stage renal disease (ESRD), 578
Enrollee, 9
Entitlement, 254
Environment, 53
Environmental factors, 72
Environmental health, 63
Epidemics, 76
Epidemiology Triangle, 53, 53f
Equitable access, 542
Equitable distribution of health care, 82–83
ERISA. *See* Employee Retirement Income Security Act (ERISA)
ESRD. *See* End-stage renal disease (ESRD)
E-therapy, 200
Ethics committees, 379
Ethics in Patient Referrals Act of 1989, 205
Ethnic Health Disparities, 589
European health systems, 620
EVD. *See* Ebola virus disease (EVD)
Evidence-based care, 435–436, 627
Evidence-based health care, 643–644
Evidence-based medicine (EBM), 643
E-visits, 200–201
Evolution of healthcare services, 105–136
  ACA, 131–132
  autonomy and organization, 115
  blanket insurance policies, 120
  Blue Cross plans, 121
  Blue Shield, 121
  combined hospital/physician coverage, 121
  commercial insurance, 122
  corporate era medical care, 128–129
  cultural authority, 113
  dependency, 114–115
  economic necessity and Baylor plan, 120–121
  educational reform, 116
  globalization of health care, 129–131
  healthcare reform era, 131–136
  health services for veterans, 119
  institutionalization, 114
  licensing, 115–116
  medical practice in disarray, 108
  medical specialization, 116–117
  Medicare and Medicaid, 126–127
  mental healthcare reform, 117–118
  missing institutional core, 109–110
  national healthcare initiatives, 122–125
  patchy legacy of ACA, 132–133
  postindustrial era, 112–128
  preindustrial era, 107–112, 107e
  primitive medical procedures, 108–109
  private health insurance, rise of, 120–122
  professional sovereignty, 112–116
  public health development, 118–119
  science and technology, 113–114, 113e
  substandard medical education, 111–112
  technological, social, and economic factors, 120
  unstable demand, 110–111
  urbanization, 112–113
  worker's compensation, 119–120
Exclusive provider plan, 404
Executive committee, 375
Expenditures on research and development, 206–207
Experience rating, 242
Extension for Community Healthcare Outcomes, 634–635

Index

F

Face-to-face clinical time, 634
Families First Coronavirus Response Act, 67, 281
Family Medicine for America's health, 629
FDA. *See* Food and Drug Administration (FDA)
Federal Emergency Management Agency (FEMA), 66
Federal Medical Assistance Percentage (FMAP), 263
Federal poverty level (FPL), 578
Federal Register, 587
Fee-for-service, 111, 268
   flaws in, 393
   focus on illness rather than wellness, 393
   uncontrolled prices and payment, 393
   uncontrolled utilization, 393
Fee schedule, 268, 390
FEMA. *See* Federal Emergency Management Agency (FEMA)
Fertility, 78
Fidelity, 377
Financing, 5. *See also* Health services financing
Financing and payment, 204–205
Flat of the curve, 223
Flexner, Abraham, 116
FMAP. *See* Federal Medical Assistance Percentage (FMAP)
Food and Drug Administration (FDA), 591
   drug from overseas, 212–213
   drug regulation and approval process, 209–212
   drug shortages, 213–215
   legislation, 209t–210t
   regulation of biologics, 216
   regulation of medical devices and equipment, 215–216
Food and Drug Administration Modernization Act, 211
Food and Drug Administration Safety and Innovation Act, 213
Food, Drug, and Cosmetic Act (FD&C Act), 209t, 210, 216
Forand, Aime, 126
Forces of future change, 614–615
   cultural-anthro forces, 621–622
   ecological forces, 620
   economic forces, 616–618
   global forces, 620–621
   informational forces, 620
   political forces, 618–619
   social and demographic forces, 615–616
   technological forces, 619–620
Formal care, 438
Formulary, 399
Founding Fathers, 577
FPL. *See* Federal poverty level (FPL)
Fragmented policies, 577–578
Framework Convention on Tobacco Control (FCTC), 603
Fraud, defined, 531
Free clinics, 327
Free market, 11, 12
Freestanding facilities, 317–318
Full extent of practice, 631
Funds, disbursement of, 277

G

Gatekeeping, 117, 297, 397, 397f
General hospitals, 366
Generalists, 149–150
Gene therapy, 641
Genetic factors, 73
Genetic medicine, 641
Geographic maldistribution, 156
Geriatrics Academic Career Award Program, 634
Geriatrics, training in, 634–635
Geriatrics Workforce Enhancement Program, 634
Germany, 28–29
GHSA. *See* Global Health Security Agenda (GHSA)
Global Action Plan for Healthy Lives and Well-being for All (SDG3 GAP), 603
Global budgets, 10
Global forces, 620–621
Global health, 130
   challenges and reform, 34–35
Global Health Initiative, 600
Global health measures, 80–81
Global Health Security Agenda (GHSA), 637
Global Health Security (GHS) Index, 69
   main categories of, 69
   strengths and limitations of, 70f
Global Initiative on Digital Health (GIDH), 603
Globalization, 190, 621
   of health care, 129–131
Global medical practice, technology impact on, 221
Global public health policies, 600
Global threats, 636–641
   COVID-19, case of, 637–638
   historical context, 636–637
   public health threats, 639–641
Government as subsidiary, to private sector, 577
Government-insured-and-financed system, 623
Government policy, 208
Government, role of, 352–353
Great Recession of 2007–2009, 617, 622
Gross domestic product (GDP), 277
Group insurance, 244
Group model, 403
Growth-oriented policies (political forces), 614

Index

H

HAN. *See* Health Alert Network (HAN)
HCUP. *See* Healthcare Cost and Utilization Project (HCUP)
HDHPs. *See* High-deductible health plans (HDHPs)
Health
  basic concepts of, 50–56
  definitions of, 50–52
  factors affecting, 72
  promotion of, 56–61
Health Alert Network (HAN), 68
Health and Social Care Act, 29
Health care
  barriers to, 489–490
  defined, 51
  enhancing mental, 597
  equitable distribution of, 82–83
  evidence-based, 643–644
  examples of innovations in, 629*e*
  key implications, 82
  racism in, 502–504, 503*b*–504*b*
  reforms, 603–605
    Australia: Collaboratives Program, 605
    Canada: Medicare and Canada Health Act, 605
    China: Universal Health Coverage, 604
    Germany: Digital Healthcare Act, 604
    Switzerland: Universal Healthcare Coverage, 604–605
    United Kingdom: National Health Service (NHS) Model, 604
    United States: Affordable Care Act (ACA), 603–604
  robotics and, 550–551
Healthcare Common Procedures Coding System (HCPCS), 269, 272
Healthcare context, 621
Healthcare Cost and Utilization Project (HCUP), 558
Healthcare costs, 219–220
Healthcare delivery, 2
  basic components of, 5–7, 6*f*
  broad description of, 4–5
  characteristics of, 4
  complexity of, 3*t*
  continuum of services, 15, 17
  corporatization of, 129
  external forces affecting, 10*f*
  functions, 6*f*
  high technology, 15
  imperfect market, 11–13
  justice in U.S., 85–86
  litigation risks, 15
  major characteristics of, 9–17
  medical model of, 530
  medical technology impact on structure and processes of, 221
  multiple payers, 14
  no central agency, 10–11
  overview of, 2
  partial access, 11
  power balancing, 14–15
  quest for quality and value, 15–17
  significance for managers, 21–23
  significance for practitioners, 21
  third party insurers and payers, 13
  trends and directions, 17–21
Healthcare delivery infrastructure, 626–631
  patient activation, 630–631
  population health, 628–630
Healthcare Effectiveness Data and Information Set (HEDIS), 392, 575
Health care for the military, 266
Healthcare managers, 21–23
  capturing new markets, 22
  complying with regulations, 22
  evaluating implications, 22
  following the organizational mission, 22–23
  handling threats and opportunities, 22
  planning, 22
  positioning the organization, 21–22
Health Care Quality Act, 592
Healthcare reform
  defined, 7
  insurance and, 7–8
  private insurance under Trump's, 247–248
Healthcare reform directions, 618–619
Healthcare reform era, 131–136
Healthcare reform in transition, 622–623
Healthcare systems, 622
  in Australia, 23–24
  Canada, 24–26
  children and, 480–481
  in China, 26–28
  description of, 4–5
  in developing countries, 33–34
  framework, 35–37
  in Germany, 28–29
  highly integrated, 416–420
  HIV/AIDS and, 500
  in Israel, 30–31
  in Japan, 31–32
  in other countries, 23–35 (*See also specific countries*)
  in Singapore, 32–33
  system foundations, 35
  system outcomes, 37
  system outlook, 37
  system processes, 37
  system resources, 35–37
  in United Kingdom, 29–30
  women and, 484
Healthcare teams, 172–174, 173*e*
Healthcare workforce, trends in, 170–179
  aging workforce, 171
  global challenges, 174–179, 175*e*
  healthcare teams, 172–174
  impact of health technology, 171–172
  workforce shortages, 171

Index

Health determinants, 72–73
  Blum's model of, 72–73
  contemporary models of, 73–74
  defined, 89
  factors affecting, 72
    environmental factors, 72
    genetic factors, 73
    lifestyle factors, 72–73
    medical care factors, 73
Health informatics, 194
Health information organization (HIO), 197–198, 198e
Health information technology (HIT)
  advancement in, 20
Health Information Technology for Economic and Clinical Health (HITECH) Act, 198
Health insurance, 241
  basic terminologies, 242–244
    cost sharing, 243
    covered services, 243–244
    premiums, 242
    risk rating, 242–243
  children, 479
  COVID-19 pandemic and, 7
  employment-based enrollment, 407, 407f
  employment-based trends, 251–253
  fee-for-service, 393
  function of, 240–242
  fundamental principles of, 241
  for long-term care, 454–455
  private, 120–122, 242–251
  public, 253–267, 352–353
  types of, 241f
  women, 482, 484
Health insurance expansion, 599
Health Insurance Portability and Accountability Act (HIPAA), 199, 550, 583
Health maintenance organization (HMO), 401–404
  employees enrolled in, 402f
  group model, 403
  IPA model, 403–404
  mixed model, 402
  network model, 403
  staff model, 402–403
Health Maintenance Organization Act (HMO Act), 128, 403, 583
Health maintenance organizations (HMOs), 4, 582, 591
Health Outcomes Survey (HOS), 392
Health planning, 9, 533–535
  CON statutes, 534–535
  experiments in United States, 533–534
Health policy, 574–605
  critical policy issues, 587–588
    access to care, 588–590
    cost of care, 591–592
    quality of care, 592–593
  defined, 574
  domestic health policy, 593–599
    current domestic health policy initiatives, 593–597
    health insurance expansion, 599
    rural health transformation, 597–599
  forms of, 575–576
  initiatives
    ARPA, 596
    enhancing mental health care, 597
    expanding access to medicaid, 596
    telehealth and home care, 596–597
    value-based payment agenda, 596
  international health policy, 600–605
    health reforms, 600–601
    WHO health initiatives, 601–603
  legislative health policy, development of, 584–587
    legislative committees and subcommittees, 585–586
    legislative process, 586–587
    policy cycle, 584–585
    policy implementation, 587
  principal features of, 576–577
    decentralized role of the states, 581–582, 581e
    fragmented policies, 577–578
    government as subsidiary, to private sector, 577
    incremental and piecemeal policies, 578
    interest groups, demanders of policy, 578–580, 579e
    pluralistic suppliers of policy, 580–581
    politics of Affordable Care Act, 583–584
    presidential leadership, 582–583
    research in policy development, role of, 593
  uses of, 575
Health problems, 616, 620
Health professional shortage areas (HPSA), 485–486, 590
Health Professions Educational Assistance Act, 485
Health protection
  and environmental health, 63
  during global pandemic, 64–66
  and One Health, 63–64
  and preparedness in the United States, 67–69
Health reforms, 600–601
  cost containment under, 539
Health reimbursement arrangement vs. health savings account, 246e
Health-related measures, 75–81
Health-related quality of life (HRQL), 223, 553

Health Resources and Services Administration, 634
Health risk appraisal, 56
Health risks among persons 20 years and older, 472t
Health savings account, health reimbursement arrangement vs., 246e
Health Security Act (1993), 125
Health services administrators, 169–170
Health services delivery
American College of Physicians, 621
evidence-based health care, 643–644
forces of future change, 614–615
cultural-anthro forces, 621–622
ecological forces, 620
economic forces, 616–618
global forces, 620–621
informational forces, 620
political forces, 618–619
social and demographic forces, 615–616
technological forces, 619–620
frontiers in clinical technology, 641–643
global threats and international cooperation, 636–641
COVID-19, case of, 637–638
historical context, 636–637
international cooperation, future of, 638–639
public health threats, 639–641
healthcare reform in transition, 622–623
American College of Physicians (ACP), 623
third option, 623–625
infrastructure, innovations in, 626–631
patient activation, 630–631
population health, 628–630
introduction, 614
long-term care, 635–636
new frontiers in clinical technology, 641–643
nursing profession, 631
paradigm shift of, 626e
third option, 623–625
workforce challenges, 631–635
Campaign for Action, 631–632
nursing profession, 631
primary-care physicians, 632–634
training in geriatrics, 634–635
Health services financing, 238–282. *See also* Health insurance
COVID-19 pandemic and, 279–282
financing and cost control, 239–240, 240f
health reimbursement arrangement vs. health savings account, 246e
influence on delivery of health services, 240f
insurance function, 240–242
Medicaid, 263–265
Medicare, 254–262
national health expenditures, 277–279
nation's healthcare dollars, 279, 280f
payment function, 268–277
role and scope of, 238–239
Health services for special populations, 461–515
Health services for veterans, 119
Health services professionals
allied health professionals, 166–169
chiropractors, 162
dentists, 159–161
doctoral nursing degrees, 162
employed in heath service sites, 147t
health services administrators, 169–170
nonphysician providers, 164–166
nurses, 162–164
optometrists, 162
pharmacists, 161
physicians, 146–159
podiatrists, 162
psychologists, 162
trends in healthcare workforce, 170–179
Health services utilization measures, 79–80
crude measures of, 80
institution-specific measures, 80
specific measures of, 80
Health status
disability, 77
longevity, 75–76
measures of, 75–78
morbidity, 75
mortality, 77–78
Health technology assessment (HTA), 222
Health Transformation Alliance, 595
Healthy Kids Corporation, 582
Healthy People 2010, 558
Healthy People 2020, 68, 88–92, 88–92, 326
achievement of, 91–92
measurement of, 89–90
overarching goals, 88–89
Healthy People 2030, 92–93
foundational principles, 92
overarching goals, 92
plan of action, 92–93
Healthy People 2010: Healthy People in Healthy Communities, 88
Healthy people initiatives, 87–88
Healthy People 2000: National Health Promotion and Disease Prevention Objectives, 87

Index

HEDIS. *See* Healthcare Effectiveness Data and Information Set (HEDIS)
Heredity, 73
HHS Action Plan to Reduce Racial, 589
High-deductible health plans (HDHPs), 245, 625
Higher levels of education, 631
Highly integrated healthcare systems, 416–420
High-risk pools, 625
Hill-Burton Act, 352, 575, 583
HIPAA. *See* Health Insurance Portability and Accountability Act (HIPAA)
Hispanic Americans, 471–473
HIT. *See* Health information technology (HIT)
HIV/AIDS, 65, 177, 219, 462, 494–495
  in children, 495, 497
  cost of, 499–500
  discrimination issues and, 498
  federal spending for, 499f
  need for research, 497
  provider training, 498–499
  public health concerns, 497–498
  related issues, 497–499
  in rural communities, 495
  U.S. healthcare system and, 500
  in women, 497
  women with, 483
HMOs. *See* Health maintenance organizations (HMOs)
H1N1, 64
H3N2, 64
Holistic care, 434
Holistic health, 51
  dimensions of, 51f
Holistic medicine, 51
Home-based services, 443–448
  adult daycare, 444–445
  adult foster care, 445
  continuing care at home, 446–447
  housekeeping services, 446
  senior centers, 446
Home-delivered and congregate meals, 446
Home health care, 316–317, 319–320, 444, 444f, 445f
  demographic characteristics of, 320f
  estimated payments for, 321f
  and hospice care patients, 322t–323t
  organizational characteristics of, 321t–322t
Homeland Security Act of 2002, 67
Homelessness, 487–489
Homophobia, 498
Horizontal integration, 415
Hospice services, 320–325, 323f
Hospital Association's Annual Survey of Hospitals, 543
Hospital-based outpatient services, 275, 314–317
Hospital Care Structure Reform Act, 29
Hospital Financing Reform Act, 29
Hospital metrics, 376e
Hospitals, 348
  access and utilization, 357, 358t
  accreditation of, 376
  board of trustees, 374–375
  CEO, 375
  certification of, 376
  changes in number of beds, average size, and occupancy rates, 365t
  children's, 369
  church-affiliated, 371–372
  classification
    by length of stay, 369
    by location, 369–370
    by size, 370–371
  closures, 354
  community, 365
  critical access, 370
  demand/employment, 359–363
  expenditures, 359–361, 360t, 361f
  general, 366
  governance, 374–376, 374f
  international cost comparisons, 361–363, 362f
  investor-owned, 364
  largest U.S. multihospital chains, 366t
  licensure, 376
  long-term care, 369
  magnet, 377
  management concepts, 373–376
  medical staff, 375–376
  Medicare-dependent, 370
  by multiunit affiliation, 365–366
  nonprofit, expectations for, 372–373
  osteopathic, 372
  outpatient care, 314–317
  by ownership, 363–364
  pharmaceutical care in, 359
  private for-profit, 364
  private nonprofit, 364
  profitability, 361
  proprietary, 364
  psychiatric, 367–368
  public, 363–364
  by public access, 365, 365f
  rehabilitation, 368
  rural, 369
  short-stay, 369
  sole community, 370
  specialty, 366–367
  swing bed, 370
  teaching, 371
  transformation of United States, 348–351
  by type of service, 366–369
  urban, 369
  voluntary, 349
Host, 53
House Committees, 585–586
Housekeeping services, 446
Housing, 439–441
  private, 439–440
  public, 440–441
Housing subsidies, 118
HPSA. *See* Health professional shortage areas (HPSA)

Index

HRQL. *See* Health-related quality of life (HRQL)
Human-animal-ecosystems interface, 620
Human immunodeficiency virus (HIV), 326
Hurricane Katrina (2005), 67
Hurricane Sandy (2012), 67

I

IADLs. *See* Instrumental activities of daily living (IADLs)
Iatrogenic illnesses, 58
IDEA. *See* Individuals with Disabilities Education Act (IDEA)
IDS. *See* Integrated delivery systems (IDS)
IHCIA. *See* Indian Health Care Improvement Act (IHCIA)
IHR treaty. *See* International Health Regulations (IHR) treaty
IHTSG. *See* Interior Health Thoracic Surgical Group (IHTSG)
Imaging technologies, 642
IME. *See* Indirect Medical Education (IME)
Immigration, 78
Immunotherapy, 642
Imperfect market, 527
Incidence, 76
Incremental health policy, 578
Indemnity insurance, 393
Independent Hospital Pricing Authority, 24
Independent practice association (IPA) model, 403–404, 403*f*
Indian Health Care Improvement Act (IHCIA), 475
Indian Health Service, 267, 475
Indian Self-Determination and Education Assistance Act, 267
Indirect Medical Education (IME), 155
Individual private health insurance, 245
Individuals with Disabilities Education Act (IDEA), 325
Individuals with intellectual disabilities, intermediate care facilities for, 452
Inequitable access, 542
Infant mortality rate, 77, 78
Infant, neonatal, and postneonatal mortality rates by mother's race, 470*t*
Infection control committee, 376
Inflation Reduction Act (IRA), 619
Influenza, 64
Informal care, 438
Informational forces, 620
Information technology (IT), 191–199, 620
Informed consent, 378
Infrastructure, innovations, 626–628
  patient activation, 630–631
  population health, 628–630
Innovation and diffusion factors driving
  anthro-cultural beliefs and values, 204
  expenditures on research and development, 206–207
  factors driving, 203–208, 203*t*
  financing and payment, 204–205
  government policy, 208
  medical specialization, 204
  Stark Law Regulation, 206*e*
  supply-side controls, 207–208
  technology-driven competition, 205–206
Innovative programs, 634
Inpatient days, 356
Inpatient facilities and services, 347–380. *See also* Hospitals
  advanced institutions of medical training and research, 350–351
  average daily census, 358
  average length of stay, 356–357
  capacity, 357–358, 358*f*
  consolidated systems of health services delivery, 351
  discharges, 355–356
  distinct institutions of care for sick, 349–350
  downsizing phase, 353–354
  ethical and legal issues in patient care, 377–379
  expansion phase, 351–353
  government role, 352–353
  hospital closures, 354
  hospitals transformation of United States, 348–351
  hospital types, 363–372, 363*f*
  inpatient days, 356
  key utilization and operational concepts, 355–359
  magnet recognition program, 377
  managed care impact, 354
  occupancy rate, 358–359, 359*f*
  organized institutions of medical practice, 350
  primitive institutions of social welfare, 349
  private health insurance, growth of, 352
  public health insurance, 352–353
  reimbursement changes, 354
Inpatient psychiatric DRG-based payment, 275
Inpatient Quality Indicators, 558
Institute of Medicine (IOM), 298–300, 592, 631
  COPC and, 307
Institutionalization, 114
Institutional services, 439, 440*f*
Institutional trends, 453–454
Institution-related quality of life, 553
Institution-specific utilization measures, 80

Index

Instrumental activities of daily living (IADLs), 77, 431
Insurance, 5. *See also* Health insurance
  commercial, 122
  employment-based health, 122
  indemnity, 393
Insurance risk pools, 581
Insured, 241
Insurer, 240
Integrated access, 588–589
Integrated delivery systems (IDS), 17–18, 417–418
  core functions, 18–19
Integrated Team Effectiveness Model (ITEM), 174
Integration
  alliance, 414–415
  basic forms of, 415–416
  horizontal, 415
  of individual and population health, 86–87
  joint venture, 414
  management services organization (MSO), 415
  mergers and acquisitions, 413–414
  model for holistic health, 88f
  networks, 414
  provider-sponsored organization (PSO), 416
  service strategies, 415
  strategies, 413–415, 413f
  vertical, 415
  virtual, 414–415
  virtual organizations, 414–415
Intellectual disability (ID), 441
Interest groups, demanders of policy, 578–580, 579e
Interior Health Thoracic Surgical Group (IHTSG), 202
Intermediate care facilities for individuals with intellectual disabilities, 452
Internal Revenue Code, 122
Internal Revenue Service (IRS), 575

International Conference on Primary Health Care (1978), 307
International cooperation
  COVID-19, case of, 637–638
  future of, 638–639
  historical context, 636–637
  public health threats, 639–641
International health policy, 600–605
  health reforms, 600–601
  WHO health initiatives, 601–603
International Health Regulations (IHR) treaty, 637, 640
International Medical Device Regulators Forum, 216
International medical graduates, 159
International treaties, 640
Interoperability, 196
Investor-owned hospitals, 364
IOM. *See* Institute of Medicine (IOM)
IPA model, 403
IRS. *See* Internal Revenue Service (IRS)
Israel, 30–31
IT. *See* Information technology (IT)

J

Japan, 31–32
Johns Hopkins Hospital, 130
Johns Hopkins Primary Care Policy Center, 304
Johns Hopkins University, 116
Johnson, Lyndon, 126, 583, 585
Joint Commission, 575
  Primary Care Medical Home Designation Standards, 303
Justice in U.S. health delivery system, 85–86
Justification for social determinants, 74

K

Kaiser Permanente, 18
Kefauver-Harris Drug Amendments, 210
Kennedy, Edward, 127, 586
Kennedy, John F., 117, 585
Kerr-Mills Act, 126
King v. Burwell, 134

L

Laboratory Response Network (LRN), 68
Leading causes of death, 2017, 63t
Legal rights, 378–379
Legislative committees and subcommittees, 585–586
Legislative health policy, development of, 584–587
  legislative committees and subcommittees, 585–586
  legislative process, 586–587
  policy cycle, 584–585
  policy implementation, 587
Legislative process, 586–587
Legislators, 574
Licensed practical nurses (LPNs), 163
Licensing, 115–116
Licensure, 376
Life expectancy, 76t
  at birth, 467f
Lifestyle factors, 72–73
Liquid biopsies, 642
Living will, 379
Longevity, 75–76
Long-term care (LTC), 429–456, 635–636. *See also* Nursing home(s)
  age, functional deficits and, 430–431, 431t, 432f
  Alzheimer's facilities, 452
  ambulatory, 325
  assisted living facility, 449–450

Index

community-based and institutional services, 439
continuing care retirement community (CCRC), 452–453
end-of-life care, 441
evidence-based care, 435–436
extended period of care, 433–434
holistic care, 434
home- and community-based services, 443–448
housing, 439–441
individualized services, 433
informal and formal, 438
institutional, 448–452
institutional trends, utilization, and expenditures, 453–454, 453t
insurance for, 454–455
intermediate care facilities for individuals with intellectual disabilities, 452
level of care continuum, 442–443
medical care, nursing, and rehabilitation, 436
mental health services and dementia care, 436–438
nature of, 431, 433–436
preventive and therapeutic, 438
quality of life, 434–435
range of services for individuals in, 440f
residential and personal care facilities, 449
residual function, maintenance of, 433
respite care, 439
services, 436–441
skilled nursing facilities, 450–451
social support, 438
specialized care facilities, 452
subacute care facilities, 451–452
total care, 433, 434f
use of current technology, 435
users of, 441–442
variety of services, 433
Long-term care hospitals (LTCHs), 275, 369
Low income, access and, 590
LPNs. *See* Licensed practical nurses (LPNs)
LRN. *See* Laboratory Response Network (LRN)
LTC. *See* Long-term care (LTC)
LTCHs. *See* Long-term care hospitals (LTCHs)

M

MACRA. *See* Medicare Access and CHIP Reauthorization Act of 2015 (MACRA)
Magnet hospital, 377
Magnetic resonance imaging (MRI), 642
Magnet recognition program, 377
Maldistribution, 156–159
 geographic, 156
 specialty, 156–159
Malpractice reform, 592–593
Managed care, 387–420. *See also* Integrated delivery systems; Integration
 accreditation of, 392
 care coordination, 397–399, 398f
 case management, 397–399, 398f
 choice restriction, 397
 cost control methods in, 396–401
 defined, 389
 delivery, 390
 disease management, 399
 efficiencies and inefficiencies in, 395–396
 employment-based health insurance enrollment, 407, 407f
 evolution of, 390–392, 391e
 financing, 389
 gatekeeping, 397
 historical backlash and aftermath, 411–412
 historical growth of, 392–394
  employers' response to rise in premiums, 393–394
  flaws in fee-for-service model, 393
  weakened economic position of providers, 394
 HMO, 401–404
 impact of, 354
 impact on cost/access/quality, 408–411
 insurance, 390
 integration of healthcare delivery functions, 389f
 Medicaid enrollment, 407–408, 408f
 mental health and, 492
 panel of, 397
 payment, 390
 pharmaceutical management, 399
 point-of-service (POS) plan, 404–406
 practice profiling, 401
 preferred provider organization (PPO), 404
 quality assessment in, 392
 role of, 8–9
 transition to, 388
 trends in, 406–408
 types of, 401–406
 utilization review, 399–401
Managed care approaches, 270
Managed care organizations (MCOs), 129, 575
Managed care plans, 245
Management services organization (MSO), 415
Market justice, 86
 limitations of, 86
 social justice vs., 84t
Maryland Health Care Commission (MHCC), 559
Master of Health Administration (MHA), 170

Master of Health Services
Administration (MHSA),
170
Master of Public Administration,
170
Master of Public Health, 170
Mayo Clinic, 18, 130
McCarran-Ferguson Act of
1945, 625
MCOs. *See* Managed care
organizations (MCOs)
Meals-on-wheels, 446
Means-tested program, 126, 263
Mechanisms for ethical decision
making, 379
Medicaid, 4, 7, 82, 86, 127,
198, 263–265, 576,
577, 583, 615–624,
618–619, 622–624
under ACA, 263–264
CHIP, 265–266
creation of, 126–127
dually eligible beneficiaries,
263
eligibility rules, 263
enrollment, 407–408, 408f
expanding access to, 596
expansion of, 127–128
Indian Health Service and,
267
issues with, 264
military health care and, 266
spending, 265
Veterans Health
Administration and,
266–267
Medicaid managed care
organizations (MCOs),
299
Medicaid maximization, 582
Medicaid waiver program, 499
Medical care, 436
Medical Care Act, 24
Medical care factors, 73
Medical Expenditure Panel
Survey (MEPS), 543
Medical home, 302
Medically underserved areas
(MUAs), 299, 486
Medically underserved
designation, 326

Medical model, 50
of healthcare delivery, 530
Medical nutrition therapy
(MNT), 167
Medical records committee, 375
Medical specialization,
116–117, 204
Medical staff, 375–376
Medical staff committee, 375
Medical technology, 190–226,
579, 580
assessment of, 222–225
defined, 190
e-health, 200
e-therapy, 200
e-visits, 200–201
examples of, 192t–193t
government's role in
technology diffusion,
208–217
impact, 217–222
on access, 220–221
on bioethics, 221–222
on economic value, 220
on global medical practice,
221
on healthcare costs,
219–220
on quality of care, 217–218
on quality of life, 218–219
on structure and processes
of healthcare delivery,
221
information technology and
informatics, 191–199
innovation/diffusion/
utilization of, 203–208
M-health, 200
MRI units available in
selected countries,
203–208
regulation of drugs, devices,
and biologics, 208–216
telemedicine, telehealth, and
remote monitoring,
201–203
Medical tourism, 129, 621
Medicare, 4, 7, 24, 82, 86, 127,
198, 578, 579, 583, 619,
622–624, 624e
beneficiaries, 325

certification, 324
creation of, 126–127
enrolled population and total
expenditures, 260, 261t
expansion of, 127–128
financing and spending for
services, 260–261, 261f,
262f
HI and SMI trust funds, 262t
hospital insurance (Part A),
254–255, 255e
Medicare Advantage (Part C),
257–258, 259e
Medicare Advantage Special
Needs Plans, 257–258
out-of-pocket costs, 259–260
Part D benefits and individual
out-of-pocket costs for
2023, 260e
prescription drug coverage
(Part D), 258–259, 260e
in public health insurance,
254–262
supplementary medical
insurance (Part B),
256–257, 256e–257e
Medicare Access and CHIP
Reauthorization Act of
2015 (MACRA), 590
Medicare Advantage
Prescription Drug plans,
257–258
Medicare and Medicaid Patient
Protection Act, 531
Medicare-dependent hospitals,
370
Medicare Payment Advisory
Commission (MedPAC),
254
Medicare Physician Fee
Schedule (MPFS), 269
Medicare Prescription Drug,
Improvement, and
Modernization Act
(MMA), 579, 592
Medicare Shared Savings
Program (MSSP), 18,
270, 419–420, 626
Medicare's Outpatient
Prospective Payment
System (OPPS), 275

Index

Medigap, 246–247
Mental asylum, 110
Mental health, 490–493
   barriers to, 491
   of children, 490–491
   insured and, 492
   managed care and, 492
   professionals, 492–493
   system, 491
   uninsured and, 492
Mental healthcare reform, 117–118
Mental health measures, 78
Mental health parity act (1996 and 2008), 118
Mental Health Parity and Addiction Equity Act (MHPAEA), 118, 597
Mental health services, 436–438, 437b
Mental Health Study Act of 1955, 117
Merger, 413–414
Merit-based Incentive Payment System (MIPS), 596
Mexico City Policy, 600
MHCC. *See* Maryland Health Care Commission (MHCC)
M-health, 200
MHS. *See* Multihospital system (MHS)
Middle East respiratory syndrome (MERS), 65
Mid-level healthcare professionals, 20
Migrant workers, 486–487
Military Health System (MHS), 266
Minimally invasive surgery, 642
Minnesota's statewide multipayer Health Care Home Certification standards, 303
Minorities, access and, 589
Missing institutional core, 109–110
   Almshouse and Pesthouse, 109
   dispensaries, 109
   dreaded hospital, 110
   mental asylum, 110

Mixed model, 402
MMA. *See* Medicare Prescription Drug, Improvement, and Modernization Act (MMA)
Mobile communication devices, 628
Mobile medical/diagnostic/ screening services, 318–319
Money Follows the Person (MFP), 448
Mongan, James J., 125
Moral agent, 379
Moral hazard, 13, 239
Morbidity, 75
Mortality, 77–78
Most Favored Nation (MFN), 619
MSSP. *See* Medicare Shared Savings Program (MSSP)
Multihospital system (MHS), 365, 366t
Multipayer system and administrative costs, 530–531
Multiple-target drugs, 642

N

Nanomedicine, 191
Nanotechnology, 642
NAPBC. *See* National Action Plan on Breast Cancer (NAPBC)
NASMHPD. *See* National Association of State Mental Health Program Directors (NASMHPD)
Natality, 78
National Academy of Medicine, 592
National Action Plan on Breast Cancer (NAPBC), 483
National Association of Boards of Examiners of Long-Term Care Administrators, 170

National Association of State Mental Health Program Directors (NASMHPD), 117
National Biosurveillance Strategy for Human Health, 68
National Center for Health Statistics (NCHS), 76
National Committee for Quality Assurance (NCQA), 303, 575, 932
National debt, 617
National Diabetes Prevention Program (NDPP), 61
National Disaster Medical System (NDMS), 68
National Evaluation System for Health Technology (NEST), 216
National Federation of Independent Business v. Sebelius, 133
National Governors Association, 594
National Guideline Clearinghouse (NGC), 555
National healthcare initiatives, failure of, 122–125
   ideological differences, 124–125
   institutional and public opposition, 124
   political inexpediency, 123
   tax aversion, 125
National healthcare program, 622
National health expenditures (NHE), 127, 277–279, 278e, 520
   and growth, 278
   percentage distribution of, 279t
   vs. personal, 278–279
   trends in, 520–525
National health insurance (NHI), 23
National health insurance card, 601

Index

National Health Interview Survey (NHIS), 328, 543
National Health Performance Authority, 24
National Health Planning and Resources Development Act of 1974, 216, 583
National Health Reform Act (2011), 24
National Health Security Strategy (NHSS), 68
National Health Service Corps (NHSC), 485, 590
National health system (NHS), 23, 621
National Home and Hospice Care Survey, 543
National Institute for Health and Clinical Excellence (NICE), 203
National Institute of Diabetes and Digestive and Kidney Diseases (NIDDK), 57
National Institute of Mental Health (NIMH), 117
National Institutes of Health (NIH), 56, 206, 575, 576, 619
National Nursing Home Survey, 543
National policies and programs, 576
National Prevention Strategy, 61
National Primary Health Care Strategy, 24
National Quality Forum, 556–557
National Quality Strategy (NQS), 559
National Stakeholder Strategy for Achieving Health Equity, 589
National Standards for Culturally and Linguistically Appropriate Service in Health, 589
National Survey of Children's Health, 477
Nation's healthcare dollars, 279, 280f
Natural disasters, 620
NCHS. See National Center for Health Statistics (NCHS)
NCMS. See New Cooperative Medical Scheme (NCMS)
NCQA. See National Committee for Quality Assurance (NCQA)
NDMS. See National Disaster Medical System (NDMS)
NDPP. See National Diabetes Prevention Program (NDPP)
Need, defined, 13
Neonatal intensive care units (NICUs), 204
NEST. See National Evaluation System for Health Technology (NEST)
The Netherlands, 601
Network model, 403
Networks, 414
New Cooperative Medical Scheme (NCMS), 26, 27
New frontiers in clinical technology, 641–643
NHE. See National health expenditures (NHE)
NHS. See National Health System (NHS)
NHSC. See National Health Service Corps (NHSC)
NHSS. See National Health Security Strategy (NHSS)
NICE. See National Institute for Health and Clinical Excellence (NICE)
NICUs. See Neonatal intensive care units (NICUs)
NIDDK. See National Institute of Diabetes and Digestive and Kidney Diseases (NIDDK)
NIH. See National Institutes of Health (NIH)
NIMH. See National Institute of Mental Health (NIMH)
Nixon, Richard, 127, 583
Noncertified facilities, 451
Nonphysician providers (NPPs), 164–166, 299
Nonprofit hospitals, 372–373
Nonurgent conditions, 316
Normative authority, 638
Novel couple-oriented insurance scheme, 599
NPPs. See Nonphysician providers (NPPs)
NPs. See Nurse practitioners (NPs)
NQS. See National Quality Strategy (NQS)
Nurse practitioners (NPs), 164, 299
Nurses, 162–164
　advanced practice, 163
　certified nurse-midwives, 165–166
　licensed practical, 163
　nurse practitioners, 164
　registered, 163
Nursing, 436
　Campaign for Action, 631–632
　development of professional, 351–352
　facility, 450
Nursing facility (NF), 450
Nursing home(s). See also Long-term care
　sources of payment for, 454f
　use of, by age groups, 454t
Nursing Home Compare, 451
Nursing Home Reform Act, 450
Nursing profession, 631

O

Obama, Barack, 131, 582, 583, 600
Obamacare, 618
OBRA. See Omnibus Budget Reconciliation Act (OBRA)
Occupancy rate, 358–359, 359f
Occupational therapists, 167
Office of Minority Health, 589
Office on Women's Health, 483

Index

Oklahoma's SoonerCare (Medicaid) PCMH standards, 303
Old Age Assistance program, 576
Older Americans Act, 443
Older people, access and, 589
Olmstead v. L.C., 117, 443, 577
Omnibus Budget Reconciliation Act (OBRA), 205, 269
Open-panel, 397
Opportunistic infection (OI), 498
Optometrists, 162
Organizational integration, 412–415. *See also* Integration
Organized institutions of medical practice, 350
Organized medicine, 115
Orphan Drug Act of 1983, 210
Orphan drugs, 210
Osteopathic hospitals, 372
Osteopathic medicine, 147
Ottawa Charter, 87
Outcomes, 520
Outliers, 272
Outpatient care
    ambulatory long-term care, 325
    clinical services, 315
    community health centers, 326–327
    DME, 317
    emergency services, 315–316
    emergent conditions, 316
    factors influencing, 311–312
    free clinics, 327
    freestanding facilities, 317–318
    growth in services, 310–328
    home health care, 316–317, 319–320
    hospice services, 320–325
    hospital-based, 314–317, 315*f*
    mobile medical/diagnostic/ screening services, 318–319
    nonurgent conditions, 316
    other clinics, 327
    owners/providers, 295*t*
    physician characteristics, 330*t*–331*t*
    physician practice factors, 312
    primary care (*See* Primary care)
    private practice, 313–314, 313*f*
    reimbursement, 311–312
    retail clinics, 318
    scope of, 295–296
    service settings, 295
    social factors, 312
    surgical services, 315
    surgicenters, 317
    technological factors, 312
    telephone access, 327–328
    types of settings and delivery methods, 312–328
    urgent care centers, 317
    urgent conditions, 316
    utilization control factors, 312
    utilization of services, 330–331
    walk-in clinics, 317
    women's health centers, 317
Outpatient services, 295
    payment systems, 275
Overutilization, 555

P

PACE. *See* Program of All-Inclusive Care for the Elderly (PACE)
Package pricing, 13
PAHPA. *See* Pandemic and All Hazards Preparedness Act (PAHPA)
Pain management, 219
Palliation, 324, 435
Pandemic and All-Hazards Preparedness Act (PAHPA), 67
Paraprofessionals, 442
Part A of Medicare, 127
Part B of Medicare, 127
PASRR. *See* Preadmission Screening and Resident Review (PASRR)
Patient activation, 630–631
Patient care, ethical and legal issues in, 377–379
Patient-centered care, 19, 378, 630
Patient-centered medical home (PCMH), 174, 302–303, 626
    assessment tools, 303
Patient-Centered Outcomes Research Institute (PCORI), 225, 562
Patient Driven Payment Model (PDPM), 276
Patient Protection and Affordable Care Act, 574
Patients accountability, 299
Patient Safety Indicators, 558
Patient's bill of rights, 378
Patient Self-Determination Act, 378
Patient skepticism, 627
Payer-driven price competition, 538
Pay-for-value, 18
Payment for home health services, 276–277
Payment for outpatient rehabilitation, 275
Payment function, 6, 268–277
    bundled payments, 268–269
    case-mix-based reimbursement, 272–277
    cost-plus reimbursement, 270–271
    disbursement of funds, 277
    fee for service, 268
    managed care approaches, 270
    MSSP, 270
    quality payment program, 269
    resource-based relative value scale, 269
Payments to inpatient rehabilitation facilities, 276
Payment system
    acute-care hospital, 272–275
    long-term care hospital, 275
    outpatient services, 275
    skilled nursing facility, 276

PBMs. *See* Pharmacy benefits managers (PBMs)
PCCM. *See* Primary care case management (PCCM)
PCORI. *See* Patient-Centered Outcomes Research Institute (PCORI)
PDMPs. *See* Prescription drug monitoring programs (PDMPs)
Pediatric Quality Indicators, 558
Peer review, 537
Pelosi, Nancy, 583
Pence, Mike, 66
PERS. *See* Personal emergency response system (PERS)
Personal care, 442
Personal emergency response system (PERS), 435
Personal health expenditures, national *vs.*, 278–279
Personalized medicine, 641
Personal protective equipment (PPE), 66
Person-centered care, 435
Pesthouse, 109
Phantom providers, 13
Pharmaceutical care, 161
Pharmaceutical management, 399
  drug formularies, 399
  pharmacy benefits managers, 399
  tiered cost sharing, 399
Pharmaceutical Research and Manufacturers of America (PhRMA), 579
Pharmacists, 161
Pharmacy benefits managers (PBMs), 399
PhRMA. *See* Pharmaceutical Research and Manufacturers of America (PhRMA)
Physical health measures, 75–78
Physical therapists, 167
Physician
  characteristics, 330t–331t
  reason for visiting, 331
Physician assistants (PAs), 165, 299

Physician-hospital organization (PHO), 415–416
Physician-owned specialty hospitals, 367, 368e
Physician Practice Connections—Patient-Centered Medical Home (PPC-PCMH) tool, 303
Physician practice factors, 312
Physicians, 146–159
  compensation for, 157t
  generalists and specialists, 149–150
  international medical graduates, 159f
  maldistribution, 156–159
  MDs and DOs compared, 148–149
  medical specialties/subspecialties, 149e–150e
  medical training, 154–155
  for a National Health Program, 579
  number of active, 147
  percentage of students enrollment by race, 158t
  Physician Specialty, 151t–152t
  primary *vs.* specialty care, 153
  supply of medical professionals, 155–156, 155f
  trend in primary care generalists of medicine, 157f
  work settings and practice patterns, 150–153
Piecemeal health policy, 578
Plan, 241
Planned rationing, 85
Play-or-pay mandate, 247
Pluralistic suppliers of policy, 580–581
Pluralistic U.S. system, 623
Pocket veto, 587
Podiatrists, 162
Point-of-service (POS) plan, 404–406, 406f
Policy cycle, 584–585

Policy-for-politics approach, 574
Policy implementation, 587
Policymakers, 574
Political forces, 614, 618–619
Politics of Affordable Care Act, 583–584
Population at risk, 76
Population, concept of, 75
Population health, 628–630
Positron emission tomography (PET), 218
Potential access, 542
Power balancing, 14–15
PPE. *See* Personal protective equipment (PPE)
PPHF. *See* Prevention and Public Health Fund (PPHF)
PPS. *See* Prospective payment system (PPS)
Practice profiling, 401
Preadmission Screening and Resident Review (PASRR), 447
Precision medicine, 191, 641, 642
Preexisting conditions, 240–241
Preferred provider organization (PPO), 404, 405e, 406f, 582
Premium cost sharing, 7
Premiums, 242
Prepaid plan, 121
Prescription drug monitoring programs (PDMPs), 594
Prescription Drug User Fee Act, 211
Presidential leadership, 582–583
Prevalence, 76
Prevention and Public Health Fund (PPHF), 61
Prevention Quality Indicators, 558
Price controls, 535–537
Primary care, 11, 296–310
  ACA and, 301–302
  ambulatory care visits to, 152f
  assessment tools, 303–304
  community-oriented, 307
  diagnosis group, 332t

elements of, 300
examples of questions in, 305t–306t
hospitalists, role of, 153–154
Institute of Medicine's (IOM) definition of, 298–299
   nonphysician providers, 299
   primary-care providers, 299–300
integration of public health, 300–301
models of, 334–335
new directions in, 302–310
in other countries, 331–334
pandemics and, 307
patient-centered medical homes, 302–303
providers, 299–300
vs. specialty care, 153
WHO definition of, 297–298
   coordination of care, 297–298, 298f
   essential care, 298
   point of entry, 297
Primary care case management (PCCM), 407
Primary care, four pillars of, 633–634
Primary health care, 297
Primary prevention, 57, 58f
Primitive institutions of social welfare, 349
Principle of beneficence, 378
Principle of confidentiality, 378
Principle of justice, 378
Principle of nonmaleficence, 378
Principle of respect, 377
Principles of ethics, 377–378
Private for-profit hospitals, 364, 365t
Private health insurance, 242–251
   under ACA, 247–248
   blanket insurance policies, 120
   Blue Cross plans, 121
   Blue Shield, 121
   combined hospital/physician coverage, 121
   commercial insurance, 122
   COVID-19 pandemic and, 251
   economic necessity and the Baylor plan, 120–121
   employment-based health insurance, 122
   group insurance, 244
   growth of, 352
   high-deductible health plans and savings options, 245
   individual, 245
   Medigap, 246–247
   rise of, 120–122
   self-insurance, 244–245
   short-term COBRA coverage, 245–246
   technological, social, and economic factors, 120
   under Trump's healthcare reform, 247–248
   types of, 244–247
Private housing, 439–440
Private insurers, 627
Private nonprofit hospitals, 364
Private-pay residents, 451
Professional sovereignty, growth of, 112–116
Program of All-Inclusive Care for the Elderly (PACE), 447–448
Promoting health, 19
Proprietary hospitals, 364
Prospective payment system (PPS), 576
Prospective reimbursement, 271–272
Prospective utilization review, 400
Provider-induced demand, 13, 393
Providers, 588
Provider-sponsored organization (PSO), 416
Psychiatrists, 492
Psychological distress, 620
Psychologists, 162, 493
Public-financed coverage option, 623
Public health, 61–69
   core functions, 62f
   COVID-19 pandemic, 66–67
   GHS index and, 69
   practices of medicine vs., 62
   protection and environmental health, 63
   protection and One Health, 63–64
   protection and preparedness in the United States, 67–69
   protection during global pandemics, 64–66
   security in action, COVID-19 and, 69–71
Public health development, 118–119
Public Health Emergency of International Concern (PHEIC), 638–639
Public health insurance, 253–267, 352–353, 353f
   Medicare, 254–262
Public health integration, primary care and, 300–301
Public Health Security and Bioterrorism Preparedness Response Act of 2002, 67
Public Health Service Act of 1944, 216, 586
Public health threats, 637, 639–641
Public hospitals, 363–364
Public housing, 440–441
Public option model, 623
Public policies, 574
Public–private insurance model, 600
Public reporting on quality, 556–559
   AHRQ quality indicators, 558
   CMS programs on quality, 557–558
   National Quality Forum, 556–557
   states', 559

Index

Q

QIOs. *See* Quality improvement organizations (QIOs)
Quad-function model, 5
Quality-adjusted life year (QALY), 224
Quality assessment, 553–556
   Donabedian model, 554–555, 554f
   process, 555–556
     clinical practice guidelines, 555
     cost-efficiency, 555–556
     critical pathways, 556
     risk management, 556
Quality assessment in managed care, 392
Quality assurance, 553
Quality improvement committee, 376
Quality improvement organizations (QIOs), 537, 575
Quality, IOM definition of, 551
Quality of care, 217–218, 551–553, 592–593
   ACA and, 559–562
   dimensions of, 551–552
   IOM definition of, 551
   micro view of, 552–553
     clinical aspects, 552
     interpersonal aspects, 552–553
Quality of care, managed care influence on, 410–411
Quality of life, 52–53, 218–219, 435, 560–561
   health-related, 553
   institution-related, 553
Quality payment program, 269

R

Racial and ethnic minorities, 463–467, 464f–466f, 464t–465t
Racism in health care, 502–504, 503b–504b
Radiogenomics, 641
Rate, 268
Rational drug design, 641–642
RBRVS. *See* Resource-based relative value scale (RBRVS)
Reagan, Ronald, 127, 583, 583, 600
Realign and rebalance demands, 634
Realized access, 542
Redistributive policies, 575
Refined Medicare severity DRGs, 273–275
Regenerative medicine, 642
Registered nurses (RNs), 163
Regulation of biologics, 216
Regulation of medical devices and equipment, 215–216
Regulatory tools, 575
Rehabilitation, 436
Rehabilitation hospitals, 368
Rehabilitation robots, 550
Reid, Harry, 583
Reimbursement, 6, 311–312
   case-mix-based, 272–277
   changes in, 354
   cost-plus, 270–271
   DRG-based, overview of, 272–273
   prospective, 271–272
   retrospective, 271
Reinsurance, 244
Relative value units (RVUs), 269
Remote monitoring, 201–203
Republicans, 595
Research and development expenditures on, 206–207, 207t
Research in policy development, role of, 593
Residency, 147
Residual function, maintenance of, 433
Resource-based relative value scale (RBRVS), 269, 579
Respite care, 439
Restorative care, 442
Retail clinics, 318
Retrospective reimbursement, 271
Retrospective utilization review, 400–401
Right to Try Act (2018), 211
Risk, 240
Risk factors, 53–56
   behavioral, 53
   and disease, 53–56
Risk management, 556
Risk rating, 242–243
RNs. *See* Registered nurses (RNs)
Robot-assisted surgery, 218
Robotics, health care and, 550–551
Robotic surgery, 642
Rural Action Plan, 598
Rural areas, access in, 589–590
Rural health, 484–486
Rural Health Clinics Act, 485, 487
Rural health transformation, 597–599
Rural hospitals, 369

S

Safe Medical Devices Act of 1990, 215
Safety assessment, 223
SAMHSA. *See* Substance Abuse and Mental Health Services Administration (SAMHSA)
SARS. *See* Severe acute respiratory syndrome (SARS)
SARS-CoV-2. *See* Severe acute respiratory syndrome coronavirus 2 (SARS-CoV-2)
Science and technology, 113–114
Scope of health policy, 576
Secondary care, 296
Secondary prevention, 58, 58f
Section 701 of the Public Health Service Act, 166
Self-insurance plan, 244

Index

Self-referral, 205–206
Self-regulatory, 575
Senate Committees, 586
Senior centers, 446
Sensor technology, 635
Severe acute respiratory syndrome (SARS), 26, 65, 86, 636
Severe acute respiratory syndrome coronavirus 2 (SARS- CoV-2), 637
SHI. *See* Socialized health insurance (SHI)
Short-stay hospitals, 369
Short-term COBRA coverage, 245–246
Singapore, 32–33
Single-payer system, 14, 622, 624e
Single-photon emission computed tomography (SPECT), 218
Single state-based ACO, 630
Skilled nursing care, 442–443
Skilled nursing facility (SNF), 450–451, 451f
Skilled Nursing Facility Payment System, 276
Small area variations (SAVs), 531
Smart cards, 620
SNF. *See* Skilled nursing facility (SNF)
Social and cultural factors, 616
Social and demographic forces, 615–616
Social contacts, 79
Social factors, 312
Social health measures, 79
  dimensions of, 79
Socialized health insurance (SHI), 23
Socialized medicine, 125, 622
Social justice, 84–85
  market justice *vs.*, 84t
  principle of, 84–85
Social media, use of, 60
Social resources, 79
Social Security Act of 1935, 575
Social Security Disability Insurance, 118, 578
Social Security legislation, 574
Social Security taxes, 576
Social welfare programs, 574
Society for Academic Emergency Medicine, 51
Society of Thoracic Surgeons, 579
Sole community hospitals, 370
Specialists, 149–150
Specialization in medicine, 116–117
Special populations, 461–515
  Alaska Natives, 474–475
  American Indians, 474–475
  Asian Americans, 473–474
  Black Americans, 467–471, 467t–470t, 469f, 471f, 476f
  children, 478–481
  chronically ill and, 493–494
  COVID-19 effects, 504–505
  Hispanic Americans, 471–473
  homelessness, 487–490
  mental health, 490–493
  migrant workers, 486–487
  racial/ethnic minorities, 463–467, 464f–466f, 464t–465t
  rural health, 484–486
  uninsured, 477–478
  vulnerability framework, 462–463, 462e, 463e
  women, 481–484
Specialty care, primary care *vs.*, 153
Specialty hospitals, 366–367
  physician-owned, 367, 368e
Specialty maldistribution, 156–159
Spiritual health measures, 79
Staff model, 402
Stand-alone prescription drug plans, 259
Standards of participation, 11
Stark laws, 205–206
Stark, Pete, 205
State-based risk pools, 581
State-initiated programs, 582
State mental health institutions, 368
Subacute care, 443
  facilities, 451–452
Subacute condition, 54
Subpopulations, addressing disparities across, 500–502
Substance Abuse and Mental Health Services Administration (SAMHSA), 483
Supplemental Security Income, 118
Supply-side controls, 207–208
Supply-side rationing, 85
Supply-side regulation, 538
Surge capacity, defined, 68
Surgicenters, 317
Swing bed hospitals, 370
Synchronous technology, 201
System foundations, 35
System outcomes, 37
System outlook, 37
System processes, 37
System resources, 35–37

T

Taiwan, 601
Targeted drug delivery, 642
Task Force on National Health Reform, 125
Tax aversion, 125
Teaching hospitals, 371
Tea Party movement, 580
Technological factors, 312
Technological forces, 619–620
Technology(ies), 635
  economic value of, 220
  growth of, 528
Technology diffusion, 203
  government's role in, 208–217
  certificate of need, 216–217
  regulation of drugs, devices, and biologics, 208–216
Technology-driven competition, 205–206
Telehealth, 548–549
  telemedicine *vs.*, 201

Index

Telehealth and health information technology, 20
Tele-ICU, 202–203
Telemedicine, 627
   access to care and, 548–550
   characteristics of, 201–202
   vs. telehealth, 201
   tele-ICU, 202–203
Telephone access, 327–328
Telephone triage, 327
Tertiary care, 296
Tertiary prevention, 58, 58f
Texas v. United States, 134
The Future of Nursing: Leading Change, Advancing Health, 631
Therapists, 167
   occupational, 167
   physical, 167
Third party, 9
Third-party administrator (TPA), 277
Third party insurers and payers, 13
Third-party payers, 268
Third-party payment, 527
1983 Amendments to Social Security Act, 576
3-D bioprinting, 642
Three-dimensional (3D) technology, 642
Tiered cost sharing, 399
Title 18 of the Social Security Act, 254
Title XIX, 127
Title XVIII, 127
Title XX Social Services Block Grants, 443
Top-down control, 532
Tornadoes in Oklahoma (2013), 67
Total care, 433, 434f
Total quality management (TQM), 554
TQM. *See* Total quality management (TQM)
Training in geriatrics, 634–635
TransforMED's Medical Home Implementation Quotient, 303
Travel ban, 66
Trial-and-error method, 641
TRICARE, 266
Triple-option plans, 401
Truman, Harry, 117, 124, 125, 582
Trump administration, 618–619
   Families First Coronavirus Response Act and, 281
   healthcare reform under, 248–249
Trump, Donald, 8, 106, 591, 593, 594, 614
Tuberculosis (TB), 65
21st Century Cures Act of 2016, 118, 211, 619
Two-tiered healthcare system, 627
Type 2 diabetes, 55
Typical distributive policies, 575

U

UHC. *See* Universal health coverage (UHC)
Uncontrolled prices and payment, 393
Uncontrolled utilization, 393
Underutilization, 555
Underwriting, 240
Uninsured
   in health care, 7
   special populations, 477–478
United Kingdom, 29–30
Universal access, 11
Universal coverage, 8
Universal health care, 621
Universal health coverage (UHC), 602
Universal Health Coverage Partnership, 602
Upcoding, 531
URAC's Patient-Centered Health Care Home (PCHCH) Program Toolkit, 303
Urban hospitals, 369
Urbanization, 112–113
Urgent care centers, 317
Urgent conditions, 316
USA PATRIOT Act, 208
U.S.–China Economic and Security Review Commission (USCC), 213
U.S. Constitution, 577
U.S. culture, 635
U.S. debt, 617
U.S. demographic landscape, 645
U.S. Department of Defense (DOD), 266
U.S. Department of Health and Human Services (DHHS), 575, 598
U.S. Department of Labor (DOL), 248
U.S. Department of the Treasury, 575
U.S. government agencies, 74
U.S. gross domestic product, 616
U.S. healthcare delivery, 605, 614, 615
U.S. healthcare system, 615, 645
U.S. hospitals, 621
U.S. media, 583
U.S. Perspective, 71
U.S. policy making, 583
U.S. population, 615, 616, 634
U.S. society, 616
Utilization, 9, 79–80
   controls, 539
   crude measures of, 80
   institution-specific measures, 80
   in long-term care, 453–454
   of outpatient services, 330–331
   review, 399–401
   specific measures of, 80
   uncontrolled, 393
Utilization control factors, 312
Utilization management
   care coordination, 397–399, 398f
   choice restriction, 397
   disease management, 399
   pharmaceutical management, 399
   practice profiling, 401

Utilization review (UR), 399–401
   concurrent, 400
   prospective, 400
   retrospective, 400–401
Utilization review committee, 375

V

Vaccines, 642
Value, 205
Value analysis, 223–225
Value-based payments, 268, 634
VA MISSION Act of 2018, 267
Vector-borne diseases, 620
Vella-Brodrick, D. A., 79
Vermont Blueprint for Health, 630
Vertical integration, 415
Veterans Health Administration (VHA) system, 202, 299, 635
Veterans, health services for, 119
Veterans Integrated Service Networks (VISNs), 267
VHA system. *See* Veterans Health Administration (VHA) system
Violence Against Women Act, 483
Virtual integration, 414
Virtual Thoracic Surgical Clinics (VTSC), 202
Voluntary health insurance, 120, 242
Voluntary hospitals, 349
VTSC. *See* Virtual Thoracic Surgical Clinics (VTSC)

Vulnerability framework, 462–463, 462*e*, 463*e*

W

Wagner-Murray-Dingell bill, 125
Walk-in clinics, 317
Washington, George, 108
Ways and Means Committee, 586
Weakened economic position of providers, 394
Welch, William H., 116
Well-coordinated total care, 433
Wennberg, John, 531
WHO. *See* World Health Organization (WHO)
Wofford, Harris, 125
Women, 481–484
   death, 482
   and healthcare system, 484
   health insurance, 482–484
   with HIV/AIDS, 483
   HIV/AIDS in, 497
   morbidity, 482
   Office on Women's Health, 483
   overweight and obesity in, 482
Women's health centers, 317
Worker's compensation, 119–120
Workforce challenges, 631–635
   Campaign for Action, 631–632
   nursing profession, 631
   primary care physicians, 632–634

   training in geriatrics, 634–635
World Health Organization (WHO), 51, 297, 594, 636
   access to COVID-19 tools (ACT) accelerator, 602–603
   Commission on Social Determinants of Health framework, 73–74
   coordination of care, 297–298
   COPC and, 307
   enforcement mechanisms, 639
   essential care, 298
   health initiatives, 601–603
   HIV/AIDS and, 65
   point of entry, 297
   Special Initiative for Mental Health, 601
   TB and, 65
   World Malaria Report, 65
Wuhan virus, 637

X

Xenotransplantation, 642

Z

Zero-Markup Drug policy, 27
Zika virus, 64
Zoonoses, 620
Zoonotic diseases, 63–64